Integrated, Cutting-Edge Technology Furthers Student Understanding

SMART FINANCE Discover all the review and reinforcement tools students need. This exciting online tool reinforces learning and helps students earn the grade they want with animated tutorials, step-by-step reviews, videos, interactive practice and more for each chapter.

Cengage Learning

Tom Cole, Managing Director of Leveraged Finance, Citigroup

"To be good at finance you have to understand how businesses work."

See the entire interview at **SMART|finance**

Smart Practices Video

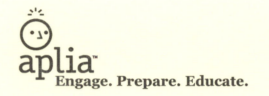

Aplia™ Finance is an online, auto-graded homework system that improves learning by increasing student effort and engagement. You'll find a digital copy of the text, access to Smart Finance tools, and a trusted homework solution.

CengageNOW for Finance supports your course goals and saves you significant preparation and grading time with such features as an algorithmic homework management system, testing, and an intuitive grade book.

Cengage Learning's The Watch helps bring pivotal, current financial events into the classroom—through a powerful, continuously updated online suite of content, discussion forums, testing tools, and more.

THOMSON ONE | Business School Edition

Thomson ONE- Business School Edition from Thomson Reuters gives students the power to do financial analysis and research using real company data and drawing from the same financial data sources that professionals access every day in their research. Six month access is included with the purchase of each new book.

news assignments for FINANCE

KnowNOW! brings news that's making a difference in the world directly to you. Discipline-specific, online pages provide instant access to breaking news with expert-developed concept questions and applications.

Cengage Learning's Finance CourseMate brings course concepts to life with interactive learning, study, and exam preparation tools that support the printed text. Watch student comprehension soar as your class works with the printed book and the textbook-specific website.

DON'T THROW THIS CARD AWAY!
THIS MAY BE REQUIRED FOR YOUR COURSE!

6 MONTHS ACCESS FREE WITH THIS TEXT!

THOMSON ONE Business School Edition

 THOMSON REUTERS

Congratulations!

Your purchase of this NEW textbook includes complimentary access to Thomson ONE – Business School Edition for Finance. Thomson ONE – Business School Edition is a Web-based portal product that provides integrated access to Thomson Reuters Financial content for the purpose of financial analysis. This is an educational version of the same financial resources used by Wall Street analysts on a daily basis!

For hundreds of companies, this online resource provides seamless access to:

- **Current and Past Company Data:**
  Worldscope which includes company profiles, financials and accounting results, market per-share data, annual information, and monthly prices going back to 1980.

- **Financial Analyst Data and Forecasts:** I/B/E/S Consensus Estimates which provides consensus estimates, analyst-by-analyst earnings coverage, and analysts' forecasts.

- **SEC Disclosure Statements:** Disclosure SEC Database which includes company profiles, annual and quarterly company financials, pricing information, and earnings.

- **And More!**

 **SOUTH-WESTERN**
CENGAGE Learning

THOMSON ONE
Business School Edition

THOMSON REUTERS

ACCESS CODE

PMFDTKXPPHZ9G2

HOW TO REGISTER YOUR ACCESS CODE

1. Launch a web browser and go to **http://www.cengage.com/thomsonone**

2. Click the "Register" button to enter your access code.

3. Enter your access code **exactly** as it appears here and create a unique User ID, or enter an existing User ID if you have previously registered for a different South-Western product via an access code.

4. When prompted, create a password (or enter an existing password, if you have previously registered for a different product via an access code.) Submit the necessary information when prompted. **Record your User ID and password in a secure location.**

5. Once registered, return to the URL above and select the "Enter" button; have your User ID and password handy.

Note: The duration of your access to the product begins when registration is complete.

For technical support, contact **1-800-423-0563** or email **support@cengage.com**.

Third Edition

Introduction to Corporate Finance

John R. Graham
Duke University

Scott B. Smart
Indiana University

SOUTH-WESTERN
CENGAGE Learning®

Australia • Brazil • Japan • Korea • Mexico • Singapore • Spain • United Kingdom • United States

![SOUTH-WESTERN CENGAGE Learning]

Introduction to Corporate Finance, Third Edition
John R. Graham and Scott B. Smart

Vice President of Editorial, Business: Jack W. Calhoun

Editor-in-Chief: Joe Sabatino

Executive Editor: Mike Reynolds

Sr. Developmental Editor: Susanna C. Smart

Sr. Editorial Assistant: Adele Scholtz

Marketing Manager: Nathan Anderson

Sr. Content Project Manager: Martha Conway

Media Editor: Scott Fidler

Manufacturing Planner: Kevin Kluck

Marketing Communications Manager: Jim Overly

Production Service: MPS Limited, a Macmillan Company

Sr. Art Director: Michelle Kunkler

Cover and Internal Designer: Jen2Design

Cover and Special Page Image: © Altus Plunkett/Flickr/Getty Images, Inc.

Rights Acquisitions Specialist: John Hill

Photo Researcher: Sara Golden, PreMedia Global

Text Permissions Researcher: Jennifer Wagner, PreMedia Global

For product information and technology assistance, contact us at
Cengage Learning Customer & Sales Support, 1-800-354-9706

For permission to use material from this text or product,
submit all requests online at **www.cengage.com/permissions**
Further permissions questions can be emailed to
permissionrequest@cengage.com

Library of Congress Control Number: 2011940952

Student Edition ISBN 13: 978-1-111-22226-0

Student Edition ISBN 10: 1-111-22226-6

Student Edition package ISBN 13: 978-1-111-22228-4

Student Edition package ISBN 10: 1-111-22228-2

South-Western
5191 Natorp Boulevard
Mason, OH 45040
USA

Cengage Learning products are represented in Canada by Nelson Education, Ltd.

For your course and learning solutions, visit **www.cengage.com**

Purchase any of our products at your local college store or at our preferred online store **www.cengagebrain.com**

Printed in the United States of America
1 2 3 4 5 6 7   15 14 13 12 11

Preface

Finance matters! All business students need to understand finance. Whether you are evaluating alternative marketing campaigns or making a new product decision, you must understand introductory finance. Likewise, in your personal life, whether you want to estimate the amount to save to buy a new car or home or want to decide whether to buy stocks, bonds, or both for your retirement account, you must understand finance.

As instructors (and former students), however, we realize that finance can be an intimidating subject, especially for students who struggle with quantitative material. Our initial goal in writing this book was to change that perception by reducing the intimidation factor and clearly communicating the excitement and relevance that finance holds for each of us.

Over the past few years we've received two types of feedback suggesting that we achieved our objective of creating an effective, user-friendly text. First, many users told us about their positive experiences with the book. Second, the book continues to experience strong and growing success in the market. Our challenge in this new third edition was to build on our earlier success and become the market-leading introductory corporate finance text. We strongly feel that this edition contains state-of-the-art pedagogy and features necessary to achieve these goals.

Distinguishing Features of the Book

This book shows students how the concepts they've learned in their prerequisite courses—like economics, statistics, and accounting—directly connect to finance. Understanding these linkages will allow them to quickly realize that *they already know more than they think they do about finance!* To help students realize the practicality of the concepts covered in this book, most chapters include one or more "Finance in Your Life" illustrations of how students might utilize key chapter ideas in their own lives. We believe that the student's grasp of the link between financial concepts and practice will be greatly improved by demonstrating how the book's key ideas might apply to the student's professional or personal lives.

Every student needs some extra explanation or support at different points in this course. Consequently, a truly outstanding technology package accompanies this book—a package that will allow students to learn and absorb material at their own pace. Computer animations review important concepts and techniques to help students re-examine complex material until they can grasp the ideas with confidence. They can view each animation as many times as needed to understand the concept or technique. Our students tell us that these animations, found at CourseMate with SmartFinance Tools at www.cengagebrain.com, are more helpful than any other single feature in the book.

Students can also visit the Smart Finance Web site to view nearly 100 video clips of finance professionals and scholars, each of whom contributes to the picture of just how often financial issues affect today's world.

Core Principles and Features

To accomplish our goal of making this the most effective, student-friendly introductory finance textbook in the market today, we followed five core principles when writing and revising the text and designing its support package.

1. **Pique student interest and demonstrate the relevance of important concepts and techniques.** We feel that it's important to begin each chapter with a recent practical illustration that stimulates student interest in the chapter. Every chapter of this book begins with a story pulled from recent headlines that illustrates a key chapter concept in an applied setting.

   In order to make it clear to students that the concepts and techniques presented in this text are not merely academic abstractions, but rather are used by practicing CFOs, we have included in most chapters a feature called "What CFOs Do." This feature summarizes survey findings that disclose the preferences of and methods used by practicing CFOs. It adds reality to the student's learning experience by providing insight into how senior financial executives apply many of the concepts and techniques that are presented throughout the text.

   We also strive to provide students with a smooth bridge between concepts and practice by including demonstrations that are simply labeled "EXAMPLE." These illustrations, many of which use real data from well-known companies, take concepts and make them easy to understand within an interesting and relevant context.

2. **Maximize the pedagogical and motivational value of technology.** We have often experimented with technology packaged with textbooks only to find that the included products somehow impeded learning and classroom delivery rather than facilitated student interest and understanding. At times, the mental investment required to learn enough about text technology has canceled out students' ability to absorb the most important finance concepts. In other cases, students have focused too much on what a particular technology *can* do, rather than what it *should* do. Some technology add-ons, created by subcontractors rather than the text's primary authors, seem to have borne almost no relationship to the text they were meant to support. And, of course, all too often a technology that we wanted to use inside or outside of the classroom simply hasn't worked.

   With such experiences behind us, we wanted to develop an integrated technology package that engages, motivates, and at times entertains students, while helping them master financial concepts on their own time and at their own pace. We wanted to use technology to allow students to hear firsthand about exciting developments in financial research. We wanted students to hear from business professionals why the material contained in the text is relevant after the final exam is over. Most of all, as authors of the text, we wanted to take primary responsibility for creating the technology package to ensure that we seamlessly integrated technology with the text's most important concepts and techniques.

   Tests with in-residence and online students have generated almost unanimous praise for these features. In fact, the most common complaint we have heard from students is, "Why can't we see more of this?" Visit CourseMate with SmartFinance Tools at www.cengagebrain.com to see a sample of the rich content that students can access on the Smart Finance Web site. Access to the Smart Finance Web site is available to students at no additional cost with each new text. Some examples of the fully integrated technology include:

   - **Animated Review Tutorials** that explain key concepts;
   - **Problem-Solving Animations** that illustrate numerical solution methods as well as develop students' problem-solving intuition; and

- **Video Clips** of well-known American and international academics and finance practitioners that illustrate the conceptual bases of theory, concepts in practice, and ethical issues that financial professionals routinely face.

3. **Provide a truly global perspective.** The economic world is shrinking—particularly with regard to financial transactions. Formerly centrally planned economies are moving toward market economies. Many developing nations are making rapid economic progress using markets-based methods. Financial markets play an increasingly important role in the ongoing globalization of business and finance. Rather than grouping international issues into a chapter or two, we have integrated a global perspective throughout the text. Every chapter has a unique feature that we call "What Companies Do Globally" designed to highlight similarities and differences among corporate finance practices around the world.

4. **Consider students' prerequisites and connect the courses they have taken to finance.** Experienced financial managers consistently tell us that they need people who can see the big picture and who can recognize connections across functional disciplines. To help students develop a larger sense of what finance is about, why it is relevant to their business studies, and to ease their transition into their own chosen fields, we highlight concepts that most students learn in their introductory economics, statistics, and accounting courses. We then connect these concepts to finance.

5. **Help students prepare for finance-related job interview questions.** We expect that most students taking this course will eventually enter the job market. To help them prepare for job interviews, throughout the text we have included in the margin near the related discussion, two different kinds of financially-focused job interview questions. Those questions labeled "? Job Interview QUESTION" were shared with us by both the recruiters who ask the questions and students confronted by them, and are intended to help students see that firms expect them to apply financial concepts that they have learned. The second type of question, labeled "? What to ASK," are questions that an interested job candidate can ask during an interview in order to learn how a firm operates and subtly convey her interest in the firm. Not only will these questions help students interview well, but they also serve the purpose of motivating students to master the related material.

Several video clips early in the book also emphasize connections between finance and other disciplines. Beginning with what students know and building on that foundation allows us to use an approach that we have used successfully in our own teaching for many years. We wanted our book to reflect that teaching philosophy.

Additional Learning Enhancements

Thomson ONE—Business School Edition Problems: Thomson ONE-BSE is an online database that draws from the industry-leading Thomson Financial's data sources, including Disclosure, Datastream, and Securities Data Corporation databases. Analysts and other finance professionals use this tool every day to conduct research. To help motivate students to perform basic research and analysis without creating extra work for the instructor, the authors have written end-of-chapter problems that require students to use Thomson ONE-BSE.

Learning Objectives highlight the key ideas of each chapter; they appear at the beginning of each chapter.

Concept Review Questions conclude each section within chapters and test students' retention of material. These Concept Review Questions tie directly to the learning objectives that open the chapters.

Major Content Improvements

Based on reviewer and user feedback along with our own experience using the Second Edition, we made numerous content improvements aimed at enhancing the text pedagogy, smoothing out and streamlining many discussions, updating all data and discussions in response to economic, institutional, and regulatory changes, and seamlessly incorporating the many new features noted earlier. We made sure that relevant discussions accurately capture the impact of the recent financial crisis on important corporate finance decisions. The key areas receiving greatest attention were:

- Capital Structure–Consistent with survey evidence indicating that capital structure is the finance function that adds the most value to the firm, we devoted a lot of attention to improving Chapter 12 on capital structure. The chapter has been restructured to compactly describe the traditional and new approaches to capital structure.
- Payout Policy–Chapter 14 on payout policy was revised to reflect the latest thinking on dividend and stock repurchase decisions as reflected in recent CFO surveys related to these decisions.
- Investment Banking–The discussion of investment banking in Chapter 11 on raising long-term financing captures the impact of the recent upheaval in the investment banking industry in its description of how the industry currently operates.

Text Supplements

Instructor's Manual Revised by Jana Cook of Oklahoma Christian University, this comprehensive Instructor's Manual is designed to support novice instructors and finance veterans alike, and includes chapter overviews, lecture guides organized by section, enrichment exercises, answers to concept review questions, answers to end-of-chapter questions, and solutions for end-of-chapter problems.

Test Bank Revised by R. Daniel Pace, University of West Florida, the Test Bank has been expanded for this edition. In addition, each question includes AACSB competency designation.

ExamView ExamView Computerized Testing Software contains all of the questions in the printed test bank. This program is an easy-to-use test creation software compatible with Microsoft Windows®. Instructors can add or edit questions, instructions, and answers and select questions randomly, by number, or by previewing them on screen. Instructors can also create and administer quizzes online, whether over the Internet, a local area network (LAN), or a wide area network (WAN).

PowerPoint Slides PowerPoint slides, revised by Peggy Ward of Wichita State University, are available for instructors for enhancing their lectures. They are available as downloads from the product support Web site at www.cengage.com/finance/graham.

Instructor's Resource CD-ROM (IRCD) A CD-ROM is available to instructors and contains electronic versions of all print instructor supplements—Instructor's Manual, Test Bank in Microsoft Word and in ExamView, and PowerPoint slides.

Product Support Website at www.cengage.com/finance/graham Access to the Web site and study tools is available to students at no additional cost with each new text. Some examples of the integrated technology materials include:

- Smart Concepts. These animated concept review tutorials, organized by chapter, explain key topics step by step, offering students opportunities to review more difficult chapter material at their own pace and at convenient times. Students can also decide how much or what parts of the review they want to cover. An icon in the text directs students to CourseMate with SmartFinance Tools at www.cengagebrain.com to explore.

- **Smart Solutions.** The Smart Solutions feature helps improve students' problem-solving skills by demonstrating animated solution steps and offering coaching about how to identify the right technique to apply to particular problems. An icon in the text directs students to CourseMate with SmartFinance Tools at www.cengagebrain.com to explore Smart Solutions.

- **Smart Ideas Videos.** Introduce your students to the leading academic researchers behind the theory or concepts you are discussing in class with Smart Ideas Videos. Each clip runs approximately two to three minutes. Video clips feature John Graham (Duke University), Robert Schiller (Yale), Elroy Dimson (London School of Business), Andrew Karolyi (Ohio State University), Kenneth French (Dartmouth College), and many, many more. An icon in the text directs students to CourseMate with SmartFinance Tools at www.cengagebrain.com to view these short video clips, which instructors can also embed in their PowerPoint presentations.

- **Smart Practices Videos.** Business and industry leaders discuss how they maximize their companies' financial performance using cutting-edge practices. These videos can help show students why corporate finance is a vital topic regardless of their functional areas. Presidents and CFOs of major corporations, such as Andy Bryant, CFO of Intel Corp., as well as corporate recruiters, are featured interviewees. An icon in the text directs students to CourseMate with SmartFinance Tools at www.cengagebrain.com, or instructors can embed these 2- to 3-minute video clips within their PowerPoint lectures.

- **Smart Ethics Videos.** These videos show how both academics and business executives view ethics and the impact that ethical or unethical behavior can have on the company's bottom line. An icon in the text directs students to CourseMate with SmartFinance Tools at www.cengagebrain.com to view these clips, or instructors can embed these 2- to 3-minute video clips within their PowerPoint presentations.

- **Smart Quizzing.** The Smart Finance Web site provides true/false and multiple-choice quiz questions for each chapter to test student knowledge.

Aplia™ for Finance! The best-selling homework solution in education today, Aplia is trusted by more than 600,000 students at over 700 institutions worldwide. **Aplia for Finance** offers an online homework system that improves learning by increasing student effort and engagement—without requiring more work from the instructor. Aplia's original, auto-graded finance assignments ensure that students grasp the skills and concepts presented in the text through interactive problem sets, news analyses, tutorials in math, accounting, statistics, economics, and financial calculators. Visit www.aplia.com for a full **Aplia for Finance** demonstration online.

CengageNOW™ Designed by instructors for instructors, **CengageNOW** mirrors your natural workflow and provides time-saving, performance-enhancing tools for you and your students—all in one program!

CengageNOW takes the best of current technology tools including online homework management, fully customizable algorithmic end-of-chapter problems and test bank, and course management.

- **Plan** student assignments with an easy online homework management component
- **Manage** your grade book with ease
- **Teach** today's student using valuable course support materials
- **Reinforce** student comprehension with Personalized Study
- **Test** with customizable algorithmic end-of-chapter problems and test bank
- **Grade** automatically for seamless, immediate results

This powerful, fully integrated online teaching and learning system provides you with the ultimate in flexibility, ease of use, and efficient paths to success to deliver the results you want—NOW!

THOMSON REUTERS | Business School Edition

Do you want to bring concepts to life with real data? Do you assign research projects? Would you like your students to conduct research on the Internet? Thomson ONE-Business School Edition meets all of these needs! This tool gives students the opportunity to use a business school version of an Internet-based database that financial analysts and professionals around the world use every day. Relevant chapters include problems specifically for use with Thomson ONE-BSE so that your students find answers in real time. Thomson ONE-BSE includes access to 10-year financial statements downloadable to Excel; one-click Peer Set analysis; indices that students can manipulate or compare; and data for international, as well as domestic, companies. This resource is included FREE with each new text. See http://tobsefin.swlearning.com for more information, including an animated demonstration.

Textbook Web Site Instructors can find electronic resources, including the Test Bank, Instructor's Manual, and PowerPoint lecture slides, at www.cengage.com/finance/graham, and students can link to CourseMate with SmartFinance Tools at www.cengagebrain.com.

Acknowledgments

Most people realize that creating a textbook is a collaborative venture. What only authors can truly appreciate is just how many people are involved in planning, writing, editing, producing, and launching a new book. In the paragraphs that follow, we thank the many people who have made significant contributions to this book. Although only two people are listed as authors on the title page, we wish to acknowledge the debt we owe to those who have worked so closely with us. We are forever grateful to Bill Megginson for his numerous significant contributions to the first two editions of this book. Much of Bill's work is woven into the fabric of this book.

We thank the people at Cengage Learning who pushed us to deliver a top-quality product. This list includes Joe Sabatino, Editor-in-Chief; Mike Reynolds, Executive Editor; and Martha Conway for her patience and professionalism as Content Project Manager. Nate Anderson deserves special thanks for his marketing efforts. We would especially like to thank our Senior Developmental Editor, Susanna Smart, for managing the difficult task of coordinating authors and supplement contributors, essential to the successful completion of a textbook package of this magnitude.

Several people made written contributions to the book and its supplements. We are particularly grateful to Lance Nail, David Whidbee, John Yeoman, Dubos Masson, and Richard Shockley for their written contributions to specific chapters.

Technology is an extremely important part of this book, and we wish to express our deep appreciation to Cengage Learning for their financial and professional support. In particular, we have been honored to work with a technical professional as competent and supportive as Scott Fidler. Many other people have also contributed to creating what we believe to be an outstanding technology package. This list begins with Jack Koning, who made truly amazing contributions in developing the flash animations, and Don Mitchell, whose audio work made the animations come to life. Deryl Dale, Candace Decker, Rebecca Loftin, Neil Charles, Murray McGibbon, Andrew Ellul, Anne Kibler, Doug Hoffman, and Richard Fish all contributed their voices to the animations, and Rebecca Barrett and Joy Hudyma helped create the text's graphics.

Though it would be nice to pretend that our skills as authors are so advanced that we did not have to make repeated passes at writing the chapters you see today, in fact this book has benefited immeasurably from the feedback we have received from reviewers. We would like to thank the following people for their insightful comments and constructive criticism of the text:

Michael H. Anderson
University of Massachusetts, Dartmouth
Tom Arnold
University of Richmond
Thomas Bates
University of Delaware
Gary Benesh
Florida State University
Mark Bertus
Auburn University
Vigdis Boasson
Ithaca College
Elizabeth Booth
Michigan State University

William Chittenden
Texas State University
Alex Deshkovski
University of North Carolina, Chapel Hill
Amy Dittmar
University of Michigan
Scott Ehrhorn
Liberty University
Kathy Fogel
Northern Kentucky University
Jennifer Foo
Stetson University
Gary Gray
Penn State University

Andrea Hueson
University of Miami, Florida
M. Zafar Iqbal
Cal Poly U San Luis Obispo
John W. Kensinger
University of North Texas
Kenneth Kim
SUNY at Buffalo
Chun Lee
Loyola-Marymount
Wendell Licon
Arizona State University

Nathaniel Manning
  Southern University at Shreveport
Terry Nixon
  Miami University, Ohio
Jonatan Jelen
  Parsons The New School for Design
Christopher Pope
  University of Georgia
Amy V. Puelz
  Southern Methodist University
Robert Puelz
  Southern Methodist University

Andreas Rauterkus
  Siena College
Todd Roberson
  Indiana University, Indianapolis
Jim Robinson
  University of Wyoming
Adina Schwartz
  Lakeland College
John Stansfield
  University of Missouri
Stanford Storey
  University of California, Irvine

Michael J. Sullivan
  University of Nevada, Las Vegas
Brian Tarrant
  Central Michigan University
Noemy Wachtel
  Kean University
J. George Wang
  Staten Island College
Ata Yesilyaprak
  Columbus State University
Jean Yu
  Oakland University

A key feature of our book is that we integrate video clips of academics and finance professionals throughout the text. The following academics provided critical contributions to this text by explaining their important contributions to modern financial thought. Our interviews with them appear in SMART IDEAS videos and SMART ETHICS videos:

Anup Agrawal
  University of Alabama
Franklin Allen
  University of Pennsylvania
Ed Altman
  New York University
Utpal Bhattacharya
  Indiana University
James Brickley
  University of Rochester
Robert Bruner
  University of Virginia
Jennifer Conrad
  University of North Carolina
Francesca Cornelli
  London Business School
Claire Crutchley
  Auburn University
David Denis
  University of Pittsburgh
Diane Denis
  University of Pittsburgh
Elroy Dimson
  London Business School
Kenneth Eades
  The University of Virginia
Ben Esty
  Harvard University
Kenneth French
  Dartmouth College
Jon Garfinkel
  University of Iowa

Tim Jenkinson
  Oxford University
Steven Kaplan
  University of Chicago
Andrew Karolyi
  Cornell University
Laurie Krigman
  Babson College
Scott Lee
  Texas A&M University
Ike Mathur
  Southern Illinois University at Carbondale
David Mauer
  University of Texas at Dallas
William Megginson
  University of Oklahoma
Chris Muscarella
  Penn State University
Mitchell Petersen
  Northwestern University
Mike Pinegar
  Brigham Young University
Annette Poulsen
  University of Georgia
Manju Puri
  Duke University
Raghu Rajan
  University of Chicago
Bruce Resnick
  Wake Forest University

Jay Ritter
  University of Florida
Antoinette Schoar
  MIT
Myron Scholes
  Stanford University and Chairman of Oak Hill Platinum Partners
Lemma Senbet
  University of Maryland
William Sharpe
  Stanford University and cofounder of Financial Engines
Robert Shiller
  Yale University
Betty Simkins
  Oklahoma State University
Laura Starks
  University of Texas
Anjan Thakor
  Washington University, St. Louis
Sheridan Titman
  University of Texas
Greg Udell
  Indiana University
Theo Vermaelen
  INSEAD
Rohan Williamson
  Georgetown University
Kent Womack
  University of Toronto

We are also grateful to the following individuals who shared their insights based on their experience practicing corporate finance. Our interviews with them appear in SMART PRACTICES videos and SMART ETHICS videos.

Beth Acton
Vice President and Treasurer (former), Ford Motor Company, currently Chief Financial Officer, Comerica

David Baum
Co-head of M&A for the Americas, Goldman Sachs

Andy Bryant
Executive Vice President, Chief Administrative Officer, Intel Corp.

Beverly Caen
Vice President (former), Instinet Corporation

Daniel T. Carter
Vice President of Finance, BevMo!

David Childress
Asset Liability Manager (former), Ford Motor Co.

Tom Cole
Leveraged Finance Group, Deutsche Bank

John Eck
President of Broadcast and Network Operations, NBC

Bill Eckmann
Investment Banker

Jay Goodgold
Managing Director, Equities Division, Goldman Sachs

David Haeberle
Chief Executive Officer, Command Equity Group

Joshua Haines
Senior Credit Analyst, The Private Bank

Jeff Kauffman
Portfolio Manager, Managing Director, Omega Advisors

Vern LoForti
VP, CFO, & Corporate Secretary, InfoSonics

David Nickel
Controller, Intel Communications Group, Intel Corp.

Jon Olson
Vice President of Finance (former), Intel Corp, currently Chief Financial Officer, Xilinx Corp.

Frank Popoff
Chairman of the Board (retired), Dow Chemical

Todd Richter
Managing Director, Head of Equity Healthcare Research, Bank of America Securities

Pam Roberts
Executive Director of Corporate Services, Cummins Inc.

Paul Savastano
Director of Information Technology, Sprint Corp.

Jackie Sturm
Director of Finance for Technology and Manufacturing, Intel Corp.

Keith Woodward
Vice President of Finance, General Mills

Last, but certainly not least, the authors wish to thank their families and friends who provided invaluable support and assistance. Finally, Suzanne Graham and Susan Smart deserve special thanks for their love and support throughout the long process of creating this book.

September 15, 2011

John Graham
D. Richard Mead Professor of Finance
The Fuqua School of Business
Duke University

Scott Smart
Eli Lilly Finance Faculty Fellow
Department of Finance
Kelley School of Business
Indiana University

About the Authors

John R. Graham is the D. Richard Mead Professor of Finance at Duke University where he also serves as the Director of the CFO Global Business Outlook survey. He is coeditor of the Journal of Finance and has published more than four dozen scholarly articles in journals such as the Journal of Financial Economics, the Review of Financial Studies, the Journal of Finance, the Journal of Accounting and Economics, and many others. His papers have won multiple research awards, including the Jensen Prize for the best corporate finance paper published in the Journal of Financial Economics and the Brattle prize for the best corporate finance paper in the Journal of Finance. Professor Graham is also a Research Associate with the National Bureau of Economic Research, Vice President of the Western Finance Association, and has been recognized for outstanding teaching and faculty contributions at Duke and the University of Utah.

Scott B. Smart is the Whirlpool Finance Faculty Fellow at the Kelley School of Business at Indiana University. He has published articles in scholarly journals such as the Journal of Finance, the Journal of Financial Economics, the Journal of Accounting and Economics, the Accounting Review, and the Review of Economics and Statistics. His research has been cited by the Wall Street Journal, The Economist, Business Week, and other major newspapers and periodicals. Professor Smart holds a Ph.D. from Stanford University and has been recognized as a master teacher, winning more than a dozen teaching awards. Some of his many consulting clients include Intel and Unext.

Brief Contents

Contents

3 **The Time Value of Money 66**

PART 2 VALUATION, RISK, AND RETURN 113

4 Valuing Bonds 114

5   Valuing Stocks   150

6   The Trade-Off Between Risk and Return   180

Smart Ideas Video

Andrew Karolyi, Cornell University p221

William Sharpe, Stanford University, Co-founder, Financial Engines p225

Smart Practices Video

Todd Richter, Managing Director, Head of Equity Healthcare Research, Bank of America Securities p228

SMART concepts p220
SMART concepts p226
SMART concepts p228

Smart Practices Video

Daniel Carter, Vice President of Finance, BevMo! p245

Chris Muscarella, Professor of Finance and L.W. 'Roy' and Mary Lois Clark Teaching Fellow, Pennsylvania State University p249

Beth Acton, Vice President and Treasurer of Ford Motor Co. (former) p264

SMART concepts p263
SMART solutions p273
SMART solutions p277

12 Capital Structure 370

Smart Ideas Video

Annette Poulsen, University of Georgia p403

Benjamin Esty, Harvard University p407

Ed Altman, New York University p412

Smart Ethics Video

Scott Lee, Texas A&M University p437

Smart Ideas Video

John Graham, Duke University p438

Kenneth Eades, University of Virginia p449

Smart Practices Video

Andy Bryant, Executive Vice President of Finance and Enterprise Systems, Chief Financial Officer, Intel Corp. p438

Cynthia Lucchese, Chief Financial Officer, Hillenbrand Industries p439

Frank Popoff, Chairman of the Board (retired), Dow Chemical p448

SMART concepts p442

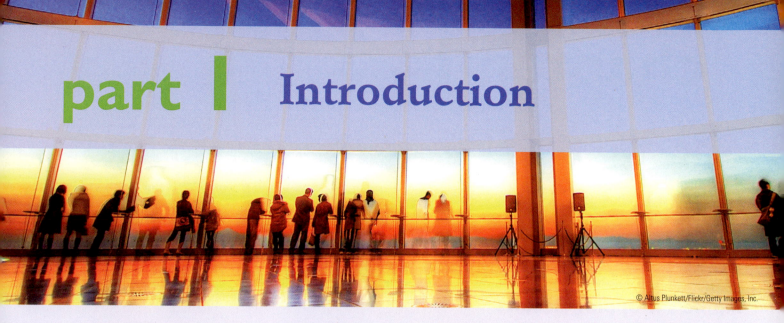
© Altus Plunkett/Flickr/Getty Images, Inc.

part 1 Introduction

Welcome to the study of *corporate finance*. In this book, you will learn the key concepts, tools, and practices that guide the decisions of financial managers. Our goal is not only to introduce you to corporate finance, but also to help you explore career opportunities in this exciting field.

Chapter 1 describes the roles that corporate finance experts play in a variety of businesses and industries. Most of what corporate finance professionals do involves one or more of the five basic functions described in the chapter. As you progress through your finance course, occasionally looking back at the five functions will help you understand how the various topics covered in this textbook fit together.

It has been said that accounting is the language of business, and it is certainly true that financial managers need to master accounting concepts and principles to do their jobs well. Chapter 2 offers a broad overview of the most important sources of accounting information: firms' financial statements. Our focus in this chapter is not on how accountants construct these statements (we leave that to your accounting professors). Instead, our goal is to illustrate how these statements serve as inputs to financial decisions and why finance emphasizes cash flow rather than earnings. We also demonstrate how companies can use financial-statement information to track their performance over time and to benchmark their results against those of other firms.

Chapter 3 introduces the time value of money, one of the most fundamental concepts in finance. Simply put, a dollar today is worth more than a dollar in the future. That's because a dollar invested today will grow to more than a dollar in the future. Managers need tools that allow them to make appropriate comparisons between costs and benefits that, in most business situations, are spread out over time. For example, a firm spends $1 million today to purchase an asset that will generate a stream of cash receipts of $225,000 over the next several years. Do the benefits of this investment outweigh its costs, or are the costs too high to justify making this investment? Chapter 3 explains how managers can make valid cost/benefit comparisons when cash flows occur at different times and using different interest rates.

chapter 1

The Scope of Corporate Finance

What Companies Do

Apple's iPopping Results

On July 19, 2011, Apple® Inc. announced its financial results for the third quarter of its 2011 fiscal year. The company posted revenue of $28.6 billion and a net quarterly profit of $7.3 billion, both new record highs. Compared to the same quarter in 2010, Apple's revenues were up 82% and profits increased 125%. The quarter's financial results were driven by sales of 3.95 million Mac computers, 20.34 million iPhones, 7.54 million iPods, and 9.25 million iPads.

Stories in the popular press tend to focus on the success of Apple's products. However, financial managers behind the scenes at Apple played a number of crucial roles in driving the success of the business. For example, prior to the iPad's launch, financial experts at Apple evaluated the potential market for such a device, estimated the cost of producing it, and calculated the unit volume that the company would have to achieve to earn a satisfactory rate of return. Because components of the iPad and other Apple devices are made abroad, financial managers in Apple's Treasury department developed a plan to manage the risks that Apple would confront when making transactions in foreign currencies. In this chapter, we explain how financial specialists interact with experts in fields as diverse as engineering, marketing, communications, and law to help companies create wealth for their shareholders. We describe the types of activities that occupy financial managers day to day, and highlight some of the most promising career opportunities for students who major in finance. The work that financial analysts do is intellectually challenging, as well as economically rewarding. We hope our overview of the field piques your interest and inspires you to learn more.

Sources: Apple Inc. Website (www.apple.com), 10-Q released on July 19, 2011. www.apple.com/pr/library/2011/07/19Apple-Reports-Third-Quarter-Results.html.

Learning Objectives

After studying this chapter, you will be able to:

- Appreciate how finance interacts with other functional areas of any business and see the diverse career opportunities available to finance majors.

- Describe how companies obtain funding from financial intermediaries and markets, and discuss the five basic functions that financial managers perform.

- Assess the costs and benefits of the three principal forms of business organization and explain why limited liability companies, with publicly traded shares, dominate economic life in most countries.

- Define agency costs and explain how shareholders monitor and encourage corporate managers to maximize shareholder wealth.

1-1 The Role of Corporate Finance in Business

Apple's recent history illustrates the positive results of good management in a highly competitive, technology-driven industry. It also reflects favorably on the vital role that financial managers play in creating wealth. Business involves people with many different skills and backgrounds working together toward common goals. Financial experts play a major role in achieving these goals and in creating value for the firm's shareholders.

This book focuses on the practicing financial manager who is a key player in the management team of a modern corporation. Throughout this text, we highlight one simple question that managers should ask when contemplating all business decisions: Does this action create value for the shareholders? **By taking actions that generate benefits in excess of costs, firms generate wealth for their investors.** Clearly, managers should take only those actions in which the benefits exceed the costs.

Cengage Learning

Tom Cole, Managing Director of Leveraged Finance, Citigroup

"To be good at finance you have to understand how businesses work."

See the entire interview at **SMART|finance**

Smart Practices Video

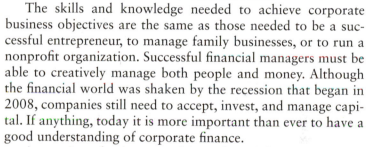

The skills and knowledge needed to achieve corporate business objectives are the same as those needed to be a successful entrepreneur, to manage family businesses, or to run a nonprofit organization. Successful financial managers must be able to creatively manage both people and money. Although the financial world was shaken by the recession that began in 2008, companies still need to accept, invest, and manage capital. If anything, today it is more important than ever to have a good understanding of corporate finance.

As an introduction to what a financial manager's job entails, the next section discusses how various functional disciplines interact with financial managers, and it describes the kinds of jobs that people with financial training generally take.

1-1a How Finance Interacts with Other Functional Business Areas

Financial professionals interact with experts in a wide range of disciplines to operate successful businesses. Working with Apple's engineers, designers, and marketers, financial managers analyzed the business potential of the iPad. Financial managers:

- Studied the opportunity and competition in the market for mobile media and computing devices;
- Evaluated the costs of producing, marketing, and distributing iPads;
- Analyzed the potential demand for the iPad;
- Used the above information to develop a pricing strategy consistent with sales projections and the creation of value for shareholders; and
- Made recommendations to the firm's top management regarding the financial viability of iPads.

In sum, although Apple's iPad was primarily a marketing- and technology-driven product, the firm's financial organization played pivotal roles in every stage of the product's life cycle—from the initial assessment and funding of research, through the initial product launch, to the management of cash flows generated by iPad sales. In all of these activities, Apple's financial analysts worked with people in other functional areas to gather the data needed to analyze the iPad's financial impact. So, in many ways, corporate finance helps make innovative technology possible.

Cengage Learning

Joshua Haines, Senior Credit Analyst, The Private Bank

"Most of the basic finance concepts that I learned in my first finance class I still use today."

See the entire interview at **SMART** | finance

Smart Practices Video

1-1b Career Opportunities in Finance

This section briefly surveys career opportunities in finance. Though different jobs require different specialized skills, financial professionals employ the same basic tools of corporate finance, whether they work for Internet startups, in industrial corporations, on Wall Street, or in the offices of a commercial bank or life insurance company. Three other skills that virtually all finance jobs require are:

- Good written and verbal communication skills
- An ability to work in teams
- Proficiency with computers and the Internet

Additionally, for an increasing number of finance jobs, managers need an in-depth knowledge of international business to achieve career success.

We classify finance career opportunities as follows[1]:

- Corporate finance
- Commercial banking
- Investment banking
- Money management
- Consulting

Typical U.S. business graduates who major in finance can expect average starting salaries of $40,000 to $60,000 per year (or more), depending upon their academic credentials and the industry in which they begin their careers.[2] The exact salary you can attain will depend not only on the economic environment but also on your personal negotiating skills and how well you master the knowledge that we present in this text.

Corporate Finance *Corporate finance* is concerned with the duties of financial managers in business. These professionals handle the financial affairs of many types of businesses—financial and nonfinancial, private and public, large and small, profit seeking and not-for-profit. They perform such varied tasks as budgeting, financial forecasting, cash management, credit administration, investment analysis, and funds procurement. In recent years, changing economic and regulatory environments have increased the importance and complexity of the financial manager's duties. The globalization of business has also increased demand for people who can assess and manage the risks associated with volatile exchange rates and rapidly changing political environments. Table 1.1 summarizes primary activities of various corporate finance positions.

---

[1]The basic job descriptions and duties are generally taken from the online resource *Careers in Finance* (www.careers-in-finance.com) and other career Web sites such as Monster.com (www.monster.com) that highlight the finance profession. Students seeking more detailed descriptions of the varying careers open to finance graduates, as well as in-depth analyses of the specific jobs and responsibilities of different positions, should join the Financial Management Association and obtain a copy of the paperback book titled *Careers in Finance* (Financial Management Association International: Tampa, Florida, 2003).

[2]Detailed starting salary information for graduates with a bachelor's degree in business administration (BBA) is available at various Web sites, including *Careers in Finance* (www.careers-in-finance.com), Careers.com (www.careers.com), the *Wall Street Journal* (www.careerjournal.com), *Jobs in the Money* (www.jobsinthemoney.com), and *Wage Access Compensation Survey* (www.wageaccess.com/start_page.asp).

Table 1.1

Career Opportunities in Corporate Finance

Position	Primary Activities
Financial analyst	Prepares and analyzes the firm's financial plans and budgets.
Capital budgeting manager	Evaluates and recommends proposed asset investments.
Cash manager	Maintains and controls the firm's cash flow and short-term investments.
Project finance manager	Arranges financing for approved asset investments.
Credit analyst/manager	Analyzes and manages all aspects of the firm's credit-granting activities.
Treasurer	Oversees all financial management activities.
Controller	Manages all aspects of the firm's accounting activities.
Chief Financial Officer (CFO)	Develops financial policies and strategies and oversees the activities of the Treasurer and Controller.

© Cengage Learning 2012

chief financial officer (CFO)
Top management position charged with developing financial policies and strategies covering all aspects of a firm's financial management and accounting activities.

Commercial Banking Commercial banking in the United States has consolidated rapidly, with the total number of banks shrinking from over 14,400 in 1980 to 6,369 at the end of the first quarter of 2011. Nonetheless, banks continue to hire large numbers of new business and finance graduates each year, and banking remains a fertile training ground for managers who later migrate to other fields. The key aptitudes required in most entry-level banking jobs are the same as in other areas. In addition to communication, people, computer, and international skills, apprentice bankers must master cash flow valuation, as well as financial and credit analysis.

Most commercial banks offer at least two basic career tracks: consumer or commercial banking. *Consumer banking* serves the financial needs of a bank's individual customers in its branch network, increasingly via electronic media such as the Internet. *Commercial banking*, on the other hand, involves extending credit and other banking services to corporate clients, ranging from small, family-owned businesses to *Fortune 500* behemoths. In addition, a great many technologically intensive support positions in banking require excellent finance skills and intimate knowledge of telecommunications and computer technology. Table 1.2 describes career opportunities in commercial banking.

Investment Banking Along with consulting, investment banking is the career of choice for many highly qualified finance students because of its high income potential

Table 1.2

Career Opportunities in Commercial Banking

Position	Primary Activities
Credit analyst	Analyzes the creditworthiness of corporate and individual loan applicants.
Corporate loan officer	Develops new loan business for the bank, makes loan recommendations, and services existing loans.
Branch manager	Manages personnel and operation of a bank branch and markets bank services to attract new depositors and borrowers.
Trust officer	Provides investment, tax, and estate advice and products to wealthy bank customers.
Mortgage banker	Originates and services mortgage loans to homebuyers and businesses.
Leasing manager	Manages banks' equipment-leasing operations and develops related products and services.
Operations officer	Responsible for a number of possible activities, such as electronic banking, internal data processing, security of electronic transactions, and coordination of computer links to ATMs, other banks, and the Federal Reserve Bank.

© Cengage Learning 2012

and the interesting nature of the work. *Investment banking* involves three main types of activities:

- Helping corporate customers obtain funding by selling securities, such as stocks and bonds, to investors
- Providing advice to corporate clients on strategic transactions, such as mergers and acquisitions
- Trading debt and equity securities for customers or for the firm's own account

Except during the recent financial crisis, investment banking has been extraordinarily profitable since the early 1990s, and the top firms (J. P. Morgan Chase, Bank of America, Morgan Stanley, Goldman Sachs, Citigroup, Barclays, Credit Suisse, Deutche Bank, and a few others) have a global presence. It remains a highly volatile industry. For example, from October 2007 to November 2008, Goldman Sachs' stock price lost three quarters of its value, an experience shared by most of the large U.S. investment banks. Investment banking is also notorious for being extremely competitive and for demanding long working hours from its professionals (especially the junior ones).

Bill Eckmann, Principal, Solar Capital

"Besides finance, there are three subject areas that have really helped me at the beginning of my career in investment banking."

See the entire interview at **SMART | finance**

Smart Practices Video

Investment banking offers lucrative rewards for those who master the game. Most undergraduates hired by investment banks are assigned duties as financial analysts. Starting salaries for entry-level analyst positions range from $60,000 to more than $75,000, plus signing bonuses of $10,000 or more and performance bonuses that, for highly ranked analysts, might equal their base salaries in a good year. Employees who advance in the investment banking business find that their incomes often rise rapidly. Success in this industry demands good analytical and communication skills, while social and networking skills also pay handsome dividends. Much of the growth in investment banking over the foreseeable future is likely to come from two sources: the ongoing development of new financial products and services, and the continued internationalization of corporate finance.

Money Management The 1980s and 1990s were very good for stock market investors and finance professionals employed in the money management industry, but working in that industry has been challenging over the last decade due to a highly volatile market that has produced very low returns on average. This industry includes investment advisory firms, mutual fund companies, pension fund managers, trust departments of commercial banks, and the investment arms of insurance companies. In fact, the money management industry encompasses any person or institution that acts as a fiduciary—a person who invests and manages money on another's behalf.

Two powerful trends have during recent years created a rapidly growing demand for money management services in the United States and other industrialized countries. First, the baby boomers (those born between 1946 and 1964) have entered their peak earning years and are beginning to invest large sums to prepare for retirement. Because many baby boomers lack the financial expertise to handle their own finances, the demand for professional money managers has surged.

The second major force fueling the growth of the money management industry has been the *institutionalization of investment*. Whereas in the past individuals held most financial assets (especially common stocks), today institutional investors dominate the markets. Of course, these money managers are not the owners of the securities they invest in, but they do hold securities and make investment decisions for their clients. This trend toward professional management of institutionally held financial assets continues to create employment opportunities in the money management industry. Table 1.3 describes career opportunities in money management.

Consulting Management consulting jobs are highly prized by business school graduates. Consultants are hired by companies to analyze firms' business problems, processes, and strategies, to make and, possibly, to implement associated recommendations.

fiduciary
A person who invests and manages money on another's behalf.

? WHAT TO ASK

What day-to-day tasks do you assign to your junior financial analysts? What opportunities for advancement are available to those who perform well in their first two years?

Table 1.3

Career Opportunities in Money Management

Position	Primary Activities
Securities analyst	Prepares company-specific and industry-wide analyses and recommendations for various classes of publicly traded securities (especially common stock and bonds).
Portfolio management, sales	Markets mutual fund shares to individual and/or institutional investors.
Portfolio manager	Selects financial assets for inclusion in portfolios designed to meet specific investment objectives (growth, income, international, emerging market bonds).
Pension fund manager	Manages assets held by a pension fund by diversifying them, allocating them to investment managers, and controlling administrative costs.
Financial planner	Provides budgeting, tax, borrowing, insurance, investment, retirement planning, and estate planning advice to individuals.
Investment adviser	Provides investment advice, performance evaluation, and quantitative analysis services to both the money management industry and wealthy individual investors.

© Cengage Learning 2012

Consulting positions offer a unique opportunity early in your career to work with a broad range of businesses on a wide range of issues, and compensation in this industry often rivals pay in the investment banking field. The nature of the work means that consultants can expect to spend much of their time on the road.

You can establish a rewarding and satisfying finance career using the corporate finance concepts, tools, and practices covered in this text. In the next section, we answer the question: What basic concepts are involved in the financial management of a corporation?

1-1 Concept Review Questions

1. Think of another company or product besides Apple's iPad, and note that company's connections between other functional areas and finance.

2. List and briefly describe five main career paths open to finance graduates.

1-2 Corporate Finance Essentials

In this section, we present several basic concepts involved in managing a corporation's finances. We begin with a discussion of the five basic corporate finance functions that managers perform, then describe debt and equity, the two principal types of long-term funding used by business, and conclude with a brief discussion of the role of financial intermediaries in corporate finance.

1-2a The Five Basic Corporate Finance Functions

corporate finance
The activities involved in managing cash (money) that flows through a business.

Although corporate finance is defined generally as the activities involved in managing cash (money) that flows through a business, a more precise description notes that the practice of corporate finance involves five basic functions: financing, financial management, capital budgeting, risk management, and corporate governance. Nearly every topic covered in this text focuses on one or more of these five functions.

financing function
Raising capital to support a company's operations and investment programs.

Financing The financing function involves raising capital to support a company's operations and investment programs. A key aspect of this activity, known as the *capital structure decision*, involves determining and maintaining the mix of debt and equity securities that maximizes the firm's overall market value. Businesses raise money either externally from creditors or shareholders or internally by retaining and reinvesting profits. Both U.S. and non-U.S. companies raise about two-thirds of their required financing internally each year, but the financing function focuses primarily on *external financing*. Large corporations enjoy varied opportunities to raise money externally, either by selling *equity* (common or preferred stock), or by issuing *debt*, which involves borrowing money from creditors. When corporations are young and small, they usually must raise equity capital privately, from friends and family, or from professional investors such as *venture capitalists*. Venture capitalists specialize in making high-risk/high-return investments in rapidly growing entrepreneurial businesses. After firms reach a certain size, they may "go public" by conducting an initial public offering (IPO) of stock—selling shares to outside investors and listing them for trade on a stock exchange. After going public, companies can raise funds by selling additional stock.

Financial Management The financial management function involves managing the firm's operating cash flows as efficiently as possible. A key responsibility of the financial management function is to ensure that the firm has enough funds on hand to support day-to-day operations. This involves obtaining seasonal financing, building adequate inventories to meet customer demand, paying suppliers, collecting from customers, and investing surplus cash, all while maintaining adequate cash balances. Effectively managing the day-to-day financial activities of the firm requires not only technical and analytical skills, but also people skills, since almost every aspect of this activity involves building and maintaining relationships with customers, suppliers, lenders, and others.

Capital Budgeting The capital budgeting function, often called the *investment function*, involves selecting the best projects in which to invest the firm's funds based on their expected risk and return. It is a critical function for two reasons. First, the scale of capital investment projects is often quite large. Second, companies can prosper in a competitive economy only by seeking out the most promising new products, processes, and services to deliver to customers. Companies such as Intel, General Electric, Deutsche Telecom, and Toyota regularly make huge capital investments, the outcomes of which drive the value of their firms and the wealth of their owners. For these and other companies, the annual capital investment budget can total several billion dollars.

The capital budgeting process breaks down into three steps:

1. Identifying potential investments
2. Analyzing the set of investment opportunities and selecting those that create shareholder value
3. Implementing and monitoring the selected investments

The long-term success of most firms depends on mastering all three steps. Not surprisingly, capital budgeting is also the area where managers have the greatest opportunity to create value for shareholders by acquiring assets that yield benefits greater than their costs.

Risk Management The risk management function involves identifying, measuring, and managing the firm's exposure to all types of risk to maintain an optimal risk-return tradeoff and therefore maximize share value. Common risks include losses that can result from adverse interest-rate movements, changes in commodity prices, and fluctuations in currency values. The techniques for managing these risks are among the most sophisticated of all corporate finance practices. The risk management task begins with quantifying the sources and size of a firm's risk exposure and deciding whether to simply accept these risks or to actively manage them.

Some risks are easily insurable, such as the risk of loss due to fire, employee theft, or product liability. Firms can reduce some other risks by *diversifying*. For example, rather than use a sole supplier for a key production input, a firm might choose to contract with several suppliers, even if doing so means purchasing the input above

venture capitalists
Professional investors who specialize in making high-risk/high-return investments in rapidly growing entrepreneurial businesses.

initial public offering (IPO)
Corporations offer shares for sale to the public for the first time by selling shares to outside investors and listing them for trade on a stock exchange.

financial management function
The activities involved in managing the firm's operating cash flows as efficiently as possible.

capital budgeting function
The activities involved in selecting the best projects in which to invest the firm's funds based on their expected risk and return. Also called the *investment function*.

risk management function
The activities involved in identifying, measuring, and managing the firm's exposure to all types of risk to maintain an optimal risk-return trade-off and therefore maximize share value.

SMART concepts
See the concept explained step-by-step at SMART|finance

hedge
To use complex financial instruments to offset market risks such as interest-rate and currency fluctuations.

the lowest attainable price. However, most firms' risk management practices focus on market-driven risks. Risk managers, who typically work as part of a company's treasury staff, use complex financial instruments to **hedge**, or offset, market risks such as interest-rate and currency fluctuations.

corporate governance function
The activities involved in developing company-wide structures and incentives that influence managers to behave ethically and make decisions that benefit shareholders.

Corporate Governance The **corporate governance function** involves developing company-wide structures and incentives that influence managers to behave ethically and make decisions that benefit shareholders. The existence of a well-functioning corporate governance system is extremely important. Good management does not occur in a vacuum. Instead, it results from a corporate governance system that hires and promotes qualified, honest people and that structures employees' financial incentives to motivate them to maximize firm value.

An optimal corporate governance system is extremely difficult to develop in practice, not least because the incentives of stockholders, managers, and other stakeholders often conflict. A firm's stockholders want managers to work hard and to protect shareholders' interests, but it is rarely profitable for any *individual* stockholder to expend time and resources monitoring managers to see if they are acting appropriately. An individual stockholder would personally bear all the costs of monitoring management, but the benefit of such monitoring would accrue to all shareholders.

collective action problem
When individual stockholders bear all the costs of monitoring management, but the benefit of such monitoring accrues to all shareholders.

This is a classic example of the **collective action problem** that arises in most relationships between stockholders and managers. Likewise, managers may feel the need to increase the wealth of owners, but they also want to protect their own jobs. Managers rationally do not want to work harder than necessary if others will reap most of the benefits. Finally, managers and shareholders may effectively run a company to benefit themselves at the expense of creditors or other stakeholders who do not have a direct say in corporate governance.

As you might expect, several mechanisms have been designed to mitigate these problems. A strong board of directors is an essential element in any well-functioning governance system, because it is the board's duty to hire, fire, pay, and promote senior managers. The board develops *fixed* (salary) and *incentive* (bonus and stock-based) compensation packages to align managers' and shareholders' incentives. Auditors play a governance role by certifying the validity of firms' financial statements.

Securities and Exchange Commission (SEC)
The federal agency, established in 1934, charged with oversight of the fair reporting of financial information to investors in public companies (those whose shares are listed for trading in a public securities market).

The **Securities and Exchange Commission (SEC)**, a federal agency established in 1934, is charged with oversight of the fair reporting of financial information to investors in public companies (those whose shares are listed for trading in a public securities market). In the United States, accounting scandals and concerns about auditors' conflicts of interest prompted the SEC to require the CFOs of large firms to personally certify their firms' earnings numbers. Despite the efforts of the SEC, corporate scandals near the turn of the century revealed numerous shortcomings in U.S. corporate governance practices. In response, Congress passed the **Sarbanes–Oxley Act of 2002 (SOX)**, which we discuss in more depth in Section 1-4.

Sarbanes–Oxley Act of 2002 (SOX)
Act of Congress that established new corporate governance standards for U.S. public companies.

Just as companies struggle to develop an effective corporate governance system, so do countries. Governments establish legal frameworks that either encourage or discourage the development of competitive businesses and efficient financial markets. For example, a legal system should permit efficiency-enhancing mergers and acquisitions but should block business combinations that significantly restrict competition. It should provide protection for creditors and minority shareholders by limiting the opportunities for managers or majority shareholders to expropriate wealth.

We will discuss each of the five major finance functions at length in this textbook, and we hope you come to share our excitement about the career opportunities that corporate finance provides. Never before has finance been as fast-paced, as technological, as international, as ethically challenging, or as rigorous as it is today. These trends have helped make it one of the most popular majors for undergraduate students in U.S. and international business schools.

What Companies Do

Which Finance Functions Add the Most Value?

Financial managers spend their days engaged in one or more of the five key finance functions. The chart below shows the results from a recent survey of CFOs who were asked to assess the value to their firms of different activities performed by the finance staff. This is by no means an exhaustive list, but it illustrates the scope of corporate finance as well as the relative importance of different roles in which financial professionals are engaged. What kinds of problems confront managers in each of the five functions?

Notice that three of the four items rated by CFOs as "most valuable" to their companies involve the financing function. At the top of the list is "capital structure," meaning the mix of debt and equity securities issued by the company. Next is "debt issuance and management," with "bank relationships" listed fourth. It may be surprising that "equity issuance" appears near the bottom of the list, but in fact most firms rarely issue new shares to investors. Doing so is costly, and typically the market reacts negatively to a new equity offering.

CFOs cite "working capital management" as the third most valuable thing that they do for their companies. "Financial analysis and planning," which includes planning for and monitoring working capital needs, is cited as being quite important, and "cash management" appears about halfway down the list.

The chart also reports that CFOs cite "making investment decisions" as the sixth most valuable activity in which they are engaged. Of course, one of the biggest investments that a firm can undertake is buying another firm, and CFOs also say that "merger, acquisition, and disposal decisions" have a large effect on firm value.

Finally, note in the chart the importance that CFOs assign to tasks such as "external financial reporting," "regulatory compliance," and "internal audit," all of which are related to how the firm is governed. Virtually every chapter in this textbook focuses on one or more of the tasks mentioned in the graph below.

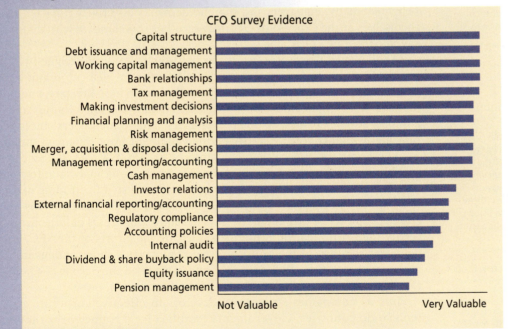

Source: Henri Servaes and Peter Tufano, "CFO Views on the Importance and Execution of the Finance Function," Deutsche Bank (2006).

1-2b Debt and Equity: The Two Flavors of Capital

debt capital
Long-term borrowed money.

Companies have access to two broad types of capital: debt and equity. Debt capital includes all of a company's long-term borrowing from creditors. The borrower is obliged to pay *interest*, at a specified annual rate, on the full amount borrowed (called the loan's *principal*), as well as to repay the principal at the debt's maturity. All of these payments must be made according to a predetermined schedule, and creditors have a legally enforceable claim against the firm. If the company defaults on any of its debt payments, creditors can take legal action to force repayment. In some cases, this means that creditors can push the borrowing firm into bankruptcy, forcing them out of business and into selling (liquidating) their assets to raise the cash needed to satisfy creditor claims.

equity capital
An ownership interest purchased by an investor, usually in the form of common or preferred stock, that is expected to remain permanently invested.

Investors contribute equity capital in exchange for ownership interests in the firm. Equity remains permanently invested in the company. The two basic sources of equity capital are common stock and preferred stock. *Common stockholders* bear most of the firm's risk, because they receive returns on their investments only after creditors and preferred stockholders are paid in full. Similar to creditors, *preferred stockholders* are promised a specified annual payment on their invested capital. Unlike debt, preferred stockholders' claims are not legally enforceable, so these investors cannot force a company into bankruptcy if a scheduled preferred stock dividend is not paid. If a company falls into bankruptcy and has to be liquidated, preferred stockholders' claims are paid off before any money is distributed to common stockholders.

1-2c The Role of Financial Intermediaries in Corporate Finance

financial intermediary
An institution that raises capital by issuing liabilities against itself, and then uses the capital raised to make either loans to corporations and individuals or to buy various types of investments.

In the United States, companies can obtain debt capital by selling securities either directly to investors or through financial intermediaries. A financial intermediary is an institution that raises capital by issuing liabilities against itself, and then uses the capital raised to make either loans to corporations and individuals or to buy various types of investments. Financial intermediaries include banks, insurance companies, savings and loan institutions, credit unions, mutual funds, and pension funds. But the best-known U.S. financial intermediaries are commercial banks, which issue liabilities such as demand deposits (checking accounts) to companies and individuals and then loan these funds to corporations, governments, and households. Banks in the United States are prohibited from making equity investments, but in many other countries they are allowed to purchase the common stock of corporate customers.

In addition to making corporate loans, financial intermediaries provide a variety of financial services to businesses. By accepting money in demand deposits received from companies and individuals, banks eliminate their depositors' need to hold large amounts of cash for use in purchasing goods and services. Banks also act as the backbone of a nation's payments system by facilitating the transfer of money between payors and payees, providing transaction information, and streamlining large-volume transactions such as payroll disbursements.

The Growing Importance of Financial Markets The role of traditional intermediaries such as banks as providers of debt capital to corporations has been declining for decades. During the years 2007–2010 this source of debt capital contracted severely due to both the collapse of the mortgage market and near-collapse of the U.S. economy. Figure 1.1 shows the value from May 2007 to May 2011 of a share

Figure 1.1

From May 2007 to February 2009, the banking sector suffered its most serious contraction since the Great Depression. One barometer of the stress on banks during this period is the price of the Powershares Dynamic Banking Portfolio Exchange Traded Fund, which fell from almost $22 per share to less than $11 in less than two years.

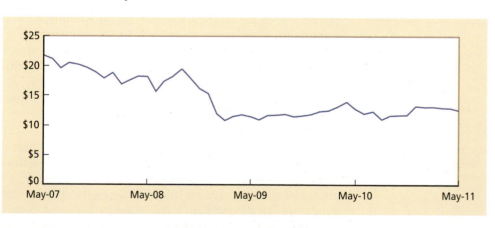

Bank Stocks Fall by Half

Source: Prices for Powershares Dynamic Banking Portfolio Exchange Traded Fund obtained from Yahoo! Finance.

primary-market transactions
Cash sales of securities to investors by a corporation to raise capital.

secondary-market transactions
Trades between investors that generate no new cash flow for the firm.

in Powershares Dynamic Banking Portfolio Exchange Traded Fund—a portfolio of bank stocks. Clearly, the price decline over that period reflects the impact of the crisis in banking.

For several decades, nonfinancial corporations have increasingly turned to capital markets for external financing. This shift toward greater reliance on market-based external funding has resulted in the growth of mutual funds and pension funds—both financial intermediaries that are major purchasers of the securities of nonfinancial corporations.

When corporations sell securities to investors in exchange for cash, they raise capital in primary-market transactions. In such transactions, firms actually receive the proceeds from issuing securities, so these are true capital-raising events. Once firms issue securities, investors can sell them to other investors. Trades between investors, called secondary-market transactions, generate no new cash flow for the firm, so they are not true capital-raising events. Most stock market trades are secondary-market trades, whereas a large fraction of all bond market trades are capital-raising primary-market transactions. Primary stock and bond offerings by both U.S. companies and worldwide have grown dramatically—more than thirteenfold—since the early 1990s.

1-2 Concept Review Questions

3. List and briefly describe the five basic corporate finance functions. What is the general relationship among them?

4. Which of the five basic corporate finance functions might be considered nontraditional? Why do you think these functions have become so important in recent years?

5. What is a *financial intermediary*? Why have these institutions been steadily losing market share to capital markets as the principal source of external financing for corporations?

1-3 Legal Forms of Business Organization

Companies exist so that people can organize to pursue profit-making ventures. This section examines how companies organize themselves legally and discusses the costs and benefits of each major form. We begin with the most popular forms of business organization in the United States and then look at popular non-U.S. forms.

1-3a Business Organizational Forms in the United States

The three key legal forms of business organization in the United States have historically been the sole proprietorship, the partnership, and the corporation. These have recently been joined by a fourth type, the limited liability company. The sole proprietorship is the most common form of organization. The largest businesses tend to be organized as corporations, and they account for a large fraction of total U.S. business sales and profits. In addition to these forms, there are two very important hybrid organizational forms: the limited partnership and the S corporation. The principles and tools that financial analysts use to do their jobs apply to all of these organizational forms.

sole proprietorship
A business with a single owner.

Sole Proprietorships A sole proprietorship is a business with a single owner. In fact, there is no legal distinction between the business and the owner. The business is the owner's personal property; it exists only as long as the owner lives and chooses to operate it, and all business assets belong to the owner. Furthermore, the owner bears personal liability for all the company's debts and pays income taxes on its earnings. Sole proprietorships are the most common type of business in the United States, accounting for about three-fourths of all business tax returns filed each year. However, proprietorships receive less than 6% of all business income and employ less than 10% of the workforce.

Simplicity and ease of operation constitute the principal benefits of the proprietorship. However, this organizational form suffers from weaknesses that in most cases limit the firm's long-term growth potential. These include the following:

- *Limited life* By definition, a proprietorship ceases to exist when the founder retires or dies. Although the founder/entrepreneur can pass the assets of the business on to a third party, most of what makes the business valuable is tied to the proprietor personally. Furthermore, changes in ownership of successful companies can trigger large tax liabilities.
- *Limited access to capital* A proprietorship can obtain operating capital from only two sources: reinvested profits and personal borrowing by the entrepreneur. In practice, both of these sources are easily exhausted.
- *Unlimited personal liability* A sole proprietor is personally liable for all the debts of the business, including judgments awarded a plaintiff in a successful lawsuit. The United States is the most litigious society in history (each year, some 20 million lawsuits are filed in state courts alone), and a single jury verdict can destroy even the most successful business.

partnership
A proprietorship with two or more owners who have joined their skills and personal wealth.

joint and several liability
A legal concept that makes each partner in a partnership legally liable for all the debts of the partnership.

Partnerships A (general) partnership is essentially a proprietorship with two or more owners who have joined their skills and personal wealth. As in a sole proprietorship, there is no legal distinction between the business and its owners, each of whom can execute contracts binding on all the other(s) and each of whom is personally liable for all the partnership's debts. This sharing of legal responsibility is known as joint and several liability.

Although nothing requires the owners to formalize the terms of their partnership in a written *partnership agreement*, most partnerships create such a document. In the absence of a partnership agreement, the business dissolves whenever one of the partners retires or dies. Furthermore, unless there is a partnership agreement specifying otherwise, each partner shares equally in business income and each has equal management authority. As with a proprietorship, partnership income is taxed only once: at the personal level.

In addition to the tax benefits and ease of formation that partnerships share with proprietorships, the partnership allows a large number of people to pool their expertise and capital to form a much larger enterprise. Partnerships enjoy more flexibility than proprietorships in that the business need not automatically terminate following the retirement or death of one partner. Industries in which partnerships are usually the dominant form of organization include accounting, consulting, engineering, law, and medicine.

The drawbacks of the partnership form resemble those of the sole proprietorship:

limited partnership (LP)
A partnership in which most of the participants (the *limited partners*) have the limited liability of corporate shareholders, but their share of the profits from the business is taxed as partnership income.

- *Limited life* The life of the firm can be limited, particularly if only a few partners are involved. Problems may also result from the instability inherent in long-term, multi-person business associations.
- *Limited access to capital* For operating capital, the firm is still limited to retained profits and personal borrowings.
- *Unlimited personal liability* This disadvantage is accentuated because the partners are subject to joint and several liability. As firms grow larger, the competitive disadvantages of the proprietorship and partnership organizational forms tend to become extremely burdensome. Almost all successful companies eventually adopt the corporate organizational form.

general partners
One or more participants in a limited partnership who operate the business and have unlimited personal liability.

limited partners
One or more totally passive participants in a limited partnership, who do not take any active role in the operation of the business and who do not face personal liability for the debts of the business.

Limited Partnerships In many ways, a limited partnership (LP) combines the best features of the (general) partnership and the corporate organizational forms (we cover the corporate form next). In any limited partnership, there must be one or more general partners, each of whom has unlimited personal liability. Because only the general partners operate the business and are legally exposed, they usually receive a greater-than-proportional (in terms of their capital contribution) share of partnership income. Most of the participants in the partnership are limited partners. They have the limited liability of corporate shareholders, but their share of the profits from the business is taxed as partnership income. The limited partners, however, must be totally passive. They contribute capital to the partnership but cannot have their names associated with the business;

neither can they take an active role in the operation of the business, even as employees. In return for this passivity, the limited partners face no personal liability for business debts. This means that, although limited partners can lose their equity investment in the business, tax authorities (or other plaintiffs) cannot sue the limited partners personally for payment of their claims. It should be emphasized that limited partners share in partnership income, which is taxed as ordinary personal income for the partners.

Limited partnerships are ideal vehicles for funding long-term investments that generate large noncash operating losses in the early years of the business, because these losses *flow through* directly to the limited partners. This means the limited partners can (under specified conditions) use the tax losses to offset taxable income from other sources. Disadvantages of LPs include a shallow secondary market for securities and difficulties with monitoring and disciplining the general partner(s). In some cases, registering an LP with the SEC allows secondary-market trading of partnership interests; this can reduce or eliminate the illiquidity problem.

Corporations Under U.S. law, a corporation is a legal entity, owned by the shareholders who hold its common stock, with many of the economic rights and responsibilities enjoyed by individuals. A corporation can sue and be sued, it can own property and execute contracts in its own name, and it can be tried and convicted for crimes committed by its employees.

The corporate organizational form has several key competitive advantages over other forms, including the following:

- *Unlimited life* Once created, a corporation has perpetual life unless it is explicitly terminated.
- *Limited liability* The firms' shareholders cannot be held personally liable for the firm's debts.
- *Separable contracting* Corporations can contract individually with managers, suppliers, customers, and ordinary employees, and each individual contract can be renegotiated, modified, or terminated without affecting other stakeholders.
- *Improved access to capital* The company itself, rather than its owners, can borrow money from creditors, and it can also issue various classes of common and preferred stock to equity investors. Furthermore, the ownership claims themselves (shares of common and preferred stock) can be freely traded among investors, without obtaining the permission of other investors, if the corporation is a public company—that is, one whose shares are listed for trading in a public securities market.

The shares of corporate common stock carry voting rights, and shareholders vote at an annual meeting to elect the firm's directors. The *directors* include key corporate personnel as well as outsiders who are typically successful private businesspeople or executives of other major corporations. The board of directors is responsible for hiring and firing managers and for setting overall corporate policies. The rules dictating voting procedures and other parameters of corporate governance appear in the firm's corporate charter, the legal document created at the corporation's inception to govern its operations. The charter can be changed only by a vote of the shareholders.

Also, in contrast to the practice in almost all other countries, incorporation in the United States is executed at the state rather than the national level and is governed primarily by state law, not federal law. Nonetheless, all fifty states have broadly similar rules for incorporation and corporate governance. At the federal level, of course, it is the SEC's job to regulate the financial reporting of corporations. Corporations may issue two forms of stock—*common* and *preferred*—each with slightly different rights and privileges. Shareholders of common and preferred stock, as owners of the firm's equity securities, are often called equity claimants. Shareholders of preferred stock typically have higher-priority access to the corporation's earnings and bear less risk than shareholders of common stock. In exchange, they generally do not have the right to vote. Therefore, we refer to common stockholders as the firm's ultimate owners. Common stockholders vote periodically to elect the members of the board of directors and, occasionally, to amend the firm's corporate charter.

---

corporation
A legal entity, owned by the shareholders who hold its common stock, with many of the economic rights and responsibilities enjoyed by individuals.

shareholder
Owner of common or preferred stock in a *corporation*.

public company
A corporation, the shares of which can be freely traded among investors without obtaining the permission of other investors and whose shares are listed for trading in a public securities market.

board of directors
Elected by shareholders to be responsible for hiring and firing managers and for setting overall corporate policies.

? JOB INTERVIEW QUESTION

What are the pros and cons of organizing a business as a corporation rather than as a partnership?

corporate charter
The legal document created at the corporation's inception to govern its operations.

equity claimants
Owners of a corporation's equity securities.

president or chief executive officer (CEO)
The top company manager with overall responsibility and authority for managing daily company affairs and carrying out policies established by the board.

agency costs
Costs that arise from conflicts of interest between shareholders and managers.

double-taxation problem
Taxation of corporate income at both company and personal levels—traditionally a significant disadvantage of the corporate form.

It is important to note the division between owners and managers in a large corporation. The top part of Figure 1.2 depicts the relationships among these important parties in a corporation. The **president or chief executive officer (CEO)** is responsible for managing day-to-day operations and carrying out policies established by the board. The board expects regular reports from the CEO regarding the firm's current status and future direction. However, the CEO and the board serve at the will of the shareholders. The separation between owners and managers, as shown by the red dashed horizontal line in Figure 1.2, leads to **agency costs**, the costs that arise from conflicts of interest between shareholders (owners) and managers. These costs—and the agency problems that cause them—are discussed in greater depth in Section 1-4b.

Although corporations dominate economic life around the world, this form has some competitive disadvantages. Many governments tax corporate income at both company and personal levels. This treatment, commonly called the **double-taxation problem**, has traditionally been a significant disadvantage of the corporate form in the United States. But the Jobs and Growth Tax Relief Reconciliation Act of 2003 (hereafter, the Tax Relief Act of 2003) substantially reduced this problem by lowering personal tax rates on dividends and capital gains.

Figure 1.2

In a corporation, stockholders own the company, and they elect a board of directors to hire managers responsible for day-to-day operations of the business.

The Finance Function in the Organizational Structure of a Typical Large Corporation

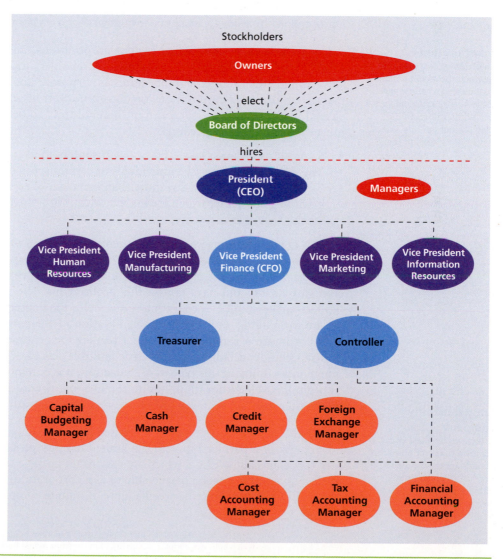

Table 1.4	**Taxation of Business Income for Corporations and Partnerships *after* Passage of the Jobs and Growth Tax Relief Reconciliation Act of 2003**	
	Partnership	**Corporation**
Operating income	$100,000	$100,000
Less: Corporate profits tax ($T_c = 0.35$)	0	35,000
Net income	$100,000	$ 65,000
Cash dividends or partnership distributions	$100,000	$ 65,000
Less: Personal tax on dividends ($T_{div} = 0.15$)		9,750
Less: Personal tax on partnership income ($T_p = 0.35$)	35,000	
After-tax disposable income	$ 65,000	$ 55,250

© Cengage Learning 2012

Table 1.4 illustrates the double-taxation problem by comparing the tax burden faced by investors in a corporation with the taxes owed by the owners of a partnership. Both businesses earn $100,000 of pre-tax income. We assume that the corporation in our example is taxed at the top corporate income-tax rate of 35% ($T_c = 0.35$) and that the partnership's investors face the top personal income-tax rate, which is also 35% ($T_p = 0.35$). The tax law now applies the same tax rate to both dividends and capital gains, and we will assume that shareholders face the top personal capital gains tax rate of 15% ($T_{div} = 0.15$). As the law currently stands, the partners receive after-tax disposable income of $65,000 [$100,000 × (1 − 0.35)] and shareholders receive net disposable income of $55,250 [$100,000 × (1 − 0.35) × (1 − 0.15)]. As this example shows, a partnership (or a proprietorship) enjoys a small tax advantage over a corporation.

S corporation

An ordinary corporation in which the stockholders have elected to allow shareholders to be taxed as partners while still retaining their limited-liability status as corporate stockholders.

S Corporations In contrast to regular corporations, an S corporation (previously called *Subchapter S corporation*) allows shareholders to be taxed as partners while still retaining their limited-liability status as corporate stockholders. This type of company is an ordinary corporation (or C *corporation*) in which the stockholders have elected to be treated as S-corporation shareholders. To be eligible for S status, a firm must meet the following criteria:

- S corporations must have 100 or fewer shareholders.
- The shareholders must be individuals or certain types of trusts (not corporations).
- S corporations cannot issue more than one class of equity security, and cannot be a *holding company*, which means that it cannot hold a controlling fraction of the stock in another company.

If a corporation meets these requirements, then S-corporation status allows the company's operating income to escape separate taxation at the corporate level.[3] Instead, each shareholder claims as personal income a proportionate fraction of total company profits and pays tax on this profit at his own personal tax rate. As with limited partnerships, S-corporation status yields the limited liability benefit of the corporate form along with the favorable taxation of the partnership form. In addition, an S corporation can easily become a regular C corporation should it outgrow the 100-shareholder ceiling or need to issue multiple classes of equity securities. Given the inherent flexibility of this type of organization, it is common for successful companies to begin life as S corporations and to retain S status until they decide to go public, at which time they are required to become regular corporations.

limited liability company (LLC)

A form of business organization that combines the tax advantages of a partnership with the limited liability protection of a corporation.

Limited Liability Companies The limited liability company (LLC) combines the tax advantages of a partnership with the limited liability protection of a corporation. All fifty U.S. states allow LLCs, which are easy to set up. The IRS allows an LLC's owners to elect taxation as either a partnership or as a corporation, and many states allow one-person LLCs and a choice between a finite or infinite company life. Even though LLCs

---

[3]According to the Internal Revenue Service, *IRS.gov Tax Stats at a Glance* (www.irs.gov/taxstats/article/0,,id=102886,00 .html, accessed June 1, 2010), more than 61% (3.99 million of 6.53 million) of all corporations filing 2007 tax returns were S corporations, which indicates both the popularity of this organizational form and the relatively small *average* size of U.S. businesses.

can be taxed as partnerships, their owners face no personal liability for other partners' malpractice, making this type of company especially attractive for professional service firms. Given the limited liability feature and the flexibility of LLCs, we expect that they will continue to gain significant organizational market share in the years to come.

1-3b Forms of Business Organization Used by Non-U.S. Companies

Here we briefly review the most important organizational forms used by non-U.S. companies. Almost all capitalist economies allow some form of limited liability business organization, with ownership shares that are freely traded on national stock markets. Similar to the United States, these companies tend to dominate economic life in the countries where these organizations exist.

Limited Liability Companies in Other Industrialized Countries Although limited liability companies exist around the world, they have different names in different countries. In Britain, they are called public limited companies (plc); in Germany, *Aktiengesellschaft* (AG); in France, *Société Générale* (SG); and in Spain, Mexico, and elsewhere in Latin America, *Sociedad Anónima* (SA). Details vary, but all of these structures are similar to publicly traded corporations in the United States. Key differences between international and U.S. companies revolve around tax treatment of business income and the amount of information that publicly traded companies must disclose. Tax rules are typically, though not always, harsher in the United States than elsewhere, and disclosure requirements are invariably greater for U.S. than for non-U.S. companies.

Many countries also distinguish between limited liability companies that can be traded publicly and those that are privately held. In Germany, *Gesellschaft mit beschränkten Haftung* (GmbH) are privately owned, unlisted limited-liability stock companies. In France, these are called *Société à Responsibilité Limitée* (SARL). Private (unlisted) companies, particularly family-owned firms, play important roles in all market economies. For example, Germany's phenomenal post-WW II growth was propelled by midsized, export-oriented companies that pursued niche marketing strategies at home and abroad. These *Mittelstand* (middle market) firms still account for about three quarters of all German economic activity. A similar set of relatively small, entrepreneurial companies has helped propel Taiwan, Singapore, and other Asian nations to growth rates consistently higher than those achieved in the industrialized West.

1-3 Concept Review Questions

6. What are the costs and benefits of each of the three major organizational forms in the United States? Why do you think the various hybrid forms of business organization have proven so successful?

7. Comment on the following statement: "Sooner or later, all successful private companies that are organized as proprietorships or partnerships must become corporations."

1-4 The Corporate Financial Manager's Goals

In widely held corporations, the owners typically do not manage the firm. This raises the interesting question: Whose interests should managers serve? Shareholders? Creditors? Customers? Employees? The traditional answer given in finance textbooks is that managers should operate the firm in a way that maximizes shareholder wealth. As a practical matter, that recommendation is difficult to implement, partly because managers may be tempted to pursue their own interests rather than shareholders' interests.

In the sections that follow, we first evaluate profit maximization and then describe shareholder wealth maximization. Next, we discuss the *agency costs* arising from potential conflicts between stockholders, managers, and other stakeholders (such as bondholders). Finally, we consider the role of ethics in corporate finance, including a brief look at how the Sarbanes–Oxley Act affects financial management.

1-4a What Should a Financial Manager Try to Maximize?

Should a financial manager try to maximize corporate profits, shareholder wealth, or something else? Here we hope to convince you that managers should seek to maximize shareholder wealth.

Maximize Profit?   Some people believe that the manager's objective is to maximize profits, and it is common to see compensation plans designed so that managers receive larger bonuses for increasing reported earnings. To achieve profit maximization, the financial manager takes those actions that make a positive contribution to the firm's profits. Thus, for each alternative, the financial manager should select the one with the highest expected profit. From a practical standpoint, this objective translates into maximizing *earnings per share (EPS)*, the amount earned on behalf of each outstanding share of common stock. Although it seems a plausible objective, profit maximization suffers from several flaws.

- Earnings per share figures are inherently backward-looking, reflecting what has happened rather than what will happen.
- Some short-run decisions (e.g., forgoing maintenance) to boost EPS can actually destroy value in the long run. Even if managers strive to maximize profits over time, they should not ignore the timing of those profits. A large profit that arrives many years in the future may be less valuable than a smaller profit earned today. As we'll learn in Chapter 3, money has a time value; simply put, a dollar today is worth more than a dollar in the future.
- A manager cannot maximize profits without knowing how to measure them, and conventional barometers of profit come from accrual-based accounting principles rather than a focus on cash flows. In finance, we place more emphasis on cash— the true currency of business—than on profits or earnings.

Focusing solely on earnings ignores risk. When comparing two investment opportunities, managers should not always choose the one they expect to generate the highest profits. They must consider the risks of the investments as well. As we will learn in Part 2, a trade-off exists between *risk and return, the two key determinants of share prices*. Higher cash flow generally leads to higher share prices, whereas higher risk results in lower share prices. Therefore, an investment project with high profits and high risk could be less valuable than one with lower profits and lower risk.

Maximize Shareholder Wealth?   Modern finance asserts that *the proper goal of firms is to maximize the wealth of shareholders*, where wealth is measured by the firm's stock price. This stock price reflects the timing, magnitude, and risk of the *cash flows* that investors expect a firm to generate over time. When considering alternative strategies, financial managers should undertake only those actions that they expect will increase the firm's share price.

Why does finance preach the wisdom of maximizing share value as the primary corporate objective? Why not focus instead on satisfying the desires of corporate stakeholders such as customers, employees, suppliers, and creditors? A firm's shareholders are sometimes called its residual claimants, meaning that they can exert claims only on the firm's cash flows that remain after all other claimants, such as customers, employees, suppliers, creditors, and governments are satisfied in full. It may help to visualize a queue with all the firm's stakeholders standing in line to receive their share of the firm's cash flows. Shareholders stand at the end of this line. If the firm cannot pay its employees, suppliers, creditors, and the tax authorities, then shareholders

? JOB INTERVIEW QUESTION

What problems might be encountered if a firm ties its employee bonuses to earnings per share?

stakeholders
Customers, employees, suppliers, and creditors of a corporation.

residual claimants
Corporate investors— typically, common stockholders—who have the right to receive cash flows after all other claimants have been satisfied in full.

What Companies Do Globally

Views on Corporate Goals and Stakeholder Groups

Although the perspective of maximizing shareholder value has enjoyed widespread acceptance in the United States, it has not been universally embraced by foreign companies. However, the chart below, which reports results from a survey of Chief Financial Officers (CFOs) conducted during the recent financial crisis, reveals a strong tilt toward shareholder wealth maximization among companies in Europe and Asia as well as North America. The survey asked CFOs to rank the importance of shareholders compared to other stakeholders. A ranking of 0 means that the CFO believes that companies should focus exclusively on shareholders, and a score of 100 means that the CFO focuses exclusively on other stakeholder groups. A score of 50 would mean that the CFO rates shareholders and other stakeholders as being equally important. On average, it is clear that CFOs from around the world place more emphasis on shareholders than on other stakeholders.

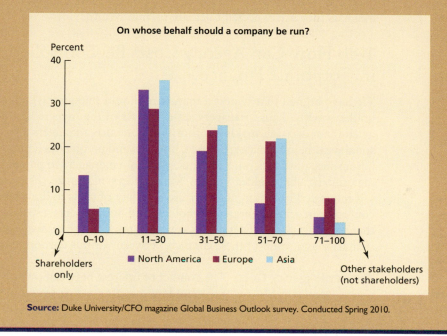

On whose behalf should a company be run?

Percent

North America   Europe   Asia

Shareholders only

Other stakeholders (not shareholders)

Source: Duke University/CFO magazine Global Business Outlook survey. Conducted Spring 2010.

receive nothing. Shareholders earn a return on their investment only after all other stakeholders' claims have been met. In other words, maximizing shareholder returns usually implies that the firm must also satisfy customers, employees, suppliers, creditors, and other stakeholders first.

Furthermore, by accepting their position as residual claimants, shareholders agree to bear more risk than do other stakeholders. If firms did not operate with the goal of maximizing shareholder wealth in mind, then shareholders would have little incentive to accept the risks necessary for a business to thrive. To understand this point, consider how a firm would operate if it were run solely in the interests of its creditors. Given that creditors receive only a fixed return, would such a firm be inclined to make risky investments, no matter how profitable? Only shareholders have the proper incentives to make risky, value-increasing investments.

Focus on Stakeholders? Although the primary goal of managers should be to maximize shareholder wealth, many firms have broadened their focus to include the interests of other stakeholders—such as customers, employees, suppliers, creditors, tax authorities, and the communities where firms operate. A firm with a stakeholder focus consciously avoids actions that would harm stakeholders by transferring their wealth to shareholders. The goal is not so much to maximize others' interests, as it is to preserve

David Nickel, Controller for Intel Communications Group, Intel Corp. (former)

"Finance's primary role is to try to drive the right business decisions to increase shareholder value."

See the entire interview at **SMART | finance**

Smart Practices Video

those interests. Considering other constituents' interests is part of the firm's social responsibility, and keeping other affected groups happy provides long-term benefit to shareholders. Such relationships minimize employee turnover, conflicts, and litigation. In most cases, taking care of stakeholders translates into maximizing shareholder wealth. But conflict between these two objectives sometimes arises. When it does, the firm should ultimately be run to benefit stockholders while preserving stakeholder interests. For example, it is important to put customers first, but obviously making customers happy enough to do repeat business is also part of maximizing shareholder value.

Interestingly, even though U.S. corporations are generally expected to act in a socially responsible way, they are rarely *required* by law to do so. The situation is much different in many Western European countries, where corporations are expected to contribute to social welfare almost as much as they are expected to create private wealth.

1-4b How Can Agency Costs Be Controlled in Corporate Finance?

We have argued that financial managers should pursue the goal of maximizing shareholder wealth. Thus, managers act as *agents* of the owners who have hired them and given them decision-making authority. In practice, managers also care about their personal wealth, job security, lifestyle, prestige, and perquisites (country club memberships, limousines, posh offices). Such concerns cause managers to pursue objectives other than maximizing shareholder wealth. Shareholders recognize the potential for managers' self-interested behavior, and they use a variety of tools to limit this behavior. Similarly, conflicts can arise between shareholders and bondholders, especially regarding the risks that the firm takes when it makes new investments. The term *agency costs* refers to costs that arise as a result of these conflicts between various corporate stakeholders.

agency problems
The conflict of interest between the goals of a firm's owners and its managers.

Types of Agency Costs   The conflict of interest between owners and managers gives rise to **agency problems**. Shareholders can attempt to overcome these agency problems by various means:

- Relying on market forces to exert managerial discipline
- Incurring the monitoring and bonding costs necessary to assure that executive compensation packages fairly align the interests of managers and stockholders

Several market forces constrain the behavior of a firm's managers. In recent years, large investors have become more active in management. This is particularly true for *institutional investors* such as mutual funds, life insurance companies, and pension funds, which often hold large blocks of stock. Activist institutional investors use their influence to put pressure on underperforming management teams, occasionally applying enough pressure to replace the CEO.

hostile takeover
The acquisition of one firm (the *target*) by another (the *acquirer*) through an open-market bid for a majority of the target's shares if the target firm's senior managers do not support (or, more likely, actively resist) the acquisition.

An even more powerful form of market discipline is the **hostile takeover**, which involves the acquisition of one firm (the *target*) by another (the *acquirer*) through an open-market bid for a majority of the target's shares. By definition, a takeover attempt is *hostile* if the target firm's senior managers resist (or simply do not support) the acquisition. Bidders in hostile deals may believe that they can improve the value of the target company, and thereby make a profit on their investment, by replacing incumbent management. Managers naturally find this threatening and erect a variety of barriers to thwart potential acquirers. Nevertheless, the constant threat of a takeover provides additional motivation for managers to act in the interests of the firm's owners.

In addition to these market forces, other devices exist that encourage managers to behave in the shareholders' interests or that limit the consequences when managers misbehave. *Monitoring expenditures* pay for audits and control procedures that alert shareholders when managers pursue their own interests too aggressively. *Bonding expenditures* protect against the potential consequences of dishonest acts by managers. Directors can make bonding expenditures, or managers can themselves make these expenditures to reassure the firm's directors of their benevolent intentions. This can be done, for example, by accepting a portion of their total pay in the form of delayed compensation.

Use of Compensation Plans to Control Agency Costs Another way to align managerial and stockholder interests is through executive compensation plans. The objective is to design such plans to give managers the incentive to act in the best interests of the owners. Incentive compensation plans tie managerial wealth to the firm's share price by paying managers with shares of stock or stock options. Stock options give the manager the right to purchase stock at a fixed price, usually the market price of the stock at the time the manager receives the options. The key idea is that managers will have an incentive to take actions that maximize the stock price, because this will increase their wealth along with that of the other shareholders.

Although tying management compensation to performance seems like an effective way to motivate managers, compensation plans have come under intense scrutiny in recent years. Individual and institutional investors, as well as the SEC, have publicly questioned whether the multimillion-dollar compensation packages granted to executives really are linked to performance. It is not hard to find examples of CEOs who receive millions in compensation when their firms are underperforming. In addition, average levels of CEO compensation in other developed countries tend to be much lower—a fact that critics of CEO pay in the United States do not miss.

1-4c Why Ethics Are Important in Corporate Finance

In recent years, the media and others have questioned the legitimacy of actions taken by certain businesses. Examples range from the $1.2 million that former Merrill Lynch CEO John Thain spent redecorating his office, shortly after Bank of America acquired Merrill in 2008, to the billions stolen by Bernard Madoff through his massive Ponzi scheme. The global financial crisis focused attention on a wide range of ethical issues. Did mortgage lenders lower their credit standards in order to make a quick profit on loan originations while passing on the risk of subprime mortgages to other investors? Did a lack of due diligence by rating agencies cause them to fail to warn investors of the risks of exotic mortgage-backed securities and credit default swaps? Should financial institutions like American International Group (AIG) pay bonuses to managers even after receiving billions in federal bailout dollars?

The last time ethical concerns received as much attention in the media was after the Enron collapse in late 2001. In response to a series of corporate scandals, Congress passed the Sarbanes–Oxley Act of 2002, a law that requires firms to provide extensive documentation of the internal controls they put in place to protect investors from fraud. Among other things, Sarbanes–Oxley requires the CFO to personally vouch for the accuracy of numbers in the financial statements. In all likelihood, one response to the current global financial crisis will be the enactment of new laws placing limits on the risks that financial institutions can take.

More and more firms are now directly addressing the issue of ethics by establishing corporate ethics policies and guidelines and by requiring employee compliance with them. Frequently, employees are required to sign a formal pledge to uphold the firm's ethics policies. Such policies typically apply to employee actions in dealing with all corporate stakeholders, including the public at large. *Ethical behavior is therefore viewed as both necessary and perfectly consistent with achieving the firm's goal of maximizing shareholder wealth.*

Andy Bryant, Executive Vice President of Technology, Manufacturing, and Enterprise Services, Intel Corp.

"I never thought that ethics would be a value add to a company, but today I believe it counts as part of your market cap."

See the entire interview at SMART|finance

Smart Ethics Video

1-4d How the Sarbanes–Oxley Act Is Changing How Corporate America Conducts Business

The failure of Enron's auditor, Arthur Andersen LLP, to alert shareholders to the company's problems (in the late 1990s) resulted in the failure of both companies after the turn of the century. In response to several accounting scandals and concerns about auditors' conflicts of interest, the U.S. Congress passed the Sarbanes–Oxley Act of 2002 (SOX). The act established a new Public Company Accounting Oversight Board (PCAOB), with the power to license auditing firms and regulate accounting and auditing standards. SOX also gave the SEC greater powers to supervise corporate governance practices in companies that have shares listed for trading on public stock exchanges. Among many other changes, this act requires both CEOs and CFOs of all large companies to *personally* certify their firms' financial statements. Thus, the CEOs and CFOs can be held personally liable for any questionable or misleading numbers reported to public investors. SOX also prevents auditing firms from providing other services—such as consulting, valuation, and tax advisory work—to the companies they are auditing, and mandates that lead auditing partners must rotate off the audit every five years. Perhaps the most crucial internal change, guidelines mandated by the act give the firm's audit committee much greater power, responsibility, and independence.

Vern LoForti, V.P., CFO, and Corporate Secretary, InfoSonics

"Sarbanes–Oxley has certainly impacted our company in many ways from operations all the way to the board."

See the entire interview at **SMART | finance**

Smart Practices Video

1-4 Concept Review Questions

8. What are *agency costs?* Why do these tend to increase in severity as a corporation grows larger?

9. What are the relative advantages and disadvantages of using sophisticated management compensation packages to align the interests of managers and shareholders?

10. Why are *ethics* important in corporate finance? What is the likely consequence of unethical behavior by a corporation and its managers?

11. Why did Congress pass the Sarbanes–Oxley Act of 2002, and what are its key provisions?

Summary

- When making financial decisions, managers should seek to create value for the firm's owners, its shareholders. The most important way to do this is to take actions that generate benefits in excess of costs, which should generate wealth for the firm's owners.

- Finance graduates must interact with professionals trained in all other business disciplines. The five most important career paths for finance professionals are in corporate finance, commercial banking, investment banking, money management, and consulting.

- Corporate finance activities can be grouped into five basic functions: the financing function, the financial management function, the capital budgeting function, the risk management function, and the corporate governance function.

- Firms can obtain capital either by borrowing (debt capital) or by selling stock (equity capital), which represents permanent ownership in the firm. Companies can obtain debt capital either by selling securities to investors or from a financial intermediary, such as a commercial bank. The initial sale of securities is called a primary-market transaction, whereas all subsequent trades between investors are considered secondary-market transactions.

- The three key legal forms of business organization in the United States are sole proprietorships, partnerships, and corporations. Sole proprietorships are most common, but corporations dominate economically. Limited partnerships and S corporations are hybrid forms, combining the limited liability of corporations with the favorable tax treatment of partnerships. A new, fourth form, the limited liability company, has become popular due to its flexibility and favorable tax treatment. Similar forms of business organization exist in other industrialized economies.

- The goal of the firm's managers should be to maximize shareholder wealth, not to maximize profits. Maximizing profits focuses on the past rather than the future, ignores the timing of profits, relies on accounting values rather than future cash flows, and ignores risk. Maximizing shareholder wealth is socially optimal because shareholders are residual claimants who profit only after all other claims are paid in full.

- Agency costs that result from the separation of ownership and management must be addressed satisfactorily for companies to prosper. These costs can be overcome (or at least reduced) by relying on the workings of the market for corporate control, incurring monitoring and bonding costs, and using executive compensation contracts designed to align the interests of shareholders and managers.

- Ethical behavior is viewed as necessary for achievement of the firms' goal of maximizing owner wealth. The Sarbanes–Oxley Act of 2002 established rules and procedures aimed at eliminating the potential for unethical acts and conflicts of interest in public corporations.

Key Terms

agency costs, 15
agency problems, 20
board of directors, 14
capital budgeting function, 8
chief financial officer (CFO), 5
collective action problem, 9
corporate charter, 14
corporate finance, 7
corporate governance function, 9
corporation, 14
debt capital, 10
double-taxation problem, 15
equity capital, 11
equity claimants, 14
executive compensation plans, 21

fiduciary, 6
financial intermediary, 11
financial management function, 8
financing function, 7
general partners, 13
hedge, 9
hostile takeover, 20
initial public offering (IPO), 8
joint and several liability, 13
limited liability company (LLC), 16
limited partners, 13
limited partnership (LP), 13
partnership, 13
president or chief executive officer (CEO), 15

primary-market transactions, 12
public company, 14
residual claimants, 18
risk management function, 8
S corporations, 16
Sarbanes–Oxley Act of 2002 (SOX), 9
secondary-market transactions, 12
Securities and Exchange Commission (SEC), 9
shareholder, 14
sole proprietorship, 12
stakeholders, 18
stock options, 21
venture capitalists, 8

Questions

Q1-1. Why must a financial manager have an integrated understanding of the five basic finance functions? Why has the risk-management function become more important in recent years? Why is the corporate governance function considered a finance function?

Q1-2. Enter the home page of the Careers in Business Web site (www.careers-in-business.com) and page through the finance positions listed and their corresponding salaries. What skill sets or job characteristics lead to the variation in salaries? Which of these positions generally require previous work experience?

Q1-3. What are the advantages and disadvantages of different legal forms of business organization? Could the limited liability advantage of a corporation also lead to an *agency problem*? Why? What legal form would an upstart entrepreneur likely prefer?

Q1-4. Can there be a difference between *maximizing profit* and *maximizing shareholder wealth*? If so, what could cause this difference? Which of the two should be the goal of the firm and its management?

Q1-5. Define a corporate *stakeholder*. Which groups are considered stakeholders? Would shareholders also be considered stakeholders? Compare, in terms of economic systems, the principle of maximizing shareholder wealth with the principle of satisfying stakeholder claims.

Q1-6. What is meant by an *agency cost* or *agency problem*? Do these interfere with maximizing shareholder wealth? Why or why not? What mechanisms minimize these costs/problems? Are executive compensation contracts effective in mitigating them?

Q1-7. Are *ethics* critical to the financial manager's goal of maximizing shareholder wealth? How are the two related? Is establishing corporate ethics policies and requiring employee compliance enough to ensure ethical behavior by employees?

Q1-8. What are the key provisions of the *Sarbanes–Oxley Act of 2002*? How has this act changed the way corporate America conducts business?

Problems

Legal Forms of Business Organization

P1-1. a. Calculate the tax disadvantage to organizing a U.S. business today as a corporation, as compared to a partnership, under the following conditions. Assume that all earnings will be paid out as cash dividends. Operating income (operating profit before taxes) will be $500,000 per year under either organizational form. The tax rate on corporate profits is 35% ($T_c = 0.35$), the average personal tax rate for the partners is also 35% ($T_p = 0.35$), and the capital gains tax rate on dividend income is 15% ($T_{div} = 0.15$).

   b. Now recalculate the tax disadvantage using the same income but with the maximum tax rates that existed before 2003. (These rates were 35% ($T_c = 0.35$) on corporate profits and 38.6% ($T_p = 0.386$) on personal investment income.)

P1-2. a. Calculate the tax disadvantage to organizing a U.S. business as a corporation versus a partnership under the following conditions. Assume that all earnings will be paid out as cash dividends. Operating income (operating profit before taxes) will be $3,000,000 per year under either organizational form. The tax rate on corporate profits is 30% ($T_c = 0.30$), the average personal tax rate for the partners is 35% ($T_p = 0.35$), and the capital gains tax rate on dividend income is 15% ($T_{div} = 0.15$).

   b. Now recalculate the tax disadvantage using the same income but with the maximum tax rates that existed before 2003. (These rates were 35% ($T_c = 0.35$) on corporate profits and 38.6% ($T_p = 0.386$) on personal investment income.)

The Corporate Financial Manager's Goals

P1-3. Consider the following simple corporate example involving one stockholder and one manager. There are two mutually exclusive projects in which the manager may invest and two possible manager compensation plans that the stockholder may choose to employ. The manager may be paid a flat $300,000 or receive 10% of corporate profits. The stockholder receives all profits net of manager compensation. The probabilities and associated gross profits associated with each project are given below:

Project #1		Project #2	
Probability	**Gross Profit**	**Probability**	**Gross Profit**
33.33%	$0	50.0%	$600,000
33.33%	$3,000,000	50.0%	$900,000
33.33%	$9,000,000		

   a. Which project maximizes shareholder wealth? Which compensation plan does the manager prefer if this project is chosen?

   b. Which project will the manager choose under a flat compensation arrangement?

   c. Which compensation plan aligns the interests of the stockholders and the manager so that the manager will act in the best interest of the stockholders?

   d. What do the answers tell you about structuring management compensation plans?

THOMSON REUTERS | Business School Edition

Access financial information from the Thomson ONE – Business School Edition Web site for the following problem(s). Go to **www.tobsefin.swlearning.com/**. If you have already registered your access serial number and have a username and password, click **Enter**. Otherwise, click **Register** and follow the instructions to create a username and password. Register your access serial number and then click **Enter** on the aforementioned Web site. When you click Enter, you will be prompted for your username and password (please remember that the password is case sensitive). Enter them in the respective boxes and then click **OK** (or hit **Enter**). From the ensuing page, click **Click Here to Access Thomson ONE – Business School Edition Now!** This opens up a new window that gives you access to the Thomson ONE – Business School Edition database. You can retrieve a company's financial information by entering its ticker symbol (provided for each company in the problem[s]) in the box below "Name/Symbol/Key." For further instructions on using the Thomson ONE – Business School Edition database, please refer to the online Help.

P1-4. Examine the insider activities of Johnson & Johnson (ticker symbol, JNJ). Under the Filings tab, click on the Daily 144 List in the Insider Analytics box. Does there appear to be a preponderance of proposed buying or selling of JNJ shares? Does this suggest that an *agency problem* exists?

| Overview | Prices | Financials | Estimates | Filings | News | Peers | People | ReportWriter |

Content Profile | Filings List | Conduct a Filings Search

Content Profile

Johnson & Johnson   Symbol: JNJ-N (C000002564)
Johnson & Johnson -NYSE - JNJ-N

New Brunswick, NEW JERSEY 08933 USA
http://www.jnj.com

Exchange: NYSE   CUSIP: 478160104   S&P GICS: 35202010
Sector: Health Care   SEDOL: 2475833   Pharmaceuticals
Industry: Pharmaceuticals   Company Status: Active

Filings	View Filings List		Spreadsheet Financials	
10-K	1/2/2005		US 10K Current Financials	1/2/2005
10-Q	10/2/2005		US 10Q Current Financials	10/2/2005
US Annual Report	1/2/2005		Proxy Executive Comp	4/28/2005
Int'l Annual Report	12/29/1996		US 10Q Historical Financials	1/9/2006
Proxy	4/28/2005		US 10K Historical Financials	1/9/2006
Registration	12/23/2005		WS 10K Historical Financials	12/9/2005

Insider Analytics			Recent News	More News
Daily 144 List	12/1/2005		Items: 1-20 of 51 Page: 1 of 3	
Daily Purchase & Sale	12/19/2005		9:56 AM	Elliott Associates Believes Guidant Bid by Boston Scientific Superior to Johnson & Johnson Offer Shareholder Views	PR Newswire via Comtex
Flash 144	11/29/2005			
Flash Purchase & Sale	12/17/2005			
	Source: Thomson Financial			

Smart Ethics Video

Andy Bryant, Executive Vice President of Technology, Manufacturing, and Enterprise Services, Intel Corp.

"I never thought that ethics would be a value add to a company, but today I believe it counts as part of your market cap."

Smart Practices Video

Tom Cole, Managing Director of Leveraged Finance, Citigroup

"To be good at finance you have to understand how businesses work."

Joshua Haines, Senior Credit Analyst, The Private Bank

"Most of the basic finance concepts that I learned in my first finance class I still use today."

Bill Eckmann, Principal, Solar Capital

"Besides finance, there are three subject areas that have really helped me at the beginning of my career in investment banking."

David Nickel, Controller for Intel Communications Group, Intel Corp. (former)

"Finance's primary role is to try to drive the right business decisions to increase share-holder value."

Vern LoForti, V.P., CFO, and Corporate Secretary, InfoSonics

"Sarbanes–Oxley has certainly impacted our company in many ways from operations all the way to the board."

SMART concepts

See risk management explained step-by-step.

Mini-Case

The Scope of Corporate Finance

The potential career paths for an individual with expertise in finance are varied and exciting. Career possibilities include the areas of corporate finance, commercial banking, investment banking, money management, and consulting.

Think of ways that the skills described as being vital to success in this chapter can be applied in each career listed. How will the ongoing trends of globalization and increased technological sophistication likely impact these jobs over the next decade?

Assignment

Find descriptions for these and other finance-related careers on the following Web site: **www.wetfeet.com**

chapter 2

Financial Statement and Cash Flow Analysis

What Companies Do

Financial Signs of an Improving Economy

How can a financial manager see the effects of a recession on her company? One of the best indicators of an economic downturn is an increase in the time that customers take to pay their bills. A clear signal that the U.S. economy was slumping was provided by the release of a 2009 survey of U.S. companies. The study—conducted by REL, a consulting firm, and *CFO Magazine*—documented a sharp increase in the average "days' sales outstanding," that is, the average number of days' sales that are outstanding as uncollected accounts receivable. The survey found that average days' sales outstanding increased from 37.5 days in 2008 to 41.8 days in 2009. Although this may not seem like a dramatic increase, days' sales outstanding rarely change by more than a day from one year to the next. Thus the 4.3-day increase was a worrisome sign that U.S. companies were experiencing difficulty in collecting on the credit they had extended.

Source: "Working It Out: The 2010 Working Capital Scorecard," by David M. Katz, CFO Magazine, June 1, 2010, CFO.com, **www.cfo.com/article.cfm/14499542**

Learning Objectives

After studying this chapter you will be able to:

- Understand the key financial statements that firms are required to provide to their shareholders;
- Evaluate the firm's cash flows using its financial statements, including the statement of cash flows;
- Calculate and interpret liquidity, activity, and debt ratios;
- Review the popular profitability ratios and the role of the DuPont system in analyzing the firm's returns;
- Compute and interpret the price/earnings and market/book ratios;
- Discuss the basics of corporate taxation of both ordinary income and capital gains.

Accounting is called the language of business. Corporate finance relies heavily on accounting concepts and language, but the primary focus of finance professionals and accountants differs significantly. Accountants apply *generally accepted accounting principles (GAAP)* to construct financial statements using an *accrual-based approach*. This means that accountants record revenues at the point of sale and costs when they are incurred, not necessarily when a firm receives or pays out cash.

In contrast, finance professionals use a *cash flow approach* that focuses on current and prospective inflows and outflows of cash. The financial manager must convert relevant accounting and tax information into cash inflows and cash outflows so that companies and investors can use this information for analysis and decision making.

This chapter describes how finance professionals use accounting information and terminology to analyze the firm's cash flows and financial performance. We begin with a brief review of the four major financial statements, then use them to demonstrate some of the key concepts involved in cash flow analysis. We give special emphasis to the firm's cash flows, free cash flows, the classification of inflows and outflows of cash, and the development and interpretation of statements of cash flows. Then, we discuss some popular financial ratios used to analyze the firm's financial performance. Finally, we review the basics of corporate taxation.

2-1   Financial Statements

accrual-based approach
Revenues are recorded at the point of sale and costs when they are incurred, not necessarily when a firm receives or pays out cash.

cash flow approach
Used by financial professionals to focus attention on current and prospective inflows and outflows of cash.

Jon Olson, Chief Financial Officer, Xilinx Corp.

"It is really important that you know some of the basics of accounting."

See the entire interview at **SMART**|finance

Smart Practices Video

Although our discussion in this chapter is based on U.S. accounting, the principles covered are quite general. Many national governments require public companies to generate financial statements based on widely accepted accounting rules. In the United States, these rules are the generally accepted accounting principles (GAAP) developed by the Financial Accounting Standards Board (FASB). The FASB is a nongovernmental, professional standards body that examines controversial accounting topics and issues standards that, in terms of their effect on accounting practices, almost have the force of law.

The Securities and Exchange Commission (SEC) regulates publicly traded U.S. companies as well as the nation's stock and bond markets. Every industrialized country has an agency similar to the SEC, and most developed countries mandate that companies generate financial statements that follow international accounting standards (IAS). These are broadly similar to GAAP, although GAAP rules tend to place greater emphasis on public information disclosure than IAS rules. Also, in response to the accounting scandals of 2001 and 2002, the Sarbanes–Oxley Act of 2002 (SOX) established the Public Company Accounting Oversight Board (PCAOB), which effectively gives the SEC authority to oversee the accounting profession's activities.

Reporting financial information, both externally to investors and internally to managers, is clearly an activity that is very important to senior financial executives. The following *What CFOs Do* feature shows that financial executives spend more time on this activity than on anything else.

The SEC requires four key financial statements: (1) the balance sheet, (2) the income statement, (3) the statement of retained earnings, and (4) the statement of cash flows.[1] In

---

[1]The SEC requires *publicly held corporations*—those whose stock is traded on either a broker market, like the New York Stock Exchange, or a dealer market, like Nasdaq, and/or those with more than $5 million in assets and 500 or more stockholders—to provide their stockholders with an annual stockholders' report that includes these statements. Although these statement titles are consistently used throughout the text, it is important to recognize that in practice, companies frequently use different statement titles.

What CFOs Do

CFO Survey Evidence

Surveys of corporate financial managers show that practitioners spend a large fraction of their working time on financial reporting and analysis. The chart below shows that "management reporting/accounting" and "financial planning and analysis" are the two most time-consuming tasks that financial managers routinely perform, each accounting for almost 21 hours per month. The related tasks of "external financial reporting/accounting," "internal audit," and "accounting policies" together account for an additional 30+ hours per month, clearly demonstrating that managers continually use the analytical tools described in this chapter.

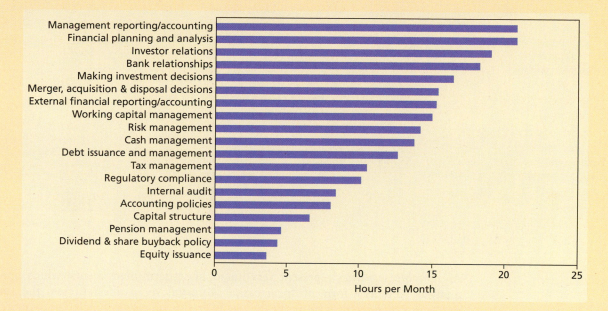

Source: Henri Servaes and Peter Tufano, "A Global Survey of Corporate Capital Structure & Treasury Risk Management Practices & Policies," Deutsche Bank (2006).

this section, we review the information these statements present using the financial statements from the 2012 stockholders' report of the Global Petroleum Corporation (GPC). Though GPC is fictional, the values constructed for it mirror those of a globally active oil company.

2-1a Balance Sheet

A firm's balance sheet presents a snapshot view of the company's financial position at a specific time. By definition, a firm's assets must equal the combined value of its liabilities and stockholders' equity. Thus creditors (lenders) or equity investors (owners) finance all of a firm's assets. A balance sheet shows assets on the left-hand side and the claims of creditors and shareholders on the right-hand side. Assets and liabilities appear in descending order of *liquidity*, the length of time it takes to convert accounts into cash during the normal course of business. The most liquid asset, *cash*, appears first, and the least liquid, *intangible assets*, comes last. Similarly, *accounts payable* represents the obligations the firm must pay with cash within the next year. The last entry on the right-hand side of the balance sheet, *stockholders' equity*, quite literally never matures—it is ongoing and is never paid in full.

Table 2.1 presents Global Petroleum Corporation's balance sheet as of December 31, 2012. As is standard practice in annual reports, the table also shows the prior year's (2011) accounts for comparison. *Cash and cash equivalents* are assets such as checking account balances at commercial banks that can be used directly as a means of payment.

Table 2.1   **Balance Sheet for Global Petroleum Corporation**

Global Petroleum Corporation Balance Sheets for the years ended December 31, 2011 and 2012 ($ in millions)

Assets	2012	2011	Liabilities and Stockholders' Equity	2012	2011
Current assets			Current liabilities		
Cash and cash equivalents	$ 440	$ 213	Accounts payable	$1,697	$1,304
Marketable securities	35	28	Notes payable	477	587
Accounts receivable	1,619	1,203	Accrued expenses	440	379
Inventories	615	530	Total current liabilities	$2,614	$2,270
Other (mostly prepaid expenses)	170	176	Long-term liabilities		
Total current assets	$2,879	$2,150	Deferred taxes	$ 907	$793
Fixed assets			Long-term debt	1,760	1,474
Gross property, plant, and equipment	$9,920	$9,024	Total long-term liabilities	$2,667	$2,267
			Total liabilities	$5,281	$4,537
Less: Accumulated depreciation	3,968	3,335	Stockholders' equity		
			Preferred stock	$ 30	$ 30
Net property, plant, and equipment	$5,952	$5,689	Common stock ($1 par value)	179	185
			Paid-in capital in excess of par	442	386
Intangible assets and others	758	471	Retained earnings	4,271	3,670
Net fixed assets	$6,710	$6,160	Less: Treasury stock	614	498
Total assets	**$9,589**	**$8,310**	Total stockholders' equity	$4,308	$3,773
			Total liabilities and stockholders' equity	**$9,589**	**$8,310**

Marketable securities represent very liquid, short-term investments, which financial analysts view as a form of "near cash." *Accounts receivable* represent the amount customers owe the firm from sales made on credit. *Inventories* include raw materials, work in process (partially finished goods), and finished goods held by the firm.

The entry for *gross property, plant, and equipment* is the original cost of all real property, structures, and long-lived equipment owned by the firm. *Net property, plant, and equipment* represents the difference between their original value and *accumulated depreciation*—the cumulative expense recorded for the depreciation of fixed assets since their purchase. On their financial statements, firms do not deduct the full cost of fixed assets when these assets are purchased. Instead, they deduct a portion of the cost, called depreciation, over several years. The only fixed asset that is not depreciated is land, because it seldom declines in value. Finally, *intangible assets* include items such as patents, trademarks, copyrights, or (in the case of petroleum companies) mineral rights entitling the company to extract oil and gas on specific properties. Although intangible assets are usually nothing more than legal rights, they are often extremely valuable—as demonstrated by our discussion of the market value of global brands in this chapter's *What Companies Do Globally* feature.

Now turn your attention to the right-hand side of the balance sheet. Current liabilities include *accounts payable*, amounts owed for credit purchases by the firm; *notes payable,* outstanding short-term loans, typically from commercial banks; and *accrued expenses,* costs incurred by the firm that have not yet been paid. Examples of accruals include taxes owed to the government and wages due employees. Accounts payable and accruals are often called "spontaneous liabilities" because they tend to change directly with changes in sales.

In the United States and many other countries, laws permit firms to construct two sets of financial statements, one for reporting to the public and one for tax purposes. For example, when a firm purchases a long-lived asset, it can choose to depreciate this asset rapidly for the purpose of obtaining large, immediate tax write-offs. When the firm constructs financial statements for release to the public, however, it may choose

deferred taxes
An account that reflects the difference between the taxes that firms actually pay and the tax liabilities they report on their public financial statements.

long-term debt
Debt that matures more than one year in the future.

preferred stock
A form of ownership that has preference over common stock when the firm distributes income and assets.

common stock
The most basic form of corporate ownership.

par value (common stock)
An arbitrary value assigned to common stock on a firm's balance sheet.

paid-in capital in excess of par
The number of shares of common stock outstanding multiplied by the original selling price of the shares, net of the par value.

retained earnings
The cumulative total of the earnings that a firm has reinvested since its inception.

treasury stock
Common shares that were issued and later reacquired by the firm through share repurchase programs and are therefore being held in reserve by the firm.

WHAT TO ASK

Does your company place a great deal of importance on hitting specific earnings targets?

common-size income statement
An income statement in which all entries are expressed as a percentage of sales.

a different depreciation method—perhaps one that results in higher reported earnings in the early years of the asset's life. The deferred taxes entry is a long-term liability that reflects the difference between the taxes that firms actually pay and the tax liabilities they report on their public financial statements. Long-term debt represents debt that matures more than one year in the future.

The stockholders' equity section provides information about the claims against the firm held by investors who own preferred and common stock. The preferred stock entry shows the proceeds from the sale of preferred stock ($30 million for GPC), which is a form of ownership that has preference over common stock when the firm distributes income and assets. Next, two entries show the amount paid in by the original purchasers of common stock, the most basic form of corporate ownership. The common stock entry equals the number of outstanding common shares multiplied by the par value per share, which is an arbitrary value with little or no economic significance. Paid-in capital in excess of par equals the number of shares outstanding multiplied by the original selling price of the shares, net of the par value. The combined value of common stock and paid-in capital in excess of par equals the proceeds the firm received when it originally sold shares to investors. Retained earnings are the cumulative total of the earnings that the firm has reinvested since its inception. Be sure you know that retained earnings are not a reservoir of unspent cash. When the retained earnings vault is empty, it is because the firm has already reinvested the earnings in new assets.

Finally, the treasury stock entry records the value of common shares that the firm currently holds in reserve. Usually, treasury stock appears on the balance sheet because the firm has reacquired previously issued stock through a share repurchase program.

GPC's balance sheet (Table 2.1) shows that the firm's total assets increased by $1,279 million, from $8,310 million in 2011 to $9,589 million in 2012. As expected, the total liabilities and shareholders' equity exactly match these totals in 2011 and 2012.

2-1b Income Statement

Table 2.2 presents Global Petroleum Corporation's income statement (also called the "profit-and-loss statement," or "P&L") for the year ended December 31, 2012. As with the balance sheet, GPC's income statement includes data from 2011 for comparison.[2] In the vocabulary of accounting, income (also called *profit*, *earnings*, or *margin*) equals revenue minus expenses. A firm's income statement, however, has several measures of "income" appearing at different points. The first income measure is *gross profit*, the amount by which *sales revenue* exceeds the *cost of goods sold* (the direct cost of producing or purchasing the goods sold). Next, a firm deducts from gross profits various operating expenses, including selling expense, general and administrative expense, and depreciation expense.[3] The resulting *operating profit* ($1,531 million for GPC) represents the profits earned from the sale of products, although this amount does not include financial and tax costs. *Other income*, earned on transactions not directly related to producing and/or selling the firm's products, is added to operating income to yield *earnings before interest and taxes (EBIT)* of $1,671 million. When a firm has no "other income," its operating profit and *EBIT* are equal. Next, the firm subtracts *interest expense*—representing the cost of debt financing—from *EBIT* to find *pretax income*. For example, GPC subtracts $123 million of interest expense from *EBIT* to find *pretax income* of $1,548 million.

The final step is to subtract taxes from pretax income to arrive at *net income*, or *net profits after taxes*, ($949 million for GPC). Net income is the proverbial bottom line and the single most important accounting number for both corporate managers and external financial analysts. Note that GPC incurred a total tax liability of $599 million during 2012, but only the $367 million *current* portion must be paid

---

[2]When reporting to shareholders, firms typically also include a so-called common-size income statement that expresses all income statement entries as a percentage of sales.
[3]Companies frequently include depreciation expense in manufacturing costs—the cost of goods sold—when calculating gross profits. In this text, we show depreciation as an expense in order to isolate its effect on cash flows.

Table 2.2   **Income Statement for Global Petroleum Corporation**

Global Petroleum Corporation Income Statements for the Years Ended December 31, 2011 and 2012 ($ in millions)

	2012	2011
Sales revenue	$12,843	$9,110
Less: Cost of goods sold[a]	8,519	5,633
Gross profit	$ 4,324	$3,477
Less: Operating and other expenses	1,544	1,521
Less: Selling, general and administrative expenses	616	584
Less: Depreciation expense	633	608
Operating profit	$ 1,531	$ 764
Plus: Other income	140	82
Earnings before interest and taxes (*EBIT*)	$ 1,671	$ 846
Less: Interest expense	123	112
Pretax income	$ 1,548	$ 734
Less: Taxes		
Current	367	158
Deferred	232	105
Total taxes	599	263
Net income (net profits after taxes)	$ 949	$ 471
Less: Preferred stock dividends	3	3
Earnings available for common stockholders	$ 946	$ 468
Less: Dividends	345	326
To retained earnings	$ 601	$ 142
Per share data[b]		
Earnings per share (*EPS*)	$ 5.29	$ 2.52
Dividends per share (*DPS*)	$ 1.93	$ 1.76
Price per share	$ 76.25	$71.50

[a] Annual purchases have historically represented about 80% of cost of goods sold. Using this relationship, its credit purchases in 2012 were $6,815 and in 2011, they were $4,506.

[b] Based on 178,719,400 and 185,433,100 shares outstanding as of December 31, 2012 and 2011, respectively.

© Cengage Learning 2012

earnings available for common stockholders
Net income net of preferred stock dividends.

earnings per share (*EPS*)
Earnings available for common stockholders divided by the number of shares of common stock outstanding.

dividend per share (*DPS*)
The portion of the earnings per share paid to stockholders.

immediately. The remaining $232 million in deferred taxes must be paid eventually, but these are noncash expenses for year 2013.

From its net income, GPC paid $3 million in dividends on its $30 million of preferred stock outstanding during both 2011 and 2012. Net income net of preferred stock dividends is **earnings available for common stockholders**. Dividing earnings available for common stockholders by the number of shares of common stock outstanding results in **earnings per share (*EPS*)**. Earnings per share represents the amount earned during the period on each outstanding share of common stock. Because there are 178,719,400 shares of GPC stock outstanding on December 31, 2012, its *EPS* for 2012 is $5.29, which represents a significant increase from the 2011 *EPS* of $2.52. The cash **dividend per share (*DPS*)** paid to GPC's common stockholders during 2012 is $1.93, up slightly from the 2011 *DPS* of $1.76.

2-1c Statement of Retained Earnings

The statement of retained earnings is a shortened form of the statement of stockholders' equity that reconciles the net income earned during a given year, and any cash dividends paid, with the change in retained earnings between the start and end of

What Companies Do Globally

Assessing the Market Value of Global Brands

How much is a global brand name worth? Interbrand Corporation, a New York–based consulting firm, has been trying to answer this question for several years. The table below details what this firm considers the 20 most valuable brands of 2010 and also lists the value of those brands in 2009. The total brand values are large and are dominated by brands of U.S.-based companies. Additionally, the rankings are remarkably stable from year to year; the 2010 ranking listed all 20 brands included in 2009, though the ranking of some (particularly Google, Nokia, Toyota, and Apple) changed significantly.

Although American companies are not required to disclose estimated brand values in their financial statements, large publicly traded British and Australian firms must do so. Brand values do, however, have a major impact on U.S.

accounting rules in one important area: accounting for the "goodwill" created when a firm is acquired by another company for more than the acquired firm's book value. This premium over book value represents the higher market (versus book) value of intangible assets such as patents, copyrights, and trademarks as well as brand names and business relationships that are not accounted for at all. The Financial Accounting Standards Board requires acquirers to periodically assess the fair value of assets they purchase through acquisitions. If the fair value of those assets declines significantly over time the firm must recognize "goodwill impairment," meaning that the value of its intangible assets has also declined. Charges arising from goodwill impairment can have a dramatic effect on reported earnings.

© Cengage Learning 2012

Rank 2010	Rank 2009	Brand	2010 Brand Value ($ Million)	2009 Brand Value ($ Million)	Percent Change	Country of Ownership
1	1	Coca-Cola	70,452	68,734	2%	U.S.
2	3	Microsoft	60,895	56,647	7%	U.S.
3	2	IBM	64,727	60,211	8%	U.S.
4	7	Google	43,557	31,980	36%	U.S.
5	4	GE	42,808	47,777	−10%	U.S.
6	6	McDonald's	33,578	32,275	4%	U.S.
7	9	Intel	32,015	30,636	4%	U.S.
8	5	Nokia	29,495	34,864	−15%	Finland
9	10	Disney	28,731	28,447	1%	U.S.
10	11	HP	26,867	24,096	12%	U.S.
11	8	Toyota	26,192	31,330	−16%	Japan
12	12	Mercedes-Benz	25,169	23,867	6%	Germany
13	13	Gillette	23,298	22,841	2%	U.S.
14	14	Cisco	23,219	22,030	5%	U.S.
15	15	BMW	22,322	21,671	3%	Germany
16	16	Louis Vuitton	21,860	21,120	4%	France
17	20	Apple	21,143	15,433	37%	U.S.
18	17	Marlboro	19,961	19,010	5%	U.S.
19	19	Samsung	19,491	17,518	11%	Korea
20	18	Honda	18,506	17,803	4%	Japan

What CFOs Do

CFO Survey Evidence

In a recent study, Graham, Harvey, and Rajgopal (2005) asked CFOs to identify the most important financial measures that they reported to outside investors. The pie chart to the right shows that the overwhelming response was earnings. The study also reported that CFOs believed that reporting higher earnings than the same quarter in the prior year was the most important earnings "benchmark" for firms to achieve, even more important than beating Wall Street analysts' earnings forecasts. The importance of earnings stands in contrast to our recommendation that managers focus on cash flows.

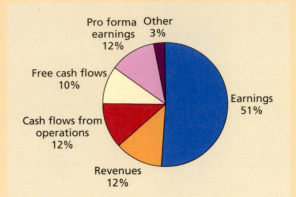

Source: Reprinted from *Journal of Accounting and Economics*, 40, John R. Graham, Campbell R. Harvey, and Shiva Rajgopal, Figure 2 and Table 9 of "The Economic Implications of Corporate Financial Reporting," pp. 3–73, Copyright © 2005, with permission from Elsevier.

that year. Table 2.3 presents this statement for Global Petroleum Corporation for the year ended December 31, 2012. It shows that the company began the year with $3,670 million in retained earnings and had net income after taxes of $949 million. From its net income, GPC paid a total of $348 million in preferred and common stock dividends. At year-end, retained earnings were $4,271 million. Thus, in 2012 the net increase for GPC was $601 million ($949 million net income minus $348 million in dividends).

2-1d Statement of Cash Flows

The statement of cash flows summarizes the inflows and outflows of cash during a given period, typically a year. This statement isolates the firm's operating, investment, and financing cash flows and reconciles them with changes in its cash and marketable securities during the year. Table 2.5 presents GPC's statement of cash flows for the year ended December 31, 2012. This statement is discussed in greater depth in Section 2-2, where we present some important cash flow concepts and measures and then show how to use those data to develop and interpret the statement of cash flows.

Table 2.3 **Statement of Retained Earnings for Global Petroleum Corporation**

Global Petroleum Corporation Statement of Retained Earnings for the Year Ended December 31, 2012 ($ in millions)

Retained earnings balance (January 1, 2012)		$3,670
Plus: Net income (for 2012)		949
Less: Cash dividends (paid during 2012)		
Preferred stock	$ 3	
Common stock	345	
Total dividends paid		348
Retained earnings balance (December 31, 2012)		$4,271

2-1e Notes to Financial Statements

A public company's financial statements include explanatory notes keyed to the relevant accounts in the statements. These notes provide detailed information on the accounting policies, calculations, and transactions that underlie entries in the financial statements. For example, the notes to Hasbro Inc.'s financial statements cover 34 of the 107 pages in its annual report. Notes typically provide additional information about a firm's revenue recognition practices, income taxes, fixed assets, leases, and employee compensation plans. Professional security analysts find this information particularly useful, and they routinely scour the notes when evaluating a firm's performance and value.

2-1 Concept Review Questions

1. What role do the FASB and SEC play with regard to GAAP?

2. Are balance sheets and income statements prepared with the same purpose in mind? How are these two statements different, and how are they related?

3. Which statements are of greatest interest to creditors? Which would be of greatest interest to stockholders?

2-2 Cash Flow Analysis

Although financial managers are interested in the information in the firm's accrual-based financial statements, their primary focus is on cash flows. Without adequate cash to pay obligations on time, to fund operations and growth, and to compensate owners, the firm will fail. The financial manager and other interested parties can gain insight into the firm's cash flows over a given time period by using some popular measures of cash flow and by analyzing the firm's statement of cash flows.

2-2a The Firm's Cash Flows

operating flows
Cash inflows and outflows directly related to the production and sale of a firm's products or services.

investment flows
Cash flows associated with the purchase or sale of fixed assets.

financing flows
Cash flow that result from debt and equity financing transactions.

free cash flow (*FCF*)
The net amount of cash flow remaining after the firm has met all operating needs including working capital commitments and capital expenditures. Represents the cash amount that a firm could distribute to debt and equity investors after meeting all its other obligations.

Figure 2.1 illustrates the firm's cash flows. Note that in the process of evaluating a firm's cash flows, analysts view cash and marketable securities as perfect substitutes. Both represent a reservoir of liquidity that increases with *cash inflows* and decreases with *cash outflows*.

A firm's total cash flows can conveniently be divided into (1) operating flows, (2) investment flows, and (3) financing flows. The operating flows are cash inflows and outflows directly related to the production and sale of products or services. Investment flows are cash flows associated with the purchase or sale of fixed assets. Clearly, purchases result in cash outflows, whereas sales generate cash inflows. The financing flows result from debt and equity financing transactions. Taking on new debt (short term or long term) results in a cash inflow; repaying existing debt requires a cash outflow. Similarly, the sale of stock generates a cash inflow, whereas the repurchase of stock or payment of cash dividends results in a cash outflow. In combination, the operating, investment, and financing cash flows during a given period affect the firm's cash and marketable securities balances.

Monitoring cash flow is important for financial managers and for outside analysts trying to estimate a firm's worth. Managers and analysts track a variety of cash flow measures. Among these one of the most important is *free cash flow*.

Free Cash Flow   The measure of free cash flow (*FCF*) is the amount of cash flow available to investors—the providers of debt and equity capital. It represents the net amount of cash flow remaining after the firm has met all operating needs including working capital commitments and capital expenditures. Free cash flow for a given period can be calculated in two steps.

Figure 2.1   **The Pattern of Cash Flows Through a Firm**

The firm's reservoir of liquidity, containing both cash and marketable securities, is impacted by changes in (1) operating flows, (2) investment flows, and (3) financing flows.

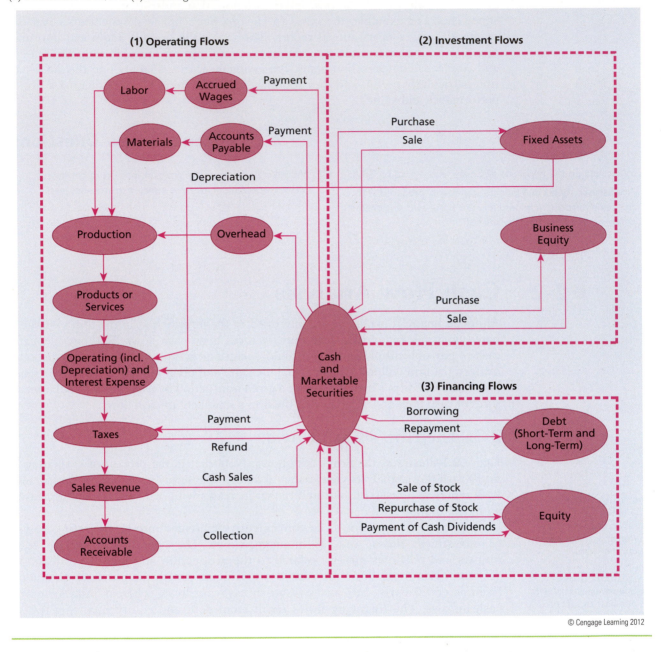

© Cengage Learning 2012

net operating profits after taxes (NOPAT)
The amount of earnings before interest and after taxes, which equals EBIT × (1 − *T*), where EBIT is earnings before interest and taxes and *T* equals the corporate tax rate.

First, we find the firm's **net operating profits after taxes (NOPAT)**, the firm's earning before interest and after taxes:[4]

(Eq. 2.1)	$\text{NOPAT} = \text{EBIT} \times (1 - T)$

where

EBIT = earnings before interest and taxes
   T = corporate tax rate

---

[4]A related indicator of a firm's financial performance is *earnings before interest, taxes, depreciation, and amortization* (EBITDA). Analysts use EBITDA to compare profitability of companies because it measures revenue minus all expenses other than interest, taxes, depreciation, and amortization. It thereby eliminates the effects of financing and accounting decisions. Although EBITDA is a good measure of profitability, it does not measure cash flows.

operating cash flow (OCF)
The amount of cash flow generated by a firm from its operations. Mathematically, earnings before interest and taxes (*EBIT*) minus taxes plus depreciation.

noncash charges
Expenses, such as depreciation, amortization, and depletion allowances, that appear on the income statement but do not involve an actual outlay of cash.

Adding depreciation back into NOPAT yields **operating cash flow (OCF)**, which is the amount of cash flow generated by the firm's operations.

> **(Eq. 2.2)** $$OCF = NOPAT + Depreciation$$

Note that because depreciation is a noncash charge, we add it back when determining *OCF*. **Noncash charges**—such as depreciation, amortization, and depletion allowances—are expenses that appear on the income statement but do not involve an actual outlay of cash. Almost all firms list depreciation on their income statements, so we focus on depreciation in our presentation. But when amortization or depletion occur in a firm's financial statements, they are treated in a similar manner.

Substituting Equation 2.1 for NOPAT into Equation 2.2, we obtain a single equation for operating cash flow:

> **(Eq. 2.3)** $$OCF = [EBIT \times (1 - T)] + Depreciation$$

Substituting the values from GPC's 2012 income statement (from Table 2.2) and assuming a 38.70% tax rate ($T = 38.70\%$), as implied by GPC's 2012 income statement, we get GPC's operating cash flow:

$$OCF = \$1,671 \times (1.00 - 0.3870) + \$633 = \$1,024 + \$633 = \$1,657$$

Hence, GPC's *OCF* was $1,657 million.

Next we convert this operating cash flow to free cash flow (*FCF*). To do so, we deduct the firm's net investments (denoted by Delta, the "change" symbol Δ) in fixed and current assets from operating cash flow, as shown in the following equation:

> **(Eq. 2.4)** $$FCF = OCF - \Delta FA - \Delta WC$$

where

ΔFA = change in gross fixed assets
ΔWC = change in working capital
$\quad = \Delta CA - \Delta A/P - \Delta accruals$

where

ΔCA = change in current assets,
$\Delta A/P$ = change in accounts payable
$\Delta accruals$ = change in accrued expenses

Spontaneous current liability changes occur automatically with changes in sales. They must therefore be deducted from current assets in order to find the net change in working capital investment. From the preceding calculation, we know that GPC's *OCF* in 2012 was $1,657 million. Using GPC's 2011 and 2012 balance sheets (Table 2.1), we can calculate the changes in gross fixed assets, current assets, accounts payable, and accruals between 2011 and 2012:

$$\Delta FA = \$9,920 - \$9,024 = \$896$$
$$\Delta CA = \$2,879 - \$2,150 = \$729$$
$$\Delta A/P = \$1,697 - \$1,304 = \$393$$
$$\Delta accruals = \$440 - \$379 = \$61$$
$$\Delta WC = \$729 - \$393 - \$61 = \$275$$

Substituting these values into Equation 2.4, yields the following expression:

$$FCF = \$1,657 - \$896 - \$275$$
$$= \$486$$

Table 2.4   **The Inflows and Outflows of Corporate Cash**

Inflows	Outflows
Decrease in any asset	Increase in any asset
Increase in any liability	Decrease in any liability
Net income (profit after tax)	Net loss
Depreciation and other noncash charges	Dividends paid
Sale of common or preferred stock	Repurchase or retirement of stock

? WHAT TO ASK

How much emphasis does your firm place on cash flow as compared to earnings?

The first line of this *FCF* calculation shows that, after subtracting $896 million in fixed asset investment and $275 million in current asset investment net of accounts payable and accruals from its *OCF* of $1,657, GPC had free cash flow in 2012 of $486 million available to pay its investors. We will use free cash flow in Chapter 5 to estimate the value of a firm. At this point, suffice it to say that *FCF* is an important measure of cash flow used by corporate finance professionals.

Inflows and Outflows of Cash Table 2.4 classifies the basic inflows and outflows of cash for corporations (assuming other things are held constant). For example, a $1,000 increase in accounts payable would be an *inflow of cash*. A $2,500 increase in inventory would be an *outflow of cash*.

Two additional points about the classifications in Table 2.4 are worth noting:

1. A *decrease* in an asset (such as inventory) is an *inflow of cash* because cash that has been tied up in the asset is released and can be used for some other purpose, such as repaying a loan. In contrast, an *increase* in inventory (or any other asset) is an *outflow of cash* because additional inventory ties up more of the firm's cash. Similar logic explains why an increase in any liability is an inflow of cash and why a decrease in any liability is an outflow of cash.

2. Our earlier discussion noted why depreciation and other noncash charges are considered cash inflows. Logic suggests that if net income is a cash inflow then a *net loss* (negative net profits after taxes) is a cash outflow. The firm must balance its losses with an inflow of cash from, say, selling off some of its fixed assets (reducing an asset) or increasing external borrowing (increasing a liability). Can a firm have a *net loss* (negative NOPAT) and still have positive operating cash flow? Yes, as Equation 2.2 indicates, this can occur when depreciation and other noncash charges during the period are greater than the net loss. The statement of cash flows treats net income (or net losses) and depreciation and other noncash charges as separate entries.

EXAMPLE

On December 31, 2010, and on September 30, 2010, Procter & Gamble Co.® (P&G) reported the following balances, in millions of dollars, in certain current asset and liability accounts.

Account	December 31, 2010	September 30, 2010
Cash	$ 3,249	$ 2,603
Accounts receivable	7,514	7,050
Inventory	7,423	7,277
Accounts payable	16,083	16,128
Short-term debt	11,158	11,512

All current asset accounts increased during the last quarter of 2010, causing outflows of cash for P&G. It may seem strange to think of an increase in cash balances as a *use* of cash, but it simply means that P&G used some of its cash flow to invest in liquid resources. On the liabilities side, accounts payable and short-term debt both decreased, representing more cash outflows for P&G.

2-2b Developing and Interpreting the Statement of Cash Flows

Accountants construct the statement of cash flows by using the income statement for a given year along with the beginning- and end-of-year balance sheets. The procedure involves classifying balance sheet changes as inflows or outflows of cash; obtaining income statement data; classifying the relevant values into operating, investment, and financing cash flows; and presenting them in the proper format.

Global Petroleum Corporation's statement of cash flows for the year ended December 31, 2012, appears in Table 2.5. Note that the statement assigns positive values to all cash inflows and negative values to all cash outflows. Notice that the calculation of "Cash provided by operating activities" includes more detail than the *OCF* calculation in Equation 2.1, and therefore these two measures differ. Notice also that, in the investment activities section, the statement of cash flows records the increase in *gross* fixed assets—rather than *net* fixed assets—as a cash outflow. Depreciation accounts for the difference between changes in gross and net fixed assets, but depreciation expense appears in the operating activities section of the statement. The focus on changes in gross fixed assets avoids double-counting depreciation in the statement. For a similar reason, the statement does not show a specific entry for the change in retained earnings as an inflow (or outflow) of cash. Instead, the factors that determine the change in retained earnings (i.e., profits or losses and dividends) appear as separate entries in the statement.

By adding up the items in each category—operating, investment, and financing activities—we obtain the net increase (or decrease) in cash and marketable securities for the year. As a check, this value should reconcile with the actual yearly change in cash and marketable securities, obtained from the beginning- and end-of-year balance sheets.

Table 2.5   **Statement of Cash Flows for Global Petroleum Corporation**

This statement is constructed using the firm's income statements and two most recent balance sheets. It groups cash flow into (1) cash flow from operations, (2) cash flow from investments, and (3) cash flow from financing. The net change at the bottom of the statement should match the net change in the cash and marketable securities balance shown between the firm's most recent two balance sheets.

Global Petroleum Corporation Statement of Cash Flows for the Year Ended December 31, 2012 ($ in millions)		
Cash flow from operating activities		
Net income (net profit after tax)	$949	
Depreciation	633	
Increase in accounts receivable	(416)	
Increase in inventories	(85)	
Decrease in other current assets	6	
Increase in accounts payable	393	
Increase in accrued expenses	61	
Cash provided by operating activities		$1,541
Cash flow from investment activities		
Increase in gross fixed assets	($896)	
Increase in intangible and other assets	(287)	
Cash provided (consumed) by investment activities		($1,183)
Cash flow from financing activities		
Decrease in notes payable	($110)	
Increase in deferred taxes	114	
Increase in long-term debt	286	
Changes in stockholders' equity	(66)	
Dividends paid	(348)	
Cash provided (consumed) by financing activities		($124)
Net increase in cash and marketable securities		**$234**

By applying this procedure to GPC's 2012 income statement and 2011 and 2012 balance sheets, we obtain the firm's 2012 statement of cash flows (see Table 2.5). It shows that GPC experienced a $234 million increase in cash and marketable securities in 2012. Looking at GPC's 2011 and 2012 balance sheets in Table 2.1, we see that the firm's cash increased by $227 million and that its marketable securities increased by $7 million. The $234 million net increase in cash and marketable securities from the statement of cash flows reconciles with the total change of $234 million in these accounts during 2012. Therefore, GPC's statement of cash flows reconciles with the balance sheet changes.

The statement of cash flows allows the financial manager and other interested parties to analyze the firm's cash flow over time. Unusual changes in either the major categories of cash flow or in specific items offer clues to problems a firm may be experiencing. For example, an unusually large increase in accounts receivable or inventory, resulting in major cash outflow, may signal credit or inventory problems. Financial managers and analysts can also prepare a statement of cash flows developed from projected, or pro forma, financial statements. They use this approach to determine if the firm will need additional external financing or will generate excess cash that could be reinvested or distributed to shareholders. After you learn the concepts, principles, and practices of corporate finance presented in the text, you will be able to glean a good amount of useful information from the statement of cash flows.

2-2 Concept Review Questions

4. How do depreciation and other noncash charges act as sources of cash inflow to the firm? Why does a depreciation allowance exist in the tax laws? For a profitable firm, is it better to depreciate an asset quickly or slowly for tax purposes? Explain.

5. What is *operating cash flow (OCF)*? How does it relate to net operating profits after taxes (NOPAT)? What is *free cash flow (FCF)*, and how is it related to *OCF*?

6. Why is the financial manager likely to have great interest in the firm's *statement of cash flows*? What type of information can interested parties obtain from this statement?

2-3 Assessing Financial Performance Using Ratio Analysis

ratio analysis
Calculating and interpreting financial ratios to assess a firm's performance and status.

Assessing a firm's financial statements is of interest to shareholders, creditors, and the firm's own management. A firm often wants to compare its financial condition to that of similar firms, but doing so can be very tricky. For example, suppose you are introduced to a man named Bill who tells you that he runs a company that earned a profit of $10 million last year. Would you be impressed by that? What if you knew that Bill's last name was Gates? Most people would agree that a profit of $10 million would be a great disappointment for Microsoft, the firm run by Bill Gates, because Microsoft's annual profit is typically in the billions.

The point here is that the amounts of sales, profits, and other items that appear on a firm's financial statements are difficult to interpret unless we have some way to put the numbers in perspective. To analyze financial statements, we need relative measures that, in effect, normalize size differences. Effective analysis of financial statements is thus based on the use of *ratios* or *relative values*. Ratio analysis involves calculating and interpreting financial ratios to assess a firm's performance and status.

2-3a Using Financial Ratios

Different constituents will focus on different types of financial ratios. Creditors are primarily interested in ratios that measure the firm's short-term liquidity and its ability to make interest and principal payments. A secondary concern of creditors is profitability; they want assurance that the business is healthy and will continue to be successful. Present and prospective shareholders focus on ratios that measure the firm's current and future levels of risk and return, because these two dimensions directly affect share price. The firm's managers use ratios to generate an overall picture of the company's financial health and to monitor its performance from period to period. They carefully examine unexpected changes in order to isolate developing problems.

An additional complication of ratio analysis is that a normal ratio in one industry may be highly unusual in another. For example, the net profit margin ratio measures the net income generated by each dollar of sales. (We will show later how to compute the ratio.) Net profit margins vary dramatically across industries. An outstanding net profit margin in the retail grocery industry would look paltry in the software business. Therefore, when making subjective judgments about the health of a given company, analysts usually compare the firm's ratios to two benchmarks. First, they compare the financial ratios in the current year with previous years' ratios. In doing so, they hope to identify trends that will aid in evaluating the firm's prospects. Second, they compare the ratios of one company with those of other benchmark firms in the same industry (or to an industry average obtained from a trade association or third-party provider).

We will use the 2012 and 2011 balance sheets and income statements for Global Petroleum Corporation, presented earlier in Tables 2.1 and 2.2, to demonstrate ratio calculations. (To simplify the presentation, we have deleted the *millions* after GPC's values.) The ratios presented in this chapter can be applied to nearly any company. Of course, many companies in different industries use ratios that focus on aspects peculiar to their industry.[5] We will cover the most common financial ratios, which are grouped into five categories: *liquidity, activity, debt, profitability,* and *market* ratios.

2-3b Liquidity Ratios

Liquidity ratios measure a firm's ability to satisfy its short-term obligations *as they come due*. Because a common precursor to financial distress or bankruptcy is low or declining liquidity, liquidity ratios are good leading indicators of cash flow problems. The two basic measures of liquidity are the *current ratio* and the *quick (acid-test) ratio*.

The **current ratio**, one of the most commonly cited financial ratios, measures the firm's ability to meet its short-term obligations. It is defined as current assets *divided* by current liabilities. The current ratio presents in ratio form what **net working capital** measures by *subtracting* current liabilities from current assets. The current ratio for GPC on December 31, 2012, is computed as follows:

$$\text{Current ratio} = \frac{\text{current assets}}{\text{current liabilities}} = \frac{\$2,879}{\$2,614} = 1.10$$

How high should the current ratio be? The answer depends on the type of business and on the costs and benefits of having too much versus not enough liquidity. For example, a current ratio of 1.0 would be acceptable for a utility but might be unacceptable for a manufacturer. The more predictable a firm's cash flows, the lower the acceptable current ratio. Because the business of oil exploration and development has notoriously unpredictable annual cash flows, GPC's current ratio of 1.10 indicates that the firm takes a fairly aggressive approach to managing its liquidity.

The **quick (acid-test) ratio** is similar to the current ratio except that it *excludes* inventory, which is usually the least-liquid current asset. The generally low liquidity of inventory results from two factors. First, many types of inventory cannot be easily sold because they are partially completed items, special-purpose items, and the like. Second, inventory is typically sold on credit, so it becomes an account receivable before being converted into cash. The quick ratio is calculated as follows:

$$\text{Quick ratio} = \frac{\text{current assets} - \text{inventory}}{\text{current liabilities}} = \frac{\$2,879 - \$615}{\$2,614} = 0.866$$

The quick ratio for GPC in 2012 is 0.866.

The quick ratio provides a better measure of overall liquidity *only* when a firm's inventory cannot be easily converted into cash. If inventory is liquid, then the **current** ratio is a preferred measure. Because GPC's inventory is mostly petroleum and refined

---

WHAT TO ASK

Does your firm focus on certain financial ratios to assess its performance? Which ones are most important?

---

liquidity ratios
Measure a firm's ability to satisfy its short-term obligations *as they come due*.

current ratio
A measure of a firm's ability to meet its short-term obligations, defined as current assets *divided* by current liabilities.

net working capital
A measure of a firm's liquidity calculated by *subtracting* current liabilities from current assets.

quick (acid-test) ratio
A measure of a firm's liquidity that is similar to the current ratio except that it *excludes* inventory, which is usually the least-liquid current asset.

---

[5]For example, airlines pay close attention to the ratio of revenues to passenger miles flown. Retailers diligently track the growth in same-store sales from one year to the next.

products that can be readily converted into cash, the firm's managers will probably focus on the current ratio.

2-3c Activity Ratios

activity ratios
A measure of the speed with which a firm converts various accounts into sales or cash.

Activity ratios measure the speed with which the firm converts various accounts into sales or cash. Analysts use activity ratios as guides to assess how efficiently the firm manages its assets and its accounts payable.

Inventory turnover provides a measure of how quickly a firm sells its goods. Here is the calculation for GPC's 2012 *inventory turnover ratio*:

inventory turnover
A measure of how quickly a firm sells its goods.

$$\text{Inventory turnover} = \frac{\text{cost of goods sold}}{\text{inventory}} = \frac{\$8{,}519}{\$615} = 13.85$$

In the numerator we used cost of goods sold, rather than sales, because firms value inventory at cost on their balance sheets. Note also that, in the denominator, we use the *ending* inventory balance of \$615. If inventories are growing over time or exhibit seasonal patterns then analysts sometimes use the *average* level of inventory throughout the year, rather than the ending balance, to calculate this ratio.

The resulting turnover of 13.85 indicates that the firm basically sells outs its inventory 13.85 times each year, or slightly more than once per month. This value is most meaningful when compared with that of other firms in the same industry or with the firm's past inventory turnover. An inventory turnover of 20.0 is not unusual for a grocery store, whereas a common inventory turnover for an aircraft manufacturer is 4.0. GPC's inventory turnover is in line with those for other oil and gas companies, and it is slightly above the firm's own historic norms.

average age of inventory
A measure of inventory turnover, calculated by dividing the turnover figure into 365, the number of days in a year.

We can easily convert inventory turnover into an **average age of inventory** by dividing the turnover figure into 365 (the number of days in a year). For GPC, the average age of inventory is 26.4 days (365 ÷ 13.85), meaning that GPC's inventory balance turns over about every 26 days.

> **EXAMPLE**
>
> Inventory ratios, like most other financial ratios, vary a great deal from one industry to another. For example, on December 31, 2010, Anheuser-Busch Companies reported inventory of \$2.4 billion and cost of goods sold of \$16.2 billion. This implies an inventory turnover ratio for Anheuser-Busch of about 6.75 and an average age of inventory of about 54 days. With the limited shelf life of beer, its primary product, Anheuser-Busch cannot afford to hold inventory too long.
>
> In contrast, for the year ended December 25, 2010, Intel Corp., a major computer hardware manufacturer, reported cost of goods sold of \$15.1 billion and inventory of \$3.8 billion. Intel's inventory turnover ratio is thus 3.97, and its average age of inventory is about 92 days.
>
> Clearly, the differences in these inventory ratios reflect differences in the economic circumstances of the industries. Apparently, beer loses its value much faster than do semiconductors.

average collection period
The average amount of time that elapses from a sale on credit until the payment becomes usable funds for a firm. Calculated by dividing accounts receivable by average daily sales. Also called the *average age of accounts receivable*.

The **average collection period**, or *average age of accounts receivable*, is useful in evaluating credit and collection policies.[6] It measures the average amount of time that elapses from a sale on credit until the payment becomes useable funds for a firm. To compute the measure, we divide the firm's average daily sales into the accounts receivable balance. As shown in the following equations, in 2012 it takes GPC on average 46.0 days to receive payment from a credit sale:

$$\text{Average daily sales} = \frac{\text{annual sales}}{365} = \frac{\$12{,}843}{365} = \$35.19$$

$$\text{Average collection period} = \frac{\text{accounts receivable}}{\text{average daily sales}} = \frac{\$1{,}619}{\$35.19} = 46.0 \text{ days}$$

The average collection period is meaningful only in relation to the firm's credit terms. If GPC extends 30-day credit terms to customers, then an average collection period of

---

[6]The average collection period is sometimes called the *days' sales outstanding (DSO)*. As with the inventory turnover ratio, the average collection period can be calculated using end-of-year accounts receivable or the average receivables balance for the year. We discuss the evaluation and establishment of credit and collection policies in Chapter 16.

46.0 days may indicate a poorly managed credit or collection department (or both). On the other hand, a longer collection period could be the result of an intentional relaxation of credit-term enforcement in response to competitive pressures. If the firm had offered customers 45-day credit terms then the 46.0-day average collection period would be quite acceptable. Clearly, one would need additional information to evaluate the effectiveness of the firm's credit and collection policies.

average payment period
The average length of time it takes a firm to pay its suppliers. Calculated by dividing the firm's accounts payable balance by its average daily purchases.

Firms use the average payment period to evaluate their payment performance. This metric measures the average length of time it takes a firm to pay its suppliers. The average payment period equals the average daily purchases divided into the accounts payable balance. Before calculating average daily purchases an analyst may need to estimate the firm's annual purchases, because they are not reported on a firm's published financial statements. Instead, annual purchases are included in its cost of goods sold. GPC's annual purchases in 2012 were estimated at 80% of the cost of goods sold, as shown in footnote (a) to its income statement in Table 2.2.

Using the annual purchase estimate of $6,815, GPC's average payment period in 2012 indicates that the firm usually takes 90.9 days to pay its bills:

$$\text{Average daily purchases} = \frac{\text{annual purchases}}{365} = \frac{\$6,815}{365} = \$18.67$$

$$\text{Average payment period} = \frac{\text{accounts payble}}{\text{average daily purchases}} = \frac{\$1,697}{\$18.67} = 90.9 \text{ days}$$

Like the average collection period, the average payment period is meaningful only in light of the actual credit terms the firm's suppliers offer. If GPC's suppliers extend, on average, 60-day credit terms, then the firm's average payment period of 90.9 days suggests that the firm is slow in paying its bills. Paying suppliers 30 days later than the agreed-upon terms could damage the firm's ability to obtain additional credit and could raise the cost of any credit that it does obtain.

However, if suppliers grant GPC average credit terms of 90 days, then its 90.9-day average payment period is very good. Clearly, an analyst would need further information to draw definitive conclusions about the firm's overall payment policies from the average payment period measurement.

fixed asset turnover
A measure of the efficiency with which a firm uses its *fixed assets,* calculated by dividing sales by the number of dollars of net fixed asset investment.

The fixed asset turnover measures the efficiency with which a firm uses its *fixed assets.* The ratio tells analysts how many dollars of sales the firm generates per dollar of investment in fixed assets. The ratio equals sales divided by net fixed assets:

$$\text{Fixed asset turnover} = \frac{\text{sales}}{\text{net fixed assets}} = \frac{\$12,843}{\$6,710} = 1.91$$

GPC's fixed asset turnover in 2012 is 1.91. Stated another way, GPC generates almost $2 in sales for every dollar of fixed assets. As with other ratios, the level of fixed asset turnover considered normal varies widely from one industry to another.

total asset turnover
A measure of the efficiency with which a firm uses *all its assets* to generate sales; calculated by dividing the dollars of sales a firm generates by the dollars of total asset investment.

The total asset turnover ratio indicates the efficiency with which a firm uses *all its assets* to generate sales. Like the fixed asset turnover ratio, total asset turnover indicates how many dollars of sales a firm generates per dollar of asset investment. All other factors being equal, analysts favor a high turnover ratio: it indicates that a firm generates more sales (and, ideally, more cash flow for investors) from a given investment in assets.

GPC's total asset turnover in 2012 equals 1.34, calculated as follows:

$$\text{Total asset turover} = \frac{\text{sales}}{\text{total assets}} = \frac{\$12,843}{\$9,589} = 1.34$$

When using the fixed asset and total asset turnover ratios, an analyst must be aware that these are calculated using the *historical costs* of fixed assets. Because some firms have significantly newer or older assets than do others, comparing fixed asset turnovers of those firms could be misleading. Firms with newer assets tend to have lower turnovers than those with older assets, which have lower book (accounting) values. A naive comparison of fixed asset turnover ratios for different firms may lead an analyst to conclude that one firm operates more efficiently than another when, in fact, the firm that appears to be more efficient simply has older (i.e., more fully depreciated) assets on its books.

2-3d Debt Ratios

Firms finance their assets from two broad sources, equity and debt. Equity comes from stockholders, whereas debt comes in many forms from many different lenders. Firms borrow from suppliers, banks, and investors who buy publicly traded bonds. *Debt ratios* measure the extent to which a firm uses money from creditors rather than from stockholders to finance its operations. Because creditors' claims must be satisfied before firms can distribute earnings to stockholders, current and prospective investors pay close attention to the debt on the balance sheet. The more indebted the firm, the higher the probability that it will be unable to satisfy the claims of all its creditors.

financial leverage
Using fixed-cost sources of financing, such as debt and preferred stock, to magnify both the risk and the expected return on a firm's securities.

Fixed-cost sources of financing, such as debt and preferred stock, create **financial leverage** that magnifies both the risk and the expected return on the firm's securities.[7] In general, the more debt a firm uses in relation to its total assets, the greater its financial leverage. That is, the more a firm borrows, the riskier its outstanding stock and bonds and the higher the return that investors require on those securities. In Chapter 12, we discuss in detail the effect of debt on the firm's risk, return, and value. This explains our focus on the use of debt ratios when assessing a firm's indebtedness and its ability to meet the fixed payments associated with debt—a way of quantifying financial leverage.

coverage ratio
A debt ratio that uses data from the *income statement* to assess the firm's ability to generate sufficient cash flow to make scheduled interest and principal payments.

Broadly speaking, there are two types of debt ratios. One type focuses on how much debt (relative to other sources of financing) appears on a firm's balance sheet. The other type, known as **coverage ratios**, uses data from the *income statement* to assess the firm's ability to generate sufficient cash flow to make scheduled interest and principal payments. Investors and credit-rating agencies use both types of ratios to assess a firm's creditworthiness.

debt ratio
A measure of the proportion of total assets financed by a firm's creditors.

The **debt ratio** measures the proportion of total assets financed by the firm's creditors. The higher this ratio, the greater is the firm's reliance on borrowed money to finance its activities. The ratio equals total liabilities divided by total assets. GPC's debt ratio in 2012 was 0.551, or 55.1%:

$$\text{Debt ratio} = \frac{\text{total liabilities}}{\text{total assets}} = \frac{\$5,281}{\$9,589} = 0.551 = 55.1\%$$

This figure indicates that the company has financed more than half of its assets with debt.

A close cousin of the debt ratio is the **assets-to-equity (A/E) ratio**, sometimes called the **equity multiplier**:

assets-to-equity (A/E) ratio
A measure of the proportion of total assets financed by a firm's equity. Also called the *equity multiplier*.

$$\text{Assets-to-equity ratio} = \frac{\text{total assets}}{\text{common stock equity}} = \frac{\$9,589}{\$4,278} = 2.24$$

equity multiplier
A measure of the proportion of total assets financed by a firm's equity. Also called the *assets-to-equity (A/E) ratio*.

Note that the denominator of this ratio uses only common stock equity of $4,278 ($4,308 of total equity – $30 of preferred stock equity). The resulting value indicates that GPC's assets in 2012 were 2.24 times greater than its equity. This value seems reasonable given that the debt ratio indicates slightly more than half (55.1%) of GPC's assets in 2012 were financed with debt. The high equity multiplier indicates high debt and low equity, whereas a low equity multiplier indicates low debt and high equity.

debt-to-equity ratio
A measure of the firm's financial leverage, calculated by dividing long-term debt by stockholders' equity.

An alternative measure that focuses solely on the firm's long-term debt is the **debt-to-equity ratio**. It is calculated as long-term debt divided by stockholders' equity. The 2012 value of this ratio for GPC is calculated as follows:

$$\text{Debt-to-equity ratio} = \frac{\text{long-term debt}}{\text{stockholders' equity}} = \frac{\$1,760}{\$4,308} = 0.409 = 40.9\%$$

GPC's long-term debts were therefore only 40.9% as large as its stockholders' equity. A word of caution: Both the debt ratio and the debt-to-equity ratio use book values

---

[7]By *fixed cost* we mean that the cost of this financing source does not vary over time in response to changes in the firm's revenue and cash flow. For example, if a firm borrows money at a variable rate, then the interest cost of that loan is *not* fixed through time, although the firm's *obligation* to make interest payments is "fixed" regardless of the level of the firm's revenue and cash flow.

of debt, equity, and assets. Analysts should be aware that the *market values* of these variables may differ substantially from their book values.

times interest earned ratio
A measure of the firm's ability to make contractual interest payments, calculated by dividing earnings before interest and taxes by interest expense.

The times interest earned ratio measures the firm's ability to make contractual interest payments. It equals earnings before interest and taxes divided by interest expense. A higher ratio indicates a greater capacity to meet scheduled payments. The times interest earned ratio for GPC in 2012 was equal to 13.59, indicating that the firm could experience a substantial decline in earnings and still meet its interest obligations:

$$\text{Times interest earned} = \frac{\text{earnings before interest and taxes}}{\text{interest expense}} = \frac{\$1,671}{\$123} = 13.59$$

2-3e Profitability Ratios

Several measures of profitability relate a firm's earnings to its sales, assets, or equity. *Profitability ratios* are among the most closely watched and widely quoted financial ratios. Many firms link employee bonuses to profitability ratios, and stock prices react sharply to unexpected changes in these measures.

gross profit margin
A measure of profitability that represents the percentage of each sales dollar remaining after a firm has paid for its goods.

The gross profit margin measures the percentage of each sales dollar remaining after the firm has paid for its goods. The higher the gross profit margin, the better. GPC's gross profit margin in 2012 is 33.7%:

$$\text{Gross profit margin} = \frac{\text{gross profit}}{\text{sales}} = \frac{\$4,324}{\$12,843} = 0.337 = 33.7\%$$

operating profit margin
A measure of profitability that represents the percentage of each sales dollar remaining after deducting all costs and expenses *other than* interest and taxes.

The operating profit margin measures the percentage of each sales dollar remaining after deducting all costs and expenses *other than* interest and taxes. As with the gross profit margin, the higher the operating profit margin, the better. This ratio tells analysts what a firm's bottom line looks like before deductions for payments to creditors and tax authorities. GPC's operating profit margin in 2012 is 11.9%:

$$\text{Operating profit margin} = \frac{\text{operating profit}}{\text{sales}} = \frac{\$1,531}{\$12,843} = 0.119 = 11.9\%$$

net profit margin
A measure of profitability that represents the percentage of each sales dollar remaining after all costs and expenses, *including* interest, taxes, and preferred stock dividends, have been deducted.

The net profit margin measures the percentage of each sales dollar remaining after deducting all costs and expenses *including* interest, taxes, and preferred stock dividends. GPC's net profit margin of 7.4% in 2012 is calculated as follows:

$$\text{Net profit margin} = \frac{\text{earnings available for common stockholders}}{\text{sales}}$$
$$= \frac{\$946}{\$12,843} = 0.074 = 7.4\%$$

Frank Popoff, Chairman of the Board (retired), Dow Chemical

"Overstating or understating the performance of the enterprise is anathema . . . it's just not on."

See the entire interview at **SMART** | finance

Smart Ethics Video

For the quarter that ended on December 31, 2010, Microsoft reported a net profit margin of 33.2%, more than six times larger than the 5.2% net profit margin reported by Wal-Mart one month later. This example shows how net profit margins vary widely across industries.

Probably the most closely watched financial ratio of them all is *earnings per share (EPS)*, which the investing public considers to be an indicator of corporate success. The earnings per share measure represents the number of dollars earned on behalf of each outstanding share of common stock. Many firms tie management bonuses to specific *EPS* targets. Earnings per share are calculated as follows:

$$\text{Earnings per share} = \frac{\text{earnings available for common stockholders}}{\text{number of shares of common stock outstanding}}$$
$$= \frac{\$946}{178.7} = \$5.29$$

John Graham, Duke University

"We asked companies, 'Do you manage your earnings?'"

See the entire interview at **SMART|finance**

Smart Ideas Video

return on total assets (ROA)
A measure of the overall effectiveness of management in generating returns to common stockholders with its available assets.

return on common equity (ROE)
A measure that captures the return earned on the common stockholders' (owners') investment in a firm.

DuPont system
An analysis that uses both income statement and balance sheet information to break the *ROA* and *ROE* ratios into component pieces.

The value of GPC's earnings per share in 2012 is $5.29.[8] This figure represents the dollar amount *earned* on behalf of each share of common stock outstanding. Note that *EPS* is not the same as dividends. The amount of earnings actually *distributed* to each shareholder is the *dividend per share*; as noted in GPC's income statement (Table 2.2), this value rose to $1.93 in 2012 from $1.76 in 2011.

The **return on total assets (ROA)**, often called the *return on investment (ROI)*, measures management's overall effectiveness in using the firm's assets to generate returns to common stockholders.[9] The return on total assets for GPC in 2012 was equal to 9.9%:

$$\text{Return on total assets} = \frac{\text{earnings available for common stockholders}}{\text{total assets}}$$

$$= \frac{\$946}{\$9,589} = 0.099 = 9.9\%$$

A closely related measure of profitability is the **return on common equity (ROE)**, which captures the return earned on the common stockholders' (owners') investment in the firm. For a firm that uses only common stock to finance its operations, the *ROE* and *ROA* figures will be identical. With debt or preferred stock on the balance sheet, these ratios will usually differ. When the firm earns a profit, even after making interest payments to creditors and paying dividends to preferred stockholders, the firm's *ROE* will exceed its *ROA*. Conversely, if the firm's earnings fall short of the amount it must pay to lenders and preferred stockholders, the *ROE* will be less than *ROA*. For GPC, the return on common equity for 2012 was 22.1%, substantially above GPC's return on total assets:

$$\text{Return on common equity} = \frac{\text{earnings available for common stockholders}}{\text{common stock equity}}$$

$$= \frac{\$946}{\$4,278} = 0.221 = 22.1\%$$

DuPont System of Analysis   Financial analysts sometimes conduct a deeper analysis of the *ROA* and *ROE* ratios using the **DuPont system**. This approach uses both income statement and balance sheet information to break the *ROA* and *ROE* ratios into component pieces. It highlights the influence of both the net profit margin and the total asset turnover on a firm's profitability. In the DuPont system, the return on total assets equals the product of the net profit margin and total asset turnover:

$$ROA = \text{net profit margin} \times \text{total asset turnover}$$

By definition, the net profit margin equals earnings available for common stockholders divided by sales, and total asset turnover equals sales divided by total assets. When we multiply these two ratios together, the sales figure cancels, resulting in the familiar *ROA* measure:

$$ROA = \frac{\text{earnings available for common stockholders}}{\text{sales}} \times \frac{\text{sales}}{\text{total assets}}$$

$$= \frac{\$946}{\$12,843} \times \frac{\$12,843}{\$9,589} = 0.074 \times 1.34 = 0.099 = 9.9\%$$

$$ROA = \frac{\text{earnings available for common stockholders}}{\text{total assets}} = \frac{\$946}{\$9,589} = 0.099 = 9.9\%$$

---

[8]We state per-share values strictly in dollars and cents, as do company reports. Per-share values are not stated in millions, unlike the dollar values used to calculate these and other ratios.

[9]Naturally, all other things being equal, firms prefer a high *ROA*. However, as we will see later, analysts must be cautious when interpreting financial ratios. We recall an old Dilbert comic strip in which Wally suggests boosting his firm's *ROA* by firing the security staff. The reduction in expenses would boost the numerator while the reduction in security would lower the denominator.

Finance in Your Life

Analyzing Your Personal Financial Statements

Imagine that in early 2013, you prepare an abbreviated personal balance sheet and income statement for the year just ended, December 31, 2012. You also prepare some "Notes" and then analyze the statements using some popular personal finance ratios, which are shown below. A review of the statements and ratios should disclose great similarity between personal and corporate financial statements and ratios.

Balance Sheet (December 31, 2012)

Assets		Liabilities and Equity	
Total liquid assets	$ 2,225	Total current liabilities	$ 905
Total investments	$ 5,750	Total long-term liabilities	$104,850
Total real and pers. prop.	$139,200	(2) Total liabilities	$105,755
(1) Total assets	$147,175	Net worth [(1)–(2)]	$ 41,420
		Total liab. and net worth	$147,175

Income Statement (Year Ended December 31, 2012)

(1) Total income	$73,040
(2) Total expenses	$61,704
Cash surplus (deficit) [(1)–(2)]	$11,336

Notes:

1. Total current debts = **$22,589**
2. Total income taxes = **$15,430**
3. Total monthly loan payments = **$1,807**
4. Monthly gross (before-tax) income = **$6,807**

Ratios

Ratio	Formula	Calculation	Interpretation
Solvency ratio	$\dfrac{\text{Total net worth}}{\text{Total assets}}$	$\dfrac{\$41,420}{\$147,175} = 0.281 = $ **28.1%**	You could tolerate about a 28% decline in asset values before becoming insolvent.
Liquidity ratio	$\dfrac{\text{Tot. liquid assets}}{\text{Tot. current debts}}$	$\dfrac{\$2,225}{\$22,589} = 0.099 = $ **9.9%**	You can cover only about 10% of 1-year debts with current liquid assets.
Savings ratio	$\dfrac{\text{Cash surplus}}{\text{Income after taxes}}$	$\dfrac{\$11,336}{\$73,040 - \$15,430} = 0.197 = $ **19.7%**	You saved 19.7% of your after-tax income during the year.
Debt service ratio	$\dfrac{\text{Total monthly loan payments}}{\text{Monthly gross (before-tax) income}}$	$\dfrac{\$1,807}{\$6,087} = 0.297 = $ **29.7%**	Your monthly loan payments account for about 30% of monthly gross income.

© Cengage Learning 2012

SMART concepts
See the concept explained step-by-step at SMART | finance

Naturally, the *ROA* value for GPC in 2012 obtained using the DuPont system is the same value we calculated before. Yet now, seeing its two component parts, we can think of the *ROA* as a product of how much profit the firm earns on each dollar of sales and the efficiency with which the firm uses its assets to generate sales. Holding the net profit margin constant, an increase in total asset turnover increases the firm's *ROA*. Similarly, holding total asset turnover constant, an increase in the net profit margin increases *ROA*.

We can push the DuPont system one step further by multiplying the *ROA* by the *assets-to-equity (A/E) ratio*, or the *equity multiplier*. The product of these two ratios equals the return on common equity.

$$ROE = ROA \times A/E$$

For a firm that uses no debt and has no preferred stock, the assets-to-equity ratio equals 1.0, and so the *ROA* equals the *ROE*. For all other firms, the assets-to-equity ratio exceeds 1.

We can apply this version of the DuPont system to GPC and thereby recalculate its return on common equity in 2012:

$$ROE = \frac{\text{earnings available for common stockholders}}{\text{total assets}} \times \frac{\text{total assets}}{\text{common stock equity}}$$

$$= \frac{\$946}{\$9,589} \times \frac{\$9,589}{\$4,278} = 0.099 \times 2.24 = 0.221 = 22.1\%$$

$$ROE = \frac{\text{earnings available for common stockholders}}{\text{common stock equity}} = \frac{\$946}{\$4,278} = 0.221 = 22.1\%$$

Observe that GPC's assets-to-equity ratio is 2.24. This means that GPC's return on common equity was more than twice as large as its return on total assets. Note also that if GPC's return on total assets were a *negative* number then the firm's return on common equity would be even more negative than its *ROA*.

The advantage of the DuPont system is that it allows the firm to break its return on common equity into three components tied to the financial statements: (1) a profit-on-sales component (net profit margin) that ties directly to the income statement; (2) an efficiency-of-asset-use component (total asset turnover) that ties directly to the balance sheet; and (3) a financial leverage use component (assets-to-equity ratio) that also ties directly to the balance sheet. Analysts can then study the effect of each of these factors on the overall return to common stockholders, as demonstrated in the following example.[10]

EXAMPLE

The 2012 ratio values for the *ROE, ROA,* assets-to-equity ratio, total asset turnover, and net profit margin calculated earlier for GPC are shown below, along with the 2012 industry averages for globally active oil companies.

Ratio	GPC	Industry Average
Return on common equity (*ROE*)	22.1%	19.7%
Return on total assets (*ROA*)	9.9%	12.1%
Assets-to-equity (A/E) ratio	2.24	1.63
Totals asset turnover	1.34	1.42
Net profit margin	7.4%	8.5%

We begin the analysis of GPC's performance during 2012 with its return on common equity of 22.1%, which is noticeably above the industry average of 19.7%. To learn why GPC's *ROE* outperformed the industry, we look at two components of *ROE: ROA* and the assets-to-equity (A/E) ratio. We see that GPC's *ROA* of 9.9% was well below the industry average of 12.1%. But thanks to its *greater use of leverage*—an A/E ratio of 2.24 for GPC versus 1.63 for the industry—GPC was able to generate a higher *ROE* than the average firm.

---

[10] Keep in mind that the ratios in the DuPont system are interdependent and that the equation is just a mathematical identity. It is easy to draw questionable conclusions about lines of causality using the DuPont system. For example, consider this farcical version of the formula:

$$ROA = \frac{\text{earnings available for common stockholders}}{\text{sales}} \times \frac{\text{sales}}{\text{assets}} \times \frac{\text{assets}}{\text{CEO age}} \times \frac{\text{CEO age}}{\text{common stock equity}}$$

In this equation, we might interpret the third term on the right as the efficiency with which a CEO of a given age manages the firm's assets. If a younger CEO manages the same quantity of assets, then this ratio would increase and, holding all other factors constant, we could say that the firm's *ROE* would increase. This is clearly silly, but mathematically this expression ultimately gives you the firm's *ROE*.

continued

Looking further at the two components of *ROA* (the net profit margin and the total asset turnover), we see that GPC's total asset turnover of 1.34 is very close to the industry average of 1.42. However, *its net profit margin of 7.4% is below the industry average of 8.5%*, which caused GPC's *ROA* to be below the industry average, too. This suggests that GPC was less able than its competitors to manage costs and generate a profit on sales.

In summary, GPC compensated for its below-average *ROA* by using significantly more leverage than its competitors. Clearly, GPC took greater risk in order to compensate for low profits on sales. The firm should focus on its income statement to improve its profitability and also should consider reducing its leverage to moderate its risk. It appears that GPC has problems in both its income statement (net profit margin) and its balance sheet (assets-to-equity ratio).

? JOB INTERVIEW QUESTION

What financial ratios might you review in order to gain insight into how investors think a firm is performing?

price/earnings (P/E) ratio
A measure of a firm's long-term growth prospects that represents the amount investors are willing to pay for each dollar of a firm's earnings.

2-3f Market Ratios

Market ratios relate the firm's market value, as measured by its current share price, to certain accounting values. These ratios provide insight into how investors think the firm is performing, and they also reflect the common stockholders' assessment of the firm's past and expected future performance. Here we consider two popular market ratios, one that focuses on earnings and another that considers book value.

The **price/earnings (P/E) ratio** measures the amount investors are willing to pay for each dollar of the firm's earnings. Investors often use the P/E ratio, the most widely quoted market ratio, as a barometer of a firm's long-term growth prospects and of investor confidence in the firm's future performance. A high P/E ratio indicates investors' belief that a firm will achieve rapid earnings growth in the future; hence, companies with high P/E ratios are referred to as *growth stocks*. Simply stated, investors who believe that future earnings are going to be higher than current earnings are willing to pay a lot for today's earnings, and vice versa.

Using the per-share price of $76.25 for Global Petroleum Corporation on December 31, 2012, and its 2012 *EPS* of $5.29, the P/E ratio at year-end 2012 is:

$$\text{Price/earnings (P/E) ratio} = \frac{\text{market price per share of common stock}}{\text{earnings per share}}$$

$$= \frac{\$76.25}{\$5.29} = 14.41$$

This figure indicates that investors were paying $14.41 for each dollar of GPC's earnings. GPC's price/earnings ratio one year before (on December 31, 2011) had been almost twice as high at 28.37 ($71.50 per share stock price ÷ $2.52 earnings per share).

The **market/book (M/B) ratio** provides another assessment of how investors view the firm's performance. It relates the market value of the firm's shares to their book value. The stocks of firms that investors expect to perform well in the future—improving profits, growing market share, launching successful products, and so forth—typically sell at higher M/B ratios than firms with less attractive prospects. Firms that investors expect to earn high returns relative to their risk typically sell at higher M/B multiples than those expected to earn low returns relative to risk.

market/book (M/B) ratio
A measure used to assess a firm's future performance by relating its market value per share to its book value per share.

To calculate the M/B ratio for GPC in 2012, we first need to find its *book value per share* of common stock:

$$\text{Book value per share} = \frac{\text{common stock equity}}{\text{number of shares of common stock outstanding}}$$

$$= \frac{\$4,278}{178.7} = \$23.94$$

We then compute the M/B ratio by dividing the book value into the current price of the firm's stock:

$$\text{Market/book (M/B) ratio} = \frac{\text{market value per share of common stock}}{\text{book value per share of common stock}}$$

$$= \frac{\$76.25}{\$23.94} = 3.19$$

Investors are currently paying $3.19 for each $1.00 of book value of GPC's stock. Clearly, investors expect GPC to continue to grow in the future: they are willing to pay more than book value for the firm's shares.

2-3 Concept Review Questions

7. Which of the categories and individual ratios described in this chapter would be of greatest interest to each of the following parties?
   a. Existing and prospective creditors (lenders)
   b. Existing and prospective shareholders
   c. The firm's management

8. How could analysts use the availability of cash inflow and cash outflow data to improve on the accuracy of the liquidity and debt coverage ratios presented previously? What specific ratio measures—using cash flow rather than financial statement data—would you calculate to assess the firm's liquidity and debt coverage?

9. Assume that a firm's total assets and sales remain constant. Would an increase in each of the following ratios be associated with a cash inflow or a cash outflow?

   a. Current ratio
   b. Inventory turnover
   c. Average collection period
   d. Average payment period
   e. Debt ratio
   f. Net profit margin

10. Use the DuPont system to explain why a slower-than-average inventory turnover could cause a firm with an above-average net profit margin to have a below-average return on common equity.

11. How can you reconcile investor expectations for a firm with an above-average M/B ratio and a below-average P/E ratio? Could the age of the firm have any effect on this ratio comparison?

2-4   Corporate Taxes

Taxation is one of the key measurement challenges facing financial decision makers. In GPC's income statement (Table 2.2) we can see that its taxes for 2012 totaled $599 million on pretax income of $1,548 million—a significant cash outflow. The financial manager needs to understand the basics of corporate taxation in order to estimate the after-tax benefits and costs required by proposed actions. Such understanding also allows consultation with tax experts, such as corporate tax counsel or a tax consultant.

Here we briefly review the most basic corporate tax concepts—the taxation of ordinary income and capital gains. Keep in mind that (1) the tax code is frequently revised and (2) corporations are subject to tax rates that differ from the personal tax rates applicable to noncorporate businesses such as sole proprietorships and partnerships.

2-4a Ordinary Corporate Income

ordinary corporate income
Income resulting from the sale of the firm's goods and services.

Ordinary corporate income is income resulting from the sale of the firm's goods and services. Under current tax laws, the applicable tax rates are subject to the somewhat progressive tax rate schedule shown in Table 2.6. The purpose of the progressive rates

Table 2.6

Corporate Income Tax Rates

Taxable Income Over	Not Over	Tax Rate
$ 0	$ 50,000	15%
50,000	75,000	25%
75,000	100,000	34%
100,000	335,000	39%
335,000	10,000,000	34%
10,000,000	15,000,000	35%
15,000,000	18,333,333	38%
18,333,333	....	35%

(lower rates on lower taxable amounts) at the bottom of the schedule is to give small corporations a better chance to grow. The following example illustrates application of the corporate tax rates.

EXAMPLE

First Vehicle Corporation (FVC), during 2012, earned pretax income of $2,800,000. What is FVC's tax liability for the year? Using the corporate tax rate schedule, FVC's tax liability is calculated as follows:

$$
\begin{aligned}
\$50,000 \times 0.15 &= \$ \quad 7,500 \\
(\$75,000 - \$50,000) \times 0.25 &= \quad 6,250 \\
(\$100,000 - \$75,000) \times 0.34 &= \quad 8,500 \\
(\$335,000 - \$100,000) \times 0.39 &= \quad 91,650 \\
(\$2,800,000 - \$335,000) \times 0.34 &= \underline{\quad 838,100} \\
\text{Tax liability} \quad &\quad \underline{\underline{\$952,000}}
\end{aligned}
$$

FVC's tax liability for 2012 on its pretax income of $2,800,000 is therefore $952,000.

---

average tax rate
A firm's tax liability divided by its pretax income.

Average Tax Rate A useful measure is the firm's average tax rate, which is calculated by dividing its tax liability by its pretax income. For example, the average tax rate for FVC in the preceding example would be exactly 34% ($952,000 ÷ $2,800,000). During 2012, FVC paid an average of 34 cents on each dollar of pretax income earned.

marginal tax rate
The tax rate applicable to a firm's next dollar of earnings.

Marginal Tax Rate More relevant to financial decision making is the marginal tax rate, which is the tax rate applicable to the firm's next dollar of earnings. This rate is important because new decisions consider incremental benefits and costs, and therefore, the tax rate used in the analysis should likewise be an incremental, rather than an average rate. Again, referring to the FVC discussions above, we can see that the firm's 2,800,001st dollar of pretax income would be taxed at a 34% rate. Therefore, 34% is FVC's marginal tax rate at its current level of operations. *Note that because this book focuses on incremental decision making, we almost always deal in marginal tax rates.*

capital gain
The difference between the sale price and the initial purchase price of a capital asset, such as equipment or stock held as an investment.

2-4b Corporate Capital Gains

Corporations experience capital gains when they sell capital assets, such as equipment or stock held as an investment, for more than their original purchase price. The amount of the capital gain is equal to the difference between the sale price and initial purchase price. If the sale price is less than the asset's book, or accounting, value, the difference is called a capital loss. Under current tax law, corporate capital gains are merely added to operating income and taxed at the ordinary corporate tax rates. The tax treatment of capital losses on depreciable business assets involves a deduction from pretax ordinary income, whereas any other capital losses must be used to offset capital gains. The following example demonstrates the tax treatment of a capital gain.

capital loss
The loss resulting from the sale of a capital asset, such as equipment or stock held as an investment, at a price below its book, or accounting, value.

EXAMPLE

Assume that First Vehicle Corporation (FVC), introduced previously, decided to sell an entire production line for $850,000. If the firm had originally purchased the line two years earlier for $700,000, how much in capital gain taxes would FVC owe on this transaction if it was in the 34% marginal tax bracket on ordinary corporate income? The firm would have realized a $150,000 ($850,000 − $700,000) capital gain on this transaction, which would result in $51,000 ($150,000 × 0.34) of taxes.

2-4 Concept Review Questions

12. How are corporations taxed on ordinary income? What is the difference between the *average tax rate* and the *marginal tax rate* on ordinary corporate income?

13. What are corporate *capital gains* and *capital losses*? How are they treated for tax purposes?

Summary

- The four key financial statements are (1) the balance sheet, (2) the income statement, (3) the statement of retained earnings, and (4) the statement of cash flows. Companies typically include with these statements detailed notes describing the technical aspects of the financial statements.

Table of Important Equations

1. $NOPAT = EBIT \times (1 - T)$
2. $OCF = NOPAT + Depreciation$
3. $OCF = [EBIT \times (1 - T)] + Depreciation$
4. $FCF = OCF - \Delta FA - \Delta WC$

- A firm's total cash flows can be conveniently divided into (1) operating flows, (2) investment flows, and (3) financing flows. Operating cash flow (*OCF*) measures the amount of cash flow generated by the firm's operations; it is calculated by adding any noncash charges (the main one being depreciation) to the firm's net operating profits after taxes (NOPAT). The value of NOPAT is calculated as earnings before interest and taxes (EBIT) multiplied by 1 minus the tax rate.

- More important than *OCF* to financial analysts is free cash flow (*FCF*), the amount of cash flow available to investors. Free cash flow equals operating cash flow less the firm's net investments in fixed and current assets.

- The statement of cash flows summarizes the firm's cash flows over a specified period of time, typically one year. It presents operating, investment, and financing cash flows. When interpreting the statement, an analyst typically looks for unusual changes in either the major categories of cash flow or in specific items to find clues to problems that the firm may be experiencing.

- Financial ratios are a convenient tool for analyzing the firm's financial statements to assess its performance over a given period. Analysts use various financial ratios to assess a firm's liquidity, activity, debt, profitability, and market value. The DuPont system is often used to assess various aspects of a firm's profitability and market value. The DuPont system uses both income statement and balance sheet data to assess a firm's profitability, particularly the returns earned on both the total asset investment and the owners' common stock equity in the firm.

- Financial decision makers must be conversant with basic corporate tax concepts, because taxes affect both benefits and costs. Taxes are a major outflow of cash to the profitable firm; they are levied on both ordinary income and capital gains. The marginal tax rate is more relevant than the average tax rate in financial decision making.

Key Terms

accrual-based approach, 28
activity ratios, 42
assets-to-equity (A/E) ratio, 44
average age of inventory, 42
average collection period, 42
average payment period, 43
average tax rate, 51
capital gains, 51
capital loss, 51
cash flow approach, 28
common stock, 31
common-size income
  statement, 31
coverage ratio, 44
current ratio, 41
debt ratio, 44
debt-to-equity ratio, 44
deferred taxes, 31
dividend per share (DPS), 32
DuPont system, 46

earnings available for common
  stockholders, 32
earnings per share (EPS), 32
equity multiplier, 44
financial leverage, 44
financing flows, 35
fixed asset turnover, 43
free cash flow (FCF), 35
gross profit margin, 45
inventory turnover, 42
investment flows, 35
liquidity ratios, 41
long-term debt, 31
marginal tax rate, 51
market/book (M/B) ratio, 49
net operating profits after taxes
  (NOPAT), 36
net profit margin, 45
net working capital, 41
noncash charges, 37

operating cash flow (OCF), 37
operating flows, 35
operating profit margin, 45
ordinary corporate income, 50
paid-in capital in excess of par, 31
par value (common stock), 31
preferred stock, 31
price/earnings (P/E) ratio, 49
quick (acid-test) ratio, 41
ratio analysis, 40
retained earnings, 31
return on common
  equity (ROE), 46
return on total assets (ROA), 46
times interest earned ratio, 45
total asset turnover, 43
treasury stock, 31

Self-Test Problems

Answers to Self-Test Problems and the Concept Review Questions throughout the chapter appear in CourseMate with Smart-Finance Tools at **www.cengagebrain.com**.

ST2-1. Use the financial statements below to answer the questions about M&M Manufacturing's financial position at the end of the calendar year 2012.

M&M Manufacturing, Inc.
Balance Sheet
At December 31, 2012 ($000)

Assets		Liabilities and Equity	
Current assets		Current liabilities	
Cash	$ 140,000	Accounts payable	$ 480,000
Marketable securities	260,000	Notes payable	500,000
Accounts receivable	650,000	Accruals	80,000
Inventories	800,000	Total current	
Total current assets	$1,850,000	liabilities	$1,060,000
Fixed assets		Long-term debt	
Gross fixed assets	$3,780,000	Bonds outstanding	$1,300,000
Less: Accumulated		Bank debt (long-term)	260,000
depreciation	1,220,000	Total long-term debt	$1,560,000
Net fixed assets	$2,560,000	Total liabilities	$2,620,000
Total assets	$4,410,000	Stockholders' equity	
		Preferred stock	$ 180,000
		Common stock (at par)	200,000
		Paid-in capital	
		in excess of par	810,000
		Retained earnings	600,000
		Total stockholders' equity	$1,790,000
		Total liabilities and equity	**$4,410,000**

M&M Manufacturing, Inc.
Income Statement
For Year Ended December 31, 2012 ($000)

Sales revenue		$6,900,000
Less: Cost of goods sold		4,200,000
Gross profits		$2,700,000
Less: Operating expenses		
Sales expense	$ 750,000	
General and administrative expense	1,150,000	
Leasing expense	210,000	
Depreciation expense	235,000	
Total operating expenses		2,345,000
Earnings before interest and taxes		$ 355,000
Less: Interest expense		85,000
Net profit before taxes		$ 270,000
Less: Taxes		81,000
Net profits after taxes		$ 189,000
Less: Preferred stock dividends		10,800
Earnings available for common stockholders		$ 178,200
Less: Dividends		75,000
To retained earnings		$ 103,200
Per share data		
Earnings per share (EPS)	$	1.43
Dividends per share (DPS)	$	0.60
Price per share	$	15.85

a. How much cash and near cash does M&M have at year-end 2012?

b. What was the original cost of all of the firm's real property that is currently owned?

c. How much in total liabilities did the firms have at year-end 2012?

d. How much did M&M owe for credit purchases at year-end 2012?

e. How much did the firm sell during 2012?

f. How much equity did the common stockholders have in the firm at year-end 2012?

g. What is the cumulative total of earnings reinvested in the firm from its inception through the end of 2012?

h. How much operating profit did the firm earn during 2012?

i. What is the total amount of dividends paid out by the firm during the year 2012?

j. How many shares of common stock did M&M have outstanding at year-end 2012?

ST2-2. The partially complete 2012 balance sheet and income statement for Challenge Industries are given below, followed (on page 55) by selected ratio values for the firm based on its completed 2012 financial statements. Use the ratios along with the partial statements to complete the financial statements. *Hint:* Use the ratios in the order listed to calculate the missing statement values that need to be installed in the partial statements.

Challenge Industries, Inc., Balance Sheet
At December 31, 2012 (in $ thousands)

Assets		Liabilities and Equity	
Current assets		Current liabilities	
Cash	$ 52,000	Accounts payable	$150,000
Marketable securities	60,000	Notes payable	?
Accounts receivable	200,000	Accruals	80,000
Inventories	?	Total current liabilities	?
Total current assets	?	Long-term debt	$425,000
Fixed assets (gross)	?	Total liabilities	?
Less: Accumulated		Stockholders' equity	
depreciation	240,000	Preferred stock	?
Net fixed assets	?	Common stock (at par)	150,000
Total assets	?	Paid-in capital in excess of par	?
		Retained earnings	390,000
		Total stockholders' equity	?
		Total liabilities and stockholders' equity	?

Challenge Industries, Inc.
Income Statement
For the Year Ended December 31, 2012 (in $ thousands)

Sales revenue		$4,800,000
Less: Cost of goods sold		?
Gross profits		?
Less: Operating expenses		
Sales expense	$690,000	
General and administrative expense	750,000	
Depreciation expense	120,000	
Total operating expenses		1,560,000
Earnings before interest and taxes		?
Less: Interest expense		35,000
Earnings before taxes		?
Less: Taxes		?
Net income (Net profits after taxes)		?
Less: Preferred dividends		15,000
Earnings available for common stockholders		?
Less: Dividends		60,000
To retained earnings		?

Challenge Industries, Inc.
Ratios
For the Year Ended December 31, 2012

Ratio	Value
Total asset turnover	2.00
Gross profit margin	40%
Inventory turnover	10
Current ratio	1.60
Net profit margin	3.75%
Return on common equity	12.5%

ST2-3. Use the corporate income tax rate schedule in Table 2.6 to calculate the tax liability for each of the following firms, with the amounts of 2012 pretax income noted.

Firm	2012 Pretax Income	Tax Liability
A	$12,500,000	?
B	200,000	?
C	80,000	?

a. What tax rate—average or marginal—is relevant to financial decisions for these firms?
b. Calculate, compare, and discuss the *average tax rates* for each of the firms during 2012.
c. Find the *marginal tax rates* for each of the firms at the end of 2012.
d. What relationship exists between the average and marginal tax rates for each firm?

Questions

Q2-1. What information (explicit and implicit) can be derived from financial statement analysis? Does the standardization required by GAAP add greater validity to comparisons of financial data between companies and industries? Are there possible shortcomings to relying solely on financial statement analysis to value companies?

Q2-2. Distinguish between the types of financial information contained in the various financial statements. Which statements provide information on a company's performance over a reporting period, and which present data on a company's current position? What sorts of valuable information may be found in the notes to financial statements? Describe a situation in which the information in the notes would be essential to making an informed decision about the value of a corporation.

Q2-3. If you were a commercial credit analyst charged with the responsibility of making an accept/reject decision on a company's loan request, with which financial statement would you be most concerned? Which financial statement is most likely to provide pertinent information about a company's ability to repay its debt?

Q2-4. What is *operating cash flow (OCF)?* How is it calculated? What is *free cash flow (FCF)?* How is it calculated from *OCF?* Why do financial managers focus attention on the value of *FCF?*

Q2-5. Describe the common definitions of "inflows of cash" and "outflows of cash" used by analysts to classify certain balance sheet changes and income statement values. What three categories of cash flow are used in the statement of cash flows? To what value should the net value in the statement of cash flows reconcile?

Q2-6. What precautions must one take when using ratio analysis to make financial decisions? Which ratios would be most useful for a financial manager's internal financial analysis? For an analyst trying to decide which stocks are most attractive within an industry?

Q2-7. How do analysts use ratios to analyze a firm's *financial leverage?* Which ratios convey more important information to a credit analyst—those revolving around the levels of indebtedness or those measuring the ability to meet the contractual payments associated with debt? What is the relationship between a firm's levels of indebtedness and risk? What must happen for an increase in financial leverage to be successful?

Q2-8. How is the *DuPont system* useful in analyzing a firm's *ROA* and *ROE?* What information can be inferred from the decomposition of *ROE* into contributing ratios? What is the mathematical relationship between each of the individual components (net profit margin, total asset turnover, and assets-to-equity ratio) and *ROE?* Can *ROE* be raised without affecting *ROA?* How?

Q2-9. Provide a general description of the tax rates applicable to U.S. corporations. What is the difference between the *average tax rate* and the *marginal tax rate?* Which is relevant to financial decision making? Why? How do *capital gains* differ from *ordinary corporate income?*

Problems

Financial Statements

P2-1. Obtain financial statements for Microsoft for the last five years either from its Web site (www .microsoft.com) or from the SEC's online EDGAR site (www.sec.gov/edgar/searchedgar/webusers .htm). First, look at the statements without reading the notes. Then, read the notes carefully, concentrating on those about executive stock options. Do you have a different perspective after analyzing these notes?

Cash Flow Analysis

SMART solutions

See the problem and solution explained step-by-step at **SMART | finance**

P2-2. Given the balance sheets and selected data from the income statement of SMG Industries that follow, answer parts (a)–(c).

a. Calculate the firm's *operating cash flow (OCF)* for the year ended December 31, 2012, using Equation 2.2.

b. Calculate the firm's *free cash flow (FCF)* for the year ended December 31, 2012, using Equation 2.4.

c. Interpret, compare, and contrast your cash flow estimates in parts (a) and (b).

SMG Industries Balance Sheets ($ in millions)					
Assets	**December 31, 2012**	**December 31, 2011**	**Liabilities and Stockholders' Equity**	**December 31, 2012**	**December 31, 2011**
Cash	$ 3,500	$ 3,000	Accounts payable	$ 3,600	$ 3,500
Marketable securities	3,800	3,200	Notes payable	4,800	4,200
			Accruals	1,200	1,300
Accounts receivable	4,000	3,800	Total current liabilities	$ 9,600	$ 9,000
Inventories	4,900	4,800	Long-term debt	$ 6,000	$ 6,000
Total current assets	$16,200	$14,800	Common stock	$11,000	$11,000
			Retained earnings	6,400	5,800
Gross fixed assets	$31,500	$30,100	Total stockholders' equity	$17,400	$16,800
Less: Accumulated depreciation	14,700	13,100	Total liabilities and stockholders' equity	$33,000	$31,800
Net fixed assets	$16,800	$17,000			
Total assets	$33,000	$31,800			

Income Statement Data (2012, $ in millions)	
Depreciation expense	$1,600
Earnings before interest and taxes (*EBIT*)	4,500
Taxes	1,300
Net profits after taxes	2,400

P2-3. Classify each of the following items as an inflow (I) or an outflow (O) of cash, or as neither (N).

Item	Change ($)	Item	Change ($)
Cash	+600	Accounts receivable	−900
Accounts payable	−1,200	Net profits	+700
Notes payable	+800	Depreciation	+200
Long-term debt	−2,500	Repurchase of stock	+500
Inventory	+400	Cash dividends	+300
Fixed assets	+600	Sale of stock	+1,300

Tables © Cengage Learning 2012

Analyzing Financial Performance Using Ratio Analysis

P2-4. Manufacturers Bank is evaluating Aluminum Industries, Inc., which has requested a $3 million loan in order to assess the firm's financial leverage and risk. On the basis of the debt ratios for Aluminum, along with the industry averages and Aluminum's recent financial statements (which follow), evaluate and recommend appropriate action on the loan request.

Aluminum Industries, Inc., Income Statement for the Year Ended December 31, 2012

Sales revenue		$30,000,000
Less: Cost of goods sold		21,000,000
Gross profit		$ 9,000,000
Less: Operating expenses		
Selling expense	$3,000,000	
General and administrative expenses	1,800,000	
Lease expense	200,000	
Depreciation expense	1,000,000	
Total operating expense		6,000,000
Operating profit		$ 3,000,000
Less: Interest expense		1,000,000
Net profit before taxes		$ 2,000,000
Less: Taxes (rate = 40%)		800,000
Net profits after taxes		**$ 1,200,000**

Aluminum Industries, Inc., Balance Sheet as of December 31, 2012

Assets		Liabilities and Stockholders' Equity	
Current assets		Current liabilities	
Cash	$ 1,000,000	Accounts payable	$ 8,000,000
Marketable securities	3,000,000	Notes payable	8,000,000
Accounts receivable	12,000,000	Accruals	500,000
Inventories	7,500,000	Total current liabilities	$ 16,500,000
Total current assets	$23,500,000	Long-term debt	
Fixed assets		(including financial	
(at cost)		leases)	$ 20,000,000
Land and buildings	$11,000,000	Total liabilities	$ 36,500,000
Machinery and		Stockholders' equity	
equipment	20,500,000	Preferred stock	
Furniture and fixtures	8,000,000	(25,000 shares,	
Gross fixed assets	$39,500,000	$4 dividend)	$ 2,500,000
Less: Accumulated		Common stock	
depreciation	13,000,000	(1 million shares,	
Net fixed assets	$26,500,000	$5 par)	5,000,000
Total assets	$50,000,000	Paid-in capital	
		in excess of par	4,000,000
		Retained earnings	2,000,000
		Total stockholders' equity	$ 13,500,000
		Total liabilities and	
		stockholders' equity	**$50,000,000**

Industry Averages

Debt ratio	0.51
Debt-equity ratio	1.07
Times interest earned ratio	7.30

P2-5. Use the information below to answer the questions that follow.

Income Statement for the Year Ended December 31, 2012

	Heavy Metal Manufacturing (HMM)	Metallic Stamping Inc. (MS)	High-Tech Software Co. (HTS)
Sales	$75,000,000	$50,000,000	$100,000,000
−Operating expenses	65,000,000	40,000,000	60,000,000
Operating profit	$10,000,000	$10,000,000	$ 40,000,000
−Interest expenses	3,000,000	3,000,000	0
Earnings before taxes	$ 7,000,000	$ 7,000,000	$ 40,000,000
−Taxes	2,800,000	2,800,000	16,000,000
Net income	$ 4,200,000	$ 4,200,000	$ 24,000,000

Tables © Cengage Learning 2012

Balance Sheets as of December 31, 2012			
	Heavy Metal Manufacturing (HMM)	Metallic Stamping Inc. (MS)	High-Tech Software Co. (HTS)
Current assets	$ 10,000,000	$ 5,000,000	$ 20,000,000
Net fixed assets	90,000,000	75,000,000	80,000,000
Total assets	$100,000,000	$80,000,000	$100,000,000
Current liabilities	$ 20,000,000	$10,000,000	$ 10,000,000
Long-term debt	40,000,000	40,000,000	0
Total liabilities	$ 60,000,000	$50,000,000	$ 10,000,000
Common stock	$ 15,000,000	$10,000,000	$ 25,000,000
Retained earnings	25,000,000	20,000,000	65,000,000
Total common equity	$ 40,000,000	$30,000,000	$ 90,000,000
Total liabilities and common equity	$100,000,000	$80,000,000	$100,000,000

a. Use the *DuPont system* to compare the two heavy metal companies shown above (HHM and MS) during 2012. Which of the two has a higher return on common equity? What is the cause of the difference between the two?

b. Calculate the return on common equity of the software company, HTS. Why is this value so different from those of the heavy metal companies calculated in part (a)?

c. Compare the leverage levels between the industries. Which industry receives a greater contribution from return on total assets? Which industry receives a greater contribution from the financial leverage as measured by the assets-to-equity (A/E) ratio?

d. Can you make a meaningful DuPont comparison across industries? Why or why not?

P2-6. Refer to Problem 2-5, and perform the same analysis with real data. Download last year's financial data from Ford Motor Company (**www.ford.com**), General Motors (**www.gm.com**), and Microsoft (**www.microsoft.com**). Which ratios demonstrate the greatest difference between Ford and General Motors? Which of the two is more profitable? Which ratios drive the greater profitability?

P2-7. A *common-size income statement* for Aluminum Industries' 2011 operations follows. Using the firm's 2012 income statement presented in Problem 2-4, develop the 2012 common-size income statement (see footnote 2) and compare it with the 2011 statement. Which areas require further analysis and investigation?

Aluminum Industries, Inc. Common-Size Income Statement for the Year Ended December 31, 2011		
Sales revenue ($35,000,000)		100.0%
Less: Cost of goods sold		65.9
Gross profit		34.1%
Less: Operating expenses		
Selling expense	12.7%	
General and administrative expenses	6.3	
Lease expense	0.6	
Depreciation expense	3.6	
Total operating expense		23.2
Operating profit		10.9%
Less: Interest expense		1.5
Net profit before taxes		9.4%
Less: Taxes (rate = 40%)		3.8
Net profits after taxes		**5.6%**

P2-8. Use the following financial data for Greta's Gadgets, Inc., to determine the effect of using additional debt financing to purchase additional assets. Assume that an additional $1 million of assets is purchased with 100% debt financing with a 10% annual interest rate.

Greta's Gadgets, Inc.
Income Statement for the Year Ended December 31, 2012

Sales	$4,000,000
− Costs and expenses @ 90%	3,600,000
Earnings before interest & taxes	$ 400,000
− Interest (0.10 × $1,000,000)	100,000
Earnings before taxes	$ 300,000
− Taxes @ 40%	120,000
Net income	$ 180,000

Greta's Gadgets, Inc.
Balance Sheet as of December 31, 2012

Assets		Liabilities and stockholders' equity	
Current assets	$ 0	Current liabilities	$ 0
Fixed assets	2,000,000	Long-term debt @ 10%	1,000,000
Total assets	$2,000,000	Total liabilities	$1,000,000
		Common stock equity	$1,000,000
		Total liabilities and	
		stockholders' equity	$2,000,000

a. Calculate the current (2012) net profit margin, total asset turnover, assets-to-equity ratio, return on total assets, and return on common equity for Greta's Gadgets.

b. Now, assuming no other changes, determine the effect of purchasing the $1 million in assets using 100% debt financing with a 10% annual interest rate. Further assume that the newly purchased assets generate an additional $2 million in sales and that the costs and expenses remain at 90% of sales. For purposes of this problem, further assume a tax rate of 40%. What is the effect on the ratios calculated in part (a)? Is the purchase of these assets justified on the basis of the return on common equity?

c. Assume that the newly purchased assets in part (b) generate only an extra $500,000 in sales. Is the purchase justified in this case?

d. Which component ratio(s) of the *DuPont system* is (are) not affected by the change in sales? What does this imply about the use of financial leverage?

P2-9. Tracey White, owner of the Buzz Coffee Shop chain, has decided to expand her operations. Her 2012 financial statements follow. Tracey can buy two additional coffeehouses for $3 million, and she has the choice of completely financing these new coffeehouses with either a 10% (annual interest) loan or the issuance of new common stock. She also expects these new shops to generate an additional $1 million in sales. Assuming a 40% tax rate and no other changes, should Tracey buy the two coffeehouses? Why or why not? Which financing option results in the better *ROE*?

Buzz Coffee Shops, Inc. 2012 Financial Statements

Balance Sheet		Income Statement	
Current assets	$ 250,000	Sales	$500,000
Fixed assets	750,000	− Costs and expenses	
Total assets	$1,000,000	@ 40%	200,000
		Earnings before	$300,000
Current liabilities	$ 300,000	interest and taxes (*EBIT*)	
Long-term debt	0	− Interest expense	0
Total liabilities	$ 300,000	Net profit before taxes	$300,000
Common equity	$ 700,000	− Taxes @ 40%	120,000
Total liabilities and		Net income	$180,000
stockholders' equity	$1,000,000		

P2-10. The financial statements of Access Corporation for the year ended December 31, 2012, follow.

Access Corporation Income Statement for the Year Ended December 31, 2012

Sales revenue		$160,000
Less: Cost of goods sold*		106,000
Gross profit		$ 54,000
Less: Operating expenses		
Sales expense	$16,000	
General and administrative expense	10,000	
Lease expense	1,000	
Depreciation expense	10,000	
Total operating expense		37,000
Operating profit		$ 17,000
Less: Interest expense		6,100
Net profit before taxes		$ 10,900
Less: Taxes @ 40%		4,360
Net profits after taxes		**$ 6,540**

*Access Corporation's annual purchases are estimated to equal 75% of cost of goods sold.

Access Corporation Balance Sheet as of December 31, 2012

Assets		Liabilities and Stockholders' Equity	
Cash	$ 500	Accounts payable	$ 22,000
Marketable securities	1,000	Notes payable	47,000
Accounts receivable	25,000	Total current liabilities	$ 69,000
Inventories	45,500	Long-term debt	$ 22,950
Total current assets	$ 72,000	Total liabilities	$ 91,950
Land	$ 26,000	Common stock[a]	$ 31,500
Buildings		Retained earnings	26,550
and equipment	90,000	Total stockholders' equity	$ 58,050
Less:		Total liabilities and	
Accumulated		stockholders' equity	$150,000
depreciation	38,000		
Net fixed assets	$ 78,000		
Total assets	**$150,000**		

[a]The firm's 3,000 outstanding shares of common stock closed 2012 at a price of $25 per share.

a. Use the preceding financial statements to complete the following table. Assume that the industry averages given in the table are applicable for both 2011 and 2012.

b. Analyze Access Corporation's financial condition as it relates to (1) liquidity, (2) activity, (3) debt, (4) profitability, and (5) market value. Summarize the company's overall financial condition.

Access Corporation's Financial Ratios

	Industry Average	Actual Ratio 2011	Actual Ratio 2012
Current ratio	1.80	1.84	_____
Quick (acid-test) ratio	0.70	0.78	_____
Inventory turnover	2.50	2.59	_____
Average collection period[a]	37 days	36 days	_____
Average payment period[a]	72 days	78 days	_____
Debt-to-equity ratio	50%	51%	_____
Times interest earned ratio	3.8	4.0	_____
Gross profit margin	38%	40%	_____
Net profit margin	3.5%	3.6%	_____
Return on total assets (ROA)	4.0%	4.0%	_____
Return on common equity (ROE)	9.5%	8.0%	_____
Market/book (M/B) ratio	1.1	1.2	_____

[a]Based on a 365-day year and on end-of-year figures.

P2-11. Given the following financial statements, historical ratios, and industry averages, calculate the UG Company's financial ratios for 2012. Analyze its overall financial situation both in comparison with industry averages and over the period 2010–2012. Break your analysis into an evaluation of the firm's liquidity, activity, debt, profitability, and market value.

UG Company Income Statement for the Year Ended December 31, 2012		
Sales revenue		$10,000,000
Less: Cost of goods sold[a]		7,500,000
Gross profit		$ 2,500,000
Less: Operating expenses		
Selling expense	$300,000	
General and administrative expense	650,000	
Lease expense	50,000	
Depreciation expense	200,000	
Total operating expense		1,200,000
Operating profit (EBIT)		$ 1,300,000
Less: Interest expense		200,000
Net profits before taxes		$ 1,100,000
Less: Taxes (rate = 40%)		440,000
Net profits after taxes		**$ 660,000**
Less: Preferred stock dividends		50,000
Earnings available for common stockholders		**$ 610,000**
Earnings per share (EPS)		$ 3.05

[a]Annual credit purchases of $6.2 million were made during the year.

UG Company Balance Sheet as of December 31, 2012				
Assets			**Liabilities and Stockholders' Equity**	
Current assets			Current liabilities	
Cash	$ 200,000		Accounts payable	$ 900,000
Marketable securities	50,000		Notes payable	200,000
Accounts receivable	800,000		Accruals	100,000
Inventories	950,000		Total current liabilities	$ 1,200,000
Total current assets	$ 2,000,000		Long-term debt	
Gross fixed assets	$12,000,000		(including financial leases)	$ 3,000,000
Less: Accumulated			Stockholders' equity	
depreciation	3,000,000		Preferred stock	
Net fixed assets	$ 9,000,000		(25,000 shares, $2 dividend)	$ 1,000,000
Other assets	$ 1,000,000		Common stock	
Total assets	$12,000,000		(200,000 shares, $3 par)[a]	600,000
			Paid-in capital in excess of par	5,200,000
			Retained earnings	1,000,000
			Total stockholders' equity	$ 7,800,000
			Total liabilities and stockholders' equity	**$12,000,000**

[a]On December 31, 2012, the firm's common stock closed at $27.50.

© Cengage Learning 2012

Historical and Industry Average Ratios for UG Company			
Ratio	Actual 2010	Actual 2011	Industry Average 2012
Current ratio	1.40	1.55	1.85
Quick (acid-test) ratio	1.00	0.92	1.05
Inventory turnover	9.52	9.21	8.60
Average collection period[a]	45.0 days	36.4 days	35.0 days
Average payment period[a]	58.5 days	60.8 days	45.8 days
Fixed asset turnover	1.08	1.05	1.07
Total asset turnover	0.74	0.80	0.74
Debt ratio	0.20	0.20	0.30
Debt-to-equity ratio	0.25	0.27	0.39
Times interest earned ratio	8.2	7.3	8.0

Continued

Historical and Industry Average Ratios for UG Company

Ratio	Actual 2010	Actual 2011	Industry Average 2012
Gross profit margin	0.30	0.27	0.25
Operating profit margin	0.12	0.12	0.10
Net profit margin	0.067	0.067	0.058
Return on total assets (ROA)	0.049	0.054	0.043
Return on common equity (ROE)	0.066	0.073	0.072
Earnings per share (EPS)	$1.75	$2.20	$1.50
Price/earnings (P/E) ratio	12.0	10.5	11.2
Market/book (M/B) ratio	1.20	1.05	1.10

ªBased on a 365-day year and on end-of-year figures.

SMART
solutions
See the problem and solution explained step-by-step at **SMART**|finance

P2-12. Choose a company that you would like to analyze and obtain its financial statements. Now, select another firm from the same industry and obtain its financial data from the Internet. Perform a complete ratio analysis on each firm. How well does your selected company compare with its industry peer? Which components of your firm's *ROE* are superior, and which are inferior?

Corporate Taxes

P2-13. Thomsonetics, Inc., a rapidly growing early-stage technology company, had the pretax income noted below for calendar years 2010–2012. The firm was subject to corporate taxes consistent with the rates shown in Table 2.6.

Year	Pretax Income
2010	$ 87,000
2011	312,000
2012	760,000

a. Calculate Thomsonetics' tax liability for each year 2010, 2011, and 2012.
b. What was the firm's *average tax rate* in each year?
c. What was the firm's *marginal tax rate* in each year?
d. If in addition to its ordinary pretax income, Thomsonetics realized a capital gain of $80,000 during calendar year 2011, what effect would this have on its tax liability, average tax rate, and marginal tax rate in 2011?
e. Which tax rate—average or marginal—should Thomsonetics use in decision making? Why?

P2-14. Trish Foods, Inc. had pretax ordinary corporate income during 2012 of $2.7 million. In addition, during the year Trish Foods sold a group of non-depreciable business assets that it had purchased for $980,000 three years earlier. Because the assets were not depreciable, their book value at the time of sale was also $980,000. The firm pays corporate income taxes at the rates shown in Table 2.6.

a. Calculate Trish Foods's 2012 tax liability, average tax rate, and marginal tax rate, assuming the group of assets was sold for $1,150,000.
b. Calculate Trish Foods's 2012 tax liability, average tax rate, and marginal tax rate, assuming the group of assets was sold for $890,000.
c. Compare, contrast, and discuss your findings in parts (a) and (b).

THOMSON REUTERS | Business School Edition

Access financial information from the Thomson ONE – Business School Edition Web site for the following problem(s). Go to **www.tobsefin.swlearning.com/**. If you have already registered your access serial number and have a username and password, click **Enter**. Otherwise, click **Register** and follow the instructions to create a username and password. Register your access serial number and then click **Enter** on the aforementioned Web site. When you click Enter, you will be prompted for your username and password (please remember that the password is case sensitive). Enter them in the respective boxes and then click **OK** (or hit **Enter**). From the ensuing page, click **Click Here to**

Access Thomson ONE – Business School Edition Now! This opens up a new window that gives you access to the Thomson ONE – Business School Edition database. You can retrieve a company's financial information by entering its ticker symbol (provided for each company in the problem(s)) in the box below "Name/Symbol/Key." For further instructions on using the Thomson ONE – Business School Edition database, please refer to the online Help.

P2-15. Compare the profitability of Delta Air Lines (ticker: U:DAL) and United Airlines (U:UAL) for the latest year. Using the *return on common equity (ROE)*, determine which firm is more profitable. Use the *DuPont system* to determine what drives the difference in the profitability of the two.

P2-16. Analyze the financial condition of Carter's, Inc., (ticker: CRI) over the last five years. Use financial ratios that relate to its liquidity, activity, debt, profitability, and market value. In which areas has the company improved, and in which areas has the company's financial position worsened?

Since these exercises depend upon real-time data, your answers will change continuously depending upon when you access the Internet to download your data.

Smart Ethics Video

Frank Popoff, Chairman of the Board (retired), Dow Chemical

"Overstating or understating the performance of the enterprise is anathema . . . it's just not on."

Smart Ideas Video

John Graham, Duke University

"We asked companies, 'Do you manage your earnings?'"

Smart Practices Video

Jon Olson, Chief Financial Officer, Xilinx Corp.

"It is really important that you know some of the basics of accounting."

SMART concepts

See DuPont analysis of familiar companies such as Microsoft, Walmart, Kroger, and Robert Mondavi.

SMART solutions

See the solutions to Problems 2-2 and 2-12 explained step-by-step.

Mini-Case

Financial Statement and Cash Flow Analysis

You have been hired as a financial analyst by First Citizens Bank. One of your first job assignments is to analyze the present financial condition of Bradley Stores, Incorporated. You are provided with the following 2012 balance sheet and income statement information for Bradley Stores. In addition, you are told that Bradley Stores has 10,000,000 shares of common stock outstanding, currently trading at $9 per share, and has made annual purchases of $210,000,000.

Your assignment calls for you to calculate certain financial ratios and to compare these calculated ratios with the industry average ratios that are provided. You are also told to base your analysis on five categories of ratios: (a) liquidity ratios, (b) activity ratios, (c) debt ratios, (d) profitability ratios, and (e) market ratios.

Continued

Balance Sheet (in 000s)			
Cash	$ 5,000	Accounts payable	$ 15,000
Accounts receivable	20,000	Notes payable	20,000
Inventory	40,000	Total current liabilities	$ 35,000
Total current assets	$ 65,000	Long-term debt	$100,000
Net fixed assets	135,000	Stockholder equity	$ 65,000
Total assets	**$200,000**	**Total liabilities and equity**	**$200,000**

Income Statement (in 000s)	
Net sales (all credit)	$300,000
Less: Cost of goods sold	250,000
Earnings before interest and taxes	$ 50,000
Less: Interest	40,000
Earnings before taxes	$ 10,000
Less: Taxes (40%)	4,000
Net income	**$ 6,000**

Industry Averages for Key Ratios	
Net profit margin	6.4%
Average collection period (365 days)	30 days
Debt ratio	50%
P/E ratio	23
Inventory turnover ratio	12.0
ROE	18%
Average payment period (365 days)	20 days
Times interest earned ratio	8.5
Total asset turnover	1.4
Current ratio	1.5
Assets-to-equity ratio	2.0
ROA	9%
Quick ratio	1.25
Fixed asset turnover ratio	1.8

Assignment

Use the following guidelines to complete this job assignment. First, identify which ratios you need to use to evaluate Bradley Stores in terms of its (a) liquidity position, (b) business activity, (c) debt position, (d) profitability, and (e) market comparability. Next, calculate these ratios. Finally, compare these ratios to the industry average ratios provided in the problem and answer the following questions.

1. Based on the provided industry average information, discuss Bradley Stores's liquidity position. Discuss specific areas in which Bradley compares positively and negatively with the overall industry.

2. Based on the provided industry average information, what do Bradley Stores's activity ratios tell you? Discuss specific areas in which Bradley compares positively and negatively with the overall industry.

3. Based on the provided industry average information, discuss Bradley Stores's debt position. Discuss specific areas in which Bradley compares positively and negatively with the overall industry.

4. Based on the provided industry average information, discuss Bradley Stores's profitability position. As part of this investigation of firm profitability, include a DuPont analysis. Discuss specific areas in which Bradley compares positively and negatively with the overall industry.

5. Based on the provided industry average information, how is Bradley Stores, viewed in the marketplace? Discuss specific areas in which Bradley compares positively and negatively with the overall industry.

6. Overall, what are Bradley's strong and weak points? Knowing that your boss will approve new loans only to companies in a better-than-average financial position, what is your final recommendation (approval or denial of loan)?

chapter 3

The Time Value of Money

What Companies Do

Take the Money and ... Park?

Facing a huge projected 2009 budget deficit, Chicago Mayor Richard Daley struck a deal to lease the city's 36,000 parking meters to an investor group that included Morgan Stanley. Morgan and its partners would pay Chicago $1.2 billion up front; in return, they would collect revenue from parking meters for the next 75 years. The deal also allowed for increases in meter rates. The least expensive parking rates would rise from $1 per hour to $2 by 2013, while fees for the choice, downtown spots would rise from $3 to $6.50.

Asked to vote on approval for the deal with just 72 hours notice, Chicago City Aldermen voted 40-5 in favor of the deal. Alderman Richard Mell, whose son-in-law Governor Rod Blagojevich was under investigation for allegedly trying to sell Barack Obama's Senate seat to the highest bidder, explained his vote by arguing that the deal was a "once-in-a-lifetime shot to grab this pool of money." Another alderman called it "an unbelievable deal."

But was it an unbelievable deal for the city of Chicago or for Morgan Stanley (who coincidentally employed Richard Daley's son) and its partners? To answer that question, you must know how to compare an up-front payment with a long-term stream of cash payments. This chapter will show you how to make that comparison.

Learning Objectives

After studying this chapter you will be able to:

- Understand how to find the future value of a lump sum invested today;
- Calculate the present value of a lump sum to be received in the future;
- Find the future value of cash flow streams, both mixed streams and annuities;
- Determine the present value of future cash flow streams, including mixed streams, annuities, and perpetuities;

- Apply time-value techniques that account for compounding more frequently than annually, stated versus effective annual interest rates, and deposits needed to accumulate a future sum;
- Use time-value techniques to find implied interest or growth rates for lump sums, annuities, and mixed streams, and an unknown number of periods for both lump sums and annuities.

3-1 Introduction to the Time Value of Money

time value of money
Financial concept that explicitly recognizes that $1 received today is worth more than $1 received in the future.

future value
The value of an investment made today measured at a specific future date accounting for interest earned over the life of the investment.

present value
The value today of a cash flow to be received at a specific date in the future, accounting for the opportunity to earn interest at a specified rate.

In business, most decisions that financial managers face involve trading off costs and benefits that are spread out over time. Just as Morgan Stanley and its partners had to determine whether it was wise to pay Chicago $1.2 billion up front for the right to collect parking fees for the next 75 years, companies have to decide whether the initial cost of building a new factory or launching a new advertising campaign is justified by the long-term benefits that result from the investment. Financial managers need a quantitative framework for evaluating cash inflows and outflows that occur at different times. It turns out that this framework is just as useful to typical consumers in their everyday lives as it is to executives in huge, multinational corporations.

The most important idea in Chapter 3 is that money has time value. This simply means that it is better to have $1 today than to receive $1 in the future. The logic of this claim is straightforward—if you have $1 in hand today, you can invest it and earn interest, which means that you will have more than $1 in the future. Thus, the time value of money is a financial concept recognizing that the value of a cash receipt (or payment) depends not just on how much money you receive, but also on when you receive it.

A simple example illustrates the essence of the time value of money. Suppose you have $100 today, and you can put that sum into an investment that pays 5% interest per year. If you invest $100 now, by the end of one year you will earn $5 in interest ($0.05 \times $100 = 5). Your $100 initial investment will have grown to $105 in one year ($5 in interest plus the original $100 investment). In a sense, then, receiving $100 now is equivalent to receiving $105 in one year. Whether you receive $100 now and invest it at 5%, or whether you have to wait a year to receive $105, you wind up with the same amount of cash. In this case, we would say that *$105 is the future value of $100 invested for one year at 5%.* More generally, the future value is the value of a cash receipt or payment as of some future date.

We can reframe the example above to illustrate another dimension of the time value of money. Suppose you have no money today, but you expect to receive $105 in one year. Suppose also that a bank is willing to lend you money, charging an interest rate of 5%. How much would they lend you today if you promise to pay them the $105 that you will receive next year? From the calculations above, you can probably guess that the answer is $100. The bank will give you $100 today in exchange for a payment next year of $105. Here, *$100 is the present value of $105 to be received in one year when the interest rate is 5%.* More generally, the present value is just the value of a future cash receipt or payment in terms of today's dollars.

On an almost daily basis, managers use time value of money methods to compare the costs and benefits of important business decisions. Homebuyers can use the same techniques to evaluate the terms of different mortgage products. Consumers do likewise when they compare offers to purchase durable goods (like automobiles or furniture) that offer either an immediate cash discount or a low-interest financing plan. The rest of this chapter shows you how to apply time value of money analytics to a wide variety of problems that you may encounter either in your career or in your personal financial transactions.

3-1 Concept Review Questions

1. Why is it better to receive $1 today than at some point in the future?

2. During the recent recession, interest rates in the United States on relatively safe investments such as bank deposits were just barely above zero. If the interest rate is actually zero, what is the relationship between the present value and the future value of money?

3-2 Future Value of a Lump Sum Received Today

3-2a The Concept of Future Value

Saving today allows investors to earn interest on their savings and enjoy higher future consumption. We have already seen that a person who invests $100 today at 5% interest expects to receive $105 in one year, representing $5 interest plus the original $100 investment. Now let's examine how much money investors can earn when they set aside money for more than a single year.

We can calculate the future value of an investment made today by applying either *simple interest* or *compound interest* over a specified period of time. Simple interest is interest paid only on the initial principal of an investment. Principal is the amount of money on which the interest is paid. To demonstrate, if the investment in our previous example pays 5% simple interest, then the future value in any year equals $100 plus the product of the annual interest payment and the number of years. In this case, its future value would be $110 after two years [$100 + (2 × $5)], $115 in three years [$100 + (3 × $5)], $120 at the end of the fourth year [$100 + (4 × $5)], and so on.

Compound interest is interest earned both on the initial principal and on the interest earned in previous periods. To demonstrate compound interest, assume that you have the opportunity to deposit $100 into an account paying 5% annual interest. After one year, your account will have a balance of $105. This sum represents the initial principal of $100 plus 5% ($5) in interest. This future value is calculated as follows:

$$\text{Future value after one year} = \$100 \times (1 + 0.05) = \$105$$

If you leave this money in the account for another year, the investment will pay interest at the rate of 5% on the *new principal* of $105. In other words, you will receive 5% interest both on the initial principal of $100 and on the first year's interest of $5. At the end of this second year, there will be $110.25 in your account, representing the principal at the beginning of year 2 ($105) plus 5% of the $105, or $5.25, in interest.[1] The future value at the end of the second year is computed as follows:

$$\text{Future value after two years} = \$105 \times (1 + 0.05) = \$110.25$$

Substituting the first equation into the second one yields the following:

$$\begin{aligned} \text{Future value after two years} &= \$100 \times (1 + 0.05) \times (1 + 0.05) \\ &= \$100 \times (1 + 0.05)^2 \\ &= \$110.25 \end{aligned}$$

Therefore, $100 deposited at 5% *compound* annual interest will be worth $110.25 at the end of two years.

simple interest
Interest paid only on the initial *principal* of an investment, not on the interest that accrues in earlier periods.

principal
The amount of money on which interest is paid.

compound interest
Interest earned both on the initial *principal* and on the interest earned in previous periods.

---

[1]Said differently, compound interest includes the beneficial effect of "earning interest on your interest." In this example, during the second year you earn $5 interest on your initial $100 principal, plus you earn another $0.25 interest on the interest you earned (and saved) the first period. All total, in the second period you earn $5.25 in interest ($5 + $0.25).

It is important to recognize the difference in future values that results from compound versus simple interest. Although the difference between the account balances for simple versus compound interest in this example ($110 versus $110.25) seems rather trivial, the difference grows exponentially over time. With simple interest, this account would have a balance of $250 after 30 years [$100 + (30 × $5)]; with compound interest, the account balance after 30 years would be $432.19.

3-2b The Equation for Future Value

Because financial analysts routinely use compound interest, we generally use compound rather than simple interest throughout this book. Equation 3.1 gives the general algebraic formula for calculating the *future value*, at the end of *n* periods, *of a lump sum invested today* at an interest rate of *r*% per period:

(Eq. 3.1)	$FV = PV \times (1 + r)^n$

where

FV = future value of an investment,
PV = present value of an investment (the lump sum),
r = interest rate per period (typically 1 year),
n = number of periods (typically years) that the lump sum is invested.

The following example illustrates how you might use the concept of future value to evaluate an investment in a bank savings account.

EXAMPLE

You have an opportunity to invest $100 cash in a bank savings account that pays 6% annual interest. You would like to know how much money you will have at the end of five years.

Substituting PV = $100, r = 0.06, and n = 5 into Equation 3.1 gives the future value at the end of year 5:

$$FV = \$100 \times (1 + 0.06)^5 = \$100 \times (1.3382) = \$133.82$$

Your account will have a balance of $133.82 at the end of the fifth year, so your investment grew by $33.82.

time line
A graphical representation of cash flows over a given period of time.

An easy way to visualize how time value of money problems work is by drawing a time line like the one shown in Figure 3.1. A **time line** is a simple diagram that illustrates the value of a single cash flow or a series of cash flows as of a particular date. Figure 3.1 demonstrates that if you invest $100 today (time 0) at 6% interest, in five years (time 5), the future value of the initial $100 will grow to $133.82.

In practice, when analysts solve problems like these, they don't solve for the future value algebraically. Instead, they use a financial calculator or a spreadsheet program such as Excel to do the calculations. Figure 3.1 illustrates how to solve the previous example using a financial calculator and Excel. With a calculator, you enter the value -$100 and press the PV key. Next, enter the number of periods, 5, and press the N key. Then enter the interest rate, 6, and press the I key. Now you are ready to calculate the answer. Instruct the calculator to compute (press CPT) the future value (press FV), and you will have the same answer we reached before, $133.82.

If you are using Excel rather than a calculator to solve this problem, you will make use of the =*fv function*. The format of that function is =fv(rate,nper,pmt,pv,type). In this function, the symbols "pmt" and "type" refer to inputs that you need when solving problems involving multiple cash flows over time. Because the problem you are solving involves a single, up-front investment, you can enter the value zero for both "pmt" and "type." The only other inputs required are the interest rate, the number of periods, and the present value (i.e., the initial investment). Therefore, in Excel you could type, =fv(0.06,5,0,-100,0), and when you enter this formula in Excel, Excel will produce the answer you seek, $133.82.

Figure 3.1   **Future Value of $100 Invested for Five Years at 6% Annual Interest**

This figure illustrates how $100 invested today grows to $133.82 over five years if the annual interest rate is 6%. The time line at the top shows the initial deposit as well as the accumulated value after five years. The lower left portion of the figure shows how to calculate the future value using a calculator. Keystrokes will vary from one calculator model to another. The lower right portion of the figure shows how to calculate the future value using Excel.

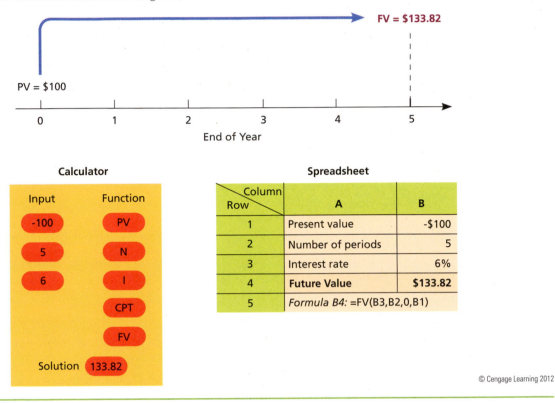

© Cengage Learning 2012

Notice that whether you use a financial calculator or Excel, you enter the initial $100 investment as a negative number. You can interpret this as taking money *out* of your wallet or paycheck to put it into the bank savings account. Five years later, you *receive* the future value, $133.82, which appears as a positive number.

EXAMPLE

Suppose the interest rate on a bank savings account is only 3%, half the rate in our earlier example. How much money will be in the account in five years, and how much growth does that represent on the initial investment?

By using a spreadsheet or financial calculator to solve Equation 3.1 using the inputs given here, we can quickly determine that the future value of a $100 investment for five years is $115.93.

$$FV = \$100 \times (1 + 0.03)^5 = \$115.93$$

In this case, the investment grew by $15.93. Notice that while the interest rate used in this calculation was half the rate we used before (3% rather than 6%), the growth in the account's value was less than half of what it was before ($15.93 versus $33.82). This is the effect of compound interest. When the interest rate on an investment increases, the value of the investment rises at an increasing rate.

3-2c A Graphic View of Future Value

Remember that we measure future value at the *end* of the given period. Figure 3.2 shows how quickly a $1.00 investment grows over time at various annual interest rates. The figure shows that (1) the higher the interest rate, the higher the future value, and (2) the longer the period of time, the higher the future value. Note that for an interest rate of 0%, the future value always equals the present value ($1), but for any interest rate greater than zero, the future value is greater than $1.

Figure 3.2   **The Power of Compound Interest:**
Future Value of $1 Invested Today at Different Annual Interest Rates

The figure shows that the future value of $1 invested today increases over time as long as the interest rate is greater than 0%. Notice that each line gets steeper the longer the money remains invested because the future value grows at an increasing rate. This is the power of compound interest. For the same reason, the future value grows faster at higher interest rates. (Observe how the lines get steeper as the interest rates increase.)

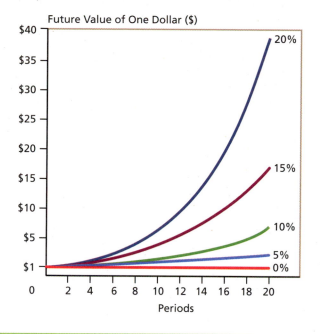

© Cengage Learning 2012

3-4 Concept Review Questions

3. If compounding occurs once per year, will a deposit made in an account paying compound interest yield a higher future value after one period than an equal-size deposit in an account paying simple interest? What about future values for investments held longer than one period?

4. How would the future value of a deposit be affected by (a) a *decrease* in the interest rate or (b) an *increase* in the holding period? Why?

● 3-3   Present Value of a Lump Sum Received in the Future

So far we have examined how to project the amount of cash that builds over time as an initial investment earns interest. Now we reverse that focus, asking what an investor would pay today in exchange for receiving a lump-sum payment at some point in the future. In other words, we want to know the *present value* of the future cash flow.

3-3a The Concept of Present Value

discounting
The process of calculating present values.

In finance, we use the term **discounting** to describe the process of calculating present values. The technique of discounting helps us to answer this question: If I can earn $r\%$ on my money, then what is the most I would be willing to pay *now* for the opportunity to receive *FV* dollars n periods from today? This process is actually the inverse of compounding interest:

- Compounding *tells us the future value of present dollars invested at a given interest rate;*

- Discounting *helps us determine the present value of a future amount, assuming an opportunity to earn a given return (r) on the money.*[2]

To see how this works, suppose an investment will pay you $300 one year from now. How much would you be willing to spend today to acquire this investment if you can earn 6% on an alternative investment of equal risk? To answer this question, you must determine how many dollars you would have to invest at 6% today in order to have $300 one year from now. Let *PV* equal this unknown amount, and use the same notation as in our discussion of future value:

$$PV \times (1 + 0.06) = \$300$$

Solving this equation for *PV* gives us

$$PV = \frac{\$300}{(1 + 0.06)} = \$283.02$$

The present value of $300 one year from today is $283.02 in today's dollars. That is, $283.02 invested today at a 6% interest rate would grow to $300 at the end of one year. Therefore, today you would be willing to pay no more than $283.02 for an investment that pays you $300 in one year.

3-3b The Equation for Present Value

We can find the *present value of a lump sum* mathematically by solving Equation 3.1 for *PV*. In other words, the present value *(PV)* of some future amount *(FV)* to be received *n* periods from now, assuming an opportunity cost of *r*, is given by Equation 3.2:

(Eq. 3.2)
$$PV = \frac{FV}{(1 + r)^n} = FV \times \frac{1}{(1 + r)^n}$$

Investors use Equation 3.2 to determine the value today of an investment that pays off in the future. There are many applications of this formula. One application helps companies determine how much money they need to charge a customer today to cover a liability looming in the future.

EXAMPLE

Equipment Rental, Inc., leases packaging machines to manufacturing firms. Their leases run for eight years, which corresponds to the useful life of the equipment. Part of their standard lease agreement dictates that at the end of the lease, Equipment Rental must remove the old equipment, and fulfilling that requirement costs Equipment Rental about $1,700 per machine. Managers at Equipment Rental want to know the present value of this cost so that they can add it to the list of up-front fees that they charge when they sign a new lease with a client. Assuming that the relevant discount rate is 8%, what is the present value of a $1,700 payment that occurs eight years in the future?

Substituting *FV* = $1,700, *n* = 8, and *r* = 0.08 into Equation 3.2 yields the following:

$$PV = \frac{\$1,700}{(1 + 0.08)^8} = \frac{\$1,700}{(1.85093)} = \$918.46$$

Figure 3.3 provides a time line illustrating the cash flows in this example as well as the calculator and spreadsheet solution methods. The format of Excel's present value function is =pv(rate,nper,pmt,fv,type). The arguments of this function are nearly identical to those of the future value function. As before, the arguments "pmt" and "type" apply only to problems with cash-flow streams, not lump sums, so for those two arguments you enter the value 0. To solve the preceding example using Excel, you could simply enter =fv(0.08,8,0,-1700,0), and Excel would provide the answer, $918.46. Notice that if you *enter the $1,700 as a negative number* (either in the

---

[2]This interest rate, *r*, is variously referred to as the *discount rate*, the *required return*, the *cost of capital*, the *hurdle rate*, or the *opportunity cost of capital*.

Figure 3.3   **Present Value of $1,700 to Be Received in Eight Years at an 8% Discount Rate**

To calculate the present value of $1,700 received in year 8, we must discount it to reflect the lost opportunity to earn 8% interest on the money for eight years. In this example, the discounted value of $1,700 equals just $918.46.

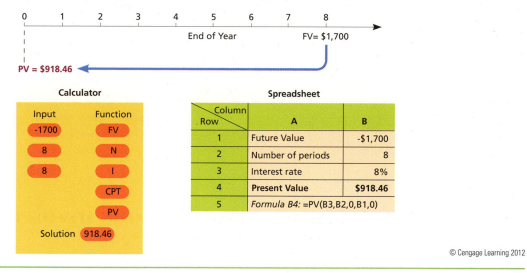

© Cengage Learning 2012

calculator or the spreadsheet) the solution for PV comes back as a positive number. In other words, the $1,700 represents an outflow when the company pays to remove the equipment in eight years, and the $918.46 represents an inflow when the firm charges this fee to its customer at the beginning of the lease.[3]

3-3c A Graphic View of Present Value

Figure 3.4 illustrates the relationship between the present value of a future lump sum, the discount rate, and the "waiting time" before the future lump sum is paid. For investors

Figure 3.4   **The Power of Discounting:**
Present Value of $1 Discounted at Different Interest Rates

This figure shows the present value of receiving $1 at various points in the future, discounted at different discount rates. For example, if the discount rate is 5%, the present value of $1 received in six years is about $0.75. Note that the present value of $1.00 falls as the interest rate rises. For example, the present value of $1 received in year six is only $0.75 if the discount rate is 5%, but only $0.43 if the discount rate is 15%. Similarly, the longer one must wait to receive a $1.00 payment, the lower the present value of that payment.

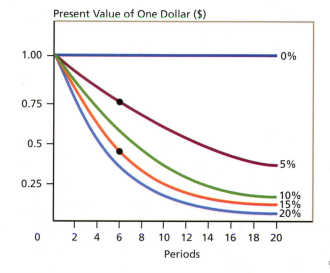

© Cengage Learning 2012

---

[3]Just remember that when using a calculator or spreadsheet, the PV and FV will have opposite signs. Which sign you use really doesn't matter. In this example, for instance, if you enter the FV ($1,700) as a positive number, then the answer you get back for PV will be negative (−$918.46).

who expect to receive cash in the future, Figure 3.4 contains two important messages. First, the present value of a future cash payment declines the longer investors must wait to receive it. Second, the present value declines as the discount rate rises. Note that for a discount rate of 0%, the present value always equals the future value ($1). However, for any discount rate greater than zero, the present value falls below the future value.

3-3 Concept Review Questions

5. How are the present value and the future value of a lump sum related definitionally? Mathematically?

6. How would the present value be affected by (a) an *increase* in the discount rate or (b) a *decrease* in the time period until the cash flow is received? Why?

3-4 Additional Applications Involving Lump Sums

Equations 3.1 and 3.2 are just two ways of writing a mathematical relationship linking the present and future value of cash flows to each other and to the interest rate and investment horizon. In many situations, the objective is not to find the present or future value of a cash payment, but to answer a question about the interest rate or the investment horizon instead. The series of examples that follows illustrates other kinds of problems that can be solved by using some form of Equation 3.1.

EXAMPLE

You saved $1,000, and you plan to put it into an investment earning 8% interest. *How many years* will it take you to triple your money? To solve this problem, start with Equation 3.1:

$$FV = PV(1 + r)^n$$

In this case, we know $PV = \$1,000$ and $r = 0.08$. We also know that $FV = \$3,000$ because the goal is to triple the initial $1,000 investment. The unknown quantity is n, the number of years needed for $1,000 to grow to $3,000 if the interest rate is 8%. Therefore, we have

$$\$3,000 = \$1,000(1 + 0.08)^n$$

Dividing both sides by $1,000 leaves a simplified equation

$$3.0 = (1.08)^n$$

To solve this last expression algebraically, we take the natural logarithm of each side and then simplify terms as follows

$$\ln(3.0) = \ln(1.08)^n$$
$$\ln(3.0) = \ln(1.08)$$
$$\ln(3.0) \div \ln(1.08) = n$$
$$1.0986 \div 0.0770 = n$$
$$14.3 \text{ years} = n$$

Figure 3.5 illustrates the calculator and spreadsheet solutions for this problem.

continued

Figure 3.5

Calculator

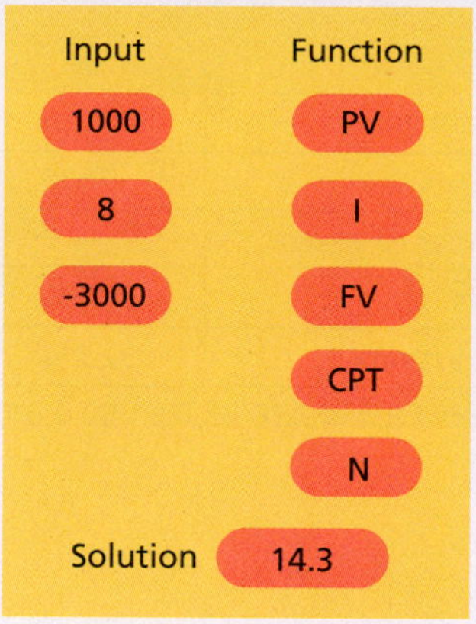

Input	Function
1000	PV
8	I
-3000	FV
	CPT
	N
Solution	14.3

Spreadsheet

Row \ Column	A	B
1	Present value	$1,000
2	Interest rate	8%
3	Future value	-$3,000
4	**Number of years**	**14.3**
5	*Formula B4:* =NPER(B2,0,B1,B3,0)	

© Cengage Learning 2012

In the preceding example, we solved for the number of periods required for a lump sum to grow to a particular future value at a particular interest rate. Here again, Excel offers a quick way to find the answer. You can use the "number of periods" function in Excel, which has the syntax, =nper(rate,pmt,pv,fv,type). In the previous problem, $1,000 is the present value, $3,000 is the future value, and 8% is the rate (the arguments "pmt" and "type" still do not apply, so enter 0). For Excel to solve this problem, the values you enter for present value and future value must have opposite signs (it doesn't matter which is positive and which is negative). Therefore, in Excel you could enter, =nper(0.08,0,1000,-3000,0), and Excel would provide the answer, 14.3 years. Alternatively, you could use a financial calculator, inputting the keystrokes shown in the margin to obtain the same answer.

Another common type of business problem requires analysts to determine the rate of return on a particular investment or to calculate the rate of growth over time in a firm's sales or profits.

EXAMPLE

Google, Inc., became a public company when it conducted an initial public offering (IPO) of common stock in August 2004. Originally priced at $85 per share, Google stock soared after the IPO. By August 2011, Google shares stood at $600. *What annual rate of return* did the investors who bought Google shares at the IPO and held them through August 2011 earn? Once again, start with Equation 3.1

$$FV = PV(1 + r)^n$$

In this case we know $FV = \$600$, $PV = \$85$, and $n = 7$ years. Plug those values into Equation 4.1 and solve for r.

$$\$600 = \$85(1 + r)^7$$

$$\$600 \div \$85 = (1 + r)^7$$

$$(\$600 \div \$85)^{(1 \div 7)} = (1 + r)$$

$$1.322 = 1 + r$$

$$r = 0.322 = 32.2\%$$

continued

Figure 3.6

Calculator

Input	Function
85	PV
-600	FV
7	N
	CPT
	I
Solution	32.2

Spreadsheet

Column / Row	A	B
1	Present value	$85
2	Future value	-$600
3	Number of years	7
4	Guess	10%
5	**Interest rate**	**32.2%**
6	*Formula B5:* =RATE(B3,0,B1,B2,0,B4)	

© Cengage Learning 2012

Google investors earned more than 32% per year in the company's first seven years. Figure 3.6 illustrates how to solve this problem using a calculator or spreadsheet. The Excel function that solves this type of problem is the "rate" function, and its syntax is =rate(nper,pmt,pv,fv,type,guess). All but one of the arguments of this function should be familiar by now. The new argument is "guess," which is not a value that is part of the problem, but rather is a numerical value that you provide just to "get Excel started" as it tries to find the solution. By default, Excel assumes a value of "guess" of 0.10 or 10%. You can leave that argument blank or enter any interest rate that you like—the value of "guess" that you submit rarely has any impact on the solution that Excel obtains. To find the rate of return on Google's stock in its first seven years, you could type into Excel, =rate(5,0,85,-600,0.10), and Excel would give you 32.2% as the answer. You could also solve the problem using the calculator keystrokes shown in Figure 3.6.

How did Google's stock achieve such spectacular performance? At least in theory, a company's stock price ought to reflect the underlying performance of the firm (as well as investor's expectations about future performance). The next example shows how to use Equation 3.1 to develop a simple measure of how Google performed as a company from 2004–2011.

EXAMPLE

In 2004, the year of its IPO, Google generated total revenue of about $3.2 billion. Seven years later, the firm reported 2011 revenues of about $37 billion. What was *the annual growth rate* in Google's revenues during this period? Again we apply Equation 3.1, substituting the values that we know as follows

$$FV = PV(1 + r)^n$$

$$\$37 = \$3.2(1 + r)^7$$

$$(\$37 \div \$3.2)^{(1 \div 7)} = (1 + r)$$

$$1.419 = 1 + r$$

$$r = 0.419 = 41.9\%$$

Notice here that we are still solving for *r*, just as we did in the previous example. In this case, the *interpretation of r is a little different*. It is not the rate of return (or the rate of interest) on some investment, but rather the compound annual growth rate between Google's 2004 and 2011 revenues. It is a simple measure of how fast the company was growing during this period. Repeating the algebraic manipulations (or the calculator or spreadsheet keystrokes) from the prior example, we can determine that Google's revenues increased at an annual rate of 41.9% from 2004 to 2011.

A final example illustrates how you might use Equation 3.1 to make a wise decision when confronted with *different options for borrowing money to purchase* a consumer durable good.

EXAMPLE

You are thinking of treating yourself to a nice graduation present, the latest and greatest laptop designed specifically for gamers. It has a huge screen with ultra fast graphics capabilities. Fully equipped, the laptop costs $3,000. The problem is that you do not have any money today. In a few months, you will be working full time, and by the end of the year you believe you will have enough money to purchase the laptop. Of course, you want it now.

As a promotion, a local electronics retailer is offering a special deal. Consumers can either buy the laptop at a discount, paying just $2,700, or they can take the laptop home today and wait one year before paying the full asking price, $3,000. Though you don't have $2,700 in cash on hand, you could charge that amount to your credit card and pay 10% interest. Which is the better option—buying the laptop today for $2,700 and paying interest to the credit card company, or paying nothing today and writing a check to the retailer for $3,000 a year later?

Once again, let's write down Equation 3.1 and plug in values that we know. You can spend $2,700 today and pay 10% interest for a year. In this case, we could write Equation 3.1 as follows:

$$FV = \$2,700(1 + 0.10)^1 = \$2,970$$

Borrowing $2,700 today on your credit card will cost you $2,970 in one year. The second option is to pay nothing today and pay the retailer $3,000 at the end of the year. You save $30 by using your credit card and repaying the credit card company $2,970 next year rather than paying the retailer $3,000. Another way to frame this problem is to determine the *implicit interest rate* that the retailer is charging if you accept the offer to pay $3,000 in one year. The retailer is essentially lending you $2,700 today (the amount that you would be charged if you paid up front), but you have to pay the full price at the end of one year. In this case, Equation 3.1 looks like this:

$$\$3,000 = \$2,700(1 + r)^1$$

$$(\$3,000 \div \$2,700) - 1 = r$$

$$0.1111 = 11.11\% = r$$

Solving for r, the implicit interest rate charged by the retailer, we obtain a rate of 11.11%. If you can borrow at a rate of 10% using your credit card, then that is preferable to accepting the retailer's loan that carries a rate of 11.11%.

3-4 Concept Review Questions

7. In the first example in this section, we saw that a $1,000 investment earning 8% would triple in 14.3 years. Suppose the investment earns just 4%, half as much as originally anticipated. A lower rate of return means that it will take more time for the investment to triple. Will it take exactly twice as long (28.6 years) to triple, more than that, or less than that? Why?

3-5 | Future Value of Cash Flow Streams

Financial managers frequently need to evaluate *streams* of cash flows that occur in future periods. Though this is mechanically more complicated than computing the future or present value of a single cash flow, the same basic techniques apply.

Two types of cash flow streams are possible: the mixed stream and the annuity. A **mixed stream** is a series of unequal cash flows reflecting no particular pattern. An **annuity** is a stream of equal periodic cash flows over a stated period of time. Either of these cash flow patterns can represent *inflows* of returns earned on investments or *outflows* of funds invested to earn future returns. Because certain shortcuts are possible when evaluating an annuity, we discuss mixed streams and annuities separately.

mixed stream
A series of unequal cash flows reflecting no particular pattern.

annuity
A stream of equal periodic cash flows over a stated period of time.

3-5a Finding the Future Value of a Mixed Stream

The future value of any stream of cash flows measured at the end of a specified year is merely the sum of the future values of the individual cash flows at that year's end.

This future value is sometimes called the *terminal value*. The following example demonstrates such a calculation.

EXAMPLE

Assume that we want to determine the balance in an investment account earning 9% annual interest, given the following five end-of-year deposits: $400 in year 1, $800 in year 2, $500 in year 3, $400 in year 4, and $300 in year 5. These cash flows appear on the time line at the top of Figure 3.7, which also depicts the future-value calculation for this mixed stream of cash flows, followed by the financial calculator and spreadsheet solutions.

Note that the first cash flow, which occurs at the end of year 1, earns interest for four years (end of year 1 to end of year 5). Similarly, the second cash flow, which occurs at the end of year 2, earns interest for three years (end of year 2 to end of year 5), and so on. Summing the future values of the five deposits yields the total future value of the mixed stream, which is $2,930.70.[4] The five deposits, which total $2,400 before interest, have grown by nearly $531 at the end of five years as a result of the interest earned.

Figure 3.7 **Future Value at the End of Five Years of a Mixed Cash Flow Stream Invested at 9%**

The future value of a mixed stream of cash flows equals the sum of the future values of the individual cash flows. For the cash flows shown on the timeline, the individual future values compounded at 9% interest to the end of year 5 are shown at the end of the arrows. Their total of $2,930.70 represents the future value of the mixed stream.

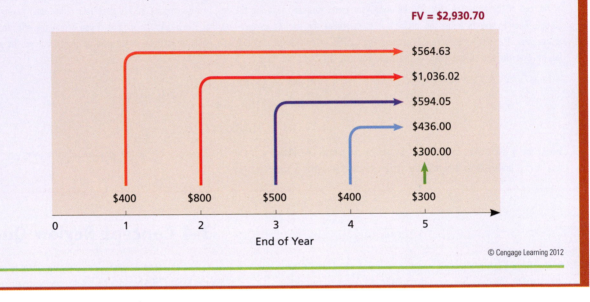

© Cengage Learning 2012

Letting CF_t represent the cash flow at the end of year t, the *future value of* an n-year <u>mixed stream of cash flows</u> (FV) is shown in Equation 3.3:

$$(\text{Eq. 3.3}) \quad FV = CF_1 \times (1 + r)^{n-1} + CF_2 \times (1 + r)^{n-2} + \cdots + CF_n \times (1 + r)^{n-n}$$

Substituting the annual cash flows and the 9% interest rate into Equation 3.3, we would calculate the value for each year (shown to the right of the time line). These values would total $2,930.70.

We can simplify the notation for Equation 3.3, as shown in Equation 3.3a, by using summation notation, which uses the Greek letter sigma (Σ), as a shorthand way of saying that the future value of this n-year mixed stream is equal to the sum of the future values of individual cash flows from periods 1, 2, 3, . . . , n:

$$(\text{Eq. 3.3a}) \qquad FV = \sum_{t=1}^{n} CF_t \times (1 + r)^{n-t}$$

? JOB INTERVIEW QUESTION

Our company invests money each month to pay future retirement benefits that are fixed contractually. If the return on our investment goes up, how does that affect the amount we must set aside each month?

---

[4]There is a $0.01 rounding difference between the future value given on the time line compared with the future-value calculation using a calculator or spreadsheet.

Although summations economize on the notation needed to express most of the equations presented in this chapter, for clarity we present equations in their non-condensed format wherever possible, and we use the summation notation sparingly.

Sometimes it is necessary to blend the techniques that we have covered thus far to solve a problem. The following example illustrates how this works.

EXAMPLE

The time line below shows a mixed stream of cash flows that has a future value in four years of $846.95 if the interest rate is 7%. The mixed stream starts with an immediate cash flow of $100, but the question mark in year 2 indicates that you do not know the value of the cash flow that arrives in that period. How can you find that *value of the missing piece of the mixed stream?*

FV of mixed stream in year 4 = $846.95 ($r = 7$%)

Cash flow	$100	$150	?	$200	$175
	0	1	2	3	4

Year

First, calculate the future value of the four cash flows that you know using Equation 3.3:

$$FV = \$100(1 + 0.07)^4 + \$150(1 + 0.07)^3 + \$200(1 + 0.07)^1 + \$175 = \$703.84$$

If the future value of the entire stream is $846.95, and the future value of the four cash flows shown on the time line is $703.84, then the difference must be the future value of the missing cash flow in year 2. That difference is $143.11. In other words, the cash flow in year 2 must grow to $143.11 after earning interest for two years. We could also say that the missing cash flow on the time line equals the present value in year 2 of $143.11 to be received in year 4. Therefore we can use Equation 3.2 as follows:

$$PV = \frac{\$143.11}{(1 + 0.07)^2} = \$125$$

These techniques allow you to calculate the future value of any cash flow stream. However, one category of cash flow, known as annuities, is very common in finance, and there are some helpful shortcuts that you can use to calculate the future value of an annuity.

3-5b Types of Annuities

ordinary annuity
An annuity for which the payments occur *at the end of each period.*

annuity due
An annuity for which the payments occur *at the beginning of each period.*

Before looking at future-value computations for annuities, we distinguish between the two basic types of annuities: the ordinary annuity and the annuity due. An ordinary annuity is an annuity for which the payments occur *at the end of each period*, whereas an annuity due is one for which the payments occur *at the beginning of each period.*

To demonstrate these differences, assume that you wish to choose the better of two annuities as a personal investment opportunity. Both are five-year, $1,000 annuities. Annuity A is an ordinary annuity and annuity B is an annuity due. Although the amount of each annuity totals $5,000, the timing of the cash flows differs; each cash flow arrives one year sooner with the annuity due than with the ordinary annuity. As you might expect (given the core principle of the time value of money), for any positive interest rate, *the future value of an annuity due is always greater than the future value of an otherwise identical ordinary annuity.*[5] Why? Because you receive the first cash flow today in the annuity due, giving you a longer time to earn interest.

3-5c Finding the Future Value of an Ordinary Annuity

The future value of an ordinary annuity can be calculated using the same method demonstrated earlier for a mixed stream.

EXAMPLE

You wish to save money on a regular basis to finance an exotic vacation in five years. You are confident that, with sacrifice and discipline, you can force yourself to deposit $1,000 annually, at the *end of each* of the next five years, into a savings account paying 7% annual interest. This situation is depicted graphically at the top of Figure 3.8.

---

[5]Because ordinary annuities arise frequently in finance, we use the term *annuity* throughout this book to refer to ordinary annuities, unless otherwise specified.

continued

Figure 3.8   Future Value at the End of Five Years of an Ordinary Annuity of $1,000 Per Year Invested at 7%

The future value of the five-year, $1,000 ordinary annuity at 7% interest at the end of year 5 is $5,750.74, which is well above the $5,000 sum of the annual deposits.

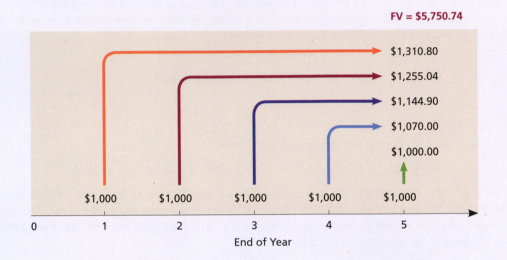

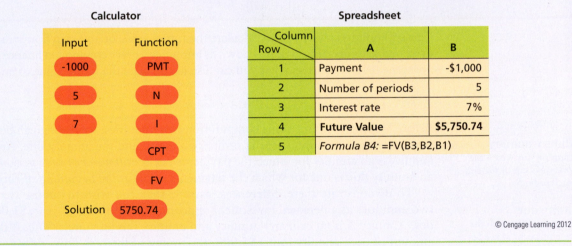

Compute the *future value (FV) of this ordinary annuity*, using Equation 3.3. Use the assumed interest rate (r) of 7% and plug in the known values of each of the five yearly ($n = 5$) cash flows (CF_1 to CF_5), as follows:

$$FV = CF_1 \times (1 + r)^{n-1} + CF_2 \times (1 + r)^{n-2} + \cdots + CF_n \times (1 + r)^{n-n}$$

$$FV = CF_1 \times (1 + r)^{5-1} + CF_2 \times (1 + r)^{5-2} + \cdots + CF_n \times (1 + r)^{5-5}$$

$$= \$1,000(1.07)^4 + \$1,000(1.07)^3 + \$1,000(1.07)^2 + \$1,000(1.07)^1 + \$1,000$$

$$= \$1,310.80 + \$1,225.04 + \$1,144.90 + \$1,070 + \$1,000 = \$5,750.74$$

The year 1 cash flow of $1,000 earns 7% interest for four years, the year 2 cash flow earns 7% interest for three years, and so on. The future value of the ordinary annuity is $5,750.74.

Making this calculation for a longer annuity would become cumbersome. Fortunately, a shortcut formula exists that simplifies the future-value calculation of an ordinary annuity. Using the symbol *PMT* to represent the annuity's annual payment,

Equation 3.4 gives the *future value of an annuity* that lasts for *n* years (*FV*), assuming an interest rate of *r*%:

(Eq. 3.4)
$$FV = PMT \times \left\{ \frac{[(1 + r)^n - 1]}{r} \right\}$$

EXAMPLE

We can demonstrate that Equation 3.4 yields the same answer obtained in the previous model by plugging in the values *PMT* = $1,000, *n* = 5, and *r* = 0.07:

$$FV = \$1,000 \times \left\{ \frac{[(1.07)^5 - 1]}{0.07} \right\} = \$1,000 \times \left[\frac{1.4026 - 1}{0.07} \right]$$
$$= \$1,000 \times 5.75074 = \$5,750.74$$

Once again, we find the future value of this ordinary annuity to be $5,750.74. You could also obtain this value using Excel's future value function. Recall that the syntax of that function is, =fv(rate,nper,pmt,pv,type). Now that you are dealing with problems involving cash flow streams rather than lump sums, you need to input particular values for the arguments "pmt" and "type." The value for "pmt" is simply the periodic cash flow that the annuity provides, and the value for "type" equals 0 if the problem you're solving is an ordinary annuity ("type" equals 1 for an annuity due). For an annuity problem, the argument "pv" requires some additional explanation. Excel will interpret any value entered for this argument as a lump sum payment that comes before the annuity begins. In this example, there is no initial lump sum (pv=0), so you can obtain the future value of the annuity by entering =fv(0.07,5,-1000,0,0).

Next, consider a slight variation on the vacation saving problem that requires you to integrate what you've learned about finding the future value of both a lump sum and an annuity.

EXAMPLE

As in the previous example, you plan to save $1,000 at the end of each of the next five years to accumulate money for a vacation, and you expect to earn 7% on the money that you save. In addition, you just received a bonus at work, which gives you another $5,000 to invest immediately. How much can you accumulate in five years if you invest your bonus in addition to the $1,000 per year that you originally intended to save?

Previously, we found that the future value of a $1,000 annuity invested over five years at 7% was $5,750.74. To that total, we now want to add the future value of a $5,000 lump sum invested immediately. Using Equation 3.1 we have:

$$\$5,000(1 + 0.07)^5 = \$7,012.76$$

Adding that to the future value of the annuity gives you a total of $12,763.50 ($7,012.76 + $5,750.74) for your vacation. A quick way to solve this is to enter into Excel =fv(0.07,5,-1000,-5000,0). Notice here that you enter both the $1,000 deposits and the initial $5,000 lump sum as negative numbers. These inputs have the same sign because they both represent money flowing in the same direction (out of your wallet into your savings account). Entering the values this way causes Excel to report the answer as a positive $12,763.50.

Sometimes consumers know that they want to accumulate a certain amount of money by making regular deposits into a savings account. In this situation, the uncertainty is not the future value of the annuity, but rather the *amount of time needed to accumulate* that *future value*.

EXAMPLE

Jim and Mary Cummings just had their first child, and they want to begin saving for college expenses. They estimate they will need a college fund worth $100,000 to pay for four years of college costs. They plan to set aside $2,700 at the end of each of the next 18 years, investing the money to earn 8% interest. Given that plan, how long will it take Jim and Mary to accumulate the money they need?

continued

One way to solve this problem is to modify Equation 3.4 to solve for the value n, the number of periods in the annuity. A little algebra transforms Equation 3.4 as follows:

$$\ln\left(\frac{FV \times r}{PMT} + 1\right) \div \ln(1 + r) = n$$

Plug in $100,0000 for FV, 0.08 for r, and $2,700 for PMT and you obtain:

$$\ln\left(\frac{\$100,000 \times 0.08}{\$2,700} + 1\right) \div \ln(1 + 0.08) = 17.9 \text{ years}$$

Apparently, Jim and Mary will have the money they need just in time.

As we did with lump sums, we can employ Excel's "number of periods" function to obtain a quick solution to this problem. To apply this function, enter, $=$nper(0.08,-2700,0,100000,0), and Excel will provide the answer, 17.9 years. In this syntax of this function, we use 0 for pv because Jim and Mary are just starting to save for college and have accumulated nothing so far. Notice also that the payment ($-$2,700) and the desired future value ($100,000) have opposite signs.

3-5d Finding the Future Value of an Annuity Due

The calculations required to find the future value of an annuity due involve only a slight change to those already demonstrated for an ordinary annuity. For the annuity due, the question is: How much money will you have at the end of five years (to finance your exotic vacation) if you deposit $1,000 annually at the *beginning of each year* into a savings account paying 7% annual interest?

Figure 3.9 graphically depicts this scenario on a time line. Note that the ends of years 0 through 4 are respectively equivalent to the beginnings of years 1 through 5. As expected, the $6,153.29 future value of the annuity due is greater than the $5,750.74 future value of the comparable ordinary annuity.[6] Because the cash flows of the annuity due occur at the beginning of the year, the cash flow of $1,000 at the beginning of year 1 earns 7% interest for five years, the cash flow of $1,000 at the beginning of year 2 earns 7% interest for four years, and so on. Comparing this to the ordinary annuity, you can see that each $1,000 cash flow of the annuity due earns interest for one more year than the comparable ordinary annuity cash flow. As a result, the future value of the annuity due is greater than the future value of the comparable ordinary annuity.

We can convert the equation for the future value of an ordinary annuity, Equation 3.4, into an expression for the *future value of an annuity due*, denoted FV (annuity due). To do so, we must take into account that each cash flow of an annuity due earns an additional year of interest. Therefore, we simply multiply Equation 3.4 by $(1 + r)$, as shown in Equation 3.5:

> (Eq. 3.5) $\qquad FV(\text{annuity due}) = PMT \times \left\{\dfrac{[(1 + r)^n - 1]}{r}\right\} \times (1 + r)$

Equation 3.5 demonstrates that the future value of an annuity due always exceeds the future value of a similar ordinary annuity (for any positive interest rate) by a factor of 1 plus the interest rate. We can check this by comparing the results from the two different five-year vacation savings plans presented earlier. We determined that, given a 7% interest rate, after five years the value of the ordinary annuity was $5,750.74, and that of the annuity due was $6,153.29. Multiplying the future value of the ordinary annuity by 1 plus the interest rate yields the future value of the annuity due:

$$FV \text{ (annuity due)} = \$5,750.74 \times (1.07) = \$6,153.29$$

---

[6]You can use the same Excel function to obtain the future value of an annuity due that you used to calculate the future value of an ordinary annuity, except that the value of "type" changes from 0 to 1. If you enter into Excel, $=$fv(0.07,5, -1000,0,1), then Excel produces the value $6,153.29.

Figure 3.9   **Future Value at the End of Five Years of an Annuity Due of $1,000 Per Year Invested at 7%**

The future value at the end of five years of a five-year, $1,000 annuity due that earns 7% annual interest is $6,153.29, which exceeds the $5,750.74 future value of the otherwise identical ordinary annuity (see Figure 3.8). Each deposit in the annuity due earns one more year of interest than the comparable deposit into the ordinary annuity.

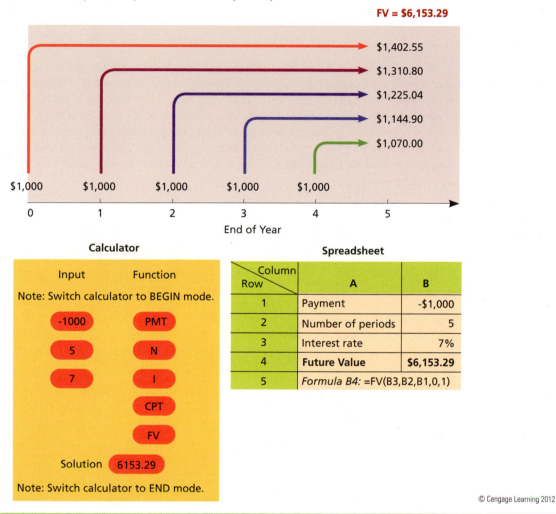

The future value of the annuity due is greater because its cash flow occurs at the beginning of each period, not at the end. In our illustration, by shifting each saving date one year earlier, you earn about $400 more with the annuity due and could enjoy a somewhat more luxurious vacation.

3-5 Concept Review Questions

8. Why is the future value of an ordinary annuity generally less than the future value of an identical annuity due?

9. Once you know the future value of an ordinary annuity, it is easy to calculate the future value of an identical annuity due. Explain.

3-6 Present Value of Cash Flow Streams

Many decisions in corporate finance require financial managers to calculate the present values of cash flow streams that occur over several years. In this section, we show how to calculate the present values of mixed cash flow streams and annuities. We also demonstrate the present-value calculation for a very important cash flow stream, known as a perpetuity.

3-6a Finding the Present Value of a Mixed Stream

The present value of any cash flow stream is merely the sum of the present values of the individual cash flows. To calculate the present values of all kinds of cash-flow streams, we can apply the same techniques we used to calculate present values of lump sums.

EXAMPLE

Shortly after graduation, you receive an inheritance that you use to purchase a small bed-and-breakfast inn. Your plan is to sell the inn after five years. The inn is an old mansion, so you know that appliances, furniture, and other equipment will wear out and need to be replaced or repaired on a regular basis. You estimate that these expenses will total $4,000 during year 1, $8,000 during year 2, $5,000 during year 3, $4,000 during year 4, and $3,000 during year 5, the final year of your ownership. For simplicity, assume that these expenses will be paid at the end of each year.

Because you have some of your inheritance left over after purchasing the inn, you want to set aside a lump sum today from which you can make annual withdrawals to meet these expenses when they come due, as shown on the time line in Figure 3.10. Suppose you invest the lump sum in a bank account that pays 9% interest. To determine the amount of money you need to put into the account, you must calculate the *present value of the stream of future expenses*, using 9% as the discount rate.

Figure 3.10   **Present Value of a Five-Year Mixed Stream Discounted at 9%**

The present value of the mixed stream is the sum of the present values of the individual cash flows discounted at the 9% rate. The present values of the individual cash flows shown at the end of the arrows are summed to find the $19,047.58 present value of the stream of cash flows.

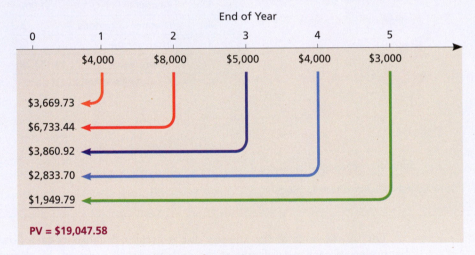

Spreadsheet

Column / Row	A	B
1	Cash flow 1	-$4,000
2	Cash flow 2	-$8,000
3	Cash flow 3	-$5,000
4	Cash flow 4	-$4,000
5	Cash flow 5	-$3,000
6	Interest	9%
7	Number of periods	5
8	**Net Present Value**	**$19,047.58**
9	*Formula B8:* =NPV(B6,B1,B2,B3,B4,B5)	

continued

Figure 3.10 (*continued*)

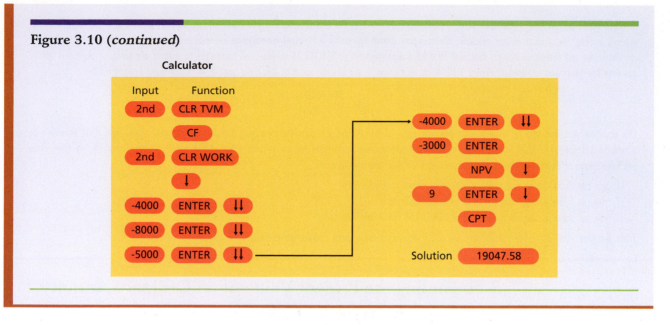

As you no doubt suspect, there is *a general formula for computing the present value of a stream of future cash flows*. Continuing to let CF_t represent the cash flow at the end of year t, the present value of an *n*-year mixed stream of cash flows (*PV*) is expressed as Equation 3.6:

$$(\text{Eq. 3.6}) \quad PV = \left[CF_1 \times \frac{1}{(1+r)^1} \right] + \left[CF_2 \times \frac{1}{(1+r)^2} \right] + \cdots + \left[CF_n \times \frac{1}{(1+r)^n} \right]$$

$$= \sum_{t=1}^{n} CF_t \times \frac{1}{(1+r)^t}$$

Substitute the cash flows shown on the time line in Figure 3.10 and the 9% discount rate into Equation 3.6 to obtain the present value, \$19,047.58.[7]

Let's stop and consider the big picture for a moment. In the previous example, we are given a series of cash flows that are spread out over time, and *we want to place a value on the entire cash-flow stream as of a specific date*. When we calculate the *present value* of the stream, we are determining *the value of the stream as of today*. When we calculate the *future value* of the stream, we are determining the *value of the stream as of a specific date in the future*. In both cases, we are placing a single value on the entire stream. The following example illustrates how the present and future values of cash-flow streams are related.

EXAMPLE

Refer once more to the cash-flow stream illustrated on the time line in Figure 3.10. We've already seen that the stream's present value is \$19,047.58. Now let's review what we covered in section 3-5a and calculate the future value of this stream. Recall that the \$4,000 cash flow could earn 9% interest for four years, the \$8,000 cash flow could earn interest for three years, and so on. Applying Equation 3.3 to this stream, we obtain:

$$FV = \$4{,}000 \times (1 + 0.09)^4 + \$8{,}000 \times (1 + 0.09)^3 + \$5{,}000(1 + 0.09)^2 + \$4{,}000$$
$$\times (1 + 0.09)^1 + \$3{,}000$$

$$FV = \$5{,}646.33 + \$10{,}360.23 + \$5{,}940.50 + \$4{,}360.00 + \$3{,}000.00 = \$29{,}307.06$$

---

[7]A simple way to perform this calculation in Excel is to use the =function. To use that function, you simply enter the interest rate followed by the series of annual cash flows. For example, entering =npv(0.09,-4000,-8000,-5000,-4000, -3000) into Excel will generate the desired result, \$19,047.58.

continued

In other words, $29,307.06 is the amount of money you would have at the end of year 5 if you made annual deposits (shown in Figure 3.10) into an account earning 9% interest. In our example, the cash-flow stream represents a series of maintenance expenditures, not deposits. In that context, the calculation we just completed implies that making a lump sum payment of $29,307.06 in year 5 is equivalent to making the series of payments spread out over five years and depicted in Figure 3.10. Next, let's calculate the present value of this lump sum as of today using Equation 3.2:

$$PV = \frac{FV}{(1 + r)^n} = \frac{\$29,307.06}{(1 + 0.09)^5} = \$19,047.58$$

This equation says that making a lump sum payment today of $19,047.58 is equivalent to paying $29,307.06 five years from now. That shouldn't be a surprise because $19,047.58 is precisely the value that we obtained previously for the present value of the mixed stream. Therefore, we have three equivalent ways of expressing the costs of maintaining the bed and breakfast inn:

(1) you can make the annual series of payments shown in Figure 3.10
(2) you can make a lump sum payment of $19,047.58 today
(3) you can make a lump sum payment of $29,307.06 five years from today

What the time value of money calculations are telling us is that these three options are equivalent as long as the interest rate is 9%.

3-6b Finding the Present Value of an Ordinary Annuity

The present value of an ordinary annuity is found in a manner similar to that used for a mixed stream. Discount each payment and then add up each term to find the annuity's present value.

EXAMPLE

An equipment supplier has approached Braden Company, a producer of plastic toys, with an intriguing offer for a service contract. Extruding Machines Corporation (EMC) offers to take over all of Braden's equipment repair and servicing for five years in exchange for a one-time payment today. Braden's managers know their company spends $7,000 at the end of every year on maintenance, so EMC's service contract would reduce Braden's cash outflows by this $7,000 annually for five years.

Because these are equal annual cash benefits, Braden can determine what it should be willing to pay for the service contract by valuing it as a five-year ordinary annuity with a $7,000 annual cash flow. If Braden requires a minimum return of 8% on all its investments, how much is it willing to pay for EMC's service contract? The time line in Figure 3.11 shows the present value calculation for this annuity.

We find the present value of this ordinary annuity by using the same method used in the preceding section to find the present value of a mixed stream. That is, we discount each end-of-year $7,000 cash flow back to time 0, and then sum the present values of all five cash flows. As Figure 3.11 shows, the present value of this annuity (EMC's service contract) is $27,948.97. If Braden were to initially deposit $27,948.97 into an account paying 8% annual interest, then it could withdraw $7,000 at the ends of years 1 through 5. After the final withdrawal (at the end of year 5), the account balance would exactly equal zero.

Therefore, if EMC offers the service contract to Braden for a lump-sum price of $27,948.97 or less, Braden should accept the offer. Otherwise, Braden should continue to perform its own maintenance.

Figure 3.11   **Present Value of a Five-Year Ordinary Annuity Discounted at 8%**

The present value of the five-year, $7,000 ordinary annuity discounted at 8% is $27,948.97, which is merely the sum of the present values of the individual cash flows shown at the end of the arrows.

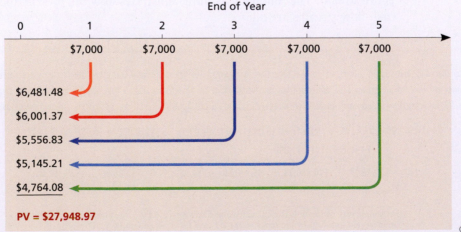

continued

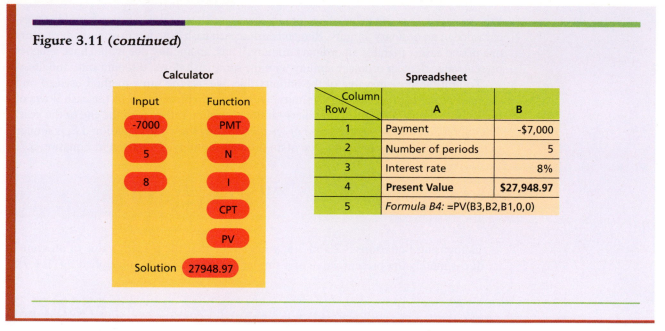

Figure 3.11 (continued)

As was the case with the future value of an annuity, a shortcut formula is available to simplify the present-value calculation for an annuity. Using the symbol *PMT* to denote the annual cash flow, the formula for the *present value of an n-year ordinary annuity (PV)* appears in Equation 3.7:

(Eq. 3.7)
$$PV = \frac{PMT}{r} \times \left[1 - \frac{1}{(1+r)^n}\right]$$

EXAMPLE

We can use Equation 3.7 to calculate the present value of the service contract EMC has offered to the Braden Company. Substituting in $n = 5$ years, $r = 0.08$, and $PMT = \$7,000$, find the present value (*PV*) of this ordinary annuity to be \$27,948.97, as shown below:

$$PV = \frac{\$7,000}{0.08} \times \left[1 - \frac{1}{(0.08)^5}\right] = \frac{\$7,000}{0.08} \times [1 - 0.680583] = \$27,948.97$$

Alternatively, we could use Excel's present value function, entering 8% for the rate, 5 for the number of periods, negative \$7,000 for the payment, and 0 for the future value and type of annuity (=pv(0.08,5,-7000,0,0) yields the answer \$27,948.97).

In some applications, the present value of the annuity is known, along with the number and size of the annual payments. What is missing is the rate of return.

EXAMPLE

You have picked out a new car that costs \$30,000. You need to borrow the full amount, and a bank has offered you a 5-year loan with annual end-of-year payments of \$7,121.89. What is the interest rate that the bank is charging on this loan?

In this case we have a five-year annuity with annual payments of \$7,121.89. Because these payments fully repay the loan, we know that the present value of the annuity is equal to the amount borrowed, \$30,000. In principle, we could try to solve Equation 3.7 for the missing value *r*. Solving that equation algebraically is extremely difficult, so you can use a financial calculator, or you can use the "rate" function in Excel. To use that function, enter, =rate(5,-7121.89,30000,0,0,0), and Excel will reveal that the interest rate on the loan is 6%. In the syntax of the rate function, you enter the payment as a negative number and the present value (the amount that must be repaid) as a positive value.

3-6c Finding the Present Value of an Annuity Due

We can find the present value of an annuity due in much the same way we found the present value of an ordinary annuity. Remember that each cash flow for an annuity due occurs one period earlier than for an ordinary annuity. Thus, an annuity due would have a higher present value than an ordinary annuity with the same cash flows, discount rate, and life.

To find the present value of the annuity due, we use the same method used to find the present value of an ordinary annuity, with one difference: each of the cash flows of the annuity due occurs one year earlier—at the beginning rather than the end of the year. The expression for the *present value of an annuity due*, shown in Equation 3.8, is similar to the equation for the present value of an ordinary annuity (*PV*) given in Equation 3.7.

$$\text{(Eq. 3.8)} \qquad PV(\text{annuity due}) = \frac{PMT}{r} \times \left[1 - \frac{1}{(1+r)^n} \right] \times (1+r)$$

Comparing Equations 3.7 and 3.8, you can see that the present value of an annuity due is merely the present value of a similar ordinary annuity multiplied by $(1+r)$.

EXAMPLE

To demonstrate, assume that the Braden Company wishes to determine the present value of the five-year, $7,000 service contract at an 8% discount rate, and assume also that each of the maintenance expenditures occurs *at the beginning of the year*. This means that the first payment for maintenance expenses would occur today.

The present value of this annuity due is simply $(1 + r)$ times the value of the ordinary annuity: $PV(\text{annuity due}) = \$27{,}948.97 \times (1.08) = \$30{,}184.89$. If Braden pays its maintenance costs at the start of each year, the most it is willing to pay EMC for the service contract increases by more than $2,000 to $30,184.89.

3-6d Finding the Present Value of a Perpetuity

perpetuity
A level cash flow stream that continues forever.

A **perpetuity** is an annuity with an infinite life; it promises to pay the same amount at the end of every year *forever*. One of the first, and certainly the most famous, perpetuities in modern history was the massive "consol" bond issue sold by the British government after the Napoleonic Wars ended in 1815. This bond issue got its name because it consolidated all the existing British war debts into a single issue that paid a constant annual amount of interest into perpetuity. The issue itself never matured, meaning that the principal was never to be repaid.

Currently, not many corporations or governments issue perpetual bonds.[8] Perhaps the simplest modern example of a perpetuity is preferred stock issued by corporations. Preferred shares promise investors a constant annual (or quarterly) dividend payment forever. Therefore, we simply express the lifetime (*n*) of this security as infinity (∞), and modify our basic valuation formulation for an annuity accordingly. For example, we wish to determine the present value of an annuity (*PV*) that pays a constant annual dividend amount (*PMT*) for a perpetual number of years ($n = \infty$) discounted at a rate *r*. Here, the Greek summation notation is helpful in expressing the formula in Equation 3.9:

$$\text{(Eq. 3.9)} \qquad PV = PMT \times \sum_{t=1}^{\infty} \frac{1}{(1+r)^t}$$

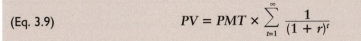

[8]Some long-term bonds are nearly perpetuities. In July 1993, the Walt Disney Company sold $300 million of bonds that matured in the year 2093, 100 years after they were issued. The market dubbed these "Sleeping Beauty bonds" because their maturity matched the amount of time that Sleeping Beauty slept before being kissed by Prince Charming in the classic story.

Fortunately, Equation 3.9 also comes in a simplified version, which says that the present value of a perpetuity equals the annual, end-of-year payment divided by the discount rate. Equation 3.10 gives this straightforward expression for the *present value of a perpetuity* (PV):

(Eq. 3.10)

$$PV = PMT \times \frac{1}{r} = \frac{PMT}{r}$$

It is important to make a subtle point here. Equations 3.9 and 3.10 calculate the present value of a perpetuity that makes its first payment one year from today. We may need to make an adjustment to these equations if we want to know the present value of a perpetuity that begins sooner or later than one year from now.

EXAMPLE

In September 2008, following a series of tumultuous events that included the bankruptcy of Lehman Brothers and the bailout of insurance giant AIG, Warren Buffett expressed his faith in the U.S. markets by purchasing perpetual preferred stocks from Goldman Sachs. These shares had no maturity and promised to pay $500 million annually in dividends. Assuming that Buffett wanted a 10% annual return on his investment, the purchase price would be:

$$PV = \$500{,}000{,}000 \div 0.10 = \$5 \text{ billion}$$

A $5 billion purchase price makes sense because each year Buffett would receive $500 million in dividends, exactly the 10% return that he sought.

Even though preferred stock usually offers the promise of paying dividends every year forever, sometimes companies are unable to make those dividend payments. When a firm has to suspend preferred dividends, it usually must make up lost dividends before it can pay dividends on common shares. The following example illustrates that even when firms pay extra preferred dividends to make up for dividends that they previously skipped, preferred shareholders must endure some loss in value of their shares.

EXAMPLE

Big Oil Corp. (BO) is a public utility that has had preferred stock outstanding for many years. BO's preferred stock promises an annual dividend payment of $4. Assuming that investors require an 8% return on those shares, the market price of the stock should be $50:

$$PV = \$4 \div 0.08 = \$50$$

Unfortunately, BO recently suffered large losses and has had to suspend its preferred dividends for the next two years. The company says that it expects to begin paying preferred dividends again three years from now. To make up for the dividends that it skipped, BO will pay a one-time dividend of $12 in three years ($8 for the dividends it skipped plus $4 for the normal dividend in year 3), and after that preferred shareholders will continue to receive the annual $4 dividend that they had come to expect. What is the present value of the dividend stream that BO is now promising? Stated differently, what price would investors be willing to pay today for BO preferred shares (assume that their required return is still 8%).

The best way to approach this problem is to break it into two parts. First, there is the $12 dividend payment expected in three years. Second, there is a perpetuity paying $4 per year starting four years from now. We need to take the present value of each part and then add them together. The market value of the preferred stock should equal the present value of the entire dividend stream.

We can find the present value of the $12 dividend by using Equation 3.1:

$$PV = \$12 \div (1 + 0.08)^3 = \$9.53$$

Next, we will use Equation 3.10 to find the present value of the perpetuity. However, remember that Equation 3.10 calculates the present value of a perpetuity that *makes its first payment one year in the future.* If we apply this equation to the perpetuity that begins in year 4, we will actually be calculating the value of the perpetuity *as of year 3.* Once we have that value, we must discount it 3 more periods to find the *present value* of the perpetuity.

$$PV(\text{year 3}) = \$4 \div 0.08 = \$50$$

$$PV = \$50 \div (1 + 0.08)^3 = \$39.69$$

continued

At last we are ready to calculate the present value of the entire BO preferred dividend stream, or equivalently, the market value of BO's preferred shares.

Value of preferred shares = value of $12 dividend + value of $4 perpetuity

Value of preferred shares = $9.53 + $39.69 = $49.22

Under normal circumstances, when BO's preferred shareholders expect to receive their $4 dividend annually, the preferred shares sell for $50. In this case, even though BO promises to eventually make up for the dividend payments that it must skip in the next two years, the value of the preferred stock dips slightly.

You might wonder why anyone would continue to hold BO preferred stock if it pays no dividends for three years. It turns out that as time goes by, and the date on which BO's dividend stream will begin again draws near, the market value of the preferred shares will rise. In other words, a preferred shareholder can expect the shares to increase in value even if they are not paying dividends.

EXAMPLE

Imagine that two years and 364 days have gone by and Big Oil Corp. has announced that it will pay the one-time $12 dividend tomorrow. After that, the company expects the annual $4 preferred dividends to resume. What is the present value now of the expected dividend stream?

As before, we can break the dividend stream into two parts. First, there is the $12 dividend *which will be paid immediately*. Clearly, its present value is $12. Second, there is the perpetual $4 dividend stream that starts in one year. From Equation 3.10 we know that the value of this perpetuity is $50 ($4 ÷ 0.08). Just add these two components together to find the value of BO's stock today:

Value of preferred shares = $12 + $50 = $62

Now consider the position of a BO preferred shareholder who purchased the stock three years ago when the firm suspended its dividends. In the previous example we determined that the value of BO preferred stock at that time was $49.22, and we have just discovered that its value today is $62. What rate of return did the investor earn over this period? Again we can apply Equation 3.1:

$$FV = PV(1+r)^n$$

$$\$62 = \$49.22(1+r)^3$$

We solved a problem like this in section 3-4. To find the answer you can use Excel's "rate" function, you can use a financial calculator, or you solve algebraically as follows:

$$r = \left(\frac{\$62}{\$49.22}\right)^{\frac{1}{3}} - 1 = 0.08 = 8\%$$

An investor who purchased BO shares for $49.22 three years ago and held it until it recently reached $62 would have earned 8% per year, exactly the required return. The return comes entirely from price appreciation in the shares because no dividends were paid during this period.

3-6e Finding the Present Value of a Growing Perpetuity

By definition, perpetuities pay a constant periodic amount forever. However, few aspects of modern life are constant, and most of the cash flows we care about have a tendency to grow over time. This is true for items of income such as wages and salaries, dividend payments from corporations, and Social Security payments from governments.[9] Inflation is only one factor that drives increasing cash flows. Because of this tendency for cash flows to grow over time, we must determine how to adjust the present value of a perpetuity formula to account for expected growth in future cash flows.

Suppose we want to calculate the present value (PV) of a stream of cash flows growing forever ($n = \infty$) at rate g. Given a discount rate of r, the *present value of the*

---

[9]Unfortunately, this is also true for expense items such as rent and utility expenses, car prices, and tuition payments.

growing perpetuity
A cash flow stream that grows each period at a constant rate and continues forever.

Gordon growth model
The valuation model that views cash flows as a *growing perpetuity*.

SMART
concepts

See the concept explained step-by-step at **SMART**|finance

growing perpetuity is given by the following equation, which is sometimes called the Gordon growth model:[10]

(Eq. 3.11)
$$PV = \frac{CF_1}{r - g} \qquad r > g$$

Note that the numerator in Equation 3.11 is CF_1, the first year's cash flow that occurs exactly one year from today. This cash flow is expected to grow at a constant annual rate (g) from now to the end of time. We can determine the cash flow for any specific future year (t) by applying the growth rate (g) as follows:

$$CF_t = CF_1 \times (1 + g)^{t - 1}$$

EXAMPLE

Assume that Gil Bates is a philanthropist wishing to endow a medical foundation with sufficient money to fund ongoing research. Gil is particularly impressed with the research proposal submitted by the Smith Cancer Institute (SCI). The institute requests an endowment sufficient to cover its expenses for medical equipment, which will total $10 million next year, and then grow by 3% in perpetuity afterwards.

Assume the institute can earn an 11% return on Gil's contribution. How much must Gil contribute to finance the institute's medical equipment expenditures in perpetuity? Equation 3.11 tells us that the present value of these expenses equals $125 million, computed as follows:

$$PV = \frac{\$10,000,000}{0.11 - 0.03} = \frac{\$10,000,000}{0.08} = \$125,000,000$$

Gil would have to make an investment of only $90,909,091 ($10,000,000 ÷ 0.11, using Equation 3.10) to fund a non-growing perpetuity of $10 million per year. The remaining $34.1 million supports the 3% annual growth in the payout to SCI.

3-6 Concept Review Questions

10. You are given a mixed cash-flow stream and an interest rate, and you are asked to calculate both the present and future value of the stream. Explain how the two numbers you calculate are related.

11. How is the present value of an annuity due related to the present value of an identical ordinary annuity?

12. Does a perpetuity pay an infinite amount of cash? Why is the present value of a perpetuity not infinite?

13. How would you calculate the present value of a perpetuity that had payments that were declining by a fixed percentage each year?

3-7   Advanced Applications of Time Value

The techniques we've studied thus far have many different applications in business as well as personal finance. Some of those applications involve compounding interest more frequently than once per year. When interest compounds more often, the stated interest rate on a loan or an investment doesn't always accurately measure the *true rate of return*, or the *effective rate* of interest. In this section, we relax the assumption maintained so far that interest compounds once per year, and we examine several additional applications of the time value of money.

3-7a Compounding More Frequently Than Annually

In many applications, interest compounds more frequently than once a year. Financial institutions compound interest semiannually, quarterly, monthly, weekly, daily,

---

[10]For this formula to work, the discount rate must be greater than the growth rate. When cash flows grow at a rate equal to or greater than the discount rate, the present value of the stream is infinite.

or even continuously. This section explores how the present-value and future-value techniques change if interest compounds more than once a year.

semiannual compounding
Interest compounds twice a year.

Semiannual Compounding The semiannual compounding of interest involves two compounding periods within the year. Instead of the stated interest rate being paid once per year, one-half of the rate is paid twice a year.

To demonstrate, consider an opportunity to deposit $100 in a savings account paying 8% interest with semiannual compounding. After the first six months, your account grows by 4% to $104. Six months later, the account again grows by 4% to $108.16. Notice that after one year, the total increase in the account value is $8.16, or 8.16% ($8.16 ÷ $100.00). This return slightly exceeds the stated rate of 8% because semiannual compounding allows you to earn *interest on interest* during the year, increasing the overall rate of return. Table 3.1 shows how the account value grows every six months for the first two years. At the end of two years, the account value reaches $116.99.

Table 3.1

The Future Value from Investing $100 at 8% Interest Compounded Semiannually Over Two Years

Period	Beginning Principal (1)	Future Value Factor (2)	Future Value at End of Period [(1) × (2)] (3)
6 months	$100.00	1.04	$104.00
12 months	104.00	1.04	108.16
18 months	108.16	1.04	112.49
24 months	112.49	1.04	116.99

quarterly compounding
Interest compounds four times per year.

Quarterly Compounding As the name implies, quarterly compounding describes a situation in which interest compounds four times per year. An investment with quarterly compounding pays one-fourth of the stated interest rate every three months.

For example, assume that after further investigation, you find an institution that pays 8% interest compounded quarterly. After three months, your $100 deposit grows by 2% to $102. Three months later, the balance again increases 2% to $104.04. By the end of the year, the balance reaches $108.24. Table 3.2 tracks the growth in the account every three months for two years. At the end of two years, the

Table 3.2

The Future Value from Investing $100 at 8% Interest Compounded Quarterly Over Two Years

Period	Beginning Principal (1)	Future Value Factor (2)	Future Value at End of Period [(1) × (2)] (3)
3 months	$100.00	1.02	$102.00
6 months	102.00	1.02	104.04
9 months	104.04	1.02	106.12
12 months	106.12	1.02	108.24
15 months	108.24	1.02	110.41
18 months	110.41	1.02	112.62
21 months	112.62	1.02	114.87
24 months	114.87	1.02	117.17

account is worth $117.17, which is greater than the sum attained after two years with semiannual compounding.

As you should expect by now, *the more frequently that interest compounds, the greater the amount of money that accumulates.*

A General Equation We can generalize the preceding examples in a simple equation. Suppose that a lump sum, denoted by *PV*, is invested at *r*% for *n* years. If *m* equals the number of times per year that interest compounds, the future value grows as shown in the following equation:

$$\text{(Eq. 3.12)} \qquad FV = PV \times \left(1 + \frac{r}{m}\right)^{m \times n}$$

Notice that if $m = 1$, this reduces to Equation 3.1. The next several examples verify that this equation yields the same ending account values after two years, as shown in Tables 3.1 and 3.2.

EXAMPLE

We have calculated the amount that you would have at the end of two years if you deposited $100 at 8% interest compounded semiannually and quarterly. For semiannual compounding, $m = 2$ in Equation 3.12; for quarterly compounding, $m = 4$. Substituting the appropriate values for semiannual and quarterly compounding into Equation 3.12 yields the following results.

For semiannual compounding:

$$FV = \$100 \times \left(1 + \frac{0.08}{2}\right)^{2 \times 2} = \$100 \times (1 + 0.04)^4 = \$116.99$$

For quarterly compounding:

$$FV = \$100 \times \left(1 + \frac{0.08}{4}\right)^{4 \times 2} = \$100 \times (1 + 0.02)^8 = \$117.17$$

Continuous Compounding As we switch from annual, to semiannual, to quarterly compounding, the interval during which interest compounds gets shorter, while the number of compounding periods per year gets larger. Theoretically, there is almost no limit to this process—interest could be compounded daily, hourly, or second by second. Continuous compounding, the most extreme case, occurs when interest compounds literally at every moment as time passes. In this case, *m* in Equation 3.12 would approach infinity, and Equation 3.12 converges to this expression:

continuous compounding
Interest compounds literally at every moment as time passes.

$$\text{(Eq. 3.13)} \qquad FV(\text{continuous compounding}) = PV \times (e^{r \times n})$$

The number *e* is an irrational number, like the number π from geometry, which is useful in mathematical applications involving quantities that grow continuously over time. The value of *e* is approximately 2.7183.[11] As before, increasing the frequency of compounding, in this case by compounding as frequently as possible, increases the future value of an investment.

---

[11]In one of the more esoteric uses of the Internet, the first 2 million digits of the number *e* appear at the URL www.antwrp.gsfc.nasa.gov/htmltest/rjn_dig.html. Only the first million will be covered on the exam.

To find the value at the end of two years of your $100 deposit in an account paying 8% annual interest compounded continuously, substitute $PV = \$100$, $r = 0.08$, and $n = 2$ into Equation 3.13:

$$FV\text{(continuous compounding)} = \$100 \times (e^{0.08 \times 2}) = \$100 \times 2.7183^{0.16}$$

$$= \$100 \times 1.1735 = \$117.35$$

The future value with continuous compounding therefore equals $117.35, which, as expected, is larger than the future value of interest compounded semiannually ($116.99) or quarterly ($117.17).[12]

3-7b Stated versus Effective Annual Interest Rates

stated annual rate
The contractual annual rate of interest charged by a lender or promised by a borrower.

effective annual rate (EAR)
The annual rate of interest *actually* paid or earned, reflecting the impact of compounding frequency. Also called the *true annual return*.

Both consumers and businesses need to make objective comparisons of loan costs or investment returns over different compounding periods. To put interest rates on a common basis for comparison, we must distinguish between *stated* and *effective annual interest rates*. The stated annual rate is the contractual annual rate of interest charged by a lender or promised by a borrower. The effective annual rate (*EAR*), or the *true annual return*, is the annual rate of interest *actually* paid or earned. Why the difference? The effective annual rate reflects the effect of compounding frequency; the stated annual rate does not.

Using the notation introduced earlier, we can calculate the *effective annual rate* by substituting values for the stated annual rate (r) and the compounding frequency (m) into Equation 3.14:

(Eq. 3.14)
$$EAR = \left(1 + \frac{r}{m}\right)^m - 1$$

We can apply this equation using data from preceding examples.

Find the effective annual rate associated with an 8% stated annual rate ($r = 0.08$) when interest is compounded annually ($m = 1$), semiannually ($m = 2$), and quarterly ($m = 4$). Substituting these values into Equation 3.14 obtains the following results:

For annual compounding:

$$EAR = \left(1 + \frac{0.08}{1}\right)^1 - 1 = (1 + 0.08)^1 - 1 = 1.08 - 1 = 0.08 = 8.0\%$$

For semiannual compounding:

$$EAR = \left(1 + \frac{0.08}{2}\right)^2 - 1 = (1 + 0.04)^2 - 1 = 1.0816 - 1 = 0.0816 = 8.16\%$$

For quarterly compounding:

$$EAR = \left(1 + \frac{0.08}{4}\right)^4 - 1 = (1 + 0.02)^4 - 1 = 1.0824 - 1 = 0.0824 = 8.24\%$$

The results mean that 8% compounded semiannually is equivalent to 8.16% compounded annually, and 8% compounded quarterly is equivalent to 8.24% compounded annually. These values demonstrate two important points: (1) the stated and effective rates are equivalent for annual compounding, and (2) the effective annual rate increases with increasing compounding frequency.

---

[12]The Excel function for continuous compounding is "=exp(argument)". For example, suppose you want to calculate the future value of $100 compounded continuously for five years at 8%. To find this value in Excel, first calculate the value of $e^{0.08 \times 5}$, by entering "=EXP(0.08*5)", and then multiply the result, 1.492, by $100 to obtain a future value of $149.20.

Not surprisingly, the maximum effective annual rate for a given stated annual rate occurs when interest compounds continuously. The effective annual rate for this extreme case can be found by using the following equation:

(Eq. 3.14a)	$EAR(\text{continuous compounding}) = e^r - 1$

For the 8% stated annual rate ($r = 0.08$), substitution into Equation 3.14a results in an effective annual rate of 8.33%, as follows:

$$e^{0.08} - 1 = 1.0833 - 1 = 0.0833 = 8.33\%$$

annual percentage rate (APR)

The stated annual rate calculated by multiplying the periodic rate by the number of periods in one year.

annual percentage yield (APY)

The annual rate of interest actually paid or earned, reflecting the impact of compounding frequency. The same as the *effective annual rate* (sometimes called the *effective APR*).

In the United States, truth-in-lending laws require disclosure on credit cards and loans of the **annual percentage rate (APR)**. The APR is the *stated annual rate* charged on the credit account or loan. It is calculated as the periodic rate (the interest rate per period) multiplied by the number of periods in one year. For example, a bank credit card that charges 1.5% per month has an APR of 18% (1.5% per month × 12 months per year). However, the actual cost of this credit card account is determined by calculating the **annual percentage yield (APY)**. The APY is the same as the *effective annual rate* (sometimes called the *effective APR*), which (as discussed earlier) reflects the impact of compounding frequency. For the credit card example, 1.5% per month interest has an effective annual rate of $[(1.015)^{12} - 1] = 0.1956$, or 19.56%. This means that paying interest at 1.5% per month is the same as paying 19.56% if interest were charged annually. If the stated rate is 1.75% per month, as is the case with many U.S. credit card accounts, the APY is a whopping 23.14%. If you are carrying a positive credit card balance at this interest rate, you will want to pay it off as soon as possible!

3-7c Calculating Deposits Needed to Accumulate a Future Sum

Suppose that someone wishes to determine the *annual deposit necessary to accumulate a certain amount of money at some point in the future.* Assume that you want to buy a house five years from now and estimate that an initial down payment of $20,000 will be required. You want to make equal end-of-year deposits into an account paying annual interest of 6%, so you must determine what size annuity results in a lump sum equal to $20,000 at the end of year 5. The solution can be derived from the equation for finding the future value of an ordinary annuity.

Earlier in this chapter, we found the future value of an *n*-year ordinary annuity (*FV*) by applying Equation 3.4. Solving that equation for *PMT*, in this case the annual deposit, we get Equation 3.15:

(Eq. 3.15)	$PMT = \dfrac{FV}{\left\{ \dfrac{[(1 + r)^n - 1]}{r} \right\}}$

Once this is done, we substitute the known values of *FV*, *r*, and *n* into the right-hand side of the equation to find the annual deposit required.

EXAMPLE

As a demonstration of this formula, you would need to make equal annual end-of-year deposits of $3,547.93 each year to accumulate $20,000 (the *FV*) at the end of five years ($n = 5$), given an interest rate of 6% ($r = 6\%$):

$$PMT = \frac{\$20,000}{\left\{ \dfrac{[(1.06)^5 - 1]}{0.06} \right\}} = \$3,547.93$$

As usual, Excel provides a shortcut for this calculation in the form of the payment (PMT) function. The syntax of this function is =pmt(rate,nper,pv,fv,type). To solve this particular problem using the payment function, you would enter, =pmt(0.06,5,0,20000,0), and Excel generates the result, $3,547.93. Notice that in this function you enter 0 for the present value because you start with nothing saved toward the down payment. Also, the value entered for "type" is 0 because this is an ordinary annuity—you are making equal end-of-year deposits to achieve your goal. Alternatively, you can use a financial calculator to find the answer as shown below.

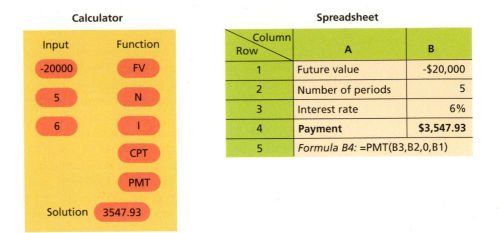

3-7d Loan Amortization

loan amortization
Occurs when a borrower pays back the principal over the life of the loan, often in equal periodic payments.

Loan amortization refers to a situation in which a borrower pays down the principal (i.e., the amount borrowed) on a loan over the life of the loan. Often, the borrower makes equal periodic payments. For instance, with a conventional, 30-year home mortgage, the borrower makes the same payment each month for 30 years until the mortgage is completely repaid. To *amortize* a loan (i.e., to calculate the periodic payment that pays off the loan), you must know the total amount of the loan (the amount borrowed), the term of the loan, the frequency of periodic payments, and the interest rate.

In terms of the time value of money, the loan amortization process involves finding a level stream of payments (over the term of the loan) with a present value (calculated at the loan interest rate) equal to the amount borrowed. Lenders use a **loan amortization schedule** to determine these payments and the allocation of each payment to interest and principal.

loan amortization schedule
Used to determine loan amortization payments and the allocation of each payment to interest and principal.

For example, suppose that you borrow $25,000 at 8% annual interest for five years to purchase a new car. To demonstrate the basic approach, we first amortize this loan assuming that you make payments at the end of years 1 through 5. We then modify the annual formula to compute the more typical monthly auto loan payments. To find the size of the annual payments, the lender determines the amount of a five-year annuity discounted at 8% that has a present value of $25,000. This process is actually the inverse of finding the present value of an annuity.

Earlier, we found the present value (*PV*) of an *n*-year ordinary annuity, using Equation 3.7. Solving that equation for *PMT*, the annual loan payment, we get Equation 3.16:

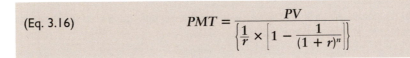

$$\text{(Eq. 3.16)} \qquad PMT = \frac{PV}{\left\{\frac{1}{r} \times \left[1 - \frac{1}{(1+r)^n}\right]\right\}}$$

Finance in Your Life

Saving for Your Retirement

It is important to begin saving for retirement when you start your first real job. Most people begin later. Let's assume that you are in your mid-thirties, have two children, and an annual income of $120,000 before taxes. You now want to get serious about retirement and have made the following estimates.

Years till retirement	30 years
Estimated years in retirement (based on actuarial tables)	27 years
Current level of household expenditures	$84,000
% of current household expenses needed in retirement	80%
Estimated annual end-of-year income in retirement from:	
Social Security	$24,000
Employer pension plan	9,000
401(k)	20,000
Total	$53,000
Expected annual inflation rate during retirement	5%
Expected annual rate of return on investments *before* retirement	8%
Expected annual rate of return on investments *during* retirement	10%

Using your estimates you wish to determine the *annual end-of-year savings needed to fund your retirement*. This value can be calculated as follows:

Estimated annual household expenditures in retirement = 0.80 × $84,000 = $67,200

Additional annual retirement income needed = $67,200 − $53,000 = $14,200

(Eq. 3.1)   Inflation-adjusted annual retirement income need = $14,200 × $(1 + 0.05)^{30}$ = $61,372

(Eq. 3.7)   Lump sum needed in 30 years to fund additional annual retirement income
        = $61,372/0.10 × {1 − $[1/(1 + 0.10)^{27}]$} = $613,720 × 0.92372 = $566,905

(Eq. 3.15)   Annual end-of-year savings required to fund lump sum
        = $566,905/{[$(1 + 0.08)^{30}$ − 1]/0.08} = $566,905/113.28321 = **$5,004**

So, in order to fund your retirement goal over your 27 years of retirement, you need to save just over $5,000 at the end of each of the next 30 years. Note that your assumed rate of return during the 30 years you are accumulating funds is 8%, and during retirement, when funds are being distributed, you are assumed to earn a 10% rate of return. If you earn lower returns, you would need to save more each year.

EXAMPLE

To find the annual payment required on the five-year, $25,000 loan with an 8% annual interest rate, we substitute the known values of $PV =$ $25,000, $r = 0.08$, and $n = 5$ into the right-hand side of the equation:

$$PMT = \frac{\$25,000}{\left\{ \frac{1}{0.08} \times \left[1 - \frac{1}{(1.08)^5} \right] \right\}} = \$6,261.41$$

Five annual payments of $6,261.41 are needed to fully amortize this $25,000 loan. We could also solve this problem using Excel's payment function. This time, the present value is $25,000, and we want the future value to be $0 (i.e., the loan balance in five years should be $0). In Excel you could enter, =pmt(0.08,5,25000,0,0), and you would obtain the same answer, $6,261.41. Finally, this problem could be solved using a financial calculator as shown on the following page.

continued

	Calculator			Spreadsheet	

Calculator

Input	Function
-25000	PV
5	N
8	I
	CPT
	PMT
Solution	6261.41

Spreadsheet

Row \ Column	A	B
1	Present value	-$25,000
2	Number of periods	5
3	Interest rate	8%
4	**Payment**	**$6,261.41**
5	*Formula B4:* =PMT(B3,B2,B1)	

Each loan payment consists partly of interest and partly of the loan principal. Columns 3 and 4 of the loan amortization schedule in Table 3.3 show the allocation of each loan payment of $6,261.41 to interest and principal. Observe that the portion of each payment representing interest (column 3) declines over the repayment period, and the portion going to principal (column 4) increases. This pattern is typical of amortized loans. With level payments, the interest component declines and a larger portion of each subsequent payment is left to repay principal.

Computing amortized loan payments is the present value formulation that people use most frequently in their personal lives to calculate auto loan and home mortgage payments. Because lenders typically require monthly payments (rather than annual) on consumer loans, we now demonstrate amortization calculations using monthly rather than annual payments. First, Equation 3.16a is simply a modified version of Equation 3.16:

$$\text{(Eq. 3.16a)} \qquad PMT = \frac{r}{[(1 + r)^n - 1]} \times (1 + r)^n \times PV$$

Table 3.3 **Loan Amortization Schedule $25,000 Principal, for 8% Interest, Five-Year Repayment Period**

End of Year	Loan Payment (1)	Beginning of Year Principal (2)	Payments		End-of-Year Principal [(2) – (4)] (5)
			Interest [0.08 × (2)] (3)	Principal [(1) – (3)] (4)	
1	$6,261.41	$25,000.00	$2,000.00	$4,261.41	$20,738.59
2	6,261.41	20,738.59	1,659.09	4,602.32	16,136.27
3	6,261.41	16,136.27	1,290.90	4,970.51	11,165.76
4	6,261.41	11,165.76	893.26	5,368.15	5,797.61
5	6,261.41	5,797.61	463.80	5,797.61	0

Second, we can generalize this formula to more frequent compounding periods by dividing the interest rate by m and multiplying the number of compounding periods by m. This changes the equation as follows:

(Eq. 3.16b)
$$PMT = \frac{\frac{r}{m}}{\left[\left(1 + \frac{r}{m}\right)^{m \times n} - 1\right]} \times \left(1 + \frac{r}{m}\right)^{m \times n} \times PV$$

EXAMPLE

Use Equation 3.16b to calculate what a *monthly* car payment will be if you borrow $25,000 for five years at 8% annual interest. Once again, PV will be the $25,000 amount borrowed, but the periodic interest rate ($r \div m$) will be 0.00667, or 0.667% per month (0.08 per year $\div$ 12 months per year). There will be $m \times n = 60$ compounding periods (12 months per year $\times$ 5 years = 60 months). Substituting these values into Equation 3.16b yields a auto loan payment of just under $507 per month:

$$PMT = \frac{\frac{0.08}{12}}{\left[\left(1 + \frac{0.08}{12}\right)^{12 \times 5} - 1\right]} \times \left(1 + \frac{0.08}{12}\right)^{12 \times 5} \times \$25,000$$

$$= \frac{0.00667}{[(1.00667)^{60} - 1]} \times (1.00667)^{60} \times \$25,000$$

$$= \$506.91$$

The monthly payment is less than one-twelfth the annual payment that we calculated in the previous example ($506.91 $\times$ 12 < $6,261.41). The reason for this is that when payments are made more frequently, less interest accrues between payments, and therefore a lower payment is required to repay the entire loan. (Note that to obtain the precise figure of $506.91, it is necessary to carry the monthly interest rate out several digits beyond where we have rounded here).

As a test of your command of the monthly payment formula, see if you can compute the monthly mortgage payment for a home purchased using a 30-year, $100,000 loan with a fixed 7.5% annual interest rate. Note that there are 360 compounding periods (12 months per year $\times$ 30 years).[13]

3-7 Concept Review Questions

14. Why is the effective annual rate often greater than the stated annual rate?

15. On a 30-year mortgage, would the total amount of money paid by the borrower over the life of the loan be greater if there were weekly payments or monthly payments?

Summary

- Financial managers can use future-value and present-value techniques to equate cash flows occurring at different times to compare decision alternatives. Managers rely primarily on present-value techniques and commonly use financial calculators or spreadsheet programs to streamline their computations.

Table of Important Equations

1. $FV = PV \times (1 + r)^n$

2. $PV = \dfrac{FV}{(1 + r)^n} = FV \times \left[\dfrac{1}{(1 + r)^n}\right]$

3. $FV = \displaystyle\sum_{t=1}^{n} CF_t \times (1 + r)^{n-t}$

---

[13]The amount of the mortgage payment is $699.21. To find this solution, just enter the formula "=pmt(0.00625,360,100000)" in Excel. The first argument in this function is the monthly interest rate, 7.5% divided by 12.

- The future value of a lump sum is found by adding the accumulated interest earned to the present value (the initial investment) over the period of concern. The higher the interest rate and the further in the future the cash flow's value is measured, the higher its future value.

- The present value of a lump sum is found by discounting the future value at the given interest rate. It is the amount of money today that is equivalent to the given future amount, considering the rate of return that can be earned on the present value. The higher the interest rate and the further in the future the cash flow occurs, the lower its present value.

- The future value of any cash-flow stream—mixed stream, ordinary annuity, or annuity due—is the sum of the future values of the individual cash flows. Future values of mixed streams are determined by valuing each cash flow separately and summing them, whereas future values of annuities are easier to calculate because they have the same cash flow each period. The future value of an ordinary annuity (end-of-period cash flows) can be converted into the future value of an annuity due (beginning-of-period cash flows) merely by multiplying it by one plus the interest rate.

$$4. \quad FV = PMT \times \left\{ \frac{[(1 + r)^n - 1]}{r} \right\}$$

$$5. \quad FV \text{ (annuity due)}$$
$$= PMT \times \left\{ \frac{[(1 + r)^n - 1]}{r} \right\} \times (1 + r)$$

$$6. \quad PV = \sum_{t=1}^{n} CF_t \times \frac{1}{(1 + r)^t}$$

$$7. \quad PV = \frac{PMT}{r} \times \left[1 - \frac{1}{(1 + r)^n} \right]$$

$$8. \quad PV \text{ (annuity due)}$$
$$= \frac{PMT}{r} \times \left[1 - \frac{1}{(1 + r)^n} \right] \times (1 + r)$$

$$9. \quad PV = PMT \times \frac{1}{r} = \frac{PMT}{r}$$

$$10. \quad PV = \frac{CF_1}{r - g} \quad r > g$$

$$11. \quad FV = PV \times \left(1 + \frac{r}{m} \right)^{m \times n}$$

$$12. \quad FV \text{ (continuous compounding)}$$
$$= PV \times (e^{r \times n})$$

$$13. \quad EAR = \left(1 + \frac{r}{m} \right)^m - 1$$

$$14. \quad EAR \text{(continuous compounding)} = e^r - 1$$

- The present value of a cash-flow stream is the sum of the present values of the individual cash flows. The present value of a mixed stream requires discounting each cash flow separately and summing them, whereas present values of annuities are easier to calculate because they have the same cash flow each period. The present value of an ordinary annuity can be converted to the present value of an annuity due merely by multiplying it by one plus the interest rate. The present value of an ordinary perpetuity—a level stream that continues forever—is found by dividing the amount of the annuity by the interest rate.

- Implied interest or growth rates can be found using the basic future-value equations for lump sums and annuities.

- Given present and future cash flows and the applicable interest rate, the unknown number of periods can be found using the basic equations for future values of lump sums and annuities.

- Some special applications of time value include compounding interest more frequently than annually, stated and effective annual rates of interest, deposits needed to accumulate a future sum, and loan amortization. The more frequently interest is compounded at a stated annual rate, the larger the future amount that will be accumulated and the higher the effective annual rate.

- The annual deposit needed to accumulate a given future sum is found by manipulating the future value of an annuity equation. Loan amortization—determination of the equal periodic payments necessary to fully repay loan principal and interest over a given time at a given interest rate—is performed by manipulating the present value of an annuity equation. An amortization schedule can be prepared to allocate each loan payment to principal and interest.

Key Terms

annual percentage rate (*APR*), 95
annual percentage yield (*APY*), 95
annuity, 77
annuity due, 79
compound interest, 68
continuous compounding, 93
discounting, 71
effective annual rate (*EAR*), 94

future value, 67
Gordon growth model, 91
growing perpetuity, 91
loan amortization, 96
loan amortization schedule, 96
mixed stream, 77
ordinary annuity, 79
perpetuity, 88

present value, 67
principal, 68
quarterly compounding, 92
semiannual compounding, 92
simple interest, 68
stated annual rate, 94
time line, 69
time value of money, 67

Self-Test Problems

ST3-1. Starratt Alexander is considering investing specified amounts in each of four investment opportunities described below. For each opportunity, determine the amount of money Starratt will have at the end of the given investment horizon.

Investment A: Invest a lump sum of $2,750 today in an account that pays 6% annual interest and leave the funds on deposit for exactly fifteen years.

Investment B: Invest the following amounts at the beginning of each of the next five years in a venture that will earn 9% annually and measure the accumulated value at the end of exactly five years:

Beginning of Year	Amount
1	$ 900
2	1,000
3	1,200
4	1,500
5	1,800

Investment C: Invest $1,200 at the *end of each year* for the next ten years in an account that pays 10% annual interest and determine the account balance at the end of year 10.

Investment D: Make the same investment as in investment C but place the $1,200 in the account at the *beginning of each year*.

ST3-2. Gregg Snead has been offered four investment opportunities, all equally priced at $45,000. Because the opportunities differ in risk, Gregg's required returns (i.e., applicable discount rates) are not the same for each opportunity. The cash flows and required returns for each opportunity are summarized below.

Opportunity	Cash Flows		Required Return
A	$7,500 at the end of 5 years		12%
B	Year	Amount	15%
	1	$10,000	
	2	12,000	
	3	18,000	
	4	10,000	
	5	13,000	
	6	9,000	
C	$5,000 at the *end of each year* for the next 30 years.		10%
D	$7,000 at the *beginning of each year* for the next 20 years.		18%

a. Find the present value of each of the four investment opportunities.
b. Which, if any, opportunities are acceptable?
c. Which opportunity should Gregg take?

ST3-3. Assume you wish to establish a college scholarship of $2,000 paid at the end of each year for a deserving student at the high school you attended. You would like to make a lump-sum gift to the high school to fund the scholarship into perpetuity. The school's treasurer assures you that they will earn 7.5% annually forever.

    a.   How much must you give the high school today to fund the proposed scholarship program?

    b.   If you wanted to allow the amount of the scholarship to increase annually after the first award (end of year 1) by 3% per year, how much must you give the school today to fund the scholarship program?

    c.   Compare, contrast, and discuss the difference in your response to parts (a) and (b).

ST3-4. Assume that you deposit $10,000 today into an account paying 6% annual interest and leave it on deposit for exactly eight years.

    a.   How much will be in the account at the end of eight years if interest is compounded

        1. annually?

        2. semiannually?

        3. monthly?

        4. continuously?

    b.   Calculate the *effective annual rate* (EAR) for (1) through (4) above.

    c.   Based on your findings in parts (a) and (b), what is the general relationship between the frequency of compounding and *EAR?*

ST3-5. Imagine that you are a professional personal financial planner. One of your clients asks you the following two questions. Use the time value of money techniques to develop appropriate responses to each question.

    a.   I need to save $37,000 over the next fifteen years to fund my three-year-old daughter's college education. If I make equal annual end-of-year deposits into an account that earns 7% annual interest, how large must this deposit be?

    b.   I borrowed $75,000, am required to repay it in six equal (annual) end-of-year installments of $16,718.98, and want to know what interest rate I am paying.

Questions

Q3-1. What is the importance to an individual of understanding *time value of money* concepts? For a corporate manager? Under what circumstance would the time value of money be irrelevant?

Q3-2. Actions that maximize profit may not maximize shareholder wealth. What role can the time value of money play in explaining the discrepancy between maximizing profits and maximizing value?

Q3-3. You are considering two investment plans. Plan A requires you to save $100 per month for ten years. Plan B requires you to save $200 per month for five years. Assuming that both plans earn the same rate of return, which plan accumulates more money?

Q3-4. Most government lotteries pay out jackpots in the form of a twenty- or thirty-year annuity, but they also give winners the option to collect their winnings as a much smaller lump sum. Explain how you would use time value of money analysis to choose between the annuity and the lump sum if you won the lottery.

Q3-5. What happens to the present value of a cash-flow stream when the discount rate increases? Place this in the context of an investment. If the required return on an investment goes up, but the expected cash flows do not change, are you willing to pay the same price for the investment, or to pay more or less for this investment than before the required return changed?

Q3-6. Look at the formula for the present value of an annuity. What happens to the present value as the number of periods increases? What distinguishes an annuity from a *perpetuity?* Why is there no formula for the future value of a perpetuity?

Q3-7. Suppose you borrow a large sum of money to buy a house, and you will pay back the loan over thirty years making fixed monthly payments. After fifteen years have passed, will you have paid off half the loan principal, more than half, or less than half? Why?

Q3-8. Under what circumstances is the effective annual rate different than the stated annual rate, and when are they the same?

Problems

Future Value of a Lump Sum Received Today

P3-1.   You have $1,500 to invest today at 7% interest compounded annually.

   a.   How much will you have accumulated in the account at the end of the following number of years?
   1.   three years
   2.   six years
   3.   nine years

   b.   Use your findings in part (a) to calculate the amount of interest earned in
   1.   years 1 to 3
   2.   years 4 to 6
   3.   years 7 to 9

   c.   Compare and contrast your findings in part (b). Explain why the amount of interest earned increases in each succeeding three-year period.

P3-2.   Dixon Shuttleworth has a large sum of money that he wants to invest to finance his retirement. He has been presented with three options. The first investment offers a 5% return for the first five years, a 10% return for the next five years, and a 20% return thereafter. The second investment offers 10% for the first ten years and 15% thereafter. The third investment offers a constant 12% rate of return. Determine which of these investments is the best for Dixon if he plans to retire in the following number of years.

   a.   fifteen years
   b.   twenty years
   c.   thirty years

Present Value of a Lump Sum Received in the Future

P3-3.   An Indiana state savings bond can be converted to $100 at maturity six years from purchase. If the state bonds pay 8% annual interest (compounded annually), at what price must the state sell its bonds? Assume no cash payments on savings bonds before redemption.

P3-4.   You have a trust fund that will pay you $1 million exactly ten years from today. You want cash now, so you are considering an opportunity to sell the right to the trust fund to an investor.

   a.   What is the least you will sell your claim for if you could earn the following rates of return on similar risk investments during the ten-year period?
   1.   6%
   2.   9%
   3.   12%

   b.   Rework part (a) under the assumption that the $1 million payment will be received in fifteen rather than ten years.

   c.   Based on your findings in parts (a) and (b), discuss the effect of both the size of the rate of return and the time until receipt of payment on the present value of a future sum.

Additional Applications Involving Lump Sums

P3-5.   You have saved $10,000 toward a down payment on a home. The money is invested in an account earning 7% interest. You will be ready to purchase the new home once your savings account grows to $25,000.

   a.   Approximately how many years will it take for the account to reach $25,000?
   b.   If the interest rate doubles to 14%, how many years will pass before you reach your $25,000 target?

P3-6.   You purchased a home for $250,000 eight years ago, and now the home is worth $300,000. What annual rate of return did you earn on your home?

P3-7.   Find the rates of return required to do the following:

   a.   Double an investment in four years
   b.   Double an investment in ten years
   c.   Triple an investment in four years
   d.   Triple an investment in ten years

P3-8.   Determine the length of time required to double the value of an investment, given the following rates of return.

a.   4%

b.   10%

c.   30%

d.   100%

P3-9.   The viatical industry offers a rather grim example of present-value concepts. A firm in this business, called a viator, purchases the rights to the benefits from a life insurance contract from a terminally ill client. The viator may then sell claims on the insurance payout to other investors. The industry began in the early 1990s as a way to help AIDS patients capture some of the proceeds from their life insurance policies for living expenses.

SMART solutions

See the problem and solution explained step-by-step at **SMART**|finance

Suppose a patient has a life expectancy of eighteen months and a life insurance policy with a death benefit of $100,000. A viator pays $80,000 for the right to the benefit and then sells that claim to another investor for $80,500.

a.   From the point of view of the patient, this contract is like taking out a loan. What is the compound annual interest rate on the loan if the patient lives exactly eighteen months? What if the patient lives thirty-six months?

b.   From the point of view of the investor, this transaction is like lending money. What is the compound annual interest rate earned on the loan if the patient lives eighteen months? What if the patient lives just twelve months?

Future Value of Cash Flow Streams

P3-10.   Liliana Alvarez's employer offers its workers a two-month paid sabbatical every seven years. Liliana, who just started working for the firm, plans to spend her sabbatical touring Europe at an estimated cost of $25,000. To finance her trip, Liliana plans to make six annual end-of-year deposits of $2,500 each, starting this year, into an investment account earning 8% interest.

a.   Will Liliana's account balance at the end of seven years be enough to pay for her trip?

b.   Suppose Liliana increases her annual contribution to $3,150. How large will her account balance be at the end of seven years?

P3-11.   Robert Williams is considering an offer to sell his medical practice, allowing him to retire five years early. He has been offered $500,000 for his practice and can invest this amount in an account earning 10% per year. If the practice is expected to generate the following cash flows, should Robert accept this offer and retire now?

End of Year	Cash Flow
1	$150,000
2	150,000
3	125,000
4	125,000
5	100,000

P3-12.   Gina Coulson has just contracted to sell a small parcel of land that she inherited a few years ago. The buyer is willing to pay $24,000 now. Alternatively, the buyer will make the series of payments shown in the following table, with each payment made at the *beginning* of the year. Because Gina doesn't really need the money today, she plans to let it accumulate in an account that earns 7% annual interest.

Beginning of Year (*t*)	Cash Flow (*CF$_t$*)
1	$ 2,000
2	4,000
3	6,000
4	8,000
5	10,000

a.   What is the future value of the lump sum at the end of year 5?

b.   What is the future value of the mixed stream at the end of year 5?

c.   Based on your findings in parts (a) and (b), which alternative should Gina take?

d.   If Gina could earn 10% rather than 7% on the funds, would your recommendation in part (c) change? Explain.

P3-13. For the following questions, assume an ordinary annuity of $1,000 and a required return of 12%.

    a.   What is the future value of a ten-year *ordinary annuity*?

    b.   If you earned an additional year's worth of interest on this annuity, what would be the future value?

    c.   What is the future value of a ten-year *annuity due*?

    d.   What is the relationship between your answers in parts (b) and (c)? Explain.

P3-14. Kim Edwards and Hiroshi Suzuki are both newly minted thirty-year-old MBAs. Kim plans to invest $1,000 per month into her 401(k) beginning next month. Hiroshi intends to invest $2,000 per month in his 401(k), but he does not plan to begin investing until ten years after Kim begins investing. Both Kim and Hiroshi will retire at age sixty-seven, and their 401(k) plans average a 12% annual return. Who will have more 401(k) money at retirement?

P3-15. To supplement your planned retirement, you estimate that you need to accumulate $220,000 in forty-two years. You plan to make equal annual end-of-year deposits into an account paying 8% annual interest.

    a.   How large must the annual deposits be to create the $220,000 fund in forty-two years?

    b.   If you can afford to deposit only $600 per year into the account, how much will you have accumulated by the end of the forty-second year?

Present Value of Cash Flow Streams

P3-16. Given the mixed streams of cash flows shown in the following table, answer parts (a) and (b):

	Cash Flow Stream	
Year	A	B
1	$ 50,000	$ 10,000
2	40,000	20,000
3	30,000	30,000
4	20,000	40,000
5	10,000	50,000
Totals	$150,000	$150,000

    a.   Find the present value of each stream, using a 15% discount rate.

    b.   Compare the calculated present values, and discuss them in light of the fact that the undiscounted total cash flows amount to $150,000 in each case.

P3-17. As part of your personal budgeting process, you have determined that at the end of each of the next five years you will incur significant maintenance expenses on your home. You'd like to cover these expenses by depositing a lump sum in an account today that earns 8%. You will gradually draw down this account each year as maintenance bills come due.

End of Year	Expense
1	$ 5,000
2	4,000
3	6,000
4	10,000
5	3,000

    a.   How much money must you deposit today to cover all of the expenses?

    b.   What effect does an increase in the interest rate have on the amount calculated in part (a)? Explain.

P3-18. Ruth Nail receives two offers for her seaside home. The first offer is for $1 million today. The second offer is for an owner-financed sale with annual payments as follows:

Year	Payment
0 (Today)	$200,000
1	200,000
2	200,000
3	200,000
4	200,000
5	300,000

Assuming that Ruth earns a return of 8% on her investments, which offer should she take?

P3-19. Melissa Gould wants to invest today to assure adequate funds for her son's college education. She estimates that her son will need $20,000 in eighteen years, $25,000 in nineteen years, $30,000 in twenty years, and $40,000 in twenty-one years. How much does Melissa have to invest in a fund today if the fund earns the following interest rate?
   a.   6% per year with annual compounding
   b.   6% per year with quarterly compounding
   c.   6% per year with monthly compounding

P3-20. Assume that you just won the state lottery. Your prize can be taken either in the form of $40,000 at the end of each of the next twenty-five years (i.e., $1 million over twenty-five years) or as a lump sum of $500,000 paid immediately.
   a.   If you expect to be able to earn 5% annually on your investments over the next twenty-five years, which alternative should you take? Why?
   b.   Would your decision in part (a) be altered if you could earn 7% rather than 5% on your investments over the next twenty-five years? Why?
   c.   At approximately what interest rate would you be indifferent when choosing between the two plans?

P3-21. For the following questions, assume an end-of-year cash flow of $250 and a 10% discount rate.
   a.   What is the present value of a single cash flow?
   b.   What is the present value of a 5-year annuity?
   c.   What is the present value of a 10-year annuity?
   d.   What is the present value of a 100-year annuity?
   e.   What is the present value of a $250 perpetuity?
   f.   Do you detect a relationship between the number of periods of an annuity and its resemblance to a perpetuity? Explain it.

P3-22. Use the following table of cash flows to answer parts (a) and (b). Assume an 8% discount rate.

End of Year	Cash Flow
1	$10,000
2	10,000
3	10,000
4	12,000
5	12,000
6	12,000
7	12,000
8	15,000
9	15,000
10	15,000

   a.   Solve for the present value of the cash flow stream by summing the present value of each individual cash flow.
   b.   Solve for the present value by summing the present value of the three separate annuities (one current and two deferred).

P3-23. Consumer Insurance, Inc., sells extended warranties on appliances that provide coverage after the manufacturers' warranties expire. An analyst for the company forecasts that the company will have to pay warranty claims of $5 million per year for three years, with the first claims expected to occur four years from today. The company wants to set aside a lump sum today to cover these costs, and money invested today will earn 10%. How much does the firm need to invest now?

P3-24. Landon Lowman, the 20-year-old star quarterback of the university football team, is approached about skipping his last two years of college and entering the professional football draft. Landon expects that his football career will be over by the time he is 32 years old. Talent scouts estimate that Landon could receive a signing bonus of $1 million today, along with a five-year contract for $3 million per year (payable at the end of each year). They further estimate that he could negotiate a contract for $5 million per year for the remaining seven years of his career. The scouts believe, however, that Landon will be a much higher draft pick if he improves by playing two more years of college football. If he stays at the university, he is expected to receive a $2 million signing bonus in two years, along with a five-year contract for $5 million per year. After that, the scouts expect Landon to obtain a five-year contract for $6 million per year to take him into retirement. Assume that Landon can earn a 10% return over this time. Should Landon stay or go?

P3-25. Matt Sedgwick, facilities and operations manager for the Birmingham Buffalo professional football team, has come up with an idea for generating income. Matt wants to expand the stadium by building sky-boxes sold with lifetime (perpetual) season tickets. Each skybox is guaranteed ten season tickets at a cost of $200 per ticket per year for life. If each skybox costs $100,000 to build, what is the minimum selling price that Matt will need to charge for the skyboxes to break even, if the required return is 10%?

P3-26. Jill Chu wants to choose the best of four immediate retirement annuities available to her. In each case, in exchange for paying a single premium today, she will receive equal annual end-of-year cash benefits for a specified number of years. She considers the annuities to be equally risky and is not concerned about their differing lives. Her decision will be based solely on the rate of return she will earn on each annuity. The key terms of each of the four annuities are shown in the following table:

Annuity	Premium Paid Today	Annual Benefit	Life (years)
A	$30,000	$3,100	20
B	25,000	3,900	10
C	40,000	4,200	15
D	35,000	4,000	12

a. Calculate to the nearest 1% the rate of return on each of the four annuities Jill is considering.
b. Given Jill's stated decision criterion, which annuity would you recommend?

P3-27. Evaluate each of the following three investments, each costing $1,000 today and providing the returns noted below, over the next five years.

Investment 1: $2,000 lump sum to be received in five years

Investment 2: $300 at the end of each of the next five years

Investment 3: $250 at the beginning of each of the next five years

a. Which investment offers the highest return?
b. Which offers the highest return if the payouts are doubled (i.e., $4,000, $600, and $500)?
c. What causes the big change in the returns on the annuities?

P3-28. Consider the following three investments of equal risk. Which offers the greatest rate of return?

	Investment		
End of Year	**A**	**B**	**C**
0	−$10,000	−$20,000	−$25,000
1	0	9,500	20,000
2	0	9,500	30,000
3	24,600	9,500	−12,600

Advanced Applications of Time Value

P3-29. You plan to invest $2,000 in an individual retirement arrangement (IRA) today at a *stated interest rate* of 8%, which is expected to apply to all future years.

a. How much will you have in the account at the end of ten years if interest is compounded as follows?
   1. annually
   2. semiannually
   3. daily (assume a 365-day year)
   4. continuously
b. What is the *effective annual rate (EAR)* for each compounding period in part (a)?
c. How much greater will your IRA account balance be at the end of ten years if interest is compounded continuously rather than annually?
d. How does the compounding frequency affect the future value and effective annual rate for a given deposit? Explain in terms of your findings in parts (a)–(c).

P3-30. Hector Garcia has shopped around for the best interest rates for his investment of $10,000 over the next year. He has found the following:

Stated Rate	Compounding
6.10%	annual
5.90%	semiannual
5.85%	monthly

    a.   Which investment offers Hector the highest *effective annual rate* of return?

    b.   Assume that Hector wants to invest his money for only six months, and the annual compounded rate of 6.10% is not available. Which of the remaining opportunities should Hector choose?

P3-31. Answer parts (a)–(c) for each of the following cases.

Case	Amount of Initial Deposit ($)	Stated Annual Rate, *r* (%)	Compounding Frequency, *m* (times/year)	Deposit Period (years)
A	2,500	6	2	5
B	50,000	12	6	3
C	1,000	5	1	10
D	20,000	16	4	6

    a.   Calculate the future value at the end of the specified deposit period.

    b.   Determine the *effective annual rate (EAR)*.

    c.   Compare the stated annual rate (*r*) to the *effective annual rate (EAR)*. What relationship exists between compounding frequency and the stated and effective annual rates?

P3-32. Tara Cutler is newly married and preparing a surprise gift of a trip to Europe for her husband on their tenth anniversary. Tara plans to invest $5,000 per year until that anniversary and to make her first $5,000 investment on their first anniversary. If she earns an 8% rate on her investments, how much will she have saved for their trip if the interest is compounded in each of the following ways?

    a.   annually

    b.   quarterly

    c.   monthly

P3-33. John Tye was hired as the new corporate finance analyst at I-Ell Enterprises and received his first assignment. John is to take the $25 million in cash received from a recent divestiture, to use part of these proceeds to retire an outstanding $10 million bond issue, and to use the remainder to repurchase common stock. However, the bond issue cannot be retired for another two years. If John can place the funds necessary to retire this $10 million debt into an account earning a 6% annual return compounded *monthly*, how much of the $25 million remains to repurchase stock?

P3-34. Find the present value of a three-year, $20,000 ordinary annuity deposited into an account that pays 12% annual interest, compounded *monthly*. Solve for the present value of the annuity in the following ways:

    a.   as three single cash flows discounted at the *stated annual rate* of interest

    b.   as three single cash flows discounted at the appropriate *effective annual rate* of interest

    c.   as a three-year annuity discounted at the *effective annual rate* of interest

P3-35. Determine the annual deposit required to fund a future annual annuity of $12,000 per year. You will fund this future liability over the next five years, with the first deposit to occur one year from today. The future $12,000 liability will last for four years, with the first payment to occur seven years from today. If you can earn 8% on this account, how much will you have to deposit each year over the next five years to fund the future liability?

P3-36. Mary Chong, capital expenditure manager for PDA Manufacturing, knows that her company is facing a series of monthly expenses associated with installation and calibration of new production equipment. The company has $1 million in a bank account right now that it can draw on to meet these expenses. Funds in this account earn 6% interest annually, with monthly compounding. Ms. Chong is preparing a budget that will require the firm to make equal monthly deposits into their bank account, starting next month, to ensure that they can pay the repair costs they anticipate over the next 24 months (shown as follows). How much should the monthly bank deposit be?

Months	Repair Costs per Month
1–4	$100,000
5–12	200,000
13–24	500,000

P3-37. Craig and LaDonna Allen are trying to establish a college fund for their son Spencer, who just turned three today. They plan for Spencer to withdraw $10,000 on his eighteenth birthday and $11,000, $12,000, and $15,000 on his subsequent birthdays. They plan to fund these withdrawals with a ten-year annuity, with the first payment to occur one year from today, and expect to earn an average annual return of 8%.

   a.   How much will the Allens have to contribute each year to achieve their goal?

   b.   Create a schedule showing the cash inflows (including interest) and outflows of this fund. How much remains on Spencer's twenty-first birthday?

P3-38. Joan Messineo borrowed $15,000 at a 14% annual interest rate to be repaid over three years. The loan is amortized into three equal annual end-of-year payments.

   a.   Calculate the annual end-of-year loan payment.

   b.   Prepare a loan amortization schedule showing the interest and principal breakdown of each of the three loan payments.

   c.   Explain why the interest portion of each payment declines with the passage of time.

P3-39. You are planning to purchase a motor home for $40,000, and you have $10,000 to apply as a down payment. You may borrow the remainder under the following terms: a ten-year loan with semiannual repayments and a stated interest rate of 6%. You intend to make $6,000 payments, applying the excess over your required payment to the reduction of the principal balance.

   a.   Given these terms, how long (in years) will it take you to fully repay your loan?

   b.   What will be your total interest cost?

   c.   What would be your interest cost if you made no prepayments and repaid your loan by strictly adhering to the terms of the loan?

P3-40. Use a spreadsheet to create amortization schedules for the following five scenarios. What happens to the total interest paid under each scenario?

   a.   **Scenario 1:** Loan amount: $1 million

      Annual rate: 5%

      Term: 360 months

      Prepayment: $0

   b.   **Scenario 2:** Same as 1, except annual rate is 7%

   c.   **Scenario 3:** Same as 1, except term is 180 months

   d.   **Scenario 4:** Same as 1, except prepayment is $250 per month

   e.   **Scenario 5:** Same as 1, except loan amount is $125,000

P3-41. You are the pension fund manager for Tanju's Toffees. The fund collects contributions (inflows) from workers each year and pays benefits (outflows) to retirees. Your CFO wants to know the minimum annual return required on the pension fund in order to make all required payments over the next five years and not diminish the existing asset base. The fund currently has assets of $500 million.

   a.   Determine the required return if outflows are expected to exceed inflows by $50 million per year.

   b.   Determine the required return with the following fund cash flows.

End of Year	Inflows	Outflows
1	$55,000,000	$100,000,000
2	60,000,000	110,000,000
3	60,000,000	120,000,000
4	60,000,000	135,000,000
5	64,000,000	145,000,000

   c.   Consider the cash flows in part (b). What will happen to your asset base if you earn 10%? 20%?

P3-42. You plan to start saving for your son's college education. He will begin college when he turns eighteen and will need $4,000 then and in each of the following three years. You will make a deposit at the end of this year in an account that pays 6% compounded annually and an identical deposit at the end of each year, with the last deposit occurring when he turns eighteen. If an annual deposit of $1,484 will allow you to reach your goal, how old is your son now?

Access financial information from the Thomson ONE – Business School Edition Web site for the following problem(s). Go to www.tobsefin.swlearning.com/. If you have already registered your access serial number and have a username and password, click **Enter.** Otherwise, click **Register** and follow the instructions to create a username and password. Register your access serial number and then click **Enter** on the aforementioned Web site. When you click Enter, you will be prompted for your username and password (please remember that the password is case sensitive). Enter them in the respective boxes and then click **OK** (or hit **Enter**). From the ensuing page, click **Click Here to Access Thomson ONE – Business School Edition Now!** This opens up a new window that gives you access to the Thomson ONE – Business School Edition database. You can retrieve a company's financial information by entering its ticker symbol (provided for each company in the problem(s)) in the box below "Name/Symbol/Key." For further instructions on using the Thomson ONE – Business School Edition database, please refer to the online Help.

P3-43. Compare the performance of Adidas AG (ticker: ADDYY) and Nike, Inc. (NKE). Calculate the five-year growth in sales and net income and determine the compound annual growth rate for each company. Does one company dominate the other in growth in both categories?

P3-44. Compare the market performance of Kimberly Clark (ticker: U:KMB) and Procter & Gamble Company (U:PG). Calculate the three-year growth in stock price and the compound annual growth rate in stock price for each company. If you had invested $10,000 in each stock three years ago, what is the current value of each investment?

Since these exercises depend upon real-time data, your answers will change continuously depending upon when you access the Internet to download your data.

SMART concepts

See time value of money concepts explained step-by-step.

SMART solutions

See the solutions to Problems 3-9 and 3-15 explained step-by-step.

Mini-Case

Present Value

Casino.com Corporation is building a $25 million office building in Las Vegas and is financing the construction at an 80% loan-to-value ratio, where the loan is in the amount of $20,000,000. This loan has a ten-year maturity, calls for monthly payments, and has a stated interest rate of 8%.

Assignment

Using this information, answer the following questions.

1. What is the monthly payment?

2. How much of the first payment is interest?

3. How much of the first payment is principal?

Continued

4. How much will Casino.com Corporation owe on this loan after making monthly payments for three years (the amount owed immediately after the thirty-sixth payment)?

5. Should this loan be refinanced after three years with a new seven-year 7% loan, if the cost to refinance is $250,000? To make this decision, calculate the new loan payments and then the present value of the difference in the loan payments.

6. Returning to the original ten-year 8% loan, how much is the loan payment if these payments are quarterly rather than monthly payments?

7. For this loan with quarterly payments, how much will Casino.com Corporation owe on this loan after making quarterly payments for three years (the amount owed immediately after the twelfth payment)?

8. What is the annual percentage rate on the original ten-year 8% loan?

9. What is the *effective annual rate* (EAR) on the original ten-year 8% loan?

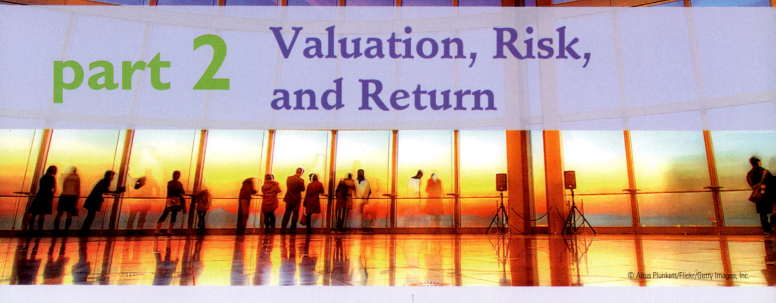

© Altus Plunkett/Flickr/Getty Images, Inc.

part 2

Valuation, Risk, and Return

A bit of wisdom attributed to the English poet Chaucer says, "nothing ventured, nothing gained." Financial markets give us ample evidence that Chaucer knew what he was talking about. Over time, high-risk investments tend to earn higher returns than do low-risk investments. When managers invest corporate funds, or when individuals decide how to allocate their money between different types of investments, they must weigh the trade-off between risk and return. The purpose of the next four chapters is to explore that trade-off in depth. We begin in Chapters 4 and 5 by describing two of the most common types of investments available in the market—bonds and stocks.

The bond market is vast, and it plays an extremely important role in the economy. Federal, state, and local governments issue bonds to finance all kinds of public works projects and to cover budget deficits. Corporations sell bonds to raise funds to meet daily operating needs and to pay for major investments. Chapter 4 describes the basic bond features and explains how investors value bonds.

Chapter 5 examines the stock market. Valuing stocks is more complex than valuing bonds because stocks do not promise fixed payment streams as do bonds. Therefore, Chapter 5 discusses methods that investors and analysts use to estimate stock values. The chapter also provides a brief explanation of how firms work with investment bankers to sell stock to the public and how investors can trade shares of stock with each other.

With the essential features of bonds and stocks in hand, Chapter 6 explores the historical returns earned by different classes of investments. The data illustrate that a fundamental trade-off between risk and return confronts investors. Chaucer was right. Investors who want to get rich have to accept risk as part of the deal.

Chapter 7 quantifies exactly what we mean by the term *risk*. The chapter also introduces one of the most important theories in finance called the Capital Asset Pricing Model, or CAPM. The CAPM attempts to quantify the risk-return trade-off, providing an estimate of the return that an investor can expect to earn on an investment with a particular level of risk. The CAPM can help investors decide how to allocate their funds across different types of investments, and it also helps corporate managers decide whether it is better to invest a firm's money in a high-risk venture, like building a manufacturing plant in a foreign country, or in a low-risk undertaking, such as upgrading old equipment.

chapter 4

Valuing Bonds

Forrest Gump Bonds

When Forrest Gump uttered the memorable line, "Life is like a box of chocolates—you never know what you're gonna get," no one could have imagined how the British candy company, Hotel Chocolat, would put that notion into practice. Founded as a catalog company nearly 20 years ago, Hotel Chocolat needed £5 million for a major expansion starting in July 2010. That sum was too small to justify the costs of a traditional bond issue. The company could have borrowed the money from a bank, but at the time lending standards were tight, and management did not want to pay the relatively high interest rate that they believed a bank would charge.

Instead, Hotel Chocolat issued its own promissory notes, raising money from its existing customers who were members of its "Tasting Club." Club members could purchase a £2,000 note paying 6.72% interest or a £4,000 note paying 7.29%. What made these notes unique was that they did not make interest payments in cash. Instead, investors received a monthly box of chocolates with a retail value equivalent to the stated interest rate. After three years, investors could redeem the notes and get their original investment back—in cash.

Sources: "Chocolate Bonds Offer a Uniquely Tasty Dividend," by Bruce Watson, *Daily Finance*, July 22, 2010. "Hotel Chocolat's Chocolate Bond," by Dean Best, *Just-Food*, May 24, 2010.

Learning Objectives

After completing this chapter you should be able to:

- Recall the fundamental concepts that determine how to value assets;

- Understand the vocabulary that describes bonds and the markets in which they trade;

- Interpret the relationship been bond prices and interest rates; and

- Explain the meaning of the "term structure of interest rates."

Perhaps the most fundamental question in finance is, "What is it worth?" In other words, finance is all about valuing things. This chapter introduces the key principle that financial analysts use to value financial assets like bonds and stocks as well as physical assets like machinery or entire manufacturing plants. That principle says that *the value of any asset equals the present value of future benefits accruing to the asset's owner.*

Our primary objective in this chapter is to describe models used to value debt securities, often called bonds. In the next chapter, we learn about pricing stocks. Why do corporate managers need to understand how to price bonds and stocks? First, firms must occasionally approach bond and stock markets to raise capital for new

investments. Understanding how investors in these markets value the firm's securities helps managers determine how to finance new projects. Second, firms periodically make investments by acquiring privately held companies, just as they unload past investments by selling divisions. In either case, knowing how the market values an enterprise guides a manager's expectations regarding the appropriate price for an acquisition or divestiture. Third, a company's stock price provides an external, independent performance assessment of top management, one that a diligent board of directors watches closely. Surely managers who will be judged (and compensated) based on the value of their firm's stock price need to understand the determinants of that price. Fourth, finance theory suggests that the objective of corporate management is to maximize the stock price by correctly weighing the marginal benefits and costs of alternative actions. How can managers take actions to maximize stock prices if they don't know what causes stock prices to rise or fall?

This chapter presents an introduction to bonds and bond valuation. We begin by laying out the principles of valuation—principles that can be applied to a wide variety of valuation problems. After that, we describe the essential features of bonds, and we show how to apply the principles of valuation to calculate bond prices.

4-1   Valuation Basics

The owner of an asset is entitled to the benefits generated by the asset. These benefits may be tangible, such as the interest payments on bonds (even when they are paid in chocolate), or intangible, such as the pleasure one experiences when viewing a beautiful painting. Either way, *the value of any asset equals the present value of all its future benefits.* Finance theory focuses primarily on tangible benefits, typically the cash flows that an asset pays over time. For instance, a landlord who owns an apartment complex receives a stream of rental payments from tenants. The landlord is also responsible for maintaining the complex, paying taxes, and covering other expenses. If the landlord wants to sell the apartment complex, what price should he expect to receive? According to our fundamental valuation principle above, the price should equal the present value of all future net cash flows. Investors value financial assets such as bonds and stocks in much the same way. First, they estimate how much cash a particular investment distributes over time. Second, investors discount the expected cash payments using the time value of money mathematics covered in Chapter 3. The investment's value, or its current market price, equals the present value of its future cash flows.

This implies that pricing an asset requires knowledge of both its future benefits and the appropriate discount rate that converts future benefits into a present value. For some assets, investors know with a high degree of certainty what the future benefit stream will be. For other investments, the future benefit stream is much harder to predict. Generally, *the greater the risk or uncertainty surrounding an asset's future benefits, the higher the discount rate investors will apply when discounting those benefits to the present.*

Consequently, the valuation process links an asset's future benefits and the risk surrounding those benefits to determine its price. Holding future benefits (cash flows) constant, an inverse relationship exists between risk and value. If two investments promise identical cash flows in the future, investors will pay a higher price for the one with the more credible promise. Or, to state that relationship another way, if a risky asset and a safe asset trade at the same price, the risky asset must offer investors higher future returns.

4-1a The Fundamental Valuation Model

required rate of return

The rate of return that investors expect or require an investment to earn given its risk.

Chapters 6 and 7 present an in-depth analysis of the relationship between risk and return. For now, take as given the market's **required rate of return**, which is the rate of return that investors expect or require a specific investment to earn, given its risk. The riskier the asset is, the higher will be the return required by investors in the marketplace. We can also say that the required rate of return on an asset is the return available in the market on another equally risky investment. When someone purchases a specific investment, they lose the opportunity to invest their money in another asset. The forgone return on the alternative investment represents an *opportunity cost*.

How do investors use this required rate of return to determine the prices of different types of securities? Equation 4.1 expresses the *fundamental valuation model* mathematically, as follows:

$$(Eq.\ 4.1) \qquad P_0 = \frac{CF_1}{(1+r)^1} + \frac{CF_2}{(1+r)^2} + \cdots + \frac{CF_n}{(1+r)^n}$$

Todd Richter, Managing Director, Head of Equity Healthcare Research, Bank of America Securities

"The concepts of value, the things that drive value, don't change."

See the entire interview at **SMART** | finance

Smart Practices Video

In this equation, P_0 represents the asset's price today (at time 0), CF_t represents the asset's expected cash flow at time t, and r is the required return—the discount rate that reflects the asset's risk. Equation 4.1 establishes a price that accounts for the asset's cash flows and the risk associated with those cash flows. The letter n stands for the asset's life, the period over which it distributes cash flows to investors, usually measured in years. As you will see, n may be a finite number, as in the case of a bond that matures in a certain number of years, or it may be infinite, as in the case of a common stock with an indefinite life span. In either case, this equation provides us with a vehicle for valuing almost any type of asset.

EXAMPLE

In July 2010, Mitchells & Butlers, Britain's largest operator of pubs, entered into a sale-leaseback transaction with real estate management firm Prupim. In this type of transaction, one party sells an asset to another and agrees to lease the asset back from the buyer. In this transaction, Mitchells & Butlers sold eight pubs, agreeing to lease them back from Prupim for £960,000 (or £120,000 per pub) per year for the next 25 years. Suppose that Prupim's required return on this deal is 10%. We can use Equation 4.1 to calculate the price Prupim would be willing to pay today in exchange for lease payments over the next 25 years.[1]

$$P_0 = \frac{£960,000}{(1+0.10)^1} + \frac{£960,000}{(1+0.10)^2} + \cdots + \frac{£960,000}{(1+0.10)^{25}} = £8,713,958$$

Remember that Equation 3.7 on page 87 provided a mathematical shortcut for solving a problem like this one. The £960,000 annual payments represent an annuity, and Equation 3.7 says that the present value of an ordinary annuity can be found as follows:

$$PV = \frac{PMT}{r} \times \left[1 - \frac{1}{(1+r)^n}\right]$$

---

[1]We can use Excel to solve for the present value of 25 annual lease payments by using the pv function. The correct syntax for this example is =pv(0.10,25,-960000,0,0).

continued

Substituting £960,000 for the annual payment (or cash flow), 10% for the interest rate, and 25 for the number of years, we can calculate the present value (or price) of this stream of payments:

$$P_0 = \frac{£960,000}{0.10} \times \left[1 - \frac{1}{(1 + 0.10)^{25}}\right] = £9,600,000 \times \left[1 - \frac{1}{10.8347}\right] = £8,713,958$$

The lease payments are worth more than £8.7 million to Prupim.

With this simple framework in hand, we turn to the problem of pricing bonds. Though bond-pricing techniques can get very complex, we focus on "plain-vanilla" bonds: those that promise a fixed stream of cash payments over a finite time period. Among the largest issuers of such fixed income securities are national governments and large, multinational corporations.

4-1 Concept Review Questions

1. Why is it important for corporate managers to understand how bonds and stocks are priced?

2. Holding constant an asset's future benefit stream, what happens to the asset's price if its risk increases?

3. Holding constant an asset's risk, what happens to the asset's price if its future benefit stream increases?

4. Discuss how one might use Equation 4.1 to determine the price per acre of farmland.

4-2 Bond Prices and Interest Rates

4-2a Bond Vocabulary

principal
The amount borrowed on which interest is paid.

maturity date
The date when a bond's life ends and the borrower must make the final interest payment and repay the principal.

par value (bonds)
The *face value* of a bond, which the borrower repays at maturity.

coupon
The periodic interest payment that a bond pays to investors.

indenture
A legal contract, between the borrower (issuer) and investor, stating the conditions under which a bond has been issued.

coupon rate
The rate derived by dividing the bond's annual coupon payment by its par value.

coupon yield
The amount obtained by dividing the bond's coupon by its current market price (which does not always equal its par value). Also called *current yield*.

Fundamentally, a bond is just a loan. Unlike car loans and home mortgages, which require borrowers to make regular payments, including both an interest component and some repayment of the original loan amount or **principal**, bonds make interest-only payments until they mature. On the **maturity date**, a bond's life formally ends, and both the final interest payment and the original principal amount are paid to investors. The *principal value* of a bond, also known as the bond's **par value** or *face value*, is typically $1,000 for corporate bonds.

Although bonds come in many varieties, most bonds share certain basic characteristics. First, many bonds promise to pay investors a fixed amount of interest, called the bond's **coupon**.[2] Most bonds make coupon payments every six months, or semiannually. Because a bond's cash flows are contractually fixed, traders often refer to bonds as *fixed-income securities*. The legal contract between the borrower who issues bonds and the investors who buy them, called the bond **indenture**, specifies the dollar amount of the coupon and when the borrower must make coupon payments. Second, a bond's **coupon rate** equals its annual coupon payment divided by its par value. Third, a bond's **coupon yield** (or *current yield*) equals the coupon divided by the bond's current market price (which does not always equal its par value).

To illustrate, suppose that a government entity or a firm issues a bond with a $1,000 par value and promises to pay investors $35 every six months until maturity. The bond's *coupon* is $70 per year, and its *coupon rate* is 7% ($70 ÷ $1,000). If the current market value of this bond is $980, then its *coupon (current) yield* is 7.14% ($70 ÷ $980).

---

[2]Historically, bond certificates were printed with coupons attached that the bondholder would literally clip (like coupons in a newspaper) and mail in to receive an interest payment. That is the origin of the term *coupon*. Not all bonds make fixed coupon payments. Some bonds make pay variable coupons that are tied to an underlying interest rate (such as the rate on U.S. Treasury bonds) or to the rate of inflation.

Bonds can have a variety of additional features, such as a *call feature* that allows the issuer to redeem the bond at a predetermined price prior to maturity, or a *conversion feature* that grants bondholders the right to redeem their bonds for a predetermined number of shares of stock in the borrowing firm. Chapter 13 discusses these and other features in detail. For now, we focus our attention on pricing ordinary bonds. We'll begin with the basic bond valuation equation and then describe its application to risk-free and risky bonds.

SMART
concepts

See the concept explained step-by-step at **SMART | finance**

4-2b The Basic Equation (Assuming Annual Interest)

We can value ordinary bonds by developing a simplified version of Equation 4.1. With annual interest, remember that a bond makes a fixed coupon payment each year. Assume that the bond makes annual coupon payments of $\$C$ for n years, and at maturity the bond makes its final coupon payment and returns the par value, $\$M$, to investors. (We will deal with the more common occurrence of semiannual coupon payments shortly.) Using these assumptions, we can replace Equation 4.1 with the following:

$$\text{(Eq. 4.2)} \qquad P_0 = \frac{C}{(1+r)^1} + \frac{C}{(1+r)^2} + \cdots + \frac{C}{(1+r)^n} + \frac{M}{(1+r)^n}$$

Equation 4.2 says that the *bond's price* equals the present value of an n-year ordinary annuity plus the present value of the lump-sum principal payment.

$$\text{Price} = PV \text{ of annuity} + PV \text{ of lump sum}$$

The annuity consists of a stream of coupon payments, and the lump sum is the bond's principal or par value. The bond's price is simply the sum of the present values of these two components:

$$\text{Price} = PV \text{ of coupons} + PV \text{ of principal}$$

Next, we modify the bond pricing equation once more, borrowing from Equation 3.7 on page 87 to highlight that the price equals the sum of the present value of an annuity and the present value of a lump-sum payment at maturity.

$$\text{(Eq. 4.2a)} \qquad P_0 = \frac{C}{r} \times \left[1 - \frac{1}{(1+r)^n} \right] + \frac{M}{(1+r)^n}$$

EXAMPLE

On January 1, 2012, Worldwide United had a bond outstanding with a coupon rate of 9.125% and a face value of $1,000. At the end of each year this bond pays investors $91.25 in interest (0.09125 × $1,000), and it matures at the end of 2022. Figure 4.1 illustrates the sequence of cash flows that the bond promises investors over time. Notice that we break up the bond's cash payments into two separate components. The first component is an eleven-year annuity of $91.25 annual payments. The second component is a lump-sum payment of $1,000 at maturity.

To calculate the price of this bond, we need to know what rate of return investors demand on bonds that are as risky as Worldwide's bonds. Assume that the market currently requires an 8% return on these bonds. Substituting the required return and the payments into Equation 4.2, we can express the current price of this bond as follows:

$$\text{Price} = \frac{\$91.25}{(1.08)^1} + \frac{\$91.25}{(1.08)^2} + \frac{\$91.25}{(1.08)^3} + \cdots + \frac{\$91.25}{(1.08)^{11}} + \frac{\$1,000}{(1.08)^{11}} = \$1,080.31$$

Figure 4.1 shows that the present value of the eleven-year coupon stream is $651.43, and the present value of the principal repayment is $428.88. That gives a combined bond value of $1,080.31 as shown below.

$$PV \text{ of coupons} = \left(\frac{\$91.25}{0.08} \right) \times \left[1 - \left(\frac{1}{1.08^{11}} \right) \right] = \$651.43$$

$$PV \text{ of principal} = \frac{\$1,000}{1.08^{11}} = \$428.88$$

$$\text{Price of bond} = \$651.43 + \$428.88 = \$1,080.31$$

continued

To calculate this value in Excel, once again we use the PV function, entering 0.08 for the rate, 11 for the number of periods, −91.25 for the payments, and −1000 for the future value (in this Excel function, the "future value" argument simply refers to any payment, above and beyond the regular annuity cash flow, coming at the very end of the final period). By entering the coupon payments and the principal repayment as negative values, we will obtain a positive value for the bond's price.

$$=\text{PV}(0.08, 11, -91.25, -1000) = 1,080.31$$

Figure 4.1 also illustrates the keystrokes one might use when solving this problem using a financial calculator.

Figure 4.1   **Time Line for Bond Valuation (Assuming Annual Interest Payments)**

Worldwide United 9.125% Coupon, $1,000 Par Value Bond, Maturing at End of 2022; Required Return Equals 8%

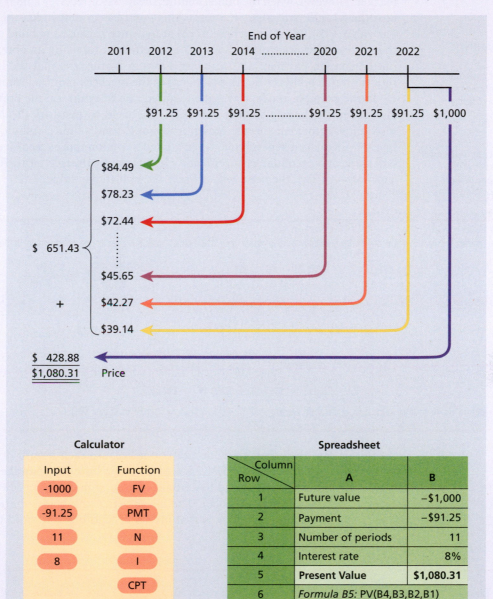

premium

A bond trades at a premium when its market price exceeds its par value.

Notice that this bond sells *above* par value because the price, $1,080.31, is greater than the $1,000 par value. When a bond sells for more than its par value, we say that the bond trades at a **premium**. Why are Worldwide's bonds trading at a premium? By assumption, the market's required return on an investment like this is just 8%, but Worldwide's bonds offer a coupon rate of 9.125%. Therefore, if Worldwide's bonds sold at par value, they would offer investors a particularly attractive return, and investors would rush to buy them. As more and more investors purchase Worldwide bonds, the market price of those bonds rises.

Think about the return that an investor earns if she purchases Worldwide bonds today for $1,080.31 and holds them to maturity. Every year, the investor receives a $91.25 cash payment. At the current market price, this represents a coupon yield of about 8.4% ($91.25 ÷ $1,080.31), noticeably above the 8% required return in the market. However, when the bonds mature, the investor receives a final interest payment plus the $1,000 par value. In a sense, this bond has a built-in loss of $80.31 ($1,000 par value − $1,080.31 purchase price) at maturity because the bond's principal is less than the current price of the bond. The net effect of receiving an above-market return on the coupon payment and realizing a loss at maturity is that the investor's overall return on this bond is exactly 8%, equal to the market's required return.

yield to maturity (YTM)

The discount rate that equates the present value of the bond's cash flows to its market price.

In the example above, 8% is the required rate of return on the bond in the market, also called the bond's **yield to maturity**. The yield to maturity (YTM) is simply the discount rate that equates the present value of a bond's future cash flows to its current market price.[3] As a general rule, when a bond's coupon rate exceeds its YTM, the bond will trade at a premium as Worldwide's bonds do. Conversely, if the coupon rate falls short of the YTM, the bond will sell at a **discount** to par value.

discount

A bond trades at a discount when its market price is less than its par value.

EXAMPLE

Suppose the market's required return on Worldwide bonds is 10% rather than 8%. In that case, the price of the bonds would be determined using this equation:

$$P_0 = \frac{\$91.25}{(1 + 0.10)^1} + \frac{\$91.25}{(1 + 0.10)^2} + \frac{\$91.25}{(1 + 0.10)^3} + \cdots + \frac{\$91.25}{(1 + 0.10)^{11}} + \frac{\$1,000}{(1 + 0.10)^{11}}$$

Breaking this calculation into the annuity and lump sum components we have:

$$\text{PV of coupons} = \left(\frac{\$91.25}{0.10}\right) \times \left[1 - \left(\frac{1}{1.10^{11}}\right)\right] = \$592.68$$

$$\text{PV of principal} = \left(\frac{\$1,000}{1.10^{11}}\right) = \$350.49$$

$$\text{Price of bond} = \$592.68 + \$350.49 = \$943.17$$

We could replicate the bond-price calculation in Excel by entering =PV(0.10,11,−91.25,−1000,0) to obtain $943.17.

In this case the bonds trade at a discount because each month investors receive a coupon yield of about 9.7% ($91.25 ÷ $943.17), a little less than the required rate of 10%. Offsetting that, the bond has a built-in gain at maturity of $56.83 ($1,000 par value − $943.17 purchase price). The net effect of the below-market coupon payments and the gain at maturity is that investors who buy and hold this bond earn a yield to maturity of exactly 10%.

EXAMPLE

Verhoeven Enterprises has an outstanding bond issue that pays a 6% annual coupon, has a $1,000 par value, and matures in five years. The current market value of one Verhoeven bond is $1,021.35. What yield to maturity do these bonds offer investors?

Because the bond sells at a premium, we can infer that the yield to maturity is less than the bond's coupon rate. We can use a financial calculator or Excel to calculate the answer very quickly, but let's try a trial-and-error approach first to strengthen our intuition about the relationship between a bond's price and its YTM. Let's start by determining the bond's value if it offers a YTM of 5%. At that rate, the price of the bond would be the following:

---

[3]The *holding period yield* is a similar measure of return used by investors to measure the realized return on a bond that is sold prior to its maturity date. It represents the compound annual return earned by the investor over the holding period for the bond. The calculation of the holding period yield is the same as that for yield to maturity except that the actual holding period and sale price are substituted into Equation 4.2 for years to maturity (*n*) and the maturity value (*M*) respectively.

continued

$$PV \text{ of coupons} = \left(\frac{\$60}{0.05}\right) \times \left[1 - \frac{1}{(1.05)^5}\right] = \$259.77$$

$$PV \text{ of principal} = \frac{\$1,000}{(1.05)^5} = \$783.53$$

$$\text{Price of bond} = \$259.77 + \$783.53 = \$1,043.30$$

Our initial guess of 5% produces a price that exceeds the market price of Verhoeven's bond. Because we initially calculated a price that is too high, we need to try again using a higher YTM. Discounting the bond's cash flows at a higher YTM results in a lower price. Suppose the YTM equals 5.5%. Now we have

$$PV \text{ of coupons} = \left(\frac{\$60}{0.055}\right) \times \left[1 - \frac{1}{(1.055)^5}\right] = \$256.22$$

$$PV \text{ of principal} = \frac{\$1,000}{(1.055)^5} = \$765.13$$

$$\text{Price of bond} = \$256.22 + \$765.13 = \$1,021.35$$

The YTM equals 5.5% because that is the discount rate that equates the present value of the bond's cash flows with its current market price. In Excel, you can find a bond's yield to maturity by using the IRR function. To calculate the yield to maturity using this function, simply enter the bond's market price as a negative number and its cash flows as positive numbers as shown below. Then type the IRR function and highlight the cells containing the values. Be sure that the cell in which you type the IRR function is formatted to show the answer to several decimal places.

Spreadsheet

Column Row	A	B
1	Price	−1021.35
2	Coupon	60
3	Coupon	60
4	Coupon	60
5	Coupon	60
6	Coupon+Principal	1060
7	IRR	5.50%
8	*Formula B7:* IRR(B1:B6)	

4-2c Semiannual Compounding

Most bonds make two interest payments per year rather than one. Adjusting our *bond-pricing* framework to handle *semiannual interest payments* is easy. A bond paying semiannual interest has twice as many coupon payments, but each payment is half as much compared to the bond with annual payments. If the bond matures in n years and the annual coupon equals C, then the bond now makes $2n$ payments equal to $C \div 2$. Similarly, if the bond's annual yield to maturity equals r, we replace that with a semiannual yield of $r \div 2$. This produces a modified version of Equation 4.2[4]:

$$(\text{Eq. 4.3}) \quad P_0 = \frac{C/2}{\left(1 + \frac{r}{2}\right)^1} + \frac{C/2}{\left(1 + \frac{r}{2}\right)^2} + \cdots + \frac{C/2}{\left(1 + \frac{r}{2}\right)^{2n}} + \frac{M}{\left(1 + \frac{r}{2}\right)^{2n}}$$

A slightly modified version of Equation 3.7 on page 87 expresses the equation above as a sum of the present value of an ordinary annuity and the present value of a lump sum:

$$(\text{Eq. 4.3a}) \quad P_0 = \left(\frac{C/2}{\frac{r}{2}}\right) \times \left[1 - \frac{1}{\left(1 + \frac{r}{2}\right)^{2n}}\right] + \frac{M}{\left(1 + \frac{r}{2}\right)^{2n}}$$

EXAMPLE

The Peterson Fishing Co. issues a three-year bond that offers a 6% coupon rate paid semiannually. This means that the annual coupon equals $60, and there are two $30 payments each year. Suppose that 6% per year is also the market's required return on Peterson bonds. The market price of the bonds equals

$$PV \text{ of coupons} = \left(\frac{\$30}{0.03}\right) \times \left[1 - \frac{1}{(1.03)^6}\right] = \$162.52$$

$$PV \text{ of principal} = \frac{\$1,000}{(1.03)^6} = \$837.48$$

$$\text{Price of bond} = \$162.52 + \$837.48 = \$1,000$$

In Excel, the solution is the same as with annual payments except that the rate and the size of the payment are cut in half and the number of periods doubles. To calculate the price of Peterson's bonds in Excel, simply type = PV(0.03,6,−30,−1000,0).

---

[4]The yield to maturity on a bond is typically quoted like an annual percentage rate. That is, the bond's annual YTM equals the semiannual yield times 2. This implies that the effective annual YTM is slightly above the quoted YTM.

FINANCING
Dental/Medical
BILLS

Finance in Your Life

How Much House Can You Afford?

Before they begin their home search, most homebuyers, particularly first-time buyers, need to estimate how expensive a home they can afford. Many lenders require that the monthly mortgage payment plus monthly payments for property taxes and homeowners insurance cannot exceed 28% of the borrower's monthly gross income. You would also like to make a down payment equal to at least 20% of your home's value. To keep things simple, we will assume that there are no closing costs, that loan payments are made at the *end* of each month, and that you have made the following estimates of the relevant values.

Monthly gross income (annual income $87,500 ÷ 12)	$7,292
Estimated monthly property taxes and insurance	$300
Approximate average monthly interest rate on mortgage loan (annual rate 7.00% ÷ 12)	0.58333%
Planned term of mortgage	360 months
Down payment	20% of purchase price
Funds available for making down payment	$50,000

Using your estimates, we can calculate *how expensive a home you can currently afford.* Remember, the amount that you borrow must equal the present value of the loan payments that you will make over the next 30 years (360 months), and the value of the home that you buy must equal the sum of your down payment and your mortgage.

Maximum allowable monthly housing expense
$$= 0.28 \times \$7,292 = \$2,042$$
Maximum monthly loan payment = housing expense − taxes and insurance
$$= \$2,042 − \$300 = \$1,742$$

[Using Eq. 3.7]   Maximum loan amount = *PV* of 360 monthly payments of $1,742
$$= (\$1,742 ÷ 0.0058333) \times [1 − (1 ÷ 1.0058333^{360})]$$
$$= \$298,630 \times 0.87679$$
$$= \$261,836$$

1. Maximum purchase price based on monthly income = $261,836 + $50,000 = $311,836
2. Maximum purchase price based on down payment = $50,000 ÷ 0.20 = $250,000

The maximum purchase price is the lower of 1 and 2 above. Although your assumed income would support a $261,836 mortgage resulting in a maximum purchase price of about $311,836, you only have enough funds for a down payment on a $250,000 home. Therefore, with the given values you can afford a $250,000 home.

Because this bond offers investors a return exactly equal to the required rate in the market, the bond sells at par value.[5]

Again, we emphasize the fundamental lesson: *the price of a bond equals the present value of its future cash flows.* We now turn to a more in-depth development of the concepts underlying bond valuation, starting with a discussion of interest rate risk.

4-2d Bond Prices and Interest Rates

A bond's market price changes frequently as time passes. Whether a bond sells at a discount or a premium, its price will converge to par value (plus the final interest payment) as the maturity date draws near. Imagine a bond that matures one day from now. The bond's final cash flow consists of its par value plus the last coupon payment. If this payment arrives just one day in the future, you determine the bond's price by discounting this payment for one day. Therefore, the price and the final payment are virtually identical.

---

[5]Notice, too, that the effective annual yield on this bond is slightly higher than the 6% coupon rate. If the semiannual yield is 3%, the effective annual yield equals 6.09% ($1.03^2 − 1$).

interest rate risk
The risk resulting from changes in market interest rates causing fluctuations in a bond's price. Also, the risk of suffering losses as a result of unanticipated changes in market interest rates.

Interest Rate Risk Between the time that a bond is issued and when it matures, a variety of economic forces can change its price, but the most important factor is the prevailing market interest rate. When the market's required return on a bond changes, the bond's price changes in the opposite direction. The higher the bond's required return, the lower its price, and vice versa. Interest rate risk is the risk resulting from changes in market interest rates causing changes in bond prices. How much a bond's price responds to changes in required returns (and therefore how much interest rate risk is associated with a particular bond) depends on several factors, especially the bond's maturity.

Figure 4.2 shows how the prices of two bonds change as their required returns change. Both bonds pay a 6% coupon, but one matures in two years, whereas the other matures in ten years. As the figure shows, when the required return equals the coupon rate, 6%, both bonds trade at par. However, as the required return increases, the bonds' prices fall. The decline in the ten-year bond's price exceeds that of the two-year bond. Likewise, as the required return decreases, the prices of both bonds increase. But the ten-year bond's price increases faster than does that of the two-year bond. The general lessons are *(1) bond prices and interest rates move in opposite directions, and (2) the prices of long-term bonds display greater sensitivity to changes in interest rates than do the prices of short-term bonds.*[6]

Forces Driving Interest Rate Risk Figure 4.2 illustrates the importance of interest rate risk—the risk that results from changes in market interest rates moving bond prices. Figure 4.3 shows just how volatile interest rates have been in the United States.

Figure 4.2   **The Relationship Between Bond Prices and Required Returns for Bonds with Differing Times to Maturity but the Same 6% Coupon Rate**

Bond prices move in the opposite direction of market interest rates. This figure shows that the prices of two-year and ten-year bonds fall as the required return rises (and vice versa), but the magnitude of this effect is much greater for the ten-year bond. Typically, long-term bond prices are much more sensitive to rate changes than short-term bond prices are.

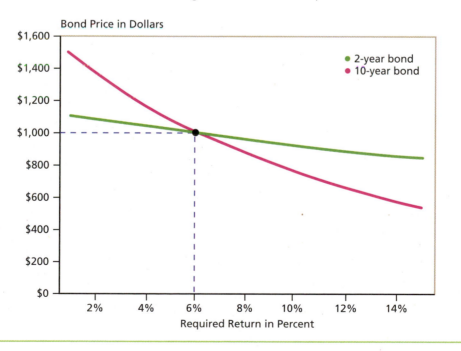

[6]Another more technical factor affecting the bond price changes in response to changes in interest rates is the magnitude of the coupon rate. All else being equal, the value of a bond with a lower coupon rate will be more responsive to changes in interest rates than will a bond with a higher coupon rate. This occurs because a given change in interest rates, say 1%, would represent a greater percentage rate change for a low coupon bond (e.g., 16.7% [1%/6%] change for a 6% coupon bond) than for a higher coupon bond (e.g., 12.5% [1%/8%] change for an 8% coupon bond).

Figure 4.3   **Treasury Bond Yields and Inflation Rates 1955–2010**

This figure shows how volatile interest rates have been over time and how inflation is one underlying cause of the volatility. The blue line shows the yield to maturity (YTM) on a ten-year Treasury bond, and the red bars show the rate of inflation each year. Bond yields are generally a little higher than inflation because investors want to earn a positive real rate of return. Because changes in interest rates cause bond prices to fluctuate, bond investors must be aware of interest rate risk.

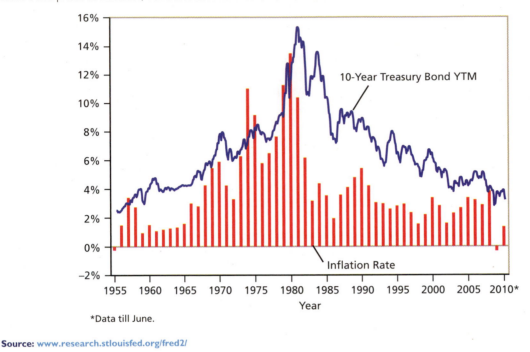

*Data till June.

Source: www.research.stlouisfed.org/fred2/

The blue line plots the historical YTM on ten-year U.S. government bonds.[7] The yields offered by these bonds peaked in 1981 at almost 14%, but recently Treasury bond yields have been much lower. The point of the graph is simple—because interest rates fluctuate widely, investors must be cognizant of the interest rate risk inherent in these instruments.

Inflation and Interest Rates One of the main factors causing interest rate movements is inflation, which is a rise in the prices of goods and services. When investors buy financial assets, they expect these investments to provide a return that exceeds the inflation rate. This is important because people want a better standard of living from saving and investing their money. If asset returns only keep up with inflation, then investors are not better off for investing their funds. To illustrate, say you want to expand your DVD collection. You have $150 to spend, and each DVD costs $15, so you can purchase ten new DVDs. Or suppose you save your money and invest it in an asset earning a 10% return. You reason that after one year, you will have $165 ($150 × 1.10), and with that you can buy eleven DVDs rather than ten. But imagine that while your money is invested, the price of DVDs increases by 10% from $15 to $16.50. Thus at the end of the year, your $165 enables you to purchase just ten DVDs, exactly what you could have purchased a year earlier. In real terms, you are no better off at the end of the year than you were at the start.

The lesson is that bond yields must offer investors a positive **real return**. The real return on an investment plus the inflation rate *approximately* equals the stated or **nominal return**. Mathematically, if *r* equals the nominal interest rate, *i* equals the inflation rate, and r_{real} equals the real rate, the *nominal interest rate formula* is:

real return
The inflation-adjusted return. Approximately equal to the difference between an investment's stated or nominal return and the inflation rate.

nominal return
The stated return offered by an investment; includes the real return plus any additional return due to expected inflation.

---

[7]We discuss the specific features of Treasury securities later in this chapter. The blue line in Figure 4.3 shows what the yield to maturity was on a newly issued ten-year Treasury bond, in each year from 1955 to 2010. In other words, at each point on the graph, you are looking at the yield on a bond with a constant maturity of ten years.

$$(1 + r) = (1 + i)(1 + r_{real})$$

(Eq. 4.4)

$$r = i + r_{real} + i \times r_{real}$$

Notice that the last term in the previous equation is the product of the inflation rate and the real interest rate. When both of these rates are relatively low, their product is very small, so we often ignore that term and simply express the nominal interest rate as (approximately) the sum of the inflation rate and the real interest rate:

(Eq. 4.4a)

$$r \approx i + r_{real}$$

In the DVD illustration, the nominal rate of return on your investment is 10%, but so is the inflation rate, so the investment's real return is zero. To earn a positive real return, the nominal return on the investment would need to be greater than 10%.

EXAMPLE

The approximation in Equation 4.4 is relatively accurate as long as neither the real rate nor the inflation rate is very high. For example, in the summer of 2010, the nominal interest rate on government bonds in Spain was about 4.25%, and the rate of inflation was about 1.25%. Plug these values into Equation 4.4 and solve for the real interest rate

$$(1 + 0.0425) = (1 + 0.0125)(1 + r_{real})$$

$$r_{real} = 0.0296 \text{ or } 2.96\%$$

This is almost exactly equal to the approximate value for the real rate obtained from Equation 4.4a

$$0.0425 \approx 0.0125 + r_{real}$$

$$r_{real} \approx 0.03 \text{ or } 3\%$$

Now consider the situation in India, where the inflation rate stood at 14% in May 2010. Suppose an investment in India offered a nominal return of 17%, so the approximate real return from Equation 4.4a would be 3%, the same real return offered on Spanish bonds at the time:

$$0.17 \approx 0.14 + r_{real}$$

$$r_{real} \approx 0.03 \text{ or } 3\%$$

However, if we use Equation 4.4 to find the exact value of the real interest rate, we find that the approximation in Equation 4.4a overstates the real rate by more than one-third of a percentage point.

$$(1 + 0.17) = (1 + 0.14)(1 + r_{real})$$

$$r_{real} = 0.0263 \text{ or } 2.63\%$$

In most cases, Equation 4.4a provides a reasonably close approximation for the real rate of return, but be aware that the quality of that approximation declines as the inflation rate or the real interest rate rises.

Look again at Figure 4.3. The red bars plot the annual rate of inflation. The graph shows that interest rates were high in 1980 because inflation was also high. Over the past two decades, as the inflation rate gradually fell, so did interest rates. Bonds are generally priced to offer a positive real return, so nominal interest rates are high when inflation is high, as was the case around 1980, and rates are low when inflation is low.[8]

Expected Inflation and Real Interest Rates Figure 4.3 clearly shows a connection between interest rates and the inflation rate. Even when the inflation rate remains constant, however, market interest rates can change. Consider the period 1992–1997. Figure 4.3 shows that during that time, the rate of inflation barely moved, hovering around 2.5% to 3.0%. Over the same time, 10-year Treasury bond yields were much more volatile. For example, from October 1993 to November 1994, bond yields rose from 5.3% to 8.0%. If inflation was essentially unchanged during this period, why did interest rates rise?

---

[8]In Figure 4.3, it appears that real interest rates were negative in 1974–75 and again in 1979–80. Keep in mind that if an investor buys a ten-year bond and holds it to maturity, the real return depends on the inflation that occurs *over* the bond's life. The figure simply plots the yields on ten-year bonds when they are issued against the inflation rate in that year.

There are at least two possible answers. First, when investors decide whether they want to purchase a bond that offers a particular interest rate, what matters to them is not what the past inflation rate *has been*, but rather what the inflation rate *will be* over the bond's life. To determine whether the nominal rate of return on a bond is high enough to provide a reasonable real return, investors must estimate how much inflation they *expect* in the future. Even if inflation in the recent past has been relatively stable, bond yields may rise if investors expect inflation to accelerate.

A second reason that interest rates may fluctuate, even when inflation remains unchanged, is that the real return required by investors may change. If the real rate rises while inflation (or expected inflation) remains steady, bond yields will increase. The real return required by investors may fluctuate with the overall state of the economy as investors' willingness to accept risk changes.

EXAMPLE

It is early 2011, and with the economy still recovering from the last recession, most investors expect very low inflation, perhaps 1% per year. Still-cautious investors are willing to buy Treasury bonds as long as they offer a real return of 2%, so using Equation 4.4a, we would expect nominal Treasury bond yields to be approximately 3% (1% inflation + 2% real return).

Imagine that by 2012 the economy is growing rapidly again. Investors still expect just 1% inflation, but now their investment alternatives are much more attractive, and they will only hold Treasury bonds if they offer a real return of 4%. Under these conditions, the nominal yield on Treasuries must rise to approximately 5% (1% inflation + 4% real return).

Changes in Issuer Risk When macroeconomic factors change, yields may change simultaneously on a wide range of bonds. But the market's required return on a particular bond can also change because the market reassesses the borrower's **default risk**, the risk that the issuer may not make all scheduled payments. For example, if investors perceive that a certain bond issuer is experiencing financial problems that could make it difficult for it to repay its debts, the required return will increase and the price of the issuer's bonds will fall. Conversely, when the market is more optimistic about a bond issuer's financial health, the required return will fall and the issuer's outstanding bonds will increase in value.

default risk
The risk that the bond issuer may not make all scheduled payments.

EXAMPLE

In the spring and summer of 2010, investors around the world became increasingly concerned about the financial condition of Greece. Large, sustained budget deficits produced an accumulated debt that was greater than the nation's Gross Domestic Product (GDP). From December 2009 to April 2010, yields on 10-year Greek government bonds rose from 4% to 7% as fears mounted that Greece would not be able to fully repay its debt. To see the impact that such an increase in yields would have on bond prices, suppose that in November 2009 Greece issued a 10-year bond paying a 4% coupon (two semiannual payments of €20). Because the coupon rate and the market's required return were both 4% in November, the bonds sold at par for €1,000. Six months later, just after the first coupon payment, investors required a 7% return on Greek bonds, so the price of the bonds issued the prior November would be (using Equation 4.3a):

$$P_0 = \frac{€20}{0.035} \times \left[1 - \frac{1}{(1 + 0.035)^{19}} \right] + \frac{€1,000}{(1 + 0.035)^{19}} = €794.35$$

In just six months, the market price of these bonds dropped €205.65, or more than 20%.

Fortunately, the same effect can work in reverse. In May 2010, the European Union announced a €100 billion rescue package for Greece. Combined with austerity measures put into place by the Greek government, the bailout plan seemed to calm the markets, at least to some extent, and Greek bond yields returned to the 4% range. That meant the price of the 10-year Greek bond sold the prior November would once again return to par value.

You might argue that this entire discussion is irrelevant if an investor holds a bond to maturity. If a bond is held to maturity, there is a good chance that the investor will receive all interest and principal payments as promised, so any price decrease (or increase) that occurs between the purchase date and the maturity date is just a "paper loss." Though the tax code may ignore investment gains and losses until investors realize them, financial economists argue that losses matter, whether investors realize them by selling assets or whether the losses exist only on paper. For example, when the Greek bond's value falls from €1,000 to €794.35, an investor holding the bond experiences an opportunity loss. Because the bond's price has fallen, the investor no longer has the opportunity to invest €1,000 elsewhere.

4-2 Concept Review Questions

5. How is a bond's coupon rate different from its *coupon (current) yield*?

6. In general, when will a bond sell at a *discount*?

7. Explain the meaning of the term *interest rate risk*.

8. Why do bond prices and bond yields move in opposite directions?

4-3 | Types of Bonds

The variety of bonds trading in modern financial markets is truly remarkable. In this section, we offer a brief description of the most common types of bonds available today. Many investors see bonds as a rather unexciting investment that provides a steady, predictable stream of income. That description fits some bonds reasonably well, but many bonds are designed with exotic features that make their returns as volatile and unpredictable as shares of common stock.

Bond trading occurs in either the primary or secondary market. *Primary market* trading refers to the initial sale of bonds by firms or government entities. Primary market trading varies depending on the type of bond being considered. For example, the U.S. Treasury sells bonds through an auction process. Most bonds sold at Treasury auctions go to a relatively small group of authorized government bond dealers, though individual investors can participate in Treasury auctions, too. When corporations and state and local government bodies issue bonds in the primary market, they do so with the help of *investment bankers*. Investment bankers assist bond issuers with the design, marketing, and distribution of new bond issues.

Once bonds are issued in the primary market, investors trade them with each other in the *secondary market*. However, many bonds issued in the primary market are purchased by institutional investors who hold the bonds for a long time. As a result, secondary market trading in bonds can be somewhat limited. For instance, if General Motors raises money by conducting a new bond offering, it is likely that their bonds will not trade as actively as General Motors common stock does. Although some specific bond issues do not trade a great deal once they are issued, the sheer size of the bond market means that investors interested in adding bonds to their portfolio have a wide range of choices. We now turn to an overview of the choices available to bond investors. There are several ways to structure an overview of the bond market, beginning with the types of bond issuers.

4-3a By Issuer

corporate bonds
Bonds issued by corporations.

Bonds come in many varieties and are classified in different ways. Perhaps the simplest classification scheme puts bonds into categories based upon the identity of the issuer. Large companies who need money to finance new investments and to fulfill other needs issue corporate bonds. Corporations issue bonds with maturities ranging from 1 to 100 years. When a company issues a debt instrument with a maturity of one to ten years, that instrument is usually called a *note* rather than a bond, but notes and bonds are essentially identical instruments. *Most corporate bonds have a par value of $1,000 and pay interest semiannually.* The corporate bond market is enormous, with more than $11 trillion outstanding in 2010.

municipal bonds
Issued by U.S. state and local governments. Interest received on these bonds is exempt from federal income tax.

Municipal bonds are bonds issued by U.S. state and local government entities. In the United States, federal law gives state and local governments a significant break by exempting interest received on municipal bonds from the bondholder's federal income tax. Obviously, this makes municipal bonds especially attractive to investors

What Companies Do Globally

Belgian CFOs Find Bond Issues Attractive

A quarterly survey by Deloitte Consulting asks Chief Financial Officers (CFOs) of Belgian firms how attractive they find various sources of funding for their firms. The graph below shows how CFOs responded during 2009 and early 2010. Specifically, the graph plots the difference between the percentage of CFOs saying that bond issues are attractive and those reporting that bond issues are unattractive in each quarter. In the first half of 2009, the global economy was in the depths of a severe recession. Not surprisingly, Belgian CFOs found it difficult to borrow money by issuing bonds in such an environment. But, as central banks took actions to lower interest rates to spark economic growth and signs of recovery began to emerge, CFOs were more interested in selling bonds. By early 2010, a majority of CFOs believed that raising funds by selling bonds was an attractive financing option for their firms.

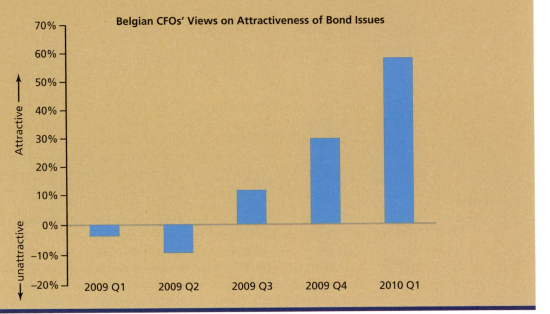

Belgian CFOs' Views on Attractiveness of Bond Issues

who face high tax rates. For instance, suppose a corporate bond selling at par offers an investor a coupon rate of 6%. If the investor's tax rate on interest income is 33%, then the after-tax return on this bond would be 4% [6% × (1 − 33%)]. Now suppose there is a municipal bond that is no more or less risky than the corporate bond, and it offers a return of 4%. Because this return is tax-free, the municipal bond's 4% return is competitive with the return offered by the corporate bond on an after-tax basis. To put this another way, the tax exemption on municipal bond interest allows state and local governments to raise money at lower interest rates than they would otherwise be able to do. State and local governments take advantage of this subsidy, with more than $2.4 trillion in municipal bonds outstanding in July 2010.

EXAMPLE

The Jobs and Growth Tax Reconciliation Act of 2003 reduced the federal income tax rate faced by most middle- and upper-income taxpayers by 2 to 3 percentage points. However, this tax cut was set to expire after 2010. What effect might we expect the return to higher tax rates in 2011 to have on the municipal bond markets?

In mid 2010, the yield on a high-quality corporate bond with a 5-year maturity was about 2.1%. For an investor whose marginal federal income tax rate was 35%, a 2.1% pre-tax yield would translate into an after-tax return of 1.365%:

$$2.1\% \times (1 - 0.35) = 1.365\%$$

This means that to the investor, the 2.1% yield on a (taxable) corporate bond was equivalent to a 1.365% yield on a (nontaxable) municipal bond.

continued

In 2011, if this investor's tax rate increased to 38.6%, the top rate in the pre-2003 tax code, then the after-tax yield on the corporate bond would fall to 1.289% (holding the pre-tax yield constant at 2.1%):

$$2.1\% \times (1 - 0.386) = 1.289\%$$

In other words, the investor is now indifferent between a corporate bond paying 2.1% and a municipal bond paying 1.289% (compared to 1.365% with the lower tax rate). In short, higher tax rates make municipal bonds more attractive, meaning that, holding all else constant, a tax increase should lower the yields and increase the prices of municipal bonds.[9]

Treasury bills

Debt instruments issued by the federal government with maturities ranging from a few days to up to 52 weeks.

Treasury notes

Debt instruments issued by the federal government with maturities ranging from two to ten years.

Treasury bonds

Debt instruments issued by the federal government that mature in thirty years.

agency bonds

Bonds issued by federal government agencies. Agency bonds are not explicitly backed by the full faith and credit of the U.S. government. Agencies issue bonds to provide credit for certain sectors of the economy such as farming, real estate, and education.

The largest single issuer of bonds is the U.S. government. The debt instruments issued by the government range in maturity from a few weeks to twenty years. Treasury bills are debt instruments with maturities of a few days up to 52 weeks. The maturities of Treasury notes range from two to ten years. The government also issues Treasury bonds that mature in 30 years. The federal government issues these instruments to raise money to cover budget deficits, and these securities are backed by the "full faith and credit" of the United States. This pledge means investors generally regard Treasury bills, notes, and bonds as very safe investments, although large, persistent budget deficits prompted one rating agency, Standard and Poor's, to lower their rating on U.S. government securities in August 2011. As with all bonds, Treasury bond prices can fluctuate as market interest rates change. Interest from Treasury securities is subject to federal income tax but not state income tax.

Some federal government agencies issue their own bonds, called agency bonds, to finance operations. Agency debt is not explicitly backed by the full faith and credit of the Treasury, so investors recognize that agency debt carries a small amount of additional risk relative to Treasury securities. In July 2010, the amount of agency debt outstanding was approximately $7.8 trillion. The government charters these agencies with the task of providing credit for certain sectors of the economy such as farming, real estate, and education. The Federal Home Loan Bank (FHLB), the Federal National Mortgage Association (FNMA or "Fannie Mae"), the Government National Mortgage Association (GNMA or "Ginnie Mae"), and the Federal Home Loan Mortgage Corporation (FHLMC or "Freddie Mac") are the major mortgage-related agencies that issue bonds. In 2007–2008, Fannie Mae and Freddie Mac experienced severe financial difficulties as defaults on home mortgages began to rise. These problems became serious enough that, in September 2008, the government effectively took over these two institutions by placing them into conservatorship. At the time, these two entities had more than $5 trillion in debt.

In this section, our focus has been on bond issues. Why do firms and government entities sell bonds? The simple answer is that bond issuers need money—money to finance a deficit, to build public infrastructure, or to pay for expanded manufacturing facilities. An important characteristic that distinguishes corporations from government entities is that when the latter group needs to issue a security to raise funds, they are essentially limited to issuing a bond or other debt instrument. Corporations, on the other hand, can issue either debt (bonds) or equity (stock).

Debt securities offer a series of cash payments that are, for the most part, contractually fixed. The cash payout that bond investors expect from a firm generally does not fluctuate each quarter as the firm's earnings do, and if a firm fails to live up to its promise to make interest and principal payments, bondholders can take legal action against the company and force it into bankruptcy court.

In contrast, common stock, which we cover in the next chapter, represents an ownership or equity claim on the firm's cash flows. Unlike bondholders, stockholders generally have the right to vote on corporate matters ranging from electing a board of directors to approving mergers and acquisitions. However, stockholders have no specific legal entitlement to receive periodic cash payments. Whether stockholders receive any cash payments at all depends on the firm's profitability and on the board of directors' decision to distribute cash to investors.

---

[9]Obviously there are many other factors that influence yields on corporate and municipal bonds, so we would stop short of predicting that a tax hike will create a rally in the municipal bond market. However, higher taxes should generally increase the difference between taxable corporate bond yields and tax-free municipal bond yields.

As we will see, some bonds have features that put them into a gray area between pure debt and equity. In the rest of this section, we discuss a wide range of bond features commonly observed in the corporate bond market.

4-3b By Features

Fixed versus Floating Rates As we have already discussed, most bonds require the borrower to make periodic coupon payments and to repay the bond's face value at maturity. The coupon payments themselves may be fixed in dollar terms over the bond's life, or the coupons may adjust occasionally, if the benchmark market interest rate changes while the bond is outstanding. Floating-rate bonds, also called *variable-rate bonds,* provide some protection against interest rate risk. If market interest rates increase, then eventually, so do the bond's coupon payments. Of course this makes the borrowers' future cash obligations somewhat unpredictable, because the *interest rate risk* of floating-rate bonds is effectively transferred from the buyer to the issuer.

The interest rate on floating-rate bonds is typically tied to a widely quoted market interest rate. Several benchmark interest rates that are often used to determine how a floating-rate bond's interest rate changes over time are the one-year Treasury rate, the prime rate, and the London Interbank Offered Rate. The prime rate is the interest rate charged by large U.S. banks to "prime" customers, usually businesses that have an excellent record of repaying their debts on time. The London Interbank Offered Rate (LIBOR) is a rate at which large banks can borrow from one another, and it is perhaps the most common benchmark interest rate for short-term debt. The equivalent of LIBOR in the United States is the federal funds rate, the rate for overnight lending between banks.

The interest rate on floating-rate bonds is typically specified by starting with one of the benchmark rates above and then adding a spread. The spread, also called the *credit spread,* is added to the benchmark interest rate, according to the risk of the borrower. Lenders charge higher spreads for less creditworthy borrowers.

floating-rate bonds
Bonds that make coupon payments that vary through time. The coupon payments are usually tied to a benchmark market interest rate. Also called *variable-rate bonds.*

prime rate
The rate of interest charged by large U.S. banks on loans to business borrowers with excellent credit records.

London Interbank Offered Rate (LIBOR)
The interest rate that large banks charge each other for overnight loans. Widely used as a benchmark interest rate for short-term floating-rate debt.

federal funds rate
The interest rate that U.S. banks charge each other for overnight loans.

EXAMPLE

In February 2010, Warren Buffett's firm, Berkshire Hathaway, issued $8 billion in floating-rate debt priced at up to 45 basis points (one basis point = 1/100th of 1%) over LIBOR. The proceeds of this offering were used to finance the acquisition of Burlington Northern Santa Fe Corp. With LIBOR at roughly 0.25%, Berkshire Hathaway would pay an interest rate starting at about 0.70%, but that rate could move up or down with changes in LIBOR.

spread
The difference between the rate that a lender charges for a loan and the underlying benchmark interest rate. Also called the *credit spread.*

Treasury Inflation-Protected Securities (TIPS)
Notes and bonds issued by the federal government that make coupon payments that vary with the U.S. inflation rate.

In addition to the fixed-rate notes and bonds, the U.S. Treasury also offers a floating-rate debt instrument called Treasury Inflation-Protected Securities (TIPS). The Treasury sells TIPS with maturities of five, ten, and thirty years. Rather than make coupon payments tied to a specific market interest rate like LIBOR, TIPS pay a variable coupon that depends on the U.S. inflation rate. Some investors find TIPS attractive because, as their name implies, they offer a return that is protected against unexpected increases in inflation. For example, suppose an investor buys a ten-year inflation-indexed note with a par value of $1,000 and a coupon rate of 2%. With no inflation, the investor will receive a coupon payment of $10 (2% × $1,000 × ½) every six months. However, say that in the first six months after the investor bought this note, the United States experienced a 10% increase in prices (i.e., a 10% inflation rate). When the first coupon payment is due, the U.S. Treasury increases the note's par value by the inflation rate, from $1,000 to $1,100. The 2% coupon rate then applies to the new principal value. The first coupon payment will be $11 (2% × $1,100 × ½). Notice that the coupon payment increases at the rate of inflation (from $10 to $11, a 10% increase). This means that TIPS offer investors a constant *real* coupon rather than the constant *nominal* coupon guaranteed by ordinary Treasury securities.[10]

---

[10]TIPS have proven to be so popular with investors that some corporations have recently offered their own inflation-indexed bonds to investors.

EXAMPLE

Earlier in this chapter, we learned that the nominal rate of interest on a bond consists of two components: the real return and the (expected) inflation rate. With most bonds, we can only observe what the nominal rate is. The rate of inflation expected by investors is an unknown and, therefore, so is the real return. However, with TIPS it is possible to see these components.

First, recognize that the coupon rate on TIPS reflects a real return because the principal value adjusts for inflation. In other words, if the TIPS coupon rate is 2%, the investors know that they will receive a 2% return after adjusting for inflation because any inflation that occurs will simply increase the principal upon which the 2% coupon is paid.

Second, if the yield on an ordinary (non-indexed) Treasury bond is a nominal yield while the yield on a TIPS is the real return, then we can estimate what rate of inflation investors expect simply by subtracting the TIPS yield from the ordinary bond yield.

$$\text{Ordinary bond yield} = \text{real return} + \text{expected inflation}$$

$$\text{TIPS bond yield} = \text{real return}$$

$$\text{Ordinary yield} - \text{TIPS yield} = \text{expected inflation}[11]$$

Figure 4.4 plots the yield on an ordinary 10-year Treasury bond (green line), the yield on a 10-year inflation-indexed bond (red line), and the difference between them (shaded area). The shaded area represents the rate of inflation expected by participants in the Treasury bond market. The graph shows that from 2003 to early the summer of 2008, yields on ordinary Treasury bonds fluctuated between 4 and 5%, while yields on indexed bonds moved between 2 and 3%. The difference in yields remained relatively steady around 2.5%, indicating that investors' inflation expectations were fairly stable. But in the second half of 2008, as the financial crisis worsened and the U.S. economy weakened, investors' inflation expectations plummeted, reaching a low point of 0.25% in December 2008. Keep in mind that the shaded area in the graph represents the rate of inflation expected over the 10-year life of these bonds. Near the end of 2008, investors were indeed very pessimistic about the state of the economy.

Figure 4.4

The figure shows yields on ordinary and inflation-indexed Treasury bonds from 2003–2010. The difference in yields between these two instruments provides a measure of investors' inflation expectations.

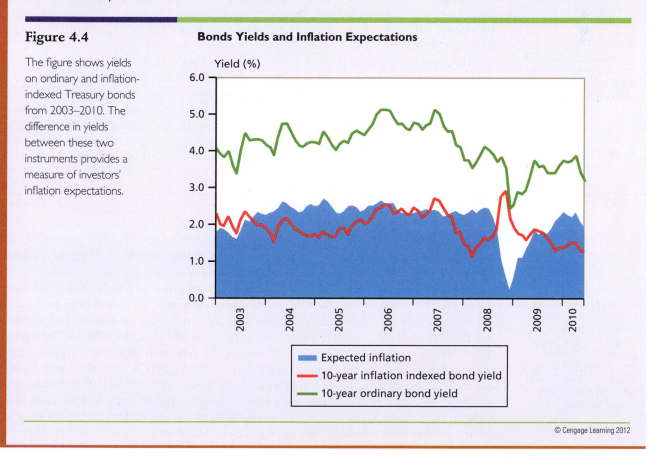

Bonds Yields and Inflation Expectations

© Cengage Learning 2012

---

[11]The difference in yields actually provides only an approximation of the expected inflation rate because other factors, such as taxes and liquidity, influence the yields of ordinary and indexed bonds. Furthermore, because investors cannot predict inflation perfectly, they should demand an inflation risk premium on ordinary Treasury bonds that do not provide inflation protection. That is, an ordinary Treasury bond's yield consists of the real return, the expected inflation rate, and a small risk premium because actual inflation may not equal expected inflation.

debenture
An unsecured bond backed only by the general faith and credit of the borrowing company.

subordinated debenture
An unsecured bond that has a legal claim inferior to, or subordinate to, other outstanding bonds.

collateral
The assets pledged to secure a loan.

mortgage bond
A bond secured by real estate or buildings.

collateral trust bond
A bond secured by financial assets held by a trustee.

equipment trust certificate
A bond often secured by various types of transporation equipment.

pure discount bond
Bonds that pay no interest and sell below par value. Also called *zero-coupon bond.*

Secured versus Unsecured What assurances do lenders have that borrowers will fulfill their obligations to make interest and principal payments on time? In the case of *unsecured debt*, the only assurance is the borrower's promise to repay, combined with the recourse offered by the legal system if the borrower does not make all promised payments. An unsecured corporate bond is usually called a debenture, which is backed only by the general faith and credit of the borrowing company. If a corporation has conducted more than one offering of debentures, some issues may have a lower priority claim than others. The term subordinated debentures refers to unsecured bonds that have legal claims inferior to, or subordinate to, other outstanding bonds. The terms *senior* and *junior* describe the relative standing of different bond issues, with senior bonds having a higher priority claim than junior bonds.

In some cases, however, firms pledge collateral when they issue bonds. Collateral refers to assets the bondholders can legally claim if a borrower defaults on a loan. When a bond is backed by collateral, we say that the bond is *secured*. Examples of secured bonds are mortgage bonds, which are bonds secured by real estate or buildings; collateral trust bonds, which are bonds secured by financial assets held by a trustee; and equipment trust certificates, which are bonds that are often secured by various types of transportation equipment.

Zero-Coupon Bonds Most bonds make periodic interest payments called coupons, but a few bonds, called *zero-coupon bonds*, pay no interest at all. Why would anyone purchase a bond that pays no interest? The incentive to purchase zero-coupon bonds is that they sell below face value. For that reason, zero-coupon bonds are also called discount bonds or pure discount bonds.[12] An investor who purchases a discount bond receives a capital gain when the bond matures and pays its face value.

The best-known example of a pure discount bond is a U.S. *Treasury bill*, or *T-bill*. T-bills are issued by the U.S. government, like Treasury notes and bonds discussed earlier, but they mature in 26 weeks or less, have a par value of $10,000, and distribute cash only at maturity. There are no intermediate coupon payments such as those paid by notes and bonds. For example, the Treasury recently sold a $10,000 face value bill that matures in six months. The selling price of this T-bill was $9,775.70. An investor who purchases the bill and holds it to maturity earns a return of 2.3% over the next six months.

$$\frac{\$10,000 - \$9,775.70}{\$9,775.70} = 0.023 = 2.3\%$$

We can convert that return to an annual rate by multiplying it by 2, so the annual (simple interest) return on the T-bill equals about 4.6%.

Treasury STRIPS
A zero-coupon bond representing a single coupon payment, or the final principal payment, made by an existing Treasury note or bond. The acronym STRIPS stands for Separate Trading of Interest and Principal Securities.

Treasury STRIPS are another example of zero-coupon bonds. The Treasury creates STRIPS by issuing an ordinary coupon-paying note or bond, then stripping off the individual coupon and principal payments the security makes, and allowing them to trade as separate securities. Suppose a five-year, $1,000 par Treasury note offers a coupon rate of 5%. This means the note will make ten coupon payments of $25 each at six-month intervals (5% $\times$ $1,000 $\times$ ½) and one $1,000 payment at maturity. The Treasury can create eleven distinct STRIP securities by selling each of these payments separately. Say an investor pays $765.13 for the right to receive the $1,000 principal payment in five years. Calculate the investor's return on this instrument by solving for its yield to maturity:

$$\$765.13 = \frac{\$1,000}{(1 + r)^5} \qquad r = 0.055, \text{ or } 5.5\%$$

---

[12]Be sure you understand the difference between a pure discount bond—a bond that makes no coupon payments at all—and an ordinary bond that sells at a discount. An ordinary bond sells at a discount when its coupon rate is below the rate of return that investors require to hold the bond.

Table 4.1   **Zero-Coupon Bond Prices and Taxable Income**

Zero-coupon bonds pay no interest, so investors earn their return by purchasing them at a discount and letting their price appreciate over time. This table illustrates how the price of a $1,000 par value discount bond rises as maturity approaches, assuming that the yield to maturity remains at 5.5%. The last column shows the investor's capital gain each year.

Years to Maturity	Yield to Maturity	Bond Price	Capital Gain
5	0.055	$ 765.13	
4	0.055	$ 807.22	$42.09
3	0.055	$ 851.61	$44.39
2	0.055	$ 898.45	$46.84
1	0.055	$ 947.87	$49.42
0	0.055	$1,000.00	$52.13

Special tax rules apply to zero-coupon bonds. In the United States, the Internal Revenue Service recognizes that capital gains, which accrue to owners of zero-coupon bonds, are a kind of implicit interest payment. An investor in zero-coupon bonds must pay taxes on this accrued interest (at ordinary income tax rates) each year, whether or not the investor sells the bond and realizes a gain. Table 4.1 shows how the price of a zero-coupon bond rises as time passes (assuming that the yield to maturity remains fixed at 5.5%) and illustrates the capital gain each year.

Convertible and Exchangeable Bonds Some bonds issued by corporations combine the features of debt and equity. Like ordinary bonds, convertible bonds pay investors a relatively safe stream of fixed coupon payments. But convertible bonds also give investors the option to convert their bonds into the common stock of the firm that issued the bonds.[13] This means that if the stock price increases, bondholders can share in that gain. An example illustrates.

convertible bond
A bond that gives investors the option to convert it into the issuer's common stock.

EXAMPLE

The world's largest maker of AIDS drugs, Gilead Sciences, Inc., announced a $2.2 billion sale of convertible notes on July 27, 2010. The notes offered a coupon rate of just 1%, but investors also received the right to convert each $1,000 par value bond into 22.1845 shares of Gilead common stock. The number of shares into which each bond is convertible is called the *conversion ratio*. At what stock price does it make sense for bondholders to exercise the right to convert their bonds into shares? Consider that each bond is worth $1,000 or 22.1845 times Gilead's stock price. The break-even point occurs when Gilead's stock price equals $45.08 ($1,000 ÷ 22.1845). At any lower price, bondholders are better off taking $1,000 in cash, but at any higher price, the shares are worth more than the bonds' face value. Moreover, there is no upper limit to the return that Gilead convertible bonds can earn. Once the price of Gilead stock exceeds $45.08, each additional $1 increase in the stock price is worth $22.1845 to bondholders. At the time the bonds were issued, Gilead's stock was valued at $33.39, so the stock price would have to rise by at least 35% before bondholders would want to convert. That 35% is known as the *conversion premium*.

exchangeable bond
Bonds issued by corporations which may be converted into shares of a company other than the company that issued the bonds.

Exchangeable bonds work in much the same way that convertible bonds do, except that exchangeable bonds are convertible into common shares of a company other than the company that issued the bonds. Exchangeable bonds' are often used when one company owns a large block of stock in another firm that it wants to divest. Although the option to convert bonds into shares generally resides with the investor who holds a convertible bond, exchangeable bonds' conversion rights can vary. Sometimes the bond indenture requires that, at maturity, bondholders accept common stock in the underlying firm. In that case, the securities are called *mandatory exchangeable bonds*.

callable (bonds)
Bonds that the issuer can repurchase from investors at a predetermined price known as the *call price*.

Callable and Putable Bonds Most corporate bonds and some government bonds are **callable**. This means that the bond issuer retains the right to repurchase the

---

[13]Some convertibles have a mandatory conversion feature, meaning that the issuer can force investors to convert their bonds into shares.

call price
The price at which a bond issuer may call or repurchase an outstanding bond from investors.

bonds in the future at a predetermined price known as the **call price**. That right is valuable when market interest rates fall. Recall that bond prices generally rise as market interest rates fall. A firm that issued noncallable bonds when rates were high may want to retire those bonds and reissue new ones after a decline in interest rates. However, retiring the outstanding bonds requires paying a significant premium over par value. With callable bonds, the call price establishes an upper limit on how much the firm must pay to redeem previously issued bonds. Investors recognize that the call feature works to the advantage of the bond issuer, so callable bonds must generally offer higher coupon rates than otherwise similar noncallable bonds.

putable bonds
Bonds that investors can sell back to the issuer at a predetermined price under certain conditions.

Putable bonds work in just the opposite way. **Putable bonds** allow investors to sell their bonds back to the issuing firm at a predetermined price under certain conditions. This option is valuable to bondholders because it protects them against a decline in the value of their bonds. Therefore, putable bonds typically have lower coupon rates than otherwise similar nonputable bonds.

Cengage Learning

Annette Poulsen, University of Georgia

"There is a trade-off between flexibility for the corporation and protection for the bondholder."

See the entire interview at **SMART | finance**

Smart Ideas Video

sinking fund
A provision in a *bond indenture* that requires the borrower to make regular payments to a third-party trustee for use in repurchasing outstanding bonds, gradually over time.

Protection from Default Risk Besides interest rate risk, bond investors also have to worry about *default risk*—the possibility that a bond issuer may not be able to make all scheduled interest and principal payments on time and in full. The *bond indenture*, the contract between a bond issuer and its creditors, usually contains a number of provisions designed to protect investors from default risk. We have already discussed some of these features, including a bond issue's seniority and whether it is secured or unsecured. Additional examples of these provisions include sinking funds and protective covenants. A **sinking fund** provision requires the borrower to make regular payments to a third-party trustee. The trustee then uses those funds to repurchase outstanding bonds. Usually sinking fund provisions require the trustee to retire bonds gradually, so that by the time a bond issue's maturity date arrives, only a fraction of the original issue remains outstanding. The trustee may purchase previously issued bonds on the open market, or the trustee may repurchase bonds by exercising a call provision, as described above.

protective covenants
Provisions in a *bond indenture* that specify requirements the borrower must meet (positive covenants) or things the borrower must not do (negative covenants).

Protective covenants, part of the bond indenture, specify requirements that the borrower must meet as long as bonds remain outstanding. *Positive covenants* specify things that the borrower must do. For example, positive covenants may require a borrower to file quarterly audited financial statements, to maintain a minimum amount of working capital, or to maintain a certain level of debt coverage ratios. *Negative covenants* specify things that the borrower must not do, such as pay unusually high dividends, sell off assets, or issue additional senior debt.

Clearly investors have a lot of choices when they consider buying bonds. The number and variety of fixed-income investments available in the market is truly astounding and far exceeds the number of common stocks available for trading. Let us turn now to the bond markets to see how bonds are traded, how bond prices are quoted, and what external information is available to bond traders to help them make investment decisions.

4-3 Concept Review Questions

9. What are the main types of issuers of bonds in the United States?

10. What is the difference between a *pure discount bond* and an ordinary bond that sells at a discount?

11. Explain who benefits from the option to *convert* a bond into shares of common stock, and who benefits from the option to *call* a bond.

4-4   Bond Markets

In terms of the dollar volume of securities traded each day, the bond market is much larger than the stock market. Though some bonds are listed on stock exchanges, most bonds trade in an electronic over-the-counter (OTC) market. The OTC market is not a single physical location where bonds are traded. It is a collection of dealers around the country and around the world who stand ready to buy and sell bonds. Dealers communicate with one another and with investors via an electronic network. Because trades are decentralized and negotiated privately, it is usually difficult to obtain accurate, up-to-date price information on most bonds. Nevertheless, it is useful to see how bond prices are quoted in different segments of the market.

4-4a Bond Price Quotations

Figure 4.5 shows representative price quotes taken from *The Wall Street Journal Online* on Tuesday, July 27, 2010, for the 10 most active investment-grade corporate bonds that traded on Monday, July 26, 2010. The first column lists the issuer's name, followed by the bond's symbol in the second column. The third column lists the bond's coupon interest rate, and the fourth column lists the month and year each bond matures. We'll consider the highlighted Citigroup bond, which has a symbol of "C.HVG," a 4.750% coupon, and maturity date in May 2015. Given the Citigroup bond's $1,000 par value, its 4.750% coupon rate implies that the bond will make two coupon payments of $23.75 each year.

The bond's ratings by each of the three major rating agencies (discussed later) appear in the fifth column. The next three columns, labeled "High," "Low," and "Last," indicate the highest, lowest, and last prices, respectively, that the bond traded on the given day. Note that *bond prices are quoted as a percentage of par values*. In the case of Citigroup, its high, low, and last price quotes on Monday, July 26, 2010, of 104.868, 102.531, and 102.617, respectively translate into

---

Figure 4.5   **Price Quotes for Most Active Investment-Grade Bonds**

The figure shows the coupon; maturity; rating; high price, low price, and last price; change in price; and yield % for the ten most active investment grade bonds traded on Monday, July 26, 2010.

Most Active Investment Grade Bonds

Issuer Name	Symbol	Coupon	Maturity	Rating Moody's/S&P/ Fitch	High	Low	Last	Change	Yield %
BANK OF AMERICA CORP	BAC.BP	5.625%	Jul 2020	A2/A/A+	104.508	102.931	103.552	−1.030	N/A
MORGAN STANLEY	MS.WB	5.625%	Jan 2012	A2/A/A	105.679	104.000	104.250	−0.747	2.607
CITIGROUP	C.HVG	4.750%	May 2015	A3/A/A+	104.868	102.531	102.617	−0.250	4.142
BANK OF AMERICA CORP	BAC.ICB	7.625%	Jun 2019	A2/A/A+	118.854	116.329	117.294	0.638	5.162
MORGAN STANLEY	MS.HPU	5.500%	Jan 2020	A2/A/A	103.750	100.175	100.868	0.514	5.382
LORILLARD TOBACCO CO	LO.GA	8.125%	Jun 2019	Baa2/BBB-/—	113.454	111.199	112.695	1.070	6.243
TIME WARNER	TWX.AY	4.700%	Jan 2021	Baa2/BBB/—	101.819	101.136	101.819	0.383	N/A
LORILLARD TOBACCO CO	LO.GB	6.875%	May 2020	Baa2/BBB-/—	105.318	102.053	103.999	0.863	N/A
WESTPAC BANKING CORP	WBK.IK	2.250%	Nov 2012	Aa1/AA/AA	102.150	101.199	101.237	−0.211	1.700
DIRECTV HLDS	DTV.GR	3.550%	Mar 2015	Baa2/BBB-/BBB-	102.398	101.939	102.335	0.274	3.005

Source: FINRA TRACE data. Reference information from Reuters DataScope Data. Credit ratings from Moody's®, Standard & Poor's, and Fitch Ratings.

$1,048.68 (104.868% × $1,000), $1,025.31 (102.531% × $1,000), and $1,026.17 (102.617% × $1,000). The next-to-last column shows how much the bond's last price has changed (in percentage points) from the previous trading day. Citigroup's bond price decreased by 0.250 percentage points, or $2.50 (0.250% × $1,000), which means its last price on Friday, July 23, 2010, was $1,028.67 ($1,026.17 + $2.50). The final column calculates the bond's yield to maturity, which for the Citigroup bond is 4.142%. To calculate this yield, we use Equation 4.3.

EXAMPLE

Figure 4.5 shows that the Citigroup bond with a coupon rate of 4.750 and maturing in May 2015 has a last price of $1,026.17. The figure lists the yield on this bond at 4.142%. To derive this yield, let us make a simplifying assumption. Figure 4.5 was taken from *The Wall Street Journal Online* on July 27, 2010. For the Citigroup bond, we assume that the most recent coupon payment was just made. This means that the next coupon payment will arrive in six months.[14] Each semiannual coupon payment equals $23.75. We assume that there are 10 coupon payments remaining between now and May 2015, plus the principal repayment at maturity. The last price in dollar terms equals $1,026.17. Now apply Equation 4.3 and use a financial calculator or Excel to find the bond's ask yield to maturity:

$$\$1,026.17 = \frac{\$23.75}{\left(1 + \frac{r}{2}\right)^1} + \frac{\$23.75}{\left(1 + \frac{r}{2}\right)^2} + \cdots + \frac{\$23.75}{\left(1 + \frac{r}{2}\right)^{10}} + \frac{\$1,000}{\left(1 + \frac{r}{2}\right)^{10}}$$

$$r = 0.04165 = 4.165\%$$

Our solution is within 0.023 percentage points (or 2.3 *basis points*) of the yield quoted in Figure 4.5. The slight difference occurs because of our simplifying assumption that the next coupon will arrive in exactly six months.

If you look closely at the ten bonds in Figure 4.5, you will notice an interesting fact: the coupon rate on the Bank of America bond (June 2019 maturity) is 7.625%, while the coupon rate on the Morgan Stanley bond (January 2020 maturity) is more than two percentage points lower at 5.500%. But the yields on these two bonds are much closer together: 5.162% for the Bank of America bond and 5.382% for Morgan Stanley. The variation in coupon rates suggests these bonds may have been issued originally at different times or in different market conditions. The Bank of America bond may have been issued during a period during which market rates were generally much higher than when the Morgan Stanley bond was issued, or perhaps Bank of America's financial condition was much weaker than Morgan Stanley's when the bonds were issued, so investors demanded a higher coupon from Bank of America. Whatever the reason for the difference, the two bonds offered similar yields in July 2010. Notice in the fifth column of Figure 4.5, the risk ratings of the two bonds are quite similar, and column 4 indicates that they mature just six months apart. If the bonds have similar risk and mature at about the same time, it should not be surprising that they offer similar returns to investors. This means that the market's current required return is around 5.25% for bonds like these and that the prices of previously issued bonds with very different coupon rates adjust until they offer competitive yields.

Also notice that all of the bonds sell at a premium. This reflects the extremely low interest rate environment prevailing in the summer of 2010. The Federal Reserve was maintaining historically low interest rates to try to spur economic growth. In Figure 4.5 the bonds selling at the highest premiums [Bank of America (June 2019 maturity) and Lorillard Tobacco (June 2019 maturity)] both had a coupon rate far above the yield to maturity. Morgan Stanley's bond (January 2020 maturity), with a coupon rate less than 12 basis points above its yield to maturity, sold slightly above par value.

yield spread
The difference in yield to maturity between a corporate bond and a Treasury bond at roughly the same maturity.

Traders often refer to the **yield spread** on a particular bond. The yield spread equals the difference in yield to maturity between a corporate bond and a Treasury bond at roughly the same maturity. By convention, yield spreads are quoted in

---

[14]By making an assumption about the timing of this bond's cash flows that is incorrect, we derive a yield that is slightly different from that reported in the figure. However, we stick with our assumption because it allows us to keep the discounting simple, with cash flows arriving exactly every six months.

basis point
1/100 of 1%; 100 basis points equal 1.000%.

terms of **basis points**, where one basis point equals 1/100 of 1% (100 basis points = 1.000%). Because corporate bonds are riskier than Treasury bonds, they offer higher yields, so the yield spread is always a positive number. For example, the yield on a Treasury bond maturing in 2015 was 1.820% on Monday, July 26, 2010. So the yield spread on the Citigroup bond would be 2.322% (4.142% – 1.820%), or 232.2 basis points.

As you might expect, bond yield spreads reflect a direct relationship with default risk. The greater the risk that the borrower may default on its debts, the higher the spread that bonds issued by the borrower must offer investors to compensate them for the risk that they take. For investors, estimating the default risk of a particular bond issue is a crucial element in determining what the required return on the bond should be. Fortunately, bond investors have several resources at their disposal to help them make this evaluation.

JOB INTERVIEW QUESTION

Yield spreads vary through time. Suppose you plot the yield spread on AAA bonds over several years. How would you expect this spread to behave during recessions vs. during economic booms?

bond ratings
Letter ratings assigned to bonds by specialized agencies that evaluate the capacity of bond issuers to repay their debts. Lower ratings signify higher default risk.

junk bonds
Bonds rated below investment grade. Also known as *high-yield bonds*.

WHAT TO ASK

Does your firm try to maintain a target rating on its outstanding debt?

4-4b Bond Ratings

For information on the likelihood that a particular bond issue may default, investors turn to bond rating agencies such as Moody's, Standard & Poor's, and Fitch. These organizations provide an independent assessment of the risk of most publicly traded bond issues, and they assign a letter **bond-rating** to each issue to indicate its degree of risk. Table 4.2 lists the major bond-rating categories provided by each of the agencies and the interpretation associated with each rating class. Bonds rated BBB− or higher by S&P and Fitch, and Baa3 or higher by Moody's fall into the investment-grade category. Bonds rated lower than that are called high-yield, speculative, or **junk bonds**. The term "junk bonds" has a derogatory connotation but simply means that these bonds are riskier than investment-grade bonds. For example, for bonds in the investment grade category, the probability of default is extremely low, perhaps as low as 1%. One study put the probability of a B-rated bond defaulting in its first year at almost 8%.[15]

Table 4.3 shows the relationship between bond ratings and yield spreads for corporate bonds at different maturities at a given point in time.[16] The yield spreads are quoted in *basis points*. The first entry in the top left corner of the table shows a corporate bond with the highest possible Aaa/AAA rating and a maturity of one year. It offered investors a yield to maturity that was just ten basis points higher than a one-year Treasury bill at the given point in time. Moving across the row, we see that yield spreads increase with time to maturity. As expected, yield spreads increase as

Table 4.2   **Bond Ratings**

Bond rating agencies such as Moody's, Standard and Poors, and Fitch assign bond ratings based on their assessment of the borrower's ability to repay. Bonds in the top four ratings categories are investment grade bonds, while those rated lower are junk bonds.

Rating Class	Moody's	S&P and Fitch	
Highest quality	Aaa	AAA	Investment-
High quality	Aa1, Aa2, Aa3	AA+, AA, AA−	grade
Upper medium	A1, A2, A3	A+, A, A−	bonds
Medium	Baa1, Baa2, Baa3	BBB+, BBB, BBB−	
Non-investment grade	Ba1, BB+		
Speculative	Ba2, Ba3	BB, BB−	Junk
Highly speculative	B1, B2, B3	B+, B, B−	bonds
Very risky, default	Caa1 or lower	CCC+ or lower	

[15]"Default Curves and the Dynamics of Credit Spreads," by Wesley Phoa, in *Professional Perspectives on Fixed Income Portfolio Management*, Frank J. Fabozzi, ed., John Wiley & Sons, 2002.
[16]We focus exclusively on corporate bonds in Table 4.3 because the yields on corporate and municipal bonds with the same rating will be quite different. As noted earlier, interest payments from municipal bonds are not subject to federal income tax. This means that investors will accept a lower yield on a municipal bond than they will accept on a corporate bond having the same rating.

Table 4.3   **The Relationship Between Bond Ratings and Spreads at Different Maturities at a Given Point in Time, Expressed in Basis Points**

The table shows the difference in yields, at given points in time, between bonds in different ratings categories and Treasury securities having the same maturity. For instance, 5-year bonds with a AAA rating offered a yield that was 29 basis points higher than the 5-year Treasury note at the given point in time. Note that yield spreads rise with maturity just as they rise as the bond rating falls.

Rating	1 yr	2 yr	3 yr	5 yr	7 yr	10 yr	30 yr
Aaa/AAA	10	12	23	29	46	58	78
Aa1/AA+	19	27	28	40	56	69	90
Aa2/AA	21	33	35	44	59	71	93
Aa3/AA−	22	36	37	49	63	75	101
A1/A+	44	49	53	61	76	90	113
A2/A	47	52	55	63	78	92	117
A3/A−	51	55	58	67	81	95	118
Baa1/BBB+	59	69	77	87	117	139	165
Baa2/BBB	62	77	5	92	124	147	172
Baa3/BBB−	69	82	87	97	129	154	177
Ba1/BB+	330	340	350	360	380	400	420
Ba2/BB	340	350	360	370	390	410	430
Ba3/BB−	350	360	370	380	400	420	440
B1/B+	470	480	490	520	560	600	650
B2/B	480	490	500	530	570	610	660
B3/B−	490	500	510	540	580	620	670
Caa/CCC	890	900	910	935	945	955	985

? JOB INTERVIEW QUESTION

A bond with a B rating offers a yield to maturity of 8%. Is the market's required return on this bond less than, equal to, or greater than 8%?

you move down the rows. The bottom row shows that the lowest-rated bonds, those that are at or near the point of default, offer yields that are 9 to 10% higher than comparable maturity Treasury securities. To illustrate an extreme case, suppose that the yield to maturity on a ten-year Treasury bond equals 3%. The last entry in Table 4.3 shows that a ten-year corporate bond rated Caa/CCC must offer a yield that is 9.55% higher than the Treasury bond, or 12.55%. If that seems like an attractive return, remember the risk dimension. An investor who buys a large number of bonds rated Caa/CCC will almost certainly not earn an average yield of 12.55%, because some of these bonds will default. When default occurs, bondholders usually do not receive all the payments they were originally promised, so the yield they realize on their bonds falls short of the promised yield to maturity.[17]

Thus far, we have maintained a simplifying assumption in our valuation models. You can see that assumption embedded in Equations 4.1 and 4.2. Both equations assume that we can apply a single discount rate, r, to determine the present value of cash payments made at any and all future dates. In other words, the models assume that investors require the same rate of return on an investment that pays cash one year from now and on one that pays cash ten years from now. In reality, required rates of return depend on the exact timing of cash payments, as the next section illustrates.

4-4 Concept Review Questions

12. Calculate a bond's yield to maturity using its last price along with its coupon rate, par value, and maturity date.

13. The price of a certain corporate bond is quoted as 97.847. What is the dollar price of this bond if its par value is $1,000?

14. Explain why the *yield spread* on corporate bonds versus Treasury bonds must always be positive. How do these spreads change (a) as the bond rating declines and (b) as the time to maturity increases?

---

[17]According to The Salomon Center for the Study of Financial Institutions, the default rate among junk bonds reached a record 12.8% in 2002. In a very rough sense, this means that one of eight junk bond issues in the market defaulted that year. The Center estimates that investors who held defaulted bonds recovered only 25% of par value. With the improving economy in 2003, the default rate fell to 4.6% and the recovery rate increased to 45%.

4-5 The Term Structure of Interest Rates

4-5a The Yield Curve

term structure of interest rates
The relationship between time to maturity and yield to maturity for bonds of equal risk.

yield curve
A graph that plots the relationship between time to maturity and yield to maturity for a group of equal-risk bonds.

A quick glance at Table 4.3 reveals an important fact: bond yields vary with maturity. The difference in the yield spread between a one-year and a thirty-year bond varies from 68 (78 – 10) basis points for Aaa/AAA bonds to 100 basis points, or more, for junk bonds. Though Table 4.3 reports yield spreads rather than yields, the data suggest that a positive relationship exists between time to maturity and yield to maturity for bonds in any risk category.

Financial experts refer to the relationship between time to maturity and yield to maturity for bonds of equal risk as the term structure of interest rates. The term structure of interest rates indicates whether yields rise, fall, or remain constant across bonds with different maturities. The simplest way to communicate information about the term structure is to draw a graph that plots yield to maturity on the *y*-axis and time to maturity on the *x*-axis. You can find a graph like this in many financial publications and on many Web sites. A graph showing the term structure of interest rates is called the yield curve.

Figure 4.6 shows how the yield curve for U.S. government bonds looked at four different dates. Usually, long-term bonds offer higher yields than do short-term bonds, and the yield curve slopes upward. That was the case in January 1983 and in July 2010. But the level of the yield curve was much higher in 1983 than in 2010. Differences in expected inflation rates in those two years largely explain why the yield curve was so much higher in 1983. In the 24 months before January 1983, the annual rate of U.S. inflation averaged about 6%. Assume that investors expected inflation to remain roughly at that level in the near term. Investors who purchased short-term Treasury bills in January 1983 earned a return of about 7.5%, slightly higher than the expected inflation rate. In contrast, in the 24 months before July 2010, the annual inflation rate was close to zero. In July 2010, T-bills offered a return of roughly 0.25%. In other words, because investors required a positive *real return* on bonds, nominal bond returns had to be higher in 1983 than in 2010 because inflation was higher in 1983.[18]

Figure 4.6 **Yield Curves for U.S. Government Bonds**

The figure shows how the yield curve looked on four different dates. Most of the time, the yield curve slopes upward because long-term bond yields exceeds short-term bond yields. But before recessions, the yield curve often inverts, as it did in November 2000.

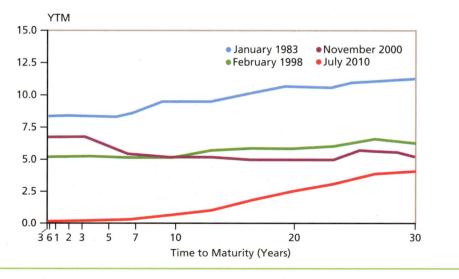

© Cengage Learning 2012

---

[18]The nominal rate of return offered by a bond or any other financial asset should include an estimate of the expected inflation rate in the future rather than merely reflect the inflation rate of the recent past. We discuss the relationship between expected inflation and returns in more depth in the next two chapters. Go to www.smartmoney.com/bonds/ to see how the yield curve has behaved in the United States since 1977. Click the link for the Living Yield Curve.

The other two lines in Figure 4.6 illustrate that the shape of the yield curve can change over time. In February 1998, the yield curve was nearly flat, with yields on short-term and long-term bonds hovering around 5%. But by November 2000, the yield curve had inverted, with short-term yields lying slightly above long-term yields. Why the yield curve sometimes slopes up and at other times slopes down is a complex problem. However, there is an interesting link between the slope of the yield curve and overall macroeconomic growth. Historically, when the yield curve inverts (i.e., switches from an upward slope to a downward slope), a recession usually follows. In fact, several research studies show that economic forecasts based on the yield curve's slope more accurately predict recessions than many forecasts produced using complex statistical models. One reason for this pattern is as follows. Suppose a firm receives new information from its sales force indicating that orders for the firm's products are likely to fall in the near term. This prompts the firm to cut back on planned investment. That means the firm's need for long-term borrowing to finance new investment is diminished. If this happens to just a few firms, it is not likely to have a noticeable effect on financial markets. But if it happens to many firms simultaneously (because demand is falling for many products at once, as happens during a recession), the aggregate demand for new financing to pay for investment will fall. Firms will not need to issue long-term bonds to borrow money for new factories or new equipment. A reduction in the demand for long-term borrowing can cause long-term interest rates to fall relative to short-term rates, and the yield curve may invert. The yield curve may also invert because short-term rates rise above long-term rates. This may occur when the Federal Reserve increases short-term rates to fight inflation.

4-5b Using the Yield Curve to Forecast Interest Rates

SMART
concepts
See the concept explained step-by-step at **SMART** finance

Economists have studied the yield curve intensely for several decades, trying to understand how it behaves and what it portends for the future. As a result of that research, we know that economic growth forecasts that include the slope of the yield curve perform well relative to forecasts that ignore the yield curve. Can the yield curve also tell us something about the direction in which interest rates are headed? The answer is a highly qualified yes. To understand the logic underlying the hypothesis that the slope of the yield curve may predict interest rate movements, consider the following example.

Russell wants to invest $1,000 for two years. He does not want to take much risk, so he plans to invest the money in U.S. Treasury securities. Consulting the Treasury Web site, Russell learns that 1-year Treasury bonds currently offer a 2% YTM, and 2-year bonds offer a 2.5% YTM. At first, Russell thinks his decision about which investment to purchase is easy. He wants to invest for two years, and the 2-year bond pays a higher yield, so why not just buy that one? Thinking further, Russell realizes that he could invest his money in a 1-year bond and reinvest the proceeds in another 1-year bond when the first bond matures. Whether that strategy will ultimately earn a higher return than that of simply buying the 2-year bond depends on what the yield on a 1-year bond will be one year from now. For example, if the 1-year bond rate rises to 4%, Russell will earn 2% in the first year and 4% in the second year, for a grand total of 6% (6.08% after compounding). Over the same period, the 2-year bond offers just 2.5% per year or 5% total (5.06% after compounding). In this scenario, Russell earns more by investing in two 1-year bonds than in one 2-year bond. But what if the yield on a 1-year bond is just 2% next year? In that case, Russell earns 4% over two years (or 4.04% after compounding), and he is better off buying the 2-year bond. If next year's yield on the 1-year bond is about 3%, then Russell will earn approximately the same return over the two years no matter which investment strategy he chooses.

expectations theory
In equilibrium, investors should expect to earn the same return whether they invest in long-term Treasury bonds or a series of short-term Treasury bonds.

This example illustrates the **expectations theory** (or expectations hypothesis): in equilibrium, investors should expect to earn the same return whether they invest in long-term Treasury bonds or a series of short-term Treasury bonds. If the yield on 2-year bonds is 2.5% when the yield on 1-year bonds is 2%, then investors must expect next year's yield on a 1-year bond to be 3%. Suppose not. If they expect a higher yield than 3%, investors are better off purchasing a series of 1-year bonds than from

Figure 4.7   **The Expectations Theory**

The expectations theory says that investors should earn the same expected return by purchasing one 2-year bond or two 1-year bonds. In this example, equilibrium occurs when the expected return on a 1-year bond next year, $E(r_2)$, is 6%. Only then do the two investment strategies provide the same expected return.

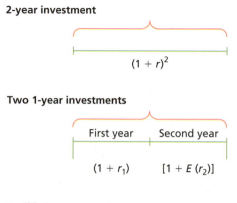

2-year investment

$$(1 + r)^2$$

Two 1-year investments

| First year | Second year |

$$(1 + r_1) \qquad [1 + E(r_2)]$$

Equilibrium occurs when

$$(1 + r_1)[1 + E(r_2)] = (1 + r)^2$$
$$(1 + 0.02)[1 + E(r_2)] = (1 + 0.025)^2$$
$$E(r_2) = 0.03003 \approx 3\%$$

buying the 2-year bond. Conversely, if investors expect next year's bond rate to be less than 3%, they will flock to the 2-year bond. Equilibrium occurs when investors' expectations are such that the expected return on a 2-year bond equals the expected return on two 1-year bonds. In this example, equilibrium occurs when investors believe that next year's interest rate will be 3%.

Figure 4.7 illustrates this idea. The first part of the figure shows that the value of $1 invested in one 2-year bond will grow to $(1 + r)^2$. In this expression, r represents the current interest rate on a 2-year bond. Next, the figure shows that investors expect $1 invested in a sequence of two 1-year bonds to grow to $(1 + r_1)$ $[1 + E(r_2)]$. Here, r_1 represents the current 1-year bond rate, and $E(r_2)$ represents the expected 1-year bond rate in the second year. Equilibrium occurs when the two strategies have identical expected returns, or when the expected 1-year interest rate is about 3%.

EXAMPLE

Suppose a 1-year bond currently offers a yield of 5%, and a 2-year bond offers a 4.5% yield. Under the expectations theory, what interest rate do investors expect on a 1-year bond next year? Remember that the expectations hypothesis says that investors should earn the same expected return by investing in either two 1-year bonds or one 2-year bond. Therefore, the break-even calculation is

$$(1 + 0.05)(1 + E(r_2)) = (1 + 0.045)^2$$

$$(1 + E(r_2)) = \frac{(1.045)^2}{(1.05)}$$

$$E(r_2) = 0.04, \text{ or } 4\%$$

The term $E(r_2)$ refers to the expected return on a 1-year bond next year (year 2). On the left-hand side of the equation, we have the return that an investor expects to earn by purchasing a 1-year bond this year and another one next year. That should equal the return earned by purchasing a 2-year bond today and holding it to maturity. Only when the expected 1-year bond rate is 4% are investors indifferent between these two strategies.

The expectations theory implies that when the yield curve is sloping upward—that is, when long-term bond yields exceed short-term bond yields—investors must expect short-term yields to rise. According to the theory, only if investors expect short-term rates to rise will they be willing to forgo the higher current yield on a long-term instrument by purchasing a short-term bond. Conversely, when the yield curve inverts, and short-term yields exceed long-term yields, investors must expect short-term rates to fall. Only then would investors willingly accept the lower yield on long-term bonds.

4-5c The Liquidity Preference and Preferred Habitat Theories

Unfortunately, the slope of the yield curve does not always provide a reliable signal of future interest rate movements, perhaps because the expectations theory ignores several factors that are important to investors and that influence the shape of the yield curve. The first factor is that investors may have a preference for investing in short-term securities. As we have seen, when market interest rates change, the prices of long-term bonds fluctuate more than the prices of short-term bonds. This added risk might deter some investors from investing in long-term bonds. To attract investors, perhaps long-term bonds must offer a return that exceeds the expected return on a series of short-term bonds. Therefore, when the yield curve slopes up, we cannot be sure whether this is the result of investors expecting interest rates to rise in the future, or simply a reflection of compensation for risk. The **liquidity preference theory** of the term structure recognizes this problem. It says that the slope of the yield curve is influenced not only by expected interest rate changes but also by the liquidity premium that investors require on long-term bonds.

A second factor clouds the interpretation of the slope of the yield curve as a signal of interest rate movements if certain investors always purchase bonds with a particular maturity. For instance, pension funds that promise retirement income to investors and life insurance companies that provide death benefits to policyholders have very long-term liabilities. These companies may have a strong desire to invest in long-term bonds (the longest available in the market) to match their liabilities, even if long-term bonds offer low expected returns relative to a series of short-term bonds. Economists use the **preferred habitat theory** (or the *market segmentation theory*) to describe the effect of this behavior on the yield curve. If short-term bond rates exceed long-term rates, the cause may be that the demand for long-term bonds is very high relative to their supply. This demand drives up long-term bond prices and drives down their yields. If the investors purchasing long-term bonds have a strong preference for investing in those securities, despite their low yields, then a yield curve that slopes down does not necessarily imply that investors expect interest rates to fall.

liquidity preference theory
States that the slope of the yield curve is influenced not only by expected interest rate changes, but also by the liquidity premium that investors require on long-term bonds.

preferred habitat theory
A theory that recognizes that the shape of the yield curve may be influenced by investors who prefer to purchase bonds having a particular maturity; also called market *segmentation theory*.

4-5d Conclusion

Valuing assets, both financial assets and real assets, is what finance is all about. In this chapter, we have learned some simple approaches for pricing bonds, which are among the most common and most important financial instruments in the market. A bond's price depends on how much cash flow it promises investors, how that cash flow is taxed, how likely it is that the issuers fulfill their promises (i.e., default risk), whether investors expect high or low inflation, and whether interest rates rise or fall over time. In the next chapter, we apply many of these same ideas to the pricing of preferred and common stock.

4-5 Concept Review Questions

15. Explain why the height of the yield curve depends on inflation.

16. Suppose the Treasury issues two 5-year bonds. One is an ordinary bond that offers a fixed nominal coupon rate of 4%. The other bond is an inflation-indexed bond (or TIPS). When the TIPS bond is issued, will it have a coupon rate of 4%, more than 4%, or less than 4%?

Summary

- Valuation is a process that links an asset's return with its risk. To value most types of assets, one must first estimate the asset's future cash flows and then discount them at an appropriate discount rate.

- Pricing bonds is an application of the general valuation framework. A bond's price equals the present value of its future cash flows, which consist of coupon and principal payments.

- The yield to maturity is a measure of the return that investors require on a bond. The YTM is the discount rate that equates the present value of a bond's cash flows to its current market price.

- Bond prices and interest rates are inversely related. When interest rates rise (fall), bond prices fall (rise), and the prices of long-term bonds are more responsive in general to changes in interest rates than are short-term bond prices.

- The return that is most important to investors is the real, or inflation-adjusted, return. The real return is roughly equal to the nominal return minus the inflation rate.

- Bonds are categorized based on who issues them or on any number of features such as convertibility, callability, maturity, and so on.

- Bond rating agencies help investors evaluate the risk of bonds. Bonds with lower ratings must offer investors higher yields.

Table of Important Equations

1. The Fundamental Valuation Model

$$P_0 = \frac{CF_1}{(1+r)^1} + \frac{CF_2}{(1+r)^2} + \cdots + \frac{CF_n}{(1+r)^n}$$

2. The Basic Equation

$$P_0 = \frac{C}{(1+r)^1} + \frac{C}{(1+r)^2} + \cdots + \frac{C}{(1+r)^n} + \frac{M}{(1+r)^n}$$

$$3.\ P_0 = \frac{C}{r} \times \left[1 - \frac{1}{(1+r)^n}\right] + \frac{M}{(1+r)^n}$$

4. Semiannual Compounding

$$P_0 = \frac{C/2}{\left(1+\frac{r}{2}\right)^1} + \frac{C/2}{\left(1+\frac{r}{2}\right)^2} + \cdots + \frac{C/2}{\left(1+\frac{r}{2}\right)^{2n}} + \frac{M}{\left(1+\frac{r}{2}\right)^{2n}}$$

$$5.\ P_0 =$$

$$\left(\frac{C/2}{\frac{r}{2}}\right) \times \left[1 - \frac{1}{\left(1+\frac{r}{2}\right)^{2n}}\right] + \frac{M}{\left(1+\frac{r}{2}\right)^{2n}}$$

- The "term structure of interest rates" describes the relationship between time to maturity and yield to maturity on bonds of equivalent risk. A graph of the term structure is called the yield curve. The slope of the yield curve is highly correlated with future economic growth.

Key Terms

agency bonds, 129	federal funds rate, 130	pure discount bond, 132
basis point, 137	floating-rate bonds, 130	putable bonds, 134
bond ratings, 137	indenture, 117	real return, 124
call price, 134	interest rate risk, 123	required rate of return, 116
callable (bonds), 133	junk bonds, 137	sinking fund, 134
collateral, 132	liquidity preference theory, 142	spread, 130
collateral trust bonds, 132	London Interbank Offered Rate	subordinated debentures, 132
convertible bond, 133	(LIBOR), 130	term structure of interest rates, 139
corporate bonds, 127	maturity date, 117	Treasury bills, 129
coupon, 117	mortgage bonds, 132	Treasury bonds, 129
coupon rate, 117	municipal bonds, 127	Treasury Inflation-Protected
coupon yield, 117	nominal return, 124	Securities (TIPS), 130
debentures, 132	par value (bonds), 117	Treasury notes, 129
default risk, 126	preferred habitat theory, 142	Treasury STRIPS, 132
discount, 120	premium, 120	yield curve, 139
equipment trust certificates, 132	prime rate, 130	yield spread, 136
exchangeable bonds, 133	principal, 117	yield to maturity (YTM), 120
expectations theory, 140	protective covenants, 134	

Self-Test Problems

Answers to Self-Test Problems and the Concept Review Questions throughout the chapter appear in CourseMate with SmartFinance Tools at **www.cengagebrain.com**.

ST4-1. A 5-year bond pays interest annually. Its par value is $1,000 and its coupon rate equals 7%. If the market's required return on the bond is 8%, what is the bond's market price?

ST4-2. A bond that matures in two years makes semiannual interest payments. Its par value is $1,000, its coupon rate equals 4%, and the bond's market price is $1,019.27. What is the bond's yield to maturity?

ST4-3. Two bonds offer a 5% coupon rate, paid annually, and sell at par ($1,000). One bond matures in two years and the other matures in ten years.
   a.   What are the YTMs on each bond?
   b.   If the YTM changes to 4%, what happens to the price of each bond?
   c.   What happens if the YTM changes to 6%?

ST4-4. The nominal rate of interest is 5% and the expected inflation rate is 2%.
   a.   What is the approximate real rate of return? What is the exact real rate?
   b.   Repeat part (a) but assume that you are in a country experiencing hyperinflation, so the nominal interest rate is 90% and the expected inflation rate is 80%.

Questions

Q4-1. What is the relationship between the price of a financial asset and the return that investors require on that asset, holding other factors constant?

Q4-2. Define the following terms commonly used in bond valuation: (a) *par value,* (b) *maturity date,* (c) *coupon,* (d) *coupon rate,* (e) *coupon yield,* (f) *yield to maturity (YTM),* and (g) *yield curve.*

Q4-3. Under what circumstances will a bond's *coupon rate* exceed its *coupon yield*? Explain in economic terms why this occurs.

Q4-4. What is the difference between a *pure discount bond* and a bond that trades at a discount? If issuers successfully sell pure discount bonds in the market, investors must want them. Can you explain why any bond purchaser might prefer to purchase a pure discount bond rather than a bond that pays interest?

Q4-5. A firm issues a bond at *par value*. Shortly thereafter, interest rates fall. If you calculate the *coupon rate*, *coupon yield*, and *yield to maturity* for this bond after the decline in interest rates, which of the three values is highest and which is lowest? Explain.

Q4-6. Twenty-five years ago, the U.S. government issued thirty-year bonds with a *coupon rate* of about 8%. Five years ago, the U.S. government sold ten-year bonds with a *coupon rate* of about 5%. Suppose that the current *coupon rate* on newly issued five-year Treasury bonds is 2.5%. For an investor seeking a low-risk investment maturing in five years, do the bonds issued twenty-five years ago with a much higher *coupon rate* provide a more attractive return than the new five-year bonds? What about the ten-year bonds issued five years ago?

Q4-7. Describe how and why a bond's *interest rate risk* is related to its maturity.

Q4-8. Explain why *municipal bonds* can offer lower interest rates than equally risky corporate bonds.

Q4-9. Explain why the *yield to maturity* on a *junk bond* is not a particularly good measure of the return you can expect if you buy it and hold it until maturity.

Q4-10. Under the *expectations theory*, what does the slope of the *yield curve* reveal about the future path of interest rates?

Q4-11. If the yield curve typically slopes upward, what does this imply about the long-term path of interest rates if the expectations theory is true?

Q4-12. Go to www.stockcharts.com/freecharts/yieldcurve.html and click on the animated yield-curve graph (be sure JAVA is enabled on your browser). Answer the following questions:
  a. Is the yield curve typically upward sloping, downward sloping, or flat?
  b. Notice the behavior of the yield curve and the S&P 500 between July 28, 1998, and October 19, 1998. In August 1998, Russia defaulted on billions of dollars of foreign debt. Then, in late September came the news that at the behest of the Federal Reserve, fifteen financial institutions would infuse $3.5 billion in new capital into hedge fund Long-Term Capital Management, which had lost nearly $2 billion in the previous month. Comment on these events as they relate to movements in the yield curve and the S&P 500 that you see in the animation.

Q4-13. At www.nber.org/cycles.html, you can find the official beginning and ending dates for U.S. business cycles, according to the National Bureau of Economic Research (NBER). For example, the NBER indicates that the U.S. economy was in recession from January 1980 to July 1980, from July 1981 to November 1982, from July 1990 to March 1991. Next, go to www.smartmoney.com/investing/bonds/the-living-yield-curve-7923/ and click on the animation of the Living Yield Curve. Pause the animation at November 1981, and click one frame at a time until August 1982. Let the animation play again until you reach March 1989. What association do you notice between the shape of the yield curve and the NBER's dates for recessions?

Q4-14. Look again at the yield-curve animation found at the SmartMoney Web site, www.smartmoney.com/investing/bonds/the-living-yield-curve-7923/. Make a note of the overall level of the yield curve from about mid-1979 to mid-1982. Compare that with the level of the curve for most of the 1990s. What accounts for the differences in yield-curve levels in these two periods?

Problems

Valuation Basics

P4-1. A best-selling author decides to cash in on her latest novel by selling the rights to the book's royalties for the next six years to an investor. Royalty payments arrive once per year, starting one year from now. In the first year, the author expects $400,000 in royalties, followed by $300,000, then $100,000, then $10,000 in the three subsequent years. If the investor purchasing the rights to royalties requires a return of 7% per year, what should the investor pay?

P4-2. An oil well produces 20,000 barrels of oil per year. Suppose the price of oil is $50 per barrel. You want to purchase the right to the oil produced by this well for the next five years. At a discount rate of 10%, what is the value of the oil rights? (You can assume that the cash flows from selling oil arrive at annual intervals.)

Bond Prices and Interest Rates

P4-3. A $1,000 par value bond makes two interest payments each year of $45 each. What is the bond's *coupon rate*?

P4-4. A $1,000 par value bond has a *coupon rate* of 8% and a *coupon yield* of 9%. What is the bond's market price?

P4-5. A bond sells for $900 and offers a *coupon yield* of 7.2%. What is the bond's annual coupon payment?

P4-6. A bond offers a *coupon rate* of 5%. If the par value is $1,000 and the bond sells for $1,250, what is the *coupon yield*?

P4-7. A bond makes two $45 interest payments each year. Given that the bond's par value is $1,000 and its price is $1,050, calculate the bond's *coupon rate* and *coupon yield*.

SMART
solutions

See the problem and solution explained step-by-step at **SMART**|finance

P4-8. Calculate the price of a five-year, $1,000 par value bond that makes semiannual payments, has a *coupon rate* of 8%, and offers a *yield to maturity* of 7%. Recalculate the price assuming a 9% YTM. What is the general relationship that this problem illustrates?

P4-9. A $1,000 par value bond makes annual interest payment of $75. If it offers a *yield to maturity* of 7.5%, what is the price of the bond?

P4-10. A $1,000 par value bond pays a *coupon rate* of 8.2%. The bond makes semiannual payments, and it matures in four years. If investors require a 10% return on this investment, what is the bond's price?

P4-11. Griswold Travel Inc. has issued six-year bonds that pay $30 in interest twice each year. The par value of these bonds is $1,000, and they offer a *yield to maturity* of 5.5%. How much are the bonds worth?

P4-12. Bennifer Jewelers recently issued ten-year bonds that make annual interest payments of $50. Suppose you purchased one of these bonds at par value when it was issued. Right away, market interest rates jumped, and the YTM on your bond rose to 6%. What happened to the price of your bond?

P4-13. You are evaluating two similar bonds. Both mature in four years, both have a $1,000 *par value*, and both pay a *coupon rate* of 10%. However, one bond pays that coupon in annual installments, whereas the other makes semiannual payments. Suppose you require a 10% return on either bond. Should these bonds sell at identical prices or should one be worth more than the other? Use Equations 4.2a and 4.3a, and let $r = 10\%$. What prices do you obtain for these bonds? Can you explain the apparent paradox?

P4-14. A bond makes annual interest payments of $75. The bond matures in four years, has a *par value* of $1,000, and sells for $975.30. What is the bond's *yield to maturity (YTM)*?

P4-15. Johanson VI Advisors issued $1,000 par value bonds a few years ago with a coupon rate of 7%, paid semiannually. After the bonds were issued, interest rates fell. Now with three years remaining before they mature, the bonds sell for $1,055.08. What YTM do these bonds offer?

P4-16. A bond offers a 6% coupon rate and sells at par. What is the bond's *yield to maturity*?

P4-17. You have gathered the following data on three bonds:

Bond	Maturity	Coupon %
A	10 yrs	9%
B	9 yrs	1%
C	5 yrs	5%

a. If the market's required return on all three bonds is 6%, what are the market prices of the bonds (you can assume annual interest payments).

b. The market's required return suddenly rises to 7%. What are the new bonds' prices, and what is the percentage change in price for each bond?

c. If the market's required return falls from the initial 6% to 5%, what are the new prices, and what is the percentage change in each price relative to the answer obtained in part (a)?

d. Which bond's price is most sensitive to interest rate movements? Does this answer surprise you? Why or why not? Can you explain why this bond's price is so sensitive to rate changes?

e. Which bond's price is least sensitive to interest rate movements? Explain.

P4-18. The rate of inflation is 5% and the *real interest rate* is 3%. What is the *nominal interest rate*?

P4-19. The *nominal interest rate* is 9% and the inflation rate is 7%. What is the *real interest rate*?

Types of Bonds

SMART solutions

See the problem and solution explained step-by-step at **SMART** | finance

P4-20. Suppose investors face a tax rate of 40% on interest received from corporate bonds. Suppose AAA-rated corporate bonds currently offer yields of about 7%. Approximately what yield would AAA-rated municipal bonds need to offer to be competitive?

P4-21. Investors face a tax rate of 33% on interest received from corporate bonds. If municipal bonds currently offer yields of 6%, what yield would equally risky corporate bonds need to offer to be competitive?

P4-22. You purchase a U.S. Treasury inflation-indexed bond at par value of $1,000. The bond offers a coupon rate of 6% paid semiannually. During the first six months that you hold the bond, prices in the United States rise by 2%. What is the new par value of the bond, and what is the amount of your first coupon payment?

P4-23. What is the price of a zero-coupon bond that has a par value of $1,000? The bond matures in thirty years and offers a *yield to maturity* of 4.5%. Calculate the price one year later, when the bond has twenty-nine years left before it matures (assume the yield remains at 4.5%). What is the return that an investor earns if they buy the bond with thirty years remaining and sell it one year later?

P4-24. A zero-coupon bond has a $1,000 face value, matures in ten years, and currently sells for $781.20.

a. What is the market's required return on this bond?

b. Suppose you hold this bond for one year and sell it. At the time you sell the bond, market rates have increased to 3.5%. What return did you earn on this bond?

c. Suppose that rather than buying the ten-year zero-coupon bond described at the start of this problem, you instead purchased a ten-year 2.5% coupon bond (assume annual payments). Because the bond's coupon rate equaled the market's required return at the time of purchase, you paid par value ($1,000) to acquire the bond. Again assume that you held the bond for one year, received one coupon payment, and then sold the bond, but at the time of sale the market's required return was 3.5%. What was your return for the year? Compare your answer here to your answer in part (b).

Bond Markets

P4-25. A corporate bond's price is quoted as 98.110. What is the price of the bond if its par value is $1,000?

P4-26. A corporate bond's price is quoted as 102.312. If the bond's par value is $1,000, what is its market price?

P4-27. A corporate bond's price is listed at 102.801. It matures in three years, has a coupon rate of 5%, and pays interest semiannually. What is the bond's yield to maturity?

P4-28. Refer back to Figure 4.5.

a. What is the yield spread in basis points between the Citigroup bond maturing in May 2015 and the DirecTV bond maturing in March 2015? Does this spread make sense given the different ratings assigned to these bonds? If not, what factors might explain the differences in yields that we observe?

b. What is the yield spread in basis points between the Morgan Stanley bond paying a 5.625% coupon and the Morgan Stanley bond paying a 5.500% coupon? Given that these two bonds have the same credit rating and similar coupons, would you expect them to offer nearly identical yields? Why or why not?

The Term Structure of Interest Rates

P4-29. A one-year Treasury security offers a 4% *yield to maturity* (YTM). A two-year Treasury security offers a 4.25% YTM. According to the *expectations theory*, what is the expected interest rate on a one-year security next year?

P4-30. A one-year Treasury bill offers a 6% *yield to maturity*. The market's consensus forecast is that one-year T-bills will offer 6.25% next year. What is the current yield on a 2-year T-bill if the *expectations theory* holds?

THOMSON REUTERS | Business School Edition

Access financial information from the Thomson ONE – Business School Edition Web site for the following problem(s). Go to **www.tobsefin.swlearning.com/**. If you have already registered your access serial number and have a username and password, click **Enter**. Otherwise, click **Register** and follow the instructions to create a username and password. Register your access serial number and then click **Enter** on the aforementioned Web site. When you click Enter, you will be prompted for your username and password (please remember that the password is case sensitive). Enter them in the respective boxes and then click **OK** (or hit **Enter**). From the ensuing page, click **Click Here to Access Thomson ONE – Business School Edition Now!** This opens up a new window that gives you access to the Thomson ONE – Business School Edition database. You can retrieve a company's financial information by entering its ticker symbol (provided for each company in the problem(s)) in the box below "Name/Symbol/Key." For further instructions on using the Thomson ONE – Business School Edition database, please refer to the online Help.

P4-31. Which of the following two companies will have a higher bond rating: Abbott Laboratories Inc (ticker: U:ABT) or Bristol Myers Squibb Company (U:BMY)? Bond rating agencies, such as Moody's, Standard and Poor's, and Fitch, investigate, among other things, a company's debt and profitability ratios (see Chapter 2 for these ratios) to rate its bonds. Examine these ratios for the two companies and explain which company's bonds are likely to have a higher rating and why.

Since these exercises depend upon real-time data, your answers will change continuously depending upon when you access the Internet to download your data.

Smart Ideas Video

Annette Poulsen, University of Georgia

"There is a trade-off between flexibility for the corporation and protection for the bondholder."

Smart Practices Video

Todd Richter, Managing Director, Head of Equity Healthcare Research, Bank of America Securities

"The concepts of value, the things that drive value, don't change."

Video photos: Cengage Learning

SMART concepts

See how to apply time value of money concepts to value stocks and bonds.
See a demonstration of the expectations theory of term structure.

SMART solutions

See the solutions to problems 4-8 and 4-20 explained step-by-step.

Mini-Case

Valuing Bonds

You go to *The Wall Street Journal* Online on the morning of March 31, 2008, and see the following bond quote under the "Most Active Investment Grade Bonds" for Procter & Gamble Co. Based on this online information, answer the following questions.

Issuer Name	Symbol	Coupon	Maturity	Rating Moody's/S&P/ Fitch	High	Low	Last	Change	Yield %
PROCTER & GAMBLE CO	PG.HD	5.550%	Mar 2037	Aa3/AA−/−	96.124	95.933	96.124	−0.245	5.825

Assignment

1. What is the YTM for this Procter & Gamble Co. corporate bond?

2. What is the coupon yield of this bond over the next year?

3. If your required rate of return for a bond of this risk-class is 6.2%, what value do you place on this Procter & Gamble Co. bond?

4. At the required rate of return of 6.2%, are you interested in purchasing this bond?

5. If you purchased this Procter & Gamble Co. bond for $961.24 yesterday and the market rate of interest for this bond increased to 6.0% today, do you have a gain or loss? How much is the gain or loss in dollars?

chapter 5

Valuing Stocks

What Companies Do

Hedge Fund Managers Like Aeropostale's Look

In early 2011, on CNBC's Fast Money program, hedge fund manager Anthony Scaramucci (aka The Hedge) made the case that Aeropostale, the teen fashion retailer, was undervalued. Scaramucci pointed out that Aeropostale had fat profit margins and generated plenty of free cash flow. Scaramucci urged investors to buy Aeropostale because of its earnings multiple. In a recent transaction, a private equity firm had purchased J Crew at a price equal to eight times that company's earnings before interest, taxes, and depreciation (EBITDA). Scaramucci noted that Aeropostale's current market price was just four times EBITDA, so to him it looked like a bargain.

Hedge fund managers, investment banking analysts, and corporate financial analysts all have to make judgments about the values of companies. Valuing an entire company or assessing whether its common stock is correctly valued is a difficult task, and there are many methods available to professionals conducting this type of analysis. Some methods rely on the discounted cash flow methods covered in Chapters 3 and 4. Other approaches rely on "market multiples" like the EBITDA multiple cited by Scaramucci. This chapter introduces you to these methods.

Source: www.cnbc.com/id/40931513/

Learning Objectives

After studying this chapter you should be able to:

- Describe the differences between preferred and common stock;

- Calculate the estimated value of preferred and common stock using zero, constant, and variable growth models;

- Value an entire company using the free cash flow approach;

- Apply alternative approaches for pricing stocks that do not rely on discounted cash flow analysis;

- Understand how investment bankers help firms issue equity securities in the primary market; and

- List the major U.S. secondary markets in which investors trade stocks.

This chapter focuses on valuing preferred and common stocks. We begin by describing the essential

features of these instruments, comparing and contrasting them with the features of bonds that we covered in the previous chapter. Next, we apply the information from this chapter's first three sections to the basic discounted cash flow valuation framework from Chapter 4 to develop a method for pricing preferred and common stock. We introduce three simple approaches—the zero, constant, and variable growth models—for valuing stocks based on the dividend streams they pay over time. We also present the free cash flow approach for valuing the entire enterprise. Then, we review some other popular stock valuation measures, including book value, liquidation value, and comparable firm multiples. Finally, we explain how firms, with the assistance of investment bankers, issue these securities to investors and how trades between investors occur on an ongoing basis once the securities have been issued.

5-1   The Essential Features of Preferred and Common Stock

How do companies raise money when they need to fund a new investment project? If a firm does not have enough internal funding (e.g., past profits), it will often turn to the capital markets to raise funds by issuing debt or equity securities. Debt securities, such as bonds, generally offer investors a legally enforceable claim to cash payments that are either fixed or vary according to a predetermined formula. Because the cash flow streams offered by bonds are typically fixed, valuing bonds is a relatively straightforward exercise as Chapter 4 demonstrated. The market price of a bond should equal the present value of the cash payments that the bond promises to make.

The same valuation principle applies to equity securities such as common stock, but investors confront a difficult challenge when they estimate the value of these securities. Firms issuing common stock make no specific promises to investors about how much cash they will receive or when. Firms may choose to make cash payments to shareholders, called **dividends**, but they are under no obligation to do so. Loosely speaking, a firm distributes cash to common stockholders if it is generating more cash from its operations than it needs to pay expenses and fund new profitable investment opportunities. For this reason, stockholders are sometimes referred to as **residual claimants**—their claim is only on the cash remaining after the firm pays all of its bills and makes necessary new investments in the business. Because it is very hard to predict the magnitude of these residual cash flows and the timing of their distribution to stockholders, valuing common stock is much more difficult than valuing bonds.

In light of this discussion, it should not surprise you to learn that debt and equity securities differ in terms of both the risks they require investors to bear and the potential rewards for taking those risks. Debt securities offer a relatively safe and predictable return, but safety comes at a price. Bond returns are rarely high enough to generate wealth quickly, and bondholders exercise almost no direct influence on corporate decisions, except when a missed payment allows bondholders to force a firm into bankruptcy court. Common stockholders accept more risk than do bondholders. For example, an investor who purchased $10,000 worth of Google stock when it debuted in August 2004 saw that investment grow to more than $60,000 in the company's first seven years of operation. In contrast, someone who

dividends
Periodic cash payments that firms make to stockholders.

residual claimants
Investors who have the right to receive the cash that remains after a firm pays all of its bills and makes necessary new investments in the business.

spent $10,000 in August 2004 to buy Citigroup common stock endured a 90% drop in the value of their shares to a little less than $1,000 in the same period. Because common stockholders are asked to take large risks, they expect higher returns on average than do bondholders.

Investors who own common shares also have opportunities to exercise some control over corporate decisions through their voting rights. Usually, investors are entitled to one vote for each share of common stock that they own, and they may exercise their right to vote at shareholders meetings. At these meetings shareholders elect the board of directors to oversee management and approve major decisions such as a large acquisition. As a practical matter, however, most investors do not attend shareholder meetings, but they can still exercise their voting rights by signing proxy statements. **Proxy statements** are documents that describe the issues that will be voted on at the shareholders meeting. By signing these documents, shareholders transfer their voting rights to another party. Usually, shareholders give their proxies to the firm's current management team, but occasionally outsiders who are dissatisfied with the firm's management or view the firm as an attractive takeover target will wage a proxy fight. In a **proxy fight**, outsiders try to acquire enough votes from shareholders to elect a new slate of directors and thereby take control of the firm, or at least effect a change in company policy.

Not all stockholders have voting rights. Preferred stock represents a kind of hybrid security, meaning that it shares some of the features of debt and some of common stock. The cash payments that preferred stockholders receive are called dividends, just like the payments that common stockholders receive, but these dividends are usually fixed, like the interest payments made to bondholders. That makes valuing preferred stock easier than valuing common stock. Like bondholders, preferred stockholders do not have voting rights, but their claims are *senior to common stock*, meaning that preferred stockholders have a higher priority claim on a firm's cash flows. For instance, companies usually must pay the dividend on preferred shares before they can pay a dividend on their common stock. Most preferred stock has a feature known as *cumulative dividends*, meaning that if a firm misses any preferred dividend payments, it must catch up and pay preferred shareholders for all the dividends they missed (along with the current dividend) before it can pay dividends on common stock. In all these instances, preferred stock seems more like debt than equity.

In other respects, preferred stock looks more like equity than debt. Dividends on preferred and common shares are not a tax deductible expense for the firm, but interest payments on debt are deductible.[1] Preferred shareholders hold a claim that is *junior to bonds,* meaning that preferred shareholders hold a lower priority claim than bondholders do, and they cannot take a firm to court for failure to pay dividends. Finally, most preferred shares do not have a specific maturity date and can remain outstanding indefinitely, similar to common stock.

Despite the differences between bonds, preferred stock, and common stock, analysts use some of the same methods to value all of these securities. The most basic valuation methods rely on the discounted cash flow techniques introduced in Chapter 3 and applied to bond valuation in Chapter 4. In the next section, we'll see how to use discounted cash flow methods to value preferred and common stock.

proxy statements
Documents that describe the issues to be voted on at an annual shareholders meeting.

proxy fight
An attempt by outsiders to gain control of a firm by soliciting a sufficient number of votes to elect a new slate of directors and effect a change in company policy.

5-1 Concept Review Questions

1. How do you think preferred shares compare to bonds and common stocks in terms of the risks that investors must face and the rewards that they expect?

2. Some companies (Google being a prime example) have two classes of common stock. The class available for outside investors to buy has one vote per share, but the other class, which is typically held by top managers, is entitled to ten votes per share. How does an arrangement like this influence the rights of outside stockholders, and what impact do you think it might have on the of the firm's common stock?

---

[1]The dividends on some kinds of "trust preferred stock" are tax deductible for the corporation.

5-2   Valuing Preferred and Common Stock

The principles involved in valuing stock mirror those we adopted to determine bond prices in Chapter 4. First, we estimate the cash flows that a stockholder expects to receive over time. Unlike bonds, preferred and common shares have no definite maturity date, so estimates of the cash flows going to stockholders must necessarily take a long-term view. Second, we determine a discount rate that reflects the risk of those cash flows. In the case of a bond, the discount rate is relatively easy to find. You simply use the yield to maturity, which is the discount rate that equates the bond's cash flows to its market price, for a similar-risk bond. Because the cash flows provided by common stock are uncertain and the maturity date is undefined, there is no mechanical calculation equivalent to a bond's yield to maturity that can provide a precise figure for the required return on stock—it has to be estimated by some other means. Third, despite the difficulties just noted, we estimate the stock's price by calculating the present value of its expected future cash flows. In other words, valuing stock is simply another application of Equation 4.1.

5-2a Preferred Stock Valuation

Preferred shares typically offer a fixed stream of cash flows with no specific maturity date. For that reason, we treat preferred stock as a security that behaves like a simple perpetuity. In Chapter 3, you learned a shortcut for valuing a *perpetuity*. For a perpetuity that makes annual cash payments, with the first payment arriving in one year, the present value equals the next payment divided by the discount rate. To find today's value of a preferred stock, PS_0, we use the equation for the present value of a perpetuity, dividing the preferred dividend, D_p, by the required rate of return on the preferred stock, r_p:

(Eq. 5.1)
$$PS_0 = \frac{D_p}{r_p}$$

EXAMPLE

Alcoa, Inc., has preferred stock outstanding that pays a dividend of $3.75 per share each year. The stock paid a dividend on September 8, 2010. If investors require a 5.5% return on this investment, what would you expect the price of these shares to be on September 9, 2010?

Recognizing that the next $3.75 dividend comes one year in the future, we can apply Equation 5.1 to estimate the value of Alcoa's preferred shares:

$$PS_0 = \frac{\$3.75}{0.055} = \$68.18$$

Equation 5.1 is valid if dividend payments arrive annually and if the next dividend payment comes in one year. In practice, most preferred stocks pay dividends quarterly. How do we modify Equation 5.1 to value a preferred stock paying quarterly dividends? One approach is to divide both the annual dividend and the required rate of return by four to obtain quarterly figures. If we apply that logic to Alcoa's preferred stock, we obtain:

$$PS_0 = \frac{(\$3.75 \div 4)}{(0.055 \div 4)} = \frac{\$0.9375}{0.01375} = \$68.18$$

Our calculations so far indicate that Alcoa's preferred stock is worth $68.18 whether it pays dividends annually or quarterly. That can't be right. The time value of money implies that investors are better off if they receive dividends sooner rather than later. In other words, if Alcoa's preferred stock pays $3.75 in dividends per year, the value of that dividend should be greater if it is paid in quarterly installments rather than in one payment per year. In fact, Alcoa stock would be worth more than $68.18 if it paid quarterly dividends, as the next example demonstrates.

When we attempted to adjust Equation 5.1 for quarterly dividends, we assumed that investors required a quarterly return of 1.375%, or one-fourth of the 5.5% required return used in the example with annual dividends. However, if the quarterly required return is 1.375%, this translates into an effective annual return that is higher than 5.5%. Using Equation 3.14 on page 94, we can calculate that a quarterly rate of 1.375% translates into an effective annual rate of about 5.6%.

$$\text{Effective annual rate} = \left(\frac{1 + 0.055}{4}\right)^4 - 1 = 0.056$$

That means our examples with annual and quarterly dividends are not making a true "apples to apples" comparison, because we have assumed a slightly higher effective discount rate in the quarterly calculations. If the effective annual required return is in fact 5.5%, then we can use Equation 3.14 to determine that the quarterly rate is just 1.35%:

$$0.055 = \left(1 + \frac{r}{4}\right)^4 - 1$$

$$\frac{r}{4} = 0.0135$$

Discounting the quarterly dividend at the appropriate quarterly rate would result in a higher value for Alcoa preferred stock.

$$PS_0 = \frac{\$0.9375}{0.0135} = \$69.44$$

Now let's turn our attention to the more challenging problem of using discounted cash flow techniques to value common stock.

5-2b Common Stock Valuation Equation

Valuing common stock is a much more difficult task than valuing preferred stock because the cash flows that common stockholders receive are not set in advance by a contract. In this section, we introduce a simple technique that connects the price of a share of stock to the dividends that the stockholder receives. In practice, the methods used by professional investors to value common shares are more complex than what we present here. Nevertheless, the simplified valuation model provides a framework that will help you understand the factors that determine common stock values. Later, we will introduce some of the alternative approaches that investors use to value shares.

When you buy a share of stock, you may expect to receive a periodic dividend payment from the firm, and you probably hope to sell the stock for more than its purchase price. But when you sell the stock, you are simply passing the rights to receive dividends to the buyer. The buyer purchases the stock from you in the belief that the dividends and capital gains justify the purchase price. This logic extends to the next investor who buys the stock from the person who bought it from you, and so on, forever. This implies that the value of common stock equals the present value of all future dividends that investors expect the stock to distribute.[2]

The easiest way to understand this argument is as follows. Suppose that an investor buys a stock today for price P_0, receives a dividend equal to D_1 at the end of one year, and immediately sells the stock for price P_1. The return on this investment is easy to calculate:

$$r = \frac{D_1 + P_1 - P_0}{P_0}$$

The numerator of this expression equals the dollar profit or loss. Dividing that by the purchase price converts the return into percentage form. Rearrange this equation to solve for the *current stock price*:

(Eq. 5.2)

$$P_0 = \frac{D_1 + P_1}{(1 + r)^1}$$

---

[2]Firms can distribute cash directly to shareholders in forms other than dividends. For instance, many firms regularly buy back their own shares. Also, when an acquiring firm buys a target, it may distribute cash to the target's shareholders. In this discussion, we assume for simplicity that cash payments always come in the form of dividends, but the logic of the argument does not change if we allow for other forms of cash payments.

This equation indicates that the value of a stock today equals the present value of cash that the investor receives in one year. But what determines P_1, the selling price at the end of the year? Use Equation 5.2 again, changing the time subscripts to reflect that the price next year will equal the present value of the dividend and selling price received two years from now:

$$P_1 = \frac{D_2 + P_2}{(1 + r)^1}$$

Now, take this expression for P_1 and substitute it back into Equation 5.2:

$$P_0 = \frac{D_1 + \dfrac{D_2 + P_2}{(1 + r)^1}}{(1 + r)^1} = \frac{D_1}{(1 + r)^1} + \frac{D_2 + P_2}{(1 + r)^2}$$

We have an expression that says that the price of a stock today equals the present value of the dividends it will pay over the next two years, plus the present value of the selling price in two years. Again we could ask, what determines the selling price in two years, P_2? By repeating the last two steps over and over, we can determine the price of a stock today, as shown in Equation 5.3:

(Eq. 5.3) $$P_0 = \frac{D_1}{(1 + r)^1} + \frac{D_2}{(1 + r)^2} + \frac{D_3}{(1 + r)^3} + \frac{D_4}{(1 + r)^4} + \frac{D_5}{(1 + r)^5} + \cdots$$

The *price of a share of common stock* today equals the present value of the entire dividend stream that the stock will pay in the future. Now consider the problem that an investor faces if she tries to determine whether a particular stock is overvalued or undervalued. In deciding whether to buy the stock, an investor needs two inputs to apply Equation 5.3: the projected dividends and the discount rate. Neither input is easy to estimate. For a stock that already pays a dividend, predicting what the dividend will be over the next few quarters is not terribly difficult, but forecasting far out into the future is another matter. For stocks that currently do not pay a dividend, the problem is even more difficult because the analyst has to estimate when the dividend stream will begin. Likewise, the discount rate, or the rate of return required by the market on this stock, depends on the stock's risk. We defer a full discussion of how to measure a stock's risk and how to translate that into a required rate of return until Chapters 6 and 7. For now, we focus on the problem of estimating dividends.[3] In most cases, analysts can formulate reasonably accurate estimates of dividends in the near future. The real trick is to determine how quickly dividends will grow over the long run. Our discussion of stock valuation centers on three possible scenarios for dividend growth: zero growth, constant growth, and variable growth.

5-2c Zero Growth

zero growth model
The simplest approach to stock valuation that assumes a constant dividend stream.

The simplest approach to dividend valuation, the **zero growth model**, assumes a constant dividend stream. That assumption is not particularly realistic for most firms, but it may be appropriate in some special cases. If dividends do not grow, we can write the following equation:

$$D_1 = D_2 = D_3 = \cdots = D$$

Plugging the constant value D for each dividend payment into Equation 5.3, you can see that the valuation formula simply reduces to the equation for the present value of a perpetuity:

$$P_0 = \frac{D}{r}$$

In this special case, the formula for valuing common stock is essentially identical to that for valuing preferred stock.

JOB INTERVIEW QUESTION

Holding all other factors constant, if investors become less risk averse, meaning that they are willing to accept lower returns when investing in risky assets, what would happen to stock values generally?

---

[3]For stocks that do not pay dividends, analysts can either estimate the value of the stock by discounting the free cash flow that the firm produces or by using a "multiples" approach. Both of these alternatives are described later in this chapter.

The computer giant, Hewlett-Packard (HP), paid a constant quarterly dividend of $0.08 per share without interruption from June 1998 to March 2011. Perhaps after receiving the same dividend for more than 12 years, investors believed that HP's dividend would remain at $0.08 (or $0.32 per year) forever. What price would they be willing to pay for HP stock?

The answer depends on investors' required rate of return. If investors demanded a 10% annual return, then the stock should be worth $0.32 ÷ 0.10 or $3.20 (making the simplifying assumption that the dividend is paid annually).[4] In fact, in the first half of 2011 HP stock actually traded close to $40 per share. This implies one of two things: either investors required a rate of return that was very low (in fact, less than 1%), which is implausible, or they expected that dividends would eventually grow, even though they had remained steady for many years. Expectations of higher dividends were realized when HP increased its dividend by 50% in the spring of 2011 and announced its intention to make double-digit dividend increases during the next few years.

5-2d Constant Growth

Of all the relatively simple stock valuation models that we consider in this chapter, the *constant growth model* probably sees the most use in practice. The model assumes that dividends will grow at a constant rate, *g*. If dividends grow at a constant rate forever, we calculate the value of that cash flow stream by using the formula for a growing perpetuity, given in Chapter 3. Denoting next year's dividend as D_1, we determine the value today of a stock that pays a dividend growing at a constant rate:[5]

Gordon growth model
Values a share of stock under the assumption that dividends grow at a constant rate forever.

(Eq. 5.4)
$$P_0 = \frac{D_1}{r - g}$$

The *constant growth model* in Equation 5.4 is commonly called the **Gordon growth model**, after Myron Gordon, who popularized this formula.

Few public companies have achieved a longer streak of uninterrupted dividend increases than Integrys Energy Group, Inc., a holding company that provides administrative support primarily to its regulated utility subsidiaries. Integrys increased its dividend in twenty consecutive years starting in 1988, with the annual dividend increase averaging 2.75% over that period. Suppose that investors expected an annual dividend of $2.79 in 2012. Although this dividend is paid quarterly, we will assume that the entire dividend arrives in July 2012 and is expected to grow at 2.75% each year. What should be the price of Integrys stock in July 2011?

Assume that the required rate of return on Integrys stock is about 10%. Substituting into the constant growth model, Equation 5.4, the result suggests that Integrys' stock price should be the following:

$$P = \frac{\$2.79}{0.10 - 0.0275} = \$38.48$$

In fact, in July 2011 Integrys stock was trading for about $50. Although the growth model's estimate of Integrys' stock price is below the firm's actual market value in 2011, it only takes small adjustments in the model's inputs to obtain an estimate that is much closer to Integrys' actual market value. For example, if we lower the required return from 10% to 9% and increase the dividend growth rate from 2.75% to 3.5%, the estimated value of Integrys stock increases from $38.48 to $50.73.

---

[4]You can apply the same formula to quarterly dividends as long as you make an appropriate adjustment in the interest rate. For example, if investors expect a 10% effective annual rate of return on HP stock, they expect a quarterly return of (1.10)0.25 2 1, or 2.41%. Using this figure, you can recalculate the stock price by dividing $0.08, the quarterly dividend, by 0.0241 to obtain $3.32. Why is HP stock more valuable in this calculation? Since HP's dividends arrive more often than once a year, the present value of the dividend stream is greater.

[5]To apply this equation, one must assume that $r > g$ and that g itself is constant. Of course, some firms may grow very rapidly for a time, so that $g > r$ temporarily. We treat the case of firms that grow rapidly for a finite period later in the discussion. In the long run, it is reasonable to assume that r must eventually exceed g.

The preceding example illustrated that by making small adjustments to the required rate of return or the dividend growth rate, we could easily obtain an estimate for Integrys Energy Group's stock that matches the actual market price. But we could also obtain a very different price with an equally reasonable set of assumptions. For instance, increasing the required rate of return from 10% to 11% and decreasing the dividend growth rate from 2.75% to 1.5% decreases the price all the way to $29.37. Obviously, analysts want to estimate the inputs for Equation 5.4 as precisely as possible, but the amount of uncertainty inherent in estimating required rates of return and growth rates makes obtaining precise valuations very difficult.

Nevertheless, the constant growth model provides a useful way to frame stock-valuation problems, highlighting the important inputs and, in some cases, providing price estimates that seem fairly reasonable. But the model should not be applied blindly to all types of firms, especially not to those enjoying rapid, albeit temporary, growth.

5-2e Variable Growth

variable growth model
Assumes that the dividend growth rate will vary during different periods of time, when calculating the value of a firm's stock.

The zero and constant growth common stock valuation models just presented do not allow for any change in expected growth rates. Many firms go through periods of relatively rapid growth, followed by a period of more stable growth. Valuing the stock of such a firm requires a **variable growth model**, one in which the dividend growth rate can vary. Using our earlier notation, let D_0 equal the last or most recent per-share dividend paid, g_1 equal the initial (rapid) growth rate of dividends, g_2 equal the subsequent (constant) growth rate of dividends, and N equal the number of years in the initial growth period. We can write the general equation for the *variable growth model* as follows:

SMART concepts
See the concept explained step-by-step at **SMART**|finance

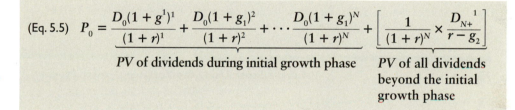

$$(\text{Eq. 5.5}) \quad P_0 = \underbrace{\frac{D_0(1 + g_1)^1}{(1 + r)^1} + \frac{D_0(1 + g_1)^2}{(1 + r)^2} + \cdots \frac{D_0(1 + g_1)^N}{(1 + r)^N}}_{PV \text{ of dividends during initial growth phase}} + \underbrace{\left[\frac{1}{(1 + r)^N} \times \frac{D_{N+1}}{r - g_2} \right]}_{\substack{PV \text{ of all dividends} \\ \text{beyond the initial} \\ \text{growth phase}}}$$

As noted by the labels, the first part of the equation calculates the present value of the dividends expected during the initial rapid-growth period. The last term, $D_{N+1} \div (r - g_2)$, equals the value, *as of the end of the rapid-growth stage*, of all dividends that arrive after year N. To calculate the *present value* of this growing perpetuity, we must multiply the last term by $1 \div (1 + r)^N$.

EXAMPLE

A food company has developed a new fat-free ice cream, and as the popularity of the product increases, the firm (unlike its customers) will grow quite rapidly—perhaps as much as 20% per year. Over time, as the market share of this new food increases, the firm's growth rate will reach a steady state. At that point, the firm may grow at the same rate as the overall economy, perhaps 5% per year. Assume that the market's required rate of return on this stock is 14%.

To value the food company's stock, you need to break the future stream of cash flows into two parts. The first part is the rapid-growth period, and the second is the constant-growth phase. Suppose that the firm's most recent (year 0) dividend was $2 per share. You anticipate that the firm will increase the dividend by 20% per year for the next three years, and after that dividends will grow at 5% per year indefinitely. The expected dividend stream for the next seven years looks like this:

Rapid-Growth Phase (g_1 = 20%)		Constant-Growth Phase (g_2 = 5%)	
Year 0	$2.00	Year 4	$3.63
Year 1	2.40	Year 5	3.81
Year 2	2.88	Year 6	4.00
Year 3	3.46	Year 7	4.20

continued

The value of the dividends during the rapid-growth phase is calculated as follows:

$$PV \text{ of dividends (initial phase)} = \frac{\$2.40}{(1.14)^1} + \frac{\$2.88}{(1.14)^2} + \frac{\$3.46}{(1.14)^3}$$

$$= \$2.11 + \$2.22 + \$2.34 = \$6.67$$

The stable-growth phase begins with the dividend paid four years from now and continues forever. The final term of Equation 5.5 is similar to Equation 5.4, which indicates that the value of a constant-growth stock at time t equals the dividend a year later, at time $t + 1$, divided by the difference between the required rate of return and the constant-growth rate. Applying that formula here means valuing the stock at the end of Year 3, just before the constant-growth phase begins:

$$P_3 = \frac{D_4}{r - g_2} = \frac{\$3.63}{0.14 - 0.05} = \$40.33$$

Don't forget that $40.33 is the estimated price of the stock *three years from now*. To express that in today's dollars, we have to discount it for three additional years as follows:

$$\frac{\$40.33}{(1.14)^3} = \$27.22$$

This represents the value today of all dividends that occur in Year 4 and beyond. To estimate the present value of the entire dividend stream, which of course represents the price of the stock today, we simply put the two pieces together:

$$\text{Total value of stock, } P_0 = \$6.67 + \$27.22 = \$33.89$$

Figure 5.1 depicts a time line for this calculation. The following single algebraic expression shows the same information in a more compact form:

$$P_0 = \frac{\$2.40}{(1.14)^1} + \frac{\$2.88}{(1.14)^2} + \frac{\$3.46 + \$40.33}{(1.14)^3} = \$33.89$$

The numerator of the last term contains both the final dividend payment of the rapid-growth phase, $3.46, and the present value *as of the end of Year 3* of all future dividends, $40.33. The value of the firm's stock using the variable growth model is $33.89.

Figure 5.1 Valuing a Stock Using the Variable Growth Model

The stock's value consists of (1) the present value of dividends during the three-year rapid-growth phase and (2) the present value of the constant-growth perpetuity which begins in four years.

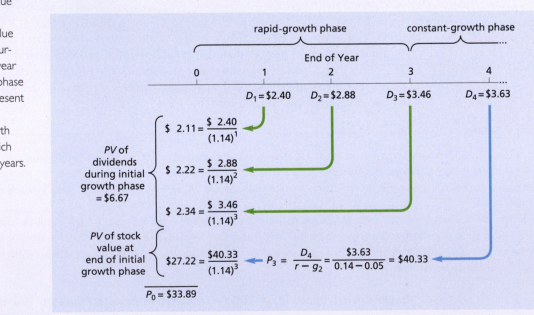

Source: www.sec.gov

As with most of our valuation models, it is possible to take the stock's market price as given and use the model to "reverse engineer" the growth rate. In other words, a stock analyst might use this model to estimate how much dividend growth investors are expecting given the price they are willing to pay for the stock.

EXAMPLE

Church & Dwight Co. is a producer of consumer products ranging from the Arm & Hammer baking soda brand to Trojan condoms. From 1999–2011, the company increased their dividend at an annual rate of about 20%, a figure roughly in line with the company's earnings growth over the same period. With total revenues in 2011 of more than $2.6 billion, Church & Dwight was hardly a consumer products giant. By comparison, Procter & Gamble's revenues in 2011 were close to $80 billion.

Even though Church & Dwight appeared to have plenty of room to grow entering 2012, no firm can sustain a 20% growth rate forever. Mature consumer products firms tend to grow at a rate that tracks overall economic growth. Let's assume that investors require a 10% return on Church & Dwight shares, and that they expect the firm to continue to increase dividends by 20% per year for a time. However, eventually annual dividend growth will settle down to 4%. Suppose that in 2011, the stock was selling for $69. If the 2011 dividend was $0.68 per share, how long would Church & Dwight have to sustain a 20% growth rate to justify the $69 stock price?

We will apply Equation 5.5 by using a trial-and-error approach to estimate how long investors expect the 20% growth rate to continue. For example, suppose they expect dividends to continue growing at that rate through 2016. The expected dividend stream would be:

Year	Dividend Calculation	
2012	$0.68(1 + 0.20)^1$	= $0.82
2013	$0.68(1 + 0.20)^2$	= $0.98
2014	$0.68(1 + 0.20)^3$	= $1.18
2015	$0.68(1 + 0.20)^4$	= $1.41
2016	$0.68(1 + 0.20)^5$	= $1.69
2017	$0.68(1 + 0.20)^5(1.04)$	= $1.76

Plugging these values into Equation 5.5 we have:

$$P = \frac{\$0.82}{(1 + 0.10)^1} + \frac{\$0.98}{(1 + 0.10)^2} + \frac{\$1.18}{(1 + 0.10)^3} + \frac{\$1.41}{(1 + 0.10)^4} + \frac{\$1.69}{(1 + 0.10)^5}$$
$$+ \left[\frac{1}{(1 + 0.10)^5} \times \frac{\$1.76}{0.10 - 0.04} \right] = \$22.66$$

Given these assumptions, the estimated price of Church & Dwight stock is less than one-third of its market value in 2011, so investors may be anticipating a more prolonged period of rapid dividend growth than assumed in our calculation. We could repeat this process, extending the rapid-growth phase a few years each time, until the estimated price is close to the actual market price. For example, if we assume that Church & Dwight dividends will grow at a 20% rate for 15 years, then the estimated stock price is $65.41.[6]

$$P = \frac{\$0.82}{(1 + 0.10)^1} + \frac{\$0.98}{(1 + 0.10)^2} + \cdots + \frac{\$10.48}{(1 + 0.10)^{15}} + \left[\frac{1}{(1 + 0.10)^{15}} \times \frac{\$10.90}{0.10 - 0.04} \right] = \$65.41$$

An investor who believes that Church & Dwight is unlikely to achieve 20% growth in dividends for such a long period of time might conclude that in 2011 the firm's stock was overvalued. Of course, some investors might believe that the company's dividends will grow rapidly for a longer period of time, and in that case the stock might seem like a bargain at $69.

5-2f How to Estimate Growth

By now, it should be apparent that a central component in many stock-pricing models is the growth rate. Unfortunately, analysts face a tremendous challenge in estimating a firm's growth rate, whether that growth rate refers to dividends, earnings, sales, or almost any other measure of financial performance. A firm's rate of growth depends on several factors. Among the most important, however, are the size of the investments it makes in new and existing projects and the rate of return those investments earn.

A simple method for estimating how fast a firm will grow uses information from financial statements. This approach acknowledges the importance of new investments in driving future growth. First, calculate the magnitude of new investments

? WHAT TO ASK

In what lines of business does your company expect to see the most growth and why?

---

[6]Notice in this equation that the dividend in 15th year equals $0.68(1.20)^{15}$, and the first dividend in the constant-growth period, i.e., the year 16 dividend, is just 4% more than the prior year's dividend.

that the firm can make by determining its *retention rate, rr*, the fraction of the firm's earnings that it retains. Second, calculate the firm's return on common equity, *ROE* (see Chapter 2), to estimate the rate of return that new investments will generate. The product of those two values is the firm's growth rate, *g*.

(Eq. 5.6)
$$g = rr \times ROE$$

EXAMPLE

In an annual report released in 2010, Church & Dwight reported net income of $243 million and total stockholders' equity of $1,602 million. Therefore, the firm's ROE was 15.2% ($243 ÷ $1,602). Church & Dwight paid $32 million in cash dividends that year, so their retention rate was 86.8% (1 — $32 ÷ $243). By taking the product of the ROE and the retention rate, we can estimate Church & Dwight's growth rate at 13.2% (0.152 × 0.868).

An alternative approach to estimating growth rates makes use of historical data. Analysts track a firm's sales, earnings, and dividends over several years in an attempt to identify growth trends. But how well do growth rates from the past predict growth rates in the future? Unfortunately, the relationship between past and future growth rates for most firms is surprisingly weak. The fact that growth rates are largely unpredictable should not come as a great surprise. One of the most fundamental ideas in economics is that competition limits the ability of a firm to generate abnormally high profits for a sustained period. When one firm identifies a profitable business opportunity, people notice, and entrepreneurs (or other companies) attempt to enter the same business. For example, consider the proliferation of smart phones and tablet devices following the success of Apple's iPhone and iPad. As more and more firms enter, profits (or the growth rate in profits) fall. At some point, if the industry becomes sufficiently competitive, profits fall to such a low level that some firms exit. As firms exit, profits for the remaining firms rise again. The constant pressure created by these competitive forces means that it is rare to observe a firm with a consistent, long-term growth trend. Perhaps one reason that companies such as Microsoft and Intel are so well known is that their histories of exceptional long-run growth are so uncommon.

Cengage Learning

Kenneth French, Dartmouth College

"Competition is one of the most pervasive forces out there in the economy."

See the entire interview at **SMART** | finance

Smart Ideas Video

5-2g What If There Are No Dividends?

After seeing the different versions of the dividend growth models, students usually ask, "What about firms that don't pay dividends?" Though many large, well-established firms in the United States pay regular dividends, many firms do not pay dividends at all. Younger firms with excellent growth prospects are less likely to pay dividends than are more mature firms, and recent decades have seen tremendous growth in the number of young, high-growth companies in the United States.

Can we apply the stock-valuation models covered thus far to firms that pay no dividends? Yes and no. On the affirmative side, firms that do not currently pay dividends may begin paying them in the future. In that case, we simply modify the equations presented earlier to reflect that the firm pays its first dividend, not in one year, but several years in the future. However, predicting when firms will begin paying dividends and what the dollar value of those far-off dividends will be is extremely difficult. Consider the problem of forecasting dividends for a company such as Yahoo! Since its IPO in April 1996, Yahoo! has paid no cash dividends even though its revenues have increased from about $19 million to more than $6.4 billion. Yahoo! has been profitable in recent years and has accumulated cash reserves close to $3 billion. Is Yahoo! ready to start paying dividends, will it continue to reinvest income to finance growth, or will it be acquired by another firm? In all likelihood, investors will have to wait several years to receive Yahoo!'s first dividend, and there is no way to determine with any degree of precision when that will happen. Consequently, analysts attempting to estimate the value of Yahoo! generally use other methods such as the free cash flow method or the "comparables" approach described in the next sections.

What happens if a company never plans to pay a dividend or otherwise to distribute cash to investors? Our answer to this question is that for a stock to have value, there must be an expectation that the firm will distribute cash in some form to investors at some point in the future. That cash could come in the form of dividends or share repurchases. If the firm is acquired by another company for cash, the cash payment comes when the acquiring firm purchases the shares of the target. Investors must believe that they will receive cash at some point in the future. If you have a hard time believing this, we invite you to buy shares in the Graham and Smart Corporation, a firm expected to generate an attractive revenue stream from selling its products and services. This firm promises never to distribute cash to shareholders in any form. If you buy shares, you will have to sell them to another investor later to realize any return on your investment. How much are you willing to pay for these shares?

5-2 Concept Review Questions

3. Why is it appropriate to use the perpetuity formula from Chapter 3 to estimate the value of preferred stock?

4. When a shareholder sells common stock, what is being sold? What gives a share of common stock value?

5. Using a dividend forecast of $2.79, a required return of 10%, and a growth rate of 2.75%, we obtained a price for Integrys Energy Group of $38.48. What would happen to this price if the market's required return on Integrys stock increased?

5-3 The Free Cash Flow Approach to Common Stock Valuation

One way to deal with the valuation challenges presented by a firm that does not pay dividends is to value the free cash flow generated by the firm. This approach makes sense because, after all, if you buy a firm, you obtain rights to all of its free cash flow. The advantage of this procedure is that it requires no assumptions about when the firm distributes cash dividends to stockholders. In practice, most analysts estimate the value of a stock using several different methods to see how widely the alternative estimates vary. Therefore, the free cash flow approach is widely used, even for stocks that do pay dividends. When using the free cash flow approach, we begin by asking, what is the total operating cash flow generated by a firm? Next, we subtract from the firm's operating cash flow the amount needed to fund new investments in both fixed assets and working capital. The difference is total free cash flow (FCF). We introduced the equation for free cash flow in Chapter 2, but here it is again:

free cash flow (FCF)
The net amount of cash flow remaining after the firm has met all operating needs, including capital expenditure and working capital needs. Represents the cash amount that a firm could distribute to investors after meeting all its other obligations.

$$FCF = OCF - \Delta FA - \Delta WC$$

Free cash flow represents the amount of cash that a firm could distribute to investors after meeting all its other obligations. Note that we used the word *investors* in the previous sentence. Total free cash flow is the amount that the firm could distribute to *all types of investors,* including bondholders, preferred shareholders, and common stockholders. Once we have estimates of the *FCFs* that a firm will generate over time, we can discount them at an appropriate rate to obtain an estimate of the total enterprise value.

Finance in Your Life

Should I Buy a 25% Interest in Sawft, Inc.?

A friend offers you the opportunity to buy into his twoyear-old software business, Sawft, Inc. Your friend will give you a 25% interest in the company for $50,000. Some of the company's key financial data are summarized below:

Free cash flow (prior year)	$27,800
Expected annual growth in free cash flow	
Next 3 years	12%
Year 4 to ∞	5%
Your required return	20%

You need to determine (1) the value of the business and (2) whether a 25% interest in the business is worth $50,000. Use the variable growth model to estimate the value of the business starting with estimates of the free cash flows (FCFs) at the end of each of the next four years:

Year 1 $FCF = \$27,800 \times 1.12 = \$31,136$

Year 2 $FCF = \$31,136 \times 1.12 = \$34,872$

Year 3 $FCF = \$34,872 \times 1.12 = \$39,057$

Year 4 $FCF = \$39,057 \times 1.05 = \$41,010$

Next, we calculate the present value (PV_0) of the FCFs for the first three years:

$$PV_0 = \$31,136 \div 1.20^1 + \$34,872 \div 1.20^2$$
$$+ \$39,057 \div 1.20^3$$
$$= \$25,947 + \$24,217 + \$22,602$$
$$= \mathbf{\$72,766}$$

Then we calculate the PV_3 (at the end of year 3) of the FCFs from year 4 to ∞.

$$PV_3 = \$41,010 \div (0.20 - 0.05)$$
$$= \frac{\$41,010}{0.15}$$
$$= \$273,400$$

Discounting the end-of-year-3 cash flow above back to time 0, we get:

$$PV_0 = \frac{\$273,400}{1.20^3}$$
$$= \mathbf{\$158,218}$$

Adding the PV_0s for the first three years to those for year 4 to ∞, we get:

(1)   **Current value of the business** = **$72,766** + **$158,218** = **$230,984**

Taking 25% of the current value of the business, we get:

(2)   **Value of a 25% interest in the business** = 0.25 × **$230,984** = **$57,746**

Assuming your estimates are correct, you should pay $50,000 for a 25% interest in Sawft, Inc., given that it's worth $57,746.

But what do we mean by "an appropriate discount rate"? This is a subtle issue that we discuss in much greater detail in Chapter 10. To understand the main idea, recall that FCF represents the total cash available for all investors. We suspect that debt is not as risky as preferred stock, and that preferred stock is not as risky as common stock.

weighted average cost of capital (WACC)
The after-tax, weighted average required return on all types of securities issued by a firm, where the weights equal the percentage of each type of financing in a firm's overall capital structure.

This means that bondholders, preferred shareholders, and common stockholders each have a different required return in mind when they buy a firm's securities. Somehow we have to capture these varying required rates of return to come up with a single discount rate to apply to free cash flow, the aggregate amount available for all three types of investors. The solution to this problem is known as the **weighted average cost of capital (WACC)**.[7] The *WACC* is the after-tax, weighted average required return on all types of securities issued by the firm, where the weights equal the percentage of each type of financing in the firm's overall capital structure. For example, suppose that a firm finances its operation with 50% debt and 50% equity. Suppose that the firm pays an after-tax return of 8% on its outstanding debt and that investors require a 16% return on the firm's shares. The *WACC* for this firm would be calculated as follows:

$$WACC = (0.50 \times 8\%) + (0.50 \times 16\%) = 12\%$$

If we obtain forecasts of the *FCFs*, and if we discount those cash flows at a 12% rate, the resulting present value is an estimate of the total value of the firm, which we denote V_{firm}.

When analysts value free cash flows, they use some of the same types of models that we have used to value other kinds of cash flow. We could assume that a firm's free cash flows will experience zero, constant, or variable growth. In each instance the procedures and equations would be the same as those introduced earlier for dividends, except we would now substitute *FCF* for dividends.

Remember, our goal in using the free cash flow approach is to develop a method for valuing a firm's shares without making assumptions about its dividends. The free cash flow approach begins by estimating the total value of the firm. To find out what the firm's shares, V_{stock}, are worth, we subtract from the total enterprise value, V_{firm}, the value of the firm's debt, V_{debt}, and the value of the firm's preferred stock, $V_{preferred}$. Equation 5.7 depicts this relationship:

(Eq. 5.7)
$$V_{stock} = V_{firm} - V_{debt} - V_{preferred}$$

We already know how to value bonds and preferred shares, so this step is relatively straightforward. Once we subtract the value of debt and preferred stock from the total enterprise value, the remainder equals the total value of the firm's shares. Simply divide this total by the number of shares outstanding to calculate the value per share, P_0.

EXAMPLE

Had a good cup of coffee lately? Probably the best-known purveyor of coffee is Starbucks Corp. By 2010, the company had nearly 17,000 coffeehouses in 50 countries, and its coffee shops had become so ubiquitous that investors wondered what prospects the firm had for additional growth. Its stock traded in the $32–$33 range during the first days of 2011. At the end of its 2010 fiscal year, Starbucks had debt with a market value of about $550 million, no preferred stock, and 743 million shares of common stock outstanding. Its fiscal year 2010 *free cash flow (FCF)*, calculated using the techniques presented in Chapter 2, was about $1.5 billion. After posting annual revenue growth rates exceeding 20% in every year from 2003–2007, Starbucks was showing signs of slowing down, with revenue growth between 2007–2010 averaging just 4.5% per year. In fact, the company was shifting its strategy away from its traditional coffeehouse business toward a consumer products focus. Given the maturation of Starbucks's traditional business and the uncertainty of its success in changing into a purveyor of coffee-related consumer products, we will assume a long-run growth rate of 4% for the company's free cash flows. We will also assume that Starbucks's WACC equals 10%.

To estimate the value of Starbucks common stock, we begin by using the constant growth model to value the entire enterprise. Our forecast for 2011 free cash flow is just 4% more than the figure generated in 2010:

$$FCF(2011) = FCF(2010) \times 1.04 = \$1.5 \times 1.04 = \$1.56 \text{ billion}$$

To calculate the present value of Starbucks' future free cash flows, we simply apply Equation 5.4:

$$V_{firm} = \frac{\$1.56}{(0.10 - 0.04)} = \$26 \text{ billion.}$$

[7]We provide only a brief sketch of the *WACC* concept at this point, deferring a deeper analysis until Chapter 10.

continued

Substituting Starbucks' enterprise value, V_{firm}, of \$26 billion, its debt value, V_{debt}, of \$550 million, and its preferred stock value, $V_{preferred}$, of \$0 into Equation 5.7, we get its total common stock share value, V_{stock}:

$$V_{stock} = \$26 - \$0.550 - \$0 = \$25.45 \text{ billion}$$

Dividing the total share value by the 743 million shares outstanding at the beginning of 2011, we get the per-share value of Starbucks' stock, P_{2011}:

$$P_{2011} = \frac{\$25,450,000,000}{743,000,000} = \$34.25$$

Our estimate of Starbucks' total common stock value at the beginning of calendar year 2011 of \$25,450,000,000, or \$34.25 per share, is slightly above its actual \$32–\$33 trading range during the first few weeks of 2011.[8]

The free cash flow approach offers an alternative to the dividend discount model that is especially useful when valuing shares that pay no dividends. As we'll see in the next section, security analysts have several alternative approaches at their disposal for estimating the value of shares. Not all of these methods involve discounted cash flow calculations, but in many cases they may arrive at similar estimates for the value of a share of stock.

5-3 Concept Review Question

6. How can the *free cash flow approach* to valuing an enterprise be used to resolve the valuation challenge presented by firms that do not pay dividends? Compare and contrast this model with the dividend valuation model.

5-4 Other Approaches to Common Stock Valuation

So far we have discussed valuation methods that require analysts to discount future dividends or free cash flows. These methods tend to work best for relatively mature, stable firms. Other methods may be used to value firms in different circumstances. For example, when a firm is performing very poorly and is on the verge of going bankrupt, the value of the firm's stock may reflect only the amount that analysts believe can be recovered by liquidating the firm's assets and paying off its debts. Or consider a relatively young, high-growth firm. Such a firm may have no dividends and negative free cash flow because the investments that it needs to make in working capital and fixed assets may exceed the company's operating cash flow. In this situation, an analyst may value the company by comparing it to other existing companies.

5-4a Liquidation Value and Book Value

liquidation value
The that remains after a firm's assets are sold and its liabilities are paid.

To calculate **liquidation value**, analysts estimate the amount of cash that remains if the firm's assets are sold and all liabilities paid. In most cases, a firm's liquidation value is far below its market value. That's because a healthy company has competitive advantages, such as brand value or intellectual property, that make it more valuable as a going concern. For instance, the total market value of Google's outstanding stock in early 2011 was almost \$200 billion, but the physical assets that the firm owned (e.g., cash, plant and equipment) could not have been sold for even half that value. Google's market value in 2011 was based primarily on its ability to generate cash in the future by developing innovative products and services.

However, there are times when it may be better to liquidate a firm than to keep operating it. For example, if a firm owns valuable assets that could be sold, but it is not able to use those assets to generate a profit, the shareholders may be better off if the firm liquidates.

---

[8]Here's an interesting postscript for this example. At the time of this analysis, the Summary screen for starbucks at the Yahoo! Finance site (www.finance.yahoo.com) showed a market capitalization of \$24 billion (versus our estimate of about \$25.45 billion) and a one-year price estimate for the stock of \$35.47 per share (versus our estimate of about \$34.25 per share). All in all, it appears that our estimates are in the ballpark.

Cengage Learning

Bill Eckmann, Investment Banker

"Besides the DCF analysis, every day I also use the comparable company analysis."

See the entire interview at **SMART**|finance

Smart Practices Video

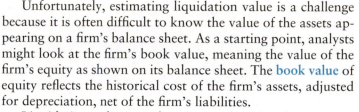

book value
The value of equity as shown on the firm's balance sheet.

comparable multiples
A valuation method that calculates a valuation ratio or multiple for each firm in a sample of similar firms, and then uses the average or median pricing multiple for the sample firms to estimate a particular firm's value.

? JOB INTERVIEW QUESTION

Our firm is contemplating an acquisition. Tell me at least two ways that you might go about estimating the value of our target company.

Cengage Learning

Robert Shiller, Yale University

"When the P/E ratio is high, it's typically justified by an argument that earnings will go up in the future."

See the entire interview at **SMART**|finance

Smart Ideas Video

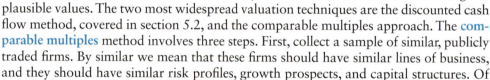

Unfortunately, estimating liquidation value is a challenge because it is often difficult to know the value of the assets appearing on a firm's balance sheet. As a starting point, analysts might look at the firm's book value, meaning the value of the firm's equity as shown on its balance sheet. The **book value** of equity reflects the historical cost of the firm's assets, adjusted for depreciation, net of the firm's liabilities.

Liquidation value may be more or less than book value, depending on the marketability of the firm's assets and the depreciation charges that have been assessed against fixed assets. For example, an important asset on many corporate balance sheets is real estate. The value of raw land appears on the balance sheet at historical cost, but, in many cases, its market value is much higher. In that instance, liquidation value may exceed book value. In contrast, suppose that the largest assets on a firm's balance sheet are highly customized machine tools, purchased two years ago. If the firm depreciates these tools on a straight-line basis over five years, the value shown on the books would equal 60% of the purchase price. However, there may be no secondary market for tools that have been customized for the firm's manufacturing processes. If the firm goes bankrupt, and the machine tools have to be liquidated, they may sell for much less than book value.

5-4b Market Multiples of Comparable Firms

Because of the uncertainty surrounding the inputs to any valuation model, analysts routinely employ different methods to analyze the same firm to estimate a range of plausible values. The two most widespread valuation techniques are the discounted cash flow method, covered in section 5.2, and the comparable multiples approach. The **comparable multiples** method involves three steps. First, collect a sample of similar, publicly traded firms. By similar we mean that these firms should have similar lines of business, and they should have similar risk profiles, growth prospects, and capital structures. Of course, no two firms are exactly alike, but an analyst using this approach attempts to gather a large number of companies that are as much alike as possible. Second, for each company in the sample, divide the firm's value (either its total value or value per share) by some measure of operating performance to get a "pricing multiple." For example, one common multiple is the price/earnings (P/E) ratio introduced in Chapter 2, where value per share is divided by the performance metric earnings per share. Other multiples frequently used by analysts include the ratio of the market value of a firm's equity to its book value (i.e., the price-to-book ratio), and the ratio of firm value (V_{firm}) to earnings before interest, taxes, and depreciation and amortization (EBITDA). Third, take the average or median pricing multiple from your sample of comparable firms, and multiply that by the operating variable (such as earnings) for the firm you want to value.

The intuition for this approach is relatively straightforward. Simply stated, the multiples method says that similar firms should sell at similar prices relative to their operating results, where operating results are often measured by sales revenue, earnings, or cash flows. For example, consider two firms which we will call Twilight and Potter. Both of these firms operate in the book publishing business, so their operating risks should be similar, which means that investors should expect about the same return from each company (we'll assume the required return is 10%). Likewise, let's assume that both firms have been growing at a steady 5% per year in the recent past. For simplicity, we will also assume that neither firm has any debt financing or preferred stock.

One big difference between the two firms is that Potter generates substantially more free cash flow than does Twilight. In fact, next year investors believe that Potter will generate $2.0 billion in free cash flow, and Twilight will deliver $1.0 billion. Let's value each company by discounting its free cash flows.

What Companies Do

How Investment Bankers Value Companies

When one firm attempts to acquire another, both the bidder and the target firm may hire an investment banker to provide fairness opinions, written reports that provide the banker's expert opinion regarding the fairness of the price offered by the bidder. Matt Cain and David Denis have investigated which methods bankers use in their fairness opinions to value target firms. As the chart shows, bankers almost always perform a discounted cash flow valuation as part of their analysis, but they sometimes use other methods. In a slight majority of acquisitions, bankers value the target company by using comparisons to public-firm multiples such as P/E ratios. Public-firm multiples are an example of valuation using the market multiples of comparable firms that we discussed in Section 5-4b. Bankers also use transaction multiples (price paid relative to target earnings in recent acquisitions) and transaction premia (what bidders have paid for targets, above and beyond their market values, in recent deals) when advising their clients.

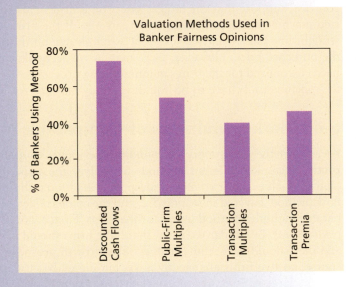

Source: Matt Cain and David Denis, "The Information Content of Fairness Opinions in Negotiated Mergers," Working paper (August 2008).

Remember, because the firms have no debt or preferred stock, the enterprise value and the stock value are one and the same.

$$V_{Twilight} = \$1,000,000,000/(0.10 - 0.05) = \$20,000,000,000$$

$$V_{Potter} = \$2,000,000,000/(0.10 - 0.05) = \$40,000,000,000$$

Potter is twice as valuable because it generates twice as much cash flow as does Twilight. However, these two companies have one more thing in common. Divide the firm value by next year's cash flow to get a value-to-cash flow multiple:

$$Twilight\ multiple = \$20,000,000/\$1,000,000 = 20$$

$$Potter\ multiple = \$40,000,000/\$2,000,000 = 20$$

The firms have the same multiple because their risks and growth prospects are identical. Another way of saying this is that in a discounted cash flow valuation of these firms, the denominator, $r\text{-}g$, is the same for Twilight and Potter (10% − 5% = 5%). For these two firms, each dollar of additional free cash flow adds $20 to firm value ($20 = $1 ÷ (10% − 5%)). Therefore, if we apply a multiple of 20 to a similar firm's cash flow, we are really just taking a shortcut to get the same answer that we would get if we did a discounted cash flow valuation for that firm. Given these results, an analyst might value a third book publishing company by forecasting its cash flows one year ahead and simply multiplying that number times 20, the multiple for comparable firms.

In practice, things do not work out as precisely as in the previous example. The next illustration shows a more realistic application of valuation using multiples.

EXAMPLE

You work for a large technology firm that is considering making an offer to buy Smart Phonz Apps, a young, privately-held startup company. By doing careful due diligence work, you have estimated that this company's revenues next year will be $195 million and its earnings before interest, taxes, depreciation and amortization (EBITDA) will be $105 million. Smart Phonz has $100 million of outstanding debt. Performing a discounted cash flow valuation of this firm would require you to estimate both the firm's WACC and its growth rate. Before doing that, you decide to conduct a public-firm multiples analysis on three similar firms. Firms A, B, and C are all companies that went public via an initial public offering (IPO) of common stock in the last few years, and each of these firms has a staff of software engineers who write programs for cell phone apps and tablet devices. The table below summarizes some key information for each of these firms.

Companies Comparable to Smart Phonz	Outstanding Shares (millions)	Stock Price	Debt Outstanding ($ millions)	Revenues ($ millions)	EBITDA ($ millions)
Company A	100	$5	$100	$100	$68
Company B	200	$2	$150	$95	$65
Company C	50	$7.50	$200	$150	$63

From this information, you calculate two multiples for each firm: (1) the ratio of total firm value to revenues, and (2) the ratio of total firm value to EBITDA. To illustrate for Company A, firm value equals the market value of outstanding equity plus the value of outstanding debt:

$$V_{Firm\ A} = V_{stock} + V_{debt} = (100{,}000{,}000 \times \$5) + \$100{,}000{,}000 = \$600{,}000{,}000$$

Next, divide this figure by total revenues or by EBITDA to obtain the desired multiple.

$$\frac{Value}{Revenues} = \frac{\$600{,}000{,}000}{\$100{,}000{,}000} = 6.0 \qquad \frac{Value}{EBITDA} = \frac{\$600{,}000{,}000}{\$68{,}000{,}000} = 8.8$$

Repeating these calculations for Companies B and C we obtain the following results.

	Equity Value ($ millions)	Firm Value ($ millions)	Value-to-Revenue Multiple	Value-to-EBITDA Multiple
Company A	$500	$600	6.0	8.8
Company B	400	550	5.8	8.5
Company C	375	575	3.8	9.1
Average			5.2	8.8

Now simply use the average value of each multiple to estimate the total firm value for Smart Phonz. Based on the multiple of firm value to revenues, Smart Phonz should be worth about $1.014 billion ($195 million times 5.2), and based on the multiple of firm value to EBITDA, the value of Smart Phonz is a bit lower at $924 million ($105 million times 8.8). You might then conduct a separate discounted cash flow valuation of Smart Phonz to see whether that estimate is also roughly in line with the estimate of about $1 billion that you just calculated based on multiples.

	Smart Phonz Valuation Based on	
	Revenues ($ millions)	EBITDA ($ millions)
Average comparable multiple	5.2	8.8
Smart Phonz Operating Metric	$195	$105
Estimated Value of Smart Phonz	$1,014	$924

If you wanted to estimate the equity value of Smart Phonz, you could just subtract its debt value from the enterprise values just calculated. This indicates that Smart Phonz's equity is worth about $900 million (= $1 billion enterprise value minus $100 million debt). Alternatively, you could calculate the equity value directly using equity comparable multiples, such as the price/earnings ratio (i.e., the price per share of common stock divided by earnings per share). It is important to recognize that if equity value is in the numerator of the ratio ("price" in the P/E ratio), then to make the ratio "apples-to-apples" the denominator must represent a flow that goes to stockholders only ("earnings" in the P/E ratio). That is, if the numerator is stock price, you should not use a number like EBITDA in the denomintor, because EBITDA can be used to pay both stockholders and bondholders.[9]

To summarize, if stock price or total equity value is in the numerator of the comparable multiple, then use a denominator that is associated only with equityholders (like earnings or book equity). In contrast, in the calculations done in the tables above, because total firm value was in the numerator of the comparable multiple, we used a denominator (EBITDA) that is associated with all investors, both bondholders and stockholders.

There is one other important consideration when you use mutiples to perform valuation analysis: When the denominator of a ratio is small, the overall ratio becomes large. For example, if earnings fall to $0.01 for one comparable firm, then its P/E ratio might be very large (if price is $20, then its P/E multiple would be 2000 (= 20 ÷ 0.01) and also vary greatly with small movements in the denominator (if earnings increased to $0.10, the PE multiple would become 200). Smart analysts watch for extreme outliers like a P/E ratio of 2000, and when extreme values appear in a sample of comparables, they exclude the outliers or use the median value for the group rather than the average.

---

[9]EBITDA (earnings before interest, taxes, depreciation and amortization) represents funds that can be used to pay bondholders (via debt interest) and stockholders (via earnings that can be paid out as dividends).

5-4 Concept Review Questions

7. Why might the terms *book value* and *liquidation value,* used to determine the value of a firm, be characterized as viewing the firm as "dead rather than alive"? Explain why those views are inconsistent with the discounted cash flow valuation models.

8. When comparing P/E ratios of different firms, analysts sometimes say that firms with higher P/E ratios are expected to grow faster than firms with lower P/E ratios. What is the discounted cash flow basis for this statement? Use a discounted cash flow argument to illustrate how two firms who are expected to grow at the same rate might still have different P/E ratios.

5-5 Primary and Secondary Markets for Equity Securities

In this section, we look at how stocks are sold to investors in the primary market and how investors trade stocks with each other in the secondary market. As previously noted, the *primary market* refers to the market in which firms originally issue new securities. Once the securities have been issued in the primary market, investors can trade them in the *secondary market.*

5-5a Investment Banking Functions and the Primary Market

Investment banks (IBs) play an important role in helping firms raise long-term debt and equity financing in the world's capital markets. **Investment banks** sell new security issues and assist and advise corporations about major financial transactions, such as mergers and acquisitions, in exchange for fees and commissions. The three principal lines of business of an investment bank are:

1. Corporate finance
2. Trading
3. Asset management

Of the three business lines, corporate finance enjoys the highest visibility and includes activities such as merger and acquisitions (M&A) advisory work and new security issues. Corporate finance tends to be the most profitable line of business, especially for more prestigious banks such as Goldman Sachs and Morgan Stanley, which can charge the highest underwriting and advisory fees. Investment banks earn revenue from trading debt and equity securities, either by acting as dealers, by facilitating trade between unrelated parties, or by holding inventories of securities that can make or lose money for the bank as inventory values fluctuate. Finally, asset management encompasses several different activities, including managing money for individuals with high net worth, operating and advising mutual funds, and managing pension funds.

When they advise corporations that want to issue common stock in the public markets, investment banks play several different roles. The complexity of the investment banker's job depends on (1) whether a firm is selling equity for the first time, and in the process, converting from private to public ownership, or (2) whether the firm has previously issued stock and is simply going back to the equity market to raise money. The first type of transaction is much more complex and is called an **initial public offering (IPO)**. The second type is known as a **seasoned equity offering (SEO)**, implying that the stock offered for sale has previously been seasoned in the market. Usually, firms hire investment bankers through a process known as a **negotiated offer**, where, as the name implies, the issuing firm negotiates the terms of the offer directly with one investment bank.[10] Firms issuing securities

investment banks
Financial institutions that assist firms in raising long-term debt and equity financing in the world's capital markets, advise corporations about major financial transactions, and are active in the business of selling and trading securities in secondary markets.

initial public offering (IPO)
A corporation offers its shares for sale to the public for the first time.

seasoned equity offering (SEO)
An equity issue by a firm that already has common stock outstanding.

negotiated offer
A process used by an issuer to hire an investment banker with whom it directly negotiates the terms of the offer.

lead underwriter
The investment bank that takes the primary role in assisting a firm in a public offering of securities.

---

[10]Less common is a competitively-bid offer in which the firm issuing securities announces the terms of its intended sale, and investment banks bid for the business.

David Baum, Co-head of M&A for Goldman Sachs in the Americas

"You sit right at the crossroads of industry and capital markets."

See the entire interview at SMART|finance

Smart Practices Video

underwrite
The investment banker purchases shares from a firm and resells them to investors.

firm-commitment offering
An offering in which the investment bank agrees to *underwrite* the firm's securities, thereby guaranteeing that the firm will successfully complete its sale of securities.

underwriting spread
The difference between the *net price* and the *offer price* of an underwritten security issue.

prospectus
A document that contains extensive details about the issuer and describes the security it intends to offer for sale.

road show
A tour of major cities taken by a firm and its bankers several weeks before a scheduled offering; the purpose is to pitch the firm's business plan to prospective investors.

Jay Goodgold, Managing Director, Equities Division, Goldman Sachs

"The goal here on the road show is to see the major institutional clients in Boston, New York, Chicago, Denver, Los Angeles, San Francisco, London, Paris, Frankfurt, and Tokyo."

See the entire interview at SMART|finance

Smart Practices Video

often enlist the services of more than one investment bank. In these cases, it is typical for one of the banks to be named the lead underwriter, and the other participating banks are known as *comanagers*.

In most equity deals, the investment bank agrees to underwrite the issue in a firm-commitment offering, which means that the bank actually purchases the shares from the firm and resells them to investors. In firm-commitment offerings, investment banks receive compensation for their services via the underwriting spread, the difference between the price at which the banks purchase shares from firms (the *net price*) and the price at which they sell the shares to institutional and individual investors (the *offer price*). Underwriting fees can be quite substantial, especially for firms issuing equity for the first time. The vast majority of U.S. initial public offerings have underwriting spreads of exactly 7%, although lower spreads are common in very large IPOs. For example, if a firm conducting an IPO wants to sell shares worth $100 million, it will receive $93 million in proceeds from the offer. The underwriter earns the gross spread of $7 million. At the other extreme, large debt offerings of well-known issuers have underwriting spreads in the 0.5% range.

Just what do investment banks do to earn their fees? Investment banks perform a wide variety of services, ranging from carrying out the analytical work required to price a new security offering, to assisting the firm with regulatory compliance, marketing the new issues, and developing an orderly market for the firm's securities once they begin trading.

Early in the process of preparing for an equity offering, an investment bank helps file the necessary documents with regulators, starting with the *registration statement*, which provides information about the securities being offered. When a firm files documents with the Securities and Exchange Commission, it must take great pains to be sure that the information provided is timely and accurate. The investment bankers also prepare a prospectus, a document containing extensive details about the issuer and the security it intends to offer. The investment bank circulates the prospectus among potential investors as a starting point for marketing the new issue. The cover of the prospectus for the November 2010 IPO of a specialty retail company, The Fresh Market, Inc., appears as Figure 5.2 on next page.

While it is preparing the necessary legal documents, the investment bank must also begin to estimate the value of the securities the firm intends to sell. Investment banks use a variety of methods to value IPO shares, including discounted cash flow models and the comparable multiples approach.

Several weeks before the scheduled offering, the firm and its bankers take a whirlwind tour of major U.S. and international cities to solicit demand for the offering from investors. Affectionately called the road show, this grueling process usually lasts a week or two. It gives managers the opportunity to pitch their business plan to prospective investors. The investment banker's goal in this process is to build a book of orders for stock that is greater (often many times greater) than what the firm intends to sell. The expressions of interest by investors during the road show are not binding purchase agreements, and the investment bank does not commit to an offer price at this point. Instead, bankers give investors a range of prices at which the offer might sell based on their assessment of demand. Given the tentative nature of the demand expressed on the road show, the banker seeks to oversubscribe the offering to minimize the bank's underwriting risk. Naturally, one way to create excess demand for an offering is to set the offer price below the market-clearing level. The vast majority of IPOs in the United States and other countries are underpriced,

Figure 5.2   Prospectus for The Fresh Market, Inc.'s Initial Public Offering

The Fresh Market IPO prospectus provides investors with information to determine if they want to buy shares in the offering. On the front page, shown here, you see that The Fresh Market planned to sell 13.175 million shares for $22 each, to trade on The Nasdaq Global Select Market.

Filed Pursuant to Rule 424(b)(4)
Registration No. 333-166473

PROSPECTUS

13,175,000 Shares

The Fresh Market, Inc.
Common Stock

This is The Fresh Market, Inc.'s initial public offering. The selling stockholders, which include certain of our officers, are selling 13,175,000 shares of our common stock. We will not receive any proceeds from the sale of shares by the selling stockholders.

The initial public offering price is $22.00 per share. Currently, no public market exists for the shares. Our common stock has been approved for listing on The NASDAQ Global Select Market under the symbol "TFM".

Investing in our common stock involves risks that are described in the "Risk Factors" section beginning on page 8 of this prospectus.

	Per Share	Total
Public offering price	$22.00	$289,850,000
Underwriting discount	$1.54	$20,289,500
Proceeds, before expenses, to the selling stockholders	$20.46	$269,560,500

The underwriters may also purchase up to an additional 1,976,250 shares from the selling stockholders, at the public offering price, less the underwriting discount, within 30 days from the date of this prospectus to cover overallotments, if any.

Neither the Securities and Exchange Commission nor any state securities commission has approved or disapproved of these securities or determined if this prospectus is truthful or complete. Any representation to the contrary is a criminal offense.

The shares will be ready for delivery on or about November 10, 2010.

Joint Book-Running Managers

BofA Merrill Lynch   **J.P. Morgan**   **Goldman, Sachs & Co.**

Morgan Stanley   William Blair & Company   BMO Capital Markets   RBC Capital Markets

The date of this prospectus is November 4, 2010.

Source: Fresh Market

---

oversubscribe
When the investment banker builds a book of orders for stock that is greater than the amount of stock the firm intends to sell.

Kent Womack, University of Toronto

"It's very easy for analysts to have conflict of interest problems."

See the entire interview at **SMART | finance**

Smart Ethics Video

meaning that once IPO shares begin trading, they do so at a price that is above the original offer price set by the firm and its bankers.

After a share offering is successfully sold, the lead underwriter often serves as the principal *market maker* for trading in the firm's stock. In this role, the lead underwriter purchases shares from investors wishing to sell, and sells shares to investors wishing to buy, thus "making a market" in the new issue. The lead underwriter also assigns one or more research analysts to cover the issuing firm. The research reports these analysts write (which naturally tend to be flattering) help generate additional interest in trading the firm's securities.

To conclude this section, we want to highlight the conflicts that investment bankers may face. Firms issuing securities, on the one hand, want to obtain the highest possible price for their shares (or bonds). Firms also want favorable coverage from securities analysts employed by their investment bankers. Investors, on the other hand, want to purchase securities at prices low enough to ensure that they will earn a high return on their investments. Investors also value dispassionate, unbiased advice from analysts. Investment bankers must therefore walk a thin line, both ethically and economically, to please their constituents. Firms issuing securities are wise to remember this. Investment bankers deal

Figure 5.3   **The Secondary Market**

On a typical trading day, the secondary market is a beehive of activity, where literally billions of shares change hands. This market consists of two parts—the *broker market* and the *dealer market*—and as can be seen, each of these markets is made up of various exchanges and trading venues.

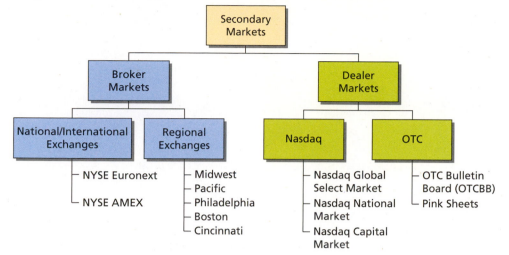

Source: From Gitman/Joehnk, *Personal Financial Planning, 12E.* © 2011 South-Western, a part of Cengage Learning, Inc. Reproduced by permission. www.cengage.com/permissions

with investors, especially large institutional investors, on a repeated basis. They must approach this group each time a new offering comes to the market. In contrast, over its entire life, a firm conducts just a single IPO.[11]

5-5b Secondary Markets for Equity Securities

The secondary markets permit investors to execute transactions among themselves—it's the marketplace where an investor can easily sell his or her holdings to someone else. Included among the secondary markets are the various *securities exchanges*, in which the buyers and sellers of securities are brought together for the purpose of executing trades. Another major segment of the market is made up of those securities that are listed and traded on the *Nasdaq market*, which employs an all-electronic trading platform to execute trades. Finally, there is the *over-the-counter (OTC) market* that deals in smaller, unlisted securities.

When you look at the secondary market *on the basis of how securities are traded*, you can essentially divide the market into two segments: broker markets and dealer markets. Figure 5.3 shows the structure of the secondary market in terms of broker or dealer markets. As you can see, the *broker market* consists of international, national, and regional securities exchanges, whereas the *dealer market* is made up of both the Nasdaq and the OTC.

The *biggest difference in the two markets is a technical point about how the trades are executed*. That is, when a trade occurs in a broker market (on one of the so-called securities exchanges), the two sides of the transaction, the buyer and the seller, are brought together and the trade takes place at that point: Investor

Jay Ritter, University of Florida

"Lots of buyers were willing to give things to the underwriters in terms of, for instance, generating extra commissions business."

See the entire interview at **SMART**|finance

Smart Ethics Video

broker market
A market in which the buyer and seller are brought together on a "securities exchange" to trade securities.

[11]A chief executive officer of a company that conducted an IPO during the 1990s told us, "You have two friends in an IPO: your lawyer and your accountant." Notice that the investment banker didn't make the list.

What Companies Do Globally

NYSE Euronext . . . on to Asia

NYSE Euronext, created by the April 4, 2007, merger of NYSE Group and Euronext N.V., is the world's largest and most liquid exchange group offering the most diverse array of financial products and services. Shortly after the merger, the heads of the merged NYSE Euronext voiced their determination to create a truly global market, including a move into China. John Thain, then chief executive of NYSE Euronext, said the company planned to expand its operations in Asia. "We want to be global, and to be global we need a bigger presence in Asia," he said.

The total capitalization of the companies listed on the exchange at the time of the merger was about $28.5 trillion, which was greater than the combined total for the next four largest exchanges in the world: the London Stock Exchange, the Tokyo Stock Exchange, Nasdaq, and the Deutsche Borse. In spite of its size, the NYSE Euronext was expected to face stiff competition from smaller and more nimble newcomers as well as from established rivals as they consolidate and as Europe introduces regulations allowing new competitors.

Not just any company can list its shares for trading on the NYSE Euronext. To qualify, a company must meet a variety of requirements that include having at least 400 stockholders with at least 100 shares each and at least 1.1 million shares outstanding worth $40 million or more. Furthermore, companies must meet minimum profitability standards in the years prior to their NYSE listing.

Sources: NYSE Euronext Web site and James Kanter, "Newly Merged NYSE Euronext has Asian Ambitions," *International Herald Tribune*, April 4, 2007, accessed from www.iht.com/bin/print.php?id=5140562.

NYSE Euronext
The largest and most prestigious broker market in the world.

dealer market
A market in which the buyer and seller are not brought together directly, but instead have their orders executed by market makers *securities dealers* who are *market makers* in the given security.

market makers
Securities dealers that "make markets" by offering to buy or sell certain securities at stated prices.

bid price
The price at which a *market maker* offers to purchase a security; the price at which an investor can sell a security.

ask price
The price at which a *market maker* offers to sell a security; the price at which one can purchase a security.

A sells his or her securities directly to the buyer, Investor B. In a sense, with the help of a *broker*, the securities change hands right there on the floor of the exchange. The largest broker market in the world is the NYSE Euronext, which was formed in 2007 by the merger of the NYSE and Euronext, a pan-European stock exchange. In contrast, when trades are made in one of the dealer markets, the buyer and seller are never brought together directly. Instead, their buy/sell orders are executed by market makers, who are *securities dealers* that "make markets" by offering to buy or sell certain securities at stated prices. Essentially, two separate trades are made: Investor A sells his or her securities to one dealer, and Investor B buys his or her securities from another, or possibly even the same, dealer. Thus, there is always a dealer involved in a dealer-market transaction. In the United States, the largest dealer market is the National Association of Securities Dealers Automated Quotation System, better known as Nasdaq.

Regardless of where a stock trade takes place, someone has to facilitate that trade, and the compensation he or she earns for doing so is the *bid-ask spread*. The bid price and ask price represent, respectively, the price at which a market maker offers to buy or sell a security. In effect, an investor pays the ask price when *buying* securities and receives the bid price when *selling* them. For example, an investor who buys 100 shares of Google stock may pay $600 per share, and another investor who sells 100 Google shares at the same time may receive just $599. The *bid-ask spread* (here, $1) represents the market maker's compensation.

5-5 Concept Review Questions

9. What is the difference between a *primary market* and a *secondary market*?

10. How are underwriters compensated?

11. What do firms and their investment bankers hope to learn on the road show?

12. When you buy a stock in the secondary market, does the firm that issued the stock receive cash?

13. Describe *broker markets* and *dealer markets* and list several differences between them.

Summary

- Preferred stock has both debt–and–equity–like features and does not convey an ownership position in the firm.

- Common stock represents a residual claim on a firm's cash flows, and common stockholders have the right to vote on corporate matters.

- The same principles apply to the valuation of preferred and common stock. The value of a share depends on the cash flow the share is expected to pay its owner over time.

- Because preferred stock pays a constant dividend with no specific expiration date, it can be valued using the perpetuity formula from Chapter 3.

- The approach used to value common stock depends on investors' expectations of dividend growth. Zero dividend growth, constant dividend growth, and variable dividend growth can all be incorporated into the basic valuation approach.

- Estimating dividend growth is very difficult. A starting point is to multiply the retention rate times the return on equity.

Table of Important Equations
1. $PS_0 = \dfrac{D_p}{r_p}$
2. $P_0 = \dfrac{D_1 + P_1}{(1 + r)^1}$
3. $P_0 = \dfrac{D_1}{r - g}$
4. $P_0 = \underbrace{\dfrac{D_0(1 + g_1)^1}{(1 + r)^1} + \dfrac{D_0(1 + g_1)^2}{(1 + r)^2} + \cdots \dfrac{D_0(1 + g_1)^N}{(1 + r)^N}}_{\text{PV of dividends during initial growth phase}}$ $\underbrace{+ \left[\dfrac{1}{(1 + r)^N} \times \dfrac{D_{N+1}}{r - g_2}\right]}_{\text{PV of all dividends beyond the initial growth phase}}$
5. $g = rr \times ROE$
6. $V_{stock} = V_{firm} - V_{debt} - V_{preferred}$

- Analysts use the free cash flow approach to value the entire enterprise. From that they derive a price per share.

- Other approaches to valuation rely on book value, liquidation value, or valuation multiples of comparable firms.

- Stock markets can be classified as either primary or secondary. Stocks are sold for the first time in the primary market, but after that, trading occurs in the secondary market.

- Investment bankers play an important role in helping firms issue new securities.

- Stocks trade both in broker markets that include national and regional securities exchanges and in dealer markets that include the Nasdaq and OTC markets.

Key Terms

ask price, 172
bid price, 172
book value, 165
broker market, 171
comparable multiple, 165
dealer market, 172
dividends, 151
firm-commitment offering, 169
free cash flow (*FCF*), 161
Gordon growth model 156

initial public offering (IPO), 168
investment banks, 168
lead underwriter, 168
liquidation value, 164
market makers, 172
negotiated offer, 168
NYSE Euronext, 172
oversubscribe, 170
prospectus, 169
proxy fight, 152

proxy statements, 152
residual claimants, 151
road show, 169
seasoned equity offering (SEO), 168
underwrite, 169
underwriting spread, 169
variable growth model, 157
weighted average cost of capital (WACC), 163
zero growth model, 155

Self-Test Problems

Answers to Self-Test Problems and the Concept Review Questions throughout the chapter appear in CourseMate with SmartFinance Tools at www.cengagebrain.com.

ST5-1. Omega Healthcare Investors pays a dividend on its Series B preferred stock of $0.539 per quarter. If the price of Series B preferred stock is $25 per share, what quarterly rate of return does the market require on this stock, and what is the effective annual required return?

ST5-2. McDonald's Corporation announced an increase of their annual dividend from $0.55 to $0.61 per share in September 2010. This continued a long string of dividend increases. McDonald's was one of a few companies that had managed to increase its annual dividend over many years, including through the financial crisis and recession from 2007–2009. Suppose you want to use the dividend growth model to value McDonald's stock. You believe the dividend will grow at 7% per year indefinitely, and you think the market's required return on this stock is 11%. Let's assume that McDonald's pays dividends annually and that the next annual dividend is expected to be $2.44 per share. The dividend will arrive in exactly one year. What would you pay for McDonald's stock right now? Suppose you buy the stock today, hold it just long enough to receive the next dividend, and then sell it. What rate of return will you earn on that investment?

Questions

Q5-1. How is preferred stock different from common stock?

Q5-2. How do you estimate the required rate of return on a share of preferred stock if you know its market price and its dividend?

Q5-3. The value of common stocks cannot be tied to the present value of future dividends because most firms don't pay dividends. Comment on the validity, or lack thereof, of this statement.

Q5-4. A common fallacy in stock market investing is assuming that a good company makes a good investment. Suppose we define a good company as one that has experienced rapid growth (in sales, earnings, or dividends) in the recent past. Explain the reasons why shares of good companies may or may not turn out to be good investments.

Q5-5. Why is it not surprising to learn that growth rates rarely show predictable trends?

Q5-6. The *book value* of a firm's common equity is usually lower than the market value of the common stock. Why? Can you describe a situation in which the *liquidation value* of a firm's equity could exceed its market value?

Q5-7. What is a *prospectus?*

Q5-8. Describe the role of the *lead underwriter* in a *firm-commitment offering*.

Q5-9. Why is the relationship between an investment banker and a firm selling securities somewhat adversarial?

Q5-10. Does secondary market trading generate capital for the company whose stock is trading?

Q5-11. Describe the basic structure of secondary markets. Be sure to differentiate between *broker markets* and *dealer markets*.

Problems

Valuing Preferred and Common Stock

P5-1. Argaiv Towers has outstanding an issue of preferred stock with a par value of $100. It pays an annual dividend equal to 8% of par value. If the required return on Argaiv preferred stock is 6%, and if Argaiv pays its next dividend in one year, what is the market price of the preferred stock today?

P5-2. Artivel Mining Corp.'s preferred stock pays a dividend of $5 each year. If the stock sells for $40 and the next dividend will be paid in one year, what return do investors require on Artivel preferred stock?

P5-3. Silaic Tools has issued preferred stock that offers investors a 10% annual return. The stock currently sells for $80, and the next dividend will be paid in one year. How much is the dividend?

P5-4. Suppose a preferred stock pays a quarterly dividend of $2 per share. The next dividend comes in exactly one-fourth of a year. If the price of the stock is $80, what is the effective annual rate of return that the stock offers investors?

P5-5. A particular preferred stock pays a $1 quarterly dividend and offers investors an effective annual rate of return of 12.55%. What is the price per share?

P5-6. The C. Alice Stone Company's common stock has paid a $3 dividend for so long that investors are now convinced that the stock will continue to pay that annual dividend forever. If the next dividend is due in one year and investors require an 8% return on the stock, what is its current market price? What will the price be immediately after the next dividend payment?

SMART | solutions

See the problem and solution explained step-by-step at **SMART** | finance

P5-7. Propulsion Sciences' (PS) stock dividend has grown at 10% per year for many years. Investors believe that a year from now the company will pay a dividend of $3 and that dividends will continue their 10% growth indefinitely. If the market's required return on PS stock is 12%, what does the stock sell for today? How much will it sell for a year from today after the stockholders receive their dividend?

P5-8. Investors believe that a certain stock will pay a $4 dividend next year. The market price of the stock is $66.67, and investors expect a 12% return on the stock. What long-run growth rate in dividends is consistent with the current price of the stock?

P5-9. Gail Dribble is analyzing the shares of Petscan Radiology. Petscan's stock pays a dividend once each year, and it just distributed this year's $0.85 dividend. The market price of the stock is $12.14. Gail estimates that Petscan will increase its dividends by 7% per year forever. After contemplating the risk of Petscan stock, Gail is willing to hold the stock only if it provides an annual expected return of at least 13%. Should she buy Petscan shares or not?

P5-10. Carbohydrates Anonymous (CA) operates a chain of weight-loss centers for carb lovers. Its services have been in great demand in recent years, and its profits have soared. CA recently paid an annual dividend of $1.35 per share. Investors expect that the company will increase the dividend by 20% in each of the next three years, and after that they anticipate that dividends will grow by about 5% per year. If the market requires an 11% return on CA stock, what should the stock sell for today?

P5-11. Hill Propane Distributors sells propane gas throughout the eastern half of Texas. Because of population growth and a construction boom in recent years, the company has prospered and expects to continue to do well in the near term. The company will pay a $0.75 per-share dividend to investors one year from now. Investors believe that Hill Propane will increase that dividend at 15% per year for the subsequent five years, before settling down to a long-run dividend growth rate of 3%. Investors expect an 8% return on Hill Propane common shares. What is the current selling price of the stock?

P5-12. Yesterday, September 22, 2012, Wireless Logic Corp. (WLC) paid its annual dividend of $1.25 per share. Because WLC's financial prospects are particularly bright, investors believe the company will increase its dividend by 20% per year for the next four years. After that, investors believe WLC will increase the dividend at a modest annual rate of 4%. Investors require a 16% return on WLC stock, and WLC always makes its dividend payment on September 22 of each year.
  a.   What is the price of WLC stock on September 23, 2012?
  b.   What is the price of WLC stock on September 23, 2013?
  c.   Calculate the percentage change in price of WLC stock from September 23, 2012, to September 23, 2013.
  d.   For an investor who purchased WLC stock on September 23, 2012, received a dividend on September 22, 2013, and sold the stock on September 23, 2013, what was the total rate of return on the investment? How much of this return came from the dividend, and how much came from the capital gain?
  e.   What is the price of WLC stock on September 23, 2016?
  f.   What is the price of WLC stock on September 23, 2017?

g.   For an investor who purchased WLC stock on September 23, 2016 received a dividend on September 22, 2017, and sold the stock on September 23, 2017, what was the total rate of return on the investment? How much of this return came from the dividend, and how much came from the capital gain? Comment on the differences between your answers to this question and your answers to part (d).

P5-13. Today's date is March 30, 2012. E-Pay, Inc., stock pays a dividend every year on March 29. The most recent dividend was $1.50 per share. You expect the company's dividends to increase at a rate of 25% per year through March 29, 2015. After that, you expect that dividends will increase at 5% a year. Investors require a 14% return on E-Pay stock. Calculate the price of the stock on the following dates: March 30, 2012; March 30, 2016; and September 30, 2013.

P5-14. One year from today, investors anticipate that Groningen Distilleries, Inc., stock will pay a dividend of $3.25 per share. After that, investors believe that the dividend will grow at 20% per year for three years before settling down to a long-run growth rate of 4%. The required rate of return on Groningen stock is 15%. What is the current stock price?

P5-15. Investors expect the following series of dividends from a particular common stock:

Year	Dividend
1	$1.10
2	$1.25
3	$1.45
4	$1.60
5	$1.75

After the fifth year, dividends will grow at a constant rate. If the required rate of return on this stock is 9% and the current market price is $45.64, what is the long-term rate of dividend growth expected by the market?

P5-16. In the constant growth model we can apply the equation $P = D \div (r - g)$, only under the assumption that $r > g$. Suppose someone tries to argue with you that for a certain stock, $r < g$ forever, not just during a temporary growth spurt. Why can't this be the case? What would happen to the stock price if this were true? If you try to answer simply by looking at the formula, you will almost certainly get the wrong answer. Think it through.

P5-17. Stephenson Technologies (ST) produces the world's greatest single-lens-reflex (SLR) camera. The camera has been a favorite of professional photographers and serious amateurs for several years. Unfortunately, the camera uses old film technology and does not take digital pictures. Ron Stephenson, owner and chief executive officer of the company, decided to let the business continue for as long as it can without making any new research and development investments to develop digital cameras. Accordingly, investors expect ST common stock to pay a $4 dividend next year and shrink by 10% per year indefinitely. What is the market price of ST stock if investors require a 12% return?

The Free Cash Flow Approach to Common Stock Valuation

P5-18. Roban Corporation is considering going public but is unsure of a fair offering price for the company. Before hiring an investment banker to assist in making the public offering, managers at Roban decide to make their own estimate of the firm's common stock value. The firm's chief financial officer gathered the following data for performing the valuation using the free cash flow valuation model.

The firm's weighted average cost of capital is 12%. It has $1,400,000 of debt at market value and $500,000 of preferred stock at its assumed market value. The estimated free cash flows over the next five years, 2013 through 2017, follow. Beyond 2017, to infinity, the firm expects its free cash flow to grow by 4% annually.

Year	Free Cash Flow
2013	$250,000
2014	290,000
2015	320,000
2016	360,000
2017	400,000

a. Estimate the value of Roban Corporation's entire company by using the *free cash flow approach*.

b. Use your finding in part (a), along with the data provided above, to find Roban Corporation's common stock value.

c. If the firm plans to issue 220,000 shares of common stock, what is its estimated value per share?

P5-19. Dean and Estevez, Inc. (D&E) is a firm that provides temporary employees to businesses. D&E's client base has grown rapidly in recent years, and the firm has been quite profitable. The firm's cofounders, Mr. Dean and Mr. Estevez, believe in a conservative approach to financial management and therefore have not borrowed any money to finance their business. A larger company in the industry has approached D&E about buying them out. In the most recent year, 2012, D&E generated free cash flow of $1.4 million. Suppose that D&E projects that these cash flows will grow at 15% per year for the next four years, and then will settle down to a long-run growth rate of 7% per year. The cofounders want a 14% return on their investment. What should be their minimum asking price from the potential acquirer?

Other Approaches to Common Stock Valuation

P5-20. Dauterive Barber Shops (DBS) specializes in providing quick and inexpensive haircuts for middle-aged men. The company retains about half of its earnings each year and pays the rest out as a dividend. Recently, the company paid a $3.25 dividend. Investors expect the company's dividends to grow modestly in the future, about 4% per year, and they require a 9% return on DBS shares. Based on next year's earnings forecast, what is DBS's price/earnings ratio? How would the price/earnings ratio change if investors believed that DBS's long-term growth rate was 6% rather than 4%? Retaining the original assumption of 4% growth, how would the price/earnings ratio change if investors became convinced that DBS was not very risky and were willing to accept a 7% return on their shares going forward?

Primary and Secondary Markets for Equity Securities

P5-21. Owners of the Internet bargain site FROOGLE.com have decided to take their company public by conducting an initial public offering of common stock. They have agreed with their investment banker to sell 3.3 million shares to investors at an offer price of $14 per share. The underwriting spread is 7%.

a. What is the net price that FROOGLE.com will receive for its shares?

b. How much money will FROOGLE.com raise in the offering?

c. How much do FROOGLE.com's investment bankers make on this transaction?

P5-22. An investor pays $101 to buy a share of Zenotrop stock. Simultaneously, a different investor sells one share of Zenotrop and receives $100 in cash. At the moment that these trades took place, what were the bid and ask prices of Zenotrop stock?

P5-23. Day trading, which typically refers to the practice of buying a stock and selling it very quickly (on the same day), was a popular activity during the Internet stock boom in the late 1990s. If a certain stock currently has a bid price of $50 and an ask price of $51, by how much would the stock price have to increase on a single day for a day trader to make a profit (assume that the bid-ask spread remains fixed throughout the day)?

THOMSON REUTERS | Business School Edition

Access financial information from the Thomson ONE – Business School Edition Web site for the following problem(s). Go to **www.tobsefin.swlearning.com/**. If you have already registered your access serial number and have a username and password, click **Enter**. Otherwise, click **Register** and follow the instructions to create a username and password. Register your access serial number and then click **Enter** on the aforementioned Web site. When you click Enter, you will be prompted for your username and password (please remember that the password is case sensitive). Enter them in the respective boxes and then click **OK** (or hit **Enter**). From the ensuing page, click **Click Here to Access Thomson ONE – Business School Edition Now!** This opens up a new window that gives you access to the Thomson ONE – Business School Edition database. You can retrieve a company's financial information by entering its ticker symbol (provided for each company in the problem(s)) in the box below "Name/Symbol/Key." For further instructions on using the Thomson ONE – Business School Edition database, please refer to the online Help.

P5-24. What rate of return do investors require on Eli Lilly & Company (LLY) common stock? Use the annual dividends per share reported for the last five years to determine the compound annual growth rate in dividends. Assume that Eli Lilly maintains this growth rate forever and has just paid a dividend. Use the latest available closing price as the current stock price. How does this required rate of return compare with the compound annual stock return over the last five years? Have investors been compensated sufficiently?

P5-25. Are shares of Eli Lilly & Company (LLY) currently under- or overpriced? Calculate the average P/E ratio over the last five fiscal years. Assuming that Eli Lilly maintains this average P/E into the future, determine the price per share using the average EPS estimate for the next fiscal year end. Is this estimate higher or lower than the latest closing price for Eli Lilly?

Since these exercises depend upon real-time data, your answers will change continuously depending upon when you access the Internet to download your data.

Smart Practices Video

Bill Eckmann, Investment Banker

"Besides the DCF analysis, every day I also use the comparable company analysis."

David Baum, Co-head of M&A for Goldman Sachs in the Americas

"You sit right at the crossroads of industry and capital markets."

Jay Goodgold, Managing Director, Equities Division, Goldman Sachs

"The goal here on the road show is to see the major institutional clients in Boston, New York, Chicago, Denver, Los Angeles, San Francisco, London, Paris, Frankfurt, and Tokyo."

Smart Ethics Video

Kent Womack, University of Toronto

"It's very easy for analysts to have conflict of interest problems."

Jay Ritter, University of Florida

"Lots of buyers were willing to give things to the underwriters in terms of, for instance, generating extra commissions business."

Smart Ideas Video

Kenneth French, Dartmouth College

"Competition is one of the most pervasive forces out there in the economy."

Robert Shiller, Yale University

"When the P/E ratio is high, it's typically justified by an argument that earnings will go up in the future."

SMART concepts

See a demonstration of the variable growth model.

SMART solutions

See the solutions to problems 5-7 and 5-14 explained step-by-step.

Mini-Case

Valuing Stocks

Your investment adviser has sent you three analyst reports for a young, growing company named Vegas Chips, Incorporated. These reports depict the company as speculative, but each one poses different projections of the company's future growth rate in earnings and dividends. All three reports show that Vegas Chips earned $1.20 per share in the year just ended. There is consensus that a fair rate of return to investors for this common stock is 14%, and that management expects to consistently earn a 15% return on the book value of equity (*ROE* = 15%).

Assignment

1. The analyst who produced report A makes the assumption that Vegas Chips will remain a small, regional company that, although profitable, is not expected to grow. In this case, Vegas Chips' management is expected to elect to pay out 100% of earnings as dividends. Based on this report, what model can you use to value a share of common stock in Vegas Chips? Using this model, what is the value?

2. The analyst who produced report B makes the assumption that Vegas Chips will enter the national market and grow at a steady, constant rate. In this case, Vegas Chips' management is expected to elect to pay out

40% of earnings as dividends. This analyst discloses news that this dividend has just been committed to current stockholders. Based on this report, what model can you use to value a share of common stock in Vegas Chips? Using this model, what is the value?

3. The analyst who produced report C also makes the assumption that Vegas Chips will enter the national market but expects a high level of initial excitement for the product that is then followed by growth at a constant rate. Earnings and dividends are expected to grow at a rate of 50% over the next year, 20% for the following two years, and then revert back to a constant growth rate of 9% thereafter. This analyst also discloses that Vegas Chips' management has just announced the pay out of 40% of the recently reported earnings to current stockholders. Based on this report, what model can you use to value a share of common stock in Vegas Chips? Using this model, what is the value?

4. Discuss the feature(s) that drive the differing valuations of Vegas Chips. What additional information do you need to garner confidence in the projections of each analyst report?

chapter 6

The Trade-Off Between Risk and Return

What Companies Do

Going Global Is Good for Your Portfolio

A report produced by the Australian financial advisory firm, Wealth Foundations, studied the performance of a portfolio invested entirely in Australian stocks and a portfolio consisting of stocks from other countries. Over the preceding 25 years, the average return on Australian stocks was 14%, while the average return on the international stock portfolio was just 12.7%. However, to earn the higher returns on Australian shares, investors had to endure greater volatility. The standard deviation (a statistical measure of volatility) of the Australian stock portfolio was 16.9% per year, compared to a standard deviation of just 15.2% for the international portfolio.

Portfolio	Return	Standard Deviation
Australia	14.0%	16.9%
International	12.7%	15.2%
Combined	13.8%	13.6%

The purpose of the Wealth Foundations report was to reinforce what finance textbooks have taught for years—diversification benefits investors. When Wealth Foundations constructed a diversified portfolio that combined stocks from Australia and other countries, they found that the diversified portfolio earned a return nearly as high as the "Australia only" portfolio (13.8%). However, the combined portfolio had less volatility than either the Australian or the international stock portfolio. In other words, by diversifying, Australian investors could substantially reduce the risk of their investments without a proportionate reduction in their returns.

Source: www.wealthfoundations.com.au/foundations-of-financial-economics-diversification.html

Learning Objectives

After studying this chapter, you should be able to:

- Calculate an investment's total return in dollar or percentage terms, identify the components of the total return, and explain why total return is a key metric for assessing an investment's performance;

- Describe the historical performance of asset classes such as Treasury bills, Treasury bonds, and common stocks, and articulate the important lessons that history provides;

- Calculate the standard deviation from a series of historical returns; and

- Distinguish between systematic and unsystematic risk, explain why systematic risk is more closely linked to returns than is unsystematic risk, and illustrate how diversification reduces volatility.

Finance teaches that investment returns are related to risk. From a purely theoretical perspective, it seems logical that risk and return should be linked, but the notion that an unavoidable trade-off between the two exists is grounded in fact. In countries around the world, historical capital market data offer compelling evidence of a positive relation between risk and return. That evidence is a major focus of this chapter.

In Chapters 4 and 5, we argued that corporate bonds are more risky than U.S. Treasury securities and that common stocks are riskier than either corporate or Treasury bonds. Based on that assessment, we should expect a relationship like that shown in Figure 6.1. If we arrange these assets from least to most risky, we expect returns to rise, as we move from left to right in the figure. Soon we will see that this is exactly the pattern revealed by historical data.

Perhaps the most important question in finance is, "What is it worth?" For an investor contemplating a stock purchase or for a corporate manager weighing a new plant construction proposal, placing a value on risky assets is fundamental to the decision-making process. The procedure for valuing a risky asset involves three basic steps:

1. Determining the asset's expected cash flows.

2. Choosing a discount rate that reflects the asset's risk.

3. Calculating the present value.

Finance professionals apply these three steps, known as *discounted cash flow (DCF) analysis*, to value a wide range of real and financial assets. Chapter 3 introduced you to the rather mechanical third step of this process—converting a sequence of future cash flows into a single number reflecting an asset's present value. Chapters 4 and 5 focused more on the first step in the process—projecting future cash flows. In this chapter and in Chapter 7, we will emphasize the second step in DCF valuation—determining a risk-appropriate discount rate.

We begin by establishing a precise measure of an investment's performance called the total return. An asset's total return captures any income that it pays as well as any changes in its price. With the definition of total return in hand, we proceed to study the historical performance of broad asset classes such as stocks and bonds. Our analysis examines both the nominal and real returns that different investments have earned over time. During the last 110 years, prices in the U.S. rose by a factor of 25. That is, the *purchasing power* of $1 in 1900 was roughly equivalent to the purchasing power of $25 today. Because inflation

---

Figure 6.1   The Trade-Off Between Risk and Return

Intuitively, we expect that investors seeking higher returns must be willing to accept higher risk. Moving along the line from safe assets such as Treasury bills to much riskier investments such as common stocks, returns should rise.

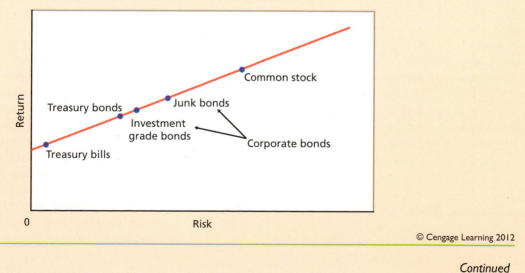

© Cengage Learning 2012

Continued

Continued

gradually erodes the value of a dollar, we focus on the real returns offered by various asset classes, not just their nominal returns. When people save their money and invest it, they do so in the hope of living more comfortably in the future. Their objective is not just to accumulate a large sum of money but to be able to spend that money to buy the necessities (and the luxuries) of life. Real returns matter because they measure the increase in buying power that a given investment provides over time.

All of this is relevant for financial managers because they work on behalf of the investors who provide money to corporations. Therefore, for managers to make value-maximizing decisions when they consider building a new plant, upgrading machinery, or launching a new product line, they have to assess each investment project's risk and then choose a discount rate that reflects the return that investors could obtain on similar investments elsewhere

in the market. Choosing a discount rate to value a specific asset requires answers to two critical questions. First, how risky is the asset, investment, or project that we want to value? Second, how much return should the project offer, given its risk? This chapter addresses the first question, showing how different ways of defining and measuring risk apply to individual assets as compared with portfolios (collections of different assets).

Building on this foundation, Chapter 7 will provide an answer to the second question. The *capital asset pricing model (CAPM)* proposes a specific way to measure risk and to determine what compensation the market expects in exchange for that risk. By quantifying the relationship between risk and return, the CAPM supplies finance professionals with a powerful tool for determining the value of financial assets such as shares of stock, as well as real assets such as new factories and equipment.

6-1 Understanding Returns

total return
A measure of the performance of an investment that captures both the income it paid out to investors and its capital gain or loss over a stated period of time.

Probably the first question that investors ask when they decide whether to undertake an investment is, "How much money will this investment earn?" In finance, we refer to the total gain or loss on an investment as the **total return**. The total return, expressed either in dollar terms or on a percentage basis, measures the change in wealth that an investor experiences from holding a particular asset such as a share of common stock or a bond.

6-1a The Components of Total Return

An investment's total return consists of two components. The first part is the income stream the investment produces. For bonds, the income stream comes in the form of interest. For common or preferred stock, dividends provide the income stream. As we learned in Chapters 4 and 5, the financial press regularly provides investment performance measures that primarily focus on an asset's income stream. For example, the *coupon yield,* which equals the coupon payment divided by the bond's market price, describes how much money the bondholder earns in interest as a percentage of the bond's price. Similarly, the *dividend yield,* equal to a stock's annual dividend payment divided by the stock price, highlights the income component of stock returns.

Measures such as the coupon yield and dividend yield may provide investors with useful information, but any performance measure that focuses entirely on an investment's income stream misses the second, and often the most important, component of total returns. That component is the change in the asset's price, called the **capital gain** or **capital loss**. For some investments, such as zero-coupon bonds and stocks that do not pay dividends, the capital gain or loss is the *only* component of total return because there is no income. For other investments, the price change may be more or less important than the income stream in determining the investment's total return.

capital gain
The increase in the price of an asset that occurs over a period of time.

capital loss
The decrease in the price of an asset that occurs over a period of time.

For example, suppose an investor spends $1,000 to purchase a newly issued ten year corporate bond that pays an annual coupon of $60. In this case, the coupon rate and the coupon yield are both 6% ($60 ÷ $1,000). Because this bond sells at par value, we know that the market requires a 6% return on the bond. Suppose we want to assess the performance of this investment after one year. To do that, we need to add up both the income paid by the bond and any price change that occurs during the year. At the end of the year, the investor receives a $60 coupon payment, but what is her bond worth? We know from Chapter 4 that the answer to that question depends on what happens to market interest rates during the year. Suppose that the market's required return has risen from 6% to 8%. At the end of the first year, the bond has nine years left until maturity. Discounting the remaining cash flows at 8%, we find that the bond's market price equals just $875.06:

$$P = \frac{\$60}{1.08^1} + \frac{\$60}{1.08^2} + \frac{\$60}{1.08^3} + \cdots + \frac{\$1,060}{1.08^9} = \$875.06$$

The investor's total return is considerably less than the 6% coupon yield. In fact, the capital loss caused by rising interest rates results in a negative total return. The investor earns income of $60, but she also experiences a capital loss of $124.94 ($1,000 − $875.06). That loss more than offsets the interest payment, and our investor ends the year with less wealth than when she started.

Note that the investor's total return this year does not depend on whether she sells the bond or continues to hold it. Selling or not selling the bond determines whether the capital loss in this example is *realized* or *unrealized*, but it has no affect on the investor's wealth (at least if we ignore taxes). At the end of the year, the investor has $60 in cash plus a bond worth $875.06. That is equivalent to owning $935.06 in cash, which would be the investor's position if she sells the bond.[1] In any case, this example illustrates that both the income and capital gain or loss components influence an investor's wealth. *The important lesson to remember is that one must focus on the total return when assessing an investment's performance.*

6-1b Dollar Returns and Percentage Returns

We can describe an investment's total return either in dollar terms or in percentage terms. Consider again the bond example in the previous three paragraphs. To calculate the *dollar return* on this investment, we simply add the income component to the capital gain or loss:

(Eq. 6.1)	**Total dollar return = income + capital gain or loss**

Earlier we defined an investment's total return as the change in wealth that it generates for the investor. In the present example, the investor begins with $1,000. A year later, she receives $60, and she owns a bond worth $875.06. Therefore, end-of-year wealth equals $935.06. The change in wealth due to this investment's performance equals −$64.94 ($935.06 − $1,000), which we can verify by plugging the appropriate values into Equation 6.1:

$$\text{Total dollar return} = \$60 + (-\$124.94) = -\$64.94$$

Dollar returns tell us, in an absolute sense, how much wealth an investment generates over time. Other things being equal, investors prefer assets that provide higher dollar returns. However, comparing the dollar returns of two different investments can be treacherous, as the following example illustrates.

EXAMPLE

Terrell purchases 100 shares of Micro-Orb stock for $25 per share. A year later, the stock pays a dividend of $1 per share and sells for $30. Terrell's total dollar return is:

Total dollar return = (number of shares) × (dividend income + capital gain)

Total dollar return = 100 × ($1 + $5) = $600

---

[1]Unrealized losses are sometimes called paper losses. This term simply means that the value of the paper that an investor holds (a bond or stock certificate) has gone down. Some investors believe that paper losses are irrelevant and that losses only matter when they are realized because an investor sells. We hope you will not be trapped by this fallacy. Sergey Brin is one of the world's richest people because he owns a large quantity of Google stock. If a stock-market crash causes Google shares to fall by half, then Brin is much less wealthy, even if he doesn't sell his stock. That his loss is only on paper does not mean that the loss is meaningless.

continued

Meanwhile, Kumar purchases 50 shares of Garcia Transportation Inc. for $15 per share. Garcia shares pay no dividends, but at the end of the year, the stock sells for $25. Kumar's total dollar return equals:

$$\text{Total dollar return} = 50 \times (\$10) = \$500$$

Based on these figures, it appears that Terrell had a better year than did Kumar. But before we reach that conclusion, we ought to recognize that at the beginning of the year, Terrell's investment was much larger than Kumar's.

The preceding example illustrates a problem we encounter when comparing dollar returns on different investments. Terrell's dollar return exceeds Kumar's by $100, but that does not necessarily mean that Terrell's stock performed better. Terrell spent $2,500 to purchase 100 Micro-Orb shares, while Kumar devoted just $750 to his investment in Garcia Transportation. Intuitively, we might expect Terrell to earn a higher dollar return than Kumar because he invested so much more than did Kumar.

Another way to compare outcomes is to calculate the *percentage return* on each investment. The total percentage return equals the total dollar return divided by the initial investment:

(Eq. 6.2)
$$\text{Total percentage return} = \frac{\text{total dollar return}}{\text{initial investment}}$$

EXAMPLE

Given that Terrell initially invested $2,500, while Kumar invested just $750, we can calculate their total returns on a percentage basis as follows:

$$\text{Terrell's return} = \frac{100 \times (\$1 + \$5)}{\$2,500} = \frac{\$600}{\$2,500} = 0.24 = 24\%$$

$$\text{Kumar's return} = \frac{50 \times (\$10)}{\$750} = \frac{\$500}{\$750} = 0.67 = 67\%$$

On a percentage basis, Kumar's investment performed better than did Terrell's, but on a dollar return basis the opposite is true. The conflict arises here because the initial amount invested by Terrell is so much larger than Kumar's up-front investment. Which investment would you rather have, one that makes you $600 richer or one that increases your initial stake by 67%? Comparing the returns on investments that involve different amounts of money is a fundamental problem to which we will return in Chapter 8. For now, we only say that dollar returns and percentage returns can lead to different relative rankings of investment alternatives.

Just as the total dollar return was the sum of an investment's income and its capital gain or loss, *the total percentage return equals the sum of the investment's yield and its percentage capital gain or loss.* Recall that the dividend yield equals a stock's dividend divided by its market price. Using the beginning-of-year price of Micro-Orb stock to calculate its dividend yield, we have:

$$\text{Micro-Orb dividend yield} = \frac{\$1}{\$25} = 0.04 = 4\%$$

Similarly, the percentage capital gain equals:

$$\text{Micro-Orb capital gain} = \frac{\$5}{\$25} = 0.20 = 20\%$$

Therefore, the total percentage return on Micro-Orb equals the sum of the dividend yield and the percentage capital gain:

$$\text{Micro-Orb total percentage return} = 4\% + 20\% = 24\%$$

Let us summarize the important points from this section:

- Measuring an investment's performance requires a focus on total return.
- The total return consists of two components, income and capital gain or loss.
- We can express total returns either in dollar terms or in percentage terms.

- When ranking the performance of two or more investments relative to each other, it is important to be careful that the amount of money initially invested in each asset is the same.
- If one asset requires a much larger up-front monetary commitment than the other, then dollar returns and percentage returns may lead to different performance rankings.

6-1 Concept Review Questions

1. In Chapter 4, we defined several bond return measures, including the *coupon*, the *coupon rate*, the *coupon yield*, and the *yield to maturity*. Indicate whether each of these measures (a) focuses on the total return or just one of the components of total return and (b) focuses on dollar returns or percentage returns.

2. You buy a stock for $40. During the next year, it pays a dividend of $2, and its price increases to $44. Calculate the total dollar and total percentage returns and show that each of these is the sum of the dividend and capital gain components.

6-2 The History of Returns (or How to Get Rich Slowly)

British writer Aldous Huxley once said, "That men do not learn very much from the lessons of history is the most important of all lessons that history has to teach." We are more optimistic. Certainly what we can learn from the history of financial markets benefits investors who study that history. Perhaps the most important lesson is this: an unavoidable trade-off exists between risk and return, so investors seeking higher returns almost always have to accept higher risk.

6-2a Nominal and Real Returns on Stocks, Bonds, and Bills

Figure 6.2 shows how a one-dollar investment in each of three different asset classes grew over the last 111 years in the United States.[2] The three types of investments shown in the figure are Treasury bills, Treasury bonds, and common stocks. Recall from Chapter 4 that *Treasury bills* mature in one year or less and thus are not highly sensitive to interest rate movements.[3] *Treasury bonds* are long-term instruments, so their prices can fluctuate dramatically as interest rates change. Common stocks are the riskiest of the three investments. As you know by now, the performance of a particular stock depends on the ability of the company to generate cash. Investors have no guarantee when they buy stock that it will perform well.

A quick glance at Figure 6.2 reveals that from 1900–2010, common stocks far outperformed Treasury bonds and bills.[4] One dollar invested in a portfolio of common stocks in 1900 grew to $21,481 by the end of 2010. In contrast, a one-dollar investment in T-bonds or T-bills grew to just $294 or $71, respectively. In comparing the values of these investments in 1900 to their 2010 levels, it is important to remember that prices of goods and services in the U.S. were not constant over this period. The fourth line in Figure 6.2 shows how inflation gradually changed the purchasing power of a dollar. The figure shows that the prices increased by a factor of 25 from 1900 to 2010, which means that the purchasing power of $1 in 1900 is roughly equivalent to the purchasing power of $25 in 2010.

---

[2]The term *asset class* simply refers to a distinct type of investment or to a group of assets that share common characteristics.

[3]Or, using terms we have learned, they carry negligible interest rate risk. In August 2011, the rating agency Standard and Poors downgraded their rating on U.S. government securities, suggesting that these securities were no longer free of default risk.

[4]The lines in this figure incorporate both the income component and the capital gain component of returns, and they assume that the initial investment and the total dollar return on each asset are reinvested each year.

Figure 6.2   **The Value of $1 Invested in Stocks, Treasury Bonds, and Bills, 1900–2010**

The figure shows that $1 invested in common stocks in 1900 would have grown to $21,481 by 2010. In comparison, one dollar invested in Treasury bonds would have grown to $294, while a dollar invested in Treasury bills would have reached just $71 by 2010.

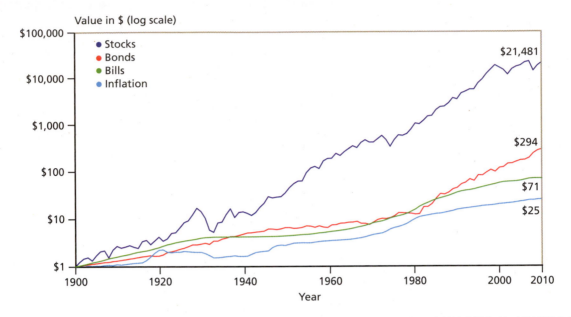

Source: "Triumph of the Optimists," by Elroy Dimson, Paul Marsh, and Mike Staunton, in *Global Investment Returns Yearbook 2010*. Published by ABN AMRO, London. Updates provided by Dimson, et al. through 2009. Authors' estimates for 2010. Reprinted with permission.

? JOB INTERVIEW QUESTION

What's the difference between an investment's nominal return and its real return? Which is more important to investors?

Figure 6.3 takes inflation out of the picture by plotting the performance of the three types of investments in *real*, inflation-adjusted terms.[5] Even after adjusting for inflation, Figure 6.3 demonstrates that common stocks outperformed other investments, increasing in real terms from $1 to $842 in 111 years. As before, the increase in wealth from investing in Treasury bonds or bills was far less. In fact, a one-dollar investment in Treasury bills grew, in real terms, to just $2.80 over this period, and this ignores taxes that investors must pay on interest, further reducing their cumulative earnings. You have to wait a long time to get rich if you are investing in Treasury bills.

6-2b The Risk Dimension

In both Figure 6.2 and Figure 6.3 another important difference between the three asset classes emerges. The line plotting the growth of one dollar invested in Treasury bills is relatively smooth. The line for bonds moves up and down a little more, and the line representing common stocks looks very jagged indeed. This implies that although a portfolio invested entirely in common stocks grows more rapidly than a portfolio invested in either bonds or bills, the common stock portfolio displays more dramatic ups and downs from year to year. In the long run, common stock investors may grow wealthier than bond investors, but their path to riches is a bumpy one. Some investors may be willing to pass up higher returns on stocks in exchange for the additional security of bonds or bills.

Table 6.1 summarizes the information in Figures 6.2 and 6.3. Both in nominal and in real terms, the average return on equities is far higher than the average return on

---

[5]Recall that the relationship between nominal returns, real returns, and inflation is given by the following equation:

$$(1 + \text{nominal}) = (1 + \text{real})(1 + \text{inflation})$$

If the nominal return on a share of stock is 15% in a certain year and the inflation rate is 10%, then we can solve for the real rate as follows:

$$(1 + 0.15) = (1 + \text{real})(1 + 0.10)$$
$$(1 + \text{real}) = (1 + 0.15) \div (1 + 0.10)$$
$$(1 + \text{real}) = 1.0455$$
$$\text{real} = 0.0455 = 4.55\%$$

Figure 6.3   **The Real Value of $1 Invested in Stocks, Treasury Bonds, and Bills, 1900–2010**

The figure shows that $1 invested in common stocks in 1900 would have grown to a real value of $842 by 2010. By comparison, a $1 investment in Treasury bonds or bills would have grown to just $8.60 or $2.80 respectively by 2010.

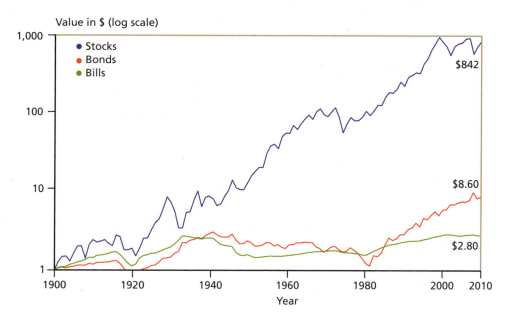

Source: "Triumph of the Optimists," by Elroy Dimson, Paul Marsh, and Mike Staunton, in *Global Investment Returns Yearbook 2010*. Published by ABN AMRO, London. Updates provided by Dimson, et al. through 2009. Author's estimates for 2010. Reprinted with permission.

Because they are both issued by the U.S. government, are the risks of Treasury bills and Treasury bonds equal? Why or why not?

Treasury bonds or bills.[6] However, notice the difference in returns between the best and worst years for common stocks, and compare that to the differences in the best and worst years for the other asset classes. In 1933, common stocks experienced their highest nominal return of 57.6%, but that outstanding performance followed on the heels of the worst year for stocks, 1931, with a nominal return of −43.9%. The difference in the best and the worst in returns is more than 100%! In contrast, Treasury bills moved within a much narrower band, with a top nominal return of 14.7% and a minimum nominal return of 0%.

Table 6.1   **Percentage Returns on Bills, Bonds, and Stocks, 1900–2010**

Stocks earn the highest average returns, but they fluctuate over a wide range. Treasury bill returns move within a fairly narrow range, but T-bills earn low average returns. Treasury bonds fall between stocks and bills along both dimensions.

Asset Class	Nominal (%)			Real (%)		
	Average	Best Year	Worst Year	Average	Best Year	Worst Year
Bills	3.9	14.7	0.0	1.0	19.7	−15.1
Bonds	5.6	40.4	−9.2	2.4	35.1	−19.4
Stocks	11.4	57.6	−43.9	8.3	56.5	−38.0

Source: "Triumph of the Optimists," by Elroy Dimson, Paul Marsh, and Mike Staunton, in *Global Investment Returns Yearbook 2010*. Published by ABN AMRO, London. Updates provided by Dimson, et al. through 2009. Author's estimates for 2010. Reprinted with permission.

[6]The formula for calculating the average return is straightforward. If there are n years of historical data and the return in any particular year t is r_t, then the average return equals the sum of the individual returns divided by n:

$$\text{Average return} = \frac{\sum_{t=1}^{n} r_t}{n}$$

Figure 6.4   **Nominal Returns on Stocks, Treasury Bonds, and Bills, 1900–2010**

The dots in the figure show the return on each asset class in every year from 1900–2010. Notice that common stock returns are riskier in that they cover a wider range than returns on Treasury bonds or bills. Common stocks also earn the highest average returns.

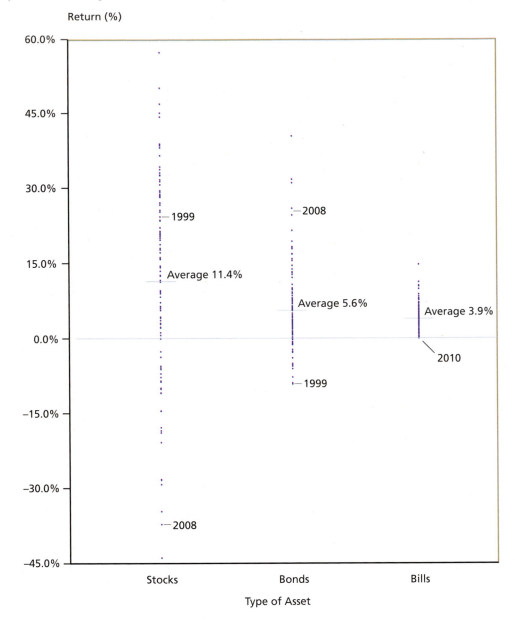

Source: "Triumph of the Optimists," by Elroy Dimson, Paul Marsh, and Mike Staunton, in *Global Investment Returns Yearbook 2010*. Published by ABN AMRO, London. Updates provided by Dimson, et al. through 2009. Author's estimates for 2010. Reprinted with permission.

Figure 6.4 shows the nominal return for each of the three asset classes in every year from 1900–2010. The wider range of outcomes on stocks relative to Treasury bonds, and likewise on bonds relative to bills, is readily apparent. But so is the tendency for stocks to earn higher average returns than T-bonds and for T-bonds to outperform T-bills. A few recent years are highlighted for comparison. For example, in 2010, returns on Treasury bills were at historically low levels, barely above 0%. Notice also that in 2008, stocks endured one of their worst years ever, while bond returns were unusually high that year. In 1999, just the reverse was true, with stock returns far above their long-term average and bond returns falling well below normal. These examples illustrate an important point to which we will return later in this chapter. Assets do not always move together. When one investment performs unusually well, other investments may earn low

Cengage Learning

Elroy Dimson, London Business School

"The worldwide average equity premium has been somewhere in the 4 to 5% range."

See the entire interview at **SMART** | finance

Smart Ideas Video

risk premium
The additional return offered by a more risky investment relative to a safer one.

returns. Investors can benefit from the fact that different assets do not always move in tandem. We will see why this is so when we discuss diversification in Section 6-4.

By now the most important lesson from the history of financial markets should be clear. *There is a positive relationship between risk and return.* Asset classes that experience more ups and downs offer investors higher returns, on average, than investments that provide more stable returns. As yet, we have not precisely defined the term risk, but you probably expect that "risk" must capture the uncertainty surrounding an investment's performance. Table 6.1 indicates that T-bill returns are more predictable than T-bond returns, and both are more predictable than stock returns.

The trade-off between risk and return leads us to an important concept known as a **risk premium**. The risk premium is the additional return offered by a more risky investment relative to a safer one. Table 6.2 reports several risk premiums by taking the differences between average stock, T-bond, and T-bill returns, as reported in Table 6.1. Common stocks offer an average 7.5% higher return than that on Treasury bills. The risk premium on equities relative to bonds averages 5.8%.

Keep in mind that the relationship between risk and return suggests that riskier assets pay higher returns *on average*, but not necessarily every single year. If it is true, on average, that riskier investments pay higher returns than safer ones, then we can use historical risk premiums as a starting point to determine what returns we might expect in the future on alternative investments. Perhaps the most important reason to study the lessons of history in financial markets is to make better guesses about what the future holds.

EXAMPLE

Suppose you want to construct a forecast for the return on U.S. stocks for the next year. One approach is to use the average historical value, 11.4% (from Table 6.1), as your forecast. A problem with this method is that 11.4% represents an average over many years, some having high inflation and some experiencing low inflation. Similarly, in some past years, interest rates on bonds and bills were relatively high; in other years, rates were much lower. You can make use of current market information to construct a better forecast than the average historical return.

For example, suppose you look at Treasury bills trading in the market at the time that you want to develop a forecast for equity returns. At that time, you find that Treasury bills offer a yield to maturity of about 1%. From Table 6.2, you see that the average risk premium on equities relative to T-bills is 7.5%. Add that premium to the current Treasury bill yield to arrive at a forecast for equity returns of 8.5% (1% + 7.5%). This should be a superior forecast compared to the simple historical average because the estimate of 8.5% reflects current market conditions (such as expected inflation rates and required returns on low-risk investments).

WHAT TO ASK

What risk premium do you think investors expect from your company, and how do you build that into your internal financial models?

Analysts use data on risk premiums for many different purposes. In Chapter 4, we saw that bonds receiving lower ratings from bond-rating agencies must pay higher yields. Bond traders know this and use data on the risk premium between relatively safe bonds (like Treasury bonds or AAA-rated corporate bonds) and riskier bonds to price complex financial instruments. As we will see in future chapters, corporate executives use the risk premium on equities relative to Treasury securities to estimate

Table 6.2   **Risk Premiums for Stocks, Bonds, and Bills, 1900–2010**

The risk premium refers to the additional return offered by an investment, relative to an alternative, because it is more risky than the alternative. Stocks offer a risk premium over Treasury bonds and bills, and T-bonds offer a risk premium over T-bills.

Comparison	Risk Premium (%)
Stocks − Bills	11.4 − 3.9 = 7.5
Stocks − Bonds	11.4 − 5.6 = 5.8
Bonds − Bills	5.6 − 3.9 = 1.7

Source: "Triumph of the Optimists," by Elroy Dimson, Paul Marsh, and Mike Staunton, in *Global Investment Returns Yearbook 2010.* Published by ABN AMRO, London. Updates provided by Dimson, et al. through 2009. Reprinted with permission.

Finance in Your Life

Planning Your Pension

Sooner than you expect, you'll graduate from college and enter the workforce. When you do, your employer will probably offer a pension plan, and you will have to decide how to allocate money in the plan between different investment options. Suppose that you plan to work for 35 years, and each year you will contribute $4,000 to the pension plan. We'll assume that these contributions occur annually starting one year from now. We will use the equation for the future value of an annuity from Chapter 3 to estimate how much money will accumulate in your account by the time you retire, exactly 35 years from now. The answer will depend on how you invest.

You can invest your money in either common stocks or bonds. Suppose that over the next 35 years the stocks earn an average annual return of 11.4% and bonds earn 5.6% annually (equal to their respective historical averages). The following table illustrates the pension account value in 35 years under three different investment allocation scenarios. The first scenario assumes you invest all contributions in stocks. The second assumes you invest exclusively in bonds, and the third assumes you split your contributions evenly between stocks and bonds. It shouldn't surprise you that the more money you invest in stocks, the greater is the future value of your retirement account. For example, if you invest everything in stocks, then by using Equation 3.4 we can calculate the account value in 35 years as follows:

$$FV = \$4,000 \times \left[\frac{(1 + 0.114)^{35} - 1}{0.114} \right] = \$1,500,013$$

Allocation Decision	Account Value in Thirty-Five Years
100% stocks	$1,500,013
100% bonds	$409,532
50% in each	$954,772

From the table, it might seem that investing all your money in stocks is obviously the best thing to do. However, there is no way for you to guarantee that your investments in stocks will earn the historical average return as our calculations assume. Consider what might happen if, in the years just before you retire, the return on the stock market was unusually low, as happened several times in the 1930s and as recently as 2008. In that case, the value of your investment account could fall by hundreds of thousands of dollars right before you need to start drawing upon those funds. Thus, the investment allocation decision involves an inevitable trade-off between the prospect of higher returns and the perils of higher risk.

the rate of return that their investors expect on major capital expenditures. We will return to the subject of the equity risk premium several times in this book, but next, we need to explore the meaning of the word *risk* in more depth.

6-2 Concept Review Questions

3. Why do investors need to pay attention to *real returns*, as well as *nominal returns*?

4. Look at Figure 6.3. The figure is drawn using a logarithmic vertical scale which means that if an investment offers a constant rate of return over time, the growing value of that investment would plot as a straight line. This implies that the steeper the line is, the higher is the rate of return

on the investment. Given this, which investment looks like it performed best in *real terms* from 1920–1930? What about from 2000–2010?

5. In Table 6.1, why are the *average real returns* lower than the *average nominal returns* for each asset class? Is it always true that an asset's nominal return is higher than its real return?

6-3 Volatility and Risk

6-3a The Distribution of Historical Stock Returns

We begin our analysis of risk with one more historical illustration. Figure 6.5 shows a histogram of stock returns since 1900. The shape of this histogram is probably familiar to you because it is somewhat reminiscent of a bell curve, also known as a

Figure 6.5   Histogram of Nominal Returns on Equities, 1900–2010

The figure illustrates the performance of stocks in the U.S. in every year from 1900–2010. For example, stock returns were between −20% and −30% in 1907, 1930, 1974, and 2002. The figure suggests that the historical distribution of stock returns is at least roughly approximated by a bell curve, also known as a *normal distribution*.

< −30	−30 to −20	−20 to −10	−10 to 0	0 to 10	10 to 20	20 to 30	30 to 40	40 to 50	> 50
						2009			
						1999			
						1998			
						1996			
				2007		1989			
				2005		1983			
				1992		1979			
				1987	2010	1976			
				1984	2006	1967			
				1978	2004	1963			
				1970	1993	1961			
				1960	1988	1955			
				1956	1986	1951	2003		
			1994	1953	1982	1950	1997		
			1990	1948	1972	1949	1995		
		2001	1981	1947	1971	1944	1991		
		2000	1977	1939	1968	1943	1985		
		1973	1966	1934	1965	1938	1980		
		1969	1946	1926	1964	1925	1975		
		1962	1941	1923	1959	1924	1945		
		1957	1940	1916	1952	1919	1936		
	2002	1929	1932	1912	1942	1909	1928		
2008	1974	1920	1914	1911	1921	1905	1927	1958	
1937	1930	1917	1913	1906	1918	1904	1922	1935	1954
1931	1907	1903	1910	1902	1901	1900	1915	1908	1933

Percent Return in a Given Year

Source: "Triumph of the Optimists," by Elroy Dimson, Paul Marsh, and Mike Staunton, in *Global Investment Returns Yearbook 2010*. Published by ABN AMRO, London. Updates provided by Dimson, et al. through 2009. Reprinted with permission.

normal distribution. In most years, stocks earned a return not far from the historical average of 11.4%. Of the 111 annual returns shown in the figure, more than half (64 to be exact) fall in a range between 0 and 30%. Extremely high or low returns occur less frequently. The only years that showed losses of 30% or more were 1931, 1937, and 2008, while 1933 and 1954 were the only two years in which stocks rose more than 50%. Collectively, these years with very high or very low returns represent about 4.5% of the data from the 111 years.

Figure 6.5 gives us a sense that stock returns can be quite volatile, and it tells us something about the relative frequencies of different outcomes in the U.S. stock market. We are interested in these frequencies not only for their historical significance but also for what they may tell us about future stock market returns. For example, a question that investors may want to ask is, "What is the probability that a portfolio of stocks will lose money in any given year?" Without a crystal ball, no one can answer that question precisely, but a close inspection of Figure 6.5 shows that returns were negative in 29 out of the last 111 years, or about 26% of the time. At least as a starting point, we can estimate a 26% probability that stocks will lose money in a particular year.

If we could list every possible outcome that might occur in the stock market and attach an exact probability to each outcome, then we would have a *probability distribution*. Some probability distributions are easy to describe. For example, the probability distribution that governs outcomes of a coin toss is given below:

Outcome	Probability
Heads	50%
Tails	50%

Unfortunately, the probability distribution for future stock returns is unknown. We rely on Figure 6.5 to give us clues about the characteristics of this distribution.

From the shape of the figure, we may conjecture that the unknown distribution of stock returns is a normal curve with a mean return (or average return) of 11.4%. A normal distribution is symmetric, so there is an equal chance of experiencing an above-average and a below-average outcome. Since 1900, the split between above-average and below-average years in the stock market is 60 to 51, very close to even. This suggests that our assumption of an underlying normal distribution may be a good approximation to reality.[7]

6-3b The Variability of Stock Returns

variance
A measure of dispersion of observations around the mean of a distribution; it is equal to the expected value of the sum of squared deviations from the mean divided by one less than the number of observations in the sample.

Every normal distribution has two key characteristics: its mean and its variance. As you may recall from statistics, the variance measures the dispersion of observations around the mean of the distribution. To be more precise, the variance is the expected value (or the average value) of squared deviations from the mean. In equations, variance is usually noted by the Greek symbol σ^2. Suppose we are estimating the variance of stock returns using n years of historical data. The return in any given year t is r_t, and the average return is $\bar{r}$. We estimate the variance using the equation below:

$$\text{(Eq. 6.3)} \qquad \text{Variance} = \sigma^2 = \frac{\displaystyle\sum_{t=1}^{n}(r_t - \bar{r})^2}{n-1}$$

Table 6.3 illustrates a variance calculation using stock returns in the U.S. from 1993–2010. Over this period, the average annual return equals 10.3%, about one percentage point less than the 11.4% historical average from 1900–2010. In the table's third column, we subtract the average return from the actual return in each year. The fourth column squares that difference. We square deviations from the mean so that both positive and negative deviations contribute to the variance calculation. If we simply added up positive and negative deviations from the mean, then the resulting sum would be zero by virtue of the definition of a mean. To find the variance, add up the numbers in the fourth column and then divide the sum by seventeen.[8] The calculations show that the variance of stock returns equals 396.1. Interpreting the number 396.1 is a little tricky because it is expressed in units of percent squared. Remember, to calculate the variance we worked with numbers in percent form and then squared them. What exactly does 396.1%² mean?

standard deviation
A measure of volatility equal to the square root of the variance.

Fortunately, we don't have to struggle to interpret these odd units. Instead, if we take the square root of the variance, we are back in percentage units, and we have the standard deviation. The standard deviation is just another measure of dispersion around the mean, but in the case of investment returns, it is easier to interpret because it is expressed in percentage terms.

$$\text{Standard deviation} = \sqrt{\text{variance}} = \sqrt{396.1} = 19.9\%$$

If we use the complete 111-year history of U.S. returns, rather than just the last eighteen years, we arrive at the following estimates of the average and standard deviation of historical returns:

$$\text{average return} = 11.4\% \qquad \text{standard deviation} = 20.0\%$$

---

[7]Extensive research on the distribution of equity return teaches us that the normal distribution is only a rough approximation of the actual returns distribution. For example, equity returns do not appear to be distributed symmetrically around the mean. This makes sense in light of the limited liability feature of the U.S. legal system. A fortunate stockholder might earn a return in excess of 100% in any given year, but no investors can experience a loss greater than 100% (unless they are buying stocks using borrowed money). When we examine historical stock returns, we do observe outcomes that are far above the mean more frequently than we see outcomes well below the mean.
[8]You may wonder why we are dividing by 17 if we have 18 years of data. The reason is technical and has to do with a statistical concept, known as degrees of freedom. The technical issue is not terribly important here, and with a very large sample, dividing by either n or $n-1$ will make little difference in the variance calculation.

Table 6.3   **Estimating the Variance of Stock Returns from 1993–2010**

To estimate the variance, first find the average return, 10.3% in this case. Next, take the difference between the actual return in each year and the average return, then square that difference. Add up the squared differences and divide the sum by one less than the number of years in the sample. The standard deviation is the square root of the variance..

Year	Return (%)	Return(%) − 10.3	(Return(%) − 10.3)^2
1993	11.3	1.0	1.0
1994	0	−10.3	106.1
1995	36.4	26.1	681.2
1996	21.2	10.9	118.8
1997	31.3	21.0	441.0
1998	23.4	13.1	171.6
1999	23.6	13.3	176.9
2000	−10.9	−21.2	449.4
2001	−11.0	−21.3	453.7
2002	−20.9	−31.2	973.4
2003	31.6	21.3	453.7
2004	12.5	2.2	4.8
2005	6.4	−3.9	15.2
2006	15.8	5.5	30.3
2007	5.6	−4.7	22.1
2008	−37.2	−47.5	2256.3
2009	28.5	18.2	331.2
2010	17.1	6.8	46.2
Sum	184.7		6733.0

Average	184.7 ÷ 18 = **10.3%**	
Variance		(6733.0 ÷ 17) = **396.1**
Standard Deviation		$\sqrt{396.1}$ = **19.9%**

Source: "Triumph of the Optimists," by Elroy Dimson, Paul Marsh, and Mike Staunton, in *Global Investment Returns Yearbook 2010*. Published by ABN AMRO, London. Updates provided by Dimson, et al. through 2009. Author's estimate for 2010. Reprinted with permission.

These figures indicate that the U.S. experience from 1993–2010 described in Table 6.3, is roughly similar to the entire twentieth century.

Let's return to our assumption that the underlying probability distribution governing stock returns is approximately normal. From the last 111 years we have estimates of the mean (11.4%) and the standard deviation (20.0%) of that distribution. Those estimates allow us to make a few other interesting descriptive statements about the behavior of common stocks. First, for any normal distribution, 68% of all observations fall between one standard deviation above and one standard deviation below the mean, and 95% of the observations should be within two standard deviations of the mean. In the present context, this implies that stock returns should fall between −8.6% and 31.4% (11.4%, plus or minus 20.0%,) in a little more than two-thirds of the years. How does that prediction compare with the historical evidence? From 1900–2010, returns fell within the range of −8.6 to 31.4% in 75 years, or 67.6% of the time. All in all, the distribution of historical returns seems close to a bell curve.

Table 6.4 shows the average annual return and the standard deviation of returns for equities (stocks), Treasury bonds, and Treasury bills during the last 111 years. We saw the average returns previously in Table 6.1, but now we have a specific measure of risk to couple with the mean returns. Once again, we see evidence that risk and return are positively linked, at least if we define risk to mean volatility (as captured by the standard deviation). The average return on stocks is more than double the average bond return, but stocks are almost 2.5 times more volatile than bonds. Bonds offer a premium over bills, but the standard deviation of bond returns is roughly three times the standard deviation for bills. Switching from nominal to real returns lowers the average returns, but it does not change the basic story. Asset classes that display greater volatility pay higher returns on average.

Table 6.4

Average Returns and Standard Deviation for Equities, Bonds, and Bills, (1900–2010)

Asset	Nominal Returns		Real Returns	
	Average (%)	Std. Dev. (%)	Average (%)	Std. Dev. (%)
Equities	11.4	20.0	8.3	20.3
Bonds	5.6	8.3	2.4	10.1
Bills	3.9	2.8	1.0	4.7

Source: "Triumph of the Optimists," by Elroy Dimson, Paul Marsh, and Mike Staunton, in *Global Investment Returns Yearbook 2010*. Published by ABN AMRO, London. Updates provided by Dimson, et al. through 2009. Author's calculations for 2010. Reprinted with permission.

Figure 6.6 plots the relationship between average returns and standard deviation for stocks, bonds, and bills. In the figure, we chose to plot nominal returns, but switching to real returns would make very little difference. The figure also includes a trend line through the three data points. Notice that the relationship shown in the figure is almost perfectly linear, meaning that the dots fall very close to the trend line.[9]

This is not the last time that we will see evidence of a straight-line relationship between risk and return. What are the implications of such a relationship? The most important implications are that (1) investors who want higher returns have to take more risk, and (2) the incremental reward from accepting more risk is constant. In other words, if an investor wants to increase his return from 5% to 10%, the additional risk that he has to accept is the same as the additional risk that another investor has to accept to increase her returns from 10% to 15%. In economics, we frequently see evidence of diminishing returns. This evidence shows up in graphs as a curve with a decreasing slope. For example, a factory can produce more output if there are more

Figure 6.6

The Relationship Between Average (Nominal) Return and Standard Deviation for Stocks, Treasury Bonds, and Bills, 1900–2010

The figure indicates that a positive relationship exists between the average returns offered by an asset class and the standard deviation of returns for that class.

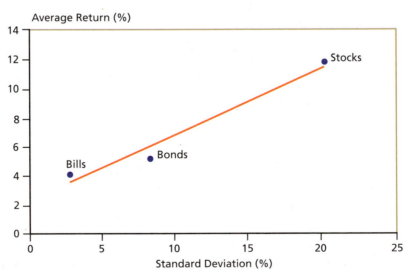

Source: "Triumph of the Optimists," by Elroy Dimson, Paul Marsh, and Mike Staunton, in *Global Investment Returns Yearbook 2010*. Published by ABN AMRO, London. Updates provided by Dimson, et al. through 2009. Author's calculations for 2010. Reprinted with permission.

[9]The trend line here is estimated using linear regression. We will discuss regression lines again in Chapter 7, but you may recall from your statistics class that a measure of "goodness of fit" for a regression line is the R-square statistic. The R-square value ranges between 0% and 100%, with a higher number indicating a stronger relationship between the two variables. In Figure 6.6, the R-square value of our line is almost 97%, indicating a very tight relationship between standard deviation and returns.

workers present, but at some point the incremental output produced by an additional worker (i.e., the marginal product) begins to fall as diminishing returns set in. With respect to risk and return, Figure 6.6 shows no similar evidence of diminishing returns to risk taking.

Thus far, we have seen that a trade-off between risk and return exists for major asset classes including stocks, Treasury bonds, and bills. Suppose we want to compare the investment performance of two specific assets such as a share of General Electric and a share of Intel. Does this same trade-off appear when we examine individual securities? As we will see in the next section, the answer is, "it depends."

6-3 Concept Review Questions

6. Use Figure 6.5 to estimate the probability that a portfolio of common stocks will earn a return of at least 20% in a given year.

7. Suppose nominal bond returns approximately follow a normal distribution. Using the data in Table 6.4, construct a range that should contain 95% of historical bond returns. (*Hint*: Use the mean and standard deviation of bond returns to calculate the endpoints of this range.) Next, refer to Figure 6.4. Is the number of years with bond returns outside the range you just calculated approximately what you expected?

8. Suppose there is an asset class with a standard deviation that lies about halfway between the standard deviations of stocks and bonds. Based on Figure 6.6, what would you expect the average return on this asset class to be?

6-4 The Power of Diversification

6-4a Systematic and Unsystematic Risk

In this section, our objective is to take the lessons we've learned about risk and return for major asset classes and apply those lessons to individual securities. As a starting point, examine Table 6.5 which shows the average annual return and the standard deviation of returns from 1993–2010 for several well-known stocks. The average return and the average standard deviation for this group of stocks appear in the table's next-to-last row. At the very bottom of the table, we show the average return and standard deviation of a portfolio of all ten of these stocks. Several observations are in order.

First, the average return for this group of stocks is higher than the average return for all stocks since 1993, as shown in Table 6.3. This group's average return is 12.1%. Perhaps one reason these firms are so familiar is because they have performed relatively

Table 6.5   **Average Returns and Standard Deviations for Ten Stocks from 1993–2010**

Compared to the figures reported for all common stocks in Table 6.3, these stocks earned slightly higher returns, but their standard deviations were also much higher.

Company	Average Return (%)	Standard Deviation (%)
Archer Daniels Midland	10.5	24.8
American Airlines	7.1	47.0
The Coca Cola Company	10.6	21.3
Exxon Mobil Corp.	13.3	16.6
General Electric Co.	12.6	29.9
Intel Corporation	22.8	50.3
Merck & Co.	11.2	32.3
Procter & Gamble	12.8	17.3
Walmart Stores	9.7	27.7
Wendy's International	10.3	46.7
Average for ten stocks	**12.1%**	**31.4%**
Equally-weighted portfolio	**12.1%**	**19.1%**

well in the recent past. Second, and more important, most of these individual stocks have a much higher standard deviation than was reported in Table 6.3, where we showed that a *portfolio* of all common stocks had a standard deviation of 19.9% from 1993–2010. Table 6.5 illustrates that eight of these ten individual stocks have a standard deviation in excess of 20%. In fact, the average standard deviation across these ten securities is 31.4%. However, observe that the standard deviation of a portfolio containing all 10 stocks is just 19.1% (comparable to the figure from Table 6.3). This raises an interesting question. *If the average stock in Table 6.5 has a standard deviation of 31.4%, how can the standard deviation of a portfolio of those stocks be 19.1%?*[10]

diversification
The act of investing in a variety of different assets rather than just one or two similar assets.

This is a key point. Individual stocks generally display much higher volatility than do portfolios of stocks.[11] Diversification, the act of investing in a variety of different assets rather than just one or two similar assets, explains why a portfolio usually has a lower standard deviation than the individual stocks that make up that portfolio. We can offer some simple intuition to explain this. In any given year, some stocks in a portfolio will have high returns, while other stocks in the portfolio will earn lower returns. Each year, the ups and downs of individual stocks at least partially cancel each other out, so the standard deviation of the portfolio is less than the standard deviations of the individual stocks. The diversification principle works not only for individual stocks but also for broad classes of investments such as stocks trading in different countries.

Figure 6.7 demonstrates the impact of diversification with just two stocks, Coca-Cola and Archer Daniels Midland (ADM).[12] In each year from 2000–2010, we plot the return on these two stocks. Recall from Table 6.5 that both Coca-Cola

Figure 6.7   **Annual Returns on Coca-Cola and Archer Daniels Midland**

The figure illustrates how diversification reduces volatility. Both Coca-Cola and ADM earned an average return of about 10.5% from 1993–2010, but the two stocks did not always move in sync. In some years, one stock had an above-average year while the other stock performed below average. The net effect of this is that a portfolio containing both Coca-Cola and ADM would be less volatile than either stock held in isolation.

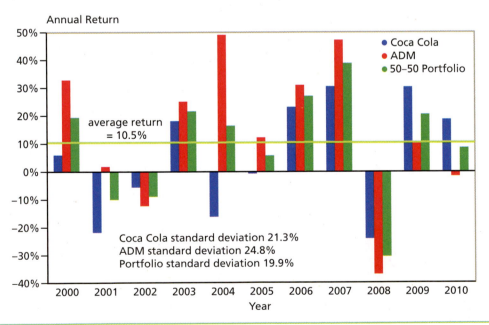

[10]The stocks in Table 6.5 are less volatile than the average stock. From 1993–2010, the standard deviation of the typical U.S. stock was about 55%, yet we know from Table 6.3 that standard deviation of the entire market is far lower than that.
[11]The same statement could be made for other types of assets (e.g., individual bonds are more volatile than a portfolio of bonds).
[12]Figure 6.7 uses data from 1993–2010, but we only show the year-by-year returns from 2000–2010.

and ADM have an average return close to 10.5%, so we have drawn a horizontal line across the bar chart to highlight the average performance for these firms. Also, recall that the standard deviation of Coke's returns is 21.3%, and for ADM the figure is 24.8%. Notice that in the years 2001–2003 and 2006–2008, Coca-Cola's returns and ADM returns were moving together in the sense that both stocks displayed above-average or below-average performance in the same year. However, in 2000, 2004, 2005, 2009, and 2010, one stock had an above-average year, while the other had a below-average year. What would have happened if we had formed a portfolio by investing some of our money in Coca-Cola and the rest in ADM?

The green bar in Figure 6.7 plots the return on an equally weighted (i.e., 50% invested in each stock) portfolio of Coca-Cola and ADM. In the years in which Coca-Cola and ADM moved together, our portfolio return was quite volatile, just as the individual stock returns were volatile. For example, our portfolio return in 2007 was very high because both stocks did well that year, and in 2008, the portfolio performed poorly because both stocks did. However, in some other years the excellent performance of one stock was partially offset by the sub-par performance of the other, and the portfolio's results were close to the average return of 10.5% (2004 and 2010 are good examples of this pattern). In other words, the portfolio's return does not deviate as far or as often from the average as the individual stock returns do. As a result, the standard deviation for the portfolio is just 19.1%, less than the standard deviation of either Coca-Cola or ADM.

Now extend that logic to portfolios containing more than two stocks. Figure 6.8 indicates that the standard deviation of a portfolio falls as the number of stocks in the portfolio rises. The dot in the upper-left corner of the graph represents a portfolio invested entirely in one randomly selected stock. As previously noted, the typical stock has a standard deviation of about 55%. Next, move down and to the right to the dot which represents a portfolio containing an equal share of two randomly selected stocks. The standard deviation of this portfolio is considerably lower.

Figure 6.8   **The Relationship Between Portfolio Standard Deviation and the Number of Stocks in the Portfolio**

The standard deviation of a portfolio tends to decline as more stocks are added to the portfolio. The standard deviation at first declines rapidly as stocks are added to the portfolio. However, at some point, adding more stocks to the portfolio does little to reduce the standard deviation. The risk that diversification eliminates is called unsystematic risk. The risk that remains, even in a well diversified portfolio, is called systematic risk.

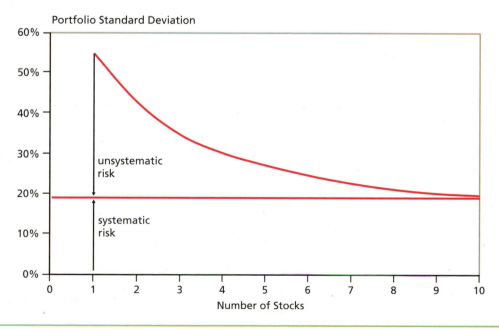

Continuing down and to the right, we continue to add randomly selected stocks, one at a time, and the resulting portfolio standard deviation declines. However, eventually adding more stocks to the portfolio does little to reduce the portfolio's standard deviation.

As you can see, there are diminishing returns to diversification. Adding more stocks to this portfolio would lower the portfolio's volatility. But even if the portfolio contains every available stock in the market, the standard deviation will not drop much more (recall that the standard deviation of the entire market is a little less than 20%). *Diversification reduces volatility, but only up to a point.* No matter how diversified the portfolio is, there will still be some volatility remaining. In finance, the risk that remains even in a well-diversified portfolio is called sys-tematic risk.[13] The term systematic risk refers to a risk that occurs systematically across many different stocks. Examples of systematic risks include the recession/expansion phases of the macroeconomy, as well as changes in inflation, interest rates, and exchange rates. On September 11, 2001, and in the days that followed, U.S. investors learned that terrorism is a type of systematic risk, as the vast majority of stocks fell in response to the attacks on the World Trade Center and the Pentagon.

Look again at the dot in Figure 6.8 showing the standard deviation of a portfolio containing just one stock. The standard deviation here is about 55%, which is a little lower than the standard deviation for the average stock trading in the U.S. market. If this stock's standard deviation equals 55%, but the standard deviation of a portfolio containing this stock (and many other assets) is roughly 20%, this suggests that most of an individual stock's risk disappears once we put that stock inside a portfolio. A substantial fraction of the volatility of an individual stock vanishes when investors hold the stock as part of a diversified portfolio. The risk of an individual stock that disappears when one diversifies is called unsystematic risk.[14] As the name implies, unsystematic risks are those risks which are not common to many securities. Instead, unsystematic risks affect just a few stocks at a time.

To understand the difference between systematic and unsystematic risk, consider the defense industry. Suppose the government announces that it will spend billions of dollars on a new high-tech weapons system. Several defense contractors submit bids to obtain the contract for this system. Investors know that each of these contractors has some chance of winning the bid, but they don't know which firm will prevail in the end. Before the government awards the contract, investors will bid up the prices of every defense stock, anticipating that for each firm there is some chance of winning the bid. However, once the government announces the winning bidder, that firm's stock price will rise even more, while the prices of other defense stocks will fall.

An investor who places an all-or-nothing bet by buying shares in only one defense contractor takes a lot of risk. Either the investor will guess the outcome of the bidding process successfully, and the investment will pay off handsomely, or the investor will bet on the wrong firm and lose money. Instead, suppose the investor diversifies and holds a position in each defense firm. That way, no matter which firm wins the contract, the investor will be sure to have at least a small claim on the value of that deal. By diversifying the investor eliminates the unsystematic risk in this situation. However, suppose there is a chance that the defense department will cancel their plans to build the weapons system. When that announcement is made,

systematic risk
Risk that cannot be eliminated through diversification.

unsystematic risk
Risk that can be eliminated through diversification.

Cengage Learning

Utpal Bhattacharya, Indiana University

"The cost of equity goes up if insider trading laws are not enforced."

See the entire interview at **SMART**|finance

Smart Ethics Video

---

[13]Other terms used to describe this type of risk are *nondiversifiable risk* and *market risk*. The meaning of non-diversifiable risk is self-evident. Market risk conveys the sense that we are concerned with risks that affect the broad market, not just a few stocks or even a few sectors in the market.
[14]Unsystematic risk is sometimes called *diversifiable risk*, *unique risk*, *firm-specific risk*, or *idiosyncratic risk*. Each of these terms implies that we are talking about risks that apply to a single firm or a few firms, not to many firms simultaneously, so this type of risk can be eliminated by holding a diversified portfolio.

Finance in Your Life

Combining Stocks and Bonds

In section 6.2 we looked at an investor's decision to invest in stocks or bonds when saving for retirement. As you might expect by now, there are likely to be advantages for the investor to hold stocks and bonds (that is, to diversify across asset classes) rather than to hold just one of these investments.

The chart below uses data on the performance of stocks and bonds from 1970–2010 to demonstrate the benefits of combining stocks and bonds in a portfolio. Remember that stocks earn higher returns, but those returns are also more volatile than are bond returns. Does this imply that investors who place a high value on safety should invest 100% of their retirement savings in bonds?

The surprising answer is no. Even investors wanting to follow a very conservative investment strategy should probably hold at least some stocks. Notice that starting from a portfolio invested entirely in bonds, increasing the allocation devoted to stocks simultaneously increases the portfolio's return and, at least up to a point, lowers the portfolio's standard deviation. In other words, the standard deviation of the portfolio is less than the standard deviations of either of the two assets in which the portfolio invests. How can this occur? The risk reduction occurs because stock and bond returns do not always move in the same direction, so sometimes their movements offset, just as is the case with ADM and Coca-Cola. In fact, by looking at the graph we can make a very strong statement. As long as investors prefer higher returns over lower returns, and less volatility rather than more, investing exclusively in bonds doesn't make much sense. Notice that the diversified portfolio containing an equal mix of stocks and bonds has about the same standard deviation as the bonds-only portfolio, but with a significantly higher return.

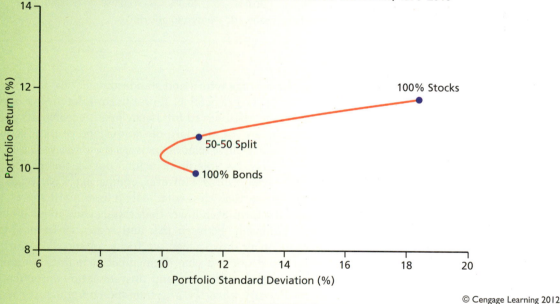

Returns and Standard Deviations of Portfolios of Stocks and Bonds, 1970–2010

© Cengage Learning 2012

all defense stocks will fall and diversifying across all of these firms will not help an investor avoid that loss.[15]

6-4b Risk and Return Revisited

Remember that our goal in this section is to be able to say something useful about the relationship between risk and return for individual assets. We already know that asset classes that pay higher returns have higher standard deviations. Is the same thing true for securities within a particular asset class? Do individual stocks with higher standard deviations earn higher returns over time?

[15]A clever reader might argue that if the government spends less on defense, then more is spent on something else. So an investor may be able to diversify this risk away by holding a broad portfolio of stocks rather than just a portfolio of defense stocks. In that case, our illustration is once again about unsystematic rather than systematic risk.

Figure 6.9   **Average Return and Standard Deviation for Ten Stocks, 1993–2010**

In contrast to the positive relationship between average returns and standard deviations for asset classes shown previously in Figure 6.6, this figure shows no such pattern for individual assets. There is no obvious tendency for the stocks that have earned the highest returns to be the most volatile. This suggests that for an individual stock, standard deviation may not be an appropriate measure of that stock's risk because it is unrelated to the stock's returns.

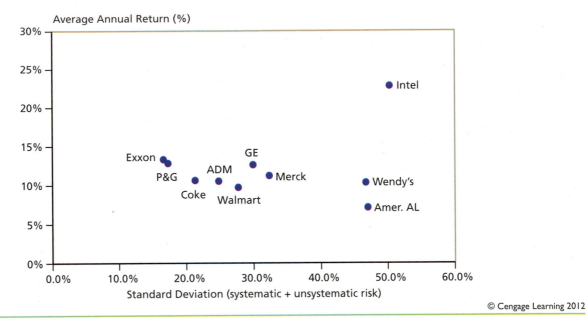

© Cengage Learning 2012

Figure 6.9 plots the average return and standard deviation for the ten stocks featured in Table 6.5. Unlike the predictable, almost linear relationship between standard deviation and returns that we observed for asset classes, no obvious pattern leaps out of this figure. If we compare the standard deviations and average returns of Intel to those of Walmart, then the positive relation between these two variables seems to hold. Clearly Walmart stock was less volatile than Intel during this period, and Walmart investors earned much lower returns. However, comparing Walmart to American Airlines, Walmart shares were actually less volatile than were AMR shares, but shareholders of the airline earned returns even lower than those achieved by Walmart.

Why does the relationship between risk and return observed for asset classes in Figure 6.6 seem to break down when we focus on specific securities? The horizontal axis in Figure 6.9 offers a clue. Remember that the standard deviation of a single stock contains both systematic and unsystematic components. *If investors are wise enough to diversify, then the unsystematic component of risk is irrelevant because diversification eliminates unsystematic risks.* How difficult is it for investors to remove exposure to unsystematic risk? In fact, it is very easy for them to do so. The mutual fund industry is built on the idea of allowing many investors to pool their money so that even people with relatively little money to invest can buy a stake in a well-diversified portfolio. This chapter's What Companies Do Globally insert shows that it is possible to eliminate some unsystematic risk by diversifying globally.

If diversification is easy, and if it eliminates unsystematic risk, then what reward should investors expect if they choose not to diversify and to bear systematic risk? Simple intuition predicts that bearing unsystematic risk offers no incremental reward. The reason is that investors can easily eliminate unsystematic risk by diversifying. In other words, investors do not have to bear this kind of risk, nor do they have to pay a lot to get rid of it. Therefore, *the market will reward investors only for bearing systematic risk.*

In Figure 6.6, we observed an almost linear relation between standard deviation and average return for three asset classes: stocks, bonds, and bills. In Figure 6.9, the relationship between standard deviation and return is not as clear. The difference between

SMART
concepts

See the concept explained
step-by-step at **SMART** | finance

What Companies Do Globally

Risk Premiums Around the World

The tendency for stocks to outperform safer investments like Treasury bills is not a phenomenon confined to the United States. As the table shows, the premium on equities relative to bills was positive in fifteen other countries from 1900–2009. The relative performance of equities vs. bills was highest in Australia and lowest in Denmark, but in all countries equities earned higher returns than bills. The equity risk premium in the United States was not especially remarkable over the last century when compared with these other nations.

The second column of numbers shows the historical standard deviation of stocks in each country. Germany, Japan, and Italy had the most volatile stock markets over the past century (What do these countries have in common

historically?), but notice how many markets around the world had a standard deviation very close to that of the U.S. market. Even more important, look at the bottom row of the table which calculates the average real return, standard deviation, and equity risk premium for a portfolio containing stocks from all sixteen countries. The world portfolio's standard deviation was just 17.8%. Only the Canadian stock market was less volatile than the world market as a whole. Here again we see the power of diversification. The average real return and the equity risk premium on the world portfolio fell in the middle of the pack relative to the individual countries, but it managed to achieve those average returns with very low volatility.

Real Equity Returns and Risk Premiums Around the World 1900–2009			
Country	Average Real Return on Equities	Standard Deviation	Risk Premium vs. Bills
Australia	7.5%	18.2%	6.8%
Belgium	2.5	23.7	2.9
Canada	5.8	17.3	4.1
Denmark	4.9	20.8	2.5
France	3.1	23.6	6.1
Germany	3.0	32.4	5.8
Ireland	3.8	23.2	3.1
Italy	2.1	29.1	5.9
Japan	3.8	29.9	5.9
South Africa	7.2	22.5	6.1
Spain	3.8	22.2	3.4
Sweden	6.2	22.9	4.2
Switzerland	4.3	19.9	3.4
The Netherlands	4.9	21.9	4.2
United Kingdom	5.3	20.1	4.2
United States	6.2	20.4	5.2
World	**5.4**	**17.8**	**4.4**

Source: "Triumph of the Optimists," by Elroy Dimson, Paul Marsh, and Mike Staunton, in *Global Investment Returns Yearbook 2010*. Published by ABN AMRO, London. Updates provided by Dimson, et al. Reprinted with permission.

the figures is that in one case (Figure 6.6), we are looking at portfolios of assets, and in the other case (Figure 6.9), we are looking at individual assets. A well-diversified portfolio contains very little unsystematic risk. This is why the standard deviation of a portfolio of stocks is typically so much lower than the standard deviation of a single stock. For a portfolio, the standard deviation of returns consists almost entirely of systematic risk. For an individual asset, the standard deviation contains both types of risk. Therefore, if the market rewards systematic risk only, then in Figure 6.6, we see a nice linear relationship between portfolio standard deviation (systematic risk) and average returns, but in Figure 6.9, standard deviation (systematic + unsystematic risk) seems almost unrelated to average returns.

To conclude this chapter, let us take a step back and think about our original objective. The fundamental goal of finance is to value things. Usually, valuation involves projecting an asset's future cash flows, choosing a discount rate that is appropriate, given the asset's risk, then calculating the present value of the asset's future cash flows. In this chapter, we have made some progress in understanding the second step of the valuation process. We know that what really matters is an investment's total return, and we want to know how that return relates to risk. But not all risks are equal, so we need to focus on an asset's systematic risk because that is what should drive the asset's return. Diversified portfolios contain very little unsystematic risk; thus a measure like the standard deviation of the portfolio's return provides a good measure of the portfolio's systematic risk. As expected, a portfolio's standard deviation and its return are closely linked.

But complications arise for individual assets because their fluctuations reflect both systematic and unsystematic factors. Therefore, the standard deviation of returns for a single stock does not focus exclusively on the stock's systematic risk. As a result, when we compare standard deviations and average returns across many different stocks, we do not see a reliable pattern between those two variables.

This is an important problem because both managers and investors have to assess the risk of individual investments, not just portfolios. They need a way to measure the systematic risk, and only the systematic risk, of each and every asset. If it is possible to quantify an individual asset's systematic risk, then we should expect that measure of risk to be reliably related to returns. This is precisely our focus in Chapter 7.

6-4 Concept Review Questions

9. Why is the standard deviation of a portfolio usually smaller than the standard deviations of the assets that comprise the portfolio?

10. In Figure 6.8, why does the line decline steeply at first and then flatten out?

11. Explain why the dots in Figure 6.9 appear to be almost randomly scattered.

Summary

- An important measure of an investment's performance is its total return. The total return is the sum of the income that the investment pays out to investors, plus any change in the price of the investment.

- Total returns can be expressed either in dollar or percentage terms.

- Historically, stocks have earned higher average returns than bonds, and bonds have earned higher returns than bills. However, higher returns come at the price of higher volatility.

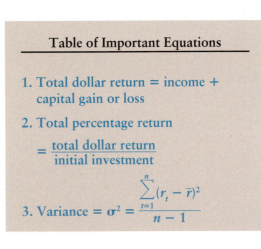

Table of Important Equations

1. Total dollar return = income + capital gain or loss

2. Total percentage return
$$= \frac{\text{total dollar return}}{\text{initial investment}}$$

3. Variance $= \sigma^2 = \dfrac{\sum_{t=1}^{n}(r_t - \bar{r})^2}{n-1}$

- Real returns measure the change in purchasing power over time, whereas nominal returns measure the change in dollars accumulated. Investors who care about what they can consume with their wealth should focus on real returns.

- Historically, stock returns are approximately normally distributed.

- One measure of risk is standard deviation, which captures deviations from the average outcome. For broad asset classes, the relationship between average returns and standard deviation is nearly linear.

- The volatility (standard deviation) of individual stocks is generally higher than the volatility of a portfolio. This suggests that diversification reduces risk.

- There is a point beyond which additional diversification does not reduce risk. The risk that cannot be eliminated through diversification is called systematic risk, whereas the risk that disappears in a well-diversified portfolio is called unsystematic risk. The variance or standard deviation of any investment equals the sum of the systematic and unsystematic components of risk.

- Because investors can easily eliminate unsystematic risk by diversifying, the market should only reward investors based on the systematic risk that they bear.

- For individual investments, there is no strong linear relationship between average returns and standard deviation. This is the case, because standard deviation includes both systematic and unsystematic risk, and returns should only be linked to systematic risk.

Key Terms

capital gain, 182	risk premium, 189	total return, 182
capital loss, 182	standard deviation, 192	unsystematic risk, 198
diversification, 196	systematic risk, 198	variance, 192

Self-Test Problems

Answers to Self-Test Problems and the Concept Review Questions throughout the chapter appear in CourseMate with SmartFinance Tools at www.cengagebrain.com.

ST6-1. Using Table 6.3, calculate the standard deviation of stock returns from 2006–2010. Over the last five years, were stocks more or less volatile than they were over the last eighteen years?

ST6-2. Table 6.3 shows that the average return on stocks from 1993–2010 was 10.3%. Not shown in the table are the average returns on bonds and bills over the same period. The average return on bonds was 10.0%, and for bills the average return was 3.3%. From these figures, calculate the risk premiums for 1993–2010 and compare recent history to the long-run numbers in Table 6.2.

ST6-3. Suppose that Treasury bill returns follow a normal distribution with a mean of 4.1% and a standard deviation of 2.8%. This implies that, 68% of the time, T-bill returns should fall within what range?

Questions

Q6-1. Why is it important to focus on *total returns* when measuring an investment's performance?

Q6-2. Why do *real returns* matter more than *nominal returns*?

Q6-3. Under what conditions will the components of a bond's return have the opposite sign?

Q6-4. Explain why dollar returns and percentage returns can sometimes send conflicting signals when comparing two different investments.

Q6-5. Do the rankings of investment alternatives depend on whether we rank based on *nominal returns* or *real returns*?

Q6-6. Look at Table 6.1. Compare the best and worst years for T-bills in terms of their *nominal returns*, and then compare the best and worst years in terms of *real returns*. Comment on what you find.

Q6-7. Over the last 111 years, 1981 was the top year for nominal bill returns, and 1982 was the top year for nominal bond returns. Why do you think that these two years saw such high returns on bonds and bills?

Q6-8. Table 6.2 calculates the risk premiums on stocks and bonds relative to T-bills by taking the difference in average nominal total returns on each asset class. Would these risk premiums be much different if we calculated them using real rather than nominal returns?

Q6-9. When measuring the volatility of an investment's returns, why is it easier to focus on standard deviation rather than variance?

Q6-10. Are there diminishing returns to risk taking?

Q6-11. Notice in Table 6.5 that the average standard deviation among the ten stocks is 31.4%, yet Figure 6.8 shows that a portfolio comprised of ten stocks has a standard deviation of about 20%. Explain why these two figures are not equal.

Q6-12. Look at Figure 6.9. Suppose you had to invest all of your money in just one of these stocks (excluding Intel). Which one seems most attractive and why? Which stock seems least attractive?

Q6-13. Classify each of the following events as a source of *systematic* or *unsystematic* risk.
   a.   Ben Bernanke retires as Chairman of the Federal Reserve and Arnold Schwarzenegger is appointed to take his place.
   b.   Martha Stewart is convicted of insider trading and is sentenced to prison.
   c.   An OPEC embargo raises the world market price of oil.
   d.   A major consumer products firm loses a product liability case.
   e.   The Supreme Court rules that no employer can lay off an employee without first giving thirty days notice.

Problems

Understanding Returns

P6-1. You purchase 1,000 shares of Spears Grinders, Inc. stock for $45 per share. A year later, the stock pays a dividend of $1.25 per share, and it sells for $49.
   a.   Calculate your total dollar return.
   b.   Calculate your total percentage return.
   c.   Do the answers to parts (a) and (b) depend on whether you sell the stock after one year or continue to hold it?

P6-2. A financial adviser claims that a particular stock earned a total return of 10% last year. During the year the stock price rose from $30 to $32.50. What dividend did the stock pay?

P6-3. D. S. Trucking Company stock pays a $1.50 dividend every year without fail. A year ago, the stock sold for $25 per share, and its total return during the past year was 20%. What does the stock sell for today?

P6-4. Nano-Motors Corp. has stock outstanding which sells for $10 per share. Macro-Motors, Inc. shares cost $50 each. Neither stock pays dividends at present.
   a.   An investor buys 100 shares of Nano-Motors. A year later, the stock sells for $15. Calculate the total return in dollar terms and in percentage terms.
   b.   Another investor buys 100 shares of Macro-Motors stock. A year later, the stock has risen to $56. Calculate the total return in dollar terms and in percentage terms.
   c.   Why is it difficult to say which investor had a better year?

P6-5. David Rawlings pays $1,000 to buy a five-year Treasury bond that pays a 6% coupon rate (for simplicity, assume annual coupon payments). One year later, the market's required return on this bond has increased from 6% to 7%. What is Rawlings, total return (in dollar and percentage terms) on the bond?

P6-6. G. Welch purchases a corporate bond that was originally issued for $1,000 several years ago. The bond has four years remaining until it matures, the market price now is $1,054.45, and *the yield to maturity (YTM)* is 4%. The bond pays an annual coupon of $55, with the next payment due in one year.
   a.   What is the bond's *coupon rate*? Its *coupon yield*?
   b.   Suppose Welch holds this bond for one year and the YTM does not change. What is the total percentage return on the bond? Show that on a percentage basis, the *total return* is the sum of the interest and capital gain/loss components.
   c.   If the yield to maturity decreases during the first year from 4% to 3.5%, what is the total percentage return that year?

P6-7. In this advanced problem, let's look at the behavior of ordinary Treasury bonds and inflation-indexed bonds, or TIPS. We will simplify by assuming annual interest payments rather than semiannual. Suppose over the next five years, investors expect 3% inflation each year. The Treasury issues a five-year ordinary bond that pays $55 interest each year. The Treasury issues a five-year TIPS that pays a coupon rate of 2%. With TIPS, the coupon payment is determined by multiplying the coupon rate times the inflation-adjusted principal value. Like ordinary bonds, TIPS begin with a par value or principal value of $1,000. However, that principal increases over time as inflation occurs. Assuming that inflation is in fact equal to 3% in each of the next five years, then the cash flows associated with each bond would look like this:

Year	T-bond Pays	TIPS Pays	Inflation-adjusted Principal (TIPS)	Coupon pymt calculation
0 (cost)	−1,000.00	−1,000.00	−1,000.00	NA
1	55.00	20.60	1,030.00	1,000.00(1.03) × 2%
2	55.00	21.22	1,060.90	1,030.00(1.03) × 2%
3	55.00	21.85	1,092.73	1,060.90(1.03) × 2%
4	55.00	22.51	1,125.51	1,092.73(1.03) × 2%
5	1,055.00	1,182.46	1,159.27	1,125.51(1.03) × 2%

In the last row of the table, notice the final TIPS payment includes the return of the inflation-adjusted principal ($1,159.27), plus the final coupon payment.

a. Calculate the *yield to maturity (YTM)* of each bond. Why is one higher than the other? Show that the TIPS YTM equals the product of the real interest rate and the inflation rate.

b. What is the *real return* on the T-bond?

c. Suppose the *real return* on the T-bond stays constant, but investors expect 4% inflation rather than 3%. What happens to the required return on the T-bond in nominal terms?

d. Imagine that during the first year, the inflation that actually occurred was 3%, as expected. However, suppose that by the end of the first year, investors had come to expect 4% inflation for the next four years. Fill out the remaining cash flows for each bond in the table below.

Year	T-bond Pays	TIPS Pays	Inflation-adjusted Principal (TIPS)	Coupon pymt calculation
0 (cost)	−1,000.00	−1,000.00	−1,000.00	NA
1	55.00	20.60	1,030.00	1,000.00(1.03) × 2%
2				
3				
4				
5				

e. Now calculate the market price of the Treasury bond as of the end of the first year. Remember to discount the bond's remaining cash flows, using the nominal required return that you calculated in part (c). Given this new market price, what is the total return offered by the T-bond in the first year?

f. Next, calculate the market price of the TIPS bond. Remember, at the end of the first year, the YTM on the TIPS will equal the product of one plus the real return (2%) and one plus the inflation rate (4%). What is the total nominal return offered by TIPS the first year?

The History of Returns (or How to Get Rich Slowly)

P6-8. Refer to Figure 6.2. At the end of each line, we show the nominal value in 2010 of a $1 investment stocks, bonds, and bonds. Calculate the ratio of the 2010 value of $1 invested in bonds divided by the 2010 value of $1 invested in bills. Now recalculate this ratio, using the real values in Figure 6.3. What do you find?

P6-9. The U.S. stock market hit an all-time high in October 1929 before crashing dramatically. Following the market crash, the U.S. entered a prolonged economic downturn dubbed "The Great Depression." Using Figure 6.2, estimate how long it took for the stock market to fully rebound from its fall which began in October 1929. How did bond investors fare over this same period? (Note: A precise answer is hard to obtain from the figure, so just make your best estimate.)

P6-10. Refer again to Figure 6.2, which tracks the value of $1 invested in various assets starting in 1900. At the stock market peak in 1929, look at the gap that exists between equities and bonds. At the end of 1929, the $1 investment in stocks was worth about five times more than the $1 investment in bonds. About how long did investors in stocks have to wait before they would regain that same performance edge? Again, getting a precise answer from the figure is difficult, so make an estimate.

P6-11. The *nominal return* on a particular investment is 11% and the inflation rate is 2%. What is the *real return*?

P6-12. A bond offers a *real return* of 5%. If investors expect 3% inflation, what is the *nominal rate of return* on the bond?

P6-13. If an investment promises a nominal return of 6% and the inflation rate is 1%, what is the real return?

P6-14. The following data shows the rate of return on stocks and bonds for several recent years. Calculate the *risk premium* on equities vs. bonds each year and then calculate the average risk premium. Do you think that, at the beginning of 2007, investors expected the outcomes we observe in this table?

Year	2007	2008	2009	2010
Return on stocks (%)	5.6	−37.2	28.5	17.1
Return on bonds (%)	9.9	25.9	14.5	6.4
Risk premium (%)				

P6-15. The table below shows the average return on U.S. stocks and bonds for 25-year periods ending in 1925, 1950, 1975, and 2000. Calculate the *equity risk premium* for each quarter century. What lesson emerges from your calculations?

Ave. Return	1925	1950	1975	2000
Stocks	9.7%	10.2%	11.4%	16.2%
Bonds	3.5%	4.1%	2.4%	10.6%
Risk Premium				

Source: Dimson, Elroy, *Triumph of the Optimists.* © 2002 Elroy Dimson, Paul Marsh, and Mike Staunton. Published by Princeton University Press. Reprinted by permission of Princeton University Press.

P6-16. The current yield to maturity on a one-year Treasury bill is 2%. You believe that the expected risk premium on stocks vs. bills equals 7.7%.
   a. Estimate the expected return on the stock market next year.
   b. Explain why the estimate in part (a) may be better than simply assuming that next year's stock market return will equal the long-term average return.

Volatility and Risk

P6-17. Using Figure 6.5, how would you estimate the probability that the return on the stock market will exceed 30% in any given year?

P6-18. In this problem, use Figure 6.5 to estimate the expected return on the stock market. To estimate the expected return, create a list of possible returns and assign a probability to each outcome. To find the expected return, multiply each possible return by the probability that it will occur and then add up across outcomes. Notice that Figure 6.5 divides the range of possible returns into intervals of 10% (except for very low or very high outcomes). Create a list of potential future stock returns by taking the midpoint of the various ranges as follows:

Possible Stock Returns (%)									
−35	−25	−15	−5	5	15	25	35	45	55
$\frac{3}{111}$	$\frac{4}{111}$							$\frac{3}{111}$	$\frac{2}{111}$

$$\text{Expected return} = \left(\frac{3}{111}\right)(-35) + \left(\frac{4}{111}\right)(-25) + \cdots + \left(\frac{3}{111}\right)(45) + \left(\frac{2}{111}\right)(55) = ?$$

Figure 6.5 shows that four years out of 111 had returns of between −20% and −30%. Let us capture this fact by assuming that if returns do occur inside that interval that the typical return would be −25%

(in the middle of the interval). The probability associated with this outcome is 4/111 or about 3.6%. Fill in the missing values in the table and then fill in the missing parts of the equation to calculate the expected return.

P6-19. Here are the nominal returns on stocks, bonds, and bills for the 1920s and 1930s. For each decade, calculate the standard deviation of returns for each asset class. How do those figures compare with the more recent numbers for stocks presented in Table 6.3 and the long-run figures for all three asset types in Table 6.4?

	Nominal Returns (%) on Stocks, Bonds, and Bills						
	1920s				**1930s**		
	Stocks	**Bonds**	**Bills**		**Stocks**	**Bonds**	**Bills**
1920	−17.9	5.8	7.6	1930	−28.3	4.7	2.4
1921	11.6	12.7	7.0	1931	−43.9	−5.3	1.1
1922	30.6	3.5	4.7	1932	−9.8	16.8	1.0
1923	3.0	5.7	5.2	1933	57.6	−0.1	0.3
1924	27.0	6.4	4.1	1934	4.4	10.0	0.2
1925	28.3	5.7	4.1	1935	44.0	5.0	0.2
1926	9.5	7.8	3.3	1936	32.3	7.5	0.2
1927	33.1	8.9	3.1	1937	−34.6	0.2	0.3
1928	38.7	0.1	3.6	1938	28.2	5.5	0.0
1929	−14.5	3.4	4.7	1939	2.9	5.5	0.0

Source: Dimson, Elroy, *Triumph of the Optimists*. © 2002 Elroy Dimson, Paul Marsh, and Mike Staunton. Published by Princeton University Press. Reprinted by permission of Princeton University Press.

P6-20. Use the data below to calculate the standard deviation of *nominal* and *real* Treasury bill returns from 1972–1982. Do you think that when they purchased T-bills, investors expected to earn negative real returns as often as they did during this period? If not, what happened that took investors by surprise?

Year	Nominal Return (%)	Real Return (%)
1972	3.8	0.4
1973	6.9	−1.7
1974	8.0	−3.7
1975	5.8	−1.1
1976	5.1	0.3
1977	5.1	−1.5
1978	7.2	−1.7
1979	10.4	−2.6
1980	11.2	−1.0
1981	14.7	5.3
1982	10.5	6.4

Source: Dimson, Elroy, *Triumph of the Optimists*. © 2002 Elroy Dimson, Paul Marsh, and Mike Staunton. Published by Princeton University Press. Reprinted by permission of Princeton University Press.

P6-21. Based on Figure 6.6, about what rate of return would a truly risk-free investment (i.e., one with a standard deviation of zero) offer investors?

The Power of Diversification

P6-22. Troy McClain wants to form a portfolio of four different stocks. Summary data on the four stocks follows. First, calculate the average standard deviation across the four stocks and then answer this question: If Troy forms a portfolio by investing 25% of his money in each of the stocks in the table, it is very likely that the standard deviation of this portfolio's return will be (more than, less than, equal to) 43.5%. Explain your answer.

Stock	Return	Std. Dev.
1	14%	71%
2	10%	46%
3	9%	32%
4	11%	25%

P6-23. The table below shows annual returns on Archer Daniels Midland (ADM) and Walmart. The last column of the table shows the annual return that a portfolio invested 50% in ADM and 50% in Walmart would have earned in 1993. The portfolio's return is simply a weighted average of the returns of ADM and Walmart.

Year	ADM	Walmart	50-50 portfolio
1993	1.5%	−22.7%	−10.6% = (0.5 × 1.5% + 0.5 × −22.7%)
1994	37.4%	−24.6%	
1995	−11.2%	−5.5%	
1996	31.1%	8.0%	
1997	10.0%	50.7%	
1998	−15.3%	76.8%	
1999	−23.5%	61.2%	
2000	32.9%	9.5%	
2001	1.9%	15.6%	
2002	−12.1%	−18.1%	
2003	25.1%	11.1%	
2004	49.1%	−10.5%	
2005	12.3%	−8.2%	
2006	31.0%	3.3%	
2007	47.2%	0.3%	
2008	−36.9%	15.0%	
2009	10.8%	10.9%	
2010	−1.5%	1.4%	

a. Plot a graph similar to Figure 6.7 showing the returns on ADM and Walmart each year.
b. Fill in the blanks in the table above by calculating the 50-50 portfolio's return each year from 1994–2010 and then plot this on the graph you created for part (a). How does the portfolio return compare to the returns of the individual stocks in the portfolio?
c. Calculate the standard deviation of ADM, Walmart, and the portfolio and comment on what you find.

P6-24. The table below shows annual returns for Merck and one of its major competitors, Eli Lilly. The final column shows the annual return on a portfolio invested 50% in Lilly and 50% in Merck. The portfolio's return is simply a weighted average of the returns of the stocks in the portfolio, as shown in the example calculation at the top of the table.

Year	Eli Lilly	Merck	50-50 portfolio
Year 1	15.4%	14.9%	15.1% = (0.5 × 15.4% + 0.5 × 14.9%)
Year 2	77.2%	76.4%	
Year 3	32.6%	24.0%	
Year 4	93.6%	35.5%	
Year 5	29.1%	41.2%	
Year 6	−24.3%	−7.4%	
Year 7	41.9%	41.7%	
Year 8	−14.4%	−35.9%	
Year 9	−17.6%	−1.1%	
Year 10	13.1%	−11.2%	
Std. Dev.			

a. Plot a graph similar to Figure 6.7 showing the returns on Lilly and Merck each year.

b. Fill in the blanks in the table above by calculating the 50-50 portfolio's return each year from Year 2 to Year 10 and then plot this on the graph you created for part (a). How does the portfolio return compare to the returns of the individual stocks in the portfolio?

c. Calculate the standard deviation of Lilly, Merck, and the portfolio and comment on what you find.

P6-25. In this problem, you will generate a graph similar to Figure 6.8. The table below shows the standard deviation for various portfolios of stocks listed in Table 6.5. Plot the relationship between the number of stocks in the portfolio and the portfolio's standard deviation. Comment on how the resulting graph is similar to and different from Figure 6.8.

Stocks in the Portfolio	Std. Deviation (%)
Exxon	16.6
Exxon + P&G	15.2
Exxon + P&G + Coke	15.4
Exxon + P&G + Coke + ADM	14.7
Exxon + P&G + Coke + ADM + Walmart	12.5
Exxon + P&G + Coke + ADM + Walmart + Wendy's	14.5

THOMSON REUTERS | Business School Edition

Access financial information from the Thomson ONE – Business School Edition Web site for the following problem(s). Go to **www.tobsefin.swlearning.com/**. If you have already registered your access serial number and have a username and password, click **Enter**. Otherwise, click **Register** and follow the instructions to create a username and password. Register your access serial number and then click **Enter** on the aforementioned Web site. When you click Enter, you will be prompted for your username and password (please remember that the password is case sensitive). Enter them in the respective boxes and then click **OK** (or hit **Enter**). From the ensuing page, click **Click Here to Access Thomson ONE – Business School Edition Now!** This opens up a new window that gives you access to the Thomson ONE – Business School Edition database. You can retrieve a company's financial information by entering its ticker symbol (provided for each company in the problem(s)) in the box below "Name/Symbol/Key." For further instructions on using the Thomson ONE – Business School Edition database, please refer to the online Help.

P6-26. Compare the average annual returns and standard deviations of annual returns of Coca-Cola (KO), FedEx Corp. (FDX), and Motorola Solutions, Inc. (MSI) to those of a portfolio containing the three companies' stocks. Calculate the average and standard deviation of annual returns for each company. Now assume that you form a portfolio by investing equal amounts of money in each stock. Determine the annual returns for this portfolio. To calculate the portfolio's return in each year, simply calculate a weighted-average of the returns of the stocks in the portfolio. The weight given to each stock is one-third. For example, if the returns on KO, FDX, and MSI are 10%, –3%, and 20% in a certain year, then the portfolio return for that year equals:

$$\left(\frac{1}{3}\right)(10\%) + \left(\frac{1}{3}\right)(-3\%) + \left(\frac{1}{3}\right)(20\%) = 9\%$$

After calculating the portfolio's return in each year, then calculate the average and standard deviation of the portfolio's annual returns.

How do these compare to the average and standard deviation of annual returns of the three firms taken separately? What can you infer about the risk and return of the portfolio compared to those of the individual firms? Does your answer change if you invest 40% of your capital in Motorola, 35% in Coca-Cola, and the remaining funds in FedEx?

P6-27. Compare the *nominal* and *real* annual returns for Oracle Corp. (ORCL). Determine the annual nominal rate of return for Oracle over the last ten years. Use the CPI inflation calculator at the Bureau of Labor Statistics Web site (**www.data.bls.gov/cgi-bin/cpicalc.pl**) to determine annual inflation rates over the last ten years. Calculate the real annual rates of return for Oracle. Is the real rate of return less than the nominal rate of return every year? Why? What do you think will happen to this relationship if the inflation in any given year were negative?

Smart Ideas Video

Elroy Dimson, London Business School

"The worldwide average equity premium has been somewhere in the 4 to 5% range."

Smart Ethics Video

Utpal Bhattacharya, Indiana University

"The cost of equity goes up if insider trading laws are not enforced."

SMART concepts

See key risk and return concepts explained step-by-step.

SMART solutions

See the solution to Problem 6–5 explained step-by-step.

Mini-Case

The Trade-Off Between Risk and Return

Assignment

Use the following information to compare the performance of the S&P 500 Index, the Nasdaq Index, and the Treasury Bill Index from 1983–2003. Each of these index numbers is calculated in a way that assumes that investors reinvest any income they receive, so the total return equals the percentage change in the index value each year. The last column shows the level of the Consumer Price Index (CPI) at the end of each year, so the percentage change in the index indicates the rate of inflation for a particular year. Note that because the data start on December 31, 1983, it is not possible to calculate returns or an inflation rate in 1983.

For the S&P 500, the Nasdaq, and the T-bill series calculate (a) the cumulative return over twenty years, (b) the average annual return in *nominal* terms, (c) the average annual return in *real* terms, and (d) the standard deviation of the nominal return. Based on these calculations, discuss the risk/return relationship between these indexes. Which asset class earned the highest average return? For which asset class were returns most volatile? Plot your results on a graph with the standard deviation of each asset class on the horizontal axis and the average return on the vertical axis.

Date	S&P 500	Nasdaq	T-Bills	CPI
12/31/1983	164.93	278.60	681.44	101.3
12/31/1984	167.24	247.35	748.88	105.3
12/31/1985	211.28	324.39	806.62	109.3
12/31/1986	242.17	348.81	855.73	110.5
12/31/1987	247.08	330.47	906.02	115.4
12/31/1988	277.72	381.38	968.89	120.5
12/31/1989	353.40	454.82	1050.63	126.1
12/31/1990	330.22	373.84	1131.42	133.8
12/31/1991	417.09	586.34	1192.83	137.9
12/31/1992	435.71	676.95	1234.36	141.9
12/31/1993	466.45	776.80	1271.78	145.8
12/31/1994	459.27	751.96	1327.55	149.7
12/31/1995	615.93	1052.13	1401.97	153.5
12/31/1996	740.74	1291.03	1473.98	158.6
12/31/1997	970.43	1570.35	1550.49	161.3
12/31/1998	1229.23	2192.68	1625.77	163.9
12/31/1999	1469.25	4069.31	1703.84	168.3
12/31/2000	1320.28	2470.52	1805.75	174.0
12/31/2001	1148.08	1950.40	1865.85	176.7
12/31/2002	879.82	1335.51	1895.83	180.9
12/31/2003	1111.92	2003.37	1915.29	184.3

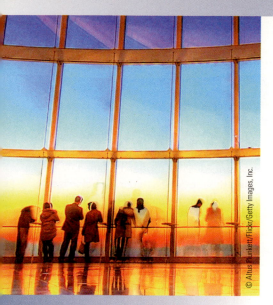
© Altus Plunkett/Flickr/Getty Images, Inc.

chapter 7

Risk, Return, and the Capital Asset Pricing Model

What Companies Do

High Beta Stocks Soar in Rising Market

As 2010 drew to a close, stock market prognosticators turned bullish. A panel of Wall Street strategists polled by Barron's expected a 10% market gain in 2011, and a forecast produced by the investment banking firm Goldman Sachs predicted a 16% increase in the value of U.S. stocks. In light of their forecast for a rising stock market, Goldman recommended that investors buy high beta stocks. High beta stocks are stocks that are riskier than average and tend to earn higher than average returns when the overall market is rising. For example, according to Zachs Investment Research, from March 2009 to the end of 2010 the S&P500 stock index rose more than 81%, but a portfolio of high beta stocks rose more than 200% over the same period.

The notion that a stock's beta is an important measure of risk and is linked to an investment's return is fundamental to one of the most important theories in all of finance—the Capital Asset Pricing Model (CAPM). The CAPM gives investors a way to judge the risks and rewards of almost any investment, and managers rely on the model when they analyze capital investment projects for their firms.

Source: www.online.barrons.com/article/SB5000142405297020451720457603183350 1901092 .html?mod=BOL_twm_col

Learning Objectives

After studying this chapter you will be able to:

- Illustrate three different approaches for estimating an asset's expected return;
- Calculate a portfolio's expected return and its beta;
- Explain how the Capital Asset Pricing Model (CAPM) links an asset's beta to its expected return; and
- Describe the concept of market efficiency and its important lessons for investors.

In this chapter, we continue our study of the relationship between risk and return. We will see that a stock's beta, a measure of how much a stock's return varies in response to variations in overall market returns, *is an important determinant of its expected return.* This is the central insight of the Capital Asset Pricing Model (CAPM), one of the most important ideas in modern finance. The scholars who developed the model earned a Nobel Prize in Economics in 1990 for their research. The CAPM is useful not only for investors in financial markets but also for managers who need to understand what returns stockholders expect on the money they contribute to corporate ventures.

 7-1

Expected Returns

expected return
A forecast of the return that an asset will earn over some future period of time.

Ultimately, people want to know what return they should expect from an investment. Investors and corporate managers decide upon investments based on their best judgments about what the future will hold. In finance, when we use the term expected return, we have in mind a "best guess" estimate of how an investment will perform. For example, in Chapter 6 we saw ample evidence that investors should expect higher returns on stocks than on bonds. Intuitively, that makes sense because stocks are riskier than bonds, and investors should expect a reward for bearing risk. However, the claim that expected returns should be higher for stocks than for bonds does not imply that stocks will actually outperform bonds every year. Rather, it means that it is more likely that stocks will outperform bonds than vice versa.

In this chapter, we want to establish a link between risk and expected returns. To establish that link, we must deal with a major challenge. *Expected returns are inherently unobservable.* Analysts have many techniques at their disposal to form estimates of expected returns, but it is important to remember that the numbers produced by these models are just estimates. As a starting point, let's see how analysts might use historical data to make educated guesses about the future.

7-1a The Historical Approach

Analysts employ at least three different methods to estimate an asset's expected return. The first method relies on historical data and assumes that the future and the past share much in common. Chapter 6 reported an average risk premium on U.S. stocks relative to Treasury bills of 7.5% over the last 111 years. If a Treasury bill currently offers investors a 2% yield to maturity, then the sum of the bill yield and the historical equity risk premium (2.0% + 7.5% = 9.5%) provides one measure of the expected return on stocks.

Can we apply that logic to an individual stock to estimate its expected return? Consider the case of Ford Motor Co. Ford stock traded in the U.S. for many years, so we can calculate its long-run average return, just as we did for the U.S. stock market. Suppose that over many decades, Ford's return has averaged 15.0%. Suppose also that over the same time period, the average return on Treasury bills was 4.0%. Thus, Ford stockholders have enjoyed a historical risk premium of 11.0%. Therefore, we might estimate Ford's expected return as follows:

$$\text{Ford expected return} = \text{Current T-bill rate} + \text{Ford historical risk premium}$$

$$\text{Ford expected return} = 2\% + 11\% = 13\%$$

Although simple and intuitively appealing, this approach suffers from several drawbacks. First, over its long history, Ford has experienced many changes, including executive turnover, technological breakthroughs in manufacturing, increased competition from domestic and foreign rivals, and even bankruptcy during the last recession. This suggests that the risks of investing in Ford have changed dramatically over time, so the risk premium on Ford shares has fluctuated too. Calculating Ford's historical risk premium over many years blends all these changes into a single number, and that number may or may not reflect Ford's current status. Thus, the historical approach yields merely a naïve estimate of the expected return. Investors need to know whether Ford's shares today are more risky, less risky, or just as risky as the long-term premium indicates.

A second flaw in applying this approach broadly is that most stocks in the market do not have as long a history as Ford does to forecast the expected return. In the last decade, more than 1,000 new firms listed their stock on U.S. markets. These firms have no long-run track record to learn from—only a few years of rather volatile recent history.

7-1b The Probabilistic Approach

A second method for estimating expected returns uses statistical concepts. When statisticians want to estimate the expected value of some unknown quantity, they first list all *possible* values that the variable of interest might take, as well as the probability that each outcome will occur. In principle, analysts can use the same approach to calculate the expected return on stocks and other financial assets. A potential advantage of this approach is that it does not require an analyst to assume that the future will look just like the past. Professional judgment plays a larger role here.

Ford Motor Co. falls into a category of stocks that traders call "cyclicals," because these stocks' fortunes rise and fall dramatically with the business cycle. To project the expected return on Ford stock, an analyst can estimate the probabilities associated with different states of the overall economy. The table below illustrates how this can work. The analyst assumes that the economy will be in one of three possible states next year: boom, expansion, or recession. The current climate presents a 20% chance that the economy will experience a recession, and the probabilities of a normal expansion or a boom are 70% and 10%, respectively. Next, the analyst projects that if the economy slips into recession, Ford stockholders will experience a 30% loss. If the economy continues to expand normally, then Ford's stock return will be 15%. If the economy booms, Ford stock will do very well, earning a total return of 55%.

Outcome	Probability	Ford Return
Recession	20%	−30%
Expansion	70%	15%
Boom	10%	55%

To calculate the expected return on Ford shares, multiply each possible return times the probability that it will occur and then add up the returns across all three possible outcomes:

Ford expected return = $0.20(-30\%) + 0.70(15\%) + 0.10(55\%) = 10\%$[1]

With an estimate of the expected return in place, the analyst can estimate the variance and standard deviation of Ford stock. To do so, subtract the 10% expected return from the actual return on Ford stock in each state of the economy. Then, square that difference and multiply it by the probability of recession, expansion, or boom. The accompanying table illustrates the calculation.

---

[1]It is easy to generalize this equation. Rather than assuming that there are just three possible outcomes for Ford stock, suppose that there are n distinct states, where n can be any number. Each state occurs with a particular probability $(p_1 + p_2 + \cdots p_n = 1.0)$ and results in a specific return on Ford shares $(r_1, r_2, r_3, \ldots)$. In this case, the expected return equals:

$$E(r) = p_1 r_1 + p_2 r_2 + p_3 r_3 + \cdots + p_n r_n$$

Outcome	Probability	Ford Return	Return − 10%	(Return − 10%)^2
Recession	20%	−30%	−40%	1,600%^{2}
Expansion	70%	15%	5%	25%^{2}
Boom	10%	55%	45%	2,025%^{2}

$$\text{Variance} = (0.20)(1{,}600\%^2) + (0.70)(25\%^2) + (0.10)(2{,}025\%^2) = 540\%^2$$
$$\text{Standard Deviation} = \sqrt{540\%^2} = \mathbf{23.2\%}$$

The analyst can apply the same model to any stock with returns tied to the business cycle. For example, purchases of Coca-Cola do not vary over the business cycle as much as car purchases do, so Coke stock should be less sensitive to economic conditions than is Ford's stock. Perhaps when the economy is booming, Coke shareholders earn 36%. Under normal economic conditions, Coke stock earns 12%, but during an economic slump, the return on Coke shares equals −15%. Maintaining the same assumptions about the probabilities of recession, expansion, and boom, estimates of Coke's expected return, variance, and standard deviation can be constructed as follows:

Outcome	Probability	Coke Return	Return − 9%	(Return − 9%)^2
Recession	20%	−15%	−24%	576%^{2}
Expansion	70%	12%	3%	9%^{2}
Boom	10%	36%	27%	729%^{2}

$$\text{Expected return} = (0.20)(-15\%) + (0.70)(12\%) + (0.10)(36\%) = 9\%$$
$$\text{Variance} = (0.20)(576\%^2) + (0.70)(9\%^2) + (0.10)(729\%^2) = 194.4\%^2$$
$$\text{Standard Deviation} = \sqrt{194.4\%^2} = \mathbf{13.9\%}$$

But the probabilistic approach has its own drawbacks. To calculate expected returns for Ford and Coca-Cola, we started with a simplifying assumption that only three possible outcomes or scenarios were possible. Clearly, the range of potential outcomes is much broader than this. Similarly, we assumed that we knew the probability of each scenario in advance. Where did those probabilities come from? Analysts can draw from historical experience, for example, by estimating the probability of a recession by studying past recession frequencies. If history shows that recessions occur in roughly one year out of every five, then 20% might be a reasonable estimate of the probability of a future recession; then again, it might be well off the mark. In any case, the probabilistic approach involves a high degree of subjectivity. It requires analysts to specify possible future outcomes for stock returns and to attach a probability to each outcome. Once again, these assumptions about possible states of the economy can be somewhat naïve if the assumptions are based on historical data.

7-1c The Risk-Based Approach

A third approach to estimate an asset's expected return is more theoretically sound and is used in practice by most corporate finance professionals. It requires an analyst to first measure the risk of the asset and then to translate that risk measure into an expected return estimate. This approach involves a two-step process. The first step is to define what we mean by risk and to measure it, and the second step is to quantify how much return we should expect on an asset with a given amount of risk.

Measuring the Risk of a Single Asset Recall that Chapter 6 introduced the notions of systematic and unsystematic risk. Remember these concepts:

- *Systematic risks* simultaneously affect many different securities, whereas unsystematic risks affect just a few securities at a time. Systematic risk refers to events, such as unexpected changes in the overall health of the economy, interest rate movements, or changes in inflation. Events that we classify as examples of *unsystematic risk* include the failure of a firm's new product to gain market share, a scandal involving top management at a particular company, or the loss of a key employee.[2]

- Investors *can eliminate unsystematic risk by diversifying,* but diversification cannot eradicate systematic (or market) risk. Because it is easy for investors to shed one type of risk but not the other, the *market pays investors for bearing systematic risk.* That is, assets with more exposure to systematic risk generally offer investors higher returns than assets with less exposure to systematic risk. We see evidence of that proposition in the historical record, such as the higher long-term average return on stocks compared to T-bonds or T-bills.

- The standard deviation of an asset's returns measures how much returns fluctuate around the average. The standard deviation calculation makes no distinction between a movement in returns caused by systematic factors, such as an increase in oil prices, and movements associated with unsystematic factors, such as the outcome of a product liability lawsuit filed against one firm. In other words, *the standard deviation measures an asset's total risk, equal to the sum of its systematic and unsystematic components.* Because only the systematic component of risk influences an asset's expected return, an asset's standard deviation is an unreliable guide to its expected return.

If systematic risk means risk that affects the entire market, then for an individual stock, we need to know the extent to which the stock moves when the market moves. We need a measure that captures *only* the systematic component of a stock's volatility, because *only* that component should be related to the asset's expected return. When an event having a positive (or negative) effect on the overall market also has a pronounced positive (or negative) effect on a particular stock, then that stock has a high degree of systematic risk and should also have a high expected return.

For a visual explanation of this idea, examine Figures 7.1A and 7.1B. The figures show scatter plots of monthly stock returns for two companies, Saks Incorporated (operators of the luxury goods chain Saks Fifth Avenue) and food producer ConAgra, versus the weekly return on the Standard and Poors 500 Stock Index (S&P 500).[3] For example, each dot in Figure 7.1A shows the return on Saks stock and the return on the S&P 500 in a particular month. Through each scatter plot we have drawn a trendline, estimated by using the method of linear regression. This trendline shows the average tendency for each stock to move with the market. However, clearly Saks stock does not track the market perfectly, which is evidence that there are unsystematic risks that affect Saks stock returns.

These two stocks respond differently, on average, to market movements. The Saks trendline's slope equals 2.3. Thus, *on average,* if the market's return one week moves by 1%, then the return on Saks stock moves in the same direction by 2.3%. ConAgra shares behave quite differently, displaying a much lower tendency to move in conjunction with the market. With a 0.6 slope, ConAgra's trendline tells us that if the market return moves up or down 1%, *on average,* ConAgra's return moves just 0.6% in response. These differences in responsiveness lead to an important conclusion. Because returns on Saks are more sensitive to overall market movements, Saks common stock has more systematic risk than does ConAgra stock. In other words, when a macro-economic event such as an unexpected shift in interest rates moves the entire market, Saks shares typically respond more sharply than do ConAgra shares.

The slopes of the trendlines in Figure 7.1A and 7.1B have a special designation in finance, known as beta. A stock's beta measures the sensitivity of its return to movements in the overall market return. Thus, beta is a measure of systematic risk. The return on a high-beta stock like Saks typically experiences dramatic up-and-down swings when the market return moves. Because Sak's beta equals 2.3, we can say that the return on Sak's shares moves, on average, 2.3 times as much as does

beta

A standardized measure of the risk of an individual asset that captures only the systematic component of its volatility; it measures the sensitivity of the asset's return to movements in the overall market.

---

[2]Notice that all these examples are negative events, in the sense that we expect them to cause the firm's stock price to fall. Of course, risk means that outcomes can be surprisingly good, just as they can be surprisingly bad.

[3]The S&P 500 is a market index consisting of 500 large U.S. stocks. It is one of the most widely watched barometers of the overall U.S. stock market, so we use it here as a proxy for the entire market.

Figure 7.1A   **Scatter Plot of Monthly Returns on Saks Inc. and the S&P 500 Stock Index**

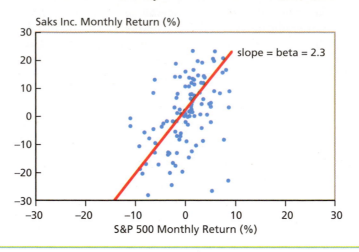

Figure 7.1B   **Scatter Plot of Monthly Returns on ConAgra Foods and the S&P 500 Stock Index**

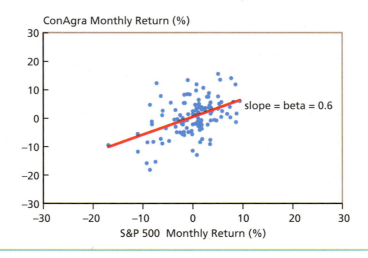

Figure 7.1C   **Scatter Plot of Monthly Returns on a Portfolio Invested Equally in Saks and ConAgra**

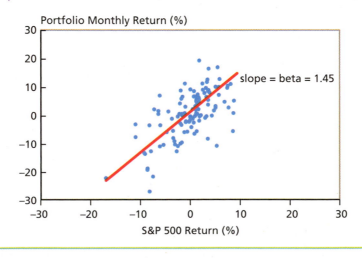

Note: The figure shows a scatter plot of monthly returns on Saks stock (Figure 7.1A), ConAgra stock (Figure 7.1B), and an equally-weighted portfolio of those two stocks (Figure 7.1C) versus the monthly return on the S&P 500 stock index.

the market return. In contrast, with a beta of just 0.6, the return on ConAgra stock moves much less on average when the overall stock market fluctuates. *This is not the same thing as saying that ConAgra is not a volatile stock.* The individual dots in Figure 7.1B show that monthly returns on ConAgra usually fall in a range between positive and negative 10%. Clearly, a stock that can gain or lose 10% in a month is volatile, but ConAgra's return does not move sharply in the same direction as the overall market return. Hence, the systematic risk of ConAgra is relatively low.

Think about the businesses that Saks and ConAgra engage in, and the reason for the wide disparity between their betas becomes clear. ConAgra produces food, and people have to eat in good times and bad. Food consumption varies little with economic fluctuations, so ConAgra's stock return is not very sensitive to market movements. To a large extent, ConAgra stock is affected by factors such as weather and government farm policies that would not affect the wider stock market very much. On the other hand, Saks sells designer fashions, expensive shoes and handbags, and other luxury products. People indulge in these products much more in good times than in bad. Consequently, the return on Saks shares moves sharply up and down in response to changing macroeconomic conditions.

Finally, look at Figure 7.1C, which plots monthly returns produced by a portfolio invested equally in Saks and ConAgra. Two important points emerge from this figure. First, notice that the slope of the line, which is the beta of the portfolio, is 1.45. That is actually equal to the average of the betas of Saks (2.3) and ConAgra (0.6). *In other words, the beta of a portfolio is a weighted average of the betas of the stocks in the portfolio.* Second, observe how in Figure 7.1C the dots cluster a little closer to the trend line than they do in Figures 7.1A and 7.1B. This occurs because in the portfolio, some of the unsystematic risk of the individual stocks has been diversified away.

Risk and Expected Returns The risk-based approach to calculating expected returns involves two steps. The first step is to develop a measure of a particular asset's systematic risk. In *beta* we have such a measure. The second step involves translating the asset's beta into an estimate of expected return. To see how that process works, examine Figure 7.2.[4]

In Figure 7.2, we plot the beta against the expected return for two important assets. First, suppose an asset is available that pays a given return with certainty, in this case, 4%. We designate this as the risk-free asset. It's return is not subject to systematic risk (therefore its beta equals zero) or default risk. In reality, no asset can promise a completely risk-free return, but a U.S. Treasury bill comes very close. In 2011 at least one rating agency downgraded the U.S. government's credit rating due to persistent budget deficits. Even so, think of a T-bill each time we refer to a risk-free asset. In Figure 7.2, the risk-free rate is 4%.

The second asset plotted in Figure 7.2 is an average stock. The term "average stock" means that this security's sensitivity to market movements is neither especially high, like Saks, nor especially low, like ConAgra. By definition, *the beta of the average stock equals 1.0.* On average, its return goes up or down by 1% when the market return goes up or down by 1%. Assume for a moment that the expected return on this stock equals 10%.

By drawing a straight line connecting the two points in Figure 7.2, we gain some insight into the relationship between beta and expected returns. An investor who is unwilling to accept any systematic risk at all can hold the risk-free asset and earn 4%. An investor who is willing to bear an average degree of systematic risk, by investing in a stock with a beta equal to 1.0, expects to earn 10%. In general, investors may expect higher or lower returns based on the betas of the stocks they hold, as the following example illustrates.

[4]Notice that Figure 7.2 is conceptually different from Figures 7.1A and 7.1B. The earlier figures compared actual returns on particular stocks to actual returns on a market index. In Figure 7.2 we are establishing a connection between risk, as measured by beta, and expected returns.

Figure 7.2   **Beta and Expected Returns**

An investor willing to accept an average level of systematic risk, by holding a stock with a beta of 1.0, expects a return of 10%. By holding only the risk-free asset, an investor can earn 4% without having to accept any systematic risk at all.

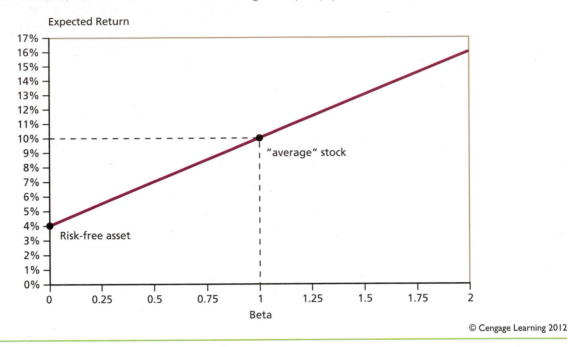

EXAMPLE

We can derive an algebraic expression for the line in Figure 7.2. Recognize that the vertical axis (y-axis) in the figure is measuring the expected return of some investment, which we will denote as E(r). The horizontal axis (x-axis) is measuring the investment's beta (β). The y-intercept is the risk-free rate, which we assume to be 4%. Because we have plotted two points on the line, we can use the "rise over run" formula to calculate the line's slope.

$$\text{slope} = \frac{\text{rise}}{\text{run}} = \frac{(10\% - 4\%)}{(1.0 - 0.0)} = 6\%.$$

Because we now know both the intercept (4%) and the slope (6%) of the line, we can express the relation between an investment's expected return and its beta as follows:

$$E(r) = 4\% + (6\% \times \beta)$$

Now consider an investor who wants to take an intermediate level of risk by holding a stock with a beta of 0.5. The expected return on this stock is 7%:

$$E(r) = 4\% + (6\% \times 0.5) = 7\%$$

On the other hand, an investor who is willing to take a lot of risk by holding a stock with a beta of 1.5 can expect a much higher return:

$$E(r) = 4\% + (6\% \times 1.5) = 13\%$$

The line in Figure 7.2 plays a very important role in finance, and we will return to it later in this chapter. For now, the important lesson is that *beta measures an asset's systematic risk, a risk that has a direct relationship with expected returns.*

7-1 Concept Review Questions

1. What is the difference between an asset's *expected return* and its *actual return*? Why are expected returns so important to investors and managers?

2. Contrast the historical approach to estimating expected returns with the probabilistic approach.

3. Why should *stock betas* and expected returns be related, while no such relationship exists between stock standard deviations and expected returns?

4. Why is the risk-based approach the best method for estimating a stock's expected return?

7-2 Risk and Return for Portfolios

In Chapter 6, we saw that investors can reduce risk dramatically by holding diversified portfolios rather than individual stocks. An investor who chooses to diversify will be more concerned with how her portfolio performs than with the performance of each individual security in the portfolio. Therefore, we need a way to measure risk and return for portfolios.

7-2a Portfolio Expected Return

Suppose an individual has $10,000 to invest, and she decides to divide that money between two different assets. Asset 1 has an expected return of 8%, and Asset 2 has an expected return of 12%. Our investor puts $4,000 in Asset 1 and $6,000 in Asset 2. What is the expected return on the portfolio?

portfolio weights
The percentage invested in each of several securities in a portfolio. Portfolio weights must sum to 1.0 (or 100%).

To begin, we must calculate the fraction of the individual's wealth invested in each asset, known as the **portfolio weights**. The fraction invested in Asset 1 equals 0.40 ($4,000/$10,000), and the fraction invested in Asset 2 equals 0.60 ($6,000/$10,000). Notice that the portfolio weights add up to 1.0.

The portfolio's expected return equals the weighted average of the expected returns of the securities in the portfolio. In this case, the expected return equals:

$$\text{Expected return} = (0.40)(8\%) + (0.60)(12\%) = 10.4\%$$

We can write a more general expression describing a portfolio's expected return. Suppose a portfolio contains different securities. The expected returns on these securities are $E(r_1)$, $E(r_2)$, . . . , $E(r_n)$. The portfolio weights are w_1, w_2, . . . , w_n. The portfolio expected return $E(r_p)$ is given by this equation:

(Eq. 7.1)
$$E(r_p) = w_1 E(r_1) + w_2 E(r_2) + \cdots + w_n E(r_n)$$
$$w_1 + w_2 + \cdots + w_n = 1$$

EXAMPLE

Calculate the expected return on the portfolio described in the following table.

Stock	E(r)	$ Invested
IBM	10%	$ 2,500
GE	12%	5,000
Sears	8%	2,500
Pfizer	14%	10,000

First, calculate the portfolio weights. The total dollar value of the portfolio is $20,000. The weights for the investments in Pfizer and Sears are 0.125 ($2,500/$20,000). The fraction invested in GE is 0.25, and the weight associated with Pfizer is 0.50. Now multiply those weights times the expected return for each stock and add up:

$$E(r_p) = (0.125)(10\%) + (0.25)(12\%) + (0.125)(8\%) + (0.5)(14\%) = 12.25\%$$

selling short
Borrowing a security and selling it for cash at the current market price. A short seller hopes that either (1) the price of the security sold short will fall, or (2) the return on the security sold short will be lower than the return on the asset in which the proceeds from the short sale were invested.

Short Selling We noted that the portfolio weights must add up to one. It is natural to assume that these weights also fall in a range between zero and one, meaning that an investor can invest nothing or everything in any particular asset. However, a more exotic arrangement is possible, one that results in a negative portfolio weight for a particular asset. A negative portfolio weight means that rather than investing in the given asset, an individual is borrowing that asset, selling it, and using the proceeds to invest more in something else. When investors borrow a security and sell it, they are **selling short**. Here's how shorting works.

Consider two assets in the market, Rocket.com and BricksNMortar Inc. Both stocks currently sell for $10 and pay no dividends. You are optimistic about Rocket's prospects, and you expect its return next year to be 25%. In contrast, you believe that BricksNMortar will earn just 5%. You have $1,000 to invest, but you'd like to invest more than that in Rocket.com. To do this, you phone a friend who owns 50 shares of BricksNMortar and persuade him to let you borrow the shares, by promising that you'll return them in one year. Once you receive the shares, you sell them in the market, immediately raising $500 (50 shares × $10 per share). Next, you combine those funds with your own money and purchase $1,500 (150 shares) of Rocket.com. Your portfolio expected return looks like this:

SMART
concepts
See the concept explained step-by-step at **SMART | finance**

$$E(r_p) = (-0.5)(5\%) + (1.5)(25\%) = 35\%$$

In this equation, the weight invested in Rocket.com equals 1.5 ($1,500 ÷ $1,000), or 150% of your total wealth. You can invest more than 100% of your wealth (i.e., more than $1,000) because you borrowed from someone else. The weight invested in BricksNMortar equals -0.5 because you took out a $500 loan equivalent to half your wealth. If you are right and BricksNMortar shares go up from $10 to $10.50 during the year (an increase of 5%), then you will effectively pay your friend 5% interest when you repurchase the BricksNMortar shares and return them next year. This loan will be very profitable if Rocket.com stock increases as rapidly as you expect. For example, in one year's time, if BricksNMortar sells for $10.50 (up 5%) and Rocket.com sells for $12.50 (up 25%), your position will look like this:

Beginning of Year		
Initial investment	$1,000	
Borrowed funds	500	(50 shares @ $10)
Rocket shares	$1,500	(150 shares @ $10)
End of Year		
Sell Rocket shares	$1,875	(150 shares @ $12.50)
Return borrowed shares	− 525	(50 shares @ $10.50)
Net cash earned	$1,350	

Rate of return = ($1,350 − $1,000)/$1,000 = 0.35 = 35%

Notice that the expected return on this portfolio exceeds the expected return of either stock in the portfolio. When investors take a short position in one asset to invest more in another asset, they are using *financial leverage*. As noted in Chapter 12, leverage magnifies expected returns, but it also increases risk.

EXAMPLE

Suppose you are wrong about these two stocks, and Rocket.com goes down by 10% during the year (to $9), while BricksNMortar increases by 10% (to $11). At the end of the year, your situation is as follows:

Sell Rocket shares	$1,350	(150 shares @ $9.00)
Return borrowed shares	$ 550	(50 shares @ $11.00)
Net cash earned	$ 800	

Rate of return = ($800 − $1,000)/$1,000 = −0.20 = −20%

The 150 shares of Rocket are worth just $1,350, and you must return 50 BricksNMortar shares, which are now worth $550, to the lender. That leaves you with just $800 of your original $1,000 investment, a loss of 20%.

Finance in Your Life

Why Portfolio Weights Shift

In Chapter 6 we looked at how your decision to allocate funds between stocks and bonds would affect the amount of money you saved for retirement. No matter how you initially allocate your savings between stocks and bonds, over time the portfolio weights will shift toward the asset earning the highest returns.

Repeating the example from page 189 of Chapter 6, suppose you invest $4,000 each year for 35 years, and you invest half of each contribution in bonds and half in stocks. Assume that bonds earn 5.6% per year and stocks earn 11.4%. The table below shows how your portfolio weights tilt toward common stocks, even though you divide your contributions equally between stocks and bonds. Because stocks earn a higher return than bonds, the stock portfolio grows faster each year, increasing the portfolio weight invested in stocks as time goes by.

| Year | Total Amount Invested | | % Invested in Stocks |
	Bond Portfolio	Stock Portfolio	
1	$ 2,000	$ 2,000	50.0%
2	4,112	4,228	50.7%
5	11,184	12,555	52.9%
10	25,872	34,095	56.9%
15	45,158	71,050	61.1%
30	147,416	429,841	74.5%

7-2b Portfolio Risk

Based on the calculation of a portfolio's expected return, you may expect that a portfolio's risk is equal to a weighted average of the risks of the assets that comprise the portfolio. That statement is partly right and partly wrong. When we shift our focus from expected return to risk, we must be very careful about the measure of risk that we use in our calculations.

For instance, in Table 6.5 in the previous chapter, we estimated the standard deviation of returns for Archer Daniels Midland (ADM) to be 24.8%. The same table reported a standard deviation for American Airlines (AMR) of 47.0%. Suppose we form a portfolio invested equally in ADM and AMR shares. With portfolio weights of 0.50, you might guess that the standard deviation of this portfolio equals:

$$\text{Portfolio standard deviation} = (0.50)(24.8\%) + (0.50)(47.0\%) = 35.9\%$$

As reasonable as that guess seems, it is wrong. It turns out that a portfolio invested in equal proportions of ADM and AMR has a standard deviation of just 28%! As a general rule, *the standard deviation of a portfolio is almost always less than the weighted average of the standard deviations of the stocks in the portfolio.* This is diversification at work. Combining securities together eliminates some of their unsystematic risk, so the portfolio is less volatile than the average stock in the portfolio.[5]

However, diversification does not eliminate systematic risk. Therefore, if we redefine portfolio risk and focus on systematic risk only, not on the standard deviation, which includes both

Andrew Karolyi, Cornell University

"Investors who seek to diversify internationally to reduce their global risk can leave money on the table if they ignore the unique industrial compositions of markets."

See the entire interview at **SMART | finance**

Smart Ideas Video

---

[5]You can also see this effect of diversification in Table 6.5 on page 195. The average standard deviation of the ten stocks listed in that table is 31.4%, but the standard deviation of a portfolio containing all ten stocks is just 19.1%.

What Companies Do Globally

How Risky Are Emerging Markets?

Over the past twenty-five years, many developing countries adopted market-oriented reforms and opened their economies to foreign capital. Despite the success these countries have enjoyed in attracting new investors, a recent report by McKinsey & Company argues that most multinational corporations overestimate the risk of investing in emerging markets. According to McKinsey, companies routinely assign a risk premium to projects in emerging markets that is more than double the risk premium that they assign to similar projects in the United States and Europe. By overstating the risks, multinational firms understate the value of investments in emerging markets. McKinsey & Company believes that this leads firms to pass up profitable investment opportunities in these countries.

If it is true that firms overstate the risks of investing in emerging markets, what is the cause of that error? McKinsey proposes that firms do not take the proper portfolio view of the businesses they engage in around the world. Rather than looking at each business unit's contribution to overall firm risk (i.e., the contribution of each unit to the firm's portfolio of businesses), companies place too much emphasis on the unsystematic risks associated with individual countries.

To demonstrate that point, McKinsey calculates a beta for each emerging market relative to a world market index. By definition, the world market's beta equals 1.0. Especially risky countries should have betas much greater than 1.0, while supposedly "safe" countries like the United States should have betas below 1.0. The bar chart below shows betas for the United States, Europe, and twenty-two emerging markets. Ten emerging markets have a beta below that of the U.S. market, and in only one country, Russia, does the market beta justify a risk premium double that of the United States. Investments that seem to be very risky when considered in isolation look much less risky as part of a portfolio. That's a lesson that applies to individual investors as well as to multinational corporations.

Betas of Markets Around the World

Source: "Are Emerging Markets as Risky as You Think?" by Marc H. Goedhart and Peter Haden, *McKinsey on Finance*, Spring 2003.

? WHAT SHOULD I ASK

Do you use the same methods to assess the risk of foreign and domestic investments that your firm makes?

systematic and unsystematic risk, then the simple weighted average formula works. For example, suppose ADM stock has a beta of 0.8 and AMR's beta equals 1.4. The beta of a portfolio with equal investments in each stock is:

$$\text{Portfolio Beta} = \beta_p = (0.50)(0.8) + (0.50)(1.4) = 1.1$$

EXAMPLE

Calculate the beta of the portfolio described in the following table.

Stock	Beta	$ Invested
IBM	1.00	$ 2,500
GE	1.33	$ 5,000
Sears	0.67	$ 2,500
Pfizer	1.67	$10,000

The portfolio weights here are the same as in the example on page 219, so the portfolio beta equals:

$$\beta_p = (0.125)(1.00) + (0.25)(1.33) + (0.125)(0.67) + (0.50)(1.67) = 1.38$$

The insert on what companies do globally illustrates why distinguishing between systematic and unsystematic risk is important, not just for investors who buy stocks and bonds, but also for corporations that build factories, invest in distribution networks, and make other kinds of investments in physical assets.

7-2 Concept Review Questions

5. How can the weight given to a particular stock in a portfolio exceed 100%?

6. Why is the standard deviation of a portfolio typically less than the weighted average of the standard deviations of the assets in the portfolio, while a portfolio's beta equals the weighted average of the betas of the stocks in the portfolio?

7-3 Pulling It All Together: The CAPM

Now we are ready to tie together the concepts of risk and return for portfolios as well as for individual securities. Once again we will begin by considering a portfolio consisting of just two assets. One asset pays a risk-free return equal to r_f. We already know that the beta of the risk-free asset equals zero. The other asset is a broadly diversified portfolio. Imagine a portfolio that is so diversified that it invests in every available risky asset in the economy. Because such a portfolio represents the overall market, we refer to it as the market portfolio. Designate the expected return on the market portfolio as $E(r_m)$.

market portfolio
A portfolio that invests in every asset in the economy.

The beta of the market portfolio must equal 1.0. To see why, reconsider the definition of beta. An asset's beta describes how the asset moves in relation to the overall market. The market portfolio will mimic the overall market perfectly. Because the portfolio's return moves exactly in sync with the market, its beta must be 1.0. Figure 7.3 plots the beta and the expected return of the risk-free asset and the market portfolio.

Suppose we combine the risk-free asset, let's call it a T-bill, and the market portfolio to create a new portfolio. We know that the expected return on this new portfolio must be a weighted average of the expected returns of the assets in the portfolio. Similarly, we know that the beta of the portfolio must be a weighted average of the betas of a T-bill and the market. This implies that the new portfolio we've created must lie along the line connecting the risk-free asset and the market portfolio in Figure 7.3. What are the properties of this line?

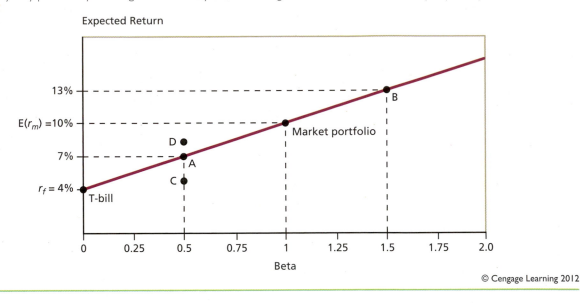

Figure 7.3   **The Security Market Line**

The Security Market Line plots the relationship between an asset's beta and its expected return. The line shows how an investor can construct a portfolio of T-bills and the market portfolio to achieve the desired level of risk and return. One investor might choose a relatively conservative portfolio, mixing T-bills and the market portfolio in equal proportions (see point A). Another investor could construct a very risky portfolio by investing his own money and borrowing more to invest in the market (see point B).

With two points identified on the line, the T-bill and the market portfolio, we can calculate the line's slope by taking the rise over the run, just as we did in the example on page 218:

$$\text{Slope} = \frac{E(r_m) - r_f}{1 - 0} = E(r_m) - r_f$$

The difference in returns between a portfolio of risky securities and a risk-free asset is the **market risk premium**. The market risk premium indicates the reward that investors receive if they hold the market portfolio.[6]

market risk premium
The additional return earned (or expected) on the market portfolio over and above the risk-free rate.

The intercept of the line in Figure 7.3 equals r_f. From elementary algebra we know that the equation for a straight line is y = b + mx where b is the intercept and m is the slope. In Figure 7.3, the variable we measure on the y-axis is the expected return on some portfolio of T-bills and the market portfolio. The variable we measure on the x-axis is the beta of this portfolio. Therefore, the equation of the line plotted in this figure is

$$E(r_p) = r_f + \beta_p [E(r_m) - r_f]$$

The equation says that the expected return on any portfolio consisting of T-bills and the market portfolio depends on three things: the risk-free rate, the portfolio beta, and the market risk premium. It's easy to verify that this equation works with a numerical illustration.

What if an investor is willing to hold a position that is even more risky that the market portfolio? One option is to borrow money. When investors buy T-bills, they are essentially loaning money to the government. Suppose investors

[6]Conceptually, the market portfolio invests in every risky asset available in the market. No such portfolio exists in practice, so to estimate the market risk premium, analysts typically use the risk premium on a well diversified stock portfolio.

EXAMPLE

Suppose the risk-free rate is 4% and the expected return on the market portfolio is 10%. This implies that the market risk premium is 6%. What is the expected return on a portfolio invested equally in T-bills and stocks? There are actually several ways to get the answer. First, we know that the expected return on the portfolio is simply the weighted average of the expected returns of the assets in the portfolio, so we have:

$$E(r_p) = (0.5)(4\%) + (0.5)(10\%) = 7\%$$

Alternatively, we could begin by calculating the beta of this portfolio. The portfolio beta is a weighted average of the betas of T-bills and the market portfolio, so we obtain:

$$\beta_p = (0.5)(\text{T-bill beta}) + (0.5)(\text{market beta}) = (0.5)(0) + (0.5)(1.0) = 0.5$$

Now, using the equation of the line in Figure 7.3, we calculate the portfolio's expected return as follows:

$$E(r_p) = 4\% + (0.5)[10\% - 4\%] = 7\%$$

The position of this portfolio appears as point A in Figure 7.3.

William Sharpe, Stanford University, Co-founder, Financial Engines

"To the extent that there is a premium for bearing risk, it is a premium for bearing the risk of doing badly in bad times."

See the entire interview at **SMART** | finance

Smart Ideas Video

also borrow money at the risk-free rate. To be more precise, suppose a certain investor has $10,000 to invest, but he raises an additional $5,000 by borrowing. The investor then puts all $15,000 in the market portfolio. The portfolio weight on T-bills becomes −0.50, and the weight invested in the market portfolio increases to 1.50. The investor now holds a portfolio with a beta greater than one and an expected return greater than 10%, as confirmed in the following calculations:

$$\beta_p = -(0.5)(0) + (1.5)(1.0) = 1.5$$
$$E(r_p) = 4\% + (1.5)[10\% - 4\%] = 13\%$$

In Figure 7.3, the investor's portfolio lies up and to the right of the market portfolio at point B.

At this point, we must stop and make a crucial observation. If it is true, as the preceding example shows, that a portfolio with a beta of 0.5 offers an expected return of 7%, then in equilibrium it must also be true that any individual security with a beta of 0.5 offers the same return. To understand this claim, examine point C in Figure 7.3. This point represents a stock with a beta of 0.5 and an expected return of less than 7%. Rational investors who own C will sell it, because they can create an equally risky portfolio that offers a higher return, by combining T-bills and the market portfolio. As investors sell asset C, its price will fall. We know that prices and returns of financial assets move in opposite directions (e.g., if a bond's price falls, its yield rises), so as the price of C falls, its expected return rises until it reaches 7%.

Similarly, consider point D in the figure. Point D represents an asset with a beta of 0.5 but an expected return greater than 7%. This asset is a true bargain because it offers investors a higher rate of return than they can earn on a 50-50 portfolio of T-bills and stocks, without requiring them to take on extra risk. Investors will rush to buy stock D, and their buying pressure will drive up the price and push down the return of stock D. As soon as the expected return on D reaches 7%, the market once again reaches equilibrium.

Figure 7.3 therefore plots the relationship between betas and expected returns for individual securities as well as for portfolios. This relationship is called The Security Market Line, and the equation of this line is the fundamental risk and return relationship predicted by the **Capital Asset Pricing Model (CAPM)**. *The CAPM says that the*

Capital Asset Pricing Model (CAPM)

States that the expected return on a specific asset equals the risk-free rate plus a premium that depends on the asset's beta and the expected risk premium on the market portfolio.

What Companies Do

CFO Forecasts of the Market Risk Premium

The expected risk premium on the market is an important component of the CAPM, but how does one know what the expected market risk premium is? One way to estimate that premium is to ask CFOs what return they expect stocks to earn relative to safe assets such as Treasury bonds or bills. The chart below shows the market risk premium that CFOs said they expected (looking ten years into the future) when they responded to the quarterly Duke University CFO Survey. From 2001 to 2011 (1st quarter), CFOs' estimates of the market risk premium averaged about 3.5%, but their forecasts fluctuated over time, ranging from a low of about 2.4% to a high of 4.75%. In general, these forecasts suggest that CFOs expect a lower market risk premium than the long-run historical average of 7.5% presented in Chapter 6.

Market Risk Premium Expected by Corporate CFOs

© Cengage Learning 2012

*expected return on any asset i, denoted by E(r*ᵢ*), depends on the risk-free rate, the security's beta, and the market risk premium:*

(Eq. 7.2) $$E(r_i) = r_f + \beta_i(E(r_m) - r_f)$$

SMART concepts

See the concept explained step-by-step at **SMART** | finance

? JOB INTERVIEW QUESTION

How would you estimate the rate of return that our shareholders expect from our company's stock?

The Capital Asset Pricing Model stands as one of the most important ideas in all of finance. Financial managers in nearly all large corporations know the model's key predictions, and they use the CAPM to estimate the rate of return that shareholders require on the firm's stock. Managers use the required return on their firm's stock (along with other information) to calculate the company's weighted average cost of capital (WACC). The WACC is important because most companies only make new investments when they believe those investments will earn returns that exceed the WACC.

As useful as it is, however, the CAPM is not a crystal ball. It gives us some insights about expected returns, but that is not the same thing as predicting how the future will unfold. In the next section, we explore the extent to which actual stock returns, rather than expected returns, may be predictable.

What Companies Do Globally

Do Companies Use the CAPM?

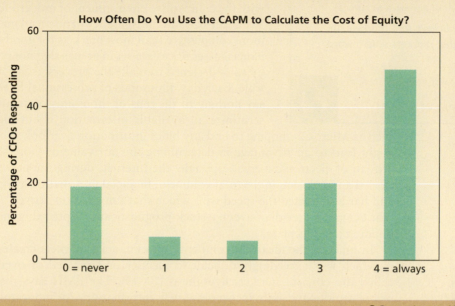

How Often Do You Use the CAPM to Calculate the Cost of Equity?

© Cengage Learning 2012

Graham and Harvey (2001) asked nearly 400 CFOs about the method they used to determine the cost of equity for their firms. As the accompanying chart indicates, nearly three-quarters of these CFOs said that their firms almost always or always (responses 3 and 4 in the survey) used the CAPM to determine the return that the market required on their stock. The second most common method for estimating the cost of equity—using the historical average return—was used by roughly half as many CFOs.

The CAPM sees widespread use in firms around the world, although the model's popularity is not as strong outside the United States. In the United Kingdom and France, roughly 45% of CFOs say that their firms use the CAPM, whereas closer to one-third of German CFOs reported doing so. However, this pattern is changing over time. The percentage of firms using the CAPM has been rising for years in the United States, and that trend seems likely to continue abroad.

7-3 Concept Review Questions

7. List the three factors that influence a stock's expected return according to the CAPM.

8. If a particular stock had no systematic risk, only unsystematic risk, what would be its expected return?

7-4 | Are Stock Returns Predictable?

Microsoft Corp. debuted as a public company with its initial public offering (IPO) on March 13, 1986. On that day, one Microsoft share sold for $21. In the twenty-four years that followed, stock splits turned a single share purchased at the IPO into 288 shares, worth an amazing $7,200 by August 2011. That represents a compound annual return of roughly 26% per year! The purpose of this section is to investigate whether such a spectacular outcome could have been anticipated by smart investors.

Suppose upon graduating from business school you decide to open your own business. The question is, what kind of business should you start? A friend suggests opening a pizza restaurant. Having learned a few valuable lessons in school, you respond that the pizza business is a terrible place to start. Most communities are already

Todd Richter, Managing Director, Head of Equity Healthcare Research, Bank of America Securities

"I don't necessarily believe that markets are efficient. I believe that markets tend toward efficiency."

See the entire interview at **SMART | finance**

Smart Practices Video

efficient markets hypothesis (EMH)
Asserts that financial asset prices rapidly and fully incorporate new information.

SMART concepts

See the concept explained step-by-step at **SMART | finance**

passively managed
A strategy in which an investor makes no attempt to identify overvalued or undervalued stocks, but instead holds a diversified portfolio.

actively managed
A strategy in which an investor does research in an attempt to identify undervalued and overvalued stocks.

index fund
A passively managed fund that tries to mimic the performance of a market index, such as the S&P 500.

saturated with pizza parlors, and most offer similar varieties of pizza with a similar ambience, or lack thereof. You want to find a niche that is less competitive. You reason that getting rich selling pizzas is nearly impossible.

As competitive as the pizza business is, it hardly compares with the competitive environment of modern financial markets. The sheer size and transparency of financial markets make them more competitive than most markets for goods and services. Financial asset prices are set in arenas that are typically governed by rules designed to make the process as fair and open as possible. Each day, thousands of professional financial analysts (to say nothing of the tens of thousands of amateurs) worldwide scrutinize all available information about high-profile stocks such as Microsoft, hoping to find any bit of information overlooked by the crowd that might lead to an advantage in determining the fair value of those shares. The rapid growth of electronic media, especially the Internet, during the past two decades has caused an explosion in the total volume of financial information available to investors and has accelerated the speed with which that information arrives. All of this means that being a better-than-average stock prognosticator is probably more difficult than building a better pizza.

In finance, the idea that competition in financial markets creates an equilibrium in which it is exceedingly difficult to identify undervalued or overvalued stocks is called the **efficient markets hypothesis (EMH)**. The EMH says that financial asset prices rapidly and fully incorporate new information. An interesting implication of this prediction is that asset prices move almost randomly over time. We must use the qualifier, "almost" in the previous sentence because there is a kind of baseline predictability to asset returns that is related to risk. For example, over time, we expect stocks to earn higher returns than bonds, because stocks are riskier. Indeed, the historical record confirms this prediction. But in any given year, stocks may do very well or very poorly relative to bonds. The efficient markets hypothesis says that it is nearly impossible to predict exactly when stocks will do well relative to bonds or when the opposite outcome will occur.

The seemingly random changes in stock prices occur because prices respond only to new information, and new information is almost by definition unpredictable. Numerous trading strategies have been devised and tested in an attempt to earn above average returns in the stock market. Some strategies suggest buying companies with the highest market share in their industry. Other strategies propose buying stocks of new companies with new technologies that could revolutionize an industry. Still others suggest buying or selling stocks based upon patterns in stock charts that allegedly repeat over time.

Of course, there is no end to the number of trading strategies like these that can be tested using the historical data. In the vast majority of cases, these trading strategies do not generate significantly higher returns than a simple buy-and-hold approach. This suggests that stock prices are indeed nearly unpredictable.

The most compelling evidence that markets are efficient is a comparison of **passively managed** versus **actively managed** mutual funds. A mutual fund that adopts a passive management style is called an **index fund**. Index fund managers make no attempt to analyze stocks to determine which ones will perform well and which ones will do poorly. Instead, these managers try to mimic the performance of a market index, such as the S&P 500, by buying the stocks that make up the index. In contrast, fund managers adopting an active management style do extensive analysis to identify mispriced stocks. Active managers trade more frequently than do passive managers and in the process generate higher expenses for their shareholders. Though there are notable exceptions (such as legendary managers Peter Lynch, Warren Buffett, and Bill Gross), most research indicates that active funds earn lower returns, after expenses, than do passive funds. Buy-and-hold wins again.

If this section concludes with the statement that stock returns are essentially unpredictable, then it is fair to ask why we place so much emphasis on the CAPM. After all, the CAPM's purpose is to provide an estimate of how a stock will perform in the future. If stock returns move essentially at random, then does the CAPM have any place in the practice of corporate finance?

It is true that the CAPM provides only an estimate of a stock's expected return and that actual outcomes deviate considerably (and unpredictably) from that estimate in any given year. Even so, the CAPM gives analysts a tool for measuring the systematic risk of any particular asset. Because assets with high systematic risk should, on average, earn a higher return than assets with low systematic risk, the CAPM offers a framework for making educated guesses about the risk and return of investment alternatives. Though it is hardly infallible, that framework enjoys widespread use in corporate finance, as we will see in subsequent chapters.

7-4 Concept Review Questions

9. If the stock market is *efficient*, what makes it efficient?

10. If prices move almost at random, then why should we place any value on the CAPM, which makes predictions about expected asset returns?

Summary

- Investors and managers make decisions based on expected returns.
- Estimates of expected returns may be obtained from historical data, from probabilistic calculations, or from a risk-based approach.

Table of Important Equations
1. $E(r_p) = w_1 E(r_1) + w_2 E(r_2) + \cdots + w_n E(r_n)$
$w_1 + w_2 + \cdots + w_n = 1$
2. $E(r_i) = r_f + \beta_i (E(r_m) - r_f)$

- An asset's beta measures its systematic risk, and it is this risk that should be linked to expected returns.
- The expected return of a portfolio equals a weighted average of the expected returns of the assets in the portfolio. The same can be said of the portfolio's beta.
- The standard deviation of a portfolio usually does not equal the weighted average of the standard deviation of the stocks in the portfolio. This is because some of the unsystematic fluctuations of individual stocks cancel each other out in a portfolio. A fully diversified portfolio contains only systematic risk.
- The CAPM predicts that the expected return on a stock depends on the stock's beta, the risk-free rate, and the market risk premium.
- In an efficient market, competition for information makes asset prices nearly unpredictable.

Key Terms

actively managed, 228
beta, 215
Capital Asset
   Pricing Model
   (CAPM), 225

efficient markets
   hypothesis (EMH), 228
expected return, 212
index fund, 228
market portfolio, 223

market risk
   premium, 224
passively managed, 228
portfolio weights, 219
selling short, 219

Self-Test Problems

Answers to Self-Test Problems and the Concept Review Questions throughout the chapter appear in CourseMate with SmartFinance Tools at **www.cengagebrain.com**.

ST7-1. Calculate the mean, variance, and standard deviations for a stock with the probability distribution outlined in the following table:

Outcome	Probability	Stock Return
Recession	10%	−40%
Expansion	60%	20%
Boom	30%	50%

ST7-2. You invest $25,000 in T-bills and $50,000 in the market portfolio. If the risk-free rate equals 2% and the expected market risk premium is 6%, what is the expected return on your portfolio?

ST7-3. The risk-free rate equals 4%, and the expected return on the market is 10%. If a stock's expected return is 13%, what is the stock's beta?

Questions

Q7-1. Based on the charts below, which stock has more *systematic risk*, and which stock has more *unsystematic risk*?

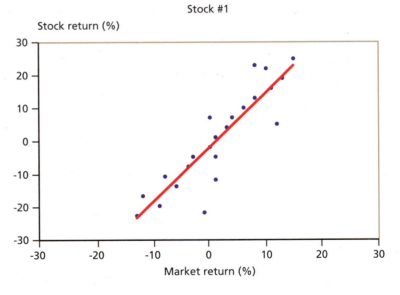

Stock #1

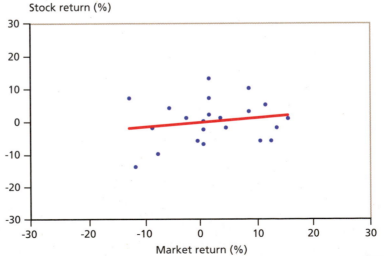

Stock #2

Q7-2. The table below shows the expected return and standard deviation for two stocks. Is the pattern shown in the table possible? Explain your answer.

Stock	Beta	Std. Dev.
1	1.5	22%
2	0.9	35%

Q7-3. Which type of company do you think will have a higher beta: a fast-food chain or a cruise-ship firm? Why?

Q7-4. Is the data in the following table believable? Explain your answer.

Stock	Std. Dev.
1	40%
2	60%
50-50 Portfolio	50%

Q7-5. How can investors hold a portfolio with a weight of more than 100% in a particular asset?

Q7-6. According to the *Capital Asset Pricing Model,* is the following data possible? Explain your answer.

Asset	Return	Std. Dev.
1	4%	0%
2	2%	20%

Q7-7. Stock A has a beta of 1.5, and Stock B has a beta of 1.0. Determine whether each statement below is true or false.
a. Stock A must have a higher standard deviation than Stock B.
b. Stock A has a higher expected return than Stock B.
c. The expected return on Stock A is 50% higher than the expected return on B.

Q7-8. If an asset lies above the security market line, is it overpriced or underpriced? Explain why.

Q7-9. A stock has a beta equal to 1.0. Is the standard deviation of the stock equal to the standard deviation of the market? Explain your answer.

Q7-10. If stock prices move unpredictably, does this mean that investing in stocks is just gambling? Why or why not?

Q7-11. Explain why *the efficient markets hypothesis* implies that a well-run company is not necessarily a good investment.

Problems

Expected Returns

P7-1. a. Suppose that over the long run, the risk premium on stocks relative to Treasury bills has been 7.6% in the United States. Suppose also that the current Treasury bill yield is 1.5%, but the historical average return on Treasury bills is 4.1%. Estimate the expected return on stocks and explain how and why you arrived at your answer.
b. Suppose that over the long run, the risk-premium on stocks relative to Treasury bonds has been 6.5%. The current Treasury bond yield is 4.5%, but the historical return on T-bonds is 5.2%. Estimate the expected return on stocks and explain how and why you arrived at your answer.
c. Compare your answers above and explain any differences.

P7-2. The table below shows the difference in returns between stocks and Treasury bills and the difference between stocks and Treasury bonds at ten-year intervals.

Years	Stocks vs. Bonds	Stocks vs. Bills
1964–73	3.7%	8.3%
1974–83	0.2%	8.6%
1984–93	7.5%	5.4%
1994–2003	4.8%	2.1%

a. At the end of 1973, the yield on Treasury bonds was 6.6% and the yield on T-bills was 7.2%. Using these figures and the historical data on the previous page from 1964—1973, construct two estimates of the expected return on equities as of December 1973.

b. At the end of 1983, the yield on Treasury bonds was 6.6% and the yield on T-bills was 7.2%. Using these figures and the historical data on the previous page from 1974—1983, construct two estimates of the expected return on equities as of December 1983.

c. At the end of 1993, the yield on Treasury bonds was 6.6% and the yield on T-bills was 2.8%. Using these figures and the historical data on the previous page from 1984—1993, construct two estimates of the expected return on equities as of December 1993.

d. At the end of 2003, the yield on Treasury bonds was 5.0% and the yield on T-bills was 1.0%. Using these figures and the historical data on the previous page from 1994—2003, construct two estimates of the expected return on equities as of December 2003.

e. What lessons do you learn from this exercise? How much do your estimates of the expected return on equities vary over time, and why do they vary?

P7-3. Use the information below to estimate the expected return on the stock of Bieber Corporation.
 Long-run average stock return = 10%
 Long-run average T-bill return = 4%
 Current T-bill return = 2%

P7-4. Calculate the expected return, variance, and standard deviation for the stocks in the table below.

		Stock Returns in Each Scenario		
Product Demand	**Probability**	**Stock 1**	**Stock 2**	**Stock 3**
High	20%	30%	20%	15%
Medium	60%	12%	14%	10%
Low	20%	−10%	−5%	−2%

P7-5. Calculate the expected return, variance, and standard deviation for each stock listed below.

		Stock Returns in Each State		
State of the Economy	**Probability**	**Stock A**	**Stock B**	**Stock C**
Recession	15%	−20%	−10%	−5%
Normal Growth	65%	18%	13%	10%
Boom	20%	40%	28%	20%

P7-6. Refer to Figure 7.2 and answer the following questions.
 a. What return would you expect on a stock with a beta of 2.0?
 b. What return would you expect on a stock with a beta of 0.66?
 c. What determines the slope of the line in Figure 7.2?

Risk and Return for Portfolios

P7-7. Calculate the portfolio weights implied by the dollar investments in each of the asset classes below.

Asset	$ Invested
Stocks	$10,000
Bonds	$10,000
T-bills	$ 5,000

P7-8. Wendi Deng recently inherited $1 million and has decided to invest it. Her portfolio consists of the following positions in several stocks. Calculate the portfolio weights to fill in the bottom row of the table.

	Intel	General Motors	Procter & Gamble	Exxon Mobil
Shares	7,280	5,700	5,300	6,000
Price per share	$25	$45	$55	$45
Portfolio weights				

P7-9. Victoria Goldman is a financial advisor who manages money for high-net-worth individuals. For a particular client, Victoria recommends the following portfolio of stocks.

	Global Recording Artists (GRA)	Soccer Intl. (SI)	Liquid Oxygen Corp. (LO)	Viva Mfg. (VM)	Wannabe Travel (WT)
Shares	8,000	9,000	7,000	10,500	4,000
Price per share	$40	$36	$45	$30	$60
Portfolio weights					

   a. Calculate the portfolio weights implied by Ms. Goldman's recommendations. What fraction of the portfolio is invested in GRA and SI combined?
   b. Suppose that the client purchases the stocks suggested by Ms. Goldman, and a year later the prices of the five stocks are as follows: GRA($60), SI($50), LO($38), VM($20), WT($50). Calculate the portfolio weights at the end of the year. Now what fraction of the portfolio is held in GRA and SI combined?

P7-10. Calculate the expected return, variance, and standard deviation for the stocks in the table below. Next, form an equally weighted portfolio of all three stocks and calculate its mean, variance, and standard deviation.

State of the Economy	Probability	Returns in Each State of the Economy		
		Cycli-Cal Inc.	Home Grown Crop.	Pharma-Cel
Boom	20%	40%	20%	20%
Expansion	50%	10%	10%	40%
Recession	30%	−20%	−10%	−30%

P7-11. You analyze the prospects of several companies and come to the following conclusions about the expected return on each:

Stock	Expected Return
Starbucks	18%
Sears	8%
Microsoft	16%
Limited Brands	12%

You decide to invest $4,000 in Starbucks, $6,000 in Sears, $12,000 in Microsoft, and $3,000 in Limited Brands. What is the expected return on your portfolio?

P7-12. Calculate the expected return of the portfolio described in the accompanying table.

Stock	$ Invested	Expected Return
A	$40,000	10%
B	20,000	14%
C	25,000	12%

P7-13. Calculate the portfolio weights based on the dollar investments in the table below. Interpret the negative sign on one investment. What is the size of the initial investment on which an investor's rate of return calculation should be based?

Stock	$ Invested
1	$10,000
2	−5,000
3	5,000

P7-14. Pete Pablo has $20,000 to invest. He is very optimistic about the prospects of two companies, 919 Brands Inc. and Diaries.com. However, Pete has a very pessimistic view of one firm, a financial institution known as Lloyd Bank. The current market price of each stock and Pete's assessment of the expected return for each stock appear below.

Stock	Price	Expected Return
919 Brands	$60	10%
Diaries.com	80	14%
Lloyd Bank	70	−8%

a. Pete decides to purchase 210 shares of 919 Brands and 180 shares of Diaries.com. What is the expected return on this portfolio? Can Pete construct this portfolio with the amount of money he has to invest?

b. If Pete sells short 100 shares of Lloyd Bank, how much additional money will he have to invest in the other two stocks?

c. If Pete buys 210 shares of 919 Brands and 180 shares of Diaries.com, and he simultaneously sells short 100 shares of Lloyd Bank, what are the resulting portfolio weights in each stock? (Hint: The weights must sum to one, but they need not all be positive.)

d. What is the expected return on the portfolio described in part (c)?

P7-15. Shares in Springfield Nuclear Power Corp. (SNP) currently sell for $25. You believe that the shares will be worth $30 in one year, and this implies that the return you expect on these shares is 20% (the company pays no dividends).

a. If you invest $10,000 by purchasing 400 shares, what the expected value of your holdings next year?

b. Now suppose that you buy 400 shares of SNP, but you finance this purchase with $5,000 of your own funds and $5,000 that you raise by selling short 100 shares of Nader Insurance Inc. Nader Insurance shares currently sell for $50, but next year you expect them to be worth $52. This implies an expected return of 4%. If both stocks perform as you expect, how much money will you have at the end of the year after you repurchase 100 Nader shares at the market price and return them to your broker? What rate of return on your $5,000 investment does this represent?

c. Suppose you buy 400 shares of SNP and finance them as described in part (b). However, at the end of the year SNP stock is worth $31. What was the percentage increase in SNP stock? What is the rate of return on your portfolio (again, after you repurchase Nader shares and return them to your broker)?

d. Finally, assume that at the end of one year, SNP shares have fallen to $24. What was the rate of return on SNP stock for the year? What is the rate of return on your portfolio?

e. What is the general lesson illustrated here? What is the impact of short selling on the expected return and risk of your portfolio?

P7-16. You are given the following data on several stocks:

State of the Economy	Probability	Returns in Each State of Economy		
		Gere Mining	Reubenfeld Films	DeLorean Automotive
Boom	25%	40%	24%	−20%
Expansion	50%	12%	10%	12%
Recession	25%	−20%	−12%	40%

a. Calculate the expected return and standard deviation for each stock.

b. Calculate the expected return and standard deviation for a portfolio invested equally in Gere Mining and Reubenfeld Films. How does the standard deviation of this portfolio compare to a simple 50-50 weighted average of the standard deviations of the two stocks?

c. Calculate the expected return and standard deviation for a portfolio invested equally in Gere Mining and DeLorean Automotive. How does the standard deviation of this portfolio compare to a simple 50-50 weighted average of the standard deviations of the two stocks?

d. Explain why your answers regarding the portfolio standard deviations are so different in parts (b) and (c).

P7-17. In an odd twist of fate, the return on the stock market has been exactly 1% in each of the last eight months. The return on Simon Entertainment stock in the past eight months has been as follows: 8%, 4%, 16%, −10%, 26%, 22%, 1%, −55%. From this information, estimate the beta of Simon stock.

P7-18. Petro-Chem Inc. stock has a beta equal to 0.9. Digi-Media Corp.'s stock beta is 2.0. What is the beta of a portfolio invested equally in these two stocks?

Putting It All Together: The CAPM

P7-19. The risk-free rate is currently 5%, and the expected risk premium on the market portfolio is 7%. What is the expected return on a stock with a beta of 1.2?

P7-20. The expected return on the market portfolio equals 12%. The current risk-free rate is 6%. What is the expected return on a stock with a beta of 0.66?

P7-21. The expected return on a particular stock is 14%. The stock's beta is 1.5. What is the risk-free rate if the expected return on the market portfolio equals 10%?

P7-22. If the risk-free rate equals 4% and a stock with a beta of 0.75 has an expected return of 10%, what is the expected return on the market portfolio?

P7-23. You believe that a particular stock has an expected return of 15%. The stock's beta is 1.2, the risk-free rate is 3%, and the expected market risk premium is 6%. Based on this, is your view that the stock is overvalued or undervalued?

P7-24. A particular stock sells for $30. The stock's beta is 1.25, the risk-free rate is 4%, and the expected return on the market portfolio is 10%. If you forecast that the stock will be worth $33 next year (assume no dividends), should you buy the stock or not?

P7-25. Currently the risk-free rate equals 5% and the expected return on the market portfolio equals 11%. An investment analyst provides you with the following information:

Stock	Beta	Expected Return
A	1.33	12%
B	0.70	10%
C	1.50	14%
D	0.66	9%

a. Indicate whether each stock is overpriced, underpriced, or correctly priced.

b. For each stock, subtract the risk-free rate from the stock's expected return and divide the result by the stock's beta. For example, for asset A this calculation is (12% − 5%) ÷ 1.33. Provide an interpretation for these ratios. Which stock has the highest ratio and which has the lowest?

c. Show how a smart investor could construct a portfolio of stocks C and D that would outperform stock A.

d. Construct a portfolio consisting of some combination of the market portfolio and the risk-free asset such that the portfolio's expected return equals 9%. What is the beta of this portfolio? What does this say about stock D?

e. Divide the risk premium on stock C by the risk premium on stock D. Next, divide the beta of stock C by the beta of stock D. Comment on what you find.

THOMSON REUTERS | Business School Edition

For instructions on using Thomson ONE, refer to the instructions provided with the Thomson ONE problems at the end of Chapters 1–6.

P7-26. Determine the beta of a portfolio consisting of Priceline.com Inc. (PCLN), Johnson & Johnson (JNJ), Home Depot (HD), and Goodyear Tire & Rubber Company (GT:US). You invest equal amounts of capital in each stock. How does the beta of this portfolio compare with the individual betas? Explain. Instead of investing equal amounts of capital in each stock, you decide to short shares worth $1,000 in each of the two least risky stocks (of the above four stocks) and invest $2,000 each in the two most risky stocks. How do you think the beta of this new portfolio will compare with the individual stock betas? Calculate the beta of this new portfolio and check if it matches your expectations. Consider another alternate portfolio. Now you short shares worth $1,000 in each of the two most risky stocks and invest $2,000 each in the two least risky stocks. How do you think the beta of this new portfolio will compare with the individual stock betas? Calculate the beta of this new portfolio and check if it matches your expectations. Do you think this portfolio will ever be profitable? If so, when?

P7-27. Determine whether the stock of Hershey Company (ticker: HSY) was mispriced (either underpriced or overpriced) at any time over the last five years. Assume that the beta for Hershey stayed constant over the last five years and use the latest available beta. Further, assume that the S&P 500 Composite Index (DSMnemonic: S&PCOMP) proxies for the market portfolio and calculate the annual returns for the index over the last five years. You can access the three month T-bill yields from Yahoo! Finance (www.finance.yahoo.com).[7] Use the Capital Asset Pricing Model (CAPM) to estimate the expected annual stock returns for Hershey for each year. Compare the expected stock returns to the actual annual returns for each year and determine if the stock was mispriced.

---

[7] Click the Investing tab at the top of the page. On the left-hand side, near the bottom of the page, click U.S. Market Indices. Click the Treasury tab at the top of the Major U.S. Indices box. Click ^IRX on the left-hand side of the box. Click Historical Prices, located under Quotes on the left-hand side of the page.

Smart Ideas Video

Andrew Karolyi, Cornell University

"Investors who seek to diversify internationally to reduce their global risk can leave money on the table if they ignore the unique industrial compositions of markets."

William Sharpe, Stanford University, Co-founder, Financial Engines

"To the extent that there is a premium for bearing risk, it is a premium for bearing the risk of doing badly in bad times."

Smart Practices Video

Todd Richter, Managing Director, Head of Equity Healthcare Research, Bank of America Securities

"I don't necessarily believe that markets are efficient. I believe that markets tend toward efficiency."

SMART concepts

See a discussion of portfolio theory short selling.
See a demonstration of the CAPM.
Learn more about market efficiency.

Mini-Case

Risk, Return, and the Capital Asset Pricing Model

On your first day as an intern at Tri-Star Management Incorporated the CEO asks you to analyze the following information pertaining to two common stock investments, Tech.com Incorporated and Sam's Grocery Corporation. You are told that a one-year Treasury Bill will have a rate of return of 5% over the next year. Also, information from an investment advising service lists the current beta for Tech.com as 1.68 and for Sam's Grocery as 0.52. You are provided a series of questions to guide your analysis.

| Economy | Probability | Estimated Rate of Return | | |
		Tech.com	Sam's Grocery	S&P 500
Recession	30%	−20%	5%	−4%
Average	20%	15%	6%	11%
Expansion	35%	30%	8%	17%
Boom	15%	50%	10%	27%

Continued

Assignment

1. Using the probabilistic approach, calculate the expected rate of return for Tech.com Incorporated, Sam's Grocery Corporation, and the S&P 500 Index.

2. Calculate the standard deviations of the estimated rates of return for Tech.com Incorporated, Sam's Grocery Corporation, and the S&P 500 Index.

3. Which is a better measure of risk for the common stock of Tech.com Incorporated and Sam's Grocery Corporation—the standard deviation you calculated in Question 2 or the beta?

4. Based on the beta provided, what is the expected rate of return for Tech.com Incorporated and Sam's Grocery Corporation for the next year?

5. If you form a two-stock portfolio by investing $30,000 in Tech.com Incorporated and $70,000 in Sam's Grocery Corporation, what is the portfolio beta and expected rate of return?

6. If you form a two-stock portfolio by investing $70,000 in Tech.com Incorporated and $30,000 in Sam's Grocery Corporation, what is the portfolio beta and expected rate of return?

7. Which of these two-stock portfolios do you prefer? Why?

© Altus Plunkett/Flickr/Getty Images, Inc.

part 3 Capital Budgeting

The long-run success or failure of most businesses depends critically on the quality of its investment decisions. For many firms, the most important investment decisions are those that involve the acquisition of fixed assets like manufacturing plants and equipment. In finance, we refer to the process of making these investment decisions as *capital budgeting*. This part of the text focuses exclusively on capital budgeting.

Chapter 8 describes some of the methods that firms use to evaluate investment opportunities. The preferred approach is the net present value (or *NPV*) method. In an *NPV* analysis, a financial manager derives the incremental cash flows associated with a particular investment and discounts those cash flows at a rate that reflects the investment's risk. If the present value of the discounted cash flows exceeds the cost of the project, the project has a positive *NPV*. The investment rule is to invest when the *NPV* is positive.

Chapter 9 goes deeper into *NPV* analysis by showing how analysts derive the cash flow estimates necessary to calculate a project's *NPV*. Experienced analysts know that certain types of cash flows occur in almost any investment project, so Chapter 9 lists several categories of cash flows and explains how to treat them properly in an *NPV* calculation.

Chapter 10 focuses on the second step in calculating *NPVs*—choosing the rate at which the investment's cash flows will be discounted. Conceptually, the discount rate should reflect the risk of the investment being analyzed. Analysts should use higher discount rates when they evaluate riskier investment projects. Furthermore, managers should "look to the market" to estimate what rate of return investors expect the firm to achieve. The market rates on debt and equity can be combined to determine the underlying required return on a company's assets, which is the weighted average cost of capital (or *WACC*) for their firm. The *WACC* establishes an important "hurdle rate" for firms. On average, if the firm purchases assets that generate returns greater than the firm's *WACC*, then the firm's investors earn a positive risk-adjust return, which creates wealth for shareholders.

239

chapter 8

Capital Budgeting Process and Decision Criteria

What Companies Do

Investment in Peru Pays Big for Candente

A January 2011 feasibility study reported good news for Candente Copper Corp., a Canadian mining company. The study estimated that Candente's mines in in Peru could produce 262 million pounds of copper, 39,000 ounces of gold, and 91,000 ounces of silver annually over the mine's 22-year life.

The financial implications of that production were substantial. Candente's investment in the Peruvian mines had an estimated net present value (*NPV*) of nearly $1 billion and an internal rate of return (*IRR*) of more than 17%. Investors reacted positively to the report, and Candente's shares rose 18% in a single day.

Sources: www.stockhouse.com/Community-News/2011/Jan/22/Canadian-small-micro-cap-weekend-roundup; www.steelguru.com/metals_news/Candente_Copper_update_on_Canariaco_Norte_Copper_Project/187165.html; www.marketwire.com/press-release/Candente-Copper-Announces-Positive-Pre-Feasibility-Progress-Report-Canariaco-Norte-Copper-TSX-DNT-1381223.htm

Learning Objectives

After studying this chapter you should be able to:

- Understand capital budgeting procedures and the ideal characteristics of a capital budgeting technique;

- Evaluate the use of the payback period, the discounted payback, and the accounting rate of return to evaluate capital expenditures;

- Discuss the logic, calculation, and pros and cons of the net present value (*NPV*) method;

- Describe the logic, calculation, advantages, and problems associated with the internal rate of return (*IRR*) technique;

- Differentiate between the *NPV* and *IRR* techniques by focusing on the scale and timing problems associated with mutually exclusive capital budgeting projects; and

- Discuss the profitability index and recent findings with regard to the actual use of *NPV* and *IRR* in business practice.

Many decisions that managers make have a long-term impact on the firm and can be very difficult to unwind once started. Major investments in plant and equipment fit this description, and so does spending on advertising designed to build brand awareness and loyalty among consumers. The terms *capital investment* and *capital spending* refer to investments in these kinds of long-lived assets, and **capital budgeting** refers to the process of determining which of these investment projects a firm should undertake.

The capital budgeting process involves these basic steps:

1. Identify potential investments;

2. Estimate the incremental inflows and outflows of cash associated with each investment;

3. Estimate a fair rate of return on each investment given its risk;

4. Analyze and prioritize the investments utilizing various decision criteria; and

5. Implement and monitor the performance of accepted projects.

Rarely is there a shortage of ideas for how a firm should invest its capital. Compelling proposals to modernize production equipment, expand research and development programs, upgrade information technology, or launch new advertising campaigns pour in from all of the firm's functional areas. The financial analyst's job is to analyze these investment opportunities, weighing their risks and returns to determine which projects create the most value for shareholders.

In this chapter we describe the different decision criteria that firms use to make capital investment decisions, highlighting the strengths and weaknesses of alternative methods. In the end, the preferred technique for evaluating most capital investments is called "net present value."

8-1   Introduction to Capital Budgeting

8-1a Traits of an Ideal Investment Criteria

capital budgeting
The process of determining which long-lived investment projects a firm should undertake.

Firms use a variety of techniques to evaluate capital investments. Some techniques involve very simple calculations and are intuitively easy to grasp. Financial managers prefer (1) an easily applied technique that (2) considers cash flow, (3) recognizes the time value of money, (4) fully accounts for expected risk and return, and (5) when applied, leads to higher firm value for any company (and higher stock prices in public firms). Easy application accounts for the popularity of some simple capital budgeting methods such as the *payback period* and *accounting rate of return* (both defined later).

Unfortunately, when comparing simple capital budgeting methods with more complex ones, other things are decidedly not equal. More complex methods such as *net present value (NPV), internal rate of return (IRR),* or the *profitability index (PI)* generally lead to better decision making because they take into account issues 1–5 cited above, factors that are neglected or ignored by simpler methods. Moreover, we will learn that the net present value approach provides a direct estimate of the change in share value resulting from a particular investment. Managers who seek to maximize share value must understand not only how to use various techniques but also the logic that explains why some methods are better than others. As challenging as that sounds, there is no reason to worry. We have already used these tools to value bonds and stocks, and now we will apply the discounted cash flow apparatus to real assets such as plant and equipment.

What CFOs Do

CFO Survey Evidence

Table 8.1 lists several of the capital budgeting methods covered in this chapter and indicates how widely they are used, according to a survey of U.S. CFOs. We argue in this chapter that the *net present value (NPV)* and *internal rate of return (IRR)* are theoretically preferable to methods such as *payback, discounted payback,* or *accounting rate of return.* Apparently CFOs agree, because most of them say that the IRR and NPV methods are their preferred tools for evaluating investment opportunities. The payback approach is also widely used. It is interesting that the popularity of NPV and IRR is particularly high among large firms and firms with CFOs who have MBA training, whereas the payback approach sees wider use in smaller firms. The payback approach, as the name suggests, focuses on how quickly an investment produces sufficient cash flow to recover its up-front costs. Smaller firms probably have less access to capital than large firms, which may explain why smaller firms rely so heavily on the payback method.

Table 8.1

Popularity of Capital Budgeting Techniques

Technique	Percent of CFOs Routinely Using Technique[a]
Internal rate of return	76%
Net present value	75%
Payback	57%
Discounted payback	29%
Accounting rate of return	20%
Profitability index	12%

[a]Note that these rounded percentages are drawn from the responses of a large number of CFOs and that many respondents use more than one technique.

Source: Reprinted from *Journal of Financial Economics*, 60, J.R. Graham and C.R. Harvey, "The Theory and Practice of Corporate Finance: Evidence from the Field," pp. 187–243, Copyright 2001, with permission from Elsevier.

? WHAT TO ASK

What methods does your firm use to analyze the financial merits of investment opportunities?

8-1b A Capital Budgeting Problem

We apply each of the decision-making techniques in this chapter to a single, simplified business problem currently facing Global Wireless Incorporated, a (fictitious) U.S.-based worldwide provider of wireless telephony services. Wireless carriers are scrambling to attract and retain customers in this highly competitive market. According to customer surveys, the number one reason for selecting a given carrier (or for switching to a new one) is the quality of service. Customers who lose calls as they commute to work or travel from one business location to another are apt to switch if another carrier offers fewer service interruptions.

Against this backdrop, Global Wireless is contemplating a major expansion of its wireless network in two different regions. Figure 8.1 depicts the projected cash inflows and outflows of each project over the next five years. By investing $250 million, Global Wireless could add up to 100 new cell sites to its existing base in Western Europe, giving it the most comprehensive service area in that region. Company analysts project that this investment could generate year-end net after-tax cash inflows that could grow over the next five years, as outlined below:

Initial Outlay	−$250 million
Year 1 inflow	$ 35 million
Year 2 inflow	$ 80 million
Year 3 inflow	$130 million
Year 4 inflow	$160 million
Year 5 inflow	$175 million

Figure 8.1   **Global Wireless Investment Proposals**

The time lines depict the cash flows for Global Wireless's proposed expansion projects—the Western Europe expansion, and the Southeastern U.S. toehold.

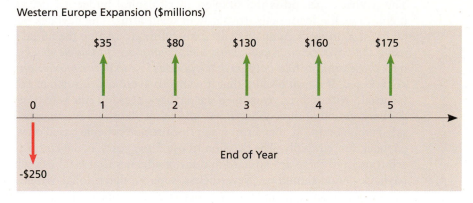

Western Europe Expansion ($millions)

Southeastern U.S. Toehold ($millions)

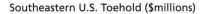

Alternatively, Global Wireless could make a much smaller investment to establish a toehold in a new market in the Southeastern United States. For an initial investment of $50 million, Global Wireless believes it can create a southeastern network, with its hub centered in Atlanta, Georgia. The projected end-of-year cash flows associated with this project are as follows:

Initial Outlay	−$50 million
Year 1 inflow	$18 million
Year 2 inflow	$22 million
Year 3 inflow	$25 million
Year 4 inflow	$30 million
Year 5 inflow	$32 million

Which investment should Global Wireless make? If the company can undertake both investments, should it do so? If it can make only one investment, which one is better for shareholders? We will see how different capital budgeting techniques lead to different investment choices, starting with the payback method.

8-1 Concept Review Question

1. What characteristics does management desire in a capital budgeting technique?

8-2 Payback Methods

8-2a The Payback Decision Rule

payback period
The amount of time it takes for a project's cumulative net cash inflows to recoup the initial investment.

The payback method is the simplest of all capital budgeting decision-making tools; it enjoys widespread use, particularly in small firms. The payback period is the time it takes for a project's cumulative net cash inflows to recoup the initial investment. *Firms using the payback approach define a maximum acceptable payback period and accept only those projects that have payback periods less than the maximum; all other projects are rejected.* If a firm decides that it wants to avoid any investment that does not "pay for itself" within three years, then the payback decision rule is to accept projects with a payback period of three years or less and reject all other investments. If several projects satisfy this condition, then firms may prioritize investments based on which ones achieve payback more rapidly. The decision to use three years as the cutoff point is somewhat arbitrary, and there are no hard-and-fast guidelines that establish what the "optimal" payback period should be. Nevertheless, suppose that Global Wireless uses three years as its cutoff when applying payback analysis. What investment decision would it make?

EXAMPLE

The investment to expand the wireless network in Western Europe requires an initial outlay of $250 million. According to the firm's cash flow projections, this project will bring $245 million in its first three years ($35 million in year 1 + $80 million in year 2 + $130 million in year 3) and $405 million after four years ($245 million in the first 3 years + $160 million in year 4). So the firm will fully recover its $250 million initial outlay sometime during year 4. Because the firm only needs to recover $5 million ($250 million initial outlay − $245 million recovered in the first 3 years) in year 4, assuming cash flow occurs at a constant rate throughout the year, we can estimate the fraction of year 4 as 0.03, by dividing the $5 million that needs to be recovered in year 4 by the $160 million expected to be recovered in that year. *The payback period for Western Europe is therefore 3.03 years, so Global Wireless would reject the investment because this payback period is longer than the firm's maximum three-year payback period.*

The toehold investment in the Southeastern U.S. project requires just $50 million. In its first two years, this investment generates $40 million in cash flow ($18 million in year 1 + $22 million in year 2). By the end of year 3, it produces a cumulative cash flow of $65 million ($40 million in the first 2 years + $25 million in year 3). Thus, the project earns back the initial $50 million at some point during year 3. It needs to recover $10 million ($50 million initial outlay − $40 million recovered in the first 2 years) in year 3. We can estimate the fraction of year 3 as 0.40, by dividing the $10 million that needs to be recovered in year 3 by the $25 million expected to be recovered that year. *The payback for the Southeastern U.S. project is therefore 2.40 years. Global Wireless would undertake the investment because this payback period is shorter than the firm's maximum three-year payback period.*

8-2b Pros and Cons of the Payback Method

Arguments For the Payback Method Simplicity is payback's main virtue. Once a firm estimates a project's cash flows, it is simply a matter of addition to determine when the cumulative net cash inflows equal the initial outlay. The intuitive appeal of the payback method is strong. It sounds reasonable to expect a good investment to pay for itself in a fairly short time. Indeed, the time value of money suggests that, other things being equal, a project that brings in cash flow faster ought to be more valuable than one with more distant cash flows. Small firms, which typically operate with limited financing, tend to favor payback because it is simple and because receiving more cash flow sooner allows them more financial flexibility. Some managers say that establishing a short payback period is one way to account for a project's risk exposure. They argue that projects that take longer to pay off are intrinsically riskier than those that recoup the initial investment more quickly, partly because forecast errors tend to increase with the length of the payback time period. The payback period is a popular decision-making technique in highly uncertain situations, where it is frequently used as the primary technique. It is used frequently for international investments made in unstable economic/political environments and in risky domestic investments such as oil drilling and new business ventures.

Another justification given for using the payback method is that some firms face financing constraints. Advocates of the payback rule argue that it makes sense for cash-strapped firms to use payback because it indicates how quickly the firm can generate cash flow to repay debt or to pursue other investment opportunities. Career concerns may also

Cengage Learning

Daniel Carter, Vice President of Finance, BevMo!

"It's a metric that frankly most of our operators can truly appreciate."

See the entire interview at **SMART** | finance

Smart Practices Video

lead managers to prefer the payback rule. Particularly in large companies, managers rotate quite often from one job to another. To obtain promotions and to enhance their reputations, managers want to make investments that enable them to point to success stories at each stage of their careers. A manager who expects to stay in a particular position in the firm for just two or three years may prefer to undertake investments that recover costs quickly rather than projects that have payoffs far into the future.

Arguments Against the Payback Method Though the payback method has apparent virtues, it suffers from two serious problems. First, the payback cutoff period is simply a judgment with no direct connection to share value maximization. How can we be sure that accepting projects that pay back within three years will maximize shareholder wealth? What if a project has an enormous payoff in year 3 or year 4? Payback ignores cash flows beyond the cutoff point. Second, the way that the payback method accounts for the time value of money is crude. The payback method assigns a 0% discount rate to cash flows that occur before the cutoff point. That is, if the payback period is three years, then cash flows that occur in years 1, 2, and 3 receive equal weight in the payback calculation. Beyond the cutoff point, the payback method ignores all cash flows. In other words, cash flows in year 4 and beyond receive zero weight (or have zero present value) as if the discount rate were infinite.

8-2c Discounted Payback

discounted payback period
The amount of time it takes for a project's discounted cash flows to recover the initial investment.

The **discounted payback period** is the same as the payback period except that in calculating the former, managers discount cash flows first. In other words, the discounted payback method calculates how long it takes for a project's discounted cash flows to recover the initial investment. This represents a minor improvement over the simple payback method in that it does a better job of accounting for the time value of cash flows that occur within the payback cutoff period. As with the ordinary payback rule, discounted payback totally ignores cash flows that occur beyond the cutoff point, and the chosen cutoff is often arbitrary.

EXAMPLE

Suppose that Global Wireless uses the discounted payback method, with a discount rate of 18% and a cutoff period of three years. The following schedules show the present value (*PV*) of each project's cash flows during the first three years.[1] For example, $29.7 million is the present value of the $35 million that the Western Europe investment is expected to earn in its first year, $57.5 million is the present value of the $80 million that the project is expected to earn in its second year, and so on.

Year	Western Europe Project ($ millions)		Southeastern U.S. Project ($ millions)	
	PV of Cash Flow	Cumulative PV	PV of Cash Flow	Cumulative PV
1	29.7	29.7	15.3	15.3
2	57.5	87.2	15.8	31.1
3	79.1	166.3	15.2	46.3

Recall that the initial outlay for the Western Europe expansion project is $250 million but is only $50 million for the Southeastern U.S. toehold project. After three years, neither project's cumulative present value of cash flows exceeds its initial outlay. Neither investment satisfies the condition that the discounted cash flows recoup the initial investment within three years. Therefore, Global Wireless would reject both projects.

Before presenting the more sophisticated methods of capital budgeting, in the next section we present a simple method often used to evaluate projects from an accounting perspective.

---

[1]We are assuming here that the first year's cash flows occur one year after the initial investment (end of year 1), the second year's cash flows occur two years after the initial investment (end of year 2), and so on.

8-2 Concept Review Questions

2. What factors account for the popularity of the *payback method*? In what situations is it often used as the primary decision-making technique? Why?

3. What are the major flaws of the *payback period* and *discounted payback period* approaches?

8-3 Accounting-Based Methods

8-3a Accounting Rate of Return

For better or worse, managers in many firms focus as much on how a given project will influence reported earnings as on how it will affect cash flows. Managers justify this focus by pointing to the positive (or negative) stock-price response that occurs when their firms beat (or fail to meet) earnings forecasts made by Wall Street securities analysts. Managers may also overemphasize a project's accounting-based earnings because their compensation is based on meeting accounting-based performance measures such as earnings-per-share or return-on-total-assets targets. Consequently, some firms base their investment decisions on accounting-based rate of return measures.

accounting rate of return
Return on investment calculated by dividing net income by the book value of assets.

Companies have many different ways of defining a *hurdle rate* for their investments in terms of accounting rates of return. Almost all these metrics involve two steps: (1) to identify the project's net income each year and (2) to measure the project's invested capital requirements, as shown on the balance sheet, each year. Given these two figures, a firm may calculate an **accounting rate of return** by dividing net income by the book value of assets, either on a year-by-year basis or by taking an average over the project's life. Note that this measure is comparable to *return on total assets (ROA)*, also called *return on investment (ROI)*, introduced in Chapter 2, for measuring a firm's overall effectiveness in generating returns with its available assets. Companies will usually establish some minimum accounting rate of return, the hurdle rate, that projects must earn before they can be funded. When more than one project exceeds the minimum standard, firms prioritize projects based on their accounting rates of return and invest in projects with higher returns first.

What CFOs Do

CFO Survey Evidence

In a recent study, Graham, Harvey, and Rajgopal (2005) asked CFOs to identify the most important financial measures that they reported to outside investors. The pie chart to the right shows that the overwhelming response was earnings. The study also reported that CFOs believed that reporting earnings in the current quarter that are higher than earnings in the same quarter in the prior year was the most important earnings "benchmark" for firms to achieve, even more important than beating Wall Street analysts' earnings forecasts. The importance of earnings stands in contrast to our recommendation that managers focus on cash flows.

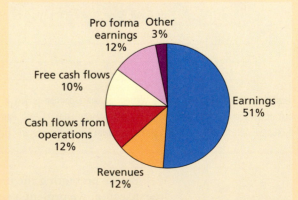

Source: John R. Graham, Campbell R. Harvey, and Shiva Rajgopal, "The Economic Implications of Corporate Financial Reporting," *Journal of Accounting and Economics* 40 (2005), pp. 3–73.

EXAMPLE

Suppose that the practice at Global Wireless is to calculate a project's accounting rate of return by taking the project's average contribution to net income and dividing by its average book value. Global Wireless ranks projects based on this measure and accepts those that offer an accounting rate of return of at least 25%. So far, we have been given the cash flows from each of the two projects that Global Wireless is evaluating. Chapter 9 discusses in more depth the differences between cash flow and net income, but for now, the net income figures for each project appear below. We will assume that the company depreciates fixed assets on a straight-line basis over five years.

	Net Income ($ in millions)	
Year	**Western Europe Project**	**Southeastern U.S. Project**
1	−15	8
2	30	12
3	80	15
4	110	20
5	125	22

Therefore, the Western Europe project will have an annual depreciation charge of $50 million (one-fifth of $250 million), and the Southeastern U.S. project will have an annual depreciation charge of $10 million (one-fifth of $50 million). The Western Europe project begins with a book value of $250 million. After five years of depreciation it has a book value of $0. Therefore, the average book value of that project is $125 million [($250 − $0) ÷ 2]. The project's average net income equals $66 million [(−$15 + $30 + $80 + $110 + $125) ÷ 5], so its average accounting rate of return is an impressive 52.8% ($66 ÷ $125). The same steps applied to the Southeastern U.S. project yield an average book value of $25 million [($50 − $0) ÷ 2], an average net income of $15.4 million [($8 + $12 + $15 + $20 + $22) ÷ 5], and an accounting rate of return of 61.6% ($15.4 ÷ $25). Because both projects earn more than the required 25% minimum return, Global Wireless should be willing to invest in either project, and it would rank the Southeastern U.S. investment above the Western Europe expansion.

8-3b Pros and Cons of the Accounting Rate of Return

Because of their convenience, ease of calculation, and ease of interpretation, accounting-based measures are used by many firms to evaluate capital investments. However, these techniques have serious flaws. First, as the preceding example demonstrates, the decision about what depreciation method to use has a large effect on both the numerator and the denominator of the accounting rate of return formula. Second, this method makes no adjustment for the time value of money or project risk. Third, investors should be more concerned with the market value than the book value of the assets that a firm holds. After five years, the book value of Global Wireless's investment (in either project) is zero, but the market value will almost certainly be positive and may be even greater than the initial amount invested. Fourth, as explained in Chapter 2, finance theory teaches that investors should focus on a company's ability to generate cash flow rather than on its net income. Fifth, the choice of the 25% accounting return hurdle rate is essentially arbitrary. This rate is not based on rates available on similar investments in the market, but reflects a purely subjective judgment on the part of management.

By now you may have noticed some common themes in our discussion of the pros and cons of different approaches to capital budgeting. None of the methods discussed thus far consider all of a project's cash flows in the decision-making process. Each of these methods fails to properly account for the time value of money, and none of them deal adequately with risk. Most importantly, none of the methods discussed so far are consistent with the goal of shareholder wealth maximization. We now turn our attention to a method that solves all these difficulties and therefore enjoys widespread support from both academics and business practitioners.

8-3 Concept Review Questions

4. Why do managers focus on the effect that an investment will have on reported earnings rather than on the investment's cash flow consequences?

5. What factors determine whether the annual *accounting rate of return* on a given project will be high or low in the early years of the investment's life? In the latter years?

●8-4   Net Present Value

8-4a Net Present Value Calculations

net present value (NPV)
The sum of the present values of all of a project's cash flows, both inflows and outflows, discounted at a rate consistent with the project's risk. Also, the preferred method for valuing capital investments.

The **net present value (NPV)** of a project is the sum of the present values of all its cash flows, both inflows and outflows. The rate used to discount the cash flows must be consistent with the project's risk. Calculating an investment project's *NPV* is relatively straightforward. First, write down the net cash flows that the investment will generate over its life. Second, discount these cash flows at a rate that reflects the degree of risk inherent in the project. (Note: The choice of discount rate is discussed in Chapter 10.) Third, add up the discounted cash flows to obtain the *NPV*, and invest in the project only when that value exceeds zero.

$$\text{(Eq. 8.1)} \quad NPV = CF_0 + \frac{CF_1}{(1 + r)^1} + \frac{CF_2}{(1 + r)^2} + \frac{CF_3}{(1 + r)^3} + \cdots + \frac{CF_n}{(1 + r)^n}$$

In this expression, CF_t represents net cash flow in year t, r is the discount rate, and n represents the project's life. Each year's cash flows could be positive or negative, though typically projects generate cash outflows initially and cash inflows later on. For example, suppose that the initial cash flow, CF_0, is a negative number representing the outlay necessary to get the project started, and suppose that all subsequent cash flows are positive. In this case, the *NPV* can be defined as the *present value of future cash inflows minus the initial outlay*. The *NPV* decision rule says that firms should invest when the sum of the present values of future cash inflows exceeds the initial project outlay. That is, $NPV > \$0$, when the following occurs:

$$-CF_0 < \frac{CF_1}{(1 + r)^1} + \frac{CF_2}{(1 + r)^2} + \frac{CF_3}{(1 + r)^3} + \cdots + \frac{CF_n}{(1 + r)^n}$$

Simply stated, *the NPV decision rule is*:

$NPV > \$0$ invest
$NPV < \$0$ do not invest

Notice that for a project to have a positive *NPV*, the present value of its cash inflows must exceed the present value of its cash outflows. Therefore, any project that meets the discounted payback criterion will also have a positive *NPV*. But is the opposite true? Some projects with positive *NPV*s have large cash flows beyond the payback cutoff period. So we can say that a firm using the discounted payback approach will never accept a project with a negative *NPV*, and it may reject some projects with positive *NPV*s. Another way to say this is that the discounted payback approach is overly conservative relative to the *NPV* method.

Why Does the *NPV* Rule Generally Lead to Good Investment Decisions?
Remember that the firm's goal in choosing investment projects is to maximize shareholder wealth. Conceptually, the discount rate, r, in the *NPV* equation represents an opportunity cost, the highest return that investors can obtain in the marketplace on an investment with risk equal to the risk of the project under consideration. When the *NPV* equals zero, the investment provides a rate of return equal to shareholders' required return; all investors should be satisfied by a project with a zero *NPV*, but no extra "economic profit" is earned. Therefore, a project with a positive *NPV* earns a return that exceeds shareholders' expectations.

A firm that consistently finds positive *NPV* investments expects to surpass the shareholders' requirements and enjoy a rising stock price. Clearly, the acceptance of positive *NPV* projects is consistent with the firm's value-creation goal. Conversely, if the firm makes an investment with a negative *NPV*, the investment will decrease value and shareholder wealth. A firm that regularly makes negative *NPV* investments will see its stock price lag as it generates lower-than-required returns for stockholders.

Drawing on what we already know about valuing bonds, we can develop an analogy to drive home the point about the relationship between stock prices and the *NPV* rule. Suppose that, at a given moment in time, investors require a 5% return on five-year Treasury bonds. Of course, this means that if the U.S. Treasury issues five-year, $1,000 par value bonds paying an annual coupon of $50, the market price of these bonds will be $1,000, equal to par value.[2]

$$\$1,000 = \frac{\$50}{1.05^1} + \frac{\$50}{1.05^2} + \cdots + \frac{\$1,050}{1.05^5}$$

Now apply *NPV* logic. If an investor purchases one of these bonds for $1,000, the *NPV* equals zero because the bond's cash flows precisely satisfy the investor's expectation of a 5% return.

$$NPV = \$0 = -\$1,000 + \frac{\$50}{1.05^1} + \frac{\$50}{1.05^2} + \cdots + \frac{\$1,050}{1.05^5}$$

Next, imagine that in a fit of election-year largesse, the U.S. Congress decrees that the coupon payments on all government bonds will double, so this bond now pays $100 in interest per year. If the bond's price remains fixed at $1,000, this investment's *NPV* will suddenly switch from zero to positive. At a price of $1,000, the bond is underpriced if Congress raises the bond's coupon to $100:

$$NPV = \$216.47 = -\$1,000 + \frac{\$100}{1.05^1} + \frac{\$100}{1.05^2} + \cdots + \frac{\$1,100}{1.05^5}$$

Of course, the bond's price will not remain at $1,000. Investors will quickly recognize that—with a price of $1,000 and a coupon of $100—the return offered by these bonds substantially exceeds the required rate of 5%. Investors will flock to buy the bonds, rapidly driving up bond values until prices reach the point at which buying bonds becomes a zero *NPV* investment once again.[3] In the new equilibrium, the bond's price will rise by $216.47, exactly the amount of the *NPV* that was created when Congress doubled the coupon payments:

$$NPV = \$0 = -\$1,216.47 + \frac{\$100}{1.05^1} + \frac{\$100}{1.05^2} + \cdots + \frac{\$1,100}{1.05^5}$$

NPV and Stock Price The same forces that drove up the bond's price in the previous section will drive up a firm's stock price when it makes a positive *NPV* investment, as shown in Figure 8.2. The figure depicts a firm that investors believe will pay an annual dividend of $4 in perpetuity. If investors require a 10% return on this firm's stock, the price will be $40.[4] What happens if the firm makes a new investment that is as risky as the stock just described? If the return on this investment is greater than 10% then it will have a positive *NPV*. Investors will recognize that the firm has made an investment that exceeds their expectations and so will raise their forecast of future dividends, perhaps to $4.10 per year. At that level, the new stock price will be $41. The same thing happens in reverse if the firm makes an investment that earns a return below 10%. At this rate, the project has a negative *NPV*. Shareholders recognize that this investment's cash flows fall below their expectations, so they lower their estimates of future dividends to $3.90 per year. As a consequence, the stock price falls to $39.

Chris Muscarella, Professor of Finance and L.W. 'Roy' and Mary Lois Clark Teaching Fellow, Pennsylvania State University

Cengage Learning

"We look at the impact on stock prices of firms' capital budgeting decisions."

See the entire interview at **SMART** | finance

Smart Practices Video

---

[2]Though Treasury bonds pay interest semiannually, we assume annual interest payments here to keep the example simple.
[3]Recall that in Chapter 7, we said that an underpriced stock would lie above the security market line. The same thing is happening here. At a price of $1,000, the bond is underpriced if Congress raises the bond's coupon to $100. Recognizing the underpricing, investors will buy the bonds, causing their price to rise and the expected return to fall.
[4]Remember that the price of a stock that pays a constant dividend in perpetuity equals the annual dividend divided by the required rate of return—in this case, $4 ÷ 0.10 = $40.

Figure 8.2   The *NPV* Rule and Shareholder Wealth

If a firm invests in a project that earns more than its required return, its expected dividends and stock price are expected to rise. If the project earns less than the required return, the expected dividends and stock price are expected to fall.

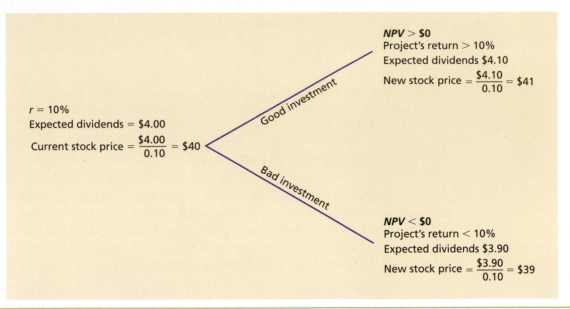

Now apply this thought process to Global Wireless. Suppose that its shareholders demand an 18% return on their shares. According to the principles we discussed in Chapter 5, the price of Global Wireless stock will reflect the value of all future cash distributions that investors expect from the company, discounted at a rate of 18%. But what if Global Wireless discovers that it can make an investment that offers a return substantially above 18%? By definition, such an investment has a positive *NPV*; by undertaking it, Global Wireless will increase its stock price (just as Candente Copper did; see page 240) as investors realize that the investment will enable the firm to distribute higher-than-expected cash flows as a result of the investment. How far will the price of each share rise? Simply divide the project's *NPV* (which represents the wealth the project is expected to create) by the number of outstanding shares. The result is the amount by which Global Wireless's stock price should increase.

EXAMPLE

What are the *NPV*s of each of the investment opportunities now facing Global Wireless? Time lines depicting the *NPV* calculations for Global Wireless's projects appear in Figure 8.3. Discounting each project's cash flows at 18% yields the following results:

$$NPV_{WesternEurope} = -\$250 + \frac{\$35}{(1.18)^1} + \frac{\$80}{(1.18)^2} + \frac{\$130}{(1.18)^3} + \frac{\$160}{(1.18)^4} + \frac{\$175}{(1.18)^5} = \$75.3$$

$$NPV_{Southeastern\ U.S.} = -\$50 + \frac{\$18}{(1.18)^1} + \frac{\$22}{(1.18)^2} + \frac{\$25}{(1.18)^3} + \frac{\$30}{(1.18)^4} + \frac{\$32}{(1.18)^5} = \$25.7$$

Both projects increase shareholder wealth, so both are worth undertaking. One could say that both projects outearn the firm's 18% required return and are therefore acceptable. However, if the company can make only one investment, it should choose to expand its presence in Western Europe. That investment increases shareholder wealth by $75.3 million, whereas the Southeastern U.S. investment increases wealth by only about one third as much. If Global Wireless has 100 million common shares outstanding, then accepting the Western Europe project should increase the stock price by about $0.75 ($75.3 million ÷ 100 million shares). Accepting the Southeastern U.S. investment would increase the stock price by almost $0.26 ($25.7 million ÷ 100 million shares).

continued

Figure 8.3a

NPV of Global Wireless's Projects at 18% ($millions)

Western Europe Project

The net present value (NPV) of Global Wireless's Western Europe Project is $75.3 million, which means that it is acceptable (NPV > $0) and therefore creates wealth for shareholders.

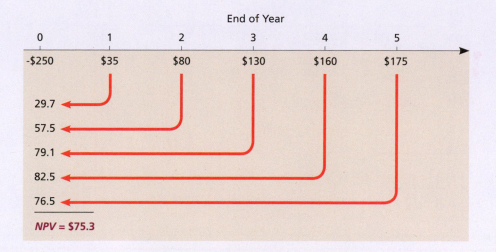

Spreadsheet

Row \ Column	A	B
1	Cash flow 0	-250
2	Cash flow 1	35
3	Cash flow 2	80
4	Cash flow 3	130
5	Cash flow 4	160
6	Cash flow 5	175
7	Interest	18%
8	**Net Present Value**	**$75.3**
9	*Formula B8:* -250 + NPV(B7,B2,B3,B4,B5,B6)	

Calculator

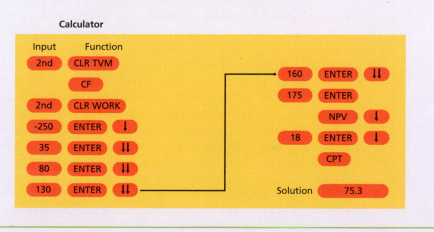

continued

Figure 8.3b   ***NPV* of Global Wireless's Projects at 18% ($millions)**

Southeastern U.S. Project

The net present value (*NPV*) of Global Wireless's Southeastern U.S. Project is $25.7 million, which means that it is acceptable (*NPV* > $0) and therefore creates value for shareholders.

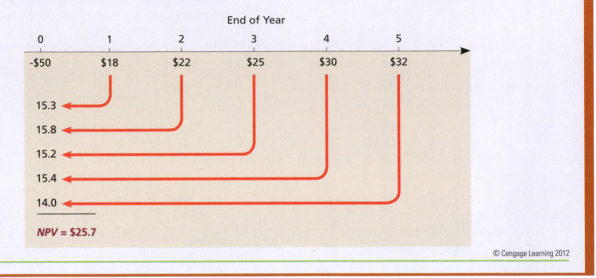

8-4b Pros and Cons of *NPV*

The net-present-value method solves all the problems we have identified with the payback and discounted payback rules, as well as the problems associated with decision rules that are based on the accounting rate of return. First, the *NPV* rule focuses on cash flow, not accounting earnings. Second, when properly applied, the net-present-value method makes appropriate adjustments for the time value of money. Third, the decision rule to invest when *NPV*s are positive and to refrain from investing when *NPV*s are negative reflects the firm's need to compete for funds in the marketplace and have its projects outearn projects of similar risk. Fourth, the *NPV* approach offers a relatively straightforward way to control for differences in risk among alternative investments. Cash flows on riskier investments should be discounted at higher rates. Fifth, the *NPV* method incorporates all the cash flows that a project generates over its life, not just those that occur in the project's early years. Sixth, the *NPV* gives a direct estimate of the change in shareholder wealth resulting from a given investment.

We are enthusiastic supporters of the *NPV* approach, especially when compared with the other decision methods examined thus far. However, there is one subtle drawback to the *NPV* rule, and it results from our inability to incorporate the value of managerial flexibility when calculating a project's *NPV*. What we mean by "managerial flexibility" are options that managers can exploit to increase the value of an investment. For example, if a firm makes an investment that turns out better than expected, managers have the option to expand that investment, making it even more valuable. Conversely, if a firm invests in a project that does not generate as much positive cash flow as anticipated, then managers have the option to scale back the investment and redeploy resources to more productive uses. The *NPV* method (like the other methods studied in this chapter) does a poor job of capturing the value of managerial flexibility. Incorporating the value of these options into the analysis requires a highly sophisticated approach that relies on the use of decision trees and the principles of option pricing. We offer a brief introduction to valuing investment with option-like characteristics in Chapter 10.

The NPV method enjoys widespread use in large corporations, but there are two other popular capital budgeting tools that are closely related to NPV. One of these alternative approaches, called *economic value added*, essentially calculates an investment's NPV on a year-by-year basis. The other approach, known as the *internal rate of return*, summarizes the economic merits of an investment in a single number which represents the compound annual rate of return that an investment earns over its life. In most cases (but not all) these techniques lead to the same investments decision that NPV analysis does, although there are some important, subtle differences between the three approaches.

8-4c Economic Value Added

economic value added (EVA)
A method of analyzing capital investments which determines whether an investment produces net cash flow sufficient to cover the firm's cost of capital

economic profit
A profit that exceeds a normal, competitive rate of return in an industry or line of business.

Net present value analysis is appealing for making capital budgeting decisions because it is both theoretically sound and easy to implement. In recent years, a variant of *NPV* analysis called economic value added (EVA®), or, more generically, shareholder value added (SVA), has become popular with many firms. A registered trademark of Stern Stewart & Company, EVA is based on the century-old idea of economic profit. In accounting, we say that a firm earns a profit if its revenues are greater than its costs. But when economists use the term *economic profit* they refer to how much profit a firm earns relative to a competitive rate of return. If a firm earns zero economic profit, then its accounting profits are positive and just sufficient to satisfy the returns required by the firm's investors. If a firm's economic profits are positive then its stock price will rise because it is out-earning its cost of capital and investor expectations. Similarly, a firm may be earning a positive *accounting* profit, but if that profit does not cover the firm's cost of capital then *economic* profits are negative.

EXAMPLE

On April 23, 2009, Microsoft reported an accounting profit of $2.98 billion. Just prior to that disclosure, Microsoft's market capitalization was roughly $170 billion, so reported earnings represented a return of just 1.75% relative to the value of shareholders' investment in the company—a rate of return similar to what investors in AAA-rated corporate bonds were earning at the time. Microsoft's economic profits for the quarter were therefore negative because they were lower than the company's cost of capital (one component of which was shareholders' required return for investing in Microsoft stock).

EVA establishes a benchmark for managers that measures an investment's performance in each period based on whether it earns an economic profit. The EVA metric subtracts "normal profit" from an investment's cash flow to determine whether the investment is adding value for shareholders. As we have already explained, *NPV* also provides a measure of value added, so it should not be surprising that these methods are quite similar.

To illustrate how the EVA method works, consider an investment that requires $5 million of capital funding. For simplicity, assume that the invested capital never depreciates and generates annual cash flow of $600,000 in perpetuity. Finally, assume that the firm making this investment has a 12% cost of capital. The formula used to calculate EVA for a particular year is:

$$\text{EVA} = \text{Cash flow} - [(\text{Cost of capital}) \times (\text{Invested capital})]$$
$$= \$600,000 - 0.12 \times (\$5,000,000) = \$0$$

An EVA of zero means that the project earns exactly its cost of capital. That is, the project covers all costs including the cost of funds—but does not earn any economic profit above and beyond that amount.

To determine whether the project should be undertaken, an analyst would calculate the EVA in every year and then discount the future EVAs back to the present at the cost of capital; if the resulting value is positive, then the investment is worthwhile. In this case, because EVA every year is zero (and the present value of all future EVAs is also zero), we conclude that this investment provides a breakeven return for shareholders. What would the *NPV* method say? Using the perpetuity shortcut to value the investment's inflows, we find that the *NPV* is also zero,

$$NPV = -\$5,000,000 + \frac{\$600,000}{0.12} = \$0$$

so the two methods yield the same conclusion.

EVA uses the same basic cash flows as *NPV* and evaluates the economics of an investment "one year at a time," whereas *NPV* compares the incremental net cash inflows over the investment's life (discounted to the present at the firm's cost of capital) to the net cash outflows required by the investment. Technically, discounting the time series of annual EVAs at the firm's cost of capital should result in the project's *NPV*. Thus *NPV* and EVA are fully compatible and yield the same capital budgeting decisions. The appeal of EVA is its integration of *NPV* analytical techniques into day-to-day managerial decision making.

8-4 Concept Review Questions

6. What does it mean if a project has an *NPV* of $1 million?

7. Why might the discount rates used to calculate the *NPVs* of two competing projects differ?

8. What do *NPV* and EVA have in common, and how do they differ?

8-5 Internal Rate of Return

8-5a Finding a Project's *IRR*

As methods used for evaluating investment projects, payback, discounted payback, and accounting-based methods suffer from common problems—the complete or partial failure to make adjustments for the time value of money and for risk. Alternative methods, such as *NPV*, correct these shortcomings.

Perhaps the most popular and intuitive of these alternatives is the **internal rate of return (*IRR*)** method. An investment's internal rate of return is analogous to a bond's *yield-to-maturity* (*YTM*), a concept we introduced in Chapter 4. Recall that a bond's *YTM* is the discount rate that equates the present value of its future cash flows to its market price. The *YTM* measures the compound annual return that an investor earns by purchasing a bond and holding it until maturity (provided that all payments are made as promised and that interest payments can be reinvested at the same rate). Likewise, an investment project's *IRR* is the compound annual rate of return on the project, given its up-front costs and subsequent cash flows.

In mathematical terms, the *IRR* is the discount rate, *r*, that makes the net present value of all project cash flows equal to zero:

$$\text{(Eq. 8.2)} \quad NPV = \$0 = CF_0 + \frac{CF_1}{(1+r)^1} + \frac{CF_2}{(1+r)^2} + \frac{CF_3}{(1+r)^3} + \cdots + \frac{CF_n}{(1+r)^n}$$

To find a project's *IRR*, we must begin by specifying the project's cash flows. Next, using a financial calculator, a spreadsheet, or even trial and error, we find the discount rate that equates the present value of cash flows to zero. Once we have calculated the *IRR*, we compare it with a prespecified hurdle rate established by the firm. The hurdle rate represents the firm's minimum acceptable return for a given project, so *the IRR decision rule is to invest only if the project's IRR exceeds the hurdle rate; otherwise reject the project.*

But where does the hurdle rate come from? How do firms decide whether to require projects to exceed a 10% hurdle or a 20% hurdle? The answer provides insight into another advantage of *IRR* over relying on a project's payback period or accounting rate of return. A company should set the hurdle rate equal to market returns on similar investments. For example, if the project at hand involves expanding a fast-food restaurant chain then the hurdle rate should reflect the returns that fast-food businesses of similar risk offer investors. Therefore, the *IRR* method, like the *NPV* method, establishes a hurdle rate or a decision criterion that is *market-based,* unlike

internal rate of return (*IRR*)
The compound annual rate of return on a project, given its up-front costs and subsequent cash flows.

? JOB INTERVIEW QUESTION

What's the relationship between a project's *NPV* and its *IRR*?

Finance in Your Life

The *IRR* of a Master's Degree

A decision that many people face is whether to invest the time and money necessary to earn a graduate degree. Suppose that you are trying to evaluate the financial merits of staying in school for one more year to earn a graduate degree. You decide that you will undertake this investment if it earns a return greater than 10% (i.e., 10% is your hurdle rate). You determine that the costs of obtaining the degree, which include tuition, books, and lost wages that you would have earned from working during the next year, add up to about $50,000 in present value terms. This represents your initial outlay. However, once you have the degree in hand, you estimate that your starting salary will be $5,000 higher than it otherwise would have been, and that the difference between your earnings with the degree and what you would have earned without the degree will

grow at 5% per year over the next 30 years. That is, the cash flows associated with this decision are as follows:

Today	−$50,000
Year 1	$ 5,000
Year 2	$ 5,250
Year 3	$ 5,512
......	
Year 29	$19,601
Year 30	$20,581

Plugging these values into equation 8.2 and solving for the discount rate that results in a zero present value, we find that the *IRR* associated with the master's degree program is 14.2%. Given that this return exceeds the 10% hurdle rate, you decide to enroll in the master's program.

the payback and accounting-based approaches that establish arbitrary thresholds for investment approval. In fact, *for a given project, the hurdle rate used in* IRR *analysis should be the discount rate used in* NPV *analysis.*

net present value (NPV) profile

A plot of a project's *NPV* (on the y-axis) against various discount rates (on the x-axis). It is used to illustrate the relationship between the *NPV* and the *IRR* for the typical project.

Figure 8.4 is a **net present value (NPV) profile**, which plots a project's *NPV* (on the y-axis) against various discount rates (on the x-axis). The *NPV* profile illustrates the relation between a typical project's *NPV* and its *IRR*. By "typical," we mean a project with initial cash outflows followed by cash inflows. In this case, the *NPV* declines as the discount rate used to calculate the *NPV* increases. Not all projects have this feature, as we will soon see. The green line in Figure 8.4 shows that when the discount rate is relatively low, the project has a positive *NPV*. When the discount rate is high, the project has a negative *NPV*. *At some discount rate, the* NPV *equals zero, and that rate is the project's* IRR.

Figure 8.4   *NPV* Profile

The *NPV* is positive when the *IRR* is greater than the hurdle (i.e., discount) rate, and the *NPV* is negative when the *IRR* is less than the hurdle rate.

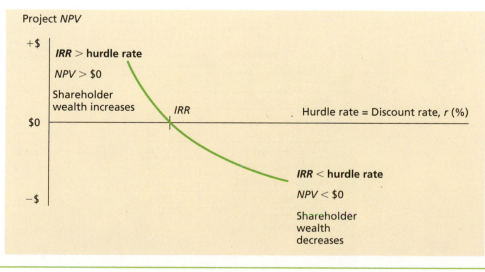

Suppose that Global Wireless requires its analysts to calculate the *IRR* of all proposed investments. The company agrees to undertake only those investments that offer an *IRR* exceeding 18%, a rate that Global Wireless believes to be an industry standard. Figures 8.5a and 8.5b present time lines depicting the *IRR* calculations for Global Wireless's two projects. To obtain the *IRR* for each project under consideration, just solve these two equations:

$$\$0 = -\$250 + \frac{\$35}{(1 + r_{WE})^1} + \frac{\$80}{(1 + r_{WE})^2} + \frac{\$130}{(1 + r_{WE})^3} + \frac{\$160}{(1 + r_{WE})^4} + \frac{\$175}{(1 + r_{WE})^5}$$

$$\$0 = -\$50 + \frac{\$18}{(1 + r_{SE})^1} + \frac{\$22}{(1 + r_{SE})^2} + \frac{\$25}{(1 + r_{SE})^3} + \frac{\$30}{(1 + r_{SE})^4} + \frac{\$32}{(1 + r_{SE})^5}$$

Here, r_{WE} is the *IRR* for the Western Europe project, and r_{SE} is the *IRR* for the Southeastern U.S. project. Solving these expressions yields the following:[5]

$$r_{WE} = 27.8\%$$

$$r_{SE} = 36.7\%$$

Because both investments exceed the hurdle rate of 18%, Global Wireless would like to undertake both projects. But what if it can invest in only one project or the other? Should the company invest in the Southeastern U.S. project because it offers the higher *IRR*, or should they invest in the Western Europe project because it has a higher *NPV*? In this case, the *NPV* and *IRR* methods provide conflicting project rankings.

Figure 8.5a   *IRR of Global Wireless's Projects ($millions)*

Western Europe Project

The internal rate of return (*IRR*) for Global Wireless's Western Europe Project is 27.8%, which is the discount rate that causes the project's cash flows to have an *NPV* of $0. The project is acceptable because its *NPV* is greater than the firm's 18% hurdle rate.

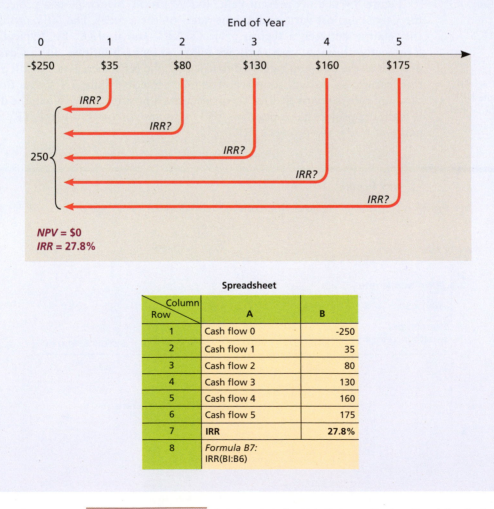

Row \ Column	A	B
1	Cash flow 0	-250
2	Cash flow 1	35
3	Cash flow 2	80
4	Cash flow 3	130
5	Cash flow 4	160
6	Cash flow 5	175
7	**IRR**	**27.8%**
8	*Formula B7:* IRR(B1:B6)	

[5]Of course, you can make this calculation using a financial calculator or Excel, as shown below the time lines in Figure 8.5a.

continued

Figure 8.5a (continued)

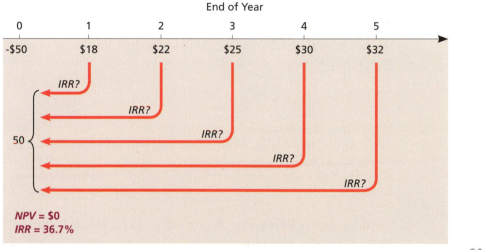

Calculator

© Cengage Learning 2012

Figure 8.5b *IRR* **of Global Wireless's Projects ($millions)**

Southeastern U.S. Project

The internal rate of return (*IRR*) for Global Wireless's Southeastern U.S. Project is 36.7%, which is the discount rate that causes the project's cash flow to have an *NPV* of $0.

© Cengage Learning 2012

8-5b Advantages of the *IRR* Method

The question of how to rank investments that offer different *IRR*s points to an important potential weakness of this method. However, before considering the problems associated with *IRR* analysis, let us discuss the advantages that make it one of the most widely used methods for evaluating capital investments.

First, the *IRR* makes an appropriate adjustment for the time value of money. The value of a dollar received in the first year is greater than the value of a dollar received in the second year. Even cash flows that arrive several years in the future receive some weight in the analysis (unlike payback, which totally ignores distant cash flows). Second, the hurdle rate is based on market returns obtainable on similar investments. This takes away some of the subjectivity that creeps into other analytical methods, like the arbitrary threshold decisions that must be made when using payback or accounting rate of return, and it allows managers to make explicit, quantitative adjustments for differences in risk across projects. Third, because the "answer" that comes out of an *IRR* analysis is a rate of return, its meaning is easy for both financial and nonfinancial managers to grasp intuitively. As we will see, however, the intuitive appeal of the *IRR* approach has its drawbacks, particularly when ranking investments with different *IRR*s. Fourth, the *IRR* technique focuses on cash flow rather than on accounting measures of income.

Despite its advantages, the *IRR* technique has some quirks and problems that in certain situations should concern analysts. Some of these problems arise from the mathematics of the *IRR* calculation, but other difficulties come into play only when companies must rank **mutually exclusive projects**. Two or more projects are mutually exclusive if accepting one project implies that the others cannot be undertaken. If the *IRR*s of several projects exceed the hurdle rate, but only a subset of those projects can be undertaken, how does the firm choose? It turns out that the intuitive approach, selecting those projects with the highest *IRR*s, sometimes leads to bad decisions.

mutually exclusive projects
Two or more projects for which accepting one project implies that the others cannot be undertaken.

8-5c Problems with the Internal Rate of Return

There are two classes of problems that analysts encounter when evaluating investments using the *IRR* technique. The first class can be described as "mathematical problems," which are difficulties in interpreting the numbers that one obtains from solving an *IRR* equation. These problems occur infrequently in practice, but you should be aware of them. For example, consider a simple project with cash flows at three different points in time:

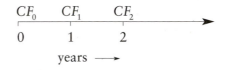

CF_0 is the immediate cash flow when the project begins, and CF_1 and CF_2 are cash flows that occur at the end of years 1 and 2, respectively. Note that conceptually the values of CF_0, CF_1, and CF_2 could be either positive or negative. Solving for this project's *IRR* means setting the net present value of all these cash flows equal to zero:

$$NPV = \$0 = CF_0 + \frac{CF_1}{(1 + r)^1} + \frac{CF_2}{(1 + r)^2}$$

Notice that this equation involves terms such as $[1 \div (1 + r)]^1$ and $[1 \div (1 + r)]^2$. In other words, this is a quadratic equation. Solving a quadratic equation can result in outcomes including (1) a unique solution, (2) multiple solutions, and (3) no real solution. The following examples illustrate the problems with multiple *IRR*s and no real solution.

Lending versus Borrowing A firm establishes a hurdle rate of 20% for new investments. Consider two projects with cash flows occurring at just two dates: now and one year from now.

Project	Cash Flow Now	Cash Flow in One Year	IRR	NPV (@20%)
1	−$100	+$150	50%	+$25
2	+$100	−$150	50%	−$25

The first project displays the familiar pattern of an initial cash outflow followed by a cash inflow. Most investment projects probably fit this profile. But the second project begins with a cash inflow followed by a cash outflow. What kinds of projects in the real world follow this pattern? Think of a firm that is cutting timber. The timber is cut and sold immediately at a profit, but when harvesting is complete, the company must replant the forest at considerable expense. Similarly, consider an optional warranty sold with a new car. The warranty seller receives payment up front but may have to pay claims later on.

Both projects described in the table have a 50% *IRR*, but are the two projects equally desirable? It should be intuitive to you that project 1 is superior because it generates net cash inflows over time whereas project 2 generates net cash outflows. Indeed, the *NPV*s bear this out: project 1 generates a positive $25 *NPV* and project 2 yields a negative $25 *NPV*.

The problem we are confronting here is known as the *lending-versus-borrowing problem*. We can think of project 1 as analogous to a loan. Cash flows out today in exchange for a larger amount of cash in one year. When we lend money, a higher interest rate (or a higher internal rate of return) is preferable, other things held constant. In contrast, project 2 is analogous to borrowing money. We receive cash up front but have to pay back a larger amount later. When borrowing money, a lower interest rate (or a lower *IRR*) is preferred, other factors held constant. Therefore, we can modify the internal rate of return decision rule as follows:

1. When projects have initial cash outflows and subsequent cash inflows, invest when the project *IRR* exceeds the hurdle rate.

2. When projects have initial cash inflows and subsequent cash outflows, invest when the project *IRR* falls below the hurdle rate.

Figure 8.6 illustrates this situation. The *NPV* of project 1 falls when the discount rate rises, as we would expect. This means that if the *IRR* exceeds the hurdle rate then the project's *NPV* is positive, but if the *IRR* falls below the hurdle rate then the *NPV* is negative. So in this case it makes sense to follow the usual rule of accepting projects when the *IRR* exceeds the hurdle rate. In contrast, the *NPV* of project 2 actually rises as the discount rate rises. This counterintuitive relationship holds because the firm is essentially borrowing money in project 2. The higher the rate at which the firm discounts the amount it will have to repay, the lower the present value of that payment and the higher the *NPV* of the project. In this case, it makes sense to accept projects only when the *IRR* falls short of the firm's hurdle rate.

Multiple *IRR*s A second difficulty with the *IRR* method can occur when a project's cash flows alternate between negative and positive values—that is, when the project

Figure 8.6   **Lending versus Borrowing**

The green line is the *NPV* profile for project 1, which is a loan made by the firm; it shows that as the *IRR* exceeds the hurdle rate, the loan's *NPV* is positive. The orange line is the *NPV* profile for project 2, which involves the firm borrowing money; it shows that the higher the rate at which the loan payments are discounted, the higher the *NPV*.

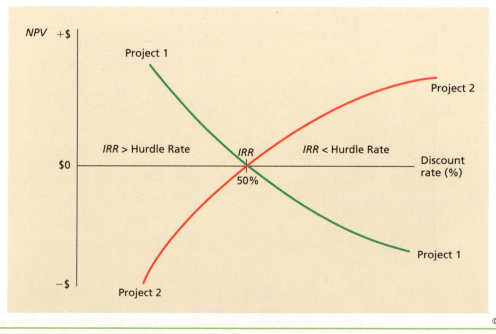

generates an alternating series of net cash inflows and outflows. In that case, there may be more than one solution to the *IRR* equation. As an example, consider a project with the following stream of cash flows:

Year	CF ($ in millions)
0	+100
1	−460
2	+791
3	−602.6
4	+171.6

Admittedly, this project has a rather strange sequence of alternating net cash inflows and outflows, but it is not hard to think of real-world investments that generate cash flow streams that flip back and forth like this. Consider, for example, high-technology products. A new product costs money to develop. It generates plenty of cash for a year or two, but it quickly becomes obsolete. Obsolescence necessitates more spending to develop an upgraded version of the product, which then generates cash again. The cycle continues indefinitely.

Figure 8.7 presents the *NPV* profile for a project with the cash flows just described at various discount rates. Notice that there are four points on the graph at which the project's *NPV* equals zero. In other words, there are several *IRR*s for this project, including 0%, 10%, 20%, and 30%. How does one apply the *IRR* decision rule in a situation such as this? Suppose that the hurdle rate for this project is 15%. Two of the four *IRR*s on this project exceed the hurdle rate, and two fall below the hurdle rate. Should the firm invest or not? The only way to know for sure is to check the *NPV*. On the graph, we see that at a discount rate of 15%, the project's *NPV* is positive, so the firm should invest.

The general rule of thumb is that the maximum number of *IRR*s that a project can have equals the number of sign changes in the cash flow stream. Therefore, in the

Figure 8.7 **NPV Profile for a Project with Multiple IRRs**

This project with alternating cash inflows and outflows has an *NPV* profile that reflects multiple *IRR*s. At each discount rate for which the *NPV* = $0, there is an *IRR*. In this case, *IRR*s occur at 0%, 10%, 20%, and 30%.

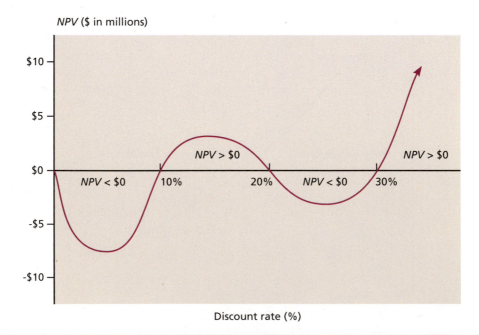

typical project with one negative cash flow up front and only positive cash flows later on, there is just one sign change, and there will be at most one *IRR*. In the previous example, there are four sign changes in the cash flow stream and four different *IRR*s. *In the event that you have to evaluate a project with more than one sign change in the cash flows, beware of the multiple* IRR *problem.* In this situation, the *NPV* profile must be analyzed because use of the *IRR* typically does not result in the correct decision.

No Real Solution After entering the cash flows from a particular investment into a calculator or a spreadsheet, you may receive an error message indicating that there is no solution to the problem. For some cash flow patterns, it is possible that there is no real discount rate that equates the project's *NPV* to zero. In these cases, the only solution to the *IRR* equation involves imaginary numbers, hardly something that we can compare with a firm's hurdle rate.

EXAMPLE

When we first looked at the Global Wireless Western Europe expansion project, we examined cash flows over a five-year project life. Let's modify the example a little. Suppose that the project life is six years rather than five, and in the sixth year the firm must incur a large negative cash outflow. The modified cash flow projections look like this:

Year	Western Europe Project ($ in millions)
0	−250
1	35
2	80
3	130
4	160
5	175
6	−355

When we attempt to calculate the *IRR* for this stream of cash flows, we find that our financial calculator (or Excel) returns an error code. The problem is that for this stream of cash flows, there is no real solution to the *IRR* equation. That is, there is no (real) interest rate at which the present value of cash flows equals zero. If we cannot determine the *IRR* of this project, how can we determine whether the project meets the firm's hurdle rate of 18%?

The last three examples illustrate problems that analysts may encounter when using the *IRR* decision rule. In practice, these problems arise infrequently because most investments generate cash outflows up front and cash inflows later on. Hence, most investments have a unique *IRR*. However, two additional problems may arise when analysts use the *IRR* method to prioritize projects or to choose between mutually exclusive projects. We examine these problems in the next section.

8-5d *IRR, NPV,* and Mutually Exclusive Projects

The Scale Problem Suppose a friend promises to pay you $2 tomorrow if you lend him $1 today. If you make the loan and your friend fulfills his end of the bargain, then you will have made an investment with a 100% *IRR*.[6] Now consider a different case. Your friend asks you to lend him $100 today in exchange for $150 tomorrow. The *IRR* on that investment is 50%, exactly half the *IRR* of the first example. Both of these loans offer very high rates of return. Assuming that you trust the friend to repay you in either case, which investment would you choose if you could choose only one? The first investment increases your wealth by $1, and the second increases your wealth by $50. Even though the rate of return is lower on the second investment, most

---

[6]The *IRR* is 100% per day in this example, which is not a bad return if you annualize it.

people would prefer to lend the larger amount because of its substantially greater monetary payoff.

The point of these examples is to illustrate the *scale problem* inherent in *IRR* analysis. When choosing between mutually exclusive investments, we cannot conclude that the one offering the highest *IRR* will necessarily create the most wealth. When several alternative investments offer *IRR*s that exceed a firm's hurdle rate, choosing the investment that maximizes shareholder wealth involves more than picking the highest *IRR*. For example, take another look at the investment opportunities faced by Global Wireless, opportunities that vary dramatically in scale.

EXAMPLE

Here again are the *NPV* and *IRR* figures for the two investment alternatives.

Project	IRR	NPV (@18%)
Western Europe	27.8%	$75.3 million
Southeastern U.S.	36.7	25.7 million

If we had to choose just one project on the basis of *IRR*, then we would (erroneously) choose to invest in the Southeastern U.S. project. But we have also seen that the Western Europe project generates a much higher *NPV*, meaning that it creates more wealth for Global Wireless shareholders. Hence, the *NPV* criterion tells us to expand in Western Europe rather than in the Southeastern United States. Why the conflict? It is because the scale of the Western Europe expansion is roughly five times that of the Southeastern U.S. project. Even though the Southeastern U.S. project provides a higher rate of return, the opportunity to make the much larger Western Europe investment (an investment that also offers a return well above the firm's hurdle rate) is more attractive.

The Timing Problem Managers of public corporations often receive criticism for neglecting long-term investment opportunities for the sake of meeting short-term financial performance goals. We refrain from commenting on whether corporate managers, as a rule, put too much emphasis on short-term performance. However, we do agree with the proposition that a naive reliance on the *IRR* method can lead to investment decisions that unduly favor investments with short-term payoffs over those that offer returns over a longer horizon. The following example illustrates the problem we have in mind.

EXAMPLE

A company wants to evaluate two investment proposals. The first involves a major effort in new product development. The initial cost is $1 billion, and the company expects the project to generate relatively meager cash flows in the first four years, followed by a big payoff in year 5. The second investment is a significant marketing campaign to attract new customers. It too has an initial outlay of $1 billion, but it generates significant cash flows almost immediately and lower levels of cash in the later years. A financial analyst prepares cash flow projections and calculates each project's *IRR* and *NPV* as shown in the following table (the firm uses 10% as its hurdle rate):

Cash Flow	Product Development ($ in millions)	Marketing Campaign ($ in millions)
Initial Outlay	−1,000	−1,000
Year 1	0	450
Year 2	50	350
Year 3	100	300
Year 4	200	200
Year 5	1,500	100
Technique		
IRR	14.1%	15.9%
NPV (@10%)	$ 184.44	$ 122.44

The analyst observes that the first project generates a higher *NPV*, whereas the second offers a higher *IRR*. Bewildered, he wonders which project to recommend to senior management.

Figure 8.8   ***NPV Profiles Demonstrating the Timing Problem***

The timing problem can lead to *NPVs* and *IRRs* that yield different investment recommendations. At any discount rate below 12.5%, product development is preferred due to its higher *NPV*, although the marketing campaign has a higher *IRR*.

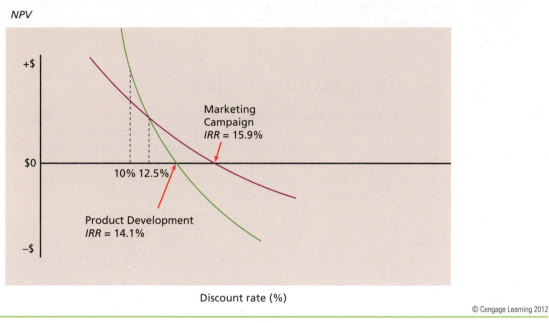

JOB INTERVIEW QUESTION

Does *IRR* always rank projects the same as *NPV*?

SMART concepts

See the concept explained step-by-step at **SMART** | finance

Even though both projects require the same initial investment and both last for five years, the marketing campaign generates more cash flow in the early years than the product development proposal. Therefore, in a relative sense, the payoff from product development occurs later than the payoff from marketing. We know from our discussion of interest-rate risk in Chapter 4 that when interest rates change, long-term bond prices move more than do short-term bond prices. The same phenomenon is at work here. Figure 8.8 plots the *NPV* profiles for the two projects on the same set of axes. Notice the line plotting *NPVs* for the product development idea is much steeper than the other. In simple terms, this means the *NPV* of that investment is much more sensitive to the discount rate than is the *NPV* of the marketing campaign.

Each investment's *IRR* appears in Figure 8.8 where the *NPV* lines cross the *x*-axis. Figure 8.8 shows that both *IRRs* exceed the hurdle rate of 10% and that the marketing campaign has the higher *IRR*. The two lines intersect at a discount rate of 12.5%. At that discount rate, the *NPVs* of the projects are equal. At discount rates below 12.5%, product development, which has a longer-term payoff, has the higher *NPV*. At discount rates above 12.5%, the investment in the marketing campaign offers a larger *NPV*. Given that the required rate of return on investments for this particular firm is 10%, the firm should choose to spend the $1 billion on product development. However, if the firm bases its investment decision solely on achieving the highest *IRR*, it will choose the marketing campaign instead.

In summary, when the timing of cash flows is very different from one project to another, the project with the highest *IRR* may or may not have the highest *NPV*. As in the case of the scale problem, the timing problem can lead firms to reject investments that they should accept. We want to emphasize that this problem (and the scale problem) occurs only when firms must choose between mutually exclusive projects. In the previous example, if the firm can invest in both projects, then the analyst should recommend that it do so. If the firm must choose between two acceptable projects, it should rely on *NPV* analysis to identify the better project.

8-5 Concept Review Questions

9. Describe how the *IRR* and *NPV* approaches are related.

10. If the *IRR* for a given project exceeds a firm's hurdle rate, does that mean that the project necessarily has a positive *NPV*? Explain.

11. Describe the "scale problem" and the "timing problem." Explain the potential effects of these problems on using *IRR* versus *NPV* to choose among mutually exclusive projects.

● 8-6 Profitability Index

profitability index (*PI*)
A capital budgeting tool, defined as the present value of a project's cash inflows divided by the absolute value of its initial cash outflow.

Calculating the Profitability Index A final capital budgeting tool to discuss is the profitability index (*PI*). Like the *IRR*, the profitability index is a close cousin of the *NPV* approach. For simple projects that have an initial cash outflow (CF_0) followed by a series of inflows (CF_1, CF_2,...,CF_n), the *PI* is expressed mathematically as the present value of a project's cash inflows divided by the the absolute value of its initial cash outflow.[7]

(Eq. 8.3)
$$PI = \frac{\frac{CF_1}{(1+r)^1} + \frac{CF_2}{(1+r)^2} + \cdots + \frac{CF_n}{(1+r)^n}}{|CF_0|}$$

The decision rule to follow when evaluating investment projects using the *PI* is to invest when the *PI* is greater than 1.0 (i.e., when the present value of cash inflows exceeds the initial cash outflow) and to refrain from investing when the *PI* is less than 1.0. Note that if the *PI* is above 1.0, then the *NPV* is greater than $0. This means that the *NPV* and *PI* decision rules will always yield the same investment recommendation when we are simply trying to decide whether to accept or reject a single project.

EXAMPLE

To calculate the *PI* for each of Global Wireless's investment projects, calculate the present value of its cash inflows from years 1–5 and then divide by the absolute value of the initial cash outflow to obtain the following result:

Project	PV of *CF* (1–5) ($ in millions)	Initial Outlay ($ in millions)	PI
Western Europe	325.3	250	1.3
Southeastern U.S.	75.7	50	1.5

Both projects have a *PI* greater than 1.0, so both are worthwhile. However, if we rank projects based on the *PI*, then the Southeastern U.S. project looks better.

Beth Acton, Vice President and Treasurer of Ford Motor Co. (former)

"*We look at capital investments in a very similar fashion whether they're routine or large investments.*"

See the entire interview at **SMART** | finance

Smart Practices Video

Because the *NPV*, *IRR*, and *PI* methods are so closely related, they share many of the same advantages relative to payback or accounting rate of return analysis, and there is no need to reiterate those advantages here. However, it is worth pointing out that the *PI* and the *IRR* share an important flaw. Both suffer from the *scale problem* described earlier. Recall that our *NPV* calculations suggested that the Western Europe project created more value for shareholders than the Southeastern U.S. endeavor, whereas the *IRR* and *PI* comparisons suggest just the opposite project ranking. The latter two analyses identify the Southeastern U.S. project as the superior investment because

---

[7]Because the initial cash flow is usually negative, we divide by the absolute value of that cash flow in equation 8.3.

What Companies Do Globally

CFO Survey Evidence

Surveys of corporate financial managers around the world reveal both major similarities and significant differences in the use of various capital budgeting techniques. The graph below documents how frequently managers in the United States, the United Kingdom, Germany, France, Brazil, and Australia use internal rate of return, net present value, payback period, real option analysis, and accounting rate of return. Internal rate of return and *NPV* are used by over 70% of managers of U.S companies and a majority or near-majority of Australian, Brazilian, and British managers, but the propensity to use either of these theoretically preferred methods of capital budgeting decision making is below 50% in all other countries. In fact, payback is the most frequently employed decision-making tool in all countries besides the United States.

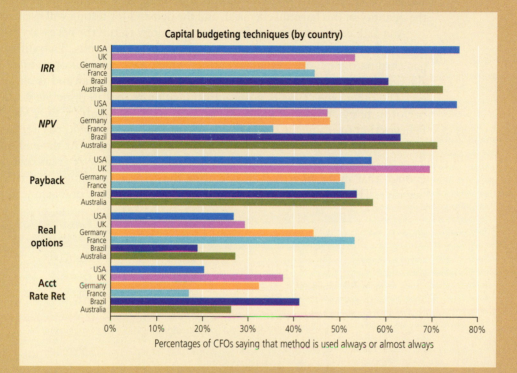

Capital budgeting techniques (by country)

Percentages of CFOs saying that method is used always or almost always

Sources: John R. Graham and Campbell R. Harvey, "The Theory and Practice of Corporate Finance: Evidence from the Field," *Journal of Financial Economics* 60 (2001), pp. 187–243; Dirk Brounen, Abe de Jong, and Kees Koedijk, "Corporate Finance in Europe: Confronting Theory with Practice," *Financial Management* 33 (Winter 2004), pp. 71–101; "Narratives in Managers' Corporate Finance Decisions," Les Coleman, Krishnan Maheswaran, and Sean Pinder, Working Paper, University of Melbourne, 2008.

the differences in scale between the two projects are ignored. For the Southeastern U.S. project, the *PI* indicates that project cash inflows exceed the initial cash outflow by 50% on a present-value basis. The present value of cash inflows for the Western Europe investment exceeds the initial cash outflow by just 30%. But the Western Europe project is much larger, and as our *NPV* figures reveal, it generates considerably more wealth for Global Wireless stockholders.[8]

8-6 Concept Review Questions

12. How are the *NPV*, *IRR*, and *PI* approaches related?

13. What important flaw do both the *IRR* and *PI* share? Explain.

[8]The use of the profitability index in *capital rationing*, which occurs when the firm has more acceptable projects than it can fund from its current budget, is discussed in Chapter 9.

8-7   A New Investment Problem

We conclude with an investment problem that illustrates many of the issues that we introduced earlier in this chapter.

The Ana-Lab Corporation conducts chemical analysis of water, soil, and industrial wastes as mandated by the Environmental Protection Agency (EPA). Ana-Lab's customers include local governmental bodies, who are responsible for insuring that local water supplies are safe for drinking, and manufacturing companies, who must verify that the wastes that they release into water or landfills comply with strict regulatory standards.

A new regulation recently imposed by the EPA sets limits on the amount of a certain chemical that can be released in industrial waste water. In the next few years, Ana-Lab expects many of its customers to ask for new tests that monitor the presence of this chemical. However, over time Ana-Lab's clients will change their production processes to reduce the quantity of this harmful chemical, and the demand for testing will eventually decline.

Ana-Lab does not currently have the technology to run the necessary tests, so it will have to buy several new machines called gas chromatographs. Two different types of gas chromatograph are available, both of which have a useful operating life of about six years. One type, Type A, is less expensive than the other and is cheaper to operate. The other type, Type B, costs a great deal more, but in principle it can be used to perform many additional kinds of chemical tests. Ana-Lab's CEO, Mr. Whitehead, believes that over time he could find new customers who would pay for the additional types of tests that the Type B chromatographs can perform. At the end of its life, the Type B machine must be removed from Ana-Lab's facility at great cost, a cost large enough that in the final year of operating the Type B machines, the net cash flow is negative. The estimated cash flows associated with each type of machine appear below:

Year	Type A Chromatograph	Type B Chromatograph
0	−$1,000,000	−$3,200,000
1	450,000	500,000
2	350,000	550,000
3	250,000	1,000,000
4	200,000	1,500,000
5	150,000	2,000,000
6	125,000	−600,000

Mr. Whitehead asks you to provide analysis to help him determine which chromatograph to purchase. He is particularly interested in knowing how quickly each machine will pay back its initial cost and the rate of return that each machine offers. He tells you that if he does not spend money on new gas chromatographs, he will probably replace some existing equipment in the lab, and he would expect to earn a return of about 10% on that type of investment. As you sit down to begin your analysis, a number of questions come to mind.

What is the payback period of each machine?

What are the pros and cons of focusing on payback as a decision criterion in this particular case?

What is the internal rate of return provided by each machine?

What problems could arise if Mr. Whitehead chooses the machine with the highest IRR?

What hurdle rate ought to be applied to an investment like this?

Payback Period   The Type A machine produces cash flow of $800,000 in its first two years and $250,000 in its third year. Therefore, it pays back the initial $1,000,000 cost about four-fifths of the way through year three ($200,000 ÷ $250,000 = 0.8).

Its payback period is 2.8 years. The Type B machine generates cash flow of $2,050,000 during its first three years and $1,500,000 in its fourth year. Therefore, it earns back the initial $3,200,000 cost in 3.77 years ($1,150,000 ÷ $1,500,000 = 0.77). Based on payback analysis, the Type A chromatograph seems more attractive.

You recall that the payback approach fails to account for the time value of money and completely ignores cash flows beyond the payback period. The Type A machine produces most of its cash flows early in its life, while the Type B machine generates larger cash flows in the later years (but it also has a significant negative cash flow in year six). Because the timing of the cash flows generated by each machine is so different, you worry that a simple payback analysis might lead to a decision that is not best for the company in the long run.

Internal Rate of Return Next, you calculate the rate of return earned by each machine by solving for the *IRR* as follows:

Type A:

$$-\$1,000,000 + \frac{\$450,000}{(1 + r)} + \frac{\$350,000}{(1 + r)^2} + \frac{\$250,000}{(1 + r)^3} + \frac{\$200,000}{(1 + r)^4} + \frac{\$150,000}{(1 + r)^5} + \frac{\$125,000}{(1 + r)^6} = 0$$

$r = IRR = 0.18 = 18\%$

Type B:

$$-\$3,200,000 + \frac{\$500,000}{(1 + r)} + \frac{\$550,000}{(1 + r)^2} + \frac{\$1,000,000}{(1 + r)^3} + \frac{\$1,500,000}{(1 + r)^4} + \frac{\$2,000,000}{(1 + r)^5} - \frac{\$600,000}{(1 + r)^6} = 0$$

$r = IRR = 0.139 = 13.9\%$

The Type A machine seems to be the best choice because it offers an 18% return compared to 13.9% for the Type B machine. You feel somewhat relieved that the *IRR* analysis favors the Type A machine, consistent with the conclusion from your payback period analysis. You also feel reassured that *both* machines earn a return well in excess of the 10% return that Mr. Whitehead said he could earn by replacing existing equipment. However, you wonder if an investment in gas chromatographs should earn more than 10%. Perhaps the demand for the tests that the chromatograph can perform is very sensitive to economic conditions, and if so, the investment may have higher systematic risk than Ana-Lab's existing business.

Additional Analysis Before reporting back to Mr. Whitehead, you decide to calculate the *NPV* for each machine using the 10% hurdle rate that he suggested as well as a higher rate, 13%, to adjust for the higher risk of these new machines. Given that *IRRs* of both machines exceed even the higher of these two hurdle rates, you expect to find that both machines create value (i.e., have a positive *NPV*) for Ana-Lab. Your calculations are summarized below:

	Type A Chromatograph	Type B Chromatograph
NPV at 10%	$186,476	$388,084
NPV at 13%	$109,712	$ 83,566

What previously seemed to be an easy decision to invest in the Type A machine now appears to be less clear cut. When you discount the cash flows at the 10% rate suggested by Mr. Whitehead, the *NPV* of the Type B machine is more than twice as large as the alternative. But at a 13% discount rate, the Type A machine looks like the better choice. You wonder, what accounts for the conflicting rankings?

Conclusion Notice that the cash flows associated with each machine differ in three important ways. First, Ana-Lab must invest a lot more money to purchase the Type B machine. Second, the Type A machine produces most of its cash flow in the early years, while the Type B machine produces higher cash flows later in its life. Third, the Type B machine has net cash outflows up front and in year 6, but the Type A machine only has an outflow in the initial year.

With respect to the differences in the up-front investments required to purchase each machine, recall that the *NPV* and *IRR* rankings may conflict because it is sometimes better to accept a lower return on a larger investment compared to a higher return on a smaller investment. The *IRR* of the Type A machine is 18%, but Ana-Lab earns that return on an investment of just $1 million. It is possible that the company could make more money if it earned a lower rate of return on a much larger investment. That is precisely what the *NPV* analysis is telling you, at least when the discount rate is 10%. If 10% is the proper hurdle rate to apply to this investment decision, then buying the Type B machine creates $388,084 in additional wealth for the company, even though the rate of return is higher on the other machine.

But if Type B is the right choice at 10%, why is it not correct based on a 13% discount rate? Because the Type B machine produces so much of its cash flows in years four and five, its *NPV* is very sensitive to the discount rate. Figure 8.9 demonstrates this. At relatively low discount rates, the Type B chromatograph produces a higher *NPV* compared to the Type A machine, but for higher rates, the *NPV* of the Type A machine is higher. The two curves in Figure 8.9 intersect at a discount rate of roughly 12.64%, meaning that the *NPVs* of the two machines are equal at that point. Therefore, your advice to Mr. Whitehead should be to purchase the Type B machine if the appropriate hurdle rate is 12.64% or lower and purchase the Type A machine if the appropriate hurdle rate is greater than 12.64% but less than 18%. This suggests that the company should spend the necessary time to carefully calculate the correct discount rate for this project.

A final consideration is the impact of multiple sign changes in the cash flows associated with the Type B machine. Recall that when the cash flows change sign more than once, it is possible that an investment can have more than one *IRR*. In that case it is helpful to plot the investment's *NPV* for a range of discount rates. In Figure 8.9 you can see that the *NPV* for the Type B chromatograph is positive for any discount rate between 0% and 13.9%, and at higher rates (at least up to 20%) the *NPV* is negative. Thus, over a range of discount rates that represent plausible hurdle rates for this investment, there is only one *IRR*. Still, when cash flows change signs more than once, as they do for the Type B machine, you should check to see if the investment has more than one *IRR* by plotting a graph like Figure 8.9.[9]

Figure 8.9

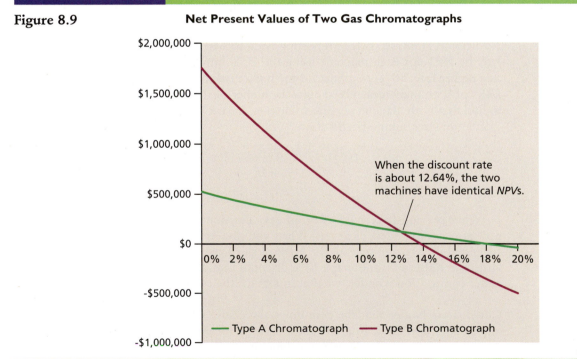

Net Present Values of Two Gas Chromatographs

When the discount rate is about 12.64%, the two machines have identical *NPVs*.

— Type A Chromatograph   — Type B Chromatograph

© Cengage Learning 2012

---

[9] The Type B machine does in fact have another *IRR*. The second *IRR* is approximately −75.38%.

Summary

- The capital budgeting process involves generating, reviewing, analyzing, selecting, and implementing long-term investment proposals that are consistent with the firm's strategic goals.

- Other things being equal, managers would prefer an easily applied capital budgeting technique that considers cash flow, recognizes the time value of money, fully accounts for expected risk and return, and when applied, leads to higher stock prices.

Table of Important Equations
1. $NPV = CF_0 + \dfrac{CF_1}{(1+r)^1} + \dfrac{CF_2}{(1+r)^2}$ $+ \dfrac{CF_3}{(1+r)^3} + \cdots + \dfrac{CF_n}{(1+r)^n}$
2. $NPV = \$0 = CF_0 + \dfrac{CF_1}{(1+r)^1} + \dfrac{CF_2}{(1+r)^2}$ $+ \dfrac{CF_3}{(1+r)^3} + \cdots + \dfrac{CF_n}{(1+r)^n}$; $r = IRR$
3. $PI = \dfrac{\dfrac{CF_1}{(1+r)^1} + \dfrac{CF_2}{(1+r)^2} + \cdots + \dfrac{CF_n}{(1+r)^n}}{\lvert CF_0 \rvert}$

- Though simplicity is a virtue, the simplest approaches to capital budgeting do not always lead firms to make the best investment decisions.

- Capital budgeting techniques include the payback period, discounted payback period, and the accounting rate of return, which are less-sophisticated techniques because they do not explicitly deal with the time value of money and are not tied to the firm's wealth-maximization goal. More-sophisticated techniques include net present value (*NPV*), internal rate of return (*IRR*), and profitability index (*PI*). These methods often give the same accept-reject decisions but do not necessarily rank projects the same.

- Using the *IRR* approach can occasionally lead to poor investment decisions when projects have cash flow streams alternating between negative and positive values. The *IRR* technique may provide suboptimal project rankings when different investments have very different scales or when the timing of cash flows varies dramatically from one project to another.

- Although the *NPV* and *IRR* techniques give the same accept or reject decisions, these techniques do not necessarily agree in ranking mutually exclusive projects. Because of its lack of mathematical, scale, and timing problems, the most straightforward and, theoretically, the best decision technique is net present value (*NPV*).

- The profitability index is a close cousin of the *NPV* approach, but it suffers from the same scale problem as the *IRR* approach.

Key Terms

Self-Test Problems

Answers to Self-Test Problems and the Concept Review Questions throughout the chapter appear in CourseMate with SmartFinance Tools at www.cengagebrain.com.

ST8-1. Nader International is considering investing in two assets—A and B. The initial outlay, annual cash flows, and annual depreciation for each asset appears in the following table for the assets' assumed five-year lives. Nader will use straight-line depreciation over each asset's five-year life. The firm requires a 12% return on each of those equally risky assets. Nader's maximum payback period is 2.5 years, its maximum discounted payback period is 3.25 years, and its minimum accounting rate of return is 30%.

	Asset A		Asset B	
Year	Cash Flow	Depreciation	Cash Flow	Depreciation
0	−$200,000	–	−$180,000	–
1	$ 70,000	$40,000	$ 80,000	$36,000
2	80,000	40,000	90,000	36,000
3	90,000	40,000	30,000	36,000
4	90,000	40,000	40,000	36,000
5	100,000	40,000	40,000	36,000

a.   Calculate the *payback period* for each asset, assess its acceptability, and indicate which asset is best, using the payback period.

b.   Calculate the *discounted payback* for each asset, assess its acceptability, and indicate which asset is best, using the discounted payback.

c.   Assuming that each year's net income equals cash flow minus depreciation, calculate the *accounting rate of return* from each asset, assess its acceptability, and indicate which asset is best, using the accounting rate of return.

d.   Compare and contrast your findings in parts (a), (b), and (c). Which asset would you recommend to Nader, assuming that they are mutually exclusive? Why?

ST8-2. JK Products, Inc. is considering investing in either of two competing projects that will allow the firm to eliminate a production bottleneck and meet the growing demand for its products. The firm's engineering department narrowed the alternatives down to two—Status Quo (SQ) and High Tech (HT). Working with the accounting and finance personnel, the firm's CFO developed the following estimates of the cash flows for SQ and HT over the relevant six-year time horizon. The firm has an 11% required return and views these projects as equally risky.

	Project SQ	Project HT
Year	Cash Flows	
0	−$670,000	−$940,000
1	$250,000	$170,000
2	200,000	180,000
3	170,000	200,000
4	150,000	250,000
5	130,000	300,000
6	130,000	550,000

a.   Calculate the *net present value* (NPV) of each project, assess its acceptability, and indicate which project is best, using NPV.

b.   Calculate the *internal rate of return* (IRR) of each project, assess its acceptability, and indicate which project is best, using IRR.

c.   Calculate the *profitability index* (PI) of each project, assess its acceptability, and indicate which project is best, using PI.

d.   Draw the NPV *profile* for project SQ and HT on the same set of axes, and use this diagram to explain why the NPV and the IRR show different preferences for these two mutually exclusive projects. Discuss this difference in terms of both the "scale problem" and the "timing problem."

e.   Which of the two mutually exclusive projects would you recommend that JK Products undertake? Why?

Questions

Q8-1.   Can you name some industries where the payback period is unavoidably long?

Q8-2.   In statistics, you learn about Type I and Type II errors. A Type I error occurs when a statistical test rejects a hypothesis when the hypothesis is actually true. A Type II error occurs when a test fails to reject a hypothesis that is actually false. We can apply this type of thinking to capital budgeting. A Type I error occurs when a firm rejects an investment project that would actually enhance shareholder wealth. A Type II error occurs when a firm accepts a value-decreasing investment, which should have been rejected.

    a. Describe the features of the payback rule that could lead to Type I errors.

    b. Describe the features of the payback rule that could lead to Type II errors.

    c. Which error do you think is more likely to occur when firms use payback analysis? Does your answer depend on the length of the cutoff payback period? You can assume a "typical" project cash flow stream, meaning that most cash outflows occur in the early years of a project.

Q8-3. Holding the cutoff period fixed, which method has a more severe bias against long-lived projects, payback or discounted payback?

Q8-4. For a firm that uses the *NPV* rule to make investment decisions, what consequences result if the firm misestimates shareholders' required returns and consistently applies a discount rate that is "too high"?

Q8-5. "Cash flow projections more than a few years out are not worth the paper they're written on. There-fore, using payback analysis, which ignores long-term cash flows, is more reasonable than making wild guesses as one has to do in the *NPV* approach." Respond to this comment.

Q8-6. "Smart analysts can massage the numbers in *NPV* analysis to make any project's *NPV* look positive. It is better to use a simpler approach like payback or accounting rate of return that gives analysts fewer degrees of freedom to manipulate the numbers." Respond to this comment.

Q8-7. In what way is the *NPV* consistent with the principle of shareholder wealth maximization? What hap-pens to the value of a firm if a positive *NPV* project is accepted? If a negative *NPV* project is accepted?

Q8-8. A particular firm's shareholders demand a 15% return on their investment, given the firm's risk. How-ever, this firm has historically generated returns in excess of shareholder expectations, with an average return on its portfolio of investments of 25%.

    a. Looking back, what kind of stock-price performance would you expect to see for this firm?

    b. A new investment opportunity arises, and the firm's financial analysts estimate that the project's return will be 18%. The CEO wants to reject the project because it would lower the firm's aver-age return and therefore lower the firm's stock price. How do you respond?

Q8-9. What are the potential faults in using the *IRR* as a capital budgeting technique? Given these faults, why is this technique so popular among corporate managers?

Q8-10. Why is the *NPV* considered to be theoretically superior to all other capital budgeting techniques? Rec-oncile this result with the prevalence of the use of *IRR* in practice. How would you respond to your CFO if she instructed you to use the *IRR* technique to make capital budgeting decisions on projects with cash flow streams that alternate between inflows and outflows?

Q8-11. Outline the differences between *NPV, IRR,* and *PI.* What are the advantages and disadvantages of each technique? Do they agree with regard to simple accept or reject decisions?

Q8-12. Under what circumstances will the *NPV, IRR,* and *PI* techniques provide different capital budgeting decisions? What are the underlying causes of the differences often found in the ranking of mutually exclusive projects using *NPV* and *IRR*?

Problems

Payback Methods

P8-1. Suppose that a thirty-year U.S. Treasury bond offers a 4% coupon rate, paid semiannually. The market price of the bond is $1,000, equal to its par value.

    a. What is the *payback period* for this bond?

    b. With such a long payback period, is the bond a bad investment?

    c. What is the *discounted payback period* for the bond, assuming its 4% coupon rate is the required return? What general principle does this example illustrate regarding a project's life, its discounted payback period, and its *NPV*?

P8-2. The cash flows associated with three different projects are as follows:

Cash Flows	Alpha ($ in millions)	Beta ($ in millions)	Gamma ($ in millions)
Initial Outflow	−1.5	−0.4	−7.5
Year 1	0.3	0.1	2.0
Year 2	0.5	0.2	3.0
Year 3	0.5	0.2	2.0
Year 4	0.4	0.1	1.5
Year 5	0.3	−0.2	5.5

a. Calculate the *payback period* of each investment.
b. Which investments does the firm accept if the cutoff payback period is three years? Four years?
c. If the firm invests by choosing projects with the shortest payback period, which project would it invest in?
d. If the firm uses *discounted payback* with a 15% discount rate and a four-year cutoff period, which projects will it accept?
e. One of these almost certainly should be rejected, but may be accepted if the firm uses payback analysis. Which one?
f. One of these projects almost certainly should be accepted (unless the firm's opportunity cost of capital is very high), but may be rejected if the firm uses payback analysis. Which one?

Accounting-Based Methods

P8-3. Kenneth Gould is the general manager at a small-town newspaper that is part of a national media chain. He is seeking approval from corporate headquarters (HQ) to spend $20,000 to buy some Macintosh computers and a laser printer to use in designing the layout of his daily paper. This equipment will be depreciated using the straight-line method over four years. These computers will replace outmoded equipment that will be kept on hand for emergency use.

HQ requires Kenneth to estimate the cash flows associated with the purchase of new equipment over a four-year horizon. The impact of the project on net income is derived by subtracting depreciation from cash flow each year. The project's average accounting rate of return equals the average contribution to net income divided by the average book value of the investment. HQ accepts any project that (1) has an average accounting rate of return that exceeds the cost of capital of 15%, and (2) returns the initial investment within four years (on a cash flow basis). The following are Kenneth's estimates of cash flows:

	Year 1	Year 2	Year 3	Year 4
Cost Savings	$7,500	$9,100	$9,100	$9,100

a. What is the average contribution to net income across all four years?
b. What is the average book value of the investment?
c. What is the average *accounting rate of return*?
d. What is the *payback period* of this investment?
e. Critique the company's method for evaluating investment proposals.

Net Present Value

P8-4. Calculate the *net present value (NPV)* for the following twenty-year projects. Comment on the acceptability of each. Assume that the firm has an opportunity cost of 14%.
a. Initial cash outlay is $15,000; cash inflows are $13,000 per year.
b. Initial cash outlay is $32,000; cash inflows are $4,000 per year.
c. Initial cash outlay is $50,000; cash inflows are $8,500 per year.

P8-5. Michael's Bakery is evaluating a new electronic oven. The oven requires an initial cash outlay of $19,000 and will generate after-tax cash inflows of $4,000 per year for eight years. For each of the costs of capital listed, (1) calculate the *NPV*, (2) indicate whether to accept or reject the machine, and (3) explain your decision.
a. The cost of capital is 10%
b. The cost of capital is 12%.
c. The cost of capital is 14%.

P8-6. Using a 14% cost of capital, calculate the *NPV* for each of the projects shown in the following table and indicate whether or not each is acceptable.

Year	Project A	Project B	Project C	Project D	Project E
			Cash Flows		
0	−$20,000	−$600,000	−$150,000	−$760,000	−$100,000
1	$3,000	$120,000	$ 18,000	$185,000	$ 0
2	3,000	145,000	17,000	185,000	0
3	3,000	170,000	16,000	185,000	0
4	3,000	190,000	15,000	185,000	25,000
5	3,000	220,000	15,000	185,000	36,000
6	3,000	240,000	14,000	185,000	0
7	3,000		13,000	185,000	60,000
8	3,000		12,000	185,000	72,000
9	3,000		11,000		84,000
10	3,000		10,000		

P8-7. Scotty Manufacturing is considering the replacement of one of its machine tools. Three alternative replacement tools—A, B, and C—are under consideration. The cash flows associated with each are shown in the following table. The firm's cost of capital is 15%.

Year	A	B	C
		Cash Flows	
0	−$95,000	−$50,000	−$150,000
1	$20,000	$10,000	$58,000
2	20,000	12,000	35,000
3	20,000	13,000	23,000
4	20,000	15,000	23,000
5	20,000	17,000	23,000
6	20,000	21,000	35,000
7	20,000	—	46,000
8	20,000	—	58,000

a. Calculate the *NPV* of each alternative tool.
b. Using *NPV*, evaluate the acceptability of each tool.
c. Rank the tools from best to worst, using *NPV*.

P8-8. Erwin Enterprises has 10 million shares outstanding with a current market price of $10 per share. There is one investment available to Erwin, and its cash flows are provided below. Erwin has a cost of capital of 10%. Given this information, determine the impact on Erwin's stock price and firm value if capital markets fully reflect the value of undertaking the project.

Year	Cash Flow
0	−$10,000,000
1	$3,000,000
2	$4,000,000
3	$5,000,000
4	$6,000,000
5	$9,800,000

P8-9. A certain investment requires an initial outlay of $12 million and subsequently produces annual cash inflows of $1.4 million in perpetuity. A firm evaluating this investment uses a discount rate of 10%. What is the investment's *NPV*? What is the *EVA* each period? What is the present value of the stream of *EVAs*?

Internal Rate of Return

P8-10. For each of the projects shown in the following table, calculate the *internal rate of return* (*IRR*).

Year	Project A	Project B	Project C	Project D
		Cash Flows		
0	−$72,000	−$440,000	−$18,000	−$215,000
1	$16,000	$135,000	$ 7,000	$108,000
2	20,000	135,000	7,000	90,000
3	24,000	135,000	7,000	72,000
4	28,000	135,000	7,000	54,000
5	32,000	—	7,000	—

P8-11. William Industries is attempting to choose the better of two mutually exclusive projects for expanding the firm's production capacity. The relevant cash flows for the projects are shown in the following table. The firm's cost of capital is 15%.

Year	Project A	Project B
	Cash Flows	
0	−$550,000	−$358,000
1	$110,000	$154,000
2	132,000	132,000
3	165,000	105,000
4	209,000	77,000
5	275,000	55,000

a. Calculate the *IRR* for each of the projects.

b. Assess the acceptability of each project based on the *IRR*s found in part (a).

c. Which project is preferred, based on the *IRR*s found in part (a)?

P8-12. Contract Manufacturing, Inc. is considering two alternative investment proposals. The first proposal calls for a major renovation of the company's manufacturing facility. The second involves replacing just a few obsolete pieces of equipment in the facility. The company will choose one project or the other this year, but it will not do both. The cash flows associated with each project appear below, and the firm discounts project cash flows at 15%.

Year	Renovate	Replace
0	−$9,000,000	−$1,000,000
1	3,500,000	600,000
2	3,000,000	500,000
3	3,000,000	400,000
4	2,800,000	300,000
5	2,500,000	200,000

a. Rank these investments based on their *NPV*s.

b. Rank these investments based on their *IRR*s.

c. Why do these rankings yield mixed signals?

P8-13. Consider a project with the following cash flows and a firm with a 15% cost of capital.

Year	Cash Flow
0	−$20,000
1	50,000
2	−10,000

a. What are the two *IRR*s associated with this cash flow stream?

b. If the firm's cost of capital falls between the two *IRR* values calculated in part (a), should it accept or reject the project?

P8-14. A certain project has the following stream of cash flows:

Year	Cash Flow
0	$17,500
1	−80,500
2	138,425
3	−105,455
4	30,030

a.   Fill in the following table:

Cost of Capital (%)	Project *NPV*
0	_____
5	_____
10	_____
15	_____
20	_____
25	_____
30	_____
35	_____
50	_____

b.   Use the values developed in part (a) to draw an *NPV profile* for the project.
c.   What is this project's *IRR*?
d.   Describe the conditions under which the firm should accept this project.

Profitability Index

P8-15. Evaluate the following three projects, using the profitability index. Assume a cost of capital of 15%.

Cash Flows	Project		
	Liquidate	Recondition	Replace
Initial Cash Outflow	−$100,000	−$500,000	−$1,000,000
Year 1 cash inflow	50,000	100,000	500,000
Year 2 cash inflow	60,000	200,000	500,000
Year 3 cash inflow	75,000	250,000	500,000

a.   Rank these projects by their *PI*s.
b.   If the projects are independent, which would you accept according to the *PI* criterion?
c.   If these projects are mutually exclusive, which would you accept according to the *PI* criterion?
d.   Apply the *NPV* criterion to the projects, rank them according to their *NPV*s, and indicate which you would accept if they are independent and mutually exclusive.
e.   Compare and contrast your answer from part (c) with your answer to part (d) for the mutually exclusive case. Explain this result.

P8-16. You have a $10 million capital budget and must make the decision about which investments your firm should accept for the coming year. Use the following information on three mutually exclusive projects to determine which investment your firm should accept. The firm's cost of capital is 12%.

Cash Flows	Project 1	Project 2	Project 3
Initial Cash Outflow	−$4,000,000	−$5,000,000	−$10,000,000
Year 1 cash inflow	1,000,000	2,000,000	4,000,000
Year 2 cash inflow	2,000,000	3,000,000	6,000,000
Year 3 cash inflow	3,000,000	3,000,000	5,000,000

a.   Which project do you accept on the basis of *NPV*?
b.   Which project do you accept on the basis of *PI*?
c.   If these are the only investments available, which one do you select?

P8-17. Both Old Line Industries and New Tech, Inc., use the *IRR* to make investment decisions. Both firms are considering investing in a more efficient $4.5 million mail-order processor. This machine could generate after-tax savings of $2 million per year over the next three years for both firms. However, due to the risky nature of its business, New Tech has a much higher cost of capital (20%) than does Old Line (10%). Given this information, answer parts (a)–(c).

    a.   Should Old Line invest in this processor?

    b.   Should New Tech invest in this processor?

    c.   Based on your answers in parts (a) and (b), what can you infer about the acceptability of projects across firms with different costs of capital?

P8-18. Butler Products has prepared the following estimates for an investment it is considering. The initial cash outflow is $20,000, and the project is expected to yield cash inflows of $4,400 per year for seven years. The firm has a 10% cost of capital.

    a.   Determine the *NPV* for the project.

    b.   Determine the *IRR* for the project.

    c.   Would you recommend that the firm accept or reject the project? Explain your answer.

P8-19. Reynolds Enterprises is attempting to evaluate the feasibility of investing $85,000 in a machine having a five-year life. The firm has estimated the *cash inflows* associated with the proposal as shown below. The firm has a 12% cost of capital.

Year	Cash Inflows
1	$18,000
2	22,500
3	27,000
4	31,500
5	36,000

    a.   Calculate the *payback period* for the proposed investment.

    b.   Calculate the *NPV* for the proposed investment.

    c.   Calculate the *IRR* for the proposed investment.

    d.   Evaluate the acceptability of the proposed investment using *NPV* and *IRR*. What recommendation would you make relative to implementation of the project? Why?

P8-20. Sharpe Manufacturing is attempting to select the best of three mutually exclusive projects. The initial cash outflow and after-tax cash inflows associated with each project are shown in the following table.

Cash Flows	Project X	Project Y	Project Z
Initial Cash Outflow	$80,000	$130,000	$145,000
Cash Inflows Years 1–5	27,000	41,000	43,000

    a.   Calculate the *payback period* for each project.

    b.   Calculate the *NPV* of each project, assuming that the firm has a cost of capital equal to 13%.

    c.   Calculate the *IRR* for each project.

    d.   Summarize the preferences dictated by each measure and indicate which project you would recommend. Explain why.

P8-21. Wilkes, Inc., must invest in a pollution-control program in order to meet federal regulations to stay in business. There are two programs available to Wilkes: an all-at-once program that will be immediately funded and implemented, and a gradual program that will be phased in over the next three years. The immediate program costs $5 million, whereas the phase-in program will cost $1 million today and $2 million per year for the following three years. If the cost of capital for Wilkes is 15%, which pollution-control program should Wilkes select?

P8-22. A consumer product firm finds that its brand of laundry detergent is losing market share, so it decides that it needs to "freshen" the product. One strategy is to maintain the current detergent formula but to repackage the product. The other strategy involves a complete reformulation of the product in a way that will appeal to environmentally conscious consumers. The firm will pursue one strategy or the other but not both. Cash flows from each proposal appear below, and the firm discounts cash flows at 13%.

Year	Repackage	Reformulate
0	−$3,000,000	−$25,000,000
1	2,000,000	10,000,000
2	1,250,000	9,000,000
3	500,000	7,000,000
4	250,000	4,000,000
5	250,000	3,500,000

a. Rank these investments based on their *NPV*s.
b. Rank these investments based on their *IRR*s.
c. Rank these investments based on their *PI*s.
d. Draw *NPV profiles* for the two projects on the same set of axes and discuss these profiles.
e. Do these investment rankings yield mixed signals?

P8-23. Lundblad Construction Co. recently acquired ten acres of land and is weighing two options for developing the land. The first proposal is to build ten single-family homes on the site. This project would generate a quick cash payoff as the homes are sold over the next two years. Specifically, Lundblad estimates that it would spend $2.5 million on construction costs immediately, and it would receive $1.6 million as cash inflows in each of the next two years.

The second proposal is to build a strip shopping mall. This project calls for Lundblad to retain ownership of the property and to lease space to retail businesses that would serve the neighborhood. Construction costs for the strip mall are also about $2.5 million, and the company expects to receive $350,000 annually (for each of fifty years, starting one year from now) in net cash inflows from leasing the property. Lundblad's cost of capital is 10%.

a. Rank these projects based on their *NPV*s.
b. Rank these projects based on their *IRR*s.
c. Rank these projects based on their *PI*s. Do these rankings agree with those based on *NPV* or *IRR*?
d. Draw *NPV profiles* for these projects on the same set of axes. Use this graph to explain why, in this case, the *NPV* and *IRR* methods yield mixed signals.
e. Which project should Lundblad choose?
f. Which project should Lundblad choose if its cost of capital is 13.5%? 16%? 20%?

Mini-Case

Capital Budgeting Process and Techniques

Contact Manufacturing, Inc., is considering two alternative investment proposals. The first proposal calls for a major renovation of the company's manufacturing facility. The second involves replacing just a few obsolete pieces of equipment in the facility. The company will choose one project or the other this year, but it will not do both. The cash flows associated with each project appear below and the firm discounts project cash flows at 15%.

Year	Renovate	Replace
0	−$9,000,000	−$2,400,000
1	3,000,000	2,000,000
2	3,000,000	800,000
3	3,000,000	200,000
4	3,000,000	200,000
5	3,000,000	200,000

Assignment

1. Calculate the *payback period* of each project, and based on this criteria, indicate which project you would recommend for acceptance.

2. Calculate the *net present value* (NPV) of each project, and based on this criteria, indicate which project you would recommend for acceptance.

3. Calculate the *internal rate of return* (IRR) of each project, and based on this criteria, indicate which project you would recommend for acceptance.

4. Calculate the *profitability index* (PI) of each project, and based on this criteria, indicate which project you would recommend for acceptance.

5. Overall, you should find conflicting recommendations based on the various criteria. Why is this occurring?

6. Chart the *NPV profiles* of these projects. Label the intersection points on the x- and y-axis and the crossover point.

7. Based on this *NPV profile* analysis and assuming the WACC is 15%, which project would you recommend for acceptance? Why?

8. Based on this *NPV profile* analysis and assuming the WACC is 25%, which project would you recommend for acceptance? Why?

9. Discuss the important elements to consider when deciding between these two projects.

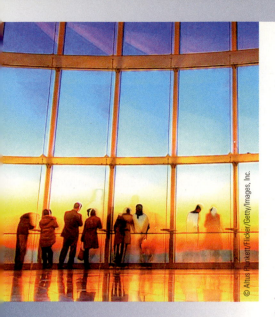

chapter 9

Cash Flow and Capital Budgeting

What Companies Do

Will the Tax Relief Act Stimulate Investment?

On December 17, 2010, President Obama signed into law the Tax Relief, Unemployment Insurance Reauthorization, and Job Creation Act of 2010. Among the law's many provisions were several affecting the speed with which business could take deductions for new investments. Historically, the tax law required business to depreciate long-lived assets such as plant and equipment gradually over several years rather than deducting the entire cost of these investments from income in the year they were purchased. Because writing off the cost of new equipment reduces the income that is subject to taxation (and thereby decreases firms' tax bills), businesses generally prefer to deduct those costs as soon as possible.

The 2010 act allowed companies to take "bonus depreciation" on certain kinds of assets, and that bonus was substantial—firms could deduct up to 50% of the cost of a new asset in the year it was purchased and put into service. Many small businesses qualified for an even sweeter tax break enabling them to deduct the entire cost of new assets immediately.

In passing this legislation, policy makers recognized that changes to depreciation rules alter the incentives that businesses have to make new investments. All else being equal, allowing companies to write off the cost of new assets more rapidly increases the net present value of these investments. Congress and the president hoped that by allowing businesses to depreciate their assets more rapidly, firms would invest more and hire more workers to get the economy moving again.

Source: www.lexology.com/library/detail.aspx?g=e848405b-0cf5-4d9b-a7cb-fcb5a7c027d1

279

Learning Objectives

After studying this chapter you should be able to:

- Differentiate between cash flow and accounting profit with regard to incremental cash flow, financing costs, taxes, and noncash expenses;

- Discuss depreciation, fixed asset expenditures, working capital expenditures, and terminal value;

- Understand relevant cash flows and the effects of sunk costs, opportunity costs, and cannibalization;

- Demonstrate the procedures for determining the relevant cash flows for a capital budgeting problem;

- Analyze capital rationing decisions, competing replacement projects with unequal lives, and excess capacity utilization projects; and

- Describe how the human element can affect the capital budgeting process and its outcomes.

Chapter 8 described various capital budgeting techniques that analysts use to evaluate and rank investment proposals. Each of the examples in Chapter 8 began with a sequence of cash flows, although we did not discuss the origins of those cash flow numbers. This chapter describes how to determine the relevant cash flows. We begin with an overview of the kinds of cash flows that may appear in almost any type of investment. Next, we present an extended capital budgeting example and we discuss special problems and situations that frequently arise in the capital budgeting process. The chapter concludes with a brief discussion of the human element in capital budgeting.

9-1 Types of Cash Flows

9-1a Cash Flow vs. Accounting Profit

When accountants prepare financial statements for external reporting, they have a very different purpose in mind than financial analysts have when they evaluate the merits of an investment. Accountants want to produce financial statements that fairly and accurately represent the state of a business at any given time, as well as over a period of time. Given this purpose, accountants measure the inflows and outflows of a business's operations on an *accrual basis* rather than on a *cash basis*. For example, accountants typically credit a firm for earning revenue once a sale is made, even though customers may not pay cash for their purchases for several weeks or months. Similarly, accountants typically do not record the full cost of an asset as an expense if they expect the asset to confer benefits to the firm over several years. If a firm spends $1 billion on an asset that it plans to use over ten years, accountants may count only one tenth of the purchase price, or $100 million, as a current-year depreciation expense.

In contrast, when they analyze an investment's merits, *financial analysts focus on the actual cash inflows and outflows that the investment produces*. In part this is because no matter what earnings a firm may show on an accrual basis, it cannot survive for long unless its investments generate enough cash to pay its bills. Furthermore, the emphasis that sound financial analysis places on cash flow reflects the time value of money. If a firm sells a product for $1,000, the value of that sale is greater if the customer pays immediately rather than 30 or 90 days in the future.

This chapter shows you how to calculate the cash flows needed to estimate an investment's net present value (*NPV*). The key principles involved are:

- Include only the investment's incremental cash flows;
- Ignore an investment's financing costs;
- Focus on after-tax cash flows; and
- Adjust for non-cash expenses such as depreciation

The following sections illustrate these principles.

Focusing on Incremental Cash Flows For capital budgeting purposes, financial analysts and companies focus on *incremental* cash inflows and outflows. Cash flows triggered by a particular investment that would not have otherwise occurred are incremental cash flows. The cost of building and operating a new plant and the revenues from selling the products produced at the plant are clear examples of incremental cash flows. However, some incremental cash flows are more subtle and can be easy to miss. For example, when a firm launches a new product line, revenues from older products may decline, and those lost sales represent an incremental cash outflow. We will discuss **incremental cash flows** in more depth later in this chapter. For now, recognize that identifying the cash flows that directly result from a proposed investment is a key step in the analysis of investment opportunities.

incremental cash flows
Cash flows triggered by an investment that would not have otherwise occurred.

Ignoring Financing Costs Much of this chapter focuses on which cash flows to include in calculating a project's *NPV*. We should also mention an important category of cash flows that should be excluded—financing cash flows. When calculating a project's *NPV*, analysts should ignore the costs of raising the money to finance the project, whether those costs are in the form of interest expense from debt financing or dividend payments to equity investors. It may seem counterintuitive to exclude costs such as interest expense from an investment's cash-flow calculations, but it is necessary to do so because they are accounted for in the process of discounting future cash flows. When analysts discount a project's cash flows, the chosen discount rate takes into account the opportunity that investors have to invest in other firms or projects. Therefore, if an analyst deducted cash outflows to investors, such as interest and dividend payments, the analyst would, in effect, double-count the financing costs of the investment.

 **JOB INTERVIEW QUESTION**

If we finance an investment project with debt, how should we handle interest expenses in the *NPV* calculation?

EXAMPLE

Suppose that a company has an investment project that costs $1 million to undertake. Half of this money will come from stockholders who require a 12% return, and half will come from bondholders who demand 8%. In Chapter 5 we introduced the concept of a firm's weighted average cost of capital (WACC), a rate that blends the cost of equity and the after-tax cost of debt. This is often the rate that firms use to discount cash flows in *NPV* calculations. If the firm faces a 40% corporate tax rate, then its after-tax cost of debt is 4.8% [8% pretax $\times$ (1 − 40%)] and its WACC is:

$$\text{WACC} = 50\% \times 12\% + 50\% \times [8\% \times (1 - 40\%)] = 8.4\%$$

Suppose that the firm's investment project will generate annual sales of $440,000 in perpetuity, as well as $300,000 in annual operating expenses. The company must also pay $40,000 in annual interest expenses ($500,000 $\times$ 8%).[1] Is this investment worth undertaking?

One of the company's financial analysts calculates that the project will generate $60,000 each year in after-tax cash, but this calculation includes both the investment's operating cash flows and its financing cash flows (i.e., interest expense) as shown below:

Sales	$ 440,000
Operating expenses	−300,000
Interest expense	− 40,000
Pre-tax cash flow	$ 100,000
Taxes (40%)	− 40,000
After-tax cash flow	$ 60,000

Now, let's see whether the firm would accept or reject this project based on these cash flow numbers. If the project costs $1 million up front and generates cash inflows of $60,000 per year (in perpetuity), its NPV is negative:

$$NPV = -\$1,000,000 + \frac{\$60,000}{0.084} = -\$285,714$$

Is rejecting this investment the right decision? One way to answer this question is to ask whether stockholders and bondholders are satisfied with the payments they receive as a result of the investment. Each year bondholders receive $40,000, which represents an 8% return on their investment ($40,000 ÷ $500,000). In addition, the investment generates $60,000 per year for shareholders, and that represents a 12% return on their investment ($60,000 ÷ $500,000). It appears that investors receive exactly what they require, so the investment is just worth making and its *NPV* should be zero.

Why does the calculation above show a negative *NPV?* By deducting interest expenses from cash flows *and* discounting cash flows at a rate that also reflects the after-tax cost of debt, the analyst's *NPV* calculation double counts that financing cost. If we ignore the project's financing cash flows and recalculate the *NPV*, it becomes apparent that the investment indeed just satisfies investors.

Sales	$ 440,000
Operating expenses	−300,000
Pre-tax cash flow	$ 140,000
Taxes (40%)	−56,000
After-tax cash flow	$ 84,000
NPV = −$1,000,000 + $84,000 ÷ 0.084 = $0	

[1]For simplicity, we assume that there is no depreciation expense associated with this investment.

In an operational sense, when using the income statement to develop an investment's relevant cash flows, we ignore financing costs by focusing on *earnings before interest* rather than earnings after deduction of interest expense. Given the structure of an income statement, earnings before interest also excludes all dividends paid to preferred and/or common stockholders. The deduction of interest expense and dividends would double-charge the firm for its financing costs—once in the cash flows and again in the discount rate used to find present value. As we demonstrate later in this chapter, *you should ignore both interest and dividends when developing an investment's relevant cash flows.*

Considering Taxes When determining cash flows, it is important to account for taxes paid to the government. Remember, we evaluate a project from the perspective of the stockholder. Taxes reduce the cash flows that firms can pay to their shareholders; therefore, when performing a capital budgeting analysis, all cash flows should be measured on an after-tax basis.

In the previous example we demonstrated that interest expense and other financing cash flows should be excluded from a project's cash flow projections. Similarly, it is necessary to calculate the taxes that a firm must pay on an investment's cash flows as if the firm had no debt. In other words, the after-tax cash flows used in capital budgeting are those for an all-equity project. The discount rate used in the NPV calculation captures the effects of the tax break that firms receive when they use debt financing, just as it accounts for the interest payments that firms make to bondholders.

The existence of different tax jurisdictions (local, state, national, international) means that determining taxes paid can be somewhat complicated in practice. To keep you focused on the important issues, in this chapter we use simplified illustrations to emphasize the principles involved in measuring after-tax cash flows. Also, to minimize distraction, throughout the chapter we assume that the corporate income tax rate equals 40%.

noncash expenses
Tax-deductible expenses for which there is no corresponding cash outflow in the current period. They include depreciation, amortization, and depletion.

Adjusting for Noncash Expenses Though we have emphasized that managers must focus on the cash flows that an investment generates, they cannot totally ignore noncash expenses (tax-deductible expenses for which there is no corresponding cash outflow in the current period) when projecting cash flows. Noncash expenses, such as depreciation or amortization, affect an investment's cash flows because they reduce the taxes that firms pay. Remember, depreciation deductions reflect the accounting professions' reliance on the accrual method to portray a firm's financial condition. Therefore, when a firm's income statement shows a deduction for depreciation, that does not mean that the firm has actually incurred a cash charge for depreciation. Nevertheless, the depreciation expense reduces income subject to government taxation, and therefore it reduces the firm's tax bill. In other words, the depreciation deduction itself does not represent a cash outflow, but it does produce a real cash flow by shielding some of the firm's cash flows from taxes.

There are two ways to calculate cash flows that take this effect into account. First, we can add noncash expenses back to *net income before interest and after taxes.* Alternatively, we can ignore noncash expenses when calculating *net income before interest and after taxes*, and then add back the tax savings created by noncash deductions.

EXAMPLE

Let's examine two ways to treat noncash expenses to obtain cash flow numbers for a simple project. Suppose a firm spends $30,000 in cash to purchase a fixed asset today that it plans to fully depreciate on a straight-line basis over three years. After acquiring this machine, the firm can produce 10,000 units of some product each year. Each unit costs $1 to make and sells for $3. Given this information, we can construct an income

continued

statement for this project. In each of the next three years, the project income statement would look like this (note that the $30,000 initial investment does not appear here):

Sales	$30,000
Less: Cost of goods	10,000
Gross profit	$20,000
Less: Depreciation	10,000
Pretax income	$10,000
Less: Taxes (40%)	4,000
Net income after taxes	$ 6,000

After the firm spends $30,000 to make this investment, how much cash flow will it generate in each of the subsequent three years? There are two ways to arrive at the answer. First, take net income after taxes and add back depreciation, for which there was no cash outlay:

$$\text{Cash flow} = \text{net income after taxes} + \text{depreciation}$$
$$= \$6,000 + \$10,000 = \underline{\$16,000}$$

Second, calculate net income after taxes, ignoring depreciation expense, and then add back the tax savings generated by the depreciation deduction:

Sales	$30,000	
Less: Cost of goods	10,000	
Pretax income	$20,000	
Less: Taxes (40%)	8,000	
After-tax income	$12,000	
Plus: Depreciation tax savings	4,000	(40% × $10,000)
Total cash flow	$16,000	

? JOB INTERVIEW QUESTION

When calculating the net present value of a project, we can either depreciate the cost of the investment on a straight-line basis or on an accelerated schedule. Which depreciation method should we use?

modified accelerated cost recovery system (MACRS)
Defines the allowable annual depreciation deductions for various classes of assets.

9-1b Depreciation

The largest noncash item for most investment projects is depreciation. Analysts must know the magnitude and timing of depreciation deductions for a given project because these deductions affect the taxes that the firm will pay. Treating depreciation properly is complicated because the law allows firms to use several different depreciation methods. For example, in the United States and the United Kingdom, firms keep separate sets of books, one for tax purposes and one for financial reporting purposes, using different depreciation methods. Their goal is to show low taxable income to the taxing authorities and stable, growing income to investors. As a result, most U.S. and UK firms use accelerated depreciation methods for tax purposes and straight-line depreciation for financial reporting. In contrast, in nations such as Japan, Sweden, and Germany, the law requires that the income firms report to the tax authorities be substantially the same as the income they report to investors. Because we are interested in the cash flow consequences of investments, and because depreciation only affects cash flow through taxes, *we consider only the depreciation method that a firm uses for tax purposes when determining project cash flows.*

Table 9.1 illustrates the tax depreciation allowed in the United States on various classes of equipment. The **modified accelerated cost recovery system (MACRS)** defines the allowable annual depreciation deductions for various classes of assets. IRS rules identify the specific types of equipment that make up each asset class, and it is not always obvious why a particular asset is placed in one class versus another. For example, on the same automobile assembly line you may find equipment in both the three-year and seven-year classes, and the automobiles themselves fall under the five-year class (if they are used for business purposes). A quick glance at the table reveals that U.S. tax laws allow firms to take larger depreciation deductions in the

What Companies Do Globally

Depreciation Rules and Gas Prices

In the spring of 2007, gas prices in the U.S. reached then-record levels. Consumers complained about what it cost them to fill up, and politicians threatened to remove special tax breaks that benefited "big oil."

One widely cited explanation for the jump in gas prices was limited refining capacity in the U.S. To what extent do U.S. tax laws create incentives for new refining capacity? A 2007 study by Ernst and Young compared investment incentives in the oil refining companies embedded in the tax codes of the U.S. and 11 other countries. Essentially, Ernst and Young looked at the depreciation allowances granted to investments in refining plant and equipment and calculated what fraction of an initial investment in refining capacity could be recovered during the investment's first five years. The table below reports their findings. In the U.S., less than two-thirds of the up-front cost could be recovered in five years, compared to almost 80% in Canada and Taiwan, and roughly 90% in Korea and Malaysia. In only three countries were the recovery rates slower than they were in the U.S. Aggravating the problem, the U.S. has one of the highest corporate tax rates among these nations. The report concluded that, combining the high tax rates with relatively long write-off periods for new investments, the U.S. lags much of the world in the incentives it provides for new investments in energy.

Country	Percentage of Capital Costs Recovered after 5 Years Petroleum Refining
Malaysia	90.0%
Korea	89.0%
Canada	79.6%
Taiwan	78.5%
Germany	72.3%
Japan	72.3%
India	66.1%
Brazil	63.1%
U.S.	63.1%
Indonesia	45.0%
China	39.8%
Mexico	32.3%

Source: International Comparison of Depreciation Rules and Tax Rates for Selected Energy Investments, Prepared for American Council on Capital Formation, Ernst and Young, May 2007.

Table 9.1   **U.S. Tax Depreciation Allowed for Various MACRS Asset Classes. Figures Represent the Percentage of an Asset's Depreciable Basis That Is Depreciable in Each Year.**

	Tax Depreciation Schedules by Asset Class					
Year(s)	3-Year	5-Year	7-Year	10-Year	15-Year	20-Year
1	33.33	20.00	14.29	10.00	5.00	3.75
2	44.45	32.00	24.49	18.00	9.50	7.22
3	14.81	19.20	17.49	14.40	8.55	6.68
4	7.41	11.52	12.49	11.52	7.70	6.18
5		11.52	8.93	9.22	6.93	5.71
6		5.76	8.92	7.37	6.23	5.28
7			8.93	6.55	5.90	4.89
8			4.46	6.55	5.90	4.52
9				6.56	5.91	4.46
10				6.55	5.90	4.46
11				3.28	5.91	4.46
12					5.90	4.46
13					5.91	4.46
14					5.90	4.46
15					5.91	4.46
16					2.95	4.46
17–20						4.46
21						2.23

Source: IRS Publication 946

early years of an asset's life. The cash flow effect of this system is to accelerate the tax benefits associated with depreciation.[2]

9-1c Fixed Asset

Many capital budgeting decisions involve the acquisition of a fixed asset. The cost of this investment often appears as the initial cash outflow for a project. Additional factors that influence the cash consequences of asset acquisitions include installation costs and after-tax proceeds from sales of any existing assets that are being replaced.

In many cases, the cost of installing new equipment can be a significant part of a project's initial outlay. For tax purposes, firms combine the asset's purchase price and its installation cost to arrive at the asset's *depreciable basis*, which is often recognized as an immediate cash outflow. In future years, though depreciation itself is not a cash outflow, we have seen that depreciation deductions affect future cash flows by reducing taxes. Depreciation deductions influence taxes through another channel when firms sell old fixed assets. Specifically, when a firm sells an old piece of equipment, there is a tax consequence if the selling price differs from the old equipment's *book value*. If the firm sells an asset for more than its book value, the firm must pay taxes on the gain. If a firm sells an asset for less than its book value, then it can treat the loss as a tax deductible expense.

EXAMPLE

Electrocom Manufacturing purchased $100,000 worth of new computers three years ago. Now it is replacing these machines with newer, faster computers. The firm has a 40% tax rate. Because computers qualify as five-year equipment under MACRS depreciation rules, the company has depreciated 71.20% (20.00% in year 1 + 32.00% in year 2 + 19.20% in year 3) of the old machines' cost, leaving a book value of $28,800. Electrocom sells its old computers to another firm for $10,000. This allows Electrocom to report a loss on the sale of $18,800 ($28,800 book value − $10,000 sale price). Assuming that Electrocom's business is otherwise profitable, it can deduct this loss from other pretax income, resulting in a tax savings of $7,520 (0.40 × $18,800). In the analysis of the new investment project, this $7,520 is treated as a cash inflow.

9-1d Net Working Capital

Consider a retail firm evaluating the opportunity to open a new store. Part of the cash outflow of this investment involves expenditures on fixed assets such as shelving, cash registers, and merchandise displays, but stocking the store with inventory constitutes another important cash outflow. A portion of this cash outflow may be deferred if the firm can purchase inventory from suppliers on credit. By the same token, cash inflows from selling the product may be delayed if the firm sells to customers on credit.

net working capital
The difference between a firm's current assets and its current liabilities.

Just as a firm must account for cash flows on fixed assets, it must also weigh the cash inflows and outflows associated with *changes* in net working capital. The definition of net working capital is simply the difference between current assets and current liabilities. *An increase in net working capital represents a cash outflow.* Net working capital increases if current assets rise (e.g., if the firm buys more inventory) or if current liabilities fall (e.g., if the firm pays down accounts payable). As noted in Chapter 2 (see Table 2.5), any increase (decrease) in a current asset account or any

---

[2]That is, the tax benefits accrue faster than would be the case under straight-line depreciation. An observant reader of Table 9.1 will notice that the law grants four years of depreciation deductions on the three-year asset class, six years of deductions for assets in the five-year class, and so on. There appears to be one "extra year" of depreciation for each asset class because the first year's deduction reflects an assumption that, on average, investments in fixed assets are in service for just one half of the first year. The last half-year of depreciation deductions for an asset falling in the N-year class occurs in year $N + 1$. This is the same as assuming the equipment is put into service on July 1 of the first year. Note also that special rules apply to real estate assets. In general, land is not depreciable. The law does allow depreciation deductions for structures, with the depreciable life of the structure depending on whether it is a commercial or residential property.

decrease (increase) in a current liability account results in a cash outflow (inflow).[3] Net working capital decreases when current assets fall (as when a firm sells inventory) or when current liabilities increase (as when the firm borrows from suppliers). Therefore, *a decrease in net working capital represents a cash inflow.*

EXAMPLE

Have you ever noticed the cottage industries that temporarily spring up around certain big events? Think about the booths that open in shopping malls near the end of each year and sell nothing but calendars. Suppose you are evaluating the opportunity to operate one of these booths from November through January. You begin by ordering (on credit) $15,000 worth of calendars. Your suppliers require a $5,000 payment on the first day of each month, starting in December. You anticipate that you will sell (entirely on a cash basis) 30% of your inventory in November, 60% in December, and 10% in January. You plan to keep $500 in the cash register until you close the booth on February 1. Your balance sheet at the beginning of each month looks like this:

	Oct. 1	Nov. 1	Dec. 1	Jan. 1	Feb. 1
Cash	$ 0	$ 500	$ 500	$ 500	$ 0
Inventory	0	15,000	10,500	1,500	0
Accounts payable	0	15,000	10,000	5,000	0
Net working capital	0	500	1,000	−3,000	0
Monthly net working capital *change*	NA	+500	+500	−4,000	+3,000

The cash flows associated with *changes* in net working capital are as follows:

$500 cash outflow from October to November

$500 cash outflow from November to December

$4,000 cash inflow from December to January

$3,000 cash outflow from January to February

Notice that at the start of November, purchases of inventory are entirely on credit, so the increase in inventory is exactly offset by an increase in accounts payable. The only working capital cash outflow occurs because you must raise $500 to put in the cash register. During November, sales reduce your inventory by $4,500 (inflow), but you pay suppliers $5,000 (outflow). You still have the same amount in the cash register as before, $500, so on net you have an outflow of $500, exactly equal to the increase in net working capital from the prior month. During the month of December, sales reduce your inventory by $9,000 (inflow), and you pay $5,000 to suppliers (outflow). That leaves you with cash inflow of $4,000, equal to the decrease in net working capital during the month. By February 1, sales reduce your inventory by the remaining $1,500 in calendars (inflow), you empty $500 from the cash register (inflow), and you pay the last $5,000 to suppliers (outflow). The net effect is a $3,000 cash outflow during January.[4]

9-1e Terminal Value

Some investments have a well-defined life span. The life span may be determined by the physical life of a piece of equipment, by the length of time until a patent expires, or by the period of time covered by a leasing or licensing agreement. Often, however, investments have an indefinite life. For example, when a company acquires another company as a going concern, as noted in the stock valuation discussion in Chapter 5, it generally expects the acquired company's assets to continue to generate cash flow for a very long period of time.

---

[3]Of course, one important current asset account is cash. It may seem counterintuitive to argue that if the balances in the cash account increase, then that should be treated as a cash outflow. However, consider again the example of a new retail store. If the company opens a new store, a small amount of cash will have to be held in that store for transactions purposes. Holding fixed the amount of cash that the firm maintains in all of its other stores and in its corporate accounts, opening a new store requires a net increase in the firm's cash holdings. If the firm did not open the new store, then it could invest the cash that it would have held in reserve in the new store in a different project. Likewise, consider what happens if the company decides to close one of its stores. The cash kept in reserve at that location can be redeployed for another use, so reducing cash at that store represents a cash inflow to the firm as a whole. As we will see in Chapter 17, cash management tools have become so sophisticated today that few investments require significant changes in cash holdings. Changes in the other working capital items, such as inventory, receivables, and payables, typically have a much greater cash flow impact than changes in cash balances.

[4]In this section we are looking only at the working capital cash flows associated with this project. We have not considered any fixed asset investment up front, nor have we included the profits from selling calendars at a markup, or the labor costs of operating the booth. These issues would certainly be considered in a complete analysis of the investment.

? WHAT TO ASK

How far out into the future do you take financial projections for major investments?

terminal value
The value of all of a project's cash flows beyond a certain date in the future.

When managers invest in an asset with a long life span, they typically do not construct cash flow forecasts more than five to ten years into the future. These long-term forecasts can be inaccurate to the point that the fine detail in an item-by-item cash flow projection is not very meaningful. Instead, managers project detailed cash flow estimates for five to ten years, then calculate a project's terminal value, the value of all of a project's cash flows beyond a certain date in the future. There are a number of ways to calculate terminal value.

Perhaps the most common approach to calculate the terminal value is to take the final year of cash flow projections and make an assumption that all future cash flows will grow at a constant rate. For example, in valuing a large acquisition, many acquiring firms project the target company's cash flows for five to ten years in the future. After that, they assume that cash flows will grow at a rate equal to the growth rate in gross domestic product (GDP) for the economy.[5]

EXAMPLE

Suppose that analysts at JDS Inc. are analyzing the potential acquisition of SDL Inc. They project that the acquisition of SDL Inc. will generate the following new stream of cash flows:

Year 1	$0.50 billion
Year 2	1.00 billion
Year 3	1.75 billion
Year 4	2.50 billion
Year 5	3.25 billion

In year 6 and beyond, analysts believe that cash flows will continue to grow at 5% per year. What is the terminal value of this investment? Recall that in Chapters 3 and 5, we learned that we can determine the present value, at a discount rate r, of a stream of cash flows growing at a perpetual rate, g, by using the following formula:

$$PV_t = \frac{CF_{t+1}}{r - g}$$

We know that the year-6 cash flow is 5% more than in year 5, or $3.41 billion ($1.05 \times$ $3.25 billion). Put that number in the numerator of the equation. We also know that $g = 5\%$. Suppose that JDS Inc. discounted the cash flows of this investment at 10%. Using the formula above, we can determine that the present value, *as of year 5*, of cash flows in years 6 and beyond equals the following:

$$PV_5 = \frac{\$3.41}{0.10 - 0.05} = \$68.20$$

This means that the terminal value, the value of the project at the end of year 5, equals $68.20 billion. To determine the entire value of the project, discount this figure along with all the other cash flows at 10% to obtain a total value of $48.67 billion:[6]

$$\frac{\$0.5}{1.10^1} + \frac{\$1}{1.10^2} + \frac{\$1.75}{1.10^3} + \frac{\$2.5}{1.10^4} + \frac{\$3.25}{1.10^5} + \frac{\$68.2}{1.10^5} = \$48.67$$

Given this set of assumptions, the most JDS Inc. should pay to acquire SDL Inc. is about $48.67 billion. Notice that the terminal value is enormous relative to the cash flows that occur in years 1 through 5. This highlights that accurately estimating terminal value is very important.

Notice in the preceding example that the terminal value was very large relative to all the other cash flows. If we discount the terminal value for five years at 10%, we find that $42.35 billion of the project's total $48.67 billion present value comes from the terminal-value assumptions. Those proportions are not uncommon for long-lived investments, illustrating just how important estimates of terminal value can be in assessing an investment's merit. Analysts must think very carefully about the assumptions they make when calculating terminal value.

---

[5]We emphasize that when companies assume that an investment's cash flows will grow at some rate in perpetuity, the rate of growth in nominal GDP, either in the local economy or the world economy, serves as a maximum potential long-run growth rate. Why? If an investment generates cash flows that grow forever at a rate that exceeds the growth of nominal GDP, then mathematically, that one investment eventually becomes the entire economy.

[6]Notice that this is the gross present value, not the *NPV*, because in this example we are not deducting any up-front costs incurred to acquire SDL Inc.

For example, the growth rate used to calculate a project's terminal value does not always equal the long-run growth rate of the economy. A factory with fixed capacity might offer zero growth in cash flows, or growth that just keeps pace with inflation, once the firm hits the capacity constraint.

Several other methods maintain widespread application in terminal-value calculations. One method calculates terminal value by multiplying the final year's cash flow estimate by a market multiple such as a *price-to-cash-flow ratio* (price-to-earnings and price-to-sales ratios are also used at times) for publicly traded firms with characteristics similar to those of the investment. For example, the last specific cash flow estimate for the SDL Inc. acquisition was $3.25 billion in year 5. JDS Inc. may observe that the average price-to-cash-flow ratio for companies in this industry is 20. Multiplying $3.25 billion by 20 results in a terminal value estimate of $65 billion, quite close to the estimate obtained from the perpetual growth model. One hazard in using this approach is that market multiples fluctuate through time, which means that when year 5 finally arrives, even if SDL Inc. generates $3.25 billion in cash flow as anticipated, the market may place a much lower value on that cash flow than it did when the acquisition originally took place.

Other approaches to this problem use an investment's book value or its expected liquidation value to estimate the terminal-value figure. Using *book value* is most common when the investment involves physical plant and equipment with a limited useful life. In such a case, firms may plausibly assume that after a number of years of depreciation deductions, the asset's book value will be zero. Depending on whether the asset has fairly standard characteristics that would enable other firms to use it, its *liquidation value* may be positive or it may be zero.[7] Finding liquidation value often involves inclusion of the tax cash flows that result from selling the asset for a price that differs from its book value at the time of sale. Some assets may even have negative terminal values if disposing of them entails substantial costs. Projects that involve the use of substances hazardous to the environment fit this description. When an investment has a fixed life span, part of the terminal value or terminal cash flow may also include recovery of working capital investments. When a retail store closes, for example, the firm realizes a cash inflow from liquidating inventory.

9-1 Concept Review Questions

1. Why is it important for the financial analyst to (a) focus on incremental cash flows, (b) ignore financing costs, (c) consider taxes, and (d) adjust for noncash expenses when estimating a project's relevant cash flows?

2. Why do we consider *changes* in net working capital associated with a project to be cash inflows or outflows rather than consider the absolute level of net working capital?

3. For what kinds of investments does terminal value account for a substantial fraction of the total project *NPV*, and for what kinds of investments is terminal value relatively unimportant?

9-2 | Incremental Cash Flows

We have seen that many investment problems have similar types of cash flows that analysts must estimate: initial outlays on fixed assets and working capital, operating cash flow, and terminal value. But in a broader sense, there is only one type of cash flow that matters in capital budgeting analysis—*incremental cash flow*. To rephrase the oath that witnesses take in television courtroom dramas, analysts must focus on "all incremental cash flow and nothing but incremental cash flow." Determining

---

[7]It has been estimated that firms can expect to recover no more than 20–50% of the original purchase cost of a new machine, once it has been installed. This finding is applicable even for assets with reasonably active secondary markets.

Finance in Your Life

The Value of an MBA

You earn $60,000 per year working as an engineer for a software developer, and you pay taxes at a flat rate of 35%. You expect salary increases each year of about 5%. Lately, you have been thinking about going back to school to earn an MBA. A few months ago, you spent $1,000 to enroll in a Graduate Management Admission Test (GMAT) study course, and $2,000 visiting various MBA programs in the United States. From your research on MBA programs, you have learned a great deal about the costs and benefits of the degree. At the beginning of each of the next two years, your out-of-pocket costs for tuition, fees, and textbooks will be $35,000. You expect to spend roughly the same amount on room and board in graduate school that you spend now. At the end of two years, you anticipate that you'll get a job offer with a salary of $90,000, and you expect that your pay will increase by 8% per year over your career (spanning roughly the next 30 years). The schedule of incremental cash flows for the next few periods looks like this:

Year 0	−$35,000
Year 1	− 35,000
Year 2	+ 15,503
Year 3	+ 18,032

Observe that we did not include the $1,000 spent studying for the GMAT and the $2,000 spent visiting MBA programs in the cash outflow for year 0. Those costs have already been incurred, and they cannot be recovered even if you decide not to get an MBA, so they are not incremental. The cash inflow figures for years 2 and 3 require some explanation. Had you stayed at your current job for the next two years, rather than go back to school, your pay would have increased to $66,150 [$60,000 × (1 + 0.05)²]. Therefore, the difference between that figure and your $90,000 post-MBA salary represents a net cash inflow of $23,850. Assuming that you pay about 35% of your earnings in taxes, the after-tax inflow would be $15,503 [$23,850 × (1.00 − 0.35)]. In year 3, you expect to earn 8% more, or $97,200, compared with what you would have earned at your old job, $69,458 [$66,150 × (1 + 0.05)]. The after-tax cash inflow in year 3 equals $18,032 [($97,200 − $69,458) × (1.00 − 0.35)]. If you carry these steps out for 30 years, you will quickly see that the MBA has a substantial positive *NPV* at almost any reasonable discount rate.

? WHAT TO ASK

When you are evaluating a new investment proposal, how do you try to quantify potential reactions by competitors and factor those into your financial analysis?

which cash flows are incremental and which are not for a given project can become complicated at times.

For example, suppose you complete your undergraduate degree, work for a few years, and then consider quitting your job to return to school to pursue an MBA degree. Many of the incremental outflows associated with going back to school are fairly obvious, such as tuition and fees, the cost of textbooks, and possibly relocation expenses. What about expenditures on room and board? Whether or not you decide to pursue an MBA, you still have to eat and have a place to sleep at night. Therefore, room and board expenditures are not incremental to your decision to go back to school.[8]

The cash inflows associated with an investment in an MBA degree are more difficult to estimate. You believe that obtaining an MBA degree offers the opportunity to earn higher pay after graduation than you earned before returning to school. Furthermore, you hope that, after obtaining an MBA, your salary will increase at a much faster rate than it otherwise would have. The net cash flow equals the difference in the salary that you earn with an MBA versus the salary that you would have earned without an MBA, after taxes, of course.

Incremental cash flows should be calculated relative to what the world would be like if the project were not pursued. For example, one of the largest investments that companies make is acquiring another business. In an acquisition, the bidder evaluates the incremental cash flows from making the acquisition relative to what the bidder's cash flows would be if the target firm remained independent or was acquired

---

[8]Of course, you may spend more on housing and food while you're working than when you're in graduate school. In that case, the difference in spending would be an incremental cash inflow.

**Paul Savastano, Director
of Information Technology,
Sprint Nextel Corp.**

*"So the challenge becomes, how do you quantify
the benefits when a big piece of the investment is
going to be for things that people never see?"*

See the entire interview at **SMART | finance**

Smart Practices Video

sunk costs
Costs that have already
been paid and are therefore
not recoverable.

opportunity costs
Forgone cash flows on an
alternative investment that
the firm or individual decides not to make.

by another firm. Indeed, managers often state that one of
their motivations for buying other companies is to keep them
out of the hands of competitors. If a bidding firm believes
that its existing business would be negatively impacted if a
competitor purchased the target company, then the reduction
in cash flows that a successful acquisition prevents represents
a cash inflow from the acquisition. As you can imagine, estimating the consequences of a competitor's actions on a firm's
existing business is very difficult.

9-2a Sunk Costs

A sunk cost is a cost that has already been paid and is therefore
not recoverable; thus, it is irrelevant to the investment deci-
sion. For instance, in the *Finance in Your Life* example, your cash outflows did not
include the money you had already spent on the GMAT review and on visits to MBA
programs. Clearly, these costs are not recoverable whether or not you ultimately decide to give up your job and return to school. The money has already been spent and
therefore has no bearing on your investment decision. Simply stated, *sunk costs are
irrelevant and therefore should be ignored when determining an investment's relevant
cash flows.*

9-2b Opportunity Costs

In the *Finance in Your Life* box, we made a number of simplifying assumptions in
our analysis of the decision to pursue an MBA. For instance, we assumed that you
received your pay in a lump sum each year and that you faced a flat tax rate. Of
course, the incremental salary that you earn arrives monthly, and your higher earnings may be taxed at a higher rate. All these effects are easy to account for, although
the calculations become a bit more tedious.

However, there is one major error in our analysis of your investment problem.
We ignored a significant opportunity cost. Undertaking one investment frequently
means passing on an alternative. In capital budgeting, the opportunity costs of an
investment are the cash flows that the firm (or in this case, you) will not receive
from other investments (or actions) as a result of undertaking the proposed investment. If you did not attend school, you would earn $60,000 [$39,000 after
taxes ($60,000 × (1.00 − 0.35))] the first year and $63,000 [$40,950 after taxes
($63,000 × (1.00 − 0.35))] the second year. This is your *opportunity cost* of
getting an MBA, and it is just as important in the overall calculation as your out-
of-pocket expenses for tuition, fees, and books. Though it is still true, given the
assumptions of our example, that the *NPV* of an MBA is positive, the value of
the degree falls substantially once we recognize opportunity costs. As every MBA
student knows, opportunity costs are real, not just hypothetical numbers from
a textbook. Directors of MBA programs all over the world know that MBA applications are countercyclical. That is, the number of students applying to MBA
programs increases during economic downturns and falls during booms. The most
plausible explanation of this phenomenon is that potential MBA students face
higher opportunity costs when the economy is strong.

Probably the most common type of opportunity cost encountered in capital budgeting problems involves the alternative use of an asset owned by a firm. Suppose
that a company owns raw land that it purchased some years ago in anticipation of an
expansion opportunity. Now the firm is ready to expand by building new facilities on
the raw land. Even though the firm may have paid for the land many years ago, using
the land for expansion entails an incremental opportunity cost. The opportunity cost
is the cash that would be received if the firm sold the land or leased it for another
purpose today. That cost (the cash inflows given up) should be factored into the *NPV*
calculation for the firm's expansion plans.

9-2c Cannibalization

cannibalization
Loss of sales of a firm's existing product when a new product is introduced.

Scott Lee,
Texas A&M University

"We have found evidence that the market punishes firms that were involved in defense procurement fraud."

See the entire interview at **SMART** | finance

Smart Ethics Video

Incremental cash flows can show up in surprising forms. One type of incremental cash outflow that firms must be careful to measure when launching a new product is called **cannibalization**. This involves the "substitution effect" that frequently occurs when a firm introduces a new product. Typically, some of the new product's sales come at the expense of the firm's existing products. In the food products industry, sales of a low-fat version of a popular product may reduce sales of the original (presumably, high-fat) version. Some consumers may effectively substitute purchase of the new "improved" product for purchase of the original product, which has the effect on net of reducing the incremental cash flows of the new project.[9] Firms carefully consider the incremental cash outflows from existing product sales that are cannibalized by a newer product.[10]

In the next section, we work through an extended example of a capital budgeting project, illustrating how to apply the principles from this section to calculate the project's cash flows each year. Before getting into the details, we want to remind you of the overall picture. Cash flows are important because they are necessary to calculate a project's *NPV*. Estimating the *NPV* is important because it provides an estimate of the increase or decrease in shareholder value that will occur if the firm invests. Research has demonstrated the connection between capital investment decisions and shareholder value by showing that stock prices rise on average when firms publicly announce significant new capital investment programs. This suggests that, on average, companies invest in positive *NPV* projects.

9-2 Concept Review Questions

4. What are *sunk costs* and *cannibalization*, and do they affect the process of determining a proposed investment's incremental cash flows?

5. A real estate development firm owns a fully leased forty-story office building. A tenant recently moved its offices out of two stories of the building, leaving the space temporarily vacant. If the real estate firm considers moving its own offices into this forty-story office building, what cost should it assign for the space? Is the cost of the vacant space zero because the firm paid for the building long ago, a cost that is *sunk*, or is there an incremental *opportunity cost*?

6. Suppose that an analyst makes a mistake and calculates the *NPV* of an investment project by discounting the project's *contribution to net income* each year rather than by discounting its *relevant cash flows*. Would you expect the *NPV* based on net income to be higher or lower than the *NPV* calculated using the relevant cash flows?

9-3 Cash Flows for Protect IT, Incorporated

Protect IT, Inc., is a (fictitious) company that makes protective cases for smart phones such as the iPhone. The company is considering a proposal to expand its product selection to include protective covers for tablet devices like the iPad, and so far the firm has spent $10,000 analyzing the potential market for such a product. Management

---

[9]But it's even more complicated than that. If this company does not introduce a low-fat product line, a competitor might, which would reduce sales of high-fat products anyway. Thus, this company needs to consider the incremental cash flows from introducing a new, low-fat product line relative to what cash flows would be if this company did not introduce low-fat products, considering that someone else might.

[10]On a capital budgeting exam problem, one of our students mentioned that a firm needed to be wary that its new product should not "cannibalize the existing sales force." Needless to say, that is not the kind of cannibalization that we have in mind, although should it occur, it would certainly represent an incremental cash outflow.

believes that many purchasers of cell phone cases will also buy tablets, and so the company has a built-in clientele for the new product line. If the company decides to undertake this project, it will begin selling new products next month when its new fiscal year begins. The company would therefore make the required investment before the end of the current fiscal year (year 0). The company accepts projects with positive *NPVs*, and it uses a 15% discount rate to calculate *NPV*.

Up-front costs include $50,000 in computer equipment that the firm will depreciate for five years on a straight-line basis starting in year 1. Protect IT must also make an immediate investment of $4,500 in inventory, though $2,500 of that can be purchased on credit. For transactions purposes, the firm plans to increase its cash balance by $1,000 immediately. Managers expect the average selling price of its new tablet covers to be $13.50, and they expect that price to remain constant indefinitely. Protect IT expects to finance this investment using the cash flow generated from its existing business.

Managers expect unit sales volume to start at 4,500 and to grow rapidly for a few years. In the long run, they predict that unit sales will increase by 4% per year. Cost of goods sold will equal 72% of sales revenue, with selling, general, and administrative expenses at 10% of sales.

As sales grow, Protect IT will hold slightly larger cash balances and make additional investments in inventory and receivables. Each year accounts receivable will be equivalent to one-month's sales, and inventory balances will be about 12.5% of sales. We assume that after the initial purchase of new computers, no additional fixed asset investments will be necessary. In addition, Protect IT's suppliers will provide trade credit on terms such that the accounts payable balance will equal about 10% of cost of goods sold for each year.

Table 9.2 shows various projections for the investment project. The top two lines list anticipated selling prices and unit volumes in each of the next six years. Below that appears a series of projected income statements for the next six years. Top-line revenue equals the product of expected selling price and unit volume each year. Next, the table subtracts cost of goods sold, SG&A expenses, and depreciation to arrive at pre-tax profit. Taxes constitute 40% of pre-tax profit.

Beneath the income statement appears a series of abbreviated projected balance sheets. Each shows the project's total asset requirements (including both current and fixed assets) as well as the financing available from suppliers in the form of accounts payable. As mentioned previously, any additional financing the project requires will come from internally generated funds from the already profitable cell phone cover business.

To determine whether this is an investment opportunity worth taking, we determine the project's cash flows through time and discount them at 15% to calculate the project's *NPV*. As part of this calculation, we have to estimate the value of the endeavor beyond the sixth year. In other words, we have to estimate the project's terminal value.

9-3a Year 0 Cash Flow

The firm will have cash outlays of $50,000 for computer equipment immediately (year 0). The firm will also have a cash outlay of $3,000 for its net investment in working capital. That consists of outflows of $1,000 to increase the cash balance and $4,500 to purchase inventory, and an inflow of $2,500 from an increase in trade credit. Therefore, the net cash flow for year 0 is:

Increase in fixed assets	−$50,000
Increase in working capital	−$ 3,000
Total cash outflow	−$53,000

Notice that we do not include the $10,000 that Protect IT spent studying the potential market for covers for tablet devices. That is a sunk cost that cannot be

Table 9.2   **Projections for Protect IT's Investment Project**

Year	0	1	2	3	4	5	6
Price per unit	$13.50	$13.50	$13.50	$13.50	$13.50	$13.50	$13.50
Units	0	4,500	10,000	16,000	22,000	24,000	25,000
Abbreviated Project Income Statement							
Revenue	$ 0	$60,750	$135,000	$216,000	$297,000	$324,000	$337,500
Less: Cost of goods sold	0	43,740	97,200	155,520	213,840	233,280	243,000
Gross profit	$ 0	$17,010	$ 37,800	$ 60,480	$ 83,160	$ 90,720	$ 94,500
Less: SG&A expense	0	6,075	13,500	21,600	29,700	32,400	33,750
Less: Depreciation	0	10,000	10,000	10,000	10,000	10,000	0
Pretax profit	$ 0	$ 935	$ 14,300	$ 28,880	$ 43,460	$ 48,320	$ 60,750
Taxes	0	374	5,720	11,552	17,384	19,328	24,300
$After-tax profit	$ 0	$ 561	$ 8,580	$ 17,328	$ 26,076	$ 28,992	$ 36,450
Abbreviated Project Balance Sheet							
Cash	$ 1,000	$ 2,000	$ 2,500	$ 3,000	$ 3,200	$ 3,300	$ 3,500
Accounts receivable	0	5,063	11,250	18,000	24,750	27,000	28,125
Inventory	4,500	7,594	16,875	27,000	37,125	40,500	42,188
Current assets	$,500	$14,657	$30,625	$48,000	$65,075	$70,800	$73,813
Gross P&E	$50,000	$50,000	$50,000	$50,000	$50,000	$50,000	$50,000
Less: Accumulated depr.	0	10,000	20,000	30,000	40,000	50,000	50,000
Net P&E	$50,000	$40,000	$30,000	$20,000	$10,000	$ 0	$ 0
Total assets	$55,500	$54,657	$60,625	$68,000	$75,075	$70,800	$73,813
Accounts payable	$ 2,500	$ 4,374	$ 9,720	$15,520	$21,384	$23,328	$24,300

recovered, even if the company decides not to pursue this investment, so it is not an incremental cash flow.

9-3b Year 1 Cash Flow

In year 1, the project earns after-tax income of $561. To determine cash flows, we add back the noncash depreciation charge of $10,000. There is no new investment in fixed assets in year 1, but the net working capital balance rises from $3,000 to $10,283. This represents a cash outflow of $7,283, which consists of the following components:

	Year 0	Year 1
Cash	$1,000	$ 2,000
Receivables	0	5,063
Inventory	4,500	7,594
Payables	−2,500	−4,374
Net Working Capital	$3,000	$10,283

You can calculate the net cash outflow from new investments in working capital on an item-by-item basis as follows:

Outflows
Increase in cash	$1,000
Increase in receivables	5,063
Increase in inventory	3,094
Total working capital outflows	$9,157

Inflows
Increase in payables	$1,874

Net cash flow from working capital = inflows − outflows = −$7,283

Summing up, the incremental cash flows for year 1 are as follows:

Net income	$ 561
Depreciation	10,000
Net working capital	−7,283
Net cash flow	$ 3,278

9-3c Year 2 Cash Flow

In year 2 we simply repeat the steps we followed to arrive at year 1's cash flow numbers. Net income equals $8,580. To that, add back the $10,000 noncash depreciation deduction. Next, determine the change in working capital. The working capital balance increased from $10,283 in year 1 to $20,905 in year 2, so this represents a cash outflow of $10,622. As in year 1, there are no new investments in fixed assets to consider, so the net cash flow in year 2 equals:

Net income	$ 8,580
Depreciation	10,000
Increase in working capital	−10,622
Net cash flow	$ 7,958

Table 9.3 illustrates the annual net cash flows for the investment project all the way through the sixth year. Several interesting patterns emerge from this table. First, the project's cash flows grow rapidly for the first five years, primarily because sales volume is growing. However, notice that in year 6 two interesting things happen. First, tax savings from depreciation deductions run out, so an important source of cash inflows stops. Second, the change in working capital in year 6 is relatively small compared to the other years. Remember that the thing driving Protect IT to invest in more working capital each year was sales growth. By year 6, sales growth has slowed to the long-run rate of 4%, so the firm doesn't need to increase working capital items as fast as it had in the project's first five years.

Because this project starts generating net cash inflows as early as year 1, it is probably not representative of most investment projects that firms undertake. Many projects, especially those that involve launching new ventures or product lines, take several years before they produce positive cash flow. If Protect IT discounts the project's cash flows at 15%, it has a positive *NPV* of $12,824, counting only the first six years' cash flows. But that probably understates the investment's true value because Protect IT will surely operate this business beyond year 6. Therefore, to complete the analysis, we need to estimate this venture's terminal value.

9-3d Terminal Value

We produce two different terminal-value estimates for this project. In the first, we assume that by year 6 the project has reached a steady state, meaning that cash flows will grow at 4% per year indefinitely. In the second, we assume that the firm sells its

Table 9.3	Annual Net Cash Flow Estimates for Protect IT's Investment Project						
	Year 0	Year 1	Year 2	Year 3	Year 4	Year 5	Year 6
New fixed assets	$50,000	$ 0	$ 0	$ 0	$ 0	$ 0	$ 0
Change in working capital	−3,000[a]	−7,283	−10,622	−11,575	−11,211	−3,781	−2,041
Net income	0	561	8,580	17,328	26,076	28,992	36,450
Depreciation	0	10,000	10,000	10,000	10,000	10,000	0
Net cash flow	−$53,000	$3,278	$ 7,958	$15,753	$24,865	$35,211	$34,409

[a]Represents the initial working capital investment.

investment at the end of year 6 and receives a cash payment equal to the project's book value.

In year 6, the project generates a net cash inflow of $34,409. Assuming that cash flows beyond the sixth year grow at 4% per year, and discounting those cash flows at 15%, we can use the equation for a growing perpetuity (Equation 3.11) to determine the terminal value of the project *as of the end of year 6,* as follows:

$$\text{Terminal value} = \frac{\$35,785}{0.15 - 0.04} = \$325,318$$

Notice that the numerator of $35,785 in the expression above is the estimated year 7 cash flow, which is 4% greater than the cash flow in year 6 (i.e., $1.04 \times \$34,409 = \$35,785$). Remember (from Chapter 3, Equation 3.11, and Chapter 5, Equation 5.4), when valuing a stream of cash flows that grows at a perpetual rate, the *value today* equals *next year's cash flow* divided by the difference between the discount rate and the growth rate. Thus, to determine the terminal value in year 6, we must use the cash flow in year 7 in the numerator.

As a second approach, assume that the terminal value of the project simply equals the book value at the end of year 6. At that time, the firm has fully depreciated its investment in computers, so its only assets are cash ($3,500), receivables ($28,125), and inventory ($42,188). Offsetting those assets are $24,300 in accounts payable, so the book value of the venture is just $49,513, a far cry from our prior terminal value estimate. The magnitude of that difference should not surprise us too much. In general, as noted in Chapter 5, a profitable, growing business will have a market value that exceeds its book value.

A third way to estimate the project's terminal value is to use a market multiple approach. A Protect IT analyst could multiply the project's expected sales, earnings, or cash flow in year 6 times a market multiple based on comparable companies. For example, suppose that at the present time, companies that make accessories for the iPad sell at a price-to-sales ratio of about 1.5. Table 9.2 projects that in six years the line of protective covers will generate $337,500 in revenue. Multiplying this times 1.5 suggests that the product line could be worth $506,250 at the end of year 6. Clearly, different methods of calculating a project's terminal value can lead to very different estimates.

9-3e Protect IT Project *NPV*

Putting all this together, we arrive at different estimates of the project's *NPV*, depending on which estimate of terminal value we use. Assuming that this business will continue to increase profits forever, we arrive at the following *NPV*:

$$NPV = -\$53,000 + \frac{\$3,278}{1.15^1} + \frac{\$7,958}{1.15^2} + \frac{\$15,753}{1.15^3} + \frac{\$24,865}{1.15^4} + \frac{\$35,211}{1.15^5}$$
$$+ \frac{\$34,409 + \$325,318}{1.15^6} = \$153,468$$

On the other hand, if we assume that the terminal value is only equal to book value after six years, then we arrive at the following *NPV*:

$$NPV = -\$53,000 + \frac{\$3,278}{1.15^1} + \frac{\$7,958}{1.15^2} + \frac{\$15,753}{1.15^3}$$
$$+ \frac{\$24,865}{1.15^4} + \frac{\$35,211}{1.15^5} + \frac{\$34,409 + \$49,513}{1.15^6}$$
$$= \$34,230$$

In this example, the project yields a positive *NPV*, no matter which terminal-value estimate we choose, so investing in the new product line will increase shareholder wealth. However, in many real-world situations, especially those involving

David Nickel, Controller for Intel Communications Group, Intel Corp.

"Capital budgeting is the key theme for deciding which programs get funded."

See the entire interview at **SMART | finance**

Smart Practices Video

long-lived investments, the "go" or "no-go" decision will depend critically on terminal-value assumptions. It is not at all uncommon for the perpetual growth and market multiple approaches to yield positive *NPVs*, while the book value approach shows a negative *NPV*. In that case, managers have to think more deeply and realistically about the long-run value of their enterprise.

9-3 Concept Review Questions

7. We did not discuss the possibility that the new product line might cannibalize sales of existing products. Is that likely to be a problem in this situation? Why or why not?

8. What are three ways that Protect IT might estimate the *terminal value* of this project?

9. Suppose Congress passes legislation that allows Protect IT to depreciate its investment in computers over three years rather than five. In general, what impact would this legislation have on the project's *NPV*?

9-4 Special Problems in Capital Budgeting

Though our objective in writing this book was to provide the most real-world focus possible, real business situations are more complex and occur in more varieties than any textbook can reasonably convey. In this section, we examine common business decisions with special characteristics that make them more difficult to analyze than the examples we have covered thus far. We will see that whereas the analysis may require a little more thinking, the principles involved are the same ones discussed throughout this chapter and Chapter 8.

9-4a Capital Rationing

In Chapter 8, we asked the following question: If a firm must choose between several investment opportunities, all worth taking, how does it prioritize projects? We learned that the *IRR* and *PI* methods sometimes rank projects differently than the *NPV* does, although properly applied, all three techniques generate the same accept or reject decisions.

? WHAT TO ASK

At your firm, how is the overall budget for capital investments established?

A Fundamental Question There is a fundamental question that we have avoided until now. If the firm has many projects with positive *NPVs* (or investments with acceptable *IRRs*), why not accept all of them? One possibility is that the company may be constrained by the availability of trained and reliable personnel—especially managers. This prevents the firm from growing extremely rapidly, especially because adding a new product or project would require managerial talent of the highest order. Another possibility is that the firm simply does not have enough money to finance all its attractive investment opportunities. But why couldn't a large, publicly traded firm raise money by issuing new shares to investors and using the proceeds to undertake any and all appealing investments?

If you watch firms closely over time, you notice that most do not often issue new common stock. As Chapter 11 discusses more fully, firms generally prefer to finance investments with internally generated cash flow and will only infrequently raise money in the external capital markets by issuing new equity. There are several possible reasons for this reluctance to issue new equity. First, when firms announce their plans to raise new equity capital, they may send an unintended negative signal to the market. Perhaps investors may interpret the announcement as a sign that the firm's existing investments are not generating acceptable levels of cash flow. Perhaps investors may see the decision to issue new shares as an indication that managers believe the firm's stock is overvalued. In either case, investors may react negatively to this announcement, causing the stock price to fall. Undoubtedly, managers try to persuade investors that the funds being raised will be invested in profitable projects, but convincing investors that this is the true motive for the issue is an uphill struggle.

A second reason why managers may avoid issuing new equity is that by doing so, they dilute their ownership stake in the firm (unless they participate in the offering by purchasing some of the new shares). A smaller ownership stake means that managers control a shrinking block of votes, raising the potential of a corporate takeover or other threat to their control of the firm.

In conversations with senior executives, we often hear a third reason why firms do not fund every investment project that looks promising. Behind every idea for a new investment is a person, someone who may have an emotional attachment to the idea, or a career-building motivation for proposing the idea in the first place. Upper-level managers are wise to be a little skeptical of the cash flow forecasts they see on projects with favorable *NPVs* or *IRRs*. It is a given that every cash flow forecast will prove to be wrong. If the forecasting process is unbiased, half the time forecasts will be too pessimistic, and half the time they will be too optimistic. Which half is likely to surface on the radar screen of a CFO or CEO in a large corporation? (Answer: The optimistic ones.) Establishing an annual budget constraint on capital expenditures to ration capital is one mechanism by which senior managers impose discipline on the capital budgeting process. By doing so, they hope to weed out some of the investment proposals with an optimistic bias built into the cash flow projections.

capital rationing
The situation where a firm has more positive *NPV* projects than its available budget can fund. It should choose the combination of those projects that maximizes shareholder wealth.

Selecting the Best Projects Under Rationing Regardless of their motivation, managers cannot always invest in every project that offers a positive *NPV*. In such an environment, capital rationing occurs. Given a set of attractive investment opportunities, managers must choose the combination of projects that maximizes shareholder wealth, subject to the constraint of limited funds. The following example demonstrates the application of this approach for selecting investments under capital rationing.

EXAMPLE

Assume that a particular firm has five projects to choose from as shown in Table 9.4. Note that all of the projects require an initial cash outflow in year 0 that is followed by four years of cash inflows. All of the projects have positive *NPVs*, *IRRs* that exceed the firm's 12% required return, and *PIs* greater than 1.0. Notice that the first project has the highest *IRR* and the highest *PI*, but project 5 has the largest *NPV*. This is again the familiar *scale problem* discussed in Chapter 8. Suppose that this firm can invest no more than $300 million this year. What portfolio of investments maximizes shareholder wealth?

Notice that there are several combinations of projects that satisfy the constraint of investing no more than $300 million. If we begin by accepting the project with the highest *PI*, then continue to accept additional projects until we bump into the $300 million capital constraint, we will invest in projects 1, 2, and 3. With these three projects, we have invested just $250 million, but that does not leave us with enough capital to fund either project 4 or 5. The total *NPV* obtainable from the first three projects is $170.8 ($59.2 + $52.0 + $59.6) million. No other combination of projects that satisfies the capital constraint yields a higher aggregate *NPV*. For example, investing in projects 3 and 5, thereby using up the full allotment of $300 million in capital, generates a total *NPV* of just $130.6 ($59.6 + $71.0) million. Likewise, investing in projects 1, 2, and 4, another combination that utilizes all $300 million in capital, generates an aggregate *NPV* of $149.6 ($59.2 + $52.0 + $38.4) million.[11]

? JOB INTERVIEW QUESTION

How would you decide between two machines, one that costs more and last longer versus another one that is less expensive but must be replaced more often?

9-4b Equipment Replacement and Equivalent Annual Cost

Assume that a firm must purchase an electronic control device to monitor its assembly line. Two types of devices are available. Both meet the firm's minimum quality standards, but they differ in three dimensions. First, one device is less costly than the other. Second, the cheaper device requires higher maintenance expenditures. Third, the less expensive device (three-year life) does not last as long as the more expensive one (four-year life), so it will have to be replaced sooner. The sequence of expected

---

[11]Reviewing Table 9.4, we see that the *IRR* and *PI* result in identical project rankings. Therefore, had we used the *IRR* rather than the *PI* we would have selected the same set of projects. These two decision techniques generally result in similar, but not necessarily identical, project rankings.

Table 9.4

Capital Rationing and the Profitability Index (12% required return)

Year	Projects				
	1	**2**	**3**	**4**	**5**
0	−$ 70	−$ 80	−$ 100	−$ 150	−$ 200
1	30	30	40	50	90
2	40	35	50	55	80
3	50	55	60	60	80
4	55	60	65	90	110
NPV	$59.2	$52.0	$59.6	$38.4	$71.0
IRR	44%	36%	36%	23%	28%
PI	1.8	1.6	1.6	1.3	1.4

cash outflows (we have omitted the negative signs for convenience) for each device are as follows:

Device	End of Year (all values are *outflows*)				
	0	**1**	**2**	**3**	**4**
A	$12,000	$1,500	$1,500	$1,500	
B	14,000	1,200	1,200	1,200	1,200

Notice that to keep the example simple, the maintenance costs do not rise over time. Suppose this firm uses a discount rate of 7%. Following is the *NPV* cost of each stream of cash outflows:

Device	*NPV* Cost of Cash Outflows
A	$15,936
B	18,065

Purchasing and operating device A seems to be much cheaper than using device B (remember that we are looking for a lower *NPV*, because these are *cash outflows*). But this calculation ignores the fact that using device A will necessitate a large replacement expenditure in year 4, one year earlier than device B must be replaced. We need a way to capture the value of replacing device B less frequently than device A.

One way to do this is to look at both machines over a twelve-year time horizon. Over the next twelve years, the firm will replace device A four times (4 × 3 years = 12 years) and device B three times (3 × 4 years = 12 years). At the end of the twelfth year, both machines have to be replaced, and thus begins another twelve-year cycle. Table 9.5 shows the streams of cash flows over the cycle, assuming that when either control device wears out it can be replaced and maintained at the same costs that initially applied (i.e., all future costs remain the same). Notice that in the replacement years, the firm must pay both the maintenance cost on the old device (to keep it running through the year) and the purchase price of the new device. The present value cost (using a 7% discount rate) of the cash outflows for the devices over the entire twelve-year period follows:

Device	NPV
A	$48,233
B	42,360

Taking into account the greater longevity of device B, it is the better choice. Remember, *our objective is to find the minimum-cost alternative*, which, in this case, is device B.

Table 9.5   **Operating and Replacement Cash Flows for Two Devices (all values are *outflows*)**

Year	Device A	Device B
0	$ 12,000	$ 14,000
1	1,500	1,200
2	1,500	1,200
3	13,500	1,200
4	1,500	15,200
5	1,500	1,200
6	13,500	1,200
7	1,500	1,200
8	1,500	15,200
9	13,500	1,200
10	1,500	1,200
11	1,500	1,200
12	1,500	1,200
NPV (@7%)	**$48,233**	**$42,360**

Note: At the end of twelve years, the firm has to replace equipment, regardless of whether it chooses device A or B; thus, a new twelve-year cycle begins.

equivalent annual cost (EAC) method
Represents the annual expenditure over the life of each asset that has a present value equal to the present value of the asset's annual cash flows over its lifetime.

An alternative approach to this problem is called the **equivalent annual cost (EAC) method**. The EAC method begins by calculating the present value of cash flows for each device over its lifetime. We have already seen that the *NPV* for operating device A for three years is $15,936, and the *NPV* for operating device B for four years is $18,065. Next, the EAC method asks, what annual expenditure over the life of each machine would have the same present value? That is, the EAC solves each expression as follows:

$$\$15,936 = \frac{X}{1.07^1} + \frac{X}{1.07^2} + \frac{X}{1.07^3} \qquad X = \$6,072$$

$$\$18,065 = \frac{Y}{1.07^1} + \frac{Y}{1.07^2} + \frac{Y}{1.07^3} + \frac{Y}{1.07^4} \qquad Y = \$5,333$$

In the first equation, the variable X represents the annual cash flow from a three-year annuity that has the same present value as the actual purchase and operating costs of device A. If the firm purchases device A and keeps replacing it every three years for the indefinite future, the firm will incur a sequence of cash flows over time with the same present value as a perpetuity of $6,072. In other words, $6,072 is the *equivalent annual cost (EAC)* of device A. Likewise, in the second equation, Y represents the annual cash flow from a four-year annuity with the same present value as the purchase and operating costs of device B. If the firm buys device B and replaces it every four years, then it will incur a sequence of cash flows having the same present value as a perpetuity of $5,333. The firm should choose the alternative with the lower EAC, which is device B.

Our approaches for solving the problem of choosing between equipment with unequal lives both assume that the firm will continue to replace worn-out equipment with similar machines for a long period of time. That may not be a bad assumption in some cases, but new technology often makes old equipment obsolete. For example, suppose that the firm in our example believes that in three years a new electronic device will be available that is more reliable, less costly to operate, and longer lived. If this new device becomes available in three years, the firm will replace whatever device it is using at the time with the newer model. Furthermore, the superior attributes of the new model imply that the salvage value for the old device will be zero. How should the firm proceed?

Knowing that it will replace the old device with the improved device in three years, the firm can simply discount cash flows for three years:

$$NPV_A = \$12,000 + \frac{\$1,500}{1.07^1} + \frac{\$1,500}{1.07^2} + \frac{\$1,500}{1.07^3} = \$15,936$$

$$NPV_B = \$14,000 + \frac{\$1,200}{1.07^1} + \frac{\$1,200}{1.07^2} + \frac{\$1,200}{1.07^3} = \$17,149$$

In this case, the best device to purchase is A rather than B. Remember that B's primary advantage was its longevity. In an environment in which technological developments make old machines obsolete, longevity is not much of an advantage.

9-4c Excess Capacity

Companies often operate at less than full capacity. In such situations, managers encourage alternative uses of the excess capacity because they view it as a free asset. Although it may be true that the marginal cost of using excess capacity is zero in the very short run, using excess capacity today may accelerate the need for more capacity in the future. When that is so, to fully account for incremental cash flow effects, managers should charge the cost of accelerating new capacity development against the current proposal for using excess capacity. This procedure can be demonstrated by the following example.

EXAMPLE

Imagine a retail department store chain with a regional distribution center in the southeastern United States. At the moment, the distribution center is not fully utilized. Managers know that in two years, as new stores are built in the region, the firm will have to invest $2 million (cash outflow) to expand the distribution center's warehouse. A proposal surfaces to lease all the excess space in the warehouse for the next two years at a price that would generate beginning-of-year cash inflow of $125,000 per year. If the firm accepts this proposal, it will have no excess capacity. In order to hold inventory for new stores coming on line in the next few months, the firm will have to begin expansion immediately. The incremental investment in this expansion is the difference between investing $2 million now versus investing $2 million two years from today. The incremental cash inflow is, of course, the $125,000 lease cash flows that are received today and one year from today. Should the firm accept this offer? Assuming a 10% discount rate, the *NPV* of the project is shown as follows:

$$NPV = \$125,000 - \$2,000,000 + \frac{\$125,000}{1.1^1} + \frac{\$2,000,000}{1.1^2} = -\$108,471$$

Notice that we treat the $2 million investment in the second year as a cash inflow in this expression. By building the warehouse today, the firm avoids having to spend the money two years later. Even so, the *NPV* of leasing excess capacity is negative. However, a clever analyst could propose a counteroffer derived from the following equation:

$$NPV = X - \$2,000,000 + \frac{X}{1.1^1} + \frac{\$2,000,000}{1.1^2} = \$0$$

The value of *X* represents the amount of the lease cash inflow (one received today and the other received in one year) that would make the firm indifferent to the proposal. Solving the equation, we see that if the lease cash inflows are $181,818, the project *NPV* equals zero. Therefore, if the firm can lease its capacity for a price above $181,818, it should do so.

9-4 Concept Review Questions

10. When a firm is faced with *capital rationing*, how can the *profitability index* (*PI*) be used to select the best projects? Why does choosing the projects with the highest *PI* not always lead to the best decision?

11. Under what circumstance is the use of the *equivalent annual cost* (*EAC*) *method* to compare substitutable projects with different lives clearly more efficient computationally than using multiple investments over a common period where both projects terminate in the same year?

12. In almost every example so far, firms must decide to invest in a project immediately or not at all. But suppose that a firm could invest in a project today or it could wait one year before investing. How could you use *NPV* analysis to decide whether to invest now or later?

13. Can you articulate circumstances under which the cost of excess capacity is zero? Think about why the cost of excess capacity normally is not zero.

9-5 The Human Face of Capital Budgeting

? WHAT TO ASK

How does the approval process for new investment ideas work at your company?

This chapter illustrates which cash flows analysts should discount and which cash flows they should ignore when valuing real investment projects. There are relatively simple rules of thumb that guide managers in this task; however, executing these rules appropriately in practice is an obvious challenge. Deciding which costs are incremental and which are not, incorporating the myriad of tax factors that influence cash flows, and measuring opportunity costs properly are much more complex maneuvers than we or anyone else can convey in a textbook. The nuances of capital budgeting are best learned through practice.

There is another factor that makes real-world capital budgeting more complicated than textbook examples—the *human element*. Neither the ideas for capital investments nor the financial analysis used to evaluate them occurs in a vacuum. Almost every investment proposal important enough to warrant a thorough financial analysis has a champion behind it, someone who believes that the project is a good idea and perhaps will advance the individual's own career. When companies allocate investment capital across projects or divisions, they must recognize the potential for an optimistic bias to creep into the numbers. This bias can arise through intentional manipulation of the cash flows to make an investment look more attractive, or it may simply arise if the analyst calculating the *NPV* is also the cheerleader advocating the project in the first place.

One way that companies attempt to control this bias is by putting responsibility for analyzing an investment proposal under an authority independent from the individual or group proposing the investment. For example, it is common in large firms for a particular group to have the responsibility of conducting the financial analysis required to value any potential acquisition targets. In this role, financial analysts play a gatekeeper role, protecting shareholders' interests by steering the firm away from large, negative *NPV* investments. Naturally, these independent analysts face intense pressure from the advocates of each project to portray the investment proposal in its best possible light. Consequently, financial experts need to know more than just which cash flows count in the *NPV* calculation. They also need to have a sense of what is reasonable when forecasting a project's profit margin and its growth potential. Analysts must also prepare to defend their assumptions, explaining why their (often more conservative) projections do not line up with those offered by the managers advocating a given investment.

Raghu Rajan,
University of Chicago

"Capital budgeting is not just about estimating cash flows and discount rates, but is also a lot about horse trading."

See the entire interview at **SMART|finance**

Smart Ideas Video

Many experienced managers say that they have never seen an investment with a negative *NPV*. They do not mean that all investments are good investments, but rather that all analysts know enough about *NPV* analysis to recognize how to make any investment look attractive. In this environment, another skill comes into play in determining which project receives funding. We refer to this skill as storytelling, as opposed to number crunching. Most good investments have a compelling story behind them—a reason, based on sound economic logic, that the *investment's NPV should be positive*. The best financial analysts not only provide the numbers to highlight the value of a good investment but also explain why the investment makes sense. We return to this storytelling element of capital budgeting in Chapter 10.

9-5 Concept Review Question

14. What role does the *human element* play in the capital budgeting decision process? Could it cause a negative *NPV* project to be accepted?

What CFOs Do

CFO Survey Evidence

Throughout this chapter we have stressed that managers should focus on cash flows rather than accounting earnings, both in intrafirm financial analysis (including capital budgeting assessments) and in the financial data they report to external stakeholders. Do practicing managers actually follow this advice? Unfortunately, survey evidence clearly suggests that financial managers place far greater emphasis on accounting earnings, especially earnings per share, than they do on any other financial metric. The following graph describes how 401 financial executives ranked the importance of company metrics provided to outsiders. Over half (51%) of the respondents listed earnings as the most important metric they report, with pro forma earnings and revenues the two next most important measures reported. Cash flows from operations and free cash flows,

two of the metrics we stress in this chapter, were selected by only 12% and 10% of respondents, respectively.

The researchers conducting this survey also reported the disquieting fact that 78% of responding managers admitted a willingness to sacrifice firm value to smooth reported earnings. In response to the question, "How large a sacrifice in value would your firm make to avoid a bumpy earnings path?" 52% of managers reported a willingness to make a small sacrifice, 24% said they would make a moderate sacrifice, and 2% said they would make a large sacrifice to smooth reported profits. This clearly suggests that many managers will forgo positive-NPV investment opportunities so as not to disrupt reported earnings per share.

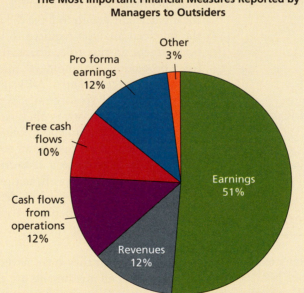

The Most Important Financial Measures Reported by Managers to Outsiders

- Other 3%
- Pro forma earnings 12%
- Free cash flows 10%
- Cash flows from operations 12%
- Revenues 12%
- Earnings 51%

Source: Reprinted from *Journal of Accounting and Economics*, 40, John R. Graham, Campbell R. Harvey, and Shiva Rajgopal, Figure 2 and Table 9 of "The Economic Implications of Corporate Financial Reporting," pp. 3–73, Copyright 2005, with permission from Elsevier.

Summary

- To estimate an investment's relevant cash flows, the analyst focuses on incremental cash flows, ignores financing costs, considers taxes, and adjusts for any noncash expenses such as depreciation.
- The costs of financing an investment, such as interest paid to lenders and dividends paid to shareholders, should not be counted as part of a project's cash outflows.

The discount rate captures the financing costs, so deducting interest expense and dividends from a project's cash flows would be double counting.

- Certain types of cash flow are common to many different kinds of investments. These include fixed asset cash flow, working capital cash flow, operating cash flow, and terminal cash flow.

- To find working capital cash flow, calculate the change in net working capital from one period to the next. Increases in net working capital represent cash outflows, whereas decreases in net working capital represent cash inflows.

- To find operating cash flow, calculate after-tax net income (as if the firm had no debt) and add back any noncash expenses.

- To find terminal value, or terminal cash flow, employ one of several methods, including the perpetual growth model and the use of book value, or market multiples.

- Only the incremental cash flows associated with a project should be included in *NPV* analysis. The analyst should avoid including sunk costs in estimates of incremental cash flows.

- Opportunity costs and any cannibalization should be reflected in an investment's cash flow projections.

- When capital rationing exists, managers should analyze all combinations of projects that satisfy the budget constraint and choose the combination that has the highest overall *NPV*.

- When evaluating alternative equipment purchases with unequal lives, determine the equivalent annual cost (*EAC*) of each type of equipment and choose the one that is least expensive.

- When confronted with proposals to use excess capacity, think carefully about the true cost of that capacity. It is rarely zero.

- When analyzing capital budgeting projects, it is important to consider human factors and make sure that the project, in addition to having a positive *NPV*, makes sense.

Key Terms

cannibalization, 291
capital rationing, 297
equivalent annual cost (EAC)
    method, 299
incremental cash flows, 281

modified accelerated cost
   recovery system
   (MACRS), 283
net working capital, 285
noncash expenses, 282

opportunity costs, 290
sunk cost, 290
terminal value, 287

Self-Test Problems

Answers to Self-Test Problems and the Concept Review Questions throughout the chapter appear in CourseMate with SmartFinance Tools at www.cengagebrain.com.

ST9-1. Claross Inc. wants to determine the relevant operating cash flows associated with the proposed purchase of a new piece of equipment that has an installed cost of $10 million and falls into the five-year MACRS asset class. The firm's financial analyst estimated that the relevant time horizon for analysis is six years. She expects the revenues attributable to the equipment to be $15.8 million in the first year and to increase at 5% per year through year 6. Similarly, she estimates all expenses, other than depreciation attributable to the equipment, to total $12.2 million in the first year and to increase by 4% per year through year 6. She plans to ignore any cash flows after year 6. The firm has a marginal tax rate of 40% and its required return on the equipment investment is 13%. (Note: Round all cash flow calculations to the nearest $0.01 million.)

a. Find the *relevant incremental cash flows* for years 0 through 6.
b. Using the cash flows found in part (a), determine the *NPV* and *IRR* for the proposed equipment purchase.
c. Based on your findings in part (b), would you recommend that Claross Inc. purchase the equipment? Why?

ST9-2. Atech Industries wants to determine whether it would be advisable for it to replace an existing, fully depreciated machine with a new one. The new machine will have an after-tax installed cost of $300,000 and will be depreciated under a three-year MACRS schedule. The old machine can be sold today for $80,000, after taxes. The firm is in the 40% tax bracket and requires a minimum return on the replacement decision of 15%. The firms' estimates of its revenues and expenses (excluding depreciation) for both the new and the old machine (in $ thousands) over the next four years are given below.

	New Machine		Old Machine	
Year	Revenue	Expenses (excluding depreciation)	Revenue	Expenses (excluding depreciation)
1	$ 925	$740	$625	$580
2	990	780	645	595
3	1,000	825	670	610
4	1,100	875	695	630

Atech also estimates the values of various current accounts that could be impacted by the proposed replacement. They are shown below for both the new and the old machine over the next four years. Currently (at time 0), the firm's net investment in these current accounts is assumed to be $110,000 with the new machine and $75,000 with the old machine.

	New Machine Year			
	1	2	3	4
Cash	$20,000	$25,000	$ 30,000	$ 36,000
Accounts Receivable	90,000	95,000	110,000	120,000
Inventory	80,000	90,000	100,000	105,000
Accounts Payable	60,000	65,000	70,000	72,000

	Old Machine Year			
	1	2	3	4
Cash	$15,000	$15,000	$15,000	$15,000
Accounts Receivable	60,000	64,000	68,000	70,000
Inventory	45,000	48,000	52,000	55,000
Accounts Payable	33,000	35,000	38,000	40,000

Atech indicates that after four years of detailed cash flow development, it will assume, in analyzing this replacement decision, that the year 4 incremental cash flows of the new machine over the old machine will grow at a compound annual rate of 2% from the end of year 4 to infinity.

a. Find the incremental *operating cash flows* (including any working capital investment) for years 1 to 4, for Atech's proposed machine-replacement decision.
b. Calculate the *terminal value* of Atech's proposed machine replacement at the end of year 4.
c. Show the *cash flows* (initial outlay, operating cash flows, and terminal cash flow) for years 1 to 4, for Atech's proposed machine replacement.
d. Using the cash flows from part (c), find the *NPV* and *IRR* for Atech's proposed machine replacement.
e. Based on your findings in part (d), what recommendation would you make to Atech regarding its proposed machine replacement?

ST9-3. Performance Inc. is faced with choosing between two mutually exclusive projects with differing lives. It requires a return of 12% on these projects. Project A requires an initial outlay at time 0 of $5,000,000 and is expected to require annual maintenance cash outflows of $3,100,000 per year over its two-year life. Project B requires an initial outlay at time 0 of $6,000,000 and is expected to require annual maintenance cash outflows of $2,600,000 per year over its three-year life. Both projects are acceptable investments and provide equal quality service. The firm assumes that the replacement and maintenance costs for both projects will remain unchanged over time.

a. Find the *NPV* of each project over its life.

b. Which project would you recommend, based on your finding in part (a)? What is wrong with choosing the best project, based on its *NPV*?

c. Use the *equivalent annual cost (EAC) method* to compare the two projects.

d. Which project would you recommend, based on your finding in part (c)? Compare and contrast this recommendation with the one you gave in part (b).

Questions

Q9-1. In capital budgeting analysis, why do we focus on *cash flow* rather than *accounting profit?*

Q9-2. To finance a certain project, a company must borrow money at 10% interest. How should it treat interest payments when it analyzes the project's cash flows?

Q9-3. Does depreciation affect cash flow in a positive or negative manner? From a net present-value perspective, why is accelerated depreciation preferable? Is it acceptable to utilize one depreciation method for tax purposes and another for financial reporting purposes? Which method is relevant for determining project cash flows?

Q9-4. In what sense does an increase in accounts payable represent a cash inflow?

Q9-5. List several ways to estimate a project's *terminal value.*

Q9-6. What are the tax consequences of selling an investment asset for more than its book value? Does this have an effect on project cash flows that must be accounted for? What is the effect if the asset is sold for less than its book value?

Q9-7. Why must *incremental, after-tax, cash flows,* rather than total cash flows, be evaluated in project analysis?

Q9-8. Differentiate between *sunk costs* and *opportunity costs.* Which of these costs should be included in incremental cash flows and which should be excluded?

Q9-9. Why is it important to consider *cannibalization* in situations where a company is considering adding substitute products to its product line?

Q9-10. Before entering graduate school, a student estimated the value of earning an MBA at $300,000. Based on that analysis, the student decided to go back to school. After completing the first year, the student ran the *NPV* calculations again. How would you expect the *NPV* to look after the student has completed one year of the program? Specifically, what portion of the analysis must be different than it was the year before?

Q9-11. Punxsutawney Taxidermy Inc. (PTI) operates a chain of taxidermy shops across the Midwest, with a handful of locations in the South. A rival firm, Heads Up Corp., has a few Midwestern locations, but most of its shops are located in the South. PTI and Heads Up decide to consolidate their operations by trading ownership of a few locations. PTI will acquire four Heads Up locations in the Midwest, and will relinquish control of its southern locations in exchange. No cash changes hands up front. Does this mean that an analyst working for either company can evaluate the merits of this deal by assuming that the project has no initial cash outlay? Explain.

Q9-12. What is the only relevant decision for independent projects if an unlimited capital budget exists? How does your response change if the projects are mutually exclusive? How does your response change if the firm faces *capital rationing*?

Q9-13. Explain why the *equivalent annual cost (EAC) method* helps firms evaluate alternative investments with unequal lives.

Q9-14. Why isn't excess capacity free?

Problems

Types of Cash Flows

P9-1. Calculate the present value of depreciation tax savings on a depreciable asset with a purchase price of $5 million and zero salvage value, assuming a 10% discount rate, a 34% tax rate, and the following type of depreciation:

    a.   The asset is depreciated over a three-year life, according to Table 9.1.

    b.   The asset is depreciated over a seven-year life, according to Table 9.1.

    c.   The asset is depreciated over a twenty-year life, according to Table 9.1.

P9-2. A certain piece of equipment costs $32 million, plus an additional $2 million to install. This equipment qualifies under the five-year MACRS category. For a firm that discounts cash flows at 12% and faces a tax rate of 34%, what is the present value of the depreciation tax savings associated with this equipment? By how much would that number change if the firm could treat the $2-million installation cost as a deductible expense rather than include it as part of the depreciable cost of the asset?

P9-3. The government is considering a proposal to allow even greater accelerated depreciation deductions than those specified by MACRS.

    a.   For which type of company would this change be more valuable, a company facing a 10% tax rate or one facing a 30% tax rate?

    b.   If companies take larger depreciation deductions in the early years of an investment, what will be the effect on reported earnings? On cash flows? On project *NPVs*? How do you think the stock market might respond if the tax law changes to allow greater accelerated depreciation?

P9-4. Taylor United is considering overhauling its equipment to meet increased demand for its product. The cost of the equipment overhaul is $3.8 million, plus $200,000 in installation costs. The firm will depreciate the equipment modifications under MACRS using a five-year recovery period. Additional sales revenue from the overhaul should amount to $2.2 million per year, and additional operating expenses and other costs (excluding depreciation) will amount to 35% of the additional sales. The firm has an ordinary tax rate of 40%. Answer the following questions about Taylor United, for each of the next six years.

    a.   What additional earnings, before depreciation and taxes, will result from the overhaul?

    b.   What additional earnings after taxes will result from the overhaul?

    c.   What incremental operating cash flows will result from the overhaul?

P9-5. Wilbur Corporation is considering replacing a machine. The replacement will cut operating expenses by $24,000 per year for each of the five years that the new machine is expected to last. Although the old machine has a zero book value, it has a remaining useful life of five years. The depreciable value of the new machine is $72,000. Wilbur will depreciate the machine under MACRS using a five-year recovery period, and is subject to a 40% tax rate on ordinary income. Estimate the incremental operating cash flows attributable to the replacement. Be sure to consider the depreciation in year 6.

P9-6. Advanced Electronics Corporation is considering purchasing a new packaging machine to replace a fully depreciated packaging machine that will last five more years. The new machine is expected to have a five-year life and depreciation charges of $4,000 in year 1; $6,400 in year 2; $3,800 in year 3; $2,400 in both year 4 and year 5; and $1,000 in year 6. The firm's estimates of revenues and expenses (excluding depreciation) for the new and the old packaging machines are shown in the following table. Advanced Electronics is subject to a 40% tax rate on ordinary income.

	New Packaging Machine		Old Packaging Machine	
Year	Revenue	Expenses (excluding depreciation)	Revenue	Expenses (excluding depreciation)
1	$50,000	$40,000	$45,000	$35,000
2	51,000	40,000	45,000	35,000
3	52,000	40,000	45,000	35,000
4	53,000	40,000	45,000	35,000
5	54,000	40,000	45,000	35,000

a. Calculate the operating cash flows associated with each packaging machine. Be sure to consider the depreciation in year 6.

b. Calculate the incremental operating cash flows resulting from the proposed packaging machine replacement.

c. Depict on a time line the incremental operating cash flows found in part (b).

P9-7. Premium Wines, a producer of medium-quality wines, has maintained stable sales and profits over the past eight years. Although the market for medium-quality wines has been growing by 4% per year, Premium Wines has been unsuccessful in sharing this growth. To increase its sales, the firm is considering an aggressive marketing campaign that centers on regularly running ads in major food and wine magazines and airing TV commercials in large metropolitan areas. The campaign is expected to require an *annual* tax-deductible expenditure of $3 million over the next five years. Sales revenue, as noted in the following income statement for 2011, totaled $80 million. If the proposed marketing campaign is not initiated, sales are expected to remain at this level in each of the next five years, 2012–2016. With the marketing campaign, sales are expected to rise to the levels, shown in the sales forecast table, for each of the next five years. The cost of goods sold is expected to remain at 75% of sales; general and administrative expense (exclusive of any marketing campaign outlays) is expected to remain at 15% of sales; and annual depreciation expense is expected to remain at $2 million. Assuming a 40% tax rate, find the *cash flows* over the next five years associated with Premium Wines' proposed marketing campaign.

Premium Wines Income Statement For the Year Ended December 31, 2011		
Sales revenue		$80,000,000
Less: Cost of goods sold (75%)		60,000,000
Gross profits		$20,000,000
Less: Operating expenses		
General and administrative expense (15%)	$12,000,000	
Depreciation expense	2,000,000	
Total operating expense		14,000,000
Net profits before taxes		$ 6,000,000
Less: Taxes (rate = 40%)		2,400,000
Net profits after taxes		$ 3,600,000

Premium Wines Sales Forecast

Year	Sales Revenue
2012	$82,000,000
2013	84,000,000
2014	86,000,000
2015	90,000,000
2016	94,000,000

Incremental Cash Flows

P9-8. Identify each of the following situations as involving *sunk costs, opportunity costs,* and/or *cannibalization.* Indicate what amount, if any, of these items would be relevant to the given investment decision.

a. The investment requires use of additional computer storage capacity to create a data warehouse containing information on all your customers. The storage space you will use is currently leased to another firm for $37,500 per year, under a lease that can be canceled without penalty by you at any time.

b. An investment that will result in producing a new lighter-weight version of one of the firm's best-selling products. The new product will sell for 40% more than the current product. Because of its high price, the firm expects the old product's sales to decline by about 10% from its current level of $27 million.

c. An investment of $8 million in a new venture that is expected to grow sales and profits. To date, you have spent $135,000 researching the venture and performing feasibility studies.

d. Subleasing 100 parking spaces in your firm's parking lot to the tenants in an adjacent building that has inadequate off-street parking. You pay $20 per month for each space under a noncancelable fifty-year lease. The sublessee will pay you $15 per month for each space. You have advertised the spaces for over a year with no other takers, and you do not anticipate needing the 100 spaces for many years.

e.   The firm is considering launching a completely new product that can be sold by your existing sales force, which is already overburdened with a large catalog of products to sell. On average, each sales rep sells about $2.1 million per year. You expect that, given the extra time involved in selling the new product, your sales reps will likely devote less time to selling existing products. Although you forecast that the average sales rep will sell about $300,000 of the new product annually, you project a decline of about 7% per year in existing product sales.

P9-9.   Barans Manufacturing is developing the incremental cash flows associated with the proposed replacement of an existing stamping machine with a new, technologically advanced one. Given the following costs related to the proposed project, explain whether each would be treated as a *sunk cost* or an *opportunity cost* in developing the incremental cash flows associated with the proposed replacement decision.

a.   Barans could use the same dies and other tools (with a book value of $40,000) on the new stamping machine that it used on the old one.

b.   Barans could link the new machine to its existing computer system to control its operations. The old stamping machine did not have a computer control system. The firm's excess computer capacity could be leased to another firm for an annual fee of $17,000.

c.   Barans needs to obtain additional floor space to accommodate the new, larger stamping machine. The space required is currently being leased to another company for $10,000 per year.

d.   Barans can use a small storage facility, built by Barans at a cost of $120,000 three years earlier, to store the increased output of the new stamping machine. Because of its unique configuration and location, it is currently of no use to either Barans or any other firm.

e.   Barans can retain an existing overhead crane, which it had planned to sell for its $180,000 market value. Although the crane was not needed with the old stamping machine, it can be used to position raw materials on the new stamping machine.

P9-10.   Blueberry Electronics is exploring the possibility of producing a new handheld device that will serve both as a basic PC, with Internet access, and as a cell phone. Which of the following items are incremental costs for the project's analysis?

a.   Research and development funds that the company has spent while working on a prototype of the new product.

b.   The company's current-generation product has no cell phone capability. The new product may therefore make the old one obsolete in the eyes of many consumers. However, Blueberry expects that other companies will soon bring to market products combining cell phone and PC features, which will also reduce sales on Blueberry's existing products.

c.   Costs of ramping up production of the new device.

d.   Increases in receivables and inventory that will occur as production increases.

P9-11.   New York Pizza is considering replacing an existing oven with a new, more sophisticated oven. The old oven was purchased three years ago at a cost of $20,000, and this amount was being depreciated under MACRS using a five-year recovery period. The oven has five years of usable life remaining. The new oven being considered costs $30,500, requires $1,500 in installation costs, and would be depreciated under MACRS using a five-year recovery period. The old oven can currently be sold for $22,000, without incurring any removal or cleanup costs. The firm pays taxes at a rate of 40% on both ordinary income and capital gains. The revenues and expenses (excluding depreciation) associated with the new and the old machines for the next five years are given in the following table.

	New Oven		Old Oven	
Year	Revenue	Expenses (excluding depreciation)	Revenue	Expenses (excluding depreciation)
1	$300,000	$288,000	$270,000	$264,000
2	300,000	288,000	270,000	264,000
3	300,000	288,000	270,000	264,000
4	300,000	288,000	270,000	264,000
5	300,000	288,000	270,000	264,000

a. Calculate the initial cash outflow associated with replacement of the old oven with a new one.

b. Determine the incremental cash flows associated with the proposed replacement. Be sure to consider the depreciation in year 6.

c. Depict on a time line the incremental cash flows found in parts (a) and (b), associated with the proposed replacement decision.

P9-12. Speedy Auto Wash is contemplating the purchase of a new high-speed washer to replace the existing washer. The existing washer was purchased two years ago at an installed cost of $120,000; it was being depreciated under MACRS using a five-year recovery period. The existing washer is expected to have a usable life of five more years. The new washer costs $210,000 and requires $10,000 in installation costs; it has a five-year usable life and would be depreciated under MACRS using a five-year recovery period. The existing washer can currently be sold for $140,000, without incurring any removal or cleanup costs. To support the increased business resulting from purchase of the new washer, accounts receivable would increase by $80,000, inventories by $60,000, and accounts payable by $116,000. At the end of five years, the existing washer is expected to have a market value of zero; the new washer would be sold to net $58,000 after removal and cleanup costs, and before taxes. The firm pays taxes at a rate of 40% on both ordinary income and capital gains. The estimated *profits before depreciation and taxes* over the five years for both the new and the existing washer are shown in the following table.

	Profits Before Depreciation and Taxes	
Year	New Washer	Existing Washer
1	$86,000	$52,000
2	86,000	48,000
3	86,000	44,000
4	86,000	40,000
5	86,000	36,000

a. Calculate the initial cash outflow associated with the replacement of the existing washer with the new one.

b. Determine the incremental cash flows associated with the proposed washer replacement. Be sure to consider the depreciation in year 6.

c. Determine the terminal cash flow expected at the end of year 5 from the proposed washer replacement.

d. Depict on a time line the incremental cash flows associated with the proposed washer-replacement decision.

P9-13. TransPacific Shipping is considering replacing an existing ship with one of two newer, more efficient ones. The existing ship is three years old, cost $32 million, and is being depreciated under MACRS using a five-year recovery period. Although the existing ship has only three years (years 4, 5, and 6) of depreciation remaining under MACRS, it has a remaining usable life of five years. Ship A, one of the two possible replacement ships, costs $40 million to purchase and $8 million to outfit for service. It has a five-year usable life and will be depreciated under MACRS using a five-year recovery period. Ship B costs $54 million to purchase and $6 million to outfit. It also has a five-year usable life and will be depreciated under MACRS using a five-year recovery period. Increased investments in net working capital will accompany the decision to acquire ship A or ship B. Purchase of ship A would result in a $4-million increase in net working capital; ship B would result in a $6-million increase in net working capital. The projected *profits before depreciation and taxes* for each alternative ship and the existing ship are given in the following table.

	Profits Before Depreciation and Taxes		
Year	Ship A	Ship B	Existing Ship
1	$21,000,000	$22,000,000	$14,000,000
2	21,000,000	24,000,000	14,000,000
3	21,000,000	26,000,000	14,000,000
4	21,000,000	26,000,000	14,000,000
5	21,000,000	26,000,000	14,000,000

The existing ship can currently be sold for $18 million and will not incur any removal or cleanup costs. At the end of five years, the existing ship can be sold to net $1 million before taxes. Ships A and B can be sold to net $12 million and $20 million before taxes, respectively, at the end of the five-year period. The firm is subject to a 40% tax rate on both ordinary income and capital gains.

a. Calculate the initial outlay associated with each alternative.

b. Calculate the operating cash flows associated with each alternative. Be sure to consider the depreciation in year 6.

c. Calculate the terminal cash flow at the end of year 5, associated with each alternative.

d. Depict on a time line the incremental cash flows associated with each alternative.

P9-14. The management of Kimco is evaluating replacing their large mainframe computer with a modern network system that requires much less office space. The network would cost $500,000 (including installation costs) and due to efficiency gains, would generate $125,000 per year in operating cash flows (accounting for taxes and depreciation) over the next five years. The mainframe has a remaining book value of $50,000 and would be immediately donated to a charity for the tax benefit. Kimco's cost of capital is 10% and the tax rate is 40%. On the basis of *NPV*, should management install the network system?

P9-15. Pointless Luxuries Inc. (PLI) produces unusual gifts targeted at wealthy consumers. The company is analyzing the possibility of introducing a new device designed to attach to the collar of a cat or dog. This device emits sonic waves that neutralize airplane engine noise, so that pets traveling with their owners can enjoy a more peaceful ride. PLI estimates that developing this product will require up-front capital expenditures of $10 million. These costs will be depreciated on a straight-line basis for five years. PLI believes that it can sell the product initially for $250. The selling price will increase to $260 in years 2 and 3, before falling to $245 and $240 in years 4 and 5, respectively. After five years the company will withdraw the product from the market and replace it with something else. Variable costs are $135 per unit. PLI forecasts sales volume of 20,000 units the first year, with subsequent increases of 25% (year 2), 20% (year 3), 20% (year 4), and 15% (year 5). Offering this product will force PLI to make additional investments in receivables and inventory. Projected end-of-year balances appear in the following table.

	Year 0	Year 1	Year 2	Year 3	Year 4	Year 5
Accounts receivable	$0	$200,000	$250,000	$300,000	$150,000	$0
Inventory	0	500,000	650,000	780,000	600,000	0

The firm faces a tax rate of 34%. Assume that cash flows arrive at the end of each year, except for the initial $10-million outlay.

a. Calculate the project's contribution to net income each year.

b. Calculate the project's cash flows each year.

c. Calculate two *NPVs*, one using a 10% discount rate and the other using a 15% discount rate.

d. A PLI financial analyst reasons as follows: "With the exception of the initial outlay, the cash flows from this project arrive in more or less a continuous stream rather than at the end of each year. Therefore, by discounting each year's cash flow for a full year, we are understating the true *NPV*. A better approximation is to move the discounting six months forward (e.g., discount year 1 cash flows for six months, year 2 cash flows for eighteen months, and so on), as if all the cash flows arrive in the middle of each year rather than at the end." Recalculate the *NPV* (at 10% and 15%) maintaining this assumption. How much difference does it make?

P9-16. TechGiant Inc. (TGI) is evaluating a proposal to acquire Fusion Chips, a young company with an interesting new chip technology. This technology, when integrated into existing TGI silicon wafers, will enable TGI to offer chips with new capabilities to companies with automated manufacturing systems. TGI analysts have projected income statements for Fusion five years into the future. These projections appear in the following income statements, along with estimates of Fusion's asset requirements and accounts payable balances each year. These statements are designed assuming that Fusion remains an independent, stand-alone company. If TGI acquires Fusion, analysts believe that the following changes will occur.

1. TGI's superior manufacturing capabilities will enable Fusion to increase its gross margin on its existing products to 45%.

2. TGI's massive sales force will enable Fusion to increase sales of its existing products by 10% above current projections (for example, if acquired, Fusion will sell $110 million, rather than $100 million, in 2012). This increase will occur as a consequence of regularly scheduled conversations between TGI salespeople and existing customers and will not require added marketing expenditures. Operating expenses as a percentage of sales will be the same each year as currently forecasted (ranges from 10% to 12%). The fixed asset increases currently projected through 2016 will be sufficient to sustain the 10% increase in sales volume each year.

3. TGI's more efficient receivables and inventory management systems will allow Fusion to increase its sales as previously described, without making investments in receivables and inventory beyond those already reflected in the financial projection. TGI also enjoys a higher credit rating than Fusion, so after the acquisition, Fusion will obtain credit from suppliers on more favorable terms. Specifically, Fusion's accounts payable balance will be 30% higher each year than the level currently forecast.

4. TGI's current cash reserves are more than sufficient for the combined company, so Fusion's existing cash balances will be reduced to $0.

5. Immediately after the acquisition, TGI will invest $50 million in fixed assets to manufacture a new chip that integrates Fusion's technology into one of TGI's best-selling products. These assets will be depreciated on a straight-line basis for eight years. After five years, the new chip will be obsolete, and no additional sales will occur. The equipment will be sold at the end of year 5 for $1 million. Before depreciation and taxes, this new product will generate $20 million in (incremental) profits the first year, $30 million the second year, and $15 million in each of the next three years. TGI will have to invest $3 million in net working capital up front, all of which it will recover at the end of the project's life.

6. Both companies face a tax rate of 34%.

Fusion Chips Income Statements ($ in thousands for Years Ended December 31)					
	2012	**2013**	**2014**	**2015**	**2016**
Sales	$100,000	$150,000	$200,000	$240,000	$270,000
− Cost of goods sold	60,000	90,000	120,000	144,000	162,000
Gross profit	$ 40,000	$ 60,000	$ 80,000	$ 96,000	$108,000
− Operating expenses	12,000	17,250	22,000	25,200	27,000
− Depreciation	12,000	18,000	24,000	28,800	32,400
Pretax income	$ 16,000	$ 24,750	$ 34,000	$ 42,000	$ 48,600
− Taxes	5,440	8,415	11,560	14,280	16,524
Net income	$ 10,560	$ 16,335	$ 22,440	$ 27,720	$ 32,076

Fusion Chips Assets and Accounts Payable ($ in thousands on December 31)						
	2011	**2012**	**2013**	**2014**	**2015**	**2016**
Cash	$ 400	$ 400	$ 525	$ 600	$ 600	$ 600
Accounts receivable	6,000	7,000	10,500	14,000	16,800	18,900
Inventory	10,000	12,500	18,750	25,000	30,000	33,750
Total current assets	$16,400	$ 19,900	$ 29,775	$ 39,600	$ 47,400	$ 53,250
Plant and equipment						
Gross	$80,000	$113,000	$166,500	$226,000	$283,200	$336,900
Net	$50,000	$ 71,000	$106,500	$142,000	$170,400	$191,700
Total assets	$66,400	$ 90,900	$136,275	$181,600	$217,800	$244,950
Accounts payable	$ 7,500	$ 13,500	$ 20,250	$ 27,000	$ 32,400	$ 36,450

Note: The 2011 figures represent the balances currently on Fusion's balance sheet.

a. Calculate the cash flows generated by Fusion as a stand-alone entity in each year from 2012 to 2016.

b. Assume that by 2016, Fusion reaches a "steady state," which means that its cash flows will grow by 5% per year in perpetuity. If Fusion discounts cash flows at 15%, what is the present value as of the end of 2016 of all cash flows that Fusion will generate from 2017 forward?

c. Calculate the present value, as of 2011, of Fusion's cash flows from 2012 forward. What does this *NPV* represent?

d. Suppose TGI acquires Fusion. Recalculate Fusion's cash flows from 2012 to 2016, making all the changes previously described in items 1–4 and 6.

e. Assume that after 2016, Fusion's cash flows will grow at a steady 5% per year. Calculate the present value of these cash flows, as of 2016, if the discount rate is 15%.

f. Ignoring item 5 in the list of changes, what is the *PV*, as of 2011, of Fusion's cash flows from 2012 forward? Use a discount rate of 15%.

g. Finally, calculate the *NPV* of TGI's investment to integrate its technology with Fusion's. Considering this in combination with your answer to part (f), what is the maximum price that TGI should pay for Fusion? Assume a discount rate of 15%.

P9-17. A project generates the following sequence of cash flows over six years:

Year	Cash Flow ($ in millions)
0	−59.00
1	4.00
2	5.00
3	6.00
4	7.33
5	8.00
6	8.25

a. Calculate the *NPV* over the six years. The discount rate is 11%.

b. This project does not end after the sixth year, but instead will generate cash flows far into the future. Estimate the *terminal value,* assuming that cash flows after year 6 will continue at $8.25 million per year in perpetuity, and then recalculate the investment's *NPV*.

c. Calculate the *terminal value,* assuming that cash flows after the sixth year grow at 2% annually in perpetuity, and then recalculate the *NPV*.

d. Using market multiples, calculate the *terminal value* by estimating the project's market value at the end of year 6. Specifically, calculate the terminal value under the assumption that at the end of year 6, the project's market value will be ten times greater than its most recent annual cash flow. Recalculate the *NPV*.

Special Problems in Capital Budgeting

P9-18. You have a $10-million capital budget and must make the decision about which investments your firm should accept for the coming year. Projects 1, 2, and 3 are mutually exclusive, and Project 4 is independent of all three. The firm's cost of capital is 12%.

	Project 1	Project 2	Project 3	Project 4
Initial cash outflow	−$4,000,000	−$5,000,000	−$10,000,000	−$5,000,000
Year 1 cash inflow	1,000,000	2,000,000	4,000,000	2,700,000
Year 2 cash inflow	2,000,000	3,000,000	6,000,000	2,700,000
Year 3 cash inflow	3,000,000	3,000,000	5,000,000	2,700,000

a. Use the information on the *three mutually exclusive projects* to determine which of those three investments your firm should accept on the basis of *NPV*.

b. Which of the *three mutually exclusive projects* should the firm accept on the basis of *PI?*

c. If the *three mutually exclusive projects* are the only investments available, which one do you select?

d. Now given the availability of Project 4, the independent project, which of the mutually exclusive projects do you accept? (Note: Remember, there is a $10 million budget constraint.) Is the better technique in this situation the *NPV* or the *PI?* Why?

P9-19. Semper Mortgage wishes to select the best of three possible computers, each expected to meet the firm's growing need for computational and storage capacity. The three computers—A, B, and C—are equally risky. The firm plans to use a 12% cost of capital to evaluate each of them. The initial outlay and the annual cash outflows over the life of each computer are shown in the following table.

	Cash Outflows (CF_t)		
Year (t)	Computer A	Computer B	Computer C
0	−$50,000	−$35,000	−$60,000
1	7,000	5,500	18,000
2	7,000	12,000	18,000
3	7,000	16,000	18,000
4	7,000	23,000	18,000
5	7,000	—	18,000
6	7,000	—	18,000

a. Calculate the *NPV* for each computer over its life. Rank the computers in descending order, based on *NPV*.

b. Use the *equivalent annual cost (EAC) method* to evaluate and rank the computers in descending order, based on the EAC.

c. Compare and contrast your findings in parts (a) and (b). Which computer would you recommend that the firm acquire? Why?

P9-20. Seattle Manufacturing is considering the purchase of one of three mutually exclusive projects for improving its assembly line. The firm plans to use a 14% cost of capital to evaluate these equal-risk projects. The initial outlay and the annual cash outflows over the life of each project are shown in the following table.

	Cash Outflows (CF_t)		
Year (t)	Project X	Project Y	Project Z
0	−$156,000	−$104,000	−$132,000
1	34,000	56,000	30,000
2	50,000	56,000	30,000
3	66,000	—	30,000
4	82,000	—	30,000
5	—	—	30,000
6	—	—	30,000
7	—	—	30,000

a. Calculate the *NPV* for each project over its life. Rank the projects in descending order based on *NPV*.

b. Use the *equivalent annual cost (EAC) method* to evaluate and rank the projects in descending order based on the EAC.

c. Compare and contrast your findings in parts (a) and (b). Which project would you recommend that the firm purchase? Why?

SMART solutions

See the problem and solution explained step-by-step at **SMART** | finance

P9-21. As part of a hotel renovation program, a company must choose between two grades of carpet to install. One grade costs $22 per square yard, and the other, $28. The costs of cleaning and maintaining the carpets are identical, but the less expensive carpet must be replaced after six years, whereas the more expensive one will last nine years before it must be replaced. The relevant discount rate is 13%. Which grade should the company choose?

P9-22. Gail Dribble is a financial analyst at Hill Propane Distributors. Gail must provide a financial analysis of the decision to replace a truck used to deliver propane gas to residential customers. Given its age, the truck will require increasing maintenance expenditures if the company keeps it in service. Similarly, the market value of the truck declines as it ages. The current market value of the truck, as well as the market value and the required maintenance expenditures for each of the next four years, appears below.

Year	Market Value	Maintenance Cost
Current	$7,000	$ 0
1	5,500	2,500
2	3,700	3,600
3	0	4,500
4	0	7,500

The company can purchase a new truck for $40,000. The truck will last fifteen years and will require end-of-year maintenance expenditures of $1,500. At the end of fifteen years, the new truck's salvage value will be $3,500.

a. Calculate the *equivalent annual cost (EAC)* of the new truck. Use a discount rate of 9%.

b. Suppose the firm keeps the old truck one more year and sells it then rather than now. What is the opportunity cost associated with this decision? What is the present value of the cost of this decision as of today? Restate this cost in terms of year-1 dollars.

c. Based on your answers to (a) and (b), is it optimal for the company to replace the old truck immediately?

d. Suppose the firm decides to keep the truck for another year. Gail must analyze whether replacing the old truck after one year makes sense or whether the truck should stay in use another year. As of the end of year 1, what is the present value of the cost of using the truck and selling it at the end of year 2? Restate this answer in year-2 dollars. Should the firm replace the truck after two years?

e. Suppose the firm keeps the old truck in service for two years. Should it replace it rather than keep it in service for the third year?

P9-23. A firm that manufactures and sells ball bearings currently has excess capacity. The firm expects that it will exhaust its excess capacity in three years. At that time, it will spend $5 million, which represents the cost of equipment as well as the value of depreciation tax shields on that equipment, to build new capacity. Suppose that this firm can accept additional manufacturing work as a subcontractor for another company. By doing so, the firm will receive net cash inflows of $250,000 immediately, and in each of the next two years. However, the firm will also have to spend $5 million two years earlier than originally planned to bring new capacity on line. Should the firm take on the subcontracting job? The discount rate is 12%. What is the minimum cash inflow that the firm would require (per year) to accept this job?

THOMSON REUTERS | Business School Edition

For instructions on using Thomson ONE, refer to the instructions provided with the Thomson ONE problems at the end of Chapters 1–6.

P9-24. Compute the annual depreciation tax savings for BASF (BASFY) over the last five years. Use an average tax rate (income taxes divided by pretax income from the income statement) for each year. How has depreciation tax savings changed for BASF over these years?

P9-25. Calculate changes in net working capital for Best Buy Co., Inc. (BBY) over the last five years. For each year, determine if the change represents a cash inflow or a cash outflow for the company. From the balance sheet, identify source(s) for this change.

Smart Ideas Video

Raghu Rajan, University of Chicago

"Capital budgeting is not just about estimating cash flows and discount rates, but is also a lot about horse trading."

Smart Practices Video

Paul Savastano, Director of Information Technology, Sprint Nextel Corp.

"So the challenge becomes, how do you quantify the benefits when a big piece of the investment is going to be for things that people never see?"

David Nickel, Controller for Intel Communications Group, Intel Corp.

"Capital budgeting is the key theme for deciding which programs get funded."

Smart Ethics Video

Scott Lee, Texas A&M University

"We have found evidence that the market punishes firms that were involved in defense procurement fraud."

SMART concepts

See an NPV analysis of the decision to open a laser eye surgery center.

SMART solutions

See the solution to Problem 9-1.
See the solution to Problem 9-21.

Mini-Case

Cash Flow and Capital Budgeting

ACE Rental Cars, Incorporated (ACE) is analyzing whether to enter the discount used rental car market. This project would involve the purchase of 100 used, late-model, mid-sized automobiles at the price of $9,500 each. In order to reduce their insurance costs, ACE will have a LoJack Stolen Vehicle Recovery System installed in each automobile at a cost of $1,000 per vehicle. ACE will also utilize one of their abandoned lots to store the vehicles. If ACE does not undertake this project they could lease this lot to an auto repair company for $80,000 per year. The $20,000 annual maintenance cost on this lot will be paid by ACE whether the lot is leased or used for this project. In addition, if this project is undertaken, net working capital will increase by $50,000.

The automobiles will qualify as a 5-year class asset under the modified accelerated cost recovery system (MACRS). Each car is expected to generate $4,800 a year in revenue and have operating costs of $1,000 per year. Starting 4 years from now, one-quarter of the fleet is expected to be replaced every year with a similar fleet of used cars. This is expected to result in a net cash flow (including acquisition costs) of $100,000 per year continuing indefinitely. This discount rental car business is expected to have a minimum impact on ACE's regular rental car business where the net cash flow is expected to fall by only $25,000 per year. ACE expects to have a marginal tax rate of 32%.

Based on this information, answer the following questions.

Assignment

1. What is the initial cash flow (fixed asset expenditure) for this discount used rental car project?

2. Is the cost of installing the LoJack System relevant to this analysis?

3. Are the maintenance costs relevant?

4. Should you consider the change in net working capital?

5. Estimate the depreciation costs incurred for each of the next 4 years.

6. Estimate the net cash flow for each of the next 4 years.

7. How are possible cannibalization costs considered in this analysis?

8. How does the opportunity to lease the lot affect this analysis?

9. What do you estimate as the terminal value of this project at the end of year 4 (use a 12% discount rate for this calculation)?

10. Applying the standard discount rate of 12% that ACE uses for capital budgeting, what is the NPV of this project? If ACE adjusts the discount rate to 14% to reflect higher project risk, what is the NPV?

chapter 10

Risk and Capital Budgeting

What Companies Do

Hershey Tastes Sweeter to Deutsche Bank

Firms like The Hershey Company finance capital investment programs by raising capital through public issues of debt and equity securities and by plowing cash flows earned from previous investments back into the business. Virtually all public companies have a weighted average cost of capital (or *WACC*) that they set as a hurdle rate for new investment projects. Investments that offer returns greater than the *WACC* move forward, while managers typically reject projects that generate lower returns. Similarly, Wall Street analysts use a company's *WACC* to estimate the value of a company's stock. When the stock's market price is below analysts' estimates, they issue a "buy" signal to investors. With so many decisions influenced by the *WACC*, companies put much effort into estimating their cost of capital. But where does that number come from?

A recent report by Deutsche Bank provides an answer. On April 27, 2011, Deutsche Bank raised its estimate of the value of Hershey by about 4%. The report explained that the bank's decision to upgrade its outlook on Hershey was based on a discounted cash flow model which employed a *WACC* for Hershey of 9%. To calculate Hershey's *WACC*, Deutsche Bank needed to know the returns that Hershey's lenders and its shareholders expected on their investments as well as the amount of debt and equity financing employed by the company. In most cases, the yield to maturity on a company's bonds is a good indication of the return that lenders expect, but how did Deutsche Bank determine the returns expected by Hershey's stockholders? In their report, Deutsche Bank explained that they used the Capital Asset Pricing Model to estimate Hershey's expected return on equity. For their analysis, Deutsche Bank estimated that Hershey's stock beta was 0.8, the risk-free rate was 4.5%, and the market risk premium was 6%. Those figures implied an expected return on Hershey stock of 9.3% [4.5% + (0.8 × 6%)]. Hershey had a modest amount of long-term debt outstanding that offered a yield of about 6%. Combining the costs of equity and debt and weighting by the proportion of each in the firm's overall financial structure produced a *WACC* of 9%.

Source: benzinga.com (**www.benzinga.com/analyst-ratings/analyst-color/11/04/1036039/
update-deutsche-bank-raises-pt-on-the-hershey-company-to**)

Learning Objectives

After studying this chapter you should be able to:

- Understand operating leverage and financial leverage, and the potential effect each of them has on a firm's cost of capital;

- Estimate the firm's weighted average cost of capital, both with and without the allowed tax-deductibility of interest payments to bondholders;

- Review the roles of breakeven analysis and sensitivity analysis in evaluating investment opportunities;

- Explain how scenario analysis, Monte Carlo simulation, and decision trees can be used to assess an investment's risk;

- Describe the types of real options and their role in valuing potential investments; and,

- Discuss the strategic aspects of capital budgeting with regard to competition and the role of real options in improving the quality of decisions.

This chapter concludes our coverage of capital budgeting. Chapter 8 preached the virtues of *NPV* analysis, and Chapter 9 showed how to generate the cash flow estimates required to calculate a project's *NPV*. This chapter focuses on the risk dimension of project analysis. To calculate *NPV*, an analyst must evaluate the risk of a project and decide what discount rate adequately rewards investors for bearing that risk. Often, the best place to discover clues for use in estimating the discount rate is the market for the firm's securities.

The chapter begins with a discussion of how managers can look to the market to calculate a discount rate that properly reflects the risk of a firm's investment projects. Even when managers are confident that they have estimated project cash flows carefully and have chosen a proper discount rate, they should perform additional analysis to understand the causes and effects of a project's risk. Their tools include breakeven analysis, sensitivity analysis, scenario analysis, simulation, and decision trees—all covered in this chapter. We conclude with sections on real options and on strategy that describe the sources of value in investment projects and illustrate how rudimentary application of *NPV* analysis can understate the value of certain investments.

10-1 Choosing the Right Discount Rate

10-1a Cost of Equity

What discount rate should managers use to calculate a project's *NPV*? This is a difficult question and is at times the source of heated discussions when firms evaluate capital investment proposals. *A project's discount rate must be high enough to compensate investors for the project's risk*. Thus, conceptually, the discount rate should reflect the return on an alternative (or "opportunity") project of equal risk. One implication of this statement is that if a firm undertakes many different investment projects of various degrees of risk, then managers err if they apply a single, companywide discount rate to value each investment. In principle, the appropriate discount rate to use in *NPV* calculations should vary from one investment to another if the risks vary across investments. Interestingly, survey data suggests that companies do not always follow this principle: CFOs appear to be fairly evenly split regarding the use of companywide versus project-specific discount rates in *NPV* calculations.

To simplify things a little, we initially consider a firm that finances its operations using only equity and invests in only one industry. Because the company has no debt, its investments must provide returns sufficient to satisfy just one type of investor: common stockholders. Because the firm invests in only one industry, we will assume that all its investments are *equally risky*. Therefore, when calculating the *NPV* of any project that this firm might undertake, its managers can use the required return on equity, often called the *cost of equity*, as the discount rate. If the company uses the cost of equity as its discount rate then, by definition, any project with a positive *NPV* will generate returns that exceed shareholders' required returns.

To quantify shareholders' return expectations, managers look to the market. Recall from Chapter 7 that, according to the CAPM, the expected or required return on

? JOB INTERVIEW QUESTION

How would you estimate the cost of capital for our company?

Figure 10.1   **Risk Adjustments to Cash Flows and Discount Rates**

More than 70% of CFOs always or almost always adjust cash flows or discount rates for market ("beta") risk. Also popular among CFOs are adjustments for interest rate, foreign exchange, and business cycle risks.

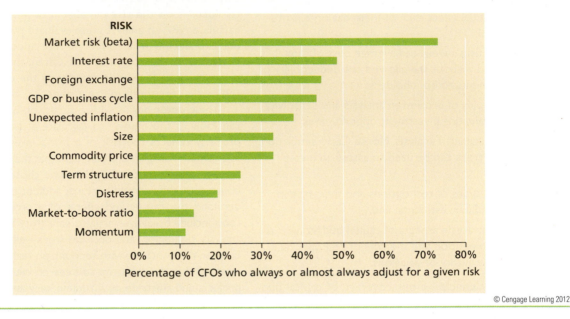

© Cengage Learning 2012

any security equals the risk-free rate *plus* the security's beta multiplied by the expected market risk premium:

(Eq. 10.1) $$E(r_i) = r_f + \beta_i(E(r_m) - r_f)$$

WHAT TO ASK

How does your firm estimate your cost of equity? Do you benchmark this against other firms in your industry?

Managers can estimate the return that shareholders require if they know (1) their firm's equity beta, (2) the risk-free rate, and (3) the expected market risk premium. Research has shown that most managers use the CAPM to compute their firm's cost of equity this way.

Figure 10.1 summarizes the responses of 392 CFOs to a survey question of Graham and Harvey (2001) regarding the types of risk they feel are important when adjusting cash flows or discount rates. Note the primary importance given to market risk as measured by beta in the CAPM.

EXAMPLE

Carbonlite, Inc., manufactures bicycle frames that are both extremely strong and very light. The firm finances its operations 100% with equity and is now evaluating a proposal to build a new manufacturing facility that will enable it to double its output within three years. Because Carbonlite sells a luxury good, its fortunes are sensitive to macroeconomic conditions; its stock has a beta of 1.5. Carbonlite's financial managers observe that the current interest rate on risk-free government bonds is 5%, and they expect that the return on the overall stock market will be about 11% per year in the future. Given this information, Carbonlite should calculate the *NPV* of the expansion proposal using a discount rate of 14%:

$$E(r) = 5\% + 1.5(11\% - 5\%)$$

$$= 14\%$$

To reiterate, Carbonlite should use its cost of equity capital, 14%, to discount cash flows because we have assumed both that the company has no debt on its balance sheet and that undertaking any of Carbonlite's investment proposals will not alter the firm's risk. If either assumption is invalid, then the cost of equity may not be the appropriate discount rate.

In the preceding example, Carbonlite's stock beta is 1.5 because sales of premium bicycle frames are highly correlated with the overall economy. Therefore, Carbonlite's investment in new capacity is riskier than an investment in new capacity by some other firm producing a product whose sales are relatively insensitive to economic conditions. For example, managers of a food-processing company might apply a lower discount rate to an expansion project than would Carbonlite's managers because the stock of a food processor has a lower beta. The general lesson is that the same type of capital investment project (such as capacity expansion, equipment replacement, or new product development) may require different discount rates in different industries. The level of *systematic (nondiversifiable) risk* varies from one industry to another; so, too, should the discount rate used in capital budgeting analysis.

Cost Structure and Operating Leverage Several other factors affect betas, which in turn affect project discount rates. One of the most important factors is a firm's cost structure—specifically, its mix of fixed and variable costs. The greater the importance of fixed costs in a firm's overall cost structure, the more volatile will be its cash flows and the higher will be its stock beta (all other factors held constant). Operating leverage measures the tendency of operating cash flow volatility to increase with fixed operating costs. Mathematically, the definition of operating leverage can be expressed as

operating leverage
Measures the tendency of operating cash flow volatility to increase with fixed operating costs.

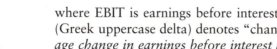

$$(\text{Eq. } 10.2) \qquad \text{Operating leverage} = \frac{\left(\dfrac{\Delta EBIT}{EBIT}\right)}{\left(\dfrac{\Delta \text{sales}}{\text{sales}}\right)}$$

where EBIT is earnings before interest and taxes (see Chapter 2) and the symbol Δ (Greek uppercase delta) denotes "change in." *Operating leverage equals the percentage change in earnings before interest and taxes divided by the percentage change in sales.* When a small percentage increase (decrease) in sales leads to a large percentage increase (decrease) in EBIT, the firm has high operating leverage. The connection between operating leverage and costs is easy to see in the next example.

EXAMPLE

Carbonlite, Inc., uses robotic technology to paint its finished bicycle frames, whereas its main competitor, Fiberspeed Corp., offers customized, hand-painted finishes. Robots represent a significant fixed cost for Carbonlite, but robots help keep variable costs low. Fiberspeed incurs very low fixed costs, but it has high variable costs because of the time required to paint frames by hand. Both firms sell their frames at an average price of $1,000 apiece. Last year each firm made a profit (EBIT) of $1 million on sales of 10,000 bicycle frames, as shown in Table 10.1. Suppose that next year both firms experience a 10% increase in sales volume to 11,000 frames, holding constant all the other figures. Carbonlite's fixed costs do not change, and its EBIT will increase by $600 ($1,000 price minus $400 variable costs) per additional frame sold. Thus Carbonlite's EBIT will increase 60% from $1 million to $1.6 million, so its operating leverage is 6.0 (60% ÷ 10%). Fiberspeed's EBIT grows from $1 million to $1.3 million, an increase of just 30%, so it's operating leverage is 3.0 (30% ÷ 10%).

Because Carbonlite has higher fixed costs and lower variable costs, its profits increase more rapidly in response to a given increase in sales than do Fiberspeed's profits. In short, Carbonlite has more operating leverage. Figure 10.2 shows this graphically. The figure shows two lines, one tracing out the relationship between sales growth (from the base of 10,000 frames per year) and EBIT growth (from the $1 million EBIT base) for Carbonlite, the other illustrating the same linkage for Fiberspeed.[1] Because of its greater operating leverage, the line for Carbonlite is much steeper than the one for Fiberspeed. Even though Carbonlite and Fiberspeed compete in the same industry, they may well use different discount rates in their capital budgeting analysis because operating leverage increases the risk of Carbonlite's cash flows relative to Fiberspeed's.

Financial Structure and Financial Leverage We have seen that Carbonlite's sales are extremely sensitive to the business cycle because the firm produces a luxury item. We have also observed that, because of its high operating leverage, Carbonlite's profits are quite sensitive to changes in sales. These factors contribute to Carbonlite's relatively high stock beta of 1.5 and its correspondingly high cost of equity of 14%. One other factor looms large in determining whether firms have high or low stock betas. Remember that Carbonlite's financial structure is 100% equity. In practice it is much more common to see both debt and equity on the right-hand side of a firm's balance

---
[1]These comparisons are based on a reference point of 10,000 frames per year sold for $1,000 per frame and an EBIT of $1 million. All changes described and shown in Figure 10.2 assume these points of reference in each case. Clearly, the sensitivity of these values to change will vary depending on the point of reference utilized.

Table 10.1

Financial Data for Carbonlite, Inc., and Fiberspeed Corp.

Item	Carbonlite	Fiberspeed
Fixed cost per year	$5 million	$2 million
Variable cost per bike frame	$400	$700
Sale price per bike frame	$1,000	$1,000
Contribution margin[a] per bike frame	$600	$300
Last year's sales volume	10,000 frames	10,000 frames
EBIT[b]	$1 million	$1 million

[a]The **contribution margin** is the sale price per unit minus the variable cost per unit.
For Carbonlite: $1,000 − $400 = $600 per bike.
For Fiberspeed: $1,000 − $700 = $300 per bike.
[b]EBIT equals sales volume multiplied by the contribution margin *minus* fixed costs.
For Carbonlite: (10,000 × $600) − $5,000,000 = $1,000,000
For Fiberspeed: (10,000 × $300) − $2,000,000 = $1,000,000

Figure 10.2

Operating Leverage for Carbonlite and Fiberspeed

The higher operating leverage of Carbonlite is reflected in its steeper slope, demonstrating that its *EBIT* is more responsive to a given change in sales than is the *EBIT* of Fiberspeed.

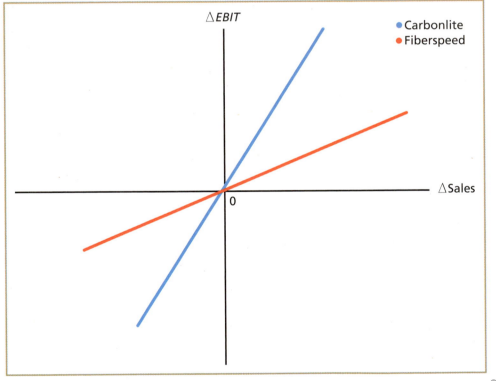

financial leverage
The magnification of both risk and expected return that results from the fixed cost associated with the use of debt. As a result, it leads to a higher stock beta.

sheet. When firms finance their operations with debt and equity, the presence of debt creates **financial leverage**, which leads to a higher stock beta. The effect of financial leverage on stock betas is much the same as the effect of operating leverage. When a firm borrows money, it creates a fixed cost that it must repay regardless of whether sales are high or low.[2] As was the case with operating leverage, an increase (decrease) in sales will lead to sharper increases (decreases) in earnings for a firm with financial leverage than for a firm that has only equity on its balance sheet.

---

[2]We use the term *fixed cost* here to mean a cost that does not vary with sales rather than simply a cost that is constant over time. Even when a firm agrees to a loan with a variable interest rate, which means that interest payments are not constant over time, the cost of repaying the debt does not generally vary as a function of sales.

Table 10.2

The Effect of Financial Leverage on Shareholder Returns

Account	Firm A	Firm B
Assets	$100 million	$100 million
Debt (interest rate = 8%)	$ 0 (0%)	$50 million (50%)
Equity	$100 million (100%)	$50 million (50%)
When Return on Assets Equals 20%		
EBIT	$20 million	$20 million
Less: Interest	0	4 million (0.08 × $50 million)
Cash to equity	$20 million	$16 million
ROE	$20 million/$100 million = 20%	$16 million/$50 million = 32%
When Return on Assets Equals 5%		
EBIT	$5 million	$5 million
Less: Interest	0	4 million (0.08 × $50 million)
Cash to equity	$5 million	$1 million
ROE	$5 million/$100 million = 5%	$1 million/$50 million = 2%

Table 10.2 illustrates the effect of financial leverage on the volatility of a firm's cash flows and on its beta. The table compares Firms A and B, which are identical in every respect except that Firm A finances its operations with 100% equity while Firm B uses 50% equity and 50% long-term debt with an interest rate of 8%. For simplicity, we assume that neither firm pays taxes. These firms sell identical products at the same price, they both have $100 million in assets, and they face the same production costs. Suppose that over the next year both firms generate EBIT equal to 20% of total assets, or $20 million. Firm A pays no interest, so it can distribute all $20 million to its shareholders, a 20% return on their $100 million equity investment. Firm B pays 8% interest on $50 million ($4 million). After paying interest, Firm B can distribute $16 million to shareholders, which represents a 32% return on their equity investment of $50 million. Suppose that under a different scenario both firms have EBIT equal to just 5% of assets, or $5 million. Firm A pays out all $5 million to its shareholders, a return of 5%. Firm B pays $4 million in interest, leaving just $1 million for shareholders, a return of only 2%. Thus, when business is good, the debt that it uses causes shareholders of Firm B to earn higher returns than shareholders of Firm A, and the opposite happens when business is bad.

When companies use debt to finance operations, discount-rate selection becomes complicated in two ways. First, debt creates financial leverage, which increases a firm's stock beta relative to the value it would have if the firm financed investments only with equity. Second, when a firm issues debt, it must satisfy two groups of investors rather than one. Cash flows generated from capital investment projects must be sufficient to meet the return requirements of bondholders as well as stockholders. Therefore, a firm that issues debt cannot discount project cash flows using only its cost of equity capital: it must choose a discount rate that reflects the expectations of both investor groups. Fortunately, finance theory offers a way to find that discount rate.

10-1b Weighted Average Cost of Capital (*WACC*)

In Chapter 7, we learned that the expected return on a portfolio of two assets equals the weighted average of the expected returns of each asset in the portfolio. We can apply that idea to the problem of selecting an appropriate discount rate for a company that has both debt and equity in its capital structure. Imagine that Lox-in-a-Box, Inc., a chain of kosher fast-food stores, has $100 million worth of common stock outstanding on which investors require a return of 15%. In addition, the firm has $50 million

Table 10.3	Cash Distributions to Lox-in-a-Box Investors	
	Total cash flow available to distribute (13% × $150 million)	$19.5 million
	Less: Interest owed on bonds (9% × $50 million)	4.5 million
	Cash available to shareholders ($19.5 million − $4.5 million)	$15.0 million
	Rate of return earned by shareholders ($15 million ÷ $100 million)	15%

in bonds outstanding that offer a 9% return.[3] To simplify our discussion, we hold the firm's overall risk constant by *assuming that the investments being considered do not change either the firm's cost structure or its financial structure.* Using this information, we can answer the question: What rate of return must the firm earn on its investments to satisfy both groups of investors?

weighted average cost of capital (WACC)
The after-tax weighted-average required return on all types of securities issued by a firm, in which the weights equal the percentage of each type of financing in a firm's overall capital structure.

The Basic Formula The answer lies in a concept known as the weighted average cost of capital (*WACC*). Let D and E denote the *market value* of the firm's debt and equity securities, respectively, and let r_d and r_e represent the rate of return that investors require on bonds and shares. The *WACC* is the simple weighted average of the required rates of return on debt and equity, where the weights equal the percentage of each type of financing in the firm's overall capital structure.[4]

(Eq. 10.3)
$$WACC = \left(\frac{D}{D+E}\right)r_d + \left(\frac{E}{D+E}\right)r_e$$

Plugging in the values from our example, we find that the *WACC* for Lox-in-a-Box is 13%:

$$WACC = \left(\frac{\$50}{\$50 + \$100}\right) \times 9\% + \left(\frac{\$100}{\$50 + \$100}\right) \times 15\% = 13\%$$

How can Lox-in-a-Box managers be sure that earning a 13% return on its investments will satisfy the expectations of both bondholders and shareholders? Here's a simple way to see the answer. Assume the company invests in a project that does not alter the firm's overall risk and earns exactly 13%. It therefore has a zero *NPV* if the company uses the *WACC* as its hurdle rate. Lox-in-a-Box has $150 million in assets. A project that offers a 13% return will generate $19.5 million in cash flow each year (13% × $150 million). Suppose that the company distributes this cash flow to its investors. Will they be satisfied? Table 10.3 illustrates that the cash flow the company generates is just enough to meet the expectations of bondholders and stockholders. Bondholders receive $4.5 million, or exactly the 9% return they expected when they purchased bonds. Shareholders receive $15 million, representing a 15% return on their $100-million investment in the firm's shares.

The *WACC* has a large impact on the value of a firm's investments, and hence, on the value of the firm itself. Holding an investment's cash flows constant, a lower

---

[3]The return we have in mind here is the yield to maturity (YTM)—developed in Chapter 4—on the firm's bonds. Unless the bonds sell at par, the coupon rate and the YTM will be different, and the YTM provides a better measure of the return that investors who purchase the firm's debt can expect.

[4]As a practical matter, firms in many countries, including the United States, can deduct interest payments to bondholders when they calculate taxable income. If a firm's interest payments are tax deductible, and if the corporate tax rate equals T_c, we have the following:

$$WACC = \left(\frac{D}{D+E}\right)(1 - T_c)r_d + \left(\frac{E}{D+E}\right)r_e$$

We address this important adjustment for tax-deductible interest later in this chapter, after we have fully developed the key concepts.

What Companies Do Globally

Can Foreign Investors Reduce the Cost of Capital?

What happens to the cost of capital when a nation that has been closed to foreign financial investment opens up to foreign investors? Finance theory suggests that allowing foreign capital in should reduce the cost of external financing for the country's publicly traded companies by increasing the supply of potential lenders and equity investors. Academic research strongly supports this idea.

A relatively recent study found that three economically important things happen when emerging economies open their stock markets to foreign investors. First, the aggregate dividend yield on publicly traded stocks falls by 240 basis points (2.4%). This drop will lower the cost of equity capital, r_e, and the *WACC*. The figure below demonstrates how dividend yields change in the five years before (-5 to -1) and five years after ($+1$ to $+5$) opening stock markets, which occurs in year 0 in the figure. Second, the nation's overall stock of capital increases by an average of 1.1 percentage point per year, meaning that companies invest more in productive assets. Third, the growth rate of output per worker rises by 2.3 percentage points per year. Together these three outcomes make a clear policy statement: let foreign financial investment in!

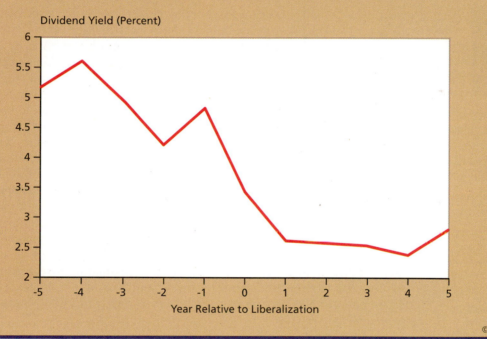

Dividend Yield (Percent)

Year Relative to Liberalization

© Cengage Learning 2012

WACC implies that the investment has a higher value. Thus, policies that reduce the cost of capital in an economy encourage companies to undertake new projects. The What Companies Do Globally insert explains that when countries open their financial markets to foreign investors, the cost of capital falls and companies respond by investing more.

Modifying the Basic WACC Formula The *WACC* formula can be modified to accommodate more than two sources of financing. For instance, suppose a firm raises money by issuing long-term debt, D, equity, E, and preferred stock, P. Denoting the respective required return on each security by r_d, r_e, and r_p, we can determine the *WACC* (still ignoring taxes) as follows:

$$WACC = \left(\frac{D}{D+E+P}\right)r_d + \left(\frac{E}{D+E+P}\right)r_e + \left(\frac{P}{D+E+P}\right)r_p$$

The S. D. Williams Company has 1 million shares of common stock outstanding, which currently trade at a price of $50 per share. The market value of the common stock is therefore $50 million ($50 per share × 1 million shares). The company believes that its stockholders require a 15% return on their investment. The company also has $47.1 million (par value) in five-year, fixed-rate notes with a coupon rate of 8% and a yield to maturity of 7%. Because the yield on these bonds is less than the coupon rate, they trade at a premium. The current market value of the five-year notes is $49 million. Lastly, the company has 200,000 outstanding preferred shares, which pay an $8 annual dividend and currently sell for $80 per share. The market value of the preferred stock is therefore $16 million ($80 per share × 200,000 shares) and the rate of return on the preferred stock is 10% ($8 annual dividend ÷ $80 current price). What is the company's *WACC*?

Begin by calculating the market value of each security. S. D. Williams has $50 million in common stock, $49 million in long-term debt, and $16 million in preferred stock for a total capitalization of $115 million. Next, determine the required rate of return on each type of security. The rates on common stock, long-term debt, and preferred stock are 15%, 7%, and 10%, respectively. Plug all these values into the *WACC* equation to obtain 10.9%:

$$WACC = \left(\frac{\$49}{\$115}\right) \times 7\% + \left(\frac{\$50}{\$115}\right) \times 15\% + \left(\frac{\$16}{\$115}\right) \times 10\% = 10.9\%$$

Beth Acton, former Vice President and Treasurer of Ford Motor Co.

"For us, it's a very critical calculation because we use it to assess product programs, to assess other capital investments, and to analyze acquisitions."

See the entire interview at **SMART**|finance

Smart Practices Video

? JOB INTERVIEW QUESTION

A firm has $100 million in publicly traded debt outstanding. How would you calculate the CAPM beta for this debt?

Kenneth Eades, University of Virginia

"Some of the big things that are hard to convince students to do in fact are widely used in practice."

See the entire interview at **SMART**|finance

Smart Ideas Video

An Important Proviso Now we have seen two approaches for determining the correct discount rate to apply when addressing capital budgeting problems. A firm that uses only equity should discount project cash flows using the cost of equity, and a firm that uses both debt and equity should discount cash flows using the *WACC*. Both recommendations are subject to the important proviso (noted earlier) that the company makes investments in only one line of business—or, stated differently, that the firm discounts cash flows using the *WACC* only when the project under consideration is very similar to the risk and financing choices of the firm's existing assets. For example, assuming an unchanged financing mix, if managers at Lox-in-a-Box believe that the firm should vertically integrate by investing in a salmon fishing fleet, they should not discount cash flows from that investment at the firm's *WACC*. The risks of salmon fishing hardly resemble those of running a fast-food chain, and it is the risk of the fast-food chain that is reflected in the firm's current *WACC*. Evaluating investments that deviate significantly from a firm's existing investments requires a different approach. To better understand that approach, we need to revisit the CAPM and see how it is related to the *WACC*.

10-1c The *WACC*, CAPM, and Taxes

The CAPM states that the required return on any asset is directly linked to the asset's beta. By now, we are used to thinking about betas of shares of common stock, but there is nothing about the CAPM that restricts its predictions to common stock. When a firm issues preferred stock or bonds, the required returns on those securities should reflect their systematic risks (i.e., their betas) just as the required returns on the firm's common shares should. We could use the same procedure to estimate the beta of a preferred share or a bond that we use to estimate a stock's beta. However, preferred stocks and bonds generally make fixed, predictable cash payments over time, so measuring the rate of return that investors require on these securities is relatively easy, even without knowing their betas. *For preferred stock, the dividend yield (annual dividend ÷ price) provides a good measure of required returns; for debt, the yield to maturity (YTM) does the same, at least for high-grade debt with relatively low default risk.*

The Main Lessons Summarizing the main lessons we have learned thus far, we offer the following rules about finding the right discount rate for an investment project:

1. If an all-equity firm invests in an asset that is similar to its existing assets, then the cost of equity is the appropriate discount rate to use in *NPV* calculations.

2. If a firm with both debt and equity invests in an asset that is similar to its existing assets, then the *WACC* is the appropriate discount rate to use in *NPV* calculations, as long as the firm's financial structure remains unchanged.

3. The *WACC* reflects the return that the firm must earn on average across all its assets in order to satisfy investors, but using the *WACC* to discount cash flows of any one investment can lead to mistakes. The reason for this is that a particular investment may be more or less risky than the firm's average investment and so, in return, require a higher or lower discount rate than the *WACC*, assuming an unchanged financial structure.

? **WHAT TO ASK**

How does your firm handle the effects of taxes on the cost of capital given the many different tax jurisdictions that you are subject to?

Considering Taxes Nothing in the real world is as simple as it is portrayed in textbooks. One important item that we have neglected thus far is the effect of taxes on project discount rates. In the United States and many other countries, interest payments to bondholders are tax deductible. This results in a lower cost of debt. For example, a firm with a before-tax cost (r_d) of debt of 7% and a tax rate (T_c) of 30% would have an after-tax cost of debt [$r_d \times (1 - T_c)$] of 4.9% [7.0% $\times (1 - 0.30)$]. The tax-deductibility of interest lowers a firm's tax payments and therefore effectively reduces its cost of debt. So the opportunity to deduct interest payments reduces the after-tax cost of debt and changes the basic *WACC* formula:

$$(Eq.\ 10.4) \qquad WACC = \left(\frac{D}{D + E}\right)(1 - T_c)r_d + \left(\frac{E}{D + E}\right)r_e$$

where T_c is the marginal corporate tax rate.

Fortunately, the three main lessons listed previously do not change when we add taxes to the picture. Only the calculations change. When a firm is making an "ordinary" investment, it can use Equation 10.4 to determine its after-tax *WACC*, which serves as the discount rate in *NPV* calculations.

10-1 Concept Review Questions

1. Why is using the cost of equity to discount project cash flows inappropriate when a firm uses both debt and equity in its capital structure?

2. Two firms in the same industry have very different equity betas. Offer two reasons why this could occur.

3. For a firm considering expansion of its existing line of business, why is the *WACC*, rather than the cost of equity, the preferred discount rate if the firm has both debt and equity in its capital structure?

4. The cost of debt, r_d, is generally less than the cost of equity, r_e, because debt is a less risky security. A naive application of the *WACC* formula might suggest that a firm could lower its cost of capital (thereby raising the *NPV* of its current and future investments) by using more debt and less equity in its capital structure. Give one reason why using more debt might not reduce a firm's *WACC*, even if $r_d < r_e$.

10-2   A Closer Look at Risk

Thus far, the only consideration we have given to risk in our capital budgeting analysis is selecting the right discount rate. But it would be simplistic to say that, given a stream of cash flows, an analyst's work is done after he has discounted those cash flows using a risk-adjusted discount rate to determine the *NPV*. Managers generally want to know more about a project than just its *NPV*. They want to know the sources of uncertainty and the downside risk as well as the quantitative importance of each source. Managers need this information to decide whether a project requires additional analysis, such as market research or product testing. Managers also want to identify a project's key value drivers, so they can closely monitor them after an investment is made. Next, we explore techniques that give managers deeper insights into the uncertainty structure of capital investments.

10-2a Breakeven Analysis

breakeven point (BEP)
The level of sales or production that a firm must achieve in order to fully cover all costs. Sales or production above the BEP results in profits.

contribution margin
The sale price per unit (SP) minus variable cost per unit (VC).

When firms make investments, they do so with the objective of earning a profit. But another objective that sometimes enters the decision process is avoiding losses. Therefore, managers often want to know what is required for a project to break even. Breakeven analysis can be expressed in many different ways. For instance, when a firm introduces a new product, it may want to know the level of sales at which incremental net income turns from negative to positive. When evaluating a new product launch over several years, managers might ask what growth rate in sales the firm must achieve in order to reach a project *NPV* of zero. Perhaps the most common form of breakeven analysis focuses on the minimum sales volume needed for a firm to fully cover all costs. The standard equation for the breakeven point (BEP) is found by dividing the fixed costs (FC) by the contribution margin, which is the sale price per unit (SP) minus variable cost per unit (VC).

$$\text{(Eq. 10.5)} \qquad \text{BEP} = \frac{\text{fixed costs}}{\text{contribution margin}} = \frac{\text{fixed costs}}{\text{SP} - \text{VC}}$$

EXAMPLE

Take another look at Table 10.1 on page 320, which shows price and cost information for Carbonlite, Inc., and Fiberspeed Corp. How many bicycle frames must each firm sell to achieve a breakeven point with EBIT equal to zero? We can obtain the answer by substituting the data for each firm into Equation 10.5.

$$\text{Carbonlite breakeven point} = \frac{\$5,000,000}{(\$1,000 - \$400)} = 8,333 \text{ frames}$$

$$\text{Fiberspeed breakeven point} = \frac{\$2,000,000}{(\$1,000 - \$700)} = 6,667 \text{ frames}$$

Figures 10.3a and 10.3b illustrate the breakeven point (BEP) for each firm. Despite its $600 contribution margin, Carbonlite's high fixed costs result in a breakeven point at higher sales volume than Fiberspeed's breakeven point. This should not surprise us, as we already know that Carbonlite's production process results in higher operating leverage than Fiberspeed's.

Breakeven analysis is popular in part because it provides clear targets. From breakeven calculations, managers can derive specific goals for different functional areas in the firm (e.g., produce at least 10,000 units, gain at least a 5% market share, hold variable costs to no more than 65% of the selling price). As always, we encourage managers to use breakeven analysis in the context of net present values rather than earnings targets. A project that reaches the breakeven point in terms of net income would still destroy shareholder value if it does not recover the firm's cost of capital. A firm that exceeds the NPV breakeven point will create shareholder value.

? JOB INTERVIEW QUESTION
How would you determine the best output mix for a factory producing at full capacity?

10-2b Sensitivity Analysis

Most capital budgeting problems require analysts to make many different assumptions before arriving at a final *NPV*. For instance, forecasting project cash flows may require assumptions about the selling price of output, costs of raw materials, market

Figure 10.3a   **Breakeven Point for Carbonlite**

The breakeven point (BEP) for Carbonlite is 8,333 units, which occurs at the point where its total costs equal its total revenue.

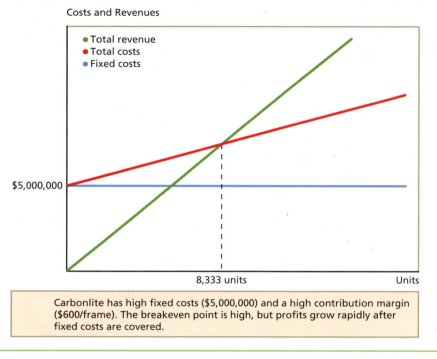

Costs and Revenues

- Total revenue
- Total costs
- Fixed costs

$5,000,000

8,333 units   Units

Carbonlite has high fixed costs ($5,000,000) and a high contribution margin ($600/frame). The breakeven point is high, but profits grow rapidly after fixed costs are covered.

© Cengage Learning 2012

Figure 10.3b   **Breakeven Point for Fiberspeed**

The breakeven point (BEP) for Fiberspeed is 6,667 units, which occurs at the point where its total costs equal its total revenue.

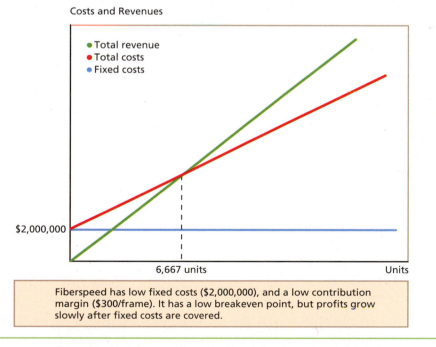

Costs and Revenues

- Total revenue
- Total costs
- Fixed costs

$2,000,000

6,667 units   Units

Fiberspeed has low fixed costs ($2,000,000), and a low contribution margin ($300/frame). It has a low breakeven point, but profits grow slowly after fixed costs are covered.

© Cengage Learning 2012

sensitivity analysis
Exploration of the impact of individual assumptions on a decision variable, such as a project's *NPV*, by determining the effect of changing one assumption while holding all others fixed.

share, and many other unknown quantities. Managers use **sensitivity analysis** to explore the importance of each individual assumption, holding all other assumptions fixed, on the project's *NPV*. A common way of conducting sensitivity analysis is first to establish a base case set of assumptions for a particular project and then to calculate its *NPV* based on those assumptions. Next, managers allow one assumption to change while holding all others fixed, recalculating the *NPV* based on that one change. By repeating this process for all the uncertain variables in an *NPV* calculation, managers can see how sensitive the *NPV* is to changes in baseline assumptions. The following example illustrates this procedure.

EXAMPLE

Imagine that Greene Transportation Incorporated (GTI) has developed a new skateboard equipped with a gyroscope for improved balance. GTI estimates that *this project has a positive NPV of $236,000* under the following base-case assumptions:

1. The project's life is five years.
2. The project requires an up-front investment of $7 million.
3. GTI will depreciate the initial investment on a straight-line basis for five years.
4. One year from now, the skateboard industry will sell 500,000 units.
5. Total industry unit volume will increase by 5% per year.
6. GTI expects to capture 5% of the market in the first year.
7. GTI expects to increase its market share by one percentage point each year after year 1.
8. The selling price will be $200 in year 1.
9. The selling price will decline by 10% annually after year 1.
10. All production costs are variable and will equal 60% of the selling price.
11. GTI's tax rate is 30%.
12. The appropriate discount rate is 14%.

Under the base-case assumptions, the project has a small (relative to the $7 million investment) but positive *NPV* ($236,000), so GTI's managers may want to explore how sensitive the *NPV* is to changes in the assumptions. Analysts often begin a sensitivity analysis by developing both pessimistic and optimistic forecasts for each of the model's important assumptions. These forecasts may be based on subjective judgments about the range of possible outcomes or on historical data drawn from the firm's past investments. For example, a firm with historical data available on output prices might set the pessimistic and optimistic forecasts at one standard deviation below and above their expected price.

Table 10.4 shows pessimistic and optimistic forecasts for several of the *NPV* model's key assumptions. Next to each assumption is the project *NPV* that results from changing one (and only one) assumption from the base-case scenario. For example, if GTI can sell its product for $225 rather than $200 per unit the first year, the project *NPV* increases to $960,000. If, however, the selling price is less than expected—say, $175 per unit—then the project *NPV* declines to −$488,000. A glance at Table 10.4 reveals that small deviations in assumptions about market share generate large *NPV* changes whereas assumptions about market size have less impact.

Table 10.4

Sensitivity Analysis of the Gyroscope Skateboard Project (Base-case *NPV* = $236) (all dollar values in thousands, except initial selling price)

NPV	Pessimistic	Assumption	Optimistic	*NPV*
−$558	$8,000	Initial investment	$6,000	$1,030
−343	450,000 units	Market size in year 1	550,000 units	815
−73	2% per year	Growth in market size	8% per year	563
−1,512	3%	Initial market share	7%	1,984
−1,189	0%	Growth in market share	2% per year	1,661
−488	$175	Initial selling price	$225	960
−54	62% of sales	Variable costs	58% of sales	526
−873	−20% per year	Annual price change	0% per year	1,612
−115	16%	Discount rate	12%	617

© Cengage Learning 2012

10-2c Scenario Analysis and Monte Carlo Simulation

scenario analysis
A variation of *sensitivity analysis* that provides for calculating the decision variable, such as net present value, when a whole set of assumptions changes in a particular way.

Scenario analysis is a variation of sensitivity analysis. Rather than adjust a single assumption up or down, analysts conduct scenario analysis by calculating the project's *NPV* when a whole set of assumptions changes in a particular way. For example, what if consumer interest in GTI's new skateboard is low, leading to a lower market share and a lower selling price than originally anticipated. If production volume falls short of expectations, cost as a percentage of sales may also be higher than expected.

Monte Carlo simulation
A sophisticated form of sensitivity analysis that calculates the decision variable, such as *NPV*, using a range or distribution of potential outcomes for each of a model's assumptions.

David Nickel, Controller for Intel Communications Group, Intel Corp.

"One of the key things we try to do is to try to understand key scenarios."

See the entire interview at **SMART** | finance

Smart Practices Video

Pam Roberts, former Executive Director of Corporate Services, Cummins Inc.

"We recognize that we can't predict each parameter with great accuracy."

See the entire interview at **SMART** | finance

Smart Practices Video

decision tree
A visual representation of the sequential choices that managers face with regard to a particular investment.

Developing realistic scenarios requires a great deal of thinking about how an *NPV* model's assumptions are related to each other. Analysts must ask questions, such as: "If the market doesn't grow as fast as we expect, which other of our assumptions might also be wrong?" As with sensitivity analysis, firms often construct a base-case scenario along with more optimistic and pessimistic ones. For instance, consider a worst-case scenario for GTI's new skateboard. Suppose Murphy's Law kicks in, and every pessimistic assumption from Table 10.4 becomes reality. In that case, the project's *NPV* is a disastrous negative $4.9 million. On the other hand, if all the optimistic assumptions turn out to be correct, then the *NPV* is a positive $11.7 million. Although extreme, these scenarios are still useful in that they illustrate the range of possible *NPVs*.

There is also an even more sophisticated form of sensitivity analysis. In **Monte Carlo simulation**, analysts specify a range or a distribution of potential outcomes for each of the model's assumptions. For example, a simulation might specify that GTI's skateboard price is a random variable drawn from a normal distribution with a mean of $200 and a standard deviation of $30. Similarly, the analyst could dictate that the skateboard might achieve an initial market share anywhere between 1% and 10%, with each outcome being equally likely (i.e., a uniform distribution). It is even possible to specify the degree of correlation between key variables. The model could be structured in such a way that when the demand for skateboards is unusually high, the likelihood of obtaining a high price increases.

Analysts enter all the assumptions about distributions of possible outcomes into a spreadsheet. Next, a simulation software package takes random draws from these distributions, calculating the project's cash flows (and perhaps its *NPV*) over and over again under different scenarios, perhaps thousands of times. After completing these calculations, the software package produces statistical output that includes the distribution of project cash flows (and *NPVs*) as well as sensitivity figures for each of the model's assumptions.

The use of Monte Carlo simulation has grown dramatically during the last twenty-five years because of steep declines in the costs of computer power and simulation software.[5] Its fundamental appeal is that it provides decision makers with a probability distribution of *NPVs* rather than a single point estimate of the *expected NPV*. This improves the information available to decision makers by allowing them to consider the risk (probability distribution) as well as the expected value of *NPV*.

The bottom line is that Monte Carlo simulation is a powerful tool when used properly and tempered with common sense. Using simulation to explore the distribution of a project's cash flows—and the major sources of risk driving that distribution—should result in better investment decisions, but be wary of *NPV* distributions produced by a simulation program.

10-2d Decision Trees

Most important investment decisions are much more complex than simply forecasting cash flows, discounting at the appropriate rate, and investing if the *NPV* exceeds zero. In the real world, managers face a sequence of future decisions that influence an investment's value. These decisions might include whether to expand or abandon a project, whether to alter a marketing program, when to upgrade manufacturing equipment, and, most important, how to respond to the actions of competitors. A **decision tree** is

---

[5]Just a few of the companies that we know have used Monte Carlo simulation include Merck, Intel, Procter & Gamble, General Motors, Pfizer, Owens-Corning, and Cummins.

a visual representation of the sequential choices that managers face with regard to a particular investment. Sketching out a decision tree is somewhat like thinking several moves ahead in a game of chess. The value of decision trees is that they force analysts to think through a series of *if-then* statements that describe how they will react as the future unfolds. The following example illustrates the use of decision trees.

EXAMPLE

Imagine that Trinkle Foods Limited of Canada has invented a new salt substitute, Odessa, which it plans to use in snack foods such as potato chips and crackers. The company is trying to decide whether to spend 5 million Canadian dollars (C$) to test-market, in Vancouver, British Columbia, a new line of potato chips flavored with Odessa. Depending on the outcome of that test, Trinkle may spend an additional C$50 million one year later to launch a full line of snack foods across Canada. If consumer acceptance in Vancouver is high, the company predicts that its full product line will generate net cash inflows of C$12 million per year for ten years.[6] If consumers in Vancouver respond less favorably, Trinkle expects cash inflows from a nationwide launch to be just C$2 million per year for ten years. Trinkle's cost of capital is 15%.

Figure 10.4 shows the decision tree for this problem. Initially, the firm can choose whether or not to spend the C$5 million on test-marketing. If Trinkle goes ahead with the market test, it estimates the probability of high and low consumer acceptance to be 50%. After the company sees the test results, it will decide whether to invest C$50 million for a major product launch.

The proper way to work through a decision tree is to begin at the end and work backward to the initial decision. Suppose that Trinkle learns one year from now that the Vancouver market test was successful. At that point, Trinkle calculates the *NPV* (in millions of Canadian dollars) of launching the product as follows:

$$NPV = -C\$50 + \frac{C\$12}{1.15^1} + \frac{C\$12}{1.15^2} + \frac{C\$12}{1.15^3} + \cdots + \frac{C\$12}{1.15^{10}} = C\$10.23$$

Clearly, Trinkle will invest if it winds up in this part of the decision tree, but what if initial test results are unfavorable and it still launches the product? In that situation, the *NPV* is

$$NPV = -C\$50 + \frac{C\$2}{1.15^1} + \frac{C\$2}{1.15^2} + \frac{C\$2}{1.15^3} + \cdots + \frac{C\$2}{1.15^{10}} = -C\$39.96$$

Thus, the product should not launch if the test marketing is unfavorable. The best decision to make if the initial test does not go well is to walk away. After the test has been done, its cost is a *sunk cost*. As of time 1, the *NPV* of doing nothing is zero.

A decision tree helps to create a set of simple if-then decision rules. If initial test results indicate high consumer acceptance of Odessa, then Trinkle should go ahead with the full product launch to capture a positive *NPV* of C$10.23 million. But if initial results show that consumers do not like foods flavored with Odessa, Trinkle should not invest the additional C$50 million.

With this information in hand, we now step back and evaluate the project at time 0. We can evaluate today's decision about whether or not to spend the C$5 million on testing. Recall that we calculated the *NPVs* in terms of year-1 dollars—that is, as of the date of the decision on whether or not to launch the product nationwide. In terms of today's Canadian dollars (millions), the expected *NPV* of conducting the market test is determined to be

$$NPV = -C\$5 + 0.5 \left(\frac{C\$10.23}{1.15} \right) + 0.5 \left(\frac{C\$0}{1.15} \right) = -C\$0.55$$

Spending the money for test-marketing does not appear to be worthwhile.

Subtle Decision Tree Issues There is a subtle flaw in our analysis of Trinkle. Can you spot it? Currently, when Trinkle must decide whether or not to invest in test-marketing, it does not know what the test results (unavailable for another year) will indicate. So at the end of one year, when the firm chooses whether or not to invest C$50 million for a major product launch, it knows a great deal more. If the market research in Vancouver indicates a high demand for Odessa, then the risk that it will flop elsewhere in Canada is probably very low. If so, does it make sense to use a discount rate of 15% when calculating the *NPV* of the product launch decision? A mere one-percentage point reduction in the discount rate, from 15% to 14%, would be enough to cause the expected *NPV* of conducting the market test to increase from −C$0.55 to C$0.52, thereby suggesting that Trinkle's test marketing *would* be worthwhile.

Though decision trees are useful to sharpen strategic thinking, the previous example illustrates a potentially serious flaw. The risk of many investments changes as you move from one point in the decision tree to another. Worse, analysts rarely attempt

---

[6]Note that the test begins immediately, the C$50 million investment starts one year later, and the stream of C$12 million annual cash inflows begins one year after that.

Figure 10.4   **Decision Tree for Odessa Investment**

The decision tree depicts the sequence of decisions facing Trinkle Foods' decision whether to spend C$5 million to test market Odessa, a new salt substitute. If the test market is successful, the *NPV* of launching the product is C$10.23 million; if the initial test results are negative, and it launches the product, it will have an *NPV* of −C$39.96 million. By working backwards (from right to left on the tree), Trinkle can decide whether to conduct the test in the first place.

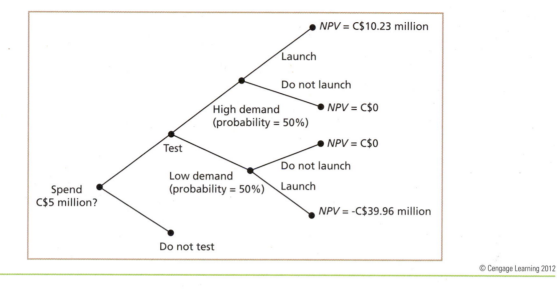

© Cengage Learning 2012

to make adjustments to the discount rate to reflect these risk changes. This makes it difficult to know whether the final *NPV* obtained from a decision tree is correct.

Another practical difficulty in using decision trees is determining the probabilities for each branch of the tree. Unless firms have a great deal of experience with similar "bets," estimating these probabilities is more art than science. How does Trinkle Foods know that the probability of a successful Vancouver market test is 50%? Why not 80% or 10%? The only way to form useful estimates of these probabilities is to rely on experience—yours or the experience of others. For example, large pharmaceutical companies have enough experience investing in potential drug compounds to make reasonable estimates of the odds that any particular drug will make it to market.

10-2 Concept Review Questions

5. Why might a project that reaches the *breakeven point (BEP)* in terms of net income be bad for shareholders?

6. Which variable do you think would be more valuable to examine in a project *sensitivity analysis*: the growth rate of sales or the allowable depreciation deductions each year? Explain.

7. You work for an airline that is considering a proposal to offer a new, nonstop flight between Atlanta and Tokyo.

Senior management asks a team of analysts to run a *Monte Carlo simulation* of the project. Your job is to advise the group on what assumptions they should put in the simulation regarding the distribution of the ticket price your airline will be able to charge. How would you go about this task?

8. Why might the discount rate vary as you move through a *decision tree*?

10-3   Real Options

10-3a Why *NPV* May Not Always Give the Right Answer

Only a few decades ago, the net present value method was essentially absent from the world of corporate practice. Today it has become the standard tool for evaluating capital investments, especially in very large firms. Even so, *NPV* can systematically overstate or understate the value of certain types of investments. These systematic errors occur because the *NPV* method is essentially static. That is, *NPV* calculations

? JOB INTERVIEW QUESTION

Under what conditions might an *NPV* calculation recommend the wrong investment decision?

real option
The right, but not the obligation, to take a future action (e.g., cancel or delay) when implementing a project. Note that these actions can change an investment's value.

random walk
When next period's value for a variable equals this period's value plus or minus a random shock. When financial asset prices follow a random walk, future and past prices are statistically unrelated, and the best estimate of the future price is simply the current price.

do not typically take into account potential future actions by managers that may increase the value of an investment once it has been made. When managers can react to changes in the environment in ways that alter an investment's value, we say that the investment has an embedded real option. A real option is the right, but not the obligation, to take a future action (e.g., cancel or delay) when implementing a project. Note that these actions can change an investment's value. We will present an in-depth analysis of how option-pricing techniques can be used to improve capital budgeting processes in Chapter 19, so only an overview is presented here. Hopefully, this will be enough to convince you that identifying and valuing—even if only conceptually— the real options embedded in most capital investment projects can help managers make better investment decisions.

A simple example shows where *NPV* can go wrong. Suppose that you are bidding on the rights to extract oil from a proven site over the next year. You expect extraction costs from this field to run about $79 per barrel. Currently, oil sells for $75 per barrel. You know that oil prices fluctuate over time, but you do not possess any unique ability to predict where the price of oil is headed next. Accordingly, you assume that the price of oil follows a random walk, meaning that next period's value equals this period's value plus or minus a random shock. Because future and past oil prices are statistically unrelated, your best estimate of the future price of oil is simply the current price. How much would you bid?

An *NPV* analysis would tell you not to bid at all. If your best forecast of the future price of oil is $75 per barrel, then you cannot make money when extraction costs are $79 per barrel. The expected *NPV* of this investment is negative, no matter how much oil you can pump out of the ground.

A real options approach to the problem yields a different answer. If you own the rights to extract oil, you are not obligated to do so if the price is too low. You reason that you will pump oil only when the market price is high enough to justify incurring the extraction costs. Predicting exactly when the price of oil will be high enough to make pumping profitable is impossible, but historical price fluctuations persuade you that the price of oil will be higher than extraction costs at least some of the time. Therefore, extraction rights at this site are worth more than zero.[7]

The oil extraction problem is analogous to the test-marketing problem in the previous section. In both cases, managers have the option of spending additional resources at a future date. These options add to a project's value in a way that traditional *NPV* analysis often ignores because of its static approach to decision making. In general, we can say that the value of a project equals the sum of two components—the part captured by *NPV* and the remaining value of real options:

$$\text{Project value} = NPV \pm \text{Option value}$$

The *NPV* may either understate or overstate a project's value, depending on whether the proposed investment creates or destroys future options for the firm. In the oil drilling example, buying extraction rights creates an option—to pump or not to pump oil in the future—and the *NPV* understates the investment's value. But it is just as easy to imagine projects that eliminate options rather than create them. For instance, by signing a long-term contract to supply a refinery with a certain quantity of crude oil each month, a firm loses its flexibility in the extraction decision.

? WHAT TO ASK

Does your company use real options analysis when making capital investment decisions?

10-3b Types of Real Options

Like Monte Carlo simulation, real options analysis is growing in popularity in many industries. We now turn to a description of common types of real options encountered in capital budgeting decisions: expansion, follow-on investment, abandonment, and flexibility options.

---

[7]To determine exactly how much these rights are worth, we must use techniques that are presented later, in Chapter 19.

Expansion Options What do companies do when one of their investments becomes a huge success? They look for new markets in which to expand that investment. For instance, once Blu-Ray technology gained significant popularity, consumers could rent Blu-Ray DVDs in video stores, grocery stores, and many other places where they were previously unavailable. Likewise for Blu-Ray players: the number of retail outlets selling them also expanded dramatically.

Naturally, companies invest in expansion only for their most successful investments. As mentioned in the decision-tree problem, the risk of expanding an already successful project is much less than the risk when the project first begins. A traditional *NPV* calculation misses both of these attributes—the *option to expand* or not, depending on initial success, and the change in risk that occurs when the initial outcome is favorable.

Follow-On Investment Options A *follow-on investment option* is similar to an expansion option. It entitles a firm to make additional investments should earlier investments prove to be successful. The difference between this and the expansion option is that here the subsequent investments are more complex than a simple expansion of the earlier ones.

Hollywood offers an excellent example of follow-on options. Did you know that the rights to movie sequels are sometimes bought and sold before the original movie is completed? By purchasing the right to produce a sequel, a studio obtains the opportunity to make an additional investment should the first film become a commercial success.

Abandonment Options Just as firms have the right to invest additional resources to expand projects that enjoy early success, they also can withdraw resources from projects that fail to live up to short-run expectations. In an extreme case, a company may decide to withdraw its entire commitment to a particular project and exercise its *option to abandon*.

In legal systems that provide limited liability to corporations, shareholders have the ultimate abandonment option. A firm may borrow money to finance its operations, but if it cannot generate cash flow sufficient to pay back its debts then management may declare bankruptcy, turn over the company's assets to its lenders, and let the shareholders walk away. Though declaring bankruptcy is not what shareholders hope for when they invest, it means that the most shareholders can lose is their initial investment. Put another way, investors who buy shares are willing to pay a little more because of the embedded option to abandon (in this case, the *default option*) than they would be willing to pay without that option. We can express this mathematically as follows:

$$\text{Share value} = NPV + \text{Value of default option}$$

Consider the same situation from the lender's perspective. When lenders commit funds to a corporation, they know that the borrower may default and that the lenders' ability to recover the associated losses does not extend to the shareholders' personal assets. We could even say that an investor who buys a bond from a corporation is simultaneously selling an option to the firm—the option to default. So the price paid by the investor for the bond is effectively net of the proceeds from the option to default. We typically assume that an option to default is essentially absent in U.S. Treasury securities (although Moody's downgrade of U.S. debt raises some doubt about that assumption). If a Treasury bond and a corporate bond offer the same interest payments to investors, which one would sell at a higher price? Treasuries, because

$$\text{Corporate bond value} = \text{Treasury bond value} - \text{Value of firm's default option}$$

Abandonment options crop up in unexpected places, and it is important for managers to recognize whether a given investment has an attached abandonment option or grants another party the right to abandon. Consider refundable and nonrefundable airline tickets. With a refundable ticket, the traveler has the right to abandon travel plans without incurring a penalty. Such a ticket is more valuable than one that requires a traveler to pay a penalty if plans change.

Flexibility Options   Other options that have recently come to prominence in capital budgeting analyses are collectively known as *flexibility options*. Three examples illustrate the nature of flexibility options. First, the ability to use multiple production inputs creates option value. An example of such *input flexibility* is a boiler that can switch between oil or gas as a fuel source, enabling managers to switch from one type of fuel to another as prices change. Second, having a flexible production technology capable of producing (and switching between) a variety of outputs using the same basic plant and equipment can be useful. For example, an oil refiner can switch its output between different grades/types of fuel such as 87 or 91 octane gas or kerosene. This type of *output/operating flexibility* creates value when output prices are volatile.

Finally, option value can be created by maintaining excess production capacity that can quickly be used to meet peak demand. Though costly to purchase and maintain, this *capacity flexibility* can be quite valuable in capital-intensive industries subject to wide swings in demand and long lead times for building new capacity. For example, consider the profit opportunities a multinational company can employ if it has the excess capacity needed to move production around the world in response to movements in the real exchange rate.

10-3c The Surprising Link Between Risk and Real Option Values

Until now, the approach presented for every valuation problem covered in this text satisfies the following statement: Holding other factors constant, an increase in an asset's risk decreases its price. If two bonds offer the same coupon but investors perceive one to be riskier than the other, then the safer bond will sell at a higher price. If two investment projects have identical cash flows but one is riskier, then analysts will discount the cash flows of the riskier project at a higher rate, resulting in a lower *NPV*.

A surprising fact is that this relationship does not hold for options. For an explanation, we go back to the oil extraction problem. The current price of oil is $75 per barrel and extraction costs are $79. The expected future price of oil is the same as the current price so an *NPV* calculation would say that this investment is worthless.

Cengage Learning

Andy Bryant, Executive Vice President and Chief Administrative Officer, Intel Corp.

"Option theory was always used to show why we should do something. I never saw an analysis that said why we should not do something."

See the entire interview at **SMART|finance**

Smart Practices Video

Consider two different scenarios regarding the future price of oil. In the low-risk scenario, the price of oil in the future will be $79 or $71, with each price equally probable. This means that the expected price of oil is still $75. However, both an *NPV* and an options analysis would conclude that bidding on the rights to this site is not a good idea because the price of oil will never be above the $79 extraction cost.

Next, think about the high-risk scenario. The price of oil may be $90 or $60 with equal probability, so again we have an expected price of $75. If the price turns out to be $60, extracting the oil clearly does not make sense. But if the price turns out to be $90, extracting oil generates a profit of $11 per barrel ($90 sale price − $79 extraction cost). Therefore, a real options analysis would say that bidding for the right to extract the oil is a sensible decision.

Why does more risk lead to higher option values? Observe that in these two scenarios the payoff from extracting oil equals zero whether the price of oil falls to $71 or all the way to $60. At either price, an oil producer would simply decline to incur extraction costs; thus, a huge decrease in the price of oil is no more costly than a small decrease. On the other hand, the payoffs on the upside increase as the price of oil rises. This all means that options are characterized by asymmetric payoffs. When the price of oil is extremely volatile, the potential benefits if prices rise are quite large. Yet if oil prices fall precipitously then there is no additional cost relative to a slight decline in prices, since in either case the payoff is zero.

9. Give a real-world example of an *expansion option* and an *abandonment option*.

10. We know that riskier firms must pay higher interest rates when they borrow money. Explain this using the language of *real options*.

●10-4 Strategy and Capital Budgeting

10-4a Competition and *NPV*

Finance textbooks tend to focus on the mechanics of project evaluation: how to estimate cash flows, how to select the right discount rate, how to calculate an *NPV* or *IRR*, and so on. This emphasis on technique is intentional. Knowing how to apply quantitative discipline to the project selection process is crucial. Nevertheless, experienced managers rarely make major investment decisions based solely on *NPV* calculations. The best managers have a well-honed intuition that tells them why a particular project would or would not be a good investment. Their business acumen helps them to recognize projects that will create shareholder value, even if the *NPV* numbers from financial analysts are negative, and to avoid investments that will destroy value, even when the *NPV* calculations are positive.

Jon Olson, Chief Financial Officer, Xilinx Corp.

"Our job at the company is to test the limits, not just create financial analysis that ratifies peoples' intuition."

See the entire interview at **SMART | finance**

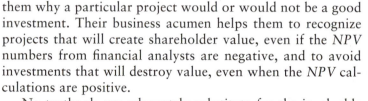

Smart Ethics Video

No textbook can adequately substitute for the invaluable experience of making many investment decisions over several years and then watching some of them succeed and others fail. However, there are certain common characteristics shared by projects that enhance shareholder value.

Recall some of the most basic lessons from microeconomics about a perfectly competitive market. In such a market, there are many buyers and sellers trading a similar product or service. Because every player in the market is small relative to the whole market, everyone behaves as if their decisions and actions will not affect prices. Competition and the lack of entry or exit barriers ensures that in the long run the product's market price equals the marginal cost of producing it, and no firm earns pure economic profit.[8] In a market with zero economic profits, the *NPV* of any investment equals zero: every project earns just enough to recover the cost of capital, no more and no less.

Therefore, how can any project earn a positive *NPV*? The answer: A project can earn a positive *NPV* *only when markets are not perfectly competitive*. For example, if the project calls for production of a new good, is there something about this good that clearly differentiates it from similar goods already in the market? If the new product is genuinely unique, is there some kind of entry barrier (e.g., patents, limited access to production inputs, etc.) that will prevent other firms from producing their own, nearly identical versions of the product, competition that would eventually preclude any pure economic profits?

Competitive advantages of this sort can come in many forms. One firm may have superior engineering or R&D talent that generates a continuous stream of innovative products. Another may excel at low-cost manufacturing processes. Still another may create a sustainable competitive advantage through its unique marketing programs.

? JOB INTERVIEW QUESTION

How can a project earn a positive *NPV* in the long run? Why doesn't competition drive all projects to *NPV* = $0?

---

[8]Remember that the notion of "economic profit" is very different from accounting profit. If a firm makes a *zero economic profit*, then it earns just enough to pay competitive prices for the labor and capital that it employs to produce a good or service. Zero economic profit is equivalent to an *NPV* of zero.

The main point is that *if any project is to have a positive NPV, then advocates of that project should be able to articulate its lasting competitive advantage even before running the numbers.* No matter how positive the project's *NPV* appears to be on paper, if no one can explain its main competitive advantage in the market then the firm should probably think twice about investing. Similarly, when an investment proposal has a compelling reason for its competitive edge but the *NPV* numbers come out negative, it may be worth sending the financial analysts back to their desks to take a second look at their assumptions.

We want to emphasize here that, although the numbers are extremely important, they should line up with experienced intuition. When the two are in conflict, managers need to think hard about whether the *NPV* model is in error or whether the project lacks a true competitive advantage.

10-4b Strategic Thinking and Real Options

We conclude this chapter with a return to the topic of real options. The technical aspects of calculating the real option value of a given project (which we cover in Chapter 19) can be quite complex. Real options techniques are still relatively new and are used extensively by firms in only a few industries. Though we expect an increasing number of firms to include real options analysis as part of their standard capital budgeting approach, we believe that just thinking about a project from a real options perspective can be valuable even if coming up with a dollar value for a real option proves to be elusive.

Investments generally have option value as long as they are not all or nothing bets. Almost all investments fit this description. Managers usually have opportunities subsequent to the initial investment to make decisions that can increase or decrease the value of the investment—decisions that create (or destroy) an investment's option value. To maximize, or at least recognize, an investment's option value, managers should try to describe—before the firm commits to an investment—all the subsequent decisions they will make as events unfold. In other words, managers must articulate their strategy for a given investment. This strategy may consist of a series of statements like these:

- *If sales in the first year exceed our expectations, then we plan to commit another $50 million to ramp up production.*
- *If consumers enjoy sending and receiving files on their cell phones, then we will be prepared to invest additional resources so that our cell phones will be capable of performing other tasks on the Internet.*
- *If our MP3 player cannot hold as many songs as the leading model, then the unit must weigh at least one ounce less than the market leader or we will not commit the resources necessary to manufacture it.*

This series of *if-then statements* is necessary to value a real option, but it also has intangible value in that it forces managers to think through their strategic options before they invest. Identifying a real option is tantamount to identifying future points at which it may be possible for managers to create and sustain competitive advantages.

10-4 Concept Review Questions

11. Why must manager intuition be part of the investment-decision process regardless of a project's *NPV* (or *IRR*)?

12. Why is it helpful to think about *real options* when making an investment decision?

Summary

- All-equity firms can discount their "standard" investment projects at the cost of equity. Managers can estimate the cost of equity using the CAPM.

- The cost of equity is influenced by a firm's cost structure (operating leverage) as well as by its financial structure (financial leverage).

- Firms with both debt and equity in their capital structures can discount their "standard" investments using the companywide weighted average cost of capital, or *WACC*.

- The *WACC* is the companywide weighted average of the cost of each source of financing used by a firm, where the weights are equal to the proportion of the market value represented by each source of financing.

Table of Important Equations
1. $E(r_i) = r_f + \beta_i(E(r_m) - r_f)$
2. Operating leverage $= \left(\dfrac{\Delta EBIT}{EBIT}\right) \div \left(\dfrac{\Delta sales}{sales}\right)$
3. $WACC = \left(\dfrac{D}{D+E}\right)r_d + \left(\dfrac{E}{D+E}\right)r_e$
4. WACC when interest on debt is tax deductible $WACC = \left(\dfrac{D}{D+E}\right)(1 - T_c)r_d + \left(\dfrac{E}{D+E}\right)r_e$

- A company's *WACC* and CAPM are connected in that the cost of equity and debt (and any other financing source) are driven by the betas of the firm's equity and debt. Rather than calculate betas for preferred stock and debt, we can estimate their returns using dividend yield for preferred stock and yield to maturity (YTM) for debt.

- The *WACC* can be calculated on both a pretax and an after-tax basis. Because in the United States interest payments to bondholders are tax deductible, we focus on the after-tax *WACC* formula.

- Several tools exist to assist managers in understanding the sources of uncertainty in a project's cash flows. These tools include breakeven analysis, sensitivity analysis, scenario analysis, Monte Carlo simulation, and decision trees. The value of many investments includes not just the *NPV* but also the investment's option value. As a static analytical tool, *NPV* analysis often misses the value of management's ability to alter an investment in response to environmental changes that may occur after it is made.

- Types of real options include the option to expand, the option to make follow-on investments, the option to abandon, and flexibility options related to production inputs, outputs, and capacity.

- An investment's option value, unlike its *NPV*, increases as risk increases.

- For an investment to have a positive *NPV*, it must have a competitive advantage—something that distinguishes it from the economic ideal of perfect competition.

- Valuing an investment's option value requires strategic thinking. Articulating the strategy may be as important as calculating the project's value.

Key Terms

breakeven point (BEP), 326
contribution margin, 326
decision tree, 329
financial leverage, 320

Monte Carlo simulation, 329
operating leverage, 319
random walk, 332
real option, 332

scenario analysis, 328
sensitivity analysis, 327
weighted average cost of capital (WACC), 322

Self-Test Problems

Answers to Self-Test Problems and the Concept Review Questions throughout the chapter appear in CourseMate with SmartFinance Tools at **www.cengagebrain.com**.

ST10-1. A financial analyst for Quality Investments, a diversified investment fund, has gathered the following information for the years 2012 and 2013 on two firms—A and B—that it is considering adding to its portfolio. Of particular concern are the operating and financial risks of each firm.

	2012		2013	
	Firm A	**Firm B**	**Firm A**	**Firm B**
Sales ($ million)	10.7	13.9	11.6	14.6
EBIT ($ million)	5.7	7.4	6.2	8.1
Assets ($ million)			10.7	15.6
Debt ($ million)			5.8	9.3
Interest ($ million)			0.6	1.0
Equity ($ million)			4.9	6.3

a. Use the data provided to assess the *operating leverage* of each firm (using 2012 as the point of reference). Which firm has more operating leverage?

b. Use the data provided to assess each firm's *ROE* (cash to equity/common stock equity), assuming the firm's return on assets is 10% and 20% in each case. Which firm has more *financial leverage*?

c. Use your findings in parts (a) and (b) to compare and contrast the operating and financial risks of Firms A and B. Which firm is more risky? Explain.

ST10-2. Sierra Vista Industries (SVI) wishes to estimate its cost of capital for use in analyzing projects that are similar to those that already exist. The firm's current capital structure, in terms of market value, includes 40% debt, 10% preferred stock, and 50% common stock. The firm's debt has an average yield to maturity of 8.3%. Its preferred stock has a $70 par value, an 8% dividend, and is currently selling for $76 per share. SVI's beta is 1.05, the risk-free rate is 4%, and the return on the S&P 500 (the market proxy) is 11.4%. SVI is in the 40% tax bracket.

a. What are SVI's pretax costs of debt, preferred stock, and common stock?

b. Calculate SVI's weighted average cost of capital (*WACC*) on both a pretax and an after-tax basis. Which *WACC* should SVI use when making investment decisions?

c. SVI is contemplating a major investment that is expected to increase both its operating and financial leverage. Its new capital structure will contain 50% debt, 10% preferred stock, and 40% common stock. As a result of the proposed investment, the firm's average yield to maturity on debt is expected to increase to 9%, the market value of preferred stock is expected to fall to its $70 par value, and its beta is expected to rise to 1.15. What effect will this investment have on SVI's *WACC*? Explain your finding.

Questions

Q10-1. Explain when firms should discount projects using the cost of equity. When should they use the *WACC* instead? When should they use neither?

Q10-2. If a firm takes actions that increase its *operating leverage*, we might expect to see an increase in its equity beta. Why?

Q10-3. Firm A and Firm B plan to raise $1 million to finance identical projects. Firm A finances the project with 100% equity, whereas firm B uses a 50-50 mix of debt and equity. The interest rate on the debt equals 7%. At what rate of return on the investment (i.e., assets) will the rate of return on equity be the same for Firms A and B? (*Hint:* Think through Table 10.2.)

Q10-4. Why do you think it is important to use the market values of debt and equity, rather than their book values, when calculating a firm's *WACC*?

Q10-5. Assuming that there are no corporate income taxes, how can the costs of preferred stock and debt be estimated?

Q10-6. What are the three main lessons learned about choosing the right discount rate for use in evaluating capital budgeting projects?

Q10-7. How does the calculation of the after-tax *WACC* differ from that of the before-tax *WACC*? Which method is typically applied in the United States? Why?

Q10-8. In what sense could one argue that, if managers make decisions using breakeven analysis, then they are not maximizing shareholder wealth? How can breakeven analysis be modified to solve this problem?

Q10-9. Explain the differences between *sensitivity analysis* and *scenario analysis*. Offer an argument for the proposition that scenario analysis offers a more realistic picture of a project's risk than does sensitivity analysis.

Q10-10. In Chapter 9, we discussed how one might calculate the *NPV* of earning an MBA. Suppose you are asked to perform a sensitivity analysis on the MBA decision. Which of the following factors do you think would have the greatest impact on the degree's *NPV*?
   a. The ranking of the school you choose to attend
   b. Your choice of a major
   c. Your GPA
   d. The state of the job market when you graduate

Q10-11. Suppose you want to model the value of an MBA degree with *decision trees*. What would such a decision tree look like?

Q10-12. If you decide to invest in an MBA, what is your *follow-on investment option?* Your *abandonment option?*

Q10-13. Your company is selling the mineral rights to several hundred acres of land it owns that are believed to contain silver deposits. The current price of silver is $18 per ounce but, of course, future prices are uncertain. Would you expect the mineral rights to sell for more or for less if investors believe that silver prices will be more volatile in the future than they have been in the past? Explain.

Problems

Choosing the Right Discount Rate

P10-1. Puritan Motors has a capital structure consisting almost entirely of equity.
   a. If the beta of Puritan stock equals 1.6, the risk-free rate equals 6%, and the expected return on the market portfolio equals 11%, then what is its cost of equity?
   b. Suppose that a 1% increase in expected inflation causes a 1% increase in the risk-free rate. Holding all other factors constant, what will this do to the firm's cost of equity? Is it reasonable to hold all other factors constant? What other part of the calculation of the cost of equity is likely to change if expected inflation rises?

P10-2. Fournier Industries, a publicly traded waste disposal company, is a highly leveraged firm with 70% debt, 0% preferred stock, and 30% common equity financing. Currently the risk-free rate is about 4.5%, and the return on the S&P 500 (the market proxy) is 12.7%. The firm's beta is currently estimated to be 1.65.
   a. What is Fournier's current cost of equity?
   b. If the firm shifts its capital structure to a less highly leveraged position by selling preferred stock and using the proceeds to retire debt, it expects its beta to drop to 1.20. What is its cost of equity in this case?
   c. If the firm shifts its capital structure to a less highly leveraged position by selling additional shares of common stock and using the proceeds to retire debt, it expects its beta to drop to 0.95. What is its cost of equity in this case?
   d. Discuss the potential impact of the two strategies discussed in parts (b) and (c) above on Fournier's weighted average cost of capital (*WACC*).

P10-3. In its 2009 annual report, The Coca-Cola Company reported sales of $30.99 billion for fiscal year 2009 and $31.94 billion for fiscal year 2008. The company also reported operating income (roughly equivalent to EBIT) of $8.23 billion in 2009 and $8.45 billion in 2008. Meanwhile, arch rival PepsiCo,

SMART
solutions
See the problem and solution explained step-by-step at **SMART** | finance

Inc., reported sales of $43.23 billion in 2009 and $43.25 billion in 2008. PepsiCo's operating income was $8.04 billion in 2009 and $6.96 billion in 2008. Based on these figures, which company had higher operating leverage?

P10-4. Gail and Company had the following sales and EBIT during the years 2012 through 2014.

	2012	2013	2014
Sales ($ million)	75.2	82.7	95.1
EBIT ($ million)	26.3	30.5	36.0

   a. Use the data provided to assess Gail and Company's operating leverage over the following periods
      (1) 2012–2013
      (2) 2013–2014
      (3) 2012–2014
   b. Compare, contrast, and discuss the firm's operating leverage between the 2012–2013 period and the 2013–2014 period. Explain any differences.
   c. Compare the operating leverage for the entire 2012–2014 period to the values found for the two subperiods and explain the differences.

P10-5. Firm 1 has a capital structure with 20% debt and 80% equity. Firm 2's capital structure consists of 50% debt and 50% equity. Both firms pay 7% annual interest on their debt. Finally, suppose both firms have invested in assets worth $100 million. Calculate the *return on equity* (ROE) for each firm, assuming the following:
   a. The return on assets is 3%.
   b. The return on assets is 7%.
   c. The return on assets is 11%.
   What general pattern do you observe?

P10-6. Firm A's capital structure contains 20% debt and 80% equity. Firm B's capital structure contains 50% debt and 50% equity. Both firms pay 7% annual interest on their debt. The stock of Firm A has a beta of 1.0, and the stock of Firm B has a beta of 1.375. The risk-free rate of interest equals 4%, and the expected return on the market portfolio equals 12%.
   a. Calculate the *WACC* for each firm, assuming there are no taxes.
   b. Recalculate the *WACC* for each firm, assuming that they face a tax rate of 34%.
   c. Explain how taking taxes into account in part (b) changes your answer found in part (a).

P10-7. A firm has a capital structure containing 60% debt and 40% common stock equity. Its outstanding bonds offer investors a 6.5% yield to maturity. The risk-free rate currently equals 5%, and the expected *risk premium* on the market portfolio equals 6%. The firm's common stock beta is 1.20.
   a. What is the firm's required return on equity?
   b. Ignoring taxes, use your finding in part (a) to calculate the firm's *WACC*.
   c. Assuming a 40% tax rate, recalculate the firm's *WACC* found in part (b).
   d. Compare and contrast the values for the firm's *WACC* found in parts (b) and (c).

P10-8. Dingel, Inc., is attempting to evaluate three alternative capital structures—A, B, and C. The following table shows the three structures along with relevant cost data. The firm is subject to a 40% tax rate. The risk-free rate is 5.3% and the market return is currently 10.7%.

Item	Capital Structure		
	A	B	C
Debt ($ million)	35	45	55
Preferred Stock ($ million)	0	10	10
Common Stock ($ million)	65	45	35
Total Capital ($ million)	100	100	100
Debt (yield to maturity)	7.0%	7.5%	8.5%
Annual Preferred Stock Dividend	—	$2.80	$ 2.20
Preferred Stock (Market Price)	—	$30.00	$21.00
Common Stock Beta	0.95	1.10	1.25

a. Calculate the after-tax cost of debt for each capital structure.
b. Calculate the cost of preferred stock for each capital structure.
c. Calculate the cost of common stock for each capital structure.
d. Calculate the weighted average cost of capital (*WACC*) for each capital structure.
e. Compare the *WACC*s calculated in part (d) and discuss the impact of the firm's financial leverage on its *WACC* and its related risk.

P10-9. A firm has a capital structure containing 40% debt, 20% preferred stock, and 40% common stock equity. The firm's debt has a yield to maturity of 8.1%, its annual preferred stock dividend is $3.10, and the preferred stock's current market price is $50.00 per share. The firm's common stock has a beta of 0.90, and the risk-free rate and the market return are currently 4.0% and 13.5%, respectively. The firm is subject to a 40% tax rate.
a. What is the firm's cost of preferred stock?
b. What is the firm's cost of common stock?
c. Calculate the firm's after-tax *WACC*.
d. Recalculate the firm's *WACC*, assuming that its capital structure is deleveraged to contain 20% debt, 20% preferred stock, and 60% common stock.
e. Compare, contrast, and discuss your findings from parts (c) and (d).

A Closer Look at Risk

P10-10. Alliance Pneumatic Manufacturing, a specialty machine-tool producer, has fixed costs of $200 million per year. Across all the firm's products, the average contribution margin equals $1,200. What is Alliance's breakeven point in terms of units sold?

P10-11. See Table 10.4 on page 328. Determine which of the following has the greater effect on the *NPV* of the gyroscope skateboard project—an increase in the initial selling price of 12.5% (compared to the base case) or an increase in the size of the market of 10% in year 1 (compared to the base case).

P10-12. JK Manufacturing is considering a new product and is unsure about its price as well as the variable cost associated with it. JK's marketing department believes that the firm can sell the product for $500 per unit, but feels that if the initial market response is weak, the price may have to be 20% lower in order to be competitive with existing products. The firm's best estimates of its costs are fixed costs of $3.6 million and variable cost of $325 per unit. Concern exists with regard to the variable cost per unit due to currently volatile raw material and labor costs. Although the firm expects this cost to be about $325 per unit, it could be as much as 8% above that value. The firm expects to sell about 50,000 units per year.
a. Calculate the firm's *breakeven point* (*BEP*) assuming its initial estimates are accurate.
b. Perform a sensitivity analysis by calculating the breakeven point for all combinations of the sale price per unit and variable cost per unit. (*Hint*: There are four combinations.)
c. In the best case, how many units will the firm need to sell to break even?
d. In the worst case, how many units will the firm need to sell to break even?
e. If each of the possible price/variable cost combinations is equally probable, what is the firm's expected breakeven point?
f. Based on your finding in part (e), should the firm go forward with the proposed new product? Explain why or why not.

P10-13. Consumer Products Inc. (CPI) can pay one of its foreign suppliers $20 million to obtain exclusive marketing rights to a new product. Demand for this product is uncertain, but CPI's preliminary estimates indicate that there is a 50% chance of strong product demand, which will result in cash inflows of $5.2 million per year for eight years; there is a 20% chance of moderate product demand, which will result in cash inflows of $4.5 million per year for eight years; and there is a 30% chance of weak demand, which will result in cash inflows of $4.0 million per year for eight years. For $2 million, CPI can conduct a feasibility study that will confirm whether product demand will be strong, moderate, or weak, and then CPI can decide whether to purchase rights to the product. CPI's cost of capital applicable to the proposed new product decision is 12%.
a. Draw the *decision tree* associated with CPI's proposed feasibility study.
b. Calculate the *NPV* associated with each of the possible product demand outcomes—strong, moderate, and weak.
c. Find the expected *NPV* of performing the feasibility study.

d.   Based on your findings in part (c), what recommendation would you give CPI about the proposed feasibility study? Explain.

Real Options

P10-14.   Stanley Marcus, a financial intern at Mega Manufacturing Company (MMC), was asked by the CFO to review the *NPV* calculations on a major new product investment. After analyzing the cash flows and other calculations, Stanley confirmed that the *NPV* was $1.5 million. In the process of investigating all aspects of the project and its cash flows, Stanley learned that should the new product be successful, it would open the door to a number of opportunities to further expand the firm's product line. Using option valuation techniques that he learned in an advanced finance course, he estimated the value of these expansion options to be $0.45 million.

a.   Based on Stanley's analysis, what is the value of the proposed new product investment?

b.   How can Stanley explain the value found in part (a) to the CFO, who is unfamiliar with the concept of *real options*?

P10-15.   Tech Industries, a contract manufacturer of circuit boards, is evaluating an investment in a new production line to handle the growing demand from its customers, who produce consumer electronic products. Based on reasonable growth assumptions, the *NPV* of the new production line was found to be −$2.3 million. Management feels obligated to therefore reject the project. It recognizes that the production line would provide a high degree of output flexibility because it could be repurposed easily and inexpensively to produce circuit boards for numerous other applications. The firm's project analyst estimated the value of this *output flexibility option* to be $3.3 million.

a.   Based on the information provided, what is the true value of Tech Industries' proposed new production line?

b.   What recommendation would you give Tech Industries regarding the proposed new production line? Explain.

For instructions on using Thomson ONE, refer to the instructions provided with the Thomson ONE problems at the end of Chapters 1–6.

P10-16.   Compare the *operating leverage* of Toyota Motor Corp. (TM) with that of Nissan Motor Company Limited (NSANY), using financial information from the last five years. Which company has the higher operating leverage and why? Which company do you expect will have the higher beta? Check the reported betas on Thomson ONE to see if they match your expectations.

P10-17.   Conduct a similar analysis on *financial leverage* for the same two companies evaluated in Problem 10–16.

Smart Ethics Video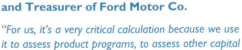

Jon Olson, Chief Financial Officer, Xilinx Corp.

"Our job at the company is to test the limits, not just create financial analysis that ratifies peoples' intuition."

Smart Ideas Video

Kenneth Eades, University of Virginia

"Some of the big things that are hard to convince students to do in fact are widely used in practice."

Smart Practices Video

Beth Acton, former Vice President and Treasurer of Ford Motor Co.

"For us, it's a very critical calculation because we use it to assess product programs, to assess other capital investments, and to analyze acquisitions."

David Nickel, Controller for Intel Communications Group, Intel Corp.

"One of the key things we try to do is to try to understand key scenarios."

Smart Practices Video

Pam Roberts, former Executive Director of Corporate Services, Cummins Inc.

"We recognize that we can't predict each parameter with great accuracy."

Andy Bryant, Executive Vice President and Chief Administrative Officer, Intel Corp.

"Option theory was always used to show why we should do something. I never saw an analysis that said why we should not do something."

Videos photos: Cengage Learning

SMART concepts

See the continuation of the *NPV* analysis—with scenario analysis—of the decision to open a laser eye surgery center.

SMART solutions

See the solution to Problem 10-3.

Mini-Case

Cost of Capital and Project Risk

Cascade Water Company (CWC) currently has 30,000,000 shares of common stock outstanding that trade at a price of $42 per share. CWC also has 500,000 bonds outstanding that currently trade at $923.38 each. CWC has no preferred stock outstanding and has an equity beta of 2.639. The risk-free rate is 3.5%, and the market is expected to return 12.52%. The firm's bonds have a 20-year life, a $1,000 par value, a 10% coupon rate, and pay interest semiannually.

CWC is considering adding to its product mix a healthy bottled water geared toward children. The initial outlay for the project is expected to be $3,000,000, which will be depreciated using the straight-line method to a zero salvage value, and sales are expected to be 1,250,000 units per year at a price of $1.25 per unit. Variable costs are estimated to be $0.24 per unit, and fixed costs of the project are estimated at $200,000 per year. The project is expected to have a 3-year life and a terminal value (excluding the operating cash flows in year 3) of $500,000. CWC has a 34% tax rate. For the purposes of this project, working capital effects will be ignored. Bottled water targeted at children is expected to have different risk characteristics from the firm's current products. Therefore, CWC has decided to use the "pure play" approach to evaluate this project. After

researching the market, CWC managed to find two pure-play firms. The specifics for those two firms are:

Firm	Equity Beta	D/E	Tax Rate
Fruity Water	1.72	0.43	34%
Ladybug Drinks	1.84	0.35	36%

Assignment

1. Determine the current weighted average cost of capital for CWC.

2. Determine the appropriate discount rate for the healthy bottled water project.

3. Should the firm undertake the healthy bottled water project? As part of your analysis, include a sensitivity analysis for sales price, variable costs, fixed costs, and unit sales at ±10%, 20%, and 30% from the base case. Also perform an analysis of the following two scenarios:

    a. *Best case:* Selling 2,500,000 units at a price of $1.24 per unit, with variable production costs of $0.22 per unit.

    b. *Worst case:* Selling 950,000 units at a price of $1.32 per unit, with variable production costs of $0.27 per unit.

© Altus Plunkett/Flickr/Getty Images, Inc.

The previous chapters provided a framework for deciding how a firm should invest its money. In this part, we examine the related questions: How should managers finance the investments they undertake? Should managers pay for new investments by using cash that the firm generates internally, or should external sources of funds be tapped? Is it better to finance with equity or with debt? If the firm's investments are successful, should the company return capital to shareholders by paying a dividend or should it repurchase shares instead?

Chapter 11 describes the trade-offs firms face when they choose between internal or external financing or between debt and equity. The chapter explains how firms work with investment bankers to issue equity. Because investment bankers serve two masters—firms that want to sell securities and investors who must be persuaded to buy them—the investment banking business is fraught with potential conflicts of interest. Chapter 11 describes some of the conflicts that arise in this industry.

In Chapter 12, we explore the question of whether managers can increase the value of a firm by financing its operations with an optimal mix of debt and equity. A classic and important line of argument suggests that such an optimal capital structure may not exist, but the chapter offers useful guidelines that managers can consult when deciding what type of funding to raise for their companies.

Chapter 13 looks at long-term debt and leasing. It may seem odd to put debt and leasing together, but a lease is a fixed obligation just like the obligation firms undertake when they borrow money by issuing bonds. Managers evaluate lease financing in a fashion similar to that used when deciding how much long-term debt to issue.

Chapter 14 examines how managers can affect the value of a firm through its dividend payout policy. In Chapter 5, we presented a model that showed that the value of any stock can be viewed as the present value of all dividends that the stock will pay through time. We explore the ways that dividends may, or may not, affect firm value.

chapter 11

Raising Long-Term Financing

What Companies Do

Financial Engines Revved Up

What comes to mind when you think about a firm "going public" by conducting an initial public offering (IPO) of common stock? Most people would probably think about hot technology stocks like Google, or emerging social networking companies like Facebook, but excitement in the IPO market isn't limited to glamorous firms. On March 16, 2010, Financial Engines, Inc., (founded in 1996 by William Sharpe, Nobel laureate and finance professor) completed its IPO, selling 10.6 million shares at $12 and raising more than $125 million. The company, which provides services to nearly one-quarter of all Fortune 500 companies, advises clients on 401(k) retirement account investing decisions. Financial Engines's computer programs decide how investors should allocate their retirement savings among different types of assets. That business model may not excite many people, but the company's initial returns were very exciting for its investors.

The initial buyers of Financial Engines's stock paid $12 per share, but shares began trading in the secondary market at $15 and kept climbing higher, ending the first trading day up 44%. With millions of baby boomers (those born between 1946 and 1964) struggling to manage their retirement nest eggs, Wall Street apparently felt that Financial Engines's retirement investment advisory business is a growth business. With the equity that they raised in their IPO, Financial Engines seemed well positioned to achieve rapid growth in the next few years.

Source: "Hot IPO: Retirement-savings advisor Financial Engines soars in debut," Business: Money & Company, *Los Angeles Times*, March 16, 2010, accessed at **www.latimesblogs.latimes.com/money_co/2010/03/financial -engines.html**, June 8, 2010 and Rick Aristotle Munarriz, "Finally! A Hot IPO!," *The Motley Fool, Fool.com*, March 17, 2010, accessed at **www.fool.com/investing/general/2010/03/17/finally-a-hot-ipo.aspx**, June 8, 2010

Learning Objectives

After studying this chapter you should be able to:

- Discuss the basic choices that corporations face in raising long-term financing;

- Describe the costs and benefits of raising long-term funds by issuing securities rather than by borrowing from a financial intermediary;

- Understand how investment banks help corporations issue securities, and describe the services investment banks provide before, during, and after a security issue;

- Explain the basic issuance and pricing patterns observed in the initial public offering (IPO) market in the United States;

- Describe the basic issuance and pricing patterns observed in the U.S. market for seasoned equity offerings (SEOs), and explain why so few large companies issue seasoned common stock; and

- Explain some important aspects of international common stock offerings, including the role of American Depositary Receipts (ADRs).

This chapter introduces the primary instruments that companies around the world use for long-term financing: common stock, preferred stock, and long-term debt. Although the types of securities are similar, significant differences exist across countries in terms of how corporations use them and in the degree to which firms obtain financing in capital markets rather than through financial intermediaries. For example, countries such as Canada, the United States, Britain, and Australia are characterized by large, highly liquid stock and bond markets. Other industrialized countries, particularly those in continental Europe, have much smaller capital markets and rely primarily on commercial banks for financing. Despite these differences in financial systems, corporations around the world display certain common tendencies; most importantly, they universally rely on internally generated cash flow (principally retained profits) as the dominant source of new financing. Funding a company's operations this way—by retaining rather than paying out corporate profits—is called *internal financing*. The alternative, *external financing*, refers to raising money from sources external to the firm, such as banks or capital markets.

11-1 The Basic Choices in Long-Term Financing

Debt and equity constitute the two main sources of corporate long-term financing. Equity capital represents an ownership interest that is junior to debt, because debt capital represents a legally enforceable claim, with cash flows that can be either fixed or varied, according to a predetermined formula. These basic financial instruments exist in most countries, and the rights and responsibilities of the holders of these instruments are very similar. Companies around the world face the same basic financing problem: how to fund projects and activities that will allow the firm to grow and prosper. This section examines the firm's financing alternatives, particularly the choice between internal and external financing, and surveys key issues related to raising external financing either through financial intermediaries or in capital markets.

11-1a The Need to Fund a Financial Deficit

financial deficit
Occurs when a corporation requires more financial capital for investment than it supplies in the form of retained earnings.

Corporations everywhere are net dissavers, which is an economic way of saying they demand more financial capital for investment than they supply in the form of retained earnings. Corporations must close this financial deficit by borrowing or by issuing new equity securities. Every major firm confronts four key financing decisions on an ongoing basis:

1. How much capital must the company raise each year?

2. How much should be raised externally rather than through retained earnings?

3. How much of the external funding should be raised through borrowing from a bank or another financial intermediary, and how much should be raised externally by selling securities directly to investors?

4. What proportion of the external funding should be structured as long-term debt, common stock, or preferred stock?

The answer to the first question depends on the capital budgeting process of a firm. A company would ideally raise enough capital to fund all its positive-*NPV* investment projects and to cover its working capital needs.

11-1b The Choice between Internal and External Financing

At first glance, the internal/external choice in Question 2 seems to be a decision that firms can make mechanically. The difference between the firms' total financing needs and its internally generated funding equals the external financing requirement. Its *internally generated funds* are its cash flow from operations, calculated as net income plus depreciation and other noncash charges minus dividends. So the *external financing requirement* would equal the firm's capital expenditures plus change in net working capital minus its internally generated funding.

The external financing decision is not simple, however. Management may want to build up or reduce net working capital over time, and besides, its dividend policy is not fixed, except in the very short term. Additionally, there are higher legal and transactions costs to raising capital externally than by retaining internally generated funds. Not surprising, the residual nature of external financing needs implies that the amount required by a given company will be highly variable from year to year.

Internal cash flow is the dominant source of corporate funding in the United States, with businesses regularly financing two-thirds to three-quarters of all their capital spending needs internally. Over time, other countries have also moved in the same direction. Chinese corporations still meet well over half of their total financing needs externally, primarily through bank borrowing, largely because they are growing faster than they can finance internally.

11-1c Raising Capital from Financial Intermediaries or on Capital Markets

Does it matter whether a company raises capital by dealing with a financial intermediary or by selling securities directly to investors? Shouldn't a bank's money and an investor's money be perfect substitutes? In reality, a corporation's choice between intermediated and security market financing significantly influences its ownership structure. Before analyzing this issue, we define a financial intermediary and briefly describe what it does.

What Is a Financial Intermediary, and What Does It Do? A financial intermediary (FI) is an institution, such as a bank, that raises capital by issuing liabilities against itself—for example, checking accounts or savings accounts. The intermediary pools the capital that's been raised and uses it to make loans to borrowers or, where allowed, to make equity investments in nonfinancial firms. Borrowers repay their loans to the intermediary and have no direct contact with the individual savers who provided funds to the intermediary. In other words, both borrowers and savers deal directly with the intermediary. Because of their role in serving both borrowers and savers, intermediaries specialize in credit analysis and collection. They offer financial products tailored to the particular needs of borrowers and savers.

The Role of Financial Intermediaries in U.S. Corporate Finance A general distrust of concentrated, private economic power has dramatically influenced U.S. financial regulation. Throughout most of the 20th century, policymakers discouraged the growth of large intermediaries (especially commercial banks), in part by imposing on them severe geographical restrictions. Congress passed the McFadden Act in 1927 to prohibit interstate banking. The tide began to change when enormous financial institutions formed overseas, making it more difficult for U.S. institutions to compete. After numerous failed attempts to repeal the McFadden Act, in July 2004, Congress finally approved a bill allowing full interstate branch banking. As a result, the number of U.S. banks has significantly declined, primarily through mergers.

cash flow from operations
Cash inflows and outflows directly related to the production and sale of a firm's products and services. Calculated as net income plus depreciation and other noncash charges.

SMART concepts
See the concept explained step-by-step at SMART | finance

financial intermediary (FI)
An institution, such as a bank, that raises capital by issuing liabilities against itself and lending to borrowers.

McFadden Act
Congressional act of 1927 that prohibited interstate banking.

Glass-Steagall Act
Congressional act of 1933 mandating the separation of investment and commercial banking.

Gramm-Leach-Bliley Act
Act that allowed commercial banks, securities firms, and insurance companies to join together.

primary issues
Initial sale of securities by a firm to raise capital.

secondary offerings
The sale of previously issued securities, which are typically held in large blocks by one or more investors, raises no additional funds for the initial issuer.

securitization
The repackaging of loans and other traditional bank-based credit products into securities that can be sold to public investors.

initial public offering (IPO)
The first public sale of a company's common stock to outside investors.

seasoned equity offerings (SEOs)
Common stock sales by companies who shares already trade in the market.

Eurobond
A bond issued by an international borrower and sold to investors in countries with currencies other than that in which the bond is denominated.

The second pivotal law affecting American U.S. markets was the Glass-Steagall Act, passed in 1933 in response to perceived banking abuses during the Great Depression. This legislation mandated the separation of investment and commercial banking: it prohibited commercial banks from underwriting corporate security issues, from providing security brokerage services to their customers, or even owning voting equity securities on their own account. Banking's corporate financing role was effectively restricted to making commercial loans and providing closely related services, such as leasing. As with the McFadden Act, there were repeated attempts to repeal Glass-Steagall, and these finally succeeded when Congress passed the Gramm-Leach-Bliley Act in November 1999.

Nonbank FIs, such as insurance companies, pension funds, and specialized finance companies such as General Electric Credit Corporation and General Motors Acceptance Corporation also play important roles in U.S. corporate finance, both as creditors and as equity investors.

The Corporate Finance Role of Non-U.S. Financial Intermediaries In markets outside the United States, commercial banks typically play much larger roles in corporate finance. In most countries, a handful of very large banks service most large firms, and the size and competence of these banks give them tremendous influence over corporate financial and operating policies. This power is further strengthened by the ability of most non-U.S. banks to underwrite corporate security issues and to make direct equity investments in commercial firms. Most countries other than the United States also allow commercial banks to provide a full range of financial services.

11-1d The Expanding Role of Securities Markets in Corporate Finance

No trend in modern finance is as clear or as transforming as the worldwide shift toward corporate reliance on securities markets rather than intermediaries for external financing. Important observations related to external financing and the shift toward securities financing include:

1. Primary issues, the initial sale of a security by a firm to raise capital, have increased by a factor of more than 15 over the last 20 years.

2. Secondary offerings, the sale of previously issued securities, which are typically held in large blocks by one or more investors, raise no additional funds for the initial issuer.

3. The increase in security market financing reflects a trend toward securitization, which involves the repackaging of loans and other traditional bank-based credit products into securities that can be sold to public investors.

4. U.S. companies tend to issue far more debt than equity each year.

5. Initial public offerings (IPOs), which are the first public sales of a company's common stock to outside investors, generally represent less than one-third of all common stock sold in a given year. The remaining common stock sales are seasoned equity offerings (SEOs), which are new issues of common stock by companies who have previously conducted an IPO and therefore a have existing shares trading in the market.

6. The credit crisis that began in 2008 caused the volume of almost every type of security issued to fall sharply. Issuances have rebounded somewhat since then.

7. International corporate issuers show the same preference as U.S. companies by issuing far more debt than equity.

8. Certain securities, most notably *Eurobonds*, cannot be offered in the United States but can be sold to international investors. A Eurobond issue is a single-currency bond that

Frank Popoff, Chairman of the Board (retired), Dow Chemical

"A Samurai bond is just an exercise in matching exposure and income."

See the entire interview at SMART|finance

Smart Practices Video

foreign bond
A bond issued in a host country's financial market, in the host country's currency, by a nonresident corporation.

Yankee bonds
Bonds sold by foreign corporations to U.S. investors.

international common stock
Equity issues sold in more than one country by non-resident corporations.

is sold in several countries simultaneously. An example is a dollar-denominated bond issued by a U.S. corporation and sold to European investors.

9. A foreign bond is an issue that is sold by a nonresident corporation in a foreign country and is denominated in the host country's currency. An example is a Swiss franc-denominated bond sold in Switzerland by a Japanese corporate issuer. In most years Yankee bonds, dollar-denominated bonds issued by foreign firms in the U.S. market, are the single largest category of foreign bonds.

10. International common stock, issues that are sold in more than one country by non-resident corporations, typically represents between 5 and 10% of all worldwide offerings.

11.1 Concept Review Questions

1. What are *financial intermediaries*, and what role do these firms play in providing long-term capital to publicly traded U.S. nonfinancial corporations?

2. What patterns are observed in U.S. security issues each year? How do these patterns compare to those in international security issues?

11-2 Investment Banking and the Public Sale of Securities

investment bank
A bank that helps firms acquire external capital.

bulge bracket
Consists of firms that generally occupy the lead or co-lead manager's position in large, new security offerings.

underwriting spread
The difference between the price at which an investment bank sells shares to investors and the price at which the bank purchases shares from the issuing firm.

prospectus
The first part of a registration statement; it is distributed to all prospective investors.

Although corporations around the world rely on internal financing for most of their funding, companies also raise large amounts of capital externally each year. Once corporate managers have decided to raise external capital and to raise equity rather than debt, they usually enlist an investment bank to help sell the firm's securities. Issuing firm managers can either negotiate privately with individual banks regarding the terms of the equity sale, or they can solicit competitive bids for the business. On behalf of firms, investment banks can issue shares to a small group of sophisticated investors in a private placement, they can issue new shares to existing shareholders through a rights offering, or they can engage in a much broader public share offering that reaches domestic as well as international investors.

The investment banks that are ranked highest each year in terms of the total amount of money raised typically includes the same group of firms. Among them are Bank of America Merrill Lynch, JP Morgan, Barclays Capital, Citigroup, Deutsche Bank, Goldman Sachs, Morgan Stanley, Credit Suisse, and UBS. These firms are perennial members of investment banking's prestigious bulge bracket, firms that generally occupy the lead or co-lead manager's position in large, new security offerings, meaning that they take primary responsibility for the new offering (even though other banks participate as part of a *syndicate*). As a result, they earn higher fees. Investment banks are compensated with an underwriting spread, the difference between the price at which the banks sell shares to investors and the price at which they purchase shares from firms. You can readily identify the lead investment bank in a security offering by looking at the offering prospectus, the legal document that describes the terms of the offering. The lead bank's name appears on the front page, usually in larger, bolder print than the names of other participating banks.

EXAMPLE

Figure 11.1 presents the prospectus title page for the March 2010, initial public share offering by Financial Engines, Inc., a leading provider of independent, technology-enabled portfolio management services, investment advice, and retirement help to participants in employer-sponsored defined contribution retirement plans. The lead underwriters were Goldman Sachs and UBS Investment Bank. Both firms are perennial members of investment banking's *bulge bracket*. Piper Jaffray and Cowen and Company are also important underwriters for this offering, though these companies are not routinely members of investment banking's bulge bracket. The title page also shows an underwriting discount of $0.84 per share and an offer price of $12.00 per share, for a percentage discount of 7.00% ($0.84 ÷ $12.00). The underwriters thus stood to receive total compensation of $8,904,000 for their efforts in this underwriting. This represented a fairly normal underwriting discount for an offering of this size.

Figure 11.1

10,600,000 Shares

Common Stock

This is an initial public offering of shares of common stock of Financial Engines, Inc.

Financial Engines is offering 5,868,100 of the shares to be sold in the offering. The selling stockholders identified in this prospectus are offering an additional 4,731,900 shares. Financial Engines will not receive any of the proceeds from the sale of the shares being sold by the selling stockholders.

Prior to this offering, there has been no public market for the common stock. Our common stock has been approved for listing on The Nasdaq Global Market under the symbol "FNGN."

See "Risk Factors" on page 15 to read about factors you should consider before buying shares of the common stock.

Neither the Securities and Exchange Commission nor any state securities commission has approved or disapproved of these securities or determined if this prospectus is truthful or complete. Any representation to the contrary is a criminal offense.

	Per Share	Total
Initial public offering price	$ 12.00	$127,200,000
Underwriting discounts and commissions	$ 0.84	$ 8,904,000
Proceeds, before expenses, to Financial Engines	$ 11.16	$ 65,487,996
Proceeds, before expenses, to the selling stockholders	$ 11.16	$ 52,808,004

To the extent that the underwriters sell more than 10,600,000 shares of common stock, the underwriters have the option to purchase up to an additional 1,590,000 shares from Financial Engines at the initial public offering price less the underwriting discounts and commissions.

The underwriters expect to deliver the shares against payment in New York, New York on March 19, 2010.

Goldman, Sachs & Co.

UBS Investment Bank

Piper Jaffray   **Cowen and Company**

Prospectus dated March 15, 2010

Underwriting spreads vary considerably depending on the type of security being issued. Banks charge higher spreads on equity issues than on debt issues. They also charge higher spreads for *unseasoned equity offerings* (i.e., IPOs) than they do for *seasoned equity offerings*. In general, the riskier the security being offered, the higher the spread charged by the underwriter. Securities that have both debt- and equity-like features, such as convertible bonds and preferred stock, have spreads that are higher than those of ordinary debt but lower than those of common stock.

Spreads on international IPOs are significantly lower than on U.S. initial offers. In part, this reflects differences in underwriting practices across countries. To assess

book building
A process in which underwriters ask prospective investors to reveal information about their demand for the offering.

fixed-price offer
An offer in which the underwriters set the final offer price for a new issue weeks in advance.

Cengage Learning

Tim Jenkinson, Oxford University

"There are basically three ways of doing an IPO."

See the entire interview at **SMART** | finance

Smart Ideas Video

Securities Act of 1933
The most important federal law governing the sale of new securities.

full disclosure
Requires issuers to reveal all relevant information concerning the company selling the securities and the securities themselves to potential investors.

Securities Exchange Act of 1934
Act that established the U.S. Securities and Exchange Commission (SEC) and laid out specific procedures for both the public sale of securities and the governance of public companies.

due diligence
Examination of potential security issuers in which investment banks are legally required to search out and disclose all relevant information about an issuer before selling securities to the public.

demand for a company's shares and to set the offer price, U.S. underwriters typically use a process known as book building, in which underwriters ask prospective investors to indicate their demand for the offering. Through conversations with investors, the underwriter tries to measure the demand curve for a given issue, and the investment bank sets the offer price after gathering all the information it can from investors. Book building has become increasingly common in international markets, but a method called a fixed-price offer also survives. In fixed-price offers, underwriters set the final offer price for a new issue weeks in advance. This imposes more risk on the underwriters, for which they must either charge higher spreads or price the shares far below the expected post-offer price. Thus the observed spreads are actually lower on fixed-price offers than in book-built offerings.

11-2a Conflicts of Interest Facing Investment Banks

The institutional arrangements for selling securities to the public, as described above, confront investment banks with potential conflicts of interest. Banks are providing advice and underwriting services to companies that want to issue securities. On the one hand, issuing firms want to obtain the highest possible price for their shares. But they also want favorable coverage from their investment banks' research analysts, who produce reports that are intended to advise clients on whether securities are fairly priced. Investors, on the other hand, want to purchase securities at the lowest price possible, but they also value dispassionate, unbiased advice from analysts. Investment bankers must therefore walk a thin line, in terms of both ethics and economics, when attempting to please their constituents. Firms issuing securities are wise to bear this in mind. Investment bankers deal with investors, particularly institutional investors such as mutual funds, on a repeated basis. They must approach this group each time they bring a new offering to market. In contrast, over the life of a firm, there is just one IPO and perhaps a few SEOs.

Banks struggle with these conflict-of-interest problems; instead, they must price new security issues to strike a balance between the revenue maximization goal of the issuing firms and the profit maximization objective of their investing clients. Of course, lawmakers and regulators recognize that the investment banking business susceptible to conflict-of-interest problems, and so there is an extensive set of rules that impose constraints on how securities may be sold. Now we turn to a brief overview of the legal environment surrounding security issues.

11-2b Legal Rules Governing Public Security Sales in the United States

Security issues in the United States are regulated at both the state and federal levels. The most important federal law governing the sale of new securities is the Securities Act of 1933 and its amendments. The basis for federal regulation of the sale of securities is the concept of full disclosure, which means that issuers must reveal all relevant information concerning the company selling the securities and the securities themselves to potential investors. The other major federal law governing securities issues is the Securities Exchange Act of 1934, which established the U.S. Securities and Exchange Commission (SEC) and laid out specific procedures for the public sale of securities and the governance of public companies.

Given the emphasis that U.S. securities law places on disclosure, it is not surprising that investment banks are required to perform due diligence examinations of potential security issuers. This means that they must search out all relevant information about an issuer before selling securities to the public. Investors can sue underwriters if they do not perform adequate due diligence; of course, in such cases the underwriter's reputation suffers as well. The fact that investment banks are willing to underwrite an

certification
Assurance that the issuing company is in fact disclosing all material information.

registration statement
The principal disclosure document for all public security offerings.

effective (offering)
Status of an offering before any shares can actually be sold to public investors.

supplemental disclosures
The second part of the *registration statement*, which is filed with the SEC.

issue provides valuable **certification** that the issuing company is in fact disclosing all material information.

The principal disclosure document for all public security offerings is the **registration statement**. Firms must file this highly detailed document with the SEC before they can solicit investors. A final revised version must be approved by the commission before an offering can become **effective** and shares can be sold to public investors. There are two basic parts to the registration statement: Part I, the *prospectus*, is distributed to all prospective investors; Part II, **supplemental disclosures**, is filed only with the SEC, although investors can obtain a copy from the commission.

If the purpose of the offering is to allow an existing shareholder to sell a large block of stock to new investors, the issue is a *secondary offering* and raises no capital for the firm. If the shares offered for sale are newly issued shares, which increase the number of outstanding shares and raise new capital for firms, the issue is a *primary offering*. If some of the shares come from existing shareholders and some are new, the issue is a *mixed offering*.

EXAMPLE

The Financial Engines IPO was a mixed offering. The company itself was issuing 5,868,100 new shares to raise $70.42 million, and intended to use the net proceeds from this offering for general corporate purposes, including working capital and capital expenditures. A group of existing shareholders sold an additional 4,731,900 shares, netting themselves $56.78 million.

shelf registration (Rule 415)
Allows a qualifying company to file a master registration statement, a single document summarizing planned financing over a two-year period.

Shelf Registration (Rule 415) As an alternative to filing a lengthy registration statement and awaiting SEC approval, firms with more than $150 million in outstanding common stock can use a procedure, known as **shelf registration** (or **Rule 415**) for the issue. This procedure allows a qualifying company to file *a master registration statement*, a single document summarizing planned financing over a two-year period. Once the SEC approves the issue, it is placed on the shelf, and the company can sell the new securities to investors out of inventory (off the shelf) as needed any time during the next two years. This has proven to be immensely popular with issuing corporations, which previously had to incur the costs (including costs of delay) of filing separate SEC registrations for each new security issue. In addition to saving time and money, shelf registration allows firms to issue securities in response to changing market conditions.

Ongoing Regulatory Requirements for a Publicly Traded Firm Once a company successfully completes an IPO and lists its shares for trading on an exchange, it becomes subject to all the costs and reporting requirements of a public company. These include cash expenses such as exchange-listing fees and the cost of preparing and distributing proxies, annual reports, and other documents to shareholders. Additionally, public companies must hold general shareholders' meetings at least once each year and must obtain shareholder approval for important decisions, such as approving a merger, authorizing additional shares of stock, and approving new stock option plans. The most costly regulatory constraints on public companies are the disclosure requirements for the firm, its officers and directors, and its principal shareholders. In essence, the company must report any material change in its operations, ownership, or financing. Once a firm goes public, life becomes very public indeed.

? JOB INTERVIEW QUESTION

What role does *shelf registration* play in meeting a firm's ongoing long-term financing needs?

11-2 Concept Review Questions

3. What does the phrase *bulge bracket* mean?

4. What is the guiding principle behind most of the important U.S. securities legislation? What role does the security registration process play in implementing this philosophy?

5. What is *shelf registration*? Why do you think this has proven to be so popular with issuing firms?

11-3 The U.S. Market for Initial Public Offerings (IPOs)

Given its role in providing capital market access to entrepreneurial growth companies, the U.S. initial public offering market has long been considered a vital economic and financial asset. Indeed, a welcoming IPO market has been a key building block of American success in high-technology industries. At least for the last twenty years, IPO markets have been growing around the world, and the U.S. market share of global IPOs has been in decline. According to recent research by Doidge, Karolyi, and Stulz, the U.S. share of the worldwide IPO market (in terms of the number of IPOs) fell from close to 60% in 1990 to roughly 20% in 2007. Even so, the U.S. share of IPO activity still ranks near the top.

11-3a Patterns Observed in the U.S. IPO Market

To the uninitiated, some quick facts about the U.S. IPO market reveal some very interesting patterns.

1. The IPO market is highly cyclical. Over time, aggregate IPO volume shows a very distinct pattern of boom and bust.

2. There is a tendency for firms going public in a certain industry to cluster in time. It is common to see bursts of IPO activity in fairly narrow industry sectors, such as energy, biotechnology, and communications, and more recently, social networking companies. Perhaps the most famous of these industry IPO waves occurred in the late 1990s when the market witnessed an incredible boom in both the number of Internet companies going public and the valuations assigned to them by the market.

EXAMPLE

The short-term stock-price increases for Internet-related IPOs had financial experts scratching their heads in 1999, none more so than the December 9, 1999, debut of VA Linux. The company went public with an offer price of $30 per share; after one trading day, the stock closed at almost $240 per share. For investors who bought shares at the offer price and sold them as soon as possible, the one-day return was an astronomical 700%. Investors who held on for the long term did not fare as well. After the IPO, the stock closed above $240 only once, and it fell to an intraday low of 54 cents on July 24, 2002. By August 2011, the company, now renamed Geeknet, Inc., saw its stock trading at less than 1% of its original IPO date value.

3. As recently as the early 1980s, investment banks targeted initial offerings almost exclusively at individual investors, particularly at retail customers of the brokerage firms involved in the underwriting syndicate. Since the mid-1980s, however, institutional investors have grown in importance, and they generally receive half to three-quarters of the shares offered in the typical IPOs and up to 90% or more of the hot issues.

4. Over the last two decades, numerous international companies raised capital in the U.S. IPO market. Both established international companies and non-U.S. entrepreneurial firms frequently make initial stock offerings to U.S. investors, either publicly via a straight IPO or to institutional investors through a **Rule 144A offering**. This special type of offering allows issuing companies to waive some disclosure requirements by selling stock only to sophisticated institutional investors, who may then trade the shares among themselves.

Rule 144A offering
A special type of offering, first approved in April 1990, that allows issuing companies to waive some disclosure requirements by selling stock only to sophisticated institutional investors, who may then trade the shares among themselves.

11-3b Advantages and Disadvantages of an IPO

The decision to convert from private to public ownership is not an easy one. The benefits of having publicly traded shares are numerous, but so, too, are the costs. This section describes the costs and benefits of IPOs for U.S. firms. As we discuss more fully in Section 11-5, the motivations for going public are significantly different for continental European business owners than for their U.S. counterparts.

Benefits of Going Public Chapter 2 of the accounting firm KPMG Peat Marwick's publication *Going Public: What the CEO Needs to Know* (1998) suggests the following advantages of an IPO to an entrepreneur.

1. **New capital for the company.** An initial public offering gives the typical private firm access to a larger pool of equity capital than is available from any other source. Whereas venture capitalists can provide perhaps $10 million to $40 million in funding throughout a company's life as a private firm, an IPO allows the company to raise many times that amount in one offering. An infusion of common equity not only permits the firm to pursue profitable investment opportunities, it also improves the firm's overall financial condition and provides additional borrowing capacity. Furthermore, if the firm's stock performs well, the companies will be able to raise additional equity capital in the future.

2. **Publicly traded stock for use in acquisitions.** Unless a firm has publicly traded stock, the only way it can acquire another company is to pay in cash. After going public, a firm has the option of exchanging its own stock for that of the target firm. Not only does this minimize cash outflow for the acquiring firm, but such a payment method may be free from capital gains tax for the target firm's owners. This tax benefit may reduce the price that an acquirer must pay for a target company.

3. **Listed stock for use as a compensation vehicle.** Having publicly traded stock allows the company to attract, retain, and provide incentives for talented managers by offering them stock options and other stock-based compensation. Going public also offers liquidity to managers who were awarded options while the firm was private.

4. **Personal wealth and liquidity.** Entrepreneurship almost always violates finance's basic dictum about diversification: entrepreneurs generally have most of their financial wealth and their human capital tied up in their companies. Going public allows entrepreneurs to reallocate cash from their businesses and to diversify their portfolios. Entrepreneurial families also frequently execute IPOs during times of transition—for example, when the company founder wishes to retire and provide a method of allocating family assets among those heirs who do and do not wish to remain active in the business.

In addition to these benefits, the act of going public generally results in a blaze of media attention, which often helps promote the company's products and services. Being a public company also increases a firm's overall prestige. However, the often massive costs must be weighed against the obvious benefits of an IPO.

Drawbacks to Going Public KPMG Peat Marwick's *Going Public* publication also includes the drawbacks of an IPO for a firm's managers.

1. **The financial costs of an IPO.** Few entrepreneurs are truly prepared for just how costly the process of going public can be in terms of out-of-pocket cash expenses and opportunity costs. Total cash expenses of an IPO, such as printing, accounting, and legal services, frequently approach $1 million, and most of this must be paid even if the offering is postponed or canceled. Additionally, the combined costs associated with the underwriter's fees (usually 7%) and the initial underpricing of the firm's stock (roughly 15% on average) represent a large transfer of wealth from current owners to the underwriters and to the new stockholders.

2. **The managerial costs of an IPO.** As costly as an IPO is financially, many entrepreneurs find the continuous demands made on their time during the IPO process to be even more burdensome. Rarely can CEOs and other top managers delegate these duties, which grow increasingly intense as the offering date approaches. There are also severe restrictions on what an executive can say or do during the immediate pre-offering period, and because the process can take months to complete, the

distraction costs of going public are very high. Top executives must also take time to meet with important potential stockholders before completing the IPO and indefinitely thereafter.

3. **Stock price emphasis.** Owners/managers of private companies frequently operate their firms in ways that balance competing personal and financial interests. This includes seeking profits, but it can also include employing family members in high positions as well as other personal benefits. Once a company goes public, however, external pressures build to maximize the firm's stock price; as managerial shareholdings fall, managers become vulnerable to job loss either through takeover or through dismissal by the board of directors.

4. **Life in a fishbowl.** Public shareholders have the right to a great deal of information about a firm's internal affairs, and releasing this information to stockholders also implies releasing it to competitors and potential acquirers as well. Managers must disclose, especially in the IPO prospectus, how and in what markets they intend to compete, information that is obviously valuable to competitors. Additionally, managers who are also significant stockholders are subject to binding disclosure requirements and face serious constraints on their ability to buy or sell company stock.

In spite of these drawbacks, often several hundred management teams each year decide that the benefits of going public outweigh the costs and begin the process of planning for an IPO. In addition to these standard IPOs, four special types of IPOs warrant attention.

11-3c Specialized Initial Public Offerings: ECOs, Spin-offs, Reverse LBOs, and Tracking Stocks

The four special types of IPOs are equity carve-outs (ECOs), spin-offs, reverse LBOs, and tracking stocks. An equity carve-out (ECO) occurs when a parent company sells shares of a subsidiary corporation to the public through an initial public offering. The parent company may sell some of the subsidiary shares it already owns, or the subsidiary may issue new shares. In either event, the parent company almost always retains a controlling stake in the newly public company.

A spin-off occurs when a public parent company spins off a subsidiary to the parent's shareholders by distributing shares on a pro rata basis. Thus, after the spin-off, there will be two public companies rather than one. Conceptually, the total stock price of the parent should drop by approximately the amount that the market values the shares of the newly public spin-off. Researchers document significantly positive price reactions for the stock of divesting parent companies at the time of spin-off announcements, perhaps indicating that the market expects the two independent companies will be managed more effectively than they would have been had they remained together.

In a reverse LBO (or second IPO), a formerly public company that had previously gone private through a leveraged buyout goes public again. Reverse LBOs are easier to price than traditional IPOs because information exists about how the market valued the company when it was publicly traded. Empirical research indicates the private equity partners earn very high returns on these transactions. One reason for this is obvious: only the most successful LBOs can subsequently go public again.

The final type of specialized equity offering, tracking stocks, is a recent innovation that may well have already run its course. These are equity claims based on (and designed to mirror, or *track*) the earnings of wholly owned subsidiaries of diversified firms. They are hybrid securities because the tracking stock firm is not separated from the parent company in any way, instead remaining integrated with the parent both legally and operationally. In contrast, both carve-outs and spin-offs result in legally separate firms. AT&T conducted the largest common stock offering in U.S. history when it issued $10.6 billion in AT&T Wireless tracking stock in April 2000. AT&T's stock rose significantly when it announced the wireless offering. Unfortunately, both parent and tracking stock performed horribly during the months after the issue, and in July 2001, AT&T Wireless became an independent company; it was acquired by Cingular Wireless in October 2004.

? JOB INTERVIEW QUESTION

What are the pros and cons of doing an IPO?

equity carve-out (ECO)
Occurs when a parent company sells shares of a subsidiary corporation to the public through an initial public offering.

spin-off
A parent company creates a new company with its own shares to form a division or subsidiary, and existing shareholders receive a pro rata distribution of shares in the new company.

? WHAT TO ASK

Has your firm ever done an *equity carve-out (ECO)* or a *spin-off* and, if so, why?

reverse LBO (or second IPO)
A formerly public company that has previously gone private through a leveraged buyout and then goes public again. Also called a second IPO.

tracking stocks
Equity claims based on (and designed to mirror, or track) the earnings of wholly owned subsidiaries of diversified firms.

flip
To buy shares at the offer price and sell them on the first trading day.

IPO underpricing
Occurs when the offer price in the prospectus is consistently lower than what the market is willing to bear.

Jay Ritter, University of Florida

"Every single country in the world has IPOs underpriced on average."

See the entire interview at SMART|finance

Smart Practices Video

11-3d The Investment Performance of Initial Public Offerings

Are IPOs good investments? The answer seems to depend on the investment horizon of the investor and whether or not the investor can purchase IPO shares at the offer price. If an investor can buy shares at the offer price and then flip them—sell them on the first trading day—then the returns on IPOs are on average substantial. But if the investor buys shares in the secondary market and holds them for the long term, the average returns are much less rewarding.

IPO initial return
The gain when an allocation of shares from an investment banker is sold at the first opportunity because the offer price is consistently lower than what the market is willing to pay.

Positive Initial Returns for IPO Investors (Underpricing) Year in and year out, in virtually every country around the world, the very short term returns on IPOs are surprisingly high. In the United States, the share price in the typical IPO closes roughly 15% above the offer price after just one day of trading. Researchers refer to this pattern as IPO underpricing, meaning that the offer price in the prospectus is consistently lower than what the market is willing to pay. To capture this initial return, an investor must be fortunate enough to receive an allocation of shares from the investment banker and to sell those shares at the first opportunity. Investors who buy IPO shares when open-market trading begins usually receive much smaller returns, and take on much greater risks, than do investors who participate in the initial offering.

Clearly, underpricing is a pervasive phenomenon. However, the long-run performance of IPOs presents a different puzzle.

EXAMPLE

The Indiana-based maker of fashion accessories, Vera Bradley, went public by selling stock in an IPO on October 21, 2010. Shares in the company were offered to initial investors at $16, but after one trading day the company's stock price stood at $24.85, a one-day gain of more than 55%! Even investors who purchased stock on the open market fared well as Vera Bradley's shares doubled in the six months after their IPO. Contrast that performance with the experience of Mecox Lane, an e-commerce fashion retailer in China. Mecox conducted an IPO on the Nasdaq in October 2010 and saw its stock price rise from the $11 offer price to $17.50 on its first day (a gain of 59%). However, Mecox's stock price fell by more than 50% in the firm's first six months as a public company, trading below $6 per share by May 2010.

Negative Long-Term IPO Returns Early research on the long-run performance of IPOs was not encouraging for investors. It showed that investors who buy IPO shares at the end of the first month of trading and then hold these shares for five years thereafter fare much worse than they would have by purchasing the shares of comparable, size-matched firms. On average, investors' net returns are more than 40% *below* what they would have earned after five years of alternative equity investments.

These findings are controversial because they challenge the notions that investors are rational and financial markets efficient. More recent research casts doubt on this long-run underperformance for IPO shares. Studies conclude that most IPOs do not yield significant long-run underperformance—provided that IPO returns are compared to an appropriate benchmark. In particular, a compelling case is made that much of the observed underperformance can be explained by leverage effects and risk reductions resulting from the IPO itself. Raising new equity capital via an IPO reduces the firm's leverage and its financial risk, so investors will accept a lower required return subsequent to the offering. On balance, we conclude that IPOs tend to earn normal long-term returns. Given these conflicting findings, we cannot yet draw firm conclusions about the long-run return on IPO shares.

Jay Ritter, University of Florida

"By the middle of 2001, 97% of Internet companies were trading below the offer price."

See the entire interview at SMART|finance

Smart Practices Video

11-3 Concept Review Questions

6. What patterns have been observed in the types of firms going public in the United States? Why do you think that certain industries become popular with investors at different times?

7. What are the principal benefits of going public? What are the key drawbacks?

8. Distinguish between an *equity carve-out* and a *spin-off*. How might a spin-off create value for shareholders?

9. To what does the term *underpricing* refer? If the average IPO is underpriced by about 15%, how might an unsophisticated investor who regularly invests in IPOs earn an average return of less than 15%?

10. How does underpricing add to the cost of going public?

11-4 Seasoned Equity Offerings in the United States

Seasoned equity offerings (SEOs) are surprisingly rare for both U.S. and non-U.S. companies. In fact, the typical large U.S. company will not sell new common stock even once per decade, though when an SEO is launched it tends to be much larger than the typical IPO. So what factors do managers feel are most important to consider when issuing seasoned equity? The results of a recent survey aimed at identifying these factors are shown in Figure 11.2. The figure shows that nearly two-thirds (64%) of the respondents expressed concern that an SEO will dilute earnings per share, and half of responding managers were concerned about diluting specific large shareholders. Over 60% of respondents voiced concerns regarding the size of a new issue and the likely negative effect that announcement of such an offering would have on the current price of outstanding shares. Further, about 50% stated they were considering a new stock issue to provide

Figure 11.2   **Factors that Affect SEO Issuance Decisions — CFO Survey Evidence**

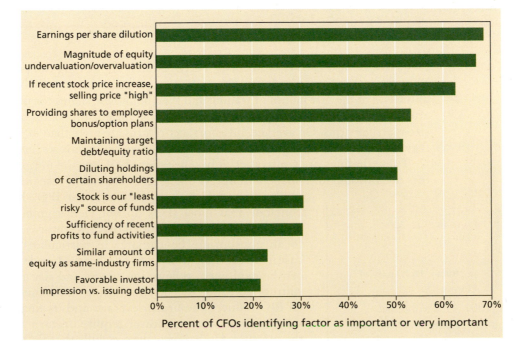

Source: Reprinted from John R. Graham and Campbell Harvey, "The Theory and Practice of Corporate Finance: Evidence from the Field," *Journal of Financial Economics*, 60, pp. 187–243, copyright © 2001, with permission of Elsevier.

shares for employee stock option programs and to maintain the firm's debt-to-equity ratio near the targeted level. Far fewer managers believed that recent firm profits would be insufficient to fund company activities, that the firm should issue stock to move toward an industry-standard leverage ratio, or that investors would prefer the company to issue stock rather than bonds.

Seasoned common stock issues must generally follow the same regulatory and underwriting procedures as unseasoned offerings. Seasoned offerings differ from unseasoned ones not just because of the former's large average size but also, and principally, because seasoned securities have an observable market value when the offering is priced, which obviously makes pricing much easier. Studies show that American SEOs tend to be priced very near the current market price. However, ease of pricing does not mean that investors welcome new equity offering announcements, as we now discuss.

11-4a Stock Price Reactions to Seasoned Equity Offerings

One reason why corporations issue seasoned equity very rarely is that stock prices usually fall when firms announce plans to conduct SEOs. On average, the price decline is about 3%. In the United States, the average dollar value of this price decline is equal to almost one-third of the dollar value of the issue itself. Clearly, the announcement of seasoned equity issues conveys negative information to investors overall, though precisely what information is transmitted is not always clear. The message may be that management, which is presumably better informed about a company's true prospects than are outside investors, believes the firm's current stock price is too high. Alternatively, the message may be that the firm's earnings will be lower than expected in the future and management is issuing stock to make up for the internal cash flow shortfall.

There is some evidence that SEOs are bad news for shareholders, not only at the time they are announced but also over holding periods of one to five years. Negative long-run returns following seasoned equity offerings have been documented in a variety of studies. As with long-run IPO returns, however, whether or not long-run returns following SEOs are unusually low depends on the comparison benchmark.

general cash offerings
Share offerings sold to all investors, not just existing shareholders.

rights offerings
A special type of seasoned equity offering that allows the firm's existing owners to buy new shares at a bargain price or to sell that right to other investors.

Most equity sales in the United States fall under the category of general cash offerings, meaning that shares are offered for sale to any and all investors. However, there is a special type of seasoned equity offering that allows firms' existing owners to buy new shares at a bargain price or to sell that right to other investors. These rights offerings are relatively scarce in the United States but are growing in importance internationally.

11-4b Rights Offerings

preemptive rights
These hold that shareholders have first claim on anything of value distributed by a corporation.

One of the basic tenets of U.S. commercial law is that shareholders have first claim on anything of value distributed by a corporation. These preemptive rights give common stockholders the right to maintain their proportionate ownership in the corporation by purchasing shares whenever the firm sells new equity. Because this strategy keeps all the gains and losses on share issues within the family, firms usually price rights offerings well below the current market price in order to ensure that the offering sells out and the firm raises the funds needed. The laws of most U.S. states grant shareholders the preemptive right to participate in new issues unless this right is removed by shareholder consent. However, the vast majority of publicly traded U.S. companies have removed preemptive rights from their corporate charter, so rights offerings by large U.S. companies are quite rare today. Rights offerings are still common in other countries, however.

11-4c Private Placements in the United States

private placement
Unregistered security offerings sold directly to accredited investors.

As noted earlier, a private placement involves the sale of securities in a transaction that is exempt from the registration requirements imposed by federal securities law. A private placement occurs when an investment banker arranges for the direct sale of a new security issue to an individual, several individuals, an institutional investor, or a

Finance in Your Life

FINANCING
Dental/Medical
BILLS

Understanding Employer Pension Plans

Selecting a pension plan is probably the last thing on your mind now, but you are likely to be asked to make that very choice when you begin your first job after graduation. Most U.S. companies and nonprofit institutions offer workers the opportunity to contribute to individual pension plans through payroll deductions, up to some maximum percentage (usually 5–6%) of the employee's annual salary. Many employers also fully or partly match employee contributions. These plans have proven very successful at building up large financial nest eggs for retiring U.S. workers, who on average will receive more from private pensions and personal savings than they do from Social Security payments.

There are two basic types of employer-sponsored pension plans: defined benefit plans and defined contribution plans. Both function much the way their names suggest. *Defined benefit plans*, which were traditionally the most common types offered by American business, promise workers payment of a fixed percentage of their final years' salary after retirement, either for a fixed number of years or for as long as they live. To meet this commitment, the employer invests each worker's personal contributions, plus any matching payments made by the employer, in a company-managed account that will eventually fund that worker's retirement payments. Importantly, it is the company that bears the risk that the value of this investment account may or may not cover the promised retirement benefits.

In *defined contribution plans*, employers only promise to make specific contributions to workers' retirement accounts rather than promising to pay a fixed percentage of their final period salary. The actual payments that a retiree will receive will be based solely on the amount of money that has been contributed to that employee's account over the years and the returns that these investments have earned. Defined contribution plans thus shift the financial risk of retirement planning from employers to employees, although workers gain control over their own retirement planning in return.

accredited investors
Individuals or institutions that meet certain income and wealth requirements.

group of institutions. The investment banker is paid a commission for acting as an intermediary in the transaction. To qualify for a private-placement exemption, the sale of the securities must be restricted to a small group of accredited investors, individuals or institutions that meet certain income and wealth requirements. The rationale for the private-placement exemption is that accredited investors are financially sophisticated agents who do not need the protection afforded by the registration process. Typical accredited institutional investors include insurance companies, pension funds, mutual funds, and venture capitalists.

Traditional Private Placements Versus Rule 144A Issues The private-placement exemption, in addition to allowing securities to be issued privately, requires that privately placed securities must be registered before they can be resold, or the subsequent sale must also qualify as a private placement. Rule 144A, adopted in 1990, provides a private-placement exemption for institutions with assets exceeding $100 million, known as qualified institutional buyers, and allows them to freely trade privately placed securities among themselves. The principal reasons for instituting Rule 144A were to increase liquidity and reduce issuing costs in the private-placement market. Another reason was to attract large foreign issuers who were unable or unwilling to conform to U.S. registration requirements for public offerings.

qualified institutional buyers
Institutions with assets exceeding $100 million.

Private placements have several advantages over public offerings. They are less costly in terms of time and money than registering with the SEC, and the issuers do not have to reveal confidential information. Also, because there are typically far fewer investors, the terms of a private placement are easier to renegotiate, if necessary. The disadvantages of private placement are that the securities have no readily available market price, they are less liquid, and there is a smaller group of potential investors than in the public market. Two features stand out in any analysis of private placements in recent years. First, debt offerings are much more common than equity offerings, although individual stock issues raise significantly larger amounts on average. Second, Rule 144A offerings account for about two thirds of the total dollars raised each year through private placements in the United States.

What Companies Do Globally

Average First-Day Returns on IPOs for 43 Countries

Significantly positive initial returns on initial public offerings are observed in many other countries besides the United States. As this figure shows, IPO underpricing is observed in at least forty-three countries; all show significant underpricing, and twenty-four of these countries have mean initial returns that are greater than the U.S. average. The average level of underpricing varies greatly across countries—from about 5% in Russia and Argentina to about 100% in India to an amazing 170% in China.

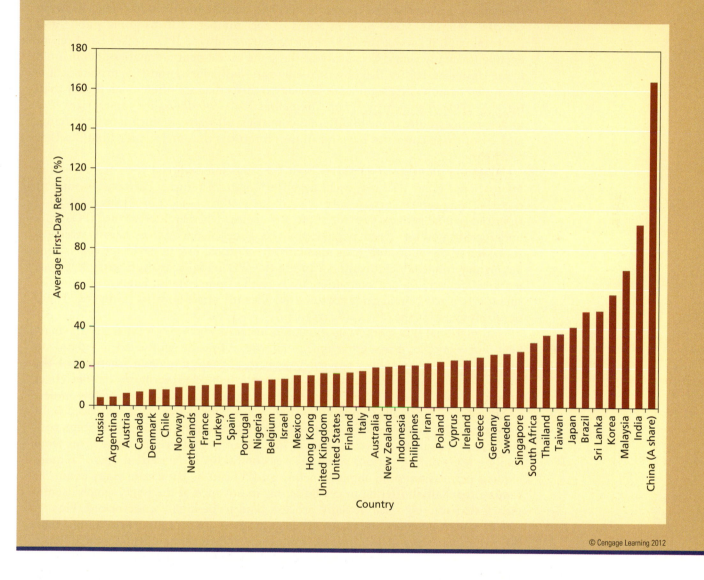

© Cengage Learning 2012

11-4 Concept Review Questions

11. What happens to a company's stock price when the firm announces plans for a seasoned equity offering? What are the long-term returns to investors following an SEO?

12. Why do you think that *rights offerings* have largely disappeared in the United States?

13. What is a *qualified institutional buyer*? How does this differ from an *accredited investor*?

14. What are the relative advantages and disadvantages of private placements compared to those of public offerings of stock and bond issues?

11-5 International Common-Stock Offerings

The international market for equity offerings can be broken down into two parts: each nation's market for domestic stock offerings and the international, or cross-border, market for equity offerings. We briefly look at each in turn, beginning with a survey of national markets.

11-5a Non-U.S. Initial Public Offerings

Relative to activity in the United States, the market for IPOs has been growing rapidly for many years. Both in terms of the number of firms going public and the total capital raised, the U.S. share of the worldwide IPO market has been in decline for many years. Yet, many of the same investment anomalies documented in the United States are also observed internationally. First, non-U.S. private-sector IPOs also demonstrate significant first-day returns that are often much higher than for U.S. IPOs. The nearby *What Companies Do Globally* figure summarizes IPO underpricing studies from 43 different countries; all show significant underpricing, and 24 of these countries have mean initial returns that are greater than the U.S. average.

A second anomaly common to both U.S. and international IPOs is that initial international offers also may yield negative long-term returns. However, studies of non-U.S. long-run returns are subject to all the methodological problems bedevilling U.S. studies (and perhaps even more), so it is unclear whether international IPOs truly underperform or not. Third, popular non-U.S. issues also tend to be heavily oversubscribed, and the allocation rules mandated by national law or exchange regulations largely determine which investors capture the IPO initial returns. Fourth, hot-issue markets are as prevalent internationally as in the United States. Finally, taxation issues (particularly capital gains tax rules) significantly affect how issues are priced and/or which investors the offers are targeting.

International IPO markets do, however, differ in important ways from U.S. markets. For example, many governments impose politically motivated mandates on firms wishing to go public, requiring them to allocate minimum fractions of the issue to their employees or to other targeted groups. Furthermore, the net effect of pricing restrictions in many countries is to ensure that IPOs are severely underpriced; this is especially common in countries where shares must be priced on a par-value basis and/or where minimum dividend payouts are mandated. Some governments (even in advanced economies like Japan's) routinely prohibit firms from making IPOs during periods when market conditions are unsettled and/or require explicit permission to be obtained before an IPO can be launched. Many countries require that initial offering prices be set far in advance of the issue, which usually means that offerings that actually proceed tend to be highly underpriced. Finally, non-U.S. entrepreneurs often have different motivations for taking firms public than do owner/managers of U.S. private companies. Whereas many U.S. companies go public in order to acquire the equity capital needed to finance rapid growth, continental European entrepreneurs go public mainly to rebalance their firms' capital structures and to achieve personal liquidity. On a more balanced note, most other countries place fewer restrictions on pre-offer marketing and dissemination of information than do U.S. regulators.

11-5b International Common-Stock Issues

Although the international market for common stock is not, and probably never will be, as large as the international market for debt securities, cross-border trading and issuance of common stock have increased dramatically since 1990. Much of this increase can be attributed to a growing desire on the part of institutional and individual investors to diversify their investment portfolios internationally. Because foreign stocks currently account for a small fraction of U.S. institutional holdings and of holdings in other developed economies, this total will surely grow in the years ahead.

Besides issuing stock to local investors, corporations have also discovered the benefits of issuing stock outside their home markets. For example, several top U.S. multinational companies have chosen to list their stock in half a dozen or more stock markets. Issuing stock internationally broadens the ownership base and helps a company integrate itself into the local business scene. A local stock listing increases local business press coverage and also serves as effective corporate advertising. Furthermore, having locally traded stock can facilitate corporate acquisitions because shares can then be used as an acceptable method of payment.

American Depositary Receipts Many foreign corporations have discovered the benefits of trading their stock in the United States, though they do so differently than do U.S. companies. The disclosure and reporting requirements mandated by the U.S. Securities and Exchange Commission have historically discouraged all but the largest foreign firms from directly listing their shares on American stock exchanges. Instead, most foreign companies tap the U.S. market through American Depositary Receipts (ADRs). These dollar-denominated claims issued by U.S. banks represent ownership of shares of a foreign company's stock held on deposit by the U.S. bank in the issuing firm's home country.

ADRs have proven to be very popular with U.S. investors, at least partly because they allow investors to diversify internationally. And because the shares are covered by American securities laws and pay dividends in dollars (dividends on the underlying shares are converted from the local currency into dollars before being paid out), U.S. investors are able to diversify at very low cost. As a result, the market value and trading volume of ADRs on the major U.S. stock exchanges has grew rapidly in the 1990s. More recently, foreign firms increasingly opt to raise capital abroad rather than in the United States.

11-5c Share Issue Privatizations

Anyone who examines international share offerings is soon struck by the size and importance of share issue privatizations in non-U.S. stock markets. A government executing a share issue privatization (SIP) will sell all or part of its ownership in a state-owned enterprise to private investors, via a public share offering. The words *public* and *private* can become confusing in this context; an SIP involves the sale of shares in a state-owned company to *private* investors via a *public* capital market share offering. Since Britain's Thatcher government first popularized privatizations in the early 1980s, there have been privatizing share offerings by more than 100 national governments. These SIPs have raised almost $2.5 trillion.

The importance of SIPs in creating new shareholders derives from the way these issues are generally priced and allocated. Governments almost always set offer prices well below their expected open-market value (they deliberately underprice), thereby ensuring great excess demand for shares in the offering. The issuing governments then allocate shares in a way that ensures maximum political benefit. Invariably, governments favor employees and other small domestic investors (who typically have never purchased common stock before) with relatively large share allocations, whereas domestic institutions and foreign investors are allocated far less than they desire. The net result of this strategy is to guarantee that most of the short-term capital gains of privatization IPOs are captured by the many citizen/investors (who vote) rather than by institutional and foreign investors (who do not). Furthermore, the long-run returns to investors who purchase privatizing share issues are typically quite high. In all, privatization share offerings have done as much as any other single factor to promote the development of international stock markets since the mid-1990s.

American Depositary Receipts (ADRs)
Dollar-denominated claims, issued by U.S. banks, that represent ownership of shares of a foreign company's stock held on deposit by the U.S. bank in the issuing firm's home country.

share issue privatization (SIP)
A government executing one of these will sell all or part of its ownership in a state-owned enterprise to private investors via a public share offering.

11-5 Concept Review Questions

15. In what ways are non-U.S. (private-sector) initial public offerings similar to U.S. IPOs, and in what ways are they different?

16. What are *American Depositary Receipts (ADRs)*, and how are these created? Why do you think ADRs have proven to be so popular with U.S. investors?

17. In what key ways do *share issue privatizations (SIPs)* differ from private-sector share offerings? Why do you think governments deliberately underprice SIPs?

Summary

- In almost all market economies, internally generated funds (primarily internally generated earnings) are the dominant source of funding for corporate investment. External financing is used only when needed, and then debt is almost always preferred to equity financing. The difference between a firm's total funding needs and its internally generated cash flow is referred to as its financial deficit.

- Financial intermediaries are institutions that raise funds by selling claims on themselves (often in the form of demand deposits, or checking accounts) and then use those funds to lend to borrowers. Intermediaries thus break, or *intermediate*, the direct link between final savers and borrowers that exists when companies sell securities directly to investors.

- Though financial intermediaries are essential to the smooth running of the U.S. economy, they play a relatively small role proportionately in financing U.S. corporations. This is especially true for large, multinational firms. However, intermediaries are important in the corporate financial systems of most other nations.

- Companies wanting to raise capital externally must make a series of decisions, beginning with whether to issue debt or equity and whether to employ an investment bank to assist with the securities sale. This chapter focuses on common stock offerings, but the decisions and issuing procedures are similar for preferred stock and debt securities.

- Firms wanting to raise new common-stock equity can sell stock to public investors, typically with the help of an investment bank. The firm must decide whether to sell stock to public investors through a general cash offering or to rely on sales to existing stockholders using a rights offering. Rights offerings are fairly rare in the United States today, though they remain common in other developed countries.

- Common stock can be sold through private placements to accredited investors, or it can be sold to the public if the securities are registered with the SEC. A company's first public offering of common stock is known as its initial public offering, or IPO. The average IPO in the United States is underpriced by about 15%, and this has held true for several decades. International IPOs are also underpriced. It is unclear whether or not IPOs are poor long-term investments.

- Subsequent offerings of common stock are known as seasoned equity offerings, or SEOs. The announcement of a seasoned equity issue tends to decrease a company's stock price, and there is evidence that firms issuing seasoned equity underperform over the long term.

- Non-U.S. firms in countries with well-functioning stock markets can raise equity capital using an IPO. Once issued, their shares can trade in the United States either by directly listing on a U.S. exchange, or more commonly through American Depositary Receipts (ADRs), which are dollar-denominated claims issued by U.S. banks against the actual foreign shares that they hold on deposit. The largest share offerings in world history have all been share issue privatizations (SIPs), which have done as much as any other single factor to promote the development of international stock markets.

Key Terms

accredited investors, 360
American Depositary Receipts (ADRs), 363
book building, 352
bulge bracket, 350
cash flow from operations, 348
certification, 353
due diligence, 352
effective (offering), 353
equity carve-out (ECO), 356
Eurobond, 349
financial deficit, 347
financial intermediary (FI), 348
fixed-price offer, 352
flip, 356
foreign bond, 350
full disclosure, 352

general cash offerings, 359
Glass-Steagall Act, 349
Gramm-Leach-Bliley Act, 349
initial public offering (IPO), 349
initial return, 357
IPO underpricing, 356
international common stock, 350
investment bank, 350
McFadden Act, 348
preemptive rights, 359
primary issues, 349
private placements, 359
prospectus, 350
qualified institutional buyers, 360
registration statement, 353
reverse LBO (or second IPO), 356

rights offerings, 359
Rule 144A offering, 354
seasoned equity offering (SEO), 349
secondary offering, 349
Securities Act of 1933, 352
Securities Exchange Act of 1934, 352
securitization, 349
share issue privatization (SIP), 363
shelf registration (Rule 415), 353
spin-off, 356
supplemental disclosures, 353
tracking stocks, 356
underwriting spread, 350
Yankee bonds, 350

Self-Test Problems

Answers to Self-Test Problems and the Concept Review Questions throughout the chapter appear in CourseMate with SmartFinance Tools at www.cengagebrain.com.

ST11-1. Last year, Guaraldi Instruments, Inc., conducted an IPO, issuing 2 million common shares with a par value of $0.25 to investors, at a price of $15 per share. During its first year of operation, Guaraldi earned net income of $0.07 per share and paid a dividend of $0.005 per share. At the end of the year, the company's stock was selling for $20 per share. Construct the equity account for Guaraldi at the end of its first year in business and calculate the firm's market capitalization.

ST11-2. The Bloomington Company needs to raise $20 million of new equity capital. Its common stock is currently selling for $42 per share. The investment bankers require an underwriting spread of 7% of the offering price, and the company's legal, accounting, and printing expenses associated with the seasoned offering are estimated to be $450,000. How many new shares must the company sell in order to net $20 million?

Questions

Q11-1. How should a corporation estimate the amount of financing that must be raised externally during a given year? Once that amount is known, what other decision must be made?

Q11-2. What is the dominant source of capital funding in the United States? Given this result and the fact that most corporations are net borrowers, what decisions must most managers face in order to address this financial deficit?

Q11-3. Define the term *financial intermediary*. What role do financial intermediaries play in U.S. corporate finance? How does this compare to the role of non-U.S. financial intermediaries?

Q11-4. Discuss the U.S. banking system regulations that have had a major impact on the development of the U.S. financial system. In what ways has the U.S. system been affected (positively and negatively) by these regulations?

Q11-5. What are the general trends regarding public security issuance by U.S. corporations? Specifically, which security type is most often sold to the public? What is the split between initial and seasoned equity offerings?

Q11-6. Distinguish between a *Eurobond*, a *foreign bond*, and a *Yankee bond*. Which of these three represents the greatest volume of security issuance?

Q11-7. What do you think are the most important costs and benefits of becoming a publicly traded firm? What questions would you ask before advising whether or not an entrepreneur's firm should go public?

Q11-8. If you were an investment banker, how would you determine the offering price of an IPO?

Q11-9. Are the significantly positive short-run returns earned by IPO shareholders compatible with market efficiency? If not, why not?

Q11-10. List and describe briefly the key services that investment banks provide to firms before, during, and after a securities offering.

Q11-11. Explain why the underwriting spread on IPOs averages about 7% of the offering price whereas the spread on a seasoned offering of common stock averages less than 5%?

Q11-12. Discuss the various issues that must be considered in selecting an investment banker for an IPO. Which type of placement is usually preferred by the issuing firm?

Q11-13. In terms of IPO investing, what does it mean to *flip* a stock? According to the empirical results regarding short- and long-term returns following equity offerings, is flipping a wise investment strategy?

Q11-14. What materials are presented in an IPO *prospectus*? In general, what result is documented regarding sales of shares by insiders and venture capitalists?

Q11-15. What are *American Depositary Receipts (ADRs)*, and why have they proven to be so popular with U.S. investors?

Q11-16. How do you explain the highly politicized nature of *share issue privatization (SIP)* pricing and share allocation policies? Are governments maximizing offering proceeds, or are they pursuing primarily political and economic objectives?

Problems

Investment Banking and the Public Sale of Securities

P11-1. West Coast Manufacturing Company (WCMC) is executing an initial public offering with the following characteristics. The company will sell 10 million shares at an offer price of $25 per share, the underwriter will charge a 7% underwriting fee, and the shares are expected to sell for $32 per share by the end of the first day's trading. Assume that this IPO is executed as anticipated.
  a. Calculate the initial return earned by investors who are allocated shares in the IPO.
  b. How much will WCMC receive from this offering?
  c. What is the total cost (underwriting fee and underpricing) of this issue to WCMC?

P11-2. Suppose you purchase shares of Engel, Inc. (EI), which recently executed an IPO at the post-offering market price of $32 per share and you hold the shares for one year. You then sell your EI shares for $35 per share. EI does not pay dividends, and you are not subject to capital gains taxation. During this year, the return on the overall stock market was 11%. What net return did you earn on your EI share investment? Assess this return in light of the overall market return.

P11-3. Norman Internet Service Company (NISC) is interested in selling common stock to raise capital for capacity expansion. The firm has consulted First Tulsa Company, a large underwriting firm, which believes that the stock can be sold for $50 per share. The underwriter's investigation found that its administrative costs will be 2.5% of the sale price and its selling costs will be 2.0% of the sale price. If the underwriter requires a profit equal to 1% of the sale price, how much spread (in dollars) is necessary to cover the underwriter's costs and profit?

P11-4. The Mitchell Company needs to raise $50 million of new equity capital. Its common stock is currently selling for $50 per share. The investment bankers require an underwriting spread of 3% of the offering price, and the company's legal, accounting, and printing expenses associated with the seasoned offering are estimated to be $750,000. How many new shares must the Mitchell Company sell in order to net $50 million?

P11-5. La Jolla Securities, Inc., specializes in the underwriting of small companies. The terms of a recent offering were as follows:

Number of shares	2 million
Offering price	$25 per share
Net proceeds	$45 million

La Jolla Securities' expenses associated with the offering were $500,000. Determine La Jolla Securities' profit on the offering if the secondary market price of the shares immediately after the offering began were as follows:

a. $23 per share
b. $25 per share
c. $28 per share

The U.S. Market for Initial Public Offerings (IPOs)

P11-6. Find an Internet site that provides data on recent IPOs, and pick 4 companies that conducted an IPO in recent weeks. Write down the ticker symbols and offer prices for the firms you select; then go to Yahoo! and download daily price quotes since the IPO date. For each firm, calculate the following:
a. The percentage return measured from the offer price to the closing price the first day.
b. The percentage return, measured from the opening price to the closing price the first day.

P11-7. Four companies conducted IPOs last month: Hot.Com; Biotech Pipe Dreams Corp.; Sleepy Tyme, Inc.; and Bricks N Mortar International. All four companies went public at an offer price of $10 per share. The first-day performance of each stock (measured as the percentage difference between the IPO offer price and the first-day closing price) was as follows:

Company	First-Day Return
Hot.Com	45%
Biotech Pipe Dreams	30%
Sleepy Tyme	5%
Bricks N Mortar	0%

a. If you submitted a bid through your broker for 100 shares of each company, if your orders were filled completely, and if you cashed out of each deal after one day, what was your average return on these investments?
b. Next, suppose that your orders were not all filled completely because of excess demand for hot IPOs. Specifically, after ordering 100 shares of each company, you were able to buy only 10 shares of Hot.Com, 20 shares of Biotech Pipe Dreams, 50 shares of Sleepy Tyme, and 100 shares of Bricks N Mortar. Recalculate your average return, taking into account that your orders were only partially filled.

Seasoned Equity Offerings in the United States

P11-8. GSM Corporation sold 20 million shares of common stock in a seasoned offering. The market price of the company's shares immediately before the offering was $14.75. The shares were offered to the public at $14.50, and the underwriting spread was 4%. The company's expenses associated with the offering were $7.5 million. How much new cash did the company receive?

P11-9. After a banner year of rising profits and positive stock returns, the managers of Raptor Pharmaceuticals Corporation (RPC) have decided to launch a seasoned equity offering to raise new equity capital. RPC currently has 10 million shares outstanding, and yesterday's closing market price was $75.00 per RPC share. The company plans to sell 1 million newly issued shares in its seasoned offering. The investment banking firm Robbum and Blindum (R&B) has agreed to underwrite the new stock issue for a 2.5% discount from the offering price, which RPC and R&B have agreed should be $0.75 per share lower than RPC's closing price the day before the offering is sold.

    a. What is likely to happen to RPC's stock price when the plan for this seasoned offering is publicly announced?

    b. Assume that RPC's stock price closes at $72.75 per share the day before the seasoned offering is launched, what net proceeds will RPC receive from this offering?

    c. Calculate the return earned by RPC's *existing* stockholders on their shares from the time before the seasoned offering was announced until it was actually sold for $72.75 per share.

    d. Calculate the total cost of the seasoned equity offering to RPC's existing stockholders as a percentage of the offering proceeds.

 THOMSON REUTERS | Business School Edition

For instructions on using Thomson ONE, refer to the instructions provided with the Thomson ONE problems at the end of Chapters 1-6.

P11-10. Determine the sources of capital for Canon Inc. (CAJ) in each of the last five years. How much capital was raised through internal sources, and how much was raised through external sources? Compare the sources of capital for Canon to those of Xerox Corp. (XRX). Does one company appear to depend more heavily on internal sources rather than external sources, or vice versa? What are some possible reasons for this?

Smart Ideas Video

 Tim Jenkinson, Oxford University

"There are basically three ways of doing an IPO."

Smart Practices Video

 Frank Popoff, Chairman of the Board (retired), Dow Chemical

"A Samurai bond is just an exercise in matching exposure and income."

Jay Ritter, University of Florida

"Every single country in the world has IPOs underpriced on average."

Jay Ritter, University of Florida

"By the middle of 2001, 97% of Internet companies were trading below the offer price."

SMART concepts

See financing options available to large corporations.

Mini-Case

Raising Long-Term Financing

Since graduation from college, you have worked at Precision Manufacturing, Incorporated, as a financial analyst. You have recently been promoted to the position of senior financial manager, with responsibilities that include capital budgeting decisions and the raising of long-term financing. Therefore, you decide to investigate the various alternatives for raising funds. Your goal is to make sure that the benefits from undertaking long-term projects are greater than the costs of raising the long-term funds needed to finance those projects. With this goal in mind, you decide to answer the following questions.

Assignment

1. What should managers consider when making the decision whether to finance internally or externally?

2. What services does an investment banker offer to corporations that choose to raise funds in the capital market?

3. What legal rules govern the issue of securities to the public in the United States?

4. What are the benefits to the corporation of going public?

5. What are the drawbacks to the corporation of going public?

6. What returns can investors in the common stock expect on the first day of trading if they commit to purchase shares through the IPO issue? What factors may affect the relative amount of these first-day returns?

7. Describe the following offers: (a) seasoned equity offer, (b) rights offer, and (c) private placement. In what circumstances would a company use each of these offerings to raise funds?

8. Discuss the differences between international public offerings and domestic (U.S.) public offerings.

chapter 12

Capital Structure

What Companies Do

Changing Capital Structures

On July 14, 2010, Target Corp., the second-largest U.S. discount retailer, sold $1 billion of debt in its first bond offering since January 2008. Target planned to use the proceeds to repay existing debt, fund capital expenditures associated with building new stores, remodel existing stores, acquire real estate, other assets, and companies, and to finance share repurchases. At the time of the offering Target's CEO, Gregg Steinhafel, stated: "Target's cash generation is well above the amount needed for optimal reinvestment in our core business. We expect to continue to return excess cash to our shareholders through a combination of regular dividends and opportunistic share repurchases." So, in this case, Target will increase debt and use some of the proceeds from the debt offering to retire some common stock.

About a month before the Target debt sale, Ambac Financial Group, a firm in the surety and title insurance business, announced the conversion of $11.8 million of its debt to 8.6 million shares of its common stock. This debt-to-equity conversion was part of Ambac's ongoing rigorous efforts to reduce its debt level and thereby lower its interest burden. This strategy was centered on Ambac's need to reduce the likelihood of a debt default and subsequent bankruptcy. Clearly, Ambac's actions are aimed at altering its capital structure by issuing equity to retire outstanding debt.

These examples illustrate that companies sometimes issue debt or equity, not only because they need the money to fund an investment project, but also because they want to alter their capital structure. This behavior suggests that managers believe that there is an optimal capital structure—in other words, one that maximizes firm value. This chapter explores whether there is such a thing as an optimal capital structure, and, if so, what factors determine the optimal mix of debt and equity for a particular firm.

Source: Sapna Maheshwari, "Target Plans $1 Billion Debt Sale, First Bond Offering Since January 2008," downloaded from www.bloomberg.com/news/2010-07-13/target-sells-1-billion-of-debt-at-80-basis-point-spread-over -treasuries.html and Zaks Equity Research, "Ambac Converts Debt to Equity Again," downloaded from www.zacks .com/stock/news/36428/Ambac+Converts+Debt+to+Equity+Again.

Learning Objectives

After studying this chapter you should be able to:

- Explain how financial leverage increases both a firm's risk and its returns;

- Understand how the Modigliani-Miller model indicates that capital structure is irrelevant in a world without taxes and other market frictions, but the use of debt is favored when debt interest is deductible from corporate income taxes. Discuss how corporate and personal taxes affect capital structure;

- Explain how the costs of bankruptcy and financial distress affect capital structure decisions and explore the questions raised by the agency cost/tax shield trade-off model of corporate leverage; and

- Describe the most important capital structure patterns observed around the world and explain what factors may be driving leverage choices.

The chapter opener demonstrated that a firm's financing decisions impact its capital structure. An important question raised by this is: Why do some firms choose to finance their operations largely with debt, while other companies issue little or no debt? Table 12.1 lists several prominent U.S. companies and their long-term debt levels in 2011. Note the prevalence of high-tech firms on the list of firms with very little debt. Firms on the high-debt list come from industries such as restaurants, food processing, and consumer products.

This chapter describes the key influences on managers' decisions to finance with debt or with equity. We begin by showing why firms may choose to substitute debt for equity capital, even in a world without corporate income taxes. We then show that the common practice of allowing companies to deduct interest payments from taxable income provides a strong incentive for corporations to substitute debt for equity.

Table 12.1

2011 Long-Term Debt-to-Assets Ratios

Low-Debt Firms		High-Debt Firms	
Accenture	0.00	Colgate-Palmolive	0.26
Apple	0.00	Procter & Gamble	0.16
eBay	0.06	Kellogg	0.41
Google	0.00	McDonald's	0.33
Microsoft	0.12	Target	0.36
Qualcomm	0.00	DIRECTV Group	0.69
Research in Motion	0.00	Waste Management	0.41
Texas Instruments	0.00	Yum! Brands	0.35
Yahoo!	0.00	Caterpillar	0.30

12-1 What Is Financial Leverage and What Are Its Effects?

When firms use debt in their capital structures we say that they are using *financial leverage*. Similarly, a company with debt on its balance sheet is a *levered firm*, and a company that finances its operations entirely with equity is an *unlevered firm*. The term *leverage* implies that debt magnifies a firm's financial performance. That effect can be either positive or negative, depending on the returns a firm earns on the money it borrows. A simple example illustrates this principle.

Consider the decision facing Susan Ruiz, chief financial officer of High-Tech Manufacturing Corporation (HTMC), a publicly traded company with no debt and 200,000 outstanding shares of common stock. Analysts expect HTMC to generate a $1,000,000 of total profits each year for the foreseeable future. Given HTMC's risk, shareholders require a 10% return on their investment. Using the present value formula for a perpetuity (Equation 3.10 on page 89), we find the company's value equals $10,000,000 ($1,000,000 ÷ 0.10). By dividing total firm value by the number of shares outstanding, we see that HTMC's stock price is $50 per share ($10,000,000 ÷ 200,000).

A shareholder suggests to Ms. Ruiz that by issuing bonds and retiring some of its outstanding stock, HTMC could increase earnings per share and thereby increase its stock price. To be more specific, the shareholder proposes that HTMC should issue $5,000,000 in long-term debt, at an interest rate of 6.0%, and use the proceeds to repurchase half the company's common stock (i.e., 100,000 shares). This

recapitalization
Alteration of a company's capital structure to change the relative mix of debt and equity financing.

recapitalization would result in a dramatic shift in the firm's financing mix. Ignoring for the time being any effects of this transaction on firm's equity value, HTMC's capital structure would change from 100% equity to 50% debt and 50% equity. In other words, this strategy would convert HTMC's debt-to-equity ratio from 0 to 1.0. Table 12.2 summarizes HTMC's current and proposed capital structures.

The shareholder suggests that this strategy will increase the expected return to HTMC's stockholders, as measured by earnings per share. Though initially dubious of this proposal, Ms. Ruiz creates Tables 12.2 and 12.3 to test the shareholder's prediction. As noted, she thinks that HTMC's earnings before interest and taxes (EBIT), will be $1,000,000 next year, if the economy continues to grow at a normal rate.[1] However, if the country falls into a recession next year, High-Tech's sales will fall, and EBIT will be only $500,000. On the other hand, if the economy booms, HTMC will enjoy rising sales, and EBIT will be $1,500,000. Ms. Ruiz believes that the probability of each outcome is one third, so the expected value of EBIT equals $1,000,000:

$$\text{Expected EBIT} = \left(\frac{1}{3}\right)\$1,500,000 + \left(\frac{1}{3}\right)\$1,000,000 + \left(\frac{1}{3}\right)\$500,000 = \$1,000,000$$

Table 12.3 summarizes HTMC's current and proposed capital structures, assuming that the economy grows at a normal rate and that EBIT equals $1,000,000. If the current capital structure is retained, earnings per share (EPS) will be $5.00. Because HTMC stock is currently worth $50 per share and the company pays out all net profits as dividends, HTMC's stockholders will earn a return on equity of 10% ($5.00 ÷ $50.00) over the coming year. If HTMC instead adopts the proposed recapitalization, the firm will have to pay $300,000 interest on the $5,000,000 debt (0.06 × $5,000,000), leaving $700,000 in net income ($1,000,000 EBIT − $300,000 interest). Only 100,000 shares

Table 12.2

Current and Proposed Capital Structures for High-Tech Manufacturing Corporation

	Current	Proposed
Assets	$10,000,000	$10,000,000
Equity	$10,000,000	$5,000,000
Debt	$0	$5,000,000
Debt-to-equity ratio	0	1.0
Shares outstanding	200,000	100,000
Share price	$50.00	$50.00
Interest rate on debt	—	6.0%

© Cengage Learning 2012

Table 12.3

Expected Cash Flows to Stockholders and Bondholders Under the Current and Proposed Capital Structures for High-Tech Manufacturing Corporation

Assuming *EBIT* = $1,000,000

	Current Capital Structure: All-Equity Financing	Proposed Capital Structure: 50% Debt: 50% Equity
EBIT	$1,000,000	$1,000,000.00
− Interest (6.0%)	$0	$(300,000)
Net income	$1,000,000	$700,000
Shares outstanding	200,000	100,000
Earnings per share (EPS)	$5.00	$7.00
Return on equity (P_0 = $50.00/share)	**10.0%**	**14.0%**

© Cengage Learning 2012

[1] For now, we assume that there are no taxes. Therefore, there is no difference between EBIT and net income for an unlevered company like HTMC. We relax this no-tax assumption in Section 12-3.

| | Table 12.4 | | Expected Cash Flows to Stockholders and Bondholders Under the Current and Proposed Capital Structures for High-Tech Manufacturing Corporation for Three Equally Likely Outcomes | | | |

| | Recession | | Normal Growth | | Boom | |
| EBIT | $500,000 | | $1,000,000 | | $1,500,000 | |
	All-Equity Financing	50% Debt: 50% Equity	All-Equity Financing	50% Debt: 50% Equity	All-Equity Financing	50% Debt: 50% Equity
– Interest (6.0%)	$0	$(300,000)	$ 0	$(300,000)	$0	$(300,000)
Net income	$500,000	$200,000	$1,000,000	$700,000	$1,500,000	$1,200,00
Shares outstanding	200,000	100,000	200,000	100,000	200,000	100,000
Earnings per share (EPS)	$2.50	$2.00	$5.00	$7.00	$7.50	$12.00
Return on shares (%) (P_0 = $50.00/share)	**5.0%**	**4.0%**	**10.0%**	**14.0%**	**15.0%**	**24.0%**

remain outstanding after the recapitalization, so EPS will be $7.00. In this scenario, the return on equity enjoyed by shareholders is 14% ($7 ÷ $50).

So far, the recapitalization plan seems to look rather attractive. But what happens if a recession or a boom occurs? Table 12.4 shows the payoffs to HTMC's investors under those economic scenarios. If the economy booms, High-Tech's EBIT will be $1,500,000. With the existing capital structure, EPS will be $7.50, and ROE will be 15.0%. If the economy booms and HTMC recapitalizes, EPS will be $12.00, and ROE will be an impressive 24.0%! It would seem that the recapitalization is particularly good for shareholders in this scenario.

So, what's the catch? What could possibly argue against HTMC adopting the recapitalization plan and increasing EPS and ROE? The answer is that the economy may well fall into a recession next year, in which case High-Tech's EBIT will only be $500,000. With the existing all-equity capital structure, the company would achieve an *EPS* of $2.50, yielding a 5.0% ROE for stockholders. However, if HTMC recapitalizes and the economy falls into a recession, net income will only be $200,000, after paying $300,000 in interest. Thus, EPS will be $2.00 and ROE only 4.0%. In other words, whether the recapitalization plan increases or decreases returns for shareholders depends on the state of the economy.

Recall that Ms. Ruiz believes that each of the three economic scenarios is equally likely. Based on that view, we already calculated the expected level of EBIT. But what about expected EPS and expected ROE? As HTMC's major shareholder claimed, the expected return to shareholders rises if HTMC adds debt to its capital structure.

$$\text{Expected } EPS \text{ (no debt)} = \left(\frac{1}{3}\right)\$7.50 + \left(\frac{1}{3}\right)\$5 + \left(\frac{1}{3}\right)\$2.50 = \$5$$

$$\text{Expected } EPS \text{ (with debt)} = \left(\frac{1}{3}\right)\$12 + \left(\frac{1}{3}\right)\$7 + \left(\frac{1}{3}\right)\$2 = \$7$$

$$\text{Expected } ROE \text{ (no debt)} = \left(\frac{1}{3}\right)15\% + \left(\frac{1}{3}\right)10\% + \left(\frac{1}{3}\right)5\% = 10\%$$

$$\text{Expected } ROE \text{ (with debt)} = \left(\frac{1}{3}\right)24\% + \left(\frac{1}{3}\right)14\% + \left(\frac{1}{3}\right)4\% = 14\%$$

12-1a How Leverage Increases the Risk of Expected Earnings per Share

Figure 12.1 illustrates how High-Tech's capital structure affects the relationship between EBIT and EPS. In good economic times, the company enjoys higher EPS with the 50% debt/50% equity capital structure than with the all-equity capital structure. However, in a recession, HTMC's shareholders earn more under the old all-equity capital structure. Now you can see how the term *leverage* applies to the decision to borrow money: Relative to the all-equity capital structure, borrowing money makes shareholders better off when times are good and worse off when times are bad. Leverage magnifies both the good outcomes and the bad ones.

Figure 12.1

When the company uses debt, it magnifies both upside gains and downside losses, as shown by the steeper "with debt" line. Earnings thus become riskier with leverage.

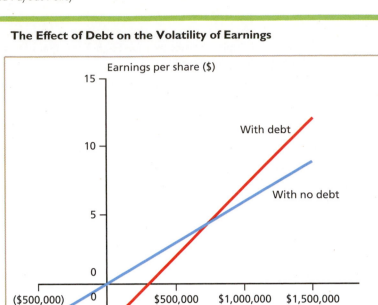

The Effect of Debt on the Volatility of Earnings

© Cengage Learning 2012

The lines in Figure 12.1 cross when EBIT equals $600,000. When EBIT exceeds $600,000, HTMC's shareholders earn more with the 50% debt/50% equity mix than with the current all-equity structure. If EBIT is below $600,000 then the reverse is true: shareholders earn higher EPS with all-equity financing than they would if HTMC were to borrow money.

For the proposed recapitalization, the *breakeven level of operating profits*—the level of EBIT yielding the same return on equity (ROE) for both capital structures—occurs when EBIT equals $600,000. It is no accident that $600,000 defines the break-even point here. Notice that if HTMC earns $600,000 on assets of $10 million then its return on assets equals 6%, the same rate that it pays on borrowed funds. If the firm can earn more on its assets than it pays on its debt, then EPS goes up relative to the all-equity case. If EBIT falls short of $600,000 then the firm earns less on its investments than it pays in interest; hence EPS goes down relative to the all-equity case. The slopes of the lines in the figure indicate that debt magnifies the effect on EPS of any change in EBIT. When EBIT changes, EPS changes faster if the firm is levered than if it is unlevered.

12-1b The Fundamental Principle of Financial Leverage

The simple example using the High-Tech Manufacturing Corporation shows why employing long-term debt financing is called applying *financial leverage*. Just as a lever magnifies the effect of a given force on an object, debt financing magnifies the impact of a change in EBIT on earnings per share. If High-Tech's realized EBIT comes in next year above $600,000, employing debt financing will increase earnings per share for the firm's shareholders. However, the reverse also holds true. If EBIT falls below $600,000, HTMC's earnings per share will be lower than they would have been with an all-equity capital structure. This yields a basic and important result:

fundamental principle of financial leverage
Substituting debt for equity increases expected returns to shareholders but also increases the risk that equity investors bear.

The **fundamental principle of financial leverage**: *substituting debt for equity increases expected returns to shareholders but also increases the risk that equity investors bear.*

What Companies Do Globally

CFO Survey: The Importance of Capital Structure Decisions

Cohen and Yagil surveyed 140 CFOs from the U.S., the UK, Germany, Canada, and Japan and asked them to rank the importance of investment policy and financing policy to their firms (5 = very important, 1 = not important). The figure below shows the unsurprising result that CFOs view both investment and financing decisions as quite important. Observe, however, that the relative importance of the two decisions varies depending on whether the CFO manages

a firm with high leverage or low leverage. In firms that rely more on debt than on equity (i.e., whose debt ratios exceed 50 %), CFOs say that managing the firm's capital structure is even more important than how the firm invests its money. Perhaps this reflects the fundamental principle of leverage. The more a firm borrows, the more volatile are its earnings, so the importance of paying close attention to capital structure increases.

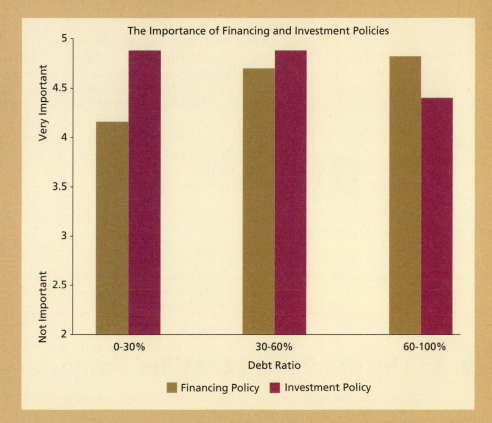

The Importance of Financing and Investment Policies

Sources: Gil Cohen and Joseph Yagil, "A Multinational Survey of Corporate Financial Policies," *Journal of Applied Finance* (Spring/Summer 2007), pp. 57–69.

? JOB INTERVIEW QUESTION

What impact would you expect on a firm's earnings if it raises its debt-to-equity ratio?

Because adding debt to the capital structure makes shareholders' claims more risky, they should demand a higher return. Therefore, whether the addition of debt to HTMC's capital structure increases the firm's stock price depends on the relative importance of two offsetting effects: the increase in expected EPS versus the increased discount rate that shareholders will apply to these earnings. In one special (but important) case, these forces offset each other exactly, which would mean that changing a firm's capital structure neither raises nor lowers its value.

12-1c Leverage Increases Expected Return—But Does It Increase Value?

Though we have demonstrated the effect that financial leverage should have on HTMC's shareholders, we haven't yet helped Ms. Ruiz decide whether to adopt the 50% debt/50% equity recapitalization or retain the company's existing all-equity capital structure. In Tables 12.1 and 12.2, and in Figure 12.1, she documents that

employing debt can increase expected EPS and ROE for HTMC's shareholders, but the added risk associated with debt makes her uncertain about the net benefit of the recapitalization.

In creating Table 12.2, we assumed that immediately after HTMC's recapitalization the remaining shares would still sell for $50. If that assumption is valid, then the total market value of HTMC equals $10 million, whether the firm finances with all equity or with some debt and some equity. Recall that if HTMC recapitalizes, its expected EPS increases from $5 to $7. Likewise, expected ROE increases from 10% to 14%. Because of the added risk that they must bear, suppose HTMC shareholders increase their required return from 10% to 14%. If shareholders believe that HTMC's earnings will be $7 per share in perpetuity, then the stock price will remain at $50 and the recapitalization will have no net impact on HTMC's total value:

$$P = \frac{\$7}{0.14} = \$50$$

From this analysis, Ms. Ruiz concludes that there is no unique, *optimal capital structure* for her company that maximizes firm value. Substituting debt for equity will increase expected EPS, but only at the cost of higher variability. With higher EPS volatility, shareholders will expect a higher return, meaning that they will discount future earnings at a higher rate. These two effects essentially cancel each other out, so shareholders are just as happy with a capital structure that includes no debt as they are with one that consists of equal proportions of debt and equity.[2]

12-1 Concept Review Questions

1. What is a *recapitalization*? Why is this considered a pure capital structure change?

2. What is the *fundamental principle of financial leverage*? What trade-offs do managers face when they consider changing a firm's capital structure?

12-2 The Modigliani & Miller Propositions

Susan Ruiz (in the preceding section) has reached the same capital structure irrelevance conclusion proposed by two economists more than half a century ago. In 1958, Franco Modigliani and Merton Miller (hereafter M&M) published a path-breaking study that challenged conventional thinking about capital structure.[3] They demonstrated that changes in the mix of debt and equity merely altered the division of a firm's cash flows between its stockholders and bondholders but did not fundamentally affect firm value. This conclusion was predicated on several important assumptions:

1. Capital markets are perfect, meaning that investors and firms face no market frictions such as taxes or transactions costs.

2. Investors can borrow and lend at the same rate that corporations can.

3. Managers and investors have identical information regarding the firm's operations and plans.

Although these assumptions clearly do not correspond to conditions in real markets, M&M's conclusions remain significant.

---

[2]This result holds for any other mix of debt and equity under the assumptions used in this example. The total market value of HTMC is the same, whether the firm uses 100% equity, 75% equity and 25% debt, or any other capital structure.

[3]See Franco Modigliani and Merton Miller, "The Cost of Capital, Corporation Finance and the Theory of Investment," *American Economic Review*, 48, no. 3 (1958), pp. 261–297.

business risk

The variability of a firm's cash flows, as measured by the variability of *EBIT*.

financial risk

How a firm's financing choices affect how its *business risk* is distributed to its stockholders and bondholders.

M&M made an important distinction between a firm's *business risk* and its *financial risk*. Business risk refers to the variability of a firm's cash flows, whereas financial risk refers to how a firm's financing choices affect how this risk is distributed to its stockholders and bondholders. HTMC's business risk is determined by how its earnings, before interest and taxes, fluctuate with the state of the economy. Notice that the volatility of EBIT is the same, whether HTMC recapitalizes or whether it finances with 100% equity. In either case, its EBIT will be $500,000; $1,000,000; or $1,500,000; depending on the state of the economy.

If HTMC retains its all-equity structure, then the financial risk that shareholders bear equals HTMC's underlying business risk. With no debt, the variations in EBIT translate directly into variations in EPS. However, under the 50-50 recapitalization, HTMC's leverage magnifies the financial risk borne by shareholders. With debt, HTMC issues a claim to bondholders that insulates them entirely from the firm's business risk. Whether the economy booms, grows normally, or falls into a recession, bondholders receive the $300,000 interest payment they are promised. In this example, because bondholders bear no risk, even though HTMC's business risk hasn't changed, the shareholders remaining after the recapitalization have to shoulder even more risk than they did before.

12-2a M&M Proposition I: Capital Structure Irrelevance

Proposition I

The famous "irrelevance proposition," which asserts that the market value of any firm equals the value of its assets and is independent of the firm's capital structure. Firm value is calculated by discounting the firm's expected EBIT at the rate r_a, appropriate for the firm's business risk.

Modigliani and Miller's Proposition I asserts the following: *The market value of any firm equals the value of its assets and is independent of the firm's capital structure.* The value of the assets, in turn, equals the present value of the cash flows generated by the assets. Because the proposition leads to the conclusion that the firm's capital structure does not matter, it is popularly known as the *irrelevance proposition*.

We can develop a simple, mathematical expression of this idea as follows. Assume that investors expect a company to generate a constant EBIT (assumed equal to *net operating income*) stream each year for the foreseeable future. The firm may have outstanding debt with market value equal to D and/or equity with a market value equal to E. By definition, the total value of the firm's outstanding securities is V, where $V = D + E$. This expression states a firm's value equals the combined value of all the securities the company issues and is invariant to the amount of debt or equity used.[4] Finally, the cash flows generated by the firm's assets are risky, and investors discount them at the rate r_a. M&M's Proposition I claims the following:

(Eq. 12.1)
$$V = (D + E) = \frac{EBIT}{r_a}$$

In terms of the firm's capital structure, Equation 12.1 indicates that *the firm's market value equals the present value of the* EBIT *it generates regardless of the capital structure it chooses*. The market value of any firm is independent of its capital structure and is calculated by discounting expected EBIT at the rate r_a, appropriate for the firm's business risk. The discount rate r_a is the required return on assets and is based on the variability of expected EBIT. This is exactly what Ms. Ruiz did for HTMC. She generated an expected level of operating profits for HTMC ($1,000,000 EBIT per year), and then discounted this stream of expected earnings, using a discount rate ($r_a = 10\%$), appropriate to the business risk that HTMC faces. Firm value is thus determined by the level of HTMC's net operating income and by the firm's degree of business risk, not by whether the EBIT stream is then allocated entirely to shareholders in the all-equity capital structure or split between debt-and-equity security holders under the proposed capitalization.

Under HTMC's current, all-equity capital structure, the return on equity is the same as the return on the firm's assets. Both ROA and ROE are 10%. But

---

[4]We are not speaking of just the value of the firm's equity here. By "value of the firm," we mean the market value of the firm's assets, not just the value of the shareholders' residual claim. Note that Equation 12.1 assume the the firm's EBIT is a perpetuity.

what happens if HTMC issues low-risk debt and uses the proceeds to repurchase half the firm's outstanding equity? The company's business risk (the variability of expected EBIT) is unchanged by this transaction, and all this risk is still borne by shareholders. However, the risk for shareholders is now magnified, because there is only half as much equity outstanding as before. By how much will the risk to HTMC's shareholders be magnified if the company adopts the proposed 50% debt/50% equity capital structure? It turns out that M&M also provided an answer to this question, with their Proposition II.

12-2b Proposition II: How Increasing Leverage Affects the Cost of Equity

Proposition II
Asserts that if we hold the required return on assets (r_a) and the required return on debt (r_d) constant, the expected return on levered equity (r_l) increases with the debt-to-equity ratio.

Modigliani and Miller's **Proposition II** asserts the following: *If we hold the required return on assets (r_a) and the required return on debt (r_d) constant, the expected return on levered equity (r_l) increases with the debt-to-equity ratio.* Equation 12.2 expresses this relationship mathematically:

(Eq. 12.2)
$$r_l = r_a + (r_a - r_d)\left[\frac{D}{E}\right]$$

Does this formula yield the same expected returns on equity for HTMC's shareholders that Susan Ruiz had calculated earlier under the current all-equity and the proposed 50% debt/50% equity capital structures? Remember that the firm's underlying business risk justifies a return, r_a, of 10% and that its cost of debt, r_d, is 6%. Clearly, under the current all-equity structure, there is no debt outstanding, and the D/E ratio is zero. Therefore, the term to the right of the plus sign in Equation 12.2 is also zero. Equation 12.2 says that the return on equity equals the return on assets, or 10%:

$$r_l = 0.10 + (0.10 - 0.06) \times \frac{\$0}{\$10,000,000} = 0.10 = 10\%$$

The proposed 50% debt/50% equity capital structure yields a debt-to-equity ratio of 1.0. We can use Equation 12.2 to calculate that the return on levered equity must be 14%, just as Ms. Ruiz had calculated previously.

$$r_l = 0.10 + (0.10 - 0.06) \times \frac{\$5,000,000}{\$5,000,000} = 0.10 + 0.04 = 0.14 = 14\%$$

Proposition II has another important interpretation. Let's rearrange the equation so that r, the return on assets, appears by itself, on the left-hand side. This results in the following expression:

$$r_a = r_l\left(\frac{E}{D+E}\right) + r_d\left(\frac{D}{D+E}\right)$$

Does this look familiar? It should. It's the expression introduced in Chapter 10 for a firm's weighted average cost of capital (WACC), if we ignore the tax deductibility of interest on debt. We have already said the value of r_a depends on a firm's business risk and is independent of the firm's capital structure. This equation might appear to contradict that claim because it might seem that changing the values of E and D on the right-hand side might change r_a. But remember, Proposition II says that as leverage increases, the required return on equity also increases. If a firm replaces equity with debt in its capital structure, the term $E \div (D + E)$ falls and the term $D \div (D + E)$ rises. However, r_l goes up because of the added financial risk borne by shareholders. The net effect of all this is to leave the WACC unchanged. For example, when HTMC uses all equity, we know that the required return on equity is 10%, so the WACC is 10%, too:

$$r_a = 10\%(1.0) + 6\%(0) = 10\%$$

Figure 12.2   **M&M Proposition II Illustrated—The Cost of Equity, Cost of Debt, and Weighted Average Cost of Capital for a Firm in a World Without Taxes**

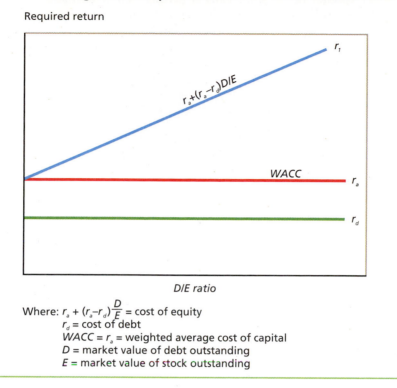

Where: $r_a + (r_a - r_d)\dfrac{D}{E}$ = cost of equity
r_d = cost of debt
$WACC = r_a$ = weighted average cost of capital
D = market value of debt outstanding
E = market value of stock outstanding

© Cengage Learning 2012

If HTMC recapitalizes, then it pays 6% to bondholders, shareholders demand a 14% return, and the WACC remains unchanged at 10%:

$$r_a = 14\%(0.50) + 6\%(0.50) = 10\%$$

If capital structure is irrelevant (if Proposition I holds), Proposition II tells us what the required return on levered equity must be to maintain the same total firm value (or the same WACC). As Figure 12.2 shows, the cost of equity will rise continuously as firms substitute debt for equity, but the weighted average cost of capital remains the same.

Remember that the value of a firm equals all of its future cash flows discounted by its cost of capital. If managers could adjust capital structure to achieve a lower overall WACC (while leaving cash flows unchanged), then that would also increase the value of the firm. Propositions I and II illustrate why this can't happen in perfect markets. Proposition I says that there is no capital structure that maximizes the value of a firm, while Proposition II says that there is no capital structure that minimizes the WACC.

12-2c Does Debt Policy Matter?

In the previous section we learned that, in a perfect market, firms' capital structure choices do not matter. That finding stands at odds with what CFOs tell us—namely, that capital structure decisions are extremely important and can have as much influence on the value of a firm as do investment decisions. If financial managers believe that capital structure is important, it must be because markets are imperfect in some important way. One of our goals in this chapter is to understand how market imperfections influence capital structure choices and affect firm value.

Is there an optimal capital structure for a particular firm? Figure 12.3 shows that, in the United States, most firms operate with target capital structures in mind. Of the

Figure 12.3

Do Firms Have Target Capital Structures?

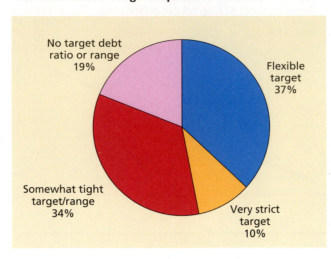

Source: Graham and Harvey (2001), "The Theory and Practice of Corporate Finance: Evidence From the Field," *Journal of Financial Economics*, 60, pp. 187–243, copyright © 2001, with permission from Elsevier.

392 CFOs surveyed by Graham and Harvey (2001), 44% said that their firm had either a "very strict" or "somewhat tight" capital structure target, and another 37% said that their firms had flexible targets. Fewer than one-fifth of CFOs said that their firm had no target debt ratio or range. In other words, most managers behave as if they believe that some capital structures are better than others, and they try to manage toward a particular target. But what factors determine the optimal capital structure, and how do managers decide what leverage policy will maximize value for their firms? One of the most important factors is the tax code.

12-2 Concept Review Questions

3. Explain how *Propositions I* and *II* are different, as well as what they have in common.

4. What is the difference between levered and unlevered equity? What effect does substituting debt for equity have on the required return on (levered) equity?

12-3 The M&M Capital Structure Model with Taxes

M&M derived their propositions by assuming that firms operate in markets without taxes or transactions costs. In this section, we look at what happens when we introduce corporate income taxes and interest deductibility into the M&M framework.

12-3a The M&M Model with Corporate Taxes

In the United States and many other countries, firms can deduct interest payments to lenders as a business expense. (Dividends paid to shareholders receive no similar tax advantage.) The interest deduction thus reduces the amount of taxes the firm must pay to the government. Intuitively, this should lead to a tax advantage for debt, meaning that managers can increase firm value by issuing debt. So returning to our High-Tech Manufacturing Corporation (HTMC) example, we now demonstrate how, with interest deductibility adding debt to the firm's capital structure could increase the firm's value by reducing the government's tax claim on the firm's cash flow.

Table 12.5

Cash Flows to Stockholders and Bondholders under the Current and Proposed Capital Structure for High-Tech Manufacturing Corporation—with Corporate Taxation

Assuming EBIT = $1,000,000 and T_c = 0.35

	Current Capital Structure: All-Equity Financing	Proposed Capital Structure: 50% Debt: 50% Equity
EBIT	$1,000,000	$1,000,000
– Interest (6.0%)	$0	$(300,000)
Taxable income	$1,000,000	$700,000
– Corporate taxes (T_c = 0.35)	$(350,000)	$(245,000)
Net income	$650,000	$455,000
Shares outstanding	200,000	100,000
Earnings per share	$3.25	$4.55

© Cengage Learning 2012

Let's begin our demonstration by assuming, as before, that the HTMC's EBIT will be $1,000,000 next year and that we are trying to decide whether to retain the firm's existing, all-equity capital structure or adopt a proposed 50% debt/50% equity capitalization. Assume that investors still require a 10% return on the firm's assets, so r_a = 0.10, as before. However, we now propose that HTMC faces a 35% corporate tax rate on earnings (T_c = 0.35). In computing taxable earnings, HTMC can deduct interest expense.[5]

Table 12.5 shows the after-tax cash flows to HTMC's shareholders and debtholders under the current and proposed capital structure, if EBIT is $1,000,000, as expected. Corporate taxes reduce the amount of money that can be distributed to security holders under both capital structures, but the effect is greater under the all-equity plan. In this case, HTMC pays taxes of $350,000, leaving only $650,000 available for distribution to shareholders. EPS thus drops to $3.25 from $5.00 under the no-tax scenario. Under the proposed capital structure, tax-deductible interest payments of $300,000 reduce taxable profits to $700,000, and HTMC only pays $245,000 in corporate taxes. This leaves $455,000 in net income that can be distributed to shareholders, yielding an EPS of $4.55 from $7.00 under the no-tax scenario. Note that under the proposed capital structure, HTMC is able to distribute $755,000 to investors ($300,000 interest to debtholders and $455,000 in dividends to shareholders). Under the all-equity capitalization, HTMC can only distribute $650,000 to investors (dividends to shareholders).

We can now compute the value of both the unlevered and levered versions of HTMC, and define these values as V_u and V_p, respectively. The basic valuation formula (Equation 12.1) used in the absence of taxes to discount EBIT must now be modified to discount after-tax net income (NI), yielding the following formula for the value of HTMC if it uses no debt (i.e., its unlevered value V_u):

$$\text{(Eq. 12.3)} \qquad V_u = \frac{[EBIT(1 - T_c)]}{r_a} = \frac{NI}{r_a} = \frac{\$650,000}{0.10} = \$6,500,000$$

The introduction of a 35% corporate profits tax causes an immediate $3,500,000 reduction (from $10,000,000 to $6,500,000) in the market value of the current all-equity structure of HTMC.

12-3b Determining the Present Value of Interest Tax Shields

Equation 12.3 reveals that corporate taxes cause a reduction in the value of an unlevered firm, compared with its value in a zero-tax environment. Now let's consider how HTMC can increase firm value by using debt financing to fund some of its investment.

---

[5]This is the same logic Modigliani and Miller used in their 1963 "modified" capital structure model, which explicitly incorporated a tax on corporate profits and interest deductibility. See Franco Modigliani and Merton Miller, "Corporate Income Taxes and the Cost of Capital," *American Economic Review* 53 (June 1963), pp. 433–443.

Remember, this increase in value occurs directly because the company can deduct interest on debt and reduce what it owes the government in taxes.

If the new debt which HTMC will issue under the proposed 50% debt/50% equity plan is assumed to be *permanent*—meaning the firm will always reissue maturing debt—the interest expense the firm pays creates a perpetual tax shield of $105,000 per year. The annual tax shield equals the tax rate times the amount of interest paid ($T_c \times r_d \times D = 0.35 \times 0.06 \times \$5,000,000 = \$105,000$). To find the present value of this perpetuity, capitalize this stream of benefits at r_d, the 6% rate of interest charged on HTMC's debt. With these assumptions, the present value of HTMC's interest tax shields is:

$$\text{(Eq. 12.4)} \quad PV \text{ Interest Tax Shields} = \frac{(T_c \times r_d D)}{r_d} = T_c \times D$$

$$= 0.35 \times (\$5,000,000) = \$1,750,000$$

In other words, the present value of interest tax shields on (perpetual) debt is equal to the tax rate times the face value of the debt outstanding. Therefore, the value of the levered version of HTMC, V_l, is equal to the value of the unlevered company plus the present value of the interest tax shields:

$$\text{(Eq. 12.5)} \quad V_l = V_u + PV \text{ Interest tax shields} = V_u + T_c D$$

$$= \$6,500,000 + \$1,750,000 = \$8,250,000$$

What a deal! In essence, the government has given HTMC's shareholders a $1,750,000 subsidy to employ debt financing rather than equity.

Figure 12.4 illustrates the impact of taxes on firm value. Panel A represents the situation in the original, no-tax case: there, the size of the pie (i.e., the value of the firm) does not depend on how you divide the pie between debt and equity claims. With a corporate income tax, though, a firm's capital structure influences its value: debt determines how much of the pie goes to the government. The more the firm borrows, the smaller is the government's claim and thus the larger are the claims held by private investors. Panel B of Figure 12.4 illustrates this point. At the limit, the government's slice (its tax claim) disappears when the firm finances its operations entirely through debt and pays all its earnings in tax-deductible interest.

EXAMPLE

In August 2010, eBay used no debt and its equity had a market value of $28.3 billion. In the absence of debt, this implies that eBay's assets were also worth $28.3 billion. What would happen to the total value of eBay if the firm issued $14.15 billion in long-term debt and used the proceeds to retire half of its equity? According to Equation 12.4, if eBay faces a corporate tax rate of 35% then the recapitalization would create an additional $4.95 billion (0.35 × $14.15 billion) in value for eBay investors!

12-3c The M&M Model with Corporate and Personal Taxes

Clearly, accounting for corporate income taxes leads us to favor the proposed 50% debt/50% equity capital structure for HTMC. However, this isn't the best possible outcome. If a 50% debt-to-capital ratio increases HTMC's total firm value by $1,750,000 more than that of the unlevered version of HTMC, and if each additional dollar of debt increases the value by $0.35, then shouldn't the *optimal* leverage ratio for the company be 100% debt? This implication, more than any other, lessened the initial acceptance of the M&M propositions. How could the theory be correct if it predicted that all firms should be highly levered, and yet, in the real world, many companies use little or no debt? Part of the answer to this question is that nontax factors partly offset the tax benefits of debt usage. Another part of the answer is that personal income taxes can cancel out some or all of the corporate-level tax benefits of debt usage.

Figure 12.4 **Pie Chart Models of Capital Structure With and Without Corporate Income Taxes**

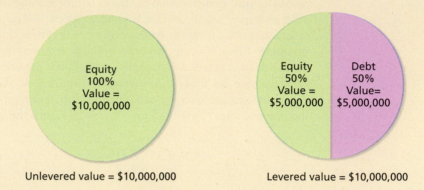

Panel A
With no taxes, the size of the pie, or the value of the firm, does not depend on the mix of debt and equity that the firm chooses. Proposition I holds, and capital structure is irrelevant.

Equity
100%
Value =
$10,000,000

Equity
50%
Value =
$5,000,000

Debt
50%
Value=
$5,000,000

Unlevered value = $10,000,000   Levered value = $10,000,000

Panel B
With a corporate income tax, a portion of the firm's cash flows goes to the government, diminishing the value of claims held by private investors. The government's slice of the pie shrinks the more debt a firm uses because the government allows a deduction for interest payments. A company could shelter nearly all of its cash flows by financing its operations almost entirely with debt. Therefore, capital structure matters because firm value is larger if the firm uses more debt.

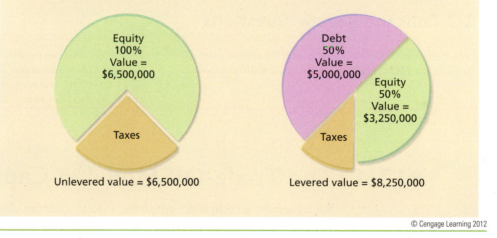

Equity
100%
Value =
$6,500,000

Taxes

Debt
50%
Value =
$5,000,000

Equity
50%
Value =
$3,250,000

Taxes

Unlevered value = $6,500,000   Levered value = $8,250,000

© Cengage Learning 2012

In 1977, Merton Miller developed a valuation model that incorporated both corporate and personal taxes.[6] Rather than using Equation 12.4, Miller provided a formula for computing the gains from using leverage, G_l, both for individual companies and for the corporate sector as a whole:

(Eq. 12.6)
$$G_l = \left[1 - \frac{(1 - T_c)(1 - T_{ps})}{(1 - T_{pd})} \right] \times D$$

where T_c = tax rate on corporate profits, as before
   T_{ps} = personal tax rate on income from stock (dividends and capital gains)
   T_{pd} = personal tax rate on income from debt (interest income)
   D = market value of a firm's outstanding debt

---

[6]See Merton Miller, "Debt and Taxes," *Journal of Finance* 32 (May 1977), pp. 261–276.

This is, in fact, a very general formulation. In a no-tax world ($T_c = T_{ps} = T_{pd} = 0$), the gains from leverage equal zero, and the original M&M irrelevance proposition holds. (See if you can verify this yourself.) In a world with only corporate income taxes ($T_c = 0.35$; $T_{ps} = T_{pd} = 0$), $G_l = T_c \times D$, and the 100% optimal debt result again emerges. If, however, personal tax rates on interest income are sufficiently high, and personal tax rates on equity income are sufficiently low, the gains to corporate leverage can be dramatically reduced, or even offset entirely. To see this, assume for a moment, as Miller did, that personal taxes on equity income are zero ($T_{ps} = 0$). This is not as wild as it may sound, as U.S. investors pay capital gains taxes only when they sell the stock, and taxes on some equity investments can be skipped entirely with careful estate planning. Investors can also hold non-dividend-paying stocks to avoid personal taxes on dividend income. Additionally, since 2003, the effective personal tax rates on dividend income for most U.S. investors is quite low. Assuming that personal taxes on equity income are zero, we can plug the (approximate) top U.S. corporate and personal income tax rates ($T_c = 0.35$ and $T_{pd} = 0.35$) into the gain-from-leverage formula:

$$G_l = \left[1 - \frac{(1 - 0.35) \times (1 - 0)}{(1 - 0.354)} \right] \times D = \left[1 - \frac{(0.65) \times (1.0)}{(0.65)} \right] \times D = 0$$

With this set of tax rates, the "gain" from leverage is actually zero, meaning that capital structure is irrelevant, just as it is in the "perfect markets" world of Modigliani and Miller! If the personal tax rate were higher than 35%, then using debt would actually reduce firm value relative to the case where the firm is financed entirely with equity.

12-3 Concept Review Questions

5. What effect does incorporating corporate income taxation have on the M&M capital structure irrelevance hypothesis? Why?

6. In 2003 the effective personal tax rates on dividend income for most U.S. investors was significantly reduced. What effect do you think these lower tax rates have had on the corporate incentive to use debt?

12-4 The Trade-Off Model of Capital Structure

We have now seen that the corporate capital structure choice is irrelevant in a world without taxes or other market frictions. We have learned not only that corporate income taxes, by themselves, give corporations a strong incentive to employ financial leverage, but also that things are much less clear-cut when personal income taxes are considered. On balance, corporate and personal taxes seem to influence the decisions that firms make regarding their capital structures, but some companies subject to the same tax code often employ very different amounts of leverage. Therefore, there must be other costs and benefits of leverage that managers trade off when they make capital structure choices. One important factor is that firms with higher debt face a greater risk of financial distress, and the costs of financial distress may be sufficiently high to discourage some firms from using debt.

12-4a Costs of Bankruptcy and Financial Distress

bankrupt
The situation that exists when a firm cannot meet its debt obligations.

bankruptcy
Describes the legal process (governed in the United States by federal law) through which the claims of a *bankrupt* firm's creditors are handled.

A firm is **bankrupt** when it cannot meet its debt obligations, and **bankruptcy** describes the legal process (governed in the United States by federal law) through which creditors' claims are handled. The threat of bankruptcy may well discourage debt financing. High leverage makes it more likely that firms will be unable to make interest and principal payments when cash flows are low. This could cause companies to default on their debts, which, in turn, could force them into bankruptcy. In principle, when a firm fails to pay its debts, creditors can force the firm into bankruptcy and claim its assets. In the U.S., managers often continue to run the firm while it is in bankruptcy, and they may choose to liquidate the firm's assets or to propose a plan to restructure the firm so that it can emerge from bankruptcy as a viable business. The firm's original shareholders generally lose their entire investment either way, and the ownership of the firm (or the firm's remaining assets) passes to bondholders and other creditors. However, the process of transferring a firm's assets from shareholders to creditors is time consuming and expensive. **Bankruptcy costs** are the direct and indirect costs of the bankruptcy process.

Direct bankruptcy costs include fees paid to attorneys, accountants, investment bankers, and other professionals involved in bankruptcy proceedings in addition to other expenses directly tied to bankruptcy filing and administration. Although direct bankruptcy costs can run into the millions of dollars, they are usually small relative to the assets of the firm, especially in high-profile cases involving large, well-known companies. **Indirect bankruptcy costs**, as the name implies, are economic losses that result from bankruptcy but are not cash outlays spent on the legal process. Indirect costs include the loss of customers and key suppliers, the time that top managers spend managing the bankruptcy process rather than focusing on their business, the loss of key employees, and missed opportunities to invest in positive-*NPV* projects. Even though indirect bankruptcy costs are inherently difficult to measure, research clearly suggests that they are significant—significant enough, in many cases, to lessen the incentive for corporate managers to employ financial leverage.

Although issuing more debt creates a larger tax shield, the more debt a firm uses, the higher is the probability that the firm will go bankrupt and incur bankruptcy costs. At low debt levels, the probability of bankruptcy is very low, so debt's tax advantages outweigh the prospect of bankruptcy costs. At higher debt levels, however, the risk of bankruptcy rises, and some firms may find that the tax advantages of debt are not sufficient to risk the costs of going bankrupt. This leads to the *trade-off model of capital structure* in which managers try to find the optimal balance between debt's various costs and benefits. The optimal balance is the one that maximizes the value of the firm. Recognition of bankruptcy costs allows us to expand the basic valuation formula first presented in Section 12-3 to express the value of a levered firm, V_l, relative to the value of an unlevered firm, V_u, the present value of the benefits from debt tax shields, and the present value of expected bankruptcy costs:

bankruptcy costs
The direct and indirect costs of the bankruptcy process.

direct bankruptcy costs
Include fees paid to attorneys, accountants, investment bankers, and other professionals involved in bankruptcy proceedings in addition to other expenses directly tied to bankruptcy filing and administration.

indirect bankruptcy costs
Include the loss of customers and key suppliers, the time that managers spend managing the bankruptcy process rather than focusing on their business, the loss of key employees, and missed opportunities to invest in positive-*NPV* projects.

$$\text{(Eq. 12.7)} \qquad V_l = V_u + PV(\textbf{Tax shields}) - PV(\textbf{Bankruptcy costs})$$

Asset Characteristics and Bankruptcy Costs   Intuitively, it seems that bankruptcy will be very costly for some types of firms and less costly for others. For example, consider a firm that sells durable goods like appliances or automobiles. Customers may hesitate to buy the firm's products if the firm is at risk of going bankrupt because a bankrupt firm might not be able to service the products that it sells. For such a firm, the loss of customers could be a very significant indirect cost of going bankrupt, so the firm has an incentive to be very careful about the amount of debt that it issues. On the other hand, few customers would worry about the long-term consequences of their local grocery store going bankrupt because not much service after the sale is required in that business. As a general rule, producers of sophisticated products or services have an incentive to use less debt than firms producing simple goods or basic services.

Companies with mostly tangible assets that have well-established secondary markets should be more willing to use debt than companies with mostly intangible assets. Firms can use tangible assets as collateral for loans, which may reduce

John Graham, Duke University

"The majority of companies follow the trade-off model."

See the entire interview at www.cengagebrain.com. **SMART**|finance

Smart Ideas Video

the cost of borrowing, and firms can sell those assets for cash if and when financial distress occurs. Therefore, trucking companies, airlines, construction firms, pipeline companies, and railroads can all employ more debt than can companies with fewer tangible assets, such as pharmaceutical manufacturers, food distributors (what is the collateral value of week-old tomatoes?), and pure service companies.

Financial distress may provide managers with perverse yet rational incentives to play a variety of games, mostly at bondholders' expense. Two such games—*asset substitution* and *underinvestment*—are especially damaging. Both games begin when managers realize that the firm will probably not fulfill its obligations to creditors.

asset substitution
When shareholders choose risky projects that benefit themselves but reduce the value of bondholders.

The Asset Substitution Problem To illustrate how asset substitution works, assume that a firm has bonds, with a face value of $10 million outstanding that mature in 30 days. These bonds were issued years ago when the firm was prospering, but since then the firm has fallen on hard times. In spite of its difficulties, the firm still has $8 million in cash on hand, and the company's managers still control the firm's investment policy. The company can invest this cash in either of two available projects, both of which require a cash investment of $8 million. Alternatively, the firm can simply hold the cash in reserve to partially repay the bond issue in 30 days. The first investment opportunity is a low-risk project (code named *Boring* by company insiders) that will return a near certain $8.15 million in 30 days. This is a monthly return of 1.88%, or an annual return of almost 25%. In other words, it is a positive-*NPV* project that will increase firm value, but it does not earn enough to fully pay off the maturing bonds.

The second investment opportunity (called project *Vegas*) is basically a gamble. It offers a 40% chance of a $12 million payoff and a 60% chance of a $4 million pay-off. Because its expected value is only $7.2 million [(0.4 × $12,000,000) + (0.6 × $4,000,000)], project *Vegas* is a negative-*NPV* "investment" that the firm's managers would reject if the firm did not have debt outstanding. However, if project *Vegas* is successful, the project's $12 million payoff will allow the company to fully pay off the bonds and pocket a $2 million profit.

Consider the incentives facing this company's managers. Clearly, bondholders want the managers to either select the low-risk project or retain the firm's cash in reserve. But because shareholders will lose control of the firm unless they can pay off the bonds in full when they mature, shareholders want the company's managers to accept project *Vegas*. If successful, the project will yield enough for shareholders to pay off the creditors and to retain ownership of the firm. However, if project *Vegas* is unsuccessful, the shareholders will simply hand over the firm and any remaining assets to bondholders, after defaulting on the maturing bonds. (Because of limited liability, the corporation's shareholders do not have to repay the bonds themselves.) This is also what will happen if the firm plays it safe by either retaining cash in the firm or accepting project *Boring*. Shareholders therefore have everything to gain and nothing to lose from accepting project *Vegas*, and their agents (the managers) control the firm's investment policy until default actually occurs.

underinvestment
When stockholders decide not to invest in a positive NPV project, and therefore "underinvest" relative to choosing all positive NPV projects.

The Underinvestment Problem The second game related to financial distress is underinvestment. To demonstrate this, assume that the firm described above gains access to a very profitable, but short-lived, investment opportunity. A longtime supplier offers to sell its excess inventory to the company at a sharply discounted price, but only if the company will pay for the inventory immediately with cash. The additional supplies will cost $9 million today but will allow the firm to increase production and profitability dramatically over the next thirty days. In fact, the firm will be able to sell the additional product so profitably that in thirty days, it will build up the $10 million cash needed to pay off the maturing bond issue. However, because the firm has only $8 million in cash on hand today, the firm's shareholders must contribute the additional $1 million needed to buy the supplier's inventory. Accepting this project would maximize overall firm value and would clearly benefit the bondholders. But the shareholders would rationally choose *not* to accept the project because the shareholders would have to finance the investment, and all the investment's payoff would accrue to the bondholders.

An all-equity firm is not vulnerable to either of these two games associated with financial distress. Managers acting in the interests of shareholders have the incentive to choose the project that maximizes firm value, in the first example, and shareholders have the incentive to choose to contribute cash for positive-*NPV* projects, in the second example. Because these costs of financial distress are related to conflicts of interest between the two groups of security holders, they are also referred to as *agency costs* of the relationship between bondholders and stockholders.

12-4b Agency Costs and Capital Structure

In addition to taxes and the costs of financial distress, several other forces influence the corporate capital structure choice. Some thirty-five years ago, Michael Jensen and William Meckling proposed an *agency cost model of financial structure*.[7] Jensen and Meckling observed that when entrepreneurs own 100% of the stock of a company, there is no separation between corporate ownership and control. Entrepreneurs bear all the costs and reap all the benefits of their actions. Once entrepreneurs sell a fraction of their stock to outside investors, they bear only a fraction of the cost of any actions they take that reduce the value of the firm. This gives entrepreneurs a clear incentive to, in Jensen and Meckling's tactful phrasing, "consume perquisites" (e.g., goof off, purchase a corporate jet, frequently tour the firm's plant in Hawaii, become a regular business commentator on television, etc.).

By selling a stake in the company to outside investors, entrepreneurs lower the cost of consuming perquisites (or perks), but this does not come free of charge. In an efficient market, investors expect entrepreneurs' performance to change after they sell stakes in their firms, so investors reduce the price they will pay for these shares. In other words, entrepreneurs are charged *in advance* for the perks they are expected to consume after the equity sale, so entrepreneurs bear the full costs of their actions. Society also suffers because these agency costs of (outside) equity reduce the market value of corporate assets. We are therefore at an impasse. Selling stock to outside investors creates agency costs of equity, which are borne solely by the entrepreneur, but which also harm society by reducing the value of corporate assets and discouraging additional entrepreneurship. On the other hand, selling external equity is vital for entrepreneurs and for society at large, because this allows firms to make investments that exceed an entrepreneur's personal wealth.

Using Debt to Overcome the Agency Costs of Outside Equity Jensen and Meckling shows how using debt financing can help overcome the agency costs of external equity in two ways. First, using debt, by definition, means that less external equity must be sold to raise a given dollar amount of external financing. Second, and more important, employing outside debt rather than equity financing reduces the amount and value of perquisites that managers can consume. The burden of having to make regular debt-service payments serves as an effective tool for disciplining corporate managers. With debt outstanding, excessive perk consumption may cost managers control of their companies if they were to default. Because taking on debt shows a manager's willingness to risk losing control of her firm, if she fails to perform effectively, shareholders are willing to pay a higher price for a firm's shares.

Agency Costs of Outside Debt If debt is such an effective disciplining device, then why don't firms use maximum debt financing? The answer is that there are also agency costs of debt. To understand these, keep in mind that, as the fraction of debt in a firm's capital structure increases, bondholders begin taking on more of the company's business and operating risk. However, shareholders and managers still control the

agency costs of (outside) equity
The value-reducing actions that managers take when ownership (by stockholders) is separated from control by managers.

agency costs of debt
Costs that arise because stockholders and bondholders have different objectives.

---

[7]See Michael C. Jensen and William H. Meckling, "Theory of the Firm: Managerial Behavior, Agency Costs, and Ownership Structure," *Journal of Financial Economics* 3 (October 1976), pp. 305–360.

Finance in Your Life

The Hidden Cost of Personal Debt

Students use borrowed money to finance their education and pay for necessities while they are in school just as corporations borrow money to finance capital investments and smooth out their working capital needs over time. Furthermore, there are important measures of personal indebtedness that are very similar to the measures of corporate leverage.

Unfortunately, many students become all too familiar with personal debt while they are in college. Today, over two-thirds of graduating American seniors have student loans outstanding, and the total amount of student loan debt is rising rapidly. Furthermore, many graduates ran up significant credit-card debt as students, so they are beginning their careers with higher debt burdens than any previous generation of American college graduates.

Many new hires soon realize, often with a shock, that they are being assigned credit ratings, whether desired or not. There are three major consumer credit rating agencies in the United States—Equifax, TransUnion, and Experian—and each of them assigns a FICO© score to every person who applies for credit. This scoring system, which was developed by and is named after Fair Isaac & Company, assigns a personal rating between 300 (very poor credit risk) and 850 (excellent credit risk). The scores are based on a person's income and overall indebtedness, the type of debt outstanding (credit cards, car loans, student loans, etc.), and the monthly payment amounts. Merchants and lenders refer to these scores to determine whether to grant an applicant credit, and the value assigned can have a massive influence on a graduate's access to and cost of credit.

A recent graduate's credit rating is typically most important when he or she applies for an auto or home mortgage loan for the first time. The average mortgage rates offered to borrowers for FICO scores between 500 and 850 typically differ by about 3.50%. People with scores below 500 would probably be denied credit altogether. So, think ahead before incurring additional debt. Those hidden costs can adversely affect both the availability and cost of future credit opportunities.

---

firm's investment and operating decisions. This gives managers a variety of incentives to effectively steal bondholder wealth for themselves and other shareholders. The easiest way to do this is to float a bond issue and then pay out the money raised to shareholders as a dividend. After default, the bondholders are left with an empty corporate shell, and limited liability prevents them from trying to collect directly from shareholders.

Bondholders are generally sophisticated enough to take steps to prevent managers from playing these games with their money. The most effective, preventive step that bond investors can take is to write very detailed loan covenants into bond contracts, which are contractual clauses that limit a borrower's ability to expropriate the bondholders' wealth. The downside of loan covenants is that they make bond agreements costly to negotiate and to enforce. In any case, the agency costs of debt are real, and they become more important as a firm's leverage ratio increases.

loan covenants
Contractual clauses that limit the actions that a borrower can take, protecting the lender's wealth from being expropriated.

12-4c The Trade-Off Model Revisited

Our discussion thus far has shown that certain real-world factors—such as corporate income taxes and agency costs of outside equity—give corporate managers an incentive to substitute debt for equity in their firms' capital structure. Other factors such as personal income taxes, bankruptcy, and agency costs of outside debt give managers an incentive to favor equity financing. We are now ready to tie together all these influences and present the trade-off model of corporate leverage. This model expresses the value of a levered firm as the value of an unlevered firm, plus the present values of tax shields and the agency costs of outside equity, minus the present value of bankruptcy costs and the agency costs of debt, as follows:

trade-off model of corporate leverage
According to this model managers trade off the costs and benefits of using debt to choose the amount of debt that maximizes firm value as expressed in Equation 12.7b.

$$(Eq.\ 12.7b)\quad V_l = V_u + PV\ \text{Tax Shields} - PV\ \text{Bankruptcy Costs} + PV\ \text{Agency Costs of Outside Equity} - PV\ \text{Agency Costs of Outside Debt}$$

Figure 12.5   **The Trade-Off Model of Corporate Leverage**

This model describes the optimal level of debt for a given firm as a trade-off between the benefits of corporate borrowing and the increasing agency and bankruptcy costs that come from additional borrowing. The optimal debt B* is chosen to maximize firm value.

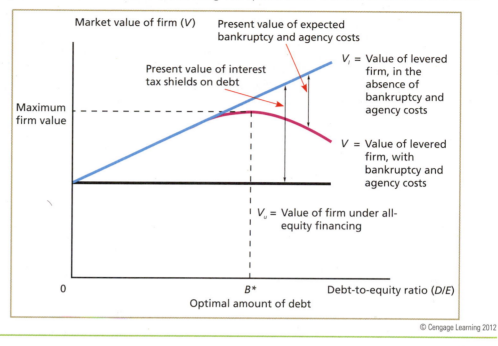

© Cengage Learning 2012

WHAT TO ASK

Does your firm manage its capital structure to achieve some optimal mix of debt and equity? If so, how is the optimum combination determined?

Figure 12.5 describes how agency costs, bankruptcy costs, and tax benefits of leverage interact to determine a typical firm's optimal debt level. Starting from a capital structure with no debt, managers can increase firm value by replacing equity with debt, thus shielding more cash flow from taxation. In the absence of bankruptcy costs and the agency costs of debt, managers would maximize firm value by borrowing as much as possible, a situation represented by the blue line in Figure 12.5. The purple line shows how bankruptcy and agency costs alter this conclusion. As a firm borrows more, it increases the probability that it will go bankrupt. Therefore, expected bankruptcy costs and agency costs of debt rise with leverage. At some point, the additional tax benefit from issuing more debt is exactly offset by the increase in expected bankruptcy and agency costs. When that occurs, the purple line reaches a maximum, and managers have found the mix of debt and equity that maximizes the value of the firm.

12-4 Concept Review Questions

7. What are the important *direct costs of bankruptcy* and *indirect bankruptcy costs*? Which of these, do you think, are the most important for discouraging maximum debt use by corporate managers?

8. Suppose someone borrows from a bank to buy a new car. A few months later, the borrower realizes that he will have to default on this loan in a few more months, after which the bank will repossess the car. What kind of *underinvestment* problem might occur here?

9. Suppose a commercial bank suffers loan losses so severe that it approaches insolvency. What kinds of asset substitution problems might arise? How might bank regulators act to prevent these problems?

10. Think of the gaudy corporate perks given to managers, such as a plush office, a company jet, or luxury box seats at professional sporting events. How can managers justify these as value-maximizing corporate expenditures that benefit the shareholders?

12-5 The Pecking-Order Theory

There are three empirical regularities that seem inconsistent with firms' choosing an optimal capital structure according to the trade-off model.

1. The most profitable firms in an industry have the lowest debt ratios.

2. Leverage-increasing events—such as stock repurchases and debt-for-equity exchange offers—almost always increase stock prices, whereas leverage-decreasing events reduce stock prices. These facts suggest that firms systematically use too little leverage and do not operate at or near the optimal, target debt ratio.

3. Firms issue debt frequently, but equity issues are rare. Announcements of new seasoned equity issues are invariably greeted with a large decline in the firm's stock price, a decline that is often equal to a third or more of the new offering's value.

How can we account for these perplexing facts? One answer was put forward in 1984 by Stewart Myers, who proposed the **pecking-order theory**.

pecking-order theory
A hypothesis that assumes managers are better informed about investment opportunities faced by their firms than are outside investors.

12-5a Assumptions Underlying the Pecking-Order Theory

The pecking-order theory is based on four facts that Myers observed about corporate financial behavior. First, dividend policy is "sticky." Managers tend to maintain a stable dividend payment, neither increasing nor decreasing dividends in response to temporary fluctuations in profits. Second, firms prefer internal financing (retained earnings and depreciation) to external financing of any sort, debt or equity. Third, if a firm must obtain external financing, it will issue the safest security first. Finally, as a firm requires more external financing, it will work down the "pecking order" of securities, beginning with safe debt, then progressing through risky debt, convertible securities, preferred stock, and finally common stock as a last resort.

Myers and Nicholas Majluf (1984) provide additional justification for the pecking order that is based on asymmetric information. The authors make two plausible assumptions about managers: (1) a firm's managers know more about the company's current earnings and investment opportunities than do outside investors; and (2) managers act in the interest of *existing* shareholders.

Why are these two assumptions crucial? The one about asymmetric information implies that managers who develop or discover a marvelous new positive-*NPV* investment opportunity cannot convey that information to the market because outside investors don't believe the managers' statements. After all, every management team has an incentive to announce wondrous new projects, and investors cannot immediately verify these claims. Skeptical investors will buy new equity issues only at a large discount from what the stock price would be without informational asymmetries. Corporate managers understand these problems, and in certain cases they will reject positive-*NPV* investments simply to avoid selling equity to new investors at a discount, which would have the effect of transferring wealth from old to new shareholders.

What a dilemma! Investors cannot trust managers, so investors place a low value on new issues of common stock. Managers forgo valuable projects because they cannot credibly convey their private information to existing shareholders. Endemic information problems in financial markets do not have easy solutions.

What, then, must managers do? According to Myers and Majluf, corporations should retain sufficient financial slack or flexibility to fund positive-*NPV* projects *internally*. **Financial slack** includes a firm's cash and marketable securities holdings in addition to its unused debt capacity. Firms with sufficient financial slack can finesse the information problem because they need never issue equity to finance investment projects. In addition, the optimal investment rule is once again in force, because managers can accept all positive-*NPV* projects without harming existing shareholders. This theory also explains why highly profitable firms might retain earnings (Intel is a classic example). Such firms are building both financial slack and financial flexibility.

The pecking-order theory also explains stock market reactions to leverage-increasing and leverage-decreasing events. Firms with valuable investment opportunities find a

Financial slack
Large cash and marketable security holdings or unused debt capacity.

What CFOs Do

Graham and Harvey (2001) asked U.S. CFOs to rate the importance of several factors in setting capital structures. Figure 12.6 shows their findings. Number one on the list is financial flexibility, which at first glance seems to support the pecking-order theory. However, Graham and Harvey find that the types of firms that value financial flexibility are not necessarily the ones predicted by the pecking-order theory—namely, firms with severe asymmetric information issues. The authors also asked CFOs if they issued equity only when issuing debt was not an option (as the pecking-order theory predicts), but CFOs did not indicate that inability to issue debt was the reason they issued equity.

Figure 12.6   **What Factors Do U.S. Companies Consider When Choosing Debt Policy?**

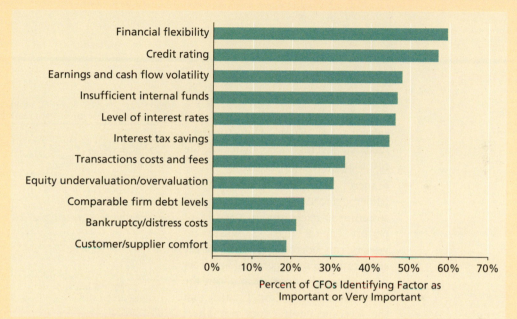

Source: Reprinted from Graham and Harvey, "The Theory and Practice of Corporate Finance: Evidence From the Field," *Journal of Financial Economics*, Volume 60, Issue 2-3, May/June, pages 187–243, Copyright 2001, with permission from Elsevier.

way to finance their projects internally, or they use the least risky securities possible (debt) if financing must be obtained externally. Therefore, only managers who consider the firm's shares to be overvalued will issue equity. Investors understand these incentives and also realize that managers are better informed about a firm's prospects. Hence investors always greet the announcement of a new equity issue as bad news: a sign that management considers the firm's shares to be overvalued.[8]

12-5b Evidence on the Pecking-Order and Trade-Off Theories

The pecking-order theory is consistent with the fact that the vast majority (roughly 90%) of corporate investments in the United States are funded internally through retained earnings. It also explains why profitable firms (which have lots of financial slack) borrow less than unprofitable firms because they rely on internal funds rather than debt. But the pecking-order theory

**Keith Woodward,
Vice President of Finance,
General Mills**

"In General Mills we have lots of discussions about what is the optimal capital structure."

See the entire interview at
www.cengagebrain.com. **SMART** | finance

Smart Practices Video

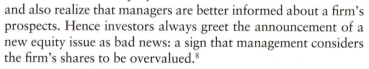

[8]This works in reverse, too. The CFO of a Fortune 500 company with billions in cash reserves told us that his company wanted to distribute some of the cash to investors, but management did not want to force investors to pay taxes on high dividend payments and were reluctant to repurchase shares because they thought the firm's stock was overvalued.

implies that firms have no target capital structure and that the debt ratios observed in the real world ought to fluctuate randomly. The theory also seems at odds with the evidence that firms owning more tangible assets typically use more leverage.

12-5 Concept Review Questions

11. If you ask senior corporate executives whether their firms' stock prices are overvalued, undervalued, or fairly valued, which do you think would be the most common response? What does this have to do with the pecking-order theory?

12. What happens to stock prices when corporate managers announce leverage-increasing transactions such as debt-for-equity exchange offers? What happens to stock prices, in response to leverage-decreasing announcements? How do you interpret these findings?

Summary

- Financial leverage means using debt financing to increase expected earnings per share. Unfortunately, financial leverage also increases the risk that equity investors bear.

- Franco Modigliani and Merton Miller (M&M) showed that capital structure is irrelevant in a world of perfect capital markets where investors can borrow and lend at the same rate and managers and investors have identical information about the firm. Their Proposition I states that the leverage choice does not affect a firm's value. M&M's Proposition II says that, even though the cost of debt is less than the cost of equity, the WACC does not decrease when a firm reduces equity and adds debt to its capital structure. This is because more debt increases the cost of equity, which exactly offsets the advantage of replacing some equity with debt.

- In a world with tax-deductible interest payments and only company-level taxation of operating profits, the optimal corporate strategy is to use the maximum possible leverage. This minimizes the government's claim on profits and maximizes income flowing to private investors.

Table of Important Equations

1. $V = (E + D) = \dfrac{EBIT}{r_a}$

2. $r_l = r_a + (r_a - r_d)\dfrac{D}{E}$

3. $V_u = \dfrac{[EBIT(1 - T_c)]}{r_a} = \dfrac{NI}{r_a}$

4. PV Interest Tax Shields
$= \dfrac{(T_c \times r_d D)}{r_d} = T_c \times D$

5. $V_l = V_u +$ PV Interest tax shields
$\quad = V_u + T_c D$

6. $G_l = \left[1 - \dfrac{(1 - T_c)(1 - T_{ps})}{(1 - T_{pd})}\right] \times D$

7. $V_l = V_u +$ PV (Tax shields)
$\quad - $ PV (Bankruptcy costs)

8. $V_l = V_u + \begin{array}{c} PV\ Tax \\ Shields \end{array} - \begin{array}{c} PV\ Bankruptcy \\ Costs \end{array}$

$+ \begin{array}{c} PV\ Agency \\ Costs\ of \\ Outside \\ Equity \end{array} - \begin{array}{c} PV\ Agency \\ Costs\ of \\ Outside \\ Debt \end{array}$

- When governments impose taxes at both the corporate and personal level, debt's tax advantage usually is lower than when there is a corporate income tax only; in some cases, higher personal taxes on interest income may lead to a net tax disadvantage for debt.

- If bankruptcy resulted in a costless transfer of ownership from shareholders to creditors, then bankruptcy would have no important consequence for a firm's capital structure. It is because the bankruptcy process triggers large direct and indirect costs that bankruptcy creates a cost to using debt.

- Creditors know that corporate managers, who operate their firms in the interests of shareholders, have incentives to expropriate creditor wealth by playing certain games with the firm's investment policy. Asset substitution is one such game, and underinvestment is another. Creditors protect themselves from these games in several ways, especially by inserting loan covenants into bond contracts.

- There are several important agency costs inherent in the relationship between corporate managers and outside investors and creditors. In some cases, using financial leverage can help overcome these agency problems; in others, using leverage introduces other agency problems. The modern *trade-off* model of corporate leverage predicts that a firm's optimal debt level is set by trading off the tax benefits of increasing leverage against the increasingly severe bankruptcy costs and agency costs of heavy debt usage.

- The pecking-order theory predicts that managers will operate their firms in such a way as to minimize the need to secure outside financing—for example, by retaining profits to build up financial slack. These same managers will use the safest source of funding, usually senior debt, when they must secure outside financing.

Key Terms

agency costs of debt, 387
agency costs of (outside) equity, 387
asset substitution, 386
bankrupt, 384
bankruptcy, 384
bankruptcy costs, 385
business risk, 377

direct bankruptcy costs, 385
financial risk, 377
financial slack, 390
fundamental principle of financial leverage, 374
indirect bankruptcy costs, 385
loan covenants, 388
pecking-order theory, 390

Proposition I, 377
Proposition II, 378
recapitalization, 372
trade-off model of corporate leverage, 388
underinvestment, 386

Self-Test Problems

Answers to Self-Test Problems and the Concept Review Questions throughout the chapter appear in CourseMate with SmartFinance Tools at www.cengagebrain.com.

ST12-1. As Chief Financial Officer of the Uptown Service Corporation (USC), you are considering a recapitalization plan that would convert USC from its current all-equity capital structure to one including substantial financial leverage. USC now has 150,000 shares of common stock outstanding, which are selling for $80.00 each.

The recapitalization proposal is to issue $6,000,000 worth of long-term debt, at an interest rate of 7.0%, and use the proceeds to repurchase 75,000 shares of common stock worth $6,000,000. USC's earnings in the next year will depend on the state of the economy. If there is normal growth, EBIT will be $1,200,000. EBIT will be $600,000 if there is a recession, and it will be $1,800,000 if there is an economic boom. You believe that each economic outcome is equally likely. Assume there are no market frictions such as corporate or personal income taxes.

a. If the proposed recapitalization is adopted, calculate the number of shares outstanding, the per-share price, and the debt-to-equity ratio for USC.
b. Calculate the earnings per share (EPS) and the return on equity (ROE) for USC shareholders, under all three economic outcomes (recession, normal growth, and boom), for both the current all-equity capitalization and the proposed mixed (debt/equity) capital structure.
c. Calculate the breakeven level of EBIT where earnings per share for USC stockholders are the same under the current and proposed capital structures.
d. At what level of EBIT will USC shareholders earn zero EPS under the current and the proposed capital structures?

ST12-2. An unlevered company operates in perfect markets and has earnings before interest and taxes (EBIT) of $2,000,000. Assume that the required return on assets for firms in this industry is 8%. The firm issues $10 million worth of debt, with a required return of 6.5%, and uses the proceeds to repurchase outstanding stock. There are no corporate or personal taxes.

    a.   What is the market value and required return of this firm's stock before the repurchase transaction, according to M&M Proposition I?

    b.   What is the market value and required return of this firm's remaining stock after the repurchase transaction, according to M&M Proposition II?

ST12-3. The EBIT of Westside Manufacturing is $10 million. The company has $60 million of debt outstanding with a required rate of return of 6.5%. The required rate of return on the industry is 10%, and the corporate tax rate is 30%. Assume there are corporate taxes but no personal taxes.

    a.   Determine the present value of the interest tax shield of Westside Manufacturing and also the firm's total value.

    b.   Determine the gain from leverage if there are personal taxes of 10% on stock income and 35% on debt income.

ST12-4. You are the manager of a financially distressed corporation with $10 million in debt outstanding that will mature in one month. Your firm currently has $7 million cash on hand. Assume that you are offered the opportunity to invest in either of the following two projects.

Project 1: The opportunity to invest $7 million in risk-free Treasury bills with a 4% annual interest rate (or a 0.333% monthly interest rate)

Project 2: A high-risk gamble that will pay $12 million in one month if it is successful (probability = 0.25) but will pay only $4,000,000 if it is unsuccessful (probability = 0.75)

    a.   Compute the expected payoff for each project. Which one you would adopt if you were operating the firm in the shareholders' best interests? Why?

    b.   Which project would you accept if the firm were unlevered? Why?

    c.   Which project would you accept if the company were organized as a partnership rather than a corporation? Why?

ST12-5. Run-and-Hide Detective Company currently has no debt and, for the foreseeable future, expects to earn $5 million in earnings before interest and taxes (EBIT) each year. The required return on assets for detective companies of this type is 10.0%, and the corporate tax rate is 35%. There are no taxes on dividends or interest at the personal level. Run-and-Hide calculates that there is a 5% chance that the firm will fall into bankruptcy in any given year. If bankruptcy does occur, it will impose direct and indirect costs totaling $8 million. If necessary, use the industry required return for discounting bankruptcy costs.

    a.   Compute the present value of bankruptcy costs for Run-and-Hide.

    b.   Compute the overall value of the firm.

    c.   Recalculate the firm's value under the assumption that firm shareholders face a 15% personal tax rate on equity income.

Questions

Q12-1. Why is the use of long-term debt financing referred to as using *financial leverage*?

Q12-2. What is the fundamental principle of financial leverage?

Q12-3. What is the basic conclusion of the original Modigliani and Miller *Proposition I*?

Q12-4. Following from the conclusion of Proposition I, what is the crux of M&M *Proposition II*? What is the natural relationship between the required returns on debt and equity that results from Proposition II?

Q12-5. In what way did M&M change their conclusion regarding capital structure choice with the additional assumption of corporate taxes? In this context, what explains the difference in value between levered and unlevered firms?

Q12-6. By introducing personal taxes into the model for capital structure choice, how did Miller alter the previous M&M conclusion that 100% debt is optimal? What happens to the gains from leverage if personal tax rates on interest income are significantly higher than those on stock-related income?

Q12-7. What is the difference between *direct bankruptcy costs* and *indirect bankruptcy costs*? Give examples of each and explain which of them is typically larger.

Q12-8. All else equal, which firm would face higher costs of financial distress: a software development firm or a hotel chain? Why would financial distress costs affect these firms so differently?

Q12-9. Describe how managers of firms that have debt outstanding and face financial distress might jeopardize the investments of creditors with the games of *asset substitution* and *underinvestment*.

Q12-10. Differentiate between direct and indirect costs of bankruptcy. Which of the two is generally more significant?

Q12-11. How can loan covenants in bond contracts be both an agency cost of debt and a way to prevent agency costs of debt?

Q12-12. What are the trade-offs in the agency cost/tax shield trade-off model? How is the firm's optimal capital structure determined under the assumptions of this model? Does research evidence support this model?

Q12-13. What is the observed relationship between debt ratios and profitability, and the perceived costs of financial distress?

Q12-14. How influential are corporate and personal taxes on capital structure?

Q12-15. What is the pecking-order theory, and what facts does it seem to explain better than the trade-off model does?

Problems

What Is Financial Leverage and What Are Its Effects?

P12-1. As chief financial officer of the Magnificent Electronics Corporation (MEC), you are considering a recapitalization plan that would convert MEC from its current all-equity capital structure to one that includes substantial financial leverage. MEC now has 500,000 shares of common stock outstanding, which are selling for $60 each. You expect the firm's earnings before interest and taxes (EBIT) to be $2,400,000 per year, for the foreseeable future.

The recapitalization proposal is to issue $15,000,000 worth of long-term debt, at an interest rate of 6.0%, and then use the proceeds to repurchase 250,000 shares of common stock worth $15,000,000. Assuming there are no market frictions such as corporate or personal income taxes, calculate the expected return on equity for MEC shareholders under the current all-equity capital structure and also under the proposed recapitalization.

P12-2. All-Star Production Corporation (APC) is considering a recapitalization plan that would convert APC from its current all-equity capital structure to one that includes some financial leverage. APC now has 10,000,000 shares of common stock outstanding, which are selling for $40.00 each. You expect the firm's EBIT to be $50,000,000 per year for the foreseeable future.

The recapitalization proposal is to issue $100,000,000 worth of long-term debt, at an interest rate of 6.50%, and then to use the proceeds to repurchase as many shares as possible at a price of $40.00 per share. Assume there are no market frictions such as corporate or personal income taxes. Calculate the expected return on equity for APC shareholders under the current all-equity capital structure and under the recapitalization plan.

  a. Calculate the number of shares outstanding, the per-share price, and the debt-to-equity ratio for APC if it adopts the proposed recapitalization.

  b. Calculate the earnings per share (EPS) and the return on equity (ROE) for APC shareholders under the current all-equity capitalization as well as under the proposed mixed (debt/equity) capital structure.

  c. Calculate the breakeven level of EBIT, where earnings per share for APC stockholders are the same under both the current and proposed capital structures.

  d. At what level of EBIT will APC shareholders earn zero EPS under the current and proposed capital structures?

P12-3. As chief financial officer of the Campus Supply Corporation (CSC), you are considering a recapitalization plan that would convert CSC from its current all-equity capital structure to one that includes substantial financial leverage. CSC now has 250,000 shares of common stock outstanding that are selling for $60.00 each. The recapitalization proposal is to issue $7,500,000 of long-term debt at an interest rate of 6.0% and use the proceeds to repurchase 125,000 shares of common stock worth $7,500,000. USC's earnings next year will depend on the state of the economy. If there is normal growth, EBIT will be $2,000,000, EBIT will be $1,000,000 if there is a recession, and EBIT will be $3,000,000 if there is an economic boom. You believe that each economic outcome is equally likely. Assume there are no market frictions such as corporate or personal income taxes.

a. Calculate the number of shares outstanding, the per-share price, and the debt-to-equity ratio for CSC if the proposed recapitalization is adopted.

b. Calculate the expected earnings per share (EPS) and return on equity (ROE) for CSC shareholders under all three economic outcomes (recession, normal growth, and boom) for both the current all-equity capitalization and the proposed mixed debt/equity capital structure.

c. Calculate the break-even level of EBIT where earnings per share for CSC stockholders are the same under the current and proposed capital structures.

d. At what level of EBIT will CSC shareholders earn zero EPS under the current and the proposed capital structures?

The Modigliani & Miller Propositions

P12-4. An unlevered company operates in perfect markets and has a earnings before interest and taxes (*EBIT*) of $250,000. Assume that the required return on assets for firms in this industry is 12.5%. Suppose that the firm issues $1 million worth of debt with a required return of 5% and uses the proceeds to repurchase outstanding stock.

a. What is the market value and required return of this firm's stock before the repurchase transaction?

b. What is the market value and required return of this firm's remaining stock after the repurchase transaction?

P12-5. Assume that capital markets are perfect. A firm finances its operations via $50 million in stock with a required return of 15% and $40 million in bonds with a required return of 9%. Assuming that the firm could issue $10 million in additional bonds at 9% and use the proceeds to retire $10 million worth of equity, what would happen to the firm's WACC? What would happen to the required return on the company's stock?

P12-6. A firm operates in perfect capital markets. The required return on its outstanding debt is 6%, the required return on its shares is 14%, and its WACC is 10%. What is the firm's debt-to-equity ratio?

P12-7. Assume that two firms, U and L, are identical in all respects except one: Firm U is debt free, whereas Firm L has a capital structure that is 50% debt and 50% equity by market value. Further suppose that the assumptions of M&M's "irrelevance" Proposition I hold (no taxes or transactions costs, no bankruptcy costs, etc.) and that each firm will have earnings before interest and taxes (EBIT) of $800,000.

If the required return on assets, r_a, for these firms is 12.5% and the risk-free debt yields 5%, calculate the following values for both Firm U and Firm L: (1) total firm value, (2) market value of debt and equity, and (3) required return on equity.

P12-8. Hearthstone Corp. and The Shaky Image Co. are companies that compete in the luxury consumer goods market. The two companies are virtually identical except that Hearthstone is financed entirely with equity and The Shaky Image uses equal amounts of debt and equity. Suppose that each firm has assets with a total market value of $100 million. Hearthstone has 4 million shares of stock outstanding worth $25 each. Shaky has 2 million shares outstanding in addition to a publicly traded debt whose market value is $50 million. Both companies operate in a world with perfect capital markets (no taxes, etc.). The WACC for each firm is 12%, and the cost of debt is 8%.

a. What is the price of Shaky stock?

b. What is the cost of equity for Hearthstone? For Shaky?

P12-9. In the mid-1980s, Michael Milken and his firm, Drexel Burnham Lambert, popularized the term *junk bonds*—bonds with low credit ratings. Many of Drexel's clients issued junk bonds to the public to raise money to conduct a leveraged buyout (LBO) of a target firm. After the LBO, the target firm would have an extremely high debt-to-equity ratio, with only a small portion of equity financing remaining.

Many politicians and members of the financial press worried that the increase in junk bonds would bring about an increase in the risk of the U.S. economy because so many large firms had become highly leveraged. Merton Miller disagreed. See if you can follow his argument by assessing whether each of the statements below is true or false.

a.   The junk bonds issued by acquiring firms were riskier than investment-grade bonds.

b.   The remaining equity in highly leveraged firms was more risky than it had been before the LBO.

c.   After an LBO, the target firm's capital structure would consist of very risky junk bonds and very risky equity. Therefore, the risk of the firm would increase after the LBO.

d.   The junk bonds issued to conduct the LBO were less risky than the equity they replaced.

The M&M Capital Structure Model with Taxes

P12-10. Herculio Mining has earnings before interest and taxes (EBIT) of $5 million. It has $50 million of debt outstanding with a required rate of return of 6%. The required rate of return on assets in this industry is 12%, and the corporate tax rate is 40%. Assume there are corporate taxes but no personal taxes.

a.   Determine the present value of the interest tax shield of Herculio Mining as well as the total value of the firm.

b.   Determine the gain from leverage if there are personal taxes of 20% on stock income and 30% on debt income.

P12-11. An all-equity firm is subject to a 30% tax rate. Its total market value is initially $3,500,000, and there are 175,000 shares outstanding. The firm announces a program to issue $1 million worth of bonds at 10% interest and to use the proceeds to buy back common stock.

a.   What is the value of the tax shield that the firm acquires through the bond issue?

b.   According to M&M, what is the likely increase in market value per share of the firm after the announcement (assuming efficient markets)?

c.   How many shares will the company be able to repurchase?

P12-12. Intel Corp. is a firm that uses almost no debt and had a total market capitalization of about $109 billion in August 2010. Assume that Intel faces a 35% tax rate on corporate earnings. Ignore all elements of the decision except the corporate tax savings.

a.   By how much could Intel managers increase the value of the firm by issuing $50 billion in bonds (which would be rolled over in perpetuity) and simultaneously repurchasing $50 billion in stock? Why do you think that Intel has not taken advantage of this opportunity?

b.   Suppose the personal tax rate on equity income, as faced by Intel shareholders, is 10% and that the personal tax rate on interest income is 40%. Recalculate the gains to Intel from replacing $50 billion of equity with debt.

P12-13. SoonerCo has $15 million of common stock outstanding, earnings before interest and taxes (EBIT) of $2.5 million per year, and $15 million of debt outstanding with a required return (interest rate) of 8%. The required rate of return on assets in this industry is 12.5%, and the corporate tax rate is 35%. Within the M&M framework of corporate taxes but no personal taxes, determine the present value of the interest tax shield of SoonerCo as well as the firm's total value. Finally, determine the gain from leverage if there are personal tax rates of 15% on stock income and 25% on debt income.

The Trade-Off Model

P12-14. Assume that you are the manager of a financially distressed corporation with $1.5 million in debt outstanding that will mature in two months. The firm currently has $1 million cash on hand. Assuming that you are operating the firm in the shareholders' best interests and that loan covenants prevent you from simply paying out the cash to shareholders as cash dividends, what should you do?

P12-15. You are the manager of a financially distressed corporation with $1.5 million in debt outstanding that will mature in three months. The firm currently has $1 million cash on hand. Assume that you are offered the opportunity to invest in either of the following two projects:

Project 1: The opportunity to invest $1 million in risk-free Treasury bills with a 4% annual interest rate (a quarterly interest rate of 1% = 4% per year ÷ 4 quarters per year)

Project 2: A high-risk gamble that will pay $1.6 million in two months if it is successful (probability = 0.4), but will only pay $400,000 if it is unsuccessful (probability = 0.6)

a. Compute the expected payoff for each project. If you were operating the firm in the shareholders' best interests, which one would you adopt, and why?

b. Which project would you accept if the firm were unlevered? Why?

c. Which project would you accept if the company were organized as a partnership rather than a corporation? Why?

P12-16. A firm has the choice of investing in one of two projects. Both projects last for one year. Project I requires an investment of $11,000; it yields $11,000 with a probability of 0.5 and $13,000 with a probability of 0.5. Project 2 also requires an investment of $11,000; it yields $5,000 with a probability of 0.5 and $20,000 with a probability of 0.5. The firm is capable of raising $10,000 of the investment required through a bond issue carrying an annual interest rate of 10%.

a. Assuming that the investors are concerned only about expected returns, which project would stockholders prefer? Why?

b. Which project would bondholders prefer? Why?

P12-17. An all-equity firm has 100,000 shares outstanding worth $10 each. The firm is considering a project requiring an investment of $400,000 that has an *NPV* of $50,000. The company is also considering financing this project with a new issue of equity.

a. At what price can the firm issue the new shares so that existing shareholders are indifferent to whether or not the firm takes on the project with this equity financing?

b. At what price would the firm issue the new shares so that existing shareholders capture the full benefit associated with the new project?

P12-18. You are the manager of a financially distressed corporation that has $5 million in loans coming due in 30 days. Your firm has $4 million cash on hand. Suppose that a long-time supplier of materials to your firm is planning to exit the business but has offered to sell your company a large supply of material at the bargain price of $4.5 million—but only if payment is made immediately in cash. If you choose not to acquire this material, then the supplier will offer it to a competitor and your firm will have to acquire the material at market prices totaling $5 million over the next few months.

a. Assuming that you are operating the firm in the shareholders' best interests, would you accept the project? Why or why not?

b. Would you accept this project if the firm were unlevered? Why or why not?

c. Would you accept this project if the company were organized as a partnership? Why or why not?

P12-19. Magnum Enterprises has earnings before interest and taxes (EBIT) of $5 million. There is $50 million of debt outstanding with a required rate of return of 6%. The required rate of return on the industry is 12%. The corporate tax rate is 40%; there are corporate taxes, but no personal taxes. Compute the value of Magnum assuming that the present value of bankruptcy costs is $10 million.

P12-20. Slash and Burn Construction Company currently has no debt and expects to earn $10 million in earnings before interest and taxes (EBIT) each year for the foreseeable future. The required return on assets for construction companies of this type is 12.5%, and the corporate tax rate is 40%. There are no taxes on dividends or interest at the personal level. Slash and Burn calculates that there is a 10% chance the firm will fall into bankruptcy in any given year and that, if bankruptcy does occur, it will impose direct and indirect costs totaling $12 million. If necessary, use the industry required return for discounting bankruptcy costs.

a. Compute the present value of bankruptcy costs for Slash and Burn.

b. Compute the overall value of the firm.

c. Recalculate the value of the company, assuming that the firm's shareholders face a 25% personal tax rate on equity income.

P12-21. Worldwide Contractors, Inc., currently has no debt and expects to earn $10 million in earnings before interest and taxes (EBIT) each year for the foreseeable future. The required return on assets for contractors of this type is 12.5%, and the corporate tax rate is 40%. There are no taxes on dividends or interest at the personal level. Worldwide calculates that there is a 10% chance the firm will fall into bankruptcy in any given year and that, if bankruptcy does occur, it will impose direct and indirect costs totaling $12 million. If necessary, use the industry required return for discounting bankruptcy costs. Assume that the managers of Worldwide are weighing two capital structure alteration proposals.

Proposal 1: Borrow $20 million at an interest rate of 6% and use the proceeds to repurchase an equal amount of outstanding stock. With this level of debt, the likelihood that Worldwide will fall into bankruptcy in any given year increases to 15%, and if bankruptcy occurs then it will impose direct and indirect costs totaling $12 million.

Proposal 2: Borrow $30 million at an interest rate of 8% and use the proceeds to repurchase an equal amount of outstanding stock. With this level of debt, the likelihood of Worldwide falling into bankruptcy in any given year rises to 25%, and the associated direct and indirect costs of bankruptcy, should it occur, increase to $20 million.

For each proposal, calculate both the present value of the interest tax shields and the overall value of the firm, assuming that there are no personal taxes on debt or equity income.

The Pecking-Order Theory

P12-22. Go to finance.yahoo.com and download recent balance sheets for Microsoft, Merck, Archer Daniels Midland, and General Mills (MSFT, MRK, ADM, and GIS, respectively). Calculate several debt ratios for each company and comment on the differences that you observe in the use of leverage. What factors do you think account for these differences?

For instructions on using Thomson ONE: Business School Edition, refer to the instructions provided with the Thomson ONE: Business School Edition problems at the end of Chapters 1–6.

P12-23. How does the value of an unlevered firm change if it takes on debt in a perfect capital market? Abercrombie & Fitch (ANF) is an all-equity firm. Using the latest year's earnings before interest and taxes (EBIT) and its weighted average cost of capital (WACC), calculate the value of ANF. If the company decides to change its debt-to-equity ratio to 0.5, by issuing debt and by using the proceeds to repurchase stock, what will ANF's value be after the change in capital structure? Assume that its cost of debt is one quarter of its cost of equity and that markets are perfect. What happens to its cost of equity after the new debt is issued? What is likely to happen to ANF's equity beta after debt is issued?

P12-24. How does the value of an unlevered firm change if it takes on debt in the presence of corporate taxes? Repeat the analysis for ANF from the previous problem, after relaxing only the "no corporate tax" assumption of perfect capital markets. Use the average tax rate (income taxes divided by pretax income from the income statement) for the latest available year. What is the value of ANF after it issues debt? What is the benefit of issuing debt when there are corporate taxes? How will the beta for a levered ANF, in the presence of corporate taxes, compare to that of an all-equity ANF and that of a levered ANF, in perfect capital markets? When capital markets are perfect, except for corporate taxes, what is the optimal level of debt the company should issue? In reality, do we observe firms that maintain this optimal level of debt? Why or why not?

Smart Ideas Video

Mitchell Petersen, Northwestern University

"When firms structure their business, they need to think about trading off operating and financial leverage."

John Graham, Duke University

"The majority of companies follow the trade-off model."

Smart Practices Video

Keith Woodward, Vice President of Finance, General Mills

"In General Mills we have lots of discussions about what is the optimal capital structure."

SMART concept

This animation presents the M&M capital structure irrelevance proposition and the effect of corporate income taxes on this proposition.

SMART solutions

See the solution to Problem 12-7.

Mini-Case

Capital Structure

A few years after being appointed financial manager at Sedona Fabricators, Inc., you are asked by your boss to prepare for your first presentation to the board of directors. This presentation will pertain to issues associated with capital structure. It is intended to ensure that some of the newly appointed, independent board members understand certain terminology and issues. As a guideline for your presentation, you are provided with the following outline of questions.

Assignment

1. What is capital structure?

2. What is financial leverage?

3. How does financial leverage relate to firm risk and expected returns?

4. Modigliani and Miller demonstrated that capital structure policy is irrelevant. What is the basis for their argument? What are their Propositions I and II?

5. How does the introduction of corporate taxes affect the M&M model?

6. How do the costs of bankruptcy and financial distress affect the M&M model?

7. What are agency costs? How can the use of debt reduce agency costs associated with equity?

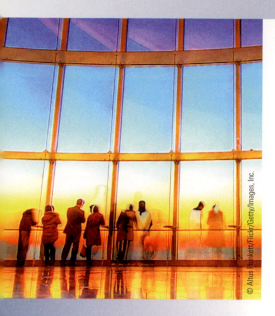

© Altus Plunkett/Flickr/Getty/Images, Inc.

chapter 13

Long-Term Debt and Leasing

What Companies Do

GE Capital's AAA-Rated Bonds Issued During the Financial Crisis

The default risk of individual corporate bond issues is routinely assessed by bond ratings agencies, which assign a rating that can range from AAA for bonds issued by the most creditworthy corporate borrowers to speculative-grade, C-rated bonds issued by extremely risky companies. AAA bonds have the lowest yield spreads of all corporate bonds. In early 2007, AAA bonds had an average yield spread of barely 100 basis points (one percentage point) above Treasuries. This welcoming environment for corporate bond issuers fundamentally changed as a result of the global financial crisis that began in the summer of 2007 and deepened throughout 2008. The average yield spread for AAA bonds rose from 204 basis points early in 2008 to 513 basis points in January 2009.

In January 2009, GE Capital made one of the first bond issues by a financial company borrower since the summer of 2008 that was not explicitly guaranteed by the Federal Deposit Insurance Corporation (FDIC). Despite carrying a AAA rating, GE Capital was forced to price its 30-year bond issue at an historically high 400-basis-point (four-percentage-point) yield spread over comparable 30-year Treasury bonds. The GE Capital bond offering demonstrated that historical pricing norms are far less relevant during a financial crisis, a time during which frightened investors must be offered substantial yield premiums to bear corporate default risk. Interestingly, as the economy was recovering in July 2010, the GE Capital bonds were selling to yield only about 175 basis points (1.75-percentage-points) above comparable U.S. Treasury bonds.

Sources: Aline van Duyn, "Corporate Bonds Find Hope from New Issues," *Financial Times* (January 8, 2009). Copyright © 2009 Financial Times Ltd. All rights reserved. Rate updates obtained from www://finance.yahoo.com/ on July 15, 2010.

Learning Objectives

After studying this chapter you should be able to:

- Describe the most important characteristics of long-term debt financing, such as the factors that influence its cost and the covenants lenders include to protect their investment;

- Discuss the differences between the two main types of loans arranged by corporate borrowers and explain why syndicated loans have become such an attractive source of debt financing;

- Describe the most important types of corporate bonds issued by U.S. corporations and compare these to bonds issued by international borrowers;

- Explain how corporations decide whether to refund an existing bond issue by exercising a call option;

- Explain the difference between operating leases and capital, or financial, leases; and

- Describe the steps involved in deciding whether to acquire an asset through a lease or by borrowing the money required to purchase the asset (the lease-versus-purchase decision).

Corporations and governments around the world issue long-term debt in order to finance capital investments or to fund current operations. As we saw in Chapter 11, the vast majority of external capital raised by companies each year is debt rather than equity, and most debt is long-term.[1] This chapter examines the key features, costs, advantages, and disadvantages of two sources of capital for business: long-term debt and leasing.

13-1 Characteristics of Long-Term Debt Financing

Long-term debt is the dominant form of long-term, external financing in all developed economies. On the balance sheet, accountants classify debt as long-term if it matures in more than one year. Firms obtain long-term debt by negotiating with a financial institution (or a syndicate consisting of several institutions) for a term loan or by selling bonds. We begin by analyzing the choice between public and private debt offerings, and then we discuss long-term debt covenants and costs.

13-1a The Choice between Public and Private Debt Issues

fixed-rate offerings
Debt issues that have a coupon interest rate that remains constant throughout the issue's life.

loans
Private debt agreements arranged between corporate borrowers and financial institutions, especially commercial banks.

private placements
Unregistered security offerings sold directly to *accredited investors*.

floating-rate issues
Debt issues with an interest (coupon) rate that is a fixed spread above a base rate that periodically changes.

Once a firm's managers decide to employ long-term debt financing, they face a series of practical choices regarding how to structure the debt. The first decision managers make is whether to issue public or private debt. In the United States, public long-term debt offerings involve selling securities (bonds and notes) directly to investors, usually with the help of investment bankers. Firms must register these offerings with the SEC. Most long-term corporate bond offerings take the form of unsecured debentures, and the vast majority of U.S. public debt offerings are fixed-rate offerings, meaning they have a coupon interest rate that remains constant.

Private debt issues usually take one of two forms. Loans are private debt agreements arranged between corporate borrowers and financial institutions, especially commercial banks, whereas private placements are unregistered security offerings sold directly to *accredited investors* (as defined in the Securities Act of 1933). The best-known and most common form of loan is a *term loan* arranged between a borrower and a single bank. However, much more funding is raised via *syndicated loans* that are arranged for a single borrower but funded by multiple banks. The overwhelming majority of both term loans and syndicated loans extended are floating-rate issues, where

---

[1] By definition, governments can raise funds only by issuing debt, because few investors would wish to purchase government equity even if such a financial creature existed. Although government debt issuance is an extremely important and interesting topic, we henceforth focus exclusively on corporate debt issuance.

the loan is priced at a fixed spread above a base interest rate, usually the London Interbank Offered Rate (*LIBOR*) or the U.S. bank *prime rate*. The interest rate paid by issuers of floating-rate debt thus moves as the base interest rate changes.

13-1b Loan Covenants

Most debt agreements include certain *loan covenants*. These are contractual clauses that place specific operating and financial constraints on the borrower. Loan covenants typically remain in force for the life of the debt agreement but do not normally place a burden on a financially sound business. Covenants allow the lender to monitor and control the borrower's activities to protect itself against the *agency problem* created by the differing objectives of owners and lenders. Without these provisions, the borrower could take advantage of the lender by investing in riskier projects or distributing cash to shareholders without compensating lenders with a higher interest rate on their loans.

There are two types of covenants. *Positive covenants* require the borrower to take a specific action, and *negative covenants* prohibit certain actions.

Positive Covenants Positive covenants specify things that a borrower must do. Some of the most common positive covenants include the following:

1. The borrower must maintain satisfactory accounting records in accordance with generally accepted accounting principles (GAAP).

2. The borrower must supply audited financial statements.

3. The borrower must pay taxes and other liabilities when due.

4. The borrower must maintain all facilities in good working order.

5. The borrower must maintain a minimum level of *net working capital*. Inadequate liquidity is a common precursor to default.

6. The borrower must maintain life insurance policies on certain key employees without whom the firm's future would be in doubt.

7. The borrower is often considered to be in default on all debts if it is in default on any debt to any lender. This is known as a **cross-default covenant**.

8. Occasionally, a covenant specifically requires the borrower to spend the borrowed funds on a specific project or financial need.

Negative Covenants Negative covenants specify what a borrower must not do. Common negative covenants include the following:

1. Borrowers may not sell receivables because doing so could cause a long-run cash shortage if the borrower uses the proceeds to meet current obligations.

2. Long-term lenders often impose fixed asset restrictions. These constrain the firm with respect to the liquidation, acquisition, and encumbrance of fixed assets because any of these actions could damage the firm's ability to repay its debt.

3. Many debt agreements prohibit borrowing additional long-term debt or require that additional borrowing be subordinated to the original loan. **Subordination** means that junior creditors must wait until all claims of the senior debt are satisfied in full before having their own claims satisfied.

4. Borrowers are prohibited from entering into certain types of leases to limit their additional fixed-payment obligations.

5. Occasionally, the lender prohibits business combinations by requiring the borrower to agree not to consolidate, merge, or combine in any way with another firm because such action could significantly change the borrower's operating and financial risk.

Cengage Learning

Annette Poulsen, University of Georgia

"The covenant is the promise about what the corporation is going to do or not do."

See the entire interview at **SMART|finance**

Smart Ideas Video

---

cross-default covenant
A positive debt covenant in which the borrower is considered to be in default on all debts if it is in default on any debt.

subordination
Agreement by all subsequent or more junior creditors to wait until all claims of the senior debt are satisfied in full before having their own claims satisfied.

? JOB INTERVIEW QUESTION
What are negative covenants and how do they benefit lenders?

What Companies Do Globally

Islamic Finance: How Do You Sell Bonds When You Cannot Charge Interest?

The past two decades have witnessed a dramatic increase in the issuance of financial securities that fulfill the principles of Islamic or Shari'ah law. While there are many nuances, three fundamental features of Shari'ah compliance stand out. First, interest cannot be charged or earned. In place of interest, loans are structured as investment partnerships—where the bank's or bondholder's return comes in the form of a share of profits—or by structuring loan payments as fees or dividends rather than interest. Second, to earn a return, lenders (e.g., banks) must bear ownership risk in real assets (i.e., not purely financial assets). Ownership risk means that the lender cannot just benefit on the upside, but must be exposed to risk that an asset can decline in value. Third, Islamic loans cannot be used to fund prohibited activities, such as gambling or adult entertainment.

In the Western World, when a firm wants to buy a machine or other asset, it often first borrows the needed funds from a bank in a purely financial transaction, paying interest on the loan. Under the rules of Islamic finance, rather than charging interest, the bank would instead (at least partially) own the machine, and charge the firm to use it. This approach is akin to leasing, where a lender (i.e., lessor) buys an asset and allows a lessee to use the asset in exchange for a rental fee. The lessor earns a return via this usage fee, rather than by charging financial interest. Interestingly, Islamic finance usage fees are often pegged to a market interest rate (e.g., LIBOR +1%), though the fee is not considered interest because the entire deal is structured to meet approval of the appropriate Shari'ah board.

Islamic bonds are known as *sukuk* and are often traded on public markets. For example, in 2009, $14 billion sukuk were listed on the London Stock Exchange. The sukuk are structured so that the investor is a partial owner in the underlying asset the bond is used to finance, and the investor's return is considered profit sharing.

Many Islamic financial institutions fared better than Western banks during the 2008–2009 financial crisis. Western banks got into trouble in part by buying or selling loans that were originated elsewhere, and by trading derivative securities. Both of these practices are forbidden under Shari'ah law (because they are purely financial in nature), and thus many Islamic financial institutions avoided the most risky of practices that later haunted Western banks.

The turbulent economic times of 2008–2009 highlighted, however, that from the Western perspective there may be political or legal risks associated with Islamic markets. For example, the Nakheel real estate partnership (a subsidiary of Dubai World[1]) announced in late 2009 that it would not be able to meet its scheduled sukuk payments. Investors worldwide wondered how they would fare if the Nakheel sukuk defaulted, and whether commercial law or Islamic law would prevail should the issue end up in bankruptcy court. The sukuk's market value quickly fell to less than $0.40 on the dollar. Eventually, in late spring of 2010, the emirate of Dubai[2] said that it would back the Nakheel bonds and make the scheduled payments, and the crisis was averted. While this addressed the short-run problem, it left unsettled how financial priorities would be decided in an Islamic bankruptcy court.

These issues notwithstanding, Islamic financial markets are likely to grow rapidly in coming decades, as Islamic nations and firms continue to grow and seek financial capital, and as Islamic investors seek to buy securities that satisfy Islamic law.

[1] Dubai World is an investment company that manages projects for the government of Dubai, including DP World, the world's third largest port operator. Nakheel is a well-known real estate subsidiary of Dubai World. Among its famous projects is the man-made palm-shaped island, Palm Jumeirah.
[2] Dubai is the second largest emirate (akin to a state in the United States) of the U.A.E. (United Arab Emirates). The largest emirate of the UAE is Abu Dhabi, also the capital city. Abu Dhabi and Dubai are the only two emirates that have veto power in the UAE's legislature.

Sources: John Burton, "Islamic Bond Issues Seen Dropping Further," *Financial Times* (January 22, 2009); Delphine Strauss, "Islamic-Style Turkish Bonds Fail to Appeal," *Financial Times* (January 29, 2009).

6. To prevent liquidation of assets through large salary payments, the lender may prohibit or limit salary increases for specified employees.

7. A relatively common provision prohibits the firm's annual cash dividend payments from exceeding 50% to 70% of net earnings or a specified dollar amount.

In the process of negotiating the terms of long-term debt, the borrower and lender must agree to an acceptable set of covenants. If a borrower violates a covenant, the lender may demand immediate repayment of the entire loan, waive the violation and continue the loan, or waive the violation but alter the terms of the original agreement.

13-1c Cost of Long-Term Debt

In addition to specifying positive and negative covenants, the long-term debt agreement specifies the interest rate, the timing of interest payments, and the size of principal repayment. The major factors affecting the cost, or interest rate, of long-term debt are loan maturity, loan size, borrower risk, and the underlying cost of money.

Loan Maturity Generally, the *yield curve* is upward sloping, which implies that long-term loans have higher interest rates than short-term loans. Factors that can cause an upward-sloping yield curve include (1) the general expectation of higher future inflation or interest rates; (2) lender preferences for shorter term, more liquid loans; and (3) greater demand for long-term rather than short-term loans relative to the supply of such loans. In a practical sense, the longer the term, the greater the default risk associated with the loan; therefore, to compensate for all these factors, the lender typically charges a higher interest rate on long-term loans.

Loan Size The size of the loan can affect the interest cost of borrowing in an inverse manner because of economies of scale. Loan administration costs per dollar borrowed are likely to decrease with increasing loan size. However, the risk to the lender increases, since larger loans result in less diversification. The size of the loan sought by each borrower must therefore be evaluated to determine the net administrative cost versus risk trade-off.

Borrower Risk The higher the firm's operating leverage, the greater the volatility of its operating cash flows. Also, the higher the borrower's financial leverage, conveniently reflected in a high financial *debt ratio* or a low *times interest earned ratio*, the greater the volatility of the shareholders' cash flows. The lender's main concern is with the borrower's ability to fully repay the loan as prescribed in the debt agreement. A lender uses an overall assessment of the borrower's operating and financial risk, along with information on past payment patterns, when setting the interest rate on a loan.

Cost of Money The cost of money is the basis for determining the actual interest rate charged. Generally, the rate on U.S. Treasury securities with equivalent maturities is considered the basic (lowest-risk) cost of money. To determine the actual interest rate to be charged, the lender will add premiums for borrower risk and other factors to this basic cost of money for the given maturity. Alternatively, some lenders determine a prospective borrower's risk class and find the rates charged on loans with similar maturities and terms to firms in the same risk class. Instead of having to determine a risk premium, the lender can use the risk premium prevailing in the marketplace for similar loans.

13-1 Concept Review Questions

1. What factors should a manager consider when deciding on the amount and type of long-term debt to be used to finance a business?

2. What factors should a manager consider when negotiating the loan covenants in a long-term debt agreement?

3. How can managers estimate their firms' cost of long-term debt prior to meeting with a lender?

13-2 Corporate Loans

Corporations can acquire debt financing by borrowing money as a loan from a financial or nonfinancial institution or by selling debt securities (like bonds). Here we describe the two most important types of corporate borrowing: term loans and syndicated loans.

13-2a Term Loans

term loan
A loan made by an institution to a business, with an initial maturity of more than 1 year, generally 5 to 12 years.

A term loan is made by a financial institution to a business and has an initial maturity of more than one year, generally five to twelve years. Term loans are often made to finance permanent working capital needs, to pay for machinery and equipment, or to liquidate other loans.

Term loans are essentially private placements of debt. Firms typically negotiate term loans directly with the lender instead of using an investment banker as an intermediary. An advantage of term loans over publicly traded debt is their flexibility. The securities (bonds or notes) in a public debt issue are usually purchased by many different investors, so it is almost impossible to alter the terms of the borrowing agreement should new business conditions make such changes desirable. With a term loan, the borrower can negotiate with a single lender for modifications to the borrowing agreement.[2]

Characteristics of Term Loan Agreements The actual term loan agreement is a formal contract ranging from a few to a few hundred pages. The following items commonly appear in the document: the amount and maturity of the loan, payment dates, interest rate, positive and negative covenants, collateral (if any), purpose of the loan, action to be taken in the event the agreement is violated, and stock purchase warrants. Of these, payment dates, collateral requirements, and stock purchase warrants require some discussion.

balloon payment
A large lump-sum payment that pays back the entire loan principal at the maturity of a term loan that during its life requires only periodic interest payments.

Payment Dates Term loan agreements usually specify whether the loan payments are made monthly, quarterly, or annually. Generally, these equal payments fully repay the interest and principal over the life of the loan. Occasionally, a term loan agreement will require periodic interest payments over the life of the loan followed by a large lump-sum payment at maturity. This so-called balloon payment pays back the entire loan principal if the periodic payments represent only interest.

collateral
The specific assets pledged to secure a loan.

Collateral Requirements Term lending arrangements may be unsecured or secured. Secured loans have specific assets pledged as collateral. The collateral often takes the form of an asset such as machinery and equipment, plant, inventory, pledges of accounts receivable, and pledges of securities. Unsecured loans are obtained without pledging specific assets as collateral. Whether lenders require collateral depends in part on the lender's evaluation of the borrower's financial condition.

Term lending is often referred to as *asset-backed lending*, though term lenders in reality are primarily cash flow lenders. They hope and expect to be repaid out of cash flow but require collateral both as an alternative source of repayment and as ransom to decrease the incentive of borrowing firms to default (because a defaulting borrower would lose the use of valuable corporate assets). Most pledged assets

lien
A legal contract specifying under what conditions a lender can take title to an asset if a loan is not repaid and prohibiting the borrowing firm from selling or disposing of the asset without the lender's consent.

are secured by a lien, which is a legal contract specifying under what conditions the lender can take title to the asset if the loan is not repaid and prohibiting the borrowing firm from selling or disposing of the asset without the lender's consent. The liens serve two purposes: to establish clearly the lender's right to seize and liquidate collateral if the borrower defaults; and to serve notice to subsequent lenders of a prior claim on the asset(s). Not all assets can be readily used as collateral, of course. For an asset to be useful as collateral, it should (1) be nonperishable, (2) be relatively homogeneous in quality, (3) have a high value relative to its physical size, and (4) have a well-established secondary market where seized assets can be turned into cash without a severe price penalty.

stock purchase warrants
Instruments that give their holder the right to purchase a certain number of shares of a firm's common stock at a specified price during a certain period of time.

Stock Purchase Warrants The corporate borrower sometimes gives the lender certain financial benefits, usually stock purchase warrants, in addition to the payment of

---

[2]Companies typically arrange loans with commercial banks as part of a larger, ongoing banking relationship. Large companies often have dozens of these banking relationships, but a critical decision for smaller firms is whether to maintain one large banking relationship or several smaller ones in order to minimize the risk of being unable to arrange financing during an emergency.

Benjamin Esty, Harvard University

"The syndicated loan market is now the largest single source of corporate funds in the world."

See the entire interview at SMART|finance

Smart Ideas Video

interest and repayment of principal. Warrants are instruments that give their holder the right to purchase a certain number of shares of the firm's common stock at a specified price during a certain period of time. They are designed to entice institutional lenders to make long-term loans, possibly under relatively favorable terms. Warrants are also frequently used as sweeteners for corporate bond issues.

Term Lenders There is a wide array of sources for term loans. The primary lenders making term loans to businesses are commercial banks, insurance companies, pension funds, regional development companies, the U.S. federal government's Small Business Administration, small business investment companies, commercial finance companies, and equipment manufacturers' financing subsidiaries.

13-2b Syndicated Loans

syndicated loan

A large-denomination credit arranged by a group (a *syndicate*) of institutional lenders, commonly commercial banks, for a single borrower.

A syndicated loan is a large-denomination credit arranged by a group (a *syndicate*) of institutional lenders, commonly commercial banks, for a single borrower. Although syndicated lending has been a fixture of U.S. and international finance for over three decades, syndicated loans have increased dramatically in size, volume, and importance during the last twenty years.

The syndicated loan market appeals to borrowers who need to arrange very large loans quickly. Loans for top-tier corporate borrowers are floating-rate credits with very narrow spreads (10−75 basis points) over LIBOR. Typically, lenders structure these loans as *lines of credit* that borrowers can draw down as needed over several years. After that time, the loans generally convert to term credits that firms must repay on a set schedule. One increasingly important use of syndicated lending is to fund debt-financed acquisitions by corporate borrowers, where the ability to borrow large sums quickly and (relatively) discreetly is especially valuable.

Though syndicated loans are used for virtually all types of corporate finance, there are two uses that merit special discussion: Eurocurrency lending and project finance.

Eurocurrency loan market

A large number of international banks that stand ready to make floating-rate, hard-currency loans to international corporate and government borrowers.

Eurocurrency Lending The Eurocurrency loan market consists of a large number of international banks that stand ready to make floating-rate, hard-currency loans (typically, U.S.-dollar denominated) to international corporate and government borrowers. For example, a British bank that accepts a dollar-denominated deposit in London is creating a *Eurodollar deposit*, and by then relending that deposit to another bank or corporate borrower it is making a *Eurodollar loan*. These loans are often structured as *lines of credit* on which borrowers can draw. Most large loans (over $500 million) are syndicated, thereby providing a measure of diversification to the lenders. Eurocurrency syndicated loans sometimes exceed $10 billion, and loans of $1 billion or more are quite common. Furthermore, in total size, the Eurocurrency market dwarfs all other international corporate financial markets.

project finance (PF) loans

Loans usually arranged for infrastructure projects such as toll roads, bridges, and power plants.

stand-alone companies

Companies created for the sole purpose of constructing and operating a single project.

Project Finance Project finance (PF) loans are typically arranged for infrastructure projects—such as toll roads, bridges, power plants, seaports, tunnels, and airports—that require large sums to construct but that, once built, generate significant amounts of free cash flow for many years. Although project finance lending almost always involves the use of syndicated loans, project finance differs from other types of syndicated credits in two vital ways. First, PF loans are made to stand-alone companies, sometimes called *vehicle companies*, created for the sole purpose of constructing and operating a single project. Second, PF loans are almost always limited or *nonrecourse loans*, backed only by the assets and cash flows of the project, so the parent firm that sponsors the project does not guarantee payment of the loan. Project finance loans have been employed in many famous projects, such as the Eurotunnel under the English Channel, Euro Disneyland in France, the Athens International Airport, the Seoul-Pusan High-Speed Rail Project in Korea, and the Philippines' Power Project.

13-2 Concept Review Questions

4. Suppose that a specialty retail firm takes out a term loan from a bank. Which do you think the bank would prefer to receive as collateral: a claim on the firm's inventory or on its receivables?

5. A problem with *collateral* is that its value is positively correlated with the borrower's ability to repay. Explain.

6. What aspect of syndicated lending is most attractive to the lenders?

7. Why are *syndicated loans* especially useful for financing takeovers?

8. How do *project finance (PF) loans* differ from other types of syndicated loans?

13-3 Corporate Bonds

? WHAT TO ASK

What types of long-term debt does your company use?

debentures
Unsecured bonds backed only by the general faith and credit of the borrowing company.

subordinated debenture
An unsecured bond on which the creditors' claims are not satisfied until the senior debtholders' claims have been fully satisfied.

income bonds
An unsecured bond that pays interest only when the debtor company has positive earnings.

mortgage bonds
A secured bond, where the security is real estate.

collateral trust bonds
A bond secured by stock and/or bonds that are owned by the issuer.

equipment trust certificates
A secured bond used to finance transportation equipment.

A *corporate bond* is a debt instrument that allows a corporation to borrow money from institutions or individuals and promises to repay it in the future under clearly defined terms. Firms issue bonds with maturities of ten to thirty years (debt securities with an original maturity of one to ten years are called *notes*) and with a par value (face value) of $1,000. The coupon interest rate on a bond represents the percentage of the bond's par value that the firm will pay to investors each year. In the United States, companies typically pay interest semiannually in two equal coupon payments. Bondholders receive the par value back when the bonds mature.

13-3a Popular Types of Bonds

Bonds can be classified in a variety of ways. Here we break them into traditional bonds, the basic types that have been around for years, and new, innovative bonds. Table 13.1 summarizes the traditional types of bonds issued by corporations in terms of their key characteristics and priority of lender's claim in the event of default. Note that the first three types, debentures, subordinated debentures, and income bonds, are unsecured; whereas the last three, mortgage bonds, collateral trust bonds, and equipment trust certificates, are secured (backed by specific assets pledged as collateral). The majority of U.S. corporate bonds are debentures, where the debt is backed by the faith and credit of the issuing corporation itself rather than by specific pledged collateral.[3]

Over the years, corporations have developed many new debt instruments designed to attract a unique clientele of bond investors who, it is presumed, would be willing to pay a higher price for a given special feature. A detailed discussion of these new offerings is beyond the scope of an overview chapter, but Table 13.2 surveys the characteristics of a few of them.

13-3b Legal Aspects of Corporate Bonds

When they issue bonds, corporations typically raise hundreds of millions of dollars from many unrelated investors. The dispersion in the investor base creates a need for special legal arrangements to protect lenders.

---

[3]Although not a direct source of financing for individual corporations, the market for mortgage-backed securities (MBS) grew rapidly through mid-2007, at which point it was a $500 billion annual business in the United States alone. MBS offerings are created by pooling large numbers of home mortgage loans and then selling securities backed by these mortgages directly to investors. This market revolutionized home mortgage lending in the United States because it allowed financial institutions to economize on the use of their capital by originating mortgage loans and then selling them to MBS specialists. Unfortunately, the credit crisis that gripped the world during 2007–2009 was triggered by rapidly rising default rates in the U.S. mortgage-backed securities market—especially in the subprime (low borrower quality) segment.

Table 13.1

Characteristics and Priority of Lender's Claims of Traditional Types of Bonds

Bond Type	Characteristics	Priority of Lender's Claim
Debentures	Unsecured bonds that only creditworthy firms can issue. Most *convertible bonds* are debentures.	Seniority is the same as that of any general creditor. May have other unsecured bonds subordinate to them.
Subordinated debentures	Claims are not satisfied until those of the creditors holding senior debts have been fully satisfied.	Claim is that of a general creditor, but not as high as a senior debt claim.
Income bonds	Payment of interest is required only when earnings are available from which to make such payment. Sometimes issued in reorganization of a failed or failing firm.	Seniority is that of a general creditor. Not in default when interest payments are missed, because they are contingent only on earnings being available.
Mortgage bonds	Secured by real estate or buildings. Can be *open-end* (additional bonds issued against collateral), *limited open-end* (a specified amount of additional bonds can be issued against collateral), or *closed-end*; may contain an *after-acquired clause* (property subsequently acquired becomes part of mortgage collateral).	Seniority is on proceeds from sale of mortgaged assets; if not fully satisfied, the lender becomes a general creditor. The *first mortgage* claim must be satisfied before distribution of proceeds to *second mortgage* holders. A number of mortgages can be issued against the same collateral.
Collateral trust bonds	Secured by stock and/or bonds that are owned by the issuer. Collateral value is generally 25–35% higher than bond value.	Claim is on proceeds from stock and/or bond collateral; if not fully satisfied, the lender becomes a general creditor.
Equipment trust certificates	Used to finance transportation equipment—airplanes, trucks, boats, and railroad cars. A trustee buys such an asset with funds raised through the sale of trust certificates and then leases it to the firm, which, after making the final scheduled lease payment, receives title to the asset.	Claim is on proceeds from the sale of the asset; if proceeds do not fully satisfy outstanding debt, trust certificate lenders become general creditors.

indenture
A legal document stating the conditions under which a bond has been issued.

Bond Indenture A bond **indenture** is a complex and lengthy legal document stating the conditions under which a bond has been issued. It specifies both the rights of the bondholders and the duties of the issuing corporation. In addition to specifying the interest and principal payment dates and containing various positive and negative covenants, the indenture frequently contains *sinking fund requirements* and, if the bond is secured, provisions with respect to a security interest.

Sinking Fund Requirements A positive covenant often included in a bond indenture is a **sinking fund** requirement. Its objective is to provide for the systematic retirement of bonds prior to their maturity. To carry out this requirement, the corporation makes semiannual or annual payments to a trustee who uses the payments to retire bonds by purchasing them in the marketplace. This process is simplified by the inclusion of a limited *call feature*, which permits the issuer to repurchase a fraction of outstanding bonds each year at a call price. The trustee will exercise this option only when sufficient bonds cannot be purchased in the marketplace or when the bond's market price exceeds its call price.

sinking fund
A positive covenant included in a bond indenture, the objective of which is to provide for the systematic retirement of bonds prior to their maturity.

　　The typical life of a U.S. corporate bond is far shorter than its stated maturity implies. The reasons for this are the ability of companies to call (and then refinance) bonds and the pervasiveness of mandated sinking funds in long-term U.S. debt security issues. Sinking funds work in such a way that the typical bond issue with, say,

Table 13.2 **Characteristics of Some Newer Types of Debt Instruments**

Bond Type	Characteristics[a]
Zero (or low) coupon bonds	Issued with no (zero) or very low coupon (stated interest) rate and sold at a large discount from par. A significant portion (or all) of the investor's return therefore comes from gain in value (i.e., par value minus purchase price) and is paid at maturity. Generally callable at par value. Because the issuer can deduct the current year's interest accrual without having to actually pay the interest until the bond matures (or is called), its cash flow each year is increased by the amount of the tax shield provided by the interest deduction. Although interest is not actually paid, the investor must pay taxes on the implicit interest payments.
Junk (or high-yield) bonds	Debt rated Ba or lower by Moody's or below BBB- by Standard & Poor's. Beginning in the mid-1980s, commonly used by rapidly growing firms to obtain growth capital, most often as a way to finance mergers and takeovers of other firms. High-risk bonds with high yields—typically yielding at least 3 percentage points more than high-quality corporate debt.
Floating-rate bonds	Stated interest rate is adjusted periodically within stated limits in response to change in specified money or capital market rates. Popular when future inflation and interest rates are uncertain. Tend to sell at close to par as a result of the automatic adjustment to changing market conditions. Some issues provide for annual redemption at par at the option of the bondholder.
Extendible notes	Debt instruments with short maturities, typically 1 to 5 years, which can be redeemed or renewed for a similar period at the option of the holders. Similar to a floating-rate bond. An issue might be a series of 3-year renewable notes over a period of 15 years; every 3 years, the notes could be extended for another 3 years at a new rate that is competitive with market interest rates prevailing at the time of renewal.
Putable bonds	Bonds that can be redeemed at par (typically, $1,000) at the option of their holder either at specified dates, such as 3 to 5 years after the date of issue and every 1 to 5 years thereafter, or when and if the firm takes specified actions such as being acquired, acquiring another company, or issuing a large amount of additional debt. In return for the right to put the bond at specified times or actions by the firm, the bond's yield is lower than that of a nonputable bond.

[a]The claims of lenders (i.e., bondholders) against issuers of each of these types of bonds vary, depending on their other features. Each of these bonds can be unsecured or secured.

$100 million principal amount and a fifteen-year maturity will probably have only a few million dollars' worth of bonds still outstanding when the last bonds are redeemed fifteen years after issuance. Depending on the terms of the sinking fund, the actual average maturity of this issue (the weighted average years outstanding) will probably be less than ten years, not the fifteen years originally stated.

Because sinking funds force corporations to redeem some bonds early, they reduce the risk of default for two reasons. First, sinking funds increase the likelihood that investors will become aware of any financial difficulties encountered by the issuing firm early (when it misses a sinking fund payment) rather than late. This will trigger the demand for effective corrective action, up to and including the removal of the issuing firm's incumbent management team. Second, because at maturity only a fraction of a given bond issue will remain outstanding, the issuing firm's managers will have less incentive to default on the issue or attempt to expropriate bondholder wealth by filing for bankruptcy protection.

Security Interest The bond indenture is similar to a loan agreement in that any collateral pledged against the bond, the lenders' *security interest*, is specifically identified in the document. Usually, the title to the collateral is attached to the indenture, which also describes the collateral's disposition under various circumstances. The protection of bond collateral is crucial to increasing the safety—and thus to enhancing the marketability—of a bond issue.

trustee (bond)
A third party to a bond *indenture* that acts as a watchdog on behalf of the bondholders, making sure that the issuer does not default on its contractual responsibilities.

Trustee A trustee is a third party to a bond *indenture* and can be an individual, a corporation, or, most often, a commercial bank trust department. The trustee, whose services are paid for by the issuer, acts as a watchdog on behalf of the bondholders, making sure that the issuer does not default on its contractual responsibilities. The trustee is empowered to take specified actions on behalf of bondholders if the borrower violates any indenture terms.

13-3c Methods of Issuing Corporate Bonds

Public issues of corporate bonds in the United States must be registered with the Securities and Exchange Commission, and large offerings are generally underwritten by an investment banking syndicate. However, there is tremendous variation in actual offering procedures, and these differences have increased over time as new debt securities have developed. In particular, two financial and regulatory innovations transformed U.S. bond-issuance patterns. First, the introduction of *shelf registration* in the early 1980s allowed corporations to register large blocks of debt securities and then sell them in discrete pieces over the subsequent two years as market conditions warranted. Shelf registration can be used for both debt and equity offerings, but not all companies use this technique for selling stock. In contrast, most companies that can use shelf registration for debt offerings do so.

The second major innovation occurred in 1990, when the SEC created a new private-placement market by implementing *Rule 144A*. This allowed qualified institutional investors (those with assets exceeding $100 million) to trade nonregistered securities among themselves, and corporate issuers soon found this was an attractive market for new equity and, especially, new debt issues. Because Rule 144A issues offer investors much greater liquidity than do traditional private placements and are less costly than traditional public offerings, U.S. and international corporations sell a total of between $400 billion and $500 billion in securities most years under this rule.

13-3d General Characteristics of a Bond Issue

Three characteristics commonly observed in a U.S. bond issue are (1) a call feature, (2) a conversion feature, and (3) stock purchase warrants. Each of these features grants an option, either to the issuer or the investor, that can have a significant impact on a bond's value.

Call Feature The call feature is included in most corporate bond issues and gives the issuer the opportunity to repurchase bonds prior to maturity. The *call price* is the stated price at which bonds may be repurchased. Sometimes the call privilege is exercisable only during a certain period, and usually bonds are not callable in the first few years. Typically, the initial call price exceeds the par value of a bond by an amount equal to one year's interest. For example, a $1,000 bond with a 10% coupon interest rate would be callable for around $1,100 [$1,000 + (0.10 × $1,000)]. The amount by which the call price exceeds the bond's par value is commonly referred to as the *call premium*. This premium compensates bondholders for having the bond called away from them and is the cost to the issuer of calling the bonds.

The call feature is generally advantageous to the issuer because it enables the issuer to retire outstanding debt prior to maturity. Thus, when interest rates fall, an issuer can call an outstanding bond and reissue a new bond at a lower interest rate. When interest rates rise, the call privilege will not be exercised, except possibly to meet sinking fund requirements. Of course, to issue a callable bond, the firm must pay a higher coupon interest rate than that on noncallable bonds of equal risk in order to compensate bondholders for the risk of having the bonds called away.

? JOB INTERVIEW QUESTION

Should a callable bond have a lower or higher yield than a similar noncallable bond? Why would a firm want to issue callable bonds?

convertible bonds
Bonds that allow bondholder to exchange each bond for a stated number of shares of common stock.

Conversion Feature The conversion feature of convertible bonds allows bondholders to exchange each bond for a stated number of shares of common stock. Bondholders will convert their bonds only when the market price of the stock is greater than the *conversion price*, hence providing a profit to the bondholder. Because the option to convert into stock is valuable, the interest rate paid on convertible bonds is usually lower than the rate on traditional bonds, all else being equal. (The valuation of convertible bonds is discussed in detail in Chapter 19.)

Stock Purchase Warrants   Like term loans, bonds occasionally have warrants attached as sweeteners to make them more attractive to prospective investors. As we noted previously, a *stock purchase warrant* gives its holder the right to purchase a certain number of shares of common stock at a specified price during a certain period of time.

13-3e High-Yield Bonds

The risk of publicly traded bond issues is assessed by independent agencies such as Moody's and Standard & Poor's (S&P). Both agencies have ten major *bond ratings* derived by using financial ratio and cash flow analyses. Bonds rated Baa or higher by Moody's (BBB- or higher by S&P) are known as investment-grade bonds. Bonds rated below investment-grade are known as junk bonds, high-yield bonds, or speculative bonds. As the name suggests, junk bonds carry a much higher default risk than do investment-grade bonds, but they also offer higher yields. Prior to the late 1970s, such issues were quite rare. Historically, most of these speculative bonds trading in the market were fallen angels, bonds that received investment-grade ratings when they were first issued but later fell to junk status.

Junk bond default rates typically peak during recessions. When junk bond default rates rose sharply during the 1990–1991 recession, many commentators wrote off high-yield debt as a viable financing tool. As Figure 13.1 shows, the speculative bond market has prospered since then, at least in terms of the par value of junk bonds outstanding. Default rates rose from 1999 to 2002 and, not surprisingly, rose again during the global recession in 2008. Junk bond investors recognize that they are assuming much of the issuing firm's operating (business) risk when they purchase high-yield debt, but they are willing to do so in return for promised yields that approach the returns earned by stockholders. Of course, a higher *promised* yield may or may not result in a higher *realized* return, because the higher yield reflects a higher likelihood that the borrower will default (in whole or in part) on the bond sometime during its life. In other words, owing to the risk of default and the probability that investors experience losses when default occurs, the expected return on junk bonds is generally well below the promised return (i.e., the yield to maturity).

Bonds are essentially unmarketable without a rating. After a bond is rated, the rating is not changed unless the likelihood of the company's defaulting on the bond issue changes. It is perhaps surprising that bond issuers themselves pay the ratings companies to issue ratings on newly issued bonds. Additionally, in its discussions with the rating agency the issuing firm can communicate sensitive information privately to the rating agency. This information can then be usefully reflected via the bond rating without being directly disclosed to competitors.

Cengage Learning

Ed Altman, New York University

"Probably about 75% of the bonds are investment grade; that's BBB or higher."

See the entire interview at **SMART|finance**

Smart Ideas Video

13-3f International Corporate Bond Financing

Companies can sell bonds internationally by tapping the *Eurobond* or *foreign bond* markets. Both of these provide established, creditworthy borrowers the opportunity to obtain large amounts of long-term debt financing quickly and efficiently, in their choice of currency, and with flexible repayment terms.

Eurobonds   A Eurobond is issued by an international borrower and sold to investors in countries with currencies other than the currency in which the bond is denominated. A dollar-denominated bond issued by a U.S. corporation and sold to European

Figure 13.1   **Par Value Amounts Outstanding and Default Rates for High-Yield Bonds (Junk Bonds), 1971–2008Q3.**

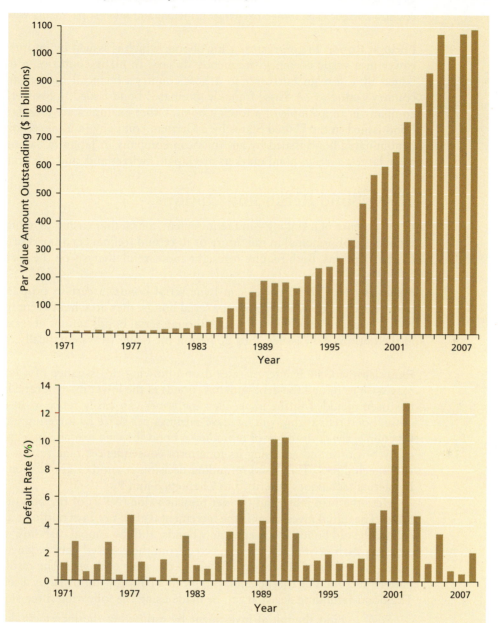

Source: Edward I. Altman and Gaurav Bana, "Report on Defaults and Returns on High Yield Bonds: The Year 2002 in Review and Market Outlook." NYU Salomon Center, February 2008, Figure 1. Updates provide by Edward Altman.

bearer bonds
Bonds that pay interest to the bearer and both shelter investment income from taxation and provide protection against exchange-rate risk.

investors is an example of a Eurobond. The Eurobond market first developed in the early 1960s, when several European and U.S. borrowers discovered that many European investors wanted to hold dollar-denominated **bearer bonds**. Investors wanted bearer bonds because they would both shelter investment income from taxation—because coupon interest payments were made to the bearer of the bond and names were not reported to tax authorities—and provide protection against exchange-rate risk.

Until the mid-1980s, blue-chip U.S. corporations were the largest single class of Eurobond issuers, and many of these companies were able to borrow in this market at interest rates below those the U.S. government paid on Treasury bonds. As the market matured, issuers were able to choose the currency in which they borrowed. Later, the Eurobond market became much more balanced in terms of the mix of borrowers, total issue volume, and currency of denomination. Most Eurobond issues, in fact, were executed as part of a complicated financial engineering transaction known as a *currency swap*, wherein companies headquartered in different countries issue bonds in their home-country currencies and then exchange principal and interest payments with each other.

Foreign Bonds In contrast to a Eurobond, which is issued by an international borrower in a single currency (frequently dollars) in many countries, a foreign bond is issued by a foreign borrower in a host country's financial market and in the host country's currency. A Swiss franc-denominated bond issued in Switzerland by a U.S. company is an example of a foreign bond. Other examples are a dollar-denominated bond issued in the United States by a German company (a Yankee bond) and a yen-denominated bond issued by an American company in Japan (a Samurai bond). The three largest foreign bond markets are Japan, Switzerland, and the United States.

> **foreign bond**
> A bond issued in a host country's financial market, in the host country's currency, by a foreign borrower.

13-3g Bond Refunding Options

In the absence of a sinking-fund requirement, a firm that wishes to avoid a large single repayment of principal in the future or to refund (refinance) a bond prior to maturity has two options. Both require foresight and careful analysis on the part of the issuer.

> **refund**
> To refinance a debt with new bonds.

Serial Issues The borrower can issue serial bonds, a certain proportion of which mature each year. When firms issue serial bonds, they attach different interest rates to bonds maturing at different times. Although serial bonds cannot necessarily be retired at the option of the issuer, they do permit the issuer to systematically retire the debt.

> **serial bonds**
> Bonds of which a certain portion mature each year.

Exercising a Call If interest rates drop following the issuance of a bond, the issuer may wish to refund the debt with new bonds at the lower interest rate. If a call feature has been included in the issue, then the issuer can easily retire it. In an accounting sense, bond refinancing will increase earnings per share by lowering interest expense. Of course, the desirability of refunding a bond through exercise of a call is not necessarily obvious, and assessing its long-term consequences requires the use of present value techniques. This bond refunding decision is another application of the capital budgeting techniques described in Chapters 8 and 9.

Here the firm must find the net present value (*NPV*) of the bond-refunding cash flows. The initial investment is the incremental after-tax cash outflows associated with calling the old bonds and issuing new bonds, and the annual cash flow savings are the after-tax cash savings that are expected from the reduced debt payments on the new lower-interest bond. These cash flows are the same each year. The resulting cash flow pattern surrounding this decision is typical: an outflow followed by a series of inflows. The bond-refunding decision can be made using the following three-step procedure.

Step 1. **Find the initial investment** by estimating the incremental after-tax cash outflow required at time 0 to call the old bond and issue a new bond in its place. Any overlapping interest resulting from the need to pay interest on both the old and new bonds is treated as part of the initial investment.

Step 2. **Find the annual cash flow savings,** which is the difference between the annual after-tax debt payments with the old and new bonds. This cash flow stream will be an annuity, with a life equal to the maturity of the old bond.

Step 3. Use the after-tax cost of the new debt (as the discount rate) to **find the net present value (*NPV*)** by subtracting the initial investment from the present value of the annual cash flow savings. The annual cash flow savings is a contractually fixed cash flow stream that represents the difference between two contractual debt-service streams, the old bond and the new bond. Therefore, the appropriate discount rate should reflect the risk of the firm's debt (which is tied to these same contractually fixed cash flows). That is, we discount these cash flows at the firm's cost of debt. Moreover, we follow convention and *use the after-tax cost of debt as the discount rate.* If *NPV* is positive then the proposed refunding is recommended;

otherwise, the bonds should not be refunded. Application of this bond refunding decision procedure is illustrated in the Example that follows. First, however, a few tax-related points must be clarified.

call premium
The amount by which the call price exceeds the par value of a bond. Paid by corporations to buy back outstanding bonds prior to maturity.

Call Premiums The amount by which the call price exceeds the par value of the bond is the **call premium**. It is paid by the issuer to the bondholder to buy back outstanding bonds prior to maturity. The call premium is treated as a tax-deductible expense in the year of the call.

Bond Discounts and Premiums When bonds are sold at a discount or at a premium, the firm is required to amortize (write off) the discount or premium in equal portions over the life of the bond. The amortized discount is treated as a tax-deductible expenditure, whereas the amortized premium is treated as taxable income. If a bond is retired prior to maturity, any unamortized portion of a discount or premium is deducted from or added to pretax income at that time.

Floatation or Issuance Costs Any costs incurred in the process of issuing a bond must be amortized over the life of the bond. The annual write-off is therefore a tax-deductible expenditure. If a bond is retired prior to maturity, then any unamortized portion of this cost is deducted from pretax income at that time.

EXAMPLE

The Davis Corporation, a manufacturer of industrial piping, is contemplating calling $50 million of 30-year, $1,000 par value bonds (50,000 bonds) issued five years ago with a coupon interest rate of 9%. The bonds have a call price of $1,090 and initially netted proceeds of $48.5 million due to a discount of $30 per bond (50,000 bonds × $970 net per bond). The initial flotation cost was $400,000. The company intends to sell $50 million of 25-year, $1,000 par value bonds with a 7% (coupon) interest rate to raise funds for retiring the old bonds. The flotation costs on the new issue are estimated to be $450,000. The firm is currently in the 30% tax bracket and estimates its after-tax cost of debt to be 4.9% [0.07 × (1 − 0.30)]. Because the new bonds must first be sold and their proceeds then used to retire the old bonds, the firm expects a two-month period of overlapping interest during which interest must be paid on both the old and the new bonds.

Step 1. *Find the initial investment.* Finding the initial investment requires a number of calculations.

a. *Call premium.* The call premium per bond is $90 ($1,090 call price − $1,000 par value). Because the total call premium is deductible in the year of the call, its after-tax cost is calculated as follows:

Before tax ($90 × 50,000 bonds)	$4,500,000
Less: Taxes (0.30 × $4,500,000)	$1,350,000
After-tax cost of call premium	$3,150,000

b. *Flotation cost of new bond.* This cost was given as $450,000.

c. *Overlapping interest.*[4] The after-tax cost of the overlapping interest on the old bond is treated as part of the initial investment and calculated as follows:

Before tax [0.09 × (2 ÷ 12) × $50,000,000]	$750,000
Less: Tax shield (0.30 × $750,000)	$225,000
After-tax cost of overlapping interest	$525,000

d. *Unamortized discount on old bond.* The firm was amortizing the $1,500,000 discount ($50,000,000 par value − $48,500,000 net proceeds from sale) on the old bond over 30 years. Because only five of the 30 years' amortization of the discount has been applied, the firm can deduct the remaining 25 years of unamortized discount as a lump sum, thereby reducing taxes by $375,000 [(25 ÷ 30) × $1,500,000 × 0.30].

e. *Unamortized flotation cost of old bond.* The firm was amortizing the $400,000 initial flotation cost on the old bond over 30 years. Because only five of the 30 years' amortization of this cost has been applied, the firm can deduct the remaining 25 years of unamortized flotation cost as a lump sum, thereby reducing taxes by $100,000 [(25 ÷ 30) × $400,000 × 0.30].

Summarizing these calculations in Table 13.3, we find the initial investment to be $3,650,000. This means that the Davis Corporation must pay out $3,650,000 now to implement the proposed bond refunding.

---

[4]Technically, the after-tax amount of overlapping interest could be reduced by the after-tax interest earnings from investment of the average proceeds available from the sale of the new bonds during the interest overlap period. To simplify, we ignore any interest earned on the proceeds from sale of the new bonds during the overlap period.

continued

Table 13.3   **Finding the Initial Investment for the Davis Corporation's Bond Refunding Decision**

a. Call premium

Before tax [($1,090 − $1,000) × 50,000 bonds]	$4,500,000	
Less: Taxes (0.30 × $4,500,000)	(1,350,000)	
After-tax cost of call premium		$3,150,000

b. Flotation cost of new bond   450,000

c. Overlapping interest

Before tax [0.09 × (2 ÷ 12) × $50,000,000]	$ 750,000	
Less: Taxes (0.30 × $750,000)	(225,000)	
After-tax cost of overlapping interest		525,000

d. Tax savings from unamortized discount on old bond
[(25 ÷ 30) × ($50,000,000 − $48,500,000) × 0.30]   (375,000)

e. Tax savings from unamortized flotation cost of old bond
[(25 ÷ 30) × $400,000 × 0.30]   (100,000)

Initial investment   **$3,650,000**

Step 2. *Find the annual cash flow savings.* Finding the annual cash flow savings requires a number of calculations.

a. *Interest cost of old bond.* The after-tax annual interest of the old bond is calculated as follows:

Before tax (0.09 × $50,000,000)	$4,500,000
Less: Taxes (0.30 × $4,500,000)	$1,350,000
After-tax interest cost	$3,150,000

b. *Amortization of discount on old bond.* The firm was amortizing the $1,500,000 discount ($50,000,000 par value − $48,500,000 net proceeds from sale) on the old bond over 30 years, resulting in an annual write-off of $50,000 ($1,500,000 ÷ 30). Because it is a tax-deductible noncash charge, the amortization of this discount results in an annual tax savings of $15,000 (0.30 × $50,000).

c. *Amortization of flotation cost on old bond.* The firm was amortizing the $400,000 flotation cost on the old bond over 30 years, resulting in an annual write-off of $13,333 ($400,000 ÷ 30). Because it is a tax-deductible noncash charge, the amortization of the flotation cost results in an annual tax savings of $4,000 (0.30 × $13,333).

d. *Interest cost of new bond.* The after-tax annual interest cost of the new bond is calculated as follows:

Before tax (0.07 × $50,000,000)	$3,500,000
Less: Taxes (0.30 × $3,500,000)	$1,050,000
After-tax interest cost	$2,450,000

e. *Amortization of flotation cost on the new bond.* The firm will amortize the $450,000 flotation cost on the new bond over 25 years, resulting in an annual write-off of $18,000 ($450,000 ÷ 25). Because it is a tax-deductible noncash charge, the amortization of the flotation cost results in an annual tax savings of $5,400 (0.30 × $18,000).

Table 13.4 summarizes these calculations. Combining the first three values [(a), (b), and (c)] yields the annual after-tax debt payment for the old bond of $3,131,000. When the values for the new bond [(d) and (e)] are combined, the annual after-tax debt payment for the new bond is $2,444,600.

Subtracting the new bond's annual after-tax debt payment from that of the old bond, we find that implementation of the proposed bond refunding will result in an annual cash flow savings of $686,400 ($3,131,000 − $2,444,600).

Table 13.4   **Finding the Annual Cash Flow Savings for the Davis Corporation's Bond Refunding Decision**

Old Bond

a. Interest cost

Before tax (0.09 × $50,000,000)	$4,500,000	
Less: Taxes (0.30 × $4,500,000)	(1,350,000)	
After-tax interest cost		$3,150,000

b. Tax savings from amortization of discount
[($1,500,000 ÷ 30) × 0.30]   (15,000)

continued

Table 13.4	**(Continued)**		
	c. Tax savings from amortization of flotation cost		
	[($400,000 ÷ 30) × 0.30]		(4,000)
	(1) Annual after-tax debt payment		$3,131,000
	New Bond		
	d. Interest cost		
	Before tax (0.07 × $50,000,000)	$3,500,000	
	Less: Taxes (0.30 × $3,500,000)	(1,050,000)	
	After-tax interest cost		$2,450,000
	e. Tax savings from amortization of flotation cost		
	[($450,000 ÷ 25) × 0.30]		(5,400)
	(2) Annual after-tax debt payment		$2,444,600
	Annual cash flow savings [(1) − (2)]		**$ 686,400**

Step 3. Find the net present value (NPV). Table 13.5 shows the calculations for determining the *NPV* of the proposed bond refunding. The present value of the annual cash flow savings of $686,400 at the 4.9% after-tax cost of debt over 25 years is computed (using Equation 3.7 on page 87) to be $9,771,792. Subtracting the initial investment of $3,650,000 from the present value of the annual cash flow savings results in a net present value of $6,121,792. Because a positive *NPV* results, the proposed bond refunding is recommended.

Table 13.5   **Finding the Net Present Value of the Davis Corporation's Bond Refunding Decision**

Present value of annual cash flow[a]

$$\$686,400 \times \frac{1}{r}\left[1 - \frac{1}{(1+r)^n}\right] = \$686,400 \times \frac{1}{0.049}\left[1 - \frac{1}{(1.049)^{25}}\right]$$

$$= \$686,400 \times 14.2363 = \qquad \$9,771,792$$

Less: Initial investment (from Table 13.3)	(3,650,000)
Net present value (NPV) of refunding	**$6,121,792**

Decision: The proposed refunding is recommended because the *NPV* of refunding of $6,121,792 is greater than $0.

[a]Annual cash flow savings from Table 13.4 multiplied by a 25-year, 4.9% annuity (Equation 3.7).

13-3 Concept Review Questions

9. What factors should a manager consider when choosing between a term loan and a bond issue for raising long-term debt?

10. What factors might influence the choice between a *serial bond issue* and an issue with a *sinking fund* requirement?

11. What factors, other than the current interest rate at which new debt could be sold, should a manager consider when deciding to refund a bond issue?

13-4 Leasing

leasing
Acquiring use of an asset by agreeing to make a series of periodic, tax-deductible payments.

lessee
Under a lease, the user of the underlying asset who makes regular payments to the *lessor*.

Leasing, like long-term debt, obligates a company to make a series of periodic, tax-deductible payments that may be fixed or variable. You can think of a lease as being comparable to secured long-term debt because in both cases there is an underlying asset tied to the firm's financial obligation. The lessee uses the underlying asset and makes regular payments to the lessor, who retains ownership of the asset. For example, many companies (lessees) lease copy machines from companies like Xerox (lessors), which legally owns the machines residing with the lessees. Leasing can take a number of forms. Here we discuss the basic types of leases, lease arrangements, the lease contract, the lease-versus-purchase decision, the effects of leasing on future financing, and the advantages and disadvantages of leasing.

13-4a Basic Types of Leases

lessor
Under a lease, the owner of the asset who receives regular payments for its use from the *lessee*.

The two basic types of leases available to a business are *operating leases* and *financial leases*. Accountants also use the term *capital leases* to refer to financial leases.

operating lease
A contractual arrangement whereby the lessee agrees to make periodic payments to the lessor, often for five years or less, to obtain an asset's services. The lessee generally receives an option to cancel, and the asset has a useful life longer than the lease term.

Operating Leases   An operating lease is a contractual arrangement whereby the lessee agrees to make periodic payments to the lessor, often for five years or less, to obtain an asset's services. The lessee has the option to cancel the lease by paying a cancellation fee. Assets that are leased under operating leases have useful lives that are longer than the lease's term, although (as with most assets) the economic usefulness of the assets declines over time. Computer systems are prime examples of assets whose relative efficiency diminishes with new technological developments. The operating lease is a common arrangement for obtaining such systems as well as for other relatively short-lived assets, such as copiers or automobiles. When an operating lease expires, the lessee returns the asset to the lessor, who may lease it again or sell it. In some instances, the lease contract will give the lessee the option to purchase the asset when the contract ends. In operating leases, the underlying asset usually has significant market value when the lease ends, and the lessor's original cost generally exceeds the total value of the initial lessee's payments.

financial (or capital) lease
A noncancelable contractual arrangement whereby the lessee agrees to make periodic payments to the lessor, typically for more than five years, to obtain an asset's services. Also called a *capital lease*.

Financial or Capital Leases   A financial (or capital) lease is generally for a longer term than an operating lease. Financial leases are noncancelable and therefore obligate the lessee to make payments over a predefined period. Even if the lessee no longer needs the asset, payments must continue until the lease expires. Financial leases are commonly used for leasing land, buildings, and large pieces of equipment. The noncancelable feature of the financial lease makes it quite similar to certain types of long-term debt, and therefore financial leases are often shown as long-term debt on the lessee's balance sheet. As is the case with debt, failure to make the contractual lease payments can result in bankruptcy for the lessee.

Another distinguishing characteristic of the financial lease is that the total payments over the lease period are greater than the lessor's initial cost. In other words, the lessor earns a return by receiving more than the asset's purchase price. Technically, under Financial Accounting Standards Board (FASB) Standard No. 13, "Accounting for Leases," a financial (or capital) lease is defined as having one of the following elements:

1. The lease transfers ownership of the property to the lessee by the end of the lease term.

2. The lease contains an option to purchase the property at a bargain price. Such an option must be exercisable at a fair market value for the lease to be classified as an operating lease.

3. The lease term is equal to 75% or more of the estimated economic life of the property (exceptions exist for property leased toward the end of its usable economic life).

4. At the beginning of the lease, the present value of the lease payments is equal to 90% or more of the fair market value of the leased property.

Financial leases result in long-term financial commitments by the firm.

13-4b Lease Arrangements

direct lease
A lessor acquires the assets that are leased to a given lessee.

sale-leaseback arrangement
One firm sells an asset to another for cash, then leases the asset back from its new owner.

Lessors use three primary techniques for obtaining assets for leasing. The method selected depends largely on the desires of the prospective lessee. A direct lease results when a lessor acquires the assets to lease out. In other words, the lessee did not previously own the assets that it is leasing. In a sale-leaseback arrangement, one firm sells an asset to another for cash and then leases the asset back from its new owner. You can see the resemblance of this arrangement to a collateralized loan. In such a loan, the lender gives the firm cash up front in exchange for a stream of future payments. If the borrower defaults on those payments, the lender keeps the collateral. In a sale-leaseback, the lessee receives cash immediately (by giving up ownership of the asset) and effectively repays this loan by leasing back the underlying asset. Sale-leaseback arrangements are therefore akin to borrowing and are attractive to firms that need cash for operations.

Leasing arrangements that include one or more third-party lenders are **leveraged leases**. Unlike in direct and sale-leaseback arrangements, the lessor in a leveraged lease acts as an equity participant, supplying on average about 20% of the asset's cost and borrowing the balance of the funds. In recent years, leveraged leases have become especially popular in connection with very expensive assets.

A lease agreement usually specifies whether or not the lessee is responsible for maintenance of the leased assets. Both operating and financial leases generally include **maintenance clauses** specifying who is to maintain the assets and make insurance and tax payments. Under operating leases these costs are typically the lessor's responsibility (for example, a Xerox technician comes to repair a broken copier), whereas under financial leases the lessee is typically responsible for these costs. The lessee often has the option to renew a lease at its expiration. **Renewal options** are especially common in operating leases because their term is generally shorter than the useful life of the leased assets. **Purchase options**, which allow the lessee to purchase the leased asset when the lease expires, occur in both operating and financial leases.

The lessor can be one of a number of parties. With operating leases, the lessor is quite likely to be a manufacturer's leasing subsidiary or an independent leasing company. Financial leases are frequently handled by independent leasing companies or by the leasing subsidiaries of large financial institutions, such as commercial banks and life insurance companies. Life insurance companies are especially active in real estate leasing. Pension funds and commercial banks have recently increased their leasing activities.

13-4c The Lease Contract

The key items in a lease contract generally include a description of the leased assets, the term or duration of the lease, provisions for cancellation, lease payment amounts and dates, provisions for maintenance and associated costs, renewal options, purchase options, and other provisions specified in the lease negotiation process. Furthermore, lease contracts spell out the consequences of the violation of any lease provision by either the lessee or the lessor.

13-4d The Lease-Versus-Purchase Decision

Companies often have to make the **lease-versus-purchase (or lease-versus-buy) decision** when contemplating the acquisition of new assets. The alternatives available are to (1) lease the assets, (2) borrow funds to purchase the assets, or (3) purchase the assets using available liquid resources. Similar financial analysis applies to alternatives (2) and (3). Even if the firm has the liquid resources with which to purchase the assets, using these resources is viewed as equivalent to borrowing. Therefore, we will compare only the leasing and purchasing alternatives.

The lease-versus-purchase decision involves application of the capital budgeting methods presented in Chapters 8 and 9. The analysis can be framed in two different ways, but both approaches yield the same answer if done correctly. In one approach, we first list the cash flows associated with the purchase option and the lease option; then we take the differences in cash flows between the two options and calculate the *NPV* of the incremental cash flow stream discounting at the after-tax cost of debt. The alternative approach is simply to calculate the *NPVs* of the purchase and lease options separately (discounting each at the after-tax cost of debt) and then compare them. Note that either method can be used to determine whether the lease option or the purchase option is better, but neither method addresses whether leasing or purchasing is worthwhile in the first place. (You should perform this analysis separately.)

leveraged lease
A lease under which the lessor acts as an equity participant, supplying on average about 20% of the cost of the asset, and borrowing the balance of the funds.

maintenance clause
A clause in a lease that specifies who is to maintain the assets and make insurance and tax payments.

renewal option
In an operating lease, an option that allows the lessee to renew the lease at its expiration.

purchase option
An option allowing the lessee to purchase the leased asset when the lease expires.

? WHAT TO ASK

Has your firm considered leasing rather than buying some of its fixed assets?

lease-versus-purchase (or lease-versus-buy) decision
The alternatives available are to (1) lease the assets, (2) borrow funds to purchase the assets, or (3) purchase the assets using available liquid resources. Even if the firm has the liquid resources with which to purchase the assets, the use of these funds is viewed as equivalent to borrowing.

That is, the lease-versus-purchase analysis merely allows us to make statements about the *relative* merits of leasing versus buying.

The following Example demonstrates application of both approaches—(1) calculating the *NPV* of the incremental lease-versus-purchase cash flows and (2) separately calculating the *NPV*s of the lease and purchase option cash flows and comparing them.

EXAMPLE

ClumZee Movers has already conducted a standard *NPV* analysis and determined that acquiring a new delivery truck would increase firm value. Now, ClumZee needs to decide whether to lease or purchase the truck.

The truck costs $25,000 and will reduce operating costs by $4,500 annually over its five-year life. If ClumZee buys the truck, then it will be depreciated on a straight-line basis, and the truck will have no resale value after five years. Alternatively, the firm can lease the truck for $6,300 per year (with payments at the end of each year). The lease payments are tax-deductible. ClumZee faces a 35% tax rate, and its pre-tax cost of debt is 8%.

Table 13.6 shows the cash flows for both the lease and the purchase option. Under either scenario, the firm realizes $4,500 in savings each year, or $2,925 after taxes [$4,500 × (1 − 35%)]. Under the purchase option, the firm has a large initial cash outflow, but it can deduct $5,000 per year in depreciation, saving $1,750 in taxes each year ($5,000 × 35%). With the lease option, the firm pays $6,300 per year before taxes, or $4,095 after taxes [$6,300 × (1 − 35%)]. Subtracting the net cash flows associated with the purchase option from those tied to the leasing decision and then discounting them at the after-tax cost of debt of 5.2% [8% × (1 − 35%)], we obtain the following incremental *NPV* of leasing versus purchasing:

$$NPV = \$25,000 - \frac{\$5,845}{(1.052)^1} - \frac{\$5,845}{(1.052)^2} - \frac{\$5,845}{(1.052)^3} - \frac{\$5,845}{(1.052)^4} - \frac{\$5,845}{(1.052)^5}$$

$$= -\$166$$

The *NPV* is negative and so the incremental benefits of purchasing exceed those of leasing. Therefore, ClumZee *should purchase the truck* they need.

Table 13.6 **Lease vs. Purchase Analysis for ClumZee Movers: After-Tax Cash Flows ($)**

	Lease Option			Purchase Option				Lease-Purchase Option
Year	Cost Savings	Lease Payment	Net Cash Flow	Purchase Price	Cost Savings	Depreciation Tax Shield	Net Cash Flow	Net Cash Flow
0	$0	$0	$0	−$25,000	$0	$0	−$25,000	$25,000
1	$2,925	−$4,095	−$1,170		$2,925	$1,750	$ 4,675	−$ 5,845
2	$2,925	−$4,095	−$1,170		$2,925	$1,750	$ 4,675	−$ 5,845
3	$2,925	−$4,095	−$1,170		$2,925	$1,750	$ 4,675	−$ 5,845
4	$2,925	−$4,095	−$1,170		$2,925	$1,750	$ 4,675	−$ 5,845
5	$2,925	−$4,095	−$1,170		$2,925	$1,750	$ 4,675	−$ 5,845

We could reach the same decision by calculating the NPVs of the lease option and the purchase option separately and choosing the one with the higher *NPV*.

$$NPV(\text{Lease}) = -\frac{\$1,170}{(1.052)^1} - \frac{\$1,170}{(1.052)^2} - \cdots - \frac{\$1,170}{(1.052)^5} = -\$5,037$$

$$NPV(\text{Purchase}) = -25,000 + \frac{\$4,675}{(1.052)^1} + \frac{\$4,675}{(1.052)^2} + \cdots + \frac{\$4,675}{(1.052)^5} = -\$4,871$$

The purchase option is $166 [−$5,037 − (−$4,871)] less expensive than the lease option. Because the purchase option's *NPV* is $166 larger and the benefits are the same for both options, the purchase option is less costly and therefore, ClumZee should purchase the truck rather than lease it. (Note: ClumZee initially stated that acquiring the new delivery truck would increase firm value, so here the firm has merely determined the least expensive method of financing the purchase.)

It is worth noting that if the lessee and lessor have the same discount rate and same tax rates, then leasing strictly for financial reasons is a zero-sum game between lessee and lessor. Cash outflows for the lessee represent inflows for the lessor, and vice versa. Only when the two parties have different tax rates or costs of capital can leasing increase aggregate value purely for financial reasons. Therefore, the lower cost of leasing or buying results from factors such as the differing tax brackets of the

Finance in Your Life

Should I Lease or Buy the Car?

Once you have done the necessary research, found the best car to buy, and negotiated the lowest purchase price, you must decide how best to pay for it. For most buyers this financing decision involves a choice between (1) leasing the car or (2) borrowing to buy the car. Let's assume that you are buying a new car, have no trade-in, have negotiated an out-the-door price of $24,500, and that you can safely earn 5% annual interest net of taxes paid on that interest. In addition, you have gathered the following data on the lease and the purchase alternatives.

Lease	
Down payment	$2,000
Lease term	48 months
Lease payment	$375 per month

Purchase	
Down payment	$3,000
Loan maturity	48 months
Loan payment	$525 per month
Estimated trade-in value of car at end 48 months	$10,750

Using the above data, we can perform a lease-versus-purchase analysis for the car. To simplify, we ignore sales tax differences and explicit consideration of the time value of money, and we assume that under the purchase alternative the car will be sold at the end of four years (48 months).

Lease Cost	
Down payment	$ 2,000
Total lease payments (48 months × $375 per month)	18,000
Opportunity cost of down payment (0.05 × $2,000 × 4 years)	400
Total Cost of Lease	**$20,400**

Purchase Cost	
Down payment	$ 3,000
Total loan payments (48 months × $525 per month)	25,200
Opportunity cost of down payment (0.05 × $3,000 × 4 years)	600
Estimated trade-in value of car at end of 48 months	−10,750
Total Cost of Purchase	**$18,050**

Comparing the total lease and total purchase costs, we see that the purchase cost of $18,050 is well below the lease cost of $20,400. Therefore, **you should purchase the car; as a result, you will save about $2,350 ($20,400 lease cost − $18,050 purchase cost) over the four years.**

lessor and the lessee, different tax treatments for leases versus purchases, and differing risks and borrowing costs for the lessor and the lessee. Moreover, when making a lease-versus-purchase decision, the firm will find that inexpensive borrowing opportunities and high required lessor returns increase the attractiveness of purchasing. Likewise, leasing decisions are affected by many nonfinancial factors such as the risk of obsolescence and the experience and expertise of the lessor. Subjective factors like these must be included in the decision-making process. Like most financial decisions, the lease-versus-purchase decision requires a certain degree of judgment and consideration of qualitative factors.

13-4e Effects of Leasing on Future Financing

Because leasing is considered a type of debt financing, it affects a firm's future financing ability. Lease payments are shown as a tax-deductible expense on the firm's income statement. Anyone analyzing the income statement would probably recognize that assets are being leased, although the actual details of the amounts and terms of the leases might be unclear. The following sections discuss the lease disclosure requirements established by the Financial Accounting Standards Board (FASB) and the effect of leases on financial ratios.

Lease Disclosure Requirements Standard No. 13 of the FASB, "Accounting for Leases," requires explicit disclosure of financial (capital) lease obligations on the firm's balance sheet. Such a lease must be shown as a *capitalized lease*, meaning that the present value of all its payments is included as an asset and corresponding liability on the firm's balance sheet. An operating lease, on the other hand, need not be capitalized, but its basic features must be disclosed in a footnote to the financial statements. Standard No. 13, of course, establishes detailed guidelines to be used in capitalizing leases to reflect them as an asset and corresponding liability on the balance sheet. Subsequent standards have further refined lease capitalization and disclosure procedures, as the following Example shows.

EXAMPLE

Altmont Company, a manufacturer of printing equipment, is leasing an asset under a ten-year lease requiring annual beginning-of-year payments of $15,000. The lease can be capitalized merely by calculating the present value of the lease payments over the life of the lease. However, the rate at which the payments should be discounted must be determined.[5] If a 10% discount rate is used, then the present (or capitalized) value of the lease is found by multiplying the annual lease payment by the expression for a ten-year, 10% annuity due (Equation 3.8 on page 88). This value of

$$\$101,385 \left[\$15,000 \times \frac{1}{0.10} \times \left[1 - \frac{1}{(1.10)^{10}} \right] \times (1.10) \right]$$ would be shown as an asset and corresponding liability on the firm's balance sheet to

reflect the firm's financial position.

Leasing and Financial Ratios Because the consequences of missing a financial lease payment are the same as those for missing an interest or principal payment on debt, a financial analyst must view the lease as a long-term financial commitment of the lessee, analogous to debt. With FASB Standard No. 13, the inclusion of each financial (capital) lease as an asset and corresponding liability (i.e., long-term debt) provides for a balance sheet that more accurately reflects the firm's financial status. It thereby permits various types of financial ratio analyses to be performed directly on the statement in a manner that captures all of the firm's fixed obligations and indebtedness. Note also that because $1 of leasing commitment is very similar to $1 of debt financing, we can think of lease financing as being similar to using 100% debt to finance the acquisition of a given asset. The cost of capital associated with 100% debt financing is the after-tax cost of debt (to see this, consider the weighted average cost of capital formula, found in Equation 10.4 in Chapter 10, when only debt is used). Therefore, because of this similarity between leasing and using 100% debt financing, the after-tax cost of debt is often used as the discount rate when calculating present values in lease analysis, like our analysis in Section 13-4d above.

13-4f Advantages and Disadvantages of Leasing

Leasing has a number of commonly cited advantages and disadvantages that should be considered when making a lease-versus-purchase decision. Although not all these advantages and disadvantages hold in every case, several of them may apply in any given situation.

---

[5]In Standard No. 13, the FASB established certain guidelines for the appropriate discount rate to use when capitalizing leases. Most commonly, the rate used is equal to the rate the lessee would have incurred if funds were borrowed to buy the asset with a secured loan under terms similar to the lease repayment schedule. This simply represents the before-tax cost of a secured loan.

Commonly Cited Advantages

1. Leasing allows the lessee, in effect, to depreciate land, which is prohibited if the land were purchased. Because the lessee who leases land is permitted to deduct the total lease payment as an expense for tax purposes, the effect is analogous to the firm purchasing the land and then depreciating it.

2. The use of sale-leaseback arrangements may permit the firm to increase its liquidity by converting an asset into cash, which can then be used as working capital. A firm short of working capital or in a liquidity bind can sell an owned asset to a lessor and then lease the asset back for a specified number of years.

3. Leasing provides 100% financing. Most loan agreements for the purchase of fixed assets require the borrower to pay a portion of the purchase price as a down payment. Therefore, the borrower is able to borrow (at most) only 90% to 95% of the purchase price of most assets and often less. Of course, this extra borrowing through leasing may reduce the firm's remaining borrowing capacity.

4. When a firm becomes bankrupt or is reorganized, the maximum claim of lessors against the corporation is three years of lease payments—and the lessor, of course, reclaims the asset. If debt is used to purchase an asset, the creditors have a claim that is equal to the total outstanding loan balance. The lessor also has higher priority in bankruptcy than do most of the lessee's other creditors, and, therefore, the lessor can initially charge a little bit less for bankruptcy risk than other creditors would have to charge.

5. In a lease arrangement, the firm may avoid the cost of obsolescence if the lessor fails to accurately anticipate the obsolescence of assets and sets the lease payment too low. This is especially true in the case of operating leases, which generally have relatively short lives. Of course, the lessee may pay for this expected benefit in the form of a higher lease payment.

6. A lessee avoids many of the negative covenants that are usually included as part of a long-term loan. Requirements with respect to the sale of accounts receivable, subsequent borrowing, business combinations, and so on are not generally found in lease agreements.

7. In the case of low-cost assets that are infrequently acquired, leasing—especially through operating leases—may provide the firm with needed financing flexibility. That is, the firm does not have to arrange other financing for these assets and can obtain them with relative convenience through a lease.

Commonly Cited Disadvantages

1. A lease does not have a stated interest cost. In cases where the return to the lessor is quite high, the firm might be better off borrowing to purchase the asset.

2. At the end of the term of the lease agreement, the lessor realizes the asset's salvage value, if any. If the lessee had purchased the asset, it could have claimed the asset's salvage value. Of course, in a competitive leasing market, if the lessor expects a higher salvage value then the lease payments would be lower.

3. Under a lease, the lessee is generally prohibited from making improvements to the leased property or asset without the lessor's approval. If the property were owned outright, this difficulty would not arise. Of course, lessors generally encourage leasehold improvements that are expected to enhance the asset's salvage value.

4. If a lessee leases an asset that subsequently becomes obsolete, it still must make lease payments over the remaining term of the lease. This is true even if the asset is unusable.

13-4 Concept Review Questions

12. Why is it considered important whether a lease is classified as an *operating lease* or as a *financial (or capital) lease*?

13. What factors should be considered when deciding between leasing an asset or borrowing funds to purchase the asset?

Summary

- Long-term debt and leasing are important sources of capital for businesses. Long-term debt can take the form of term loans or bonds. The characteristics of each can be tailored to meet the needs of both the borrower and the lender.

- The conditions of a term loan are specified in the loan agreement. This agreement specifies the rights and responsibilities of both lender and borrower, and the agreement typically lists several positive and negative covenants that the borrower must not violate.

- Syndicated loans are large-denomination credits arranged for a single borrower by a syndicate of institutional lenders, primarily commercial banks. These have been increasing in importance in recent years because very large loans can be arranged quickly and inexpensively and can have flexible borrowing terms.

- The conditions of a bond issue are specified in the bond indenture and are enforced by a trustee. These legal agreements are highly detailed and not easily modified, because bonds are held by many investors. In contrast, privately placed loan terms can be modified rather easily, because the borrower can negotiate directly with one creditor or a relatively small number of creditors.

- Frequently when interest rates drop, bond issuers make refunding decisions, which involve determining the *NPV* associated with calling outstanding bonds and issuing new bonds with lower-interest-coupons to replace the refunded bonds.

- Leasing serves as an alternative to borrowing funds to purchase an asset. Operating leases are described in a footnote to a firm's balance sheet, whereas financial lease obligations must be shown on the balance sheet as an asset and corresponding liability. Firms often make lease-versus-purchase decisions, which involve choosing the alternative with the lower present value of cash outflows.

- Leasing affects a firm's future financing ability. Financial analysts view leases as long-term financial commitments. A variety of advantages and disadvantages of leasing are commonly cited.

Key Terms

balloon payment, 406
bearer bonds, 413
call premium, 415
collateral, 406
collateral trust bonds, 408
convertible bonds, 411
cross-default covenant, 403
debentures, 408
direct lease, 418
equipment trust certificates, 408
Eurobond, 412
Eurocurrency loan market, 407
fallen angels, 412
financial (or capital) lease, 418
fixed-rate offerings, 402
floating-rate issues, 402
foreign bond, 414

high-yield bonds, 412
income bonds, 408
indenture, 409
investment-grade bonds, 412
junk bonds, 412
lease-versus-purchase (or
    lease-versus-buy) decision, 419
leasing, 417
lessee, 417
lessor, 418
leveraged lease, 419
lien, 406
loans, 402
maintenance clause, 419
mortgage bonds, 408
operating lease, 418
private placements, 402

project finance (PF) loans, 407
purchase option, 419
refund, 414
renewal option, 419
sale-leaseback arrangement, 418
serial bonds, 414
sinking fund, 409
speculative bonds, 412
stand-alone companies, 407
stock purchase warrants, 406
subordinated debenture, 408
subordination, 403
syndicated loan, 407
term loan, 406
trustee (bond), 411

Self-Test Problems

Answers to Self-Test Problems and the Concept Review Questions throughout the chapter appear in CourseMate with SmartFinance Tools at **www.cengagebrain.com**.

ST13-1. The initial proceeds per bond, the size of the issue, the initial maturity of the bond, and the years remaining to maturity are shown in the following table for a number of bonds. Each bond has a $1,000 par value, and the issuing firm is in the 35% tax bracket.

Bond	Proceeds per Bond	Size of Issue	Initial Maturity of Bond	Years Remaining to Maturity
A	$ 975	50,000 bonds	10 years	5 years
B	1,020	25,000	20	15
C	1,000	100,000	25	12

a. Indicate whether each bond was sold at a discount, at a premium, or at its par value.
b. Determine the total discount or premium for each issue.
c. Determine the annual amount of discount or premium amortized for each bond.
d. Calculate the unamortized discount or premium for each bond.
e. Determine the after-tax cash flow associated with the retirement now of each of these bonds, using the values developed in part (d).

ST13-2. The principal, coupon interest rate, and interest overlap period are shown in the following table for several different bonds.

Bond	Principal	Coupon Interest Rate	Interest Overlap Period
A	$ 15,000,000	6.5%	2 months
B	20,000,000	7.0	3
C	15,000,000	6.0	4
D	100,000,000	8.0	6

a. Calculate the dollar amount of interest that must be paid for each bond during the interest overlap period.
b. Calculate the after-tax cost of overlapping interest for each bond if the firm is in the 40% tax bracket.

ST13-3. Well-Sprung Corporation is considering offering a new $100 million bond issue to replace an outstanding $100 million bond issue. The firm wishes to take advantage of the decline in interest rates that has occurred since the original issue. The two bond issues are described in what follows. The firm is in the 30% tax bracket.

Old bonds. The outstanding bonds have a $1,000 par value and an 8.5% coupon interest rate. They were issued five years ago with a twenty-year maturity. They were initially sold at a $30 per bond discount, and a $750,000 floatation cost was incurred. They are callable at $1,085.

New bonds. The new bonds would have a fifteen-year maturity, a par value of $1,000, and a 7.0% coupon interest rate. It is expected that these bonds can be sold at par for a floatation cost of $600,000. The firm expects a three-month period of overlapping interest while it retires the old bonds.

a. Calculate the initial investment that is required to call the old bonds and issue the new bonds.
b. Calculate the annual cash flow savings, if any, expected from the proposed bond-refunding decision.
c. If the firm uses its 4.9% after-tax cost of debt to evaluate low-risk decisions, find the net present value (NPV) of the bond-refunding decision. Would you recommend the proposed refunding? Explain your answer.

ST13-4. Strident Corporation is attempting to determine whether to lease or purchase a new telephone system. The firm is in the 40% tax bracket, and its after-tax cost of debt is currently 4.5%. The terms of the lease and the purchase are as follows:

Lease. Annual beginning-of-year lease payments of $22,000 are required over the five-year life of the lease. The lessee will exercise its option to purchase the asset for $30,000, to be paid along with the final lease payment.

Purchase. The $100,000 cost of the telephone system can be financed entirely with a 7.5% loan (pre-tax) requiring annual end-of-year payments of $24,716 for five years. The firm in this case will depreciate the equipment using the straight-line method over five years. The firm plans to keep the equipment and use it beyond its five-year recovery period.

a. Calculate the after-tax cash outflows associated with each alternative.

b. Calculate the present value of each cash outflow stream using the after-tax cost of debt.

c. Which alternative—lease or purchase—would you recommend? Why?

Questions

Q13-1. Comment on the following proposition: The use of floating-rate debt eliminates interest rate risk (the risk that interest payment amounts will change in the future) for both the borrower and the lender.

Q13-2. What purpose do *loan covenants* serve in a debt agreement? What factors should a manager consider when negotiating covenants?

Q13-3. List and briefly discuss the key features that distinguish long-term debt issues from each other.

Q13-4. Define the following: term loan, balloon payment, collateral, and stock purchase warrants.

Q13-5. What is a *syndicated loan*? Why have these loans proven so popular with corporate borrowers?

Q13-6. What is a *project finance (PF) loan*? What role does a stand-alone company play in the typical project finance deal?

Q13-7. What is a *debenture*? Why do you think that this is the most common form of corporate bond in the United States but is much less commonly used elsewhere?

Q13-8. How do *sinking funds* reduce default risk?

Q13-9. What is a *trustee*? Why do bondholders insist that a trustee be included in all public bond offerings? Why are these less necessary in private debt placements?

Q13-10. What impact has adoption of *Rule 144A* had on debt-issuance patterns in the United States?

Q13-11. Why are most corporate bonds callable? Who benefits from this feature, and what is the cost of adopting a call provision in a public bond issue?

Q13-12. Why do corporations have their debt rated? Compare the role played by rating agencies and a company's outside auditors.

Q13-13. What does *investment grade* mean in the context of corporate bond issues? How do these bonds differ from *junk bonds*, and why have the latter proven so popular with investors?

Q13-14. What is a *Eurobond*? Why did these bonds come into existence? Why do Eurobond investors like the fact that these are typically "bearer bonds"? What risk does an investor run from holding bearer bonds rather than registered bonds?

Q13-15. Explain how uncertainty concerning future interest rates would affect the decision to refund a bond issue.

Q13-16. Define the following: direct lease, sale-leaseback arrangement, leveraged lease, and financial (capital) lease. What elements must be included in a lease in order for it to be considered a financial (capital) lease?

Q13-17. How would the availability of floating-rate debt affect the lease-versus-purchase decision?

Q13-18. For acquiring an asset, what are the key advantages of leasing as compared to borrowing? What are the key disadvantages of leasing?

Problems

Corporate Bonds

P13-1. The initial proceeds per bond, the size of the issue, the initial maturity of the bond, and the years remaining to maturity are shown in the following table for a number of bonds. In each case the bond has a $1,000 par value, and the issuing firm is in the 40% tax bracket.

Bond	Proceeds per Bond	Size of Issue	Initial Maturity of Bond	Years Remaining to Maturity
A	$ 985	10,000 bonds	20 years	15 years
B	1,025	20,000	25	16
C	1,000	22,500	12	9
D	960	5,000	25	15
E	1,035	10,000	30	16

a. Indicate whether each bond was sold at a discount, at a premium, or at its par value.
b. Determine the total discount or premium for each issue.
c. Determine the annual amount of discount or premium amortized for each bond.
d. Calculate the unamortized discount or premium for each bond.
e. Determine the after-tax cash flow associated with the retirement now of each of these bonds, using the values developed in part (d).

P13-2. For each of the callable bond issues in the following table, calculate the after-tax cost of calling the issue. Each bond has a $1,000 par value, and the various issue sizes and call prices are shown in the following table. The issuing firm is in the 40% tax bracket.

Bond	Size of Issue	Call Price
A	12,000 bonds	$1,050
B	20,000	1,030
C	30,000	1,015
D	50,000	1,050
E	100,000	1,045
F	500,000	1,060

P13-3. The floatation cost, the initial maturity, and the number of years remaining to maturity are shown in the following table for a number of bonds. The issuing firm is in the 40% tax bracket.

Bond	Floatation Cost	Initial Maturity of Bond	Years Remaining to Maturity
A	$250,000	30 years	22 years
B	500,000	15	5
C	125,000	20	10
D	750,000	10	1
E	650,000	15	6

a. Calculate the annual amortization of the flotation cost for each bond.
b. Determine the tax savings, if any, expected to result from the unamortized floatation cost of each bond if it were called today.

P13-4. The principal, coupon interest rate, and interest overlap period are shown in the following table for five different bonds.

Bond	Principal	Coupon Interest Rate	Interest Overlap Period
A	$ 5,000,000	8.0%	3 months
B	40,000,000	7.0	2
C	50,000,000	6.5	3
D	100,000,000	9.0	6
E	20,000,000	5.5	1

a.   Calculate the dollar amount of interest that must be paid for each bond during the interest over-lap period.

b.   Calculate the after-tax cost of overlapping interest for each bond if the firm is in the 40% tax bracket.

P13-5.   Schooner Company is contemplating offering a new $50 million bond issue to replace an outstanding $50 million bond issue. The firm wishes to take advantage of the decline in interest rates that has occurred since the initial bond issuance. The old and new bonds are described in what follows. The firm is in the 40% tax bracket.

Old bonds. The outstanding bonds have a $1,000 par value and a 9% coupon interest rate. They were issued five years ago with a twenty-year maturity. They were initially sold for their par value of $1,000, and the firm incurred $350,000 in flotation costs. They are callable at $1,090.

New bonds. The new bonds would have a $1,000 par value, a 7% coupon interest rate, and a fifteen-year maturity. They could be sold at their par value. The flotation cost of the new bonds would be $500,000. The firm does not expect to have any overlapping interest.

a.   Calculate the tax savings that are expected from the unamortized portion or the old bonds' flotation cost.

b.   Calculate the annual tax savings from the floatation cost of the new bonds, assuming the fifteen-year amortization.

c.   Calculate the after-tax cost of the call premium that is required to retire the old bonds.

d.   Determine the initial investment that is required to call the old bonds and issue the new bonds.

e.   Calculate the annual cash flow savings, if any, that are expected from the proposed bond refunding decision.

f.   If the firm has a 4.2% after-tax cost of debt, find the net present value (*NPV*) of the bond refunding decision. Would you recommend the proposed refunding? Explain your answer.

P13-6.   High-Gearing Incorporated is considering offering a new $40 million bond issue to replace an outstanding $40 million bond issue. The firm wishes to thereby take advantage of the decline in interest rates that has occurred since the original issue. The two bond issues are described in what follows. The firm is in the 40% tax bracket.

Old bonds. The outstanding bonds have a $1,000 par value and a 10% coupon interest rate. They were issued five years ago with a twenty-five-year maturity. They were initially sold at a $25 per bond discount, and a $200,000 flotation cost was incurred. They are callable at $1,100.

New bonds. The new bonds would have a twenty-year maturity, a par value of $1,000, and a 7.5% coupon interest rate. It is expected that these bonds can be sold at par for a flotation cost of $250,000. The firm expects a three-month period of overlapping interest while it retires the old bonds.

a.   Calculate the initial investment that is required to call the old bonds and issue the new bonds.

b.   Calculate the annual cash flow savings, if any, expected from the proposed bond refunding decision.

c.   If the firm uses its 4.5% after-tax cost of debt to evaluate low-risk decisions, find the net present value (*NPV*) of the bond refunding decision. Would you recommend the proposed refunding? Explain your answer.

P13-7.   Web Tools Company is considering using the proceeds from a new $50 million bond issue to call and retire its outstanding $50 million bond issue. The details of both bond issues are outlined in what follows. The firm is in the 40% tax bracket.

Old bonds. The firm's old issue has a coupon interest rate of 10%, was issued four years ago, and had a twenty-year maturity. The bonds sold at a $10 discount from their $1,000 par value, floatation costs were $420,000, and their call price is $1,100.

New bonds. The new bonds are expected to sell at par ($1,000), have a sixteen-year maturity, and have floatation costs of $520,000. The firm will have a two-month period of overlapping interest while it retires the old bonds.

a.   What is the initial investment that is required to call the old bonds and issue the new bonds?

b.   What are the annual cash flow savings, if any, from the proposed bond refunding decision if the new bonds have an 8% coupon interest rate? If the new bonds have a 9% coupon interest rate?

c.   Construct a table showing the net present value (*NPV*) of refunding under the two circumstances given in part (b) when (1) the firm's after-tax cost of debt is 4.8% $[0.08 \times (1 - 0.40)]$ and (2) this cost is 5.4% $[0.09 \times (1 - 0.40)]$.

d. Given the circumstances described in part (c), discuss when refunding would be favorable and when it would not.

e. If the four circumstances summarized in your answer to part (d) were equally probable (each had a probability of 25%), would you recommend refunding? Explain your answer.

Leasing

P13-8. Given the lease payments and terms shown in the following table, determine the yearly after-tax cash outflows for each firm. Assume that lease payments are made at the *beginning of each year*, that the firm is in the 40% tax bracket, and that no purchase option exists.

Firm	Annual Lease Payment	Term of Lease
A	$ 250,000	5 years
B	160,000	12
C	500,000	8
D	1,000,000	20
E	25,000	6

P13-9. GMS Corporation is attempting to determine whether to lease or purchase research equipment. The firm is in the 40% tax bracket, and its after-tax cost of debt is currently 6%. The terms of the lease and the purchase are as follows:

Lease. Annual beginning-of-year lease payments of $93,500 are required over the three-year life of the lease. The lessee will exercise its option to purchase the asset for $25,000, to be paid along with the final lease payment.

Purchase. The $250,000 cost of the research equipment can be financed entirely with a 10% loan (pre-tax) requiring annual end-of-year payments of $100,529 for three years. The firm in this case will depreciate the equipment using the straight-line method for three years. The firm plans to keep the equipment and use it beyond its three-year recovery period.

a. Calculate the after-tax cash outflows associated with each alternative.

b. Calculate the present value of each cash outflow stream using the after-tax cost of debt.

c. Which alternative—lease or purchase—would you recommend? Why?

P13-10. Eastern Trucking Company needs to expand its facilities. In order to do so, the firm must acquire a machine costing $80,000. The machine can be leased or purchased. The firm is in the 40% tax bracket, and its after-tax cost of debt is 5.4%. The terms of the lease and purchase plans are as follows:

Lease. The leasing arrangement requires beginning-of-year payments of $16,900 over five years. The lessee will exercise its option to purchase the asset for $20,000, to be paid along with the final lease payment.

Purchase. If the firm purchases the machine, its cost of $80,000 will be financed with a five-year, 9% loan (pre-tax) requiring equal end-of-year payments of $20,567. The machine will be depreciated on a straight-line basis for five yeas. The firm plans to keep the equipment and use it beyond its five-year recovery period.

a. Determine the after-tax cash outflows of Eastern Trucking under each alternative.

b. Find the present value of the after-tax cash outflows for each alternative using the after-tax cost of debt.

c. Which alternative—lease or purchase—would you recommend? Why?

P13-11. Given the lease payments, years remaining until the leases expires, and discount rates shown in the following table, calculate the capitalized value of each lease. Assume that lease payments are made at the beginning of each year.

Lease	Lease Payment	Remaining Term	Discount Rate
A	$ 40,000	12 years	10%
B	120,000	8	12
C	9,000	18	14
D	16,000	3	9
E	47,000	20	11

THOMSON REUTERS | Business School Edition

For instructions on using Thomson ONE, refer to the instructions provided with the Thomson ONE problems at the end of Chapters 1–6.

P13-12. Analyze the long-term debt of General Electric Company (ticker: GE), Caterpillar, Inc. (CAT), and Ford Motor Company (F) relative to total assets over the last ten years. How has long-term debt changed over this period? Do the companies appear to maintain a certain level of long-term debt?

Since these exercises depend upon real-time data, your answers will change continuously depending upon when you access the Internet to download your data.

Smart Ideas Video

Ed Altman, New York University

"Probably about 75% of the bonds are investment grade; that's BBB or higher."

Annette Poulsen, University of Georgia

"The covenant is the promise about what the corporation is going to do or not do."

Benjamin Esty, Harvard University

"The syndicated loan market is now the largest single source of corporate funds in the world."

Mini-Case

Long-Term Debt and Leasing

The CFO of your firm asks you to review the long-term debt position of the company to decide if the company should make any changes in its borrowing arrangements. Before conducting this review, you decide to bring yourself up to date on terminology and types of long-term borrowing arrangements. Therefore, as a start, you decide to answer the following questions.

Assignment

1. What types of debt covenants might managers consider?

2. What are the major factors that affect the cost or interest rate of a debt instrument?

3. What are *term loans,* and what are their characteristics?

4. What are *syndicated loans,* and what are their primary applications?

5. What are some of the legal arrangements used to protect lenders related to corporate bonds?

6. What are some of the general features of corporate bonds?

7. What options are available for a firm that wishes to avoid a large single repayment of principal in the future or to refund a bond prior to maturity?

8. In what ways are leases similar to long-term debt?

9. What are the two basic types of leases?

10. What are the advantages and disadvantages of leasing?

chapter 14

Payout Policy

What Companies Do

Dividend Payouts Are Growing: Starbucks Announces Its First Dividend

In the first quarter of 2010, companies included in the Standard & Poors 500 Index posted the biggest gain in dividend rates in over two years. The gain was attributed to improving confidence following the economy's big downturn in 2008 and 2009. During the quarter, the S&P companies announced planned dividend payments in excess of $4.4 billion, the largest amount since they announced $6.7 billion in the fourth quarter of 2007. One cause of the increased payouts was believed to be that a build up of cash relative to the market values of many firms led them to return a portion of profits to their shareholders.

Starbucks is a good example of one of these dividend payers. After two years of layoffs and store closings, in the first quarter of 2010, it issued its first-ever dividend. Howard Schultz, company founder and CEO at the time, announced that the firm's ambitious turnaround had sliced $580 million from its expenses and that the turnaround was taking hold. He also indicated that beyond the announced 10 cent per share dividend, the company planned to ultimately boost that payment to as much as 40% of its annual profit and expand its effort to buy back its own shares. As many analysts suggest, it appears that Starbucks has matured beyond the fast-growth stage and as a result will likely implement plans to distribute cash to its shareholders through both dividends and share repurchases. This behavior exemplifies that of a long-term profitable firm that has matured.

Sources: "S&P 500 Dividend Rates Post Biggest Gain in Over Two Years," *The Wall Street Journal*, March 19, 2010, WSJ.com, www.blogs.wsj.com/marketbeat/2010/03/19/sp-500-dividend-rates-post-biggest-gain-in-over-two-years/tab/print/; "After Starbucks Dividend, Who's Next?", *The Wall Street Journal*, March 24, 2010, WSJ.com, www.blogs.wsj.com/marketbeat/2010/03/24/after-starbucks-dividend-whos-next/; Ashley M. Heher, "Starbucks to Pay First Dividend, Expands Buyback," Associated Press, March 24, 2010, www.finance.yahoo.com/news/Starbucks-to-pay-first-apf-954916568.html?x=0&.v=6.

Learning Objectives

After studying this chapter you should be able to:

- Discuss the fundamentals of payout policy, including cash dividend payment procedures, types of policies, and share repurchases;
- Describe some of the key factors affecting dividend and share repurchase decisions;
- Understand why payout policy is irrelevant in a world with perfect capital markets;
- Review the arguments for dividend relevance in the imperfect (real) world, including agency and signaling models;
- Review real-world influences on payout policy such as taxes, transactions costs, and uncertainty; and,
- Summarize key lessons regarding payout policy.

A firm's payout policy describes the choices its managers make about distributing cash to shareholders. These choices include whether to pay shareholders a regular (recurring) dividend or a one-time "special" dividend, whether to repurchase outstanding shares, and what size the cash distribution should be. In firms with a history of paying dividends, managers must decide if their firm should maintain their current payouts or change them. Managers tend to increase regular dividends only when they expect that future cash flow will be sufficient to pay the dividends and to meet their firm's other financial needs. Firms must also weigh the stock market's reaction to changes in dividend policy. Influencing that reaction are factors such as the current level of a firm's dividends, the volatility of the dividend stream over time, and the income taxes investors must pay when they receive dividends. As you can see, the many dimensions of this problem can make payout policy decisions quite difficult.

In recent years phenomenal growth has been observed in both the number of firms implementing share repurchase programs and in the total value of these programs. Companies that announce a share repurchase program state that they will buy some of their own shares over a period of time. Firms usually repurchase shares through purchases on the open market, though targeted repurchases directly from large shareholders are also possible. In executing a repurchase program, firms distribute some of the cash they have accumulated to investors who want to sell their shares. Therefore, dividends and share repurchases are alternative means by which firms pay out cash to investors. In fact, the annual value of share repurchases in the United States sometimes exceeds that of cash dividends.

It is important to keep in mind that a firm's dividend policy is not independent from its other financing and investment decisions. For example, for a firm that has at least some debt, paying a dividend decreases the firm's equity and therefore raises its debt ratio. A firm that decides to distribute cash to shareholders via a dividend or share repurchase may increase the likelihood that it will have to raise external financing in the future. In fact, it is not unusual for the same firm to pay a dividend, repurchase shares, borrow money, and issue new common stock all in the same year. It should be no surprise then that some of the same issues that arise when we think about capital structure decisions are also important in setting dividend policy.

Our objective in this chapter is to answer two basic questions. First, does payout policy matter? (Can managers increase or decrease the total market value of a firm's securities by changing its payouts?) Second, if payout policy does matter, how should managers set payouts to maximize firm value? Before attacking these questions, in Section 14-1 we provide a brief overview of payout policy fundamentals and in Section 14-2 we discuss the factors affecting dividend and share repurchase decisions. Section 14-3 shows that payouts are irrelevant in a world of perfect (frictionless) capital markets, which suggests that dividends and share repurchases exist because of some imperfection in markets or human nature. Section 14-4 describes various real-world market imperfections that affect actual payout policy decisions. Finally, Section 14-5 presents a payout policy checklist and summarizes key payout policy lessons.

●14-1 Payout Policy Fundamentals

payout policy
The choices managers make about distributing a firm's cash—paying regular or "special" dividends or repurchasing stock—to shareholders.

share repurchase programs
Programs in which companies will buy some of their own shares over a period of time, usually on the open market.

In Chapter 5, we argued that the value of a share of stock equals the present value of the cash flows the shareholder receives over time. Even though a company is not paying dividends or repurchasing shares today, its market value reflects the likelihood that the firm will either pay dividends or repurchase shares in the future or be acquired by another company, at a price that reflects a higher stream of cash payments. To provide an understanding of the fundamentals of payout policy, we begin with a discussion of the procedures for paying cash dividends and the factors affecting dividend policy.

14-1a Cash Dividend Payment Procedures

In the United States, as in most countries, shareholders do not have a legal right to receive dividends. Instead, a firm's board of directors must decide whether to pay

dividend yield
Annual cash dividend per share divided by the current stock price.

dividend payout ratio
The percentage of current earnings available for common stockholders paid out as dividends. Calculated by dividing the firm's cash dividend paid per share by its earnings per share in a given period.

dividends. The directors usually meet to evaluate the firm's recent financial performance and future outlook and to determine whether, and in what amount, dividends should be paid. The payment date of the cash dividend, if one is declared, must also be established.

Payment Patterns and Measures Most U.S. firms that pay dividends do so once every quarter. Firms adjust the size of their dividends periodically, but not necessarily every quarter. Figure 14.1 provides evidence suggesting that most firms adjust their dividends infrequently, "smoothing" dividends over time rather than adjusting them up or down each quarter as earnings fluctuate. The figure plots average earnings, dividends, and share repurchases for U.S. nonfinancial firms from 1990 to 2009.[1] Observe that the earnings and repurchases lines dip significantly during the recessions in the early 1990s and in 2001–2002, but in both cases the change in dividends was muted. However, a modest reduction in dividends occurred as earnings fell dramatically during the recession that began with the financial crisis in 2007.

Investors closely track two ratios related to corporate dividend payments. The first is the dividend yield, which equals the annual cash dividend divided by the current stock price. The second ratio related to dividend payments is the dividend payout ratio, which equals dividends paid per share divided by earnings per share in a given period.

EXAMPLE

On May 18, 2011, Intel Corp. (INTC) announced a 16% increase in its quarterly dividend to $0.21 per share ($0.84 annually). On the day of that announcement, Intel's stock traded for $23.50, so its *dividend yield* was 3.6% [($0.21 × 4) ÷ $23.50]. Intel's earnings during the prior quarter were $0.56 per share, which implies a *dividend payout ratio* of about 37.5% ($0.21 ÷ $0.56).

Figure 14.1   **Payouts through 2009. Dividends, Repurchases, Earnings**

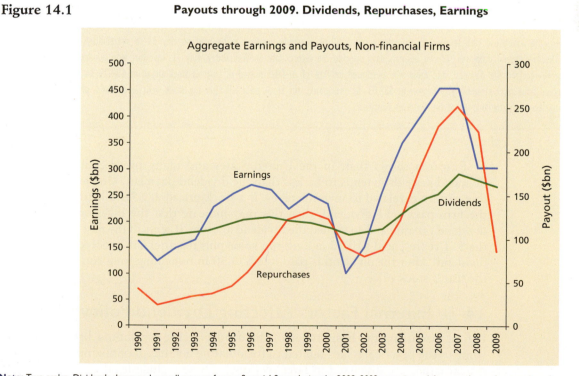

Note: Two scales. Dividends decreased a small amount for nonfinancial firms during the 2008–2009 recession, while repurchases decreased much more.

---

[1]We thank Mark T. Leary of Washington University in St. Louis for providing data for the figure.

Figure 14.2

A Timeline Illustrating Important Dates in the Dividend Process

| Board of directors announces dividend | Stock goes ex-dividend | Record date | Payment date |

announcement date
The day a firm declares the amount of the dividend, plus the dividend record and payment dates to the public.

date of record
The date on which the names of all persons who appear as stockholders are entitled to receive a dividend.

ex-dividend date
Date on or after which a purchaser of a stock does not receive the current dividend. Usually two business days prior to the *date of record.*

payment date
The actual date on which a firm mails the dividend payment to the holders of record.

Relevant Dates When firms announce dividends, they also establish certain dates that determine which shareholders receive the dividends. The day on which firms release this information to the public is the announcement date. *Shareholders of record,* all persons whose names appear as stockholders on the date of record, are entitled to the dividend. However, because it takes time to make bookkeeping entries after stocks trade, investors who buy stock on the *record date* will miss the dividend payment. To receive the dividend, an investor must own the stock before the ex-dividend date, usually two business days prior to the date of record. Firms distribute dividends on the payment date, which usually comes a few weeks after the record date. Figure 14.2 shows a timeline illustrating these events.

In a perfect market (no taxes and transactions costs) and in the absence of any new information, when a stock "goes ex-dividend," its price should drop by the amount of the dividend. To see why, consider that an investor who buys a stock just prior to the ex-dividend date will receive the dividend a few days later, whereas an investor who buys on the ex-dividend date misses this payment. Therefore, investors who buy on the ex-dividend date will pay less for the stock. For example, suppose a stock that pays a $1 dividend sells for $51 just before going ex-dividend. Once the ex-dividend date passes, the price should drop to $50 (ignoring market imperfections like income taxes).

EXAMPLE

On April 26, 2011, the warehouse club retailer, Costco, announced a $0.24 quarterly dividend to be paid on May 27 to shareholders of record as of Friday, May 13. The ex-dividend date was set two business days prior to the record date on Wednesday, May 11. Investors who purchased Costco stock on or before May 10 received the dividend, and those who purchased on May 11 or later missed it. Costco's stock closed at $82.23 on the afternoon of May 10, and it opened the next morning $0.20 lower at $82.03. As anticipated, the stock price fell after the stock went ex-dividend, although the price decline was slightly less than the amount of the dividend payment.

Research shows that, in the United States and many other countries, the ex-dividend price drop tends to be less than the dividend payment. One explanation for this pattern is related to investor taxes. If a stock priced at $51 falls to $50.30 when the firm pays a $1 dividend, then this may indicate that the investor faces a 30% dividend tax rate and so valued the dividend at only 70 cents in the first place. That is, the $51 represented $50.30 in long-run value plus the after-tax proceeds from the $1 dividend. After the dividend is paid, the $50.30 in remaining long-run value dictates the firm's stock price.

14-1b External Factors Affecting Dividend Policy

Before discussing the basic types of dividend policies, we should briefly consider some of the practical issues related to formulating a value-maximizing policy (theoretical issues are discussed in later sections). These include legal constraints, contractual constraints, internal constraints, the firm's growth prospects, and owner considerations.

Table 14.1

Calculating the Maximum Amount a Firm Can Pay in Cash Dividends

The stockholders' equity account of the Omega Corporation is presented in the table below.

Omega Corporation's Stockholders' Equity	
Common stock at par	$100,000
Paid-in capital in excess of par	200,000
Retained earnings	140,000
Total stockholders' equity	$440,000

In states where a firm's legal capital is defined as the par value of its common stock, the firm could pay out a maximum of $340,000 ($200,000 + $140,000) in cash dividends without impairing its capital. In states where a firm's capital includes all paid-in capital, the firm could pay out only $140,000 in cash dividends.

Most U.S. states prohibit corporations from paying out as cash dividends any portion of their "legal capital," which is measured by the par value of common stock, as described in Section 2-1 of Chapter 2. Other states define legal capital to include not only the par value of the common stock but also any paid-in capital in excess of par. States establish these *capital-impairment restrictions* to provide a sufficient equity base to protect creditors' claims. The example presented for the Omega Corporation in Table 14.1 clarifies the varying definitions of capital.

An earnings requirement limiting the amount of dividends to the sum of a firm's present and past earnings is sometimes imposed. In other words, Omega cannot pay more in cash dividends than the sum of its current earnings plus historic retained earnings. However, *laws do not prohibit a firm from paying more in dividends than its current earnings*.

If a firm has overdue liabilities or is legally insolvent (if the fair market value of all its assets is less than its total liabilities), most states prohibit cash dividends. In addition, the Internal Revenue Service prohibits firms from accumulating earnings for the sole purpose of reducing the owners' taxes. A firm's owners must pay income taxes on dividends when they are received, but the owners pay no tax on capital gains until they sell the stock. A firm might retain a large portion of earnings to delay the payment of taxes by its owners. If the IRS can determine that a firm has accumulated excess earnings to allow owners to delay paying ordinary income taxes, it may levy an **excess earnings accumulation tax** on any retained earnings above a specified amount. This rarely occurs in practice, however.

Negative covenants in loan agreements sometimes constrain a firm's ability to pay cash dividends. Generally, these constraints prohibit cash dividends until the firm achieves a certain level of earnings, or they may limit dividends to a certain dollar amount or percentage of earnings. Constraints on dividend payments help protect creditors from losses due to insolvency. If a firm violates one of these contractual restrictions, creditors generally have the right to demand immediate repayment of their loans.

14-1c Types of Dividend Payout Policies

The following sections describe three basic payout dividend policies, but bear in mind that the constant dollar payout dividend policy dominates in every major economy. A particular firm's cash dividend payout policy may incorporate elements of each policy type.

Constant Payout Ratio Policy One type of dividend policy rarely adopted by firms is a constant payout ratio. As noted earlier, the *dividend payout ratio* indicates the percentage of each dollar earned that is distributed to the owners. With a **constant payout ratio dividend policy**, the firm establishes that a certain percentage of earnings is paid to shareholders in each dividend period. The problem with this policy is that if

excess earnings accumulation tax
A tax levied by the IRS on a firm that has accumulated sufficient excess earnings to allow owners to delay paying ordinary income taxes.

constant payout ratio policy
Dividend policy in which a firm establishes that a certain percentage of earnings is paid to owners in each dividend period.

the firm's earnings drop or if a loss occurs in a given period, the dividends may be low or even nonexistent, making them as volatile as the firm's earnings.

constant dollar payment policy
Dividend policy based on the payment of a fixed-dollar dividend in each period.

Constant Dollar Payout Policy Another type of dividend policy, the constant dollar payout dividend policy, is based on the payment of a fixed-dollar dividend in each period. Using this policy, firms often increase the regular dividend once a *proven* increase in long-term earnings has occurred. Under this policy, firms almost never cut dividends unless they face a true crisis.

target dividend payout ratio
A policy under which a firm attempts to pay out a specified percentage of earnings by paying a stated dollar dividend adjusted slowly toward the target payout as proven earnings increase.

Firms that pay a steady dividend may build their policy around a target dividend payout ratio. Under this policy, the firm attempts to pay out a specified percentage of earnings. Rather than let dividends fluctuate, however, it pays out a stated dollar dividend and slowly adjusts it toward the target payout, as proven earnings increases occur. This is known as a *partial-adjustment strategy*, and it implies that at any given time, firms may be in a transition between two dividend payout levels.

low-regular-and-extra payout policy
Policy of a firm paying a low regular dividend supplemented by an additional cash dividend when earnings warrant it.

Low-Regular-and-Extra Payout Policy Some firms establish a low-regular-and-extra payout policy that pays out a low regular dividend, supplemented by an additional cash dividend when earnings warrant it. If earnings are higher than normal in a given period, the firm may pay out this additional dividend, which is designated an extra dividend or a special dividend. By designating the amount—by which the current dividend exceeds the regular payment—as an extra dividend, the firm avoids giving shareholders false hopes. The use of the "extra" or the "special" designation is more common among companies that experience temporary shifts in earnings.

EXAMPLE

An exception is National Presto Industries (NPI), primarily a housewares and small appliance manufacturer with an unbroken 66-year dividend history, that regularly pays "extra" dividends. Every year, NPI pays a base $1 per share dividend plus an extra dividend based on profits. In 2011, NPI announced its $1.00 per share regular dividend plus an extra dividend of $7.25 per share, resulting in a total annual dividend of $8.25 per share. Its resulting *dividend yield* for 2011 was a very attractive 7.4%.

extra dividend/special dividend
An additional dividend that a firm may pay if earnings are higher than normal in a given period.

14-1d Stock Dividends and Stock Splits

In addition to paying cash dividends, firms sometimes issue *stock dividends*. A transaction that is essentially identical to a stock dividend is a *stock split*.

stock dividends
The payment to existing shareholders of a dividend in the form of stock.

Stock Dividends A stock dividend is the payment to existing shareholders of a dividend in the form of stock. For example, if a firm declares a 20% stock dividend, it will issue twenty new shares for every one hundred shares that an investor owns. Firms often pay stock dividends as a replacement for, or a supplement to, cash dividends. However, a stock dividend does not necessarily increase a shareholder's wealth. If a firm pays a 20% stock dividend, and nothing else about the firm changes, then the number of outstanding shares increases by 20%, and the stock price drops by about 16.7% to 83.3% of its original price ($100\% \div 120\% = 83.3\%$). Thus, the net effect on shareholder wealth is neutral; the stock dividend neither increases nor decreases the value of investors' shareholdings, that is, 120% shares × 83.3% price = 100% of original value. In other words, shareholders receiving stock dividends maintain a constant proportional share of the firm's equity.

stock split
A transaction in which a firm increases the number of outstanding shares by issuing new shares to existing stockholders.

Stock Splits Stock splits, like stock dividends, should have mostly cosmetic effects on a firm. When a firm executes a stock split, its share price declines because the number of outstanding shares increases. For example, in a 2-for-1 split, the firm doubles the number of shares outstanding but the stock price falls to approximately half its previous level. Managers who implement stock splits generally say they are trying to restore the per-share price of the firm's stock to within a "preferred" trading range that individual investors desire. Such managers believe that they can achieve a higher overall firm value by keeping the stock price low enough to appeal to retail investors.

Intuition suggests that stock splits should not create value for shareholders. After all, if someone gives you two $5 bills in exchange for one $10 bill, you are no better off. A stock split should also have no effect on the firm's capital structure because it changes the number rather than the value of outstanding shares. In spite of this logic, research shows that stock splits increase the market value of a firm's equity by about 2.5%. In other words, if a firm whose stock trades for $100 announces a 2-for-1 split, research shows that the stock price will fall to roughly $51.25 (so two shares are worth $102.50).

EXAMPLE

Most established U.S. public companies routinely split their shares to keep the price within a perceived optimal range. General Electric (GE), a company that has paid a cash dividend each quarter for over one hundred years, is perhaps the best example of this policy. GE's stock was first offered for sale at $108 per share in 1892. Had GE not split its stock repeatedly over the years, the price per share would have been over $92,000 by 2011. The price of the voting shares (A shares) of the most famous company that refuses to split its voting stock, Berkshire Hathaway, was $119,164 on May 18, 2011.

reverse stock splits
Occurs when a firm replaces a certain number of outstanding shares with just one new share to increase the stock price.

Most stock splits increase the number of shares outstanding, but firms sometimes conduct **reverse stock splits**, replacing a number of outstanding shares with just one new share. For example, in a 1-for-2 split, one new share replaces two old shares; in a 2-for-3 split, two new shares replace three old shares; and so on. A firm whose stock sells at a very low price may initiate a reverse stock split to increase its stock price and avoid being delisted due to the minimum share price requirement of the exchange where the stock trades.

14-1e Share Repurchases

Companies can also pay out cash to shareholders by repurchasing some of their outstanding stock. Comparing the dividend and share repurchase values in Figure 14.1 on page 433 we can see that share repurchases have grown in importance relative to dividends, and that in many recent years, aggregate repurchases have exceeded aggregate dividends. The repurchase boom began in part because an SEC ruling in 1982 clarified when companies could and could not repurchase their shares without fear of being charged with insider trading or price manipulation.

In addition to paying out cash to shareholders, the practical motives for stock repurchases include obtaining shares to be used in acquisitions, having shares available for employee stock-option plans, and retiring shares. From a broader perspective, the rising importance of share repurchases suggests that they may enhance shareholder value, perhaps because they have traditionally been a tax-advantaged method of paying out cash. Although it is not clear exactly what managers are trying to achieve through repurchases, frequently mentioned rationales include: sending a *positive signal* to investors in the marketplace that management believes the stock is undervalued, thus reducing the number of shares outstanding and raising earnings per share (*EPS*). A recent study argues convincingly that share repurchases have grown rapidly since the early 1990s, largely to offset the dilution effects of the exercise of stock options.[2] As the number and the value of options granted to (and exercised by) top executives have increased in importance, companies have been buying back shares to keep the total number outstanding from rising too sharply, thus reducing earnings per share.

Cengage Learning

Scott Lee, Texas A&M University

"Generally associated with repurchase announcements is a fairly strong market response."

See the entire interview at **SMART**|finance

Smart Ethics Video

Taxes Today both dividends and capital gains are taxed at either 5% or 15%. In spite of the parity of these rates, share

---

[2]See J. Fred Weston and Juan A. Siu, "Changing Motives for Share Repurchases," *Finance* Paper 3 (2003), Anderson Graduate School of Management, UCLA.

Andy Bryant, Executive Vice President of Finance and Enterprise Systems, Chief Financial Officer, Intel Corp.

"Dividends are probably not the most effective way to return cash to shareholders."

See the entire interview at **SMART** | finance

Smart Practices Video

? WHAT TO ASK

How does your firm decide whether to distribute cash to investors by paying dividends or by conducting share repurchases?

repurchases still give investors the option to participate or not (to sell or to retain their shares). Therefore, capital gains taxes can be deferred, whereas taxes on cash dividends must be paid in the year the dividends are received.

Repurchase Methods Companies can use several methods to repurchase shares. In the most common approach, an *open-market share repurchase*, firms buy back their shares in the open market. In a *tender offer*, or *self-tender*, firms offer to buy back a certain number of shares, usually at a premium above the current market price. In a *Dutch auction repurchase*, firms ask investors to submit prices at which they are willing to sell their shares. If the firm wants to buy back 2 million shares, it reviews the offers submitted by shareholders and determines the lowest price at which shareholders will tender a total of 2 million shares. In a Dutch auction, all investors receive the same price when they sell back their shares, even if they expressed a willingness to sell at a lower price in their original offer. When firms announce plans to repurchase shares, their stock prices typically rise, and the positive reaction is much greater for tender offers and Dutch auctions than for open-market share repurchases.

Having reviewed the basic mechanics and issues surrounding payout policy, we can now look more closely at the factors affecting dividend and share repurchase decisions.

14.1 Concept Review Questions

1. What policies and payments comprise a firm's *payout policy*? Why is determining payout policy more difficult today than in decades past?

2. Why should we expect a firm's stock price to decline by approximately the amount of the dividend payment on the ex-dividend date? Why do U.S. stock prices generally fall by less than the amount of the dividend payment?

3. Define and differentiate between *stock dividends* and *stock splits*. Are they both forms of payout by the firm? Explain.

4. Why are share repurchases considered an alternative to cash dividend payments? Compare the tax consequences to the recipient of a cash dividend versus an equal-dollar share repurchase.

14-2 Factors Affecting Dividend and Share Repurchase Decisions

Here we begin with a look at some survey evidence on the views of CFOs on dividends and share repurchases in order to better understand payout policy practices. In addition, we consider some other important evidence regarding dividend and share repurchase decisions.

14-2a CFO Views on Dividends and Repurchases

John Graham, Duke University

"Why do companies hesitate to initiate a dividend or to increase a dividend?"

See the entire interview at **SMART** | finance

Smart Ideas Video

The findings from a 2005 survey of 384 CFOs and treasurers along with extensive one-on-one interviews with two dozen additional CFOs and treasurers provide insight into how financial executives approach payout policy decisions. Figure 14.3 compares and contrasts executive views on dividends and repurchases. For example, an overwhelming percentage of CFOs agree with the statement that "there are negative consequences to reducing dividends," but fewer than 30% agree with that statement when applied to share repurchases. In other words, CFOs believe that investors view dividends as a commitment made by the firm that must be fulfilled, whereas share repurchases are more discretionary. In that spirit, nearly 80% of CFOs say that they make repurchase decisions *after* investment plans are in place, but fewer than 35% make the same claim about dividends.

Figure 14.3   **CFOs, Views on Dividends and Repurchases**

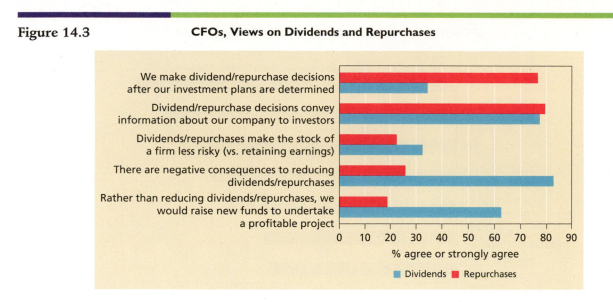

Source: Reprinted from Brav, Graham, Harvey, Michaely, "Payout Policy in the 21st Century," *Journal of Financial Economics,* volume 77, pg. 483–527, copyright 2005, with permission from Elsevier.

Apparently, dividend decisions are as important (or perhaps more important) than at least some investment decisions for these executives. This view is confirmed by the question asking whether CFOs would raise external capital to fund a new investment rather than cutting payout to shareholders. More than 60% of the CFOs say that they would raise external funds rather than cut dividends to finance a profitable new investment, but fewer than 20% say that they would raise capital to avoid cutting repurchases.

14-2b Further Evidence on Dividend and Share Repurchase Practices

A key advantage of share repurchases is their flexibility as a form of payout. Managers don't feel that their firm is penalized if repurchases are reduced from one year to the next; they curtail repurchases in order to pursue attractive investments; and they are not generally inclined to raise external funds to maintain repurchase programs. Figure 14.4 reports CFO responses to a set of questions that address separate issues related to corporate share repurchase policy. An overwhelming majority of CFOs (87%) said that they repurchased shares when their stock was a good value (i.e., when the share price was relatively low). Similarly, CFOs said they repurchased shares when buying their own stock was a better investment than other alternatives available to them at the time. But several other factors were important in repurchase decisions, such as trying to increase EPS, offsetting dilution from stock option programs, and having excess cash on the balance sheet.

Cynthia Lucchese, Chief Financial Officer, Hillenbrand Industries

"We have to decide how much cash to return as a dividend versus share repurchases."

See the entire interview at **SMART**|finance

Smart Practices Video

Repurchase Effects When a firm buys back shares, it reduces the denominator in the earnings per share (EPS) calculation, and more than 75% of the CFOs reported in Figure 14.4 that raising EPS was an important part of their thinking on share repurchases. So, does increasing EPS by decreasing shares outstanding sound like an easy way to create value? After all, won't shareholders place a higher value on a firm's stock if its earnings are higher? The answer is no, value will not necessarily increase due solely to an increase in EPS. Why? Because as the firm distributes cash to shareholders, not only does the number of outstanding shares fall but also the mix of assets held by the firm changes. For simplicity, assume that a firm owns just two kinds of assets, low-risk cash and high-risk plant and equipment. When the firm distributes some of its cash to investors, its subsequent asset mix is riskier than it was prior to

Figure 14.4

CFOs, Views on Why Firms Repurchase Shares

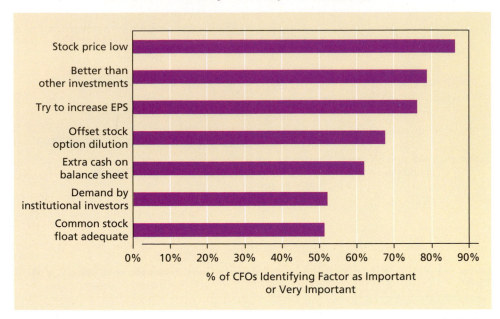

Source labels (left to right on chart): Stock price low; Better than other investments; Try to increase EPS; Offset stock option dilution; Extra cash on balance sheet; Demand by institutional investors; Common stock float adequate

X-axis: % of CFOs Identifying Factor as Important or Very Important (0% to 90%)

Source: Reprinted from *Journal of Financial Economics*, 77, Brav, Graham, Harvey, Michaely, "Payout Policy in the 21st Century," pg. 483–527, Copyright © 2005, with permission from Elsevier.

the repurchase, so shareholders will demand a higher rate of return. Moreover, as equity is retired through share repurchases the company's ratio of debt to equity increases, and so financial risk increases as well. The effect of increasing the risk borne by shareholders offsets the reduction in shares outstanding, so even though EPS rises after a share repurchase, that alone does not lead to an increase in firm value because the earnings are riskier.

Dividend Effects The evidence presented above indicates that dividend decisions are made very conservatively. That is, companies are hesitant to start paying dividends (or to increase the amount of dividends they pay) in part because they know they'll be reluctant to reduce them in the future. In one of the earliest research studies on dividends, John Lintner[3] documented several patterns with respect to firms' dividend policies, patterns that are roughly consistent with this conservative view of dividends. In particular:

1. Firms have long-run target dividend payout ratios.
2. Dividend changes follow shifts in long-run, sustainable earnings (not short-run changes in earnings).
3. Managers are reluctant to increase dividends if they might have to be cut later.
4. Managers focus on dividend changes rather than on dividend levels.

Lintner developed a simple model that captured these patterns and estimated firms' target payout ratios as well as the speed with which firms adjusted to those ratios. A slower adjustment speed simply means that firms smooth dividends more as earnings change. You might guess—because firms are placing more importance in recent years on share repurchases and because managers view them as a more flexible tool than dividends for paying cash to shareholders—that firms' target dividend payouts are now lower (and that adjustments to the target now occur more slowly) than when Lintner published his findings. Indeed, recent research by Leary and Michaely[4] finds that, for the period 1950–1983, firms that paid dividends had a target of distributing a little more than one-third of their earnings as dividends; moreover, when their dividend

---

[3] See John Lintner, "The Distribution of Incomes of Corporations among Dividends, Retained Earnings, and Taxes." *American Economic Review* 46(May 1956), pp. 97–113.
[4] See Mark T. Leary and Roni Michaely, "Why Firms Smooth Dividends: Empirical Evidence." Working paper (February 17, 2009), Johnson Graduate School of Management, Cornell University, Ithaca, NY.

payouts deviated from the desired target, firms made adjustments to close about one-third of that gap each year. But from 1984 to 2002, the target payout ratio appears to have fallen to just 20% of earnings, and likewise the speed of adjustment to that target is much slower. In other words, dividend smoothing increased in recent years.

14-2 Concept Review Questions

5. Describe some of the key survey findings regarding dividend and share repurchase decisions. What is the key advantage of share repurchases over dividend payouts?

6. Well-diversified investors are willing to tolerate great volatility in the prices of stocks they own. Why do you think they might value a constant dividend payment even though the underlying corporate profits on which dividends are ultimately based are highly variable?

7. What appears to have happened to *dividend payout ratios* and the speed of dividend smoothing during recent years? How has management's use of share repurchases affected these behaviors?

14-3 Dividends in Perfect and Imperfect Worlds

14-3a Payout Policy Irrelevance in a World with Perfect Capital Markets

Just as they did with capital structure, Miller and Modigliani demonstrated that—in a world of perfect and frictionless capital markets—payout policy does not affect a firm's market value. Value derives solely from the profitability of the firm's assets and the competence of its management team. If payout policy does affect firm value, then it must be because markets are imperfect.

The notion that dividends are irrelevant appears to be a contradiction. After all, we argued in Chapter 5 that a stock's value equals the present value of all its future dividend payments. How, then, do we arrive at a dividend "irrelevance" result? As with capital structure, the answer emerges that a firm's value derives solely from its current and expected future operating profits. As long as the firm accepts all positive-*NPV* investment projects and has *costless* access to capital markets, it can pay any level of dividends it desires. But if a firm pays out its earnings as a dividend, then it must issue new shares to raise the cash required to finance its ongoing investments. So a company can either retain its profits and finance its investments with internally generated cash flow, or it can pay out its earnings as dividends and raise the cash needed for investment by selling new shares. This dividend irrelevance is best explained with an example.

Consider two firms, Retention and Payout, that are the same size today (January 1, 2012), are in the same industry, and have access to the same investment opportunities. Suppose both companies have assets worth $20 million that will generate a net cash inflow of $2 million by December 31, 2012. Each firm thus earns a 10% return on investment. Furthermore, assume investors require a return, r, of 10% per year and that, at the end of this year, each company will have the opportunity to invest $2 million in a positive-*NPV* project. Each company currently has 1 million shares outstanding, implying a share price of $20 ($P_{\text{Jan12}} = \$20$). Payout's managers want to pay out the firm's earnings as dividends and finance the $2 million investment by issuing new shares. Retention's managers prefer to retain the firm's earnings to fund the $2 million investment program. If each management team pursues its preferred strategy, assuming perfect and frictionless capital markets, will the two firms still have identical values next year?

Yes. To see how, we first examine Retention's strategy. Retention's managers finance the $2 million investment project by retaining $2 million in profits. Retention's market value on December 31, 2012, equals the $20 million beginning value, plus the $2 million ($2 per share) in reinvested earnings, plus the investment's net present value. For simplicity, assume that the project's *NPV* is positive but small enough to be ignored. Retention's year-end 2012 value is $22 million ($20 million + $2 million), or $22 per share ($P_{Dec12} = \$22$), because the firm did not have to issue any new shares in order to finance its investments. Plugging these data into our basic valuation equation from Chapter 5 verifies that Retention's shareholders indeed earn their required 10% return on investment:

$$r = \frac{D_{2012} + P_{Dec12} - P_{Jan12}}{P_{Jan12}} = \frac{\$0 + \$22 - \$20}{\$20} = 10\%$$

We can extend this example indefinitely into the future. In each period, Retention commits to reinvesting all its annual profits (10% return on assets), and shareholders earn an acceptable return because their share values increase 10% each year. Retention never issues new shares, so the number of outstanding shares remains fixed at 1 million.

So far, so good. But what about firm Payout? This company's managers decide to pay a $2 million dividend at the end of the year, so they must raise the $2 million needed for investment by selling new shares. But how many shares must they sell? To answer that, we must deduce what the price of Payout's shares will be on December 31, 2012. After it distributes the dividend, Payout will have assets worth $20 million, exactly what it started with on January 1. With 1 million shares outstanding, the share price will still be $20, so Payout must issue 100,000 new shares to raise the $2 million it needs to undertake its investment project. After the company issues new shares and invests the proceeds, Payout's total market value will equal $22 million ($20 per share × 1.1 million shares outstanding). Payout's market value of $22 million on December 31, 2012, matches Retention's value. We can verify that Payout's original shareholders earn the same 10% return earned by Retention's investors:

$$r = \frac{D_{2012} + P_{Dec12} - P_{Jan12}}{P_{Jan12}} = \frac{\$2 + \$20 - \$20}{\$20} = 10\%$$

Once again, we can repeat this process indefinitely. Each year, Payout distributes all of its net cash flow as a dividend, issuing new shares to finance new investments.

We have shown that the market values of Retention and Payout are equal on December 31, 2012, even though they follow radically different dividend policies. Retention has 1 million shares outstanding worth $22 each, while Payout has 1.1 million shares outstanding worth $20 each. Because both companies have a total value of $22 million, we can say that dividend policy is irrelevant to valuing a firm, at least when markets are frictionless. But what if Retention's investors prefer that the company pay out earnings rather than reinvest them, or if Payout's shareholders prefer that the company reinvest earnings rather than issue new shares? We reinforce dividend policy irrelevance by demonstrating in the following Example that investors can unwind firms' dividend policy decisions. In the end, what is true for the firm as a whole is true for each investor: *Dividend policy is irrelevant when capital markets are perfect.*

SMART concepts

See the concept explained step-by-step at **SMART|finance**

EXAMPLE

Consider two investors, Bert and Ernie. On January 1, 2012, Bert owns an 11% stake (110,000 shares) in Retention, whereas Ernie holds an 11% stake (also 110,000 shares) in Payout. By the end of 2012, Bert has received no dividend but he still owns 11% of Retention's outstanding shares, which are now worth $22 each. In contrast, Ernie receives a $220,000 dividend during 2012 but, because Payout issues 100,000 shares to finance its investment opportunity, the shares Ernie owns now represent only a 10% stake in Payout (110,000 ÷ 1,100,000).

If either Bert or Ernie is unhappy with the dividend policy of the firm in which he has invested, he can unwind that policy. For example, suppose Bert wishes to receive cash like he would from a dividend. At the end of 2012, Bert can sell 10,000 of his shares for $22 each, generating a cash inflow of $220,000, exactly equal to the dividend that Ernie receives on his investment. In selling some of his shares, Bert creates *homemade dividends*. By the end of the year, Bert owns just 10% of Retention's equity, but that's exactly equal to the ownership stake that Ernie holds in Payout.

Conversely, suppose that Ernie prefers that Payout did not pay dividends. The solution to Ernie's problem is simple. When he receives the $220,000 dividend, he simply reinvests the money by purchasing 11,000 new Payout shares. That would bring his total ownership to 121,000, or 11%, of Payout's shares (121,000 ÷ 1,100,000). In other words, Ernie's position is just like Bert's.

This may seem complex, but the essential points of these examples are simple. If there were no frictions or imperfections in capital markets, then investors would not care whether the firm (1) retains earnings to fund positive-*NPV* investments or (2) pays dividends and sells new shares to finance investments. In either case, cash flows from the firm's investments—not dividend decisions—determine shareholders' returns.

14-3b Miller and Modigliani Meet the (Imperfect) Real World

In the previous section, we saw that when capital markets are perfect and frictionless, payout decisions do not affect firm value. The core of the idea behind Miller and Modigliani's argument is that operational and investment decisions, not financial policies, are what create value. However, in Figure 14.3 we saw that corporate managers say that maintaining the existing dividend payment ranks *ahead* of investment decisions at many companies. This is the starkest possible rejection of the Miller and Modigliani irrelevance argument because it implies that a financial decision (of maintaining dividends) is more important than the investment decision.

How can this be the case? Here we discuss several academic theories that explain why payout decisions do matter. Each of these theories describes why a certain market imperfection (taxes, agency costs, etc.) affects payout decisions in general or the choice between dividends and repurchases.

Dividends, Repurchases, and Taxes Prior to 2003, there was a substantial tax advantage to distributing cash to shareholders via share repurchases rather than dividends. Dividends were taxable as ordinary income when received (at tax rates as high as 40%). In contrast, the only taxpayers who might have an immediate tax liability resulting from a share repurchase were those who sold their shares back to the firm. For these investors, only the difference between the selling price and the original purchase price was taxable, and the applicable tax rate was the relatively low capital gains rate, not the rate on ordinary income. Therefore, the market imperfection of high dividend taxation (relative to share repurchase taxation) encouraged firms to shift payout toward share repurchases.

The Jobs and Growth Tax Relief Reconciliation Act of 2003 reduced the tax advantage for share repurchases by equalizing tax rates on dividends and capital gains at 15% beginning in May 2003. As a consequence, the friction of dividend taxation decreased, and some firms that had not previously paid dividends began doing so. A spike in the number of new dividend initiations occurred after May 2003 and continued for several subsequent quarters, but the number of firms initiating dividends slowly fell back to pre-2003 levels just two years after the tax cuts took effect.

CFO surveys conducted before and after the 2003 tax cuts confirm that tax rates affected the dividend decisions of some firms but certainly not the majority. In February 2003, CFOs of firms that paid dividends and of firms that did not were asked whether impending reductions in the dividend tax rate would cause them to initiate or increase dividend payments. A large majority of both dividend payers and nonpayers said that the tax cut would probably not, or definitely not, prompt them to change their dividend policies. Another survey in June 2003 (one month after the tax cut took effect) produced similar results, with more than 80% of dividend payers and nearly 70% of nonpayers responding that they would not increase or initiate dividends in response to the tax changes. A final survey taken two years later found that a majority of firms still claimed that the dividend tax cut had not influenced their dividend decisions. Only 5% of dividend payers and about 20% of nonpayers said that the tax cut had greatly affected their dividend policy. Thus, taxes do matter, but only for a small number of firms.

At the time of this writing it seems possible that dividends will again be taxed at ordinary income levels (which may be as high as 40%) whereas capital gains tax rates will increase less. If future tax rates were to rise dividends would again be at a material tax disadvantage compared to capital gains, and corporations would resume shifting payout away from dividends and toward increased share repurchases.

Agency Cost and Signaling Models of Payout There are several nontax market imperfections that may make corporate payout decisions relevant. This section begins by describing how agency costs (misaligned incentives between managers and stakeholders) can lead to a positive role for payout activities. We concentrate on the *agency cost/contracting model* of dividends (or, more simply, the *agency cost model*).

What Companies Do Globally

EU Firm Payout Policy Survey Evidence

Von Eije and Megginson (2008) studied the payout policies of firms in the 15 nations of the European Union for the period 1989–2006. They found that the fraction of European firms paying dividends declined during this period, whereas the total value of dividends and repurchases increased. Those patterns mirror what happened in the United States during the same period. Figure 14.5 also shows that in Europe (as in the United States) share repurchases grew more rapidly than dividends, although repurchases in Europe accelerated much later than they did in the United States.

Figure 14.5   **Dividends and Repurchases in the European Union, 1989–2006**

As a percentage of total cash payouts to shareholders, from 1989 through 2006 share repurchases rose relative to dividends in Europe, just as they did in the United States.

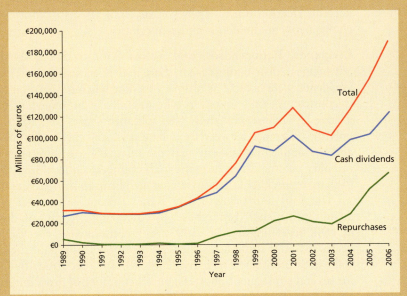

Source: Reprinted from *Journal of Financial Economics 89* (2), Henk von Eije and William Megginson, "Dividends and Share Repurchases in the European Union," pp. 347–374, Copyright © 2008, with permission from Elsevier.

agency cost/ contracting model
A theoretical model that explains empirical patterns in dividend payment and share repurchase data based on the belief that paying dividends allows a firm to overcome agency problems between managers and shareholders.

Agency Cost/Contracting Model The agency cost/contracting model assumes that firms begin paying dividends in order to overcome the *agency problems* resulting from a separation of corporate ownership and control. In privately held companies with tight ownership structures, there is little separation between ownership and control. Because agency problems in these firms are minimal, dividends are not very important. Even after a company goes public, it rarely begins paying dividends immediately because ownership remains concentrated for several years after an IPO. Eventually, ownership becomes more widely dispersed as firms raise new equity capital and as the original owners diversify their holdings. With dispersed ownership, few investors have the incentive or the ability to monitor corporate managers, so agency problems can become severe in large, mature firms that generate substantial *free cash flow*. Managers naturally face temptation to hoard this cash, possibly even spending it on perquisites or negative-*NPV* projects. Investors understand these temptations and will pay a low price for management-controlled firms that hoard excessive amounts of cash. In contrast, shareholders pay higher prices for companies with more responsive managers who commit to pay out free cash flow by initiating dividend payments (or aggressively repurchasing shares). This model thus explains why initiating or increasing dividend payments also increases stock prices, at least among firms otherwise subject to agency issues.

The agency cost model predicts that dividend-paying firms are older, larger, and generate more cash than nonpaying companies. It also predicts that dividend payers have fewer growth opportunities. The data for U.S. firms is consistent with these predictions. If we compare U.S. firms that pay dividends with firms that do not, we find that (1) the average market value of dividend payers is much greater than that of nonpayers and (2) payers grow much more slowly. The average age of dividend payers is more than twice the average age of nonpayers.

signaling model

Assumes that managers use dividends to convey positive information to poorly informed shareholders.

asymmetric information

The situation that exists when managers of the firm have more information about the firm and its prospects than do investors.

Signaling Model The signaling model of dividends addresses another market imperfection that makes payout policy relevant: asymmetric information—managers of the firm have more information about the firm and its prospects than do investors. If managers know that their firm is strong when investors for some reason do not know this, then managers can pay dividends (or aggressively repurchase shares) in hopes of signaling their firm's quality to the marketplace. For a signal to effectively separate strong firms from weak firms (so that a strong firm can signal its type to the market), it must be costly for a weak firm to mimic the action taken by the strong firm.

According to the signaling model, it is costly for a firm (especially a weak firm) to initiate or increase dividends. For example, a firm that pays out will likely face greater scrutiny from the capital markets if it needs to raise capital in the future, or the firm must expect positive internal cash flow in the near future (as did Starbucks in the chapter-opening story); in both of these scenarios, the strong firm has an advantage over the weak firm. An alternative signaling story is based on investors having to pay higher taxes on dividend income, with the weak firm being less able to withstand this cost to their investors. Thus, dividends help investors solve the asymmetric information problem of distinguishing between high-quality and low-quality firms, because high-quality firms are more able to pay dividends. Like the agency cost model, the signaling model predicts that stock prices should rise in response to dividend increases (and fall in response to dividend decreases). However, the signaling model also predicts that firms with high-growth opportunities will pay higher dividends, contrary to the empirical evidence.

There is some evidence supporting the agency and signaling theories; however, the views of corporate managers don't line up too closely with these theories. Recall that the agency cost theory says that dividends solve the agency problems that arise between shareholders and managers due to the separation of ownership and control. In a 2005 survey of CFOs by Brav, et. al.,[5] fewer than 15% of the CFOs responding agreed that these agency-related issues influence dividend policy. Of course, the crux of agency theory is that managers do not always behave in shareholders' best interests, so it may not be surprising that CFOs do not acknowledge the importance of the agency theory in surveys. Our view is that signaling probably does play a role in explaining some payout decisions (e.g., perhaps Starbucks's first-ever dividend in 2010) but is less relevant in many cases, so averaged across all firms the survey support for signaling is modest.

14-3 Concept Review Questions

8. Imagine a firm that has an intermediate dividend policy compared to Payout and Retention. This firm pays out half its earnings to shareholders and finances new investment partially through new share issues and partially through retained profits. Describe how dissatisfied shareholders in this firm could unwind the dividend policy if they preferred either higher or lower dividends.

9. Managers of slow-growing but profitable firms (e.g., tobacco companies) may pay out earnings as dividends. What can they choose to do instead?

10. How do Miller and Modigliani arrive at their conclusion that dividend policy is irrelevant in a world of perfect and frictionless capital markets?

11. What effect would the fact that, for the recipient, dividends are taxed at higher rates than gains made on stock sales have on a firm's decision with regard to paying out cash to its shareholders?

12. Why are both the *agency model* and *signaling model* consistent with the observation that stock prices fall for firms that decrease dividends?

[5]See Alon Brav, John R. Graham, Campbell R. Harvey, and Roni Michaely, "Payout Policy in the 21st Century," *Journal of Financial Economics* 77, pp. 483–527.

14-4 Real-World Influences on Payout Policy

Few of us have ever traded in perfect and frictionless capital markets, so our next task is to examine whether dividend policy continues to be irrelevant when we account for real-world factors such as taxes, trading costs, and information differences between managers and investors. Our final goal for this section is to determine whether a given firm has an optimal (value-maximizing) payout policy and, if so, how that policy should be set. As we proceed, you may notice a puzzling fact. Almost all the real-world issues we incorporate—such as taxes, transactions costs for issuing new securities, and uncertainty about a firm's investment opportunities—argue *against* the payment of cash dividends. Yet U.S. corporations pay out over half their annual earnings in most years.

14-4a Personal Income Taxes

When the personal tax rate on dividends is higher than the tax rate on capital gains, the result is clear-cut: firms wishing to distribute cash to shareholders should not pay cash dividends, but instead should repurchase stock. This offers investors the choice of either receiving cash in a tax-favored form (as a capital gain) or foregoing the cash altogether by not selling shares, and thus seeing their share values increase as their fractional ownership increases.

Why don't we see more companies substituting share repurchase programs for cash dividend payments? There are three answers to this question. First, as we have seen, many U.S. companies *have* been repurchasing their shares during the past ten years. Increasing numbers of non-U.S. companies are beginning to do so as their national laws allow. Second, the firms that initiate share repurchase programs are the same companies that also make large cash dividend payments. Finally, the IRS has the power to rule that a given company's share repurchase program is merely an attempt to avoid taxes. The IRS can impose the higher personal income tax rates on all income received by investors. The actual importance of this rule in deterring repurchases is questionable, however, because the IRS almost never invokes it.

On balance, incorporating personal taxes into our model does not help us understand why firms pay dividends. However, tax effects may account for some of the patterns we observe, such as the rise in share repurchase programs in the United States and other industrialized countries.

14-4b Trading and Other Transactions Costs

If personal taxes cannot explain observed dividend payments, what about transactions costs of issuing and trading stocks? Trading costs affect expected dividend payouts in two potentially offsetting ways. First, if investors find it costly to sell just a few shares to generate cash (i.e., to create homemade dividends), then they may be willing to pay a premium for stocks that regularly pay dividends. Regular cash dividend payments are a costless way to receive a cash return on an investor's stock portfolio. This cash could be used either for consumption or for rebalancing the investor's portfolio. In spite of this, a transactions cost argument cannot easily explain why aggregate dividend payouts in the United States have remained fairly high, even as U.S. stock markets have become vastly more efficient and the costs of trading have declined dramatically.

The second effect of transactions costs on dividend payments is completely negative. This relates to a corporation's need to replace cash paid out as dividends with cash obtained through new share sales. Remember that dividend irrelevance depends critically on a company being able to fund its investment either by retaining corporate profits or by paying out profits as dividends and replacing the cash by issuing new shares. As long as share issues are costless, investors are indifferent about whether

Finance in Your Life

To Dividend or Not to Dividend

Like many business students, you may be an active investor already or plan to become one soon. And, you may have wondered whether it is better to buy the stock of companies that pay dividends or to purchase stock of similar companies that do not pay cash dividends but instead reinvest all profits in the firm. So should you buy dividends or not?

To show how taxes impact your investment decision, let's assume that you invest $10,000 today into either of two stocks that are very similar, except that one company (High Pay, or HP) pays out all its earnings as dividends, while the second company reinvests all profits and pays no dividends (No Pay, or NP). Further assume that you plan to hold these shares for five years, that each stock currently sells for $10/share (so you buy 1,000 shares in either stock that you choose), and that the expected annual, pre-tax return on each stock will be 7% per year over your five-year holding period. Finally, assume that your personal income tax rate on dividends and capital gains is currently 5% but will jump to 15% in two years and remain at 15% for the final three years of your investment horizon. Which investment will yield the most money in five years when you are ready to buy your first dream house?

Computing the net payoff ten years from now for the non-dividend-paying stock NP is very easy—you will make only one investment (today) and will only pay (capital gains) tax once, at a 15% rate, five years from now on the stock appreciation.

Pre-tax payoff for NP in 5 years
$$= \$10,000.00 \times (1.07)^5$$
$$= \underline{\$14,025.52}$$

After-tax payoff for NP in 5 years
$$= \$14,025.52 - [(\$4,025.52) \times (0.15)]$$
$$= \underline{\$13,421.69}$$

Computing the net payoff five years from now for the dividend-paying stock HP is mechanically more difficult because each year you will receive a cash dividend that will be taxed at your personal tax rate of 5% for years 1 and 2, and then 15% for years 3–5. For simplicity, assume that dividends are paid once per year, at year end, and that you reinvest all after-tax net dividends received in new shares of HP at $10/share (assume you can buy fractional shares). The equations below detail the end-of-year (EOY) after-tax value of your HP investment for years 1–5.

EOY1 after-tax value = $10,000.00 + $700.00 × (0.95)
$$= \$10,665.00$$
EOY2 after-tax value = $10,665.00 + $746.55 × (0.95)
$$= \$11,374.22$$
EOY3 after-tax value = $11,374.22 + $796.20 × (0.85)
$$= \$12,050.99$$
EOY4 after-tax value = $12,050.99 + $843.57 × (0.85)
$$= \$12,768.02$$

EOY5 after-tax value of HP investment
$$= \$12,768.02 + \$893.76 \times (0.85)$$
$$= \underline{\$13,527.72}$$

This process shows that you would have $106.03 ($13,527.72 − $13,421.69) more in total after-tax value at the end of five years from investing in the high-pay-dividend stock than you would if you invested in the no-pay-dividend stock, if all the assumptions are valid. So HP is the preferred investment.

to receive returns in the form of capital gains (on non-dividend-paying shares) or as cash dividends on shares. If issuing securities entails large costs, however, all parties should prefer a full-retention strategy. In theory, a corporation should never both pay dividends and raise funds for investment by issuing new stock. Because many large corporations do just that, it is obvious that transactions costs alone do not explain observed dividend policy.

14-4c The Residual Theory of Dividends

The previous discussion suggests another possible explanation of observed dividend payments. Might dividends simply be a residual, the cash left over after corporations have funded all their positive-*NPV* projects? If that's the case, it would help explain why firms in rapidly growing industries retain almost all their profits, whereas firms in mature, slow-growing industries tend to have very high dividend payouts. It would also explain the "life-cycle" pattern of dividend payments for individual firms, where young, fast-growing companies rarely pay any dividends. But those same companies

Frank Popoff, Chairman of the Board (retired), Dow Chemical

"The decision specific to dividends is one that boards wrestle with on a regular basis."

See the entire interview at **SMART | finance**

Smart Practices Video

residual theory of dividends
Observed dividend payments are simply a residual, the cash left over after corporations have funded all their positive-*NPV* investments.

typically transition to a high-payout strategy as they mature and their growth rate slows.

This **residual theory of dividends** probably has some merit, but it suffers from one problem. Actual dividend payments are not as variable as they would be if firms strictly treated them as residual cash flows. In fact, over time dividend payments exhibit very stable patterns of cash flow. As noted earlier, evidence suggests that corporate managers smooth dividends, and that they are very cautious about changing established dividend payout levels. Clearly, the residual theory does not fully explain how firms make their dividend policy decisions.

14-4d Paying Dividends as a Means of Communicating Information

Sooner or later, most people who study the dividend puzzle recognize that firms may pay dividends to convey information to investors. Managers, who have a better understanding of the firm's true financial condition than do shareholders, can convey this information to shareholders through the dividend policy they select. Dividend payments have what accountants call "cash validity," meaning that dividend payments are believable and are hard for weaker firms to duplicate. Phrased in economic terms, in a world characterized by *asymmetric information* between managers and investors, cash dividend payments serve as credible information sent from corporate insiders (officers and directors) to the company's shareholders. Viewed in this way, every aspect of a firm's dividend policy conveys significant new information.

14-4e What Type of Information Is Being Communicated?

When a company begins paying dividends (a dividend initiation), it is conveying management's confidence that the firm is now profitable enough to both fund its investment projects and pay out cash. Investors and managers know that reducing or eliminating dividend payments, after they have begun, results in negative market reaction. Therefore, dividend initiations send a strong signal to the market about management's assessment of the firm's long-term ability to generate cash.

The same logic applies to dividend increases. Because everyone understands that dividend decreases should be avoided, management's willingness to increase dividend payments clearly implies confidence that its profits will remain high enough to support the new payment level. Dividend increases suggest a *permanent* increase in a firm's normal level of profitability. In other words, dividends change only when the level of *permanent earnings* changes. Unfortunately, this logic applies even more strongly to dividend decreases. Dividend cuts are viewed as very bad news. Managers reduce dividend payments only when they have no choice, such as when there is a cash flow crisis or when the financial health of the firm is declining and no turnaround is in sight. Therefore, it is no surprise that when managers decrease dividends, the market reaction is often severe.

14-4f Dividend Payments as Solutions to Agency Problems

When firms are small and growing rapidly, they not only have tight ownership structures, but also tend to have many profitable investment opportunities. These growth firms can profitably use all the cash flow that they generate internally. Thus, they have no reason to pay cash dividends. In time, successful growth firms establish secure,

Kenneth Eades, University of Virginia

"It's an earnings story, not a dividend story."

See the entire interview at **SMART** | finance

Smart Ideas Video

often dominant, market positions. They begin to generate operating cash flows that are much larger than the amounts needed to invest in the remaining positive-*NPV* investment opportunities open to them. Managers of firms with cash flow in excess of that needed to fund all positive *NPV* projects *should* begin to pay dividends to ensure that they will not invest that cash flow in negative-*NPV* projects. However, managers may prefer to retain cash and spend it, because of the increased status attained from running a larger (though not necessarily more valuable) company.

If managers are given the proper incentives, it is believed that they will initiate dividend payments as soon as the firm begins generating excess cash flow. Managerial contracts that tie compensation to the firm's stock price performance are designed to ensure that managers pay out excess cash flow rather than invest it unwisely. The larger the excess cash flow generated, the larger the dividend payout should be. This is the essential prediction of what is known as the agency cost/contracting model of dividend payments, which was introduced in Section 14-3b. The central predictions of this model are threefold. First, it predicts that dividend initiations and increases should be viewed as good news by investors and thus should lead to stock price increases upon announcement. Second, the agency cost model predicts that firms (and industries) that generate the largest amounts of excess cash flow should also have the highest dividend payout ratios. Finally, this model predicts that managerial compensation contracts will not only be designed to entice managers to pursue a value-maximizing dividend policy, but will also be effective.

14-4 Concept Review Questions

13. In what way can managers use dividends to convey pertinent information about their firms in a world of asymmetric information? Why would a manager choose to convey information via a dividend policy? Is there evidence supporting or refuting the informational role of dividends?

14. Why is it difficult for a firm with weaker cash flows to mimic a dividend increase undertaken by a firm with stronger cash flows?

15. According to the *residual theory of dividends*, how does a firm set its dividend? With which dividend policy is this theory most compatible? Does it appear to be validated by actual corporate dividend payment data?

14-5 Payout Policy: Key Lessons

In this chapter, we have learned that firms take a conservative approach to paying dividends. The key factor driving dividend payments is the stability of long-run cash flows. Dividends are smoothed and do not vary as much as earnings do from year to year, and once firms start paying dividends they are reluctant to reduce them. Firms that pay dividends tend to be older and larger and produce ample cash flows, and they grow more slowly than firms that do not pay dividends.

Share repurchases, on the other hand, are viewed by managers as being more flexible. Managers say that they are willing to cut back on share repurchases if necessary to finance new investments, whereas managers say that they would raise external capital to fund new investments before cutting dividends.

Not surprisingly, as a percentage of total cash paid to shareholders, repurchases have been gaining ground for many years. In addition to valuing the flexibility of share repurchases, managers appear to engage in repurchases most actively when they perceive their stock to be undervalued.

We also learned that taxes have some influence on dividend decisions, but changes in tax rates do not generally bring about radical and widespread changes in dividend payout. The agency and signaling payout theories help explain payout decisions at some firms, but research findings so far do not offer a lot of support of these theories explaining payout policies for the broad cross-section of companies.

Summary

- Large publicly traded corporations almost invariably choose to pay regular cash dividends to their shareholders. These payments are generally a fairly stable dollar amount per period, rather than a constant fraction of the firm's earnings. In the United States, dividends are usually paid on a quarterly basis.

- Share repurchases have grown relative to dividends for several decades. Today share repurchases and dividends are subject to the same tax rates. The appeal of share repurchase programs is that they are much more flexible than dividend payout commitments.

- Dividend payout decisions are made conservatively. Companies do not initiate or increase dividend payments until they are comfortable that long-run earnings will be stable and reliable. Repurchases may be paid out of stable earnings or when a firm has a temporary increase in cash flows or cash on the balance sheet.

- Stock dividends and stock splits are used by companies that want to reduce the per-share price of their stock in the open market. In a 2-for-1 stock split, for example, two new shares are distributed for every existing share an investor holds, and the price of the stock falls by roughly half.

- CFOs believe that investors view dividends as a commitment made by the firm that must be fulfilled, whereas share repurchases are more discretionary. Most CFOs would raise external funds rather than cut dividends to finance a profitable new investment, but most would not raise capital to avoid cutting repurchases. Dividend decisions are typically made very conservatively: Companies are hesitant to start paying dividends (or to increase the amount of dividends they pay) in part because they will be reluctant to reduce them in the future.

- In a perfect and frictionless world (one without market imperfections), dividend policy is irrelevant in the sense that it does not affect the value of a firm. However, the fact that many firms pay dividends is something of a puzzle because most real market imperfections (such as taxes) argue against paying cash dividends.

- One theory of dividend policy assumes that dividend payments serve to reduce agency costs between corporate managers and external investors by committing the firm to pay out excess profits. Managers are prevented from spending the profits on perquisites or wasting them on unwise capital investments. Most of the empirical evidence supports this agency cost model over the competing signaling model, which predicts that managers use dividend payments to convey information to investors about the firm's expected future earnings.

- In addition to ownership considerations, several other aspects of a firm's operating and regulatory environment seem to influence dividend payouts. Other things being equal, closely held corporations, which operate in a high-growth industry where large ongoing capital investments are needed to compete, have lower dividend payouts than do widely held firms in slow-growing or highly regulated industries.

- The residual theory of dividends suggests that dividends are simply a residual, the cash left over after corporations have funded all positive *NPV* projects. This theory explains why high-growth firms retain most of their profits and pay no or low dividends, whereas mature, slow-growing firms tend to have high dividend payouts. Although appealing, actual dividend payments are not as variable as they would be if firms viewed them purely as residuals from cash flow.

Key Terms

agency cost/contracting model, 444
announcement date, 434
asymmetric information, 445
constant dollar payment policy, 436
constant payout ratio policy, 435
date of record, 434
dividend payout ratio, 433
dividend yield, 433
ex-dividend date, 434

excess earnings accumulation
    tax, 435
extra dividend, 436
low-regular-and-extra payout
    dividend policy, 436
payment date, 434
payout policy, 432
residual theory of
    dividends, 448

reverse stock split, 437
share repurchase program, 432
signaling model, 445
special dividend, 436
stock dividend, 436
stock split, 436
target dividend payout ratio, 436

Self-Test Problems

Answers to Self-Test Problems and the Concept Review Questions throughout the chapter appear in CourseMate with SmartFinance Tools at www.cengagebrain.com.

ST14-1. What do *date of record*, *ex-dividend date*, and *payment date* mean, related to dividends? Why would you expect the price of a stock to drop by the amount of the dividend on the ex-dividend date? What rationale has been offered for why this does not actually occur?

ST14-2. What has happened to the total volume of share repurchases announced by U.S. public companies since 1982? Why did that year mark such an important milestone in the history of share repurchase programs in the United States?

ST14-3. What has happened to the average cash dividend payout ratio of U.S. corporations over time? What explains this trend? How would your answer change if share repurchases were included in calculating U.S. dividend payout ratios?

ST14-4. What does it mean to say that corporate managers "smooth" cash dividend payments? Why do managers do this?

ST14-5. What are the key assumptions and predictions of the signaling model of dividends? Are these predictions supported by empirical research findings?

ST14-6. What is the expected relationship between dividend payout levels and the growth rate and availability of positive-*NPV* projects, under the agency cost model of dividends? What about the expected relationship between dividend payout and the diverseness of the firm's shareholders? Consider a firm, such as Microsoft, awash in excess cash flow and available positive-*NPV* projects, and having a relatively diverse shareholder base in an industry with increasing competition. Does either the agency model or the signaling model adequately predict the dividend policy of Microsoft? Which does the better job?

Questions

Q14-1. What fraction of U.S. public companies pays regular cash dividends today? How has this changed over the past fifty years?

Q14-2. What is a firm's *dividend yield*? How does it compare to that firm's *dividend payout ratio*?

Q14-3. Compare and contrast the following dividend policies: the *constant payout ratio dividend policy* and the *constant dollar payout dividend policy*. Which policy do most public companies actually follow? Why?

Q14-4. What is a *low-regular-and-extra payout dividend policy*? Why do firms pursuing this policy explicitly label some cash dividend payments as "extra"?

Q14-5. What is a *stock dividend*? How does this differ from a *stock split*?

Q14-6.   What factors have contributed to the growth in share repurchase programs by U.S. public companies? What the effect did the Jobs and Growth Tax Relief Reconciliation Act of 2003 have on share repurchase programs?

Q14-7.   What is the average stock market reaction to: (a) a dividend initiation; (b) a dividend increase; (c) a dividend termination; and (d) a dividend decrease? Are these reactions logically consistent?

Q14-8.   What are the key assumptions and predictions of the *agency cost/contracting model* of dividend payments? Are these predictions supported by research findings?

Q14-9.   Around the world, utilities generally have the highest dividend payouts of any industry, yet they also tend to have massive investment programs, which they finance using external sources. How do you reconcile high payouts and large-scale security issuance?

Q14-10.   Why do firms with diverse shareholder bases typically pay higher dividends than private firms or public firms with concentrated ownership structures? How are fixed dividends used as a bonding (commitment) mechanism by managers of firms with dispersed ownership structures and large amounts of excess cash flow?

Q14-11.   How is the *residual theory of dividends* used to explain observed dividend payments? How is this theory in conflict with evidence suggesting that corporate managers smooth dividends?

Problems

Payout Policy Fundamentals

P14-1.   Beta Corporation has the following shareholders' equity accounts:

Common stock at par	$ 5,000,000
Paid-in capital in excess of par	2,000,000
Retained earnings	25,000,000
Total stockholders' equity	$32,000,000

    a.   What is the maximum amount that Beta Corporation can pay in cash dividends, without impairing its legal capital, if it is headquartered in a U.S. state where capital is defined as the par value of common stock?

    b.   What is the maximum amount that Beta Corporation can pay in cash dividends, without impairing its legal capital, if it is headquartered in a U.S. state where capital is defined as the par value of common stock, plus paid-in capital in excess of par?

P14-2.   What are alternative ways in which investors can receive a cash return from their investment in the equity of a company? From a tax standpoint, which of these would be preferred, assuming that investors face the same 15% tax on income and capital gains? What are the pros and cons of paying out cash dividends?

P14-3.   Delta Corporation earned $2.50 per share during fiscal year 2011 and paid cash dividends of $1.00 per share. During the fiscal year that just ended on December 31, 2012, Delta earned $3.00 per share, and the firm's managers expect to earn this amount per share during fiscal years 2013 and 2014, as well.

    a.   What was Delta's *payout ratio* for fiscal year 2011?

    b.   If Delta's managers want to follow a *constant dollar payout dividend policy*, what dividend per share will they declare for fiscal year 2012?

    c.   If Delta's managers want to follow a *constant payout ratio dividend policy*, what dividend per share will they declare for fiscal year 2012?

    d.   If Delta's managers want to follow a partial-adjustment strategy, with a target payout ratio equal to fiscal year 2011's, how could they change dividend payments during 2012, 2013, and 2014?

P14-4.   Advanced Vehicle Enterprises (AVE) follows a policy of paying out 50% of its net income as cash dividends to its shareholders each year. The company plans to do so again this year, during which AVE earned $100 million in net profits after tax. The company has 40 million shares outstanding and pays dividends annually.

a. What is the company's dollar dividend payment per share each year?

b. Assuming that AVE's stock price is $54 per share immediately before its ex-dividend date, what is the expected price of AVE stock on the ex-dividend date if there are no personal taxes on dividend income received?

P14-5. General Manufacturing Company (GMC) follows a policy of paying out 50% of its net income as cash dividends to its shareholders each year. The company plans to do so again this year, during which GMC earned $100 million in net profits after tax. The company has 40 million shares outstanding and pays dividends annually. Assume that an investor purchased GMC stock a year ago at $45. The investor, who faces a personal tax rate of 15% on both dividend income and on capital gains, plans to sell the stock soon. Transactions costs are negligible.

a. Calculate the after-tax return this investor will earn if she sells GMC stock at the current $54 stock price prior to the ex-dividend date.

b. Calculate the after-tax return the investor will earn if she sells GMC stock on the ex-dividend date, assuming that the price of GMC stock falls by the dividend amount on the ex-dividend date.

c. Calculate the after-tax return the investor will earn if she sells GMC stock on the ex-dividend date, assuming that the price of GMC stock falls by one half the dividend amount on the ex-dividend date.

P14-6. Specialty Chemicals Company (SCC) pays out 50% of its net income as cash dividends to its shareholders once each quarter. The company plans to do so again this year, during which SCC earned $100 million in net profits after tax. If the company has 40 million shares outstanding and pays dividends quarterly, what is the company's dollar dividend payment per share each quarter?

P14-7. Twilight Company's stock is selling for $60.25 per share, and the firm's managers have just announced a $1.50 per share dividend payment.

a. What should happen to Twilight Company's stock price on the ex-dividend date, assuming that investors do not have to pay taxes on dividends or capital gains and do not incur any transactions costs in trading shares?

b. What should happen to Twilight Company's stock price on the ex-dividend date, assuming that it follows the historical performance of U.S. stock prices on ex-dividend days?

c. If the historical "ex-dividend-day-price effect," observed in U.S. stock markets, was indeed a tax effect, what should happen to Twilight Company's stock price on the ex-dividend date, given the tax changes embodied in the Jobs and Growth Tax Relief Reconciliation Act of 2003?

P14-8. Global Financial Corporation (GFC) has 10 million shares outstanding, each currently worth $80 per share. The firm's managers are considering a plan to split the company's stock 2-for-1, but they are concerned about the impact this split announcement will have on the firm's stock price.

a. If GFC's managers announce a 2-for-1 stock split, what exactly will the company do, and what will GFC's stock price likely be after the split?

b. How many total shares of GFC stock will be outstanding after the stock split?

c. If GFC's managers believe that the ideal stock price for the firm's shares is $20 per share, what should they do? How many shares would be outstanding after this action?

d. Why do you think GFC's managers are considering a stock split?

P14-9. The net income for a firm is currently $1,000,000 and is projected to grow annually for the next four years as follows: $1,200,000, $1,300,000, $1,500,000, and $1,700,000. Assuming the dividend payout ratio is 20% and there are 1,000,000 shares outstanding, what is the current dividend per share? Further assuming that the firm does not change its stated dividend, what is the dividend payout ratio for the next four years? (*Note:* All figures are in thousands.)

P14-10. A firm's shares currently sell for $32.48, with 5 million shares outstanding. The firm is considering a 20% stock dividend in which 100 shares become 120 shares. After the stock dividend, at what price will the shareholders' value be unchanged? (*Hint:* Consider shareholder value to be the market capitalization, which equals the number of shares outstanding multiplied by the stock price.) If the stock price became $27.50 after the stock dividend, do the shareholders benefit?

P14-11. A firm's shares currently sell for $3.50 with 4 million shares outstanding. The firm plans to reverse split its stock by combining two shares into one share. If the price after this reverse split is $6.52, have shareholders gained or lost value? How much value is gained or lost? (*Hint:* Consider shareholder value to be the market capitalization, which equals the number of shares outstanding multiplied by the stock price.)

P14-12. Sunshine Pageants decides that it will use a Dutch auction to repurchase 2 million shares. Investors have submitted the following bids on the price and quantity they are willing to sell shares to the firm:

Price ($)	Shares
24.45	100,000
24.50	200,000
24.60	600,000
24.75	1,100,000
24.95	2,000,000
25.15	2,500,000
25.50	5,000,000

Determine the lowest price at which the firm is able to purchase 2 million shares. (*Note:* If the firm is willing to purchase shares for $25.50, then it must purchase all shares at this price; the goal is to find the lowest price at which the firm can purchase the 2 million shares.) Given the purchase price of the shares, how much extra money do the shareholders receive compared to the schedule of acceptable bids?

P14-13. Investor A recognizes $100 in dividend income that is taxed at a rate of 20%. Investor B also wants to recognize the same after-tax revenue as investor A, but investor B owns stock that does not pay dividends. If investor B's stock sells for $12 a share (originally purchased for $7 a share) and if the capital gains tax is 40%, then how many shares must investor B sell?

P14-14. Maggie Fiduciary is a shareholder in the Superior Service Company (SSC). The current price of SSC's stock is $33 per share, and there are 1 million shares outstanding. Maggie owns 10,000 shares, or 1% of the stock, which she purchased one year ago for $30 per share. Assume that SSC makes a surprise announcement that it plans to repurchase 100,000 shares of its own stock, at a price of $35 per share. In response to this announcement, SSC's stock price increases $1 per share, from $33 to $34, but this price is expected to fall back to $33.50 per share after the repurchase is completed. Assume that Maggie faces marginal personal tax rates of 15% on both dividend income and capital gains.

a. Calculate Maggie's (realized) after-tax return from her investment in SSC shares, assuming that she chooses to participate in the repurchase program and that all of the shares she tenders are purchased at $35 per share.

b. How many shares will Maggie be able to sell if all SSC's shareholders tender their shares to the firm as part of this repurchase program and the company purchases shares on a pro rata basis?

c. What fraction of SSC's total common equity will Maggie own after the repurchase program is completed if she chooses not to tender her shares?

P14-15. Go to the home page for Dogs of the Dow (**www.dogsofthedow.com**), look at the year-to-date figures, and observe the dividend yields of the thirty stocks of the Dow Jones Industrial Average. Which industries contain the higher-dividend-yielding stocks, and which contain the lower-yielding stocks? Are there differences in the growth prospects between the high- and low-yielding stocks? Is this what you expected? Explain.

P14-16. Stately Building Company's shares are selling for $75 each, and its dividend yield is 2.0%. What is the amount of Stately's dividend per share?

P14-17. The stock of Up-and-Away Inc. is selling for $80 per share and is currently paying a quarterly dividend of $0.25 per share. What is the dividend yield on Up-and-Away stock?

P14-18. Well-Bred Service Company earned $50,000,000 during 2012 and paid $20,000,000 in dividends to the holders of its 40 million shares. If the current market price of Well-Bred's stock is $31.25, calculate the following: (a) the company's dividend payout ratio; (b) the stated dividend per share, assuming Well-Bred pays dividends annually; (c) the stated dividend per share, assuming Well-Bred pays dividends in four equal quarterly payments; and (d) the current dividend yield on Well-Bred stock.

Dividends in Perfect and Imperfect Worlds

P14-19. It is January 1, 2012, and Boomer Equipment Company (BEC) currently has assets of $250 million and expects to earn a return of 10% during 2012. There are 20 million shares of BEC stock outstanding. The firm has an opportunity to invest in a positive-NPV *(minimal)* project that will cost $25 million over the course of 2012, and is trying to determine if it should finance this investment by retaining profits over the course of the year or by issuing new shares while paying the profits earned as dividends. Show that the decision is irrelevant in a world of perfect and frictionless markets.

P14-20. Swelter Manufacturing Company (SMC) currently has assets of $200 million and a required return of 10% on its 10 million shares outstanding. The firm has an opportunity to invest in positive-NPV *(minimal)* projects that will cost $20 million and is trying to determine if it should withhold this amount from dividends payable to finance the investments or if it should pay out the dividends and issue new shares to finance the investments. Show that the decision is irrelevant in a world of perfect and frictionless markets. How is the result affected if a personal income tax of 15% is introduced into the model?

P14-21. Assume that it is now January 1, 2012, and you are examining two unlevered firms that operate in the same industry, that have identical assets worth $80 million that yield a net profit of 12.5% per year, and that have 10 million shares outstanding. During 2012, and all subsequent years, each firm has the opportunity to invest an amount equal to its net income in (slightly) positive-NPV investment projects. The Beta Company wants to finance its capital spending through retained earnings. The Gamma Company wants to pay out 100% of its annual earnings as cash dividends and to finance its investments with a new share offering each year. There are no taxes or transactions costs to issuing securities.

    a.   Calculate the overall and per-share market value of the Beta Company at the end of 2012 and each of the two following years (2013 and 2014). What return on investment will this firm's shareholders earn?

    b.   Describe the specific steps that the Gamma Company must take today (1/1/2012), and at the end of each of the next three years (year-end 2012, 2013, and 2014), if it pays out all of its net income as dividends and still grows its assets at the same rate as that of the Beta Company.

    c.   Calculate the number and per-share price of shares that the Gamma Company must sell today, and at the end of 2012, 2013, and 2014, if it pays out all of its net income as dividends and still grows its assets at the same rate as that of the Beta Company.

    d.   Assuming that you currently own 100,000 shares (1%) of Gamma Company stock, compute the fraction of the company's total outstanding equity that you will own three years from now if you do not participate in any of the share offerings the firm will make during this holding period.

P14-22. Investors anticipate that Sweetwater Manufacturing Inc.'s next dividend, due in one year, will be $4 per share. Investors also expect earnings to grow at 5% in perpetuity, and they require a return of 10% on their shares. Use the Gordon growth model (see Equation 5.4 on page 156) to calculate Sweetwater's stock price today.

P14-23. Super-Thrift Pharmaceuticals Company traditionally pays an annual dividend equal to 50% of its earnings. Earnings this year are $30,000,000. The company has 15 million shares outstanding. Investors expect earnings to grow at a 5% annual rate in perpetuity, and they require a return of 12% on their shares.

    a.   What is Super-Thrift's current dividend per share? What is it expected to be next year?

    b.   Use the Gordon growth model (see Equation 5.4 on page 156) to calculate Super-Thrift's stock price today.

P14-24. Casual Construction Corporation (CCC) earned $60,000,000 during 2012. The firm expects to earn $63,000,000 during 2013, in line with its long-term earnings growth rate. There are 20 million CCC shares outstanding, and the firm has a policy of paying out 40% of its earnings as cash dividends. Investors require a 10% return on CCC shares.

    a.   What is CCC's current dividend per share? What is it expected to be next year?

    b.   Use the Gordon growth model (see Equation 5.4 on page 156) to calculate CCC's stock price today.

P14-25. Hole Foods Donuts, Inc., has generated profits of $2 per share for many years and has consistently paid 100% of those profits to shareholders via a dividend. Investors do not expect Hole Foods Donuts to grow in the future. The company has 200,000 shares of stock outstanding worth $20 per share. Suppose the firm decides to eliminate its dividend and instead use the money to repurchase shares.

a. Assuming that there are no taxes and that the repurchase announcement conveys no new information to investors about the profitability or risk of Hole Foods Donuts, how do you think the stock price will react to the announcement?

b. How many shares will Hole Foods Donuts repurchase?

c. What stock price would you expect for Hole Foods Donuts one and two years after this announcement? What would the stock price have been in the next two years if the company had simply maintained its old dividend policy?

P14-26. Jasper Metals, Inc., just announced that it will pay its regular quarterly dividend of $3.50 per share.

a. Does the stock price fall to reflect this payment on the announcement date, the record date, the ex-dividend date, or the payment date?

b. Assume that there are no market imperfections. By how much will the stock price fall?

c. Suppose investors must pay a 38% tax on dividends received but pay nothing on capital gains. How would this change your answer to part (b)?

d. Now suppose that investors must pay 38% in taxes on both dividends and capital gains. In this case, how much would you expect the stock price to fall in response to the dividend?

e. Suppose that, just prior to the dividend announcement, Jasper Metals stock was worth $175 per share. Assume once again that there are no taxes. If you own 50 shares, then what is the value of your investment? How does the dividend payment affect your wealth? If Jasper Metals cancels the dividend and announces that they will repurchase 2% of their outstanding shares, what effect does that have on your wealth?

P14-27. Go to the home page of Cisco Systems, Inc. (www.cisco.com) and link to its financial reports page. Download the most recent annual report and observe the capital investment and dividend policies of Cisco Systems. Now, do the same for Chevron (www.chevron.com). Which of the two firms appears to have more high-growth, positive-*NPV* investment opportunities? Which pays the higher relative dividend? Do these results support the agency cost/contracting model? The signaling model?

Real-World Influences on Payout Policy

P14-28. Universal Windmill Company (UWC) currently has assets worth $50 million and a required return of 10% on its 2 million shares outstanding. The firm has an opportunity to invest in (minimally) positive-*NPV* projects that will cost $5 million. UWC needs to determine whether it should withhold this amount from dividends payable to finance the investments or pay out the dividends and issue new shares to finance the investments. Show that the decision is irrelevant in a world of perfect and frictionless markets. What happens if a personal income tax of 15% on dividends (but not capital gains) is introduced into the model?

P14-29. A publicly traded firm announces an increase in its dividend, with no other material information accompanying the announcement. What information is this announcement likely to convey, and what is the expected stock-price effect, as the market assimilates this information?

P14-30. Sam Sharp purchased 100 shares of Electric Lighting Inc. (ELI) one year ago for $60 per share, and he also received cash dividends of $5 per share since then. Now that ELI's stock price has increased to $64.50, Sam has decided to sell his holdings. What is Sam's gross (pretax) and after-tax return on this investment, assuming that he faces a 15% tax rate on dividends and capital gains?

THOMSON REUTERS | Business School Edition

For instructions on using Thomson ONE, refer to the instructions provided with the Thomson ONE problems at the end of Chapters 1–6.

P14-31. Compare the dividend policies of Novartis AG (ticker: S:NOVN), Astrazeneca PLC (AZN), Aventis SA (F:RPP), and Merck and Company Inc. (U:MRK) over the last five years. Determine the annual dividend payout ratios and the dividend yield for the four firms in each year. What do the dividend payout ratios tell you about investment opportunities available to each company? Do the payout ratios change significantly over time? Which of these firms, if any, follows a constant payout ratio dividend policy or a constant dollar payout dividend policy? Did any of these firms pay out an extra or special dividend over the last five years? Was it paid in a year with higher than normal earnings?

P14-32. Did any of the four companies in Problem 14-31 change dividends over the last five years? Did dividends change (in the same direction) every time earnings changed? What does this say about a manager's expectations of changes in company earnings?

Smart Ethics Video

Scott Lee, Texas A&M University

"Generally associated with repurchase announcements is a fairly strong market response."

Smart Ideas Video

John Graham, Duke University

"Why do companies hesitate to initiate a dividend or to increase a dividend?"

Kenneth Eades, University of Virginia

"It's an earnings story, not a dividend story."

Smart Practices Video

Andy Bryant, Executive Vice President of Finance and Enterprise Systems, Chief Financial Officer, Intel Corp.

"Dividends are probably not the most effective way to return cash to shareholders."

Video photos: Cengage Learning

Cynthia Lucchese, Chief Financial Officer, Hillenbrand Industries

"We have to decide how much cash to return as a dividend versus share repurchases."

Frank Popoff, Chairman of the Board (retired), Dow Chemical

"The decision specific to dividends is one that boards wrestle with on a regular basis."

SMART concepts

See what dividend irrelevance means in a world with perfect capital markets.

Mini-Case

Dividend Policy

After working for the past four years as a financial analyst for Nevada Power Corporation, you receive a well-deserved promotion. You have been appointed to work on special projects for Mr. Watkins, the chief financial officer (CFO). Your first assignment is to gather information on dividend theory and policy, because the CFO wants to reassess the firm's current dividend policy.

Assignment

1. What are the different types of dividend policies? Provide examples of situations in which each of these dividend policies could be used.

2. Describe the difference between cash dividends, stock dividends, stock splits, and share repurchases. Provide examples when each of these forms of dividends can be used.

3. Discuss the theory of dividend irrelevance. How do taxes affect the dividend irrelevance theory?

4. Discuss the payout decision in the imperfect (real) world. Be sure to include both the *agency cost/contracting model* and *signaling model* in your discussion.

5. Explain the *residual theory of dividends* and highlight its appeal as well as its major drawback.

6. How do managers use dividend policy to convey information to the marketplace? Why is dividend policy, instead of a press release, used to communicate information?

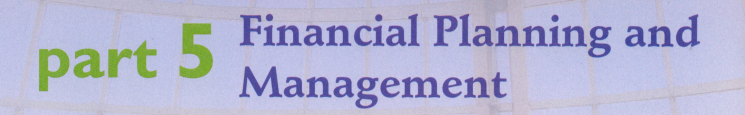

part 5　Financial Planning and Management

© Altus Plunkett/Flickr/Getty Images, Inc.

A big part of what financial managers do in large corporations might be called "the control function." By this we mean that financial managers are responsible for making sure that the firm has sufficient cash balances to operate each day. This involves checking to see that the firm pays its bills on time (but not too early) and following up on credit sales to ensure that customers pay on time as well. These are the issues that we address in Part 5.

Chapter 15 describes the financial planning process. Financial planning methods vary widely, but almost all firms' financial plans have certain characteristics in common. Most firms plan over several horizons, with the detail of the plan decreasing as the planning horizon increases. That is, firms have very detailed plans that they use to project inflows and outflows of cash, as well as earnings, over the next year or two. Most companies also develop plans that look ahead two to five years or more. Financial plans help firms focus on goal achievement, identify problems before they arise, and arrange financing before cash shortfalls become critical.

Chapter 16 takes a closer look at how cash moves through a firm. Before a manufacturing firm makes a sale, it must purchase raw materials and begin manufacturing its product. It must also maintain work-in-process as well as finished goods inventories. Most firms sell to customers on credit, so even after making a sale, no cash comes in immediately. The cash conversion cycle illustrates how managers can track the length of time that it takes a firm to generate cash from selling its goods. Clearly, the amount of time a firm's goods spend in inventory, and how long the firm must wait before its customers pay for their orders play central roles in determining how quickly a firm generates cash. As with other financial decisions, when managers determine how much to invest in items such as inventories and receivables, they must consider the cost-benefit trade-off of those investments. Over time, information technology has enabled firms to invest less and less in these types of assets.

Firms hold cash balances for many reasons, and Chapter 17 examines the factors that firms consider when they decide how much cash to hold. Part of that decision revolves around the timing of the firm's cash disbursements, and that in turn depends on the terms under which the firm's suppliers grant it credit. Chapter 17 illustrates how the credit terms granted by suppliers contain an implicit interest rate, and when the firm decides to pay its suppliers determines its effective borrowing costs.

459

chapter 15

Financial Planning

What Companies Do

Brighter Outlook for Sony

After losing 3.2 billion yen in its 2011 fiscal year, Sony released a much sunnier forecast for 2012. The company said it expected to generate 7.5 trillion yen in revenue and 80 billion yen in profit. Sony predicted that the driving force behind its improved performance would be LCD TV sales and the release of its new Next Generation Portable gaming system. However, Sony acknowledged that the revenues and profits from its music business would continue a decline that had been ongoing for several years.

Reading between the lines of Sony's 2012 forecast reveals that the company builds detailed financial plans for all of its business units. Sony uses these plans when it makes hiring decisions, enters into contracts for raw materials, schedules production runs, and communicates with the investment community. Even though Sony executives know that things do not always go according to plan (such as when a massive earthquake and tsunami in Japan cost the company 22 billion yen in 2011 sales), having a detailed financial plan in place helps the company react to changing business conditions. As Benjamin Franklin once said, "By failing to prepare, you are preparing to fail." Sony, like nearly all large corporations, puts tremendous effort into building its annual financial plans and managing to those plans.

Source: "Sony Sees Profit This Fiscal Year, Despite PSN Breach," by Don Reisinger, May 26, 2011, news.cnet.com.

Learning Objectives

After studying this chapter you should be able to:

- Understand the relationship between a firm's strategy and its plans, and the roles that finance plays in constructing strategic plans;

- Describe the impact of growth on the firm's balance sheet and the role of the sustainable growth model as a planning device;

- Discuss the role of pro forma financial statements in the financial planning process and the shorthand approach for estimating external funds required;

- Explain the "plug figure" used in constructing a pro forma balance sheet and the information it provides in the financial planning process;

- Review the conservative, aggressive, and matching financing strategies that a firm might employ to fund the long-term trend and seasonal fluctuations in its business; and

- Describe the role of the cash budget in planning and monitoring the firm's cash inflows and outflows on a short-term basis.

Financial planning is an important corporate finance activity that touches almost all functional groups in a firm. Financial planning encompasses a wide array of activities: setting long-run strategic goals, preparing quarterly and annual budgets, and managing day-to-day fluctuations in cash balances. Although most people with corporate work experience are familiar with the budgeting process, they often know little about how budgets and other financial plans are compiled at the corporate level, how they tie together sometimes competing interests within the firm, and how they interact with the firm's strategic objectives. In this chapter, we discuss various elements of a firm's financial planning processes. The chapter emphasizes both long-term and short-term financial planning. In Chapters 16 and 17 we consider the operational aspects of short-term financial decisions. The three chapters in Part 5 demonstrate how firms' financial plans must balance the interests and objectives of different business units and functional areas. For example, in setting long-term strategic and financial goals, a firm must prioritize its desires to increase sales and market share; to change or maintain its exposure to financial risk; to achieve production efficiencies; to attract and retain capable employees; and to distribute cash to shareholders. In almost every instance, making incremental progress on one of these objectives means an incremental sacrifice on one or more of the other goals.

Financial planning, particularly long-term planning, is more art than science: the connection between most financial planning models and the objective of maximizing shareholder wealth is at times tenuous.[1] The What Companies Do Globally insert on page 462 provides data that confirm the difficulty of adapting to macroeconomic forecasts. At one level, the advice we would give to a firm constructing a long-term plan is straightforward: Do whatever is necessary to invest in all positive-*NPV* projects. In practice, a variety of factors make following that advice a major challenge. CFOs usually tell us that they have many more acceptable projects than they can possibly undertake. Limits on capital, production capacity, human resources, and many other inputs make the planning process more complex than simply accepting all projects that look promising. We concede that the theoretical underpinnings of planning models are weak, so in this chapter we focus as much as possible on practice. We describe how firms *actually* build long-term and short-term financial plans rather than argue about how they *should* plan.

15-1   Overview of the Planning Process

A long-term financial plan begins with strategy. Typically, the senior management team analyzes the markets in which the firm competes. Managers try to identify ways to protect and increase the firm's competitive advantage in those markets. For example, a firm that competes by achieving the lowest production cost in an industry might seek to determine whether it should make additional investments in manufacturing facilities to achieve even greater production efficiencies. A risk to this strategy is that market demand may turn out to be such that the firm's fixed assets are underutilized. This type of firm, therefore, will try to forecast market demand and develop contingency plans for the possibility that the expected demand does not materialize. If a firm's competitive advantage derives

Cengage Learning

Jackie Sturm, Vice President of Finance, Intel Corp.

"Once the product line business plan is completed, we move into our annual planning process, which is more of a tactical exercise."

See the entire interview at **SMART** | finance

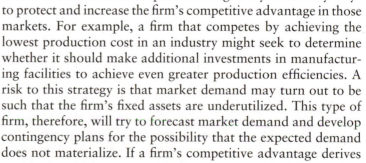

Smart Practices Video

---

[1] A number of models—such as economic value added (EVA®) and shareholder value added (SVA)—tie financial decisions and plans to shareholder value. Those widely used models, introduced in Chapter 8, are briefly discussed later in this chapter.

What Companies Do Globally

How Companies Adjust Financial Plans When a Global Recession Hits

A recession highlights the importance of clear financial and strategic operating plans, because a company's survival may hinge on how effectively it can cut costs, and match output to lower demand. This lesson was brought home to managers in 2008 as the global credit crisis cut demand for goods and services and forced the world's major economies to contract.

A 2008 survey of 1,050 chief financial officers in the United States, Europe, and Asia showed how managers were preparing to cope with the deepening recession. The survey found that managers were planning to cut research and development, marketing, and capital expenditures; to draw down their cash holdings; and to cut dividend payments. These actions are dramatic—for example, recall from Chapter 14 that companies are very reluctant to cut dividends. The survey results presented in the following figure also show that managers in Europe and the United States were planning to reduce personnel but that Asian managers expected to keep employment virtually unchanged. Managers in all three regions were planning to cut marketing expenditures significantly, while managers in Europe and the United States were planning much more drastic cuts in technology spending than were Asian managers.

U.S., European, and Asian Pro Forma Plans for 2009

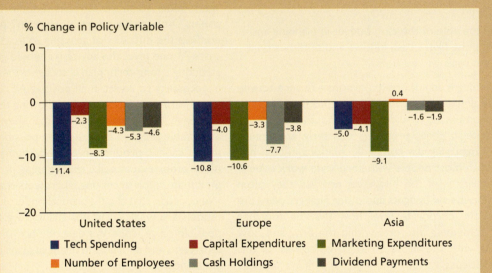

Source: Figures from Murillo Campello, John R. Graham, and Campbell R. Harvey, 2010, "The Real Effects of Financial Constraints: Evidence from the Financial Crisis," Journal of Financial Economics, Vol. 97, pp. 470–487.

from the value of its brand, it might begin by assessing whether new or expanded marketing programs might increase the value of its brand relative to competitors.

15-1a Successful Long-Term Planning

Long-term planning requires more than paying close attention to a firm's existing markets. Even more important is the ability to identify and prioritize new market opportunities. Successful long-term planning means asking and answering questions such as the following:

- In what emerging markets might we have a sustainable competitive advantage?
- How can we leverage our competitive strengths across existing markets in which we currently do not compete?
- What threats to our current business exist, and how can we meet those threats?
- Where in the world should we produce? Where should we sell?
- Can we deploy resources more efficiently by exiting certain markets and using those resources elsewhere?

As the firm's senior managers develop answers to these questions, they construct a **strategic plan**, a multiyear action plan for the major investments and competitive initiatives that they believe will drive the future success of the enterprise.

15-1b The Role of Finance in Long-Term Planning

Finance plays several roles in long-term planning. First, financial managers draw on a broad set of skills to *assess the likelihood that a given strategic objective can be achieved*. With respect to a major new investment proposal, their first questions should be "Does this investment make sense?" and "Is there good reason to expect this proposal to generate wealth for our shareholders?"

Second, the finance function *assesses the feasibility of a strategic plan*, given a firm's existing and prospective sources of funding. Though some corporate giants, such as Microsoft and Intel, hold such vast amounts of cash that they are nearly unconstrained in their ability to make large new investments, for most companies financial constraints are more limiting. Given a broad set of strategic objectives, financial managers must determine whether the firm's ability to generate cash internally, plus its ability to raise cash externally, will be sufficient to fund new spending initiatives.[2] Financial analysts generally treat expected dividend payments as a factor that limits a firm's ability to make new investments. Similarly, if fulfilling strategic objectives will require a significant increase in leverage, it is the finance group's role to communicate this trade-off to the top management team. We will see in the next section that financial managers have several tools that enable them to highlight the trade-offs firms face when setting growth targets.

Third, finance clearly *plays an important control function as firms implement their strategic plans*. Financial analysts prepare and update cash budgets to make sure that firms do not unknowingly slip into a liquidity crisis. At an even more detailed level, analysts monitor individual items in the cash budget, such as changes in inventories and receivables (our focus in Chapter 16) and changes in payables (our focus in Chapter 17). Here, too, financial managers must evaluate trade-offs.

Fourth, a major contribution of finance to the strategic planning process involves *risk management*. If a firm's strategy calls for making new investments in overseas markets (either producing or selling abroad), then the firm faces a new set of risk exposures. The finance function manages these exposures so the firm takes those risks that it believes it has a comparative advantage in taking and hedges risks for which it has no advantage. Similarly, more than in any other functional area, the job of finance is to identify problems that could develop in the future if the firm's strategic plans unfold in unexpected ways. Developing "problem scenarios" and options for dealing with them is an important part of finance's risk-management responsibility, which is covered in Chapter 23 (one of the web chapters).

In this chapter, we focus primarily on the second and third roles just described. The next section discusses the financial tools that help managers determine the trade-offs they face when setting future growth objectives.

15-1 Concept Review Questions

1. A company decides to compete by making a major investment to modernize its production facilities. Describe two ways in which meeting this objective might force a firm to sacrifice other objectives.

2. Firm A competes in a market in which the demand for its product and its selling price are highly unpredictable. Firm B competes in a market in which these factors are much more stable. Which firm probably creates cash budgets more frequently and monitors them more carefully?

---

[2]Considerations such as these are particularly important when credit market conditions are extremely tight, such as during the credit crisis of 2008–2010.

15-2 Planning for Growth

15-2a Sustainable Growth

Most firms strive to grow over time, and most firms view rapid growth as preferable to slow growth. Of course, rapid growth does not maximize wealth, since it's possible for growth to be detrimental to shareholders. Here, though, we put aside the question of whether growth is desirable. Assuming that firms seek growth, they can focus on one or a number of measures of growth.

Popular Measures of Growth Three of the most popular measures of growth are the accounting return on investment (*ROI*), economic value added (EVA), and growth in sales or assets. All of these methods rely on accounting data and are typically measured on an annual basis. We next describe *ROI* and EVA more fully.

return on investment (*ROI*)
A measure of a firm's overall effectiveness in using its assets to generate returns to common stockholders; also, return on total assets (*ROA*).

Return on Investment The accounting return on investment (*ROI*) is the firm's earnings available for common stockholders divided by its total assets. (In Chapter 2 we referred to this measure by its alternate name, *return on total assets* or *ROA*.) Return on investment measures the firm's overall effectiveness in using its assets to generate returns to common stockholders.

Firms that use this metric as a measure of growth attempt to maintain *ROI* above some minimum *hurdle rate* and often raise this standard over time. These firms frequently set hurdle rates for minimum *ROI* based on the firm's *cost of capital*. They assume that if the *ROI* is greater than the cost of capital (plus perhaps a fudge factor), then shareholder value will be created. The problem with this approach is that it compares the *accounting-based ROI* to an *economic-based* measure of the return demanded by suppliers of capital. Although use of this method has practical appeal, its theoretical roots are shallow at best.

economic value added (EVA)
A measure of the value created by an investment, a division, or an entire company, calculated as the difference between net operating profits after taxes and the cost of funds.

Economic Value Added (EVA) As noted in Chapter 8, economic value added (EVA) is the difference between *net operating profits after taxes* (*NOPAT*) and the cost of funds; when applied correctly, EVA prompts managers to make the same investment decisions that the NPV method directs them to do. The cost of funds is found by multiplying the firm's cost of capital by its investment. Analysts can apply EVA to individual investments or to the entire firm, but its use in financial planning tends to focus on the entire firm or on entire divisions.

Firms that employ EVA in the planning process typically build the EVA model into their spreadsheets and evaluate various scenarios by calculating the EVAs of the scenarios. By comparing all positive EVAs, the firm can implement the set of plans with the highest EVA, which should create the most value for shareholders. Although widely examined in the financial literature,[3] EVA's degree of positive correlation with actual share valuations remains unclear. Most agree that the measure is conceptually valid but that it is sometimes difficult to implement because it requires accrual-based accounting inputs (*NOPAT* and investment). This disconnect between theory and practice, coupled with its complex computations, tends to result in greater planning focus on growth rates.

WHAT TO ASK

What metrics does your firm use as growth targets and what role, if any, does economic value added (EVA) play in the firm's planning process?

Defining Growth Firms frequently set planning goals in terms of *target growth rates*, typically annual growth in sales or assets. For the moment, we set aside the question of whether growth creates or destroys shareholder value. We instead focus on measuring target growth rates in light of their intuitive, computational, and practical appeal. Our goal is to demonstrate a simple model that highlights the trade-offs that firms

---

[3]For some critical analyses of EVA, see Ray D. Dillon and James E. Owers, "EVA as a Financial Metric: Attributes, Utilization, and Relationship to *NPV*," *Financial Practice and Education* (Spring/Summer 1997), pp. 32–40; John D. Martin, J. William Petty, and Steven P. Rich, "A Survey of EVA and Other Residual Income Models of Firm Performance," *Journal of Finance Literature* (Winter 2005), pp. 1–20; and John M. Griffith, "The True Value of EVA," *Journal of Applied Finance* (Fall/Winter 2004), pp. 25–29.

must weigh when they choose to grow. These trade-offs depend on several factors: how rapidly the firm plans to grow; how profitable its existing business is; how much of its earnings it retains and how much it pays out to shareholders; how efficiently it manages its assets; and how much financial leverage it is willing to bear.

First, let us define what we mean by "growth." A firm's growth can be measured by increases in its market value, its asset base, the number of people it employs, or any number of other metrics. For now, let us imagine that a firm establishes a growth target in terms of sales. *Our experience suggests that most firms define and measure growth targets in terms of sales*, so we will use that convention as well. That is, when we say that a firm plans to grow by 10% next year, we mean that it hopes to achieve a 10% increase in sales revenue.

With sales growth in mind, think about what growth means for a firm in terms of its balance sheet. An increase in sales probably requires additional investments in assets. Certainly, we would anticipate that increased sales volume would require additional investments in current assets, such as inventories and receivables. Over time, increases in sales will also require new investments in fixed assets, such as production capacity and office space. As a shortcut, let us assume that a firm's total asset turnover ratio, the ratio of sales (S) divided by total assets (A), remains constant through time. In other words, any increase in sales will be matched by a comparable percentage increase in assets. Because the balance sheet equation must hold, increases in liabilities and shareholders' equity must equal the increase in assets. So how would we expect increases in liabilities and shareholders' equity to come about?

In previous chapters we learned that most companies issue new common shares very infrequently, so we will rule that out as a potential source of new financing. As with inventories and receivables, accounts payable should increase (higher sales volume means higher purchases). We might also expect to see higher accruals and higher short-term liabilities of other types. Similarly, if a firm's business is profitable then its equity account will increase (even if it does not issue any new stock) by the amount of earnings it retains. Figure 15.1 illustrates that the growth in assets must equal growth in these liability and equity accounts over time.

sustainable growth model
Derives an expression that determines how rapidly a firm can grow while maintaining a balance between its outflows (increases in assets) and inflows (increases in liabilities and equity) of cash.

Developing the Sustainable Growth Model The **sustainable growth model** starts with a balance sheet identity. It then adds a few assumptions and ultimately derives an expression that determines how rapidly a firm can grow while maintaining a balance

Figure 15.1   **Sustainable Growth Equality**

As a firm grows, it must invest in new assets to support increased sales volume. The investments in new assets must be financed with some combination of increased liabilities and increased equity.

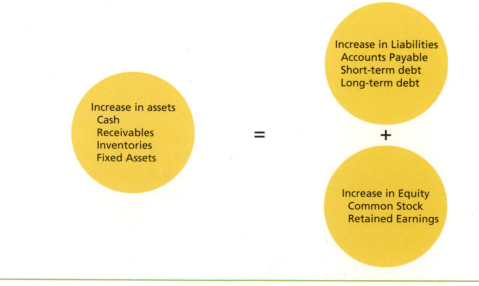

between its outflows (increases in assets) and inflows (increases in liabilities and equity) of funds. Specifically, the sustainable growth model assumes the following:

1. The firm's only form of equity is common stock (E), and it will not issue new shares of common stock next year.
2. The firm's total asset turnover ratio, S/A, remains constant.
3. The firm pays out a constant fraction, d, of its earnings as dividends.
4. The firm maintains a constant assets-to-equity ratio, A/E.
5. The firm's net profit margin, m, is constant.

Consider a firm that wants to increase sales next period by g percent. If total assets in the current period equal A, and if the total asset turnover ratio remains constant, then assets must increase in the next period by gA. This represents a change in the left-hand side of the firm's balance sheet next period—a change that must be balanced by an equal change on the right-hand side.

Given sales this period of S, a net profit margin (in this case, defined as net income divided by sales) equal to m, and a dividend payout ratio of d, we can determine the firm's retained earnings next period:

$$\text{Retained earnings} = S(m)(1 + g)(1 - d)$$

The product of S and m yields net profits in the current year. Multiplying this product by $(1 + g)$ results in next year's profits, and multiplying this result by $(1 - d)$ gives next year's retained earnings. This is the amount by which the book equity component of the balance sheet will grow. Next, observe that the ratio of assets to equity (total assets to common stock equity) equals 1 plus the ratio of total liabilities, L, to shareholders' equity:

$$A = E + L$$
$$\frac{A}{E} = \frac{E + L}{E} = 1 + \frac{L}{E}$$

Our assuming that the firm maintains a constant assets-to-equity ratio is equivalent to assuming that the ratio of liabilities to equity remains constant. Hence, for each dollar of earnings that the company retains, it can borrow an additional L/E dollars to keep the mix of debt and equity constant. For example, if a firm finances half of its assets with debt and half with equity, then the ratio L/E equals 1.0. If the firm retains $1 million in earnings in a given year, then it can afford to borrow an additional $1 million and so maintain the desired mix of debt and equity.

The increase in liabilities next year simply equals the product of next year's retained earnings and the ratio of liabilities to equity:

$$\text{Increase in liabilities} = [S(m)(1 + g)(1 - d)]\left(\frac{L}{E}\right)$$

Finally, if the increases in assets must match the increase in the sum of liabilities and equity, then we can write the following equations:

$$\underset{\uparrow \text{assets}}{gA} = \underset{\uparrow \text{ret. earnings}}{S(m)(1 + g)(1 - d)} + \underset{\uparrow \text{liabilities}}{[S(m)(1 + g)(1 - d)]\left(\frac{L}{E}\right)}$$

$$= \underset{\uparrow (\text{equity} + \text{liabilities})}{[S(m)(1 + g)(1 - d)]\left(1 + \frac{L}{E}\right)}$$

The premise of the sustainable growth model is that there will be some rate of growth, g^*, that keeps the outflows and inflows of funds in balance. This is the *sustainable growth rate*, calculated from the preceding equation and represented as follows:

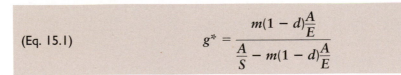

(Eq. 15.1)
$$g^* = \frac{m(1 - d)\frac{A}{E}}{\frac{A}{S} - m(1 - d)\frac{A}{E}}$$

Notice how each of the key variables in Equation 15.1 affects the sustainable growth rate:

- If a firm's net profit margin (m) increases, then the numerator rises and the denominator falls, so $g*$ increases. Therefore, generating higher profits per dollar of sales provides fuel for a higher growth rate.
- Similarly, an increase in the ratio of assets to equity (A/E)—which can occur only if the firm is willing to accept greater financial leverage—also increases the sustainable growth rate. Firms willing to borrow more can grow more rapidly.
- If a firm can increase its total asset turnover ratio (S/A), then the inverse ratio A/S falls and the sustainable growth rate rises. Firms that manage assets more efficiently and generate higher sales volume per dollar of assets can achieve more rapid growth.
- Finally, a reduction in dividend payouts (d) also tends to increase $g*$. When firms retain more earnings, they can finance faster growth.

EXAMPLE

In 2010, Yahoo! Inc. reported the following financial data:

Sales	$ 6,325 million
Net income	$ 1,232 million
Total assets	$14,928 million
Total equity	$12,558 million
Dividends	$ 0

From these figures, we can determine that Yahoo!'s net profit margin was 19.48%, its assets-to-equity ratio was 1.19, its total asset turnover ratio was 0.42 (which implies an assets-to-sales ratio of 2.36), and its dividend payout ratio was 0.0. Plugging these values into Equation 15.1 yields a sustainable growth rate of about 10.9%. For Yahoo! this meant that the company could increase sales by 10.9% without issuing new shares of common stock and without changing total asset turnover, dividend policy, profit margins, or leverage.

? JOB INTERVIEW QUESTION

What are the financial consequences of very rapid growth?

Interpreting the Sustainable Growth Model It is just as important to understand what the sustainable growth model *does not* say as it is to grasp what it does say. From the previous calculation, should we assume that Yahoo! managers should set as their firm's growth target an increase in sales of 10.9%, equal to the sustainable growth rate? Not at all. Yahoo! managers should decide what rate of growth maximizes shareholder wealth, and then they should use the sustainable growth model as a planning device to help them prepare for the consequences of their growth plans. Suppose that Yahoo! decides it is best for its shareholders if the firm grows at a more rapid rate than 10.9%. In order to do this, Yahoo! must alter one or more of the baseline assumptions of the model. It could seek ways to increase its profit margin, its asset turnover, or its leverage. Yahoo! does not pay dividends, so it cannot use a dividend cut to increase growth.

The sustainable growth model gives managers a shorthand projection that ties together growth objectives and financing needs. It provides hints about the levers that managers must pull in order to achieve growth above the sustainable rate. The model also identifies some financial benefits of growing more slowly than the sustainable rate. A firm that expects to grow at a rate less than $g*$ can plan to reduce leverage or asset turnover, or to increase dividends. Again, we emphasize that the model does not say anything about how fast the firm *should* grow.

The sustainable growth model also highlights tensions that can develop as firms pursue multiple objectives simultaneously. We have seen that one way to finance faster growth is to increase leverage, so the goals of increasing sales and maintaining the current degree of leverage may be difficult to achieve simultaneously. For the firm to achieve faster sales growth, the marketing group may agree that the firm should offer a wider array of products. Doing so may result in lower inventory turnover and reduced total asset turnover. If the firm is unwilling to increase leverage and if expanding the product line means reducing asset turnover, then meeting the sales target will depend on improving profit margins or cutting dividend payout. Compensation issues may further cloud the evaluation of competing objectives: for example, the compensation of the vice president of marketing may be tied to generating additional sales volume, whereas the CFO's compensation may depend on maintaining the firm's credit rating.

The primary advantage of the sustainable growth model is its simple way of linking together various aspects of financial planning. However, the financial planning process generally involves more complex projections. These projections are usually embodied in a set of pro forma income statements and balance sheets that firms use to provide a benchmark against which to judge future performance.

15-2b Pro Forma Financial Statements

pro forma financial statements
A forecast of what a firm expects its income statement and balance sheet to look like a year or two ahead.

Periodically, firms produce pro forma financial statements, which are forecasts of what they expect their income statement and balance sheet to look like a year or two ahead. Occasionally, firms use these statements to communicate their plans to outside investors (e.g., at the time of an IPO or earnings announcement). Most of the time, however, managers construct pro forma financial statements for purposes of internal planning and control. By making projections of sales volume, profits, fixed asset requirements, working capital needs, and sources of financing, the firm can establish goals to which compensation may be tied. The firm can also predict liquidity requirements with enough lead time to arrange additional financing when needed.

The Sales Forecast The process of creating pro forma financial statements varies from firm to firm, but there are some common elements. Most pro forma statements begin with a *sales forecast*. The sales forecast may be derived through either a "top-down" or "bottom-up" approach.

top-down sales forecast
A sales forecast that relies heavily on macroeconomic and industry forecasts.

Top-down sales forecasts rely heavily on macroeconomic and industry forecasts. Some firms use complex statistical models or subscribe to forecasts produced by econometric modeling firms. In the top-down approach, senior managers establish a firm-wide objective for increased sales. Next, individual divisions or business units receive targets that, in aggregate, collectively achieve the firm's overall growth target. Division heads pass down sales targets to product line managers and other smaller-scale units. The sales targets will vary across units within the division, but they must add up to achieve the division's goal.

bottom-up sales forecast
A sales forecast that relies on the assessment by sales personnel of demand in the coming year on a customer-by-customer basis.

Firms that use a bottom-up sales forecast begin by assessing demand in the coming year on a customer-by-customer basis. Managers add up these figures across sales territories, product lines, and divisions to arrive at the overall sales forecast for the company. Bottom-up forecasting approaches generally do not rely on mathematical or statistical models.

Not surprisingly, many firms use a blend of these two approaches. For example, a firm may generate a set of assumptions regarding the macroeconomic environment to which all divisions must adhere. It then can generate forecasts from the customer level and aggregate them to an overall forecast for the entire firm that is consistent with the macro assumptions. Some firms produce two sets of forecasts, one that uses a statistical approach and another that relies on customer feedback. Senior managers then compare the two forecasts before setting a final sales objective.

Constructing Pro Forma Statements Starting with the sales forecast, financial analysts construct pro forma income statements and balance sheets using a mix of facts and assumptions. For example, if a firm's strategic plan calls for major investments in fixed assets, then the analyst will incorporate those projections in the forecast of total fixed asset requirements as well as in the forecast of depreciation expense. In the absence of any specific knowledge of capital spending plans, an analyst may

John Eck, President of
Broadcast and Network
Operations, NBC

*"We put together assumptions . . . that we believe
the whole company should follow, and then
we leave it up to each division to give us their
forecast."*

See the entire interview at **SMART** | finance

Smart Practices Video

**percentage-of-sales
method**
Method of constructing
pro forma statements by
assuming all items grow in
proportion to sales.

plug figure
A line item on the pro
forma balance sheet that
represents an account that
can be adjusted after all other
projections are made.

assume that total fixed assets will remain at a fixed percentage relative to sales or total assets; this assumption would, in turn, drive the depreciation line item on the income statement.

Similarly, an analyst can make projections for line items that vary with sales volume. For example, by assuming a constant gross profit margin, the analyst can estimate cost of goods sold directly from the sales forecast. When firms construct pro forma statements by assuming that all items grow in proportion to sales and by extending that percentage to all income statement and balance sheet accounts, they are using the percentage-of-sales method. This is a convenient way to construct pro forma statements, and it is usually a good starting point when making financial projections. Such balance sheet items as receivables, inventory, and payables do typically increase with sales, although not always in a linear fashion. For example, a company with $100 billion in sales may not need 100 times as much inventory as a firm with $1 billion in sales.

In constructing pro forma statements, analysts usually leave one line item on the balance sheet as a plug figure, which is adjusted after making all other projections. For example, the analyst may make projections for all asset, liability, and equity accounts except for the cash balance; then, after the projections are complete, the analyst simply adjusts the cash account to make the balance sheet balance. Alternatively, the analyst might leave a short-term liability account open to serve as the plug figure. The analyst could, for example, use the line item representing the amount borrowed on a bank line of credit to make the right-hand and left-hand sides of the balance sheet equal. If this

EXAMPLE

Table 15.1 shows the 2012 balance sheet and income statement for Zinsmeister Shoe Corporation. We will use this historical information plus some assumptions to generate pro forma financial statements for 2013. We make the following assumptions:

1. Zinsmeister plans to increase sales by 30% in 2013.
2. The company's gross profit margin will remain at 35%.
3. Operating expenses will equal 10% of sales, as they did in 2012.
4. Zinsmeister pays 10% interest on both its long-term debt and its credit line.
5. Zinsmeister will invest an additional $20 million in fixed assets in 2013, which will increase depreciation expense from $10 million to $15 million in 2013.
6. The company faces a 35% tax rate.
7. The company plans to increase cash holdings by $1 million next year.
8. Accounts receivable equal 8.5% of sales.
9. Inventories equal 10% of sales.
10. Accounts payable equal 12% of cost of goods sold.
11. The company will repay an additional $5 million in long-term debt in 2013.
12. The company will pay out 50% of its net income as a cash dividend.
13. The company plans to use its credit line as the plug figure.

From this set of assumptions and the data in Table 15.1, we can construct the pro forma statements for 2013 shown in Table 15.2. To build the pro forma income statement, we first note that Zinsmeister's sales increase to $325 million. Cost of goods sold and operating expenses increase 30% over the prior year (hitting the percentage-of-sales assumptions above). Interest expense is a tricky item. To begin, assume that Zinsmeister will maintain a $5 million balance on its credit line and will retire the current portion of long-term debt. This means that its total outstanding debt during 2013 will be $25 million. At 10%, interest expense should equal $2.5 million. (We shall see that this assumption may change as we continue to build the statements.)

Putting these figures together in the pro forma income statement, we see that Zinsmeister earns a net profit of just over $41 million, half of which it pays out to shareholders.

Next, we build the pro forma balance sheet. Cash is given at $11 million ($10 million in 2012 plus a $1 million increase). Accounts receivable and inventory increase with sales as stated, so current assets increase to $71,125 million. With the additional investment in fixed assets of $20 million (less 2013's depreciation expense), net fixed assets grow to $65 million. Total assets equal $136,125 million.

continued

Table 15.1

Financial Statements for 2012 ($ thousand)

Zinsmeister Shoe Corporation Balance Sheet as of December 31, 2012

Assets		Liabilities and Equity	
Cash	$ 10,000	Accounts payable	$ 19,500
Accounts receivable	21,250	Credit line	5,000
Inventory	25,000	Current long-term debt	5,000
Current assets	$ 56,250	Current liabilities	$ 29,500
Gross fixed assets	$ 80,000	Long-term debt	20,000
Less: Accumulated depreciation	20,000	Common stock	20,200
Net fixed assets	$ 60,000	Retained earnings	46,550
Total assets	$116,250	Total liabilities and equity	$116,250

Zinsmeister Shoe Corporation Income Statement for the Year Ended December 31, 2012

Sales	$250,000
Less: Cost of goods sold	162,500
Gross profit	$ 87,500
Less: Operating expenses	25,000
Less: Interest expense	3,000
Less: Depreciation	10,000
Pre-tax income	$ 49,500
Less: Taxes	17,325
Net income	$ 32,175

Table 15.2

Pro Forma Financial Statements for 2013 ($ thousand)

Zinsmeister Shoe Corporation Pro Forma Balance Sheet as of December 31, 2013

Assets		Liabilities and Equity	
Cash	$ 11,000	Accounts payable	$ 25,350
Accounts receivable	27,625	Credit line	3,306
Inventory	32,500	Current long-term debt	5,000
Current assets	$ 71,125	Current liabilities	$ 33,656
Gross fixed assets	$100,000	Long-term debt	15,000
Less: Accumulated depreciation	35,000	Common stock	20,200
Net fixed assets	$ 65,000	Retained earnings	67,269
Total assets	$136,125	Total liabilities and equity	$136,125

Zinsmeister Shoe Corporation Pro Forma Income Statement for the Year Ended December 31, 2013

Sales	$325,000
Less: Cost of goods sold	211,250
Gross profit	$113,750
Less: Operating expenses	32,500
Less: Interest expense	2,500
Less: Depreciation	15,000
Pre-tax income	$ 63,750
Less: Taxes	22,312
Net income	$ 41,438
Dividends	$ 20,719

On the liabilities/equity side, accounts payable increase with sales, the current portion of long-term debt remains at $5 million, total long-term debt declines by $5 million, and common stock does not change. The retained earnings figure for 2013 equals the 2012 figure plus half of 2013's net income. Zinsmeister uses its credit line as the plug figure. That is, given all the assumptions so far, the credit line will decline from $5 million to $3,306 million because otherwise the assets will not balance with the sum of liabilities and equity.

continued

> Yet, because the credit line declines, our estimate of interest expense in the income statement is too high. Recall that we predicted interest expense of $2.5 million based on a 10% interest rate on total outstanding debt of $25 million. The pro forma balance sheet now shows long-term and short-term debt of just $23,306 million, so interest expense falls to $2.33 million. A decline in interest expense leads to an increase in profits and retained earnings. Higher retained earnings means that the firm can reduce the line of credit even more, and the cycle repeats. To find the amount of borrowing on the credit line and the corresponding interest expense that reconciles the balance sheet with the income statement, an analyst would need to use an iterative approach, such as Excel's "Solver" feature.

WHAT TO ASK

With what frequency does your firm construct pro forma financial statements for planning purposes?

external funds required (EFR)
The expected shortage or surplus of financial resources, given the firm's growth objectives.

assumed amount of borrowing on the credit line seems unreasonable, the company may need to recalculate the other assumptions underlying its planning process.

The bottom line for Zinsmeister is that its pro forma outlook is quite good. If the company achieves its sales growth target and keeps expenses and current asset and current liability accounts in line with historical norms, then it can invest $20 million in new fixed assets while reducing its outstanding interest-bearing debt.

In one sense, this conclusion is hardly surprising. If we take the 2012 data for Zinsmeister and plug it into Equation 15.1, we find that the company's sustainable growth rate is 31.8%. Therefore, the firm's target growth rate of 30% should leave it with some "financial slack." Going through the added steps to build pro forma statements provides the firm with much more information than does the sustainable growth rate alone. With the figures in Tables 15.1 and 15.2 programmed into a spreadsheet, analysts could easily study the effects of changes in any of the assumptions—such as Zinsmeister's ability to pay down debt—or they could identify a need to increase the credit line balance.

A Shorthand Approach for Estimating External Funds Required We can use the notation defined earlier to present another shorthand approach for estimating the amount of external funds required (EFR)—the external financing that a firm will require. Equation 15.2 states that the EFR is a function of three factors. The first term in the equation, $(A/S)\Delta S$, indicates the additional investment in assets required for a firm if it plans to maintain its total asset turnover ratio and increase the dollar volume of sales by ΔS. The second term measures the inflow of funds available to finance this growth. The inflow represented by the second term assumes that the relationship between a firm's sales and its spontaneous liabilities (in this case, accounts payable) remains constant. The third term captures the additional financing inflows that the firm creates internally through retained earnings. Thus, we have

$$(\text{Eq. } 15.2) \qquad EFR = \frac{A}{S}\Delta S - \frac{AP}{S}\Delta S - mS(1+g)(1-d)$$

If we apply this shorthand calculation to Zinsmeister, we can determine its external funds requirement (in thousands of dollars):

$$EFR = \frac{\$116,250}{\$250,000} \times (\$75,000) - \frac{\$19,500}{\$250,000} \times (\$75,000)$$

$$- \left(\frac{\$32,175}{\$250,000}\right) \times \$250,000 \times (1 + 0.30) \times (1 - 0.50) = \$8,111$$

Under the assumptions of this model, Zinsmeister will require additional external funding of $8.1 million. In the pro forma projections in Table 15.2, Zinsmeister's total external financing actually declines by $6.7 million.[4] Why the discrepancy? Closer

---

[4]Table 15.2 includes a $5 million reduction in long-term debt and a $1.7 million ($5.0 million – $3.3 million) reduction in the line of credit. The figures are imprecise because the interest expense and outstanding debt figures in Table 15.2 are not fully reconciled.

Daniel Carter, Vice President of Finance, BevMo!

"We use information on our expectations to manage expectations of investors."

See the entire interview at **SMART|finance**

Smart Practices Video

examination of the pro forma statements reveals that several of the assumptions in Equation 15.2 do not hold in a more complete analysis. For instance, from 2012 to 2013, Zinsmeister's ratio of assets to sales is not constant, as the equation assumes; instead, the ratio declines from 0.465 to 0.419. Zinsmeister is increasing sales more rapidly than assets, so its funding needs are actually less than Equation 15.2 assumes. When we build projections on an account-by-account basis, the apparent need for external funding predicted by Equation 15.2 turns into a financial surplus, highlighting that Equation 15.2 is just an approximation.

Some Concluding Remarks This discussion has presented two important points. First, shorthand approaches—such as the sustainable growth model or the equation for determining *external funds required (EFR)*—help managers predict whether they should expect a scarcity or a surplus of financial resources, given the firm's growth objectives. Second, firms can construct a more complete picture of their funding requirements by building pro forma income statements and balance sheets. Managers can use any of these models to reduce the risk of experiencing unpleasant financial surprises a year or two ahead.

Besides planning for growth that will occur over a period of years, companies also construct financial plans with shorter time horizons. These plans generally focus on temporary cash surpluses or deficits due to seasonal fluctuations in transactions volume. The next section examines this dimension of financial planning.

15-2 Concept Review Questions

3. Describe and evaluate the use of *return on investment* (*ROI*) and *economic value added* (*EVA*) as growth targets in financial planning. Why do firms often use annual growth in sales or in assets as a target growth rate?

4. Explain the difference between a firm's *sustainable* growth rate and its *optimal* growth rate. In what circumstances is a firm's optimal growth rate likely to exceed its sustainable growth rate? Under what conditions would you expect the opposite to be true?

5. Current asset accounts, especially cash and inventory, usually increase at a rate that is slightly less than the growth rate in sales. Why? What is the implication of this fact for the sustainable growth model?

15-3 Planning and Control

15-3a Short-Term Financing Strategies

In the previous section we observed that most firms establish growth as one of their long-term objectives. So it is not unusual to observe a distinct upward trend in any company's historical sales volume. However, in a single year many firms experience sharp quarter-to-quarter sales changes due to seasonal factors. Construction-related businesses generate much higher volume in the summer than they do in the winter. In contrast, toy companies experience peak volume in the winter.

Because sales volume tends to fluctuate around a long-term upward trend, we expect to observe the same pattern when we examine a firm's total assets over time. As sales volume grows, so does the firm's need for current and fixed assets. During the year, a firm's investment in current assets will tend to rise and fall with sales. This seasonal pattern creates temporary cash surpluses and deficits that the firm must manage. In the remainder of this section, we use data for Hershey Foods to demonstrate alternative financing strategies.

Hershey Foods Quarterly Sales and Total Current Assets Panel A of Figure 15.2 plots quarterly sales figures for The Hershey Company from 1992 through the fourth quarter of 2009. Hershey's fiscal year matches the calendar year, so its quarterly income statements report sales for quarters ending in March, June, September, and December each year. For Hershey, sales usually peak in the third or fourth quarter of each year. Sales troughs typically occur in the second quarter. Panel A of Figure 15.2 also reveals a gradual upward trend in Hershey sales from 1992 to 1999. That growth trend leveled off from 2000 to 2003 with the U.S. economic recession; it then resumed growth from 2004 through 2006 before leveling off again beginning in 2007.

Panel B of Figure 15.2 plots Hershey's quarterly total current assets over the same period. You can see that the patterns closely match those in Panel A. Hershey's total current assets show the same seasonal pattern (with a lag of one quarter) and the same upward trend of the company's sales. Hershey builds current assets, mostly inventory and receivables, during the third and fourth quarters of each year, and it draws down these items during the first and second quarters.

Because Hershey's total current assets fluctuate around a long-term upward trend, we can think of the company's current assets as containing both a temporary and a

Figure 15.2

Quarterly Sales and Total Current Assets for The Hershey Company (1992 through the fourth quarter of 2009)

Panel A shows the seasonal pattern in Hershey's sales, and Panel B shows a similar pattern for current assets. The straight lines represent different levels of long-term financing. The purple line represents an *aggressive strategy* in the sense that Hershey does not secure enough long-term financing to cover the permanent component of the growth in current assets. The blue line is *a conservative strategy* because Hershey has sufficient long-term financing to pay for both the permanent upward trend and the seasonal fluctuations in assets. The red line is a *matching strategy,* a middle-of-the-road approach in which Hershey finances permanent assets (fixed assets plus the permanent component of current assets) with long-term funding sources, and finances temporary or seasonal asset requirements with short-term debt.

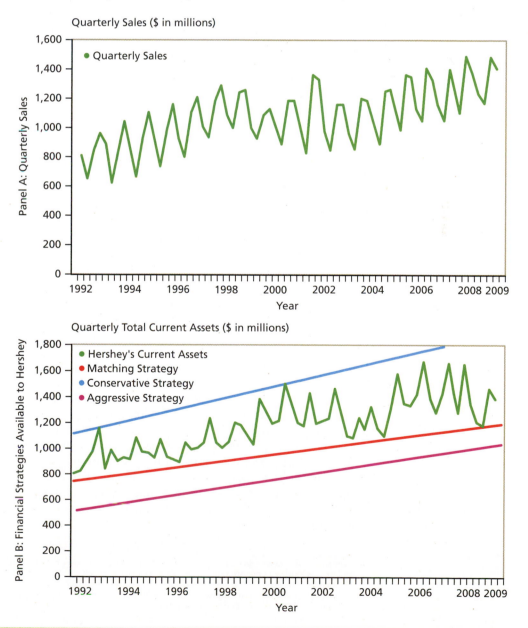

permanent component. The temporary component reflects the differences between the seasonal peaks and troughs of Hershey's business. The permanent component represents the sizeable investment in current assets that Hershey maintains even during the quarters when business is slow.

Hershey's fixed assets (not shown in the figure) do not exhibit the seasonal pattern of sales and current assets. However, its fixed assets do follow the long-term upward trend, essentially following the long-term growth in Hershey's sales.

Financing Strategies What financing strategies might Hershey employ to fund both the long-term trend and the seasonal fluctuations in its total current assets? First, Hershey might adopt a conservative strategy, one in which the firm makes sure it has enough long-term financing to cover its permanent and seasonal investments in current assets. For example, Hershey might issue long-term bonds to generate enough cash to cover all its cash needs for several years. This strategy is represented graphically by the blue line in Panel B of Figure 15.2. By using this strategy, Hershey has a cash surplus for much of the year, drawing down that surplus only when total current assets reach their peak during the third and fourth quarters each year. Hershey will invest its excess cash balances in marketable securities. We describe this strategy as conservative because it minimizes the risk that Hershey will experience a liquidity crisis during peak quarters. However, keep in mind that large investments in cash and marketable securities are not likely to make Hershey shareholders rich.[5] Furthermore, because the term structure of interest rates (the *yield curve*) is typically upward sloping, Hershey will generally pay higher interest rates on its long-term debt than it would pay if it were willing to borrow on a short-term basis.

The second strategy that Hershey might adopt is much more aggressive. In this aggressive strategy, Hershey relies heavily on short-term borrowing not only to meet the seasonal peaks each year but also to finance a portion of the long-term growth in total current assets. In Panel B of Figure 15.2, the purple line represents the aggressive strategy. The difference between that line and the one representing Hershey's total current assets indicates how much short-term debt Hershey has outstanding at any moment in time. During peak quarters, Hershey increases its short-term borrowings. But even during the first and second quarters, when business is relatively slow, Hershey continues to finance at least part of its operations with short-term debt. Thus Hershey uses short-term financing to fund a portion of its long-term, or permanent, growth in total current assets. With this strategy, the company takes advantage of short-term interest rates, which are usually lower than long-term rates. However, if short-term rates rise then Hershey will face increased interest expense. The firm also faces a significant *refinancing risk* in this strategy. That is, if Hershey's financial condition weakens, it may not be able to roll over short-term debt as it had in the past.

A third strategy is the matching strategy. Firms that follow the matching strategy finance the permanent component of current assets with long-term financing and finance the temporary or seasonal portion of current assets with short-term debt. The matching strategy is represented by the red solid line in Panel B of Figure 15.2. In the figure, notice that Hershey will increase short-term borrowing during peak periods. It will repay those loans as it reduces its investment in total current assets during slow periods.

The matching strategy is a middle-of-the-road approach. If Hershey finances its short-term assets with short-term debt, then it will have smaller cash surpluses than under the conservative approach but its borrowing costs will be lower, on average. (Because short-term debt is usually lower cost than long-term debt.) Hershey's interest costs will be higher under the matching strategy than with the aggressive strategy, but it will face less exposure to refinancing risk and its interest costs will not fluctuate as much from quarter-to-quarter.

---

conservative strategy
Financing strategy in which a company makes sure that it has enough long-term financing to cover its permanent investments in fixed and current assets as well as the additional seasonal investments in current assets that it makes during the various quarters each year.

aggressive strategy
Financing strategy in which a company relies heavily on short-term borrowing, not only to meet the seasonal peaks each year but also to finance a portion of the long-term growth in sales and assets.

matching strategy
Financing strategy in which a company finances permanent assets (fixed assets plus the permanent component of current assets) with long-term funding sources and finances its temporary or seasonal asset requirements with short-term debt.

? JOB INTERVIEW QUESTION

What are the risks of financing a long-term need with a short-term line of credit?

---

[5]Companies sometimes argue that a large cash reserve is a strategic asset because it enables the firm to make acquisitions quickly as opportunities arise. We agree that, in principle, a cash reserve could have strategic value, but it also enables managers to make value-reducing investments without facing the discipline that comes with raising money in the capital markets. As you will see in Chapter 21, research evidence suggests that managers of acquiring firms generally do not create wealth for their shareholders.

Regardless of which strategy Hershey decides to pursue, the company will pay careful attention to short-term inflows and outflows of cash. Doing so will allow the company to invest unanticipated cash surpluses and cover unexpected deficits. The primary tool for managing cash flow on a short-term basis is the cash budget.

15-3b The Cash Budget

Managers use the tools in the section on planning for growth (Section 15-2) to make financial projections over horizons of a year or more. However, they also need to monitor the firm's financial performance over shorter horizons. Because it takes cash to operate on a day-to-day basis, firms monitor their cash inflows and outflows very closely, and the primary tool they use for this purpose is the cash budget.

A **cash budget** is a statement of the firm's planned inflows and outflows of cash. Firms use the cash budget to ensure they will have enough cash available to meet short-term financial obligations. Any surplus cash resources can be invested quickly and efficiently. Typically, the cash budget spans a one-year period, with more frequent breakdowns provided as components of the budget. The CFO of Finish Line Inc., a specialty retailer, once described his company to us as a "cash and inventory business." What he meant was that running a successful retail enterprise requires close attention to managing cash flows and inventory. A company like Finish Line needs to know its exact cash position at the end of every business day. For other firms, monitoring cash positions on a weekly or monthly basis may be sufficient. Besides the volume of cash transactions, other factors that determine the frequency with which firms construct cash budgets include the volatility of prices and sales volume, and the importance of seasonal fluctuations.

Running out of cash is an ever-present threat at small and medium-size companies. Vulnerable companies include those that are growing rapidly and those that are in distress. Even in large corporations, though, astonishing changes in cash reserves can occur over just a few years. For example, in September 2007, General Motors reported cash and marketable security holdings of $30 billion, but over the following six quarters the company's cash reserves fell to $11.6 billion. Although $11.6 billion may seem like plenty of cash, GM reported a net cash outflow of $10.2 billion in just the first quarter of 2009! With the possibility of such dramatic swings in cash holdings, even large firms must monitor their cash positions closely.

As is the case with pro forma financial statements, the key input required to build a cash budget is the firm's sales forecast. On the basis of this forecast, the financial manager estimates the monthly cash inflows from cash sales, receivable collections, and other sources. Naturally, a complete cash budget also contains estimates of cash outflows; some of these vary directly with sales and some do not. Cash outlays include purchases of raw materials, labor and other production expenses, selling expenses, and investments in fixed assets. A cash budget usually presents projected inflows (cash receipts) first. Next come the projected outflows (cash disbursements). Finally, the cash budget shows whether the firm expects a net cash inflow or outflow for the period. Depending on the firm's cash balance at the start of the period, the cash budget will either reveal a need for additional financing or demonstrate that the firm will have surplus cash to invest in short-term marketable securities.

Cash Receipts Cash receipts include all the firm's cash inflows in a given period. The most common components of cash receipts are cash sales, collections of accounts receivable, and other cash receipts. The firm estimates collections of accounts receivable using the past payment patterns of its customers.[6]

SMART concepts
See the concept explained step-by-step at SMART|finance

cash budget
A statement of a firm's planned inflows and outflows of cash.

Beth Acton, Vice President and Treasurer of Ford Motor Co. (former)

"Because there is a long cycle of developing product from concept to customer, it is critical that we understand what the business implications are for the business planning period."

See the entire interview at SMART|finance

Smart Practices Video

? WHAT TO ASK
What group in your firm is responsible for putting together cash budgets and monitoring the firm's cash needs?

cash receipts
All of a firm's cash inflows in a given period.

---
[6]We discuss payment patterns more fully in Chapter 16.

Consider the cash receipts projections of Farrell Industries, a candy manufacturer, which is developing a cash budget for October, November, and December. Farrell's sales in August and September were $300,000 and $600,000, respectively. The firm forecasts sales of $1,200,000, $900,000, and $600,000 for October, November, and December, respectively. Typically, 10% of Farrell's sales are cash sales and 90% are credit sales; Farrell collects about 60% of each month's sales within the next month but must wait two months to collect the remaining 30% of sales. Bad debts have been negligible. In December, the firm expects to receive a $90,000 dividend from stock it holds in a subsidiary.

As a first step in preparing a cash budget, Farrell prepares a schedule of projected cash receipts (see Table 15.3). The first row shows total sales in each month. Remember, the figures for October–December are projections. The second row lists cash sales in each month, which (by assumption) equal 10% of total monthly sales. The third and fourth rows report the expected cash inflows from collecting receivables from the previous two months' sales. The next line reports cash receipts not related to sales, and the final line shows total cash receipts each month.

Table 15.3	Schedule of Projected Cash Receipts for Farrell Industries ($ thousand)				
	August	**September**	**October**	**November**	**December**
Forecast sales:	$300	$600	$1,200	$900	$ 600
Cash sales (10%)	$ 30	$ 60	$ 120	$ 90	$ 60
Collection of accounts receivable					
Previous month (60%)		$180	$ 360	$720	$ 540
Two months prior (30%)			$ 90	$180	$ 360
Other cash receipts			—	—	$ 90
Total cash receipts			$ 570	$990	$1,050

© Cengage Learning 2012

For example, consider the month of November. Projected sales are $900,000, implying that expected cash sales equal $90,000 (0.10 × $900,000). During November, Farrell expects to collect receivables equal to 60% of October's $1,200,000 sales, or $720,000. Farrell also expects to collect the 30% of September's $600,000 sales still on the books as receivables, or $180,000. The firm expects no other cash flows in November, so total cash receipts equal $990,000 ($90,000 + $720,000 + $180,000).

cash disbursements
All outlays of cash by a firm in a given period.

Cash Disbursements Cash disbursements include all outlays of cash by the firm in the period. The most common cash disbursements are cash purchases, fixed asset outlays, payments of accounts payable, wages, interest payments, taxes, and rent and lease payments. Cash disbursements may also include items such as dividend payments and share repurchases. It is important to remember that depreciation and other noncash expenses are *not* included in the cash budget. They are not outlays of cash, but represent a scheduled write-off of an earlier cash outflow. (Depreciation does have a cash outflow effect through its impact on tax payments.)

Farrell Industries has gathered the following data needed for the preparation of a cash disbursements schedule for October, November, and December.

Purchases: The firm's purchases average 70% of sales. Of this amount, Farrell pays 20% in cash, 60% in the month following the purchase, and the remaining 20% two months following the purchase. Thus, October purchases are $840,000 (0.70 × $1,200,000). Of that amount, Farrell pays $168,000 (0.20 × $840,000) in cash and then puts $504,000 (0.60 × $840,000) on account to pay in November and $168,000 (0.20 × $840,000) on account to pay in December.

Rent payments: Farrell will pay rent of $20,000 each month.

Wages and salaries: The firm's wages and salaries equal 10% of monthly sales plus $30,000. Thus, October's wages and salaries will be $150,000 [(0.10 × $1,200,000) + $30,000]. The figures for November and December are calculated in the same manner.

Tax payments: Farrell must pay taxes of $75,000 in December.

Fixed asset outlays: The firm will purchase new machinery costing $390,000 and pay for it in November.

continued

Interest payments: An interest payment of $30,000 is due in December.

Cash dividend payments: Farrell will pay cash dividends of $60,000 in October.

Principal payments: A $60,000 principal payment is due in December.

Table 15.4 presents the firm's schedule of projected cash disbursements, based on the preceding data.

Table 15.4	Schedule of Projected Cash Disbursements for Farrell Industries ($ in thousands)				
	August	**September**	**October**	**November**	**December**
Purchases (70% of sales)	**$210**	**$420**	**$840**	**$630**	**$420**
Cash purchases (20%)	$ 42	$ 84	$168	$126	$ 84
Payments of accounts payable:					
Previous month (60%)		126	252	504	378
Two months prior (20%)			42	84	168
Rent payments			20	20	20
Wages and salaries			150	120	90
Tax payments					75
Fixed asset outlays				390	
Interest payments					30
Cash dividend payments			60		
Principal payments					60
Total cash disbursements			$692	$1,244	$905

© Cengage Learning 2012

Net Cash Flow, Ending Cash, Financing Needs, and Excess Cash We can calculate the firm's net cash flow by subtracting its cash disbursements from its cash receipts for each period. By adding the beginning cash balance to the firm's net cash flow, we determine the ending cash balance for each period.

Like most companies, Farrell does not want its cash balance to dip below some minimum level at any time. Therefore, by subtracting the desired minimum cash balance from the ending cash balance, we arrive at one of two results: the required total financing or the excess cash balance. If the ending cash balance is less than the desired minimum cash balance, then the firm has a short-term financing need. The firm meets this need with short-term borrowing, typically notes payable. If the ending cash balance exceeds the desired minimum cash balance, then the firm has an excess cash balance that it can invest in short-term marketable securities.

EXAMPLE

Table 15.5 presents the cash budget for Farrell Industries based on the cash receipt and disbursement schedules developed in earlier Examples together with the following additional information: (1) Farrell's cash balance at the end of September is $200,000; (2) notes payable and marketable securities are $0 at the end of September; (3) the desired minimum cash balance is $50,000.

For Farrell to maintain its desired minimum ending cash balance of $50,000, it will have notes payable (short-term borrowing) balances of $226,000 in November and $81,000 in December. In October, the firm will have excess cash of $28,000, which it can invest in marketable securities. The required total financing figures in the cash budget refer to *how much the firm will owe at the end of each month*, but the figures do not represent the monthly change in borrowing. For Farrell, the monthly financial activities are as follows:

October: Farrell invests $28,000 of excess cash.

November: The firm liquidates $28,000 of excess cash and borrows $226,000. Net cash flow of −$254,000 uses all the available cash reserves ($50,000 minimum cash balance from October plus $28,000 excess cash), leaving an ending cash balance of −$176,000. To cover that negative balance and maintain the desired minimum cash balance, Farrell must borrow $226,000 ($176,000 + $50,000).

December: Net cash flows of $145,000 reduce Farrell's end-of-month borrowing needs to $81,000 (versus November's $226,000). Thus, Farrell repays $145,000 of the amount borrowed.

Table 15.5

Cash Budget for Farrell Industries ($ in thousands)

	October	November	December
Total cash receipts[a]	$570	$ 990	$1,050
Less: Total cash disbursements[b]	692	1,244	905
Net cash flow	–$122	–$ 254	$ 145
Add: Beginning cash	200	78	– 176
Ending balance cash	$ 78	–$ 176	–$ 31
Less: Minimum cash balance	50	50	50
Required total financing (notes payable)[c]		$ 226	$ 81
Excess cash balance (marketable securities)[d]	$ 28		

© Cengage Learning 2012

[a]From Table 15.3.
[b]From Table 15.4.
[c]Values are placed on this line when the ending cash balance is *less than* the desired minimum cash balance. These amounts are typically financed by short-term arrangements and so are represented by notes payable.
[d]Values are placed on this line when the ending cash balance is *greater than* the desired minimum cash balance. These amounts are typically invested in short-term vehicles and so are represented by marketable securities.

The cash budget provides the firm with figures indicating whether a cash shortage (financing need) or a cash surplus (short-term investment opportunity) is expected in each of the months covered by the forecast. In our Example, Farrell Industries can expect a cash surplus of $28,000 in October followed by cash shortages of $226,000 in November and $81,000 in December. Each of these values is based on the internal constraint of a minimum cash balance of $50,000.

Because the firm expects to borrow as much as $226,000 during the three-month period, the financial manager should establish a line of credit to ensure the availability

Finance in Your Life

Can I Make Ends Meet?

In order to achieve your personal financial goals and meet your financial obligations in a timely manner, thereby avoiding late payments and maintaining a strong credit rating, you should regularly prepare a *personal cash budget*. Typically these budgets cover the coming year divided into months. They schedule and net out cash inflows and cash outflows in order to plan for cash surpluses and shortages. Surpluses can be invested, and shortages can be met in a variety of ways such as drawing down savings or borrowing.

To demonstrate the personal cash budget, let's look at your total Inflow and outflow estimates (detailed cash flows not shown) for the next three months.

	Month 1	Month 2	Month 3
(1) Total Inflows	$5,550	$5,555	$5,555
(2) Total Outflows	$6,265	$5,365	$6,240
Net Cash Flow [(1) − (2)]	–$ 715	$ 190	–$ 685

Reviewing your personal cash budgets for the next three months, it is clear that you need to take action in order to make ends meet. Specifically, you need to cover the deficits in months 1 and 3 ($715 + $685 = $1,400) net of the surplus in month 2 ($190), or a total of $1,210 ($1,400−$190). Your budgets can be brought into balance by (1) increasing inflows by $1,210, (2) cutting outflows by $1,210, (3) drawing down savings by $1,210, (4) borrowing $1,210, or (5) a combination of these strategies that will reduce the $1,210 gap to zero. Clearly, **the best strategy would be to reduce planned outflows by a total of $1,210 over the next three months.**

of the necessary funds. The maximum amount of borrowing available on the line of credit should actually exceed the $226,000 in order to allow for possible forecast errors.

Dealing with Uncertainty in the Cash Budget Because the cash budget provides only month-end totals, it does not ensure that the firm has sufficient credit to cover intramonth financing needs. For example, what if a firm's disbursements occur before its receipts during a particular month? In that case, its intramonth borrowing needs will exceed the monthly totals shown in its cash budget. To ensure sufficient credit, the firm may forecast its expected receipts and disbursement on a *daily* basis and use these estimates, along with its cash budget, when arranging adequate credit to cover its maximum expected cash deficit.

The monthly cash surpluses and deficits predicted in the budget are affected by virtually all facets of a firm's operations. For example, changes in receivables collection, in payment patterns, or in inventory turnover can have a dramatic impact on financing needs. Any action that slows collections from customers or accelerates payments to suppliers will increase monthly financial deficits (or reduce surpluses). In that sense, almost any functional area in the firm can affect, or be affected by, the cash budget.

In this chapter, we have emphasized the importance of financial planning and have illustrated a few of the most widely used tools of the trade. We end with a word of caution: When firms construct financial plans, they clearly hope to meet the plans' goals. But the value of planning is not just in attaining established goals. Rather, its importance derives from the thinking it forces managers to do—not only about what they expect to occur in the future but also about what they will do if their expectations are not realized.

? JOB INTERVIEW QUESTION

What impact would offering customers more generous credit terms have on the cash budget?

15-3 Concept Review Questions

6. Suppose that a firm follows the *matching financing strategy*. Does this imply that the firm's current assets will equal its current liabilities?

7. Why do firms prepare *cash budgets*? How do (a) collection patterns and (b) payment patterns affect the cash budget?

8. What can be done to deal with uncertainty in the cash budgeting process? Why might an intramonth view of the firm's cash flows cause a well-prepared cash budget to fail?

Summary

- Strategic (long-term) financial plans guide firms in preparing operating (short-term) financial plans. For most firms, strategic plans are driven by competitive forces that are not always explicitly financial in nature. However, strategic plans have important financial consequences.

- The finance function partners with other functional units in developing the firm's strategic plan. Once the firm establishes the plan, finance personnel ensure that the plan is feasible given the firm's financial resources. Finance personnel also play a crucial role in monitoring progress and in managing risks associated with financial plans.

Table of Important Equations

$$1.\ g^* = \frac{m(1-d)\frac{A}{E}}{\frac{A}{S} - m(1-d)\frac{A}{E}}$$

$$2.\ EFR = \frac{A}{S}\Delta S - \frac{AP}{S}\Delta S - mS(1+g)(1-d)$$

- Most firms strive to grow over time. Popular measurements of growth include (1) achieving accounting return on investment (*ROI*) in excess of the cost of capital; (2) undertaking only actions that result in positive economic value added (EVA); and (3) realizing a target growth rate in sales or assets. Target growth rates are widely used because of their intuitive, computational, and practical appeal.

- The sustainable growth model is a tool that is used to determine the feasibility of a target growth rate under certain conditions. When the growth rate that maximizes shareholder value does not match the sustainable rate, the firm must make adjustments to the model's inputs—such as altering leverage or dividend policy—to achieve the desired growth rate.

- Pro forma financial statements are projected, or forecasted, financial statements typically based on historical financial data about the firm. Preparation of these statements begins with a sales forecast that can be developed by using a top-down or a bottom-up approach or a blend of these two approaches. The key inputs to pro forma statements are a mix of facts and assumptions.

- Firms can prepare pro forma statements using the percentage-of-sales method, which assumes that all items grow in proportion to sales. Yet certain balance sheet accounts do not typically increase in a linear fashion. As a result, analysts typically use one line item on the balance sheet as a "plug figure" that can be used to make sure the pro forma balance sheet balances. Analysts also can estimate directly the amount of external financing required to fund a firm's anticipated growth by using the equation for external funds required (EFR). This approach, like the preparation of pro forma statements, helps managers determine if they can expect a scarcity or surplus of financial resources, given the firm's growth objectives.

- During the year, a firm's investment in current assets tends to rise and fall with sales. This seasonal pattern creates temporary cash surpluses and deficits that the firm must manage. Three basic financing strategies—conservative, aggressive, and matching—can be used to fund both the long-term trend and seasonal fluctuations in a business. The conservative strategy is generally the least risky and least profitable, the aggressive strategy is the usually most risky and most profitable, and the matching strategy falls between the other two in terms of risk and profits.

- A cash budget forecasts the short-term cash inflows and outflows of a firm. For a firm with significant seasonal variations, the financial manager typically prepares the cash budget month by month. This allows the firm to determine peak short-term financing needs and peak short-term investment opportunities, typically over an annual or quarterly period.

- The financial manager must also consider intramonth cash flows to ensure that sufficient credit is available. Changes in collection and payment periods can significantly affect the cash budget's projections.

Key Terms

aggressive strategy, 474
bottom-up sales forecast, 468
cash budget, 475
cash disbursements, 476
cash receipts, 475
conservative strategy, 474

economic value added (EVA), 464
external funds required (EFR), 471
matching strategy, 474
percentage-of-sales method, 469
plug figure, 469
pro forma financial statements, 468

return on investment (ROI), 464
strategic plan, 463
sustainable growth model, 465
top-down sales forecast, 468

Self-Test Problems

Answers to Self-Test Problems and the Concept Review Questions throughout the chapter appear in CourseMate with SmartFinance Tools at www.cengagebrain.com.

ST15-1. Use the following key financial data from the most recent annual report of Rancho Inc. to answer the following questions.

Sales	$12.7 million
Net income	$ 1.3 million
Total assets	$ 7.6 million
Total equity	$ 5.2 million
Dividends	$ 0.3 million

The firm's CFO wishes to use this data to estimate the firm's sustainable growth rate.

a. Use the data provided to calculate Rancho's net profit margin, assets-to-equity ratio, total asset turnover ratio, and its dividend payout ratio.

b. Use your findings in part (a) to find Rancho's *sustainable growth rate*.

c. Interpret the sustainable growth rate calculated in part (b). Does this rate of growth assure shareholder wealth maximization? Explain.

d. If the firm's board feels that it is best for its shareholders if the firm grows more slowly, what alterations in each of the baseline assumptions would be necessary to achieve this objective?

ST15-2. Planet Inc. wishes to construct a pro forma income statement and a pro forma balance sheet for the coming year using the following data.

1. Sales are forecast to grow by 5% from $809.5 million last year to $850 million in the coming year.
2. Cost of goods sold is expected to represent 72% of forecast sales.
3. Operating expenses are expected to represent 11% of forecast sales.
4. Depreciation expense on the firm's existing net fixed assets, which currently total $275 million, is expected to remain at $55 million per year for at least four more years.
5. Planet's marginal tax rate is expected to remain at 40%.
6. Planet is expected to continue its policy of paying out 10% of net income as dividends.
7. Planet's net profit margin last year was 5.2%.
8. Planet wishes to maintain a minimum cash balance of $8 million in the coming year.
9. The firm's accounts receivable are expected to equal about 15% of sales.
10. The firm's inventory has historically averaged about 12% of cost of goods sold.
11. Planet is planning to invest an additional $35 million in fixed assets that will be depreciated on a straight-line basis over a seven-year life.
12. The firm's accounts payable, which totaled $63.5 million at the end of last year, is expected to equal about 11% of cost of goods sold in the coming year.
13. Planet plans to maintain its notes payable of $42 million requiring annual interest of 5%, which totals $2.1 million.
14. The firm has $80 million of long-term debt that matures as a lump sum due and payable in full in five years. Annual interest of $4.8 million must be paid on this debt.
15. Planet has no preferred stock outstanding, and its retained earnings and common stock currently total $250 million.
16. Planet's total assets at the end of last year were $435 million.

a. Use the preceding data to prepare Planet's pro forma income statement for the coming year.

b. Use the data provided and your findings in part (a) to prepare Planet's pro forma balance sheet for the coming year. Use notes payable as the balancing figure and ignore any change in annual interest expense caused by the change in notes payable.

c. Explain the amount of notes payable used as the balancing figure in part (b). Indicate the resulting amount of the *plug figure* needed to create the balancing figure. Will Planet be able to fund its planned growth internally? Explain.

d. Use Equation 15.2 along with Planet's relevant data to determine its *external funds required (EFR)*. Compare this value with the *plug figure* you found in part (c), and explain in general terms why differences between these two values might result.

ST15-3. Sportif Inc.'s financial analyst has compiled sales and total cash disbursement estimates for the coming months of January through May. Historically, 60% of sales are for cash with the remaining 40% collected in the following month. The ending cash balance in January is $1,000. The firm's minimum cash balance is $1,000. The analyst plans to use this data to prepare a cash budget for the months of February through May.

Sportif Inc.		
Month	**Sales**	**Total Cash Disbursements**
January	$ 5,000	$6,000
February	6,000	8,000
March	10,000	8,000
April	10,000	6,000
May	10,000	5,000

a. Use the data provided to prepare Sportif's *cash budget* for the four months February through May.

b. How much total financing will Sportif need to meet its financial requirements for the period February to May?

c. If a pro forma balance sheet dated at the end of May was prepared from the information presented, how much would Sportif have in accounts receivable?

Questions

Q15-1. What is the financial planning process? What is a *strategic plan*? Describe the roles that financial managers play with regard to strategic planning.

Q15-2. Briefly describe the following popular growth targets: (1) accounting-based *return on investment* (*ROI*), (2) *economic value added* (*EVA*), and (3) target growth rate of sales or assets. Which is most widely used, and why?

Q15-3. In the sustainable growth model, what does the word "sustainable" mean? In what ways can the sustainable growth model highlight conflicts between a firm's competing objectives?

Q15-4. With reference to Equation 15.1, explain how each of the variables influences the firm's sustainable growth rate. If high leverage allows a firm to increase its sustainable growth rate, does that mean higher leverage is necessarily good for the firm?

Q15-5. A firm chooses to grow at a rate above its sustainable rate. What changes might we expect to see on the firm's financial statements in the next year? What changes would result from growing at a rate below the firm's sustainable rate?

Q15-6. Describe the differences between the *top-down* and the *bottom-up* sales forecast methods. Describe advantages and disadvantages of each. Do you think one approach is likely to be more accurate than the other?

Q15-7. What is the logic of the *percentage-of-sales method* for constructing *pro forma financial statements*? On a year-to-year basis, which balance sheet and income statement items do you think will fluctuate most closely with sales, and which items are not likely to vary as directly with sales volume?

Q15-8. Why does it make sense to let the firm's cash balance or a short-term liability account serve as the *plug figure* in pro forma projections? Why not use gross fixed assets as the plug figure?

Q15-9. Why might pro forma statements and the equation for *external funds required* (*EFR*) yield different projections for a firm's financing needs?

Q15-10. What is the difference between the *conservative strategy*, the *aggressive strategy*, and the *matching strategy* for funding the long-term trend and the seasonal fluctuations in a firm's total current assets? Which strategy is most risky? Which is least profitable?

Q15-11. How is a *cash budget* different from a set of pro forma financial statements? Why do you think that firms typically create cash budgets at higher frequencies than they create pro forma financial statements?

Q15-12. Explain how slower inventory turnovers, slower receivables collections, or faster payments to suppliers would influence the numbers produced by a cash budget.

Problems

Planning for Growth

P15-1. Go to www.finance.yahoo.com or another financial Web site, and download the most recent two years' balance sheets and income statements for a firm of your choice. Do not choose a firm that issued or retired a significant amount of common stock in either year.

a. Calculate the actual percentage change in sales from two years ago to last year.

b. Using the balance sheet and income statement from two years ago, calculate the firm's *sustainable growth rate*.

c.   If the sustainable growth rate does not equal the actual growth rate in sales, explain how changes in the firm's financial ratios in the second year reflected the firm's decision in the previous year to grow at a rate other than the sustainable rate.

P15-2.   Eisner Amusement Parks reported the following data in its most recent annual report:

Sales	$42.5 million
Net income	$ 3.8 million
Dividends	$ 1.1 million
Assets	$50.0 million

Eisner is financed 100% with equity. What is the company's *sustainable growth rate*? Suppose that Eisner issued bonds to the public and used the proceeds to repurchase half of its outstanding shares. This recapitalization would create additional interest expenses of $2 million. Assuming that the company faces a 35% tax rate, what impact would this restructuring have on its sustainable growth rate?

P15-3.   Review the abbreviated financial statements for the last two years for Norne Energy Corp. All values are expressed in billions of dollars.

Norne Energy Corp. Balance Sheet		
	2012	**2011**
Current assets	$2.7	$2.5
Fixed assets	3.5	3.4
Total assets	$6.2	$5.9
Current liabilities	$1.9	$1.8
Long-term debt	2.1	2.2
Shareholders' equity	2.2	1.9
Total liabilities and equity	$6.2	$5.9

Norne Energy Corp. Income Statement		
	2012	**2011**
Sales	$7.5	$7.1
Net income	0.5	0.4
Dividends	0.2	0.1

a.   What was Norne's *sustainable growth rate* at the end of 2011?
b.   How rapidly did Norne actually grow in 2012?
c.   What changes in Norne's financial condition from 2011 to 2012 can you trace to the difference between the actual and sustainable growth rates?

P15-4.   The 2013 sales forecast for Clearwater Development Co. is $150 million. Interest expense will not change in the coming year. Use Clearwater's 2012 income statement, presented below, to answer the questions that follow.

Clearwater Development Co. Income Statement ($ in thousands)	
Sales	$125,000
Less: Cost of goods sold	80,000
Gross profit	$ 45,000
Less: Operating expenses	30,000
Less: Interest	10,000
Pretax profit	$ 5,000
Less: Taxes (35%)	1,750
Net income	$ 3,250

a. Use the *percentage-of-sales* method to construct a *pro forma income statement* for 2013.

b. You learn that 25% of the cost of goods sold and operating expense figures for 2012 are fixed costs that will not change in 2013. Reconstruct the pro forma income statement.

c. Compare and contrast the statement prepared in parts (a) and (b). Which statement will likely provide the better estimate of 2013 income? Explain.

P15-5. Hill Propane Distributors wants to construct a *pro forma balance sheet* for 2013. Build the statement using the following data and assumptions:

1. Projected sales for 2013 are $35 million.
2. Hill's gross profit margin is 35%.
3. Operating expenses average 10% of sales.
4. Depreciation expense last year was $5 million.
5. Hill faces a tax rate of 35%.
6. Hill distributes 20% of its net income to shareholders as a dividend.
7. Hill wants to maintain a minimum cash balance of $3 million.
8. Accounts receivable equal 8.5% of sales.
9. Inventory averages 10% of the cost of goods sold.
10. Last year's balance sheet lists net fixed assets of $30 million. All of these assets are depreciated on a straight-line basis, and none of them will be fully depreciated for at least three years.
11. Hill plans to invest an additional $1 million in fixed assets that it will depreciate over a five-year life on a straight-line basis.
12. In 2012, Hill reported common stock and retained earnings of $20 million.
13. Accounts payable averages 9% of sales.

Will Hill Propane's cash balance at the end of 2013 exceed its minimum requirement of $3 million?

P15-6. Review the following 2012 balance sheet and income statement for T. F. Baker Cosmetics, Inc. The numerical values are in thousands of dollars.

T. F. Baker Cosmetics, Inc.			
Balance Sheet			
Cash	$ 5,000	Accounts payable	$10,000
Accounts receivable	12,500	Short-term bank loan	15,000
Inventory	10,000	Long-term debt	10,000
Current assets	$27,500	Common stock	15,000
Gross fixed assets	$65,000	Retained earnings	12,500
Less: Accum. depr	30,000	Total liabilities and equity	$62,500
Net fixed assets	$35,000		
Total assets	$62,500		

T. F. Baker Cosmetics, Inc.	
Income Statement	
Sales	$150,000
Less: Cost of goods sold	120,000
Gross profit	$ 30,000
Less: Operating expenses	15,000
Less: Depreciation	5,000
Less: Interest expense	2,000
Pretax profit	$ 8,000
Less: Taxes (35%)	2,800
Net income	$ 5,200

At a recent board meeting, the firm set the following objectives for 2013:

1. The firm would increase liquidity. For competitive reasons, the firm expects accounts receivable and inventory balances to continue their historical relationships with sales and cost of goods sold, respectively, but the board felt that the company should double its cash holdings.

2. The firm would accelerate payments to suppliers. This would have two effects: First, by paying more rapidly, the firm would be able to take advantage of early payment discounts, which would increase its gross margin from 20% to 22%. Second, by paying earlier, the firm's

accounts payable balance, which historically averaged about 8.3% of cost of goods sold, would decline to 4% of cost of goods sold.

3. The firm would expand its warehouse, which would require an investment in fixed assets of $10 million. This would increase projected depreciation expense from $5 million in 2012 to $7 million in 2013.

4. The firm would issue no new common stock during the year, and it would initiate a dividend. Dividend payments in 2013 would total $1.2 million.

5. Operating expenses would remain at 10% of sales.

6. The firm did not expect to retire any long-term debt, and it was willing to borrow up to the limit of its current bank credit line of $20 million. The interest rate on its outstanding debts would average 8%.

7. The firm set a sales target for 2013 of $200 million.

Develop a set of *pro forma financial statements* to determine whether or not T. F. Baker Cosmetics can achieve all these goals simultaneously.

Planning and Control

SMART
solutions

See the problem and solution explained step-by-step at

SMART | finance

P15-7. A firm has actual sales of $50,000 in January and $70,000 in February. It expects sales of $90,000 in March and $110,000 in both April and May. Assuming that sales are the only source of cash inflow and that 60% of these are for cash and the rest are collected evenly over the following two months, what are the firm's expected cash receipts for March, April, and May?

P15-8. Bachrach Fertilizer Corp. had sales of $2 million in March and $2.2 million in April. Expected sales for the next three months are $2.4 million, $2.5 million, and $2.7 million. Bachrach has a cash balance of $200,000 on May 1 and does not want its balance to dip below that level. Prepare a *cash budget* for May, June, and July given the following information:

1. Of total sales, 30% are for cash, 50% are collected in the month after the sale, and 20% are collected two months after the sale.

2. Bachrach has cash receipts from other sources of $100,000 per month.

3. The firm expects to purchase items for $2 million in each of the next three months. All purchases are paid for in cash.

4. Bachrach has fixed cash expenses of $150,000 per month and variable cash expenses equal to 5% of the previous month's sales.

5. Bachrach will pay a cash dividend of $300,000 in June.

6. The company must make a $250,000 loan payment in June.

7. Bachrach plans to acquire fixed assets worth $500,000 in July.

8. Bachrach must make a tax payment of $225,000 in June.

P15-9. The actual sales and purchases for White Inc. for September and October 2012, along with its forecast sales and purchases for November 2012 through April 2013, follow.

Year	Month	Sales	Purchases
2012	September	$310,000	$220,000
2012	October	350,000	250,000
2012	November	270,000	240,000
2012	December	260,000	200,000
2013	January	240,000	180,000
2013	February	280,000	210,000
2013	March	300,000	200,000
2013	April	350,000	190,000

The firm makes 30% of all sales for cash and collects 35% of its sales in each of the two months following the sale. Other cash inflows are expected to be $22,000 in September and April, $25,000 in January and March, and $37,000 in February. The firm pays cash for 20% of its purchases. It pays for 40% of its purchases in the following month and for 40% of its purchases two months later.

Wages and salaries amount to 15% of the preceding month's sales. The firm must pay lease expenses of $30,000 per month. Interest payments of $20,000 are due in January and April. A principal payment of $50,000 is also due in April. The firm expects to pay a cash dividend of $30,000 in January and April. Taxes of $120,000 are due in April. The firm also intends to make a $55,000 cash purchase of fixed assets in December.

a. Assuming that the firm has a cash balance of $42,000 at the beginning of November and that its desired minimum cash balance is $25,000, prepare a *cash budget* for November through April.

b. If the firm is requesting a line of credit, how large should the line be? Explain your answer.

P15-10. Berlin Inc. expects sales of $300,000 during each of the next three months. It will make monthly purchases of $180,000 during this time. Wages and salaries are $30,000 per month plus 5% of monthly sales. The firm expects to make a $60,000 tax payment in the first month and a $45,000 purchase of fixed assets in the second month. It expects to receive $24,000 in cash from the sale of an asset in the third month. All sales and purchases are for cash. Beginning cash and the minimum cash balance equal zero.

a. Construct a *cash budget* for the next three months.

b. Berlin is unsure of the level of sales, but all other figures are certain. If the most pessimistic sales figure is $240,000 per month and the most optimistic is $360,000 per month, what are the monthly minimum and maximum ending cash balances that the firm can expect for each month?

c. Discuss how the financial manager can use the data in parts (a) and (b).

For instructions on using Thomson ONE, refer to the instructions provided with the Thomson ONE problems at the end of Chapters 1–6.

P15-11. Calculate Kroger's (U:KR) *sustainable growth rate* at the end of each of the last five fiscal years. Compare the sustainable growth rate to its actual growth rate each year and, if different, identify changes in Kroger's financial condition each year that explain the differences in growth rates.

P15-12. Construct a pro forma income statement and balance sheet for the next year for First Solar (FSLR). Estimate the *sustainable growth rate* using the latest fiscal year-end data. Assume that sales grow at this sustainable growth rate over the next year. Use the *percentage-of-sales method* to prepare the pro forma statements. Do you need a *plug figure* to make the pro forma balance sheet balance? If so, what plug figure do you use?

Since these exercises depend upon real-time data, your answers will change continuously depending upon when you access the Internet to download your data.

Smart Practices Video

Jackie Sturm, Vice President of Finance Intel Corp.

"Once the product line business plan is completed, we move into our annual planning process, which is more of a tactical exercise."

John Eck, President of Broadcast and Network Operations, NBC

"We put together assumptions . . . that we believe the whole company should follow, and then we leave it up to each division to give us their forecast."

Daniel Carter, Vice President of Finance, BevMo!

"We use information on our expectations to manage expectations of investors."

Beth Acton, Vice President and Treasurer of Ford Motor Co. (former)

"Because there is a long cycle of developing product from concept to customer, it is critical that we understand what the business implications are for the business planning period."

SMART concepts

See a demonstration of long-term financing and short-term fluctuations in asset growth and the sustainable growth model.

SMART solutions

See the solution to Problem 15-2.
See the solution to Problem 15-7.

Mini-Case

Financial Planning

Burrito Brothers, Incorporated, a regional restaurant chain, has decided to expand nationwide and, consequently, expects rapid growth. As Burrito Brothers' new CFO, you are in charge of planning for this growth. Before starting to plan, you decide to refresh your knowledge of financial planning by answering the following questions.

Assignment

1. One method of estimating the effects of growth is the *sustainable growth model*. What assumptions are inherent with this model?

2. Another method of estimating growth is for the firm's managers to forecast *pro forma financial statements.* How are the sales forecasts that are necessary to create pro forma statements derived?

3. Why might the estimates for *external funds required* (EFR) differ between using the *percentage-of-sales* method to estimate pro forma statements and using the shorthand approach in Equation 15.2?

4. If sales volume fluctuates in the short-term around the long-term estimated trend, what alternative financing strategies might be considered?

5. Discuss how managers might monitor a company's cash inflows and cash outflows on a day-to-day basis.

chapter 16

Cash Conversion, Inventory, and Receivables Management*

What Companies Do

Apple's Superior Cash Conversion and Huge Cash Balances

For years, Apple has been a leader in cash conversion—a measure of how quickly raw materials can get through the supply chain and be converted into cash. Some refer to this metric as "cash-to-cash" and others call it the "cash conversion cycle." Regardless, shorter cash conversion cycles are preferred because they reflect more efficient cash management.

In its *2010 Supply Chain Top 25*, AMR Research ranked Apple as #1 for the third year in a row, followed by P&G, Cisco Systems, Walmart, and Dell. Apple actually achieved a negative cash conversion cycle of about 45 days, which means that Apple took less time to turn its inventory into cash than the company did to pay its vendors. Apple's suppliers provided it with about 1.5 months of financing beyond what was necessary to support its accounts receivable and inventory investments. Of course, minimizing the firm's investment in current assets—particularly inventory and accounts receivable—should allow the firm to free up cash, which can then be used for more productive purposes. But what if the cash simply accumulates rather than being reinvested or distributed to investors? In Apple's case, the firm's success in preserving cash creates concern among some investors. By March 2011, Apple's cash and short-term investments exceeded $60 billion, among the largest cash hoards in the technology sector.

Many analysts and investors cite CEO Steve Jobs's legendary insecurity over Apple's competitive position as the reason for holding the large cash position. Some believe that Apple should reduce its cash stockpile by issuing a dividend, engaging in a stock buyback, or undertaking significant M&A activity, but most are willing to accept the large cash balance in view of the need to weather the economic uncertainty and quickly respond to competitive threats.

Sources: Kevin O'Marah, and Debra Hofman, "The AMR Research Supply Chain Top 25 for 2010," www.gartner.com/DisplayDocument?ref=clientFriendlyUrl&id=1379613 (accessed May 26, 2011); Cindy Johnson, "Don't Do It Apple," www.fool.com/investing/general/2011/05/25/dont-do-it-apple.aspx (posted May 25, 2011; accessed May 26, 2011).

* Professor Dubos J. Masson, CCM, CertCM, of Pepperdine University and The Resource Alliance, assisted in preparation of this chapter. The authors very much appreciate D.J.'s important contribution.

Learning Objectives

After studying this chapter you should be able to:

- Describe the cash conversion cycle, the firm's objectives with regard to it, and the actions the firm can use to accomplish these objectives;

- Explain the cost trade-offs the firm must consider when finding the optimal levels of both operating assets and short-term financing;

- Discuss the key concerns of the financial manager with regard to inventory and some of the popular techniques used to manage it;

- Review the key aspects of a firm's credit standards, including the five C's of credit and the role of credit scoring;

- Analyze proposed changes in a firm's credit standards and its credit terms using both descriptive and quantitative techniques; and

- Understand the collection policy procedures used by firms, the techniques firms use in credit monitoring, and the cash application process.

We now switch our focus from planning to operations and in this chapter describe the firm's cash conversion and key **operating assets**—the current assets needed to support a firm's day-to-day operations. We discuss the two key operating assets—inventory and accounts receivable—in this chapter. Most firms work hard to reduce the size of

their investments in these types of assets. Of course it is necessary to keep inventory on hand to keep production flowing and to satisfy unanticipated customer needs, but a firm that invests too much in inventory is not deploying its resources efficiently. Indeed, over the last two decades, the percentage of total corporate assets tied up in inventory balances has been in decline, partly due to advances in information technology that allow firms to communicate more effectively with vendors and customers. Likewise, firms routinely sell to customers on credit (often for competitive reasons), but without careful analysis behind the decision to extend credit and monitoring to ensure that credits are collected, accounts receivable balances can become excessive.

This chapter focuses on the cash conversion cycle and the efficient management of inventory and accounts receivable. We begin with the cash conversion cycle and the actions that can be taken to manage it. Next, we describe the cost trade-offs in short-term financial management. We then briefly consider the key concerns of the financial manager with regard to inventory before reviewing some popular inventory management techniques. Next we discuss effective accounts receivable management and review two important related concepts, credit standards and credit terms. Finally, we briefly cover some other receivables management activities.

16-1 The Cash Conversion Cycle

16-1a Operating Cycle

operating assets
Cash, marketable securities, accounts receivable, and inventories that are necessary to support the day-to-day operations of a firm.

operating cycle (OC)
Measurement of the time that elapses from the firm's receipt of raw materials to begin production to its collection of cash from the sale of the finished product.

A central concept in short-term financial management is the notion of the operating cycle. A firm's **operating cycle (OC)** measures the time that elapses from the firm's receipt of raw materials to its collection of cash from the sale of finished products. As you might expect, operating cycles vary widely by industry. For instance, a bakery—which uses fresh ingredients, keeps finished goods in inventory for only a day or two, and generally sells its products for cash—will have a very short operating cycle. In contrast, semiconductor manufacturers take several months to convert raw materials into finished products, which are sold on credit. The operating cycle for such a firm may extend to six months or longer.

The operating cycle influences a company's need for internal or external financing. In general, the longer a firm's operating cycle, the greater its need for financing. For example, a bakery might pay its suppliers and its employees using the revenues generated each week. The semiconductor manufacturer probably cannot persuade suppliers and employees to wait several months for payment while the firm collects cash from chip sales. Therefore, the semiconductor firm has a greater need for financing day-to-day operations.

The operating cycle encompasses two major short-term asset categories: inventory and accounts receivable. To measure the operating cycle, we use two ratios covered in Chapter 2. First, calculate the *average age of inventory* (AAI) and the *average*

Vern LoForti, V.P., CFO, and Corporate Secretary, InfoSonics

"Working capital management is extremely important because it results in good cash flow."

See the entire interview at **SMART** finance

Smart Practices Video

Jackie Sturm, Director of Finance for Technology and Manufacturing, Intel Corp.

"Inventory loses value every day you hold it."

See the entire interview at **SMART** finance

Smart Practices Video

cash conversion cycle (CCC)
The elapsed time between the points at which a firm pays for raw materials and at which it receives payment for finished goods.

Keith Woodward, Vice President of Finance, General Mills

"What we expect of financial analysts is to be able to manage all of the complexity and moving parts of working capital utilizing different ratios."

See the entire interview at **SMART** finance

Smart Practices Video

? JOB INTERVIEW QUESTION

Why do firms try to shorten their cash conversion cycles?

collection period (ACP). Next, take the sum of these two items to determine the length of the operating cycle.

Table 16.1 presents the actual operating cycles for some well-known computer manufacturers and a number of other firms. Lines 1 through 5 present data for fiscal-year 2010, and lines 6 through 8 calculate the time periods (in days) for AAI, ACP, and average payment period (APP), respectively. Using the AAI and ACP calculated in lines 6 and 7, line 9 of the table shows the OC for each firm. Note that among the four computer manufacturers (IBM, Dell, Apple, and Hewlett-Packard), Apple and the make-to-order firm, Dell, have the shortest operating cycles, followed by Hewlett-Packard and IBM. IBM's operating cycle of 117 days is far longer than the 70- to 87-day range of operating cycles for Apple, Dell, and Hewlett-Packard, which is probably a result of IBM's more diversified computer businesses. The final four columns show the operating cycles for four non-computer firms. Clearly, the operating cycle varies greatly across industries as well as across different types of companies within a given industry.

16-1b Cash Conversion Cycle

The elapsed time between the points at which a firm pays for raw materials and at which it receives payment for finished goods is called the **cash conversion cycle (CCC)**. The difference between the operating cycle and the cash conversion cycle indicates the amount of time for which suppliers are willing to extend credit. Most firms obtain a significant amount of their financing through trade credit, as represented by accounts payable. By taking advantage of trade credit, a firm reduces the amount of financing it needs from other sources to make it through the operating cycle.

To calculate the cash conversion cycle, start with the operating cycle and then subtract the *average payment period (APP)* on accounts payable. Here is the formula for the cash conversion cycle:

(Eq. 16.1)
$$CCC = OC - APP = AAI + ACP - APP$$

As Equation 16.1 shows, the cash conversion cycle has three main components: (1) average age of the inventory, (2) average collection period, and (3) average payment period. It also shows that, by changing these time periods, a firm changes the amount of time its resources are tied up in day-to-day operations

Again referring to Table 16.1, we can see that the cash conversion cycle for each firm is calculated (in line 10) by subtracting the average payment periods (in line 8) from the operating cycle (calculated in line 9). Reviewing the CCC for the computer manufacturers, we see that IBM, Dell, Apple, and Hewlett-Packard have negative CCCs. This indicates that these firms receive cash inflows before having to make the cash outflows needed to generate those inflows. This desirable state occurs in part because these firms do not keep inventory on hand for very long, but their vendors give them several months to settle their payables. Among the other four firms, only Super Value has a positive CCC. Notice how the components of the cash conversion cycle vary considerably across firms and industries. For example, Super Value has a relatively short collection period of just over seven days and keeps less

Table 16.1 **Operating Cycle (OC) and Cash Conversion Cycle (CCC) for Selected Companies, Fiscal Year 2010**

	Computer Manufacturers				Other Companies			
	IBM (IBM)	Dell (DELL)ᵃ	Apple (APPL)	Hewlett-Packard (HPQ)	Super Value (SVU)ᵇ	Polo Ralph Lauren (RL)ᶜ	GM (GM)	McDonald's (MCD)
Data ($ millions)								
(1) Sales	$99,870	$61,494	$65,225	$126,033	$37,534	$4,979	$135,592	$24,075
(2) Cost of sales	$53,857	$50,098	$39,541	$96,089	$29,124	$2,080	$118,944	$14,437
(3) A/P	$19,060	$15,474	$17,738	$34,719	$2,661	$747	$45,541	$2,916
(4) A/R	$27,353	$10,136	$11,560	$21,467	$743	$485	$10,504	$1,179
(5) Inventory	$2,549	$1,301	$1,051	$6,466	$2,270	$504	$12,125	$110
Time periods (days)								
(6) AAI {[5] ÷ [[2] ÷ 365]}	17.3	9.5	9.7	24.6	28.4	88.4	37.2	2.8
(7) ACP {[4] ÷ [[1] ÷ 365]}	100.0	60.2	64.7	62.2	7.2	35.6	28.3	17.9
(8) APP {[3] ÷ [[2] ÷ 365]}ᵈ	129.2	112.7	163.7	131.9	33.3	131.1	139.8	73.7
(9) OC [(6) + (7)]	117.2	69.6	74.4	86.7	35.7	124.0	65.5	20.7
(10) CCC [(9) − (8)]	−11.9	−43.1	−89.3	−45.2	2.3	−7.1	−74.3	−53.1

Note that because annual purchases do not appear in published financial statements, we calculate the accounts payable period using cost of sales. ᵃFiscal year ending January 2010. ᵇFiscal year ending February 2009. ᶜFiscal year ending March 2009. ᵈ "Annual purchases" cannot be found in published financial statements and so this value is calculated using "cost of sales" (line 2), which is an approach commonly used by external analysts. Because annual purchases are likely to be smaller than the cost of sales, these APPs may be understated.

EXAMPLE

Reese Industries has annual sales of $5 billion, a cost of goods sold that is 70% of sales, and purchases that are 60% of cost of goods sold. Reese has an AAI of 70 days, an ACP of 45 days, and an APP of 40 days. The 45-day ACP can be broken into 37 days until the customer places the payment in the mail and an additional 8 days before the funds are available to the firm in a spendable form. Thus, Reese's operating cycle is 115 days (70 + 45), and its cash conversion cycle is 75 days (70 + 45 − 40). Figure 16.1 presents Reese's operating and cash conversion cycles on a time line.

Figure 16.1 **Time Line for the Operating and Cash Conversion Cycles for Reese Industries**

Reese Industries has an operating cycle of 115 days, and because it takes on average 40 days to pay its accounts payable, the firm's cash conversion cycle is 75 days.

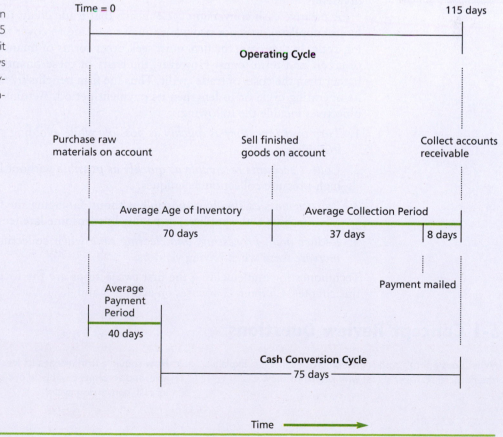

continued

Reese has invested the following resources in its cash conversion cycle, where 0.70 indicates that sales are 70% of cost of goods sold:

$$\text{Inventory} = (\$5 \text{ billion} \times 0.70) \times (70/365) = \$671.2 \text{ million}$$
$$+ \text{ Accounts receivable} = (\$5 \text{ billion}) \times (45/365) = \$616.4 \text{ million}$$
$$- \text{ Accounts payable} = (\$5 \text{ billion} \times 0.70 \times 0.60) \times (40/365)$$
$$= \$230.1 \text{ million}$$
$$= \text{Resources invested} = \$1{,}057 \text{ million}$$

If Reese could reduce from 8 days to 3 days the amount of time it takes to receive, process, and collect payments after they are mailed by its customers, then it would reduce its average collection period from 45 days to 40 days (37 + 3). This would shorten the cash conversion time line by 5 days (8 − 3) and thus reduce the amount of resources that Reese has invested in operations. For Reese, a 5-day reduction in the average collection period would reduce the resources invested in the cash conversion cycle by $68.5 million [$5 billion × (5 ÷ 365)].

than one month's worth of inventory on hand. That shouldn't be too surprising given the perishable nature of Super Value's inventory (food) and given that most of the company's sales are done on a cash basis. Also notice that Ralph Lauren's inventory age is about 90 days, or one season. Again, it should not be a surprise that fashion retailer would completely turn over its inventory about once each season.

16-1c Shortening the Cash Conversion Cycle

? WHAT TO ASK

What steps does your firm take to control the investments it makes in receivables and inventory?

In order to *maximize shareholder value, the financial manager should manage the firm's short-term activities in a way that shortens the cash conversion cycle*. This will enable the firm to operate with minimum cash investment. The firm can find alternative uses for any cash that it is not using to fund the cash conversion cycle— for example, using the cash to pursue more productive long-term investments, using it to pay down expensive long-term financing, or distributing it to the owners as dividends.

A positive cash conversion cycle means that trade credit (credit granted to a firm by its suppliers) does not provide enough financing to cover the firm's entire operating cycle. In that case, the firm must seek other forms of financing, such as bank lines of credit and term loans. However, the costs of these financing sources tend to be higher than the costs of trade credit. Thus the firm benefits by finding ways to shorten its operating cycle or to lengthen its payment period. Actions that accomplish these objectives include the following:

1. *Turn over inventory as quickly as possible* while avoiding stockouts that result in lost sales.

2. *Collect accounts receivable as quickly as possible* without losing sales because of high-pressure collection techniques.

3. *Pay accounts as slowly as possible* without damaging the firm's credit rating, its relationships with suppliers, or paying burdensome late fees.

4. *Reduce mail, processing, and clearing time* when collecting from customers but *increase* them when paying vendors.

Techniques for implementing the first two actions are the focus of the remainder of this chapter. Chapter 17 focuses on actions 3 and 4.

16-1 Concept Review Questions

1. What does a firm's *cash conversion cycle* represent? Explain the financial manager's goal with regard to the CCC.

2. How should a firm manage its inventory, accounts receivable, and accounts payable in order to reduce the length of its cash conversion cycle?

What Companies Do

A Working Capital Survey

Each year since 1997, *CFO Magazine* has published a "Working Capital Survey" that ranks 1,000 companies in 35 industries based on two measures of financial efficiency: days (of sales) of working capital and cash conversion efficiency. An article by Greg Filbeck, Thomas Krueger, and Dianna Preece assessed (1) whether stock prices of firms that ranked highly in these surveys from 1997 to 2000 rose when the results were disclosed and (2) whether annual stock returns were positively related to these firms' rankings. The authors find that stock prices of highly ranked companies increase significantly on the announcement date. But these returns reverse themselves over subsequent days, and the companies do not significantly outperform matching firms over the year following high-ranked inclusion in the "Working Capital Survey."

Professors Filbeck, Krueger, and Preece also summarize the working capital policies of the companies included in the survey. The following table describes mean, minimum, and maximum values of several financial variables for the 1,094 companies included in the surveys between 1997 and 2000. These companies are quite large on average, with annual sales of $726 million, and their stockholders earn average monthly returns of 0.53%. The companies maintain working capital equal in value to 46.12 days of sales, accounts receivable equal to 43.58 days, inventory equal to 13.53 days, and payables equal to 33.77 days. On the other hand, these average values conceal extremely wide variation in mean levels of the financial values, as shown by high standard deviations of the means and by the extreme minimum and maximum values for each variable.

Financial Data for Firms Included in *CFO Magazine's* "Working Capital Survey," 1997–2000

Variable	Number of Observations	Mean (S.D.)	Minimum	Maximum
Monthly stock return (%)	1,094	0.53% (0.28%)	−12.83%	19.69%
Sales (000)	1,094	$726,746 ($430,108)	$801	$990,701
Days of working capital	1,093	46.12 (42.74)	57.20	872.00
Accounts receivable days sales outstanding	1,092	43.58 (23.36)	0	127.50
Inventory days sales on hand	1,092	13.53 (23.54)	0.60	485.00
Payables days sales outstanding	203	33.77 (21.27)	2.00	182.00

Source: Table 3 of Greg Filbeck, Thomas Krueger, and Dianna Preece, *CFO Magazine*'s "Working Capital Survey: Do Selected Firms Work for Shareholders?" Reprinted with permission from the *Quarterly Journal of Finance and Accounting*, volume 46, no. 2 (Spring 2007), page 15.

16-2 Cost Trade-Offs in Short-Term Financial Management

When attempting to manage the firm's short-term accounts so as to minimize cash while adequately funding the firm's operations, the financial manager must focus on competing costs. Decisions with regard to the optimum levels of both operating assets and short-term financing involve cost trade-offs. For convenience, we will view the current-account decision strategies as being revenue neutral and thus will examine their cost trade-offs *solely in terms of minimizing total cost*. Clearly, with revenue neutral, minimizing total costs should increase the firm's net cash flows and therefore its value. The above What Companies Do feature summarizes the working capital policies of a large number of firms and relates them to their performance.

The optimum levels of the key operating assets—cash and marketable securities, inventory, and accounts receivable—involve trade-offs between the cost of holding the operating asset and the cost of maintaining too little of the asset. Figure 16.2 depicts the cost trade-offs and optimum level of a given operating asset. Cost 1 is the holding cost, which increases with larger operating asset account balances. Cost 2 is the cost of holding too little of the operating asset, which decreases with larger operating asset account balances. The total cost is the sum of cost 1 and cost 2 associated

Figure 16.2

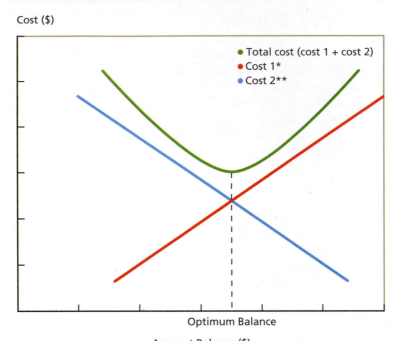

Trade-Off of Short-Term Financial Costs

Cost ($)

- Total cost (cost 1 + cost 2)
- Cost 1*
- Cost 2**

Optimum Balance

Account Balance ($)

SMART

concepts

See the problem and solution explained step-by-step at **SMART** | finance

Effect of an Increase in Account Balance

	*Cost 1	**Cost 2
Operating Assets		
Cash and marketable securities	Opportunity cost of funds and tax costs	Illiquidity and solvency costs
Inventory	Carrying cost of inventory, including financing, warehousing, obsolescence costs, etc.	Order and setup costs associated with replenishment and production of finished goods
Accounts receivable	Cost of investment in accounts receivable and bad debts	Opportunity cost of lost sales due to overly restrictive credit policy and/or terms
Short-Term Financing		
Accounts payable, accruals, and notes payable	Cost of reduced liquidity caused by increasing current liabilities	Financing costs resulting from the use of less expensive short-term financing rather than more expensive long-term debt and equity financing

© Cengage Learning 2012

with a given account balance for the operating asset. As noted, the optimum balance occurs at the point where total cost is minimized.

The table at the bottom of Figure 16.2 provides more detail on the specific costs for each operating asset. For example, consider cash and marketable securities. As the balance of these accounts *increases*, the opportunity costs and tax costs (cost 1) of the funds held in the firm rise. At the same time, the illiquidity and solvency costs (cost 2) fall; the higher the cash and marketable securities balance, the greater the firm's liquidity and the lower its likelihood of becoming insolvent. Hence, the optimum balance of cash and marketable securities is the one that minimizes the total of these two competing costs. We can evaluate the cost trade-offs for inventory and accounts receivable in a similar way, using the cost descriptions given in the table and relating them to the two cost functions in the figure. Clearly, in all cases a *decrease* in the operating asset account balance would have the opposite effect.

The optimum level of short-term financing (accounts payable, accruals, and notes payable) involves the same type of cost trade-offs as demonstrated in Figure 16.2 for operating assets. As noted in the bottom portion of the accompanying table, as the short-term financing balance *increases*, the firm faces an increasing cost of reduced liquidity (cost 1). At the same time, the firm's financing costs (cost 2) decline; short-term financing costs are lower than the alternative of using long-term debt and equity financing. The optimum amount of short-term financing is one that minimizes total cost, as shown in the graph in Figure 16.2. A *decrease* in the short-term financing balance would have the opposite effects on the competing costs.

The financial manager's primary focus when managing current accounts is to minimize total cost and thereby increase shareholder value. Each of these account balances can be evaluated quantitatively using decision models. The remainder of this chapter and the following chapter emphasize effective techniques and strategies for actively managing the current accounts over which the financial manager has direct responsibility.

16-2 Concept Review Questions

3. What general cost trade-offs must the financial manager consider when managing a firm's operating assets? How do these costs behave as a firm considers reducing its accounts receivable by, say, establishing more restrictive credit terms? How can the firm determine the optimum balance?

4. What general cost trade-offs are associated with a firm's level of short-term financing? How do these costs behave when a firm substitutes short-term financing for long-term financing? How would you quantitatively model this decision to find the optimal level of short-term financing?

16-3 Inventory Management

Inventory is an important current asset. For the typical U.S. manufacturer, inventory represents between 10% and 20% of total assets—a sizable investment. Inventory consists of the firm's stock of raw materials, work in process, and finished goods. Although inventory management is the responsibility of operations and production managers, it is also a major concern of the financial manager because of the large investments involved.

The firm's goal should be to move inventory quickly in order to minimize its investment. At the same time, it must be careful to maintain adequate inventory to meet demand and to minimize lost sales due to stock outages. The financial manager attempts to maintain optimal inventory levels that reconcile these conflicting objectives. Also, because obsolescence can severely reduce the value of inventories, the firm must carefully control inventory to avoid potential major losses in asset values.

Here we consider the aspects of inventory that concern the financial manager: the amount invested in inventory, and several popular techniques for controlling inventory.[1]

16-3a Investing in Inventory

A firm must evaluate its inventory investment in terms of associated revenues and costs. Simply stated, additional investment must be justified by additional returns. From a financial point of view, constraining inventory levels improves returns by releasing funds that the firm can use for more profitable investments. In contrast, the

---

[1]For detailed discussions of these and other inventory management techniques, see Thomas E. Vollman, William Lee Berry, David Clay Whybark, and R. Robert Jacobs, *Manufacturing Planning and Control for Supply Chain Management*, 5th Edition (Burr Ridge, IL: McGraw-Hill Irwin, 2005).

production and marketing perspectives are that expanding inventories provides for uninterrupted production runs, good product selection, and prompt delivery schedules. The firm needs to balance the conflicting preferences of finance, production, and marketing managers in order to effectively manage inventory.

The financial manager should consider several specific factors when evaluating an inventory system. On the asset side of the balance sheet, inventories represent an important short-term investment. The smaller the level of inventory needed to support the firm's sales, the faster the total asset turnover and the higher the return on total assets. (This is consistent with the DuPont system discussed in Chapter 2.) More rapid inventory turnover also reduces the potential for obsolescence and resulting price concessions. On the liability side, smaller inventories reduce the firm's short-term financing requirements and thereby lower financing costs and improve profits. The following Example illustrates the key financial trade-off associated with inventory investment.

? JOB INTERVIEW QUESTION

Why are financial managers in manufacturing firms concerned about inventory?

EXAMPLE

Kerry Manufacturing is contemplating larger production runs to reduce the high setup costs associated with a major product. The firm estimates the total annual savings in setup costs to be $120,000. It currently turns this product's inventory six times a year; with the proposed larger production runs, this turnover should drop to five times a year. If the firm's $30 million cost of goods sold for this product is unaffected by the proposal then, assuming the firm's required return on investments of similar risk is 15%, the analysis would proceed as follows.

Analysis:

Average investment in inventory	= cost of goods sold	÷ inventory turnover	
Proposed system	= $30.0 million	÷ 5 =	$6.0 million
Less: Present system	= $30.0 million	÷ 6 =	5.0 million
Increased inventory investment			$1.0 million
× required return			× 0.15
Annual cost of increased inventory investment			$150,000
Less: Annual savings in setup costs			120,000
Net loss from proposed plan			$30,000

Decision:

Don't do it; an annual loss of $30,000 will result from the proposed plan.

ABC system
An inventory control system that segregates inventory into three groups—A, B, and C. A items require the largest dollar investment and the most intensive control, B items require the next largest investment and less intensive control, and C items require the smallest investment and least intensive control.

economic order quantity (EOQ) model
A common tool used to estimate the optimal order quantity for big-ticket items of inventory. It considers operating and financial costs and determines the order quantity that minimizes overall inventory costs.

16-3b Techniques for Controlling Inventory

Although inventory control is a operations/production management task, the financial manager serves as a watchdog over this activity. This oversight is important given the firm's typically sizable investment in inventory. Firms commonly use a variety of techniques, discussed below, to control inventory. Although these techniques are typically used by operations and production managers, a good financial manager should understand them.

ABC System A firm using the ABC system segregates its inventory into three groups, A, B, and C. The A items are the most costly inventory items, and the B group consists of items accounting for the next largest investment. The C group typically consists of a large number of items accounting for a small dollar investment. Separating inventory into A, B, and C groups allows the firm to determine the level and types of inventory control procedures needed. Control of the A items should be most intensive because of the high dollar investments involved; the B and C items are subject to correspondingly less sophisticated procedures.

Basic Economic Order Quantity (EOQ) Model A popular tool for determining the optimal order quantity for an inventory item is the economic order quantity (EOQ) model. This model could be used to control the firm's big-ticket inventory items such as those included in the A group of an ABC system. The EOQ model considers order costs and carrying costs and determines the order quantity that minimizes their total. The *economic order quantity* for a given inventory item is given as

(Eq. 16.2)
$$EOQ = \sqrt{\frac{2SO}{C}}$$

total cost
The sum of the *order costs* and the *carrying costs* that is minimized using the *economic order quantity (EOQ) model.*

order cost
The *fixed dollar amount per order* that covers the costs of placing and receiving an order; used in calculating the EOQ.

carrying cost
The *variable cost per unit* of holding an item in inventory for a specified period of time. Used in calculating the EOQ.

where

S = inventory usage per period (typically one year)
O = order cost, a fixed cost associated with placing and receiving an order
C = carrying cost, a variable cost associated with holding an item in inventory

Total cost of inventory equals the sum of the fixed cost of placing each order and the variable cost of holding each item in inventory. Assuming that inventory usage is constant, the larger the order quantity, EOQ, the fewer orders placed and, therefore, the *lower the total* order cost. But placing larger orders raises the average inventory, and therefore results in *higher total* carrying cost. So the EOQ mathematically balances the trade-off between decreasing total order costs and increasing total carrying costs and calculates the order quantity that minimizes the total of these two competing costs (as in Figure 16.2).

EXAMPLE

Garrison Industries currently uses 16,000 units of an expensive inventory item each year. The firm estimates its order cost to be $500 per order and carrying cost for this item to be $100 per unit per year. Garrison wishes to estimate the optimal quantity in which to order this item. By substituting S = 16,000, O = $500, and C = $100 into Equation 16.2, we calculate the EOQ for this item as

$$EOQ = \sqrt{\frac{2 \times 16,000 \times \$500}{\$100}} = \sqrt{160,000} = 400 \text{ units}$$

By ordering this Item in quantities of 400 units, Garrison Industries will minimize its total inventory cost for this item.

Reorder Points and Safety Stock The simple EOQ model just presented assumes that inventory is instantaneously replenished precisely at the time the inventory is exhausted. This model implies perfect certainty with regard to the rate of usage and the timing of receipt from suppliers. Assuming a constant rate of usage, a firm can easily estimate a *reorder point* as follows:

Reorder Point = lead time in days × daily usage

For example, if Garrison Industries uses about 44 units per day (16,000 units per year ÷ 365 days) and if it typically takes the firm 4 days to place and receive an order, then the firm should place an order when its inventory falls to 176 units (4 days × 44 units).

To allow for faster-than-anticipated rates of usage and/or delayed deliveries, many firms maintain *safety stocks* of inventory. Management determines the size of these stocks by analyzing the probabilities of both increased usage rates and delivery delays. For example, Garrison Industries estimates that a safety stock equal to 2% of its annual usage of the given item will adequately protect against stockouts due to faster-than-anticipated usage and/or order fulfillment delays. Given that estimate, Garrison will maintain a safety stock of 320 units (0.02 × 16,000 units). A variety of more sophisticated models are available for setting both reorder points and safety stocks.

Cengage Learning

Vern LoForti, V.P., CFO, and Corporate Secretary, InfoSonics

"You have to have a high level of confidence in those suppliers who are holding that inventory at their warehouse."

See the entire interview at **SMART** | finance

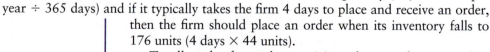

Smart Practices Video

Finance in Your Life

Should I Buy in Large Quantities?

The proliferation of superstores and warehouse clubs causes many individuals and families to buy large quantities of staple items such as paper goods, canned food, and sodas in order to try to save money. The question is: Does buying in large quantities make sense? This question can be answered by considering the cost trade-off s involved, similar to the basic EOQ model.

Let's assume that the local Costco offers a box of 200 trash bags for $12. You currently buy a box of 50 similar trash bags for $6 at the nearby grocery store every 3 months (¼ of a year), so the 200 bags should last you an entire year. Because you routinely go to both the local grocery and to Costco, your "order costs," which would be the transportation costs and the value of your time, are virtually $0. You won't have to make a special trip to either store. Assuming you have adequate storage space at home, your holding costs are strictly financial and represent the cost of having your money tied up in trash bags.

Let's assume you can earn 4% interest on your savings. Your average investment in each case would be one-half of the cost of the purchase as calculated below:

Average Investment

Costco purchase = $12/2 = $6
Nearby grocery store purchase = $6/2 = $3

The Costco purchase would therefore cause you to have on average an extra $3 ($6 − $3) invested in trash bags. Given that you can earn 4% on your money, the annual cost of tying up $3 in trash bags is $0.12 (0.04 × $3). But by buying the large quantity of trash bags at Costco, you save $12, the difference between $24 (four $6 purchases at the nearby grocery) and the $12 cost of the one-time purchase at Costco. So does it make economic sense to incur annual holding costs of $0.12 to save $12 annually? **Clearly, in this case, the large quantity purchase will save just under $12 per year.**

material requirements planning (MRP)
A computerized system used to control the flow of resources, particularly inventory, within the production-sale process.

manufacturing resource planning II (MRPII)
Expands on MRP by using a complex computerized system to integrate data from many departments and generate a production plan for the firm along with management reports, forecasts, and financial statements.

Material Requirements Planning Many manufacturing firms use computerized systems to control the flow of resources, particularly inventory, within the production process. **Material requirements planning (MRP)** is one such system. MRP uses a master schedule to ensure that the materials, labor, and equipment needed for production are at the right places, in the right amounts, and at the right times. The schedule is based on forecasts of the demand for the company's products. The schedule says exactly what will be manufactured during the next few weeks or months and when the work will take place.

Sophisticated computer programs coordinate all the elements of MRP. The computer determines material requirements by comparing production needs to the materials the company already has in inventory. The programs place orders so that items will be on hand when they are needed for production. MRP helps ensure a smooth flow of finished products.

Manufacturing resource planning II (MRPII) expands on MRP. Using a complex computer system, it integrates data from many departments, including finance, marketing, accounting, engineering, and manufacturing. MRPII can generate a production plan for the firm, as well as management reports, forecasts, and financial statements. It allows the firm to track and manage key inventory items (typically A items) on a real-time basis. The system also enables managers to assess the impact of production plans on profitability. If one department's plans change, the system transmits the effects of these changes throughout the company.

just-in-time (JIT) system
An inventory management technique used to make sure that materials arrive exactly when they are needed for production, rather than being stored on-site.

Just-in-Time System An important and widely adopted inventory management technique, imported from Japan, is the **just-in-time (JIT) system**. JIT is based on the belief that materials should arrive exactly when they are needed for production, rather than being stored on-site. Relying closely on computerized systems such as MRP and MRPII, manufacturers determine what parts will be needed and when before ordering them from suppliers so the parts arrive just in time.

Under the JIT system, inventory products are pulled through the production process in response to customer demand. JIT requires close teamwork among vendors and personnel in purchasing and production; any delay in deliveries of supplies could bring production to a halt. Clearly, unexpected events, such as 9/11, can cause problems for firms using a JIT system. In spite of such risks, a properly employed JIT system can significantly reduce inventory levels and carrying costs, thereby freeing funds for more productive uses.

16-3 Concept Review Questions

5. How might the financial manager's view of inventory differ from that of managers in production and marketing? What is the relationship between inventory turnover and inventory investment? Explain.

6. What is the *ABC system*? What role does the *EOQ model* play in controlling inventory? What basic cost trade-off does the EOQ model address?

7. From the financial manager's perspective, describe the role of reorder points, safety stock, MRP, MRPII, and a *just-in-time system* in managing a firm's inventory.

16-4 Accounts Receivable Standards and Terms

Accounts receivable (A/R) result from a company extending trade credit to its customers by selling its products or services on credit. Receivables affect the cash conversion cycle through the *average collection period (ACP)*. As noted in Chapter 2, this period is the average length of time from a sale on credit until the payment becomes usable funds for the firm. The *ACP* has two parts. The first, and generally the longer, is the credit period. It is measured as the time from the sale (or customer invoicing) until customers place their payments in the mail. The second is the time from when the customers place payments in the mail to when the firm has spendable funds in its bank account. The first part of the average collection period involves managing the credit available to the firm's customers. The second part involves receiving, processing, and collecting payments. This section discusses customer credit; the next chapter discusses receiving, processing, and collecting payments.

As with all current accounts, receivables management requires managers to balance competing interests. On the one hand, managers (generally the cash or treasury managers) prefer to receive cash payments sooner rather than later. That preference leads toward strict credit terms and strict enforcement of those terms. On the other hand, firms can use credit terms as a marketing tool to attract new customers (or to keep current customers from defecting to another firm). This objective argues for easier credit terms and more flexible enforcement.

It is also important to understand that, in many firms, the credit policy is generally not under the control of the financial (cash or treasury) managers but rather is part of the sales or customer-service functions. For many companies wishing to remain competitive, credit terms are a necessary part of determining the ultimate sales prices for their products and services.

16-4a Effective Accounts Receivable Management

Effectively managing the credit and accounts receivable process involves cooperation among sales, customer-service, finance, and accounting staffs. The key areas of concern involve:

1. Setting and communicating the company's general credit and collections policies.

2. Determining who is granted credit and how much credit is extended to each customer.

3. Managing the billing and collection process in a timely and accurate manner.

4. Applying payments and updating the accounts receivable ledger.

5. Monitoring accounts receivable on both an individual and aggregate basis.

6. Following up on overdue accounts and initiating collection procedures, if required.

In the typical company, the credit and accounts receivable departments handle most of these tasks. The cash management or treasury area will usually be responsible for managing the actual receipt of payments. The cash manager usually will also have to collect and organize the remittance data that is sent along with the payments so that the A/R department can determine what invoices have been paid. We will cover this *cash application* process in greater detail later in the chapter.

The first decision a company must make is whether it will offer trade credit at all. There are many reasons for offering credit, including increasing sales, meeting terms offered by competitors, attracting new customers, and providing general convenience. In a typical business-to-business environment, a company may have to offer trade credit just to generate sales. This is especially the case for a large company selling to smaller companies, where the smaller company literally needs the credit period in order to sell merchandise so it can pay the supplier. The small company would not usually have access to other types of credit, so if the supplier doesn't offer credit then there is no sale.

As mentioned previously, many companies see trade credit and credit terms as simply an extension of the sales price. They may use credit terms to motivate customers or to compete with other suppliers. In many cases, industry practices dictate whether firms offer credit and under what terms. The What Companies Do Globally insert on page 501 compares the level of trade credit in the United States to that in other major countries throughout the world. In today's financial environment, there are also many opportunities for companies to outsource part or all of the credit and accounts receivable process. Some outsourcing alternatives are: use of credit cards, third-party financing, and factoring, which involves the outright sale of receivables to a third-party *factor* at a discount.

factoring
The outright sale of receivables to a third-party *factor* at a discount.

Once a company has decided to offer trade credit, it must do the following:

1. Determine its credit standards: Who is offered credit and how much?

2. Set its credit terms: How long do customers have to pay, and are any discounts offered for early payment?

3. Develop its collection policy: How should delinquent accounts be handled?

4. Monitor its accounts receivable on both an individual and aggregate basis: What is the status of each customer and the overall quality of its receivables?

In addition, the firm must have effective cash application procedures in place (these are discussed in Section 16-5c).

16-4b Credit Standards

The first and most important aspect of accounts receivable management is setting credit standards. This process involves applying techniques for determining which customers should receive credit and how much credit should be granted. Much of the focus is on making sure that a company does not accept substandard customers (i.e., potential defaulters on trade credit). However, a firm must take care not to set the standards so high that potential good customers are rejected. A company's accounts receivable default rates should generally be in line with those of other companies in the same industry if it wants to remain competitive.

Granting Credit to Customers In analyzing credit requests and determining the level of credit to be offered, the company can gather information from both internal and external sources. The usual internal sources of credit information are the credit application and agreement and, if available, the company's own records of the applicant's payment history. External sources typically include financial statements, trade references, banks or other creditors, and credit-reporting agencies. Each of these

What Companies Do Globally

Trade Credit Practices Around the World

Trade credit is perhaps the single most important source of short-term external financing for U.S. businesses. But the use of trade credit varies widely across countries. The accompanying chart shows the ratio of accounts payable to sales and accounts receivable to sales for the median firm in twenty-six countries. Accounts payable is a measure of the trade credit that a firm receives from its suppliers, while accounts receivable captures the trade credit that a firm grants to its customers. As important as trade credit is in the United States, it appears to be a much more important source of financing in other countries. Italian firms use (and grant) more trade credit than firms in any other country. Heavy trade credit usage is common among the Mediterranean countries of Europe, while in northern Europe (e.g., Finland and Germany), firms use trade credit at a rate similar to that seen in the United States.

The use of trade credit varies across countries for many reasons. Probably the most important factor is whether or not a given country has well-developed markets for external capital, including a thriving banking sector. When sources of external funds are few, firms may rely more heavily on trade credit as a means of financing operations. Another factor that helps to explain cross-country differences in trade credit is firm size. Large firms have access to broader capital sources than small firms do, so in a country where firms are relatively small (e.g., Italy), trade credit may be more important.

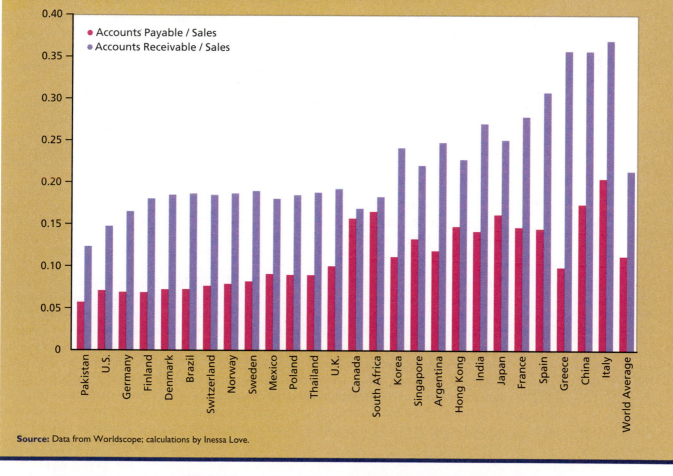

Source: Data from Worldscope; calculations by Inessa Love.

sources involves the internal costs of analyzing the data; some sources, such as credit reporting agencies, also have explicit external costs (a charge for obtaining the data).

The company must also take into account the variable costs of the products it would be selling on credit. For example, a company selling a product with a low variable cost (e.g., magazine subscriptions) will often grant credit to almost anyone without a credit check. It doesn't have much to lose if payment isn't made, but on the other hand, potential profits are great. Companies selling products with high variable costs (e.g., heavy-equipment manufacturers) will typically do extensive credit checks before granting credit and shipping merchandise.

The amount of the credit limit is also an important factor. To reduce some of the costs associated with making credit decisions, a company may routinely grant small levels of credit to new customers and then allow the credit limit to rise as the customer proves to be a good credit risk.[2]

Two popular approaches to the credit-granting process are (1) the five C's of credit and (2) credit scoring.

five C's of credit
A framework for performing in-depth credit analysis without providing a specific accept or reject decision.

Five C's of Credit   The **five C's of credit** provide a framework for performing in-depth credit analysis, but they do not provide a specific accept-or-reject decision. This credit-selection method is typically used for high-dollar credit requests. Although applying the five C's does not speed up collection of accounts, it does lower the probability of default. The five C's are defined as follows.

1. *Character* refers to the applicant's record of meeting past obligations. The lender would consider the applicant's payment history as well as any pending or resolved legal judgments against the applicant. The question addressed here is whether the applicant will pay its account, if able, within the specified credit terms.

2. *Capacity* is the applicant's ability to repay the requested credit. The lender typically assesses the applicant's capacity by using financial statement analysis focused on cash flows available to service debt obligations.

3. *Capital* refers to the financial strength of the applicant as reflected by its capital structure. In assessing capital, the lender frequently analyzes the applicant's debt relative to equity and its profitability ratios. The analysis of capital determines whether the applicant has sufficient equity to survive a business downturn.

4. *Collateral* consists of the assets the applicant has available for securing the credit. In general, the more valuable and more marketable the assets are, the more credit lenders will extend. However, trade credit is rarely a secured loan. Therefore, collateral is not the primary consideration in deciding to grant credit. Rather, it strengthens the creditworthiness of a customer who appears to have sufficient cash flows to meet its obligations.

5. *Conditions* refer to current general and industry-specific economic conditions. It also considers any unique conditions surrounding a specific transaction. For example, a firm that has excess inventory of a given item may be willing to accept a lower price or extend more attractive credit terms in order to sell that item.

credit scoring
Applies statistically derived weights for key financial and credit characteristics to predict whether or not a credit applicant with specific scores for each characteristic will pay the requested credit in a timely fashion.

Credit Scoring   Credit scoring is commonly used with high-volume–low-dollar credit requests. **Credit scoring** applies statistically derived weights for key financial and credit characteristics to predict whether a credit applicant with specific scores for each characteristic will pay the requested credit in a timely fashion. The weighted average score is the sum of the products of the applicant's score and the associated predetermined weight for each characteristic, and the resulting score determines whether to accept or reject the credit applicant. That is, the procedure results in a score that measures the applicant's overall credit strength, and the company uses that score to make the accept-or-reject decision for granting credit. Credit scoring is most commonly used by large credit card operations such as those of banks, oil companies, and department stores.

EXAMPLE

WEG Oil, a major oil company, uses credit scoring to make its consumer credit decisions. Each applicant fills out a credit application. WEG Oil inputs data from the application into an expert system, and a computer generates the applicant's final credit score, creates a letter indicating whether the application was approved, and (if approved) issues the credit card.

Table 16.2 demonstrates the scoring of a consumer credit application, and Table 16.3 describes WEG's predetermined credit standards. Because the applicant in Table 16.2 has a credit score of 83.25, he/she will be extended WEG's standard credit terms (see Table 16.3).

---

[2]The National Association of Credit Managers (NACM; see www.nacm.org) is the primary professional association for credit managers and supports several certification programs.

continued

Table 16.2

Consumer Credit Application Credit Score by WEG Oil

Financial and Credit Characteristics	Score (0 to 100) (1)	Predetermined Weight (2)	Weighted Score [(1) × (2)] (3)
Credit references	80	0.15	12.00
Home ownership	100	0.15	15.00
Income range	75	0.25	18.75
Payment history	80	0.25	20.00
Years at address	90	0.10	9.00
Years on job	85	0.10	8.50
		Total: 1.00	Credit score: 83.25

Notes: In column (1), scores are assigned by an analyst or by a computer based on information supplied on the credit application; scores range from 0 (lowest) to 100 (highest). In column (2), weights are based on the company's analysis of the relative importance of each characteristic in predicting whether or not a customer will pay its account in a timely fashion; the weights must add up to 1.00.

Table 16.3

WEG Oil's Credit Standards

Credit Score	Action
Higher than 75	Extend standard credit terms
65 to 75	Extend limited credit; if account is properly maintained, convert to standard credit terms after one year
Lower than 65	Reject application

? JOB INTERVIEW QUESTION

What financial trade-offs are typically involved when considering a change in credit standards?

contribution margin
The sale price per unit minus total variable cost per unit.

average investment in accounts receivable (AIAR)
An estimate of the actual amount of cash (variable cost) tied up in accounts receivable at any time during the year.

total variable cost of annual sales (TVC)
Calculated by multiplying the annual sales in units by the total variable cost per unit and used to estimate the *average investment in accounts receivable* under a stated policy.

Changing Credit Standards The vast majority of sales by U.S. corporations are made on credit. Thus, as a practical matter, it is important to understand how establishing and changing credit standards affect sales, costs, and overall cash flows for a given company. As we discussed earlier, it is essential that firms accurately assess the creditworthiness of individual customers who buy on credit. This does not mean that a firm should extend credit *only* to those customers who are certain to repay their debts. Following such an excessively conservative strategy will cost the company many profitable sales, especially if industry practice is to be more generous in extending credit. Instead, the firm should accept a *degree* of default risk in order to increase sales—but not so much that the additional profit from sales is overwhelmed by additional accounts receivable investment and bad debts. The financial manager is typically responsible for estimating the cash flow and financial impact of a proposed change in credit standards.

Fortunately, measuring the overall financial impact of changes in credit standards is fairly straightforward. Any change will likely yield both benefits and costs; the decision to change standards will depend on whether the benefits exceed the costs. We can describe the general impact of changes in credit standards as follows.

- **Relaxing credit standards** will generally yield increased unit sales and additional profits. (The additional profit from relaxed credit standards assumes that each unit is sold at a positive contribution margin. The contribution margin is a product's price per unit minus variable costs per unit and thus is a direct measure of gross profit per unit sold.) Relaxing credit standards will also yield higher costs from additional investment in accounts receivable and additional bad debt expense.
- **Tightening credit standards** will generally yield **reduced investment in accounts** receivable and lower bad debt expense at the cost of lower sales and profits.

It is easiest to demonstrate how to calculate the net effect of changing credit standards by giving an example.

Yeoman Manufacturing Company (YMC) produces and sells a CD organizer to music stores nationwide. YMC charges $20/unit and all of its sales are on credit, with customers selected for credit on the basis of a scoring process. With its existing credit standards, YMC expects to sell 120,000 units over the coming year, yielding total sales of $2,400,000 (120,000 units $\times$ $20/unit). Variable costs are $12/unit, and YMC has fixed costs of $240,000 per year.

YMC is contemplating a relaxation of its credit standards and expects the following effects: a 5% increase in sales to 126,000 units; an increase in the average collection period from 30 days (the current level) to 45 days; and an increase in bad debt expense from 1% (the current level) to 2% of sales. YMC plans to keep the product's sale price unchanged at $20/unit, which implies that total sales will increase to $2,520,000 (126,000 units $\times$ $20/unit). If the firm's required return on investments of equal risk is 12%, should YMC relax its credit standards?

To make this decision, YMC's managers must calculate: (1) how much profits will increase from the additional sales that relaxed credit standards are expected to generate; (2) the cost of the marginal investment in accounts receivable; (3) the cost of marginal bad debts; and (4) whether the financial benefits exceed the costs. (Note: In this and subsequent accounts receivable policy change calculations, we use a single-period approach rather than specifying all subsequent cash flows and determining their present value. Prior research has shown that for the accounts receivable decisions demonstrated in this chapter, the single-period model yields the same accept-or-reject decision as a the more detailed present value approach. We therefore choose to keep it simple.)

1. **Marginal profit contribution from sales.** We are assuming that a 5% increase in sales volume will not cause YMC's fixed costs to increase. Thus, we need to account only for changes in revenues and variable costs. Specifically, we can compute the marginal increase in profits as the increased unit sales volume times the contribution margin per unit sold:

$$
\text{(Eq. 16.3)} \qquad
\begin{aligned}
\text{Marginal profit from increased sales} &= \Delta \text{ Sales} \times \text{CM} \\
&= \Delta \text{ Sales} \times (\text{Price} - \text{VC})
\end{aligned}
$$

where

Δ Sales = change in unit sales resulting from the change in credit policies
CM = contribution margin
Price = price per unit
VC = variable cost per unit

With the assumptions just detailed for YMC, we can use Equation 16.3 to determine that relaxing credit standards as suggested will yield a marginal profit of $48,000:

$$
\begin{aligned}
\text{Marginal profit from increased sales} &= 6,000 \text{ units} \times (\$20/\text{unit} - \$12/\text{unit}) \\
&= 6,000 \text{ units} \times (\$8/\text{unit}) = \$48,000
\end{aligned}
$$

2. **Cost of the marginal investment in accounts receivable.** To determine the cost of the marginal investment in accounts receivable, we must calculate the cost of financing the current level of accounts receivable and compare it to the expected cost under the new credit standards. This is more complicated than it sounds. We must first calculate how much YMC currently has invested in accounts receivable based on its current annual sales, variable costs, and accounts receivable turnover. We then repeat this process for the level of sales expected to result from a change in credit standards. Equations 16.4, 16.5, and 16.6 present the steps required. Note that *we use variable costs in calculating investment in accounts receivable because this is the firm's actual cash expense incurred* (and tied up in receivables).

$$
\text{(Eq. 16.4)} \qquad
\begin{array}{c}
\text{Average investment in} \\
\text{accounts receivable (AIAR)}
\end{array}
= \frac{\text{total variable cost of annual sales}}{\text{turnover of accounts receivable}}
$$

$$
\text{(Eq. 16.5)} \qquad
\text{Total variable cost of annual sales (TVC)} = \text{Annual unit sales} \times \text{Variable cost/unit}
$$

$$
\text{(Eq. 16.6)} \qquad
\begin{array}{c}
\text{Turnover of} \\
\text{accounts receivable (TOAR)}
\end{array}
= \frac{365}{\text{average collection period (ACP)}}
$$

We can use these equations to compute the **average investment in accounts receivable (AIAR)** for the current, $\text{AIAR}_{\text{current}}$, and proposed, $\text{AIAR}_{\text{proposed}}$, credit standards. First, we compute the **total variable cost (TVC) of annual sales** under the current credit standards, $\text{TVC}_{\text{current}}$, and the proposed plan, $\text{TVC}_{\text{proposed}}$, using Equation 16.5:

$$
\begin{aligned}
\text{TVC}_{\text{current}} &= 120,000 \text{ units} \times \$12/\text{units} = \$1,440,000 \\
\text{TVC}_{\text{proposed}} &= 126,000 \text{ units} \times \$12/\text{units} = \$1,512,000
\end{aligned}
$$

continued

Next, we note that the 30-day average collection period under the current plan, $ACP_{current}$, is expected to rise to 45 days under the proposed plan, $ACP_{proposed}$. This allows us to use Equation 16.6 to compute the **turnover of accounts receivable (TOAR)** under the current, $TOAR_{current}$, and proposed, $TOAR_{proposed}$, credit terms:

$$TOAR_{current} = \frac{365}{ACP_{current}} = \frac{365}{30 \text{ days}} = 12.2 \text{ times/year}$$

$$TOAR_{proposed} = \frac{365}{ACP_{proposed}} = \frac{365}{45 \text{ days}} = 8.1 \text{ times/year}$$

These turnover measures suggest that, if YMC relaxes its credit standards, then the turnover of its accounts receivable will slow down from 12.2 times per year to 8.1 times per year. Clearly, this slowing is attributable to the generally slower paying additional credit customers generated by the relaxed credit standards. We now have all the inputs required to use Equation 16.4 to compute the $AIAR_{current}$ and $AIAR_{proposed}$:

$$AIAR_{current} = \frac{TVC_{current}}{TOAR_{current}} = \frac{\$1,440,000}{12.2} = \$118,033$$

$$AIAR_{proposed} = \frac{TVC_{proposed}}{TOAR_{proposed}} = \frac{\$1,512,000}{8.1} = \$186,667$$

With these measures, we can now determine the **cost of the marginal investment in accounts receivable**. This amount is the marginal investment in accounts receivable required to support the proposed change in credit policy multiplied by the required return on investment, r: *This important calculation recognizes the firm's opportunity cost—the cost of forgoing earning opportunities as a result of tying up additional money in accounts receivable.*

(Eq. 16.7)

$$\text{Cost of marginal investment in accounts receivable} = \text{Marginal investment} \times \text{Required return}$$
$$= (AIAR_{proposed} - AIAR_{current}) \times r$$
$$= (\$186,667 - \$118,033) \times 0.12$$
$$= \$68,634 \times 0.12 = \$8,236$$

This value of \$8,236 is a cost of adopting the relaxed credit standards; it represents the opportunity cost of investing an additional \$68,634 in accounts receivable rather than investing these funds in another earning asset.

3. **Cost of marginal bad debts.** YMC expects that relaxing its credit standards will increase its bad debt expense from 1% to 2% of sales. We can calculate the cost of this by subtracting the current level of bad debt expense from the expected level of bad debt expense under the proposed new credit standards. Equation 16.8 shows the calculations required to determine bad debt expense, and Equation 16.9 shows how to calculate the cost of marginal bad debts if YMC relaxes its credit standards:

(Eq. 16.8)

$$\text{Bad debt expense (BDE)} = \text{Annual sales (Sales)} \times \text{Bad debt expense rate (\% BDE),}$$
$$BDE_{proposed} = (Sales_{proposed}) \times (\%BDE_{proposed})$$
$$= \$2,520,000 \times 0.02 = \$50,400,$$
$$BDE_{current} = (Sales_{current}) \times (\% BDE_{current})$$
$$= \$2,400,000 \times 0.01 = \$24,000;$$

(Eq. 16.9)

$$\text{Cost of marginal bad debts} = BDE_{proposed} - BDE_{current}$$
$$= \$50,400 - \$24,000 = \$26,400$$

continued

4. **Net profit for the credit decision.** Now that we have calculated the individual financial benefits and costs of changing YMC's credit standards, we can use Equation 16.10 to compute the overall net profit for the credit decision:

(Eq. 16.10)

$$\text{Net profit for the credit decision} = (\text{Marginal profit from increased sales}) - (\text{Cost of marginal investment in accounts receivable})$$
$$- (\text{Cost of marginal bad debts})$$
$$= \$48{,}000 - \$8{,}236 - \$26{,}400$$
$$= \$13{,}364$$

Because relaxing YMC's credit standards is expected to yield $13,364 in increased profit, the firm should implement the proposed change. The marginal profit from additional sales will more than offset the total cost of the marginal investment in accounts receivable and marginal bad debts.

16-4c Credit Terms

turnover of accounts receivable (*TOAR*)
Three-hundred-sixty-five divided by the *average collection period (ACP)*. Used to calculate the *average investment in accounts receivable (AIAR)* when evaluating accounts receivable policies.

cost of marginal investment in accounts receivable
The marginal investment in accounts receivable required to support a proposed change in credit policy multiplied by the required return on investment.

credit terms
The terms of sale for customers.

cash discount
A method of lowering investment in accounts receivable by giving customers a cash incentive to pay sooner.

Credit terms are the terms of sale for customers. Terms of *net 30* mean that the customer has 30 days from the beginning of the credit period—typically *end of month* (EOM) or *date of invoice*—to pay the full invoice amount. Some firms offer cash discounts with terms, such as *2/10 net 30*. These terms mean the customer can take a 2% *cash discount* from the invoice amount if the payment is made within the 10-day *cash discount period*, or the customer can pay the full amount of the invoice within the 30-day *credit period*.

The nature of a firm's business influences its regular credit terms. For example, a firm selling perishable items will have very short credit terms because its items have little long-term collateral value. These firms will typically offer short terms by which the customer has 7 to 10 days to make payment. A firm in a seasonal business may tailor its terms to fit the industry cycles with terms known as *seasonal dating*. Most managers want their company's regular credit terms to be consistent with its industry's standards. A company will lose business if its terms are more restrictive than those of its competitors; if its terms are less restrictive than those of its competitors, then it will attract customers with poor financial histories that probably are unable to pay under the standard industry terms.

As briefly noted above, a popular method used to lower a firm's investment in accounts receivable is to include a **cash discount** in the credit terms. The cash discount provides a cash incentive for customers to pay sooner. By speeding collections, the discount will decrease the firm's investment in accounts receivable—which is the objective. But the discount will also decrease the per-unit profit because the customer pays less than the full invoice amount. Initiating a cash discount should reduce bad debts (because customers taking the cash discount pay a lower price for the product). Firms that consider offering a cash discount must perform a cost-benefit analysis to determine if the discount yields sufficient profits.

EXAMPLE

Masson Industries has an average collection period of 45 days: 37 days until the customers place their payments in the mail; and a further 8 days to receive, process, and collect payments. Masson is contemplating a change in its credit terms from *net 30* to *2/10 net 30*. The change is expected to reduce the average collection period to 26 days.

Masson currently sells 1,200 units of its product for $2,500 per unit. Its variable cost per unit is $2,000. It estimates that 70% of its customers will take the 2% discount and that offering the discount will increase sales by 50 units per year but will not alter its bad debt percentage for this product. Masson's opportunity cost of funds invested in accounts receivable is 13.5% per year. Should Masson offer the proposed cash discount? The cost–benefit analysis, presented in Table 16.4, shows that the *net cost* of the cash discount is $2,846. Thus, *Masson should not implement the proposed cash discount.*

continued

Table 16.4	Analysis of Offering a Cash Discount at Masson Industries		
Marginal profit from increased sales [50 units × ($2,500 − $2,000)]			$25,000
Current investment in accounts receivable ($2,000[a] × 1,200 units) × (45 ÷ 365)		$295,890	
New investment in accounts receivable ($2,000[a] × 1,250 units) × (26 ÷ 365)[b]		178,082	
Reduction in accounts receivable investment		$117,808	
Cost savings from reduced investment in accounts receivable (0.135 × $117,808)[c]			15,904
Cost of cash discount (0.02 × $2,500 × 1,250 × 0.70)			(43,750)
Net profit (cost) from proposed cash discount			$ (2,846)

[a]In analyzing the investment in accounts receivable, we use the $2,000 variable cost of the product sold, rather than its $2,500 sales price, because the variable cost represents the firm's actual cash expense incurred and tied up in receivables.

[b]The new investment in accounts receivable is tied up for only 26 days instead of the 45 days under the original terms. The 26 days is calculated as (0.70 × 10 days) + (0.30 × 37 days) + 8 days = 26.1 days, which is rounded to 26 days.

[c]Masson's opportunity cost of funds is 13.5% per year.

16-4 Concept Review Questions

8. Why do a firm's regular credit terms typically conform to its industry's standards? On what basis other than credit terms should the firm compete?

9. How are the *five C's of credit* used to perform in-depth credit analysis? Why is this framework typically used only on high-dollar credit requests?

10. How is *credit scoring* used in the credit selection process? In what types of situations is it most useful?

11. What are the key variables to consider when evaluating the benefits and costs *of changing credit standards*? How do these variables differ when evaluating the benefits and costs of *changing credit terms*?

12. Why do we include only the variable cost of sales when estimating the average investment in accounts receivable? Why do we apply an opportunity cost to this investment when estimating its cost?

13. What are the key elements of a firm's *credit terms*? What is a key determinant of the credit terms offered by a firm?

16-5 Collecting, Monitoring, and Applying Cash to Receivables

collection policy
The procedures used by a company to collect overdue or delinquent accounts receivable. The approach used is often a function of the industry and the competitive environment.

In addition to establishing the firm's accounts receivable standards and terms, the financial manager's responsibilities include collecting and monitoring receivables. The collection and monitoring process is an ongoing operating activity that is also the responsibility of finance personnel. Here we consider collection policy, credit monitoring, and cash application.

Cengage Learning

Jon Olson, Chief Financial Officer, Xilinx Corp.

"Because cash is king, we want to make sure that we have a high quality collections organization."

See the entire interview at **SMART | finance**

Smart Practices Video

16-5a Collection Policy

A company must determine what its collection policy will be and how it will implement that policy. As with credit standards and terms, the approach to collections may be a function of the industry and the competitive environment. For many delinquent accounts, a reminder, form letter, telephone call, or personal visit may initiate customer payment. At a minimum, the company should generally suspend further sales to the customer until the delinquent account is brought up to date.

If these actions fail to generate customer payment, it may be necessary to negotiate with the customer for past-due amounts and report the customer to credit bureaus. It is possible that the company sold the goods with a lien attached, obtained a pledge of collateral against the account, or had other corporate or personal guarantees from the customer. In these cases, the company should utilize these options for obtaining payment. Generally as a last resort, the account can be turned over to a collection agency or referred to an attorney for direct legal action. Obviously, a cost-benefit analysis should be made at each stage to compare the cost of further collection actions against the cost of simply writing off the account as a bad debt.

16-5b Credit Monitoring

credit monitoring
The ongoing review of a firm's accounts receivable to determine if customers are paying according to the stated credit terms.

Credit monitoring involves ongoing review of a firm's accounts receivable to determine if customers are paying according to the stated credit terms. If customers are not paying on time, credit monitoring will alert the firm to the problem. Companies must monitor credit on both an individual and an aggregate basis. Individual monitoring is necessary to determine if each customer is paying in a timely manner and to assess whether a customer is within its credit limits.

Credit monitoring on an aggregate basis indicates the overall quality of the company's accounts receivable. Slow payments are costly to a firm because they increase the average collection period and thereby the firm's investment in accounts receivable. If a company is also using its accounts receivable as collateral for a loan, then the lending institution will generally exclude any past-due accounts from those used as backup for the credit line. Therefore, changes in accounts receivable over time could diminish the company's overall liquidity and increase the need for additional financing. Analysis of accounts receivable payment patterns can also be essential for forecasting future cash receipts in the cash budget.

The three most frequently cited techniques for monitoring the overall quality of accounts receivable are: (1) the average collection period; (2) aging of accounts receivable; and (3) payment-pattern monitoring.

? JOB INTERVIEW QUESTION

What are some of the methods firms use to monitor their outstanding accounts receivable?

Average Collection Period The *average collection period* (ACP), also known as *days' sales outstanding* (DSO), is the second component of the cash conversion cycle. As noted in Chapter 2, it represents the average number of days that credit sales are outstanding. The average collection period has two components: (1) the time from sale until the customer places the payment in the mail; and (2) the time to receive, process, and collect the payment once it has been mailed by the customer. Equation 16.11 gives the formula for determining the average collection period:

$$\text{(Eq. 16.11)} \qquad \text{Average collection period} = \frac{\text{accounts receivable}}{\text{average sales per day}}$$

If we assume that the receipt, processing, and collection time is constant, then the average collection period tells the firm how many days (on average) it takes customers to pay their accounts. In applying this formula, analysts must be consistent in their use of the sales period and must adjust for known seasonal fluctuations.

EXAMPLE

P. Scofield Enterprises has an accounts receivable balance of $1.2 million. Sales during the past 90 days were $3.6 million for an average daily sales figure of $40,000. Dividing $1.2 million by $40,000 yields Scofield's average collection period of 30 days.

However, a diligent analyst at Scofield notices that sales have been increasing recently, with average sales over the last 30 days of $45,000 per day. Using this figure in the denominator of Equation 16.11 results in an average collection period of 26.7 days.

The average collection period allows the firm to determine whether there is a general problem with its accounts receivable. However, the *ACP* can also send misleading signals when daily sales fluctuate. In the preceding Example, suppose that Scofield's credit terms are net 25. Using the most recent month to calculate average daily sales results in an average collection period of 26.7 days, which is right on target given Scofield's credit terms. However, using average daily sales over the past three months yields the longer, 30-day collection period. Therefore, when using this ratio to assess the performance of the collections department, analysts have to be aware of the impact of sales fluctuations on their calculations.

If a firm believes that it has a collections problem, a first step in analyzing the problem is to age the accounts receivable. By doing so, the firm can determine if the problem exists in its accounts receivable in general or rather is attributable to a few specific accounts or to a given time period.

aging of accounts receivable
A schedule that indicates the portions of the total accounts receivable balance that have been outstanding for specified periods of time.

Aging of Accounts Receivable The aging of accounts receivable requires the firm to break down its accounts receivable into groups based on the time of origin. Aging results in a schedule indicating the portions of the total accounts receivable balance that have been outstanding for specified periods of time. The breakdown is typically made on a month-by-month basis, going back three or four months.

The purpose of aging accounts receivable is to allow the firm to pinpoint problems. For example, if a firm with terms of net 30 has an average collection period (minus receipt, processing, and collection time) of 50 days, then it will want to age its accounts receivable. If the majority of accounts are two months old, then the firm has a general problem and should review its accounts receivable operations. If the aging shows that the firm collects most accounts in about 35 days and that a few accounts are significantly past due, then the firm should analyze and pursue collection of those specific past-due accounts. If the firm has an abnormally high percentage of outstanding accounts initiated in a given month, it may be attributable to a specific event during that time period, such as hiring a new credit manager or selling a substandard product whose quality is being disputed by customers withholding payment.

Table 16.5 provides an example of an *aging schedule*. If the stated credit terms for the company in this example were net 60 days, then the aging schedule would tell us that 80% of the company's receivables are current and 20% are past due.

Payment-Pattern Monitoring The average collection period and the aging of accounts receivable are excellent monitoring techniques when sales are relatively constant. However, for cyclical or growing firms, both techniques provide potentially misleading results. For example, the average collection period divides the accounts receivable balance by the average daily sales. If the accounts receivable balance is measured during a cyclical firm's high sales period, then the average collection period will be distorted by the cyclical sales peak. Use of the firm's customer payment pattern avoids the problems of cyclical or growing sales when monitoring accounts receivable.

payment pattern
The normal timing in which a firm's customers pay their accounts, expressed as the percentage of monthly sales collected in each month following the sale.

The payment pattern is the normal timing in which a firm's customers pay their accounts; it is expressed as the percentage of monthly sales collected in each month following the sale. Every firm has a pattern in which its credit sales are paid. If the payment pattern changes, the firm should review its credit policies.

Table 16.5

Sample Aging Schedule for Accounts Receivable

Age of Accounts	Accounts Receivable	Percentage of Accounts Receivable
0–30 days	$1,200,000	50%
31–60 days	720,000	30
61–90 days	336,000	14
91+ days	144,000	6
Total accounts receivable	$2,400,000	100%

One approach to determining this pattern is to analyze a company's sales and resulting collections on a monthly basis. That is, for each month's sales, the firm computes the amount collected in the month of sale and each of the following months. By tracking these patterns over a period of time, the company can determine the average pattern of its collections using either a spreadsheet or regression analysis. For most companies, these patterns tend to be fairly stable over time—even as sales volumes fluctuate.

EXAMPLE

Consider DJM Manufacturing, which has determined that it collects, on average, 10% of credit sales in the month of sale, 60% in the month following the sale, and the remaining 30% in the second month following the sale. Thus, if sales for the month of January were $200,000, the company would expect to collect $20,000 in January, $120,000 in February, and the remaining $60,000 in March. Table 16.6 shows an example of this approach, which can be extended to develop the cash receipts portion of the cash budget.

Table 16.6

Forecasted Collections for DJM Manufacturing Using Payment-Pattern Monitoring

Sales Forecast	Forecasted Collections for DJM Manufacturing				
	January	February	March	April	May
January: $200,000	$20,000	$120,000	$ 60,000		
February: 150,000		15,000	90,000	$ 45,000	
March: 300,000			30,000	180,000	$ 90,000
April: 400,000				40,000	240,000
May: 250,000					25,000
Total projected collections for cash budget:			$180,000	$265,000	$355,000

Notes: This table is created under the assumption that the company collects 10% of each month's sales in the month of sale, 60% in the month following sale, and the remaining 30% in the second month following sale. The first column provides forecasted sales for each month; the remaining columns total up the actual cash flows for each month. In a real-life application, the remaining collections from the prior year's last quarter would be included to complete the projected cash flows in January and February.

© Cengage Learning 2012

16-5c Cash Application

cash application
The process through which a customer's payment is posted to its account and the outstanding invoices are cleared as paid.

Cash application is the process through which a customer's payment is posted to its account and the outstanding invoices are cleared as paid. In most business-to-business environments, the typical application method is known as *open item*. In this approach, the company records each customer invoice in the A/R journal and later matches received payments to the invoices in order to clear them. This task is complicated by the usual practice of paying multiple invoices with a single check. Ideally, the remittance information accompanying the check should clearly indicate any adjustments, discounts, or allowances taken related to each invoice in that remittance. Unfortunately, the remittance information is sometimes no more than barely legible copies of the invoices with handwritten notes on the adjustments stapled to the check. One of the critical tasks of the accounts receivable department, then, is to figure out what has been paid for so that the outstanding invoices can be closed out.

Some companies are able to use an alternative approach called *balance forward*. In this system, the company applies customer payments to outstanding balances and simply carries forward any unpaid amounts to the next billing period. Examples are utilities and credit card companies, where the only remittance information needed is the customer's account number, the amount of payment, and the date received. These systems generally utilize a scannable remittance document, which allows for automated capture of payment and account information. Automated processing reduces the costs of the cash application process.

16-5 Concept Review Questions

14. What is a *collection policy*? What is the typical sequence of actions taken by a firm when attempting to collect an overdue account?

15. Why should a firm actively monitor the accounts receivable of its credit customers? Describe how each of the following credit monitoring techniques works: (a) average collection period; (b) aging of accounts receivable; and (c) payment-pattern monitoring.

Summary

- The cash conversion cycle has three main components: (1) the average age of inventory (*AAI*), (2) the average collection period (*ACP*), and (3) the average payment period (*APP*). The operating cycle (*OC*) is the sum of the *AAI* and *ACP*. The cash conversion cycle (*CCC*) is *OC* minus *APP*. The length of the cash conversion cycle determines the amount of resources the firm must invest in its operations.

- The financial manager's focus when managing the firm's short-term activities is on shortening the cash conversion cycle. The basic strategies are to turn inventory quickly; collect accounts receivable quickly; pay accounts slowly; and manage mail, processing, and clearing time efficiently.

- When managing the firm's short-term accounts, the financial manager must focus on competing costs. These cost trade-offs apply to managing cash and marketable securities; accounts receivable; inventory; and accounts payable, accruals, and notes payable. The goal is to balance the cost trade-offs in a way that minimizes the total cost of each of these accounts, thereby increasing net cash flows and value.

- The large inventory investment made by most firms makes inventory a major concern of the financial manager, who must make sure that the amount of money tied up in inventory—raw materials, work in process, and finished goods—is justified by the returns generated from such investment.

- Operations/production managers use a number of techniques to control inventory. These include the ABC system, the

Table of Important Equations

1. $CCC = OC - APP$

   $= AAI + ACP - APP$

2. $EOQ = \sqrt{\dfrac{2SO}{C}}$

3. Marginal profit from increased sales $= \Delta$ Sales $\times$ CM

   $= \Delta$ Sales $\times$ (Price $-$ VC)

4. Average investment in accounts receivable (AIAR)

   $= \dfrac{\text{total variable cost of annual sales}}{\text{turnover of accounts receivable}}$

5. Total variable cost of annual sales (TVC) $=$ Annual unit sales $\times$ Variable cost/unit

6. Turnover of accounts receivable (TOAR)

   $= \dfrac{365}{\text{average collection period (ACP)}}$

7. Cost of marginal investment in accounts receivable

   $=$ Marginal investment $\times$ Required return

8. Bad debt expense (BDE)

   $=$ Annual sales (Sales) $\times$ Bad debt expense rate (% BDE),

9. Cost of marginal bad debts

   $= BDE_{proposed} - BDE_{current}$

10. Net profit for the credit decision
    $=$ (Marginal profit from increased sales) $-$ (Cost of marginal investment in accounts receivable) $-$ (Cost of marginal bad debts)

basic economic order quantity (EOQ) model, reorder points and safety stock, material requirements planning, and the just-in-time (JIT) system. Financial managers tend to serve a watchdog role over these activities.

11. Average collection period

$$= \frac{\text{accounts receivable}}{\text{average sales per day}}$$

- The objective for managing accounts receivable is to balance the competing interests of financial managers, who prefer to receive cash payments sooner, and those of sales personnel, who wish to use liberal credit terms to attract new customers. The key aspects of accounts receivable management include credit standards, credit terms, collection policy, credit monitoring, and cash application.

- When analyzing credit applicants, the firm can gather information from both internal and external sources. Two popular approaches to granting credit to customers are the five C's of credit and credit scoring (for high-volume–low-dollar requests), which is used to make relatively informed credit decisions quickly and inexpensively.

- Companies should perform a cost-benefit analysis of credit standards, credit terms, and other accounts receivable changes to ensure that such policies are profitable. Key variables involved in such an analysis include the marginal profit contribution from sales, the cost of the marginal investment in accounts receivable, and the cost of marginal bad debts. Cash discount decisions would also consider the cost of the cash discount.

- The firm's collection policy involves actions aimed at collecting delinquent accounts; these typically include reminders, form letters, telephone calls, or personal visits. If these actions are ineffective, the firm sends negative reports to credit bureaus and may turn over the account to a collection agency or an attorney.

- The three most popular techniques for credit monitoring are the average collection period, aging of accounts receivable, and payment-pattern monitoring. Firms typically make cash application of customer payments using either the open-item method or the balance-forward method.

Key Terms

ABC system, 496
aging of accounts receivable, 509
average investment in accounts
   receivable (AIAR), 503
carrying cost, 497
cash application, 510
cash conversion cycle (CCC), 490
cash discount, 506
collection policy, 507
contribution margin, 503
cost of the marginal investment in
   accounts receivable, 506

credit monitoring, 508
credit scoring, 502
credit terms, 506
economic order quantity (EOQ)
   model, 496
factoring, 500
five C's of credit, 502
just-in-time (JIT) system, 498
manufacturing resource planning II
   (MRPII), 498
material requirements planning
   (MRP), 498

operating assets, 489
operating cycle (OC), 489
order cost, 497
payment pattern, 509
total cost, 497
total variable cost of annual sales
   (TVC), 503
turnover of accounts receivable
   (TOAR), 506

Self-Test Problems

Answers to Self-Test Problems and the Concept Review Questions throughout the chapter appear in CourseMate with SmartFinance Tools at www.cengagebrain.com.

ST16-1. Aztec Products wishes to evaluate its cash conversion cycle (CCC). One of the firm's financial analysts has discovered that on average the firm holds items in inventory for 65 days, pays its suppliers 35 days after purchase, and collects its receivables after 55 days. The firm's annual sales (all on credit) are about $2.1 billion, its cost of goods sold represent about 67% of sales, and purchases represent about 40% of cost of goods sold. Assume a 365-day year.

a. What is Aztec Products's operating cycle (OC) and cash conversion cycle (CCC)?

b. How many dollars of resources does Aztec have invested in (1) inventory, (2) accounts receivable, (3) accounts payable, and (4) the total CCC?

c. If Aztec could shorten its cash conversion cycle by reducing its inventory holding period by five days, what effect would that have on its total resource investment found in part (b)?

d. If Aztec could shorten its CCC by five days, would it be best to reduce the inventory holding period, reduce the receivable collection period, or extend the accounts payable period? Why?

ST16-2. Vargas Enterprises wishes to determine the economic order quantity (EOQ) for a critical and expensive inventory item that it uses in large amounts at a relatively constant rate throughout the year. The firm uses 450,000 units of the item annually, has order costs of $375 per order, and its carrying costs associated with this item are $28 per unit per year. The firm plans to hold safety stock of the item equal to 5 days of usage, and it estimates that it takes 12 days to receive an order of the item once placed. Assume a 365-day year.

a. Calculate the firm's EOQ for the item of inventory described above.

b. How many units of *safety stock* should Vargas hold?

c. What is the firm's *reorder point* for the item of inventory being evaluated? (Hint: Be sure to include the safety stock.)

ST16-3. Belton Company is considering relaxing its credit standards to boost its currently sagging sales. It expects its proposed relaxation will increase sales by 20% from the current annual level of $10 million. The firm's average collection period is expected to increase from 35 days to 50 days, and bad debts are expected to increase from 2% of sales to 7% of sales as a result of relaxing the firm's credit standards as proposed. The firm's variable costs equal 60% of sales and its fixed costs total $2.5 million per year. Belton's opportunity cost is 16%. Assume a 365-day year.

a. What is Belton's *contribution margin*?

b. Calculate Belton's *marginal profit from increased sales*.

c. What is Belton's *cost of the marginal investment in accounts receivable*?

d. What is Belton's *cost of marginal bad debts*?

e. Use your findings in parts (b), (c), and (d) to determine the net profit (cost) of Belton's proposed relaxation of credit standards. Should it relax credit standards?

Questions

Q16-1. If you randomly chose a sample of firms and then calculated the operating cycle (OC) of each firm, what is likely to be the key cause of differences in their operating cycles? What goal should these firms attempt to achieve with regard to their OCs? How and why?

Q16-2. Why would a firm wish to minimize its cash conversion cycle (CCC) even though each of its components is important to the operation of the business? What key actions should the firm pursue to achieve this objective?

Q16-3. Describe the impact that aggressive action aimed at minimizing a firm's cash conversion cycle (CCC) would have on the following financial ratios: inventory turnover, average collection period, and average payment period. What are the key constraints on aggressive pursuit of these strategies with regard to inventory, accounts receivable, and accounts payable?

Q16-4. What are the principal cost trade-offs that the financial manager must focus on when attempting to manage short-term accounts in a manner that minimizes cash? Prepare a graph describing the general nature of these cost trade-offs and the optimal level of total cost.

Q16-5. Assume that the financial manager is considering stretching the firm's accounts payable by paying its vendors at a later date. What key cost trade-offs would be involved when making this stretching decision? How would you quantitatively model this decision?

Q16-6. What is the financial manager's primary goal with regard to inventory management? How does this goal compare with the inventory goals of production and marketing?

Q16-7. What trade-off confronts the financial manager with regard to inventory turnover, inventory cost, and stockouts? In what way is inventory viewed as an investment?

Q16-8. Why is it important for the financial manager to understand the inventory control techniques used by operations/production managers? How does controlling inventory impact a firm's profitability?

Q16-9. What role does the *ABC system* play in inventory control? What group of inventory items does the *EOQ model* focus on controlling? Describe the objective and cost trade-offs addressed by the EOQ model.

Q16-10. Why would a firm extend credit to its customers, given that such an action would lengthen its cash conversion cycle? What key cost trade-offs would be involved in this decision? What typically dictates the actual credit terms the firm extends to its customers?

Q16-11. Why is using the *five C's of credit* appropriate for evaluating high-dollar credit requests but not high-volume–low-dollar requests (e.g., department-store credit cards)?

Q16-12. What is *credit scoring*? In what types of situations is it most useful? If you were developing a credit-scoring model, what factors might be most useful in predicting whether or not a credit customer would pay in a timely manner?

Q16-13. What are the key variables to consider when evaluating potential changes in a firm's credit standards? Why are only variable costs of sales included when estimating the firm's *average investment in accounts receivable*?

Q16-14. For a firm contemplating an increase in the cash discount it offers credit customers for early payment, what key variables should be considered when quantitatively analyzing this decision? How do the variables used in this analysis differ from those considered when analyzing a potential change in the firm's credit standards?

Q16-15. What is *credit monitoring*? How can each of the following techniques be used to monitor accounts receivable? What are their attributes?
   a. Average collection period
   b. Aging of accounts receivable
   c. Payment-pattern monitoring

Problems

The Cash Conversion Cycle

P16-1. Canadian Products is concerned about managing its operating assets and liabilities efficiently. Inventories have an average age of 110 days, and accounts receivable have an average age of 50 days. Accounts payable are paid approximately 40 days after they arise. The firm has annual sales of $36 million, its cost of goods sold represents 75% of sales, and its purchases represent 70% of cost of goods sold. Assume a 365-day year.
   a. Calculate the firm's operating cycle (*OC*).
   b. Calculate the firm's cash conversion cycle (*CCC*).
   c. Calculate the amount of total resources Canadian Products has invested in its *CCC*.
   d. Discuss how management might be able to reduce the amount of total resources invested in the *CCC*.

P16-2. The cash conversion cycle is an important tool for the financial manager in managing day-to-day operations of the firm. For an investor, knowing how the firm manages its *CCC* would provide useful insights about management's effectiveness in managing the firm's resource investment in the *CCC*. Access Microsoft's annual statement at **www.microsoft.com**, and calculate Microsoft's *CCC*. Discuss any difficulties you had in obtaining adequately detailed data from Microsoft's Web site for use in calculating its *CCC*. Evaluate Microsoft's *CCC* in light of your calculations.

P16-3. A firm is weighing five plans that affect several current accounts. Given the five plans and their probable effects on inventory, receivables, and payables (as shown in the following table), which plan would you favor? Explain.

	Change		
Plan	Average Age of Inventory (days)	Average Collection Period (days)	Average Payment Period (days)
A	−35	+20	+10
B	+20	−15	+10
C	−10	+5	0
D	−20	+15	+ 5
E	+15	−15	+20

P16-4. King Manufacturing turns its inventory 9.1 times each year, has an average payment period of 35 days, and has an average collection period of 60 days. The firm's annual sales are $72 million, its cost of goods sold represents 50% of sales, and its purchases represent 80% of the cost of goods sold. Assume a 365-day year.

a. Calculate the firm's operating cycle (*OC*) and cash conversion cycle (*CCC*).

b. Calculate the firm's total resources invested in its *CCC*.

c. Assuming the firm pays 14% to finance its resource investment in its *CCC*, how much would it save annually by reducing its *CCC* by 20 days if this reduction were achieved by shortening the average age of inventory by ten days, shortening the average collection period by five days, and lengthening the average payment period by five days?

d. If the 20-day reduction in the firm's *CCC* could be achieved by a 20-day change in only one of the *CCC*'s three components, which one would you recommend? Explain.

P16-5. Bradbury Corporation turns its inventory five times each year, has an average payment period of 25 days, and has an average collection period of 32 days. The firm's annual sales are $3.6 billion, its cost of goods sold represents 80% of sales, and its purchases represent 50% of cost of goods sold. Assume a 365-day year.

a. Calculate the firm's operating cycle (*OC*) and cash conversion cycle (*CCC*).

b. Calculate the total resources invested in the firm's *CCC*.

c. Assume that the firm pays 18% to finance its resource investment. By how much could the firm increase its annual profit if (1) it reduced its *CCC* by 12 days and (2) this reduction were solely the result of extending its average payment period by 12 days?

d. If part ©'s 12-day reduction in the firm's *CCC* could alternatively have been achieved by shortening either the average age of inventory or the average collection period by 12 days, would you have recommended one of those actions rather than the 12-day extension of the average payment period specified in part (c)? Which change would you recommend? Explain.

P16-6. Go to www.finance.yahoo.com and then input the ticker symbols noted in parentheses following each of the company names listed below. Under the Financials heading in the left-hand column, click on "Income Statement" and then "Balance Sheet" to obtain the most recent income statement and balance sheet for each firm. Use the appropriate financial statement data for each firm to respond to the following instructions and questions.

Anheuser-Busch Companies, Inc. (BUD)
Coca-Cola Company (KO)
Molson Coors Brewing Company (TAP)
PepsiCo, Inc. (PEP)

a. Use the formulas given in the chapter to calculate the following time periods (in days) for each of the firms:
(1) Average age of inventory (*AAI*)
(2) Average collection period (*ACP*)
(3) Average payment period (*APP*)

b. Use the time periods calculated in part (a) to calculate each firm's operating cycle (*OC*) and cash conversion cycle (*CCC*).

c. Compare the *OC* and *CCC* calculated in part (b) for each of the following combinations:
(1) The two soft-drink companies (KO and PEP)
(2) The two beer companies (BUD and TAP)
How would you describe the differences found for each pair of firms?

d. Compare the *OC* and *CCC* for the two soft-drink companies to those of the two beer companies. Explain any differences you observe.

Cost Trade-Offs in Short-Term Financial Management

P16-7.   Geet Industries wants to install a just-in-time (JIT) inventory system in order to significantly reduce its in-process inventories. The annual cost of the system is gauged to be $95,000. The financial manager estimates that, with this system, the firm's average inventory investment will decline by 40% from its current level of $2.05 million. All other costs are expected to be unaffected by this system. The firm can earn 14% per year on investments of similar risk.

    a.   What is the annual cost savings expected to result from installation of the proposed JIT system?

    b.   Should the firm install the system?

P16-8.   Sheth & Sons Inc. is considering changing the pay period for its salaried management from every two weeks to monthly. The firm's CFO, Ken Smart, believes that such action will free up cash that can be used elsewhere in the business, which currently faces a cash crunch. In order to avoid a strong negative response from the salaried managers, the firm will simultaneously announce a new health plan that will lower managers' cost contributions without cutting benefits.

    Ken's analysis indicates that the salaried managers' bimonthly payroll is $1.8 million and is expected to remain at that level for the foreseeable future. With the biweekly system, there were 2.2 pay periods in a month. Because the managers will be paid monthly, the monthly payroll will be about $4.0 million (2.2 × $1.8 million). The annual cost to the firm of the new health plan will be $180,000. Ken believes that, because managers' salaries accrue at a constant rate over the pay period, the average salaries over the period can be estimated by dividing the total amount by 2. The firm believes that it can earn 15% annually on any funds made available through the accrual of the managers' salaries.

    a.   How much additional financing will Sheth & Sons obtain as a result of switching the pay period for managers' salaries from every two weeks to monthly?

    b.   Should the firm implement the proposed change in pay periods?

Inventory Management

P16-9.   Calculate the average investment in inventory for each of the following situations. Assume a 365-day year.

    a.   A firm's annual sales are $18 million, its gross profit margin is 32%, and its average age of inventory is 45 days.

    b.   A firm's annual sales are $325 million, its cost of goods sold is 80% of sales, and it turns its inventory ten times per year.

    c.   A firm's annual cost of goods sold totals $120 million, and it turns its inventory about every 70 days.

P16-10.   GEP Manufacturing is mulling over a plan to rent a proprietary inventory control system at an annual cost of $4.5 million. The firm predicts its sales will remain relatively stable at $585 million and its gross profit margin will continue to be 28%. GEP expects that, as a result of the new inventory control system, its average age of inventory (*AAI*) will drop from its current level of 83 days to about 46 days. The firm's required return on investments of similar risk is 12%. Assume a 365-day year.

    a.   Calculate GEP's average inventory investment both (1) currently and (2) assuming it rents the inventory control system.

    b.   Use your findings in part (a) to determine the annual savings expected to result from the proposed inventory control system.

    c.   Based on your answer to part (b), would you recommend that GEP rent the inventory control system? Explain your recommendation.

P16-11.   Iverson Industries uses 80,000 units of an "A" item of raw material inventory each year. The firm maintains level production throughout the year, given the steady demand for its finished products. The raw material order cost is $225 per order, and carrying costs are estimated to be $10.50 per unit per year. The firm wishes to maintain a safety stock of ten days of inventory, and it takes five days for the firm to receive an order once it is placed. Assume a 365-day year.

    a.   Calculate the economic order quantity (EOQ) for Iverson's raw material.

    b.   How large a *safety stock* (in units) of inventory should the firm maintain?

    c.   What is Iverson's *reorder point* for this item of inventory? (*Hint:* Be sure to include the safety stock.)

P16-12.   Litespeed Products buys 200,000 motors per year from a supplier that can fulfill orders within two days of receiving them. Litespeed transmits its orders to this supplier electronically so the lead time to receive orders is two days. Litespeed's order cost is about $295 per order and its carrying cost is about $37 per motor per year. The firm maintains a safety stock of motors equal to six days of usage. Assume a 365-day year.

    a.   What is Litespeed's economic order quantity (EOQ) for the motors?

    b.   How large a *safety stock* (in units) of motors should Litespeed maintain?

    c.   What is Litespeed's *reorder point* for motors? (*Hint:* Be sure to include the safety stock.)

    d.   If Litespeed has an opportunity to reduce either its order cost or its carrying cost by 10%, which of these would result in the lowest total cost at the associated new EOQ?

Accounts Receivable Standards and Terms

P16-13.   International Oil Company (IOC) uses credit scoring to evaluate gasoline credit card applications. The following table presents the financial and credit characteristics and weights (indicating the relative importance of each characteristic) used in the credit decision. The firm's credit standards are to accept all applicants with credit scores of 80 or higher, to extend limited credit on a probationary basis to applicants with scores higher than 70 and lower than 80, and to reject all applicants with scores at or below 70.

Financial and Credit Characteristics	Predetermined Weight
Credit references	0.25
Education	0.10
Home ownership	0.10
Income range	0.15
Payment history	0.30
Years on job	0.10

The firm needs to process three applications scored recently by one of its credit analysts. The scores for each of the applicants are summarized in the following table.

Financial and Credit Characteristics	Applicants' Scores (0 to 100)		
	X	Y	Z
Credit references	60	90	80
Education	75	80	80
Home ownership	100	90	60
Income range	70	70	80
Payment history	60	85	70
Years on job	50	60	90

    a.   Use the data presented to find the credit score for each of the applicants.

    b.   Recommend the action that the firm should take for each of the three applicants.

SMART solutions

See the problem and solution explained step-by-step at SMART | finance

P16-14.   Barans Company currently has an average collection period of 55 days and annual sales of $1 billion. Assume a 365-day year.

    a.   What is the firm's average accounts receivable balance?

    b.   If the variable cost of each product is 65% of sales, what is the *average investment in accounts receivable?*

    c.   If the equal-risk opportunity cost of the investment in accounts receivable is 12%, what is the total annual cost of the resources invested in accounts receivable?

P16-15.   Melton Electronics currently has an average collection period of 35 days and annual sales of $72 million. Assume a 365-day year.

    a.   What is the firm's average accounts receivable balance?

    b.   If the variable cost of each product is 70% of sales, what is the firm's average investment in accounts receivable?

    c.   If the equal-risk opportunity cost of the investment in accounts receivable is 16%, then what is the total annual cost of the resources invested in accounts receivable?

    d.   Suppose that Melton can shorten the average collection period to 30 days by offering a cash discount of 1% for early payment and that 60% of the customers take this discount. Should the firm offer this discount? Assume that its cost of bad debts will rise by $150,000 per year.

P16-16.   Davis Manufacturing Industries (DMI) produces and sells 20,000 units of a machine tool each year. All sales are on credit, and DMI charges all customers $500 per unit. Variable costs are $350 per unit, and DMI incurs $2 million in fixed costs each year.

DMI's top managers are evaluating a proposal from the firm's CFO that the firm relax its credit standards to increase its sales and profits. The CFO believes this change will increase unit sales by 4%. Currently, DMI's average collection period is 40 days, but the CFO expects this to increase to 60 days under the new policy. Bad debt expense is also expected to increase from 1% to 2.5% of annual sales. The firm's board of directors has set a required return of 15% on investments with this level of risk. Assume a 365-day year.

a. What is DMI's contribution margin? By how much will profits from increased sales change if DMI adopts the new credit standards?

b. Under the current credit standards, what is DMI's average investment in accounts receivable? What would it be under the proposed credit standards? What is the cost of this additional investment?

c. What is DMI's cost of marginal bad debts resulting from the relaxation of its credit standards?

d. What is DMI's net profit (or loss) from adopting the new credit standards? Should DMI relax its credit standards?

P16-17. Jeans Manufacturing thinks that it can reduce its high credit costs by tightening its credit standards. However, the firm believes that the planned tightening will result in a drop in annual sales from $38 million to $36 million. On the positive side, the firm expects its average collection period to fall from 58 to 45 days and its bad debts to drop from 2.5% to 1% of sales. The firm's variable cost per unit is 70% of its sale price, and its required return on investment is 15%. Assume a 365-day year. Evaluate the proposed tightening of credit standards, and make a recommendation to the management of Jeans Manufacturing.

P16-18. Webb, Inc., currently makes all sales on credit and offers no cash discounts. The firm is considering a 2% cash discount for payments within ten days. The firm's current average collection period is 65 days, sales are 400,000 units, selling price is $50 per unit, and variable cost per unit is $40. The firm expects that the changes in credit terms will result in a sales increase to 410,000 units, that 75% of the purchases will be paid for at the discount, and that the average collection period will fall to 45 days. Bad debts are expected to drop from 1.0% to 0.9% of sales. If Webb's required rate of return on investments of similar risk is 25%, should the firm offer the proposed discount? Assume a 365-day year.

P16-19. Microboard, Inc., a major computer chip manufacturer, is contemplating lengthening its credit period from net 30 days to net 50 days. Presently, its average collection period is 40 days; the firm's CFO believes that, with the proposed new credit period, the average collection period will be 65 days. The firm's sales are $900 million, but the CFO believes that the new credit terms will increase sales to $980 million. At the current $900 million sales level, the firm's total variable costs are $630 million. The firm's CFO estimates that, with the proposed new credit terms, bad debt expenses will increase from the current level of 1.5% of sales to 2.0% of sales. The CFO also believes that the increased sales volume and accompanying receivables will require the firm to add more facilities and personnel to its credit and collections department. The annual cost of the expanded credit operations resulting from the proposed new credit period is estimated to be $10 million. The firm's required return on similar-risk investments is 18%. Assuming a 365-day year, evaluate the economics of Microboard's proposed lengthening of the credit period and then make a recommendation to the firm's management.

Collecting, Monitoring, and Applying Cash to Receivables

P16-20. United Worldwide's accounts receivable totaled $1.75 million on August 31, 2012. The table below gives a breakdown of these outstanding accounts on the basis of the month of the initial credit sale. The firm extends credit terms of *net 30, EOM* to its credit customers.

Month of Credit Sale	Accounts Receivable
August 2012	$ 640,000
July 2012	500,000
June 2012	164,000
May 2012	390,000
April 2012 or before	56,000
Total (August 31, 2012)	$1,750,000

a. Prepare an *aging schedule* for United Worldwide's August 31, 2012, accounts receivable balance.

b. Using your findings in part (a), evaluate the firm's credit and collection activities.

c. What are some probable causes of the situation discussed in part (b)?

P16-21. Big Air Board Company, a global manufacturer and distributor of both surfboards and snowboards, is in a seasonal business. Although surfboard sales are only mildly seasonal, the snowboard sales are driven by peak demand in the first and fourth calendar quarters of each year. The following table gives the firm's monthly sales for the immediate past quarter (October through December 2012) and its forecast monthly sales for the coming year (calendar-year 2013).

Month	Sales ($ in millions)
Historic	
October 2012	$3.7
November 2012	3.9
December 2012	4.3
Forecast	
January 2013	$3.8
February 2013	2.6
March 2013	2.2
April 2013	1.6
May 2013	1.8
June 2013	1.9
July 2013	2.0
August 2013	2.2
September 2013	2.4
October 2013	4.1
November 2013	4.6
December 2013	5.1

The firm extends credit terms of *2/10 net 30, EOM* to all customers. It collects 98% of its receivables and typically writes off the other 2% as bad debts. Big Air Board's historic collection pattern, which is expected to continue through 2013, is 5% collected in the month of the sale, 65% collected in the first month following the sale, and 28% collected in the second month following the sale. Using the data given, calculate the *payment pattern* of Big Air Board's accounts receivable. Comment on the firm's monthly collections during calendar year 2013.

THOMSON REUTERS | Business School Edition

For instructions on using Thomson ONE, refer to the instructions provided with the Thomson ONE problems at the end of Chapters 1–6.

P16-22. Compute the average age of inventory, average collection period, and average payment period for Cracker Barrel Old Country Store, Inc. (CBRL), Caterpillar, Inc. (CAT), Kohl's Corp. (KSS), and Walmart Stores, Inc. (WMT) for the last four years. Also calculate the operating cycle and the cash conversion cycle for each of the firms for the same time period. Why are there differences in each of the measures across the different firms? For each firm, comment on how the CCC and each of its components have changed over the last four years. Can you conclude that one firm's cash conversion cycle is better simply because it has a lower value?

P16-23. Calculate 3M's (MMM) total annual cost of resources invested in accounts receivable in each of the last five years. Assume that there are no fixed costs, that is, all costs are variable costs (use COGS and SG&A). Calculate 3M's *average investment in accounts receivable* in each year. Using 3M's *WACC* as a measure of equal-risk opportunity cost of the investment in accounts receivable, calculate the total annual cost of resources invested in accounts receivable. Has this cost decreased or increased over the years?

Since these exercises depend upon real-time data, your answers will change continuously depending upon when you access the Internet to download your data.

Smart Practices Video

Vern LoForti, V.P., CFO, and Corporate Secretary, InfoSonics

"Working capital management is extremely important because it results in good cash flow."

Jackie Sturm, Director of Finance for Technology and Manufacturing, Intel Corp.

"Inventory loses value every day you hold it."

Keith Woodward, Vice President of Finance, General Mills

"What we expect of financial analysts is to be able to manage all of the complexity and moving parts of working capital utilizing different ratios."

Vern LoForti, V.P., CFO, and Corporate Secretary, InfoSonics

"You have to have a high level of confidence in those suppliers who are holding that inventory at their warehouse."

Video photos: Cengage Learning

Jon Olson, Chief Financial Officer, Xilinx Corp.

"Because cash is king, we want to make sure that we have a high quality collections organization."

SMART concepts

See a demonstration of the trade-offs and optimum level of a given operating asset.

SMART solutions

See the solution to Problem 16-14.

Mini-Case

Cash Conversion, Inventory, and Receivables Management

Upon graduation, you receive a job offer from Pronto Manufacturing, Inc. In this position, you will be responsible for implementing the policy and management of cash conversion, inventory, and receivables. To get ready for the start of this job, you decide to review the following topics.

Assignment

1. What is the *cash conversion cycle*, and what is the difference between it and the *operating cycle*?

2. What are some ways of shortening the cash conversion cycle?

3. Discuss techniques for controlling inventory.

4. What aspects must managers consider when deciding on a trade credit policy for the firm?

5. Describe the five C's of credit.

6. What factors should managers consider when determining the company's collection policy?

© Altus Plunkett/Flickr/Getty Images, Inc.

chapter 17

Cash, Payables, and Liquidity Management*

What Companies Do

Adopting EIPP: A Slow Move to Speed Payments

During the 1960s, a firm was considered efficient if it could process an order in 4 to 7 days, have the product delivered in 14 to 21 days, receive the invoice within a week, and pay within 45 to 60 days. Today a firm is considered old school if its customers can't order today, have it shipped to their door tomorrow, get the invoice that same day, and still have 45–60 days to pay.

To address this issue in today's e-everything world, some firms are embracing e-invoicing when making business-to-business transactions. The clunky term for this process is *electronic invoice presentment and payment*, or simply EIPP. The benefits of EIPP include elimination of paper, greatly reduced processing costs, automatic validation of invoice data, and dramatic improvement in on-time payment performance.

It is not surprising that the lack of incentive for firms to speed their payments to vendors has slowed the adoption of EIPP. Clearly, paying faster is contrary to the firm's goal of reducing its resource investment by shortening its cash conversion cycle (CCC). The strategy for increasing the adoption of EIPP being pushed by JP Morgan Xign Corp., a leader in on-demand order-to-pay business software, is for the buyer to agree to pay quickly in exchange for an attractive early-pay discount from the vendor. In addition, by making the transaction and payment electronically, the buyer and seller will reduce their manual labor costs.

Despite the fact that some major companies—such as Dell, Inc., Wells Fargo & Co., Office Depot, Inc., and Pacific Care Health Systems—have adopted EIPP, so far the acceptance of EIPP has been relatively slow. The problem is that each company that adopts it must convince its customers to sign on. Beth Robertson, a senior research analyst at research and advisory firm Tower Group, suggests that the growth in EIPP will continue to be gradual. She believes that broad technical standards must be established and security issues resolved before there will be widespread adoption of EIPP.

Source: Julie Sturgeon, "Electronic Payments," *CFO* (Winter 2003), pp. 52–53; Doug Roberts, "Giving Cash Management a Technology Boost," *Financial Executive* (December 2003), pp. 62_63; "JP Morgan Chase Closes Acquisition of Xign," Xign Corporation *Press Release,* (May 17, 2007); JP Morgan website, **www.jpmorgan.com/cm/ ContentServer?c=TS_Content&pagename=jpmorgan%2Fts%2FTS_Content%2FGeneral&cid=1159317518404** (accessed May 3, 2010).

*Professor Dubos J. Masson, CCM, CertCM, of Pepperdine University and The Resource Alliance, assisted in preparation of this chapter. The authors very much appreciate D.J.'s important contribution.

Learning Objectives

After studying this chapter you should be able to:

- Understand float, its components, and the financial manager's responsibilities with regard to cash position management;

- Review the objective of cash collections, the key types of collection systems, and the role of lockbox systems in cash collection;

- Describe the role of cash concentration and various mechanisms used by firms to transfer funds from depository banks to concentration banks;

- Explain accounts payable management with regard to the average payment period and the effect of cash discounts on timing the payment of accounts payable;

- Discuss popular disbursement products and methods and recent developments in accounts payable and disbursements; and

- Describe popular investment vehicles for short-term surpluses and the key sources of borrowing used to meet short-term deficits.

Chapter 16 described the operating and cash conversion cycles and then focused on management of the two key components of the operating cycle: inventory and accounts receivable. Here we shift focus to cash, accounts payable, and liquidity. Clearly, cash is the lifeblood of the firm. Thus it is a primary focus of the financial manager, who must conserve it by gathering cash receipts and making cash disbursements in a cost-effective manner. Additionally, the financial manager conserves cash by using efficient mechanisms for transferring it within and between the firm's operating units. As noted in Chapter 16, short-term financing decisions should result from an analysis of cost trade-offs with the goal of minimizing total costs and increasing shareholder value.

Accounts payable are also an important component of the cash conversion cycle. The firm must manage them in a way that lengthens the payment period while preserving the firm's credit reputation. This strategy will help shorten the cash conversion cycle and reduce the firm's resource requirements. The financial manager also will use other strategies and tools to slow down disbursements.

Of course, all of these cash management strategies are predicated on the firm's ability to maintain adequate liquidity to preserve the firm's solvency. Specifically, the firm must be able to both earn a positive return on idle excess cash balances and obtain low-cost financing for meeting unexpected needs and seasonal cash shortages. This important activity is commonly called **liquidity management**.

This chapter emphasizes the key procedures for managing cash, payables, and liquidity. We begin with a discussion of cash management that focuses on *float* in the cash collection and payment system and on the principles of managing the firm's cash position. Next, we consider cash collection, placing emphasis on the types of collection systems, lockbox systems, cash concentration, and various mechanisms for funds transfer. Then we review some key aspects of accounts payable and disbursements: the accounts payable process, cash discounts, disbursement products and methods, and developments in accounts payable and disbursements. Finally, we consider the firm's use of short-term investing and borrowing to maintain adequate liquidity.

17-1 Cash Management

liquidity management
Activities aimed at both earning a positive return on idle excess cash balances and obtaining low-cost financing for meeting unexpected needs and seasonal cash shortages.

cash manager
A financial specialist responsible for managing the cash flow time line related to collection, concentration, and disbursement of the company's funds.

float
Funds that have been sent by the payer but are not yet usable funds to the payee.

Many companies employ financial specialists known as **cash managers**. One of their primary roles is to manage the cash flow time line related to collection, concentration, and disbursement of the company's funds. The cash manager's job typically starts when a customer (the payer) initiates payment to the company (the payee) in any format (cash, check, or electronic). Because most business-to-business payments are still effected by sending a check in the mail, the collections process usually involves trying to reduce delays in mail, processing, and check collection.

The cash manager is also responsible for assembling or *concentrating* cash from remote collection points into a central account and for initiating payments from the company to its suppliers. The final stage of this process usually involves reconciling the company's various bank accounts and managing all the banking relationships. Any delay in timing on either the collection or disbursement side is generally referred to as *float*.

17-1a Float

Float refers to funds that have been sent by the payer but are not yet usable funds to the payee. Float is important in the cash conversion cycle because its presence increases both the firm's average collection period and its average payment period.

mail float
The time delay between when payment is placed in the mail and when payment is received.

processing float
The time that elapses between the receipt of a payment by a firm and its deposit into the firm's account.

availability float
The time between deposit of a check and availability of the funds to a firm.

clearing float
The time between deposit of the check and presentation of the check back to the bank on which it is drawn.

The primary role of the cash manager on the collections side is to *minimize collection float* wherever possible. On the payments side, trying to *maximize disbursement float* is a common practice that raises an important question: Is it ethical to intentionally pay a supplier after the term within which the firm agreed to pay? This topic will be discussed in greater detail later in the chapter.

We can view float from either the receiving party's (the payee's) perspective or the paying party's (the payer's) perspective. The following list points out that mail float and processing float are generally the same from both perspectives, though the final outcomes are different. The four components of float are defined as follows.

1. **Mail float** is the time delay between when payment is placed in the mail and when payment is received.

2. **Processing float** is the time between receipt of the payment and its deposit into the firm's account.

3. **Availability float** is the time between deposit of the check and availability of the funds to the firm.

4. **Clearing float** is the time between deposit of the check and presentation of the check back to the bank on which it is drawn.

In addition to managing the collection, concentration, and disbursement of funds, the cash manager is also responsible for the following duties:

- *Financial relationships:* Managing relationships with banks and other providers of cash management services;
- *Cash flow forecasting:* Determining future cash flows to predict surpluses or deficits (see Chapter 15);
- *Investing and borrowing:* Managing the investing of short-term surpluses or borrowing for short-term deficits; and
- *Information management:* Developing and maintaining information systems to gather and analyze cash management data.

Cash management typically resides in the firm's treasury area along with such functions as external financing and risk management. In smaller companies, accounting or clerical staffs may perform the cash management function. The staff's specific cash management tasks related to collection, concentration, and disbursement of funds are described in the following sections.

17-1b Cash Position Management

cash position management
The primary cash management tasks that are performed daily and involve the collection, concentration, and disbursement of company funds.

On a daily basis, the primary cash management tasks related to the collection, concentration, and disbursement of funds for the company are generally referred to as **cash position management**. That is, each day the cash manager must determine the amount of funds to be collected, move balances to the appropriate accounts, and fund the projected disbursements. The cash position can be managed with some degree of accuracy many weeks into the future, given proper forecasting of cash flows. Most of the cash management products and services offered by banks and other financial institutions are associated with some part of this process.

At the end of the day, the cash manager must determine (1) whether the company will have a surplus or a deficit of funds in each checking account and (2) how to manage the difference. If the company has a *surplus* of funds, then the money may be placed in some type of short-term investment, such as an interest-bearing account at its bank or a portfolio of marketable securities. However, if the firm has a *deficit*, then the cash manager must arrange either to transfer funds from investment accounts or to draw on a short-term credit agreement with the firm's bank. The management of these short-term investing and borrowing arrangements is typically the responsibility of the cash manager.

target cash balance
A cash total that is set for checking accounts to avoid engaging in *cash position management*.

Many companies, especially smaller ones, do not actively engage in cash position management but rather set a **target cash balance** for their checking accounts. The primary approach to determining these target cash balances is based on transactions

What Companies Do Globally

How Companies Determine the Amount of Excess Cash to Hold

Financial researchers have developed a clear picture of the working capital practices of U.S. corporations, but far less is known about how companies headquartered in other major countries manage their liquidity needs. A recent survey enriches our understanding of the factors that impact how much cash and marketable securities international companies hold. Professors Karl Lins, Henri Servaes, and Peter Tufano surveyed companies in twenty-nine countries, and the results highlight two important points. First, they suggest that international companies pursue liquidity management policies that are generally similar to those followed by U.S. firms. And second, they reveal that corporations everywhere make an important distinction between cash and marketable securities held for operational purposes versus cash and liquid assets held for non-operational and safety reasons.

The following table summarizes managerial responses about cash holdings. It describes the importance of various factors in determining how much excess cash—defined as holdings of cash and marketable securities in excess of operating needs—managers choose to hold. For the full sample of companies, total cash holdings amount to 9% of the book value of assets, but cash held for non-operational purposes amounts to only 40% of total cash holdings. The most important reason managers give for holding excess cash is to serve as a buffer for possible future cash flow shortfalls, while the need to maintain adequate cash to ensure efficient running of the company is the second most frequently mentioned reason. Managers are also concerned about ensuring the cost and potential availability of funds in case the firm needs to obtain working capital quickly or during an emergency.

Survey Responses to Questions about Non-operational Cash

"In deciding how much excess cash to hold, how important are the following factors?"

Factor	Percentage Responding "Important" or "Very Important"
Cash as a buffer against future cash flow shortfalls	47
Minimal cash ensures efficient running of the company	35
Difference between interest rate on cash and interest rate on debt	35
Time it takes to raise money when funds are needed	31
Level of uncertainty about future investment opportunities	31
Ability to issue debt at a "fair" price when funds are needed	30
Difference between interest rate on cash and cost of capital	26
Size of the undrawn credit facility	23
Transactions costs of raising funds	22

Source: Reprinted from *Journal of Financial Economics*, Volume 98, Issue 1, October 2010, Pages 160–176. Karl V. Lins, Henri Servaes, and Peter Tufano, "What Drives Corporate Liquidity? An International Survey of Cash Holdings and Lines of Credit," with permission from Elsevier.

requirements or a minimum balance set by the bank. The transactions requirement is determined simply by how much cash a firm needs to fund its day-to-day operations. Firms with a high volume of daily inflows and outflows will find that some balances remain in non-interest-bearing checking accounts, regardless of forecasting ability. Many banks also require a specified minimum balance in customer checking accounts. For smaller companies and banks, this minimum balance is designed to provide adequate compensation to the bank for the services it provides. For larger companies, most banks perform *account analysis*, which compares the value of the balances a firm leaves on deposit to the value of the services it receives from the bank.

A **bank account analysis statement** is a report (usually monthly) provided to a bank's commercial customers that specifies all services provided, including items processed and any charges assessed. It is basically a detailed invoice that lists all checks cleared, account charges, lockbox charges, electronic transactions, and so on. The statement also lists all balances held by the firm at the bank, and includes a

bank account analysis statement
A regular report (usually monthly) provided to a bank's commercial customers that specifies all services provided, including items processed and any charges assessed.

? WHAT TO ASK

What is the general approach used by your firm to manage cash?

computation of the credit earned by the firm on those balances. Under current federal regulations, a bank is not allowed to pay actual interest on corporate checking account balances; however, it can offer an *earnings credit* on these balances that is used to offset service charges. Most companies on account analysis will receive some credit for the transaction balances they leave in the account, and typically the credit will only partially offset the service fees. The balance of fees owed the bank will then be deducted as a service charge for the month in question.

17-1 Concept Review Questions

1. What is *float*? What are its four components? What is the difference between *availability float* and *clearing float*?

2. What activities are involved in *cash position management*? How does the cash manager monitor and take actions with regard to the end-of-day checking account balances?

3. How do smaller firms that do not engage in cash position management typically set their *target cash balance*? What is typically detailed in a *bank account analysis statement*?

17-2 Collections

The primary objective of the collections process is to quickly and efficiently collect funds from customers and others. This process includes gathering and disseminating information related to the collections, and in some cases the information may be as important as the money itself. One key requirement is ensuring that the accounts receivable department has the remittance information needed to properly post receipts and update customer files. A secondary requirement is to provide audit trails for the company's internal and external auditors.

As discussed previously, a major delay in the collections process results from *collection float*, which is a function of the mail, processing, and availability floats. The primary goal of collections is to reduce each of these float components as much as possible. Collection float is typically measured in *dollar-days*, or the number of dollars in the collection process multiplied by the number of days of float. For example, $10 million of checks with an average of five days of float would represent $50 million dollar-days of float.

It is important to understand the various payment practices in the U.S. business environment. In the United States, most business-to-business payments are still made via a check in the mail. Many consumer payments are also still made via check, whereas retail establishments must handle cash, debit, and credit cards in addition to checks.

The U.S. business environment is also characterized by a large number of financial institutions: approximately 6,400 commercial banks, 1,000 thrift institutions, and 7,500 credit unions (these figures are based on recent statistics from the FDIC and the NCUA). Historically, the United States has been lacking in true nationwide banking, but bank mergers and expansion of regional branching activities have brought this closer to reality. Speeding up collections reduces the firm's *average collection period*, which in turn reduces the investment the firm must make in its cash conversion cycle. In our example of the *cash conversion cycle* in Chapter 16 (Section 16-1), Reese Industries had annual sales of $5 billion and 8 days of total collection float (mail, processing, and availability time). If Reese can reduce its collection float time by 5 days (to 3 days), it reduces its investment in the cash conversion cycle by about $68.5 million [$5 billion × (5 days ÷ 365 days)]. A number of popular collection systems and techniques can be implemented to speed up collections.

The most recent development in the collections area is the implementation of Check 21 legislation (Check Clearing for the 21st Century Act) in 2003/2004. This allows for the creation of digital images of checks that replace the original paper checks. Such images can be cleared much more quickly and efficiently, resulting in significantly reduced clearing times for checks.

17-2a Types of Collection Systems

A firm's collection system is primarily determined by the nature of its business. Many high-volume retail establishments, such as fast-food restaurants or convenience stores, receive the bulk of their payments in cash. Other types of retail operations, such as department and variety stores, collect most of their payments by credit card, debit card, or check.

As we have noted, the typical business-to-business payment mechanism is a check mailed in response to an invoice received for products or services. What can complicate the collection process is that one check is often used to pay multiple invoices, and there may be adjustments or partial payments related to those invoices. This makes the information collected by the cash manager of critical importance to the accounts receivable department. Collection systems must take into account the information management requirements related to the payment application process.

Some types of time-critical transactions, such as real estate closings or high-dollar payments, may be received via wire transfers with same-day value. Other forms of high-volume, low-dollar receipts, especially those of a recurring nature (utility payments, insurance premiums, etc.), may come through the *automated clearinghouse (ACH) system*, which generally offers next-day settlement with fairly low transaction costs. The important thing to understand is that the type of collection system used by a company is usually a function of both the type of business and the customary methods of payment used by that business.

field banking system
Collection system characterized by many collection points, each of which may have a depository account at a local bank.

Field Banking System In a field banking system, most collections are made either over the counter (as at a retail store) or at a collection office (often used by utilities). These systems are characterized by many collection points, each of which may have a depository account at a local bank.

The main collection problem in this type of system involves transferring the funds from the local (often small) banks to the main account at the company's primary bank. Many large national retailers find they must maintain hundreds or even thousands of bank relationships as part of their collections system. Typically, the collections in a field banking system are local checks, cash, debit cards, and credit cards. Although debit card and credit card processing is usually highly automated and efficient, checks and cash must be processed and deposited at the local deposit bank. The funds must then be concentrated into the company's main account before the money can be used.

The backbone of this type of system is information management—that is, the company needs to know where the money is before the company can make use of it. Most large retailers utilize *point-of-sale (POS) information systems* that allow them to know on a daily basis how much money has been collected, in what formats (cash, check, debit card, or credit card) it was received, and how much of it was deposited at the local bank. The task of moving this money into a "concentration" account is discussed in the section on cash concentration.

One of the major developments in the area of field banking systems is the increasing use of check-conversion technology. The bulk of field banking check collections are consumer items, which are increasingly being converted into ACH debit transactions, resulting in faster collections at lower costs. Consumer checks can be converted at the point of purchase or later in the processing cycle. Consumer checks that are not converted (or business checks that are not allowed to be converted) can still be imaged (as per Check 21 guidelines) and thus processed more efficiently. Many companies are now using remote deposit capture machines to image checks as early as possible in the collections process.

mail-based collection system
Collection system in which processing centers receive the incoming mail payments, separate checks from remittance information, prepare checks for deposit, and send remittance information to the accounts receivable department.

Mail-Based Collection System In a mail-based collection system, the company typically has one or more collection points that process the incoming mail payments. These processing centers receive the mail payments, open the envelopes, separate the check from the remittance information, prepare the check for deposit, and send the remittance information to the accounts receivable department for application of payment. Companies such as utilities and credit card processors that utilize standardized, scannable remittance information can often process the payments they receive quickly and efficiently using automated equipment. Although many high-volume processors can justify the cost of the equipment needed for automated processing, other companies may find that using a *lockbox* (discussed later) is more cost effective. However, recent developments in payment processing equipment have made automated processing available to smaller companies at a reasonable price.

Electronic Systems Electronic collection systems, first patented in 2000, continue to develop rapidly as both businesses and consumers better understand their benefits. Key developments in this area are electronic invoice presentment and payment (EIPP), introduced in this chapter's opening "What Companies Do" example, in the business-to-business market and electronic bill presentment and payment (EBPP) in the business-to-consumer market. In EIPP and EBPP systems, customers are sent electronic bills that they can pay electronically. Most of these systems are Internet-based and are gradually gaining acceptance in the marketplace. The most successful of the consumer systems offer a consolidator-type service, where customers can go to one site to view and pay all their bills rather than visiting individual billing sites. Electronic payment systems have also gained acceptance in the business-to-business environment.

Some of the primary advantages of using a system such as the EIPP for business-to-business payments are (1) reduced float to the receiving party, (2) lower cost both of receivables processing for the receiver and of payment initiation and reconciliation costs for the payer, and (3) better forecasting for both parties. Though there may be a need to negotiate payment dates and possible discounts for earlier payment, companies that have implemented electronic payments report significant overall savings as a result.

The future for electronic collections systems appears to look good, as more and more companies are implementing some form of electronic invoicing and payment. Many of these systems are implemented by large companies as a means to streamline the billing of their (often smaller) customers and to automate the payment process. Companies that must pay a large number of smaller suppliers are also implementing electronic systems as a means to reduce their overall costs of running accounts payable and disbursement systems.

17-2b Lockbox Systems

A lockbox system is a popular technique for speeding up collections because it affects three components of float. It works like this: Instead of mailing payments to the company, customers mail payments to a post office box, which is emptied regularly by the firm's bank. The bank processes each payment and deposits the payments into the firm's account. The bank sends (or transmits electronically) deposit slips and enclosures to the firm so the firm can properly credit its customers' accounts.

Lockboxes are typically dispersed geographically to match the locations of the firm's customers. As a result of being near a firm's customers, lockboxes reduce mail time and clearing time. They reduce processing time to nearly zero because the bank deposits payments before the firm processes them. Obviously, a lockbox system reduces collection float, but not without a cost. Therefore, a firm must perform a cost-benefit analysis to determine whether a lockbox system should be implemented. Equation 17.1 presents a simple formula for the cost-benefit analysis of a lockbox system:

(Eq. 17.1) $\text{Net benefit or cost of lockbox} = (FVR \times r_a) - LC$

where

FVR = float value reduction in dollars
r_a = cost of capital
LC = lockbox cost (annual operating cost of the system)

Thus, if the return on the float reduction exceeds the cost of the lockbox system, then the firm should implement the lockbox system.

electronic invoice presentment and payment (EIPP)
A collection system in business-to-business transactions under which business customers are sent bills in an electronic format and can pay them via electronic means.

electronic bill presentment and payment (EBPP)
A collection system in the business-to-consumer market under which consumers are sent bills in an electronic format and can pay them via electronic means.

lockbox system
A technique for speeding up collections that affects all three components of float. Customers mail payments to a post office box, which is emptied regularly by the firm's bank, which processes and deposits the payments.

Consider Reese Industries, which has $5 billion in annual sales and eight days of customer collection float in its cash conversion cycle. Reese wants to determine if it should implement a lockbox system that reduces customer collection float to five days. The reduction in float value from decreasing customer float from eight days to five days is $41.1 million [$5 billion × (3 days ÷ 365 days)]. Reese has a cost of capital of 13.5% per year. Thus, the value to Reese of reducing customer float by three days is $5.55 million (0.135 × $41.1 million). If the annual cost of the lockbox system is less than $5.55 million, it would be beneficial to implement the system.

Although large firms whose customers are geographically dispersed commonly use a lockbox system, small firms may also find a lockbox system advantageous. The benefit to small firms often comes primarily from transferring the processing of payments to the bank.

Lockboxes are typically classified as either retail or wholesale. A *retail lockbox* uses standardized, scannable remittance documents in order to highly automate the processing of incoming payments. These types of systems are characterized by high volumes of low-dollar payments, and the key issue is processing the payments at a minimum cost per dollar collected. Given the low-dollar amounts of these payments, availability float is generally not a big issue.

Wholesale lockboxes, on the other hand, primarily process high-dollar payments with nonstandard remittance information. The key issues in this type of system are (1) reducing the availability float related to the large checks and (2) quickly forwarding the remittance information to the accounts receivable (A/R) department for application of payment. The current practice for wholesale lockboxes is to make extensive use of imaging technology to quickly and accurately relay copies of the remittance information back to the A/R department.

17-2c Cash Concentration

cash concentration
The process of bringing the lockbox and other deposits together into one bank, often called the *concentration bank*.

In the previous section, lockbox systems were discussed as a means to reduce collection float. With a lockbox system, the firm has deposits in each lockbox bank. **Cash concentration** is the process of bringing the lockbox and other deposits together into one bank, commonly called the *concentration bank*.

Cash concentration has three main advantages. First, it creates a large pool of funds for use in making short-term cash investments. Because there is a fixed-cost component in the transaction cost associated with making marketable security investments, investing a single pool of funds reduces the firm's transaction costs. The larger investment pool also allows the firm to choose from a larger variety of marketable securities. Second, concentrating the firm's cash in one account improves the tracking and internal control of that cash. Third, having one concentration bank allows the firm to implement more effective payment strategies that preserve its invested balances for as long as possible. As bank branch networks continue to expand, more and more companies are choosing banks with large geographic coverage that can simplify concentration by using deposit reconciliation services.

JOB INTERVIEW QUESTION

What are some of the advantages to a firm of using cash concentration procedures?

The configuration of a company's cash concentration system is generally a function of the collection system. That is, a company with a *field banking system* will need a way to move money quickly and efficiently from many small deposit banks into its concentration account, whereas a company with several collection centers or lockboxes will typically use wire transfers to quickly move large balances from a limited number of collection points into its concentration account. The type of disbursement system (discussed in a later section) is also an important consideration, because these accounts must be funded either by internal transfer or wire transfer.

17-2d Funds Transfer Mechanisms

There are two commonly used mechanisms for transferring cash from the depository banks to the concentration bank: automated clearinghouse debit transfers and wire transfers.

Daniel Carter, Vice President of Finance, BevMo!

"Each of our stores makes deposits into a local account, which are concentrated back into our corporate account."

See the entire interview at **SMART** | finance

Smart Practices Video

automated clearing-house (ACH) debit transfer

A preauthorized electronic withdrawal from the payer's account.

electronic depository transfer (EDT)

The term used in the cash management trade for an *automated clearinghouse (ACH) debit transfer.*

wire transfer

An electronic communication that removes funds from the payer's bank and deposits funds in the payee's bank on a same-day basis via bookkeeping entries.

Automated Clearinghouse Debit Transfers The first mechanism is an automated clearinghouse (ACH) debit transfer, which is a preauthorized electronic withdrawal from the payer's account and is generally known within the cash management field as an electronic depository transfer (EDT).

The ACH, a computerized clearing facility, makes a paperless transfer of funds between the payer and payee banks. An ACH settles accounts among participating banks; individual accounts are settled by adjustments to the respective bank balances. ACH transfers of this type generally clear in one day.

For cash concentration, an ACH debit is initiated by the concentration bank and sent to each deposit bank, with funds then moving from the deposit bank into the concentration bank. These transfers can be automatically created from deposit information and can then be centrally initiated from the company's headquarters through its concentration bank. A large nationwide retailer can easily concentrate deposits from many small deposit banks into its concentration account by using the daily deposit information gathered from its stores' point-of-sale systems.

Wire Transfers The second funds transfer mechanism is a wire transfer. In the United States, the primary wire transfer system, known as *Fedwire*, is run by the Federal Reserve System and is available to all depository institutions. A Fedwire transfer is an electronic communication that removes funds from the payer's bank and deposits funds in the payee's bank on a same-day basis via bookkeeping entries in the financial institution's Federal Reserve account. An alternative to Fedwire is the CHIPS system operated by The Clearing House (the New York clearinghouse system). This system transfers over $2 trillion a day between its members, primarily large global banks and financial institutions operating in New York.

Wire transfers can eliminate mail float and clearing float and may provide processing float reductions as well. For cash concentration, the firm moves funds using a wire transfer from each deposit account to its concentration account. Wire transfers are a substitute for ACH debit transfers, but they are generally much more expensive: both the sending and receiving banks charge significant fees for the transaction. Wire transfers are usually used only for high-dollar transfers, where the investment value of the funds outweighs the cost of the transfer.

Selecting the Best Transfer Mechanism The firm must balance the benefits and costs of concentrating cash to determine the type and timing of transfers from its lockbox accounts to its concentration account. The transfer mechanism selected should be the one that is most profitable (i.e., profit per period equals earnings on the increased funds' availability minus the cost of the transfer system). In general practice, most companies use wire transfers for large transfers of funds from lockbox deposits and use EDTs for high-volume, low-dollar transfers from small deposit banks.

EXAMPLE

To demonstrate alternative transfer methods, we consider DJM Manufacturing, which needs to transfer $120,000 from its deposit account to its concentration account. It has two choices: an electronic depository transfer (EDT) with a total cost of $1, or a wire transfer with a total cost of $15. Because this would be a midweek transfer, the funds would be accelerated by one day using a wire transfer. (*Note:* A Friday transfer would represent three days of funds acceleration.) The firm's opportunity cost for these funds is 7%.

In this Example, the value of moving the funds via wire transfer is the one day of interest that could be earned if the funds arrived in the concentration account today rather than tomorrow. This amount is calculated to be $23.01 (0.07 ÷ 365 × $120,000). Because the differential cost of wire transfer versus an EDT is $14 ($15 − $1), the company should use a wire in this case because it would result in a net benefit of $9.01 ($23.01 − $14.00).

Given the opportunity cost and transfer fees, we could also determine the minimum amount for which a wire transfer would be beneficial. Take the differential cost of a wire ($14.00) and divide by the daily interest rate (0.07 ÷ 365); in this case, the minimum transfer amount would be $73,000 [$14.00 ÷ (0.07 ÷ 365)]. If DJM were transferring funds on a Friday and thus could earn three days of interest, then the *minimum transfer amount* would be one-third of the standard amount, or $24,333 ($73,000 ÷ 3).

17-2 Concept Review Questions

4. What is the firm's objective with regard to *collection float*? What are the common types of collection systems?

5. What are the benefits of using a *lockbox system*? How does it work? How can the firm assess the economics of a lockbox system?

6. Why do firms employ *cash concentration* techniques? What are some of the popular transfer mechanisms used by firms to move funds from depository banks to their concentration banks?

7. How can the cash manager model the benefits and costs of various funds transfer mechanisms to assess their economics? How can this analysis be used to determine the *minimum transfer amount*?

17-3 Accounts Payable and Disbursements

17-3a Overview of the Accounts Payable Process

The final component of the cash conversion cycle is the *average payment period (APP)*, which has two parts: (1) the time from the purchase of raw materials until the firm places the payment in the mail and (2) payment float time (disbursement float). The payment float is the time it takes after the firm places its payment in the mail until the supplier has withdrawn funds from the firm's account. Section 17-1 addressed issues related to payment float time. In this section, we discuss the management of the time that elapses between the purchase of raw materials and mailing the payment to the supplier. This activity is called accounts payable management.

accounts payable management
A short-term financing activity that involves managing the time that elapses between the purchase of raw materials and mailing the payment to the supplier.

Purpose of the Accounts Payable Function The primary purpose of the accounts payable (A/P) function is to examine all incoming invoices and determine the proper amount to be paid. As part of this process, the cash manager matches the invoice to both the purchase order and receiving information to ensure that the goods/services were ordered by an authorized person and that they were actually received. The accounts payable clerk may make adjustments to the invoiced amount for price or quantity differences. Companies usually pay multiple invoices with a single check. A company has the right to make full use of any credit period offered, but intentionally delaying payments or increasing disbursement float is considered to be an unethical cash management practice. Once payment has been authorized (sometimes referred to as "vouchering"), the cash manager is often responsible for the actual payment itself, either managing the preparation and mailing of checks or initiating the electronic transfer of funds.

Types of Payment Systems The other issue involved with managing disbursements is the choice of a centralized or decentralized payables and payments system. In a *centralized system*, all invoices are sent to a central accounts payable department, where payment is authorized and checks or other forms of payment are initiated. Centralized systems offer many advantages, including easier concentration of funds, improved access to cash position information, better control, and reduced transaction and administrative costs. There are, however, several problems with centralized payables, such as slow payment times (which could damage relationships with vendors or cause missed opportunities for cash discounts) and the need to coordinate between central payables and field offices/managers to resolve any disputes.

Some companies utilize a more *decentralized system* to the payables and disbursement process in which payments are authorized and, in some cases, initiated at the local level. Although this approach generally helps to improve relationships with vendors and enhance local management autonomy, it makes it harder to concentrate funds and obtain daily cash position information, and it increases the chance of unauthorized disbursements.

Finance in Your Life

Finding Credit Card Finance Charges and Minimum Payments

Very few bank credit card users understand how the card issuer determines the finance charge and minimum payment. Assume that you have a SuperBank Visa card that charges a monthly interest rate of 1.5% on the *average daily balance* (the most popular method) and requires a minimum payment equal to 5% of the new balance, rounded to the nearest dollar. Assume your statement extends from October 10 through November 10—a total of 31 days—and your balance on October 10 was $582. During the period you made the following three transactions:

October 15	Purchase	$350
October 22	Purchase	54
November 6	Payment	25

As a result, you have the following account balances:

Dates	Number of Days (1)	Balance (2)	(1) × (2) (3)
Oct. 11–15	5	$582	$ 2,910
Oct. 16–22	7	$582 + $350 = 932	6,524
Oct. 23–Nov. 6	15	932 + 54 = 986	14,790
Nov. 7–10	4	986 − 25 = 961	3,844
Total	31		$28,068

Average daily balance = $28,068 ÷ 31 = $905.42
Finance charge = $905.42 × 0.015 = $13.58
New balance = $961 + $13.58 = $974.58
Minimum payment = 0.05 × $974.58 = $48.73, which rounds to $49.00

The calculations above show that your **finance charge was $13.58** (1.5% of your average daily balance of $905.42). Adding it to the end-of-month account balance of $961, your new balance was $974.58. The **minimum payment of $49** equaled 5% of the new balance—$48.73—rounded to the nearest dollar. Note that if you pay the $49 minimum payment, $13.58 of it will cover the finance charge and the remaining $35.42 ($49.00 − $13.58) will be applied to the balance outstanding when the payment is received.

17-3b Cash Discounts

When suppliers offer *cash discounts* to encourage customers to pay before the end of the credit period, it may not be in the firm's best financial interest to pay on the last day of the credit period. Accounts payable with cash discounts have stated credit terms, such as *2/10 net 30*, which means the purchaser can take a 2% *discount* from the invoice amount if the payment is made within *10 days* of the beginning of the credit period; otherwise, it must pay the full amount within *30 days* of the beginning of the credit period. The credit period begins at a specific date set by the supplier, typically either the end of the month in which the purchase is made (noted as *EOM*) or on the *date of the invoice*. Taking the discount is at the discretion of the purchaser.

When a firm is extended credit terms that include a cash discount, it has two options: (1) pay the full invoice amount at the end of the credit period, or (2) pay the invoice amount less the cash discount at the end of the cash discount period. In either case, the firm purchases the same goods. Thus, the difference between the payment amount without and with the cash discount is, in effect, the interest payment made by the firm to its supplier.

A firm in need of short-term funds must therefore compare the interest rate charged by its supplier to the best rate charged by lenders of short-term financing (typically banks) and then choose the lowest-cost option. This comparison is important because,

? JOB INTERVIEW QUESTION

What is the financial trade-off involved when a firm evaluates whether or not to take an offered cash discount?

by taking a cash discount, the firm will shorten its average payment period and thus increase the amount of resources it has invested in operating assets, which will require additional negotiated short-term financing.

To calculate the relevant cost, we assume that the firm will always render payment on the *final day of the specified payment period*—credit period or cash discount period. Equation 17.2 presents the formula for calculating the interest rate, $r_{discount}$, associated with *not taking the cash discount and paying at the end of the credit period* when cash discount terms are offered:

(Eq. 17.2)
$$r_{discount} = \frac{d}{(1 - d)} \times \frac{365}{(CP - DP)}$$

where

d = % discount (in decimal form)
CP = credit period
DP = cash discount period

EXAMPLE

Assume that a supplier to Masson Industries has changed its terms from *net 30* to *2/10 net 30*. Masson has a line of credit with a bank, and the current interest rate on that line of credit is 6.75% per year. Should Masson take the cash discount or continue to use 30 days of credit from its supplier? The interest rate from the supplier is calculated using Equation 17.2:

$$r_{discount} = \frac{0.02}{1 - 0.02} \times \frac{365}{30 - 10} = 0.372 = 37.2\% \text{ per year}$$

Thus, the annualized rate charged by the supplier to those customers not taking the cash discount is 37.2%, whereas the bank charges 6.75%. Masson should take the cash discount and obtain any needed short-term financing by drawing on its bank line of credit.

17-3c Disbursement Products and Methods

zero-balance accounts (ZBAs)
Disbursement accounts that always have an end-of-day balance of zero. The purpose is to eliminate nonearning cash balances in corporate checking accounts.

Zero-Balance Accounts Zero-balance accounts (ZBAs) are disbursement accounts that always have an end-of-day balance of zero. The purpose is to eliminate nonearning cash balances in corporate checking accounts. A ZBA is often used as a disbursement account under a cash concentration system.

A ZBA is designed as follows. Once all of a given day's checks are presented to the firm's ZBA for payment, the bank notifies the firm of the total amount to be drawn, and the firm transfers funds into the account to cover the amount of that day's checks. This leaves an end-of-day balance of $0 (zero dollars). The ZBA allows the firm to keep all operating cash in an interest-earning account, thereby eliminating idle cash balances. Thus, a firm that uses a ZBA in conjunction with a cash concentration system would need two accounts. The firm would concentrate its cash from the lockboxes into an interest-earning account and write checks against its ZBA. The firm would cover the exact dollar amount of checks presented against the ZBA with transfers from the interest-earning account, leaving the end-of-day balance in the ZBA at $0. In many cases, funding of the ZBA is made automatically and involves only an accounting entry on the part of the bank.

A ZBA is a disbursement management tool that allows the firm to *maximize the use of float on each check*. The firm accomplishes this by keeping all its cash in an interest-earning account instead of leaving nonearning balances in its checking account to cover checks that the firm has written. This allows the firm to maximize earnings on its cash balances by capturing the full float time on each check it writes.

We have discussed only ZBAs in this section. However, banks offer a variety of similar products. Another common product that achieves the same goal as a ZBA is a *sweep account*, in which the bank sweeps account surpluses into the appropriate interest-earning vehicle and liquidates similar vehicles in order to cover account shortages when they occur. Many banks also offer *multitiered ZBAs* that may be used by multidivisional companies or to segregate different types of payments (payrolls, dividends, accounts payable, etc.). This type of account allows the cash manager to better control balances and funding of the master account and associated ZBAs, thus reducing excess balances and transfers.

controlled disbursement
A bank service that provides early notification of checks that will be presented against a company's account on a given day.

Controlled Disbursement Controlled disbursement is a bank service that provides early notification of checks that will be presented against a company's account on a given day. For most large cash management banks, the Federal Reserve Bank makes two presentments of checks to be cleared each day. A bank offering controlled disbursement accounts would receive advance electronic notification from the Fed several hours prior to the actual presentment of the items. This allows the bank to let its controlled disbursement customers know as early as possible what will be presented to their accounts. This, in turn, allows customers to determine their cash position and make any necessary investment/borrowing decisions in the morning, before the checks are presented for payment. Controlled disbursement accounts are often set up as ZBAs to allow for automatic funding through a company's concentration account.

positive pay
A bank service used to combat the most common types of check fraud. A company transmits a check-issued file, designating the check number and amount of each item, to the bank when the checks are issued. The bank matches the presented checks against this file and rejects any items that do not match.

Positive Pay Positive pay is a bank service used to combat the most common types of check fraud. Given the availability of inexpensive computers, scanners, and printers, it is not difficult to create excellent copies of corporate checks or to change payees or amounts. The risk to a company issuing checks is that the bank might pay fraudulent items and the fraud would not be revealed until the account is reconciled. When using a positive pay service, the company transmits a check-issued file, designating the check number and amount of each item, to the bank when the checks are issued. The bank matches the presented checks against this file and rejects any items that do not match. It is important to note that several courts have ruled that positive pay is a "commercially reasonable" measure to prevent check fraud. This means that a company that does not use this service when available may find itself liable for fraudulent items accepted by its bank. A recent development in this area is that more companies are using payee/beneficiary verification, or reverse positive pay, to make sure that the payee or beneficiary of the check has not been altered. Earlier, more basic positive pay did not include this feature.

? WHAT TO ASK

What procedures does your firm use to manage its cash collection and payments?

17-3d Developments in Accounts Payable and Disbursements

integrated accounts payable
Provides a company with outsourcing of its accounts payable or disbursement operations. Also known as *comprehensive accounts payable.*

Integrated Accounts Payable Integrated accounts payable, also known as *comprehensive accounts payable,* provides a company with outsourcing of its accounts payable or disbursement operations. The outsourcing may be as minor as contracting with a bank to issue checks and perform reconciliations or as major as outsourcing the entire payables function. One of the most typical approaches to A/P outsourcing is to send a bank (or other financial service provider) a data file containing a listing of all payments to be made. The bank will maintain a vendor file for the company and send each vendor payment (in the preferred format) in accordance with the company's remittance advice.

purchasing card programs
Programs in which a firm issues designated employees purchasing cards with spending limits, usable only at stipulated vendors.

Purchasing/Procurement Cards Many companies are implementing purchasing (or procurement) card programs as a means of reducing the cost of low-dollar indirect purchases. Though companies have been using credit cards for travel and related expenses for many years, they have only recently begun using them to make routine purchases of supplies, equipment, or services. A firm issues purchasing cards to designated employees, but it limits the dollar amounts that may be spent and stipulates which vendors can be used. Companies that have implemented such programs report significant cost savings from streamlining the purchasing process for low-cost items. The other advantage is that the firm can pay the issuer of the purchasing card in a single, large payment that consolidates many small purchases.

Imaging Services Many disbursement services offered by banks and other vendors incorporate imaging services as part of the package. This technology allows both sides of the check, as well as remittance information, to be converted into digital images. The images can then be transmitted via the Internet or easily stored for future reference. Imaging services are especially useful when incorporated with *positive-pay* services.

imaging services
Disbursement services offered by banks and other vendors to allow both sides of the check, as well as remittance information, to be converted into digital images. The images can then be transmitted via the Internet or easily stored for future reference.

Fraud Prevention in Disbursements In recent years, disbursement fraud—especially related to check payments—has increased significantly. Fraudulent checks can be created with inexpensive scanners, computers, and laser printers. As a result, fraud prevention and control have become even more important in the accounts payable and disbursement functions. Some of the common fraud prevention measures include the following:

- Creating and disbursing checks according to written policies and procedures;
- Separating check-issuance duties (approval, signing, and reconciliation);
- Using safety features on checks (microprinting, watermarks, tamper resistance, etc.);
- Setting maximum dollar limits and/or requiring multiple signatures on checks;
- Using *positive-pay* services; and
- Increasing the use of electronic payment methods.

17-3 Concept Review Questions

8. What is the primary purpose of the accounts payable function? Describe the procedures used to manage accounts payable. What are the key differences between *centralized* and *decentralized* payables and payment systems?

9. When is it advantageous for a company to pay early and take an offered cash discount? Under what circumstance would the firm be advised to always take any offered cash discounts?

10. What is the difference between a *ZBA* and a *controlled disbursement account*? Are they direct substitutes?

11. What are some of the recent developments in the accounts payable and disbursements area? What role does new technology play in preventing disbursement fraud?

17-4 Short-Term Investing and Borrowing

After determining the company's cash position, the cash manager will generally have either surplus funds to invest or a deficit of funds to replenish via short-term borrowing. Clearly, the goal is to earn relatively safe returns on short-term surpluses and to borrow at reasonable cost to meet short-term deficits. The firm's motive for holding cash will significantly impact both its short-term investing and borrowing decisions. This section reviews the key motives for holding cash and short-term investment balances and some of the options available to the financial manager for investing short-term surpluses. In addition, it describes some key aspects of borrowing to meet short-term deficits.

17-4a Motives for Holding Cash and Short-Term Investments

There are three basic motives for holding cash and short-term investments (also called *marketable securities*). In a more general sense, these are the *motives for maintaining liquidity*. Each motive can be addressed in two ways: (1) the appropriate degree of liquidity and (2) the appropriate mix of cash and short-term investments.

transactions motive
A motive for holding cash and short-term investments in order to make planned payments for items such as materials and wages.

Transactions Motive A firm maintains cash and short-term investments to satisfy the transactions motive, which is to make planned payments for items such as materials and wages. Generally because these balances are held to make planned near-term payments, firms fulfill this motive primarily by holding cash balances. If the firm's cash inflows and cash outflows are closely matched, its transactions balances can be minimized. Although firms *must* fulfill this cash need, they typically hold liquid balances to meet the following two motives as well.

safety motive
A motive for holding cash and short-term investments in order to protect the firm against being unable to satisfy unexpected demands for cash. Sometimes called the *precautionary motive*.

Safety Motive The safety motive, sometimes called the *precautionary motive*, for holding cash and short-term investments exists to protect the firm against being unable to satisfy unexpected demands for cash. This motive is fulfilled by maintaining a pool of liquid funds that can quickly be accessed in an emergency. Generally the firm will hold highly liquid short-term investments that can immediately be converted into cash.

speculative motive
A motive for holding, typically in short-term as well as long-term investments, funds that are currently unneeded or can be used to quickly take advantage of opportunities that may arise.

Speculative Motive Firms sometimes hold cash and short-term investments for speculative reasons. This speculative motive exists because the firm has no other use for certain funds or because it wants to be able to quickly take advantage of opportunities that may arise. Typically this motive is pursued only after the firm meets its safety motive. Funds held for speculative reasons are often invested in short-term as well as long-term instruments.

17-4b Short-Term Investing

Making sure that the company has access to liquid assets when and where they are needed is one of the critical tasks for the cash manager. Although the primary form of liquidity will generally be a company's checking or demand deposit accounts at its banks, these accounts usually do not earn interest and the company should not hold excess balances in them. To earn some type of short-term return, a company will hold some near-cash assets in the form of short-term investments, often labeled *marketable securities*. These investments may be either a source of reserve liquidity or a place to maintain temporary surplus funds.[1]

Because such short-term investments are essentially a substitute for cash, *providing liquidity* and *preserving principal* should be the primary concerns. Earning a competitive return is also a consideration; however, care must be taken not to place the underlying principal at risk. Remember that the primary purpose of short-term investments is to maintain a pool of liquid assets as a substitute for cash, not to generate profits for the company. Toward this end, it is important that a company establish policies and guidelines for the management of short-term investments; they should clearly specify the purpose of the investment portfolio and provide recommendations and/or restrictions on acceptable investments and the amount of diversification.

money market mutual funds
Professionally managed short-term investment portfolios used by many small companies and some large companies.

Money Market Mutual Funds Many large companies will manage their own portfolios of short-term investments, but most companies (especially small ones) use money market mutual funds as an alternative. The money market mutual funds are professionally managed portfolios that invest in the same types of short-term instruments in which cash managers invest. They may, in fact, offer even more flexibility and stability than a self-managed fund. Using these types of funds can make sense, especially when the costs of running and managing a short-term portfolio are considered.

In most cases, these funds set their *net asset value* (NAV) at a fixed $1 per share in order to preserve the principal value of the fund. As the value of the fund increases, the fund pays investors in additional shares rather than allowing the share price to increase. Commercial money market mutual funds are available from independent companies as well as from most large banks.

[1]*Temporary surplus funds* may result from ongoing operations, seasonal performance, sales of large assets, or proceeds from a large securities issue.

Money Market Financial Instruments Short-term financial instruments are primarily fixed-income securities. They are generally issued in registered form rather than bearer form, yet they are often called marketable securities. Many of these securities are also issued in *discount form*, meaning the investor pays less than face value for the security at the time of purchase and receives the face value at maturity. Table 17.1 lists the more common securities used for money market investments.

U.S. Treasuries: U.S. Treasury bills (*T-bills*) are the benchmark of money market financial instruments. The U.S. government issues these short-term securities to finance its activities, and they appeal to a wide range of investors, both domestic and foreign. T-bills are backed by the full faith and credit of the U.S. government (making them essentially free of default risk) and have an active secondary market.

T-bills are issued in weekly auctions on a discount basis with maturities of one year or less (usually 4, 13, 26, or 52 weeks). T-bills are available in minimum denominations of $1,000 but are generally traded in round lots of $1 million. Other Treasury instruments such as *Treasury notes* (*T-notes*) and *Treasury bonds* (*T-bonds*) are initially issued as long-term securities, but they may be suitable for a short-term portfolio as they approach maturity.

All treasury securities are registered and issued in *book entry form* (a computer entry at the Federal Reserve Bank rather than a paper certificate) and are exempt from state income taxes.

Federal agency issues: These instruments have some degree of federal government backing and are issued by either federal agencies or private, shareholder-owned companies known as *government-sponsored enterprises (GSEs)*. Most of the agencies are securitized investments backed by home mortgages, student loans, or agricultural lending. Two of the agencies (Ginnie Mae and Freddie Mac) are backed by the "full faith and credit" of the U.S. government, whereas the rest are backed by the implied intervention of the government in the event of a crisis. Such a crisis actually unfolded in 2008 as U.S. real estate prices plunged, causing a steep decline in the value of mortgage-backed securities. In September of that year, the U.S. government essentially took over Freddie Mac and one of the other large GSEs, the Federal National Mortgage Association (Fannie Mae).

Bank financial instruments: U.S. and foreign banks issue short-term *certificates of deposit (CDs)* as well as *time deposits* and *banker's acceptances*. Many banks also offer money market mutual funds and sweep accounts in which their customers can invest short-term cash.

Corporate obligations: The primary corporate obligation in the short-term market is commercial paper. Highly rated corporations typically issue this investment, which is structured as an unsecured promissory note with a maturity of less than 270 days. The short maturity allows for issuance without SEC registration, and commercial paper is usually sold to other corporations rather than the general public. Most issues are also backed by credit guarantees from a financial institution and sold on a discount basis, similar to T-bills. In order to issue commercial paper, a firm must have an investment-grade credit rating, but even then access to this market is sometimes restricted. In the middle of 2007, total commercial paper outstanding in the United States exceeded $2.2 trillion. Early signs of the looming financial crisis appeared that summer, and investors began to have doubts about corporate commercial paper issuers as well as the financial institutions that backed them. Firms found it increasingly difficult to refinance maturing paper, and by April 2010 the market had declined by 50% to just $1.1 trillion outstanding.

The other corporate obligation used for short-term investments is adjustable-rate preferred stock. These stocks take advantage of the dividend exclusion (of 70% or more) for stock in one corporation held by another corporation. In order to make this investment suitable for short-term holdings, the dividend rate paid on the stock is adjusted according to some rate index. This will stabilize the price even if interest rates change during the forty-five-day holding period required to qualify for the dividend exclusion.

? JOB INTERVIEW QUESTION

What are some of the popular types of short-term investments used by firms to warehouse liquidity?

commercial paper
The primary corporate obligation in the short-term market. Typically structured as an unsecured promissory note with a maturity of less than 270 days and usually sold to other corporations rather than the general public.

adjustable-rate preferred stock
A corporate obligation used for short-term investments that takes advantage of the dividend exclusion for stock in one corporation held by another corporation; the dividend rate paid on the stock is adjusted according to some rate index.

Table 17.1   Money Market Financial Instruments

U.S. Treasuries	Interest Basis	Maturity
Treasury bills (T-bills)	Discount	4, 13, 26, or 52 weeks
Treasury notes (T-notes)	Interest bearing	2, 5, or 10 years
Treasury bonds (T-bonds)	Interest bearing	30 years

Federal Agency Issues	Underlying Assets	Backing
Government National Mortgage Association (Ginnie Mae)	Home mortgages	Full faith and credit
Department of Veterans Affairs (Vinnie Mac)	VA home loans	Full faith and credit
Federal National Mortgage Association (Fannie Mae)[a]	Home mortgages	GSE[b]-implied federal backing
Federal Home Loan Mortgage Corporation (Freddie Mac)[a]	Home mortgages	GSE[b]-implied federal backing
SLM Holding Corporation (Sallie Mae)	Student loans	Publicly traded U.S. corporation
Farm Credit Banks Funding Corporation	Agricultural loans	GSE[b]-implied federal backing
Farm Credit System Insurance Corporation	Insurer of Farm Credit Banks	GSE[b]-implied federal backing
Central Bank for Cooperatives (CoBank)	Loans to agricultural cooperatives	GSE[b]-implied federal backing
Federal Agricultural Mortgage Corporation (Farmer Mac)	Agricultural loans, rural real estate, and home mortgages	GSE[b]-implied federal backing

Bank Financial Instruments	Special Features
Certificates of deposit – CDs (domestic)	Interest-bearing deposits at financial institutions in the U.S.; may be fixed rate or floating rate with maturities from 7 days to several years
Overnight sweep accounts	Interest-bearing accounts used for investing end-of-day surplus funds
Yankee CDs	Dollar-denominated CDs issued by U.S. branches of foreign banks
Eurodollar CDs	Dollar-denominated CDs issued by banks outside the U.S.
Eurodollar time deposits	Nonnegotiable, fixed-rate time deposits issued by banks outside the U.S., with maturities ranging from overnight to several years
Banker's acceptances	Negotiable short-term instruments used for trade finance
Bank notes	Unsecured or subordinated debt of the bank (not insured)

Corporate Obligations	Special Features
Commercial paper	Unsecured promissory notes issued by corporations; maturities from 1 to 270 days; usually sold on a discount basis and backed by a credit guarantee from a bank
Adjustable-rate preferred stock	Tax advantaged for corporate holders because of dividend exclusion rule; dividend rate adjusts to maintain stable pricing

Other Short-Term Investments	Special Features
Money market mutual funds	Available directly from funds or through banks
Asset-backed securities	Debt obligations issued by companies that are secured by assets such as receivables, credit card obligations, consumer finance loans, major retailers, and automobile companies
International money market investments	Short-term bills or notes issued by foreign governments, foreign commercial paper, or other types of interest-bearing deposits in foreign currencies
Repurchase agreements (repos)	A collateralized transaction between a securities dealer or bank and an investor; generally backed by Treasuries or agency securities

[a]As of September 2008, Fannie Mae and Freddie Mac were placed under federal government conservatorship (Federal Housing Finance Agency, or FHFA).
[b]GSE denotes Government-Sponsored Enterprise.

Yield Calculations for Discount Instruments (T-Bills or Commercial Paper)[2] The yield for short-term *discount investments* such as T-bills and commercial paper is typically calculated using algebraic approximations rather than more precise present

---

[2]The calculations demonstrated in this section are the same ones we introduced in our discussion of bond prices and interest rates in Section 4-2 of Chapter 4. For convenience as well as custom, we present these formulas a bit differently here.

discount investment
An investment vehicle for which the investor pays less than face value at the time of purchase, and then receives the face value of the investment at its maturity date.

money market yield (MMY)
The yield for short-term discount instruments such as T-bills and commercial paper is typically calculated using algebraic approximations on a 360-day basis rather than more precise present value methods.

value methods. In the case of a discount investment, the investor pays less than face value at the time of purchase but then receives the investment's face value at its maturity date. There are generally no interim interest or coupon payments during the course of holding such an investment.

Determining the yield of T-bills or commercial paper generally involves a two-step process. In most cases, the rate on the investment is expressed as the discount rate, which is used to compute the dollar discount and selling price for the instrument. For example, a one-year, $100,000 T-bill sold at a 5% discount would sell for $95,000 [$100,000 × (1 − 0.05)]. The investor would pay $95,000 today and receive $100,000 in one year at the maturity date. The yield on this investment would be approximately 5.26% ($5,000/$95,000). Though the calculations for a shorter-term investment are slightly more complicated, they follow the same basic approach. Money market yield (MMY) for discount instruments is calculated on a 360-day basis but must be converted to bond equivalent yield (BEY) to compare discount instruments to interest-bearing investments, such as bank CDs. Yield calculations are illustrated in the following example.

EXAMPLE

We can use two steps to determine the yield on a 91-day, $1 million T-bill that is selling at a discount of 3.75%. Note that the convention in the discount market is to use 360 days when calculating the purchase price and money market yield.

Step 1: Calculate the dollar discount and purchase price.

Dollar discount = (Face value × Discount rate) × (Days to maturity ÷ 360)
= ($1,000,000 × 0.0375) × (91 ÷ 360) = $9,479.17

Purchase price = Face value − Dollar discount
= ($1,000,000 − $9,479.17) = $990,520.83

Step 2. Calculate MMY and BEY.

Money market yield (MMY) = (Dollar discount ÷ Purchase price) × (360 ÷ Days to maturity)
= ($9,479.17 ÷ $990,520.83) × (360 ÷ 91) = 3.786%

Bond equivalent yield (BEY) = Money market yield × (365 ÷ 360)
= 3.786% × (365 ÷ 360) = 3.839%

bond equivalent yield (BEY)
The yield equivalent used to compare discount instruments to interest-bearing investments by converting the *money market yield* from a 360-day to a 365-day year.

all-in rate
The base rate plus the spread on a short-term variable rate loan.

prime rate
The rate of interest charged by the largest U.S. banks on short-term loans to the best business borrowers.

LIBOR
The *London Interbank Offered Rate*. The rate that the most creditworthy international banks that deal in Eurodollars charge on interbank loans.

17-4c Short-Term Borrowing

For many companies, a primary source of liquidity is access to short-term lines of credit or commercial paper programs to provide needed funds. This is especially the case for companies in seasonal businesses where large amounts of operating capital may be needed for only a few months of the year. The role of the cash manager in establishing short-term borrowing arrangements is to ensure that the company has credit facilities sufficient to meet short-term cash requirements. Obviously, these arrangements should provide maximum flexibility at a minimum cost. Access to credit can be a major issue for companies in a time of financial crisis. Many creditworthy companies had difficulty getting the credit they needed as the financial and credit crisis deepened in late 2008 and early 2009. Both bank lending and access to commercial paper markets were severely constrained for most companies until early 2010 when credit markets began to thaw.

Most short-term borrowing is done on a variable-rate basis, with rates quoted in terms of a base rate plus a spread. The spread is essentially an adjustment for the relative riskiness and overall creditworthiness of the borrower. The base rate plus the spread are referred to as the all-in rate.

Typical base rates include the *prime rate* and *LIBOR* (*London Interbank Offered Rate*). The prime rate is the rate of interest charged by the largest U.S. banks on short-term loans to the best business borrowers. LIBOR is the rate that the most creditworthy international banks that deal in Eurodollars charge on interbank loans.

For bank lines of credit, lending agreements may require *commitment fees* (fees paid for the bank's agreement to make money available) and/or *compensating balance*

What CFOs Do

CFO Survey Evidence on Bank Lines of Credit

Companies obtain substantial funding from lines of credit. For example, during the first half of 2009, Campello and coauthors document that borrowing from credit lines represented about one-third of total funds (i.e., the sum of external borrowings and cash flows) used by U.S. companies. The reliance on credit lines varied greatly across firms. More than half of total funding used by unprofitable firms came from lines of credit, compared to only 18% for profitable companies. Alarmingly, in March 2009 unprofitable companies on average had drawn 63% of the maximum available on their credit lines. This extreme borrowing was part of a run on bank lines of credit that some researchers argued limited the funds that banks had available to lend through normal channels.

In early 2009 banks responded by raising the cost and reducing the availability of lines to less creditworthy firms. In the graph below constrained firms are those for which their CFOs say they are having difficulty borrowing, and unconstrained firms report they are not experiencing difficulty. As shown in the graph, authors document that financially constrained companies saw their interest rates increase in 2009 to 329 basis points above LIBOR, while the interest rate premium for unconstrained companies was only 141 basis points above LIBOR. At the same time, constrained companies saw the tenor (i.e., maturity) of their credit lines shrink from 28 months to only 22 months on average, while the tenor of credit lines for unconstrained companies remained relatively constant at nearly 30 months. This meant that financially constrained firms, the companies that most needed to borrow, would have to renegotiate with their banks or retire their credit lines eight months sooner than their unconstrained counterparts.

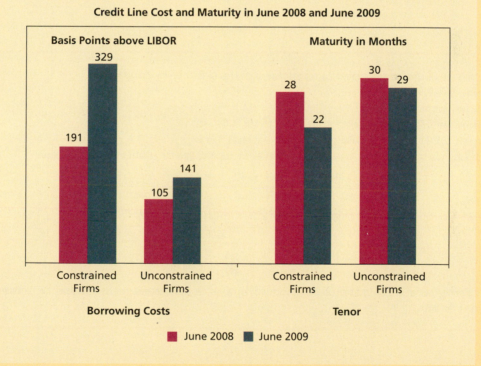

Credit Line Cost and Maturity in June 2008 and June 2009

Sources: Murillo Campello, Erasmo Giambona, John R. Graham, and Campbell R. Harvey, "Liquidity Management and Corporate Investment During a Financial Crisis," *Review of Financial Studies*, 24 (2011), pp. 1944–1979; and K. Llns, H. Servaes, and P. Tufano, "What Drives Corporate Liquidity? An International Survey of Cash Holdings and Lines of Credit," *Journal of Financial Economics*, 98 (2010), pp. 160–176.

requirements (minimum deposit balances that must be maintained by the borrower at the lending bank). These agreements may also be set up on a multiyear, revolving basis and may use current assets such as receivables or inventory as collateral. In any type of bank lending, most of the terms and conditions result from negotiations between the borrower and the bank.

line of credit
An up-front commitment by a bank to lend to a borrower in the future.

Lines of Credit A line of credit is an up-front commitment by a bank to lend to a borrower in the future. For example, a company may arrange to borrow up to $10,000,000 from a bank at any time during the next 30 months. The company must pay a commitment fee to establish this option to borrow, a fee that might cost one-quarter percent (e.g., $25,000 to establish a $10,000,000 credit line). When a firm borrows from the line, it must also pay interest on the amount borrowed, usually a variable interest rate of approximately 100 to 200 basis points (one to two percentage points) above LIBOR.

Credit lines are designed for temporary borrowing. A company experiencing slow collections one month may draw on the line to pay end-of-month payroll, rather than arrange a new, short-term loan. Or, a seasonal firm may draw on the credit line during its slow quarter, planning to pay back the borrowings plus interest the following quarter. Credit lines are also used as bridge financing for long-term investing. For example, a company may initially fund the purchase of a ten-year asset with a credit line, retiring the line quickly as longer term financing is finalized. More generally, credit lines are a fairly low-cost form of liquidity insurance, as an alternative to a company needing to accumulate large cash balances. Credit lines usually remain open for two to three years, assuming that the company does not violate a loan covenant before then.

effective borrowing rate (*EBR*)
Generally determined as the total amount of interest and fees paid, divided by the average usable loan amount.

The effective borrowing rate (*EBR*) on a bank line of credit is generally determined as the total amount of interest and fees paid, divided by the average usable loan amount. This rate is then adjusted for the actual number of days the loan is outstanding. A demonstration of this calculation follows.

EXAMPLE

We can determine the effective borrowing rate on a one-year line of credit with the following characteristics:

CL = credit line, $500,000 total
AL = average loan outstanding, $200,000
CF = commitment fee, 0.35% (35 basis points) on the *unused* portion of the line
IR = interest rate, 2.5% over LIBOR (assumed to be 5.75%), which equals 8.25%

If we use a 365-day year and assume that no compensating balances are required, then the calculations proceed as follows:

$$EBR = \frac{(IR \times AL) + [CF \times (CL - AL)]}{AL} \times \frac{365}{\text{Days loan is outstanding}}$$

$$= \frac{(0.0825 \times \$200,000) + [0.0035 \times (\$500,000 - \$200,000)]}{\$200,000} \times \frac{365}{365}$$

$$= \frac{\$16,500 + \$1,050}{\$200,000} \times \frac{365}{365} = \frac{\$17,550}{\$200,000} \times 1 = \underline{8.775\%}$$

The effective borrowing rate of 8.775% is about 50 basis points (0.50%) above the 8.25% interest rate as a result of the commitment fee paid on the unused portion of the line.

17-4 Concept Review Questions

12. What are the basic motives for holding cash and short-term investments? Why are *providing liquidity* and *preserving principal* the primary concerns in choosing short-term investments?

13. What securities are considered the benchmark for money market financial instruments, and why? What are some of the popular non-U.S. Treasury money market instruments?

14. What are the key base rates used in variable rate short-term borrowing, and how do they factor into the *all-in rate*? What other charges might be applicable to short-term borrowing? What effect do they have on the *effective borrowing rate (EBR)*?

Summary

- The cash manager's job is to manage cash flow related to collection, concentration, and disbursement of the company's funds. Float can be viewed from the perspective of either the receiving party or the paying party. Mail float and processing float are viewed the same from both perspectives. The third float component is availability float (to the receiving party) and the fourth is clearing float (to the paying party). The receiving party's goal is to minimize collection float, whereas the paying party's goal is to maximize disbursement float.

  > **Table of Important Equations**
  >
  > 1. Net benefit (cost) of lockbox
  > $$= (FVR \times r_a) - LC$$
  > 2. $$r_{discount} = \frac{d}{(1 - d)} \times \frac{365}{(CP - DP)}$$

- Cash managers are also responsible for identifying and quantifying financial relationships, forecasting cash flow, investing and borrowing, and information management. In large firms, they must manage the firm's cash position; in small firms, they set target cash balances based on transactions requirements and minimum balances set by their bank.

- In managing collections, the cash manager attempts to reduce collection float using various collection systems, which include field banking systems, mail-based systems, and electronic systems. Large firms whose customers are geographically dispersed commonly use lockbox systems, although small firms can also benefit from them.

- Firms use cash concentration to bring lockbox and other deposits together into one bank, often a concentration bank. Firms often use *automated clearinghouse (ACH) debit transfers* (also known as *electronic depository transfer [EDT]*) and *wire transfers* to transfer funds from the depository bank to the concentration bank.

- The objective of managing the firm's accounts payable is to pay accounts as slowly as possible without damaging the firm's credit rating and supplier relations. If a supplier offers a cash discount, the firm in need of short-term funds must determine the interest rate associated with *not* taking the discount (and paying at the end of the credit period) and then compare this rate with the firm's lowest-cost short-term borrowing alternative. If it can borrow elsewhere at a lower cost, the firm should take the discount and pay early; otherwise, it should not.

- Financial managers use such disbursement products and methods as zero-balance accounts (ZBAs), controlled disbursement, and positive pay. Some of the key developments in accounts payable and disbursements are integrated accounts payable, use of purchasing/procurement cards, imaging services, and a number of measures for preventing fraud.

- The cash manager will meet the firm's transactions, safety, and speculative motives by holding cash and short-term investments (often called *marketable securities*). The short-term investments allow the firm to earn a return on temporary cash balances. Investment policies and guidelines for management of short-term investments should be established.

- Small companies are likely to invest their short-term surpluses in money market mutual funds. Larger firms will invest in any of a variety of short-term, fixed-income securities; these include U.S Treasuries, federal agency issues, bank financial instruments, and corporate obligations such as commercial paper and adjustable-rate preferred stock. The yield on discount investments, such as T-bills and commercial paper, is typically approximated by calculating the money market yield (*MMY*) and converting it into a bond equivalent yield (*BEY*).

- Short-term borrowing can be obtained through the issuance of commercial paper, primarily by large firms, and through lines of credit. Most short-term borrowing occurs at a base rate—usually, the prime rate or LIBOR—plus a spread reflecting the borrower's relative riskiness. The effective borrowing rate (*EBR*) can be calculated to capture both the interest costs and other fees associated with a short-term loan.

Key Terms

accounts payable management, 530
adjustable-rate preferred stock, 536
all-in rate, 538
automated clearinghouse (ACH)
    debit transfer, 529
availability float, 523
bank account analysis statement, 524
bond equivalent yield (*BEY*), 538
cash concentration, 528
cash manager, 522
cash position management, 523
clearing float, 523
commercial paper, 536
controlled disbursement, 533
discount investment, 538

effective borrowing rate (*EBR*), 540
electronic bill presentment and
    payment (EBPP), 527
electronic depository transfer
    (EDT), 529
electronic invoice presentment and
    payment (EIPP), 527
field banking system, 526
float, 522
imaging services, 534
integrated accounts payable, 533
LIBOR, 538
line of credit, 540
liquidity management, 522
lockbox system, 527

mail float, 523
mail-based collection system, 526
money market mutual funds, 535
money market yield (*MMY*), 538
positive pay, 533
prime rate, 538
processing float, 523
purchasing (or procurement) card
    programs, 533
safety motive, 535
speculative motive, 535
target cash balance, 523
transactions motive, 535
wire transfer, 529
zero-balance accounts (ZBAs), 532

Self-Test Problems

Answers to Self-Test Problems and the Concept Review Questions throughout the chapter appear in CourseMate with Smart-Finance Tools at **www.cengagebrain.com**.

ST17-1. Gale Supply estimates that its customers' payments are in the mail for 3 days and, once received, are processed in 2 days. After the payments are deposited in the firm's bank, the bank makes the funds available to the firm in 2.5 days. The firm estimates its total annual collections from credit customers, received at a constant rate, to be $87 million. Its annual opportunity cost of funds is 9.5%. Assume a 365-day year.

    a.   How many days of *collection float* does Gale Supply have?

    b.   What is the current annual dollar cost of Gale Supply's collection float?

    c.   If the installation of an *electronic invoice presentment and payment (EIPP) system* would result in a 4-day reduction in Gale's collection float, how much could the firm earn annually on this float reduction?

    d.   Based on your findings in part (c), should Gale install the EIPP system if its annual cost is $85,000? Explain your recommendation.

ST17-2. Derson Manufacturing wishes to evaluate the credit terms offered by its four biggest suppliers of raw materials. The prime rate is currently 7.0%, and Derson can borrow short-term funds at a spread of 2.5% above the prime rate. Assume a 365-day year and that the firm always pays its suppliers on the last day allowed by their stated credit terms. The terms offered by each supplier are as follows:

Supplier 1: 2/10 net 40
Supplier 2: 1/15 net 60
Supplier 3: 3/10 net 70
Supplier 4: 1/10 net 50

    a.   Calculate the interest rate associated with not taking the discount from each supplier.

    b.   Assuming the firm needs short-term financing and considering each supplier separately, indicate whether the firm should take the discount from each supplier.

    c.   If the firm did not need any short-term financing, when should it pay each of the suppliers?

    d.   If the firm could not obtain a loan from banks and other financial institutions and needed short-term financing, when should it pay each of the suppliers?

    e.   Suppose that Derson could stretch its accounts payable to Supplier 1 (net period only) to 90 days without damaging its credit rating. What impact, if any, would this have on your recommendation with regard to Supplier 1 in part (b)? Explain you answer.

ST17-3. Rosa, Inc., has arranged a one-year, $2 million line of credit with its lead bank. The bank set the interest rate at the prime rate plus a spread of 1.50%. The prime rate is expected to remain stable at 5.25% during the coming year. In addition, the bank requires Rosa to pay a 0.50% commitment fee on the average unused portion of the line. Assume a 365-day year.

    a. Calculate the *effective borrowing rate (EBR)* on Rosa's line of credit during the coming year assuming the average loan balance outstanding during the year is $1.8 million.

    b. Calculate Rosa's *EBR* on the line of credit during the coming year assuming the average loan balance outstanding during the year is $0.8 million.

    c. Compare and contrast the *EBR*s calculated for Rosa, Inc., in parts (a) and (b). Explain the causes of the differences in *EBR*s.

Questions

Q17-1. What is *float*? What are its four basic components? Which of these components is the same from both a collection and a payment perspective? What is the difference between *availability float* and *clearing float*, and from which perspective—collection or payment—is each relevant?

Q17-2. What is *cash position management*? What types of firms set a *target cash balance*? Why? What is a bank's purpose in requiring the firm to maintain a minimum balance in its checking account? How does this relate to a *bank account analysis statement*?

Q17-3. What is the firm's goal with regard to cash collections? Describe each of the following types of collection systems:

    a. Field banking system

    b. Mail-based collection system

    c. Electronic system

Q17-4. What is a *lockbox system*? How does it typically work? Briefly describe the economics involved in performing a cost-benefit analysis of such a system.

Q17-5. Briefly describe the following funds transfer mechanisms:

    a. Automated clearinghouse (ACH) debit transfer

    b. Wire transfer

Why are wire transfers typically used only for high-dollar transfers?

Q17-6. What is the goal with regard to managing accounts payable as it relates to the *cash conversion cycle*? Briefly describe the process involved in managing the accounts payable function.

Q17-7. How can a firm in need of short-term financing decide whether or not to take a *cash discount* offered by its supplier? How would this decision change if the firm has no alternative source of short-term financing? How would it change for a firm that needs no additional short-term financing?

Q17-8. Briefly describe each of the following disbursement products/methods:

    a. Zero-balance accounts (ZBAs)

    b. Controlled disbursement

    c. Positive pay

How does a ZBA relate to the firm's *target cash balance*?

Q17-9. Briefly describe each of the following developments in accounts payable and disbursements:

    a. Integrated accounts payable

    b. Purchasing/procurement cards

    c. Imaging services

    d. Fraud prevention in disbursements

Q17-10. Briefly describe each of the three basic motives for a firm holding cash and short-term investments. For each of the motives indicate the general form in which the funds are typically held.

Q17-11. What is the firm's goal in short-term investing? How does it use *money market mutual funds*? Describe some of the popular money market financial instruments in each of the following groups:

    a. U.S. Treasuries

    b. Federal agency issues

c.   Bank financial instruments

d.   Corporate obligations

Q17-12. How is interest paid on a *discount investment*? What is the *money market yield (MMY)*? How can the *MMY* be converted into a *bond equivalent yield (BEY)*?

Q17-13. How are the rates on short-term borrowing typically set? What role does either the *prime rate* or *LIBOR* play in this process? What is the *effective borrowing rate (EBR)*? How does the *EBR* differ from the stated *all-in rate*?

Problems

Cash Management

P17-1. Nickolas Industries has daily cash receipts of $350,000. A recent analysis of the firm's collections indicated that customers' payments are in the mail an average of 2 days. Once received, the payments are processed in 1.5 days. After the payments are deposited, the receipts clear the banking system, on average, in 2.5 days. Assume a 365-day year.

a.   How much *collection float* (in days) does the firm have?

b.   If the firm's opportunity cost is 11%, would it be economically advisable for the firm to pay an annual fee of $84,000 for a lockbox system that reduces collection float by 2.5 days? Explain why or why not.

SMART solutions

See the Problem and solution explained step-by-step at **SMART** | finance

P17-2. NorthAm Trucking is a long-haul trucking company that serves customers all across the continental United States and parts of Canada and Mexico. At present, all billing activities—from preparation to collection—are handled by staff at corporate headquarters in Bloomington, Indiana. Payments are recorded and deposits are made once a day in the firm's bank, Hoosier National. You have been hired to recommend ways to reduce collection float and thereby generate cost savings.

a.   Suggest and explain at least three specific ways that NorthAm could reduce its *collection float*.

b.   Assume your preferred recommendation will cut the collection float by four days. NorthAm bills $108 million per year. If collections are evenly distributed throughout a 365-day year and if the firm's cost of short-term financing is 8%, what savings could be achieved by implementing the suggestion?

c.   Suppose the annual cost of implementing your recommendation is $100,000. In view of your answer to part (b), should NorthAm implement it?

Collections

P17-3. Qtime Products believes that using a lockbox system can shorten its accounts receivable collection period by four days. The firm's annual sales, all on credit, are $65 million and are billed on a continuous basis. The firm can earn 9% on its short-term investments. The cost of the lockbox system is $57,500 per year. Assume a 365-day year.

a.   What amount of cash will be made available for other uses under the lockbox system?

b.   What net benefit (or cost) will the firm receive if it adopts the lockbox system? Should it adopt the proposed lockbox system?

P17-4. Firm A has annual revenues of $1.6 billion and can reduce its float by four days using a lockbox system. Due to A's significant risk, A has a high cost of capital of 22%. Firm B has annual revenues of $850 million and can reduce its float by three days using a similar lockbox system. Firm B is less risky than Firm A, as evidenced by B's cost of capital of 10%. Assuming the lockbox system costs $2 million, which firm benefits more from using the system? If the two firms merge, making it necessary to have only one lockbox system for the combined firm, then how much is the net benefit of having the lockbox system under this circumstance?

P17-5. Quick Burger, Inc., a national chain of hamburger restaurants, has accumulated a $27,000 balance in one of its regional collection accounts. It wishes to make an efficient, cost-effective transfer of $25,000 of this balance to its corporate concentration account, thus leaving a $2,000 minimum balance in the regional collection account. It has the following options:

Option 1: Electronic depository transfer (EDT) at a cost of $2.50 and requiring one day to clear.

Option 2: Wire transfer at a cost of $12 and clearing the same day (zero days to clear).

a. If Quick Burger can earn 6% on its short-term investments, then which of the options would you recommend to minimize the transfer cost? (Assume a 365-day year.)

b. Compare Options 1 and 2, and determine the minimum amount that would have to be transferred in order for the wire transfer (Option 2) to be more cost-effective than the EDT (Option 1).

P17-6. Firm OPL has average daily cash inflows (Monday through Saturday) of $15,890, $13,267, $20,654, $24,956, $37,923, and $42,516, respectively. A wire transfer deposits money into a concentration account faster by one day if executed Monday through Thursday and by three days if executed Friday. Assuming that the additional cost of a wire transfer is $15.62 and that OPL has a cost of capital of 16% annually, on which days should wire transfers be considered? (*Note:* Saturday inflows should be combined with Monday inflows because banks close too early on Saturday to recognize the cash inflow.)

Accounts Payable and Disbursements

P17-7. Assume a 365-day year and that a firm receives the following credit terms from six suppliers.

Supplier 1: 2/10 net 50
Supplier 2: 1/10 net 30
Supplier 3: 2/10 net 150
Supplier 4: 3/10 net 60
Supplier 5: 1/10 net 45
Supplier 6: 1/20 net 80

a. Determine the interest rate associated with not taking the cash discount and instead paying at the end of the credit period for each of the six suppliers' credit terms.

b. In part (a), you calculated the interest rate associated with not taking the discount for each supplier's credit terms. Now you must decide whether or not to take the cash discount by paying within the discount period. To pay early, you will need to borrow from your firm's line of credit at the local bank. The interest rate on the line of credit is the prime rate plus 2.5%. You can get the most recent prime rate from the Federal Reserve at **www.federalreserve.gov/releases/ h15/update/**. For each supplier's terms, use the current prime rate to determine whether the firm should borrow from the bank or, in effect, borrow from the supplier.

P17-8. Access Enterprises is vetting four possible suppliers of an important raw material used in its production process, all offering different credit terms. The products offered by each supplier are virtually identical. The following table shows the credit terms offered by these suppliers. Assume a 365-day year.

Supplier	Credit Terms
A	1/10 net 40
B	2/20 net 90
C	1/20 net 60
D	3/10 net 75

a. Calculate the interest rate associated with not taking the discount from each supplier.

b. If the firm needs short-term funds (which are currently available from its commercial bank at 11%) and if each of the suppliers is viewed *separately*, then which, if any, of the suppliers' cash discounts should the firm *not* take? Explain why.

c. Suppose that the firm could stretch its accounts payable to supplier A (net period only) by twenty days. How would this affect your answer in part (b) concerning this supplier?

P17-9. Union Company is examining its operating cash management. One of the options the firm is considering is a *zero-balance account* (ZBA). The firm's bank is offering a ZBA with monthly charges of $1,500, and the bank estimates that the firm can expect to earn 8% on its short-term investments. Determine the minimum average cash balance that would make this ZBA a benefit to the firm. Assume a 365-day year.

Short-Term Investing and Borrowing

P17-10. Suppose Treasury bills (face value of $10,000) with maturities of thirty days, 90 days, and 180 days sell at the respective annualized discounts of 4.25%, 4.35%, and 4.92%. What are the respective *money market yields* for these T-bills? What are their respective *bond equivalent yields*?

P17-11. Sager Inc. just purchased a 91-day, $1 million T-bill that was selling at a discount of 3.25%.

a.   Calculate the dollar discount and purchase price on this T-bill.

b.   Find the *money market yield (MMY)* on this T-bill.

c.   Find the *bond equivalent yield (BEY)* on this T-bill.

d.   Rework parts (a), (b), and (c) assuming the T-bill was selling at a 3.0% discount. What effect does this drop of 25 basis points in the T-bill discount have on its *BEY*?

P17-12. Matthews Manufacturing is negotiating a one-year line of credit with its bank, Worldwide Bank. The amount of the credit line is $6.5 million with an interest rate set at 1.5% above the prime rate. A commitment fee of 0.50% (50 basis points) will be charged on the unused portion of the line. No compensating balances are required, and the loan is made on a 365-day basis.

a.   If the prime rate is assumed to be constant at 4.25% during the term of the loan and if Matthews's average loan outstanding during the year is $5.0 million, then calculate the firm's *effective borrowing rate (EBR)*.

b.   What effect would an increase in the prime rate to 4.75% for the entire year have on Matthews's *EBR* calculated in part (a)?

c.   What effect would a decrease in Matthews's average loan outstanding during the year to $4.0 million have on the *EBR* calculated in part (a)?

d.   Using your findings in parts (a), (b), and (c), discuss the effects on Matthews's *EBRs* of interest-rate changes versus changes in the average loan outstanding.

P17-13. Firm MGST is reviewing its one-year line of credit, currently with an interest rate of 9.15%. The credit line is for $1 million, but the firm intends to use only half of it throughout the year. The commitment fee is 42 basis points. Calculate MGST's *effective borrowing rate (EBR)*. MGST is considering lowering the credit line to $0.7 million. The commitment fee increases to 55 basis points, but the interest rate decreases to 9.00%. Should MGST lower the credit line based on *EBR*?

THOMSON REUTERS | Business School Edition

For instructions on using Thomson ONE, refer to the instructions provided with the Thomson ONE problems at the end of Chapters 1–6.

P17-14. Using the Statement of Cash Flows, analyze the short-term borrowing of Dell (Dell), Walmart (WMT), Honda (HMC), and Monster Worldwide (MWW). Which firms have increased and which have decreased their reliance on short-term borrowing relative to total assets? Can you explain why some of these firms might rely more or less on short-term borrowing relative to total assets?

P17-15. Using the common-size balance sheets, analyze the cash and short-term investments of Dell, Walmart, Honda, and Monster Worldwide. Which firms have increased and which firms have decreased their cash and short-term investments relative to total assets? Can you explain why some of these firms might need more or less cash relative to assets?

Since these exercises depend upon real-time data, your answers will change continuously depending upon when you access the Internet to download your data.

Smart Practices Video

Daniel Carter, Vice President of Finance, BevMo!

"Each of our stores makes deposits into a local account which are concentrated back into our corporate account."

SMART solutions

See the solution to Problem 17-1.
See the solution to Problem 17-11.

Mini-Case

Liquidity Management

Foah's Designs sells precious metal jewelry throughout the western half of the United States. It is based in Yakima, Washington, and currently all customers mail their payments to the Yakima office. The average amount of float is 6.5 days. The firm is considering implementing a lockbox system in Los Angeles. Total annual sales that are expected to be routed to the Los Angeles lockbox are $68,000,000, with an average check amount of $1,300. The lockbox system would be administered by California State Bank, which will charge a fee of $0.25 per check and an annual fixed charge of $10,000. Foah's Designs has a cost of capital of 12% per year, and the lockbox is expected to reduce float to 4 days. However, there is some chance that the lockbox will only reduce float to 5 days.

The firm must also decide between using EDT or wire transfers when transferring funds between California State Bank and its local bank, Yakima State Bank. Using the wire transfer method would cost $20 per transfer whereas the EDT method would cost only $1.50 per transfer. However, the wire transfer method would result in the funds arriving at Yakima State Bank one day sooner.

Foah's Designs is also faced with a decision concerning its accounts payable. Foah's purchases its inventory from Jewelry Findings, Inc., on credit. Jewelry Findings' terms of trade are 3/15 net 45, and Foah's Designs normally pays after exactly 45 days. However, it has been considering accessing a line of credit from Yakima State Bank to pay its accounts payable after exactly 15 days instead. The commitment fee on the unused portion of the credit line is 0.3%, and the interest rate on the loan from Yakima State Bank is 8.9%. There are no compensating balance requirements. Assume a 365-day year.

Assignment

1. Should Foah's Designs implement the lockbox system?

2. Suppose Foah's Designs plans to transfer money on a weekly basis (every Tuesday) from California State Bank to Yakima State Bank. Which transfer method should it use if the interest paid on its funds in Yakima State Bank is 0.5% higher than what they earn from California State Bank?

3. Assuming that Foah's Designs has a $2 million line of credit and that its accounts payable average $1,417,000, determine whether the firm should continuing paying Jewelry Findings, Inc., after 45 days or instead should begin accessing the line of credit from Yakima State Bank.

© Altus Plunkett/Flickr/Getty Images, Inc.

part 6 Special Topics

In the last three decades, no area of finance saw as much innovation or explosive growth as the topics covered in Part 6. In 1973, two economists provided a formula for pricing an exotic financial instrument called an option. Almost immediately, an options exchange opened, and in a few years the variety of options available, and their trading, exploded.

Over the same period, countries around the world began lowering trade barriers, resulting in a tremendous increase in exports and imports. Multinational corporations expanded their operations into foreign countries, which required them to face exposure to a new set of risks. Fortunately, options and other exotic securities provided just the tools that these corporations needed to manage the risks.

Chapter 18 deals with the unique financial issues that arise when firms do business in multiple currencies. The chapter starts with an explanation of how different countries establish an exchange rate policy, then illustrates how exchange rates are quoted and how they are linked across countries. The chapter also shows how inflation and interest rates affect exchange rates and how smart traders may find profit opportunities when markets are not in equilibrium.

Chapter 19 provides an introduction to options. We begin with a simple explanation of option contracts, how traders can use options to take risk or to reduce it, and how the price of an option depends on five key factors. Chapter 19 concludes with an introduction to the famous Black-Scholes option-pricing model.

A thriving entrepreneurial culture is one of the distinguishing features of the U.S. economy. In Chapter 20, we describe how entrepreneurs raise capital to finance their growing enterprises. The chapter describes how venture capital partnerships are structured, how they raise money to invest in new companies, and how they work with entrepreneurs to achieve success. The chapter concludes with a look at venture capital markets outside the United States.

Chapter 21 covers one of the most exciting areas of finance—mergers and acquisitions. Historically, mergers have come in waves, with some years seeing a huge volume and others experiencing very few. In the United States, mergers and acquisitions are simply part of the economic landscape—managers know that a merger is one strategic choice open to them, and that they must make choices that increase shareholder wealth. In this chapter, we also study some of the motivations for mergers and the tactics that firms use to buy other firms or defend against unwanted bids.

549

chapter 18

International Financial Management

What Companies Do

Which Yuan is Good for Business?

For many years, China controlled the value of its currency (the yuan) by imposing strict controls on how the yuan could be traded. On June 19, 2010, The People's Bank of China (PBOC) announced that it would relax some of these controls to allow more movement in the value of yuan against foreign currencies. As a result, the yuan rose against the U.S. dollar throughout the second half of 2010. In June, one yuan was worth about $0.1464, but by the end of the year the yuan's value had appreciated to $0.1515, a gain of roughly 3.5%.

Other signs that China was loosening its grip on the yuan gradually emerged. In August, McDonald's became the first nonfinancial international corporation to sell bonds denominated in yuan, and in January 2011, the Bank of China opened trading in yuan to U.S. customers through its branches in New York and Los Angeles.

Is a rising yuan good for business? Increases in the yuan's value would make goods imported from China more expensive, but it would also make U.S. exports more attractive to Chinese consumers. Fluctuations in the yuan could also create a risk for companies doing business in China.

Sources: www.efinancialnews.com/story/2011-01-12/yuan-trading-us; www.businessweek.com/news/2010 -09-06/deripaska-follows-mcdonald-s-to-yuan-bond-market-russia-credit.html

Learning Objectives

After studying this chapter you should be able to:

- Describe the difference between fixed and floating exchange rates, and interpret exchange rate quotes taken from the Web or financial newspapers;

- Explain how the four parity relationships in international finance tie together forward and spot exchange rates, interest rates, and inflation rates in different countries;

- List the types of risks that multinational corporations face when they conduct business in different countries and currencies; and

- Revise the *NPV* decision rule for capital budgeting analysis to incorporate the added complexity that arises when an investment is undertaken in a foreign currency.

Walk down the aisle of a grocery store, visit a shopping mall, go hunting for a new automobile, or check the outstanding balance of your credit card. In each of these activities, chances are that you will be dealing with products and services provided by **multinational corporations (MNCs)**, businesses that operate in many countries around the world. In recent decades, international trade in goods and services has expanded dramatically, and so too have the size and scope of MNCs. Although all the financial principles covered in this text thus far apply to MNCs, companies operating across national borders also face unique challenges. Primary among them is coping with exchange rate risk. An **exchange rate** is simply the price of one currency in terms of another, and for the past 30 years, the exchange rates of most of the world's major currencies have fluctuated daily. These movements create uncertainty for firms that earn revenues and pay operating costs in more than one currency. Currency movements also add to the pressures faced by wholly domestic companies that face competition from foreign firms.

This chapter focuses on the problems and opportunities firms face as a result of globalization, with special emphasis on currency-related issues. First, we explain the rudimentary features of currency markets, including how and why currencies trade and the rules governments impose on trading in their currencies. Second, we describe factors that drive currency values, at least for those countries that allow their currencies to float in response to market forces. Third, we discuss the special risks faced by MNCs and the strategies they employ to manage those risks. We conclude by illustrating how operating across national borders affects capital budgeting analysis.

18-1 Exchange Rate Fundamentals

multinational corporations (MNCs)
Businesses that operate in many different countries.

exchange rate
The price of one currency in terms of another currency.

floating exchange rate
An exchange rate system in which a currency's value is allowed to fluctuate in response to market forces.

fixed exchange rate
An exchange rate system in which the price of one currency is fixed relative to another currency by government authorities.

managed floating rate system
A hybrid currency system in which a government loosely fixes the value of the national currency relative to one or more other currencies.

We begin our coverage of exchange rate fundamentals by describing the "rules of the game" as dictated by national governments.

18-1a Fixed Versus Floating Exchange Rates

Since the mid-1970s, most of the world's major currencies have had a **floating exchange rate** relationship with respect to the U.S. dollar and to one another, which means that forces of supply and demand continuously move currency values up and down (the yuan being a major exception). The opposite of a floating exchange rate regime is a **fixed exchange rate** system. Under a fixed-rate system, governments fix (or *peg*) their currency's value, usually in terms of another currency such as the U.S. dollar. Once a government pegs the currency at a particular value, it must stand ready to pursue economic and financial policies necessary to maintain that value. For example, if demand for the currency increases, the government must be ready to sell currency so that the increase in demand does not cause the currency to appreciate. If demand for the currency falls, the government must buy its own currency to prevent the currency from depreciating. In many countries with fixed exchange rates, governments impose restrictions on the free flow of currencies into and out of the country. Even so, maintaining a currency peg can be quite difficult. For example, in response to mounting economic problems, the government of Argentina allowed the peso, which had been linked to the U.S. dollar, to float freely for the first time in a decade on January 11, 2002. After one day, the peso lost more than 40% of its value relative to the dollar.

Some countries have adopted hybrid currency systems in which the currency is neither pegged nor allowed to float freely. A **managed floating rate system** is a hybrid in which a nation's government loosely "fixes" the value of the national currency in relation to that of another currency, but does not expend the effort and resources

currency board arrangement
An exchange rate system in which each unit of the domestic currency is backed by a unit of some foreign currency.

that would be required to maintain a completely fixed exchange rate regime. Other countries simply choose to use another nation's currency as their own, and a handful of nations have adopted a currency board arrangement. In such an arrangement, the national currency continues to circulate, but every unit of the currency is fully backed by government holdings of another currency—usually the U.S. dollar.

The International Monetary Fund, in its *International Financial Statistics,* details the exchange rate systems in place for 186 countries. In January 2011, 32 countries had independently floating exchange rates, 36 had conventional fixed exchange rates, 36 had managed floats, 42 used another currency as their country's legal tender (including the 18 countries using the euro as their official currency), 9 maintained currency boards, and 31 maintained some other type of hybrid system. In terms of trading volume, the major currencies in international finance today are (in no particular order) the British pound sterling (£), the Swiss franc (SF), the Japanese yen (¥), the Canadian dollar (C$), the U.S. dollar (US$, or simply $), and the euro (€).

18-1b Exchange Rate Quotes

direct quote
An exchange rate quoted in terms of units of domestic currency per unit of foreign currency.

depreciate
A currency depreciates when it buys less of another currency than it did previously.

Figure 18.1 shows exchange rate values quoted in *The Wall Street Journal* for Thursday, February 10, 2011. Note that the figure states each exchange rate in two ways. The second and third columns show how much one unit of each foreign currency is worth in terms of U.S. dollars. This type of quote is called a direct quote, which is simply the dollar cost of one unit of foreign currency. At the top of the figure, for example, we see that one Argentine peso cost $0.2489. On the previous day, *The Wall Street Journal* reported that one peso cost $0.2492. Because the value of one peso in terms of U.S. currency fell slightly from Wednesday to Thursday, we say that the peso depreciated against the dollar.

indirect quote
An exchange rate quoted in terms of foreign currency per unit of domestic currency.

appreciate
A currency appreciates when it buys more of another currency than it did previously.

The last two columns of Figure 18.1 present the same information in a slightly different way. These columns show the value of each foreign currency relative to one U.S. dollar. That is, the numbers show how many units of a foreign currency you can buy with $1. This way of stating exchange rates is called an indirect quote. Again, in the first row we see that on Thursday, February 10, it cost 4.0177 pesos to purchase one dollar. On the previous day, one dollar was worth 4.0128 pesos. Because the value of one dollar in terms of pesos rose from Wednesday to Thursday, we say that the dollar appreciated against the peso. Of course, the exchange rate quotes in the second and third columns reveal exactly the same information as the quotes in the last two columns. Each of these methods of quoting exchange rates is simply the reciprocal of the other:

$$\frac{\text{dollars}}{\text{pesos}} = \frac{1}{\text{pesos/dollars}} \qquad 0.2489 = \frac{1}{4.0177}$$

Figure 18.1

Exchange Rates: New York Closing Snapshot for Thursday

Country/currency	US$ equiv Thursday	US$ equiv Wednesday	US$ vs. 1-day % chg	US$ vs. YTD % chg	Currency per US$ Thursday	Currency per US$ Wednesday
U.S.-dollar foreign-exchange rates in late New York trading						
Americas						
Argentina peso*	0.2489	0.2492	0.12	1.2	4.0177	4.0128
Brazil real	0.5993	0.6026	0.55	0.5	1.6686	1.6595
Canada dollar	1.0042	1.0062	0.2	−0.2	0.9958	0.9938
1-mos forward	1.0037	1.0057	0.2	−0.2	0.9963	0.9943
3-mos forward	1.0022	1.0043	0.21	−0.2	0.9978	0.9957
6-mos forward	0.9998	1.0018	0.2	−0.2	1.0002	0.9982
Chile peso	0.002111	0.002099	−0.57	1.2	473.71	476.42
Colombia peso	0.0005314	0.0005299	−0.28	−2	1881.82	1887.15
Ecuador US dollar	1	1	unch	unch	1	1
Mexico peso*	0.0828	0.0829	0.11	−2.1	12.0817	12.0685
Peru new sol	0.3615	0.3612	−0.08	−1.4	2.7663	2.7685

Continued

Figure 18.1 (*Continued*)

Country/currency	US$ equiv Thursday	US$ equiv Wednesday	US$ vs. 1-day % chg	US$ vs. YTD % chg	Currency per US$ Thursday	Currency per US$ Wednesday
Uruguay peso†	0.0512	0.05090	−0.59	−1.8	19.53	19.65
Venezuela b. fuerte	0.23285056	0.23285056	unch	unch	4.2946	4.2946
Asia-Pacific						
Australian dollar	1.0046	1.0117	0.71	1.7	0.9954	0.9884
China yuan	0.1518	0.1517	−0.09	−0.1	6.5869	6.5927
Hong Kong dollar	0.1284	0.1284	unch	0.2	7.7904	7.7867
India rupee	0.0219	0.02197	0.32	2.1	45.6621	45.5166
Indonesia rupiah	0.000112	0.000112	unch	−0.9	8929	8929
Japan yen	0.012007	0.01214	1.11	2.5	83.28	82.37
1-mos forward	0.01201	0.01214	1.1	2.6	83.26	82.36
3-mos forward	0.012017	0.01215	1.1	2.6	83.22	82.31
6-mos forward	0.01203	0.01216	1.1	2.6	83.13	82.22
Malaysia ringgit§	0.3284	0.3291	0.21	−1.2	3.0451	3.0386
New Zealand dollar	0.7634	0.7721	1.13	2	1.3099	1.2952
Pakistan rupee	0.01177	0.01176	−0.08	−0.8	84.962	85.034
Philippines peso	0.0229	0.023	unch	−0.1	43.592	43.573
Singapore dollar	0.7819	0.7845	0.33	−0.3	1.2789	1.2747
South Korea won	0.0008937	0.0009004	0.75	−0.2	1118.94	1110.62
Taiwan dollar	0.03454	0.03469	0.43	−0.8	28.952	28.827
Thailand baht	0.03246	0.03256	0.31	2.5	30.807	30.713
Vietnam dong	0.00005	0.00005	unch	unch	19490	19498
Europe						
Czech Rep. koruna**	0.05605	0.05667	1.11	−4.7	17.841	17.646
Denmark krone	0.1823	0.1842	1.04	−1.6	5.4855	5.4289
Euro area euro	1.3594	1.3734	1.03	−1.6	0.7356	0.7281
Hungary forint	0.00498	0.005052	1.45	−3.5	200.8	197.94
Norway krone	0.1713	0.1738	1.46	0.2	5.8377	5.7537
Poland zloty	0.3462	0.3513	1.47	−2.6	2.8885	2.8466
Romania leu	0.3189	0.3226	1.18	−1.1	3.1361	3.0994
Russia ruble‡	0.03406	0.03419	0.38	−4	29.36	29.248
Sweden krona	0.1544	0.1554	0.65	−3.6	6.4767	6.435
Switzerland franc	1.0312	1.0441	1.24	3.8	0.9697	0.9578
1-mos forward	1.0315	1.044	1.24	3.8	0.9695	0.9576
3-mos forward	1.0321	1.0449	1.24	3.8	0.9689	0.957
6-mos forward	1.033	1.0458	1.24	3.9	0.9681	0.9562
Turkey lira**	0.6289	0.6287	unch	3.1	1.5901	1.5907
UK pound	1.6092	1.6104	0.06	−3.1	0.6214	0.621
1-mos forward	1.6089	1.61	0.06	−3.1	0.6215	0.6211
3-mos forward	1.6077	1.6089	0.08	−3.1	0.622	0.6215
6-mos forward	1.6053	1.6063	0.06	−3	0.6229	0.6225
Middle East/Africa						
Bahrain dinar	2.6526	2.6525	unch	unch	0.377	0.377
Egypt pound*	0.17	0.17	unch	1.3	5.882	5.8813
Israel shekel	0.2718	0.2723	0.19	4.4	3.6792	3.6724
Jordan dinar	1.4119	1.4119	unch	unch	0.7083	0.7083
Kenya shilling	0.01232	0.01231	−0.06	0.6	81.2	81.25
Kuwait dinar	3.5705	3.5702	unch	−0.5	0.2801	0.2801
Lebanon pound	0.0006664	0.000666	−0.06	unch	1500.6	1501.5
Saudi Arabia riyal	0.2666	0.2667	unch	unch	3.7509	3.7495
South Africa rand	0.1374	0.1384	0.73	9.8	7.278	7.2254
UAE dirham	0.2723	0.2723	unch	unch	3.6724	3.6724
SDR††	1.5616	1.5616	unch	−1.4	0.6404	0.6404

*Floating rate †Financial §Government rate and ‡Russian Central Bank rate

**Commercial rate †† Special Drawing Rights (SDR); from the International Monetary Fund; based on exchange rates for U.S., British and Japanese currencies.

Note: Based on trading among banks of $1 million and more, as quoted at 4 p.m. ET by Reuters.

Source: *Wall Street Journal*, February 11, 2011. Reprinted with permission of *Wall Street Journal*, Copyright © 2011 Dow Jones & Company, Inc. All Rights Reserved Worldwide.

FINANCING
Dental/Medical
BILLS

Finance in Your Life

Pilgrimage to Mata Mata

As a devoted Lord of the Rings fan, you decide to make a trip to New Zealand to visit Mata Mata, the site of Hobbitown from The Fellowship of the Ring. After you pay for your airfare, you plan to spend $5,000 U.S. dollars on hotels, food, transportation around New Zealand, and souvenirs. At the time you put together your budget, one New Zealand dollar was worth about $0.76, so you can spend $5,000/0.76 = NZ$6,579 during your stay. However, by the time you actually travel to New Zealand, the exchange rate has moved up to $0.81/NZ$, so if you stay true to your budget to spend no more than $5,000, you have just NZ$6,173 to spend on your trip.

spot exchange rate
The exchange rate that applies to immediate currency transactions.

forward exchange rate
The exchange rate quoted for a transaction that will occur on a future date.

Notice that for a few countries, Figure 18.1 lists several different exchange rates rather than just one. For each currency, the first exchange rate listed is the spot exchange rate. The spot exchange rate is just another word for the current exchange rate. That is, if you are going to trade currencies right now, the relevant exchange rate is the spot exchange rate. In many currencies, it is possible to enter a contract today to trade foreign currency at a fixed price at some future date. The price at which that future trade will take place is called the forward exchange rate. For example, a U.S. trader wishing to exchange dollars for British pounds could do so on Thursday, February 10, at the spot exchange rate of $1.6092/£ (or equivalently, £0.6214/$). Alternatively, that trader could enter into an agreement to trade dollars for pounds one month later at the forward rate of $1.6089/£ (or equivalently, £0.6215/$). If the trader chooses to transact through a forward contract, no cash changes hands until the date specified by the contract. Though the figure only quotes forward contracts at maturities of one, three, and six months, a much richer set of forward contracts is available in the foreign exchange market.

Just as we compared movements in the spot exchange rate from one day to the next, we can also examine differences in the spot exchange rate for current transactions and the forward rate for future transactions. For example, look at the rate quotes for Japanese yen. On the spot market, one yen costs $0.012007, but the exchange rate for trades that will take place six months later is $0.012030/¥. One yen buys more dollars on the forward market than on the spot market. When one currency buys more of another on the forward market than it does on the spot market, traders say that the first currency trades at a forward premium. The forward premium is usually expressed as a percentage relative to the spot rate, so for the yen, we can calculate the six-month forward premium as follows:

forward premium
When one currency buys more of another on the forward market than it buys on the spot market.

$$\frac{F - S}{S} = \frac{\$0.012030/¥ - \$0.012007/¥}{\$0.012007/¥} = 0.0019 = 0.19\%$$

where F is the symbol for the forward rate and S stands for the spot rate, both quoted in terms of $/¥. This calculation means that one yen buys 0.19% more dollars on the six-month forward market than it buys on the spot market. Recognizing that the yen's 0.19% forward premium refers to a six-month contract, we could restate the premium in annual terms by multiplying the premium times 2, which would yield an annualized forward premium of 0.38%.

forward discount
When one currency buys less of another on the forward market than it buys on the spot market.

If the yen trades at a forward premium relative to the dollar, then the dollar must trade at a forward discount relative to the yen, meaning that one dollar buys fewer yen on the forward market than it does on the spot market. To calculate the forward discount on the dollar, we use the same equation as above, but we express the exchange rate in terms of yen per dollar:

$$\frac{F - S}{S} = \frac{¥83.13/\$ - ¥83.28/\$}{¥83.28/\$} = -0.0018 = -0.18\%$$

The dollar trades at a −0.18% forward discount for a six-month contract, or about −0.36% per year. In other words, the forward discount on the dollar is opposite in sign and similar in magnitude to the forward premium on the yen, though the discount is always smaller in absolute value than the premium. In general, to calculate the annualized forward premium or discount on a currency, based on a forward contract to be executed in N days, use the following equation:

(Eq. 18.1)
$$\frac{F - S}{S} \times \frac{360}{N}$$

EXAMPLE

Using the exchange rate quotes in Figure 18.1, we can calculate the annualized forward discount (or premium) on the Swiss franc (SF) relative to the dollar. We will calculate this based on the rate for a three-month forward contract. The spot rate equals \$1.0312/SF, and the three-month (or 90-day) forward rate equals \$1.0321/SF. Notice that the franc buys more dollars on the forward market than it does on the spot market, so it trades at a forward premium. We can determine the annualized premium as follows, given that we are using a 90-day contract:

$$\frac{\$1.0321/SF - \$1.0312/SF}{\$1.0312/SF} \times \frac{360}{90} = 0.0035 = 0.35\%$$

The forward discount or premium gives traders information about more than just the price of exchanging currencies at different points in time. The forward premium is tightly linked to differences in interest rates on short-term, low-risk bonds across countries. We explore that relationship in depth in the next section.

One last lesson remains to be gleaned from Figure 18.1. In its daily exchange rate table, *The Wall Street Journal* quotes the value of the world's major currencies relative to the U.S. dollar. But what if someone wants to know the exchange rate between British pounds and Canadian dollars? In fact, all the information needed to calculate this exchange rate appears in the figure. We simply need to calculate a **cross exchange rate** by dividing the dollar exchange rate for one currency by the dollar exchange rate for the other currency. For example, using Thursday's spot rates, we can determine the £/C\$ exchange rate:

cross exchange rate
An exchange rate between two currencies calculated by taking the ratio of the exchange rate of each currency, expressed in terms of a third currency.

$$\frac{\$1.6092/£}{\$1.0042/C\$} = C\$1.6025/£$$

triangular arbitrage
A trading strategy in which traders buy a currency in a country where the value of that currency is too low and immediately sell the currency in another country where the currency value is too high.

How can we be sure that one pound buys 1.6025 Canadian dollars simply by taking this ratio? The answer is that if the exchange rate between pounds and Canadian dollars was any other number, then currency traders could engage in **triangular arbitrage**, trading currencies simultaneously in different markets to earn a risk-free profit. Because currency markets operate virtually 24 hours per day, and because currency trades take place with lightning speed and with very low transactions costs, arbitrage maintains actual currency values in different markets relatively close to this theoretical ideal.

EXAMPLE

Suppose that on Thursday, February 10, 2011, a trader learns that the exchange rate offered by a London bank is C\$1.6100/£ rather than C\$1.6025/£ as calculated previously. What is the arbitrage opportunity? First, note that the figure C\$1.6100/£ is "too high" relative to the theoretically correct rate. This means that in London, one pound costs too much in terms of Canadian dollars. In other words, the pound is overvalued, and the Canadian dollar is undervalued. Therefore, a trader could make a profit by executing the following steps.

1. Convert U.S. dollars to British pounds in New York at the prevailing spot rate as given in Figure 18.1. Assume that the trader starts with \$1 million, which will convert to £621,427 (\$1,000,000 ÷ \$1.6092/£).

2. Simultaneously, the trader sells £621,427 in London (because pounds are overvalued there) at the exchange rate of C\$1.6100/£. The trader will then have C\$1,000,497.

3. Convert the Canadian dollars back into U.S. currency in New York. Given the spot rate of \$1.0042/C\$ in Figure 18.1, the trader will receive \$1,004,700 (C\$1,000,497 × \$1.0042/C\$).

After making these trades, all of which can occur with the touch of a keystroke, the trader winds up \$4,700 richer, all without taking risk. As long as the exchange rates do not change, the trader could keep making a profit over and over again.

Figure 18.2   **Triangular Arbitrage**

The exchange rates in New York imply that one British pound should buy 1.6025 Canadian dollars. If a bank in London offers to sell C$1.6100 for one pound, then traders can make an instant profit by selling dollars for pounds in New York, converting those to Canadian dollars in London, and then selling the Canadian dollars for U.S. dollars back in New York. The effect of these trades in New York will be to raise the dollar-pound exchange rate above 1.6092 and to push the exchange rate between U.S. and Canadian dollars below 1.0042. In London, the value of the pound will fall below C$1.6100

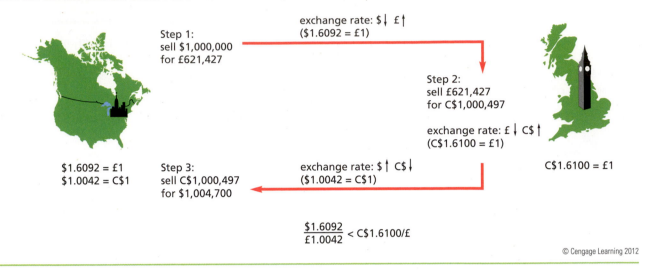

© Cengage Learning 2012

The preceding example shows that a trader could repeatedly make a profit if the exchange rates do not change. Of course exchange rates do change, and they change in a way that brings the market back into equilibrium. Figure 18.2 illustrates what happens as arbitrage takes place. As traders in New York sell U.S. currency in exchange for pounds, the pound appreciates vis-à-vis the U.S. dollar, and the exchange rate will rise from $1.6092/£ to some new, higher level. Likewise, as traders in London sell pounds in exchange for Canadian dollars, the pound will depreciate against the Canadian currency, and the exchange rate will fall below C$1.6100/£ to a lower level. Finally, as traders reap profits in New York by selling Canadian and buying U.S. currency, the exchange rate between Canadian and U.S. dollars will fall from $1.0042/C$. Though we cannot say exactly how much each of these exchange rates will move, we can say that, collectively, they will move enough to reach a new equilibrium in which the cross exchange rate in New York and the exchange rate quoted in London will be virtually identical.

With this basic understanding of foreign exchange rates in place, let us now turn to some important institutional features of the foreign exchange market.

18-1c The Foreign Exchange Market

The foreign exchange (forex) "market" is not actually a physical exchange but a global telecommunications market. In fact, it is the world's largest financial market, with total volume of more than $4 trillion *per day!* The forex market operates continuously during the business week, with trading beginning each calendar day in Tokyo. As the day evolves, trading moves westward as major dealing centers in Singapore, Bahrain (Persian Gulf), continental Europe, London, and finally North America (particularly New York and Toronto) come on-line. Prices for all the floating currencies are set by global supply and demand. Trading in fixed-rate currencies is more constrained and regulated and frequently involves a national government (or a state-owned bank) as counterparty on one side of the trade.

The players in the forex market are numerous, as are their motivations for participating in the market. We can break market participants into six distinct (but not mutually exclusive) groups: (1) exporters and importers, (2) investors, (3) hedgers, (4) speculators, (5) dealers, and at times, (6) governments.

Businesses that export goods to or import goods from a foreign country need to enter the foreign exchange market to pay bills denominated in foreign currency or to convert foreign currency revenues back into the domestic currency. Along with all the other players in the market, exporters and importers influence currency values. For instance, if Europeans develop a taste for California wines, then European importers will exchange euros (or perhaps pounds, kroner, francs, etc.) for dollars to purchase wine. Other factors held constant, these trades would tend to put upward pressure on the value of the dollar and downward pressure on European currencies.

Investors also trade foreign currency when they seek to buy and sell financial assets in foreign countries. For example, when foreign investors want to buy U.S. stocks or bonds, they must first sell their home currencies and buy dollars. Buying pressure from investors causes the dollar to appreciate against foreign currencies. In general, the pressures exerted on currencies by investors are much larger than those exerted by exporters and importers because investors account for a larger fraction of currency trading volume. For example, the total value of goods and services traded internationally each year is about $16 trillion, which is equivalent to about four days' worth of global currency trading.

EXAMPLE

In January 2011, the central bank of Peru announced that it would raise a benchmark interest rate by 0.25%. Other things being equal, higher interest rates tend to put upward pressure on a country's exchange rates due to capital inflows from foreign investors. On the same day that Peru announced the rate hike, Peru's currency, the sol, reached a 33-month high.

hedging
Trading an asset for the sole purpose of reducing or eliminating the risk associated with some other asset.

Sometimes traders in the foreign exchange market buy and sell currency to offset other risks to which they are exposed during the normal course of business. **Hedging** refers to the practice of trading an asset for the sole purpose of reducing or eliminating the risk associated with some other asset. For example, suppose that a U.S. firm expects to receive a £1,000,000 payment from a customer in the United Kingdom. The payment is due in 90 days. This receivable is risky from the U.S. firm's perspective because the exchange rate between dollars and pounds may fluctuate over the next 90 days. To hedge the risk of its pound-denominated receivable, the U.S. firm might enter a forward contract to sell pounds for dollars in 90 days. By doing so, the firm essentially locks in a dollar value for the £1,000,000 payment.

Hedgers influence currency values when they take positions to offset the risks of their existing exposures to certain currencies. In contrast, speculators take positions to make a profit. Speculators sell a currency if they expect it to depreciate, and they buy if they expect it to appreciate. Some speculators, such as George Soros, have become famous for the enormous profits (or losses) they have earned by taking large positions in certain currencies. When external pressures force a country with a pegged currency to devalue its currency, speculators often take the blame. Whether they deserve blame for causing, accelerating, or exacerbating currency crises or not, speculators can play a useful economic role by taking the opposite side of a transaction from that of hedgers. Speculators help make the foreign currency market more liquid and more efficient.

As in all financial markets, dealers play a crucial role in the foreign exchange business. Most foreign currency trades go through large, international banks in the leading financial centers around the globe. These banks provide a means for buyers and sellers to come together, and as their reward they earn a small fee, the bid-ask spread, on each transaction they facilitate. The ask price is the price at which a currency dealer is willing to sell foreign currency, and the bid price is the price at which the dealer is willing to buy currency. Because the ask price is slightly higher than the bid (hence the term, bid-ask spread), dealers make a small profit each time they buy or sell currency.

Finally, governments intervene in financial markets to put upward or downward pressure on currencies as circumstances dictate. Governments that attempt to maintain a fixed exchange rate must generally intervene more frequently than those that intervene only in times of crisis. As this chapter's Opening Focus illustrates, currency movements create winners and losers, not only across national boundaries but also within a given country. For example, a rise in the value of the U.S. dollar makes U.S. exports more expensive and foreign imports cheaper. Remember, an exchange rate is simply a price, the price of trading one currency for another. Though the financial press dramatizes changes in exchange rates by attaching adjectives such as *strong* or *weak* to a given currency, this practice is rather odd when you recognize that they are just talking about a price. For instance, if the price of apples rises and the price of bananas falls, we do not refer to apples as being strong and bananas as being weak! If the price of apples is high, that is good for apple producers and bad for apple consumers. In the same way, a rise in the value of a particular currency benefits some and harms others. Therefore, at least for the major, free-floating currencies, governments are reluctant to intervene because doing so does not unambiguously improve welfare across the board.

Even when governments want to intervene in currency markets, intervention is complicated by the fact that currency values are not set in a vacuum but are linked to other economic variables such as interest rates and inflation. In the next section, we discuss four parity relationships that illustrate the linkages that should hold in equilibrium between exchange rates and other macroeconomic variables.

18-1 Concept Review Questions

1. Explain how a rise in the euro might affect a French company exporting wine to the United States, and compare that with the impact on a German firm importing semiconductors from the United States.

2. Holding all other factors constant, how might an increase in interest rates in Britain affect the value of the pound?

3. If someone says, "The exchange rate between dollars and pounds increased today," can you know with certainty which currency appreciated and which depreciated? Why or why not?

4. Define spot and forward exchange rates. If a trader expects to buy a foreign currency in one month, can you explain why the trader might prefer to enter into a forward contract today rather than simply wait a month and transact at the spot rate prevailing then?

18-2 The Parity Conditions in International Finance

In this section, we discuss the major forces that influence the values of all the world's free-floating currencies. Theory suggests that when markets are in equilibrium, spot and forward exchange rates, interest rates, and inflation rates should be linked across countries. Market imperfections, such as trade barriers and transactions costs, may prevent these parity conditions from holding precisely at all times, but they are still powerful determinants of exchange rate values in the long run.

18-2a Forward-Spot Parity

If the spot rate governs foreign exchange transactions in the present and the forward rate equals the price of trading currencies at some point in the future, intuition suggests that the forward rate might be useful in predicting how the spot rate will change over time. For example, suppose that a British firm intends to import U.S. wheat, for which it must pay $1.5 million in one month. Imagine that the pound currently trades at a forward premium, and the prevailing spot and forward exchange rates are as follows:

$$\text{Spot} = \$1.40/£ \qquad \text{1-month forward} = \$1.50/£$$

The UK firm faces a choice. Either it can lock in the forward rate today, guaranteeing that it will pay £1 million for its wheat ($1.5 million ÷ $1.50/£), or it can wait a month and transact at the spot rate prevailing then. Let us suppose that the UK firm in this example does not care about exchange rate risk per se, so it will enter the forward contract only if it believes that trading at the forward rate will be less expensive than trading at the spot rate in 30 days.[1]

This results in a simple decision rule for the UK importer. First, it must form a forecast of what the spot exchange rate will be in one month. Let's call that the expected spot rate and denote it with the symbol $E(Spot)$. We can now determine the UK firm's decision rule:

1. Enter the forward contract today if $E(Spot) < \$1.50/£$.
2. Wait and buy dollars at the spot rate if $E(Spot) > \$1.50/£$.

For example, assume that the firm's forecast is that the spot rate will not change from its current level of $1.40/£. Given this forecast, the expected cost of purchasing $1.5 million in 30 days is £1,071,429 ($1.5 million ÷ $1.40/£); and given that the firm will need only £1 million if it locks in the forward rate, it does not pay to wait. Conversely, assume that the UK firm believes that over the next 30 days, the pound will appreciate to $1.60/£. In that case, the expected cost of paying for the wheat is just £937,500 ($1.5 million ÷ $1.60/£), and the firm should wait. Only if the firm's forecast of the expected spot rate is $1.50/£, equal to the current forward rate, will it be indifferent to whether it locks in the forward contract now or waits 30 days to transact.

If we look at this problem from the perspective of a U.S. firm that must pay in pounds in 30 days to import some product from the United Kingdom, we get just the opposite decision rule. For the U.S. firm, entering a forward contract to buy pounds makes sense if the expected spot rate in 30 days is greater than the current forward rate ($E(Spot) > \$1.50/£$). Appreciation in the pound increases the cost of importing from Britain, so if a U.S. firm expects the pound to appreciate above the current forward rate, it will lock in a forward contract immediately. On the other hand, if the U.S. firm expects the spot rate to be less than $1.50/£ in 30 days, it will choose to wait rather than lock in at the forward rate.

Now we broaden the example to include all U.S. and UK firms that face a future need to buy foreign currency. Ideally, U.S. firms that need to buy pounds to import British goods could trade with UK firms that must sell pounds and buy dollars to import U.S. goods. However, there is a problem because the circumstances under which firms in each country prefer to trade in the spot market rather than the forward market are mirror images of each other:

1. If $E(Spot) > Forward$, the UK firms do not want the forward contract, but U.S. firms do.
2. If $E(Spot) < Forward$, the UK firms want the forward contract, but U.S. firms do not.

Equilibrium will occur in this market only when the forecast of the spot rate is equal to the current forward rate. In that case, U.S. and UK firms are indifferent to whether they transact in the spot or the forward market. This yields our first parity condition, known as **forward-spot parity**. It says that the forward rate should be an unbiased predictor of where the spot rate is headed:

forward–spot parity
An equilibrium relationship that predicts that the current forward rate will be an unbiased predictor of the spot rate on a future date.

(Eq. 18.2) $$E(Spot) = Forward$$

---

[1] This is clearly an abstraction. Firms may decide to enter a forward contract, even if they think that transacting later at the spot rate might be more profitable, because they value the certainty that the forward contract gives them. In this example, we are considering the hypothetical case of a firm that does not care about uncertainty and makes currency-trading decisions solely on the basis of expected profitability.

Table 18.1

Inflation and Exchange Rate Movements, 2000–2010

	% Cumulative Inflation	% U.S. Inflation – Foreign Inflation	% Appreciation/Depreciation Against the $
United States	30	NA	NA
Japan	−2	+32	+20
United Kingdom	27	+3	+5
Mexico	93	−63	−68

It would certainly be convenient for currency traders if the forward exchange rate provided a reliable forecast of future spot rates. Unfortunately, most studies suggest that this is not the case. Changes in spot exchange rates are not closely tied to the forward exchange rate. For that matter, most researchers and practitioners agree that it is nearly impossible to predict how most exchange rates will move most of the time, at least in the short run.

If forward rates do not accurately predict movements in currency values over time, perhaps something else does. Economists have long observed a correlation between currency movements and inflation rate differentials across countries. To illustrate, Table 18.1 reports the cumulative inflation that occurred in the United States, Japan, the United Kingdom, and Mexico from 2000 to 2010. Beside those figures we show the difference between the U.S. inflation and that which occurred in the other countries, as well as the cumulative change in the values of the yen, the pound mark, and the peso against the dollar over the same period.

Notice the remarkable correspondence between the numbers in the third and fourth columns. The peso was the only currency that depreciated against the dollar from 2000–2010, and it was the only country on the list with higher inflation than the United States. Inflation rates in the United States and the UK were about equal, and the dollar-pound exchange rate was about the same in 2000 as it was in 2010. Japanese inflation was roughly 32 percentage points lower than U.S. inflation, and over the decade the yen rose relative to the dollar by about 20%.

These figures suggest that differences in inflation do a good job of explaining currency movements, at least over a long period of time. The second parity relationship reveals why.

18-2b Purchasing Power Parity

law of one price
A theory that says that the identical good trading in different markets must sell at the same price.

One of the simplest ideas in economics is that identical goods trading in different markets should sell at the same price, absent any barriers to trade. This **law of one price** has a natural application in international finance. Suppose that a DVD of a hit movie retails in the United States for $20, and the identical DVD can be purchased in Tokyo for ¥2,000. Does the law of one price hold? It depends on the exchange rate. If the spot rate of exchange equals ¥100/$, then the answer is yes. A U.S. consumer can spend $20 to purchase the DVD in the United States, or he can convert $20 to ¥2,000 and purchase the item in Tokyo. We can generalize this example as follows. Suppose that the price of an item in domestic currency is P_{dom} and the price of the identical item in foreign currency is P_{for}. If the spot exchange rate quoted in foreign currency per domestic is $Spot^{for/dom}$, then the law of one price holds if the following is true:

(Eq. 18.3)
$$\frac{P_{for}}{P_{dom}} = Spot^{for/dom}$$

Naturally, the law of one price extends to any pair of countries, not just the United States and Japan. When Equation 18.3 does not hold, traders may engage in arbitrage to exploit price discrepancies across national boundaries.

Figure 18.3   **Arbitrage and the Law of One Price**

If sunglasses sell for $200 in the U.S. and €180 in Italy, then the law of one price holds only if the exchange rate equals €0.90/$. If the exchange rate is €0.95, then traders can make a profit by purchasing the sunglasses in Italy, shipping them to the U.S. and selling them there, and converting the proceeds back into euros.

Cost of sunglasses in Italy	− €180
Revenue from selling in U.S.	+ €190
Profit	€ 10

© Cengage Learning 2012

EXAMPLE

Suppose that a pair of Maui Jim sunglasses sells for $200 in the United States and for €180 in Italy. Suppose also that the spot exchange rate between dollars and euros is €0.95/$. Does the law of one price hold? Apparently not, because Equation 18.3 says the exchange rate should be 0.90 based on the prices of sunglasses in each country, but the actual exchange rate is higher than that.

$$€180 \div \$200 = €0.90/\$ < €0.95/\$$$

How can arbitrageurs exploit this violation of the law of one price? In the equation above, the left side is less than the prevailing exchange rate, which means that the price of sunglasses in Italy is too low, or the price in the United States is too high, relative to the current exchange rate. Therefore, suppose that a trader buys sunglasses in Italy for €180 and ships them to the United States. After selling them for $200, the trader can convert back to euros, receiving €190 ($200 × €0.95/$). The arbitrage profit is €10. As long as the transactions costs of making these trades is less than €10, and as long as there are no other barriers to trade, then the process will continue until the market reaches equilibrium. Figure 18.3 illustrates how the trades of arbitragers push the market back toward an equilibrium in which the law of one price holds.

Now we will add a new wrinkle to the law of one price. Suppose that prices in different countries satisfy Equation 18.3 not just at one moment in time, but all the time. We do not necessarily expect this to be the case for every type of good sold in two countries, but if price discrepancies for similar goods become too large, the forces of arbitrage should push them back into line. Of course, the prices of goods and services change every day due to inflation (or deflation), and there is no reason to expect the inflation rate in one country to be the same as in another. If different countries are subject to different inflation pressures, how can the law of one price hold on an ongoing basis? The answer is that the exchange rate adjusts to maintain equilibrium.

EXAMPLE

Suppose that the forces of arbitrage have influenced the prices of Maui Jim sunglasses in the United States and in Italy so that the law of one price now holds. Specifically, the U.S. price is $195 and the Italian price is €185.25. If the exchange rate is still €0.95/$, then the law of one price holds because the following is true:

$$€185.25 \div \$195 = €0.95/\$$$

Now suppose that the expected rate of inflation in Italy over the next year is 12%, but no inflation is expected in the United States. One year from today, Maui Jim sunglasses will still sell for $195 in the United States, but with 12% inflation, the price in Italy will rise to €207.48 (185.25 × 1.12). If these forecasts are correct, then in a year the exchange rate must rise to €1.064/$ for the law of one price to hold:

$$€207.48 \div \$195 = €1.064/\$$$

Remember that this exchange rate is expressed in euros per dollar, so an increase from €0.95/$ to €1.064/$ represents appreciation of the dollar and depreciation of the euro.

purchasing power parity
An equilibrium relationship that predicts that currency movements are tied to differences in inflation rates across countries.

Purchasing power parity is an extension of the law of one price. Purchasing power parity says that if the law of one price holds at all times, then differences in expected inflation between two countries are associated with expected changes in currency values. Mathematically, we can express this idea as follows:

$$(Eq.\ 18.4) \qquad \frac{E(Spot^{\ for/dom})}{(Spot^{\ for/dom})} = \frac{\left[\ 1 + E(inflation_{for})\ \right]}{\left[\ 1 + E(inflation_{dom})\ \right]}$$

where, as before, the expected spot rate is $E(Spot)$, the current spot rate is S, the expected rate of inflation in the foreign country is $E(inflation_{for})$, and the expected rate of inflation in the domestic country is $E(inflation_{dom})$. Notice that the left-hand side of this equation exceeds 1.0 if traders expect the domestic currency to appreciate, and it is less than 1.0 if traders expect the foreign currency to appreciate. Likewise, the right-hand side of the equation exceeds 1.0 when expected inflation is higher abroad than it is at home, and the ratio falls below 1.0 when the opposite is true. Therefore, the equation produces the already familiar prediction that if inflation is higher in one country than another, then the currency of the country with higher inflation will depreciate. The equation advises traders who want to forecast currency movements to invest resources in forecasting inflation rates.

How accurately does purchasing power parity predict exchange rate movements? As we have already seen, over the long term there is a strong relationship between currency values and inflation rates. Countries with high inflation see their currencies depreciate over time, whereas the opposite happens for countries with lower inflation. This is no accident. If we did not observe this pattern in the data, it would signal gross violations of the law of one price and indicate that arbitrage was not working to bring prices back into line.

But purchasing power parity does not fare as well in the short run. Violations of the law of one price do occur frequently, and many studies suggest that they persist from three to four years on average. Again, arbitrage, or in this case, limits to arbitrage explain why. When goods prices in different countries are out of equilibrium, arbitrageurs must trade the goods, moving them across national borders, to earn a profit. This process cannot occur without investments in time and money, and for certain goods, trade may be impossible due to legal restrictions or the physical impediments to transporting goods. Accordingly, there is no reason to expect goods to flow from one market to the other instantaneously at any moment when the law of one price does not hold. Only if price discrepancies across markets are large enough and persistent enough will arbitrageurs find it profitable to trade. Hence, purchasing power parity does a good job of explaining long-run movements in currencies, but not day-to-day, or even year-to-year, fluctuations.

JOB INTERVIEW QUESTION

What happens to the value of the U.S. dollar when U.S. inflation increases?

18-2c Interest Rate Parity

Although it is both time-consuming and expensive to move goods across borders, the same cannot generally be said about purely financial transactions. Large institutional investors can buy and sell currencies very rapidly and at low cost, and they can buy and sell financial assets denominated in different currencies just as quickly. Interest rate parity applies the law of one price to financial assets, specifically to risk-free assets denominated in different currencies.

To illustrate, assume that a U.S. institution has $10 million that it wants to invest for 180 days in a risk-free government bill. Assume that the current annual interest rate on 180-day U.S. Treasury bills is 2% per year (1% for six months), so if the institution chooses this investment, it will have $10.1 million six months later:

$$\$10,000,000\left(1 + \frac{R_{US}}{2}\right) = \$10,000,000\left(1 + \frac{0.02}{2}\right) = \$10,100,000$$

Alternatively, the institution might choose to convert its $10 million into another currency and invest abroad. However, even if it invests in a risk-free government bill issued by a foreign government, the institution must enter into a forward contract to convert back into dollars when the investment matures. Otherwise, the return on the foreign investment is not risk-free and will depend on changes in currency values over the next six months.

For example, suppose that the annual interest rate on a six-month British government bill is 5.26% per year (2.63% for six months). Suppose also that the spot and six-month forward exchange rates are £0.5639/$ and £0.5730/$, respectively. The U.S. institution converts $10 million into £5,639,000 at the spot rate. It invests the pounds for six months at the UK interest rate and enters into a forward contract to convert those pounds back into dollars when the UK bill matures. At the end of six months, the institution has the following:[2]

$$\$10,000,000(S^{£/\$})\left(1 + \frac{R_{UK}}{2}\right)\left(\frac{1}{F^{£/\$}}\right) = \$10,000,000(£0.5639)\left(1 + \frac{0.0526}{2}\right)\left(\frac{1}{£0.5730/\$}\right)$$
$$= \$10,100,010$$

Given the prevailing interest rates on short-term, risk-free U.S. and UK bonds, and given current spot and forward exchange rates between dollars and pounds, investors are more or less indifferent to whether they invest in the United States or the United Kingdom. In other words, with respect to short-term, risk-free financial assets, the law of one price holds. This relationship is called **interest rate parity**, which simply means that risk-free investments should offer the same return (after converting currencies) everywhere. As usual, we can express interest rate parity in mathematical terms. Letting R_{for} and R_{dom} represent the risk-free rate on foreign and domestic government debt, we obtain the following equation:[3]

<table>
<tr><td>(Eq. 18.5)</td><td>$$\frac{Forward^{for/dom}}{Spot^{for/dom}} = \frac{(1 + R_{for})}{(1 + R_{dom})}$$</td></tr>
</table>

What does this expression mean? Observe that if the left-hand side of the equation is greater than 1.0, the domestic currency trades at a forward premium. If domestic investors send money abroad, when they convert back to domestic currency, they will realize an exchange loss because the foreign currency buys less domestic currency than it did at the spot rate. Domestic investors know this, so they require an incentive in the form of a higher foreign interest rate before they will send money abroad. To maintain equilibrium, the right-hand side must also be greater than 1.0, which means that the foreign interest rate must exceed the domestic rate. The bottom line is that when a nation's currency trades at a forward premium (discount), risk-free interest rates in that country should be lower (higher) than they are abroad.

As is the case with purchasing power parity, deviations from interest rate parity create arbitrage opportunities. However, these arbitrage opportunities involve buying and selling financial assets rather than physical commodities. Naturally, trade in securities can occur rapidly and much less expensively than trade in goods, so the forces of arbitrage are more powerful in maintaining interest rate parity.

The effect of all these transactions, repeated again and again, is to push exchange rates and interest rates back toward parity. As investors borrow in the United States,

---

interest rate parity
An equilibrium relationship that predicts that differences in risk-free interest rates in two countries must be tied to differences in currency values on the spot and forward markets.

JOB INTERVIEW QUESTION

If interest rates on U.S. government bonds are higher than rates on Japanese government bonds, does that mean that U.S. bonds are a better investment?

SMART concepts

See the concept explained step-by-step at **SMART** | finance

---

[2]There is a $10 difference between the return that our investor earns in the United States and the return earned in the UK. This $10 is really nothing more than a rounding error because we do not carry exchange rates past the fourth decimal place. Also, note that we first multiply the $10,000,000 times the spot exchange rate to determine the quantity of pounds available for investing. Next, we increase this amount by multiplying times one plus the UK interest rate. Finally, we have to divide the total by the forward rate to convert the currency back into dollars.

[3]Be careful to match the term of the forward rate to the term of the interest rate in this expression. For example, if you are comparing interest rates on 180-day government bills, you must use a 180-day forward rate. You can see this by going back to the example of the institution with $10 million to invest. If you set the equation representing the institution's U.S. return equal to the equation representing its UK return, the following equation results:

$$F^{£/\$}/S^{£/\$} = \frac{\left(1 + \dfrac{R_{UK}}{2}\right)}{\left(1 + \dfrac{R_{US}}{2}\right)}$$

EXAMPLE

Suppose that the six-month, risk-free rate in the United States is 2%, and in Canada it is 6%. The spot exchange rate is C$1.5855/$, and the 180-day forward rate is C$1.5937/$. Interest rate parity does not hold, as shown in the following equation:

$$\frac{C\$1.5937/\$}{C\$1.5855/\$} < \frac{\left(1 + \frac{0.06}{2}\right)}{\left(1 + \frac{0.02}{2}\right)}$$

Because the right-hand side of this equation is "too large" relative to parity, the interest rate in Canada is "too high" or the rate in the United States is "too low." The arbitrage opportunity is as follows. An investor borrows money (say $1 million) at 2% in the United States, then converts the proceeds into Canadian dollars, and invests them at 6%. Six months later, the investor converts the Canadian dollars back into U.S. currency to repay the loan. Anything left over is pure arbitrage profit.

Borrow $1 million in the U.S. at 2% for six months → must repay $1,010,000

$1 million → converted at spot rate → C$1,585,500

C$1,585,500 invested for six months at 6% → (C$1,585,500)(1.03) → C$1,633,065

C$1,633,065 converted to US$ at the forward rate → $1,024,700

$1,010,000 needed to repay U.S. loan → leaves $14,700 arbitrage profit

the U.S. interest rate will rise from 2% to a higher level. Similarly, as investors purchase Canadian government bonds, the bond prices will rise and the risk-free rate in Canada will fall. When investors sell U.S. dollars to buy Canadian dollars on the spot market, the spot rate (in terms of Canadian dollars per U.S. dollar) will rise, and just the opposite happens on the forward market as investors sell Canadian dollars to buy U.S. dollars. In terms of the interest rate parity equation, we can see how these forces drive markets to equilibrium:

$$\text{This ratio is increasing} \leftarrow \frac{C\$1.5937/\$\uparrow}{C\$1.5855/\$\downarrow} < \frac{\left(1 + \frac{0.06\downarrow}{2}\right)}{\left(1 + \frac{0.02\uparrow}{2}\right)} \rightarrow \text{This ratio is decreasing}$$

$$\downarrow$$

New equilibrium occurs when inequality becomes an equality

covered interest arbitrage
A trading strategy designed to exploit deviations from interest rate parity to earn an arbitrage profit.

The process illustrated in the preceding example is known as **covered interest arbitrage** because traders attempt to earn arbitrage profits arising from differences in interest rates across countries, and they "cover" their currency exposures with forward contracts. Implicit in this example was the assumption that investors could borrow and lend at the risk-free rate in each country. Not all investors can do this, but large, creditworthy institutions can get very close to this ideal. Moreover, they can execute the trades described in the example at very high speed and at low cost. In the real world, deviations from interest rate parity are small and transitory.

18-2d Real Interest Rate Parity (the Fisher Effect)

real interest rate parity
An equilibrium relationship that predicts that the real interest rate will be the same in every country.

If nominal rates of return on risk-free investments are equalized around the world, after adjusting for currency translation, perhaps real rates of return are also equalized. **Real interest rate parity** means that investors should earn the same real rate of return on risk-free investments no matter the country in which they choose to invest. Recall from Chapter 5 that the real rate of interest is defined as follows:

$$1 + \text{real} = \frac{1 + R}{1 + E(i)}$$

If market forces equalize real rates across national borders, then the ratio on the right-hand side should be the same in every country. Continuing to use the notation for foreign and domestic nominal interest rates and expected inflation rates, we can write the following equation:

$$\frac{1 + R_{for}}{1 + E(i_{for})} = \frac{1 + R_{dom}}{1 + E(i_{dom})}$$

Then by cross multiplying we obtain

(Eq. 18.6)
$$\frac{1 + R_{for}}{1 + R_{dom}} = \frac{1 + E(i_{for})}{1 + E(i_{dom})}$$

This equation says that if real rates are the same in the domestic and the foreign country, then the ratio of (1 plus) nominal interest rates in the two countries must equal the ratio of (1 plus) expected inflation rates. If expected inflation is higher in one country than in another, then the country with higher inflation must offer higher interest rates to give investors the same real return.

EXAMPLE

Suppose that expected inflation in the United States equals zero and expected inflation in Italy is 12%. Suppose also that the one-year, risk-free rate in the United States is 3%. What would the one-year, risk-free rate have to be in Italy to maintain real interest rate parity?

$$\frac{1 + R_{Italy}}{1 + 0.03} = \frac{1 + 0.12}{1 + 0.0} \qquad R_{Italy} = 15.36\%$$

As with purchasing power parity, real interest rate parity need not hold at all times, because when deviations from parity occur, limits to arbitrage prevent market forces from quickly reaching a new equilibrium. In the long run, we expect that real interest rate parity will hold, at least approximately, but that will not necessarily be the case in the short run.

We conclude this section with a quick review of the four parity relationships, highlighting how they are linked together. If we combine Equations 18.2, 18.4, 18.5, and 18.6, we have the following relationships:[4]

(Eq. 18.7)
$$\frac{E(S)}{S} = \frac{F}{S} = \frac{1 + R_{for}}{1 + R_{dom}} = \frac{1 + E(i_{for})}{1 + E(i_{dom})} = \frac{E(S)}{S}$$

The first equality simply restates the forward-spot parity relationship. The second equality is the expression for interest rate parity, and the third and fourth equalities define real interest rate parity and purchasing power parity, respectively. Here we see for the first time that if markets are in equilibrium, spot and forward exchange rates, nominal interest rates, and expected inflation rates are all linked internationally. If we want to understand why currency values change, Equation 18.7 gives us a number of clues. The equation also illustrates how difficult it can be for countries to manage their exchange rates. Attempts to push the exchange rate in a particular direction invariably lead to changes in other macroeconomic variables that policy makers may not desire.[5]

---

[4]Notice that to create this equation we divided equation 18.2 by S, the spot rate. This does no harm to the equality, and it allows us to highlight the connection between the four parity relationships.
[5]In October 1997, market pressure was building for a devaluation of the Hong Kong dollar. Hong Kong's currency board reacted by purchasing vast amounts of Hong Kong currency. One consequence of their activity was that overnight interest rates in Hong Kong briefly reached 280%. A year later a similar spike in short-term interest rates occurred in Russia as the government there unsuccessfully tried to prevent a sharp drop in the value of the ruble.

18-2 Concept Review Questions

5. Explain the logic behind each of the four parity relationships.

6. Explain the role of arbitrage in maintaining the parity relationships.

7. In what sense is interest rate parity an application of the law of one price?

8. An investor who notices that interest rates are much lower in Japan than in the United States borrows in Japan and invests the proceeds in the United States. This is called uncovered interest arbitrage, but is it really arbitrage? Why or why not?

18-3 Managing Financial and Political Risk

18-3a Transactions Risk

Any firm that might experience an adverse change in the value of any of its cash flows as a result of exchange rate movements faces exposure to exchange rate risk. Almost every firm is exposed to exchange rate risk to some degree, even if it operates strictly in one country and has cash flows in only one currency. Such a firm will face exchange rate risk if (1) it produces a good or service that competes with imports in the home market, or (2) it uses as a production input an imported product or service.

Nonetheless, some types of companies face greater exchange rate risk than do others. MNCs obviously face this risk in all aspects of their business, but they also have many opportunities to minimize that risk by, for example, moving production facilities to the countries where their products are sold so that costs and revenues can be in the same currency. The greatest exchange rate exposure occurs when a firm's costs and revenues are largely denominated in different currencies.

As usual, it is easiest to describe the importance of exchange rate risk to an exporter with an example. Assume that the Boeing Co. has just sold an airplane to a Japanese buyer, with the following details. First, when Boeing sells to Japanese customers, it prices its planes in yen. Boeing wants to set the yen price high enough so that the payment it receives converts back into at least \$1 million. This allows Boeing to cover costs and earn an acceptable profit. Second, assume that the current yen/dollar exchange rate is ¥100.00/\$. Boeing therefore negotiates a price of ¥100 million for the airplane. However, the company is primarily concerned with how many dollars it will collect when payment is made in yen and then converted into dollars on the foreign exchange market.

If Boeing negotiates the terms of this sale at the same time that it receives payment, it does not face any foreign exchange risk. The company will simply exchange ¥100 million for \$1 million on the spot market. In reality, Boeing will probably negotiate payment terms months before it expects payment from the Japanese customer. This simple fact creates exchange rate risk, because between the dates when Boeing sets the price in yen for the plane and when it receives payment, the exchange rate can move. Because the contract is denominated in yen, Boeing bears this exchange rate risk, but the risk would not be eliminated by denominating the sales contract in dollars—the risk would simply be shifted to the Japanese buyer.

Suppose that after Boeing agrees to a price, it must wait six months for payment. In that time, the exchange rate changes to ¥110.00/\$, meaning that the dollar has appreciated and the yen has depreciated. Boeing will still receive the same ¥100 million, but now that converts to just \$909,091. Appreciation in the dollar results in Boeing realizing an exchange rate loss of \$90,909. If the yen appreciates, say to ¥90.00/\$, Boeing will receive \$1,111,111 and will realize an exchange rate gain of \$111,111.

This exchange rate risk cannot be eliminated, but it can be hedged (transferred to a third party) using financial contracts. Assume that immediately after Boeing agrees to sell the plane for ¥100 million it enters a six-month forward contract to sell yen in exchange for dollars. Boeing's forward contract is not with its Japanese customer, but rather with a money-center bank, such as Citigroup, that serves as a dealer in the foreign exchange market. If the forward rate that Boeing agrees to equals ¥99/\$, Boeing

? WHAT TO ASK

How does your firm decide which risks to hedge, and what instruments does it use to hedge?

What Companies Do Globally

CFO Survey Evidence

In a survey of CFOs from four European countries, Brounen, de Jong, and Koedijk asked companies whether they had considered issuing debt in a foreign currency and, if so, what factors influenced that decision. A company that earns revenues in a foreign currency can offset some of that risk exposure by generating costs in the same currency, and one way to do that is by borrowing money in the foreign currency.

Apparently, the hedging motivation for issuing foreign debt is important to some firms, especially those in Britain and the United States (the U.S. figures come from Graham and Harvey 2001). More than 90% of British CFOs and almost as many American CFOs said that "providing a natural hedge" was always or almost always an important factor in their decision to issue debt in a foreign currency. In contrast, CFOs from the Netherlands and Germany put less emphasis on the hedging motive, saying instead that they considered issuing foreign debt because foreign interest rates may be lower than domestic rates.

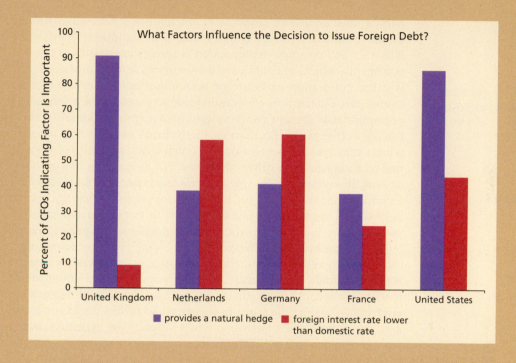

Source: Reprinted from *Journal of Banking and Finance*, 30, "Capital Structure Policies in Europe: Survey Evidence," Dirk Brounen, Abe de Jong, and Kees Koedjik, pp. 1409–1442, copyright 2006, with permission from Elsevier.

promises to deliver ¥100 million in exchange for $1,010,101 exactly six months from now. Once this forward contract is executed, Boeing is no longer exposed to exchange rate risk. The risk has not disappeared; it has simply been transferred from Boeing to Citigroup. But why would Citigroup be willing to assume this risk?

International banks—and, increasingly, other types of financial institutions—are uniquely positioned to bear exchange rate risk because they can create what amounts to a natural hedge, or offsetting risk exposure, as a normal course of their business. Offsetting risk means they are able to easily arrange mirror-image positions with other customers. To see this, consider what type of foreign exchange contract Toyota Motors might demand from Citigroup. The exchange rate risk problem for Toyota (one of Japan's biggest exporters) is the opposite of Boeing's: Toyota exports many automobiles from Japan and sells these in the United States. The company receives U.S. dollars as payment, but its costs are in yen, so it would need to *sell dollars forward* (locking in a yen price) in order to cover its costs and make an acceptable profit. Citigroup can buy dollars forward (sell yen) from Toyota and simultaneously sell dollars forward (buy yen) to Boeing, and thus net out the exchange rate exposure on its own books. This is a simplified example because Citigroup may not have a perfectly offsetting exposure for Boeing's needs, but in that case it would simply execute its own forward contract with another bank—perhaps with Toyota's main bank.

A major concern among some U.S. policymakers in the wake of the recent financial crisis is that large banks may take speculative positions in currencies and other assets, and that those positions could lead to another financial crisis. Former Federal Reserve Chairman Paul Volcker proposed a regulation to curb bank risk taking. The proposed rule would prohibit banks from engaging in "proprietary trading," meaning trading that is not on behalf of a client. In early 2011, the Volcker Rule was still under debate in Congress.

We have discussed how to measure exchange rate risk as it applies to specific transactions and have briefly discussed one method of dealing with it using a forward market hedge. However, this **transactions exposure** is but one of many types of exchange rate risk.

transactions exposure
The risk that movements in exchange rates will adversely affect the value of a particular transaction.

18-3b Translation and Economic Risk

MNCs must deal with additional complexities if they have affiliates or subsidiaries on the ground in a foreign country. One such complication arises when MNCs translate costs and revenues denominated in foreign currencies to report on their financial statements, which, of course, are denominated in the home currency. This type of risk is called **translation exposure** or **accounting exposure**. In other words, foreign exchange rate fluctuations affect individual accounts in the financial statements. A more important risk element concerns **economic exposure**, which is the overall impact of foreign exchange rate fluctuations on the firm's value. A firm faces economic exposure when exchange rate changes affect its cash flows, even those cash flows not specifically tied to transactions in other currencies. For example, a rise in the value of the dollar against the euro makes European wines less expensive to U.S. consumers, and it makes U.S. wine more expensive for European consumers. A winery operating in the United States, even one that does not sell directly to foreign customers, may realize a decline in cash flows due to competition from suddenly less expensive European vintners.

translation exposure (accounting exposure)
The risk that exchange rate movements will adversely impact reported financial results on a firm's financial statements.

economic exposure
The risk that a firm's value will fluctuate due to exchange rate movements.

What can managers do about these risks? Hedging economic exposure is more difficult than hedging transactions exposure, in part because measuring the exposure is more difficult. For instance, a U.S. winery concerned about the declining prices of foreign wines could engage in currency trades that would result in a profit if the dollar appreciates against the euro. In theory, these profits could offset the decline in earnings that occurs when European wines become less expensive, but exactly how large will these losses be for a given change in the exchange rate? Increasingly, MNCs manage their economic exposures both by using sophisticated currency derivatives and by matching costs and revenues in a given currency. For instance, a foreign company exporting to Japan might issue yen-denominated bonds, so-called **Samurai bonds**, to create a yen-based liability that would partially or fully offset the exposure resulting from yen-based receivables. However, it is important to emphasize that unless the cash inflows and outflows match exactly, some residual yen exposure will remain.

Samurai bonds
Yen-denominated bonds issued by non-Japanese corporations.

18-3c Political Risk

Another important risk facing MNCs is **political risk**, which refers to actions taken by a government that have a negative impact on the value of foreign companies operating in that country, such as raising taxes on a firm's activities or erecting barriers that prevent a firm from repatriating profits back to the home country. In its most extreme form, political risk can mean confiscation of a corporation's assets by a foreign government.

Political risk has two basic dimensions: *macro* and *micro*. *Macro political risk* means that *all* foreign firms in the country will be subject to political risk because of political change, revolution, or the adoption of new policies by a host government. In other words, no individual country or firm is treated differently. An example of macro political risk occurred when communist regimes came to power in China in 1949 and in Cuba in 1959–1960. More recently, the near collapse of Indonesia's currency in

political risk
The risk that a government will take an action that negatively affects the values of firms operating in that country.

Cengage Learning

Beth Acton, Vice President and Treasurer of Ford Motor Co. (former)

"When we look at hedging of foreign exchange exposures, we make an assessment of what kinds of risks we want to take in the business, and we are not out to second-guess the market."

See the entire interview at **SMART** | finance

Smart Practices Video

late 1997 and early 1998, plus the attendant political and economic turmoil elsewhere in Asia, highlights the real and present danger that macro political risk can pose to MNCs and international investors alike. *Micro political risk*, on the other hand, refers to a foreign government targeting punitive action against an individual firm, a specific industry, or companies from a particular foreign country. Examples include the nationalization of firms in the energy, telecommunications, and food industries by Hugo Chavez in Venezuela.

Although political risk can take place in any country, even in the United States, the political instability of many developing countries generally makes the positions of multinational companies most vulnerable there. At the same time, some of the countries in this group have the most promising markets for the goods and services being offered by MNCs. The main question, therefore, is how to engage in operations and foreign investment in such countries and yet avoid or minimize the potential political risk.

MNCs may adopt both positive and negative approaches to cope with political risk. Negative approaches include taking a trade dispute with a host country to the World Trade Organization (described later) or threatening to withhold additional investments from a country unless an MNC's demands are met. Firms may also negotiate agreements with host governments that build in costs that the host government must bear if it breaches the terms of the original agreement. Positive approaches for MNCs include working proactively to develop environmental and labor standards in a country, and generally attempting to become perceived as a domestic company by the host country's citizenry.

18-3d European Monetary Union and the Rise of Regional Trading Blocks

euro
The currency used throughout the countries that make up the European Union.

As a result of the Maastricht Treaty of 1991, 11 of the 15 European Union (EU) nations adopted a single currency, the euro, as a continent-wide medium of exchange beginning January 2, 1999. In early 2002, the national currencies of the 12 countries participating in **monetary union** disappeared and were completely replaced by the euro. Less than a decade later, 22 countries used the euro as their official currency, and membership in the European Union had grown to 27 countries, with 4 waiting to gain admission. The European Union offers both challenges and opportunities to a variety of players, including multinational firms. MNCs, especially those based in the United States, face heightened levels of competition when operating inside the EU.

monetary union
An agreement between many European countries to integrate their monetary systems including using a single currency.

Another major trading block that arose during the 1990s is the Mercosur group of countries in South America. Beginning in 1991, the nations of Brazil, Argentina, Paraguay, and Uruguay began removing tariffs and other barriers to intraregional trade. The second stage of Mercosur's development began at the end of 1994 and involved the development of a customs union to impose a common tariff on external trade while enforcing uniform and lower tariffs on intragroup trade. To date, Mercosur has been even more successful than its founders had imagined, with Venezuela joining as a member in 2006 and four other countries currently holding associate member status. Moreover, there are strong indications that some kind of economic collaboration pact between Mercosur and the European Union is likely to be negotiated in the near future.

General Agreement on Tariffs and Trade (GATT)
A trade treaty that extends free trade principles to broad areas of economic activity in many countries.

Although it may seem that the world is splitting into a handful of trading blocs, this is less dangerous than it may appear because many international treaties are in force that guarantee relatively open access to at least the largest economies. The most important such treaty is the **General Agreement on Tariffs and Trade (GATT)**, which celebrated its fiftieth anniversary in May 1998. The current agreement extends free-trading rules to broad areas of economic activity—such as agriculture, financial services, and intellectual property rights—that had not previously been covered by international treaty and that were thus

World Trade Organization (WTO)
An organization established by GATT to police world trading practices and to settle disputes between GATT member countries.

effectively off-limits to foreign competition. The 1994 revised GATT treaty also established a new international body, the World Trade Organization (WTO), to police world trading practices and to mediate disputes between member countries. The WTO began operating in January 1995, and one extremely important nation, the People's Republic of China, became a member in 2002.

18-3 Concept Review Questions

9. Distinguish between transactions, translation, and economic exposure.

10. Describe how a domestic firm might use a forward contract to hedge an economic exposure. Why does uncertainty about the magnitude of the exposure make this difficult?

11. Consider a U.S. firm that has for many years exported to European countries. How does the creation of the euro simplify or complicate the management of transactions exposure for this firm?

18-4 Long-Term Investment Decisions

Ike Mathur, University of Southern Illinois at Carbondale

"What I find very interesting is that for a long time in international finance we have talked about the first mover advantage."

See the entire interview at **SMART|finance**

Smart Ideas Video

In Chapters 8–10, we emphasized the importance of sound capital budgeting practices for a corporation's long-term survival. The same lessons covered in those chapters apply to multinational corporations. Whether investing at home or abroad, MNCs should evaluate investments based on their incremental cash flows and should discount those cash flows at a rate that is appropriate given the risk of the investment. However, when a company makes investments denominated in many different currencies, this process becomes a bit more complicated. First, in what currency should the firm express a foreign project's cash flows? Second, how does one calculate the cost of capital for an MNC, or for a given project?

18-4a Capital Budgeting

Suppose that a U.S. firm is weighing an investment that will generate cash flows in euros. The company's financial analysts have estimated the project's cash flows in euros as follows:

Initial Cost	Year 1	Year 2	Year 3
−€2 million	€900,000	€850,000	€800,000

To calculate the project's *NPV*, the U.S. firm can take either of two approaches. First, it can discount euro-denominated cash flows using a euro-based cost of capital. Having done this, the firm can then convert the resulting *NPV* back to dollars at the spot rate. For example, assume that the risk-free rate in Europe is 5%, and the firm estimates that the cost of capital (expressed as a euro rate) for this project is 10% (in other words, there is a 5% risk premium associated with the investment). The *NPV*, rounded to the nearest thousand euros, equals €122,000:

WHAT TO ASK

Does your firm use different methods to evaluate foreign as opposed to domestic investment projects?

$$NPV = -2,000,000 + \frac{900,000}{1.10^1} + \frac{850,000}{1.10^2} + \frac{800,000}{1.10^3} = 121,713$$

Assume that the current spot rate equals $0.95/€. Multiplying the spot rate times the *NPV* yields a dollar-based *NPV* of $116,000 (rounded to the nearest thousand dollars).

In this example, we did not make specific year-by-year forecasts of the future spot rates. Doing so is unnecessary because the firm can choose to hedge its currency exposure through a forward contract. Hedging the currency exposure allows the firm to separate the decision to accept or reject the project from projections of where the dollar-to-euro exchange rate might be headed. Of course, the firm may have a view on the exchange rate question, but even so, it is wise to first consider the investment on its own merits. For instance, suppose that this project has a negative *NPV*, but managers believe that the euro will appreciate over the life of the project, increasing the project's appeal in dollar terms. Given that belief, there is no need for the firm to undertake the project. Instead, it could purchase euros directly, invest them in safe financial assets in Europe, and convert back to dollars several years later. That is, if the firm wants to speculate on currency movements, it need not invest in physical assets to accomplish that objective.

A second approach for evaluating the investment project is to calculate the *NPV* in dollar terms, assuming that the firm hedges the project's cash flows using forward contracts. To begin this calculation, we must know the risk-free rate in the United States. Suppose that this rate is 3%. Recognizing that interest rate parity must hold, we can use Equation 18.5 to calculate the one-year forward rate:

$$\frac{F^{\$/euro}}{S^{\$/euro}} = \frac{1 + R_{US}}{1 + R_{euro}} \qquad F = \$0.9319/€ \qquad \frac{F}{0.95} = \frac{1.03}{1.05}$$

Similarly, we can calculate the two-year and three-year forward rates as follows:

$$\frac{F}{0.95} = \frac{1.03^2}{1.05^2} \qquad F = \$0.9142/€ \qquad \frac{F}{0.95} = \frac{1.03^3}{1.05^3} \qquad F = \$0.8967/€$$

Next, multiply each period's cash flow in euros times the matching spot or forward exchange rate to obtain a sequence of cash flows in dollars (rounded to the nearest thousand dollars):

Currency	Initial Investment	Year 1	Year 2	Year 3
€	2,000,000 × 0.95	900,000 × 0.9319	850,000 × 0.9142	800,000 × 0.8967
$	1,900,000	839,000	777,000	717,000

All that remains is to discount this project's cash flows at an appropriate risk-adjusted U.S. interest rate. But how do we determine that rate? Recall that the European discount rate used to calculate the euro-denominated *NPV* was 10%, 5% above the European risk-free rate. Intuitively, we might expect that the comparable U.S. rate is 8%, representing a 5% risk premium over the current risk-free rate in the United States. That intuition is more or less correct. To be precise, use the following formula to solve for the project's required return in U.S. dollar terms:

$$(1 + r) = (1 + 0.10)\frac{(1 + 0.03)}{(1 + 0.05)} \qquad R = 7.9\%$$

This equation takes the project's required return in euro terms, 10%, and rescales it to dollar terms by multiplying by the ratio of risk-free interest rates in each country. We can verify that discounting the dollar-denominated cash flows using this rate results in the same *NPV* (again, rounding to the nearest thousand dollars) that we obtained by discounting the cash flows in euros and converting to dollars at the spot rate.

$$NPV = -\$1,900,000 + \frac{\$839,000}{1.079^1} + \frac{\$777,000}{1.079^2} + \frac{\$717,000}{1.079^3} = \$116,000$$

These calculations demonstrate that a company does not have to "take a view" on currency movements when it invests abroad. Whether the company hedges a project's cash flows using forward contracts, or whether it calculates a project's *NPV* in local currency before converting to the home currency at the spot exchange rate, future exchange rate movements need not cloud the capital budgeting decision.

18-4b Cost of Capital

In the preceding example, we assumed that the project's cost of capital in Europe was 10%, which translated into a dollar-based discount rate of 7.9%. But where did the 10% come from? We return to the lessons of Chapter 10, namely that the discount rate should reflect the project's risk. One way to assess that risk is to calculate a beta for the investment. How should a firm calculate a beta when it makes an investment overseas?

If a firm's shareholders cannot diversify internationally, when the firm invests abroad, it should calculate a project's beta by measuring the movement of similar European investments in relation to the U.S. market, not the European market. The reason is that from the perspective of U.S. investors, the project's systematic risk depends on its relationship with the other assets that U.S. investors already own. A U.S. firm planning to build an electronics manufacturing facility in Germany might compare the returns of existing German electronics firms with returns on a U.S. stock index to estimate a project beta.

In contrast, if the firm's shareholders can diversify internationally, the firm should calculate the project's beta by comparing the relationship between its returns (or returns on similar investments) with returns on a worldwide stock index. This generates the project's "global beta." Next, to estimate the project's required return, the firm should apply the CAPM, multiplying the global market risk premium times the project's beta, and adding the risk-free rate. In all likelihood, because a globally diversified portfolio is less volatile than a portfolio containing only domestic securities, the risk premium on the global market will be less than the domestic risk premium.

EXAMPLE

A Japanese auto manufacturer decides to build a plant to make cars for the North American market. The firm estimates two project betas. The first calculation takes returns on U.S. auto stocks and calculates their betas relative to those on the Nikkei stock index. Based on these calculations, the Japanese firm decides to apply a beta of 1.1 to the investment. The risk-free rate of interest in Japan is 2%, and the market risk premium on the Nikkei index is 8%, so the project's required return is calculated as follows:

$$R_{project} = 2\% + 1.1(8\%) = 10.8\%$$

The second calculation takes the returns on U.S. auto manufacturers and determines their betas relative to those on a world stock index. It turns out that U.S. auto stocks are more sensitive to movements in the world market than they are to the Nikkei. This leads to a higher estimate of the project beta, say 1.3. However, offsetting this effect is the fact that the risk premium on the world market portfolio is just 5%. Therefore, the second estimate of the project's required return is calculated as follows:

$$R_{project} = 2\% + 1.3(5\%) = 8.5\%$$

18-4 Concept Review Questions

12. Why does discounting the cash flows of a foreign investment using the foreign cost of capital, then converting that to the home currency at the spot rate, yield the same *NPV* as converting the project's cash flows to domestic currency at the forward rate and then discounting them at the domestic cost of capital?

13. Why is it not surprising to find that the risk premium on the world market portfolio is lower than the domestic risk premium?

Summary

- Though the major currencies of the world float freely against each other, many countries have adopted exchange rate policies that fix the value of their currency relative to the currencies of other nations.

- A currency appreciates when it buys more of another currency over time. A currency depreciates when it buys less of another currency over time.

- The spot exchange rate applies to immediate currency transactions, whereas the forward exchange rate applies to trades that take place at some future time.

- The foreign exchange market is the world's largest financial market and attracts many types of participants including exporters and importers, investors, hedgers, speculators, governments, and dealers.

- The four parity relationships in international finance spell out how spot and forward exchange rates are linked to inflation and interest rates in different countries.

- When firms conduct business in other countries and currencies, they face exposure to transactions risk, translation risk, economic risk, and political risk.

- When a firm analyzes a capital investment in a foreign currency, it can either discount the foreign currency cash flows using a foreign cost of capital, or it can calculate the domestic currency equivalent of those cash flows using forward rates and discount them at the domestic cost of capital.

Table of Important Equations

1. $\dfrac{F - S}{S} \times \dfrac{360}{N}$

2. $E(Spot) = Forward$

3. $\dfrac{P_{for}}{P_{dom}} = Spot^{for/dom}$

4. $\dfrac{E(Spot^{for/dom})}{(Spot^{for/dom})} = \dfrac{\left[1 + E(inflation_{for})\right]}{\left[1 + E(inflation_{dom})\right]}$

5. $\dfrac{Forward^{for/dom}}{Spot^{for/dom}} = \dfrac{(1 + R_{for})}{(1 + R_{dom})}$

6. $\dfrac{1 + R_{for}}{1 + R_{dom}} = \dfrac{1 + E(i_{for})}{1 + E(i_{dom})}$

7. $\dfrac{E(S)}{S} = \dfrac{F}{S} = \dfrac{1 + R_{for}}{1 + R_{dom}}$

   $= \dfrac{1 + E(i_{for})}{1 + E(i_{dom})} = \dfrac{E(S)}{S}$

Key Terms

Self-Test Problems

Answers to Self-Test Problems and the Concept Review Questions throughout the chapter appear in CourseMate with SmartFinance Tools at www.cengagebrain.com.

ST18-1. Use Figure 18.1 to determine whether the British pound trades at a forward discount or a forward premium relative to the Japanese yen. Use the six-month forward rate in your calculations.

ST18-2. Suppose the spot exchange rate equals ¥100/$, and the six-month forward rate equals ¥101/$. An investor can purchase a U.S. T-bill that matures in six months and earns an annual rate of return of 3%. What would be the annual return on a similar Japanese investment?

Questions

Q18-1. Define a multinational corporation (MNC). What additional factors must be considered by the manager of an MNC that a manager of a purely domestic firm is not forced to face?

Q18-2. Who are the major players in foreign currency markets, and what are their motivations for trading?

Q18-3. Suppose that an exchange rate is quoted in terms of euros per pound. In what direction would this rate move if the euro appreciated against the pound?

Q18-4. Explain how triangular arbitrage ensures that currency values are essentially the same in different markets around the world at any given moment.

Q18-5. In what sense is it a misnomer to refer to a currency as weak or strong? Who benefits and who loses if the yen appreciates against the pound?

Q18-6. What does a spot exchange rate have in common with a forward rate, and how are they different?

Q18-7. What does it mean to say that a currency trades at a forward premium?

Q18-8. Explain how the law of one price establishes a relationship between changes in currency values and inflation rates.

Q18-9. Why does purchasing power parity appear to hold in the long run but not in the short run?

Q18-10. In terms of risk, is a U.S. investor indifferent about whether to buy a U.S. government bond or a UK government bond? Why or why not?

Q18-11. If the euro trades at a forward premium against the yen, explain why interest rates in Japan would have to be higher than they are in Europe.

Q18-12. Suppose that the U.S. Federal Reserve suddenly decides to raise interest rates. Trace out the potential impact that this action might have on (1) interest rates abroad, (2) the spot value of the dollar, and (3) the forward value of the dollar.

Q18-13. Interest rates on risk-free bonds in the United States are about 2%, whereas interest rates on Swiss government bonds are 6%. Can we conclude that investors around the world will flock to buy Swiss bonds? Why or why not?

Q18-14. A Japanese investor decides to purchase shares in a company that trades on the London Stock Exchange. The investor's plan is to hold these shares for one year, sell them and convert the proceeds to yen at year's end. During the year, the pound appreciates against the yen. Does this enhance or diminish the investor's return on the stock?

Q18-15. Suppose that the dollar trades at a forward discount relative to the yen. A U.S. firm must pay a Japanese supplier ¥10 million in three months. A manager in the U.S. firm reasons that because the dollar buys fewer yen on the forward market than it does on the spot market, the firm should not enter a forward hedge to eliminate its exchange rate exposure. Comment on this opinion.

Problems

Exchange Rate Fundamentals

P18-1. One month ago, the Mexican peso (Ps) – U.S. dollar exchange rate was Ps9.0395/$ ($0.1106/Ps). This month, the exchange rate is Ps9.4805/$ ($0.1055/Ps). State which currency appreciated and which depreciated over the last month, and then calculate both the percentage appreciation of the currency that rose in value and the percentage depreciation of the currency that declined in value.

P18-2. Using the data presented in Figure 18.1, calculate the spot exchange rate on Wednesday between Canadian dollars and British pounds (in pounds per Canadian dollar).

P18-3. On Thursday the exchange rate between the Canadian dollar and Japanese yen was C$0.0098/¥, and on Friday the exchange rate was C$0.0099/¥. Which currency appreciated and which currency depreciated?

P18-4. Go to **www.oanda.com/currency/strength-heat-map**. Follow the instructions on how to use the map, and choose the U.S. dollar as the base currency.
a. Click on the "1-month" selection to show the appreciation or depreciation of the world's currencies relative to the dollar. Does the dollar appear to be appreciating or depreciating against most of the world's currencies, or is the answer mixed?
b. Next, choose the "1-year" option, and identify two or three countries whose currencies have depreciated the most against the U.S. dollar and two or three whose currencies have appreciated the most. Search the Web to try to find out those countries' most recent inflation figures. What lesson does this reveal?

P18-5. Recently, a financial newspaper reported the following spot and forward rates for the Japanese yen (¥).

Spot:	$0.007556/¥ (¥132.34/$)
1-month:	$0.007568/¥ (¥132.14/$)
3-month:	$0.007593/¥ (¥131.71/$)

Supply the forward yen premium or discount (specify which it is) for both the one- and three-month quotes as an annual percentage rate.

P18-6. Using the data presented in Figure 18.1, specify whether the U.S. dollar trades at a forward premium or discount relative to the Canadian dollar, the Japanese yen, and the Swiss franc. Use the three-month forward rates to determine the answer.

P18-7. Using the data presented in Figure 18.1, determine the forward premium or discount on the Canadian dollar relative to the British pound, the Japanese yen, and the Swiss franc. Use the six-month forward rates to determine the answer, and express your answer as an annual rate.

P18-8. You are quoted the following series of exchange rates for the U.S. dollar ($), the Canadian dollar (C$), and the British pound (£):

$0.6000/C$	C$1.6667/$
$1.2500/£	£0.8000/$
C$2.5000/£	£0.4000/C$

Assuming that you have $1 million in cash, how can you take advantage of this series of exchange rates? Show the series of trades that would yield an arbitrage profit, and calculate how much profit you would make.

The Parity Conditions in International Finance

P18-9. The current spot exchange rate is ¥109.43/$. A particular commodity sells for $5,000 in the United States and ¥600,000 in Japan.
a. Does the law of one price hold? If not, explain how to profit through arbitrage.
b. If it costs ¥60,000 to transport the commodity from the United States to Japan, is there still an arbitrage opportunity? At what exchange rate (in yen per dollar) would buying the commodity in the United States and shipping it to sell in Japan become profitable?

    c. Given shipping costs of ¥60,000, at what exchange rate would it be profitable to buy the commodity in Japan and ship it to the United States to sell? Comment on the general lesson from parts (a)–(c).

    d. Taking the commodity prices in the United States and Japan as given, at what exchange rate (in terms of yen per dollar) would the law of one price hold ignoring shipping costs?

P18-10. If the expected rate of inflation in the United States is 1%, the one-year risk-free interest rate is 2%, and the one-year risk-free rate in Britain is 4%, what is the expected inflation rate in Britain? Use the data presented in Figure 18.1 to answer this problem.

P18-11. Go to **www.economist.com**. Under Economics, Markets & Data, find the link for the "Big Mac index." After exploring this part of the site, explain why the Big Mac index might foreshadow changes in exchange rates. What features of the Big Mac would suggest that Big Macs may not satisfy the law of one price?

P18-12. Assume that the annual interest rate on a six-month U.S. Treasury bill is 5%, and use the data presented in Figure 18.1 to answer the following:

    a. Calculate the annual interest rate on six-month bills in Canada and Japan.

    b. Suppose that the annual interest rate on a six-month bill in Japan is 0.5%. Illustrate how to exploit this via covered interest arbitrage.

    c. Suppose that the annual interest rate on a three-month UK government bond is 4%. What is the annual interest rate on a three-month government bond in Switzerland?

    d. Suppose that the actual Swiss interest rate is 0.5%. Illustrate how to conduct covered interest arbitrage to exploit this situation.

P18-13. Shortly after it was introduced, the euro traded just below parity with the dollar, meaning that one dollar purchased more than one euro. This implies

    a. that U.S. inflation was lower than European inflation

    b. that U.S. interest rates were lower than European rates

    c. that the law of one price does not hold

    d. none of the above

P18-14. Assume that the following information is known about the current spot exchange rate between the U.S. dollar and the British pound (£), inflation rates in Britain and the United States, and the real rate of interest—which is assumed to be the same in both countries:

Current spot rate, $S = \$1.4500/£$ ($£0.6897/\$$)
U.S. inflation rate, $i_{US} = 1.5\%$ per year (0.015)
British inflation rate, $i_{UK} = 2.0\%$ per year (0.020)
Real rate of interest, $real = 2.5\%$ per year (0.025)

Based on this data, use the parity conditions of international finance to compute the following:

    a. expected spot rate next year

    b. U.S. risk-free rate (on a one-year bond)

    c. British risk-free rate (on a one-year bond)

    d. one-year forward rate

Finally, show how you can make an arbitrage profit if you are offered the chance to sell or buy pounds forward (for delivery one year from now) at the current spot rate of $\$1.4500/£$ ($£0.6897/\$$). Assuming that you can borrow $1 million or £689,700 at the risk-free interest rate, what would your profit be on this arbitrage transaction?

Managing Financial and Political Risk

P18-15. Suppose that the spot exchange rate follows a random walk, which means that the best forecast of the spot rate at some future date is simply its current value. Now suppose that a U.S. firm owes €1 million to a Spanish supplier. If the U.S. firm wants to minimize the expected dollar cost of paying its Spanish supplier (without regard to currency risk), describe the circumstances under which the firm will or will not enter into a forward contract to hedge its exposure.

P18-16. Classic City Exporters (CCE) recently sold a large shipment of sporting equipment to a Swiss company—the goods will be sold in Zurich. The sale was denominated in Swiss francs (SF) and was worth SF500,000. Delivery of the sporting goods and payment by the Swiss buyer are due to occur in six months. The current spot exchange rate is $0.6002/SF (SF1.6661/$), and the six-month forward rate is $0.6020/SF (SF1.6611/$). What risk would CCE run if it remained unhedged, and how could it hedge that risk with a forward contract? Assuming that the actual exchange rate in six months is $0.5500/SF (SF1.8182/$), compute the profit or loss—and state which it is—CCE would experience if it had chosen to remain unhedged.

P18-17. A British firm will receive $1 million from a U.S. customer in three months. The firm is considering two strategies to eliminate its foreign exchange exposure. The first strategy is to pledge the $1 million as collateral for a three-month loan from a U.S. bank at 4% interest. The UK firm will then convert the proceeds of the loan to pounds at the spot rate. When the loan is due, the firm will pay the $1 million balance due by handing its U.S. receivable over to the bank. This strategy allows the UK firm to "monetize" its receivable immediately. The spot exchange rate is 0.6550 pounds per dollar.

The second strategy is to enter a forward contract at an exchange rate of 0.6450 pounds per dollar. This ensures that the UK firm will receive £645,000 in three months. If the firm wanted to monetize this payment immediately, it could take out a three-month loan from a UK bank at 8%, pledging the proceeds of the forward contract as collateral.

Which of these strategies should the firm follow?

Long-Term Investment Decisions

P18-18. A German company manufactures a specialized piece of manufacturing equipment and leases it to a UK enterprise. The lease calls for five end-of-year payments of £1 million. The German firm spent €3.5 million to produce the equipment, which is expected to have no salvage value after five years. The current spot rate is €1.5/£. The risk-free interest rate in Germany is 3%, and in the United Kingdom it is 5%. The German firm reasons that the appropriate (German) discount rate for this investment is 7%. Calculate the *NPV* of this investment in two ways.

a. First, convert all cash flows to pounds, and discount at an appropriate (UK) cost of capital. Convert the resulting *NPV* to euros at the spot rate.

b. Second, calculate forward rates for each year, convert the pound-denominated cash flows into euros using those rates, and discount at the German cost of capital. Verify that the *NPV* obtained from this approach matches (except perhaps for small rounding errors) that obtained in part (a).

THOMSON REUTERS | Business School Edition

For instructions on using Thomson ONE, refer to the instructions provided with the Thomson ONE problems at the end of Chapters 1–6.

P18-19. How do changes in exchange rates affect the consolidation of financial statements of a multinational corporation? BP PLC (BP) has operations all over the world. Look at BP's sales and operating income from U.S. operations for the last five years.[6] The default currency for all figures is BP's home currency, British pounds. Convert these numbers to U.S. dollars.[7] The bottom of the page gives you the exchange rate at which the numbers have been converted from British pounds to U.S. dollars in each year. Has the U.S. dollar strengthened or weakened over the last five years? Convert U.S. sales and operating income for each of the last five years to British pounds using both the minimum and maximum of the five exchange rates. Which of the two exchange rates gives BP the larger sales and operating income in British pounds in each year? As a multinational corporation, does BP prefer a stronger or a weaker U.S. dollar relative to the British pound?

P18-20. How do changes in exchange rates affect an international investor's returns? Calculate Deutsche Telekom's (DTEGY:US) annual stock returns using the closing stock price in euros at the end of each of the last five fiscal years. Convert the closing stock price to U.S. dollars (to determine the exchange rate at the end of each fiscal year see footnote 7 in the previous problem). Calculate the annual stock returns using U.S. dollar prices. Which years have a higher return in U.S. dollars and which years in euros? As a U.S. investor, do you prefer a strong or a weak U.S. dollar relative to the euro?

---

[6]Geographic segment data can be found under the Financial tab. Click on "More," go to Worldscope Reports & Charts, and select "Geographic Segment Review."

[7]You can change currency by clicking on the dollar sign ($) on the right side of the menu at the top and then selecting "US Dollar."

Smart Ideas Video

Ike Mathur, University of Southern Illinois at Carbondale

"What I find very interesting is that for a long time in international finance we have talked about the first mover advantage."

Smart Practices Video

Beth Acton, Vice President and Treasurer of Ford Motor Co. (former)

"When we look at hedging of foreign exchange exposures, we make an assessment of what kinds of risks we want to take in the business, and we are not out to second-guess the market."

SMART concepts

See a demonstration of interest rate parity.

SMART solutions

See the solution to Problem 18-8 explained step-by-step.

Mini-Case

International Financial Management

Five years after completing your college degree you accept an exciting new job with the multinational firm Rangsit Trading Incorporated. This new position will involve a great deal of travel, along with some other challenging responsibilities. Part of your job function is to set company policy to manage exchange rate risk. As such, you decide that you need to become fluent in the following topics.

Assignment

1. First, you decide to review basic exchange rate terminology.

    a. Describe fixed and floating exchange rate systems. What are some problems with these systems?

    b. Describe a managed floating rate system.

    c. Describe a currency board arrangement system.

2. Next, you review the following parity relationships.

    a. Describe forward-spot parity.

    b. Describe purchasing power parity.

    c. Describe interest rate parity.

    d. Describe real interest rate parity.

    e. Describe how these four parity relationships link together.

3. Finally, you review the following risks that are relevant to multinational firms.

    a. Describe transactions risk and how this risk can be alleviated.

    b. Describe translation and economic risks and how these risks can be alleviated.

    c. Describe political risk and how this risk can be alleviated.

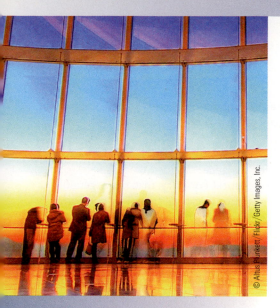

chapter 19

Options

What Companies Do

Concerns over Taxpayers' TARP Investments Warranted

In response to a growing financial crisis, the U.S. Congress passed the Emergency Economic Stabilization Act on October 3, 2008. The bill created a $700 billion Troubled Assets Relief Program (TARP) that authorized the government to make equity investments in financial institutions. By the end of January 2009, more than 300 financial institutions had participated in the program. Twenty-five of these institutions received injections of $1 billion or more from the program, with giants Bank of America, Citigroup, JP Morgan, and Wells Fargo receiving $25 billion each.

In exchange for the infusion of capital, the government received warrants granting it the right to purchase nonvoting common stock in the companies receiving assistance. This meant that if the financial sector recovered, taxpayers might earn a profit on the TARP funds. However, a Congressional Budget Office (CBO) analysis estimated that the value of taxpayers' investments fell 26% during the program's early months. To arrive at this figure, the CBO valued the TARP warrants using a modified version of the Black and Scholes option pricing model, a mathematically sophisticated tool used by option traders since the early 1970s. Despite its complexity, the Black and Scholes formula is in such widespread use today that there is even a free iPhone app that crunches the numbers automatically.

Fortunately for taxpayers, the market roared back in 2009–2010, and by November 2010, the CBO estimated that TARP's costs to taxpayers would total just $25 billion.

Sources: U.S. Treasury Department, www.online.wsj.com/public/resources/documents/st_BANKMONEY_ 20081027.html; Ronald Fink, "Taxpayers Already Down 26% on Their TARP Investments," www.financialweek .com/apps/pbcs.dll/article?AID=/20090116/REG/901169973/1028 (February 3, 2009); www.thehill.com/blogs/ on-the-money/budget/143835-tarp-costs-more-than-halved-in-new-budget.

Learning Objectives

After reading this chapter you should be able to:

- Describe the basic features of call and put options;
- Construct payoff diagrams for individual options as well as portfolios of options and other securities;
- Explain qualitatively what factors are important in determining option prices;
- Calculate the price of an option, using the binomial model; and
- List several corporate finance applications of option pricing theory.

A bit of folk wisdom says, "Always keep your options open." This implies that choices have value and that having the right to do something is better than being obligated to do it. This chapter shows how to apply that intuition to financial instruments called options. Options allow investors to buy or to sell an asset at a fixed price, for a given period of time. Having the right to buy or sell stock at a fixed price can be valuable—as long as there's a chance that the stock price can move in the right direction.

Many commentators see options merely as a form of legalized gambling for the rich. We strongly disagree with that perspective. Options exist because they provide real economic benefits that come in many different forms.

First, as part of the compensation package for managers, options provide incentives for managers to take actions that increase their firms' stock prices, thereby increasing the wealth of shareholders. Some point out that abuses may occur when firms award excessive option grants, or employees take improper actions to inflate stock prices and option values. However, we see this as a corporate governance problem, not a problem with options, per se.

Second, a wide variety of options exist, which allow holders the right to buy and to sell many different types of assets, not just common stocks. Sometimes, trading the option is more cost effective than trading the underlying asset. For example, trading a stock index option, which grants the right to buy or to sell a portfolio of stocks such as the S&P 500, enables investors to benefit from market movements while avoiding paying all of the transactions costs that would result from trading 500 individual stocks.

Third, firms use options to reduce their exposure to certain types of risk. Firms regularly buy and sell options to shelter their cash flows from movements in exchange rates, interest rates, and commodity prices. In that function, options resemble insurance much more than they resemble gambling.

Fourth, options facilitate the creation of innovative trading strategies. For instance, suppose that an investor is following a pharmaceutical company that has a genetically engineered cancer drug in clinical trials. The company has invested vast resources in this project, so much so that its future depends entirely on the outcome of these trials. If the tests are successful, the company's stock will skyrocket. If not, the firm may go bankrupt. An investor with choices limited to buying or selling the company's stock must guess whether the clinical trials will succeed or fail. As we will see, an investor who can buy and sell options can construct a trading strategy to profit from a large movement in the firm's stock price regardless of whether that movement is up or down.

Why does a chapter on options belong in a corporate finance textbook? We offer three answers. First, employees of large and small corporations regularly receive options as part of their compensation. It is valuable for both the employees and the employers to understand the value of this component of pay packages. Second, firms often raise capital by issuing securities with embedded options. For example, firms can issue bonds that are convertible into shares of common stock. Valuing these bonds requires an understanding of option pricing and is not simply a matter of calculating the present value of their interest and principal payments. Third, many capital budgeting projects have characteristics similar to options. The net present value method, discussed in Chapters 8—10, can generate incorrect accept/reject decisions for projects with downstream options. The best way to develop the ability to recognize which real investment projects have embedded options and which ones do not is to become an expert on ordinary financial options.

We begin this chapter with a brief description of the most common types of stock options and their essential characteristics. Next, we turn our attention to portfolios of options, illustrating how options can be used to construct unique trading strategies and gaining insight into how prices of different kinds of options are linked together in the market. The rest of the chapter examines factors that influence option prices, and we introduce a simple, yet powerful, tool for pricing many different kinds of options.

19-1   Options Vocabulary

derivative security
A security that derives its value from another asset.

An option is one example of a **derivative security**, a security that derives its value from another asset. An option fits this description because its value depends on the price of the underlying stock that the option holder can buy or sell. The asset from which a derivative security obtains its value is called the **underlying asset**. A **call option** grants the right to purchase a share of stock at a fixed price, on or before a certain date. The

What Companies Do Globally

CFO Survey Evidence: Options, Compensation, and Hedging Practices

The role of stock options in executive pay varies widely across countries. The following chart shows that U.S. firms are much more likely to include stock options as a significant portion of the pay package given to senior executives than are firms in other countries. Bryan, Nash, and Patel (2009) investigate differences in executive compensation practices across firms in different countries and find that stock options were more prevalent in countries that had greater institutional protections for shareholder rights and better enforcement of those protections. The study found that characteristics of firms were important, too, with equity-linked compensation such as options playing a bigger role in companies with more growth potential and in larger firms with less free cash flow.

In another 2007 study, Cohen and Yagil asked CFOs from the largest 300 companies in the United States, the United Kingdom, Canada, Germany, and Japan how often they used options to hedge financial risks. Executives in Japan reported that they were roughly 50% more likely to use options to hedge risk than their U.S. and Canadian counterparts, whereas German and British CFOs fell in the middle. CFOs from all five countries reported that they were more likely to use forward contracts (discussed in Chapter 20) than options when hedging.

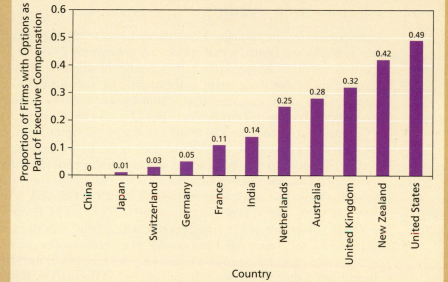

underlying asset
The asset from which an option or other derivative security derives its value.

call option
An option that grants the right to buy an underlying asset at a fixed price.

strike price
The price at which an option holder can buy or sell the underlying asset.

exercise price
The price at which an option holder can buy or sell the underlying asset.

price at which a call option allows an investor to purchase the underlying share is called the strike price or the exercise price. Because the option holder can buy the underlying stock at a fixed price, the more the market price of the stock increases, the greater the value of the call option.

Call options grant investors the right to purchase a share for a fairly short time period, usually just a few months.[1] The point at which this right expires is called the option's expiration date. An American call option gives holders the right to purchase stock at a fixed price, on or before its expiration date, whereas a European call option grants that right *only* on the expiration date. If we compare the prices of two options that are identical in every respect, except that one is American and one is European, the

---

[1] Employee stock options, which typically give workers the right to buy stock at a fixed price for up to ten years, are an important exception to this rule. Some publicly traded options have long expiration dates, too, such as the Long-Term Equity AnticiPation Securities (LEAPS) introduced by the American Stock Exchange in 1990.

Myron Scholes, Stanford University and Chairman of Oak Hill Platinum Partners

"Options markets have grown dramatically over the last thirty years."

See the entire interview at **SMART**|finance

Smart Practices Video

expiration date
The date on which the right to buy or to sell the underlying asset expires.

American call option
An option that grants the right to buy an underlying asset, on or before the expiration date.

European call option
An option that grants the right to buy the underlying asset only on the expiration date.

put option
An option that grants the right to sell an underlying asset at a fixed price.

long position
To own an option or another security.

exercise the option
Pay (receive) the strike price and buy (sell) the underlying asset.

short position
To sell an option or another security.

option premium
The market price of the option.

counterparty risk
The risk that the counterparty in an over-the-counter options transaction will default on its obligation.

price of the American option should be at least as high as the European option because of the American option's greater flexibility.

A put option grants the right to sell a share of stock at a fixed price on or before a certain date. The right to sell stock at a fixed price becomes more and more valuable as the price of the underlying stock decreases. Thus, we have the most basic distinction between put and call options—put options rise in value as the underlying stock price goes down, whereas call options increase in value as the underlying stock price goes up. Just like call options, put options specify both an exercise price at which investors can sell the underlying stock and an expiration date at which the right to sell vanishes. Also, put options come in American and in European varieties, just as call options do.

The most distinctive feature of options, both puts and calls, can be deduced from the term *option*. Investors who own calls and puts have the right to buy or sell shares, but they are not obligated to do so. This feature creates an asymmetry in option payoffs, and that asymmetry is central to understanding how to use options effectively and how to price them, as we will soon see.

19-1a Option Trading

An important feature distinguishing calls and puts from other securities we've studied, such as stocks and bonds, is that options are not necessarily issued by firms.[2] Rather, an option is a contract between two parties, neither of whom need have any connection to the company whose stock serves as the underlying asset for the contract. For example, suppose Tony and Oscar, neither of whom works for General Electric, decide to enter into an option contract. Tony agrees to pay Oscar $3 for the right to purchase one share of General Electric stock for $20 at any time during the next month. As the option buyer, Tony has a long position in a call option. He can decide at any point whether he wants to exercise the option or not. If he chooses to exercise his option, he will pay Oscar $20, and Oscar will deliver one share of GE stock to Tony. Naturally, Tony will choose to exercise the option only if GE stock is worth more than $20. If GE stock is worth less than $20, Tony will let the option expire worthless and will lose his $3 investment.

On the other side of this transaction, Oscar, as the seller of the option, has a short position in a call option.[3] If Tony decides to exercise his option, Oscar's *obligation* is to follow through on his promise to deliver one share of GE for $20. If Oscar does not already own a share of GE stock, he can buy one in the market. Why would Oscar agree to this arrangement? Because he receives the option premium, the $3 payment that Tony made at the beginning of their agreement. If GE's stock rises above $20, Oscar will lose part or all of the option premium because he must sell Tony an asset for less than what it is worth. On the other hand, if GE's stock price does not rise above $20, then Tony will not attempt to buy the asset, and Oscar can keep the $3 option premium.

Options trades do not usually occur in face-to-face transactions between two parties. Instead, options trade either on an exchange such as the Chicago Board Options Exchange in the U.S. or on the over-the-counter market. Exchanges list options on a limited number of stocks, with a limited set of exercise prices and expiration dates. By limiting the number and the variety of listed options, the exchange expects greater liquidity in the option contracts that are available for trading. Furthermore, an options exchange may serve as a guarantor, fulfilling the terms of an option contract if one party defaults. In contrast, over-the-counter (OTC) options come in seemingly infinite varieties. They are less liquid than exchange-traded options. A trader of OTC options faces counterparty risk, the risk that their counterparty on a specific trade will default on their obligation.

---

[2]This is not to say that firms cannot issue options if they want to. Firms do issue options to employees and may also sell options, as part of their risk management activities, or bundle options with other securities such as bonds and preferred shares that they sell to raise capital.
[3]We may also say that Oscar **writes an option** when he sells the option to Tony.

cash settlement
An agreement between two parties, in which one party pays the other party the cash value of its option position, rather than forcing it to exercise the option by buying or selling the underlying asset.

Most investors who trade options never exercise them. An investor who holds an option and wants to convert that holding into cash can do so in several ways. First, one investor can simply sell the option to another investor, as long as there is some time remaining before expiration. Second, an investor can receive a cash settlement for the option. To understand how cash settlement works, go back to Tony's call option to buy GE stock for $20. Suppose that the price of GE is $30 per share when the option expires. Rather than have Tony pay Oscar $20 in exchange for one share of GE, Oscar might agree to pay Tony $10, the difference between the market price of GE and the option's strike price. Settling in cash avoids the potential need for Oscar to buy one share of GE to give to Tony and the need for Tony to sell that share if he wants to convert his profit into cash. Avoiding these unnecessary trades saves transactions costs.

19-1b Option Prices

Table 19.1 shows a set of option-price quotations for Opti-Tech Corp.[4] The first column indicates that the quoted options are on Opti-Tech common stock. On the day that these option prices were obtained, the closing price of Opti-Tech was $30.00. The second column illustrates the range of expiration dates available for Opti-Tech options. The prices we've chosen to illustrate in the table are for options expiring either in April, May, or July. The third column shows the range of option strike prices available, from $27.50 to $35. The fourth and fifth columns give the most recent trading prices for calls and puts.[5] For instance, an investor who wanted to buy a call option on Opti-Tech stock, with a strike price of $27.50 and an expiration date in May, would pay $3.91. For a May put, with the same strike price, an investor would pay just $1.23. Remember, we also refer to the price of an option as the option's premium.

in the money
A call (put) option is in the money when the stock price is greater (less) than the strike price.

Options traders say that a call option is in the money if the option's strike price is less than the current stock price. For puts, an option is in the money if the strike price exceeds the stock price. Using these definitions, we can say that the call options in the upper three rows of Table 19.1 are in the money, whereas the put options in the lower six rows are in the money. Similarly, options traders say that a call option

Table 19.1 **Option Price Quotes for Opti-Tech Corp.**

The table lists prices for call and put options that expire in April, May, and July, with strike prices of $27.50, $30.00, $32.50, and $35.00.

Company	Expiration	Strike	Calls	Puts	
OPTI	April	27.50	3.26	0.67	Out-of-the-money puts, in-the-money calls
30.00	May	27.50	3.91	1.23	
30.00	July	27.50	4.91	2.04	
30.00	April	30.00	1.77	1.67	At-the-money puts and calls
30.00	May	30.00	2.53	2.33	
30.00	July	30.00	3.62	3.23	
30.00	April	32.50	0.85	3.24	In-the-money puts, out-of-the-money calls
30.00	May	32.50	1.55	3.83	
30.00	July	32.50	2.62	4.69	
30.00	April	35.00	0.36	5.24	
30.00	May	35.00	0.90	5.67	
30.00	July	35.00	1.86	6.40	

© Cengage Learning 2012

[4]This table shows only a handful of the option contracts that you may find trading at the Chicago Board Options Exchange www.cboe.com for an actively traded stock like Microsoft or General Electric. We have also chosen to exclude from the table the daily trading volume figures that are usually included.
[5]Two minor institutional details are worth mentioning here. First, at the CBOE, options expire on the third Saturday of the month. Second, an option contract grants the right to buy or to sell 100 shares of the underlying stock, even though the price quotes in the table are on a "per-share" or "per-option" basis. That is, the call price of $3.91 for the May option, with a $27.50 strike, means that for $391, an investor can purchase the right to buy 100 shares of Opti-Tech at $27.50 per share. All the examples in this chapter are constructed as if an investor can trade one option to buy or to sell one share. We make that assumption to keep the numbers simple, but it does not affect any of the main lessons of the chapter.

Finance in Your Life

"We're in the Money"

Suppose that during your final year of college, you obtain a job offer from a high-tech firm in California. Rather than offering you a cash signing bonus, they offer 400 call options with an exercise price set at the current market price of the firm's stock, $40. These options "vest" in five years, meaning that you have to wait five years before you can exercise them. How valuable might these options become?

The table below illustrates how the payoff on your options depends on the company's stock price, assuming that you plan to exercise them as soon as they vest if they are in the money.

Stock Price in Five Years	Options Payoff	Calculation
$30	$ 0	out of the money
35	0	out of the money
40	0	out of the money
45	2,000	400 × (45 − 40)
50	4,000	400 × (50 − 40)
55	6,000	400 × (55 − 40)
60	8,000	400 × (60 − 40)

What happens if the stock price is $40 or less in five years? As long as the options have not expired, you would continue to hold them in the hope that the stock price will go up. This means that although you cannot obtain any cash payoff from the options when they vest, they still have some value because you might obtain a cash payoff later.

---

out of the money
A call (put) option is out of the money when the stock price is less (greater) than the strike price.

at the money
An option is at the money when the stock price equals the strike price.

intrinsic value
The profit that an investor makes from exercising an option, ignoring transactions costs and the option premium.

time value
The difference between an option's market price and its intrinsic value.

is **out of the money** when the strike price exceeds the current stock price. Puts are out of the money when the strike price falls short of the stock price. Finally, an option is **at the money** when the stock price and the strike price are equal. In Table 19.1, the Opti-Tech options, with a strike price of $30, are at the money because the stock price is $30.00.

Take one more look at the May call option, with a strike price of $27.50. If an investor who owned this option exercised it, she could buy Opti-Tech stock for $27.50 and resell it at the market price of $30.00, a difference of $2.50. But the current price of this option is $3.91, or $1.41 more than the value the investor would obtain by exercising it. In this example, $2.50 is the option's **intrinsic value**.[6] You can think of intrinsic value as the profit an investor makes from exercising the option (ignoring transactions costs as well as the option premium). If an option is out of the money, its intrinsic value is zero. Therefore, a call option's intrinsic value equals the stock price minus the strike price ($S-X$) or zero, whichever is greater. For a put option, the intrinsic value equals either zero or the option's strike price minus the stock price ($X-S$), whichever is greater. The difference between an option's intrinsic value and its market price ($1.41, for the May call) is called the option's **time value**. At the expiration date, the time value equals zero.

Suppose you purchase the May call, with a $30 strike price for $2.53. On the option's expiration date, the price of Opti-Tech stock has grown from $30 to $35, an increase of $5, or 16.7%. What would the option be worth at that time? Because the option holder can buy stock at $30 and then immediately resell it for $35, the option should be worth $5. If the option sells for $5, that's an increase of $2.47, or a percentage increase of almost 98% from the $2.53 purchase price! Similarly, if Opti-Tech's stock price is just $25 when the option expires, then the option will be worthless. If you purchased the call for $2.53, your return on that investment would be −100%, even though Opti-Tech's stock fell just $5, or −16.7%, from the date of your purchase.

---

[6]The intrinsic value of each of the three call options, with a strike price of $30, is $0. For put options, the intrinsic value equals either X−S or $0, whichever is greater. For example, the intrinsic value of each of the three put options, with a strike price of $35, is $5 ($35−$30).

This example illustrates what may be the most important fact to know about options. *When the price of a stock moves, the dollar change of the stock is generally more than the dollar change of the option price, but the percentage change in the option price is greater than the percentage change in the stock price.* We have heard students argue that buying a call option is less risky than buying the underlying share because the maximum dollar loss that an investor can experience is much less on the option. That's only true when we compare the $30 investment required to buy one share of Opti-Tech with the $2.53 required to buy one May call. It is accurate to say that the call investor can lose, at most, $2.53, whereas an investor in Opti-Tech stock may lose $30. But there are two problems with this comparison. First, the likelihood that Opti-Tech will go bankrupt and that its stock will fall to $0 in a short time frame is negligible. The likelihood that the stock could dip below $30, resulting in a $0 value for the call option, is much greater. Second, it is better to compare an equal dollar investment in Opti-Tech stock and calls than to compare one stock to one call. An investment of $30 would purchase almost twelve Opti-Tech call options. Which position, do you think, is riskier—one share of stock or twelve call options?

19-1 Concept Review Questions

1. Explain the difference between the stock price, the exercise price, and the option premium. Which of these are market prices determined by the forces of supply and demand?

2. Explain the difference between a long position and a short position. With respect to call options, what is the maximum gain and loss possible for an investor who holds the long position? What is the maximum gain and loss for the investor on the short side of the transaction?

3. Suppose an investor holds a call option on Nestlé stock and decides to exercise the option. What will happen to the total shares of common stock outstanding for Nestlé?

4. Which of the following would increase the value of a put option—an increase in the stock price or an increase in the strike price?

19-2 Option Payoff Diagrams

So far, our discussion of options has been mostly descriptive. Now we turn to the problem of determining an option's market price. Valuing an option is an extraordinarily difficult problem, so difficult in fact that the economists who solved the problem won a Nobel Prize for their efforts. In earlier chapters, when we studied the pricing of stocks and bonds, we began by describing their cash flows. We do the same here, focusing initially on the relatively simple problem of outlining options' cash flows on the expiration date. Eventually, that will help us understand the intuition behind complex option pricing models.

19-2a Call Option Payoffs

payoff
The value received from exercising an option on the expiration date (or zero), ignoring the initial premium required to purchase the option.

payoff diagrams
A diagram that shows how the expiration date payoff from an option or a portfolio varies, as the underlying asset price changes.

We define an option's **payoff** as the price an investor would be willing to pay for the option the instant before it expires.[7] An option's payoff is distinct from its price, or premium, because the payoff only refers to the price of the option at a particular instant in time, the expiration date. Graphs that illustrate an option's payoff as a function of the underlying stock price are called **payoff diagrams**. Payoff diagrams are extremely useful tools for understanding how options behave and how they can be combined to form portfolios with fascinating properties.

Suppose an investor purchases a call option, with a strike price of $75, and an expiration date three months in the future. To acquire this option, the investor pays a premium of $8. When the option expires, what will it be worth? If the underlying stock price is less than $75 on the expiration date, the option will be worthless. No one would

---

[7]Alternatively, we could define the payoff as the value an investor would receive, ignoring transactions costs, if he or she exercised the option when it expired. If it did not make sense to exercise the option when it expired, the payoff would be zero.

pay anything for the right to buy this stock for $75 when they can easily buy it for less in the market. What if the stock price equals $76 on the expiration date? In that case, owning the right to buy the stock at $75 is worth $1, the difference between the stock's market price and the option's exercise price. Ignoring transactions costs, an investor who owns the option can buy the stock for $75 and immediately sell it in the market for $76, earning a $1 payoff. In general, the payoff of this option will equal the greater of

- $0, if the stock price is less than $75 at expiration, or
- The difference between the stock price and $75, if the stock price is more than $75 at expiration.

The red line in Figure 19.1 shows a payoff diagram for the option buyer, or the long position. This picture is a classic in finance, known as the *hockey-stick diagram*. It shows that the option, at worst, will be worth $0, and at best, the option's value is unlimited. The blue line in the figure represents the investor's **net payoff**. The net payoff line appears $8 lower than the solid line, reflecting the $8 premium the investor paid to acquire the option. On a net basis, the holder of the call option makes a profit when the price of the stock exceeds $83.[8]

Figure 19.1 also shows the call's payoff from the seller's perspective, or the short position. Options are a zero-sum game, meaning that profits on the long position

net payoff
The difference between the payoff received when the option expires and the premium paid to acquire the option.

Figure 19.1   Payoff of a Call Option with X = $75

The top graph illustrates, from the option buyer's perspective, how a call option's payoff varies as the underlying stock price changes. The red line illustrates that the call option's payoff is $0 if the stock price is $75 or less on the expiration date, but the option's payoff rises dollar for dollar with the stock price as the stock price rises above $75. The blue line illustrates the option's net payoff after taking into account the $8 premium that the buyer paid to acquire the option. The breakeven point occurs when the stock price is $83 ($75 + $8). At higher prices, the buyer earns a profit, and at lower prices, the buyer loses money. The buyer's maximum loss is $8, and the maximum gain is unlimited.

The lower graph illustrates the seller's perspective. The red line illustrates that the call option's payoff is $0 if the stock price is $75 or less on the expiration date, but the option's payoff falls dollar for dollar with the stock price as the stock price rises above $75. The blue line illustrates the option's net payoff after taking into account the $8 premium that the seller received from the buyer. The breakeven point occurs when the stock price is $83. At lower prices, the seller earns a profit, and at higher prices, the seller loses money. The seller's maximum profit is $8, and the maximum loss is unlimited.

© Cengage Learning 2012

---

[8]Notice that when the stock price is above $75 but below $83, it still makes sense for the investor to exercise his option, or to sell it, because it reduces the investor's losses. For example, if the stock price at expiration equals $80, the option payoff is $5, reducing the net loss to −$3. The careful reader may notice that we are committing a major sin, for finance professors anyway, by comparing the $8 premium paid up front to the payoff received three months later. At this point, ignoring the time value of money in the graphs is relatively harmless, but rest assured, we take that into account later when we determine the price of an option.

represent losses on the short side, and vice versa. In this part of the figure, the red line illustrates that the seller's payoff equals $0 when the stock price is below $75. It decreases as the stock price rises above $75. The incentive for the seller to engage in this transaction is the $8 premium, as shown by the blue line. If the option expires out of the money, the seller earns an $8 profit. If the option expires in the money, the seller may realize a net profit or a net loss, depending on how high the stock price is at that time. Whereas the call option buyer enjoys the potential for unlimited gains, the option seller faces exposure to the risk of unlimited losses. Rationally, if $8 is sufficient to induce someone to sell this option and thereby face the potential of huge losses, it must be the case that the seller perceives the probability of a large loss to be relatively low.

19-2b Put Option Payoffs

Figure 19.2 shows payoffs for put option buyers (long) and sellers (short). We maintain the assumption that the strike price equals $75, but, in this figure, the option premium is $7. For an investor holding a put option, the payoff rises as the stock price falls below the option's strike price. However, unlike a call option, a put option's potential gains are limited by a stock price that cannot fall below zero (because the law provides limited liability for a firm's shareholders). The maximum gain on this particular put equals $75 (or $68 on a net basis after subtracting the premium), whereas the maximum loss is the $7 option premium.

Figure 19.2   **Payoff of a Put Option with X = $75**

The top graph illustrates, from the option buyer's perspective, how a put option's payoff varies as the underlying stock price changes. The red line shows that the put option will be worthless on the expiration date if the stock price is $75 or higher. The buyer's payoff rises dollar-for-dollar as the stock price drops below $75. The blue line illustrates the put option's net payoff, which takes into account the $7 premium that the buyer paid to acquire the option. The buyer's breakeven point occurs when the stock price is $68 ($75 − $7). At lower stock prices, the buyer makes a profit, and at higher prices, the buyer loses money. The buyer's maximum profit is $68, and the maximum loss is $7.

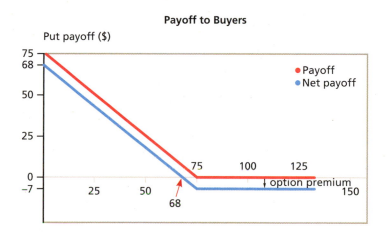

The lower graph illustrates the seller's perspective. The red line shows that the put option's payoff is $0 if the stock price is $75 or higher, but the seller loses money as the stock price falls below $75. The blue line illustrates the net payoff and reflects the $7 premium that the seller received from the buyer. The seller's breakeven point is $68. At higher stock prices, the seller makes a net profit, and at lower prices the seller loses money. The seller's maximum profit is $7, and the maximum loss is $68.

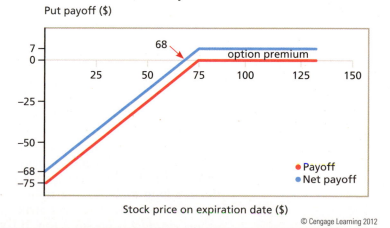

Again, the seller's perspective is just the opposite of the buyer's. The seller earns a maximum net gain of $7 if the option expires worthless, because the stock price exceeds $75 on the expiration date, and the seller faces a maximum net loss of $68 if the firm goes bankrupt and its stock becomes worthless.

EXAMPLE

Jennifer sells a put option on Electro-Lighting Systems Inc. (ELS) stock to Jason. The option's strike price is $65, and it expires in one month. Jason pays Jennifer a premium of $5 for the option. One month later, ELS stock sells for $45 per share. Jason purchases a share of ELS in the open market for $45 and immediately exercises his option to sell it to Jennifer for $65 (or Jennifer and Jason could agree to settle their contract by having Jennifer pay Jason $20). The payoff on Jason's option is $20, or $15 on a net basis. Jennifer loses $20 on the deal, or just $15, taking into account the $5 premium she received up front.

naked option position
To buy or to sell an option, without a simultaneous position in the underlying asset.

We must now clarify an important point. Thus far, all our discussions about options payoffs have assumed that each option buyer or seller had what traders refer to as a naked option position. A naked call option, for example, occurs when an investor buys or sells an option on a stock, without already owning the underlying stock. Similarly, when a trader buys or sells a put option, without owning the underlying stock, the trader creates a naked put position. Buying or selling naked options is an act of pure speculation. Investors who buy naked calls believe that the stock price will rise. Investors who sell naked calls believe the opposite. Similarly, buyers of naked puts expect the stock price to fall, and sellers take the opposite view.

But many options trades do not involve this kind of speculation. Investors who own particular stocks may purchase put options on those stocks, not because they expect stock prices to decline, but because they want protection in the event that they do. Executives who own shares of their companies' stock may sell call options, not because they think that the stock's future gains are limited, but because they are willing to give up potential profits on their shares in exchange for current income. To understand this proposition, we need to examine payoff diagrams for portfolios of options and other securities.

19-2c Payoffs for Portfolios of Options and Other Securities

Experienced options traders know that by combining different types of options, they can construct a wide range of portfolios with unusual payoff structures. Think about what happens if an investor simultaneously buys a call option and a put option on the same underlying stock and with the same exercise price. We've seen before that the call option pays off handsomely if the stock price rises, whereas the put option is most profitable if the stock price falls. By combining both into one portfolio, an investor has a position that can make money whether the stock price rises or falls.

Suppose that Cybil cannot decide whether the stock of Internet Phones Corp. (IPC) will rise or fall from its current value of $30. Suppose Cybil decides to purchase a call option and a put option on IPC stock, both having a strike price of $30 and an expiration date of April 20. Cybil pays premiums of $4.50 for the call and $3.50 for the put, for a total cost of $8. Figure 19.3 illustrates Cybil's position. The payoff of her portfolio equals $0 if IPC stock price is $30 on April 20, and if that occurs, Cybil will experience a net loss of $8. But if the stock price is higher or lower than $30 on April 20, at least one of Cybil's options will be in the money. On a net basis, Cybil makes a profit if the IPC stock either falls below $22 or rises above $38, but she does not have to take a view on which outcome is more likely.

In this example, Cybil is speculating, but not on the *direction* of IPC stock. Rather, Cybil's gamble is on the *volatility* of IPC shares. If the shares move a great deal, either up or down, she makes a net profit. If the shares do not move much by April 20, she experiences a net loss. Options traders refer to this type of position as a *long straddle*, a portfolio consisting of long positions in calls and puts on the same stock with the same strike price and expiration date. Naturally, creating a *short straddle* is possible, too. If Cybil believed that IPC stock would not move

Figure 19.3   **Payoff to Portfolio Containing One Call and One Put (X = $30)**

In this situation, the strike price is $30, the call premium is $4.50, and the put premium is $3.50. Combining a put and a call therefore costs $8. By purchasing a call (upper left graph) and a put (upper right graph) option that have the same strike price, an investor can profit from a significant change in the underlying stock price in either direction. The blue line in the lower graph shows that the investor makes a net profit if the underlying stock price falls below $22 or rises above $38.

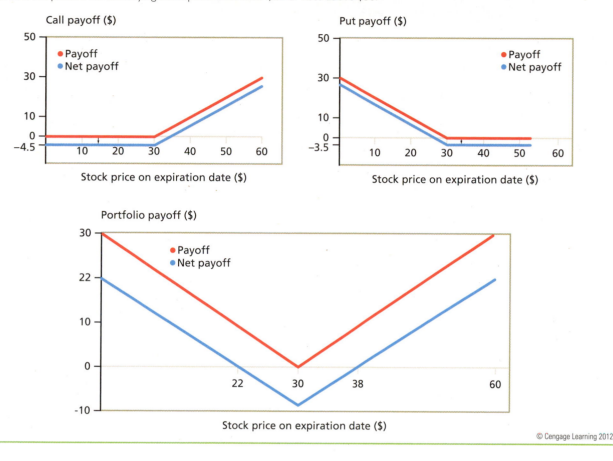

© Cengage Learning 2012

far from its current value, she could simultaneously sell a put and a call option on IPC stock, with a strike price of $30. She would receive $8 in option premiums from this trade. If IPC stock was priced at $30 on April 20, both of the options she sold would expire worthless. On the other hand, if IPC stock moved up or down from $30, one of the options would be exercised, reducing Cybil's profits from the options sale.

Now let's look at what happens when investors form portfolios by combining options with other securities such as stocks and bonds. To begin, examine Figure 19.4, which displays payoff diagrams for a long position in common stocks and bonds.[9] A payoff diagram shows the total value of a security (in this case, one share of common stock or one bond) on a specific future date on the y-axis, and the value of a share of stock on that same date on the x-axis. In Figure 19.4, the payoff diagram from holding a share of stock is a 45-degree line emanating from the origin because both axes of the graph are plotting the same thing—the value of the stock on a future date.[10]

---

[9]In Figure 19.4, we do not plot the net payoff, meaning that the diagram ignores the initial cost of buying stocks or bonds, or the revenue obtained from shorting them.

[10]Figure 19.4 also shows the payoff diagram for a short position in stock, and as always, it is just the opposite of the long payoff diagram. When investors short sell stocks, they borrow shares from other investors, promising to return the shares at a future date. Short selling therefore creates a liability. The magnitude of that liability is just the price of the stock that the short seller must return on a future date.

Figure 19.4   **Payoff Diagrams for Stocks and Bonds**

The graphs show the payoff for long (upper left) and short (upper right) positions in common stock and in risk-free, zero-coupon bonds (lower left for long bond position, lower right for short bond position). The payoff diagram for stock is a 45-degree line (upward sloping for the buyer and downward sloping for the seller) because the payoff of the stock simply equals the price of the stock. Similarly, the bond payoff lines are horizontal because the bond pays $75 to the buyer (or requires the seller to pay $75) with certainty. The bond's payoff is not affected by changes in the stock price.

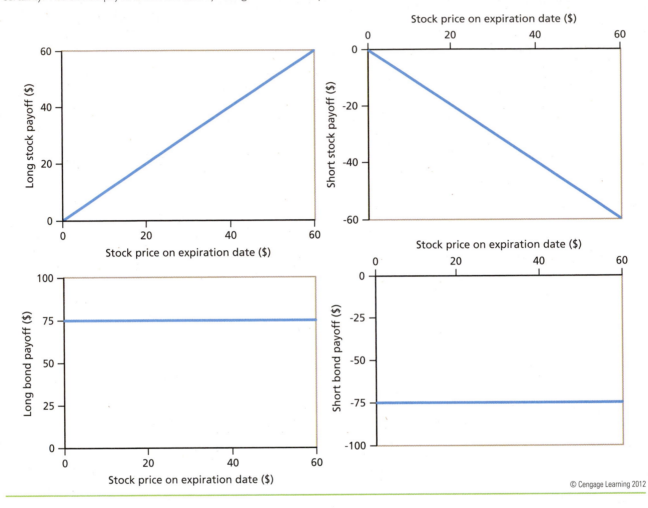

The payoff diagram for the bond requires a little more explanation. The type of bond in this example is very special. It is a risk-free, zero-coupon bond with a face value of $75. The payoff for an investor who purchases this bond is simply $75, no matter what the price of the stock underlying the put and call options turns out to be. That's why the diagram shows a horizontal line at $75 for the long bond's payoff.[11]

Next, consider a portfolio consisting of one share of stock and one put option on that share, with a strike price of $40. If, on the expiration date of the option, the stock price is $40, or more, the put option will be worthless. Therefore, the portfolio's total value will equal the value of the stock. What happens if the stock price is less than $40 on the option's expiration date? In that case, the put option has a positive payoff, which insures that the portfolio's value cannot drop below $40, even if the stock price does. Imagine that the stock price falls to $30. At that point, the put option's payoff is $10, leaving the combined portfolio value at

[11]Is it really possible to buy a risk-free bond with a face value of $75? Perhaps not, but an investor could buy 75 Treasury bills, each with a face value of $1,000, resulting in a risk-free bond portfolio with a face value of $75,000. The assumption that investors can buy risk-free bonds with any face value is just a simplification to keep the numbers in our examples manageable.

Figure 19.5   **Payoff from One Long Share and One Long Put (X = $40)**

The graph shows the payoff on a protective put, a portfolio that combines a long position in the underlying stock (upper left) and a long position in a put option (upper right) on that stock, with a strike price of $40. If the stock price increases above $40, the investor's portfolio goes up. However, if the stock falls below $40, the put option gives the investor the right to sell the stock at $40, essentially putting a floor on the portfolio's value.

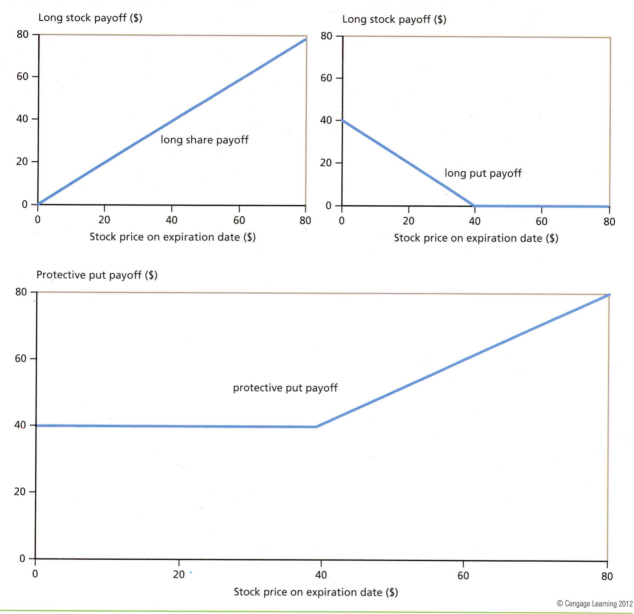

© Cengage Learning 2012

$40 ($30 from the stock + $10 from the put). Simply stated, the put option provides a kind of portfolio insurance, for it guarantees that the share of stock can be sold for at least $40. However, if the price of the stock rises, the portfolio value will rise right along with it. Though the put option will be worthless, any increase in the stock price beyond $40 increases the portfolio's value as well, as shown in Figure 19.5. This strategy is known as a **protective put**.

Investors can construct portfolios containing options, stocks, and bonds in ways that generate a wide range of interesting payoffs. We have illustrated how investors could construct a portfolio not only to profit from a stock's volatility, but to protect themselves from that volatility, using put options. As we see in the next section, no matter what kind of payoff structure an investor wants to create, there is always more than one way to form a portfolio that generates the desired payoffs.

protective put
A portfolio containing a share of stock and a put option on that stock.

19-2d Put-Call Parity

In the payoff diagrams we have studied thus far, the vertical axis shows the value of an option at a particular point in time—the expiration date. Knowing what an option is worth when it expires is important, but option traders need to know the value of options at any time, not just on the expiration date. We explore option pricing in greater depth in the next two sections, but we can gain some basic insights into the process of valuing option by examining payoff diagrams.

Suppose an investor forms a portfolio containing one risk-free, zero-coupon bond, with a face value of $75, and one call option, with a strike price of $75. The bond matures in one year, which is also when the call option expires. Figure 19.6 shows that in one year, this portfolio's payoff will be at least $75. Even if the call option expires out

Figure 19.6   **Payoff on Portfolio of One Bond (*FV* = $75) and One Call (*X* = $75)**

The diagram illustrates the payoff of a portfolio containing a call option (upper left) and a risk-free bond (upper right). In the bottom graph we see that the bond ensures that the portfolio's payoff will never be less than $75. However, if the underlying stock's price is greater than $75 on the expiration date, then the portfolio's payoff will be greater than $75 because both the bond and the call option will have a positive payoff.

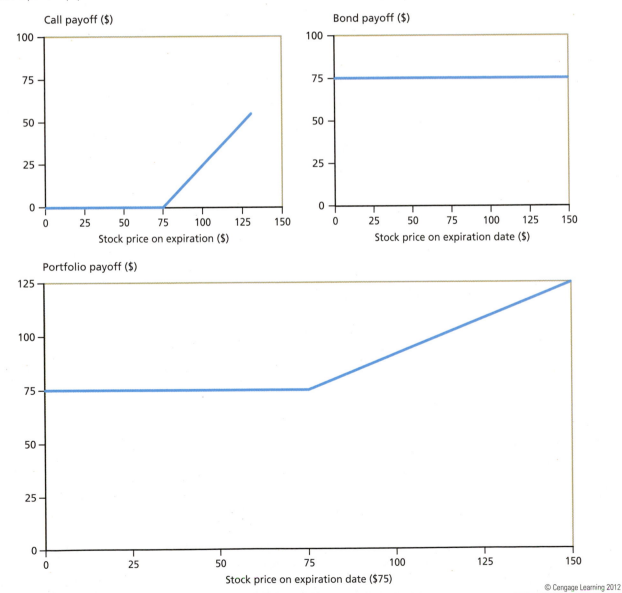

Cengage Learning

John Eck, President of Broadcast and Network Operations, NBC

"That allowed us to create some doubt around the transaction and allowed us not to have to book the gain up front but to book it as the cash came in."

See the entire interview at **SMART|finance**

Smart Ethics Video

of the money, the bond will pay $75. In addition, if the price of the underlying stock is high enough, the call option will have a positive payoff, too, and the portfolio's payoff will exceed $75.

Does this diagram look familiar? Notice that it has the same basic shape as the protective put, shown in Figure 19.5. In fact, we could create a new portfolio with exactly the same payoff as the one shown in Figure 19.6, simply by combining one put option, with a strike price of $75, and one share of the underlying stock. Both of these portfolios provide a minimum payoff in one year of $75, with additional upside potential if the stock price rises above $75.

Think carefully about what this means. An investor who wants to construct a position with a minimum payoff of $75, plus the potential for a higher payoff if the stock price rises, has two alternatives. He can either purchase a risk-free bond, with a face value of $75, and a call option, with $X = \$75$, or he can purchase one share of stock and one put option, with $X = \$75$. No matter what happens to the stock price over the next year, these portfolios have equal payoffs on the expiration date. Therefore we can write:

Payoff on bond + Payoff on call = Payoff on stock + Payoff on put

This equation applies to payoffs that occur one year in the future, when the put and call options expire and the bond matures. However, an important principle in finance says that if two assets have identical cash flows in the future, then they must sell for the same price today. If that were not true, then investors could earn unlimited risk-free profits by engaging in arbitrage, simultaneously buying the asset with the lower price and selling the asset with the higher price. *To prevent arbitrage opportunities, the price of the portfolio consisting of a bond and a call option must equal the price of the portfolio consisting of one share of stock and one put option.*

In making the previous statement, we took a subtle, but important, step forward in understanding options. Notice that the last sentence of the previous paragraph used the word "price" rather than the word "payoff." Because the future payoffs on these two portfolios will be identical on the expiration date, then the prices of the portfolios must be equal on the expiration date and on any date prior to expiration. We can express this idea algebraically, as follows:

(Eq. 19.1) $$S + P = B + C$$

put-call parity
A relationship that links the market prices of stock, risk-free bonds, call options, and put options.

In this equation, S stands for the current stock price, P and C represent the current market prices (premiums) of the put and call options, respectively, and B equals the current price of the risk-free, zero-coupon bond. Equation 19.1 describes one of the most fundamental ideas in option pricing, known as **put-call parity**. Put-call parity says that the prices of put and call options on the same underlying stock, with the same strike price and the same expiration date, must be related to each other.

EXAMPLE

Mototronics Inc. stock currently sells for $28 per share. Put and call options on Mototronics shares are available, with a strike price of $30 and an expiration date of one year. The price of the Mototronics call option is $6, and the risk-free interest rate equals 5%. What is the appropriate price for the Mototronics put option? In other words, what price would satisfy put call parity?

Examine Equation 19.1. We know that the stock price equals $28, and the call price is $6. To find the put price, we also need to know the market price of a risk-free bond. Refer once again to Figure 19.6. In that example, the face value of the bond is $75, equal to the strike price of the option. To apply put-call parity to value the Mototronics put option, we must recognize that B, in Equation 19.1, represents a risk-free bond, with a face value of $30, the same value as the option's strike price. The face value of the bond must equal the option's strike price because on the right-hand side of Equation 19.1, it is the bond that provides the "floor" on the portfolio value. On the left-hand side of Equation 19.1, the put option creates a floor on

continued

the portfolio value, and that floor is equal to the strike price of the put. That is, if the put option's strike is $30, then the left-hand side of Equation 19.1 can never be less than $30. For the right-hand side of Equation 19.1 to have the same floor, the bond's face value must equal $30.

If a risk-free bond pays $30 in one year, then the current market price of the bond equals

$$B = \$30 \div (1.05) = \$28.57$$

Plug this and the other known values into Equation 19.1 to solve for the put price:

$$S + P = B + C$$
$$\$28 + P = \$28.57 + \$6$$
$$P = \$6.57$$

SMART concepts

See the concept explained step-by-step at SMART | finance

? JOB INTERVIEW QUESTION

How are the prices of put and call options on the same underlying stock related to each other?

Pause a moment to take an inventory of the information that is required to value the Mototronics put option. To calculate the put value, we had to know the following facts:

- The strike price of the option, $30;
- The current price of the underlying stock, $28;
- The amount of time remaining before the option expires, one year;
- The risk-free interest rate, 5%; and
- The the price of the call option, $6.

It turns out that each of these items, except for the last one, are required to value an option, whether we use put-call parity to determine the option's price or an alternative method. In the next section, we provide an intuitive, qualitative explanation of how several of these factors influence option prices.

19-2 Concept Review Questions

5. What would happen if an investor who owned a share of a particular stock also bought a put option, with a strike price of $50, and sold a call option, with a strike price of $50? Try to draw the payoff diagram for this portfolio.

6. Is selling a call the same thing as buying a put? Explain why or why not.

7. A major corporation is involved in high-profile antitrust litigation with the government. The firm's stock price is somewhat depressed due to the uncertainty of this case. If the company wins, investors expect its stock price to shoot up. If it loses, the stock price will decline even more than it already has. If investors expect a resolution to the case in the near future, what affect do you think that resolution will have on put and call options on the company's stock? Hint: think about Figure 19.3.

19-3 Qualitative Analysis of Option Prices

19-3a Factors That Influence Option Values

Before getting into the rather complex quantitative aspects of pricing options, let's cultivate the intuition needed to understand the factors that influence option prices. We begin by taking a look at recent price quotes for options on Whirlpool Corporation stock. Table 19.2 shows prices of several Whirlpool option contracts, as taken from the Chicago Board Options Exchange Web site (www.cboe.com) on February 18, 2011.

You should notice a striking pattern here. The prices of both calls and puts rise the longer the time before expiration. To understand why, think about the call option that expires in March, roughly one month in the future (as of the date that we gathered the option prices). Currently this option is out of the money because it grants

Table 19.2 — Prices of Option Contracts on Whirlpool Stock, February 18, 2011

The table shows the market prices of various call and put options on Whirlpool stock, as of February 18, 2011. Both call and put prices increase as the expiration date moves from March to June to September.

Whirlpool Price	Expiration	Strike	Call	Put
$83.44	March	$85	$2.15	$4.00
83.44	June	85	5.48	7.60
83.44	September	85	7.24	8.70

© Cengage Learning 2012

the right to purchase Whirlpool stock for $85, but investors can buy Whirlpool in the open market for $83.44. Buying the March call option requires an investment of just $2.15. The option is inexpensive because there is only a small chance that, before the option expires in one month, Whirlpool's stock price will increase enough to make exercising the option profitable. If an investor pays $2.15 for the call option, then Whirlpool's stock price must reach at least $87.15 before the investor earns a net profit. That would represent a 4.4% gain on Whirlpool shares in just a few weeks, so the low price of the Whirlpool call in part reflects that investors doubt the stock will move that much in one month.

However, the price of the June call option with a strike price of $85 is two-and-a-half times greater than the price of the March call. The June option expires in about four months. For an investor who pays $5.48 to acquire this option, the stock price must rise to at least $90.48 ($85 + $5.48) in the next four months in order for exercising the option to produce a net profit. That represents an increase of about 8.4% from the current stock price. Investors must think that an 8.4% gain in four months is more likely than a 4.4% gain in one month because they are willing to pay more for the June call than the March call. The same pattern holds for puts. The June put option sells for $3.60 more than the March put option because investors recognize that the chance of a significant drop in Whirlpool stock over a one-month period is much lower than the chance of a large decrease over the next four months. In general, *holding other factors constant, call and put option prices increase as the time to expiration increases.*[12]

Next, let's examine the prices of several Whirlpool puts and calls, all which expire in March. Table 19.3 lists the market prices of these options, as of February 18, 2011. Once again, a clear pattern emerges. Call option prices fall as the strike price increases, and put option prices rise as the strike price increases. This relationship is

Table 19.3 — Prices of March Option Contracts on Whirlpool Stock

The table shows the market prices of various call and put options on Whirlpool stock, as of February 18, 2011 and February 11, 2011. The table illustrates that call prices increase and put prices decrease when the difference between the stock price and the exercise price ($S - X$) increases.

Expiration	Strike	February 18, 2011 Whirlpool = $83.44		February 11, 2011 Whirlpool = $86.70	
		Call	Put	Call	Put
March	$80	$4.80	$1.68	$7.60	$0.88
March	85	2.15	4.00	4.18	2.48
March	90	0.85	7.85	1.95	5.25
March	95	0.34	12.30	0.78	9.10

© Cengage Learning 2012

[12]There are a few exceptions to this rule. Suppose you hold a European put option on a company that is about to go bankrupt. The firm's stock price will be nearly zero, and it cannot drop much farther. In this case, you would prefer to exercise your option immediately, rather than having to wait to sell it, so the value of the option will decline as the time to expiration lengthens.

Table 19.4   **Prices of Option Contracts on Two Stocks, February 18, 2011**

On February 18, 2011, Mosaic calls were trading for more than Whirlpool calls (holding the strike prices and expiration dates equal). Mosaic options were more valuable, in part, because Mosaic stock was more volatile.

Expiration	Strike	Mosaic Call	Whirlpool Call
March	$85	$2.71	$2.15
March	90	1.24	0.85

Mosaic stock price = $83.02
Whirlpool stock price = $83.44

intuitive. A call option grants the right to buy stock at a fixed price. That right is more valuable the cheaper the price at which the option holder can buy the stock. Conversely, put options grant the right to sell shares at a fixed price. That right is more valuable the higher the price at which investors can sell.

We can see a similar relationship by looking at Table 19.3, which shows what happened to the prices of March Whirlpool options during the week from February 11–18, 2011. During that week, Whirlpool shares fell $3.26. All the call prices in Table 19.3 declined during the week, but all the put prices increased. In response to the $3.26 decline in Whirlpool stock, call prices dropped between $0.44 and $2.80, and put prices rose between $0.80 and $3.20. Combining the lessons of the last few paragraphs, we can say that *call prices increase and put prices decrease when the difference between the underlying stock price and the exercise price (S−X) increases.*

Finally, to isolate the most important, and the most subtle, influence on option prices, examine Table 19.4, which compares the prices of March options on two different stocks, Whirlpool and and Mosaic, a producer of phosphate and potash crop fertilizers. On February 18, 2011, these two stocks traded at nearly the same prices, with Whirlpool at $83.44 compared to Mosaic's $83.02. We might expect Whirlpool and Mosaic options with similar characteristics (i.e., same expiration date and strike price), to trade at nearly identical prices, but Table 19.4 shows that this was not the case. Looking at March call options with a $85 strike, we see that Whirlpool's call sold for $2.15 while Mosaic's was worth 26% more at $2.71 (despite Mosaic's stock price trading for $0.42 less than Whirlpool's). For contracts with a slightly higher strike price, $90, Mosaic's call was worth 46% more than Whirlpool's ($1.24 versus $0.85). Why were Mosaic's call options worth so much more even though its stock price was trading at a lower price than Whirlpool shares?

Figure 19.7 offers a clue about what makes Mosaic options so valuable. The figure charts weekly price movements in the two stocks from November through February 2011. Notice that the fluctuations in Mosaic are often larger than Whirlpool's movements. Mosaic is a much smaller company than Whirlpool, and its cash flows are very sensitive to movements in agricultural commodity prices (which are themselves notoriously volatile). Perhaps, then, it is not too surprising that Mosaic's stock is more volatile than Whirlpool's. But why should Mosaic's higher volatility lead to higher option prices?

The answer lies in the asymmetry of option payoffs. When a call option expires, its payoff is zero, for a wide range of stock prices. Whether the stock price falls below the option's strike price by $1, $10, or $100, the call payoff is zero. On the other hand, as the stock price rises above the strike price, the call option's payoff increases. A similar relationship holds for puts. The value of a put at expiration is zero if the stock price is greater than the strike price. Whether the stock price is just above the strike price or far above it does not change the payoff. However, the put option has a larger payoff the lower the stock price falls, once it falls below the strike price. In summary, *call and put option prices increase as the volatility of the underlying stock increases.*

Figure 19.7   **Weekly Stock Price Changes for Whirlpool and Mosaic**

From November 2010 to February 2011, Mosaic common shares exhibited larger weekly fluctuations than did Whirlpool shares.

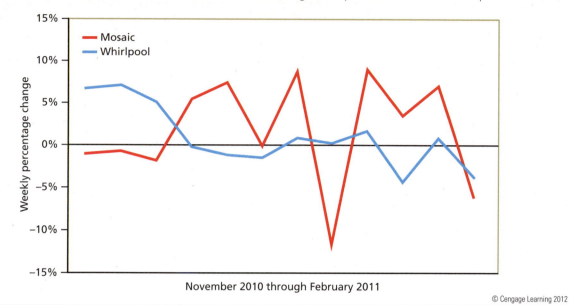

November 2010 through February 2011

EXAMPLE

Suppose you are tracking two stocks. One exhibits much more volatility than the other. Call the more volatile stock Extreme Inc. and the less volatile one Steady Corp. At present, shares of both companies sell for about $40. At-the-money put and call options are available on both stocks, with an expiration date in three months. Based on the historical volatility of each stock, you estimate a range of prices that you think the shares may attain by the time the options expire. Next to each possible stock price, you write down the option payoff that will occur if the stock actually reaches that price on the expiration date (the strike price is $40 for both options). The numbers appear in the accompanying table.

Stock	Potential Prices in Three Months	Call Payoff	Put Payoff
Extreme Inc.	$15	$0	$25
	25	0	15
	35	0	5
	45	5	0
	55	15	0
	65	25	0
Steady Corp.	$30	0	$10
	34	0	6
	38	0	2
	42	2	0
	46	6	0
	50	10	0

The payoffs of puts and calls for both companies are zero, exactly half the time. But when the payoffs are not zero, they are much larger for Extreme Inc. than they are for Steady Corp. That makes options on Extreme Inc. shares much more valuable than options on Steady Corp. stock.

Summing up, we now know that option prices usually increase as time to expiration increases. Option values also rise as the volatility of the underlying asset increases. Call option prices increase as the difference between the stock price and the strike price (S-X) grows larger, whereas put prices increase as this difference decreases. We are finally ready to tie all this together and calculate market price of puts and calls. Fortunately, simple, but powerful, tools exist for valuing options. We examine two approaches for valuing options, the binomial model and the Black and Scholes model.

19-3 Concept Review Questions

8. Throughout most of this book, we have shown that if an asset's risk increases, its price declines. Why is the opposite true for options?

9. Put options increase in value as stock prices fall, and call options increase in value as stock prices rise. How can the same movement in an underlying variable (e.g., an increase either in time before expiration or in volatility) cause both put and call prices to rise at the same time?

19-4 Option Pricing Models

19-4a The Binomial Model

binomial option pricing model
A model that uses the principle of "no arbitrage" to calculate call and put values.

Earlier in this chapter, we studied an important relationship linking the prices of puts, calls, shares, and risk-free bonds. Put-call parity establishes a direct link between the prices of these assets, a link which must hold to prevent arbitrage opportunities. A similar logic drives the binomial option pricing model. The binomial model recognizes investors can combine options (either calls or puts) with shares of the underlying asset to construct a portfolio with a risk-free payoff. Any asset with a risk-free payoff is relatively easy to value—just discount its future cash flows at the risk-free rate. But if we can value a portfolio containing options and shares, then we can also calculate the value of the options by subtracting the value of the shares from the value of the portfolio.

Let's work through an example that shows how to price an option, using the binomial method. The example proceeds in three distinct steps. First, we must find a portfolio of stock and options which generates a risk-free payoff in the future. Second, given that the portfolio offers a risk-free cash payment, we can calculate the present value of that portfolio by discounting its cash flow at the risk-free rate. Third, given the portfolio's present value, we can determine how much of the portfolio's value comes from the stock and how much comes from the option. By subtracting the value of the underlying shares from the value of the portfolio, we obtain the option's market price.

Step 1: Create a Risk-Free Portfolio Suppose the shares of Financial Engineers Ltd. currently sell for $55. We want to determine the price of a call option on Financial Engineers stock, with an exercise price of $55 and an expiration date in one year. Assume the risk-free rate is 4%.

The binomial model begins with an assumption about the volatility of the underlying stock. Specifically, the model assumes that by the time the option expires, the stock will have increased or decreased to a particular dollar value. In this problem, we assume that one year from now, Financial Engineers stock price will have risen to $70 or it will have fallen to $40. Figure 19.8 provides a simple diagram of this assumption.[13]

The call option we want to price has a strike of $55. Therefore, if the underlying stock reaches $70 in one year, the call option will be worth $15. However, if Financial Engineers stock falls to $40, the call option will be worthless.

Here is the crux of the first step. We want to find some combination of Financial Engineers stock and the call option which yields the same payoff whether the stock goes up or down over the next year. In other words, we want to create a risk-free combination of shares and calls. To begin, suppose we purchase one share of stock and h call options. At the moment, we do not know the value of h, but we can solve for it. Because our portfolio objective is to generate the same cash payment one year from now, whether our share of stock rises or falls, we can write down the portfolio's payoffs in each possible scenario and then choose h so that the payoffs are equal:

---

[13]How can we possibly know that the price of Financial Engineer's stock will be either $70 or $40? Of course we cannot know that. Almost any price is possible one year in the future. Soon, we will illustrate that this assumption, which seems completely ridiculous now, isn't really necessary in a more complex version of the binomial model. But let's understand the simple version first.

Figure 19.8

The figure shows that in one year, Financial Engineers stock will be worth $70 or $40. If there is a call option on this stock, with a strike price of $55, then it will be worth $15 or $0 when that option expires in one year.

Binomial Option Pricing

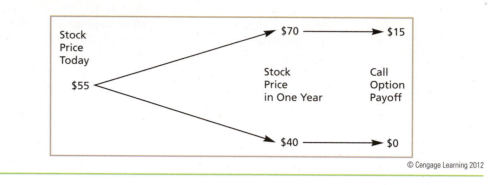

© Cengage Learning 2012

	Cash Flows One Year from Today	
	If the Stock Price Goes Up to $70	If the Stock Price Drops to $40
One share of stock is worth	$70	$40
h options are worth	$15h	$0h
Total portfolio is worth	$70 + $15h	$40 + $0h

A portfolio that contains one share of stock and h call options will have the same cash value in one year if we choose the value of h that solves this equation:

$$70 + 15h = 40 + 0h$$
$$h = -2$$

The value of h represents the number of call options in our risk-free portfolio. Because h equals -2, we must *sell two call options* and combine that position with our single share of stock to create a risk-free portfolio. Why do we sell options to achieve this objective? Remember that the value of a call option rises as the stock price rises. If we own a share of stock and a call option (or several call options) on that stock, the assets in our portfolio will move together, rising and falling at the same time. To create a portfolio that behaves like a risk-free bond, we need the movements in the stock and the call option to offset each other. If the stock's movements exactly cancel out fluctuations in the call, then the portfolio's payout will not move at all, just like a risk-free bond. Therefore, if we buy a share we must sell call options to create offsetting movements between the assets in our portfolio.

What happens to our portfolio if we buy one share and sell two calls? You can see the answer in two ways. First, just plug the value, -2, back into the equation that we used to solve for h and you get:

$$40 = 40$$

This expression says that the portfolio payoff will be $40, whether the stock price increases or decreases. Another way to see this is to lay out the payoffs of each asset in the portfolio in a table like this.

	Cash Flows One Year from Today	
	If the Stock Price Goes Up to $70	If the Stock Price Drops to $40
One share of stock is worth	$70	$40
Two short options are worth	−30	0
Total portfolio is worth	40	40

The first line of the table is self-explanatory. The second line indicates that if we sell two call options and the stock price equals $70 next year, then we will owe the holder of the calls $15 per option, or $30 total. On the other hand, if one year from now the stock price equals $40, then the call options we sold will be worthless, and we will have no cash outflow. In either case, the total cash inflow from the portfolio will be $40.

Because this portfolio pays $40 in one year, no matter what happens, we call it a perfectly hedged portfolio. The value of h is called the **hedge ratio** because it tells us what combination of stocks and calls results in a perfectly hedged position.[14]

hedge ratio
A combination of stock and options that results in a risk-free payoff.

Step 2: Calculate the Present Value of the Portfolio Because the portfolio, consisting of one share of stock and two short call options, pays $40 for certain next year, we can say that the portfolio behaves like a risk-free bond (in technical terms, the portfolio is a "synthetic" risk-free bond). The second step requires us to calculate the present value of the portfolio. Because we already know that the risk-free rate equals 4%, the present value of the portfolio equals:

$$PV = \frac{\$40}{1.04} = \$38.46$$

It is crucial at this step to understand the following point. Buying one share of stock and selling two calls yields the same future payoff as buying a risk-free, zero-coupon bond, with a face value of $40. Because both of these investments offer $40 in one year, with certainty, they should both sell for the same price today. That's the insight that allows us to determine the option's price in the next step.

Step 3: Determine the Price of the Option If a risk-free bond, paying $40 in one year, costs $38.46 today, then the net cost of buying one share of Financial Engineers stock and selling two call options must also be $38.46. Why? Both investment strategies offer the same future cash flows, so they must both sell for the same price. Therefore, to determine the price of the option, we need to write down an expression for the cost of our hedged portfolio and set that expression equal to $38.46.

From the information given in the problem, purchasing one share of stock costs $55. Partially offsetting this cost will be the revenue from selling two call options. Denoting the price of the call option, C, we can calculate the total cost of the portfolio as follows:

$$\text{Total portfolio cost} = \$55 - 2C = \$38.46$$

Solving for C, we obtain a call value of $8.27.

At this point, it is worth reviewing what we've accomplished. We began with an assumption about the future movements of the underlying stock. Next, given the type of option we wanted to value and its characteristics, we calculated the payoffs of the option for each of the two possible future stock prices. Given those payoffs, we discovered that by buying one share and selling two calls, we could generate a certain payoff of $40 in one year. Because the present value of that payoff is $38.46, the net cost of buying the share and selling the calls must also equal $38.46. That implies that we received revenue of $16.54 from selling two calls, or $8.27 each. The following example repeats the process to value an identical put option on the same underlying stock.

EXAMPLE

We begin this problem with the same set of assumptions from the last problem. Financial Engineers stock sells for $55, and it may increase to $70 or decrease to $40 in one year. The risk-free rate equals 4%. We want to use the binomial model to calculate the value of a one-year put option, with a strike price of $55. We begin by finding the composition of a perfectly hedged portfolio. As before, let's write down the payoffs of a portfolio that contains one share of stock and h put options:

---

[14]The hedge ratio can be defined as the ratio of calls to shares in a perfectly hedged portfolio (the definition we use here) or as the ratios of shares to calls. In this example, the hedge ratio equals either $-2:1$ (using our definition) or $-1:2$ (using the alternative definition). Either way, the hedge ratio defines the mix of options and shares that results in a perfectly hedged portfolio.

continued

	Cash Flows One Year from Today	
	If the Stock Price Goes Up to $70	**If the Stock Price Drops to $40**
One share of stock is worth	$70	$40
h options are worth	$0h	$15h
Total portfolio is worth	$70 + $0h	$40 + $15h

Notice that the put option pays $15 when the stock price drops, and it pays nothing when the stock price rises. Set the payoffs in each scenario equal to each other and solve for h:

$$70 + 0h = 40 + 15h$$
$$h = 2$$

To create a perfectly hedged portfolio, we must buy one share of stock and two put options. Observe that in this problem we are buying options, not selling them. Put values increase when stock values decrease, so it is possible to form a risk-free portfolio containing long positions in both stocks and puts because they move in opposite directions. By plugging the value of $h = 2$ back into the equation, we see that an investor who buys one share of stock and two put options essentially creates a synthetic bond, with a face value of $70:

$$70 + 0(2) = 40 + 15(2)$$
$$70 = 70$$

Given a risk-free rate of 4%, the present value today of $70 is $67.31. It would cost $67.31 to buy a one-year, risk-free bond paying $70, so it must also cost $67.31 to buy the synthetic version of that bond, consisting of one share and two puts. Given that the current share price is $55, and letting P denote the price of the put, we find that the put option is worth $6.16 (rounding to the nearest penny):

$$\text{Cost of one share} + 2 \text{ puts} = \$67.31 = \$55 + 2P$$
$$\$12.31 = 2P$$
$$\$6.16 = P$$

Take a moment to look over the last two examples of pricing options that use the binomial approach. Make a list of the data needed to price these options:

1. The current price of the underlying stock
2. The amount of time remaining before the option expires
3. The strike price of the option
4. The risk-free rate
5. The possible values that the underlying stock could take in the future

? JOB INTERVIEW QUESTION

What factors influence the prices of call and put options?

On this list, the only unknown is the fifth item. You can easily find the other four necessary values by looking at current market data.

At this point, we want to pause and ask one of our all-time favorite exam questions. Look back at Figure 19.8. What assumption are we making about the probability of an up and down move in Financial Engineers stock? Most people see that the figure shows two possible outcomes and guess that the probabilities must be 50-50. That is not true. At no point in our discussion of the binomial model did we make any assumption about the probabilities of up and down movements in the stock. We don't have to know what those probabilities are to value the option, which is convenient because estimating them could be very difficult.

Why are the probabilities of no concern to us? There are two answers to this question. The first answer is that the market sets the current price of the stock at a level that reflects the probabilities of future up and down movements. In other words, the probabilities are embedded in the stock price, even though no one can see them directly.

The second answer is that the binomial model prices an option through the principle of "no arbitrage." Because it is always possible to combine a share of stock with options (either calls or puts) into a risk-free portfolio, the binomial model says that the value of that portfolio must be the same as the value of a risk-free bond.

Otherwise, an arbitrage opportunity would exist because identical assets would be selling at different prices. Hence, because the portfolio containing stock and options offers a risk-free payoff, the probabilities of up and down movements in the stock price do not enter the calculations. An investor who holds the hedged portfolio doesn't need to worry about movements in the stock because they do not affect the portfolio's payoffs.

Almost all students object to the binomial model's assumption that the price of a stock can take just two values in the future. Fair enough. It is certainly true that one year from today, the price of Financial Engineers may be $70, $40, or almost any other value. However, it turns out that more complex versions of the binomial do not require analysts to specify just two final prices for the stock. The binomial model can accommodate a wide range of final prices. To see how this works, consider a slight modification to our original problem.

Rather than presume that Financial Engineers stock will rise or fall by $15 over a year's time, suppose it may rise or fall by $7.50 every six months. That's still a big assumption, but if we make it, we find that the list of potential prices of Financial Engineers stock, one year from today, has grown from two values to three. Figure 19.9 proves this claim. After one year, the price of the stock may be $40, $55, or $70. Now let's modify the assumption one more time. Suppose the price of the stock can move

---

Figure 19.9

Multistage Binomial Trees

The binomial model can be modified to allow for multiple stock price movements throughout the life of an option. The more movements we build into the model, the finer the grid of possible stock prices when the option expires.

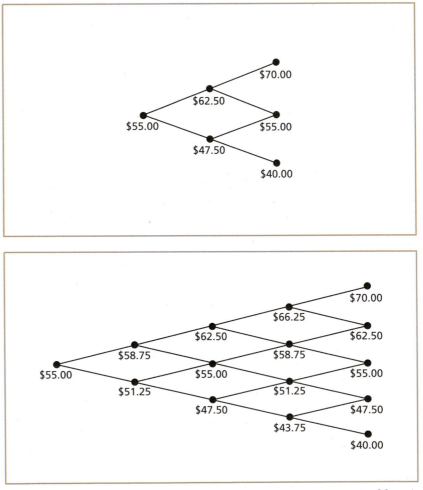

up or down $3.75 every three months. Figure 19.9 shows that in this case, the number of possible stock prices one year in the future grows to five.

Given a tree with many branches like the one in Figure 19.9, it is possible to solve for the value of a call or put option by applying the same steps we followed to value options using the simple two-step tree. Now imagine a much larger tree, one in which the stock moves up or down every few minutes, or even every few seconds. Each change in the stock price is very small, perhaps a penny or two, but as the tree unfolds and time passes, the number of branches rapidly expands, as does the number of possible values of the stock at the option's expiration date. If you imagine what this tree would look like, you can see that when the option expires in a year, the price of Financial Engineers stock can take any one of hundreds, or even thousands, of different values. Therefore, the complaint about the binomial model's artificial assumption of just two possible stock prices no longer applies. Though extremely tedious, solving for the call value involves working all the way through the tree, applying the same steps over and over again.

The binomial model is an incredibly powerful and flexible tool that analysts can use to price all sorts of options, from ordinary puts and calls, to complex real options which are embedded in capital investment projects. The genius of the model is in its recognition of the opportunity to use stock and options to mimic the payoffs of risk-free bonds, the easiest of all securities to price. That insight is also central to the second option pricing model that we discuss, the Black and Scholes Model.

19-4b The Black and Scholes Model

In 1973, Myron Scholes and Fisher Black published what might fairly be called a trillion-dollar research paper. Their research produced for the first time a formula that traders could use to calculate the value of call options, a path-breaking discovery, which had eluded researchers for decades. Black and Scholes did not have to wait long to see whether their formula would have an effect in financial markets. That same year, options began trading in the United States on the newly formed Chicago Board Options Exchange (CBOE). Traders on the floor of the options exchange used handheld calculators that were programmed with the Black-Scholes formula. From that beginning, trading in options exploded over the next two decades, hence, the trillion-dollar moniker given to the original research paper.[15]

When you first encounter it, the Black and Scholes option pricing equation looks rather intimidating. As a matter of fact, their paper was originally rejected by the editor at the prestigious academic journal in which Black and Scholes published their prize-winning formula. He felt it was too technical and not of interest to a wide audience. Although it is true that the derivation of the formula requires a rather high level of mathematics, the intuition behind the equation is fairly straightforward. In fact, the logic of the Black and Scholes model mirrors that of the binomial model.

Black and Scholes began their research by asking a question. Suppose investors can buy and sell shares of stock, options on those shares, and risk-free bonds. Does a combination of options and shares exist that provides a risk-free payoff? This should sound familiar, because this is exactly how you begin when you price an option, using the binomial model. However, Black and Scholes' approach to valuing an option differs from the binomial method in several important ways.

First, recall that the binomial model assumes that over a given time period, the stock price will move up or down by a known amount. In Figure 19.9, we showed that by shortening the length of the period during which the stock price moves, we increase the number of different prices that the stock may reach by the option's expiration date. The Black and Scholes model takes this approach to its logical extreme. It presumes that stock prices can move at every instant. If we were to illustrate this

---

[15]For this achievement, Myron Scholes won the Nobel Prize in economics in 1997, an honor he shared with Robert Merton, another researcher who made seminal contributions to options research. Fisher Black undoubtedly would have been a corecipient of the award had he not died in 1995.

assumption by drawing a binomial tree like the ones in Figure 19.9, the tree would have an infinite number of branches, and on the option's expiration date, the stock price could take on almost any value.

Second, Black and Scholes did not assume that they knew precisely what the up and down movements in stock would be at every instant. They recognized that these movements were essentially random, and therefore unpredictable. Instead, they assumed that the volatility, or standard deviation, of a stock's movements was known.

With these assumptions in place, Black and Scholes calculated the *price of a European call option* (on a nondividend-paying stock) with the following equations:

(Eq. 19.2)
$$C = SN(d_1) - Xe^{-rt}N(d_2)$$

(Eq. 19.3)
$$d_1 = \frac{\ln\left(\frac{S}{X}\right) + \left(r + \frac{\sigma^2}{2}\right)t}{\sigma\sqrt{t}}$$
$$d_2 = d_1 - \sigma\sqrt{t}$$

Let's dissect this carefully. We have seen most of the terms in the equation before:

S = current market price of underlying stock

X = strike price of option

t = amount of time (in years) before option expires

r = annual risk-free interest rate

σ = annual standard deviation of underlying stock's returns

e = 2.718 (approximately)

$N(X)$ = the probability of drawing a value less than or equal to X from the **standard normal distribution**

standard normal distribution
A normal distribution with a mean of zero and a standard deviation of one.

Does this list of variables look familiar? It should because it is nearly identical to the list of inputs required to use the binomial model. The stock price (S), the strike price (X), the time until expiration (t), and the risk-free rate (r) are all variables that the binomial model uses to price options. The new item that the Black and Scholes model requires is the standard deviation, σ, of the underlying asset's returns.

What about the term Xe^{-rt}? Recall from our discussion about continuous compounding, in Chapter 3, that the term e^{-rt} reflects the present value of $1, discounted at r percent for t years. Therefore, Xe^{-rt} simply equals the present value of the option's strike price.[16] With this in mind, look again at Equation 19.2. The first term equals the stock price, multiplied by a quantity labeled $N(d_1)$. The second term is the present value of the strike price, multiplied by a quantity labeled $N(d_2)$. Therefore, we can say that the call option value equals the "adjusted" stock price, minus the present value of the "adjusted" strike price, where $N(d_1)$ and $N(d_2)$ represent adjustment factors. Earlier in this chapter, we saw that call option values increase as the difference between the stock price and the strike price, S-X, increases. The same relationship holds here, although we must now factor in the terms $N(d_1)$ and $N(d_2)$.

In the Black and Scholes equation, d_1 and d_2 are simply numerical values (calculated using Equation 19.3) that depend on the model's inputs: the stock price, the strike price, the interest rate, the time to expiration, and volatility. The expressions $N(d_1)$ and $N(d_2)$ convert the numerical values of d_1 and d_2 into probabilities, using the standard normal distribution.[17] Figure 19.10 shows that the value, $N(d_1)$, equals the area under the standard normal curve to the left of value d_1. For example, if we calculate the value of d_1 and find that it equals 0, then $N(d_1)$ equals 0.5 because half of the area under the curve falls to the left of zero. The higher the value of d_1, the closer $N(d_1)$ gets to 1.0. The lower the value of d_1, the closer $N(d_1)$ gets to zero. The same

---

[16]Remember, this expression can be written in two ways: $Xe^{-rt} = \frac{X}{e^{rt}}$. Assuming that the continuously compounded risk-free rate of interest equals r and the amount of time before expiration equals t, this is simply the present value of the strike price.

[17]Recall from the statistics that the standard normal distribution has a mean equal to zero and a standard deviation equal to one.

Figure 19.10

Standard Normal Distribution

The expression $N(d_1)$ equals the probability of drawing a particular value, d_1, or a lower value, from the standard normal distribution. In the figure, $N(d_1)$ is represented by the shaded portion under the bell curve. Because the normal distribution is symmetric about the mean, we can write, $N(d_1) = 1 - N(-d_1)$.

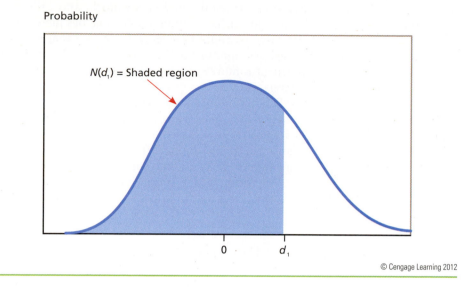

Probability

$N(d_1)$ = Shaded region

0   d_1

relationship holds between d_2 and $N(d_2)$. Given a particular value of d_1 (or d_2), to calculate $N(d_1)$ you need a table showing the cumulative standard normal probabilities, or you can plug d_1 into the *Excel* function, =normsdist(d_1). A common intuitive interpretation of $N(d_1)$ and $N(d_2)$ is that they represent the risk-adjusted probabilities that the call will expire in the money. Therefore, a verbal description of Equation 19.2 is:

> *The call option price equals the stock price, minus the present value of the exercise price, adjusted for the probability that when the option expires, the stock price will exceed the strike price (i.e., the probability that the option expires in the money).*

EXAMPLE

The stock of Cloverdale Food Processors currently sells for $40. A European call option on Cloverdale stock has an expiration date six months in the future, and a strike price of $38. The estimate of the annual standard deviation of Cloverdale stock is 45%, and the risk-free rate is 6%. What is the call worth? It's worth $6.58 as shown below.

$$d_1 = \frac{\ln\left(\frac{40}{38}\right) + \left(0.06 + \frac{0.45^2}{2}\right)\frac{1}{2}}{0.45\sqrt{\frac{1}{2}}} = \frac{(0.0513) + (0.0806)}{0.3182} = 0.4146$$

$$d_2 = d_1 - \sigma\sqrt{t} = 0.4146 - 0.45\sqrt{\frac{1}{2}} = 0.0964$$

$$N(0.4146) = 0.6608 \qquad\qquad N(0.0964) = 0.5384$$

$$C = 40(0.6608) - 38(2.718^{-(.06)(0.5)})(0.5384) = \$6.58$$

By experimenting with Equations 19.2 and 19.3, we can study the effect of changes in each of the key input variables on the price of a call option. For example, suppose we recalculate the value of the Cloverdale call option, described earlier, by adjusting just one of the required inputs each time to see the resulting effect on the option's price. After just a few experiments, we could reach the following conclusions:

- The call value increases as the price of Cloverdale stock (S) increases
- The call value increases as the time to expiration (t) increases
- The call value increases as the standard deviation of Cloverdale stock (σ) increases
- The call value increases as the strike price (X) decreases
- The call value increases as the risk-free interest rate (r) increases

? JOB INTERVIEW QUESTION

How does a stock's ex-
pected return influence
the price of a call option?

We have already discussed the first four relationships above. Call values generally increase with increases in the underlying stock price, the time to expiration, or
the volatility of the underlying stock, and calls are more valuable when the strike
price is lower. The finding that call values increase when the interest rate increases is
new. Here is an intuitive explanation for that relationship. The call option grants the
holder the right to buy something and to pay for it at a later date. The right to defer
payment is more valuable when the interest rate is high, so call values increase when
interest rates do.

Though the Black and Scholes model and the binomial model look very different
at first glance, they share the same underlying logical principles. Both models calculate option values, based on the notion that combinations of options and underlying
shares can mimic the payoffs of risk-free bonds. Both models require essentially the
same inputs (S, X, r, t, and some assumption about volatility) to calculate option values. And both models produce the same predictions about how changes in the input
variables affect option prices.

19-4 Concept Review Questions

10. To value options, using the binomial method, is it necessary
    to know the expected return on the stock? Why or why not?

11. There is an old saying that nature abhors a vacuum. The
    financial equivalent is "markets abhor arbitrage opportuni-
    ties." Explain the central role this principle plays in the
    binomial model.

19-5 Options in Corporate Finance

Thus far, our emphasis has been on stock options that trade in financial markets. The
principles we've developed to understand those options can be applied more broadly
in a wide range of corporate finance problems. We conclude this chapter with a brief
overview of the applications of option pricing techniques to the problems that corporate financial managers encounter on a regular basis.

19-5a Employee Stock Options

? WHAT TO ASK

Does your company use
options as part of its risk
management program?

Many firms use employee stock option grants (ESOs) as part of their compensation
packages. ESOs are essentially call options that give employees the right to buy shares
in the company they work for, at a fixed price. When firms distribute ESOs to their
employees, they typically set the strike price equal to the current market price, so
ESOs are typically at the money when they are issued. Like the ordinary call options that trade in financial markets, ESOs are most valuable when the price of the
underlying stock is well above the strike price. Thus, granting ESOs gives employees
an incentive to take actions that increase the firm's stock price. Aligning the interests
of employees with those of shareholders is one of the primary reasons that firms
compensate their people with options. Options do not result in a perfect alignment
of interests, however. For example, we know that option values increase if the volatility of the underlying stock increases, so paying managers in options creates at least
some incentive for them to take added risk. That added risk may or may not be in the
interests of shareholders.

ESOs differ from ordinary call options in several important ways. Whereas the
majority of options traded in financial markets expire within a few months, ESOs
grant employees the right to buy stock for as long as ten years. We know that call
option values increase as the time toward expiration grows longer, so the long life
of ESOs makes them particularly attractive to employees. However, many firms do
not allow employees to exercise their options until a vesting period has passed. For

example, a common requirement is that the employee must work for the firm for five years after receiving an ESO grant, before the option can be exercised. In a sense, ESOs are a blend of American and European options. Like European options, ESOs cannot be exercised immediately, but like American options, ESOs can be exercised at any time after the vesting period has passed.

Besides using options to give employees an incentive to increase the stock price, firms issue options because they require no immediate cash outlay. Small firms, rapidly growing firms, and firms that do not have an abundance of cash may elect to pay employees with options as a way of conserving cash.

A related motivation for firms to grant ESOs has to do with the accounting treatment of options. The Financial Accounting Standards Board (FASB) requires firms to treat the value of employee stock options grants as an expense on the income statement. To do this, firms must value the grants that they make. FASB does not specify exactly how firms should do their valuations, but they have issued statements encouraging the use of a version of the binomial model similar to the one we discussed in the last section.

Opponents of this change argued that forcing companies to create an expense category for options didn't make sense because firms paid no cash to employees at the time that ESOs were issued. Those opposed to the proposed rule also said that the binomial model was too complex and required too many assumptions to generate reliable estimates of the cost of option grants. Furthermore, they argued that many firms

Myron Scholes, Stanford University and Chairman of Oak Hill Platinum Partners

"I think that companies should expense executive stock option grants."

See the entire interview at **SMART**|finance

Smart Ideas Video

would restrict their option grants to senior executives, if the FASB forced companies to report a charge against income for ESOs. Intel, which historically granted options to nearly all of its more than 70,000 employees, joined other high-tech firms in an intense lobbying effort to persuade Congress not to require option expensing.

Proponents of expensing options, including business luminaries such as Warren Buffet and Alan Greenspan, point out that ignoring the cost of issuing ESOs when calculating net income defies economic logic. We know that options have value, even when they are not in the money. Even if a company pays employees in options rather than cash, that option-based compensation still constitutes an expense because options have value. For example, imagine that one firm pays employees in cash, whereas another firm pays in options. Employees who receive cash compensation can use that cash to purchase options on their firm's stock in financial markets, thereby achieving an economic position similar to those employees who were originally paid in options. Existing accounting rules require firms to record numerous types of transactions that involve a transfer of value but not a transfer of cash. For example, if one firm purchases the assets of another in exchange for stock, no cash changes hands, but surely the firms are exchanging something of value, and accounting statements must reflect that exchange. Proponents of treating ESOs as an expense recognize that using the binomial model, or any other model, to value ESOs involves some subjectivity. At the end of the day, the expense calculation is just an estimate of the true cost of ESOs. But accounting statements are full of estimates, ranging from reserves for bad debts to depreciation charges. Estimates are necessary to create a reasonable picture of a firm's financial condition. Where financial statements are concerned, it is better to be approximately right than precisely wrong.

19-5b Warrants and Convertibles

warrants
Securities that grant rights similar to a call option, except that when a warrant is exercised, the firm must issue a new share, and it receives the strike price as a cash inflow.

Warrants are securities that are issued by firms and that grant investors the right to buy shares of stock at a fixed price, for a given period of time. Warrants bear a close resemblance to call options, and the same factors that influence call option values affect warrant prices, too (stock price, risk-free rate, strike price, expiration date, and volatility). However, there are some important differences between warrants and calls:

1. Warrants are issued by firms, whereas call options are contracts between investors who are not necessarily connected to the firm whose stock serves as the underlying asset.

2. When investors exercise warrants, the number of outstanding shares increases and the issuing firm receives the strike price as a capital inflow. When investors exercise call options, no change in outstanding shares occurs, and the firm receives no cash.

3. Warrants are often issued with expiration dates that are several years in the future, whereas most options expire in just a few months.

4. Although call and put options trade as stand-alone securities, firms frequently attach warrants to public or privately-placed bonds, preferred stock, and sometimes even common stock. Warrants that are attached to other securities are called equity kickers, implying that they give additional upside potential to the security to which they are attached. When firms bundle warrants together with other securities, they may or may not grant investors the right to unbundle them and sell the warrants separately.

equity kickers
Warrants attached to another security offering (usually a bond offering) that give investors more upside potential.

Even though warrants and options differ in some important respects, the Black and Scholes model can be used to value warrants—provided an adjustment is made to account for the dilution that occurs when firms issue new shares to warrant holders. A simple example will illustrate how to adjust for dilution.

Assume that a small firm has 1,000 shares outstanding worth $10 each. The firm has no debt, so the value of its assets equals the value of its equity: $10,000. Two years ago, when the firm's stock price was just $8, the firm issued 100 shares of common stock to a private investor. Each share had an attached warrant granting a two-year right to purchase one share of stock for $9. The warrants are about to expire, and the investor intends to exercise them.

What would the investor's payoff be if she held ordinary call options (sold to her by another private investor) rather than warrants? Because the price of the stock is $10 and the strike price is $9, the investor would earn a profit of $1 per share, or $100 on the calls. If calls were exercised, then the firm would still have 100 shares outstanding worth $10 each. From the firm's point of view, the call exercise would generate neither a cash inflow nor a cash outflow.

JOB INTERVIEW QUESTION

How does a price of a warrant compare to the price of a call with identical characteristics?

In contrast, if the investor exercises her warrants, then two changes take place. First, the firm receives cash equal to the strike price ($9) times the number of warrants exercised (100), or a total inflow of $900. This raises the total value of the firm's assets to $10,900. Simultaneously, the firm's outstanding shares increase from 1,000 to 1,100, so the new price per share can be calculated as follows:

$$\text{New price per share} = \$10,900/1,100 = \$9.91$$

The investor's payoff on the warrants is just $0.91, compared to $1.00 on a comparable call option. Fortunately, it's easy to use the Black and Scholes model to value a call option with characteristics similar to those of a warrant and then multiply the call value times an adjustment factor for dilution. If N_1 represents the number of "old shares" outstanding and N_2 represents the number of new shares issued as a result of the warrants being exercised, then the price of the warrants equals the price of an identical call option, $\$C$, multiplied by the dilution factor, $N_1/(N_1 + N_2)$:

(Eq. 19.4) $$\text{Warrant value} = \$C(N_1/(N_1 + N_2))$$

EXAMPLE

As part of the Troubled Asset Relief Program (TARP), the U.S. government paid Wells Fargo $25 billion in exchange for preferred stock and warrants. The government received 110.3 million warrants, and Wells Fargo had 3,325 million outstanding shares at the time. We will use the Black and Scholes formula and the adjustment factor in Equation 19.4 to value the Wells Fargo warrants. To value the warrants, we must know the price of Wells Fargo stock, the expiration date of the warrants, the strike price, and the risk-free rate. We also need an estimate of Wells Fargo's volatility. Here are the relevant figures: stock price = $31.22; strike price = $34.01; risk-free rate = 2%; expiration = 10 years; standard deviation = 94.7%.

continued

$$d_1 = \frac{\ln\left(\frac{31.22}{34.01}\right) + \left(0.02 + \frac{(0.947)^2}{2}\right)10}{0.947\sqrt{10}} = \frac{(-0.086) + (4.684)}{2.995} = 1.535$$

$$d_2 = d_1 - \sigma\sqrt{t} = 1.535 - 2.995 = -1.460$$

$$N(1.535) = 0.938, \ N(-1.459) = 0.072$$

$$C = 31.22(0.938) - 34.01(2.718)^{-(.02)(10)} = \$27.28$$

$$\text{Warrant} = \frac{3,325}{3,325 + 110.3}(27.28) = \$26.40$$

convertible bond
A bond that gives investors the right to convert their bonds into shares.

A convertible bond grants investors the right to receive payment in the shares of an underlying stock rather than in cash. Usually, the stock, which investors have the right to "purchase" in exchange for their bonds, is the stock of the firm that issued the bonds. In some cases, however, a firm that owns a large amount of common stock in a different firm will use those shares as the underlying asset for a convertible bond issue. In either case, a convertible bond is essentially an ordinary corporate bond with an attached call option or warrant.

In June 2010, the software giant, Microsoft, announced a sale of four-year, zero-coupon bonds, which would generate proceeds for the company of approximately $1.25 billion. Microsoft's bonds offered investors a yield to maturity of just 1.85%, similar the yields on four-year government bonds at the time. How could a technology firm borrow money at a rate comparable to that paid by the U.S. government? Investors were willing to buy Microsoft's bonds, despite the low yield, because the bonds were convertible into Microsoft common stock. Specifically, each Microsoft bond that had a market value when issued of $1,000 could be converted into 29.94 shares of Microsoft common stock.

Convertible bonds offer investors the security of a bond and the upside potential of common stock. If Microsoft's shares increase in value, its convertible bondholders will redeem their bonds for Microsoft shares rather than cash. To see how far Microsoft's shares would have to rise before bondholders would want to convert, we divide the bond price by the conversion ratio.

conversion ratio
The number of shares bondholders receive if they convert their bonds into shares.

The conversion ratio defines how many Microsoft shares bondholders will receive if they convert. In this case, the conversion ratio is 29.94. Therefore, if bondholders choose to convert immediately, they will effectively be paying a conversion price for Microsoft of:

conversion price
The market price of a convertible bond, divided by the number of shares of stock that bondholders receive if they convert.

$$\text{Conversion price} = \frac{\$1,000}{29.94} = \$33.40$$

At the time Microsoft issued these bonds, its stock was selling for $25.11 per share. Holding the price of the bond constant at $1,000 Microsoft's shares would have to rise by 33% before bondholders would want to convert their bonds into common shares. This 33% figure equals the bond's conversion premium.

conversion premium
The percentage increase in the underlying stock that must occur before it is profitable to exercise the option to convert a bond into shares.

At a stock price of $25.11, it does not make sense for holders of Microsoft's convertible bonds to trade them for shares of stock. Nevertheless, we can still ask, what value will bondholders receive if they do convert? If Microsoft stock sells for $25.11 and each bond can be exchanged for 29.94 shares, then the conversion value of one bond equals $751.79 (29.94 × $25.11).

conversion value
The market price of the stock, multiplied by the number of shares of stock that bondholders receive if they convert.

Conversion value is important because it helps define a lower bound on the market value of a convertible bond. For example, suppose interest rates jump suddenly, and the yield on Microsoft's bonds increases, the price of the bonds cannot fall below the conversion value of $751.79. If it did, investors could exploit an arbitrage opportunity by purchasing one bond and immediately converting it into shares of stock.

In general, we can say that the price of a convertible bond will be, at a minimum, the higher of (1) the value of an identical bond without conversion rights, or (2) the

Figure 19.11

The convertible bond must sell for *at least* its value as a straight bond, or its conversion value, whichever is greater. If the bond's value is $1,000, and the conversion ratio is 20, then the conversion price equals $50. For each $1 increase in the stock price beyond $50, the bond's conversion value rises by $20.

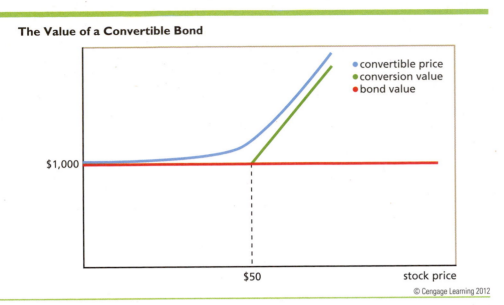

The Value of a Convertible Bond

conversion value. Figure 19.11 demonstrates this pattern for a generic convertible bond with a par value of $1,000 and a conversion ratio of 20. The horizontal line represents the present value of the convertible bond's scheduled interest and principal payments, which we simplify to be $1,000. The upward sloping line shows the bond's conversion value at different stock prices, and the curve shows the convertible bond's price. When the stock price is very low, so is the probability that the bonds will ever be worth converting into shares, so the convertible bond sells at a price comparable to an ordinary bond. As the share price rises, the value of the conversion option increases.

Most convertible bonds have another feature that slightly complicates matters. When firms issue convertibles, they almost always retain the right to call back the bonds. When firms call their outstanding bonds, bondholders can choose, within 30 days of the call, to receive either the call price in cash or a quantity of shares equal to the conversion ratio. Effectively, the call option that firms retain allows them to shorten the conversion option held by bondholders. If a firm calls its bonds, investors will choose cash if the call price exceeds conversion value, and they will choose shares if the opposite is true.

Under what circumstances should a firm call its convertible bonds? If managers are acting in the interests of shareholders, they will never call bonds that are worth less than the call price. Doing so would transfer wealth from shareholders to bondholders. Similarly, if the price of a bond rises above the call price, because the underlying stock has increased in value, then firms should call the bonds. If firms do not call the bonds and the stock price continues to increase, then when investors ultimately choose to convert their bonds into shares, firms will be selling stock at a bargain. Again, the result is a transfer of wealth from shareholders to bondholders. Therefore, the optimal policy is to call the bonds when their market value equals the call price.[18]

19-5 Concept Review Questions

12. How are employee stock options different from the options that trade on the exchanges and in the over-the-counter market?

13. What is the most important reason why firms should be required to show an expense on their income statement for employee stock options?

14. Suppose a warrant and a call option have the same strike price, the same expiration date, and the same underlying asset. Which is more valuable, the warrant or the call? Why?

[18]Actually, this would be the optimal call policy if firms could force investors to choose cash or shares immediately upon receiving the call. However, because investors have 30 days to decide whether they want cash or shares, the optimal time to call may be when the market value of the bonds slightly exceeds the call price. The reason is that if firms call the bonds precisely when the market price hits the call price, the stock price may fall during the 30 day decision period. A decline in the stock price would lower the conversion value, and firms would be forced to redeem the bonds for cash. Allowing the conversion value of the bonds to rise a little beyond the strike price gives firms a little "slack."

Summary

- Options are contracts that grant the buyer the right to buy or sell stock at a fixed price.
- Call options grant the right to purchase shares; put options grant the right to sell shares.
- Options provide a real economic benefit to society and are not simply a form of legalized gambling.
- American options allow investors to exercise their options before they expire, but European options do not.

Table of Important Equations
1. $S + P = B + C$
2. $C = SN(d_1) - Xe^{-rt} N(d_2)$
3. $d_1 = \dfrac{\ln\left(\dfrac{S}{X}\right) + \left(r + \dfrac{\sigma^2}{2}\right)t}{\sigma\sqrt{t}}$
$d_2 = d_1 - \sigma\sqrt{t}$
4. Warrant value = $\$C(N_1 / (N_1+N_2))$

- Payoff diagrams show the value of options or portfolios of options on the expiration date. Payoff diagrams can be used to illustrate how portfolios of options and other securities perform as the underlying stock price moves.
- Put-call parity establishes a link between the market prices of calls, puts, shares, and bonds.
- Call option prices rise and put option prices fall as $(S-X)$ increases.
- Calls increase in value when there is time left before expiration, whereas the effect of a longer expiration period on the value of a put can be positive or negative.
- An increase in the volatility of the underlying asset increases the values of puts and calls.
- The binomial model uses the principle of "no arbitrage" to determine the market prices of puts and calls.

Key Terms

American call option, 582
at the money, 584
binomial option pricing model, 598
call option, 581
cash settlement, 583
conversion premium, 609
conversion price, 609
conversion ratio, 609
conversion value, 609
convertible bond, 609
counterparty risk, 582
derivative security, 580

equity kickers, 608
European call option, 582
exercise price, 581
exercise the option, 582
expiration date, 582
hedge ratio, 600
in the money, 583
intrinsic value, 584
long position, 582
naked option position, 588
net payoff, 586
option premium, 582

out of the money, 584
payoff, 585
payoff diagrams, 585
protective put, 591
put option, 582
put-call parity, 593
short position, 582
standard normal distribution, 604
strike price, 581
time value, 584
underlying asset, 581
warrants, 607

Self-Test Problems

Answers to Self-Test Problems and the Concept Review Questions throughout the chapter appear in CourseMate with SmartFinance Tools at www.cengagebrain.com.

ST 19-1. Several call options on Cuban Cigars Inc. are available for trading. The expiration date, strike price, and current premium for each of these options appears below.

Strike	Expiration	Premium
$40	July	$6.00
$45	July	$3.50
$50	July	$1.75

An investor decides to purchase one call with a $40 strike, and one with a $50 strike. At the same time, the investor sells two of the calls with a $45 strike price. Draw a payoff diagram for this portfolio of options. Your diagram should have two lines, one showing the portfolio's payoff on a gross basis, and one showing the payoff net of the cost of forming the portfolio.

ST19-2. A stock currently sells for $36. In the next six months, the stock will either go up to $42 or it will fall to $31. If the risk-free rate is 4% per year, calculate the current market price of a call option on this stock, with an expiration date in six months and a strike price of $35.

Questions

Q19-1. Explain why an option is a derivative security.

Q19-2. Is buying an option more or less risky than buying the underlying stock?

Q19-3. What is the difference between an option's price and its payoff?

Q19-4. List five factors that influence the prices of calls and puts.

Q19-5. What are the economic benefits that options provide?

Q19-6. What is the primary advantage of settling options contracts in cash?

Q19-7. Suppose you want to invest in a particular company. What are the pros and cons of buying the company's shares versus buying their options?

Q19-8. Suppose you want to make an investment that will be profitable if a company's stock price falls. What are the pros and cons of buying a put option on the company's stock versus short selling the stock?

Q19-9. Suppose you own an American call option on Pfizer stock. Pfizer stock has gone up in value considerably since you bought the option, so your investment has been profitable. There is still one month to go before the option expires, but you decide to go ahead and take your profits in cash. Describe two ways that you could accomplish this goal. Which one is likely to leave you with the highest cash payoff?

Q19-10. Look at the Opti-Tech call option prices in Table 19.1. Holding the expiration month constant, call prices increase as the strike price decreases. The strike prices decrease in increments of $2.50. Do the call option prices increase in constant increments? That is, does the call price increase by the same amount as the strike price drops, from $35 to $32.50 to $30, and so on?

Problems

Options Vocabulary

P19-1. If the underlying stock price is $25, indicate whether each of the options below is in the money, at the money, or out of the money.

Strike	Call	Put
$20		
25		
30		

P19-2. The stock of Spears Entertainment currently sells for $28. A call option on this stock has a strike price of $25, and it sells for $5.25. A put option on this stock has a strike price of $30, and it sells for $3.10. What is the intrinsic value of each option? What is the time value of each option?

Option Payoff Diagrams

P19-3. Draw payoff diagrams for each of the positions below (X = strike price).
    a.   Buy a call, with $X = \$50$
    b.   Sell a call, with $X = \$60$
    c.   Buy a put, with $X = \$60$
    d.   Sell a put, with $X = \$50$

P19-4. Draw payoff diagrams for each of the portfolios below (X = strike price).
  a.   Buy a share of stock and short a call, with X = $35.
  b.   Buy a risk-free zero-coupon bond with a face value of $35 and sell a put, with X = $35.
  c.   Explain how these payoff diagrams relate to the concept of put-call parity.

P19-5. Draw payoff diagrams for each of the following portfolios (X = strike price):
  a.   Buy a call, with X = $50, and sell a call, with X = $60.
  b.   Buy a bond with a face value of $10, short a put, with X = $60, and buy a put, with X = $50.
  c.   Buy a share of stock, buy a put option, with X = $50, sell a call, with X = $60, and short a
        bond (i.e., borrow) with a face value of $50.
  d.   What principle do these diagrams illustrate?

P19-6. Draw a payoff diagram for the following portfolio. Buy two call options, one with X = $20 and one
with X = $30, and sell two call options, both with X = $25.

P19-7. Refer to the data in the table below.

Strike Price	Put Price
$30	$1.00
35	3.50
40	6.50

Suppose an investor purchases one put, with X = $30, and one put, with X = $40, and sells two puts,
with X = $35. Draw a payoff diagram for this position. In your diagram, show the gross payoff (ignor-
ing the costs of buying and selling the options) and the net payoff. In what range of stock prices does
the investor make a net profit? What is the investor's maximum potential dollar profit and maximum
potential dollar loss?

P19-8. Draw a payoff diagram for the following portfolios:
  a.   Buy a bond with a face value of $80, buy a call, with X = $80, and sell a put, with X = $80.
  b.   Buy a share of stock, buy a put, with X = $80, and sell a call, with X = $80.
  c.   Buy a share of stock, buy a put, with X = $80, and sell a bond with a face value of $80.

P19-9. Suppose that Lisa Emerson owns a share of Zytex Chemical stock, which is worth $100 per share.
Lisa purchases a put option on this stock, with a strike price of $95, and she sells a call option, with
a strike price of $105. Plot the payoff diagram for Lisa's new portfolio and explain how it relates to
this chapter's Opening Focus.

P19-10. Imagine that a stock sells for $33. A call option, with X = $35 and an expiration date in six months,
sells for $4.50. The annual risk-free rate is 5%. Calculate the price of a put option that expires in six
months and has a strike price of $35.

Qualitative Analysis of Option Prices

P19-11. Examine the data in the table below. Given that both stocks trade for $50 and both options have a
$45 strike price and a July expiration date, can we say that the option of Company A is overvalued or
that the option of Company B is undervalued? Why or why not?

Company	Stock Price	Expiration	Strike Price	Call Price
A	$50	July	$45	$7.50
B	50	July	45	6.75

P19-12. Examine the data in the table below. The call option on Company #1 is out of the money by $1 and
so is the call option on Company #2. Given that the options expire at the same time, is it surprising
that their prices are so different? Why or why not?

Company	Stock Price	Expiration	Strike Price	Call Price
#1	$49	August	$50	$6.00
#2	19	August	20	3.75

P19-13. Suppose an American call option is in the money, so S > X. Demonstrate that the market price of
this call (C) cannot be less than the difference between the stock price and the exercise price. That
is, explain why this must be true: C ≥ S − X. (Hint: consider what would happen if C < S − X.)

Option Pricing Models

P19-14.   a.   A call option expires in three months and has $X = \$40$. The underlying stock is worth $42 today. In three months, the stock may increase by $7 or decrease by $6. The risk-free rate is 2% per year. Use the binomial model to value the call option.

b.   A put option expires in three months and has $X = \$40$. The underlying stock is worth $42 today. In three months, the stock may increase by $7 or decrease by $6. The risk-free rate is 2% per year. Use the binomial model to value the put option.

c.   Given the call and the put prices you calculated in parts (a) and (b), check to see if put-call parity holds.

P19-15.   A stock is worth $20 today, and it may increase or decrease $5 over the next year. If the risk-free rate of interest is 6%, calculate the market price of the at-the-money put and call options on this stock that expire in one year. Which option is more valuable, the put or the call? Is it always the case that a call option is worth more than a put if both are tied to the same underlying stock, have the same expiration date, and are at the money? (Hint: use the put-call parity to prove the statement true or false.)

P19-16.   Explain the following paradox. A put option is a highly volatile security. If the underlying stock has a positive beta, then a put option on that stock will have a negative beta (because the put and the stock move in opposite directions). According to the CAPM, an asset with a negative beta, such as the put option, has an expected return below the risk-free rate. How can an equilibrium exist in which a highly risky security such as a put option offers an expected return below a much safer security such as a Treasury bill?

P19-17.   A particular stock sells for $27. A call option on this stock is available, with a strike price of $28 and an expiration date in four months. If the risk-free rate equals 6% and the standard deviation of the stock's return is 40%, what is the price of the call option? Next, recalculate your answer assuming that the market price of the stock is $28. How much does the option price change in dollar terms? How much does it change in percentage terms?

P19-18.   Temex Foods stock currently sells for $48. A call option on this stock is available, with a strike price of $45 and an expiration date six months in the future. The standard deviation of the stock's return is 45%, and the risk-free interest rate is 4%. Calculate the value of the call option. Next, use the put-call parity to determine the value of a Temex put option that also has a $45 strike price and six months until expiration.

Options in Corporate Finance

P19-19.   A convertible bond has a par value of $1,000 and a conversion ratio of 20. If the underlying stock currently sells for $40 and the bond sells at par, what is the conversion premium? The conversion value?

Smart Ideas Video

Myron Scholes, Stanford University and Chairman of Oak Hill Platinum Partners

"I think that companies should expense executive stock option grants."

Smart Practices Video

Myron Scholes, Stanford University and Chairman of Oak Hill Platinum Partners

"Options markets have grown dramatically over the last thirty years."

Smart Ethics Video

John Eck, President of Broadcast and Network Operations, NBC

"That allowed us to create some doubt around the transaction and allowed us not to have to book the gain up front but to book it as the cash came in."

SMART concepts

See a demonstration of put-call parity.
See how to use the binomial model to price an option.
Learn how to interpret the Black and Scholes option pricing model.

SMART solutions

See the solutions to Problems 19-6 and 19-10 explained step-by-step.

Mini-Case

Options

You have recently spent one of your Saturday afternoons at an options seminar presented by Derivatives Traders Incorporated. Interested in putting some of your new knowledge to work, you start by thinking about possible returns from an investment in the volatile common stock of PurchasePro .com, Incorporated (PPRO). Four options currently trade on PPRO. Two are call options, one with a strike price of $35 and the other with a strike price of $45. The other two are put options, which also have strike prices of $35 and $45, respectively. To help you decide which options strategies might work, evaluate the following option positions.

Assignment

1. You believe the price of PPRO will rise and are therefore considering either (a) taking a long position in a $45 call by paying a premium of $3, or (b) taking a short position in a $45 put for which you will receive a premium of $3. If the stock price is $50 on the expiration date, which position makes you better off?

2. You believe the price of PPRO will fall and are therefore considering either (a) taking a long position in a $35 put, paying a premium of $2, or (b) taking a short position in a $35 call, receiving a premium of $2. If the stock price is $30 on the expiration date, which position makes you better off?

3. Assume you can buy or sell either the call or the put options, with a strike price of $35. The call option has a premium of $3, and the put option has a premium of $2. Which of these option contracts can be used to form a long straddle? What is the payoff if the stock price closes at $38 on the option expiration date? What is the payoff if the stock price closes at $28 on the option expiration date?

4. Assume you can buy or sell either the call or the put options, with a strike price of $35. The call option has a premium of $3, and the put option has a premium of $2. Which of these option contracts can be used to form a short straddle? What is the payoff if the stock price closes at $38 on the option expiration date? What is the payoff if the stock price closes at $28 on the option expiration date?

chapter 20

Entrepreneurial Finance and Venture Capital

What Companies Do

Amazon.com Redefines e-Commerce But Follows a Typical Financing Path for an Entrepreneurial Company

Since its founding in July 1994, Amazon.com has emerged as one of the prototypical successful companies of the Internet age. It quickly established itself as the premier online marketer of published materials, offering several million titles in a variety of languages. In 1999, Amazon.com began expanding its online offerings to include music, auctions, toys, electronics, travel, and numerous other products and services. By 2011, Amazon.com was selling products to customers in over 200 countries with total revenues approaching $37 billion.

In addition to being one of the great success stories to emerge from the "dot-com bubble," Amazon.com offers a classic example of creative corporate finance. Launched with a $10,000 cash investment and a $15,000 loan from Jeffrey Bezos, the company's founder and CEO, Amazon.com's early growth was fueled, in part, by credit card loans drawn on Mr. Bezos's personal account. In July 1995, one year after Amazon.com went online, the company secured private equity funding from Silicon Valley's top venture capital firm (Kleiner Perkins Caufield & Byers), and less than two years later, the firm executed one of the splashiest initial public offerings of a very splashy decade. Investors who purchased Amazon's stock at its IPO price of $18 per share experienced a one-year return of more than 400%. The private equity investors (whose weighted average share purchase price was a mere $0.56 per share) received an astronomical total return of more than 15,000%. Amazon.com's stock surpassed the $200 mark in May 2011, which translated into a market capitalization of over $90 billion.

Sources: The information on Amazon.com is drawn from the prospectus for the company's IPO, the firm's Web site (www.amazon.com), the Web sites of CNN Money (www.money.cnn.com), Quicken (www.quicken.com), Yahoo (www.yahoofinance.com), and various published reports.

Learning Objectives

After studying this chapter you should be able to:

- Describe how the financing of entrepreneurial growth companies differs from the financing techniques used by more mature, publicly traded corporations;

- Discuss the four main types of institutional venture capital funds operating in the United States today and explain how these differ in terms of organization, financing, and investment objectives;

- Explain how venture capitalists structure their investments and why they use staged financing and generally use convertible preferred stock as their investment vehicle. Review how venture capitalists price their investments and the principal methods they use to exit an investment; and

- Describe the international markets for venture capital, particularly those in Western Europe, Canada, Israel, China, and Japan.

Beginning around 1980, no area of finance has prospered quite as much as the field of *entrepreneurial finance*. **Entrepreneurial finance** focuses on the special challenges and problems associated with the investment in and financing of risky businesses, typically start-ups. From the proliferation of *venture capital* investors, to the boom and bust in Internet-related IPOs, the financial performance of **entrepreneurial growth companies (EGCs)**, typically high-risk, technology-based start-ups, has offered spectacular theater during the past 35 years.

In this chapter, we examine the particular challenges faced by financial managers of EGCs and the ways that venture capitalists (VCs) help meet these challenges. The topic is an important one, even for students who are not aspiring venture capitalists. Formerly the near-exclusive domain of small, highly specialized venture capital limited partnerships, the financing of EGCs now affects professionals working for mutual funds, pension funds, and even Fortune 500 manufacturing concerns. Increasingly, large corporations, such as Microsoft, Pfizer, and General Electric, have internal venture capital units that spend billions annually to finance, nurture, and grow new business opportunities. By studying how VCs choose and structure EGC investments, we can learn lessons that extend well beyond the venture capital industry.

20-1 | The Challenges of Financing Entrepreneurial Growth Companies

entrepreneurial finance
Focuses on the special challenges and problems associated with the investment in and financing of risky businesses, typically start-ups.

entrepreneurial growth companies (EGCs)
Typically high-risk, start-ups that are commonly funded by venture capitalists.

Cengage Learning

Greg Udell, Indiana University

"Firms that access venture capital finance typically have loads of intangible assets on their balance sheets and very little in the way of tangible assets."

See the entire interview at **SMART**|finance

Smart Ideas Video

How does entrepreneurial finance differ from ordinary corporate finance? Entrepreneurial growth companies (EGCs) differ from large, publicly traded firms in four important ways. First, EGCs often achieve very rapid growth, at times consuming much more cash than they generate. Rapid growth requires substantial ongoing investments in fixed assets and working capital. Privately owned EGCs usually plan to convert to public ownership, either through an initial public offering (IPO) of common stock or by selling out to a larger firm. Once they become publicly traded, EGCs are much more likely to raise external equity financing through a seasoned equity offering than are older, larger firms.

Second, the most valuable assets of many of these firms are often patents and other (intangible) intellectual property rights. Because these rights are difficult to finance externally, they pose a huge challenge to the professionals who must obtain adequate funding on attractive terms. Amazon.com demonstrates this point very well. The company has total assets of only $16.9 billion, but it boasts a stock market capitalization of over $90 billion. Third, many EGCs seek to commercialize highly promising, but untested, technologies. This inevitably means that both the risk of failure and the potential payoff from success are dizzyingly high. Fourth, EGCs must attract, motivate, compensate, and retain highly skilled technical and entrepreneurial talent—but do so in a way that minimizes cash outflow, because EGCs are often severely cash constrained. Not surprisingly, they partially compensate employees with stock-option grants.

Table 20.1

Sources of Start-Up Capital for a Sample of 132 Small Companies

Capital Sources	Mean Percent[a]
Equity:	
Personal equity	35.6
Partnerships	5.2
Issuance of stock	3.2
Miscellaneous	2.7
	46.7
Debt:	
Institutional loans	43.8
Loans from individuals	5.3
Issuance of bonds	1.1
Miscellaneous	2.7
	52.9

[a]Percentages of the total start-up capital. Mean percents do not sum to 100% due to rounding.

Source: Richard B. Carter and Howard E. Van Auken, "Personal Equity Investment and Small Business Financial Difficulties," Reprinted from *Entrepreneurship Theory and Practice 15* (Winter 1990), pp. 51–60, with the permission of Baylor University. All rights reserved.

private equity
Financing provided either through capital investments by current owners or through funding by professional venture capitalists.

? WHAT TO ASK

Does your firm invest in entrepreneurial growth companies, and if so, how do you finance these firms?

The distinctive features of entrepreneurial finance are that (1) EGCs rely heavily on equity financing and (2) financial contracting between them and their financiers is fraught with information problems. As we learned in Chapter 12, growth opportunities cannot easily be financed with borrowed money, so they must be funded with equity capital. Whereas most technology- and knowledge-based companies struggle to finance growth opportunities with equity, mature firms can obtain the bulk of the equity funding they need each year by reinvesting profits. EGCs grow very rapidly. They must rely on *external* equity financing to fund investments, which vastly exceed the amount of internal funding the companies can generate. Finally, because most EGCs are privately held, they lack access to public stock markets and rely instead on private-equity financing. Private equity generally means either capital investments by current owners or funding by professional venture capitalists. The term is also used to refer to buyout funds, organizations that manage companies acquired through leveraged buyouts; discussion of these funds is beyond the scope of this text.

The vast majority of firms, even those that subsequently emerge as EGCs, begin life on a modest scale, often with little or no external equity financing other than that provided by the founder's friends and family. Only after entrepreneurs exhaust these sources of personal equity can they expect to obtain debt financing from banks or other financial institutions. Table 20.1 summarizes the results of a study examining the sources of start-up capital for a sample of 132 companies launched during 1987. The table shows that personal equity financing and loans from financial institutions represented the two most important sources of start-up capital, accounting for almost 80% of funds raised. This study does not explicitly examine whether the entrepreneurs personally guarantee the loans (rather than being limited liability loans made directly to the company). However, entrepreneurs almost always become personally liable for loans made to their newly formed businesses.

20-1 Concept Review Questions

1. What are the most important ways that *entrepreneurial finance* differs from ordinary finance? What special burdens confront financial managers of entrepreneurial growth companies (EGCs)?

2. Why must firms usually finance intangible assets with equity rather than with debt?

20-2 Venture Capital Financing in the United States

venture capital
A professionally managed pool of money raised for the purpose of making actively managed direct equity investments in rapidly growing private companies.

Venture capital is a professionally managed pool of money that is raised for the purpose of making actively managed direct equity investments in rapidly growing private companies. Many of the companies in which venture capitalists invest are involved in bringing new scientific discoveries to market. Until the mid-1990s, only the United States had an active venture capital market. This is changing rapidly, as many countries have experienced rapid growth in venture capital financing over the past 15 years.

Through the late 1970s, the total pool of venture capital in the U.S. was quite small. Most of the active funds were sponsored either by financial institutions (e.g., Citicorp Venture Capital) or nonfinancial corporations (e.g., Xerox). Most of the money raised by these funds came from their corporate backers and from wealthy individuals or family trusts. There are two features of early venture capital funds that we still observe today: (1) these funds' investments were mostly intermediate-term, equity-related investments targeted at technology-based private companies, and (2) the venture capitalists (VCs) played a unique role as active investors, contributing both capital and expertise to portfolio companies. Also, from the very start, VCs looked to invest in those rare companies that not only had the potential of going public or being acquired at a premium within a few years, but also offered investment returns of 25 to 50% per year. Over the years, reductions in tax rates and liberalized pension fund investment regulations resulted in rapid growth in VC investment from about $68 million in 1977 to more than $30 billion in 2007. After a drop to just over $19 billion during the economic downturn in 2009, VC funding rebounded to $23.7 billion in 2010.

institutional venture capital funds
Formal business entities with full-time professionals dedicated to seeking out and funding promising ventures.

20-2a Types of Venture Capital Funds

When discussing venture capital, it is important to carefully differentiate between institutional venture capital funds and angel capitalists. **Institutional venture capital funds** are formal business entities in which full-time professionals seek out and fund promising ventures, whereas **angel capitalists** (or *angels*) are wealthy individuals who make private-equity investments on a more ad hoc basis. A vibrant market for angel capital routinely provides billions per year in total equity investment to private businesses in the United States. In many years, the amount of capital provided by angel capitalists rivals that invested by venture capitalists. Nonetheless, we focus on the latter group because these firms operate nationally and provide the performance benchmark against which all private equity investment is compared.

angel capitalists
Wealthy individuals who make private equity investments on an ad hoc basis.

small business investment companies (SBICs)
Federally chartered corporations established as a result of the Small Business Administration Act of 1958.

There are four categories of institutional venture capital funds. First, **small business investment companies (SBICs)** are federally chartered corporations established as a result of the Small Business Administration Act of 1958. In 2010, SBICs invested over $2 billion in approximately 1,700 small firms. SBICs can borrow money from the U.S. Treasury, can obtain equity capital from the Treasury in the form of preferred equity interests, and can organize themselves as limited partnerships. Second, **financial venture capital funds** are subsidiaries of financial institutions, particularly commercial banks. These are generally set up both to nurture companies, which will ultimately become profitable customers of the corporate parent, and to earn high investment returns by leveraging the financial expertise and contacts of existing corporate staff. Though many financial venture capital funds are organized as SBICs, their orientation is sufficiently specialized that they are generally classified separately. Third, **corporate venture capital funds** are subsidiaries or stand-alone firms established by nonfinancial corporations, which are eager to gain access to emerging technologies by making early-stage investments in high-tech firms. Finally, **venture capital limited partnerships** are funds that are established by professional venture capital firms. These firms act as the general partners—organizing, investing, managing, and ultimately liquidating

financial venture capital funds
Subsidiaries of financial institutions, particularly commercial banks.

corporate venture capital funds
Subsidiaries or stand-alone firms established by nonfinancial corporations to gain access to emerging technologies.

venture capital limited partnerships
Funds established by professional venture capital firms, and organized as limited partnerships.

Finance in Your Life

How Do I Finance My Business Start-up?

Many business students plan to start their own business one day, and all who do struggle with the same question: How can I obtain funding needed to start my own business?

Almost all new companies are financed informally, with investments of cash and effort (sweat equity) by the entrepreneur and perhaps supplemental investments from the entrepreneur's friends and family. Although every prospective entrepreneur can and should develop a detailed business plan, this alone will not allow the entrepreneur to successfully borrow money from a bank or obtain arms-length equity capital from investors. The entrepreneur instead should concentrate on getting the business up and running and—most vitally—generating the positive cash flow that must be reinvested in the new business. Such internally generated funds are usually the only source of growth capital during a new business's very early stage of development.

Once the business has been operating successfully for many months (or years), the new entrepreneur is in a position to approach one or more angel investors for external equity capital. Angels are typically wealthy local businesspeople who can invest from $50,000 to over $200,000 in a new business, and can also offer practical advice and monitoring to the entrepreneur. Angels are looking for an attractive financial return of 20–40% per year from investments made in functioning, profitable businesses with real customers, products, and cash flow.

So if you are dreaming of starting your own business, keep the following advice in mind. First, start small, using only money that you, your friends, and your family can provide. Second, reinvest all your profits in the business, and employ any reasonably priced debt financing that may be provided by banks, suppliers, or customers (but try to avoid credit card advances). Finally, approach business angels for your first round of external funding once you have your business established—then present your business plan to them as an opportunity to invest in a growth business. Good luck and happy entrepreneuring!

? JOB INTERVIEW QUESTION

Our firm is considering establishing a corporate venture capital fund in order to gain access to emerging technologies. Why would this strategy be preferred over expanding our R&D operations?

the capital raised from the limited partners. Most limited partnerships have a single-industry focus that is determined by the expertise of the general partners.

Limited partnerships dominate the venture capital industry, partly because they make their investment decisions free from outside influences. The SBICs have been hampered by their historical reliance on inappropriate funding sources and by the myriad regulations that apply to government-sponsored companies. The financial and corporate funds tend to suffer because their ultimate loyalty rests with their corporate parents rather than the companies in which they invest. Finally, corporate funds have histories of only intermittent commitment to venture capital investing. Corporate funds tend to scale back dramatically when business conditions sour. For all these reasons, limited partnerships now control the majority of total industry resources, and their influence on fund-raising seems to be increasing.

20-2b Investment Patterns of U.S. Venture Capital Firms

Given the media attention lavished on venture capital in the United States, most people are surprised to learn that the industry invested only a few billion dollars each year before 1996. Of course, annual disbursements naturally differ from total fund-raising. The total amount of money available for investment is the sum of realized investment returns (from IPOs and mergers of companies owned by VCs) as well as new fund inflows from investors. After 1996, total investment spending surged to an astonishing $100 billion (spread over 5,608 companies) in 2000, before declining very sharply thereafter to just over $23 billion during 2010.

The bulk of venture capital funding once came either from corporate sponsors (in the case of financial or corporate funds) or wealthy individuals. However, today institutional investors have become the dominant sources of funding. Pension funds alone typically account for 25–40% of all new money raised by institutional venture capital firms. Even though few pension funds allocate more than 5% of their total assets to private-equity investments, their sheer size makes them extremely important investors.

20-2c Industrial and Geographic Distribution of Venture Capital Investment

One reason for the success enjoyed by institutional VCs is that they usually invest only in those industries where they have some competitive advantage and where their involvement in management of the companies they fund can create real economic value. The majority of VC investment flows into information-technology industries (communications and computers). Other industries receiving significant VC funding during recent years include biotechnology, telecommunications, and medical devices and equipment.

Another striking regularity in venture capital investment patterns concerns the geographical distribution of the companies funded by VCs. Firms located in California consistently receive more venture capital backing than firms in any other state. For instance, California firms have typically captured well above 40% of total annual funding, generally over three times the funding received by firms in New England. The flow of money into California has typically dwarfed that in other large, populous states such as New York and Texas, which on average each receive about 5% of total annual VC funding.

20-2d Venture Capital Investment by Stage of Company Development

The popular image of VCs holds that they specialize in making investments in start-up or very early-stage companies. This is only partly true. In fact, during recent years early-stage financing typically accounted for between 20 and 25% of total investment. Start-up seed money actually only represented less than 5% of total VC investment. Being rational investors, venture capitalists are as leery as anyone else of backing extremely risky new companies. They are more likely to invest if the entrepreneur/founder is well known to the venture capitalists or the venture is exceptionally promising, or both. Later-stage investments in more mature companies generally account for 25 to 45% of total financing, while expansion financing generally represents over half of total VC investment spending.

Although the distribution between early- and later-stage funding varies from year to year, one principle of venture capital funding never changes—the earlier the development stage of the company being financed, the higher the expected return on investment demanded by the venture capitalist. Professional VCs typically demand compound annual investment returns in excess of 50% on start-up investments. But they will accept returns of 20 to 30% per year on later-stage deals because the risk is far lower in more established companies. VCs extract a higher expected return on early-stage investments, in part, by requiring entrepreneurs to sell them a higher ownership stake for a given investment amount in these deals.

Usually, there is not a stark choice between early- and later-stage investments. Most VC funds that invest in a company during its early years remain committed to the firm as it develops. VCs typically participate in many financing rounds as the company they have initially financed matures. On average, the prices venture capitalists pay to acquire additional shares in companies in which they have made earlier investments rise in each subsequent round of financing.

20-2e The Economic Effect of Venture Capital Investment

Before examining the organizational structure of the U.S. venture capital industry, we should briefly assess whether venture capital investments have really been as large and influential as is generally believed. A recent study published by the National Venture Capital Association documented the scale and economic effect of 30 years of VC investment in the United States.[1] Over the period 1970 to 2005,

---

[1] See Jeanne Metzger and Channa Brooks, "Three Decades of Venture Capital Investment Yields 7.6 Million Jobs and $1.3 Trillion in Revenue," National Venture Capital Association (October 22, 2001), downloaded at www.nvca.org.

American venture capitalists invested over $410 billion in more than 23,000 companies in all 50 states. Venture capital-backed firms employed 10.0 million people and generated $2.1 trillion in sales during 2005, representing 9.0% of jobs and 16.6% of GDP for that year. The study also found that "venture capital-financed companies had approximately twice the sales, paid almost three times the federal taxes, generated almost twice the exports, and invested almost three times as much in R&D per $1,000 in assets as did the average non-venture capital-backed companies." Finally, the study documented that, on average, every $36,000 in VC investment created one new job.

Much the same pattern is observed in Western Europe, the other major international market for venture capital. A study by the European Private Equity and Venture Capital Association found that VC-backed European companies generated significantly higher growth rates in sales, research spending, exports, and job creation during the 1990–1995 period than did otherwise comparable non-VC-backed companies.[2] Recent updates of this study show that European private-equity funds invested €8.4 billion in 8,399 VC-stage companies during 2003. Roughly one fourth the total investment was in early-stage companies. Finally, an astonishing 95% of European venture-backed companies said that they either would not exist or would not have developed as quickly without VC investment.

20-2 Concept Review Questions

3. What is an *angel capitalist*, and how does this type of investor differ from a professional (institutional) venture capitalist?

4. Why do you think that private limited partnerships have come to dominate the U.S. venture capital industry? Can you think of any weaknesses this organizational form might have as a vehicle for financing entrepreneurial growth companies?

20-3 The Organization and Operations of U.S. Venture Capital Firms

20-3a Organization and Funding of Venture Capital Limited Partnerships

Most of the top venture capital firms are organized as general partnerships, and many of them are concentrated in California's Silicon Valley, south of San Francisco. These firms usually begin the venture financing process by creating a distinct limited partnership fund, often with a dedicated investment target, such as funding clean energy start-ups. Although some venture funds are created by public offerings of limited partnership interests (which can then be freely traded), the vast majority are organized and capitalized by private negotiation between the fund's sponsor and a well-established group of institutional investors. To say that a fund is capitalized at its inception is something of a misnomer. In practice, the limited partners make capital commitments, which the general partner then draws on over time as the fund becomes fully invested. In addition to organizing the limited partnership, the sponsoring firm acts as the general partner (and has unlimited liability) over the fund's entire life, typically ten years (though often extendable for up to three additional years). As general partner, the VC is responsible for (1) seeking out investment opportunities and negotiating the terms on which these investments will be made; (2) monitoring the performance of the portfolio companies and providing additional funding and expertise as necessary; (3) finding an attractive exit opportunity, such as an IPO or a *trade sale* of the firm

[2]The study is entitled "The Economic Impact of Venture Capital in Europe," and is available for downloading at www.evca.com. Updates of this study include the *Survey of the Economic and Social Impact of Venture Capital in Europe*, published by EVCA on June 20, 2002, and the *EVCA Final Survey of Pan-European Private Equity and Venture Capital Activity 2002*, published by EVCA on June 4, 2003.

to another company or investor group, that will allow the fund to liquidate its investments; and (4) distributing the realized cash returns from these exits to the limited partners and then terminating the fund. For its services, the general partner receives an annual management fee equal to 1% to 3% (usually 2%) of the fund's total committed capital, as well as an incentive fee, called *carried interest* and usually equal to 20%, on the realized return on the fund's investments. It is also worth emphasizing that the management fee is based on committed capital, not on total assets under management or deal value, though this fee often declines after the fund's investment period is complete.

The relationship between VCs and investors is fraught with *agency problems*. Investors must commit large amounts of money for long-term, illiquid, nontransparent investments in private partnerships, over which they can exercise no direct control without forfeiting their limited liability. Venture capitalists have many opportunities to expropriate the limited partners' wealth. They can set up new funds, which exclude the old limited partners, to finance the most promising companies, and they can make side deals with the best companies in their fund. Reputational concerns largely control these problems, but contractual covenants also play a role in curtailing agency problems. These include limiting the VC's ability to establish new funds, without granting existing investors equal access, mandating that existing investors be included in any equity sale contracts the VC negotiates, and restricting the VC's freedom to invest in foreign and in publicly traded securities, or in leveraged buyouts. These covenants restrict the VC's ability to expropriate the limited partners' wealth through side deals, as well as ensure that the VC will not make investments outside the fund manager's area of expertise.

Many senior partners at top venture capital firms are well known for their skills in finding, nurturing, and bringing to market high-tech companies. Examples include John Doerr of Kleiner Perkins Caufield & Byers, William Hambricht of Hambricht and Quist, and Sam Rosen of Rosen Partners. These industry leaders have become extraordinarily wealthy, but even "ordinary" venture capitalists did quite well during the 1995 to 2000 boom. The industry's financial rewards attract numerous would-be VCs, but jobs in the industry are notoriously difficult to obtain, particularly for newly minted business school graduates. Partners and associates in venture capital firms often are engineers or other technically trained professionals who themselves worked in high-tech companies before becoming full-time VCs. This experience gives them in-depth knowledge of both the technological and business aspects of the industries in which they invest. It is this expertise, along with capital and contacts, which entrepreneurs look for when they approach a VC for funding. For example, John Doerr of Kleiner Perkins Caufield & Byers has bachelor's and master's degrees in electrical engineering, plus an MBA from Harvard Business School. He worked for Intel Corporation for five years before becoming a venture capitalist.

Cengage Learning

Manju Puri, Duke University

"Venture capital does have a positive role for innovative companies in helping to push their product out quickly."

See the entire interview at SMART|finance

Smart Ideas Video

20-3b How Venture Capitalists Structure Their Investments

Although one should be wary of describing anything as unique as a venture capital investment contract as standard, most agreements between VCs and entrepreneurs share certain characteristics. First and foremost, venture capital contracts allocate risk, return, and ownership rights between the entrepreneur (and other existing owners of a portfolio company) and the fund. The distribution of rights and responsibilities depends on (1) the experience and reputation of the entrepreneur, (2) the attractiveness of the portfolio company as an investment opportunity, (3) the stage of the company's development, (4) the negotiating skills of the contracting parties, and (5) the overall state of the market. If, at a time of fierce competition among

Steve Kaplan, University of Chicago

"It's not just about what fraction of the company the venture capitalists are getting."

See the entire interview at **SMART**|finance

Smart Ideas Video

staged financing
Method of investing venture capital in a portfolio company in stages, over time.

cancellation option
Option held by the venture capitalist to deny or delay additional funding for a portfolio company.

VCs, a respected and experienced entrepreneur approaches a fund with an opportunity to invest in an established company with a promising technology, then the entrepreneur will secure financing on relatively attractive terms. At the other extreme, if an inexperienced entrepreneur seeks start-up funding at a time when venture capital is scarce (such as during the recent recession), the entrepreneur will have to accept fairly onerous contract terms in order to attract funding.

Early in the negotiation process, the parties must estimate the candidate company's value. The company's past R&D efforts, its current and prospective sales revenue, its tangible assets, and the present value of its expected net cash flows all enter into the valuation equation. To a large extent, this valuation will determine what fraction of the firm the entrepreneur must exchange for venture backing. Next, the parties must agree on the amount of new funding the venture capitalist will provide and the required return on that investment. Naturally, the higher the perceived risk, the higher the required return.

Venture capitalists use staged financing to minimize their risk exposure. To illustrate how staged financing works, assume that a company needs $25 million in private funding to fully commercialize a promising new technology. Rather than invest the entire amount at once, the venture capitalist initially advances only enough (say, $5 million) to fund the company to its next development stage. Both parties agree to specific performance objectives (e.g., building a working product prototype) as a condition for more rounds of financing. If the company succeeds in reaching those goals, the venture capitalist will provide funding for the next development stage, usually on terms more favorable to the entrepreneur. Staged financing is not only an efficient way to minimize risk for the venture capitalist, it also gives the venture fund an extremely valuable option to deny or delay additional funding. This cancellation option places the maximum feasible amount of business risk on the entrepreneur, but in return it allows the entrepreneur to obtain funding at a lower price than would otherwise be required. Staged financing also provides tremendous incentives for the entrepreneur to create value, because at each new funding stage the VC provides capital on increasingly attractive terms.

EXAMPLE

Paul Gompers provides two classic examples of how staged financing should work in the development of private companies: Apple Computer and Federal Express.[3] Apple received three rounds of private equity funding. In the first round, venture capitalists purchased stock at $0.09 per share, but this rose to $0.28 per share in the second round and then $0.97 per share in the third round. Needless to say, all these investments proved spectacularly profitable when Apple went public, at $22.00 per share in 1980. Investors in Federal Express, however, used staged financing with more telling effect during their three rounds of private equity financing. The investors purchased stock for $204.17 per share in the first round, but the firm's early performance was much poorer than anticipated. In the second round, shares were purchased for $7.34 each, but the company's finances continued to deteriorate, so a third financing round, at $0.63 per share, was required. As we know, FedEx eventually became a roaring success and went public at $6.00 per share, in 1978, but staged financing allowed venture capitalists to intervene decisively during the firm's problematic early development.

A recent study by Hochberg, Ljungqvist, and Lu[4], describes how venture capitalists use staged financing. The study examines 47,705 investments made by VCs and finds that roughly one-third of the companies receiving first-round investments were written off without obtaining subsequent financing, and another 6.3% were able to exit through an IPO or trade sale after only one VC funding round. However, the majority (60.5%) of first-round deals proceeded to a second financing round, and then 70.0% of these proceeded to a third round. A lower fraction of second-round companies failed (22.3%

---

[3]See Paul A. Gompers, "Optimal Investment, Monitoring, and the Staging of Venture Capital," *Journal of Finance 50* (December 1995), pp. 1,461–1,489.
[4]Yael V. Hochberg, Alexander Ljungqvist, and Yang Lu, "Whom You Know Matters: Venture Capital Networks and Investment Performance," *Journal of Finance 62* (February 2007), pp. 251–301.

write-offs) than during the first round, and a higher fraction (7.7%) achieved successful exit. This pattern of decreasing failure rates and rising exit rates continues for all subsequent rounds. In other words, if your company makes it to the third financing round, the likelihood of business failure is much reduced, and the odds of ultimately achieving a successful exit are very high.

A distinguishing characteristic of venture capital investment contracts is their extensive and sophisticated *covenants*. Some of these covenants—both positive and negative—appear in many standard debt financing contracts. For example, venture capital contracts often contain clauses that specify maximum acceptable leverage and dividend payout ratios, require the firm to carry certain types of business insurance, and restrict the firm's ability to acquire other firms or sell assets without prior investor approval. Other covenants, occur almost exclusively in private equity investment contracts. All of the economic, control, and ownership terms of an investment proposal are detailed in a **term sheet** that the venture capitalist prepares and presents to the entrepreneur.

1. **Ownership right agreements** not only specify the distribution of ownership but also allocate board seats and voting rights to the participating VC. Special voting rights often given to VCs include the rights to veto major corporate actions and to remove the management team if the firm fails to meet performance goals.

2. **Ratchet provisions** protect the venture group's ownership rights in the event that the firm sells new equity under duress. Generally, these provisions ensure that the venture capital group's share values adjust so that the entrepreneur bears the penalty of selling low-priced new stock under duress in the type of down round financing that Federal Express had to accept. For example, if the venture fund purchased shares initially for $1 each and the start-up later sells new stock at $0.50 per share, then a full ratchet provision would mandate that the venture group receive one new share for each old share, thereby protecting the value of the VC's initial stake. A partial ratchet adjusts VC share ownership only in an amount that is proportional to the amount of new capital raised. Obviously, it would not take many rounds of financing at reduced prices to completely wipe out a management team's ownership stake.

3. **Demand registration rights**, **participation rights**, and **repurchase rights** preserve exit opportunities for VCs. *Demand registration rights* give the venture fund the right to compel the firm to register shares with the SEC for a public offering—at the firm's expense. *Participation rights* give VCs the option to participate in any private stock sale that the firm's managers arrange for themselves. If a company held by the VC does not conduct an IPO or sell out to another firm within a specified time period, then *repurchase rights* give VCs the option to sell their shares back to the firm.

4. **Stock option plans** provide incentives for company managers in virtually all venture capital deals. As part of these plans, the firm sets aside a large pool of stock to compensate current managers for superior performance and to attract talented new managers as the company grows.

This listing of covenants is by no means comprehensive. Other common provisions describe the conditions for additional financing and the payoffs to entrepreneurs if the VCs decide to hire new managers. However, the most fascinating and distinguishing feature of venture capital contracts is unquestionably their nearly total reliance on convertible securities as their investment vehicle of choice.

20-3c Why Venture Capitalists Use Convertible Securities

Most people assume that when VCs invest in a firm, they receive shares of common stock in exchange for their capital. In fact, U.S. venture capitalists almost always receive some type of convertible security instead—either convertible debt or, more frequently, convertible preferred stock. There are several reasons for this marked preference. First, venture capitalists could exercise effective voting control with common stock only if

---

term sheet
An investment proposal detailing all of the economic, control, and ownership terms—including covenants—that is prepared and presented to an entrepreneur by a venture capitalist.

ownership right agreements
Agreements between venture capital investors and portfolio-company managers allocating ownership stakes and voting rights to venture capitalists.

ratchet provisions
Contract terms that adjust downward the par value of the stock venture capitalists have purchased in a company in case the firm must sell new stock at a lower price than the VC originally paid.

demand registration rights
Agreements giving the venture capitalists the right to demand that a portfolio company's managers arrange for a public offering of shares in the company.

participation rights
Agreements giving the venture capitalists the right to participate in any sale of stock that a portfolio company's managers might arrange for themselves.

repurchase rights
Give the venture capitalists the right to force the company to buy back (repurchase) the shares held by the VC.

stock option plans
Plans set up to provide stock options to newly-hired managers of portfolio companies in order to give them incentives to manage the company to create value.

they purchased a majority of the firm's common shares, which would be extremely expensive and would place far more of the firm's business risk on the venture group than on the entrepreneur. Because convertible debt or preferred stock is a distinct security class, contract terms and covenants specific to that issue are negotiable, whereas all common stockholders must be given the same per-share voting and control rights. Furthermore, because firms can create multiple classes of convertible debt or preferred stock, they can use these securities to construct extremely complex and sophisticated contracting arrangements with different investor groups.

Seniority offers a second reason why venture capitalists generally demand convertible debt or preferred stock rather than common stock: it places the VC ahead of the entrepreneur in the line of claimants on the firm's assets should the firm not succeed. However, preferred stock or subordinated debt leaves the firm the option to issue more senior debt, thereby preserving its borrowing capacity and making it easier for the firm to arrange trade credit or bank loans. The convertible securities held by VCs typically pay a low dividend, suggesting that VCs use these securities for control rather than to generate steady cash flows.

Most important, convertible securities give VCs the right to participate in the upside when companies they hold thrive. In fact, VCs are usually required to convert their preferred stock into common shares before venture-backed companies execute initial public offerings in order to present an uncluttered balance sheet to prospective investors.

20-3d The Pricing of Venture Capital Investments

As you might expect, valuing the types of young, rapidly growing companies that venture capital firms finance presents a huge challenge. How do VCs value portfolio companies? The empirical evidence suggests that VCs use a wide variety of valuation methods and that, from one deal to the next, valuations can be rather idiosyncratic. As in all other areas of financial valuation, however, venture capitalists employ the basic valuation process of investing in those ventures expected to earn returns in excess of the appropriate risk-adjusted return, which is typically in the range of 30% to 50%. The key distinction of VC investment is that the expected return must be quite high because the risk of most VC investments is also much higher than in other areas. The following example illustrates one common valuation approach.

Assume that the president and founder of the start-up company Biotech Concepts Corporation (BCC) approaches a technology-oriented venture capital fund for $5 million in new funding to support her firm's rapid growth. After intense negotiations, the parties agree that BCC is currently worth $10 million and that the risk of the firm is such that the venture capitalist is entitled to a 50% compound annual (expected) return. To arrive at the $10 million estimate, the VC may compare the candidate company's sales (or earnings, if there are any) to those of similar public companies and then apply a pricing multiple. Assume further that both parties agree that BCC should plan to execute an IPO in five years, at which time the firm is expected to have net profits of $4 million and to sell at a price/earnings multiple of 20, valuing the company at $80 million. To calculate the value of its stake in the candidate company as of the IPO date, the VC uses basic future value techniques. The initial investment, A, equals $5 million; the required rate of return, r, is 50%; and the time horizon, n, is five years. Therefore, the future value is

$$\text{(Eq. 20.1)} \quad FV = A(1 + r)^n = \$5,000,000(1.50)^5 = \$5,000,000(7.6) = \$38,000,000$$

To determine what fraction of BCC's equity it will receive now, the VC divides the future value of its stake by BCC's expected market valuation at the IPO:

$$\text{(Eq. 20.2)} \quad \text{Equity fraction} = \frac{FV}{\text{expected market valuation}} = \frac{\$38,000,000}{\$80,000,000} = 0.475$$

This means that the venture capital fund will receive 47.5% of BCC's equity in exchange for its $5 million investment. If the VC agrees to accept a lower return, say 40%, then the VC's expected IPO payoff will be $26.9 million and the VC would require a 33.6% equity stake up front to achieve this return. When the VC requires a higher return, the entrepreneur must relinquish a larger fraction of the firm.

20-3e The Profitability of Venture Capital Investments

Interpreting the data on venture capital returns is controversial, and industry assessments tend to differ significantly from those presented by academics. Figure 20.1 describes five-year rolling average annual returns for venture capital funds, the S&P 500, and the NASDAQ 100 Index over the period 1990–2008, as presented in the *National Venture Capital Association (NVCA) Yearbook 2009*. This chart suggests that VC funds outperformed U.S.-listed equities most years. Repeated examples of boom-and-bust investment cycles in which very high realized returns prompt excessive new capital inflows into venture capital funds, which in turn cause returns to drop sharply over the next harvest cycle, have been documented in the academic literature. Although a 30% compound annual return was typical for venture capital funds during the late 1970s and early 1980s, returns fell short of this every year from 1984 to 1994. Returns were again at target levels in 1995 and 1996 and then surged in 1999. However, more recent returns following the collapse of the Nasdaq market in March 2000—and then again after the financial crisis of 2008—have been uniformly negative. Even so, the returns on VC investments during 2008 were better than the −38.5% return posted by the S&P 500 that year.

Figure 20.1   **Returns to Venture Capital Investing versus Public Markets**

This figure details five-year rolling average annual returns as of December 31, 2008.

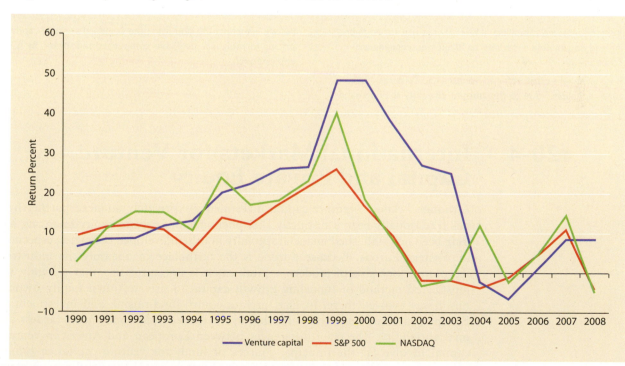

Source: *National Venture Capital Association Yearbook 2009*, National Venture Capital Association.

Comment: The returns on venture capital investments tend to outperform investments in listed stocks, according to industry sources.

Researchers have found a strong positive correlation between venture returns and returns on small stock mutual funds. This relationship highlights the importance of a healthy public stock market for new ventures in general, and for initial public offerings in particular. Because VCs prefer to exit via an IPO, and because the returns from them partially flow into new venture investments, any decline in the stock market's appetite for new issues has an immediate negative effect on the venture capital industry.

20-3f Exit Strategies Employed by Venture Capitalists

VCs are not long-term investors. They seek to add value to a private company and then to harvest their investment. VCs use three principal methods to exit an investment: (1) through an initial public offering of shares to outside investors; (2) through a sale of the company they hold directly to another company in a *trade sale*; or (3) through selling the company they hold back to the entrepreneur/founders, known as the redemption option. IPOs are by far the most profitable (and glorious) exit option for venture capitalists, though trade sales are also quite profitable on average. During 1980–2004, 3,374 venture capital–backed IPOs were executed on U.S. capital markets and raised $155.1 billion. In the wake of the financial crisis and recession in 2008–2009, IPO activity declined steeply. Only 21 VC-backed IPOs took place in 2008–2009, though a slight rebound occurred in 2010 with 39 VC-backed firms going public.

Perhaps surprisingly, VCs do not exit immediately at the time of an IPO. Instead, they retain shares for several months or even years before either distributing them to the limited partners or selling the shares on the open market and then distributing the cash proceeds to those partners. The distributions usually occur after a period of sharply rising stock prices, and the average stock price response to distribution announcements is significantly negative.

redemption option
Option for venture capitalists to sell a company back to its entrepreneur or founders.

Cengage Learning

David Haeberle, Chief Executive Officer, Command Equity Group

"If you make ten investments as a fund, you're probably going to see five write-offs."

See the entire interview at **SMART**|finance

Smart Practices Video

20-3 Concept Review Questions

5. Why do venture capitalists almost always use *staged financing* and convertible securities to finance entrepreneurial companies?

6. Entrepreneurs often refer to venture capitalists as "vulture capitalists," due to the amount of equity they demand before investing. Do you think the standard venture capital pricing formula is a justifiable compensation for risk, or is it exploitative?

20-4 International Markets for Venture Capital and Private Equity

Although "classic" venture capital investment by privately financed partnerships has traditionally been a distinctly U.S. phenomenon, private equity financing has long been an established financial specialty in other developed countries, especially in Western Europe. Because Europe is the birthplace of not only the Industrial Revolution but also of modern capitalism, it is not surprising that a highly sophisticated method of funneling growth capital to private (often family owned) businesses evolved there. In fact, private equity fund-raising and investment in Europe compared quite well with that in the United States and shows far less annual variability. The chief differences between European and American venture capital involve (1) the principal sources of funds for venture capital investing, (2) the organization of the venture funds themselves, (3) the development stage of the companies that are able to attract venture financing, and (4) the principal method of harvesting venture capital investments.

Before proceeding, we should point out a difference in the definition of the term *venture capital* in Europe and the United States. Whereas American commentators tend to refer to all professionally managed, equity-based investments in private, entrepreneurial growth companies as venture capital, European commentators apply the term only to early- and expansion-stage financing. Later-stage investments and funding for management buyouts are called *private equity investment* in Europe, whereas "private equity" refers only to buyout funds in the United States. Where necessary, we maintain this distinction, but in general we shall refer to both venture capital and private equity investment simply as *European venture capital*.

20-4a European Venture Capital and Private-Equity Fund-Raising and Investment

As in the United States, venture capital fund-raising and investment in Europe grew very rapidly during the late 1990s; since 2000, it has remained fairly stable at between €8 billion and €17 billion. As in the United States, a majority of European venture capital investment during recent years was funneled into life sciences, followed by energy and environmental services, computer and consumer electronics, and communications. In one other important respect, venture capital investment patterns in Europe and the United States have long been similar: both are highly concentrated geographically. Almost one-quarter (23.8%) of year-2008 total investment was targeted at British companies, and 59% of European private equity funding originated in the United Kingdom. Germany and France followed with (respectively) 16.3% and 16.1% of European investment; Italy came in fourth with 9.6%. As in the United States, the fraction of European venture capital allocated to early- versus later-stage companies fluctuates significantly from year to year, though truly early-stage (seed and start-up) investments rarely account for more than one-third of the VC total.

For a mix of cultural and legal reasons, European venture capital funds are rarely organized according to the U.S. model. Instead, funds are generally organized as investment companies under various national laws, and their approach to dealing with companies they hold is much more akin to the reactive style of U.S. mutual fund managers than to the proactive style of America's venture capitalists. The relative lack of a vibrant entrepreneurial high-technology sector in Europe also hampers continental VCs' efforts to attract technologically savvy fund managers or entrepreneur/founders who wish to use their expertise to develop new firms.

One of the greatest disappointments of European policymakers wishing to duplicate the success of the United States in high-technology development has been the continent's failure to establish a large, liquid market for the stock of entrepreneurial growth firms. Although several stock markets exist that collectively rival U.S. exchanges in total capitalization of listed companies, no European market emerged as a serious alternative to America's Nasdaq or NYSE as a market for IPOs until the German Neuer Markt, the pan-European Easdaq, and other markets such the French Nouveau Marche reached critical mass in the late 1990s. The number of European IPOs surged after these markets matured—especially the Neuer Markt, which had attracted over 300 listings by early 2000. Unfortunately, the Neuer Markt collapsed almost as fast as it took off. The European IPO market is now effectively closed to all but the most profitable and established firms, though a few European (and a great many Israeli) technology companies have been able to execute IPOs on U.S markets. Unfortunately, this is not a viable option for most entrepreneurial companies and, as noted previously, U.S. markets are no longer especially receptive even to home-grown IPOs.

20-4b Venture Capital Markets Outside the United States and Western Europe

The key venture capital markets outside the United States and Western Europe are Canada, Israel, Japan, China, and India. The venture capital industries of Israel and Canada differ dramatically from other advanced countries. Canadian government

What Companies Do Globally

The Role of Venture Capital and Private Equity Investment In Financing a Nation's R&D Expenditures (2005)

Country	Venture Capital and Private Equity Investment $US Billion	% of GDP	R&D Spending as a % of GDP
United States	$46.41	0.37%	2.52
United Kingdom	27.92	1.25	1.44
China	8.80	0.36	1.13[a]
France	8.55	0.40	1.89
Japan	7.95	0.17	2.59
Singapore	4.41	3.77	2.62
Sweden	3.52	0.99	3.19
Germany	3.16	0.11	2.22
Spain	3.12	0.28	1.17
Netherlands	2.74	0.44	1.52
Italy	2.56	0.14	1.01
Australia	2.32	0.31	1.57
Korea	2.10	0.27	4.08
India	1.94	0.24	0.74
Denmark	1.24	0.48	1.76
Canada	1.24	0.11	2.01
Israel	1.08	0.88	5.15
South Africa	0.89	0.37	2.00
New Zealand	0.75	0.68	0.99
Indonesia	0.56	0.19	—

This table details how a country's venture capital and private equity investment and R&D spending relate to its GDP. A review of the table shows that whereas Singapore had the highest level of venture capital and private equity investment as a percent of its GDP (3.77%), Israel had the highest levels of R&D spending as a percent of GDP 5.15%). Other countries with high levels of VC and private equity investment relative to GDP include the United Kingdom, Sweden, Israel, and New Zealand. Countries exhibiting high levels of R&D spending relative to GDP include Korea, Sweden, Singapore, Japan, and the United States. Comparing each country's VC and private equity investment as a percent of GDP to its R&D spending as a percent of GDP, it is clear that most countries finance well below half of their R&D expenditures with venture capital and private equity. Clearly, much of the R&D financing must come from company and government sources.

Sources: Venture capital and private equity investment data, PricewaterhouseCoopers, *Global Private Equity Report 2006* (www.pwcmoneytree.com), gross domestic product data for OECD countries from Organization of Economic Development (www.oecd.org); other nations' data from World Bank (www.worldbank.org), R&D spending data, OECD Statistics (www.oecd.org), except India, whose research spending value is from a report by a national science administrator.

policies led to its venture capital system that is based on funds sponsored by labor unions, though this has changed over the past decade. In a relative sense, Israel has achieved the greatest success in venture capital because it is routinely has the highest level of R&D spending as a percent of GDP. As the What Companies Do Globally box shows, in 2005 Israel's R&D spending represented slightly more that 5% of its GDP. About 17% of Israel's R&D spending was funded with venture capital. Part of Israel's success can be traced to deliberate policy decisions in the early 1990s by the Likud government, which took concrete steps to commercialize defense-related technology developed with public funding.

Venture capital fund-raising and investment in Asia grew significantly between 1995 and 2000, though much less rapidly than in Europe or the United States. Japan has a financial specialty referred to as "venture capital," but most of the firms involved are commercial or investment bank subsidiaries that make few truly entrepreneurial investments. Although China is the fastest-growing major economy in the world, venture capital and private equity play a small role in its development, mainly because the country lacks the basic legal infrastructure needed to support a vibrant VC market and because access to a listing on a Chinese stock market is severely restricted. Nonetheless, many VC-backed U.S. manufacturing ventures have a Chinese sourcing and production component. In many ways, India is the most interesting and promising private equity market in the world today. India's history as a former British colony gave it a legal system similar to U.S. multiple stock exchanges, as well as a heritage of English as the native language of its educated classes. India's rapid economic development since 1991 has been propelled both by the macroeconomic and market-opening reforms adopted that year and by relatively large inflows of foreign investment, which were attracted by India's vast potential and by the quality of the graduates of its elite universities and technical institutes. Crucially, much of India's growth has been in the information technology (IT) sector, the traditional target of venture capital investment. For all these reasons, India should become one of the five leading venture capital markets globally within a very few years.

20-4c The Outlook for Venture Capital

As this chapter is being written (June 2011), the venture capital industry is emerging from a depressed state around the world and especially in the United States. Fund-raising and investment levels fell sharply in 2008–2009, although signs of a turnaround are emerging. The history of VC suggests that the industry will probably rebound strongly once economic recovery takes hold. This same history also implies that the VC deals executed during this depressed period may well prove to be extremely profitable half a decade from now, since only the strongest and most reputable venture capitalists are actively investing today—and they have their pick of the most promising deals. As we noted early in this chapter, venture capital's fundamental economic function is to commercialize science, and this need will surely endure.

20-4 Concept Review Questions

7. Why do you think European governments and stock exchanges are so keen to promote a vibrant entrepreneurial sector? Can you think of any competitive advantages that might accrue to Europe because of its relatively late start in developing IPO markets?

8. What are some of the competitive strengths and weaknesses of venture capital as practiced in Europe, Japan, and Canada when compared with practices in the United States?

9. What type of growth in venture capital funding and investment have China and India experienced during recent years? What is their future outlook for venture capital growth?

Summary

- Entrepreneurial finance requires specialized financial management skills because entrepreneurial growth companies (EGCs) are unlike other private or publicly traded companies. In particular, EGCs must finance much higher asset growth rates than other firms and tap external financial markets much more frequently.

Table of Important Equations

1. $FV = A(1 + r)^n$

2. $Equity\ fraction = FV/expected\ market\ valuation$

- In addition to providing risk capital to entrepreneurial growth firms, professional venture capitalists (VCs) provide managerial oversight, coupled with technical and business advice, assistance in developing and launching new products, and valuable help recruiting experienced management talent.

- U.S. venture capital investments are highly concentrated both geographically and industrially. Furthermore, the most successful VC funds are almost always organized as limited partnerships and follow distinctive investment strategies (staged investment) using unique financial instruments (convertible preferred stock).

- U.S. venture capitalists endeavor to make intermediate-term, high-risk investments in entrepreneurial growth firms and then to exit these investments either by selling the companies they hold to another firm or by executing an initial public offering. Phenomenal growth in venture capital fund-raising and investment has occurred since the mid-1990s in the United States, Western Europe, and certain Asian countries but not in Japan or most developing countries. In recent years, the two largest venture capital markets (the United States and Europe) have seen significant convergence in contracting practices, investment patterns, and returns.

- Canada and Israel have had great success in venture capital funding and investment, as have China and India—but growth in venture capital elsewhere in Asia has lagged behind that in the United States and Western Europe. Venture capital investment in developing countries has been growing from a low base during recent years.

Key Terms

angel capitalists, 619
cancellation option, 624
corporate venture capital funds, 619
demand registration rights, 625
entrepreneurial finance, 617
entrepreneurial growth companies (EGCs), 617
financial venture capital funds, 619

institutional venture capital funds, 619
ownership right agreements, 625
participation rights, 625
private equity, 618
ratchet provisions, 625
redemption option, 628
repurchase rights, 625

small business investment companies (SBICs), 619
staged financing, 624
stock option plans, 625
term sheet, 625
venture capital, 619
venture capital limited partnerships, 619

Self-Test Problems

Answers to Self-Test Problems and the Concept Review Questions throughout the chapter appear in CourseMate with SmartFinance Tools at www.cengagebrain.com.

ST20-1. You are seeking $1.5 million from a venture capitalist to finance the launch of your online financial search engine. You and the VC agree that your venture is currently worth $3 million and that, when the company goes public in an IPO five years hence, it will have an expected market capitalization of $20 million. Given the company's stage of development, the VC requires a 50% return on investment. What fraction of the firm will the VC receive in exchange for its $1.5 million investment in your company?

ST20-2. An entrepreneur seeks $12 million from a VC fund. The entrepreneur and fund managers agree that the entrepreneur's venture is currently worth $30 million and that the company will likely to be ready to go public in four years. At that time, the company is expected to have a net income of $6 million and comparable firms are expected to be selling at a price/earnings ratio of 25. Given the company's stage of development, the venture capital fund managers require a 40% compound annual return on their investment. What fraction of the firm will the fund receive in exchange for its $12 million investment?

ST20-3. Suppose that six out of ten investments made by a VC fund are a total loss, meaning that the return on each is −100%. Of the remaining investments, three break even (earning a 0% return) and one pays off spectacularly by earning a 650% return. What is the realized return on the VC fund's overall portfolio?

Questions

Q20-1. List and describe the key financial differences between entrepreneurial growth companies (EGCs) and large publicly traded firms.

Q20-2. How does the financing of entrepreneurial growth companies (EGCs) differ from that of most firms in mature industries? Under what circumstances can EGCs obtain debt financing from banks or other financial institutions?

Q20-3. What is an *angel capitalist*? How do the financing techniques used by angels differ from those employed by professional venture capitalists?

Q20-4. Distinguish between the four basic types of venture capital funds. Which type has emerged as the dominant organizational form? Why?

Q20-5. What are some of the common characteristics of those entrepreneurial growth companies that are able to attract venture capital investment? In which industries and states is the majority of venture capital invested?

Q20-6. What is meant by *early-stage* and *later-stage* venture capital investment? What proportions of venture capital have been allocated between the two in recent years? Which stage requires a higher expected return? Why?

Q20-7. What are the responsibilities and typical payoff for a general partner in a venture capital limited partnership?

Q20-8. Define *staged financing*. Why is this an efficient risk-minimizing mechanism for venture capitalists?

Q20-9. List and briefly describe some of the more popular *covenants* included in venture capital investment contracts. What is their general purpose?

Q20-10. What is the most popular form of financing (or security type) required by venture capitalists in return for their investment? Why is this form of financing optimal for both the entrepreneur and the venture capitalist?

Q20-11. List the major differences between venture capital financing in the United States and in Western Europe. What major changes have been occurring recently in the European venture capital industry?

Q20-12. Why is a vibrant IPO market considered vital to the success of a nation's venture capital industry? What impact did the collapse of Germany's Neuer Markt have on the European venture capital industry?

Q20-13. Describe the recent levels of venture capital activity in Canada, Israel, China, and India. What is the outlook for each of them?

Problems

The Organization and Operations of U.S. Venture Capital Firms

P20-1. Access the National Venture Capital Association Web site at www.nvca.org. Update Figure 20.1 using the most recent data available from this Web site and its links. What general trend do you see in the returns to venture capital investing versus returns in the public markets?

P20-2. An entrepreneur seeks $4 million from a venture capitalist. They agree that the entrepreneur's venture is currently worth $12 million and that, when the company goes public in an IPO three years hence, it will have an expected market capitalization of $70 million. Given the company's stage of development, the VC requires a 40% return on investment. What fraction of the firm will the VC receive in exchange for its $4 million investment?

P20-3. An entrepreneur seeks $10 million from a VC fund. The entrepreneur and fund managers agree that the entrepreneur's venture is currently worth $25 million and that the company will likely be ready to go public in five years. At that time, the company is expected to have net income of $7.5 million, and comparable firms are expected to be selling at a price/earnings ratio of 30. Given the company's stage of development, the venture capital fund managers require a 50% compound annual return on their investment. What fraction of the firm will the fund receive in exchange for its $10 million investment?

P20-4. The venture capital fund Techno Fund II made a $4 million investment in Optical Fibers Corporation five years ago and, in return, received 1 million shares representing 20% of Optical Fibers' equity. Optical Fibers is now planning an initial public offering in which it will sell 1 million newly created shares for $50 per share. Techno has chosen to exercise its demand registration rights and will sell its shares—alongside the newly created shares—in Optical Fibers' IPO. The investment banks underwriting Optical Fibers' IPO will charge a 7% underwriting spread, so both the firm and Techno Fund II will receive 93% of the $50-per-share offer price. Assuming the IPO is successful, calculate the compound annual return that Techno will have earned on its investment.

P20-5. High-Tech Fund III made a $3 million investment in Internet Printing Company (IPC) six years ago and received 2 million shares of series A convertible preferred stock. Each of these shares is convertible into two shares of IPC common stock. Three years later, High-Tech III participated in a second round of financing for IPC and received 3 million shares of series B convertible preferred stock in exchange for a $15 million investment. Each series B share is convertible into one share of IPC common stock. Internet Printing Company is now planning an IPO, but it must convert all its outstanding convertible preferred shares into common stock before the offering. After conversion, IPC will have 20 million common shares outstanding and will create another 2 million common shares for sale in the IPO. The underwriter handling IPC's initial offering expects to sell these new shares for $45 each but has prohibited existing shareholders from selling any of their stock in the IPO. The underwriter will keep 7% of the offer as an underwriting discount. Assume that the IPO is successful and that IPC shares sell for $60 each immediately after the offering.

a. Calculate the total number of IPC common shares that High-Tech III will own after the IPO. What fraction of IPC's total outstanding common stock does this represent?

b. Using the post-issue market price for IPC shares, calculate the (unrealized) compound annual return that High-Tech III earned on its original and subsequent investments in IPC stock.

c. Now assume that the second-round IPC financing had been made under much less favorable conditions and that High-Tech III paid only $1 million instead of $15 million for the 3 million series B shares. Assuming that all the other features of IPC's initial offering described earlier hold true, calculate the (unrealized) compound annual return High-Tech III earned on this second investment in IPC stock.

P20-6. Suppose that five out of ten investments made by a VC fund are a total loss, meaning that the return on each of them is −100%. Of the ten investments, three break even, earning a 0% return. If the VC fund's expected return equals 50%, what rate of return must it earn on the two most successful deals in order to achieve a portfolio return equal to expectations?

Smart Ideas Video

Greg Udell, Indiana University

"Firms that access venture capital finance typically have loads of intangible assets on their balance sheets and very little in the way of tangible assets."

Manju Puri, Duke University

"Venture capital does have a positive role for innovative companies in helping to push their product out quickly."

Steve Kaplan, University of Chicago

"It's not just about what fraction of the company the venture capitalists are getting."

Antoinette Schoar, MIT

"We find that there's a very large amount of variation in returns of different funds."

Smart Practices Video

David Haeberle, Chief Executive Officer, Command Equity Group

"If you make ten investments as a fund, you're probably going to see five write-offs."

Mini-Case

Entrepreneurial Finance and Venture Capital

Through your financial services firm, Vestin Capital, Inc., you have raised a pool of money from clients. You intend to invest it in new business opportunities. To prepare for this endeavour, you decide to answer the following questions.

Assignment

1. What are some of the challenges of financing entrepreneurial growth companies (EGCs)?

2. What are the different types of venture capital funds?

3. What are some choices for organizing a venture capital firm?

4. In what ways should a venture capital firm structure its investments?

5. Should venture capital firms use convertible securities?

6. What are some of the exit strategies that may be available to a venture capital firm?

chapter 21

Mergers, Acquisitions, and Corporate Control

What Companies Do

The Deal That Might Have Been—BHP Billiton's Bid for Rio Tinto Collapses

Had the deal been successfully completed, Australia's BHP Billiton Ltd.'s $140 billion hostile takeover bid for fellow mining company Britain's Rio Tinto plc, launched in November 2007, would have been the third-largest takeover in history. Instead, the bid's failure and withdrawal in January 2009 resulted in the largest failed takeover attempt ever and left the shareholders of both companies feeling bruised. The merger seemed to make sense when launched at the peak of the mining industry's global business cycle. But by 2009 it had fallen victim to plunging share and commodity prices, worldwide economic contraction, opposition from powerful national and business interests intent on scuttling a merger between the world's first- and third-largest mining companies, and the desire of Rio Tinto's board and management team to remain independent.

When BHP Billiton Ltd. approached the board of directors of Britain's Rio Tinto plc on November 7, 2007, with an offer to exchange three BHP shares for each Rio Tinto share, this represented a 14% premium over Rio Tinto's share price the day before. Rio Tinto's board immediately rejected the offer as inadequate. Undeterred, BHP followed up with an identical tender offer targeted directly at Rio Tinto's shareholders. It announced that it had lined up a high-powered set of investment and commercial banks to advise BHP on its takeover strategy and to provide financing for a proposed $30 billion buyback of shares in the combined company, to be executed if and when the merger was completed. BHP also described how it would integrate the two companies and predicted that it would be able to generate synergies—cost savings, increased sales, and more productive investment spending—of $3.7 billion per year.

Unfortunately for BHP, several large mineral-consuming nations and businesses concluded that the proposed synergies would actually result from price increases for iron ore and other key products, and they challenged the proposed merger on antitrust grounds. These opponents pointed out that a merged BHP–Rio Tinto would control almost 40% of the world's supply of iron ore and would leave just two companies controlling almost 80%. The Chinese state-owned company Chinalco went so far as to pay $14.1 billion in February 2008 to buy Rio Tinto's UK-listed subsidiary to ensure that Chinese interests would be represented in a combined BHP–Rio Tinto. The European Union's Competition Commission also opened a formal investigation of the merger and signaled its plans to oppose the deal in court.

Meanwhile, the market capitalizations of both BHP and Rio Tinto fell by more than a third during 2008 as the global financial crisis pummeled stock prices and slowing growth sharply cut worldwide demand for minerals. In December 2008, BHP was forced to withdraw its offer in order to focus on cutting costs in its own operations. The takeover saga, the bid's ultimate collapse, and the recession left Rio Tinto so badly weakened that the firm was forced to cut its 2009 capital investment spending plans from $9 billion to

$4 billion and to search for ways of trimming its $37 billion in debt—which in February 2009 actually exceeded its $36 billion stock market capitalization. The year 2008 saw a record number and value of failed takeover bids, and the BHP–Rio Tinto deal that got away was the largest of them all.[1]

Learning Objectives

After studying this chapter you should be able to:

- Describe the most important forms of corporate control transactions and distinguish between transactions that integrate two businesses and those that split up an existing single business;

- Discuss the differences between horizontal, vertical, and conglomerate mergers;

- Explain the different methods of payment acquirers use to execute mergers and acquisitions, and discuss how returns to target and bidder firm shareholders differ between cash and stock mergers;

- Contrast the motivations of managers who implement value-maximizing mergers and acquisitions to those who execute non-value-maximizing combinations; and

- Describe the most important laws and regulations that govern corporate control activities in the United States, and explain why international corporate control regulations have become much more important recently.

As its name implies, corporate control refers to the monitoring, supervision, and direction of a corporation or other business organization. The most common change in corporate control results from the combination of two or more business entities into a single organization, as happens in a merger or acquisition. A change in corporate control also occurs with the consolidation of voting power within a small group of investors, as found in going-private transactions such as leveraged buyouts (LBOs) and management buyouts (MBOs). Transfer of ownership of a business unit with a divestiture and the creation of a new corporation through a spin-off are other ways to bring about such a change.

The forces effecting changes in corporate control and the resulting impact on the business community present some of the most interesting and hotly contested debates in the field of finance. For example, the corporate control contest for RJR Nabisco captivated corporate America in the fall of 1988, spawned a book and a movie about the takeover, and remains a source of debate for academics and politicians over the social benefit of corporate control activities. We address the causes and consequences of changes in corpo-rate control in this chapter, as well as provide real-world examples of the merger/acquisition process and the technical aspects a corporate manager must consider before making decisions regarding corporate control changes.

---

corporate control
The monitoring, supervision, and direction of a corporation or other business organization.

In this chapter, we study corporate control events, which are related to the monitoring, supervision, and direction of a business organization. The most common change in corporate control is the combination of two or more business entities into a single organization, as happens in mergers and acquisitions (M&A), which are the main focus of this chapter. A change in corporate control also occurs with the consolidation of voting power within a small group of investors, as found in going-private transactions, such as leveraged buyouts (LBOs) and management buyouts (MBOs). Transfer of ownership of a business unit with a divestiture and the creation of a new corporation through a spin-off are other ways to bring about such a change. The chapter concludes with a brief look at corporate governance, that is, the laws, practices, and institutions that determine how—and in whose interests—companies are operated.

takeover
A transaction in which the control of one entity is taken over by another

acquisition
The purchase of resources, assets, or another firm.

Before examining mergers and acquisitions in detail, we start by defining some basic terms. A takeover is any transaction in which the control of one entity is taken over by another. A takeover can be a friendly merger negotiated between the boards of directors of two independent corporations, or it can be an aggressive and unwanted offer by one firm to buy another. An acquisition is the purchase of resources by a business enterprise. These resources may be new assets purchased from the producer, assets (e.g., a plant or a machine) currently owned by another company, or another firm in its entirety, which is commonly known as a merger.

---

[1]We thank Anil Shivdasani, Ben Ee, Amanda Gonzales, Ray Groth, and Ged Johnson for their help and insights.

merger
A transaction in which two or more business organizations combine into a single entity.

vertical merger
Companies with current or potential buyer-seller relationships combine to create a more integrated company.

horizontal merger
A combination of competitors within the same industry.

conglomerate merger
Unrelated diversification mergers that occur between companies in completely different lines of business.

The term merger applies to a transaction in which two or more business organizations combine into a single entity. Most often the term merger is reserved for a transaction in which one corporation takes over another upon the approval of both companies' boards of directors and shareholders after terms are negotiated in a definitive merger agreement. The company making the acquisition is often called the acquirer or bidder, and the firm being acquired is the target. A vertical merger combines two companies with a current or potential buyer-seller relationship. In July 2010, Google announced plans to acquire ITA Software, a company that produces the software behind many travel sites on the Internet. This is an example of an upstream vertical merger because Google is purchasing a firm that provides a service that is necessary before consumers can use travel sites to book flights (sites that they may find through Google's search engine). The very same month, First Solar, a manufacturer of thin film solar modules, acquired NextLight Renewable Power, a company involved in the construction of large-scale solar power projects. Essentially, NextLight was a potential customer for First Solar, so that acquisition is an example of a downstream vertical merger. In contrast, a horizontal merger combines two companies in the same industry, such as the 2010 merger of Continental and United Airlines. Finally, a conglomerate merger joins two companies in different lines of business. General Electric was formed by mergers that took place over decades, with the resulting conglomerate firm producing everything from washing machines to jet engines to nuclear turbines.

21-1

JOB INTERVIEW QUESTION

What conditions contribute to a robust M&A environment (i.e., contribute to merger waves)?

JOB INTERVIEW QUESTION

Why did M&A activity shrink so dramatically during the 2007–2008 financial crisis?

Merger Waves and International Acquisition Activity

In some years, merger activity reaches such a frenzy that there seems to be daily news of another dramatic offer from one company to buy another. In other years, activity slows down, often in response to a weak economy. These ebbs and flows in acquisition activity are known as merger waves. For example, we see in Figure 21.1 that M&A activity increased dramatically throughout the 1990s, reaching all-time highs in 2000, near the peak of the Internet bubble. Acquisitions then decreased during the recession of the early 2000s, only to pick up again in the late 2000s and then drop once more during the 2008–2009 recession.

Three economy-wide explanations for the ebbing and flowing of overall merger activity have been put forth. The first explanation posits that changes in technology,

Figure 21.1

Trends in M&A: Total Value of M&A Transactions in the U.S. Hit an All-Time High in 2000

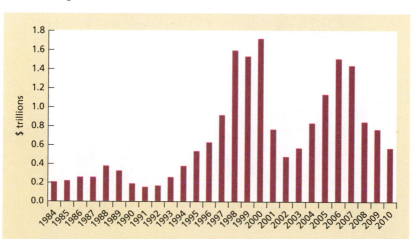

Source: SDC Platinum, Oct 2010. © Reuters. Used with permission.

such as the growing importance of Internet commerce in the 1990s, often lead to numerous alliances and acquisitions, as firms seek to strategically position themselves in the new economy. Economic or regulatory changes also can lead to a flurry of merger activity. For example, the relaxing of the Glass-Steagall banking regulations in the 1990s opened the door for commercial banks to enter sectors such as insurance and security issuance that had previously been off-limits. This naturally also led to mergers between companies in these various industries.

A second explanation of merger waves suggests financial market conditions, such as the ease with which companies can obtain funding for acquisitions or the relative strengths of currencies, will either encourage or discourage M&A activity. Merger waves often occur when the stock market is near a recent high (because when stock prices are high, companies often find it easier to issue new equity at a reasonable price) and when debt markets are very liquid (at which time the cost of debt is often relatively low). Foreign acquisition of assets in a given country also increases following a drop in home country currency values. For example, more U.S. companies became targets when the dollar depreciated in 2007, but this trend waned as the dollar grew stronger in 2008 and 2009.

A third explanation of merger waves is related to behavioral finance. When targets or entire industries are believed to be undervalued (i.e., current stock price is below its true value), these companies become attractive targets, under the assumption that the valuation will eventually correct itself. Note that this explanation implies that the market is at least sometimes inefficient and therefore incorrectly prices target stocks. Conversely, companies that believe their stocks are overvalued by the market may attempt to use their stock as currency to purchase the assets of another firm. For example, if a stock's true value is $10 but it temporarily trades at $15, if managers can purchase a fairly valued asset with their stock, the firm can, to some extent, lock in the $15 value. While heard frequently, the behavioral explanation implies that arbitrage activity does not swiftly eliminate inefficient mispricing of common stocks. Consequently, one must be cautious when considering this explanation of merger waves. (However, AOL's acquisition of Time Warner in 2000 would suggest that this occurs in at least some cases.)

International Activity The amount of cross-border merger activity has increased dramatically in recent years. Figure 21.2 presents cross-border mergers between U.S. companies and firms located in other countries. As can be seen, cross-border merger

Figure 21.2   **Value of Cross-Border Transactions Involving U.S. Firms in 2010**

Source: SDC 2011. © Reuters. Used with permission.

Figure 21.3   **Merger Transactions by Region (1998 – 2003)**

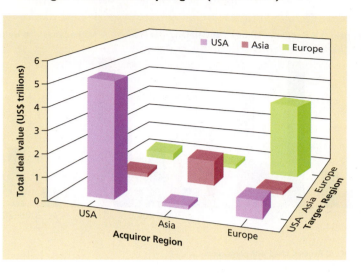

Figure 21.4   **Merger Transactions by Region (2004–2009)**

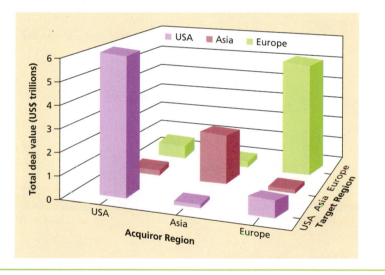

and acquisition activity is a two-way street. U.S. companies acquired more assets from UK firms in 2010 than from any other country; at the same time, Canadian firms were the most active in acquiring U.S. assets.

Figures 21.3 and 21.4 show the amount of M&A activity within the United States, Asia, and Europe, as well as between different pairs of those regions during two time periods, 1998–2003 and 2004–2009. The front row shows that U.S. firms do more acquisitions than firms in Europe and Asia do. The tallest bars indicate that most M&A activity occurs within a region; that is, companies tend to acquire other companies in the same region.

Albeit on a smaller scale, the amount of cross-border M&A activity has increased in recent years. For example, there has been an increase in European acquisitions of U.S. companies, and of U.S. acquisitions of Asian companies. Overall, the total value of cross border transactions across all three regions increased by 14.7% from US$2.86 trillion (1998 to 2003) to US$3.28 trillion (2004 to 2009).

Figure 21.5

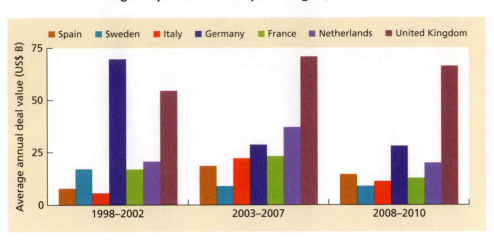

Foreign Acquisitions of European Targets, 1998–2010

Figure 21.6

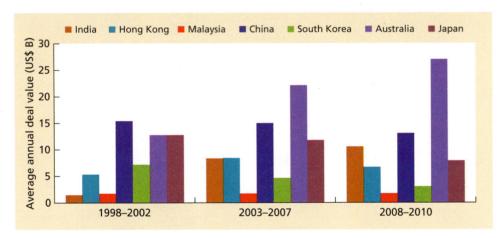

Foreign Acquisitions of Targets in Asia and Pacific Rim, 1998–2010

Though not explicitly shown in Figures 21.3 and 21.4, about one-third of the "within Europe" merger activity (the green bar in the back right corner) includes mergers that take place across country borders (e.g., a French acquisition of a UK company). Analogously, about 15% of "within Asia" merger activity involves companies located in different countries.

Figures 21.5 and 21.6 summarize cross-border M&A activity between different countries within a given region from 1998 to 2010. In Figure 21.5, the UK is particularly active due to its relatively relaxed regulations and strong commitment to open markets. At the same time, in Figure 21.6, emerging countries such as China have started to play a major role in international M&A.

As further proof of the growing importance of international M&A, Table 21.1 lists the top 15 corporate takeovers of all time. Three of the top five involve firms based outside of the United States.

Table 21.1   **Fifteen Largest Corporate Takeovers,[a] Ranked by Transaction Value**

Acquirer	Target	Transaction Value ($ billion)	Year
Vodafone AirTouch PLC (UK)	Mannesmann AG (Germany)	202.8	2000
America Online Inc. (U.S.)	Time Warner Inc. (U.S.)	164.7	2001
Royal Bank of Scotland (UK)	ABN Amro (Netherlands)	98.0	2007
Pfizer Inc. (U.S.)	Warner-Lambert Co. (U.S.)	89.2	2000
Royal Dutch Petroleum (Netherlands)	Shell Trading and Transport (UK)	80.1	2005
Exxon Corp. (U.S.)	Mobil Corp. (U.S.)	78.9	1999
Glaxo Wellcome PLC (UK)	SmithKline Beecham (UK)	76.0	2000
AT&T Inc	Bell South Corp	72.7	2006
Travelers Group Inc. (U.S.)	Citicorp (U.S.)	72.6	1998
Comcast Corp	AT&T Broadband & Internet Services	72.0	2001
Sprint (U.S.)	Nextel Communications (U.S.)	71.0	2004
Pfizer (U.S.)	Wyeth (U.S.)	68.0	2009
Sanofi (France)	Aventis (France)	65.7	2004
SBC Communications Inc. (U.S.)	Ameritech Corp. (U.S.)	62.6	1999
NationsBank Corp. (U.S.)	BankAmerica Corp. (U.S.)	61.6	1998

[a]As of December 31, 2010.

Source: Mergers & Acquisitions (SDC Publishing), Mergers and Acquisitions Report (Thomson Financial), and *Financial Times* (from **www.ft.com**).

21-1 Concept Review Questions

1. What are three explanations for merger waves? Which of these provides the best explanation for the decline in M&A activity during the recent financial crisis and recession?

2. Figures 21.3 and 21.4 show that firms are much more likely to acquire other firms in the same region than they are to acquire firms from another region. Why do you think this is the case?

21-2 Why Do Companies Make Acquisitions?

If you were in charge of the world economy, one of your goals would be to place assets into the hands of the investors or companies that value them the most. This would allow the economy to be most productive and efficient. Given that no one person organizes the economy, other means such as mergers and acquisitions are needed to accomplish this goal.

The outcome of acquisitions can often be disruptive: companies are sometimes broken up, employees are often laid off, and some divisions may be shut down. While painful in the short run, mergers and acquisitions play a very important role in helping an economy allocate resources efficiently. By moving assets to new companies or investors where they can be used more productively, M&A is often good for the economy's health in the long run. For example, mergers and acquisitions, along with resource reallocation more generally, played an important role in transforming the transportation sector from producing horse-drawn carriages in the early 1900s, to producing cars, planes, and rocket engines decades later.

Managers at a particular company are less concerned about the overall economy's efficiency than they are about their own firm's operations. How can their company operate most effectively, often in the face of intense competition? One strategy might involve acquiring a unit of another company, or perhaps an entire firm. For example, acquiring an oil refinery can help a chemical company obtain sole ownership of a key input into its production process, to guarantee smooth, on-time production that is not subject to the whims of the oil markets.

This section discusses several justifications for merger and acquisition activity. Note that in the previous section, we discussed explanations for economy-wide trends that drive merger waves. In this section, we dig deeper into explanations of mergers between two firms in any given year, even during years where overall M&A activity is low.

There are three important principles that managers must keep in mind when evaluating an acquisition opportunity. *First, does it increase shareholder value?* In previous chapters, we emphasized that shareholders are the owners of the firm, and therefore maximizing long run share price is a fundamental goal of the firm. Therefore, a merger should only be conducted if it increases long-run stockholder value.[2] *Second, what price is being paid for the acquisition?* This is of course closely related to the first principle. No matter how attractive a target, the acquiring firm can destroy value if it overpays. *Finally, is an acquisition really needed to obtain the hoped-for benefit of the merger?* For example, rather than conduct an outright acquisition, can a chemical company instead arrange a strategic alliance or partnership that allows it to reliably access oil as a key input into its production process? Acquisitions can distract management, often cause disruption, involve fees (to lawyers, bankers, etc.), and can be painful to reverse. If the sought-after outcome can be obtained in some way that is short of a full-fledged merger, it can at times be less expensive and less risky to pursue this alternative course of action. As we explore the common justifications for mergers and acquisitions, keep these three important principles in mind, because we will see that not all of the given explanations make economic sense. Note that these explanations are not mutually exclusive; that is, at times they overlap or are in other ways related to each other.

21-2a Explaining Mergers and Acquisitions

Growth A common practitioner view is that firms must grow or they will stagnate and eventually die. After all, from the equation for a growing perpetuity,

$$\text{Value} = \text{cash flow}/(r - g)$$

it may seem that if growth (g) increases, so does firm value. Mergers are a primary way for a company to grow, by acquiring another firm's customers or production capabilities. We note, however, that acquiring growth at a high price can be short-sighted. Growth only increases firm value if the acquisition price does not exceed the present value of the cash flows produced by the acquired assets.[3]

Another cautionary consideration about growth is related to managerial agency costs. Managers can increase their power, prestige, and even pay by increasing the size of the empire they oversee. Consequently, a recommendation by a divisional manager, or even a CEO, to pursue a project that they claim is central to a firm's growth strategy must be tempered by the realization that the manager may personally benefit from the transaction, and thus have personal incentive to increase firm size more than is optimal.

The important question is whether the acquisition increases firm value. This will be the case if the value of the acquired assets to the acquiring firm is greater than the price paid to purchase those assets. In other words, growth acquisitions make sense when they produce positive NPV.

synergy
A reduction in costs or increase in revenues that results from a merger.

Synergies Michael Eisner, the former CEO of Disney, provided perhaps the best definition of synergy with his view of the value created by his company's 1995 merger with Capital Cities/ABC: "1 + 1 = 4." That is, synergies occur when combining two entities produces extra value, so the combination is worth more than the sum of the two separate entities. Synergies sound good. After all, who wouldn't like to create value? However, synergies are very difficult to measure and even harder to obtain. The synergies expected to result from the Disney–Capital Cities/ABC combination were never realized in full. In fact, perhaps "1 + 1 = 1.5" in this case.

---

[2] Notice that we refer to long run shareholder value. When a merger is first announced, the initial stock market reaction is often negative, which can be interpreted to indicate that the market believes that the merger will not add value even in the long run. There may be some cases in which it is justified to pursue an acquisition even though there is an initial negative stock market reaction. However, to pursue such a merger, management must have a convincing argument for why the long-run benefits of a merger are positive, even though the stock market does not recognize this initially. Of course these arguments should be scrutinized carefully.

[3] One subtle point is that when evaluating a merger, the cash flows should be measured relative to the cash flows the firm would receive if no merger were to occur. So if, for example, a company were expected to have annual cash flows of −$1 million if no merger were to occur, and flat cash flows with the merger, then incremental cash flows due to the merger would be $1 million annually.

What Companies Do Globally

Survey Evidence: Why Pursue Mergers

What motivates corporate managers to merge with other companies? A survey of acquiring firm managers indicates that the most important acquisition motive is to capture potential synergies from combining with another firm. Exhibit 1 reveals that the desire to take advantage of synergy is easily the most popular motive for mergers among managers of firms that executed at least one merger during 1990–2001, with 37.3% of respondents listing this as their top-ranked motive. The desire to diversify ranked second, and merging to achieve a specific organizational form through restructuring ranked a distant third choice. No other motive was ranked highly by more than 8% of respondents.

And what specific synergies are managers looking for in the mergers they implement? As described in Exhibit 2, reduced operating costs resulting from greater economies of scale from combined production are by far the most common synergies that managers hope to capture. Nearly 90% of respondents listed this as the top-ranked source of synergy.

Exhibit 1   Motives for Mergers and Acquisitions

This exhibit shows the most important reasons responding firms gave for their mergers and acquisitions during 1990–2001. Respondents could indicate more than one reason, but this exhibit reports only the top-ranked motive.

Motives	n	%
Take advantage of synergy	28	37.3
Diversify	22	29.3
Achieve a specific organizational form as part of an ongoing restructuring program	8	10.7
Acquire a company below its replacement cost	6	8.0
Use excess free cash	4	5.3
Reduce tax on the combined company due to tax losses of the acquired company	2	2.7
Realize gains from breakup value of the acquired firm	0	0.0
Other	5	6.7
Totals	**75**	**100.0**

Exhibit 2   Sources of Synergy

This exhibit presents the source of synergy for those firms directly or indirectly involved in synergy-related mergers. Of the 75 total responses, 69 stated that gained synergies from economies of scale. Although respondents could indicate more than one reason, this exhibit reports only the top-ranked motive for a given respondent.

Source of Synergy	n	%
Operating economies (resulting from greater economies of scale that improve productivity or cut costs)	62	89.9
Financial economies (resulting from lower transactions costs and tax gains)	4	5.8
Increased market power (due to reduced competition)	3	4.3
Differential efficiency (due to the acquiring firm's management being more efficient)	0	0.0
Totals	**69**	**100.0**

Sources: Exhibits 2 and 3 of Tarun K. Mukherjee, Halil Kiymaz, and H. Kent Baker, "Merger Motives and Target Valuation: A Survey of Evidence from CFOs," *Journal of Applied Finance* 14 (Fall/Winter 2004), pages 7–24. Copyright © The Financial Management Association, International, University of South Florida, COBA, 4202 E. Fowler Avenue, Ste. #3331, Tampa, FL 33620-5500 www.fma.org.

Finance in Your Life

Where Mergers Go Wrong

In a Winter 2004 study entitled *Where Mergers Go Wrong*, McKinsey documented that on average, acquirers in mergers pay sellers almost all of the value created by the merger. This takes the form of a premium that usually ranges from 10 to 35% of the target company's preannouncement value. This occurs because the average acquirer in the study substantially overestimated the synergies that would result from a merger.

McKinsey found that revenue synergies are greatly overestimated, with fewer than one-fourth of merger synergies meeting incremental revenue expectations. In addition, few companies account for the revenue "dis-synergies" that befall

merging companies. These could be temporary business disruptions resulting from consolidations, employee turnover, and the like. In contrast, two-thirds of mergers achieve within 10% of projected cost savings, which are often related to lay-offs and branch closings.

The study recommends that firms should take care to maintain customer relationships during the transitional period. When formulating merger plans, assumptions of synergies and market growth should be challenged, and double checked against overall industry and economic growth. Managers would do well to apply external benchmarks as sanity checks when formulating cost savings and growth assumptions.

economies of scale
Relative operating costs are reduced for merged companies because of an increase in size that allows for the reduction or elimination of overlapping resources.

economies of scope
Value-creating benefits of increased breadth of operations for merged companies.

resource complementarities
A firm with a particular operating expertise merges with a firm with another operating strength to create a company that has expertise in multiple areas.

JOB INTERVIEW QUESTION

Do mergers on average succeed or fail from the standpoint of creating new value? If they fail, why?

Synergies can occur through *cost reductions* and *revenue enhancements*. Combining two firms can reduce costs for several reasons. One is economies of scale, which result when relative operating costs are reduced because of an increase in size that allows for the reduction or elimination of overlapping resources. A simple example is that Walmart can sell products cheaply because its huge buying power gives it economies of scale—units are cheaper because they buy so many of them. Another economy of scale can occur through workforce and related reductions after two companies are merged. For example, the combined company only needs one CFO, one billing department, and one branch on the corner of Broad and Main Streets; therefore, they can reduce workforce and branches, ultimately cutting costs. Economies of scope also create value due to increased size, in this case when a firm produces several different goods or internally houses several aspects of the supply chain. For example, a huge firm like Johnson and Johnson can afford to have an in-house graphics team at a cost that is lower than if each division individually contracted out graphics work.

Revenue enhancements can lead to synergistic gains when two business entities combined sell more products than they could sell separately. This revenue synergy is often the result of resource complementarities, which occur when a firm with a particular operating expertise merges with a firm with different strengths, to create a company that has expertise in multiple areas. A good example of such a complementarity is the 2010 merger of Disney and Marvel. Benefits of the merger include combining Marvel's deep bench of characters with Disney's well established distribution channels (for movies and collectibles). Cross-selling opportunities can also arise when an acquisition provides a company with access to markets in a new geography or a new demographic.

Cost reductions are often fairly straightforward to predict and document, and in fact, companies often realize nearly all of the predicted cost synergies. In contrast, revenue enhancements are much harder to achieve. The box on page 644 describes a McKinsey study that documents that fewer than half of mergers achieve hoped-for revenue synergies. As mentioned before, it is also important to verify that a formal merger (versus a joint venture, for example) is necessary to achieve hoped for synergies.

Market Position Mergers often occur when a company attempts to solidify or improve its position in its industry. For example, traditional grocery chain market leaders Kroger and Safeway embarked on a series of acquisitions in the late 1990s. Their objective was to solidify their leadership positions in response to a new threat to the industry: Walmart groceries. A similar phenomenon can occur in slow growth or unprofitable industries. In this case, an industry often begins to consolidate, leaving fewer firms to compete over shrinking profits. Managers often take the perspective of consolidate or be consolidated. In recent years, the drug store and domestic airline industries have consolidated.

Though market position mergers sometimes make good economic sense, there are at least two issues that may limit a potential merger's viability. First, government anti-trust regulations are designed to prohibit a single firm (or firms) from gaining sufficient market power to set prices above the competitive level. Consider the Staples–Office Depot proposed merger from several years ago. With only three firms competing in this industry before the merger, the regulatory authorities denied this acquisition on the grounds that the merged company would have the power to control prices in the office supplies market, with only one (much smaller) competitor to provide price competition. The second issue is the fundamental question of whether the merger increases firm value. From the acquirer's point of view, this means making sure not to pay more than the net present value of incremental cash flows attributable to the merger. From the seller's perspective, though it can be a hard pill to swallow, at times selling the firm may create more net present value for shareholders than the target could create if it remained independent or instead attempted to acquire another entity.

? JOB INTERVIEW QUESTION

What are more important (reliable), revenue or expense synergies?

Relative Valuation Managers often state that they acquire assets or firms that are undervalued by the market. Some argue that high value (perhaps overvalued) firms buy low value (perhaps undervalued) firms.[4] A company that uses its overpriced stock as currency to purchase undervalued assets on the cheap does, of course, create value, but keep in mind that this implies that the market is inefficient on two accounts: in overvaluing the acquiring stock and in undervaluing the target firm's stock. There are famous examples where such market mispricing seems to occur, such as AOL's famous acquisition of Time-Warner in the late '90s, where AOL's stock was priced at a stratospheric $191.00 per share in December 1999, during the height of the Internet boom (the price fell to $72 within one year). However, it seems to us that such market mispricings are fairly rare and should not often be the motivation behind a major corporate event such as an acquisition.

Diversification A diversifying or conglomerate merger occurs when a company acquires assets or an entire company that operates in another industry. For example, in 2008/9, Philips Electronics (maker of TVs and stereos) purchased a medical device company because senior management thought health care had greater growth potential.[5] Obvious questions arise from such acquisitions. Does Philips have a comparative advantage in running a medical device firm? Can this deal create new value (synergies), or are the underlying businesses too disparate? Will Philips's senior management possibly get distracted as they attempt to run a medical device company, potentially hurting the electronics division? To provide insight into the answers to these questions, we next list several possible advantages of conglomerate form, most of which also have qualifications and possible disadvantages.

Consider two companies, Y and C, one of which operates in an industry that does well in boom times (e.g., yacht building) and another that does well during recessions (e.g., coupon distribution). Combining the two companies in a diversifying merger will produce more stable cash flows because as Y goes up, C goes down, and vice versa. We learned in Chapter 6 that portfolio diversification is valuable to investors because it enables them to reduce risk for the same expected rate of return. Even so, is there any advantage to having a firm that implements the diversification for investors? Given that investors can already hold individual firms Y and C in their diversified portfolio, they will not pay more for the combined company that offers just portfolio diversification. There would need to be some other advantage to combining the companies to justify paying a premium for the combined firm.

[4]Rhodes-Kropf, Robinson, and Viswanathan (2005) measure value based on MB, the market-to-book ratio (the market value of the firm divided by the book value of assets). These authors show that targets do not in fact have low value. They argue that the more correct statement is that "high MB buys somewhat lower MB" on average. These authors show that high MB firms have a tendency to buy medium-high MB firms, while medium-to-low MB firms acquire low MB companies.

[5]An example of a conglomerate run amuck is Ling-Temco-Vought (LTV). Ling had an electrical contracting business, then bought two others, next bought Temco Aircraft, then bought Chance Vought Aerospace, then added the wire and cable company Okonite and bought Wilson, the sports equipment company—which was also involved in meat packing and pharmaceuticals. Ling later spun each of these Wilson divisions into separate companies traded on the American Stock Exchange; they soon acquired the trader nicknames "Golfball," "Meatball," and "Goofball," respectively. Ling then added Greatamerica, Post's holding company for Braniff International Airways and National Car Rental, as well as J & L Steel, and it then acquired a series of resorts in Mexico and Colorado. By 1969 LTV had purchased 33 companies, employed 29,000 workers, offered 15,000 separate products and services, and was one of the 40 largest industrial corporations. In the end, after numerous divestitures, what was left of LTV filed for bankruptcy in 2000.

Related to this point, diversifying mergers are sometimes said to reduce risk. Diversification can reduce the variance of cash flows, and yet if stock returns are priced by the CAPM (see Chapter 7), then reducing variance alone may not improve stock performance.[6] The CAPM tells us that conglomeration would need to reduce systematic risk (i.e., beta risk) or the cost of capital, while at the same time not hurting growth potential, to improve stock performance.

In some cases, the stability of a conglomerate can result in a better credit rating than would be possible for the individual divisions to obtain on their own. For example, GE maintained a AA+ credit rating even during the depths of the late 2000s recession due in larger part to the stability of the overall firm than to the stellar performance of each division. Having a high credit rating reflects the ability to borrow relatively cheaply, including providing access to certain segments of the debt markets such as the commercial paper market. Of course, having a high credit rating is not the primary goal of a corporation but rather should be viewed in the context of whether it increases firm value.

One possible advantage of conglomerate form stems from internal capital markets. That is, if one division of a firm has growth opportunities but would struggle to borrow in capital markets, a conglomerate can transfer profits from a division that produces excess cash flow. This could especially be a good thing in developing economies (where the capital markets might not be fully developed), or when capital markets freeze up, such as during the 2008-09 recession. Thus, internal capital markets potentially offer the advantage of providing capital to cash-poor, growth-rich divisions. However, internal capital markets can also lead to inefficient outcomes if, for example, management uses profits from a healthy division to prop up a failing division that is destroying overall firm value. Most evidence seems to indicate that internal capital markets do not add value in mature, well-functioning economies.

There can also be advantages to conglomerate size such as economies of scale, as discussed above. The stability of conglomerates can also increase employee job security, at least in the short run. This could be good if it increases employee productivity but could be bad if the workforce becomes too complacent or protected from competitive pressures. Moreover, it becomes harder to motivate employees in individual conglomerate business units because it is harder to tie stock compensation directly to a given division. Finally, large conglomerates can suffer from slow decision processes.

In most cases the disadvantages of operating in conglomerate form are thought to outweigh the advantages in recent years. Fewer conglomerates are formed now versus several decades ago, and if anything, existing conglomerates are often broken up.

Managerial Explanations Sometimes a company will acquire another firm in order to acquire a new management team. This is common when expanding into a new country or new industry. Managerial acquisitions can also occur within an industry to acquire young talent. For example, when JP Morgan Chase acquired Bank One in July 2004, one explanation was that it wanted to acquire a young Jamie Dimon, who became CEO and led JP Morgan Chase through the financial crisis of 2008/2009 relatively unscathed. Other managerial explanations of mergers are more ominous. We already mentioned the empire building tendencies that are sometimes linked to upper management.

Roll (1986) offers a somewhat different rationale with his overconfidence or **hubris hypothesis of corporate takeovers**. Roll contends that some managers overestimate

hubris hypothesis of corporate takeovers
A theory that contends that some managers overestimate their own managerial capabilities and pursue takeovers with the belief that they can better manage their takeover target than the target's current management.

[6] If corporate diversification reduces the volatility of taxable income, it can reduce expected taxes paid and hence increase firm value. Consider a firm that has two divisions, A and B. Division A earns $10 million in taxable income in odd years and loses $10 million in even years. Division B does the reverse (loses $10 million in taxable income in odd years and earns positive $10 million in even years). The conglomerate therefore earns exactly zero dollars every year, and never pays taxes.

Now, let's think about the taxes owed if A and B were separate companies. To keep thing simple, assume that each company had exactly $0 in taxable income each of the last few years. Assume this year is 2013 (an odd year) and company A earns $10 million and pays $3.5 million in taxes (35% tax rate). In 2014 (an even year), the company loses $10 million, and "carries back" this loss to get a refund of the $3.5 million in taxes it paid in 2013. That is, the government sends company A a $3.5 million check in 2014. What A loses by paying taxes in 2013 and getting a refund in 2014 is the time value of money on $3.5 million for one year (not to mention the hassle of filing taxes and then filing again for refunds). Assume the discount rate is 10%. A's "tax cost" is $3.5 − $3.5/(1.1) = 0.318$, that is, $318,000. This happens every two years in perpetuity, and A's 2-year discount rate is 21% (=$1.1^2 − 1$). Therefore, the present value tax cost to A (as of 2012) is $318,000/0.21 = $1.52 million. Company B never pays taxes because it loses $10 million in odd years that it carries forward to the next year, completely shielding taxes in even years. Therefore, as two stand-alone companies, A and B owe the government taxes with a present value of $1.52 million. If A and B merge into one company, they would not owe any taxes (recall the first paragraph). Therefore, expected tax obligations are lower for conglomerates, as long as the taxable income across divisions is not perfectly, positively correlated.

their own managerial capabilities and pursue takeovers in the belief that they can better manage their target than can its current management team. Acquiring managers then overbid for the target and fail to realize the expected post-merger gains, thereby diminishing shareholder wealth. Thus, the intent of the managers is not contrary to the best interests of shareholders (the managers think they will create value), but the result is still value decreasing.

EPS Accretion From Main Street to Wall Street, a common benchmark to measure the gains from a merger is how it affects the acquiring company's earnings per share. To measure this effect, you sum the earnings of the two firms and divide by the sum of the two companies' number of shares outstanding, plus a few adjustments. If the EPS of the acquiring firm goes down, the merger is said to dilute EPS (and, implicitly, hurt stock price), while if EPS increases, the deal is accretive to earnings. Sometimes analysts implicitly assume that higher EPS necessarily leads to higher stock price. But is it true that higher EPS always leads to higher stock price? For example, if EPS increases but earnings also become riskier, does stock price necessarily increase? Regardless of the answer to that question, managers of the bidding firm as well as Wall Street analysts place a great deal of importance on the effects of a merger on the firm's earnings. The next section illustrates how to measure those effects.

21-2b Calculating the Effect of a Merger on Earnings per Share

The following example illustrates how to determine what EPS will be after a merger deal is closed. The key inputs are earnings of bidder and target before the merger, shares outstanding before and new shares issued to complete the merger, and some adjustments that capture merger-related incremental changes to earnings, such as increases due to synergies. Given that earnings are earned over the year, most analysts use a weighted average of shares outstanding over the year (though others may use year-end shares outstanding). The basic calculation looks like this:

Post-merger EPS = (Bidder net income + Target net income + After-tax synergies ± Adjustments) ÷ (Bidder shares outstanding + New shares issued)

The adjustments are calculated as follows:

1. Subtract after-tax depreciation and amortization from write-ups.
2. Subtract incremental after-tax interest expense associated with new debt financing.
3. Subtract lost opportunity cost of cash balances for cash that is used to finance the acquisition.
4. Add interest expense associated with target's debt that is retired and preferred stock dividends associated with preferred stock that is liquidated or converted as part of the acquisition.
5. Adjustments are sometimes made for one-time acquisition-related charges, but we ignore those here.

EXAMPLE

Let's say Peanut Butter, Inc., decides to buy Jelly Sandwiches Corp. for $100 million. The deal should generate cost savings because both companies have similar retail markets and can tap the marketing and distribution channels of the other. Also, people tend to pay more for peanut butter and jelly sandwiches than they would for each product individually.

Peanut Butter has 10 million shares outstanding and an annual net income of $50 million, so EPS is $5. Peanut Butter's current stock price is $100. Jelly has 5 million shares outstanding and annual net income of $15 million.

After Tax Synergies: The merger results in savings of around $5 million annually. Additionally, because of increased demand due to the popularity and convenience of premade peanut butter and jelly sandwiches, Peanut Butter's bankers estimate additional synergies of $2.7 million. Total pre-tax synergies are therefore $7.7 million. At a tax rate of 35%, after tax synergies are $5 million.

continued

Financing the Acquisition: Of the $100 million purchase price, assume Peanut Butter pays Jelly's shareholders with $50 million in cash, and $50 million in Peanut Butter stock. This involves:

1. Issuing $30 million in new debt. At 10% yield to maturity, this will result in annual interest payments of $3.0 million each year. For simplicity, we are assuming that the new debt is perpetual (it never retires).

2. Withdrawing $20 million in corporate cash which was originally earning 5% per year.

3. Issuing 600,000 new shares at $100 each. Use $50 million of the proceeds to pay Jelly's shareholders, and the remainder to retire $10 million of Jelly's debt. This results in annual interest expense savings of $1.5 million, or $970,000 in after-tax savings (because interest expense is tax deductible, creating a tax shield of $530,000 = $1.5M × 35%).

Adjustments:

1. <u>After-tax depreciation and amortization from write-ups:</u>   As a result of the merger, Peanut Butter will be taking over four of Jelly's plants. Equipment in the plant was purchased for around $30.0 million, but is valued at $45.4 million in the takeover. The difference of $15.4 million is known as a write up. Assuming that Peanut Butter is able to depreciate this over ten years, it can deduct depreciation of $1.54 million per year. Applying a 35% tax rate, this translates to after-tax depreciation from write-ups of around $1 million a year.

2. <u>After-tax interest expense because of new financing:</u>   New financing results in annual interest expense of $3.0 million per year. After-tax annual interest expense is therefore $1.95 million a year (35% tax rate).

3. <u>Opportunity cost of cash balances:</u>   The $20 million used to pay for the acquisition could have been earning 5%, or $1 million a year pre-tax, $650,000 per year after-tax.

4. <u>Add interest expense associated with target's debt that is retired:</u>   Saving $970,000 million in after-tax interest expense will increase earnings going forward.

$$\text{Total adjustments} = -\$1 \text{ million} - \$1.95 \text{ million} - \$650{,}000 + \$970{,}000 = -\$2.63 \text{ million}$$

Compute Post-Merger EPS:

(Bidder net income + target net income + after-tax synergies − adjustment)/(Bidder shares outstanding + new shares issued)

= ($50 million + $15 million + $5 million − $2.63 million)/(10 million + 600,000)

= $6.36.

Given that the original Peanut Butter EPS is $5, management expects this merger to be accretive. Note that merger synergies are one important reason that this deal increases earnings. Using debt to finance part of the acquisition, instead of all stock, also increases EPS in this example, though as discussed next, this made the earnings riskier because they were levered up.

To determine the effect of a merger on stock price, it is important to consider not just the merger effects on the level of earnings but also to consider whether the merger makes the firm's cash flows and earnings riskier. Consider how the method of payment can affect earnings risk. If the acquiring company issues a lot of debt and uses the principle as cash to acquire a target's stock, then (assuming the target's profitability exceeds financing costs) the acquirer will increase its EPS via the acquisition, while the number of shares outstanding will remain constant, so earnings per share will increase. In contrast, the acquirer could instead issue its own shares to purchase the target's equity. In this case, the effect on earnings will be similar (we need to adjust for after-tax interest paid) but the number of shares will increase because of the new shares issued, which will have an effect of reducing EPS in the stock acquisition.

Does this mean that the first method (borrowing to obtain funds to make the purchase) is better than the second method (increasing the number of shares to make the purchase) because it increases EPS more? Not necessarily. As pointed out in Chapter 13, using debt levers up the transaction, splitting the gains or losses over a smaller number of acquisition shares. While this may increase expected EPS, it also increases the riskiness of EPS, which puts downward pressure on stock price and the P/E ratio. If P/E falls while EPS increases, it is not clear that stock valuation will also increase. Therefore, it is not clear that a company's stock price will increase just because a deal is EPS accretive.

Having said this, we emphasize that EPS accretion is often desirable. If an acquisition increases EPS because it cuts costs, increases revenue, or otherwise increases net present value, these are positive effects of the acquisition.

21-2 Concept Review Questions

3. What characteristics surrounding a merger would lead you to conclude that it is motivated by value-maximizing managers rather than non-value-maximizing managers?

4. What different challenges and pressures might senior management of an acquirer face if the acquiring company is a public versus a private company?

5. Given that conglomerate mergers and corporate diversification have proven to be failures in general, why would any manager pursue these objectives? Can you think of any cases where corporate diversification has worked successfully? What distinguishes these cases from the norm?

21-3 Do Mergers Create Value?

The previous section described proposed explanations of whether and how mergers might increase, or destroy, firm value. Only by looking at the data can we determine whether, on net, mergers actually add value. In this section we demonstrate that by and large, mergers do create value, but this gain accrues almost entirely to target firms, with the stockholders of acquiring firms often losing money.

For mergers to create value, it must be the case that two companies combined are worth more than the two companies are worth separately, once synergies and other merger gains and costs are considered. One way to determine whether value is added is to compare the present value of all future cash flows of the combined firm to the sum of the value of bidder's future cash flows plus the present value of target's future cash flows. This valuation and several others are discussed next.

When considering whether to attempt to acquire a target, the acquirer must determine what to bid for the target. This bid price is tied to an assessment of the bidder's fair market value. This determination is typically made using one or more of the following valuation methods briefly summarized below.

It is important, of course, to keep straight whether you are determining the equity value or the total firm value (or enterprise value) of the target. Total firm value equals the value of the target's traded securities, so in simplest terms firm value equals equity value plus debt value. Therefore, if we know debt value, it is easy to convert from equity value to firm value (by adding debt value to equity value) or vice versa. Rather than the total firm value, investment bankers and other financial professionals often determine **enterprise value**. Enterprise value is roughly firm value minus the dollar value of excess cash, where excess means cash that is not needed to efficiently operate the firm.[7] That is, enterprise value is the value of the firm's underlying operations. Given how difficult it is to determine which cash is excess versus which is needed for operational purposes, enterprise value is usually determined by subtracting all of the target's cash. This concept will be discussed further in the next section.

enterprise value
The total value of the firm (including debt, equity, and other securities) that would need to be purchased to control the whole target entity.

---

[7]More specifically, enterprise value = equity value + debt + preferred stock + minority interest − cash.

21-3a Merger Valuation Methods

Next we discuss the following common merger valuation methods:

- Discounted Cash Flow – As discussed in earlier chapters, DCF values a company based on the present value of expected future cash flows, often discounted at the weighted average cost of capital.
- Public Comparables – Observable market values of comparable companies, typically publically traded, are used to estimate the market value of the target.
- Precedent Transactions – The premiums (or discounts) paid in recent acquisitions that involve the target's competitors, or other companies exhibiting similar characteristics, are used as a benchmark for the premium above (or discount below) market value that an acquirer might be expected to pay for the target in a similar transaction. Precedent transactions are often implemented via multiples, as explained below.

As an example, the following excerpts were included in Sun Microsystem's preliminary merger proxy statement following the definitive agreement to be acquired by Oracle:

- "Credit Suisse calculated [Sun's enterprise] value as a multiple of certain financial data for selected technology companies" in similar technology sectors.
- "The calculated multiples included Fully Diluted Enterprise Value as a multiple of Revenue, EBITDA and [operating income]…The [comparable] companies were selected because they had publicly traded equity securities and were deemed to be similar to Sun in one or more respects including the nature of their business, size, diversification, financial performance and geographic concentration."
- "Credit Suisse also calculated the net present value of Sun's free cash flows using Sun's management forecasts [of cash flows] … In performing this analysis, Credit Suisse applied discount rates ranging from 10.50% to 13.00% based on Sun's estimated weighted average cost of capital."
- "Credit Suisse also calculated the premiums paid in selected technology [precedent] transactions since January 1, 2007 … four weeks and one day prior to the announcement of the technology transactions."

As we begin to think more about company valuations, it is important to discuss in more detail the difference between equity value and enterprise value. Equity value is the value available to stockholders, whereas enterprise value is the firm value available to all stakeholders including creditors, debtors, and non-controlling (minority) interest holders. This is an important distinction because often an acquisition will trigger debt covenants requiring that target firm's debt be repaid in the event of a transfer of control. So, for example, if Firm A pays $10 million for Firm B's equity but Firm B also has $6 million in debt, Firm A will then have to pay Firm B shareholders $10 million and also pay Firm B debt holders $6 million. The enterprise value of this transaction is therefore $16 million. This figure represents the takeover price, including obligations the buyer must satisfy (such as buying out existing debtholders).

Acquirers and investment bankers often use multiples to estimate enterprise value, after which they deduct the market value of the target's debt to arrive at an estimate of the value of the target's equity. It is also common to use multiples to calculate equity value. The key determining which multiples calculate equity value and which calculate enterprise value is the denominator of the multiple. A multiple with EBITDA or revenue in the denominator will calculate enterprise value (i.e., enterprise value is the numerator of the multiple) because both EBITDA and revenue are available to all stakeholders. In contrast, a multiple with earnings in the denominator will calculate equity value because earnings are available only to shareholders.[8]

---

[8] EBITDA, by definition, represents earnings before subtracting interest expense and is therefore available to all stakeholders. Specifically, EBITDA is used to pay debtholders (through principal and interest payments) as well as shareholders (through dividends or share repurchases). Earnings, or net income, are available only to shareholders because earnings are net of interest payments to debtholders.

EXAMPLE

Situation: You work in internal strategy for Taft Corp. and are preparing an acquisition bid for 100% of W. Lee Corp. Without synergies, W. Lee is expected to generate $5M, $8M, and $10M in after-tax earnings in each of the next three years, respectively. With synergies, these earnings are expected to be $6 million, $10 million and $12 million. Year 4 (t = 4) earnings inclusive of synergies will be 3% higher than t = 3 earnings, and then earnings are expected to grow by 3% in perpetuity. Taft discounts using a rate of 9%.

W. Lee has two key rivals. The first, with similar financial and operating characteristics and expected earnings of $6.1M next year, was recently acquired for $210M. The second rival is similar except that it is considered to be in a mature, low growth stage and is trading at a P/E multiple of 17.3. What acquisition bid do you recommend for W. Lee Corp?

Solution: Use each valuation method to identify an appropriate range.

- Discounted Cash Flow: Discount the next three year's earnings, including synergies, to arrive at discounted cash flows[9]: [($6 million/1.09) + ($10 million/1.09^2) + ($12 million/1.09^3)] = $23.2 million. Next, use the growing perpetuity formula and the fact that year 4 cash flows are 3% higher than the year before to find the present value (as of year 3) of all the cash flows in year 4 and beyond, then discount that back to the present time: [($12 million × 1.03)/(0.09 − 0.03) = $206 million, discounted back three years at 9% equals $159.1 million.] Finally, sum to arrive at the value for the entire firm in today's dollars: $159.1 million + $23.2 million = $182.3 million.
- Public Comparables: The public rival has a P/E multiple of 17.3 which would imply that W. Lee is worth $86.5 million (17.3 × $5 million), quite a bit lower than the DCF estimate. However, we know this rival is low growth whereas W. Lee is expecting 40% growth in year 1 and 20% growth in year 2. Therefore, the 17.3 multiple may be only appropriate for the terminal value (in year 3) when W. Lee is expected to reach a mature, low growth stage. Applying this multiple to determine the terminal value in t = 3 yields 17.3 × $12 million = $207.6 million. This is very close to our year 3 terminal value estimate above using DCF ($206 million), which reinforces the terminal value estimated in the DCF analysis.
- Precedent Transactions: Given the similarities between the companies and transactions, to apply precedent transactions we identify the acquisition multiple ($210 million/$6.1 million = 34.4) and multiply by W. Lee's earnings to arrive at an estimate: 34.4 × $5 million = $172 million. Remember, both synergies and a control premium are built into this valuation, which is the likely explanation for why the multiple is so much larger than the Public Comparable.
- Conclusion: The Public Comparable is not particularly helpful in this analysis but gives us comfort that our DCF terminal value is reasonable; the DCF and the Precedent Transactions methods imply a valuation range between $172 million and $182 million.

To determine how target and bidder shareholders fare in an acquisition, we look to the market. A positive combined bidder plus target stock market reaction implies that the market believes that a merger creates value.[10] Of course many things can change after the initial merger announcement: bids may be increased, target management may respond positively or negatively to the initial bid, the form of payment may change (or be announced), etc. Even with these considerations, studying short-term market reactions provides interesting insights into the market's perception of mergers and acquisitions.

21-3b Stockholder Gains (or Losses) in Mergers–Returns to Bidder and Target

Table 21.2 presents the returns earned by shareholders in each of the last three decades. The returns are shown for the bidding firm (i.e., the company making the acquisition) and also for the target firm (i.e., the company being taken over). These are two-day returns, for the day of the announcement and the next day. The returns are expressed net of the normal return expected over those two days, so the announcement reactions are considered abnormal returns (i.e., above and beyond what the firms would have been expected to earn on those two days).[11]

We see that targets earn significantly positive abnormal returns when a merger is announced, reflecting the large premium usually offered for target stock. Over the

[9]We are assuming earnings approximate cash flows.
[10]We are assuming that no word has leaked out in advance of the merger announcement. If information leaks out in advance, the market price may have changed prior to the announcement, and there may not be any market reaction on the day of the official announcement. In such a case, it would not be correct to conclude that there are no valuation effects from the merger.
[11]To be more precise, we use each firm's CAPM beta to determine its expected return, which is equal to the risk-free return plus beta times the market risk premium for a two-day interval. Abnormal return is the difference between actual return and expected return.

Table 21.2

	Abnormal Returns to Targets and Bidders in a Two-Day Window		
	1980–1989	**1990–1999**	**2000–2010**
Bidding Firm	0.30%	−2.43%	−1.65%
Target Firm	12.57%	11.69%	21.92%
Combined	5.1%	3.2%	1.19%

Source: SDC and authors' calculations. © Reuters. Used with permission.

past several decades, targets have experienced abnormal returns averaging about 15% in the two days surrounding the takeover announcement. Not all targets experience substantial gains. Figure 21.7 shows the distribution of returns earned since 1991, and we see that about one-fourth of targets experience a negative return upon merger announcement.

Table 21.2 also shows that bidders, in contrast, lose money on average in some decades, and barely break even in others. This implies that any value gains created by the merger are paid almost entirely (sometimes even more) to the target shareholders. In many cases, therefore, bidders appear to pay too large of an acquisition premium on average, paying up front for any gains the market expects the merger to produce. Why might bidders do this? One reason is that few companies seek to be taken over, so it is necessary to pay a control premium in order to buy out target shareholders. A related explanation is that if a bidding war occurs, with two companies both bidding for the same target, then "in the heat of the moment" bidders have a tendency to offer aggressive prices for the target. This phenomenon is sometimes called the *winner's curse*, referring to the possibility that when multiple bidders are attempting to buy an asset with an uncertain value, the ultimate winner may well pay a price that is greater than the asset's true value. A third explanation, described in the next section, relates to the frequent use by acquirers of their common stock as acquisition currency. To put these results in context, it is important to remember that

Figure 21.7

Distribution of Abnormal Returns for Targets in Two-Day Window around Announcements (1991–2010)

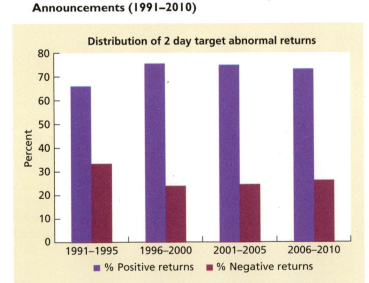

Source: SDC and authors' calculations. © Reuters. Used with permission.

Table 21.2 presents two-day returns, so it is possible that bidder shareholders eventually earn their reward in the long run (though, currently the market does not expect them to do so—if the market expected long-run gains, they would be reflected in the two-day return).

While acquiring firms may experience negative abnormal returns around the time of the merger announcement,[12] this does not mean that the merger does not create any value. To determine whether the merger creates value, we need to consider the combined bidder and target returns. For example, if a $9B firm bidder earns a 0% return when it takes over a $1B target that itself earns a 10% abnormal return, then the overall merger created a 1% abnormal return (= ($9B*0% + $1B*10%) ÷ $10B). Table 21.2 shows that on average, mergers do create value (but most of this value gain flows to target shareholders on average). This modest value creation is consistent with research by Andrade, Mitchell, and Stafford (2001), who show that there is on average a 1% improvement in abnormal operating performance (measured by an increase in return on assets) in the year after an acquisition is completed.

21-3c Method of Payment

Just like any other type of investment, a merger must be financed with capital—such as debt, accumulated profits (that is, cash on hand), or newly issued common stock. These components make up the consideration offered in a transaction and sum to the *transaction value*: the dollar value of all forms of payment offered to the target for control of the company. Cash on hand from retained earnings and/or generated from a debt issuance is used in financing a cash-only deal, where target's shareholders receive only cash for their shares in a public company or where target's owner(s) receives cash for the private enterprise. More rarely, the target receives a new issue of debt in exchange for control in a debt-only transaction.

The bidding firm's stock is the only mode of payment in a stock-swap merger, or **pure stock exchange merger**. The most common stock-swap merger involves the issuance of new shares of bidder common stock in exchange for the target's common stock, but payment may come in the form of either preferred stock or subsidiary tracking shares. The number of shares of the surviving firm's common stock that target shareholders receive is determined by the exchange ratio. For instance, if an acquirer sets an exchange ratio of 0.75 for a target with 100 million shares outstanding, the acquirer will issue 75 million new shares (0.75 × 100 million) in exchange for the target's shares. If the acquirer's current stock price is $20 and the target's stock price is $12, the transaction value of this merger would be $1.5 billion ($20 × 75 million). An investor who owns 100 shares of the target stock ($1,200) would receive acquirer stock worth $1,500 ($20 × 75 shares), a 25% control premium.[13] One advantage of this approach is that if a stock deal is structured properly, a stock exchange is tax-free even if the target shareholders experience a capital gain, while a cash offer is taxable to target shareholders if they earn a capital gain.

Mergers are often financed with a combination of cash and securities in transactions known as **mixed offerings** (see Figure 21.8). For example, in January 2005, SBC Communications offered AT&T shareholders a combination of SBC stock worth $18.41 per share plus $1.30/share in cash. Occasionally, target shareholders are also offered a choice for the medium of exchange. For example, target shareholders could be offered the choice of either $30 cash or 1.25 shares of the surviving company's shares for each share that they hold. This way, the shareholders can

? JOB INTERVIEW QUESTION

When should an acquirer pay for an acquisition with equity? When should an acquirer finance an acquisition with debt?

pure stock exchange merger
A merger in which stock is the only mode of payment.

mixed offerings
A merger financed with a combination of cash and securities.

---

[12]Negative bidder price pressure can be associated with arbitrageurs shorting the bidder's stock and going long the target's stock.

[13]We assume in this example that the bidder stock price does not change from $20 when the merger is announced.

Figure 21.8

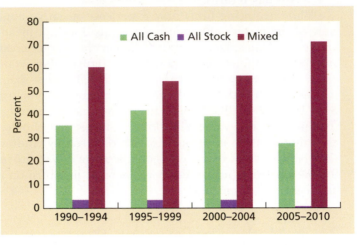

Mergers by Financing Mix

© Cengage Learning 2012

decide whether the exchange ratio is sufficient for them to remain shareholders in the surviving company or whether they should take the money and run with the cash offer.

Table 21.3 indicates that target shareholders fare well in pure stock-for-stock transactions, and even better in all-cash deals. Bidders, on the other hand, nearly break even when cash is involved in the purchase and lose on all stock deals. Note also that a higher percentage of bidders earn positive returns in all cash deals.

Several theories have been offered to explain the differential returns between cash and stock offers. The first relates to the signaling model first described in Chapter 13. In the context of this model, the mode of payment offered by acquiring firms signals inside information to the capital markets. If managers use stock to make an acquisition, it can be interpreted by the market as a signal that the firm's stock is overvalued. Receiving this signal, the capital markets downwardly revise the value of the acquirer's equity. Other theories concerning the differential returns due to financing method include the tax and preemptive bidding hypotheses. The *tax hypothesis* postulates that target shareholders must be paid a capital gains tax premium in cash offers (because they have to turn around and pay tax to the government on any profits earned), which is not required in a stock offer. The *preemptive bidding hypothesis* asserts that acquirers who wish to ward off other potential bidders for a target will offer a substantial initial takeover premium in the form of

Table 21.3

Abnormal Returns to Targets and Bidders in Two-Day Window Conditional on Method of Payment (Tender offers in SDC, 2000–2010)

	All Cash	All Stock
Target two-day returns	26.96%	12.22%
Bidder two-day returns	−0.72%	−2.24%
Combined two-day returns	2.62%	−0.50%
% Deals with positive returns for bidders	45.56%	23.08%
% Deals with positive returns for target	93.27%	81.25%

Source: SDC and authors' calculations. © Reuters. Used with permission.

cash. Finally, the lower returns for bidders in stock deals may reflect the fact that stock deals are typically dilutive to bidder EPS, which may be received negatively by the stock market.

21-3d Returns to Bondholders

Common stock is not the only security affected in corporate control activities; bonds and preferred stock can also be affected. When an acquisition increases the stability of cash flows relative to the target's historic cash flows, thereby reducing default risk, target bonds may increase in value. A 2004 study by Billet, King, and Mauer provides evidence consistent with this possibility. The bondholders' gain is a wealth transfer from the merging firms' shareholders—especially the financially healthier firm's shareholders—since cash flows that they would have received in the weaker firm's loss period are instead diverted to pay the bondholders' claims. The point is that while corporate managers may pursue mergers at least in part to reduce financial risk, the benefit sometimes accrues to fixed claimants (such as existing bondholders), possibly at the expense of shareholders.[14] The study also demonstrates that when a target is acquired by a less creditworthy bidder, target bondholders experience negative returns.[15]

Bidder bondholders can experience similar outcomes. Given that bidding firms are rarely experiencing financial distress, bidding bondholders infrequently benefit from merging with a cash flow rich target; more often, they suffer value loss as the a financially weaker target firm is acquired.

21-3e How Do Target CEOs Make Out?

Not only do stockholders of target firms do well, so do their chief executives. Research done in 2004 by Hartzell, Ofek, and Yermack documents payments received by target CEOs as their firms are sold. These target chief executives receive payments equaling 10 to 15 times their annual salary and bonus when their firms are taken over. About 55% of the payment comes in the form of stock and options, with the rest consisting of golden parachute severance payments and additional bonuses. These payments could be interpreted as a lavish perk to the outgoing executive. Alternatively, these payments may play the role of encouraging CEOs to, and rewarding them for, taking an action that creates the most value for target shareholders.

21-3 Concept Review Questions

6. In an M&A deal, both the target and the bidder typically do their own valuations. Which valuation method do you think target management favors, and which do you think managers of the bidder advocate?

7. Most bidders are much larger than the target firms that they seek to buy. When the bidder is much larger than the target, why might it appear that the bidder's shareholders do not profit much from the deal even if it creates a significant amount of value in total?

---

[14]One subtle consideration is whether the target debt can be refinanced at the bidder cost of capital. For example, if a low-risk acquirer buys a high risk target, can the target's debt be refinanced at the bidder's low cost of debt? While this possibility is often implicitly assumed in models that analyze merger consequences, the most likely outcome is that the target's securities will be refinanced not at the pre-deal financing costs of the bidder, but rather at the combined firm's post-deal costs. This combined cost may in some cases reflect cost-reducing benefits of diversification of the bidder and target but often will lie between the pre-deal costs of the bidder and target.

[15]Another situation in which there are significantly negative returns on existing target bonds occurs when a leveraged buyout occurs, loading substantial new debt on the target firm.

21-4 Merger and Acquisition Transaction Details

There are a number of ways to integrate the assets and resources of an acquired firm into the acquiring company. The following discussion describes various forms of resource integration that may be used to combine the resources of an acquirer and a target.

21-4a Types of Mergers

statutory merger
A target integration in which the acquirer can absorb the target's resources directly with no remaining trace of the target as a separate entity.

subsidiary merger
A merger in which the acquirer maintains the identity of the target as a separate subsidiary or division.

reverse triangle merger
When a subsidiary of the bidder merges with the target firm.

consolidation
A merger in which both the acquirer and target disappear as separate corporations, combining to form an entirely new corporation with new common stock.

tender offer
The structured purchase of a target's shares in which the acquirer announces a public offer to buy a minimum number of shares at a specific price.

hostile takeover
When a bidder makes an unsolicited offer for a target.

A statutory merger occurs when the acquirer absorbs the target's resources directly, with no remaining trace of the target as a separate entity. Many intrastate bank mergers are of this form. Conversely, an acquirer may wish to maintain the identity of the target as either a separate subsidiary or division. A subsidiary merger is often the integration vehicle when there is brand value in the name of the target, such as the January 2005 acquisition of Molson by Adolph Coors to form Molson Coors Brewing. In a reverse triangle merger the acquiring firm creates a subsidiary, and this subsidiary's equity merges with the target firm's stock. The target becomes a wholly owned subsidiary of the bidder, with the target's legal entity remaining intact (eliminating the need to rewrite contracts to reflect a new corporate name).

Under consolidation, both the acquirer and target disappear as separate corporations and combine to form an entirely new corporation with new common stock. This form of integration is common in so-called mergers of equals, where the market values of the acquirer and target are similar. Many of these new corporations adopt a name that is a hybrid of the former names, such as the 2001 consolidation of Chevron and Texaco to become ChevronTexaco. (In 2005, the name was changed to Chevron to convey a more unified presence around the world.) But some managers of newly created companies want a fresh start with a company name. An example of this occurred in 2000, when the Amsterdam Stock Exchange, the Paris Bourse, and the Brussels Stock Exchange merged to form Euronext.

An acquirer can also attain control of a public corporation through a non-negotiated purchase of the corporation's shares in the open market or by obtaining voting control of other stockholders' shares via a proxy contest. Theoretically, an acquirer can gain control simply through open-market purchases of a target firm's shares, though regulation severely restricts this form of creeping acquisition in most developed countries. Generally, an acquirer must explicitly bid for control through a tender offer for shares. A tender offer is a structured purchase of the target's shares in which the acquirer announces a public offer to buy a minimum number of shares at a specific price in a cash offer directly to target stockholders. Interested stockholders may then tender their shares at the offer price. If at least the minimum number of shares is tendered, then the acquirer buys those shares at the offer price. The acquirer has the option to buy the shares tendered at the offer price or of canceling the offer altogether if the minimum number of shares is not tendered. Though fairly rare, a two-step offer occurs when the acquirer offers to buy a certain number of shares at one price and, if the first step is successful, then more shares in a second step at another (typically lower) price. A *short-form merger* occurs when the bidder acquires substantially most (e.g., 90% in a company headquartered in Delaware) of the outstanding shares. In this case, the bidder can do a short-form merger the next day to own 100% of target outstanding shares, as long as the payment in the merger is the same as the payment in the tender offer.

Tender offers can be part of a hostile takeover attempt (an offer not solicited by the target board of directors that bypasses the target board and goes straight to target shareholders) or a friendly tender offer (that occurs after a deal is negotiated with the target board). Unsolicited takeover attempts are not particularly common, especially outside the United States, but many a friendly merger was completed due to the threat of an unsolicited takeover by an undesired bidder. There are of course some mergers that are friendly from the start.

merger of equals
A merger of two firms that are roughly the same size; usually friendly.

going-private transactions
The transformation of a public corporation into a private company through issuance of large amounts of debt used to buy the outstanding shares of the corporation.

management buyout (MBO)
The transformation of a public corporation into a private company by the current managers of the corporation.

employee stock ownership plan (ESOP)
The transformation of a public corporation into a private company by the employees of the corporation itself.

reverse LBO
A formerly public company that has previously gone private through a leveraged buyout and then goes public again.

dual-class recapitalization
Issuance of a new class of common shares with the intent of concentrating control of voting rights in one group of investors.

In the United States, individuals or corporations may own up to 5% of any corporation's stock before they must file a Schedule 13D form with the Securities and Exchange Commission (SEC) identifying themselves as a significant stockholder in the company. Thus, an interested potential acquirer could accumulate a substantial number of shares (known as a *foothold*) without the knowledge of the target's management, but once it crosses that 5% threshold, the takeover attempt must be declared via a 13D filing.

In recent years, the financial press uses the phrase merger of equals to describe some transactions. For example, on May 3, 2010, Continental and United Airlines announced a merger of equals, indicating in a press release that "the all-stock merger of equals brings together two of the world's premier airlines, creating a combined company well positioned to succeed in an increasingly competitive global and domestic aviation industry." Mergers of equals most often involve bidders and targets of roughly similar size and are friendly in terms of board negotiations. Oftentimes, the bidding firm promises to treat the board members, management, and employees of the target firm fairly and perhaps offer concessions in terms of the location of headquarters or company name. On average, mergers of equals result in a smaller premium paid to target shareholders. Cynics argue that the target board and management sell out shareholders by accepting a lower premium in exchange for their own well-being and remuneration. Proponents of mergers of equals argue that a smaller premium allows the bidder to proceed slowly and carefully when integrating the companies, rather than making drastic changes quickly in an effort to justify the larger premiums that usually accompany acquisitions. While there may be elements of truth to both arguments, we note that ultimately there is one surviving company, with one CEO, one CFO, one board, etc., and often this surviving entity is dominated by representatives of the bidding firm.

21-4b LBOs, MBOs, and Recapitalizations

Changes in corporate control also occur when voting power becomes concentrated in the hands of one individual or a small group. Going-private transactions are one way to achieve this concentration of control. Just as they sound, going-private transactions transform public corporations into private companies through issuance of sufficient debt to buy all of the outstanding shares of the corporation. The acquiring party may be a leveraged-buyout (LBO) or private equity firm[16]—such as Kohlberg, Kravis, and Roberts (KKR), which specializes in such deals. Other going private transactions can be driven by the current managers of the corporation (known as a management buyout, or MBO); or even the employees of the corporation itself through an employee stock ownership plan (ESOP). An LBO that sells shares to the public again in a second initial public offering is known as a reverse LBO.

Leveraged buyouts are interesting because of the high premiums often paid and due to the extensive use of debt financing. Of course, increased risk accompanies high debt levels, resulting in high costs of debt and equity (as discussed in Chapter 12, formula 12.2 can be used to lever up the cost of equity to reflect greater financial risk). Typically, high debt levels are maintained for several years in an LBO, then are gradually reduced to more normal, long-term levels. Therefore, when valuing an LBO, the discount rate is typically high in early years but gradually declines. Terminal values are very important in LBO valuation and represent the value at which an LBO investor may cash out by selling its stake in the buyout, perhaps by issuing common stock and taking the firm public again.

A dual-class recapitalization may also concentrate control. Under this form of organizational restructuring, the parties wishing to concentrate control (usually

---

[16]When a private equity firm such as KKR buys a company, it is referred to as a financial buyer. In contrast, when one company buys another company, the acquirer is often called a strategic buyer. The key difference between each buyer's acquisition strategy is that strategic buyers seek opportunities that will synergistically create short and long term value for the acquiring firm while financial buyers often seek to buy a company, operate it for a short period, and then resell it often within five years.

management) buy all the shares of a newly issued Class B stock, which carries super voting rights (100 votes per share, for example). Traditional Class A shareholders generally receive some form of compensation, such as higher dividends, for the dilution of their voting power. Dual-class companies are rare in the United States but are common in other countries (see Nenova 2003). The higher stock price typically assigned to the share class with superior voting rights, often called the *voting premium*, has been used as a measure for the private benefits of control in a publicly traded firm.

A leveraged recapitalization occurs when a company issues substantial debt to repurchase equity. The firm essentially performs a leveraged buyout on itself, except that not all of the outstanding equity is retired. The remaining stockholders, known as the stub equity, own a much more highly levered (and riskier) stake in the firm.

Just how much debt can a company manage, whether it becomes highly levered via an LBO or a leveraged recap? The typical metric considered on the street by finance professionals is based on the Debt/EBITDA ratio. By considering earnings before interest, taxes, depreciation, and amortization, analysts argue that this captures the full cash flow available to the firm to make debt interest payments. Consequently, LBO pricing and valuation is often expressed in terms of EBITDA multiples (e.g., "five times EBITDA"). One word of caution: the Debt/EBITDA ratio does not explicitly capture the capital needs of the firm. This may not be a major concern if the capital expenditure and other working capital needs of the firm do not outstrip cash inflows. If working capital needs are significant, however, overall liquidity and working capital implications should be carefully considered when determining a firm's debt capacity. More generally, we recommend that analysts and managers consider the capital structure issues presented in Chapter 12 when determining debt capacity.

21-4c Takeover Defenses and Divestitures

Takeover Defenses Takeover defenses are defensive measures that many companies rely on to ward off surprise or unwanted takeover attempts. Some of these defenses are written in company charters, and most states have extensive takeover statutes that dictate the offer and defense strategies for companies incorporated in that state. Not only might these defensive tactics prevent an unwanted takeover, they also can provide a shield that a target can use to delay a takeover attempt in a way that strengthens the target's negotiating power. Table 21.4 describes several takeover defenses. Many of these provisions have the ultimate effect of increasing the price the bidder must pay to acquire the target.

Divestitures We have explored in detail how and why a company goes about acquiring assets from another firm. But what about the other side of the transaction, when a company wants to divest (get rid of) one of its plants or business units? A company may decide to divest a unit that it feels is no longer a strategic fit with its core business, because a unit has large capital demands that the parent feels it can not afford, because a multi-segment company (e.g., a conglomerate) is priced at a discount relative to peer firms, or perhaps because the parent is in distress and needs to sell something to raise cash (e.g., Citigroup's June 2009 sale of its 51% stake in Smith-Barney). What options are available to a firm that wants to sell or otherwise separate a division or some fraction of its assets? A divestiture occurs when the assets and/or resources of a subsidiary or division are conveyed to another organization. An example of a divestiture occurred when Guaranty Financial Group, Inc., sold (on December 31, 2008) its wholly owned subsidiary, Guaranty Insurance Services, Inc., to JLT Insurance Agency Holdings, Inc.

An asset sale or sell-off occurs when a company sells a division, plant, or machinery to new owners, usually in exchange for cash. The receipt of cash makes this a taxable event, and the seller must pay tax (at the corporate income tax rate) for any capital gains above the tax basis of the sold assets. In a spin-off, the parent company distributes to its own shareholders a division or subsidiary of the parent. This spun-off company is a new entity, with equity shares that are distinct from the parent equity. Existing shareholders receive a pro rata distribution of shares in the new company.

Table 21.4

Commonly Used Antitakeover Devices

Measure	Antitakeover Effect
Fair-price amendments	Require that a fair price be paid to all shareholders in the event of a takeover, usually defined as the highest price paid to any shareholder
Golden parachutes	Large termination payments and other arrangements made to target executives that are activated after a takeover.
Greenmail	The payment of a premium price for the shares held by a potential hostile acquirer but not paid to all stockholders; prevented in some states' statutes.
Just-say-no defense	Refusal to accept a takeover offer on the grounds that management feels it is not in the long-term interests of shareholders.[17]
Pac-Man defense	The initiation of a takeover attempt for the hostile acquirer itself
Poison pills	Dilution of the value of shares acquired by a hostile bidder through the offer of additional shares to all other existing shareholders at a discounted price
Poison puts	Deterrent to hostile takeovers through put options attached to bonds that allow the holders to sell their bonds back to the company at a prespecified price in the event of a takeover or change in control
Recapitalization	A change in capital structure designed to make the target less attractive. Usually involves a substantial increase in debt.
Classified boards	Only a fraction of directors stand for election in any given year, for example due to different term lengths or staggered start/end dates, making it harder for an outsider to take control by electing a majority of the board.
Standstill agreements	Negotiated contracts that prevent a substantial shareholder from acquiring additional shares for a defined period of time.
Supermajority approvals	Require the approval of large majorities (e.g., 67% or 80%) for a takeover to occur.
White knight defense	The pursuit of a friendly acquirer to take over the company instead of a hostile acquirer.
White squire defense	The sale of a substantial number of shares to an entity that is sympathetic to current management but has no current intention of acquiring the firm.

For example, on February 11, 2009, the FCC granted approval of the separation of Time Warner Inc. and Time Warner Cable in a spin-off. On February 12, 2009, Time Warner Cable received a favorable IRS ruling, meaning that this spin-off, like most, was not taxable to shareholders.

A **split-off** is similar to a spin-off in that the parent company creates a newly independent company from a subsidiary, but ownership of the company is transferred only to certain existing shareholders in exchange for their shares in the parent. *Equity carve-outs* (described more fully in Chapter 16) bring a cash infusion to the parent from the sale of a common stock interest in a subsidiary through a partial public offering to new stockholders. One key feature of an equity carve-out is that the parent company retains some control of the decision process in the subsidiary, versus a spin-off where the parent gives up decision rights. (It is often the case that a carve-out precedes the ultimate spin-off of a unit.)

Split-ups and bust-ups are extreme corporate control events. As it sounds, the **split-up** of a corporation is the split-up and sale of all its subsidiaries so that it ceases to exist (except possibly as a holding company with few if any assets). A **bust-up** is the takeover of a company that is subsequently split up.

split-off
A parent company creates a new, independent company with its own shares, and ownership is transferred to certain shareholders only, in exchange for their shares in the parent.

split-up
The division and sale of all of a company's subsidiaries, so that it ceases to exist.

bust-up
The takeover of a company that is subsequently split up.

---

[17]The courts generally do not engage in Monday morning quarterbacking, that is, second-guessing past business decisions made by a company. The courts presume that managers and boards of directors generally make business decisions that are in the best long-run interests of shareholders, according to a case law concept known as the *business judgment rule*. Thus, at times, a board can just say no and reject what appears to an attractive takeover offer, under the logic that the board knows what is best for the shareholders in the long run, even if an offer is for a large premium, or the stock market reacts negatively to the rejection of an attractive offer. See Section 21.5 for additional discussion.

To decide among these various divestiture options, management will usually consider the after-tax proceeds received by the parent company from each option, how many bidders might exist to purchase a given unit, and whether the firm's existing shareholders are likely to hold onto, or immediately churn (i.e., sell), the divested unit if they were to receive it in a spin-off. The ultimate decision should be based on the desire to maximize long-run shareholder value, combined with the company's desire to focus its ongoing operations on business units for which it has a comparative advantage running.

21-4 Concept Review Questions

8. List several different types of merger structures. Why might different types be used in different settings?

9. How does a tender offer differ from a proxy fight? Why might these two corporate control actions be considered different ways to achieve the same objective?

10. What are the two most important methods of paying for corporate acquisitions?

11. Who wins and who loses in corporate takeovers? Why do acquiring-firm shareholders generally lose in stock-swap mergers but either benefit or at least break even in acquisitions paid for with cash?

21-5 Accounting Treatment of Mergers and Acquisitions

? JOB INTERVIEW QUESTION

How is goodwill created through a merger? Under what conditions may it be subsequently adjusted?

goodwill
An intangible asset created if the restated values of the target in a merger lead to a situation in which its assets are less than its liabilities and equity.

The newest accounting requirements for acquisitions were published by the Financial Accounting Standards Board as SFAS No. 141(R), *Business Combinations.* They became effective for fiscal years that start after December 15, 2008. Under this new standard, the acquiring firm recognizes the target's assets and liabilities in its consolidated financial statements at their fair values at the time of the acquisition.[18] (Should the target continue to prepare its own separate financial statements, the acquisition does not affect the carrying values of the target's assets and liabilities.)

The acquiring firm also determines whether there is a difference between the fair value of the target's net assets and the amount that it paid for the target. If the acquiring firm paid more than the fair value of the target's net assets (for example, because of expected synergies from combining the acquiring firm's and target's assets), it recognizes the difference as an intangible asset on its balance sheet called goodwill. If the acquiring firm paid less than the fair value of the target's net assets (a bargain purchase), it recognizes the difference as a gain in earnings at the time of the acquisition.

After the acquisition closes, the value of goodwill must be evaluated to determine if it has been impaired due to a decline in fair value relative to carrying value. In accordance with SFAS No. 142, *Goodwill and Other Intangible Assets,* if the value of goodwill is impaired, then the amount of the impairment is written down from the goodwill account on the balance sheet and charged off against earnings. Otherwise, the goodwill balance remains unchanged on the balance sheet indefinitely. Many large write-downs were taken soon after SFAS No. 142 went into effect on December 15, 2001. JDS Uniphase, AOL Time Warner, and Nortel Networks all took multibillion-dollar write-downs in 2002 for acquisitions completed in prior years, and the newly renamed MCI Inc. took a $75 billion write-down in early 2004 for acquisitions previously completed by the company (when it was named WorldCom). The following Example details the treatment of accounting for acquisitions.

---

[18]Fair value, according to SFAS No. 157, *Fair Value Measurements,* is the price that would be received to sell an asset or paid to transfer a liability in an orderly transaction between market participants at the measurement date.

EXAMPLE

Assume that a target firm has 5 million shares outstanding priced at $10 per share. The acquiring firm offers a 20% takeover premium ($12 per share), for a transaction value of $60 million. The acquiring firm wants the R&D capabilities of the target firm so that it can exploit synergies with its own assets and is willing to pay a premium to obtain those capabilities. The fair value of the target's current assets is $10 million and the fair value of its long-term assets is $60 million. Deducting the $5 million in current liabilities and $25 million in long-term liabilities, the target firm has a net asset value of $40 million. Thus, the acquiring firm is willing to pay $20 million ($60 million less $40 million) for intangible assets that represent the premium paid to acquire the R&D capabilities.

Current assets	$10,000,000
Long-term assets	60,000,000
Less: Liabilities	30,000,000
Net asset value	$40,000,000
Purchase price paid	60,000,000
Less: Net asset value	40,000,000
Goodwill	$20,000,000

	Pre-acquisition			Post-acquisition
($ in millions)	Acquirer's financial statements	Target's financial statements	Fair values of target assets and liabilities	Consolidated financial statements
Assets				
Current	100	10	10	50*
Long-term	350	50	60	410
Goodwill	0	0		20
Total assets	450	60		480**
Liabilities				
Current	50	5	5	55
Long-term	250	25	25	275
Total liabilities	300	30		330
Owners' equity	150	30		150***
Total liabilities and owners' equity	450	60		480

*If the acquirer used $60m cash to make the acquisition, consolidated current assets = 100 + 10 − 60 = 50.

**If the acquirer used $60m cash to make the acquisition, consolidated total assets = 450 + 70 + 20 − 60 = 480 (acquirer's assets + fair value of target's assets + goodwill − payment for target's shares).

***In consolidated statements, only the shares held by outside investors are shown.

Assume that the target firm is treated as a separate reporting unit after the acquisition. Going forward, the firm must evaluate its goodwill to determine whether its value has been impaired. As long as the firm can demonstrate that the goodwill's fair value has not fallen below its carrying value of $20 million on the balance sheet, then it will remain unaffected on the balance sheet. However, if the value is impaired (i.e., fair value has decreased) then the value loss must be reported, deducted from the balance sheet, and taken as a write-off against current period earnings. For example, assume that two years later the R&D capabilities of the subsidiary do not turn out to be as valuable as expected. The fair value of the reporting unit is estimated at $55 million and the fair value of the net assets is estimated at $50 million, resulting in an implied fair value of the goodwill of $5 million. Because the carrying value of the goodwill is $20 million, this represents a $15 million impairment. This $15 million will be deducted from the balance sheet and taken as an intangible asset write-down on the income statement, reducing earnings by $15 million in the year that the impairment is recognized.

An alternative scenario might arise in which the acquiring firm obtains control of the target but does not acquire all of the target's outstanding shares. For example, if the acquiring firm in the above example was able to acquire only 90% of the target's out-standing shares, there would be a 10% non-controlling interest in the target (this 10% was formerly known as a minority interest). The acquiring firm would still recognize

100% of the fair value of the target's assets and liabilities in its consolidated financial statements. In addition, it would recognize the fair value of the non-controlling interest as an equity item and would calculate goodwill as the difference between the amount it paid for the target plus the fair value of the non-controlling interest and the fair value of the target's net assets.

21-5 Concept Review Questions

12. What is *goodwill* in the context of merger accounting? What must an acquiring company do if the value of an acquired company is revealed to have declined after a merger?

13. Describe target companies you think would yield substantial goodwill once acquired.

21-6 Regulation of Mergers and Acquisitions

21-6a Antitrust Regulation

Mergers, especially horizontal mergers, present the possibility of creating corporate giants that have the potential to reduce competition. For this reason, antitrust enforcement seeks to prevent mergers that are deemed anticompetitive. Antitrust regulation began with the Sherman Antitrust Act of 1890, was reinforced by the Clayton Act of 1914, and was further strengthened by the Celler–Kefauver Act of 1950. The last major federal antitrust legislation was enacted in the Hart-Scott-Rodino Antitrust Improvements Act of 1976, but the interpretation and enforcement of antitrust laws changes through time, in part with the political orientation of the country at a point in time.

The following sections outline the major aspects of various U.S. antitrust laws, starting with the guidelines established by regulatory agencies for determining the anticompetitive potential of a merger. As discussed below, international regulation of M&A activity has increased in importance in recent decades.

Determination of Anticompetitiveness The Department of Justice established the first set of U.S. merger guidelines for determining anticompetitiveness in 1968 and modified them in 1982, 1984, and 1992. The following guidelines are those currently used by the DOJ and FTC.

The 1982 guidelines use the Herfindahl Index (HI) (also known as the Herfindahl-Hirschman Index) to determine market concentration. The HI is calculated as the sum of the squares of each company's percentage of sales within a market (i.e., industry). For example, if there are three firms in an industry, and they account for 50%, 30%, and 20% of total sales, the HI Index would be 3,800 ($50^2 + 30^2 + 20^2$). If the smaller two companies merged, the HI Index would increase to 5,000.

The HI is used by the DOJ to establish a range of concentration levels within a market or industry:

HI > 2,500	Highly concentrated
HI = 1,500 to 2,500	Moderately concentrated
HI < 1,500	Not concentrated

Mergers resulting in a highly concentrated HI measure are the most likely to be challenged. Consider the example in Table 21.5. The premerger HI of this industry is 1,750 (moderately concentrated). A merger between Company 7 and Company 8 would reduce the number of competitors in the industry, but the marginal impact of a merger between the two smallest players in the industry would increase the HI to only 1,800 and would likely not face a challenge. However, a merger between the two largest firms in the industry would result in an HI of 2,980—moving this industry from moderately to highly concentrated and likely prompting a challenge by the DOJ or FTC.

Table 21.5 **Determination of Anticompetitiveness: Using the Herfindahl Index (HI)**

Premerger Concentration			Postmerger Concentration					
Firm	Market Share (%)	Market Share Squared	Firm	Market Share (%)	Market Share Squared	Firm	Market Share (%)	Market Share Squared
1	30	900	1	30	900	1 + 2	50	2,500
2	20	400	2	20	400	3	10	100
3	10	100	3	10	100	4	10	100
4	10	100	4	10	100	5	10	100
5	10	100	5	10	100	6	10	100
6	10	100	6	10	100	7	5	25
7	5	25	7 + 8	10	100	8	5	25
8	5	25						
Sum (=HI)		1,750			1,800			2,950
Concentration		Moderate			Moderate			High

EXAMPLE

The failed 1997 merger attempt of Staples and Office Depot exemplifies the role of regulatory agencies in preventing what are deemed to be anticompetitive combinations. On September 4, 1996, Staples and Office Depot announced their intent to merge in a $3.4 billion deal. At the time, Office Depot and Staples were the largest and second-largest office supply superstores, respectively. Of the $14.0 billion in sales in this market, Office Depot had a market share of $6.6 billion, followed by Staples with $4.1 billion, and the only other major competitor was OfficeMax, with sales of $3.3 billion.

As permitted under the Hart–Scott–Rodino Act, the Federal Trade Commission (FTC) reviewed the proposed merger for anticompetitive effects and requested more information from the companies at the end of the initial review period. At the end of the second review, the FTC concluded that the proposed merger would have an anticompetitive impact if allowed to be consummated, so it rejected the merger proposal. One of the key points cited by the FTC in its rejection was the market power (the 5% rule)[19] that the merged firm would be able to wield in those markets where no stores other than Staples or Office Depot existed. In order to remedy this obstacle, Staples and Office Depot proposed to sell 63 stores to OfficeMax in the geographic markets where both Staples and Office Depot were located. The FTC again rejected the merger and threatened to sue the companies in federal court if they attempted to pursue their merger. The FTC further threatened that, even if it could not prevent the merger under the Hart–Scott–Rodino Act through its federal lawsuit, it would continue to pursue the merged firm for antitrust violations.

The managers of both companies continued to fight for their combination, despite the FTC's threats. When presenting their argument to the federal judge assigned to the case, lawyers for the companies expressed the companies' willingness to sell off stores in order to satisfy the FTC and enhance competition; they also contended that the FTC had improperly defined their industry when determining the Herfindahl Index. The FTC had limited their industry classification to office supply superstores, so there were only three main competitors and an HI of 3,634 (already highly concentrated). The HI would increase to 6,394 after the merger. Lawyers for the companies, however, stated that the appropriate industry classification should be discount retailers and should include such stores Walmart and Kmart in addition to office supply stores. The judge in the case disagreed with the companies' lawyers and sided with the FTC in barring the merger from taking place. The managers of Staples and Office Depot announced their intentions to abandon their merger plans shortly thereafter.

Although merger guidelines have evolved over time and in recent years have been less hostile toward horizontal combinations, the DOJ and FTC remain active enforcers of antitrust laws. In August 2010, the DOJ and FTC issued revised Horizontal Merger Guidelines, the first major overhaul of merger guidelines since 1992. One change is to focus more heavily on a merger's competitive effects, for example the impact with respect to consumer prices, and the potential for future price discrimination.

Other Antitrust Considerations Managers contemplating a merger now face antitrust scrutiny from regulators beyond just U.S. federal regulators. Globalization and proactive state regulators play an important role in merger approval. Individual states have become

---

[19]The 5% rule is an alternative to the HI anticompetitiveness rule presented in Table 24.5. This alternative rule is based on an elasticity measure that gauges whether a merged firm will have the market power to control prices in its market. To implement the 5% rule, the DOJ determines whether a 5% increase in price would results in a decline of more than 5% in market demand. If it would, then that market is deemed elastic and therefore unlikely to be adversely affected by a merger (and also less likely to be strictly governed by the HI measure).

more active participants in the oversight of anticompetitive business practices since the 1990s. For example, attorneys general from 14 states joined the antitrust lawsuit first lodged against Microsoft by the Justice Department in 1994. Even after the federal government abandoned its case against Microsoft in 2001 in an effort to settle the case out of court, many of the states refused to abandon their status as plaintiffs against Microsoft.

21-6b The Williams Act

During the conglomerate merger wave of the 1960s, hostile tender offers became an increasingly frequent and controversial means to facilitate takeovers. The controversy over these tender offers revolved around target shareholders' inability to evaluate the terms of the tender offers in the often short periods of time for which they were open and around the abuses of higher takeover premiums being offered to select shareholders. In response to this controversy, the Williams Act passed in 1967 and was enacted in 1968 as an amendment to the Securities and Exchange Commission Act of 1934. Section 13 of the Williams Act introduced ownership disclosure requirements, and Section 14 created rules for the tender offer process.

Ownership Disclosure Requirements Section 13D of the Williams Act requires public disclosure of stock ownership levels beyond 5%. This section of the act mandates that any individual, group of individuals acting in concert, or firm must file a Schedule 13D form within 10 calendar days of acquiring a 5% or greater stake in a publicly traded company. This disclosure serves as a warning to the managers and stockholders of a corporation that a potential acquirer might be in the wings and provides background information on that potential acquirer. Stockholders or managers of the corporation may sue for damages if any material misrepresentation (such as initiating a later takeover attempt when the stated purpose of ownership was for investment purposes) is made on the form.

Tender Offer Regulation Prior to the passage of the Williams Act, tender offers were largely unregulated, open calls to the shareholders of public companies to tender (sell) their shares at offered prices. Section 14 made the tender offer market a much more restrictive and structured process. Any party initiating a tender offer must file a Schedule TO form (a tender offer statement). Boards of directors of tender offer targets are then required to file a Schedule 14D-9 form, which contains their recommendation to shareholders on whether to accept or reject, offer no recommendation, or state that they do not have enough information to make a recommendation. Section 14 also provides structural rules and restrictions on the tender offer process. These rules include a minimum tender offer period of 20 business days, the right of target shareholders to withdraw shares already tendered at any time during the tender offer period, and the requirement that the acquirer accept all shares tendered during this period (if the offer is oversubscribed, tendered shares are purchased on a pro rated basis) and that all tendered shares receive the same price.

21-6c International Regulation of Mergers and Acquisitions

International regulatory authorities, especially in Europe, have become more proactive when dealing with global, large-scale mergers. The European Commission (EC) first signaled its more stringent antitrust regulatory authority in 1999 when it vetoed the proposed merger of U.S. communications giants WorldCom and Sprint. The EC expressed concerns about the pricing power that the combined firm could have if the second- and third-largest U.S. communications firms (behind then industry leader AT&T) merged to become the first- or second-largest communications firm in many European markets. The managers of both WorldCom and Sprint abandoned their effort to merge after the EC's decision. EC competition commissioner Mario Monti created an international stir in 2001 when he denied the petition to merge filed by General Electric and Honeywell, although the merger had already been approved by U.S. antitrust authorities. Monti's stern defense of his position and denial of the petition on appeal sent a clear message that firms with international operations that are considering a merger must take into account antitrust authorities outside the United States, even if the merger is between U.S. firms. Monti caused an even bigger stir when in early 2004 his commission sued Microsoft in an attempt to force the company to uncouple application packages from its operating system (Windows). The commission maintained that this tie gave Microsoft monopoly power. The EC won this court case in 2005, and the top European Union court upheld this ruling in September 2007. Five months later, European regulators imposed a record €899 million ($1.4 billion) fine on Microsoft for failure to comply with demands to end its alleged anticompetitive practices. Adding insult to injury, these regulators opened a new antitrust case against Microsoft in early 2009, seeking to force the company to open up its Explorer Internet software to competing firms.

More recently, the EC made headlines by signaling initial objection to an acquisition of Sun Microsystems by Oracle, suggesting that Oracle's ownership of a key Sun asset, MySQL, would be a detriment to competition. After five months of due diligence, and well after the FTC approved the transaction, the EC gave their blessing. An important implication of this process is the importance and influence of the European Commission, as well as other international securities and trade regulators, in affecting the outcome of proposed M&A transactions.

21-6d Other Legal Issues Concerning Corporate Control

Federal securities laws also regulate the actions of managers in corporate control events. The high-profile insider-trading scandals of the 1980s generated a keen interest in these laws, while the 2001 Enron and WorldCom scandals prompted Congress to pass the Sarbanes–Oxley Act of 2002. This act primarily targeted accounting practices, but it also mandated significant changes in how (and how much) information must be reported by companies to investors. Individual states have also become more interested in promoting corporate control legislation after witnessing business practices that were perceived as detrimental to the welfare of the electorate. In recent years, many states have developed antitakeover and antitrust laws designed to regulate takeovers of corporations located in their states. We describe the major elements of these other federal and state corporate control laws next.

Laws Affecting Corporate Insiders Federal securities laws govern the actions of corporate managers and corporate insiders (and generally anyone in possession of material nonpublic information) during corporate control events. These laws generally attempt to prevent informed trading on nonpublic information (i.e., inside information), such as an upcoming takeover attempt known only to the insiders of the acquiring firm. The Securities and Exchange Commission (SEC) strictly enforces the following rules. Rule 10-b-5 outlaws material misrepresentation of information used in the sale or purchase of a security. Trading on inside information about a pending merger is considered a material misrepresentation because material information (news of the merger) is being withheld. Also, SEC Rule 14-e-3 specifically forbids trading on inside information in tender offers. The Insider Trading Sanctions Act of 1984 strengthened both SEC rules with triple damage awards. Managers are also restricted from issuing misleading information regarding merger negotiations and may be sued if they deny the existence of merger negotiations that are actually taking place. Finally, Section 16 of the Securities and Exchange Act establishes a monitoring facility for the trading of corporate insiders.

State Laws Individual states have increasingly regulated corporate control activities over the years. Some states have adopted various provisions against takeovers and bust-ups and have formed antitrust agencies that restrict corporate control activities in their states beyond the level of federal regulations.

Antitakeover and anti–bust-up provisions include voting initiatives—such as supermajority voting, which requires that large majorities (usually 67%) approve a takeover—and control share provisions that require the approval of target shareholders before a potential acquirer may even buy a substantial number of shares in the target firm. Fair-price provisions also restrict tender offers by ensuring that all target shareholders receive the same price in each step of a two-step transaction.

fair-price provisions
Rules that ensure that all target shareholders receive the same offer price in any tender offers initiated by the same acquirer, limiting the ability of acquirers to buy minority shares cheaply with a two-tiered offer.

21-6 Concept Review Questions

14. Which industries do you anticipate will experience industry shocks that will spur merger activity in the near future?

15. How does the dynamic interpretation of antitrust laws affect managers' acquisition strategies? What impact does the involvement of individual states have on the acquisition decision?

16. Do you believe that increasing global competition will further heighten merger activity?

17. What is the Herfindahl Index, and what does it measure?

18. What is the purpose of classifying mergers by degree of business concentration? Why do you think these classifications have changed over time?

21-7 Corporate Governance

corporate governance
The processes and rules that determined how a company is governed.

board of directors
Representatives elected by shareholders and charged with the responsibility of overseeing management.

Corporate governance refers to how companies are governed, that is, the processes and rules that affect who ultimately makes the decisions in a company. In Chapter 1, we discussed how stockholders are the ultimate owners of any corporation, and therefore in principle have the right to make company decisions. However, any one stockholder typically owns only a small portion of any particular public company, and the ownership of any particular firm is diffuse (that is, spread across many different stockholders). Therefore, stockholders rarely have the time or insight to oversee a company and all its operations, so they elect representatives whose job is to oversee the decisions made at the firm. These representatives are known as the board of directors of the firm. This section briefly reviews corporate governance, and in particular, the duties of the board in the context of merger and acquisition transactions.

Other than in extreme circumstances, such as when a company files Chapter 11 or is a bidder or target in an acquisition, the board members are not involved in the daily activities of the firm. Instead, the firm hires professional managers and employees to perform day-to-day operations. Board members typically have four to eight meetings per year, and at these meetings upper management updates the board on key issues facing the firm, usually making recommendations of the course of action they believe the firm should follow. Ideally, the board is fully engaged and does not just rubber stamp the recommendations of upper management. However, board members are often identified and approved by the company's CEO and upper management team, which raises the possibility that the board is captured by management in the sense that the board may not fully scrutinize the company's recommendations and decisions. The number of captured boards has declined since the 2002 passage of the Sarbanes-Oxley Act because public companies are now required to have a nominating committee comprised entirely of independent directors. Corporate governance involves the study of these interrelations between the board, management, and in general the oversight of the company.

One of the primary functions of the board is to *monitor* upper management and the decisions of the firm. Another is to offer *advice*. Therefore, a board is ideally made up of experienced business veterans, bankers, and experts in the operations of the firm. A portion of the board should ideally be independent and not in any way personally tied to the CEO or upper management, to ensure that objective oversight and advice are provided.

Governance varies widely across countries. In many European countries, there are two boards of directors, a management board and a supervisory board, with the latter being selected in large part by employees and labor unions. Not surprisingly, governance in Europe is often employee-friendly. In many Asian countries, there is a pyramid structure to corporate ownership, in which company A owns a substantial portion of company B which in turn owns a substantial portion of company C, and so on. The actual decision-making process therefore involves numerous firms and is interlocked with the decisions of other companies. In Japan, such a network of companies is often organized around a main bank and is called a keiretsu. There are many other interesting aspects to corporate governance. However, because this chapter is about mergers and acquisitions, we focus the rest of this section on responsibilities of the board and governance in the context of M&A.

21-7a Duties of the Board in the Context of M&A

The board of directors' primary obligation is to shareholders, in particular to maximize long run shareholder value. When a bidder desires to acquire another firm, the bidder can make an offer directly to shareholders in the form of a tender offer. However, it is usually in the bidder's best interest to approach the target board or CEO in a friendly manner and negotiate the terms and conditions of the offer. Ultimately, the target shareholders must approve the sale of the company but the target's board plays a crucial role in interacting with the bidder and representing the shareholders' best interests.

Often, when a company is the target of a takeover bid, the outside bidder offers to buy the target's stock at a premium over current stock price. Should the board immediately agree to the first offer above current share price? Does the target board legally have to agree to a bidder's offer, even when it is extremely generous? The board has fiduciary duties (i.e., legal obligations) to shareholders in this context. The *duty of loyalty* requires the board to make decisions that are in the best interests of the company and its stockholders, not in their own personal interests. The *duty of care* requires the board to fully inform themselves, and follow a reasonable decision-process, when making business decisions. As discussed in footnote 17, the *business judgment rule* usually offers protection for the board in terms of defending their decisions, as long as there is no evidence of fraud, negligence, or illegality, and the board performs these basic duties.

If there is chance of a conflict of interest, in which the personal interest of board members might conflict with the best interests of the company or shareholders, a special committee is formed to handle merger negotiations. This special committee includes independent board members who are at arm's length and can make objective decisions about the proposed merger (because the personal jobs of inside board members, who also work at the firm, may be affected by the merger outcome).

When a company that has no plans to sell itself receives an outside bid, the board should carefully consider the bid. Is the premium offered large enough that it appears to maximize the wealth of shareholders? For example, is it likely that the target stock price will at any time in the foreseeable future exceed the offer price in a present value sense? If not, then it may be sensible for the target to accept the bid at this time, or attempt to negotiate an even higher bid. However, as long as the board satisfies the duties laid out above, it is not under obligation to recommend accepting an outside bid. One important exception occurs when the target is deemed to be in play and the sale of the firm is inevitable. In this case, *Revlon duties* apply, and the target board's obligation is to secure the highest offer price available, and takeover defenses cannot be used to thwart such an offer.[20] Note that the valuation of an offer price can still be subjective. For example, if one bidder offers $50 in cash and another bidder offers high-risk securities that it argues are worth $51 (but the target does not feel are worth $51), the lower cash bid is at times accepted by the board.

There are other interesting aspects of acquisition negotiations. Who will be the CEO of the new, combined firm? The bidder CEO, the target CEO, or someone entirely different? Often the bidder CEO becomes the new CEO, though it is not unusual for there to be a planned transition to another CEO within a couple years, and it is not uncommon for this new CEO to be the target's current CEO. Likewise, the new board of directors of the combined firm often consists of majority representation of the bidder board, along with target representation. This is one reason that boards often increase in size following mergers. The determination of the chairman of the new board often follows a transition like that just described for CEOs.

---

[20]*Revlon* refers to a famous takeover contest involving Revlon Corp. In that case, two firms were competing to acquire Revlon, and courts ultimately ruled that Revlon's board was obligated to sell the company to the highest bidder.

21-7 Concept Review Question

19. What does the term *corporate governance* mean? Can you think of any examples of deficient corporate governance during the technology bubble and the financial crisis?

Summary

- Mergers and acquisitions tend to occur in waves. Merger waves may occur due to technological or regulatory changes, fluctuations in the cost and availability of funding, or widespread misvaluations in the market. Cross-border M&A activity has been increasing over time.

- The justifications for M&A activity given by managers include driving growth, capturing synergies, improving the bidder's market position or enhancing its relative valuation, diversifying the firm's operations, and increasing earnings per share. It is important to keep in mind that whatever the motivation for a merger might be, it should only be conducted if it leads to higher value for shareholders.

- Mergers tend to create value for target shareholders but much less frequently create value for bidder shareholders.

- The most common methods used by a bidder to value a potential target include discounted cash flow valuation, the use of valuation multiples for comparable firms, or precedent transactions multiples.

- Target companies that want to remain independent have a wide range of defensive tactics that they can use to discourage bidders.

- Antitrust regulations sometimes become a barrier to the consummation of a deal if regulators believe that deal would adversely affect competition in a particular market.

Key Terms

acquisition, 636
asset sale, 658
board of directors, 666
bust-up, 659
conglomerate merger, 637
consolidation, 656
corporate control, 636
corporate governance, 666
divestiture, 658
dual-class recapitalization, 657
economies of scale, 644
economies of scope, 644
employee stock ownership plan (ESOP), 657
enterprise value, 649
fair-price provisions, 665

going-private transactions, 657
goodwill, 660
horizontal merger, 637
hostile takeover, 656
hubris hypothesis of corporate takeovers, 646
leveraged recapitalization, 658
management buyout (MBO), 657
merger, 637
merger of equals, 657
mixed offerings, 653
pure stock exchange merger, 653
resource complementarities, 644
reverse LBO, 657
reverse triangle merger, 656
spin-off, 658

split-off, 659
split-up, 659
statutory merger, 656
subsidiary merger, 656
synergy, 642
takeover, 636
takeover defenses, 658
tender offer, 656
vertical merger, 637

Questions

Q21-1. What is meant by a change in corporate control? List and describe the various ways in which a change of corporate control may occur.

Q21-2. What is a tender offer, and how can it be used as a mechanism to orchestrate a merger?

Q21-3. Distinguish between the different levels of business concentration created by mergers. Explain how the changing business environment has caused an evolution in the classification of concentration from the original FTC classification to the abbreviated FTC classification and now to the measures of overlap and focus.

Q21-4. Elaborate on the significance of the mode of payment for the stockholders of the target firm and their continued interest in the surviving firm. Specifically, which form of payment retains the stockholders of the target firm as stockholders in the surviving firm? Which payment form receives preferential tax treatment?

Q21-5. What is the signaling theory of mergers? What is the relationship between signaling and the mode of payment used in acquisitions? Is there a relationship between the mode of payment used in acquisitions and the level of insider shareholdings of acquiring firms?

Q21-6. Empirically, what are the wealth effects of corporate control activities? Who wins and who loses in corporate control contests? What explanations or theories are offered for the differences in returns of acquiring firms' common stocks? Why are higher takeover premiums paid in cash transactions than in stock transactions? How do other security holders fare in takeovers?

Q21-7. Describe several different motives for mergers. Are each of these motives likely to increase bidder value?

Q21-8. Define the types of synergy that may result from mergers. What are the sources of these synergies?

Q21-9. Explain how agency problems may lead to non-value-maximizing motives for mergers. Discuss the various academic theories offered as the rationale for motives induced by the agency problem.

Q21-10. Why does the Precedent Transactions valuation method typically yield higher valuations?

Q21-11. Would a large technology company and a large conglomerate (that operates in many industries) be good comparable firms for a multiples-based valuation? Why or why not?

Q21-12. Describe the relationship between conglomerate mergers and portfolio theory. What is the desired result of merging two unrelated businesses? Has the empirical evidence proven corporate diversification to be successful?

Q21-13. List the federal laws regulating antitrust and anticompetitive mergers. What are the actions governed by each law? How do the regulatory agencies determine anticompetitiveness?

Q21-14. What is the purpose of the Williams Act? What are the specific provisions of the act?

Q21-15. What are the restrictions faced by corporate insiders during corporate control events?

Q21-16. How have individual states become more active monitors of takeover activity?

Q21-17. To whom is the board of directors accountable, and how should this responsibility affect how the board of directors treats an acquisition bid?

Problems

Overview of Corporate Control Activities

P21-1 A firm has four divisions—food, cookware, retail, and credit services—that generate revenues of $1.5 million, $3.8 million, $5.7 million, and $3.1 million, respectively. Compute the Herfindahl Index (HI) for the firm. The firm is considering the purchase of a rival retailer, which would increase the retail division's revenues by another $3.2 million. The firm is also considering selling its credit services division. Assuming these two actions occur, what will the HI become? What is the HI if the sale of the credit division does not occur but the rival is acquired?

P21-2. HHG Consultants has been asked to analyze Carol & Carroll Co. (C&C), which has one retail division. C&C is concerned that it is not focused on its core mission of sales despite only having one division. Each store is divided into departments: casual clothing (CC), formal clothing (FC), outerwear (OW), shoes (S), and specialty items (SI). C&C's initial impression is that all of the departments contribute equally to sales. However, examination of each department's actual sales reveals that the breakdown is very different: $5.2 billion (CC), $2.7 billion (FC), $3.75 billion (OW), $4.5 billion (S), and $1.7 billion (SI). Compute a Herfindahl Index based on the departments having equal sales and based on the actual sales. Your conclusion concerning the firm's becoming unfocused will be based on the actual HI being lower than the equivalent sales HI scenario. What does your analysis find with regard to the focus of C&C's retailing division?

P21-3. Firm X has three divisions that generate revenues of $1.3 billion, $2.5 billion, and $5.2 billion. Firm Y is a competitor with three associated divisions that generate $2 billion each. Using a Herfindahl Index to measure focus, determine if both Firm X and Firm Y shareholders would see a merger as an action that would increase or rather decrease focus.

P21-4. Shareholders of the firm Up-4-Grabs (U4G) have been offered $36.00 per share in cash for each of their U4G shares currently selling for $29.53. What is the control premium being offered in this cash deal? U4G is also considering a stock-swap offer from another firm, BuyNow, Inc. (BYN). BYN will issue one share for every two shares of U4G. At what price will BYN shares be equivalent to the control premium available in the cash offer? When news leaks out about the merger, BYN shares increase to $77.00 and U4G shares increase to $35.24. What control premium does BYN offer now?

P21-5. HBABB Corp. has purchased all of the 10 million shares of BOBCO stock for $43.75 a share. BOBCO's net asset value is $350 million. How much goodwill does HBABB need to consider on its balance sheet? Suppose part of the deal requires HBABB to pay $30 million of BOBCO's debt. Refigure the net asset value (i.e., reduce the debt by $30 million) and then recalculate the goodwill. One of your accountants tells you that the net asset value should not be changed and that the $30 million used for BOBCO's debt should be added to the purchase price. Refigure the goodwill calculation and determine if there really is a difference. If there is a difference, which calculation is correct?

P21-6. Mega Service Corporation (MSC) is offering to exchange 2.5 shares of its own stock for each share of target firm Norman Corporation stock as consideration for a proposed merger. There are 10 million Norman Corp shares outstanding, and its stock price was $60 before the merger offer. MSC's pre-offer stock price was $30. What is the control premium percentage offered? Now suppose that, when the merger is consummated eight months later, MSC's stock price drops to $25. At that point, what is the control premium percentage and total transaction value?

P21-7. Bulldog Industries is offering target Blazerco, as consideration for merger, 1.5 shares of their stock for each share of Blazerco. There are 1 million shares of Blazerco outstanding, and its stock price was $50 before the merger offer. Bulldog's pre-offer stock price was $40. What is the control premium percentage offered? Now suppose that, when the merger is consummated six months later, Bulldog's stock price drops to $30. At that point, what is the control premium percentage and total transaction value?

P21-8. You are the director of capital acquisitions for Crimson Software Company. One of the projects you are considering is the acquisition of Geekware, a private software company that produces software for finance professors. Dave Vanzandt, the owner of Geekware, is amenable to the idea of selling his enterprise to Crimson, but he has certain conditions that must be met before selling. The primary condition set forth is a nonnegotiable, all-cash purchase price of $20 million. Your project analysis team estimates that the purchase of Geekware will generate the following marginal cash flow:

Year	Cash Flow
1	$1,000,000
2	3,000,000
3	5,000,000
4	7,500,000
5	7,500,000

Of the $20 million in cash needed for the purchase, $5 million is available from retained earnings with a required return of 12%, and the remaining $15 million will come from a new debt issue yielding 8%. Crimson's tax rate is 40%. Should you recommend acquiring Geekware to your CEO?

P21-9. You are the director of capital acquisitions for Morningside Hotel Company. One of the projects you are deliberating is the acquisition of Monroe Hospitality, a company that owns and operates a chain of bed-and-breakfast inns. Susan Sharp, Monroe's owner, is willing to sell her company to Morningside only if she is offered an all-cash purchase price of $5 million. Your project analysis team estimates that the purchase of Monroe Hospitality will generate the following after-tax marginal cash flow:

Year	Cash Flow
1	$1,000,000
2	1,500,000
3	2,000,000
4	2,500,000
5	3,000,000

If you decide to go ahead with this acquisition, it will be funded with Morningside's standard mix of debt and equity at the firm's weighted average (after-tax) cost of capital of 9%. Morningside's tax rate is 30%. Should you recommend acquiring Monroe Hospitality to your CEO?

P21-10. Firm A plans to acquire Firm B. The acquisition would result in incremental cash flows for Firm A of $10 million in each of the first five years. Firm A expects to divest Firm B at the end of the fifth year for $100 million. The beta for Firm A is 1.1, which is expected to remain unchanged after the acquisition. The risk-free rate, R_f, is 7%, and the expected market rate of return, R_m, is 15%. Firm A is financed by 80% equity and 20% debt, and this leverage will remain unchanged after the acquisition. Firm A pays interest of 10% on its debt, which will also remain unchanged after the acquisition.

a. Disregarding taxes, what is the maximum price that Firm A should pay for Firm B?

b. Firm A has a stock price of $30 per share and 10 million shares outstanding. If Firm B shareholders are to be paid the maximum price determined in part (a) via a new stock issue, then how many new shares will be issued, and what will be the post-merger stock price?

P21-11. Charger Incorporated and Sparks Electrical Company are competitors in the business of electrical components distribution. Sparks is the smaller firm and has attracted the attention of the management of Charger, for Sparks has taken away market share from the larger firm by increasing its sales force over the past few years. Charger is considering a takeover offer for Sparks and has asked you to serve on the acquisition valuation team that will turn into the due diligence team if an offer is made and accepted. Given the financial information and proposal assumptions that follow, how would you respond to (a) and (b)?

a. Make your recommendation about whether or not the acquisition should be pursued.

b. Assume that Sparks has accepted the takeover offer from Charger and that the new subsidiary must now be consolidated within Charger's financial statements. Taking Sparks' most recent balance sheet and a restated market value of assets of $295.6 million, calculate the goodwill that must be booked for this transaction.

Sparks Electrical Company Condensed Balance Sheet Previous Year ($ million)	
	2011
Current assets	12.2
Fixed assets	442.5
Total assets	454.7
Current liabilities	10.1
Long-term debt	150.0
Total liabilities	160.1
Shareholders' equity	294.6
Total liabilities and equity	454.7

Sparks Electrical Company Condensed Income Statement Previous Five Years ($ million)					
	2011	**2010**	**2009**	**2008**	**2007**
Revenues	1,626.5	1,614.1	1,485.2	1,380.5	1,373.4
Less: Cost of goods sold	1,488.1	1,490.9	1,359.5	1,271.4	1,268.0
Gross profit	138.4	123.2	125.7	109.1	105.4
Selling, general, & administrative expenses (SG&A)	41.1	36.8	41.2	35.0	36.1
Noncash expense (depreciation & amortization)	7.3	6.7	7.1	6.6	6.4
Less: Operating expense	48.4	43.5	48.3	41.6	42.5
Operating profit (*EBIT*)	90.0	79.7	77.4	67.5	62.9
Less: Interest expense	11.5	12.0	12.0	12.0	12.0
Earnings before taxes (*EBT*)	78.5	67.7	65.4	55.5	50.9
Less: Taxes paid	24.3	20.8	19.9	16.8	15.3
Net income	54.2	46.9	45.5	38.7	35.6

Assumptions:

- Sparks would become a wholly owned subsidiary of Charger.

- Revenues will continue to grow at 4.3% for the next five years and will level off at 4% thereafter.

- The cost of goods sold will represent 95% of revenue going forward.

- Sales-force layoffs will reduce SG&A expenses to $22 million next year, with a 2% growth rate going forward.

- These layoffs and other restructuring charges are expected to result in expensed restructuring charges of $30 million, $15 million, and $5 million (respectively) over the next three years.

- Noncash expenses are expected to remain around $7 million going forward.

- Interest expenses are expected to remain around $11.5 million going forward.

- A tax rate of 31% is assumed going forward.

- Charger's cost of equity is 12%.

- Sparks' current market capitalization is $315.7 million.

- Charger will offer Sparks a takeover premium of 20% over current market capitalization.

P21-12. Referring to Problem 21-11, assume it is now two years after the acquisition of Sparks and you must perform a goodwill impairment test of the subsidiary. Growth expectations have been lowered to 3% going forward. Using the following 5-year projection of cash flows and a 12% cost of equity, estimate the value of the subsidiary beyond year 5, the current value of the subsidiary, the current value of goodwill, and any goodwill impairment. Total assets (excluding intangibles) are now $612.5 million, and total liabilities are $175.0 million.

Cash Flow Projection for Next Five Years ($ million)					
	2014	**2015**	**2016**	**2017**	**2018**
Revenues	1,815.2	1,869.7	1,925.7	1,983.5	2,043.0
Less: Cost of goods sold @ 95% of revenue	1,724.4	1,776.2	1,829.5	1,884.3	1,940.9
Gross profit	90.8	93.5	96.2	99.2	102.1
SG&A expense @ 2% growth rate going forward	23.0	23.5	23.9	24.4	24.9
Noncash expense (depreciation & amortization)	7.0	7.0	7.0	7.0	7.0
Less: Operating expense	30.0	30.5	30.9	31.4	31.9
Operating profit (EBIT)	60.8	63.0	65.3	67.8	70.2
Less: Interest expense	11.5	11.5	11.5	11.5	11.5
Less: Restructuring charges	5.0	0.0	0.0	0.0	0.0
Earnings before taxes (EBT)	44.3	51.5	53.8	56.3	58.7
Less: Taxes paid	13.7	16.0	16.7	17.4	18.2
Net income	30.6	35.5	37.1	38.9	40.5
Free cash flow	54.1	54.0	55.6	57.4	59.0

P21-13. Firms AFD, TYU, CHG, and LAN are competitors within an industry. Their respective sales figures are $2.8 billion, $3.9 billion, $4.8 billion, and $2.1 billion. What is the Herfindahl Index (HI) for the industry? Is the industry considered highly concentrated, moderately concentrated, or not concentrated? Assuming that two more firms—QBC ($3.6 billion in sales) and RTY ($2.7 billion in sales)—are added to the industry figures, does the concentration level of the industry change? (Recompute HI to determine this.) If the three smallest firms (AFD, LAN, and RTY) merged, would the FTC be concerned? If so, why? (*Note:* The HI is measured in units of %². For example, 50% × 50% = 2,500%² (or, in decimal form, 0.50 × 0.50 = 0.25). To make the conversion from decimal to percentage form mathematically, multiply the answer by 10,000; using the same example, this yields 0.50 × 0.50 × 10,000 = 2,500.)

P21-14. Bogey Inc. (BOG), with a share price of $36 and EPS of $3, purchases Zoe Corp., with a pre-acquisition share price of $20 and EPS of $2, for a 10% premium. If the deal is financed exclusively with BOG equity and no material synergies are expected, is the deal accretive or dilutive to BOG shareholders?

P21-15. Following the previous question, what if BOG instead financed the acquisition entirely with debt at an after-tax cost of 9%? Would the deal be accretive or dilute to earnings for BOG shareholders?

P21-16. GRJ Corp. just reported $10 million in after-tax earnings and management expects to grow at 3% in perpetuity with a weighted average cost of capital of 13%:
   a. How would you value GRJ using a growing perpetuity formula?
   b. If GRJ's market capitalization is $100 million, what does this say about the market's perception of management's growth and/or cost of capital expectations?

P21-17. Posada Corp. (POS) expects to earn EBITDA of $4.2 million next year and expects slow but steady growth thereafter. POS's three key competitors (nearly identical operations and growth prospects) are JET (EBITDA of $5.1 million, Market Capitalization of $30.3 million), PET (EBITDA of $2.8 million, Market Capitalization of $15.4 million), and MO (EBITDA of $6.5 million, Market Capitalization of $40 million). What would you estimate POS's market valuation to be?

P21-18. You are assessing a potential acquisition for a client and your analyst informs you that the historic EBITDA multiple based on Public Comparables is 5.8 and the historic EBITDA multiple based on Precedent Transactions is 7.3. If the target is expecting EBITDA of $90 million, what are the valuations under each method? Can you rationalize the difference between the two?

P21-19. A given market was initially segmented evenly among 20 firms (Phase 1). Five years later, the market was still segmented evenly among competing firms, but there were now only 10 firms (Phase 2). Eventually six firms emerged with equal portions of the market (Phase 3), but a move toward deregulation of the industry has prompted two of the firms to merge. Determine the Herfindahl–Hirschman Index for the three phases. Next, determine whether the merger will cause the industry to be considered highly concentrated. In a preemptive move (fearing the FTC), the merged firms agree to sell off portions of the market to the other four firms so that the market will be equally divided among all five firms. How does this affect the HI, and is the merger viable under these circumstances?

THOMSON REUTERS | Business School Edition

For instructions on using Thomson ONE, refer to the instructions provided with the Thomson ONE problems at the end of Chapters 1-6.

P21-20. On November 18, 2005, SBC Communications, Inc., completed its acquisition of AT&T Corporation. The combined company was named AT&T Inc. (ticker symbol, T). Examine the 19-page 8-K report filed on November 18, 2005. How many shares of AT&T Inc. were exchanged for each share of AT&T Corporation? What was the total number of shares issued to the old AT&T shareholders? At the time of the merger, what percentage of the "new" AT&T was owned by old AT&T shareholders? Did old AT&T shareholders receive any additional compensation? Based on the closing stock price on November 17, 2005, what was the estimated value of the merger?

Mini-Case

Mergers, Corporate Control, and Corporate Governance

Jackson Enterprises (JE) is offering a 25% takeover premium to Michael Studios, Inc. (MSI) for the firm's 2 million outstanding shares, which are currently trading for a pre-offer price of $20 per share.

The balance sheet for MSI is:

Assets		Liabilities	
Current	$15,000,000	Current	$7,500,000
Fixed	45,000,000	Long-term	25,000,000
Total	$60,000,000	Total	$32,500,000
		Owners' equity	27,500,000
		Total liabilities and equity	$60,000,000

The market value of MSI's fixed assets is $60,000,000.

The sales (in millions) for the industry by company are:

	Sales
ABC	$89
CWC	66
DEF	35
JE	45
KOJ	42
MSI	18
SEE	76

Assignment

1. Determine the amount Jackson Enterprises is willing to pay in terms of goodwill.

2. If JE's shares are currently trading at $62.43, then how many shares should JE offer for every share of MSI?

3. Assuming that MSI will be treated as a separate reporting subsidiary following the merger, develop the balance sheet for the subsidiary.

4. Calculate the Herfindahl Index for the industry both before and after the proposed merger.

Glossary

A

ABC system An inventory control system that segregates inventory into three groups—A, B, and C. A items require the largest dollar investment and the most intensive control, B items require the next largest investment and less intensive control, and C items require the smallest investment and least intensive control.

absolute priority rules (APRs) Rules contained in *Chapter 7* of the *Bankruptcy Reform Act of 1978* that specify the procedures by which secured creditors are paid first, then unsecured creditors, then preferred shareholders, and finally common stockholders.

accounting exposure The risk that exchange rate movements will adversely impact reported financial results on a firm's financial statements.

accounting rate of return Return on investment calculated by dividing net income by the book value of assets.

accounts payable management A short-term financing activity that involves managing the time that elapses between the purchase of raw materials and mailing the payment to the supplier.

accredited investors Individuals or institutions that meet certain income and wealth requirements.

accrual-based approach Revenues are recorded at the point of sale and costs when they are incurred, not necessarily when a firm receives or pays out cash.

acquisition The purchase of resources, assets, or another firm.

actively managed A strategy in which an investor does research in an attempt to identify undervalued and overvalued stocks.

activity ratios A measure of the speed with which a firm converts various accounts into sales or cash.

adjustable-rate preferred stock A corporate obligation used for short-term investments that takes advantage of the dividend exclusion for stock in one corporation held by another corporation; the dividend rate paid on the stock is adjusted according to some rate index.

agency bonds Bonds issued by federal government agencies. Agency bonds are not explicitly backed by the full faith and credit of the U.S. government. Agencies issue bonds to provide credit for certain sectors of the economy such as farming, real estate, and education.

agency cost/contracting model A theoretical model that explains empirical patterns in dividend payment and share repurchase data based on the belief that paying dividends allows a firm to overcome agency problems between managers and shareholders.

agency costs Costs that arise from conflicts of interest between shareholders and managers.

agency costs of debt Costs that arise because stockholders and bondholders have different objectives.

agency costs of (outside) equity The value-reducing actions that managers take when ownership (by stockholders) is separated from control by managers.

agency problems The conflict of interest between the goals of a firm's owners and its managers.

aggressive strategy Financing strategy in which a company relies heavily on short-term borrowing, not only to meet the seasonal peaks each year but also to finance a portion of the long-term growth in sales and assets.

aging of accounts receivable A schedule that indicates the portions of the total accounts receivable balance that have been outstanding for specified periods of time.

all-in rate The base rate plus the spread on a short-term variable rate loan.

American call option An option that grants the right to buy an underlying asset, on or before the expiration date.

American Depositary Receipts (ADRs) Dollar-denominated claims, issued by U.S. banks, that represent ownership of shares of a foreign company's stock held on deposit by the U.S. bank in the issuing firm's home country.

angel capitalists Wealthy individuals who make private equity investments on an ad hoc basis.

announcement date The day a firm declares the amount of the dividend, plus the dividend record and payment dates to the public.

annual percentage rate (APR) The stated annual rate calculated by multiplying the periodic rate by the number of periods in one year.

annual percentage yield (APY) The annual rate of interest actually paid or earned, reflecting the impact of compounding frequency. The same as the *effective annual rate* (sometimes called the *effective APR*).

annuity A stream of equal periodic cash flows over a stated period of time

annuity due An annuity for which the payments occur *at the beginning of each period.*

appreciate A currency appreciates when it buys more of another currency than it did previously.

arbitrage The process of buying something in one market at a low price and simultaneously selling it in another market at a higher price to generate an immediate, risk-free profit. ask price The price at which a *market maker* offers to sell a security; the price at which one can purchase a security.

asset sale Assets of one company are sole to another organization, usually for cash.

asset substitution When shareholders choose risky projects that benefit themselves but reduce the value of bondholders.

assets-to-equity (A/E) ratio A measure of the proportion of total assets financed by a firm's equity. Also called the *equity multiplier.*

asymmetric information The situation that exists when managers of the firm have more information about the firm and its prospects than do investors.

at the money An option is at the money when the stock price equals the strike price.

automated clearinghouse (ACH) debit transfer A pre-authorized electronic withdrawal from the payer's account.

automatic stay Legal protection that Is given to a firm that has filed for *bankruptcy*; it prevents creditors from taking further action to collect their claims.

availability float The time between deposit of a check and availability of the funds to a firm.

average age of inventory A measure of inventory turnover, calculated by dividing the turnover figure into 365, the number of days in a year.

average collection period The average amount of time that elapses from a sale on credit until the payment becomes usable funds for a firm. Calculated by dividing accounts receivable by average daily sales. Also called the *average age of accounts receivable.*

average investment in accounts receivable (AIAR) An estimate of the actual amount of cash (variable cost) tied up in accounts receivable at any time during the year.

average payment period The average length of time it takes a firm to pay its suppliers. Calculated by dividing the firm's accounts payable balance by its average daily purchases.

average tax rate A firm's tax liability divided by its pretax income.

B

balloon payment A large lump-sum payment that pays back the entire loan principal at the maturity of a term loan that during its life requires only periodic interest payments.

bank account analysis statement A regular report (usually monthly) provided to a bank's commercial customers that specifies all services provided, including items processed and any charges assessed.

bankrupt The situation that exists when a firm cannot meet its debt obligations.

bankruptcy Describes the legal process (governed in the United States by federal law) through which the claims of a *bankrupt* firm's creditors are handled; occurs only when a company enters bankruptcy court and effectively surrenders control of the firm to a bankruptcy judge.

Bankruptcy Code Terms generally used to refer to the *Bankruptcy Reform Act of 1978.*

bankruptcy costs The direct and indirect costs of the bankruptcy process.

Bankruptcy Reform Act of 1978 The governing bankruptcy legislation in the United States today. Generally referred to as the *Bankruptcy Code.*

basis point 1/100 of 1%; 100 basis points equal 1.000%.

basis risk The possibility of unanticipated changes in the difference between the futures price and the spot price.

bearer bonds Bonds that pay interest to the bearer and both shelter investment income from taxation and provide protection against exchange rate risk.

beta A standardized measure of the risk of an individual asset that captures only the systematic component of its volatility; it measures the sensitivity of the asset's return to movements in the overall market.

bid price The price at which a *market maker* offers to purchase a security; the price at which an investor can sell a security.

binomial option pricing model A model that uses the principle of "no arbitrage" to calculate call and put values.

board of directors Representatives elected by shareholders to be responsible for hiring, firing, and overseeing managers and for setting overall corporate policies.

bond equivalent yield (*BEY*) The yield equivalent used to compare discount instruments to interest-bearing investments by converting the *money market yield* from a 360-day to a 365-day year.

bond ratings Letter ratings assigned to bonds by specialized agencies that evaluate the capacity of bond issuers to repay their debts. Lower ratings signify higher default risk.

book building A process in which underwriters ask prospective investors to reveal information about their demand for the offering.

book value The value of equity as shown on the firm's balance sheet.

bottom-up sales forecast A sales forecast that relies on the assessment by sales personnel of demand in the coming year on a customer-by-customer basis.

breakeven point (BEP) The level of sales or production that a firm must achieve in order to fully cover all costs. Sales or production above the BEP results in profits.

broker market A market in which the buyer and seller are brought together on a "securities exchange" to trade securities.

bulge bracket Consists of firms that generally occupy the lead or co-lead manager's position in large, new security offerings.

business failure A firm's inability to stay in business.

business risk The variability of a firm's cash flows, as measured by the variability of *EBIT*.

bust-up The takeover of a company that is subsequently split up.

C

call option An option that grants the right to buy an underlying asset at a fixed price.

call premium The amount by which the call price exceeds the par value of a bond. Paid by corporations to buy back outstanding bonds prior to maturity.

call price The price at which a bond issuer may call or repurchase an outstanding bond from investors.

callable (bonds) Bonds that the issuer can repurchase from investors at a predetermined price known as the *call price*.

cancellation option Option held by the venture capitalist to deny or delay additional funding for a portfolio company.

cannibalization Loss of sales of a firm's existing product when a new product is introduced.

Capital Asset Pricing Model (CAPM) States that the expected return on a specific asset equals the risk-free rate plus a premium that depends on the asset's beta and the expected risk premium on the market portfolio.

capital budgeting The process of determining which long-lived investment projects a firm should undertake.

capital budgeting function The activities involved in selecting the best projects in which to invest the firm's funds based on their expected risk and return. Also called the *investment function*.

capital gains The difference between the sale price and the initial purchase price of a capital asset, such as equipment or stock held as an investment; the increase in the price of an asset that occurs over a period of time.

capital loss The loss resulting from the sale of a capital asset, such as equipment or stock held as an investment, at a price below its book, or accounting, value; the decrease in the price of an asset that occurs over a period of time.

capital rationing The situation where a firm has more positive *NPV* projects than its available budget can fund. It should choose the combination of those projects that maximizes shareholder wealth.

carrying cost The *variable cost per unit* of holding an item in inventory for a specified period of time. Used in calculating the EOQ.

cash application The process through which a customer's payment is posted to its account and the outstanding invoices are cleared as paid.

cash budget A statement of a firm's planned inflows and outflows of cash.

cash concentration The process of bringing the lockbox and other deposits together into one bank, often called the *concentration bank*.

cash conversion cycle (CCC) The elapsed time between the points at which a firm pays for raw materials and at which it receives payment for finished goods.

cash disbursements All outlays of cash by a firm in a given period.

cash discount A method of lowering investment in accounts receivable by giving customers a cash incentive to pay sooner.

cash flow approach Used by financial professionals to focus attention on current and prospective inflows and outflows of cash.

cash flow from operations Cash inflows and outflows directly related to the production and sale of a firm's products and services. Calculated as net income plus depreciation and other noncash charges.

cash manager A financial specialist responsible for managing the cash flow time line related to collection, concentration, and disbursement of the company's funds.

cash position management The primary cash management tasks that are performed daily and involve the collection, concentration, and disbursement of company funds.

cash receipts All of a firm's cash inflows in a given period.

cash settlement An agreement between two parties, in which one party pays the other party the cash value of its option position, rather than forcing it to exercise the option by buying or selling the underlying asset.

certification Assurance that the issuing company is in fact disclosing all material information.

Chapter 11 Section of the *Bankruptcy Reform Act of 1978* that outlines the procedures to be followed when reorganizing a failed or failing firm.

Chapter 7 Section of the *Bankruptcy Reform Act of 1978* that details the procedures to be followed when liquidating a failed firm.

chief financial officer (CFO) Top management position charged with developing financial policies and strategies covering all aspects of a firm's financial management and accounting activities.

clearing float The time between deposit of the check and presentation of the check back to the bank on which it is drawn.

closing futures price The price used to settle all contracts at the end of each day's trading.

collateral The specific assets pledged to secure a loan.

collateral trust bonds A bond secured by financial assets held by a trustee.

collection policy The procedures used by a company to collect overdue or delinquent accounts receivable. The approach used is often a function of the industry and the competitive environment.

collective action problem When individual stockholders bear all the costs of monitoring management, but the benefit of such monitoring accrues to all shareholders.

commercial paper The primary corporate obligation in the short-term market. Typically structured as an unsecured promissory note with a maturity of less than 270 days and usually sold to other corporations rather than the general public.

common stock The most basic form of corporate ownership.

common-size income statement An income statement in which all entries are expressed as a percentage of sales.

comparable multiple A valuation method that calculates a valuation ratio or multiple for each firm in a sample of similar firms, and then uses the average or median pricing multiple for the sample firms to estimate a particular firm's value.

compound interest Interest earned both on the initial *principal* and on the interest earned in previous periods.

conglomerate merger Unrelated diversification mergers that occur between companies in completely different lines of business.

conservative strategy Financing strategy in which a company makes sure that it has enough long-term financing to cover its permanent investments in fixed and current assets as well as the additional seasonal investments in current assets that it makes during the various quarters each year.

consolidation A merger in which both the acquirer and target disappear as separate corporations, combining to form an entirely new corporation with new common stock.

constant dollar payment policy Dividend policy based on the payment of a fixed-dollar dividend in each period.

constant payout ratio policy Dividend policy in which a firm establishes that a certain percentage of earnings is paid to owners in each dividend period.

continuous compounding Interest compounds literally at every moment as time passes.

contribution margin The sale price per unit (SP) minus variable cost per unit (VC).

controlled disbursement A bank service that provides early notification of checks that will be presented against a company's account on a given day.

conversion premium The percentage increase in the underlying stock that must occur before it is profitable to exercise the option to convert a bond into shares.

conversion price The market price of a convertible bond, divided by the number of shares of stock that bondholders receive if they convert.

conversion ratio The number of shares bondholders receive if they convert their bonds into shares.

conversion value The market price of the stock, multiplied by the number of shares of stock that bondholders receive if they convert.

convertible bonds Bonds that allow a bondholder to exchange each bond for a stated number of shares of common stock.

corporate bonds Bonds issued by corporations.

corporate charter The legal document created at the corporation's inception to govern its operations.

corporate control The monitoring, supervision, and direction of a corporation or other business organization.

corporate finance The activities involved in managing cash (money) that flows through a business.

corporate governance The processes and rules that determine how a company is governed.

corporate governance function The activities involved in developing company-wide structures and incentives that influence managers to behave ethically and make decisions that benefit shareholders

corporate venture capital funds Subsidiaries or stand-alone firms established by nonfinancial corporations to gain access to emerging technologies.

corporation A legal entity, owned by the shareholders who hold its common stock, with many of the economic rights and responsibilities enjoyed by individuals.

cost of marginal investment in accounts receivable The marginal investment in accounts receivable required to support a proposed change in credit policy multiplied by the required return on investment.

counterparty risk The risk that the counterparty in an over-the-counter options transaction will default on its obligation.

coupon The periodic interest payment that a bond pays to investors.

coupon rate The rate derived by dividing the bond's annual coupon payment by its par value.

coupon yield The amount obtained by dividing the bond's coupon by its current market price (which does not always equal its par value). Also called *current yield.*

coverage ratio A debt ratio that uses data from the *income statement* to assess the firm's ability to generate sufficient cash flow to make scheduled interest and principal payments.

covered interest arbitrage A trading strategy designed to exploit deviations from interest rate parity to earn an arbitrage profit.

cramdown Action by the judge, at the request of the debtor that forces creditors to accept the terms of the proposed reorganization plan that they have rejected.

credit monitoring The ongoing review of a firm's accounts receivable to determine if customers are paying according to the stated credit terms.

credit scoring Applies statistically derived weights for key financial and credit characteristics to predict whether or not a credit applicant with specific scores for each characteristic will pay the requested credit in a timely fashion.

credit terms The terms of sale for customers.

cross exchange rate An exchange rate between two currencies calculated by taking the ratio of the exchange rate of each currency, expressed in terms of a third currency.

cross-default covenant A positive debt covenant in which the borrower is considered to be in default on all debts if it is in default on any debt.

cross-hedging The underlying securities in a futures contract and the assets being hedged have different characteristics.

currency board arrangement An exchange rate system in which each unit of the domestic currency is backed by a unit of some foreign currency.

currency forward contract Exchange of one currency for another at a fixed date in the future.

currency swap A swap contract in which two parties exchange payment obligations denominated in different currencies.

current ratio A measure of a firm's ability to meet its short-term obligations, defined as current assets *divided* by current liabilities.

D

date of record The date on which the names of all persons who appear as stockholders are entitled to receive a dividend.

dealer market A market in which the buyer and seller are not brought together directly, but instead have their orders executed by market makers *securities dealers* who are market *makers* in the given security.

debentures An unsecured bond backed only by the general faith and credit of the borrowing company.

debt capital Long-term borrowed money.

debt ratio A measure of the proportion of total assets financed by a firm's creditors.

debtor in possession (DIP) The firm filing a reorganization petition.

debt-to-equity ratio A measure of the firm's financial leverage, calculated by dividing long-term debt by stockholders' equity.

decision tree A visual representation of the sequential choices that managers face with regard to a particular investment.

default risk The risk that the bond issuer may not make all scheduled payments.

deferred taxes An account that reflects the difference between the taxes that firms actually pay and the tax liabilities they report on their public financial statements.

demand registration rights Agreements giving the venture capitalists the right to demand that a portfolio company's managers arrange for a public offering of shares in the company.

depreciate A currency depreciates when it buys less of another currency than it did previously.

derivative security A security that derives its value from another asset.

direct bankruptcy costs Include fees paid to attorneys, accountants, investment bankers, and other professionals involved in bankruptcy proceedings in addition to other expenses directly tied to bankruptcy filing and administration.

direct lease A lessor acquires the assets that are leased to a given lessee.

direct quote An exchange rate quoted in terms of units of domestic currency per unit of foreign currency.

discount A bond trades at a discount when its market price is less than its par value.

discount investment An investment vehicle for which the investor pays less than face value at the time of purchase, and then receives the face value of the investment at its maturity date.

discounted payback period The amount of time it takes for a project's discounted cash flows to recover the initial investment.

discounting The process of calculating present values.

diversification The act of investing in a variety of different assets rather than just one or two similar assets.

divestiture Assets and/or resources of a subsidiary or division are conveyed to another organization.

dividend payout ratio The percentage of current earnings available for common stockholders paid out as dividends. Calculated by dividing the firm's cash dividend paid per share by its earnings per share in a given period.

dividend per share (DPS) The portion of the earnings per share paid to stockholders.

dividend yield Annual cash dividend per share divided by the current stock price.

dividends Periodic cash payments that firms make to stockholders.

double-taxation problem Taxation of corporate income at both company and personal levels—traditionally a significant disadvantage of the corporate form.

dual-class recapitalization Issuance of a new class of common shares with the intent of concentrating control of voting rights in one group of investors.

due diligence Examination of potential security issuers in which investment banks are legally required to search out and disclose all relevant information about an issuer before selling securities to the public.

DuPont system An analysis that uses both income statement and balance sheet information to break the *ROA* and *ROE* ratios into component pieces.

E

earnings available for common stockholders Net income net of preferred stock dividends.

earnings per share (EPS) Earnings available for common stockholders divided by the number of shares of common stock outstanding.

economic exposure The risk that a change in prices will negatively impact the value of all cash flows of a firm; in international finance, the risk that a firm's value will fluctuate due to exchange rate movements.

economic order quantity (EOQ) model A common tool used to estimate the optimal order quantity for big-ticket items of inventory. It considers operating and financial costs and determines the order quantity that minimizes overall inventory costs.

economic profit A profit that exceeds a normal, competitive rate of return in an industry or line of business.

economic value added (EVA) A method of analyzing the value of capital investments that determines whether an investment produces net cash flow sufficient to cover the firm's cost of capital, calculated as the difference between net operating profits after taxes and the cost of funds.

economies of scale Relative operating costs are reduced for merged companies because of an increase in size that allows for the reduction or elimination of overlapping resources.

economies of scope Value-creating benefits of increased breadth of operations for merged companies.

effective (offering) Status of an offering before any shares can actually be sold to public investors.

effective annual rate (EAR) The annual rate of interest *actually paid* or earned, reflecting the impact of compounding frequency. Also called the *true annual return*.

effective borrowing rate (EBR) Generally determined as the total amount of interest and fees paid, divided by the average usable loan amount.

efficient markets hypothesis (EMH) Asserts that financial asset prices rapidly and fully incorporate new information.

electronic bill presentment and payment (EBPP) A collection system in the business-to-consumer market under which consumers are sent bills in an electronic format and can pay them via electronic means.

electronic depository transfer (EDT) The term used in the cash management trade for an *automated clearinghouse (ACH) debit transfer*.

electronic invoice presentment and payment (EIPP) A collection system in business-to-business transactions under which business customers are sent bills in an electronic format and can pay them via electronic means.

employee stock ownership plan (ESOP) The transformation of a public corporation into a private company by the employees of the corporation itself.

enterprise value The total value of the firm (including debt, equity, and other securities) that would need to be purchased to control the whole target entity.

entrepreneurial finance Focuses on the special challenges and problems associated with the investment in and financing of risky businesses, typically start-ups.

entrepreneurial growth companies (EGCs) Typically high-risk, start-ups that are commonly funded by venture capitalists.

equipment trust certificates A secured bond used to finance transportation equipment.

equity capital An ownership interest purchased by an investor, usually in the form of common or preferred stock, that is expected to remain permanently invested.

equity carve-out (ECO) Occurs when a parent company sells shares of a subsidiary corporation to the public through an initial public offering.

equity claimants Owners of a corporation's equity securities.

equity kickers Warrants attached to another security offering (usually a bond offering) that give investors more upside potential.

equity multiplier A measure of the proportion of total assets financed by a firm's equity. Also called the *assets-to-equity (A/E)* ratio.

equivalent annual cost (EAC) method Represents the annual expenditure over the life of each asset that has a present value equal to the present value of the asset's annual cash flows over its lifetime.

euro The currency used throughout the countries that make up the European Union.

Eurobond A bond issued by an international borrower and sold to investors in countries with currencies other than the currency in which the bond is denominated.

Eurocurrency loan market A large number of international banks that stand ready to make floating-rate, hard-currency loans to international corporate and government borrowers.

European call option An option that grants the right to buy the underlying asset only on the expiration date.

excess earnings accumulation tax A tax levied by the IRS on a firm that has accumulated sufficient excess earnings to allow owners to delay paying ordinary income taxes.

exchange rate The price of one currency in terms of another currency.

exchangeable bonds Bonds issued by corporations which may be converted into shares of a company other than the company that issued the bonds.

ex-dividend date Date on or after which a purchaser of a stock does not receive the current dividend. Usually two business days prior to the *date of record*.

executive compensation plans Incentives offered to a manager to encourage her to act in the best interests of the owners.

exercise price The price at which an option holder can buy or sell the underlying asset.

exercise the option Pay (receive) the strike price and buy (sell) the underlying asset.

expectations theory In equilibrium, investors should expect to earn the same return whether they invest in long-term Treasury bonds or a series of short-term Treasury bonds.

expected return A forecast of the return that an asset will earn over some future period of time.

expiration date The date on which the right to buy or to sell the underlying asset expires.

extension An arrangement wherein a firm's creditors are promised payment in full, although not immediately.

external funds required (EFR) The expected shortage or surplus of financial resources, given the firm's growth objectives.

extra dividend An additional dividend that a firm may pay if earnings are higher than normal in a given period.

F

factoring The outright sale of receivables to a third-party *factor* at a discount.

fair-price provisions Rules that ensure that all target shareholders receive the same offer price in any tender offers initiated by the same acquirer, limiting the ability of acquirers to buy minority shares cheaply with a two-tiered offer.

fallen angels Bonds that received investment-grade ratings when first issued but later fell to junk status.

federal funds rate The interest rate that U.S. banks charge each other for overnight loans.

fiduciary A person who invests and manages money on another's behalf.

field banking system Collection system characterized by many collection points, each of which may have a depository account at a local bank.

financial (or capital) lease A noncancelable contractual arrangement whereby the lessee agrees to make periodic payments to the lessor, typically for more than five years, to obtain an asset's services. Also called a *capital lease*.

financial deficit Occurs when a corporation requires more financial capital for investment than it supplies in the form of retained earnings.

financial distress The situation in which a company's cash flows are insufficient to pay its current obligations.

financial engineering The process of using the principles of financial economics to design and price financial instruments.

financial intermediary (FI) An institution, such as a bank, that raises capital by issuing liabilities against itself, and then uses the capital raised to make either loans to corporations and individuals or to buy various types of investments.

financial leverage The magnification of both risk and expected return that results from the fixed cost associated with the use of debt, which leads to a higher stock beta; the use of fixed-cost sources of financing, such as debt and preferred stock, to magnify both the risk and the expected return on a firm's securities.

financial management function The activities involved in managing the firm's operating cash flows as efficiently as possible.

financial risk How a firm's financing choices affect how its *business risk* is distributed to its stockholders and bondholders.

financial slack Large cash and marketable security holdings or unused debt capacity.

financial venture capital funds Subsidiaries of financial institutions, particularly commercial banks.

financing flows Cash flow that result from debt and equity financing transactions.

financing function Raising capital to support a company's operations and investment programs.

firm-commitment offering An offering in which the investment bank agrees to *underwrite* the firm's securities, thereby guaranteeing that the firm will successfully complete its sale of securities.

five C's of credit A framework for performing in-depth credit analysis without providing a specific accept or reject decision.

fixed asset turnover A measure of the efficiency with which a firm uses its *fixed assets*, calculated by dividing sales by the number of dollars of net fixed asset investment.

fixed exchange rate An exchange rate system in which the price of one currency is fixed relative to another currency by government authorities.

fixed-for-floating currency swap A combination of a currency swap and an interest rate swap.

fixed-for-floating interest rate swap Typically one party will make fixed-rate payments to another party in exchange for floating-rate payments.

fixed-price offer An offer in which the underwriters set the final offer price for a new issue weeks in advance.

fixed-rate offerings Debt issues that have a coupon interest rate that remains constant throughout the issue's life.

flip To buy shares at the offer price and sell them on the first trading day.

float Funds that have been sent by the payer but are not yet usable funds to the payee.

floating exchange rate An exchange rate system in which a currency's value is allowed to fluctuate in response to market forces.

floating-rate bonds Bonds that make coupon payments that vary through time. The coupon payments are usually tied to a benchmark market interest rate. Also called *variable-rate bonds*.

floating-rate issues Debt issues with an interest (coupon) rate that is a fixed spread above a base rate that periodically changes.

foreign bond A bond issued in a host country's financial market, in the host country's currency, by a foreign borrower.

forward discount When one currency buys less of another on the forward market than it buys on the spot market.

forward exchange rate The exchange rate quoted for a transaction that will occur on a future date.

forward premium When one currency buys more of another on the forward market than it buys on the spot market.

forward price The price to which parties in a forward contract agree. The price dictates what the buyer will pay to the seller on a future date.

forward rate In a currency forward contract, the forward price.

forward rate agreement (FRA) A forward contract in which the underlying asset is not an asset at all but an interest rate.

forward–spot parity An equilibrium relationship that predicts that the current forward rate will be an unbiased predictor of the spot rate on a future date.

free cash flow (FCF) The net amount of cash flow remaining after the firm has met all operating needs, including capital expenditure and working capital needs. Represents the cash amount that a firm could distribute to investors after meeting all its other obligations.

full disclosure Requires issuers to reveal all relevant information concerning the company selling the securities and the securities themselves to potential investors.

fundamental principle of financial leverage Substituting debt for equity increases expected returns to shareholders but also increases the risk that equity investors bear.

fungibility The ability to close out a position by taking an offsetting position.

future value The value of an investment made today measured at a specific future date accounting for interest earned over the life of the investment.

futures contract Involves two parties agreeing today on a price at which the purchaser will buy a given amount of a commodity or financial instrument from the seller at a fixed date sometime in the future.

G

General Agreement on Tariffs and Trade (GATT) A trade treaty that extends free trade principles to broad areas of economic activity in many countries.

general cash offerings Share offerings sold to all investors, not just existing shareholders.

general partners One or more participants in a limited partnership who operate the business and have unlimited personal liability.

Glass-Steagall Act Congressional act of 1933 mandating the separation of investment and commercial banking.

going-private transactions The transformation of a public corporation into a private company through issuance of large amounts of debt used to buy the outstanding shares of the corporation.

goodwill An intangible asset created if the restated values of the target in a merger lead to a situation in which its assets are less than its liabilities and equity.

Gordon growth model The valuation model that views cash flows as a *growing perpetuity*.

Gramm-Leach-Bliley Act Act that allowed commercial banks, securities firms, and insurance companies to join together.

gross profit margin A measure of profitability that represents the percentage of each sales dollar remaining after a firm has paid for its goods.

growing perpetuity A cash flow stream that grows each period at a constant rate and continues forever.

H

hedge To use complex financial instruments to offset market risks such as interest-rate and currency fluctuations.

hedge ratio A combination of stock and options that results in a risk-free payoff.

hedging Trading an asset for the sole purpose of reducing or eliminating the risk associated with some other asset.

high-yield bonds Bonds rated below investment grade (also known as *junk bonds* or *speculative bonds*).

horizontal merger A combination of competitors within the same industry.

hostile takeover The acquisition of one firm (the *target*) by another (the *acquirer*) through an open market bid for a majority of the target's shares if the target firm's senior managers do not support (or, more likely, actively resist) the acquisition.

hubris hypothesis of corporate takeovers A theory that contends that some managers overestimate their own managerial capabilities and pursue takeovers with the belief that they can better manage their takeover target than the target's current management.

I

imaging services Disbursement services offered by banks and other vendors to allow both sides of the check, as well as remittance information, to be converted into digital images. The images can then be transmitted via the Internet or easily stored for future reference.

in the money A call (put) option is in the money when the stock price is greater (less) than the strike price.

income bonds An unsecured bond that pays interest only when the debtor company has positive earnings.

incremental cash flows Cash flows triggered by an investment that would not have otherwise occurred.

indenture A legal contract between a borrower (issuer) and an investor, stating the conditions under which a bond has been issued.

index fund A passively managed fund that tries to mimic the performance of a market index, such as the S&P 500.

indirect bankruptcy costs Include the loss of customers and key suppliers, the time that managers spend managing the bankruptcy process rather than focusing on their business, the loss of key employees, and missed opportunities to invest in positive-*NPV* projects.

indirect quote An exchange rate quoted in terms of foreign currency per unit of domestic currency.

initial margin The minimum dollar amount required of an investor when taking a position in a futures contract.

initial public offering (IPO) The first public sale of a company's common stock, offered through the sale of shares to outside investors and listed for trade on a stock exchange.

initial return The gain when an allocation of shares from an investment banker is sold at the first opportunity

because the offer price is consistently lower than what the market is willing to pay.

insolvent The situation in which a firm's liabilities exceed its assets.

institutional venture capital funds Formal business entities with full-time professionals dedicated to seeking out and funding promising ventures.

integrated accounts payable Provides a company with outsourcing of its accounts payable or disbursement operations. Also known as *comprehensive accounts payable*.

interest differential In an interest rate swap, only the differential is exchanged.

interest rate cap A call option on interest rates.

interest rate collar A strategy involving the purchase of an interest rate cap and the simultaneous sale of an interest rate floor, using the proceeds from selling the floor to purchase the cap.

interest rate floor A put option on interest rates.

interest rate parity An equilibrium relationship that predicts that differences in risk-free interest rates in two countries must be tied to differences in currency values on the spot and forward markets.

interest rate risk The risk resulting from changes in market interest rates that cause fluctuations in a bond's price. Also, the risk of suffering losses as a result of unanticipated changes in market interest rates.

interest rate swap A swap contract in which two parties exchange payment obligations involving different interest payment schedules.

internal rate of return (IRR) The compound annual rate of return on a project, given its up-front costs and subsequent cash flows.

international common stock Equity issues sold in more than one country by nonresident corporations.

intrinsic value The profit that an investor makes from exercising an option, ignoring transactions costs and the option premium.

inventory turnover A measure of how quickly a firm sells its goods.

investment banks Financial institutions that assist firms in raising long-term debt and equity financing in the world's capital markets, advise corporations about major financial transactions, and are active in the business of selling and trading securities in secondary markets.

investment flows Cash flows associated with the purchase or sale of fixed assets.

investment-grade bonds Bonds rated Baa or higher by Moody's (BBB- or higher by S&P).

IPO underpricing Occurs when the offer price in the prospectus is consistently lower than what the market is willing to bear.

J

joint and several liability A legal concept that makes each partner in a partnership legally liable for all the debts of the partnership.

junk bonds Bonds rated below investment grade (also known as *high-yield bonds* or *speculative bonds*).

just-in-time (JIT) system An inventory management technique used to make sure that materials arrive exactly when they are needed for production, rather than being stored on-site.

L

law of one price A theory that says that the identical good trading in different markets must sell at the same price.

lead underwriter The investment bank that takes the primary role in assisting a firm in a public offering of securities.

lease-versus-purchase (or lease-versus-buy) decision The alternatives available are to (1) lease the assets, (2) borrow funds to purchase the assets, or (3) purchase the assets using available liquid resources. Even if the firm has the liquid resources with which to purchase the assets, the use of these funds is viewed as equivalent to borrowing.

leasing Acquiring use of an asset by agreeing to make a series of periodic, tax-deductible payments.

lessee Under a lease, the user of the underlying asset who makes regular payments to the *lessor*.

lessor Under a lease, the owner of the asset who receives regular payments for its use from the *lessee*.

leveraged lease A lease under which the lessor acts as an equity participant, supplying on average about 20% of the cost of the asset, and borrowing the balance of the funds.

leveraged recapitalization When a company greatly increases the portion of debt in its capital structure, often retiring equity in the process.

LIBOR The *London Interbank Offered Rate*. The rate that the most creditworthy international banks that deal in Eurodollars charge on interbank loans.

lien A legal contract specifying under what conditions a lender can take title to an asset if a loan is not repaid and

prohibiting the borrowing firm from selling or disposing of the asset without the lender's consent.

limited liability company (LLC) A form of business organization that combines the tax advantages of a partnership with the limited liability protection of a corporation.

limited partners One or more totally passive participants in a limited partnership, who do not take any active role in the operation of the business and who do not face personal liability for the debts of the business.

limited partnership (LP) A partnership in which most of the participants (the *limited* partners) have the limited liability of corporate shareholders, but their share of the profits from the business is taxed as partnership income.

line of credit An up-front commitment by a bank to lend to a borrower in the future.

liquidation value The that remains after a firm's assets are sold and its liabilities are paid.

liquidity management Activities aimed at both earning a positive return on idle excess cash balances and obtaining low-cost financing for meeting unexpected needs and seasonal cash shortages.

liquidity preference theory States that the slope of the yield curve is influenced not only by expected interest rate changes, but also by the liquidity premium that investors require on long-term bonds.

liquidity ratios Measure a firm's ability to satisfy its short-term obligations *as they come due*.

loan amortization Occurs when a borrower pays back the principal over the life of the loan, often in equal periodic payments.

loan amortization schedule Used to determine loan amortization payments and the allocation of each payment to interest and principal.

loan covenants Contractual clauses that limit the actions that a borrower can take, protecting the lender's wealth from being expropriated.

loans Private debt agreements arranged between corporate borrowers and financial institutions, especially commercial banks.

lockbox system A technique for speeding up collections that affects all three components of float. Customers mail payments to a post office box, which is emptied regularly by the firm's bank, which processes and deposits the payments.

London Interbank Offered Rate (LIBOR) The interest rate that large banks charge each other for overnight loans. Widely used as a benchmark interest rate for short-term floating-rate debt.

long position To own an option or another security.

long-term debt Debt that matures more than one year in the future.

M

mail float The time delay between when payment is placed in the mail and when payment is received.

mail-based collection system Collection system in which processing centers receive the incoming mail payments, separate checks from remittance information, prepare checks for deposit, and send remittance information to the accounts receivable department.

maintenance clause A clause in a lease that specifies who is to maintain the assets and make insurance and tax payments.

maintenance margin Margin level required to maintain an open position.

managed floating rate system A hybrid currency system in which a government loosely fixes the value of the national currency relative to one or more other currencies.

management buyout (MBO) The transformation of a public corporation into a private company by the current managers of the corporation.

manufacturing resource planning II (MRPII) Expands on MRP by using a complex computerized system to integrate data from many departments and generate a production plan for the firm along with management reports, forecasts, and financial statements.

margin account The account into which the investor must deposit the initial margin.

marginal tax rate The tax rate applicable to a firm's next dollar of earnings.

market makers *Securities dealers* that "make markets" by offering to buy or sell certain securities at stated prices.

market portfolio A portfolio that invests in every asset in the economy.

market risk premium The additional return earned (or expected) on the market portfolio over and above the risk-free rate.

market/book (M/B) ratio A measure used to assess a firm's future performance by relating its market value per share to its book value per share.

marking-to-market Daily cash settlement of all futures contracts.

matching strategy Financing strategy in which a company finances permanent assets (fixed assets plus the permanent component of current assets) with long-term funding sources and finances its temporary or seasonal asset requirements with short-term debt.

material requirements planning (MRP) A computerized system used to control the flow of resources, particularly inventory, within the production-sale process.

maturity date The date when a bond's life ends and the borrower must make the final interest payment and repay the principal.

McFadden Act Congressional act of 1927 that prohibited interstate banking.

merger A transaction in which two or more business organizations combine into a single entity.

merger of equals A merger of two firms that are roughly the same size; usually friendly.

mixed offerings A merger financed with a combination of cash and securities.

mixed stream A series of unequal cash flows reflecting no particular pattern.

modified accelerated cost recovery system (MACRS) Defines the allowable annual depreciation deductions for various classes of assets.

monetary union An agreement between many European countries to integrate their monetary systems including using a single currency.

money market mutual funds Professionally managed short-term investment portfolios used by many small companies and some large companies.

money market yield (MMY) The yield for short-term discount instruments such as T-bills and commercial paper is typically calculated using algebraic approximations on a 360-day basis rather than more precise present value methods.

Monte Carlo simulation A sophisticated form of sensitivity analysis that calculates the decision variable, such as *NPV*, using a range or distribution of potential outcomes for each of a model's assumptions.

mortgage bonds A bond secured by real estate or buildings.

multinational corporations (MNCs) Businesses that operate in many different countries.

municipal bonds Issued by U.S. state and local governments. Interest received on these bonds is exempt from federal income tax.

mutually exclusive projects Two or more projects for which accepting one project implies that the others cannot be undertaken.

N

naked option position To buy or to sell an option, without a simultaneous position in the underlying asset.

negotiated offer A process used by an issuer to hire an investment banker with whom it directly negotiates the terms of the offer.

net operating profits after taxes (NOPAT) The amount of earnings before interest and after taxes, which equals EBIT 3 (1–T), where EBIT is earnings before interest and taxes and T equals the corporate tax rate.

net payoff The difference between the payoff received when the option expires and the premium paid to acquire the option.

net present value (NPV) The sum of the present values of all of a project's cash flows, both inflows and outflows, discounted at a rate consistent with the project's risk. Also, the preferred method for valuing capital investments.

net present value (NPV) profile A plot of a project's NPV (on the y-axis) against various discount rates (on the x-axis). It is used to illustrate the relationship between the NPV and the IRR for the typical project.

net profit margin A measure of profitability that represents the percentage of each sales dollar remaining after all costs and expenses, including interest, taxes, and preferred stock dividends, have been deducted.

net working capital A measure of a firm's liquidity calculated by subtracting current liabilities from current assets.

nominal return The stated return offered by an investment; includes the real return plus any additional return due to expected inflation.

noncash charges Expenses, such as depreciation, amortization, and depletion allowances, that appear on the income statement but do not involve an actual outlay of cash.

noncash expenses Tax-deductible expenses for which there is no corresponding cash outflow in the current period. They include depreciation, amortization, and depletion.

NYSE Euronext The largest and most prestigious broker market in the world.

O

open interest The number of contracts that are currently outstanding.

opening futures price Price on the first trade of the day.

operating assets Cash, marketable securities, accounts receivable, and inventories that are necessary to support the day-to-day operations of a firm.

operating cash flow (OCF) The amount of cash flow generated by a firm from its operations. Mathematically, earnings before interest and taxes (EBIT) minus taxes plus depreciation.

operating cycle (OC) Measurement of the time that elapses from the firm's receipt of raw materials to begin production to its collection of cash from the sale of the finished product.

operating flows Cash inflows and outflows directly related to the production and sale of a firm's products or services.

operating lease A contractual arrangement whereby the lessee agrees to make periodic payments to the lessor, often for five years or less, to obtain an asset's services. The lessee generally receives an option to cancel, and the asset has a useful life longer than the lease term.

operating leverage Measures the tendency of operating cash flow volatility to increase with fixed operating costs.

operating profit margin A measure of profitability that represents the percentage of each sales dollar remaining after deducting all costs and expenses other than interest and taxes.

opportunity cost Forgone cash flows on an alternative investment that the firm or individual decides not to make.

option premium The market price of the option.

order cost The fixed dollar amount per order that covers the costs of placing and receiving an order; used in calculating the EOQ.

ordinary annuity An annuity for which the payments occur at the end of each period.

ordinary corporate income Income resulting from the sale of the firm's goods and services.

out of the money A call (put) option is out of the money when the stock price is less (greater) than the strike price.

oversubscribe When the investment banker builds a book of orders for stock that is greater than the amount of stock the firm intends to sell.

ownership right agreements Agreements between venture capital investors and portfolio-company managers allocating ownership stakes and voting rights to venture capitalists.

P

paid-in capital in excess of par The number of shares of common stock outstanding multiplied by the original selling price of the shares, net of the par value.

par value (bonds) The *face value* of a bond, which the borrower repays at maturity.

par value (common stock) An arbitrary value assigned to common stock on a firm's balance sheet.

participation rights Agreements giving the venture capitalists the right to participate in any sale of stock that a portfolio company's managers might arrange for themselves.

partnership A proprietorship with two or more owners who have joined their skills and personal wealth.

passively managed A strategy in which an investor makes no attempt to identify overvalued or undervalued stocks, but instead holds a diversified portfolio.

payback period The amount of time it takes for a project's cumulative net cash inflows to recoup the initial investment.

payment date The actual date on which a firm mails the dividend payment to the holders of record.

payment pattern The normal timing in which a firm's customers pay their accounts, expressed as the percentage of monthly sales collected in each month following the sale.

payoff The value received from exercising an option on the expiration date (or zero), ignoring the initial premium required to purchase the option.

payoff diagrams A diagram that shows how the expiration date payoff from an option or a portfolio varies, as the underlying asset price changes.

payout policy The choices managers make about distributing a firm's cash—paying regular or "special" dividends or repurchasing stock—to shareholders.

pecking-order theory A hypothesis that assumes managers are better informed about investment opportunities faced by their firms than are outside investors.

percentage-of-sales method Method of constructing pro forma statements by assuming all items grow in proportion to sales.

perpetuity A level cash flow stream that continues forever.

plug figure A line item on the pro forma balance sheet that represents an account that can be adjusted after all other projections are made.

political risk The risk that a government will take an action that negatively affects the values of firms operating in that country.

portfolio weights The percentage invested in each of several securities in a portfolio. Portfolio weights must sum to 1.0 (or 100%).

positive pay A bank service used to combat the most common types of check fraud. A company transmits a check-issued file, designating the check number and amount of each item, to the bank when the checks are issued. The bank matches the presented checks against this file and rejects any items that do not match.

preemptive rights These hold that shareholders have first claim on anything of value distributed by a corporation.

preferred habitat theory A theory that recognizes that the shape of the yield curve may be influenced by investors who prefer to purchase bonds having a particular maturity; also called market *segmentation theory*.

preferred stock A form of ownership that has preference over common stock when the firm distributes income and assets.

premium A bond trades at a premium when its market price exceeds its par value.

prepackaged bankruptcy A reorganization plan that is prepared by the company and negotiated and accepted by creditors and stockholders before the company actually files for Chapter 11 bankruptcy.

present value The value today of a cash flow to be received at a specific date in the future, accounting for the opportunity to earn interest at a specified rate.

president or chief executive officer (CEO) The top company manager with overall responsibility and authority for managing daily company affairs and carrying out policies established by the board.

price/earnings (P/E) ratio A measure of a firm's long-term growth prospects that represents the amount investors are willing to pay for each dollar of a firm's earnings.

primary issues Initial sale of securities by a firm to raise capital.

primary-market transactions Cash sales of securities to investors by a corporation to raise capital.

prime rate The rate of interest charged by large U.S. banks on short-term loans to business borrowers with excellent credit records.

principal The amount of money borrowed on which interest is paid.

private equity Financing provided either through capital investments by current owners or through funding by professional venture capitalists.

private placements Unregistered security offerings sold directly to *accredited investors*.

pro forma financial statements A forecast of what a firm expects its income statement and balance sheet to look like a year or two ahead.

processing float The time that elapses between the receipt of a payment by a firm and its deposit into the firm's account.

profitability index (PI) A capital budgeting tool, defined as the present value of a project's cash inflows divided by the absolute value of its initial cash outflow.

project finance (PF) loans Loans usually arranged for infrastructure projects such as toll roads, bridges, and power plants.

Proposition I The famous "irrelevance proposition," which asserts that the market value of any firm equals the value of its assets and is independent of the firm's capital structure. Firm value is calculated by discounting the firm's expected EBIT at the rate r_a, appropriate for the firm's business risk.

Proposition II Asserts that if we hold the required return on assets (r_a) and the required return on debt (r_d) constant, the expected return on levered equity (r_l) increases with the debt-to-equity ratio.

prospectus A document that contains extensive details about the issuer and describes the security it intends to offer for sale; the first part of a registration statement, distributed to all prospective investors.

protective covenants Provisions in a *bond indenture* that specify requirements the borrower must meet (positive covenants) or things the borrower must not do (negative covenants).

protective put A portfolio containing a share of stock and a put option on that stock.

proxy fight An attempt by outsiders to gain control of a firm by soliciting a sufficient number of votes to elect a new slate of directors and effect a change in company policy.

proxy statements Documents that describe the issues to be voted on at an annual shareholders meeting.

public company A corporation, the shares of which can be freely traded among investors without obtaining the permission of other investors and whose shares are listed for trading in a public securities market.

purchase option An option allowing the lessee to purchase the leased asset when the lease expires.

purchasing card programs Programs in which a firm issues designated employees purchasing cards with spending limits, usable only at stipulated vendors.

purchasing power parity An equilibrium relationship that predicts that currency movements are tied to differences in inflation rates across countries.

pure discount bond Bonds that pay no interest and sell below par value. Also called *zero-coupon bond.*

pure stock exchange merger A merger in which stock is the only mode of payment.

put option An option that grants the right to sell an underlying asset at a fixed price.

putable bonds Bonds that investors can sell back to the issuer at a predetermined price under certain conditions.

put-call parity A relationship that links the market prices of stock, risk-free bonds, call options, and put options.

Q

qualified institutional buyers Institutions with assets exceeding $100 million.

quarterly compounding Interest compounds four times per year.

quick (acid-test) ratio A measure of a firm's liquidity that is similar to the current ratio except that it excludes inventory, which is usually the least-liquid current asset.

R

random walk When next period's value for a variable equals this period's value plus or minus a random shock. When financial asset prices follow a random walk, future and past prices are statistically unrelated, and the best estimate of the future price is simply the current price.

ratchet provisions Contract terms that adjust downward the par value of the stock venture capitalists have purchased in a company in case the firm must sell new stock at a lower price than the VC originally paid.

ratio analysis Calculating and interpreting financial ratios to assess a firm's performance and status.

real interest rate parity An equilibrium relationship that predicts that the real interest rate will be the same in every country.

real option The right, but not the obligation, to take a future action (e.g., cancel or delay) when implementing a project. Note that these actions can change an investment's value.

real return The inflation-adjusted return. Approximately equal to the difference between an investment's stated or nominal return and the inflation rate.

recapitalization Alteration of a company's capital structure to change the relative mix of debt and equity financing.

redemption option Option for venture capitalists to sell a company back to its entrepreneur or founders.

refund To refinance a debt with new bonds.

registration statement The principal disclosure document for all public security offerings.

renewal option In an operating lease, an option that allows the lessee to renew the lease at its expiration.

repurchase rights Give the venture capitalists the right to force the company to buy back (repurchase) the shares held by the VC.

required rate of return The rate of return that investors expect or require an investment to earn given its risk.

residual claimants Investors (typically common stockholders) who have the right to receive the cash that remains after a firm pays all of its bills and makes necessary new investments in the business.

residual theory of dividends Observed dividend payments are simply a residual, the cash left over after corporations have funded all their positive-*NPV* investments.

resource complementarities A firm with a particular operating expertise merges with a firm with another operating strength to create a company that has expertise in multiple areas.

retained earnings The cumulative total of the earnings that a firm has reinvested since its inception.

return on common equity (ROE) A measure that captures the return earned on the common stockholders' (owners') investment in a firm.

return on investment A measure of a firm's overall effectiveness in using its assets to generate returns to common stockholders; also, return on total assets (*ROA*).

return on total assets (ROA) A measure of the overall effectiveness of management in generating returns to common stockholders with its available assets.

reverse LBO A formerly public company that has previously gone private through a leveraged buyout and then goes public again.

reverse LBO (or second IPO) A formerly public company that has previously gone private through a leveraged buyout and then goes public again. Also called a second IPO.

reverse stock splits Occurs when a firm replaces a certain number of outstanding shares with just one new share to increase the stock price.

reverse triangle merger When a subsidiary of the bidder merges with the target firm.

rights offerings A special type of seasoned equity offering that allows the firm's existing owners to buy new shares at a bargain price or to sell that right to other investors.

risk management The process of identifying firm-specific risk exposures and managing those exposures by means of insurance products. Also includes identifying, measuring, and managing all types of risk exposures.

risk management function The activities involved in identifying, measuring, and managing the firm's exposure to all types of risk to maintain an optimal risk-return trade-off and therefore maximize share value.

risk premium The additional return offered by a more risky investment relative to a safer one.

road show A tour of major cities taken by a firm and its bankers several weeks before a scheduled offering; the purpose is to pitch the firm's business plan to prospective investors.

Rule 144A offering A special type of offering, first approved in April 1990, that allows issuing companies to waive some disclosure requirements by selling stock only to sophisticated institutional investors, who may then trade the shares among themselves.

S

S corporations An ordinary corporation in which the stockholders have elected to allow shareholders to be taxed as partners while still retaining their limited-liability status as corporate stockholders.

safety motive A motive for holding cash and short-term investments in order to protect the firm against being unable to satisfy unexpected demands for cash. Sometimes called the *precautionary motive*.

sale-leaseback arrangement One firm sells an asset to another for cash, then leases the asset back from its new owner.

Samurai bonds Yen-denominated bonds issued by non-Japanese corporations.

Sarbanes-Oxley Act of 2002 (SOX) Act of Congress that established new corporate governance standards for U.S. public companies.

scenario analysis A variation of *sensitivity analysis* that provides for calculating the decision variable, such as net present value, when a whole set of assumptions changes in a particular way.

seasoned equity offering (SEO) An equity issue by a firm that already has common stock trading in the market.

secondary offering The sale of previously issued securities, which are typically held in large blocks by one or more investors, raises no additional funds for the initial issuer.

secondary-market transactions Trades between investors that generate no new cash flow for the firm.

Securities Act of 1933 The most important federal law governing the sale of new securities.

Securities and Exchange Commission (SEC) The federal agency, established in 1934, charged with oversight of the fair reporting of financial information to investors in public companies (those whose shares are listed for trading in a public securities market).

Securities Exchange Act of 1934 Act that established the U.S. Securities and Exchange Commission (SEC) and laid out specific procedures for both the public sale of securities and the governance of public companies.

securitization The repackaging of loans and other traditional bank-based credit products into securities that can be sold to public investors.

selling short Borrowing a security and selling it for cash at the current market price. A short seller hopes that either (1) the price of the security sold short will fall, or (2) the return on the security sold short will be lower than the return on the asset in which the proceeds from the short sale were invested.

semiannual compounding Interest compounds twice a year.

sensitivity analysis Exploration of the impact of individual assumptions on a decision variable, such as a project's *NPV*, by determining the effect of changing one assumption while holding all others fixed.

serial bonds Bonds of which a certain portion mature each year.

settlement date The future date on which the buyer pays the seller and the seller delivers the asset to the buyer.

settlement price The average price at which a contract sells at the end of a trading day.

share issue privatization (SIP) A government executing one of these will sell all or part of its ownership in a state-owned enterprise to private investors via a public share offering.

share repurchase program Programs in which companies will buy some of their own shares over a period of time, usually on the open market.

shareholder Owner of common or preferred stock in a *corporation*.

shelf registration (Rule 415) Allows a qualifying company to file a master registration statement, a single document summarizing planned financing over a two-year period.

short position To sell an option or another security.

signaling model Assumes that managers use dividends to convey positive information to poorly informed shareholders.

simple interest Interest paid only on the *initial principal* of an investment, not on the interest that accrues in earlier periods.

sinking fund A provision in a *bond indenture* that requires the borrower to make regular payments to a third-party trustee for use in repurchasing outstanding bonds, gradually over time.

small business investment companies (SBICs) Federally chartered corporations established as a result of the Small Business Administration Act of 1958.

sole proprietorship A business with a single owner.

special dividend An additional dividend that a firm may pay if earnings are higher than normal in a given period.

speculative bonds Bonds rated below investment grade (also known as *high-yield bonds* or *junk bonds*).

speculative motive A motive for holding, typically in short-term as well as long-term investments, funds that are currently unneeded or can be used to quickly take advantage of opportunities that may arise.

spin-off A parent company creates a new company with its own shares to form a division or subsidiary, and existing shareholders receive a pro rata distribution of shares in the new company.

split-off A parent company creates a new, independent company with its own shares, and ownership is transferred to certain shareholders only, in exchange for their shares in the parent.

split-up The division and sale of all of a company's subsidiaries, so that it ceases to exist.

spot exchange rate The exchange rate that applies to immediate currency transactions.

spot price The price that the buyer pays the seller in a current, cash market transaction.

spread The difference between the rate that a lender charges for a loan and the underlying benchmark interest rate. Also called the *credit spread*.

staged financing Method of investing venture capital in a portfolio company in stages, over time.

stakeholders Customers, employees, suppliers, and creditors of a corporation.

stand-alone companies Companies created for the sole purpose of constructing and operating a single project.

standard deviation A measure of volatility equal to the square root of the variance.

standard normal distribution A normal distribution with a mean of zero and a standard deviation of one.

stated annual rate The contractual annual rate of interest charged by a lender or promised by a borrower.

statutory merger A target integration in which the acquirer can absorb the target's resources directly with no remaining trace of the target as a separate entity.

stock dividend The payment to existing shareholders of a dividend in the form of stock.

stock option plans Plans set up to provide stock options to newly-hired managers of portfolio companies in order to give them incentives to manage the company to create value.

stock options Outright grants of stock to top managers, or, more commonly, giving them the right to purchase stock at a fixed price.

stock purchase warrants Instruments that give their holder the right to purchase a certain number of shares of a firm's common stock at a specified price during a certain period of time.

stock split A transaction in which a firm increases the number of outstanding shares by issuing new shares to existing stockholders.

strategic plan A multiyear action plan for the major investments and competitive initiatives that a firm's senior managers believe will drive the future success of the enterprise.

strike price The price at which an option holder can buy or sell the underlying asset.

subordinated debenture An unsecured bond on which the creditors' claims are not satisfied until the senior debtholders' claims have been fully satisfied.

subordination Agreement by all subsequent or more junior creditors to wait until all claims of the senior debt are satisfied in full before having their own claims satisfied.

subsidiary merger A merger in which the acquirer maintains the identity of the target as a separate subsidiary or division.

sunk cost Costs that have already been paid and are therefore not recoverable.

supplemental disclosures The second part of the *registration statement*, which is filed with the SEC.

sustainable growth model Derives an expression that determines how rapidly a firm can grow while maintaining a balance between its outflows (increases in assets) and inflows (increases in liabilities and equity) of cash.

swap contract Agreement between two parties to exchange payment obligations on two underlying financial liabilities that are equal in principal amount but differ in payment patterns.

syndicated loan A large-denomination credit arranged by a group (a *syndicate*) of institutional lenders, commonly commercial banks, for a single borrower.

synergy A reduction in costs or increase in revenues that results from a merger.

systematic risk Risk that cannot be eliminated through diversification.

T

tailing the hedge Purchasing enough futures contracts to hedge risk exposure, but not so many as to cause overhedging.

takeover A transaction in which the control of one entity is taken over by another.

takeover defenses Means by which a target thwarts or delays a takeover attempt.

target cash balance A cash total that is set for checking accounts to avoid engaging in *cash position management*.

target dividend payout ratio A policy under which a firm attempts to pay out a specified percentage of earnings by paying a stated dollar dividend adjusted slowly toward the target payout as proven earnings increase.

tender offer The structured purchase of a target's shares in which the acquirer announces a public offer to buy a minimum number of shares at a specific price.

term loan A loan made by an institution to a business, with an initial maturity of more than 1 year, generally 5 to 12 years.

term sheet An investment proposal detailing all of the economic, control, and ownership terms—including covenants—that is prepared and presented to an entrepreneur by a venture capitalist.

term structure of interest rates The relationship between time to maturity and yield to maturity for bonds of equal risk.

terminal value The value of all of a project's cash flows beyond a certain date in the future.

time line A graphical representation of cash flows over a given period of time.

time value The difference between an option's market price and its intrinsic value.

time value of money Financial concept that explicitly recognizes that $1 received today is worth more than $1 received in the future.

times interest earned ratio A measure of the firm's ability to make contractual interest payments, calculated by dividing earnings before interest and taxes by interest expense.

top-down sales forecast A sales forecast that relies heavily on macroeconomic and industry forecasts.

total asset turnover A measure of the efficiency with which a firm uses *all its assets* to generate sales; calculated by dividing the dollars of sales a firm generates by the dollars of total asset investment.

total cost The sum of the *order costs* and the *carrying costs* that is minimized using the *economic order quantity (EOQ) model*.

total return A measure of the performance of an investment that captures both the income it paid out to investors and its capital gain or loss over a stated period of time.

total variable cost of annual sales (TVC) Calculated by multiplying the annual sales in units by the total variable cost per unit and used to estimate the *average investment in accounts receivable* under a stated policy.

tracking stocks Equity claims based on (and designed to mirror, or track) the earnings of wholly owned subsidiaries of diversified firms.

trade-off model of corporate leverage According to this model managers trade off the costs and benefits of using debt to choose the amount of debt that maximizes firm value as expressed in Equation 12.7b.

transactions exposure The risk that a change in prices will negatively affect the value of a specific transaction or series of transactions.

transactions motive A motive for holding cash and short-term investments in order to make planned payments for items such as materials and wages.

translation exposure The risk that exchange rate movements will adversely impact reported financial results on a firm's financial statements.

Treasury bills Debt instruments issued by the federal government with maturities ranging from a few days to up to 52 weeks.

Treasury bonds Debt instruments issued by the federal government that mature in thirty years.

Treasury Inflation-Protected Security (TIPS) Notes and bonds issued by the federal government that make coupon payments that vary with the U.S. inflation rate.

Treasury notes Debt instruments issued by the federal government with maturities ranging from two to ten years.

Treasury stock Common shares that were issued and later reacquired by the firm through share repurchase programs and are therefore being held in reserve by the firm.

Treasury STRIPS A zero-coupon bond representing a single coupon payment, or the final principal payment, made by an existing Treasury note or bond. The acronym STRIPS stands for Separate Trading of Interest and Principal Securities.

triangular arbitrage A trading strategy in which traders buy a currency in a country where the value of that currency is too low and immediately sell the currency in another country where the currency value is too high.

trustee In bankruptcy, someone appointed by a judge to take over the debtor's assets with the primary objective of maximizing liquidation value.

trustee (bond) A third party to a bond *indenture* that acts as a watchdog on behalf of the bondholders, making sure that the issuer does not default on its contractual responsibilities.

turnover of accounts receivable (TOAR) Three-hundred-sixty-five divided by the *average collection period (ACP)*. Used to calculate the *average investment in accounts receivable (AIAR)* when evaluating accounts receivable policies.

U

underinvestment When stockholders decide not to invest in a positive NPV project, and therefore "underinvest" relative to choosing all positive NPV projects.

underlying asset The asset from which an option or other derivative security derives its value.

underwrite The investment banker purchases shares from a firm and resells them to investors.

underwriting spread The difference between the net price at which an investment bank sells shares to investors and the offer price at which the bank purchases shares from the issuing firm.

unsystematic risk Risk that can be eliminated through diversification.

V

variable growth model Assumes that the dividend growth rate will vary during different periods of time, when calculating the value of a firm's stock.

variance A measure of dispersion of observations around the mean of a distribution; it is equal to the expected value of the sum of squared deviations from the mean divided by one less than the number of observations in the sample.

venture capital A professionally managed pool of money raised for the purpose of making actively managed direct equity investments in rapidly growing private companies.

venture capital limited partnerships Funds established by professional venture capital firms, and organized as limited partnerships.

venture capitalists Professional investors who specialize in making high-risk/high-return investments in rapidly growing entrepreneurial businesses.

vertical merger Companies with current or potential buyer-seller relationships combine to create a more integrated company.

W

warrants Securities that grant rights similar to a call option, except that when a warrant is exercised, the firm must issue a new share, and it receives the strike price as a cash inflow.

weighted average cost of capital (WACC) The after-tax, weighted average required return on all types of securities issued by a firm, where the weights equal the percentage of each type of financing in a firm's overall capital structure.

wire transfer An electronic communication that removes funds from the payer's bank and deposits funds in the payee's bank on a same-day basis via bookkeeping entries.

workout A firm in financial distress may negotiate a solution with its creditors that enables it to bypass many of the costs involved in formally filing for bankruptcy. Requires unanimous approval from a given creditor class.

World Trade Organization (WTO) An organization established by GATT to police world trading practices and to settle disputes between GATT member countries.

Y

Yankee bonds Bonds sold by foreign corporations to U.S. investors.

yield curve A graph that plots the relationship between time to maturity and yield to maturity for a group of equal-risk bonds.

yield spread The difference in yield to maturity between a corporate bond and a Treasury bond at roughly the same maturity.

yield to maturity (YTM) The discount rate that equates the present value of the bond's cash flows to its market price.

Z

Z score The product of a quantitative model for forecasting bankruptcy that uses a blend of traditional financial ratios and a statistical technique known as *multiple discriminant analysis*. In some tests, the Z score has been found to be about 90% accurate in forecasting bankruptcy one year in the future and about 80% accurate in forecasting it two years in the future.

zero growth model The simplest approach to stock valuation that assumes a constant dividend stream.

zero-balance accounts (ZBAs) Disbursement accounts that always have an end-of-day balance of zero. The purpose is to eliminate nonearning cash balances in corporate checking accounts.

Name & Company Index

Subject Index